W9-CAO-281

Broadcasting in America

A Survey of Electronic Media

SYDNEY W. HEAD

Late of the University of Miami

CHRISTOPHER H. STERLING

The George Washington University

LEMUEL B. SCHOFIELD

University of Miami

Sponsoring Editor: Margaret Seawell
Senior Developmental Editor: Frances Gay
Project Editors: Jean Levitt, Janet Young
Senior Production/Design Coordinator: Pat Mahtani
Senior Manufacturing Coordinator: Priscilla Bailey
Marketing Manager: George Kane

Cover design by Karen Gourley Lehman
Cover image by Greg Pease/Tony Stone Worldwide

Acknowledgments for photographs on opener pages: Prologue—
© Chris Brown/SIPA-PRESS; Part 1—CBS, Inc.; Part 2—
© 1984 Norman McGrath; Part 3—Courtesy of Pepsi Cola
Company; Part 4—© 1993 Fox Broadcasting Company. All
Rights Reserved. Photo courtesy of Motion Picture & TV Photo
Archives; Part 5—AP/Wide World Photos; Part 6—Photo by
Paul Conklin; Part 7—© Jeff Zaruba 1990/Folio, Inc.

Printed in the U.S.A.

Library of Congress Catalog Card Number: 93-78634
 23456789-DH-96 95 94
ISBN: 0-395-67331-3

Brief Contents

Contents

Exhibits

Preface

Despite dramatic and continuing changes in its subject matter since *Broadcasting in America* first appeared in 1956, this seventh edition retains its original underlying goal of viewing electronic media from several broad perspectives. Broadcasting and newer media appear in context, both as a result of contemporary social forces and as social forces in their own right. They have impact on virtually all aspects of life—and on many academic disciplines, including history, engineering, economics, social science, and law. These media are fascinating in themselves, and we try here to pass on our enthusiasm for researching in and teaching about this field.

While retaining the same general chapter organization as in the previous edition, we have streamlined the presentation to assimilate more smoothly the latest trends and issues without unduly increasing the length of the seventh edition. By tightening and reorganizing the material on technology, programming, and policy, we have reduced the number of chapters from nineteen to sixteen. This edition also contains new material on the digital revolution, more thoroughly integrated coverage of cable television, including the 1992 Cable Act, and a more cohesive presentation of all material on public broadcasting in one chapter. In addition, the text explores more ethical questions than before. A second color has been added to enhance the book generally, and the exhibits specifically.

Changes in the Seventh Edition

- A new prologue introduces key concepts used throughout the book by examining the role of broadcasting and cable during Hurricane Andrew, which struck the South Florida coast in August 1992. This narrative orients readers to the more detailed chapters that follow.

- Our treatment of history in Part 1 expands its discussion of newer media as they develop histories of their own.

- Technical material in Part 2 has been reorganized and more clearly written in two instead of three chapters, reviewing the changing world of broadcasting and exploring developing results of the digital revolution—including full treatment of high-definition television.

- The business of electronic media in Part 3 features expanded coverage of cable program services, cable revenue sources, and newer technologies. Public broadcasting is now fully unified in Chapter 8, integrating program and audience material formerly scattered elsewhere.

- Our rearranged treatment of commercial programming in Part 4 appears in two chapters instead of three, and includes discussion of cable system scheduling strategies.

- Part 5 explores continuing controversies over research methods used to obtain ratings, and discusses many new examples of media's pervasive effects.

- Our discussion of policy and regulation in Part 6 has been recast into two chapters from the former three, allowing clearer emphasis on service licensing and franchising (the latter radically changed with the 1992 Cable Act, which is incorporated throughout all chapters), and the many constitutional controversies over content and ownership.

- The book concludes with a review of the rapid

and radical changes in electronic media in other countries and a wholly new chapter that looks ahead to likely future developments.

● ● ● ● ● ● ● ●

Ancillary Support

We are fortunate to have retained Dr. Louise Benjamin of the University of Georgia as author of two *Broadcasting in America* ancillary publications. She brings her many years' experience as teacher of "the BIA course" to the new *Instructor's Manual with Test Items*, which includes chapter analyses and summaries, reviews of learning objectives and key concepts, lecture and project suggestions, and a test bank. The publisher makes copies available to adopters, as it does with computerized test items for IBM and Macintosh computers.

As she did for the sixth edition, Dr. Benjamin has again written the *Study Guide* for students, which includes chapter outlines, key concepts, and practice test questions, including analyses explaining why the wrong answers are wrong and the right answers right, with specific references to the main text.

● ● ● ● ● ● ● ●

And Our Thanks To. . .

As always in this multifaceted project, we are grateful to the many people who have helped with advice and information as they attempt to keep us out of trouble. We especially appreciate the contributions of Dr. Susan Tyler Eastman of Indiana University, who authored the programming chapters in the previous two editions and who generously shared her insights, ideas, and experience throughout this edition. Dr. Paul Driscoll of the University of Miami read the prologue, and, as did Miami's Dr. Mitchell Shapiro, provided information for other chapters.

Elliot Sivowitch of the Smithsonian Institution's Division of Electricity and Nuclear Energy carefully read Chapters 4 and 5 and made many useful sugges-

tions and corrections. Dr. Richard Ducey of the National Association of Broadcasters made important publications and data available for the technology and economics chapters. Corey Flintoff of National Public Radio and Dr. Bernadette McGuire of the Association of Public Television Stations read drafts of Chapter 8 and provided source material. Dr. Sheva Farkas of Ohio University, an Arbitron researcher before returning to academe, gave us valuable comments on Chapter 11. John Dimling of Nielsen and Shelly Cagner of Arbitron supplied data and ratings examples from their firms.

The chapters dealing with controls benefitted from comments by Dr. Herbert Terry of Indiana University and from documents provided by Barry Umansky, NAB's deputy general counsel. Chapter 15 was shaped with the informed insights of both Dr. Donald Browne of the University of Minnesota and Dr. Douglas Boyd of the University of Kentucky.

The instructors listed below reviewed the draft manuscript at the publisher's request. Their unsigned comments alerted us to errors and offered useful advice on organization and contents.

Virginia Bacheler
State University of New York—Brockport

Bradley Chisholm
University of Nevada—Las Vegas

Robert G. Finney
California State University—Long Beach

Robert S. Fortner
Calvin College

Linda Fuller
Worcester State College

Geoffrey Hammill
Eastern Michigan University

Charles F. Houlberg
San Francisco State University

David C. Martin
California State University—Sacramento

Kevin O. Sauter
University of Saint Thomas, Minnesota

Robert L. Stevenson
University of North Carolina—Chapel Hill

As always, we take responsibility for the use made of the advice and ideas given by all of these people.

And special thanks to Bailey Siletchnik, who, while working on this project for Houghton Mifflin, consistently went out of her way to be helpful.

Nor can we close without acknowledging contributions by family members. Jennifer Anne Sterling labored many hours on valuable creative ideas for exhibit illustrations in the book's early stages. Brad Schofield, marketing director at Cable TV of York, Pennsylvania, patiently answered his father's many cable questions; his sister, Jennifer Schofield Peña, graciously served as conscripted proofreader. Naturally, the longest-suffering members of the *Broadcasting in America* team are our spouses. Ellen Sterling and Shirley Schofield helped read galleys, calmed frazzled author husbands, added a spot of humor (or prayer) in down moments, and in so many other behind-the-scenes ways helped us see the project through.

Christopher H. Sterling
WASHINGTON, D.C.

Lemuel B. Schofield
CORAL GABLES, FLORIDA

A Personal Note

Photo by Christopher H. Sterling.

Sydney Warren Head, 1913–1991

This edition of *Broadcasting in America* is the first to appear without the active participation of its founding author, Dr. Sydney W. Head. As he worked with us in the initial planning for the seventh edition of *Broadcasting in America*, he knew he had but a few months to live. He died on July 7, 1991, at the age of 77.

Born in England, Head grew up in central California, earned his A.B. and M.A. degrees at Stanford University and his Ph.D. at New York University. He had been professor of communication at the University of Miami, where he created and for many years led the radio/television/film program, and later served on the Temple University faculty. Head became founding president in 1955 of what is now the Broadcast Education Association and, three decades later, received that organization's highest honor, the Distinguished Education Service Award.

Head maintained lifelong interests in reading, sailing, gourmet cooking, and traveling. He had spent the 1960s in Africa, studying, conducting seminars and workshops, and helping several nations on that continent develop their broadcast systems.

A respected scholar and prodigious writer, Head authored, contributed to, or edited such works as *Broadcasting in Africa* (1974), *Broadcast/Cable Programming* (1981, revised editions since), and *World Broadcasting Systems: A Comparative Analysis* (1985), as well as many articles and research reports. Houghton Mifflin published the first edition of *Broadcasting in America* in 1956, and the second in 1972.

Sydney invited Christopher Sterling, his Temple University colleague, to write an annotated guide to further reading for *Broadcasting in America*'s third edition in 1976. Chris became a collaborator on the fourth (1982), and co-author of the fifth (1986) and sixth (1990) editions. The authors asked Lemuel Schofield, with whom Sydney had worked at the University of Miami, to write the business chapters for both the fifth and sixth editions. Lem joins this edition as co-author with primary responsibility for the prologue and the business and programming chapters, serving also as contributor and editor throughout the book.

Broadcasting in America will always bear Sydney's unique imprimatur and contain countless examples of his wisdom and insight. He set very high standards, always demanding—of his students and colleagues alike—the best-quality work and the most concise writing possible. The authors of this seventh edition have striven to maintain those standards, although doing so without Sydney's firm yet friendly guiding hand.

C.H.S. and L.B.S.

Prologue

Hurricane Andrew: Electronic Media in a Crisis

• •

"People in Dade County are dying tonight."

Bryan Norcross, chief meteorologist at a Miami television station, spoke these somber words as the eyewall of Hurricane "Andrew"—the most destructive natural disaster in American history—roared ashore a few miles south of downtown Miami, early in the morning of August 24, 1992. His voice was heard by thousands of terrified residents huddled in closets, bathrooms, and special shelters, listening to Norcross and others on battery-operated radios. (During the overnight storm, some television stations simulcast their coverage on local radio frequencies.)

Although the hurricane-related death toll—38 people—was remarkably low for such a powerful storm, all agreed that more would have died had electronic media been less thorough in preparing their audiences for Andrew's onslaught. Florida Governor Lawton Childs observed that "mass communication—primarily the broadcast media—allowed us to warn the many thousands of residents about the storm hours before it made landfall. I hate to think of the additional devastation a storm of this magnitude reaching our shores unannounced could have produced" (*Broadcasting*, 31 August 1992: 5).

Floridians had become complacent about hurricanes. The "it-won't-happen-here" mentality prevailed throughout the state. Nor did they pay much attention when, on August 14, the National Hurricane Center in Coral Gables, Florida, noted a low-pressure system off the coast of Africa. The Hurricane Center upgraded the system to tropical depression status on August 16 and to Tropical Storm Andrew the following day. On Saturday, August 22, with winds exceeding 75 mph, Andrew officially became a hurricane.

Even then, many residents expected the storm to take a traditional turn to the north. But experts thought otherwise and began to issue advisories, picked up and broadcast by radio and television stations throughout the area:

- 11:00 A.M.—"Andrew continues to strengthen rapidly."
- 2:00 P.M. (with the storm 655 miles east of

Hurricane Andrew's Path

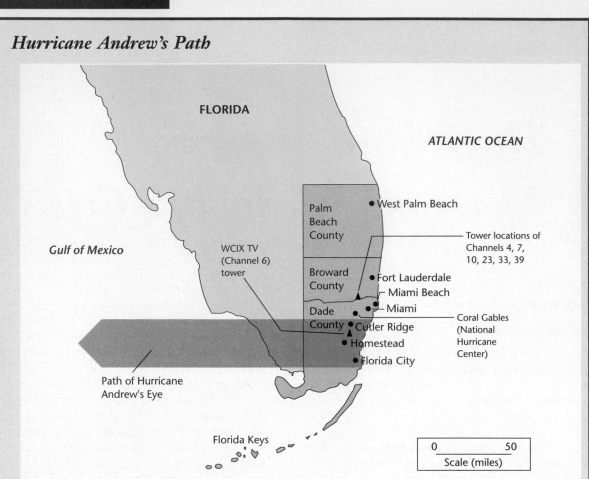

FLORIDA

ATLANTIC OCEAN

Gulf of Mexico

Palm Beach County

• West Palm Beach

WCIX TV
(Channel 6)
tower

Tower locations of
Channels 4, 7,
10, 23, 33, 39

Broward County

• Fort Lauderdale
— Miami Beach
•— Miami

Dade County

• Cutler Ridge
▲ Homestead
• Florida City

Coral Gables
(National
Hurricane
Center)

Path of Hurricane
Andrew's Eye

Florida Keys

0	50

Scale (miles)

The eye of Hurricane Andrew entered the Florida peninsula just south of Miami and north of the Keys. Winds blew down WCIX's television tower, located directly in Andrew's path, as well as the National Hurricane Center's radar in Coral Gables. Other TV towers, located at an "antenna farm" farther north on the Dade/Broward County line, were spared. Television and most radio studios are in greater Miami. Radio station transmitter sites are scattered throughout the area. Some survived; others, including those antennas co-located on the WCIX tower, were lost.

Had the storm come ashore only a few miles farther north, both overall devastation and damage to electronic communication would have been much more severe. In preparation for such a possibility, authorities stood ready to implement power increases for radio and television stations in Palm Beach County to ensure that vital information would reach the public.

Miami)—"The westward movement is expected to continue through Sunday, increasing the threat to south and central Florida."

- 5:00 P.M.—The Hurricane Center issues a hurricane watch for most of south Florida.

At last, people begin to pay attention. They pour into supermarkets, convenience stores, and building-supply firms for food, water, and batteries, as well as plywood and duct tape to protect windows.

Early Sunday morning, residents receive orders to evacuate coastal areas. Others move everything they can indoors and tape windows; a fortunate few close hurricane shutters. Everyone searches for the safest place—a room with no windows—to ride out the storm, as most radio and television stations program continuous weather and emergency information.

- 4:00 P.M.—Some emergency shelters swell to capacity; water pressure drops as thousands fill their bathtubs to store what would become a scarce commodity.
- 7:00 P.M.—Officials close Miami Beach to incoming automobile traffic.
- 8:00 P.M.—The Hurricane Center places the storm 185 miles east of Miami and describes it as "extremely dangerous."

Hurricane Center Director Bob Sheets continues his regular live reports on local radio and television.

- 3:00 A.M., Monday, August 24—Radar shows the storm's center, with 140 mph winds, just 40 miles east of Miami. In the city, and south toward the Florida Keys, winds have become strong and it is raining hard. Few can sleep. Some lie in bathtubs, covered by mattresses for protection.
- 4:28 A.M.—The eyewall enters Biscayne Bay, and two minutes later officials order all police and fire personnel off the streets.
- 5:20 A.M.—The Hurricane Center's radar unit blows over and is useless. The Center remains in telephone contact with Miami television station WTVJ, which, with its own radar, continues to track the storm's progress.

The last wind measurement, before the wind gauge also breaks, is 164 mph. Later, others would claim that winds reached nearly 200 mph.

- 7:00 A.M.—Winds begin to subside as the storm moves west toward Louisiana, and people everywhere cautiously peer out to see the devastation.

As the photographs here show, thousands suffered total loss of homes and possessions. Others were more fortunate. Countless trees were down, blocking streets. Power lines hung dangerously across sidewalks. But this was not the end of it. Now the looting began, accompanied by threats from gun-carrying homeowners. Thousands of people were without electricity, running water, sanitation, telephone, and food, as daytime humidity and temperatures soared. Inoperable traffic lights made driving a nightmare.

In the days that followed, rebuilding began. The air, which had been filled with the "freight-train" roar of Andrew's winds, then strange silence, now carried the sounds of chain saws, hammers, and helicopters and the smells of diesel fuel and roofing tar. Neighbors helped neighbors. The National Guard arrived. Tent cities sprouted. Price gouging ran rampant and con men took down-payments for roofs they would never install. But for most, the human spirit prevailed. And as weeks turned into months, Dade county returned—as closely as it could—to normalcy.

The importance of electronic media becomes vividly clear in such a crisis. Beginning several days before Andrew came ashore, radio and television stations regularly aired weather advisories. By Saturday they had intensified their coverage and by Sunday they had begun 24-hour programming devoted to Andrew updates, emergency preparations, advice on how to weather the storm, and calming reassurance that this, too, would pass. WTVJ-TV remained on the air continuously for 203 hours. At least four radio stations simulcast the signals of local television stations, whose news departments were far better equipped to provide thorough coverage. In fact, at the height of the storm, TV had more

Andrew's Power

At best, these photographs—including one showing WCIX-TV's downed transmission tower—can only suggest the devastation and personal tragedy caused by Hurricane Andrew.

Sources: Photo by Beth A. Keiser, *Miami Herald*; tower photo courtesy of WCIX.

listeners than viewers, as power failures made television screens throughout Dade County go dark, though battery-powered radios remained in use. When it was over, broadcasters refocused to assist in the massive cleanup and relief operations.

Those who experienced Hurricane Andrew first-hand (as did one of the present authors) can easily answer the question: Why study broadcasting? Because of its utter utility—its universal, enduring usefulness unmatched by any other medium.

Andrew's arrival in Florida tells us a good deal about the unique value of electronic media. As we examine that brief but terrifying event, we introduce topics discussed later in this book, offering dramatic illustrations of the otherwise everyday roles of radio, television, and cable.

Development

This was not the first time, of course, that electronic media played a major role in time of crisis. Chapter 1, for example, details telegraphic efforts made in 1912 to aid imperiled passengers on the *Titanic*. Years later, during a massive 1965 power blackout in all of New York City and much of the Northeast (when two authors were present!), AM radio explained what was happening and brought reason and order to what could have been a major disaster. And later still, television provided vivid, live descriptions of the bombing of Baghdad and the subsequent brief war in the Persian Gulf.

Nor would it be the last. When a terrorist bomb exploded in the basement of New York City's World Trade Center in February 1993, it knocked out broadcast transmitters on the roof, taking six of the city's seven VHF television stations off the air. Only WCBS-TV, with back-up equipment on the Empire State Building, was able to broadcast uninterrupted. By feeding their signals directly to area cable systems, and by using transmission facilities of public and low-power stations, TV newscasters were able to give out emergency telephone numbers and urge calm on those inside the building. And less than six months later, when floods inundated the nation's midsection, broadcasters again responded, providing not only news coverage to the nation and the

world, but also vital information and help to victims of the disaster (see Exhibit P.h).

Thus, Hurricane Andrew and these other crises serve as examples of points addressed in Part 1 of this book:

- History provides context for current events.
- By examining what has gone before, we can better understand what is happening today and what may occur tomorrow.

Technology

Broadcasters have always had to find innovative ways to serve their publics. When Andrew hit Florida on the morning of August 24, Miami's ABC affiliate, WPLG-TV, was knocked off the air for almost three hours when it lost its studio-to-transmitter microwave link. Because its studios, located only a few blocks from Biscayne Bay, could easily flood, WPLG set up an alternative studio at its transmitter. The Fox affiliate, WSVN-TV, also worried about high water (the storm's tidal surge carried a 35-foot boat from the bay to the station's nearby parking lot), so it, too, moved operations to its transmitter site.

High winds blew down the tower of the CBS affiliate WCIX-TV (see Exhibit P.b), keeping the station silent until 4:00 P.M., when it began broadcasting from an auxiliary transmitter north of Miami. Because their antennas were on the WCIX tower, three radio stations were also knocked off the air. WTVJ-TV, the NBC affiliate, rode out the storm in a special bunker that technicians had hastily constructed in its downtown studios.

And, of course, for hours (days and weeks in some places) there was no electricity. Most stations had to turn to back-up generators, which, though able to power basic equipment, could not handle all requirements—especially air conditioning. So news anchors in sports clothes became the order of the day as they read their stories under limited, yet very hot, lights. Technicians experienced difficulty locating enough diesel fuel to keep generators operating (those at one multiple transmitter site burned 300 gallons per hour).

Andrew's Magnitude

Storm-related deaths 38 (15 incurred directly during the storm, 23 indirectly during clean-up efforts that followed)

Homes destroyed 28,066
People left homeless 160,000
People out of work 86,000

Total property damage $20 billion
Insured losses At least $15 billion

Power customers who lost service 1.4 million
Telephone customers who lost service 80,000

Damage to agriculture $1 billion
Damage to parks $110.4 million
Damage to beaches $4.5 million

Recreational boats damaged or destroyed 1,500
Storm debris 3.1 million cubic yards (15 years' worth of landfill space)
Traffic lights damaged 5,000

Military troops deployed 29,300

Source: "Andrew by the Numbers," *Miami Herald*, 24 September 1992: 24A, and "Rumors of Death," *Tropic*, 20 December 1992: 13.

---

in English, Spanish, and even Creole, the station brought detailed information to storm victims within a 25-mile radius of its transmitter. To ensure that they could receive the broadcasts, the army, in cooperation with other agencies, distributed some 15,000 free battery-operated portable radios to people in areas without electricity. The federal government's Emergency Broadcast System (EBS) also helped to spread vital information and to coordinate communication activities (see Exhibit P.d).

Hardest hit were cable systems. When homeowners finally had electricity restored (for some, this took several weeks), they discovered they still had no cable reception. Some systems lost service to as many as 95 percent of their customers. One cable company alone lost more than 1,200 miles of cable lines in the blink of Andrew's eye. Because most systems string cables on utility poles, operators had to wait until power and telephone crews had finished their repair work. Even then, rebuilding went slowly. Area newspapers regularly published schedules specifying when customers could expect their cable service to be restored (although information was spotty because the papers couldn't get some systems to answer their phones). A few systems ran newspaper ads with projected completion schedules. Yet many homes were without cable even six months after the storm.

Part 2 of this book explains how broadcasting, cable, and other electronic means of mass communication work. As Hurricane Andrew illustrated:

- Electronic media depend on complex technology and (as with cable) on other services.
- Even as technology continues to advance, events can force media to return to the basics of over-the-air transmission in order to serve their audiences.

Business

As you might expect, Andrew had substantial economic impact on all electronic media. Cable systems, unable to serve customers, lost subscription fees. Broadcasters, pre-empting regular programming, lost advertising revenue. When normal pro-

---

News crews had earlier scouted locations where their expensive remote vans would have at least partial protection against high winds. Cellular telephone reports from ordinary citizens, advising listeners as the storm moved through the area, supplemented news-department coverage.

Nor were traditional broadcasters alone in their efforts to keep the public informed. The U.S. Army set up "Radio Recovery" on AM frequency 1610 (usually reserved for traffic information on Florida's turnpike). Operating at 400 watts and broadcasting

gramming resumed, some advertisers were reluctant to return to the air: their own revenues had dropped and they couldn't afford to advertise; they felt advertising was inappropriate during a crisis; potential customers had suffered losses and weren't in the mood to buy; and until electric power was fully restored, commercials would reach only a limited audience.

Television stations incurred added expense as they expanded local news coverage to 24 hours a day (calling in all personnel and assigning them to 12-hour overtime shifts). And all had costs of rebuilding facilities and replacing equipment—only some of which was covered by insurance.

But, like their audiences, broadcasters rebounded. Only two days after the storm, one trade group, the Radio Advertising Bureau, shipped to member-stations special kits that advised how to rebuild their advertising streams! Radio stations began reporting new short-term business from tree-removal services, insurance companies, and banks. As insurance companies issued settlement checks, automobile dealers, furniture stores, and others decided they had potential customers after all.

Miami's television stations, in an unusual display of cooperation, joined in sponsoring a full-page ad in the trade magazine *Broadcasting* urging advertisers and their agencies to

> Think of the Miami [market area] as the eye of a furious buying frenzy. While only 7% of the population was dramatically affected by Hurricane Andrew, these consumers will pack spending power upwards of 30 billion incremental dollars on everything from bikes to boats and bathing suits to swimming pools.

Andrew had impact on station personnel as well. Many worked 12 hours or more each day for a week or longer while maneuvering their way around fallen trees and through traffic gridlock. Weather and sports reporters were pressed into service as relief news anchors. Some staffers who were not photographers found themselves carrying camcorders with orders to get whatever pictures they could. Field reporters worked under harrowing weather and safety conditions. One photographer was attacked by looters.

As detailed in Exhibit P.e, one television station's weatherman became a local hero and in so doing turned his stalled career around. Less than a month after the storm, the same station fired its prime news anchor and replaced him with its top sportscaster. Some suggested this resulted from the anchor's decision to sit out the storm with his family, rather than join co-workers as they broadcast 24 hours a day under most difficult conditions—thus demonstrating less than full dedication to his role as journalist. (Management disagreed, saying that they had previously planned the change, and that they implemented it after the sportscaster had come through with flying colors when he co-anchored hurricane coverage with the station's meteorologist.)

Part 3 of this book examines the structures and the economic bases of broadcasting and cable:

- Most electronic media operate as "for-profit" businesses. Cable systems rely primarily on subscriber fees, broadcasters on advertising revenue. In times of crisis, however, media forgo these profit motives—and incur added expense—to serve the public.
- In the final analysis, people make broadcasting the powerful and influential medium that it is. And the success or failure of those people may often be determined by how they rise to the challenges of crisis.

Programming

Andrew presented Miami broadcasters with a series of program decisions—some easily made, others not. Affiliates of the ABC, CBS, and NBC television networks had no difficulty deciding to pre-empt network (and all other entertainment) programming in order to present 24-hour-a-day live coverage of the storm's progress and of preparations for survival. The Spanish-language affiliates of Telemundo and Univision, as well as the Fox affiliate, which bills itself as "South Florida's News Station," did the same. Radio stations with local staffs expanded their news breaks; those without such staffs

EBS: It Really Works!

"This is a test. This station is conducting a test of the Emergency Broadcast System. This is only a test. Beeeeeep . . . Beeeeeep. . . . This is a test of the Emergency Broadcast System. The broadcasters of your area in voluntary cooperation with federal, state, and local authorities have developed this system to keep you informed in the event of an emergency. . . ."

How often have radio and television stations interrupted our favorite program with this curious announcement? How often have we wondered what it all means, how the system operates, and how well it works, if at all, when an emergency really exists?

Hurricane Andrew provides some answers. First, and most important: Yes, EBS works, and very well at that.

As for how it works: EBS divides the United States into nearly 600 EBS *Operational Areas*, each containing at least one key station—called a Common Program Control Station (CPCS-1)—that authorities contact to activate EBS. After receiving an activation request, the CPCS-1 broadcasts a statement alerting the public that important instructions are forthcoming, then transmits the EBS Attention Signal, followed by the emergency announcement. Participating stations monitor their CPCS-1 and retransmit the messages. Non-participating stations leave the air after advising their audiences to tune to active frequencies.

As Andrew approached, Florida's governor activated the state's EBS at 9:30 A.M. on Sunday, August 23, 1992. Miami's primary EBS stations converted to all-news-and-information formats and provided vital information to people throughout the area—both directly and via rebroadcast by other stations. Beginning late Sunday evening and continuing through early Monday morning as Andrew roared through south Florida, even on into Tuesday, some radio stations discontinued their own programming and simulcast the EBS station signals.

EBS personnel helped arrange fuel delivery to stations when emergency generators ran low. They also coordinated EBS communication efforts with those of the Department of Defense, the National Telecommunications Administration, and the Federal Emergency Management Agency.

President Harry S Truman had established CONELRAD (Control of Electromagnetic Radiation) in 1951. It required all radio stations, during national emergencies, to broadcast only on AM frequencies 640 or 1240—a plan intended to provide information to citizens while, at the same time, preventing incoming enemy airplanes from navigating to their targets by homing in on local radio signals, as the Japanese had done a decade earlier at Pearl Harbor. By the early 1960s, however, sophisticated missile guidance systems had rendered CONELRAD obsolete, and President John F. Kennedy replaced it with EBS.

Although EBS has served the public well, it now must move into 21st century technology. Even before Andrew struck, the FCC had announced plans to overhaul the system, including (1) the use of automated equipment that would reduce human error and would continually—and silently—test itself; (2) the inclusion of such services as amateur radio, wireless cable, direct broadcast satellite, and cellular telephones in the new system; and (3) the renaming of EBS to reflect the incorporation of these new technologies.

Source: *Emergency Broadcast System*, Federal Emergency Management Agency, Washington, DC, March 1990.

How a Local EBS System Works

1
State or Local Officials Activate EBS

2
Key Station Activates EBS

3
Emergency Messages Disseminated

4
Public Receives Emergency Messages

Public Officials

Civil Defense
Local Emergency Operating Center

National Weather Service
AP, UPI, Telephone, NOAA Weather Radio or Weather Wire

Common Program Control Station

Amateur Radio, CB Radio, and Spotter Groups Support the EBS

Cable Systems

Broadcast Stations

Public

Activating the EBS

National Level

Activated by the President of the United States via control points for Radio, Cable, and TV networks, AP, UPI, and participating common carriers.

Local Level

Activated by designated local officials. For example, WDEL, Common Program Control Station (CPCS-1) for New Castle, activates that operational area.

State Level

Activated by the governor or designated state officials. WDSD (FM) is the Originating Primary Relay Station for the State Relay Network.

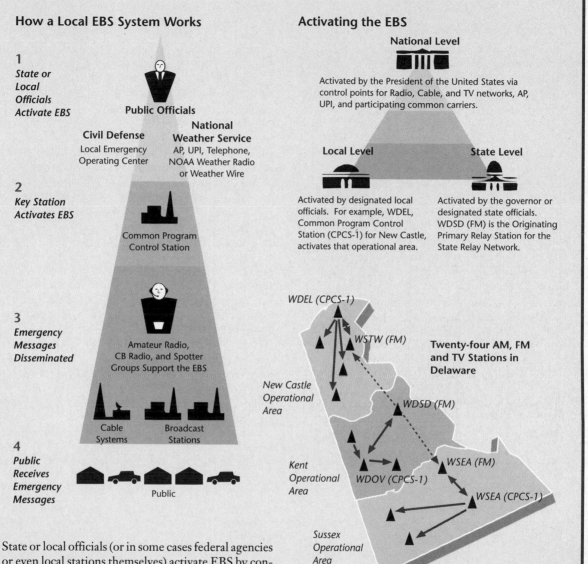

WDEL (CPCS-1)

WSTW (FM)

New Castle Operational Area

Twenty-four AM, FM and TV Stations in Delaware

WDSD (FM)

WSEA (FM)

Kent Operational Area

WDOV (CPCS-1)

WSEA (CPCS-1)

Sussex Operational Area

State or local officials (or in some cases federal agencies or even local stations themselves) activate EBS by contacting key stations—called Common Program Control Stations (CPCS-1s)—which in turn transmit emergency information to the public directly and through rebroadcast by other radio and television stations and cable systems.

Using Delaware as an example, this illustration shows that EBS can activate in any or all of the state's three Operational Areas.

Bryan Norcross: Hurricane Hero

Crises often create instant heros. Hurricane Andrew did just that for Bryan Scott Norcross, who provided the calm yet authoritative voice that helped thousands of south Floridians ride out the storm.

When, by Saturday night, August 22, 1992, it had become clear that Hurricane Andrew would strike the south Florida coast, Norcross became the focal point of the storm coverage by Miami's NBC television affiliate, WTVJ. He moved into the anchor chair at 9:00 A.M. Sunday, where he would stay—with little relief—for 12 days, and soon became the dominant authority to whom thousands turned for information, advice, and comfort.

For the next 23 hours Norcross tracked the storm, telling his audience—with incredible accuracy—what to expect and when. When the National Hurricane Center lost its radar, his took over. He performed complex calculations that allowed him to pinpoint Andrew's location and to predict with precision when and where it would hit and how long it would take to pass over. He proved instrumental in persuading people to evacuate homes that lay in harm's way, and he shamed authorities into opening toll gates on Florida's turnpike so that evacuees could pass through more quickly.

Norcross understood well that human lives, not just property, were in jeopardy. He warned, "Now is the time to find a closet in the inside of your home and get everything out of it. The last-resort place you're going to be is in the back of that closet with a transistor radio and a mattress over the top of you, and we'll tell you when it's OK to come out."

Norcross took telephone calls on the air from frantic listeners barricaded in closets and bathrooms as their homes disintegrated around them. With his voice growing more and more hoarse, he gave comforting assurance to scores of people in fear for their lives.

A Phi Beta Kappa graduate of Florida State University (FSU), Norcross began his television career first as an engineer, then as a producer and director at stations in Atlanta, Denver, and Louisville. It was in Louisville that Bryan (he had changed the "i" to "y" because he had read somewhere that "y" and "k" are the sexiest letters in the alphabet) broadcast his first weather story, going it alone by pointing a camera at his chair and giving the city its only TV report on a paralyzing snow storm. Later, as news director, he tried unsuccessfully to find a meteorologist for his station—even at a salary far higher than his own—and so returned to FSU for his own graduate degree in meteorology.

Norcross came to Miami in 1983. Working first at the ABC affiliate, he moved to WTVJ in 1990. He continued to study his craft, was the only local weatherperson regularly in attendance at the National Hurricane Conference, and persuaded station management both to outfit the facility with sophisticated weather equipment and to make hurricane-proof the station's ability to stay on the air. His preparations paid off.

At 41 years of age, and described variously as gawky, skinny, with a scratchy, nasal voice, Norcross's future with WTVJ had been uncertain before Andrew's arrival. His contract would expire at the end of the year and he worried about renewal, given the trend at some stations to use what his producer calls "weather bunnies." But his performance under stress changed all that. WTVJ planned "an expanded capacity" for him and signed him to a new, three-year contract that about doubled his annual salary to nearly $300,000.

carried the signals of other stations or, at a minimum, announcements from the National Hurricane Center.

As the storm drew closer, broadcast efforts intensified and became even more focused. Several AM and FM stations that normally programmed music converted to all-news-and-information formats. Others simulcast the audio portion of televised hurricane coverage. And non-Fox independent TV stations suspended all regular programming, carrying

In this photograph of a television screen, Norcross (left) and news anchor Tony Segreto broadcast live from a specially constructed bunker in WTVJ's studio, as the station's radar shows Hurricane Andrew's eye just off the Florida coast.

Some residents unofficially nominated him for public office, spray-painting "Norcross for Governor" on their shattered homes. He has received thousands of thank-you letters, and hoards of grateful fans have purchased T-shirts that read "When Norcross talks, everyone listens." In May 1993 NBC aired *Hurricane Andrew*, a made-for-TV movie about the disaster, although earlier consideration of having Norcross play himself in the film had been abandoned.

But mostly Bryan Norcross will be remembered for his compassion, his expertise, his soothing manner, and the service he performed when south Florida huddled in crisis. As one resident put it: "As far as I'm concerned, Bryan's the reason I'm alive."

instead a simple message that urged viewers to tune to any facility offering hurricane information.

This intensity continued for about a week following the storm: nonstop television news coverage; reporters, photographers, producers, writers—all working to the point of exhaustion; satellite news-gathering trucks, helicopters, and other equipment pushed to their limits; stations setting up temporary studios in the areas hardest hit by Andrew, from which local anchors originated stories.

Then came the first really difficult decision: when to *stop*. By the second week following the storm, personnel were exhausted, operating costs had sky-rocketed, advertising revenue had ceased. Besides, what more could be said or shown? But wait. Every day power was being restored to hundreds, sometimes thousands of homes—none of which had seen the previous coverage. So during that second week, television stations began gradual withdrawal: they carried some prime time and other entertainment shows, while continuing greatly expanded newscasts. By the third week, television programming had largely returned to normal, although the total time devoted to local news remained greater than before (affiliates continued, for example, to pre-empt network early-morning magazine programs).

ABC, CBS, and NBC, which had typically opened their evening newscasts with hurricane stories, had by the second week moved such coverage down to second or third in story lineup and, by the third week, usually didn't mention Andrew until after the first commercial break.

Radio station practices varied widely. Most resumed their normal formats soon after the storm had passed, though many included regular news updates. Others continued to broadcast nonstop news and information for more than a month. Cable systems, to the extent they were able to operate at all, had offered regular programming.

Most programs that TV stations pre-empted were lost forever to south Florida viewers. But not so for soap operas. The NBC affiliate, for example, broadcast missed episodes during the wee hours of the morning—thus making them available to fanatic viewers either during the middle of the night, or to those who knew how to program their videocassette recorders at more civilized hours.

Even a month after the storm, television stations devoted extra time to the disaster and its aftermath. The ABC affiliate, for example, set aside the Saturday 8:00 to 9:00 P.M. period for a series of news special reports, *After Andrew: Our Journey Back*. The CBS affiliate continued its expanded, one-hour, early-evening news. And the Fox affiliate planned about ten extra weekly hours devoted to storm relief efforts. Stations also increased their investigative reports on such issues as whether building codes were adequate (some were not) and whether contractor violations had contributed to the devastation (some had).

Some Florida broadcasters joined directly in the relief effort. Within a month after the storm, 15 television and 18 radio stations had raised $2.2 million in a two-hour telethon. Many others individually organized volunteers, handled cash donations, and gathered and distributed food, clothing, and emergency supplies.

But these activities were not limited to Florida. One Miami Spanish-language station joined its network, Univision, in a telethon that received pledges of $1 million locally and $3.5 million nationwide. Cash, food, and relief items came from stations all over the country. NBC radio's *Talknet* host, Bruce Williams, appealed to Kuwait, Saudi Arabia, and the United Arab Emirates for economic aid to Andrew's victims—pointing to U.S. aid given them a year earlier during the Gulf War. Within two days the network reported that the amir of Kuwait had donated $10 million to the American Red Cross; two weeks later the United Arab Emirates came through with $5 million.

In the midst of all this, stations pursued promotional possibilities. Competition for news audiences intensified. On-air announcements touted exclusive stories and pictures. Some outlets produced videocassettes for sale to the public—with proceeds to go toward relief efforts.

As detailed in Part 4 of this book:

- Programming is the essence of electronic media.
- Broadcasters and cable operators employ a wide variety of programs and program formats to attract audiences.
- During emergencies, radio and television stations can react swiftly to alter programming in ways that meet the needs of their audiences.

Effects

Andrew clearly demonstrated not only our dependence on broadcasting but also the ability of the medium both to serve and to influence its users.

Oh, How We Love That Box!

A recent survey by *TV Guide* revealed the following about the extent of America's love affair with television:

- Fewer than one in four (23 percent) of those who responded said they would agree to give up television for the rest of their lives in exchange for $25,000.
- Almost half (46 percent) said they wouldn't give it up for anything less than $1 million.
- One-quarter said they wouldn't do it even for that $1 million.

When asked which they would select—a television set or a telephone—if they and their immediate family were stranded on a deserted island for a year, about a third (34 percent) picked TV, choosing to give up all contact with anyone outside their family for 12 months.

Source: "Would You Give Up TV for a Million Bucks?" 10 October 1992: 9. Reprinted with permission from TV Guide® Magazine. Copyright © 1992 by News America Publications Inc.

Certainly our love of television has been widely documented. Exhibit P.f details a *TV Guide* survey that produced startling—and to some, distressing—results. Radio, meanwhile, continues to play an important role in the lives of many—in their cars, in their homes, and at the beach.

Andrew confirmed how much we have come to depend on television by revealing what happens when we lose it. Without TV, parents had to find new ways to entertain their children—and themselves. Frustration grew as people without telephones, stoves, or refrigerators were unable to pass the time with soap operas or football games. Some rediscovered books; others met their neighbors for the first time. Still others refused to accept deprivation; they connected TV sets to portable generators or even automobile batteries.

Cable took longer to return, producing new frustrations. Subscribers soon realized that they had allowed themselves to become totally dependent on that wire. Not only had they lost program variety and choice, but most also lacked roof antennas. And indoor "rabbit ears" (if they could be found at all, for stores soon sold all they had) simply did not produce the quality pictures to which they had become accustomed. Some wondered if manufacturers had skimped on the tuning capacity of their "state-of-the-art, cable-ready" sets. And although a lot of people desperately missed their cable service, the greater and more basic losses suffered by so many others made it socially unacceptable to complain.

In contrast to America's addiction to broadcast entertainment, the *need* for broadcasting remains less recognized. The medium has many positive roles: it entertains, it informs (even commercials sometimes do both), it educates, it serves as companion for the lonely. And in times of crisis, it becomes vital. When Andrew struck, broadcasting was the only link between citizens and those who could offer information, advice, and help. Newspapers and magazines could do nothing; those able to publish were unable to deliver their wares through impassable streets. Even word of mouth failed, as telephones went out of service and streets became closed to automobile traffic.

Only broadcasting could keep south Florida apprised of the storm's gathering strength and minute-by-minute advance. It enticed the reluctant to evacuate low-lying homes, telling them where they could find shelter. It persuaded skeptics to batten down the hatches and to collect food, water, and emergency supplies. Finally, it gave the "all clear" and then moved on to aid both directly and indirectly in efforts to rebuild and recover.

Andrew also illustrated the two-way aspect of broadcasting's impact: events and audiences not only are affected by but also have effects *on* media. Miami stations reported what they termed "fundamental changes" in the way they cover and present news. They planned less-structured programs, working more without scripts and without tightly edited video, as well as an increased number of public-service and "positive" pieces, and of photo-

South Florida Broadcasters Respond to Hurricane Andrew

Hours of Hurricane Coverage Provided During the 3 Days Prior to the Storm

91% of television stations and 98% of radio stations provided coverage. The mean number of hours of coverage provided by area television stations was 13, and the mean number of hours of coverage provided by area radio stations was 10.

Hours of Hurricane Coverage Provided During the Storm and in Its Immediate Aftermath

91% of television stations and 87%* of radio stations provided coverage. The mean number of hours of coverage provided by area television stations was 12, and the mean number of hours of coverage provided by area radio stations was 15.

In addition to providing storm coverage, all television and 87% of responding radio stations participated directly in such relief efforts as raising money, coordinating volunteer efforts, and gathering food, clothing, and supplies.

Advertising Revenue Lost Because of Storm Coverage

*4 of 7 responding stations without coverage had been blown off the air by the storm.

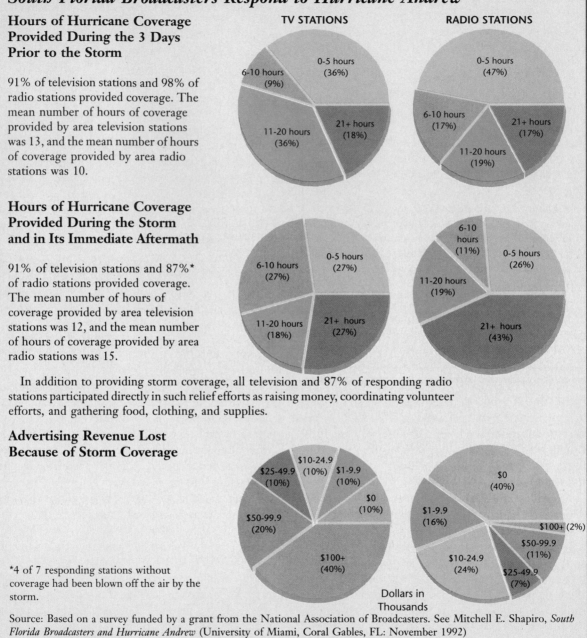

TV STATIONS

0-5 hours (36%)
6-10 hours (9%)
11-20 hours (36%)
21+ hours (18%)

RADIO STATIONS

0-5 hours (47%)
6-10 hours (17%)
21+ hours (17%)
11-20 hours (19%)

0-5 hours (27%)
6-10 hours (27%)
11-20 hours (18%)
21+ hours (27%)

6-10 hours (11%)
0-5 hours (26%)
11-20 hours (19%)
21+ hours (43%)

$10-24.9 (10%)
$25-49.9 (10%)
$1-9.9 (10%)
$0 (10%)
$50-99.9 (20%)
$100+ (40%)

$0 (40%)
$1-9.9 (16%)
$100+ (2%)
$50-99.9 (11%)
$10-24.9 (24%)
$25-49.9 (7%)

Dollars in Thousands

Source: Based on a survey funded by a grant from the National Association of Broadcasters. See Mitchell E. Shapiro, *South Florida Broadcasters and Hurricane Andrew* (University of Miami, Coral Gables, FL: November 1992)

graphic essays in which viewers see no reporter and pictures alone tell the story. Some stations inaugurated a more casual on-air appearance (anchors in shirtsleeves became the norm at the NBC affiliate). And all agreed that, although they considered themselves reasonably well prepared for Andrew, "next time" they would redouble their total preparation effort.

The storm had a significant effect on yet another aspect of the broadcast business—ratings. One specific case: When Dan Rather was the only network anchor to come to Florida to cover the story, the national audience for his *CBS Evening News* shot up by a third, moving his program into the top network-news spot for the first time in three years. Moreover, the network's episode of *48 Hours* that was devoted to Andrew came in number one in the national prime-time rankings for the first time ever. In fact, coverage of Andrew produced dramatic rating increases for all three major television networks, as well as for CNN and The Weather Channel.

At the same time, the storm presented researchers with serious rating problems locally. Because so many homes had been destroyed while thousands of others had no electricity, reliable audience sampling became virtually impossible. One major television rating organization, Arbitron, stopped calculating overnight data in the Miami market for several weeks. Later, it and the other major company, Nielsen, managed with audience sample sizes that were smaller than normal. Similarly, Arbitron published its regular summer rating report for radio, again using a smaller sample size. Broadcasters and advertisers alike welcomed the continuity but questioned the real value of these surveys.

In addition to explaining rating systems, Part 5 of this book also looks at the *impact* of electronic media:

- Broadcasting and cable have *effects*—consequences for both individuals and society.
- Broadcasting ranks as the most universal means of instant public communication, conveying information, entertainment, education, and persuasion.
- Effects run in both directions—from media to the public and from the public to media.

Controls

Chapter 13 of this book describes in detail the extent to which electronic media are controlled—mostly by the Federal Communications Commission (FCC). But even that agency can act with surprising speed to bend rules when necessary.

During the Andrew crisis the FCC operated a special 24-hour telephone service through which broadcasters could obtain emergency waivers and temporary authorizations. For example, when Miami's CBS affiliate lost its tower, the FCC issued a waiver that permitted the station to broadcast at reduced power and from a different location. It gave permission to one all-news radio station to operate temporarily at double its normal power. The Commission also worked with the Department of Defense and the National Telecommunications and Information Administration to allow the army to set up its own AM radio station to transmit relief information.

Normally, any station that goes off the air must answer to the FCC, but under the circumstances this measure presented no cause for concern to those outlets silenced temporarily by the storm. And as noted earlier, radio stations simulcast programs from other radio stations and from television—a practice already permitted by FCC rules.

As Part 6 tells us:

- In order to maintain orderly operation, with a minimum of frequency interference, and to ensure service to the "public interest, convenience, or necessity," the FCC enforces rules that govern how broadcasters and cable operators conduct their business.
- A flexible FCC stands ready to waive or modify rules, however, whenever the need arises.

Global View

As one should expect whenever a major disaster occurs, audiences around the world learned of Andrew's devastation through local electronic media.

From England to Australia, broadcasters carried extensive coverage of the storm and its aftermath—often to the relief or concern of citizens who had relatives in Florida. CNN fed stories to 210 countries. Reporters from as far away as Japan arrived soon after the storm and rented technical facilities from local broadcasters to relay their reports back to their respective countries. One Spanish-language radio station in Miami established a special short-wave hookup with Honduras, Nicaragua, and El Salvador to assist people there in their efforts to locate lost family members.

As we shall see later in Chapter 15:

- Broadcasting is everywhere. More than 200 countries and dependencies have their own radio broadcast stations; about 85 percent of these have television stations.
- Throughout the world, more homes boast radio and television receivers than any other amenity. Millions of people who lack electricity, indoor plumbing, refrigerators, telephones, even common medicines, nevertheless own radios.

Tomorrow

Exciting futures await the electronic media. Technological advances are occurring with dizzying speed. What is possible today was undreamed of only a few years ago. As discussed in Chapter 16, even experts cannot be sure what tomorrow will bring.

Yet Florida's ordeal in August 1992 produced two compelling arguments in the ongoing dialogue that will ultimately shape media in the 21st century:

- While cable offers a wondrous, if sometimes bewildering, array of program options, it can never replace over-the-air communication, so essential when power goes out and utility poles go down.
- Although direct-to-home broadcasts—whether of television or radio—offer new audience options, they can never completely replace *local* outlets, able to respond instantly and knowledgeably in emergency situations. Even the best-intentioned and most informed anchorperson in New York or Washington simply cannot replace the local personality who is able to tell frantic listeners that, because the 79th Street causeway is now under water, they should take the Julia Tuttle, go north on I-95, exit and turn right at 125th Street, go three blocks, and turn left at the gas station to find life-saving shelter.

And Then Came the Floods

In the summer of 1993 torrential rains pounded America's Midwest, overfilling the Mississippi River and its tributaries to record heights. Streets turned into streams and fields into lakes. Thousands of homes, businesses, and farms were destroyed, and countless families were without electricity or running water. Damage estimates, including crop losses, ran into the billions of dollars.

President Clinton cut short a Hawaii vacation to inspect hard-hit Davenport, IA (shown here), and other devastated cities and towns, promising federal assistance. National Guardsmen and the U.S. Army Corps of Engineers filled sandbags and provided drinking water. Florida residents, recalling aid they had received when Andrew struck, formed convoys of volunteers and supplies.

ABC's Peter Jennings, CBS's Dan Rather, and NBC's Tom Brokaw all arrived to cover the story, which led the national newscasts. But once again it was the local broadcaster who came to the immediate rescue of its audience. WGEM-AM of Quincy, IL, for example, devoted 24 hours to flood information. Station reporters, many pressed into service from the operation's business side, offered updates on river stages, bridge closings, and levee conditions. They instructed listeners on where to bring sandbags.

Fielding more than 100 calls an hour (most of them on-air), WGEM also controlled rumors—it was quick to set the record straight when a radio news network erroneously reported that a critical levee had burst.

Unlike Andrew, which came and went within hours, the flood lasted for weeks. Waters receded only to swell again as more rain fell. The storm taxed to the limit the energies of citizen and broadcaster alike.

Source: Photo courtesy the White House.

PART 1

Development

American electronic media developed over a number of decades. The next three chapters trace that evolution: the beginnings with wireless and then radio to 1927 (Chapter 1); the heyday of radio and television for the next half-century (Chapter 2); and the introduction of newer electronic media in the past decade or so (Chapter 3). We consider inventors who made electronic media possible, along with business innovators who made it universal reality. We follow the growth of systems and content from the first tentative programs and hookups of the 1920s' crystal-set era to the host of electronic media choices available in the 1990s. *Our emphasis here is on how present-day electronic media owe much of their structure and operation to decisions made years ago.*

Chapter 1

Rise of Radio

• •

While it took a century to introduce photography into general use, half a century for the telephone, and 35 years for radio technology, radio *broadcasting* took only about eight years. The preconditions for its emergence had been evolving for at least a century. Several developments intertwined: (1) emergence of social conditions favorable to the development of mass communications (urbanization, better education, more leisure time), leading to the habit of media consumption; (2) development of industrial and business institutions able to provide consumer goods in quantity (including entertainment and news); and (3) scientific progress that developed new ways of communicating that content.

• • • • • • • •

Precedents

The idea—and widespread habit—of mass media consumption had already been developed by popular newspapers, the phonograph, and the motion picture long before broadcasting began. These older media arose from the mechanical tradition of the 19th century and from fundamental social changes brought about by the Industrial Revolution (which took place from roughly 1750 to 1850). For centuries, the primary occupation of most people had been agriculture; but industrial employment increasingly drew people away from the land until by the mid-20th century, most people lived and worked in cities.

Those concentrations of city dwellers became the target of what we now call the *mass media*—those means of communication that employ print or electronic or film technology to reach thousands or millions of people, at about the same time, offering entertainment and information that most people like, at a price most can afford.

Penny Press

Urban concentration, education and rising literacy, and more leisure time all contributed to the transformation of newspapers from something primarily for the elite to a commonplace product for everyone. The "penny press" signaled this transformation. After 1833, the New York *Sun* led a trend toward mass-appeal and mass-produced papers. They sold for just a penny a copy, first in the thousands and eventually in the hundreds of thousands of copies.

Until that time, newspapers had concentrated on news of commerce, party politics, and other "serious" topics. The new penny press broadened the range of subjects covered, telling of everyday events, sensational crimes, gossip, human-interest stories, and sports—all presented in an easy, breezy style that contrasted with flowery essays of the past. Penny newspapers built their appeal by cutting across lines of class, sex, age, political party, and cherished beliefs. By the 1890s some penny papers had circulations over a million. They helped to create a habit of mass media consumption on which broadcasting would later build.

Vaudeville

Early broadcasting also drew heavily from vaudeville, itself a successor to traveling minstrel shows. Hugely popular from 1880 to 1920, vaudeville featured song-and-dance teams, short plays, Irish tenors, and ethnic comics, and filled theaters in cities large and small. New York had 37 vaudeville houses, Philadelphia 30, and Chicago 22. Hundreds operated in smaller towns across the country. By the turn of the century, vaudeville theaters began showing bits of novelty film as a filler while clearing the house between programs—"an ironic foreshadowing of impending doom" (Nye, 1970: 171). At its peak, the vaudeville circuit sold more tickets than did all other kinds of entertainment combined.

Then came movies, followed by radio. These newer media could earn more because they brought entertainers to national audiences without transporting troupes and all their baggage, scenery, and musical instruments from town to town. The new media drew on the same vaudeville talent pool. Song-and-patter teams proved especially adaptable to radio. Famous radio comics Jack Benny and Fred Allen started in vaudeville. Musical variety shows of network radio and, later, of television had their beginnings in vaudeville.

The Phonograph

A late-19th-century invention, the phonograph, like vaudeville, prepared people for broadcasting's future role. Owning a phonograph made people comfortable with investing in a piece of furniture that brought entertainment home. By the end of World War I—on the eve of broadcasting's introduction—some 200 phonograph manufacturers turned out more than two million players each year.

As broadcasting developed in the 1920s, phonograph recording still depended on obsolete acoustic methods that were little different from those used by Thomas Edison in 1878. Competition from broadcasting and the Depression devastated the phonograph industry, and by 1933 it was "practically extinct" (Gelatt, 1977: 265).

Ironically, not long after it drove many phonograph companies out of business, broadcasting increased audiences for music of all kinds while supplying technology for improved sound-recording quality.

Motion Pictures

Cinema evolved at the same time as the phonograph. In fact, Edison played a key role in both developments, marketing a "kinetoscope" motion-picture camera in 1889. He modified it slightly in the 1890s to turn it into a peep-show device that enabled viewers, one at a time, to watch brief sequences of pictures in silent motion. Like the phonograph industry, motion pictures were well established by the time broadcasting began in 1920. The movies catered to a mass audience for information as well as entertainment: news reels formed an important part of movie theater presentations until television newscasts superseded them in 1967.

Radio technology had something to teach motion pictures—the ability to talk. The need for *synchronized* sound (precise matching of sound and picture) limited progress toward "talkies." These finally began in earnest in 1928, however, with several rival sound systems competing for acceptance. One such sound system had been developed by RCA, owner of the first national radio network—an example of the many links between broadcasting and motion pictures long before the advent of television.

●●●●●●●●

1.2 Wire Communication

Although broadcasting built on prior arts of sound recording and movies, its direct technical and industrial foundations were the telegraph and the telephone—point-to-point rather than mass-oriented media. Thus it was *electronic technology*, rather than the mechanical technology of early phonographs and movies, that led to radio's invention and, eventually, to its application to mass as well as individual needs.

Telegraph

Few people needed instant communication beyond the horizon until the coming of early railroads. Then some means of signaling to distant stations became essential for safe and efficient rail operations. To meet this need, the British developed a form of *electrical telegraphy* in the 1820s.* Electrical impulses sent along a wire caused deflections of a pointer in a detecting device at the receiving end. An operator "read" messages by interpreting the pointer's movements.

An American artist, Samuel F. B. Morse, after extensive experiments in the 1830s, made significant improvements. His telegraph receiver had the great advantage of automatically recording messages on strips of paper. We still refer to *Morse code* for the system that he and a partner developed for translating letters of the alphabet into patterns of electrical impulses.

*The word *telegraphy* (which literally means "distant writing") had long referred to relaying of semaphore (visual) messages through a series of line-of-sight signaling stations. Slowly telegraphy—and a later word *telephony*—came to refer, respectively, to code and voice communication by wire. Early in this century, telegraphy or telephony, preceded by the words *wireless* or *radio*, would signal the technologies discussed here. Today, telephony usually includes voice and data technologies that—along with computers—are rapidly converging with those of broadcasting.

With assistance from federal money, Morse in 1844 installed the first U.S. operational telegraph line, linking Washington, DC, and Baltimore. The first message sent over its 40-mile line suggests the awe produced by this achievement: "What hath God wrought!"

In most countries, governments still operate national telecommunications systems. Congress, however, fearing that the Post Office would lose money if government competed with the mails by running a telegraph service as well, sold out to private investors, retaining only the right to regulate that service. By the end of the Civil War in 1865, Western Union had emerged to dominate telegraphy—the first big communications monopoly.

Underwater Cables

Laying telegraph lines underwater offered new challenges. Technological and financial limitations frustrated several early attempts to lay a cable beneath the Atlantic Ocean. Regular transatlantic cable telegraphy finally began in 1866. Soon Europe and America could exchange information in minutes instead of weeks or months. Faster international communication brought profound changes in trade, politics, diplomacy, and war.

Cables and telegraphy had an early and lasting association with news. Even before the electric telegraph became widely available, newspapers had begun to share costs of news gathering—the first form of media syndication. The British news agency Reuters "followed the cable" wherever it led, establishing one of the first international *news agencies* or *news wire services*. The Associated Press began in New York in the 1840s, and soon other nations followed suit.

Bell's Telephone

By the 1870s inventors in many countries had been seeking means of transmitting speech, eliminating the tedious business of encoding and decoding telegraph messages. Sound, of course, involves much more complex variations of electric current than do simple "on-off" telegraph signals. The problem centered on finding a sensitive *transducer*, a device able to convert complex sound energy from one medium (air) to another (electric current). Many investigators seemed close to a solution when Alexander Graham Bell filed for his key telephone patent in 1876.

Bell organized his original telephone firm a year later, when he received a second essential patent. But he and his friends could not raise enough capital to develop the new invention. Patent control soon passed to others who went on to develop what is known today as American Telephone and Telegraph (AT&T).*

AT&T as Big Business

Rather than trying to serve the entire country directly, AT&T adopted a policy of franchising regional operating companies. These firms received exclusive rights to use Bell's patents. In turn, the firms gave AT&T substantial stock holdings. By the time the Bell patents expired in 1893–1894, AT&T had controlling interests in most franchise companies. Furthermore, AT&T had developed long lines to connect central offices of telephone companies with one another. AT&T ensured its supremacy in this long-distance field in 1914 by acquiring a key radio invention, the Audion (see Section 1.3), making coast-to-coast telephone service possible. With AT&T's 1881 purchase of Western Electric as its manufacturing arm, the whole process of manufacture, installation, and servicing was integrated within the Bell companies—a vertical structure that a century later led to the breakup of what was then still a near-monopoly.

*Telephone service developing in Europe in the 1880s led to a long-lasting broadcast-like service in Budapest, Hungary. After several earlier experiments, the *Telefon Hirmondo* or "Telephonic Newspaper" began in 1893 to connect homes by telephone wire to a central office. The service soon provided a 12-hour daily schedule of news, sports, stocks, concerts, authors reading from their books, and other programming, supported in part by advertising. Subscribers listened on earphones. The Budapest service was "broadcasting" in every sense except in its use of wires. It survived into the 1930s before radio superseded its mode of delivery. Similar but smaller experiments took place in Britain and elsewhere (one lasted a few months in Newark, New Jersey, in 1911) and were widely publicized at the time.

Control of key patents led to the first great telecommunications monopolies. Western Union, when first offered the fledgling Bell patent in 1877 for a mere $100,000 (several million dollars in today's values), turned down the chance, regarding telephony as unimportant to its monopoly position. Yet in very few years telephony's expansion had carried AT&T to much greater size and scope than Western Union. Indeed, AT&T bought out its older rival in 1910 and held it until pressured by the government to sell three years later.

This near-monopoly of early telephony, plus extensive research and operating experience, allowed AT&T to dominate radio in the 1920s, when the company saw broadcasting as a form of telephony (see Section 1.8). The need for interconnecting broadcast networks gave AT&T a continuing role providing wire and microwave relays into the 1980s.

During the early 1900s, AT&T's manufacturing arm, Western Electric, ranked as one of the largest industrial concerns in the country. With General Electric (GE) and Westinghouse, it virtually dictated trends in the electrical industry and set its tone for reaction to early wireless communication. GE helped develop the vacuum tube, which was key to wireless innovation, and became a major investor in early radio stations. Even before GE did so, its great rival Westinghouse owned broadcast stations (including pioneer Pittsburgh station KDKA, discussed at Section 1.7).

Westinghouse, GE, and AT&T's Western Electric thus formed a powerful trio in electric lighting, power, and communication. Their patent control, economic power, and know-how strongly shaped development of wireless and broadcasting.

• • • • • • • •

1.3 Invention of Wireless

The notion that it should somehow be possible to send telegraph and telephone messages without costly and confining wire connections stimulated inventive juices of scientists and tinkerers late in the 19th century, and still does today.

Conflicting Claims

Inventors in many countries claimed to have been first in solving problems of wireless transmission. Most had common access to critically important scientific knowledge about electromagnetic energy that appeared in documents published by two physicists: (1) an 1873 theoretical paper by James Clerk Maxwell, predicting the existence of invisible radiant energy similar to light; and (2) an even more important 1888 report of a laboratory experiment by Heinrich Hertz, in which he proved Maxwell's theory by generating and detecting radio energy and measuring its wavelength.

Hertz's paper, *Electromagnetic Waves and Their Reflection*, led to the invention of a viable wireless system within a few years of its publication.* But Hertz sought merely to verify a scientific theory, not to innovate a new means of communication. He failed to realize practical implications of his experiments.

Marconi's "Releasing Touch"

It remained for Guglielmo Marconi—more practical inventor than theory-based scientist—to supply the "right releasing touch," as a Supreme Court justice put it (US, 1942: 65). Stimulated by Hertz's paper, young Marconi experimented with similar equipment, first indoors and then on the grounds of his father's estate near Bologna, Italy. Endless experiments with different shapes, sizes, and types of antennas, ground systems, and other components gradually improved performance of his pioneering wireless system. Fortunately, Marconi had both leisure time for experimentation and money for equipment.

Equally important, he had access through his family to necessary official and business circles. His mother (part of a wealthy British family) arranged introductions to important English postal and military officials, the most likely customers for Marconi's invention after Italian officials expressed little

*In recognition of his contribution's importance, Hertz's name, abbreviated Hz, with the meaning "one cycle per second," has been adopted internationally as the standard way to express frequency of radio waves (see Section 4.3).

Exhibit 1.a ● ● ● ● ● ● ● ● ● ● ● ● ● ●

Guglielmo Marconi (1874–1937)

In a 1902 photo, the inventor examines paper tape bearing a radiographic message in Morse code. Though radio equipment still remained very crude, well-developed wire telegraphy equipment could be readily adapted to record wireless messages. Seated is George Kemp, Marconi's most trusted engineering assistant.

Source: Photo courtesy Smithsonian Institution, Washington, DC.

interest. Marconi, by then 22, went to London and registered his patent in 1896. In 1897, he launched his own company, with help from his mother's family, to manufacture wireless equipment and to offer public wireless telegraphic service.

To a remarkable degree Marconi combined the genius of an inventor with that of a business innovator. As an inventor he persisted tirelessly, never discouraged, even by hundreds of failed attempts at solving a problem. As a business manager he had a flair for effective public relations. In the early 1900s he repeatedly staged dramatic and convincing demonstrations to prove the usefulness of wireless communication (see Exhibit 1.a). In 1909 Marconi received the Nobel prize in physics (shared with Germany's Ferdinand Braun) for achievements in wireless telegraphy.

Among Marconi's business ventures, the U.S. branch known as American Marconi had a decisive influence on the development of broadcasting in America. Founded in 1899, American Marconi began to realize substantial profits as late as 1913, when it had achieved a virtual monopoly on U.S. wireless communication: by then, it owned 17 land stations and 400 shipboard facilities. All used a wireless extension of the telegraph principle: point-to-point communication between ships and shore stations, between ships at sea, and between countries.

Technical Advances

For some 20 years, radio waves could be transmitted only in short bursts, suitable for radio telegraphy but not for speech. The *vacuum tube oscillator* finally provided a *continuous* signal effective for transmission of spoken words.

As serious a problem was the detection, or sensing, of incoming signals. Marconi and later inventors worked on a variety of approaches. In 1904 Marconi obtained a U.S. patent that enabled his transmitters to focus their radiation to a limited group of frequencies. Receivers could then select, or *tune* to, desired frequencies, excluding simultaneous signals present in other parts of the spectrum.

Early equipment also lacked any means of making incoming signals louder. Resolution of these related problems of signal generation, detection, and amplification came with invention of an improved vacuum tube, which made radio *broadcasting* possible. For that reason, its inventor, Lee de Forest, felt justified in titling his 1950 autobiography *Father of Radio*.

De Forest's Audion

After receiving a Yale Ph.D. in 1899, de Forest focused on developing inventions. Following the leads of Edison's electric light in 1883 and Marconi researcher Ambrose Fleming's vacuum tube of 1904, he experimented with creating a radio detector by using a glowing filament to heat gas within a glass enclosure. Both Edison and Fleming had patented devices based upon the then-unexplained fact that an electric current would flow between a hot filament and a nearby metal plate, both inside the lamp. Because such lamps or tubes had two elements, the filament and the plate, they were called *diodes*.

De Forest made the crucial improvement by adding a third element to the tube, creating a *triode*. He positioned his new element, the *grid*, between filament and plate. A small voltage applied to the grid could control with great precision the flow of electrons from filament to plate. Thus a weak signal could be amplified. De Forest first used the triode— or *Audion*, as one of his associates dubbed it—in 1906.

Full development of the Audion and related circuits took more than a dozen years, in part because de Forest did not fully understand his own creation. Its first practical application improved not radio but telephone service. In 1913, AT&T purchased telephone rights for Audions (to be used as amplifiers in telephone lines), making initial coast-to-coast long-distance calls possible two years later.

• • • • • • • •

1.4 Early Wireless Services

During its first two decades, wireless as a business made its money by supplying *point-to-point* and *point-to-multipoint* services at long distance, usually over water. Land wireless services had little appeal because of existing telephone and telegraph lines. Wireless manufacturing was limited to meeting needs of the few communications service companies. The mass market for thousands of broadcast transmitters and millions of receivers lay in the future.

Maritime Applications

Naturally, world maritime powers took an immediate interest in wireless technology. Wireless assisted during a maritime disaster as early as 1898. Both the British and American navies began experimenting with ship installations in 1899. And the Japanese victory in the 1904–1905 Russo-Japanese War was due in part to superiority of Japanese Marconi-supplied equipment over that used by the Russian Navy.

Commercial ships were early customers for radio services. Radio allowed them to communicate with one another over long distances and with coastal stations far beyond the horizon. In 1909, when the SS *Republic* sank off New York, wireless-alerted rescue ships saved her passengers. Each year the number of dramatic rescues increased (see Exhibit 1.b).

Transoceanic Wireless

Long-distance radio communication across oceans held commercial promise as an alternative to expensive submarine telegraph cables, but because of technical limitations this radio service did not become strongly competitive until the 1920s. In the meantime, the Marconi company, which dominated the transatlantic wireless business, had built several high-power coastal stations in North America prior to the outbreak of World War I in 1914.

In 1917 GE installed a 200-kilowatt *alternator* in its facility at New Brunswick, New Jersey. The alternator, a huge and costly machine, put out a powerful very low frequency (VLF) signal at about 20 kHz.* It represented a major improvement in long-distance radio communication, even though vacuum tube transmitters largely displaced alternators during the 1920s. This aided development of the short-wave (high-frequency) portion of the spectrum, which turned out to be much more efficient than the lower frequencies that had previously been used for long-distance communication. A sharp rise in transatlantic radio traffic followed.

*For an explanation of the "kHz" abbreviation, see Section 4.1.

Wireless Goes to War

When America entered World War I in April 1917, the U.S. Navy took over all wireless stations in the country, dismantling most "for the duration" and running the remainder for its own needs. The Army Signal Corps and Air Service also used radio. Some 10,000 soldiers and sailors received training in wireless. After the war, they helped popularize the new medium, forming a core of amateur enthusiasts, laboratory technicians, and electronics manufacturing employees. They also constituted a ready-made audience for the first broadcasting services.

To mobilize the best wireless resources of the country for war, the navy decreed a moratorium on patent lawsuits. Manufacturers agreed to "pool" patents, making them available to one another without risk of infringement. Thus wartime need brought about an important transition. Previously, wireless had been dominated mainly by inventor-entrepreneurs, struggling to market their discoveries while feverishly experimenting on new ones. After the war, big business took over. AT&T added wireless rights to its original purchase of telephone rights to de Forest's Audion. GE owned the powerful alternator patents and had the ability to mass-produce vacuum tubes. And Westinghouse, another producer of vacuum tubes, looked for new ways of capitalizing on wireless.

• • • • • • • •

1.5 Radio Experimenters

All the wireless services discussed thus far used *radiotelegraphy*, or code—not voice transmission. Throughout this period, however, eager experimenters sought the key to *radiotelephony*, the essential precursor of broadcasting.

Fessenden's 1906 "Broadcast"

Reginald Fessenden made the first-known voice broadcast. Using an ordinary telephone as a crude microphone and an alternator to generate radio

Exhibit 1.b • • • • • • • • • • • • •

Titanic *Disaster (April 1912)*

A luxury liner advertised as unsinkable, the *Titanic*, struck an iceberg and sank in the Atlantic on her maiden voyage from Britain to the United States in April 1912. One heroic Marconi radio operator stayed at his post and went down with the ship, although the second operator survived. Some 1,500 people died—among them some of the most famous names in the worlds of art, science, finance, and diplomacy—partially because each nearby vessel, unlike the *Titanic*, had but one radio operator (all that was then required), who had already turned in for the night. Only by chance did the operator on a ship some 50 miles distant hear distress calls from the *Titanic*. It steamed full speed to the disaster site, rescuing about 700 survivors.

Source: Photo from UPI/Bettmann Archive.

The fact that for days radiotelegraphy maintained the world's only thread of contact with the survivors aboard the rescue liner *Carpathia* as it steamed toward New York brought the new medium of wireless to public attention as nothing else had done. Subsequent British and American inquiries revealed that a more sensible use of wireless (such as a 24-hour radio watch) could have saved more lives. Because of such findings, the *Titanic* disaster influenced the worldwide adoption of stringent laws governing shipboard wireless stations. The *Titanic* tragedy also set a precedent for regarding the radio business as having a special public responsibility. This concept carried over into broadcasting legislation a quarter of a century later.

Exhibit 1.c •••••• • • • • • • •

Reginald Fessenden (1866–1932) at Brant Rock

Fessenden (center) stands with some of his associates in front of the building where he made the historic 1906 broadcast. The column in the background is the base of his antenna. The adjustable tower, shown complete in the distant postcard view, was taken down around 1912.

The Wireless Station-Brant Rock, Mass.
No. 1691 Moore & Gibson Co., New-York. Germany

Sources: Left photo courtesy Smithsonian Institution, Washington, DC; right photo from Christopher H. Sterling.

---

energy, Fessenden transmitted on Christmas Eve 1906 from Brant Rock, on the Massachusetts coast south of Boston (see Exhibit 1.c). He played a violin, sang, read from the Bible, and transmitted a phonograph recording. Ship wireless operators heard the transmission far out at sea, amazed to hear what some called "angel" voices and music in earphones that until then had brought them only static and the harsh staccato of Morse code. Fessenden's historic

transmission led a long string of demonstrations that culminated in the start of regular broadcasting services in 1920.

De Forest's Experiments

Audion inventor Lee de Forest, a lover of fine music, also felt the challenge of radiotelephony and naturally turned toward it. In 1907, hard on Fessenden's

Exhibit 1.d

Lee de Forest (1873–1961)

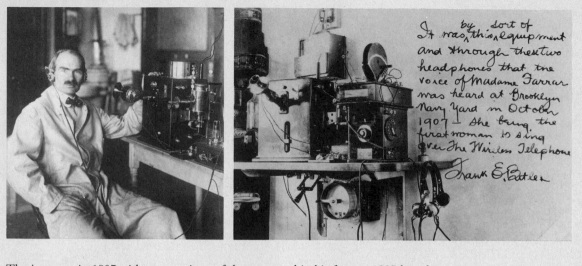

It was, by sort of this, equipment and through these two headphones that the voice of Madame Farrar was heard at Brooklyn Navy Yard in October 1907 — she being the first woman to sing over the Wireless Telephone

Frank E. Butler

The inventor in 1907 with a transmitter of the type used in his famous 1907 broadcast, along with a shipboard receiver of the type that picked up the transmission.

Sources: De Forest photo from Culver Pictures; transmission photo courtesy Smithsonian Institution, Washington, DC.

heels, he made experimental voice and music transmissions from a building in downtown New York City (see Exhibit 1.d). By 1916 de Forest had begun using his Audion as an oscillator to generate radio-frequency energy. In doing so, he chose electronic means of generation rather than the alternator's mechanical approach. He set up an experimental transmitter that year in his Bronx home and began transmitting phonograph recordings and announcements. De Forest aired election returns in November 1916 (anticipating by four years the opening broadcast of KDKA—see Section 1.7). Many others also made radiotelephone transmissions at university laboratories and in private research facilities during the early years of the century.

• • • • • • • •

1.6 Government Monopoly: The Road Not Taken

The military importance of radio during World War I raised the question as to whether temporary government control should become a permanent monopoly. Though the war ended in November 1918, the navy didn't relinquish control of radio facilities until early 1920. The critical decisions made during this 18-month period profoundly affected the future of broadcasting in America.

The Navy's Claims

Was radio too vital to entrust to private hands? The navy thought so. In fact, it had always asserted jurisdiction over radio as primarily a natural marine service. Concerned about renewed patent gridlock with the wartime emergency's end, the navy supported a bill introduced in the House of Representatives late in 1918 that proposed to make radio a permanent government monopoly. Despite strong arguments from navy brass, the bill failed to pass.

Restoration of private ownership in 1920, however, meant returning most commercial wireless communications facilities in the United States to a foreign-owned company, American Marconi. (Former German stations had already passed to American hands.) Marconi also seemed about to capture exclusive rights to an important American invention, GE's alternator, which had so greatly improved transoceanic radiotelegraphy late in the war. Disturbed at the prospect that American Marconi might consolidate a U.S. monopoly by capturing such rights, the navy strongly opposed the deal. British Marconi, as parent of the American subsidiary, found itself caught in a squeeze play—unable to expand without the alternator patents. With implied government approval, the head of GE, Owen D. Young, negotiated the purchase of American Marconi.

RCA Founded

GE created a new subsidiary in the fall of 1919 to carry on American Marconi's extensive wireless telegraphy business, calling it the Radio Corporation of America (RCA). Under RCA's charter, all its officers had to be Americans and at least 80 percent of its stock had to be in American hands. RCA took over American Marconi's assets late in 1919. Eventually RCA's name became intimately linked with broadcasting, but its initial founders had no plans to enter a field few then imagined.

Westinghouse and AT&T joined GE as investors in RCA. AT&T sold its interest in 1923; but RCA remained under GE and Westinghouse control until 1932, when an antitrust suit forced them to sell their stock, making RCA an independent corporation.

David Sarnoff, who would play the dominant RCA leadership role, had started with American Marconi as a radio code clerk and later became assistant traffic manager of the company's radiotelegraphy business. When RCA took over in 1919, he stayed on with the new firm and was promoted to commercial manager. He helped to convert the company from a limited operation into a major corporation presiding over many subsidiaries. Sarnoff became president of the company in 1930, chairperson of the board in 1947, and finally retired in 1969. As *Time* said in its 1971 obituary, his was "one of the last great autocracies in U.S. industry."

Patents Pooled

RCA and its parent companies each held important radio patents, yet each found itself blocked by patents held by the others. In the 1919–1923 period, AT&T, GE, Westinghouse, RCA, and other minor players worked out a series of *cross-licensing* agreements, modeled after the navy-run patent pool of World War I. These allowed the companies to use one another's patents—and thus to carve up the radio service and equipment market. Within just a few years, however, these carefully worked out plans fell into utter confusion because of the astonishing growth of a new use for radiotelephony— broadcasting.

● ● ● ● ● ● ● ●

1.7 The "First" Broadcast Station

Amateur Beginnings

In 1920 Dr. Frank Conrad, an engineer with Westinghouse in Pittsburgh, operated an amateur radio

Exhibit 1.e

Conrad's 8XK and Its Successor, KDKA

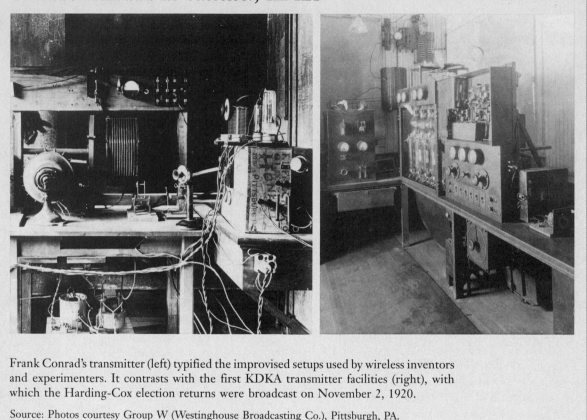

Frank Conrad's transmitter (left) typified the improvised setups used by wireless inventors and experimenters. It contrasts with the first KDKA transmitter facilities (right), with which the Harding-Cox election returns were broadcast on November 2, 1920.

Source: Photos courtesy Group W (Westinghouse Broadcasting Co.), Pittsburgh, PA.

station, 8XK, in connection with his experimental work at the factory (see Exhibit 1.e). Conrad fell into the habit of transmitting recorded music, sports results, and bits of talk in response to requests from other amateurs, or "hams." These informal "programs" built up so much interest that they were mentioned in newspapers. None of this was unusual—similar amateur transmissions had been made by others elsewhere around the world. What

made Conrad's 8XK transmissions different was the chain of events that resulted.

Horne's department store in Pittsburgh, sensing growing public interest in wireless, wondered whether people might be willing to *buy* receiving sets to pick up Conrad's broadcasts. Until then, wireless had catered to engineers and technical amateurs: if you wanted to listen in, you made your own receiver. Horne's store installed a demonstration receiver and ran a statement in its regular newspaper display advertisement of September 22, 1920: " 'Air Concert' Picked Up by Radio Here . . . . Amateur Wireless Sets made by the maker of the Set which is in operation in our store, are on sale here $10.00 up."

Opening of KDKA

Westinghouse executives saw the potential for a novel merchandising tie-in: it could manufacture radio receivers and create a demand for these products by regularly transmitting programs to the general public. Accordingly, Westinghouse ordered conversion of a radiotelegraph transmitter for broadcasting. It went on the air as station KDKA from an improvised studio at the Westinghouse factory in East Pittsburgh on November 2, 1920.

KDKA's opening coincided with the 1920 presidential election, so the maiden broadcast consisted of election returns, fed to the station by telephone from a newspaper office, interspersed with phonograph and live banjo music. Soon after the election, KDKA began a regular (one-hour-per-evening) broadcast schedule of music and talk.

First Listeners

Broadcasting would have developed much more slowly had it not been for a ready-made audience of thousands of amateur set builders who created demand for a type of radio service never before supplied as a business—entertainment. In order to appreciate 8XK and KDKA's fascination for listeners of the day, remember that, with rare exceptions, previous wireless signals had been restricted to monotonous Morse code. To hear music and voices instead was a startling and thrilling experience.

The audience quickly expanded beyond radio amateurs. Many enthusiasts built inexpensive homemade crystal sets (Exhibit 1.f). But the experience of listening-in created a huge public appetite for receiver improvements: first (after 1922) one detector vacuum tube, then another tube for an amplifier, then more tubes for a superheterodyne circuit (for greatly improved reception), then a loudspeaker. Manufacturers could not keep up with demand.

KDKA's Success

Unhampered by competing signals, KDKA's skywave signal (described at Section 4.5) could be picked up at great distances. Newspapers all over the country and even in Canada printed the station's program schedule. To assist in reception of DX signals (DX refers to long distance—meaning almost any station in another town), local stations often observed a "silent night" once a week so as not to interfere with more distant incoming signals.

In its first year of operation, KDKA pioneered many types of programs that later became standard radio fare: orchestra music, church services, public-service announcements, political addresses, sports events, dramas, and market reports. But KDKA lacked one now-familiar type of broadcast material—*commercials*. Westinghouse did not sell advertising, bearing the entire expense in order to promote sales of its own products. Manufacturers took it for granted that each firm that wanted to promote its wares over the air would open its own station.

KDKA meets five criteria that qualify it as the *oldest U.S. radio broadcasting station*, despite many other claims based on earlier experiments, demonstrations, or temporary operations. KDKA (1) used radio waves (2) to send out noncoded signals (3) in a continuous, scheduled program service (4) intended for the general public, and (5) was licensed by the government to provide such a service (Baudino & Kittross, 1977).* It was still operated by Westinghouse more than 70 years later.

Competition Begins

Westinghouse did not dominate radio for long. Broadcast operations had strong appeal for department stores, newspapers, educational institutions, churches, and electrical equipment supply dealers. Though the number of stations increased slowly in 1920, with 30 licenses issued by the end of the year,

---

*No *broadcasting* licenses as such existed in 1920. KDKA received a license equivalent to the ones issued to commercial shore stations that exchanged radiotelegraph messages with ships under the Radio Act of 1912 (see Section 1.10).

Exhibit 1.f ●●●●●●●●●●●●●●

Changing Radio Receivers

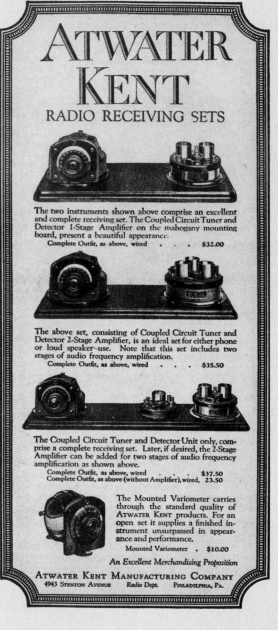

Early radio receivers, all battery-powered, either were homemade or, after 1921, could be purchased in stores. Here are ads for two better-known early brands—an inexpensive Crosley "Pup" sold from 1925 to 1928 as store-purchased sets began to outnumber homemades, and a 1923 series of Atwater Kent "breadboard" receivers (so-called for the way they appeared sitting on a flat board).

the new industry had gathered momentum by the spring of 1922. In that year alone, 100,000 receivers were sold. By May more than 200 stations had been licensed; by early 1923 some 576 were on the air.

Among those early stations, however, mortality ran high. Would-be broadcasters hastened to get in on the ground floor of—they knew not quite what. Inadequately backed stations soon fell by the wayside. Educational stations in particular lost out in this survival-of-the-fittest process.

● ● ● ● ● ● ● ●

1.8   Emergence of an Industry

No such problems of money or managerial support bothered two leading New York City stations—WJZ, flagship station of the "Radio Group" (GE, Westinghouse, and RCA), and WEAF, flagship of the "Telephone Group" (AT&T and Western Electric). These owner-groups represented two very different conceptions of broadcasting.

Rival Station Approaches

After KDKA, Westinghouse opened WJZ in October 1921. As a manufacturing member of the Radio Group, Westinghouse first saw its stations as a way to stimulate interest in its own products. Recognizing that attractive programming motivated people to buy receivers, both KDKA and WJZ took responsibility for producing programs.

As AT&T put WEAF on the air in August 1922, no expense was spared to give the station every technical advantage. Seeing broadcasting as a common carrier (merely a new form of telephony), however, AT&T made clear it would "furnish *no programs whatsoever* over that station" (Dept. of Commerce, 1922: 7, italics supplied). In a 1922 press release, AT&T emphasized its approach:

> Just as the company leases its long distance wire facilities for the use of newspapers, banks, and other concerns, so it will lease its radio telephone facilities and will not provide the matter which is sent out from this station (quoted in Banning, 1946: 68).

It soon became clear, however, that filling WEAF's schedule entirely with leased time simply would not work. Potential advertisers, to which stations might sell time to raise money, had no idea how to develop programs capable of attracting listeners. AT&T therefore found itself forced into show business after all—a decidedly uncomfortable role for a regulated monopoly extremely sensitive about maintaining a dignified public image.

Thus the two groups started with opposing ideas about how broadcasting should work. In the end, both sides had part of the answer. The Radio Group's idea that each company would own a separate station devoted exclusively to promoting that owner's goods was not practical. The Telephone Group correctly foresaw that the number of stations would have to be limited and that each would have to be used by many different advertisers. It miscalculated, however, in placing the primary emphasis on message senders rather than on the interest of the general public, whose good will (and ears) had to be earned. Thus the Radio Group's acceptance of station-centered programming responsibility prevailed. It took about four years for these conflicting ideas to sort themselves out.

"Toll" Broadcasting

WEAF called advertiser-purchased time "toll" broadcasting. It carried the first toll broadcast—a radio advertisement—on August 28, 1922 (see Exhibit 1.g). True to AT&T's concept, WEAF at first allowed advertisers to fill all their time with their own sales message. The idea that advertising would occur only through occasional announcements in programs consisting mostly of entertainment came later.

AT&T thought in terms of *institutional* advertising; nothing so crass as price would be mentioned. In 1923 the first weekly advertiser appeared on WEAF, sponsoring a musical group it called "The Browning King Orchestra"—a handy way to ensure frequent mention of the sponsor's name, though the fact that Browning King sold clothing went unmentioned.

"Toll" Radio and the Rise of Sponsorship

Broadcast advertising began at AT&T-owned WEAF in New York, on August 28, 1922, with a ten-minute talk about a new apartment development in Jackson Heights on Long Island. The ad cost $50 and led to apartment sales exceeding $27,000 (Felix, 1927: 3). The company purchased four more daytime $50 ads and the first evening spot for $100. But advertising on radio developed slowly: only two other companies—an oil company and American Express—had "rented the phone booth" by the next month (Barnouw, 1978: 16). Some Manhattan department stores also tried the microphone during the Christmas season. In the first few months WEAF earned a few hundred dollars from these fledgling "sponsors."

Most of the new advertisements were talks—simply an announcer speaking to the audience for several minutes. A few early ads offered gifts to listeners who wrote in, and the hundreds who responded gave added impetus to advertisers and ad agencies standing on the sidelines, unsure as to how they would handle this new sound medium when their only experience had been with print.

To our way of thinking, the ads were very genteel in tone and content. They mentioned neither price nor a store's specific location. In early 1923 WEAF began to carry a weekly one-hour music program named after the sponsor, Browning King men's clothes. But what the sponsor made went unmentioned—just the name of the program helped keep the advertiser in the public eye. Soon many other companies took up the same approach, dropping overt sales messages for simple company-name recognition in the program title. The first book on radio advertising, which appeared in 1927, supported such indirect approaches, arguing that radio "clearly was not an advertising medium, useful in disseminating sales arguments and selling points" (Felix, 1927: 9).

As CBS and NBC developed and the Depression increased pressure on revenues, broadcasters and ad agencies alike learned how to persuade more potential sponsors to take to the air.

"Chain" Broadcasting

AT&T interpreted the cross-licensing agreements as giving it the right to prevent other broadcasters from connecting broadcast equipment to its telephone lines. WEAF soon began to capitalize on this advantage.

Networking began in 1923 with the first permanent station interconnection between WEAF and WMAF (South Dartmouth, Massachusetts), the latter owned by a rich eccentric for his own amusement. He persuaded WEAF to feed him both toll (commercial) and nontoll (sustaining) programs, paying a fee for the latter and broadcasting the commercial programs without additional cost to the advertisers.

AT&T gradually added to its "chain" (network) of stations. In October 1924, it set up a temporary coast-to-coast chain of 22 stations to carry a speech by President Calvin Coolidge. The regular network at this time, however, consisted of only 6 stations, to which WEAF fed three hours of programming a day. At first, regular AT&T telephone lines linked stations together; but by 1926 the telephone company began setting aside special improved circuits for exclusive use of its radio network.

Refused network interconnection by AT&T, Radio Group stations turned to Western Union's telegraph lines, even though they provided too narrow a band of frequencies for satisfactory broadcast use. Despite these difficulties, in 1923 WJZ opened a station in Washington, DC, and by 1925 it had organized its own network of 14 stations.

New Cross-Licensing Agreements

The growing market for broadcasting equipment, especially receivers, upset the delicate balance of commercial interests that the original RCA cross-licensing agreements had served. Those agreements covered only point-to-point wireless and did not account for broadcasting. Thus there were no rules among the patent partners for manufacture of broadcast transmitters and receivers. The public appetite for sets was insatiable and would not be filled for years to come. Lines of customers formed in front of stores that had any sets or parts. Dealers needed a full year to catch up on orders. A federal suit alleging that the patent pool violated antitrust laws (because pool members tried to control both the manufacture and sale of all radio equipment) added urgency to the need for change. By 1926 AT&T concluded that its original concept of broadcasting as a branch of telephony had been a mistake.

Accordingly, the companies participating in cross-licensing agreements redistributed and redefined their rights to use commonly owned patents and engage in various aspects of the radio business. AT&T retained rights to use telephone facilities for station interconnection but sold WEAF and its other broadcasting assets to the Radio Group in 1926 for $1 million, agreeing as well not to manufacture radio receivers. RCA agreed to lease its network relays from AT&T.

This 1926 agreement was vital to the future of broadcasting in America. As long as the two groups of companies fought about fundamental policies, broadcasting's economic future remained uncertain. The 1926 agreements removed that uncertainty.

• • • • • • • •

1.9 How Networks Began

People first learned of the 1926 industry settlement through an announcement of something new in broadcasting.

Pioneering NBC

A few months after the agreement, the Radio Group, under Owen Young and David Sarnoff's leadership, created a new subsidiary, the National Broadcasting Company (NBC)—the first company organized solely and specifically to operate a broadcasting *network*. Its 4½-hour coast-to-coast inaugural broadcast—a prestigious variety of talks, singers, comedy, and orchestras—took place on November 15, 1926. The network's 25 stations reached an estimated five million listeners. Not until after 1928, however, did national networks operate on a regular and continuing basis.

In 1927, RCA divided NBC into two semiautonomous networks, dubbed Blue and Red. WJZ (later to become WABC) and the old Radio Group network formed the nucleus of the Blue; WEAF (later to become WNBC—today's WFAN) and the old Telephone Group network formed the nucleus of the Red. This dual network arrangement arose because NBC now had duplicate outlets in New York and other major cities. By tying up two of the best stations in major cities, and by playing one network off against the other, NBC gained a significant advantage over the rival networks that had begun to develop.

Upstart CBS

Just months after NBC began, an independent talent-booking agent, looking for an alternative to NBC as an outlet for his performers, started a rival network. It went through rapid changes in ownership, picking up along the way the name Columbia Phonograph Broadcasting System as a result of an investment by a record company. The latter soon withdrew, but it left behind the right to use the Columbia name. The network's future remained uncertain until September 1928, when William S. Paley purchased the "patchwork, money-losing little company," as he later described it. He had become interested in radio while working as advertising manager for his father's Philadelphia cigar business. When he took over, CBS had only 22 affiliates. Paley quickly turned the failing network around with a new affiliation contract. In his autobiography a half-century later, he recalled:

> I proposed the concept of free sustaining service. . . . I would guarantee not ten but twenty hours of programming per week, pay the stations $50 an hour for the commercial hours used, but with a new proviso. The network would not pay the stations for the first five hours of commercial programming time. . . . To allow for the possibility of more business to come, the network was to receive an option on additional time.
>
> And for the first time, we were to have exclusive rights for network broadcasting through the affiliate. That meant the local station could not use its facilities for any other broadcasting network. I added one more innovation which helped our cause: local stations would have to identify our programs with the CBS name. (Paley, 1979: 42)

These Paley innovations became standard practice in network contracts. Paley also simplified the firm's name to Columbia Broadcasting System (later just CBS, Inc.) and bought a New York outlet (now WCBS) as flagship station. For the next several decades, CBS seldom faltered, and Paley eventually rivaled Sarnoff as the leading broadcast executive (see Exhibit 1.h).

Network Advertisers

By 1928, under pressure of rising operating costs and advertiser interest, advertising on radio became more acceptable and common. Because most stations had not yet developed needed programming and production skills, advertising agencies took over the programming role, introducing program *sponsorship*. Sponsors did more than simply advertise—they also produced programs that carried advertising. Ad agencies thus soon controlled most major entertainment shows on behalf of their advertiser clients. In fact, they continued to do so into the 1950s, when television began to predominate.

Agencies evaded early network rules against frequent mention of sponsors by tacking trade names to performers' names. Audiences of the late 1920s heard the "Cliquot Club Eskimos," "A&P Gypsies," "Ipana Troubadours," and others. One opening billboard announcement from this period managed to add four indirect product mentions to the permissible single direct mention of sponsor and product name:

> Relax and smile, for Goldy and Dusty, the Gold Dust Twins are *here* to send their songs *there*, and "brighten the corner where you are." The Gold Dust Corporation, manufacturer of Gold Dust Powder, engages the facilities of station WEAF, New York . . . so that listeners-in may have the opportunity to chuckle and laugh with Goldy and Dusty. Let those Gold Dust Twins into your hearts and homes tonight, and you'll never regret it, for they *do* brighten the dull spots. (quoted in Banning, 1946: 262)

Anyone not already aware could hardly guess that this commercial refers to laundry soap!

• • • • • • • •

1.10 Developing Government's Role

One final foundation block remained to complete broadcasting's emergence—development of national policy through passage of legislation to impose order on radio.

Wire Regulation

The federal government's decision to return radio to private control after World War I did not mean abandonment of government oversight. From telegraphy's inception, governments throughout the world had recognized a need for both national and international regulation to ensure fair and efficient operation of telecommunication systems. In 1865, 25 European countries drew up the International Telegraphic Convention, precursor of today's International Telecommunication Union (ITU), which provides a cooperative world forum to regulate technical aspects of wire and wireless communication (see Section 15.3). This prior experience in regulation of wire services set a pattern for radio regulation.

Exhibit 1.h •••••••••••••••

Sarnoff and Paley

Both network broadcasting pioneers came from immigrant Russian families, but there the similarity ceases. Sarnoff (left) rose from direst poverty, a self-educated and self-made man. In contrast, Paley (right) had every advantage of money and social position. After earning a degree from the Wharton School of Business at the University of Pennsylvania in 1922, he joined his father's prosperous cigar company.

The differences between Sarnoff and Paley extended to their personalities and special skills. Sarnoff was "an engineer turned businessman, ill at ease with the hucksterism that he had wrought, and he did not condescend to sell, but Bill Paley loved to sell. CBS was Paley and he sold it as he sold himself" (Halberstam, 1979: 27).

Sarnoff had been introduced to radio by way of hard work at the telegraph key for American Marconi, Paley

by way of leisurely DX listening: "As a radio fan in Philadelphia, I often sat up all night, glued to my set, listening and marveling at the voices and music which came into my ears from distant places," he recalled (Paley, 1979: 32).

Paley's introduction to the business of radio came through sponsoring of programs. After becoming advertising manager of his father's cigar company in 1925, he experimented with ads on WCAU in Philadelphia. Impressed with the results, he explored getting into the radio business and late in 1928 took over the struggling CBS network.

Both men, shown here about 1930, were highly competitive and pitted their companies against each other for 40 years before Sarnoff's retirement in 1969.

Sources: Sarnoff photo courtesy RCA; Paley photo courtesy CBS, Inc.

Maritime Wireless Regulation

The first international conference specifically concerned with wireless communication took place in Berlin in 1903, only six years after Marconi's first patent. It dealt mainly with Marconi's refusal to exchange messages with rival maritime wireless systems. Nations agreed that humanitarian considerations had to take precedence over commercial rivalries in maritime emergencies. Three years later, at a second Berlin Convention, nations agreed to equip ships with suitable wireless gear and to exchange SOS messages freely among different commercial systems.*

Finally, prodded by the terrible 1912 *Titanic* disaster (see Exhibit 1.b), Congress joined the world's 1906 convention rules by modifying a 1910 wireless act requiring radio apparatus and operators on most ships at sea. A few weeks later, the Radio Act of 1912, the first comprehensive U.S. radio (though not *broadcasting*) legislation, called for federal licensing of all land transmitters. The 1912 act remained in force until 1927—throughout broadcasting's first years.

Failure of the 1912 Act

The new law worked well enough for point-to-point services for which it was designed. Broadcasting, however, introduced unprecedented demands on spectrum never imagined in 1912. The act called for the secretary of commerce to grant licenses to any U.S. citizen applying for same, giving no grounds on which applications might be rejected. In 1912 Congress had no reason to anticipate rejections. Presumably all who had need or reason to operate radio stations could be allowed to do so. After becoming secretary of commerce in 1921,

*The international distress, or SOS, frequency was set at 600 meters, what we now call 500 kHz. This decision had a bearing on the eventual allocation of the broadcasting band. It would have been more efficient to locate AM service lower in the spectrum, but this outcome was prevented to avoid interference with distress calls. The SOS signal, chosen at the 1906 Berlin international radio conference, was selected because its pattern in Morse code (... --- ...) could be recognized even by those unfamiliar with code.

Herbert Hoover required that all broadcast stations share time on the same channel. Later that year he allocated two frequencies—833 kHz for "news and entertainment" stations, and 618 kHz for "crop and weather report" stations. While time sharing worked well for ships' stations (which needed only occasional exchanges of specific messages and could wait for use of a channel), broadcast stations, with their need to transmit uninterrupted program services, needed continuous access to their channels.

The rapid growth in the number of stations soon created intolerable interference. Adding more channels didn't help because still more stations crowded on the air. Some owners then began to change frequency, power, times of operation, and even their location at will. These changes created even worse interference, of course, so that acceptable reception became impossible.

National Radio Conferences

An ardent believer in free enterprise and limited regulation, Hoover hoped radio would be able to discipline itself without government controls. To that end, he called a series of four national radio conferences in Washington. Only 22 attended the first in 1922, whereas 400 showed up for the 1925 session. In 1924 Hoover optimistically called these conferences "experiments in industrial self-government" (Dept. of Commerce, 1924: 2), but even then he must have suspected the experiment was hopeless. He commented repeatedly that here was an industry that increasingly *wanted* government regulation to eliminate interference; and, indeed, the conferees grew more explicit each year in their pleas for government action. Meanwhile, Hoover issued informal rulings and added more frequencies for stations.

The Zenith Decision

Finally, a 1926 federal court decision completely undermined Hoover's assumed powers of enforcement. A Zenith Radio Corporation station, WJAZ in Chicago, had operated at times and on frequencies different from those authorized in its license.

Hoover brought suit under the 1912 act to enforce compliance, but the court found in favor of the station, stating that "administrative rulings cannot add to the terms of an act of Congress and make conduct criminal which such laws leave untouched" (F, 1926: 618).

The Zenith case illuminates a fundamental concept of American "government by laws, not men." No government official has unlimited authority. Paradoxically, by failing to define the secretary's discretionary powers to enforce the Radio Act of 1912, Congress left him powerless.

In less than a year, 200 new broadcast stations took advantage of government's inability to enforce licensing rules. Meaningful reception had become impossible in most places—the Federal Radio Commission later noted that "the listener might suppose instead of a receiving set he had a peanut roaster with assorted whistles" (FRC, 1927: 11). In New York, 38 stations created bedlam, as did 40 in Chicago. Sales of radio sets declined noticeably—and complaints to Congress rose accordingly. Finally, in a message to Congress in late 1926, President Coolidge said, "The whole service of this most important public function has drifted into such chaos as seems likely, if not remedied, to destroy its great value. I most urgently recommend that this legislation should be speedily enacted" (Coolidge, 1926: 32).

Radio Act of 1927

Coolidge referred to a long-proposed new radio law, which after prolonged debate Congress finally passed on February 23, 1927. The Radio Act of 1927 embodied recommendations of Hoover's Fourth Radio Conference and so can be said to represent what most broadcasters themselves wanted.

The act provided for a temporary Federal Radio Commission (FRC) to put things in order. After two years, though, it became clear that broadcasting and other radio services would need continuing and detailed attention, so Congress made the FRC permanent. The radio commission defined an AM broadcast band, standardized channel designation by frequency instead of wavelength, closed down portable broadcast transmitters, and cut back on the number of stations allowed to operate at night. (Interference increases after dusk, because AM signals travel farther at night than during daylight hours. See Sections 4.5 and 4.7.)

At last, investors in broadcasting could move ahead with the assurance that signals would not be ruined by uncontrollable airwave mavericks. The Radio Act of 1927 and the resulting FRC regulation completed the foundation of broadcasting as a new communication service. A period of stable growth could now begin.

• • • • • • • •

Summary

1.1 Among preconditions for development of broadcasting were general late-19th-century trends toward urbanization, education, and development of major industries. The penny-press newspaper, vaudeville, phonograph, and motion pictures gave rise to patterns of mass media production, distribution, and consumption that would soon be followed by radio broadcasting.

1.2 The industrial context for radio was the electrical industry, dominated by AT&T's Western Electric, General Electric, and Westinghouse, each of which controlled important patents. Immediate technical precursors of wireless were the 1840s' land telegraph, the 1860's submarine cable, and the 1880's telephone.

1.3 Theories of James Clerk Maxwell in the 1860s led to experiments by Heinrich Hertz two decades later and provided the impetus for Guglielmo Marconi's development of a working wireless system in the 1890s. Only after development of the vacuum tube by Ambrose Fleming in 1904, and its major improvement two years later with Lee de Forest's Audion, did practical radiotelephony (voice signals by radio) become possible.

1.4 Wireless was first applied to maritime and transoceanic telegraphic communication early in this century. World War I accelerated development of radio technology, bringing about pooling of crucial wireless patents and development of radio manufacturing and trained radio personnel. The U.S. Navy took over control of most radio transmitters from 1917 to 1920.

1.5   Experimenters in many countries contributed to the development of radio. Two important American innovators were Reginald Fessenden, who conducted the first broadcast in 1906, and Lee de Forest, who filled both inventive and entrepreneurial roles in the first two decades of this century.

1.6   Under protest, the navy returned nonmilitary transmitters to private hands in 1920. GE formed RCA to take over and operate American Marconi holdings. Major manufacturing firms executed patent cross-licensing agreements in 1919–1923 to allow the development of wireless. All of this was directed to point-to-point long-distance service—the primary application of radio as then understood.

1.7   The foundation for broadcasting was laid between 1919 and 1927 and included the (1) concept of broadcasting to entertain a general audience, (2) acceptance of advertising as a means of financially supporting radio, (3) development of competing na-

tional networks of stations, and (4) federal regulation and licensing of stations.

1.8   Early development of broadcasting was characterized as well by a basic conflict between Radio and Telephone Groups of broadcasters. Disagreements centered on use of pooled patents, rights to sell on-air advertising, and use of telephone lines for networking.

1.9   In 1926 cross-licensing agreements drawn up prior to the development of broadcasting were replaced. AT&T withdrew from broadcasting except to provide network interconnections. RCA initiated both NBC Red and Blue networks. A rival firm, CBS, was formed in 1927 and was purchased by William Paley two years later.

1.10   Early laws concerning wireless at sea were supplemented by the more important Radio Act of 1912, which focused on point-to-point uses of radio, not on broadcasting per se. By 1926, despite efforts of Secretary Hoover, radio had fallen into a chaotic unregulated state. Congress finally passed the Radio Act of 1927 to complete the foundation of broadcasting in America.

Chapter 2

Radio to Television

Until 1950, AM radio dominated broadcasting. While FM and television slowly evolved in laboratories, broadcasting developed along patterns set in the 1920s. Networks matured and numbers of both stations and receivers increased. Radio became a central part of American life.

These "golden years" of radio's expanding popularity and success coincided with years of extreme social stress—the Great Depression, followed by World War II. For millions of listeners, radio provided both entertainment that allowed them an escape from reality, and news that described a changing world. Changes in older print, film, and recorded media were evident with radio's competition even in the 1930s and accelerated rapidly with commercial television's postwar rise. This chapter covers the transition from radio to television to about 1980, which, in turn, sets the stage for even more dramatic changes since, as discussed in the next chapter. Our focus here is on commercial broadcasting; Chapter 8 reviews parallel changes in noncommercial services.

2.1 Depression Era Radio (1929–1937)

On-air stations actually declined in number during the 1930s—a first in radio's short history (see Exhibit 2.a). This decrease resulted from Federal Radio Commission efforts to clear up interference (by forcing many stations off the air) and from a shortage of investment funds in those Depression years. On the other hand, by 1937 three-quarters of all American homes had radios, increased radio listening was prompting more advertiser interest in and expenditure on radio time, and station numbers had again begun an upward climb that continued into the 1980s.

A third of American workers lost their jobs during the Depression; national productivity fell by half. None of today's social programs existed to cushion suffering caused by unemployment and poverty. In this stressful era, radio entertainment came as a godsend, a widely available distraction from the

Exhibit 2.a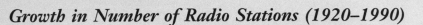

Growth in Number of Radio Stations (1920–1990)

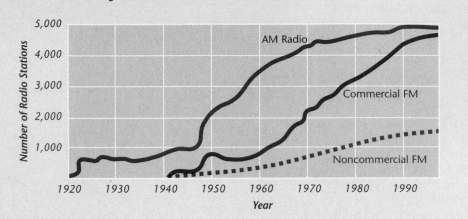

Note that the only downtrends in the growth curves occurred in 1930s AM, when the FRC imposed order on the pre-Radio Act chaos, and in 1950s FM, when its initial promise seemed not to be paying off. The sharp upward trend in the AM growth curve in the late 1940s occurred after the removal of World War II's restraints on consumer goods.

Source: Adapted from STAY TUNED: A CONCISE HISTORY OF AMERICAN BROADCASTING by Sterling, C., and Kittross, J. © 1978 by Wadsworth Publishing Company, Inc. Reprinted by permission of Wadsworth, Inc.

---

grim realities of daily struggles to survive. As little as $15 could buy a vacuum tube receiver. Listener loyalty became "almost irrational," according to historian Erik Barnouw:

> Destitute families, forced to give up an icebox or furniture or bedding, clung to the radio as to a last link to humanity. In consequence, radio, though briefly jolted by the Depression, was soon prospering from it. Motion picture business was suffering, the theater was collapsing, vaudeville was dying, but many of their major talents flocked to radio—along with audiences and sponsors. Some companies were beginning to make a comeback through radio sponsorship. In the process, the tone of radio changed rapidly. (Barnouw, 1978: 27)

Becoming president in 1933, Franklin D. Roosevelt proved to be a master broadcaster, the first national politician to exploit radio to its full potential. He lifted everyone's spirit with ringing phrases in his inaugural address ("The only thing we have to fear is fear itself"), broadcast nationwide by both CBS and NBC, the only national networks in 1933.

Soon Roosevelt's distinctive, patrician voice became familiar to every listener who tuned in his "fireside chats," a term used to suggest the informality, warmth, and directness of these presidential radio reports—a new phenomenon in American politics. "It was in the most direct sense the government reaching out and touching the citizen.

". . . Roosevelt was the first professional of the art" (Halberstam, 1979: 15).

FCC Takes Over

Roosevelt also had an important impact on communications regulation. To eliminate overlap among various agencies regulating wire and radio operations, he urged Congress to create a *communications* commission to pull all the pieces under one roof. A few months later, Congress passed a comprehensive Communications Act of 1934, which, although much amended, still governs electronic media and telecommunications operations today (see Section 13.2).

The Act created a seven-member Federal Communications Commission (reduced to five members in 1983) to regulate all interstate electronic communication, including broadcasting. Most of the Radio Act of 1927 survived, its key provisions incorporated into the new act. The FCC replaced the FRC and began operations in mid-1934 as one of many agencies established during frenetic early New Deal government activity. A half-century later, FCC Chair Mark Fowler would often call his agency "the last of the New Deal dinosaurs," referring to the FCC's formative years and one-time activism, when it used its licensing power to compel stations to act in what the agency felt was the larger public interest instead of only in their commercial self-interest.

Programming Excesses

Side by side with self-conscious correctness and conservatism of network radio, however, there existed another, quite different standard of broadcasting. In what many still feel is radio's most controversial program, *The Mercury Theater on the Air*, directed by Orson Welles and John Houseman, presented a sensational radio play called "The War of the Worlds" in October 1938. In the form of radio news reports, it simulated an alien invasion from Mars, causing widespread panic among listeners. Many began to flee imaginary Martians even though the play had been clearly identified as a Halloween prank. One reason for its extraordinary

impact was that the broadcast came shortly after radio had reported the month-long Munich crisis, foreshadowing World War II. Listeners had become so edgy, expecting radio reports of dire events, that even a Martian invasion seemed possible to many. The FCC made regulatory noises, but decided that as no overt deception had been intended, no Commission action was needed.

All across the country, radio proved irresistibly attractive to a variety of offbeat individualists who exploited it as a personal soapbox. As pioneer radio critic Ben Gross recalled it,

> Tailors, preachers, loan sharks, swamis, and physical culture men, merchants, nostrum dispensers, and frenzied advocates of odd ideas, such as Colonel Henderson of Shreveport, Louisiana, who combined primitive theology with hatred of chain stores, indulged in a saturnalia of "free speech." (Gross, 1954: 68)

In most cases the Federal Radio Commission had been able to correct abuses without withdrawing licenses (which at first had to be renewed at six-month intervals). But in two notorious instances during the early 1930s, the Commission administered the ultimate penalty. In one, the FRC objected to the broadcasting of medical advice by a "Dr." John Brinkley on his station, KFKB, in Milford, Kansas. Though not a qualified physician, Brinkley prescribed sex-rejuvenation surgery and drugs that he packaged himself and sold by number rather than by name. The FRC refused to renew KFKB's license, saying that Brinkley used his station to sell his quack medicine and attack others (especially the American Medical Association), not to serve the broader public interest.

The second case involved a religious crusader alleging municipal corruption. The Reverend Dr. Shuler of Trinity Methodist Church (South) broadcast in Los Angeles over KGEF, a small, shared-time religious station. His fire-and-brimstone personal attacks drew huge radio audiences. However, when KGEF's license came up for renewal in 1931, some 90 witnesses appeared in opposition. The FRC turned down Shuler's renewal application.

Both the KFKB and the KGEF renewal denials withstood court appeals, thus helping to establish the Commission's legal right to review a station's past programming in deciding whether license renewal would be in the public interest. As an indication of the difference between regulation of the 1930s and that of today, many communications lawyers agree that in the permissive atmosphere of the 1990s neither station would have lost its license.

The fact that Brinkley and Shuler held broadcast *licenses* made them vulnerable. Most personal exploiters of radio simply bought time on stations owned by others. Notable among this group during the 1930s was Reverend Charles Coughlin, a Catholic priest with a charismatic radio appeal. From the unlikely base of a suburban Detroit parish church, the Shrine of the Little Flower, Father Coughlin built up a fanatically loyal national radio following. His vitriolic sermons against communism, Wall Street, Jews, labor unions, and other targets generated millions of dollars in small donations from his devoted followers. He was finally silenced in 1940, not by political opponents or church superiors but by refusal of networks and most larger stations to continue selling him time (Brown, 1980). With U.S. entry into World War II imminent, his tirades became an embarrassment to broadcasters.

The downfall of Brinkley, Shuler, and Coughlin did not put other exploiters out of business; it merely caused most of them to lower their profile. Spellbinders, quacks, cultists, zealots, and get-rich-quick schemers have always been part of broadcasting. They cannot be completely suppressed without violating First Amendment guarantees of freedom of expression and of religion and the constitutional separation of church and state. Excesses of some notorious 1980s' "televangelists" illustrate the point.

Network Development

William Paley's CBS worked for years to overcome its image as a number-two network laboring in NBC's wake. Big advertisers and star performers usually preferred NBC to CBS whenever they had a choice, regardless of CBS's growing popularity. Paley claimed CBS was at the mercy of sponsors and ad agencies. "They could always take a successful show away from us and put it on NBC" (1979: 174).

NBC remained part of RCA as the latter became a giant diversified corporation with worldwide interests in communications services and manufacturing. Reflecting RCA's high corporate status, NBC assumed the role of a dignified elder among networks. It further enhanced its image in 1933 when it moved into new headquarters—the 70-story art-deco-style RCA building, part of New York's famed Rockefeller Center.*

The Mutual Broadcasting System (MBS) started on a basis different from that of CBS and NBC. In the early 1930s there were only two major-market radio stations on clear channels that were not affiliated with CBS or NBC: WGN-Chicago and WOR–New York. They arranged in 1934 to form a network organization to sell commercial time jointly with WXYZ-Detroit and WLW-Cincinnati. The four stations exchanged programs on a regional network basis. Their chief asset at the start, *The Lone Ranger,* had been introduced by WXYZ in 1933 and left Mutual two decades later.

Radio Comedy's Success

The first network radio entertainment program to achieve widespread popularity was a prime-time, five-days-a-week situation comedy, *Amos 'n' Andy.* Charles Correll ("Andy") and Freeman Gosden ("Amos") came to radio as a song-and-patter team. At a station manager's suggestion, they tried their luck at a comedy series. The two white performers developed a black dialect show in ghetto English, featuring ups and downs of the "Fresh Air Taxicab Company of America, Incorpulated."

---

* CBS achieved its own architectural monument in 1965 when it moved into a splendid Eero Saarinen–designed headquarters tower at the corner of 52nd Street and Sixth Avenue, just two blocks from NBC. Sheathed in elegant dark granite, the CBS building became known as "Black Rock," while NBC was referred to as "30 Rock" for its address, or sometimes "Big Rock." The more aggressive ABC, just down the street, became "Hard Rock" or "Little Rock."

Amos 'n' Andy became the top network show of the early 1930s. Traffic stopped on main streets of towns across the country and movies halted in midreel at 7:00 PM so that people would not miss their nightly 15 minutes of chuckles over antics of Amos, Andy, the Kingfish, Lightnin', Madam Queen, and a host of minor characters, most of whom Correll and Gosden played themselves.

Today impersonation of blacks by white actors using stereotyped dialect and comedy situations based on ghetto poverty wouldn't even be suggested. A Pittsburgh newspaper asked the Federal Radio Commission to ban the series as racist as early as 1931, but its defenders had a convincing argument: most blacks seemed to enjoy the program just as much as whites.*

Minorities and Women in Radio

The *Amos 'n' Andy* story says a lot about the early image and role of blacks in radio. All ethnic minorities had a hard time with radio programming and employment, for the industry was small, and sometimes small-minded. Prior to the 1960s, radio glaringly reflected American ideas about (and other media coverage of) minority groups. If minority characters or themes appeared in radio drama or variety shows at all, they were placed in situations that today would be labeled racist and stereotyped. Orientals were villains, Hispanics had heavy accents and were not very bright. Foreign-born persons of all types were constantly stereotyped.

> The only black shows to last on broadcast stations were those with crossover appeal to whites, like musical programs featuring the Mills Brothers, Ethel Waters, and Duke Ellington. Blacks would [also] tune in those shows. . . . However, as was true in society, they were considered a secondary audience whose support

was not vital to the show's success. (Newman, 1988: 46)

Nor could many afford radios. Of more than 12 million blacks (about a tenth of the nation's population, most were concentrated in the South and a handful of Northern cities) between 3 and 10 percent had radios in 1930, when nearly half the total population owned sets.

Stereotyping declined somewhat in World War II programs— in part because of issues over which the war was being fought, in part because of the number of black people in the armed forces—and more blacks got on-air positions at other than black-focused stations. As their number and economic power—and thus market value to advertisers—rose, so, too, did their image on radio very slowly change. In 1949 the trade-weekly *Sponsor* published its first special report on the Negro audience and "Negro-appeal radio" (segregation was alive and well on the air and across the land), updating it annually after that.

Blacks' image on the air got a boost in the 1950s from the rising popularity of rhythm and blues music underlying rock and roll. What had been narrow-appeal "race music" on records and a few black-appeal radio stations became an almost overnight craze—and with it came success for many black singers and performers. A few began to succeed on television (as discussed at Section 6.7).

From radio's inception, on the other hand, women played important performance roles—especially in music and comedy. A review of radio fan magazines even in the early 1930s reveals countless female performers on national and local programs. Network programs (such as *The Rise of the Goldbergs*, beginning in 1930, featuring, and partly written by, Molly Berg), and other comedy series carried on into the 1950s.

For most women, success in management and technical fields came only well after World War II. Women got into these areas initially through noncommercial radio outlets; they were also active in station and network public relations. Women broadcast journalists were rare until the 1960s.

---

* Opposition became more widespread in the 1950s. CBS ran a television version of *Amos 'n' Andy* (with black actors) from 1951 to 1953, but dropped it because of opposition from the National Association for the Advancement of Colored People. Syndicated showings continued until 1966, when the syndicator finally agreed to withdraw the series from both national and international syndication (Ely, 1991).

2.2 Controversies

In both music and news programming, early radio soon found itself in the midst of several disputes.

Live-Music Era

Networks and larger stations relied heavily on music from radio's very beginning. In the mid-1930s more than half of all radio programming consisted of music, three-quarters of it carried on a sustaining (nonsponsored) basis. Each network and most large stations had their own orchestras. CBS devoted a quarter of its entire schedule to music. NBC began regular Metropolitan Opera broadcasts in 1931, carrying it mostly on a sustaining basis.*

All this created vast new public appetites for music both classical and popular. However, although radio expanded music's market, it also created copyright and union-rights problems never before faced by music creators and performers.

ASCAP and BMI

When broadcasting began, no one could be sure what impact radio's use of music would have. Would radio performances harm new musical works? Or could radio enhance markets for sheet music, recordings, and in-person performances? As early as 1922, ASCAP (the American Society of Composers, Authors, and Publishers), began making substantial demands for payments by broadcasters for use of musical works in its catalog, whether broadcast live or from recordings.*

These demands imposed new and unexpectedly heavy financial burdens on radio stations, few of which had any income at the time. To better face ASCAP on an industrywide basis, station owners formed the National Association of Broadcasters (NAB) in 1923. But as radio grew, the fees collected by ASCAP also grew, and soon broadcasting was providing most of ASCAP's royalties. As the only licensing organization during this period, ASCAP controlled virtually all contemporary music. Stations could not produce popular music programs without paying for ASCAP copyrights.

For several months in 1940, however, all ASCAP music disappeared from radio (because broadcasters finally drew the line at sharply higher fees), leading to endless repetition of light classics, Stephen Foster tunes, and other music in the public domain. Broadcasters broke ASCAP's monopoly by creating their own cooperative music-licensing organization, Broadcast Music, Inc. (BMI). BMI's existence—and its own rapidly expanding list of popular music—forced ASCAP to temper its own rates. Popular music soon returned to the air.

Recorded Programs

Radio affected music in yet another way. When broadcasting began, phonograph records still used relatively primitive technology. They ran at 78 revolutions per minute, allowing time for only three or four minutes on a side. In 1929, 16-inch ETs (electrical transcriptions), running 15 minutes to a

---

* In 1940 Texaco, Inc., began to underwrite the Met broadcasts and has continued to do so ever since—making this the longest continuous program with the same sponsor in radio. Texaco, which now organizes a special 300-station radio network to carry the programs, abstains from commercial interruptions, inserting brief sponsor identifications only at intermissions. Radio's longest-running program, *Grand Ole Opry*, began in 1925 as *WSM Barndance*.

* Under copyright law, playing music (even a recording) for profit constitutes a "performance" obligating a user (such as a broadcast station) to pay copyright holders (composers, lyricists, and music publishers) for *performing rights*. As individual copyright holders cannot monitor performances at tens of thousands of concert halls, hotels, nightclubs, and broadcast stations, they rely on *music licensing* organizations—of which ASCAP is the oldest—to act on their behalf in collecting copyright fees for performances of both live and recorded music. For more on this process, see Section 14.9.

side at 33 1/3 rpm, came into use for radio program syndication and for subscription music libraries. The latter provided stations with a basic library of music on ETs, supplemented by regular recordings.

Radio networks, however, scorned recorded programs. They regarded their ability to distribute *live* programming as a major asset. Only in 1946 did ABC break the recording ban to lure Bing Crosby away from NBC. The top-rated singer hated the tension and risks of real-time broadcasting, compounded by the need to repeat each live program in New York a second time because of time-zone differences on the West Coast. Crosby himself financed a then little-known company, Ampex, to improve tape recorders based on magnetic-tape technology developed by Germany during World War II. As soon as broadcast-quality audio tape recorders became available, Crosby insisted on recording his weekly prime-time program. CBS and NBC soon followed ABC's lead in dropping the ban on recordings.

AFM's Battle Against Recordings

Still another party was unhappy with recording. Although broadcasting created many new jobs for musicians, they saw its increasing reliance on recorded music (especially the ETs used for syndicated programs) as a threat. If stations and networks used recordings heavily, many musicians would lose their jobs.

The man who would bring this issue to a head, James "Little Caesar" Petrillo, became president of the American Federation of Musicians (AFM) in 1940. He threatened to close down transcription makers, thus forcing syndication firms to pay substantial extra fees for every broadcast transcription made, with revenues going to a union slush fund that Petrillo alone controlled. He succeeded in forcing broadcasters to hire professional musicians as "platter turners" in control rooms and as librarians in station record libraries of his home town, Chicago. And he demanded that stations increase musicians' pay as much as fivefold. With unprecedented bravado, Petrillo defied the National War Labor Board,

President Roosevelt, the Supreme Court, and the Congress of the United States.

Exasperated, Congress passed the Lea Act in 1946 specifically to bring Petrillo under control. Adding a new sec. 506 to the Communications Act, the Lea Act forbade stations to hire unneeded personnel merely to satisfy union demands, banned union restrictions on transcription use, and prohibited unions from preventing broadcasts by amateur musicians—including students.

Press-Radio "War"

Like music, news depends on syndication to distribute programs from central to local points while spreading production costs over many outlets. NBC's Blue Network had begun a regular 15-minute nightly newscast by Lowell Thomas in 1930, a sign that radio might soon assume a competitive role with newspapers and news agencies. After all, who would buy a paper to read news already heard on radio—or buy advertising space in papers carrying stale news? In a panic, newspapers calculated that they could suppress radio competition by denying broadcasters access to the three major news agencies of the time: Associated Press (AP), owned cooperatively by newspapers themselves; International News Service (INS); and United Press (UP).

In response to threats that news agency access might be cut off, CBS began forming its own news-gathering organization. Newspaper publishers turned up the heat in 1933, forcing networks to agree to severe limits on radio news. Publishers set up a Press-Radio Bureau designed exclusively to protect newspaper interests.*

Acceding to news agency demands, CBS suspended its own news gathering and, with NBC, agreed to confine themselves to two five-minute news summaries from the Press-Radio Bureau. These could be aired only after morning and

---

* CBS and NBC were parties to this "Biltmore Agreement" (named for the New York hotel at which press and radio representatives met), but nonaffiliated stations were not. Relevant parts of the document are reprinted by Kahn (1984: 101).

Exhibit 2.b •••••• • • • • • • • •

Broadcasting *Magazine—*
Radio to Television

Sol Taishoff and Martin Codell began *Broadcasting*, now the standard trade weekly, in 1931, on an investment of about $11,000. It appeared biweekly for its first decade, reporting on business and programming news, and the changing regulatory scene. With its strongly pro-industry editorials and its editors who were active in broadcast and regulatory circles, *Broadcasting* often shaped the news it reported of what was then a very small radio industry. In 1935 it published its first annual directory of all stations and ancillary businesses, now called *Broadcasting/Cable Yearbook*. In January 1941, the magazine became a weekly. Taishoff bought out his partner in 1944, and a few years later Codell founded *Television Digest*, a weekly newsletter that is now the chief competitor of *Broadcasting*. Taishoff died in 1982 after more than 50 years at the helm of his magazine, which has always been headquartered in Washington, DC. In 1987, the family sold control to the Times Mirror conglomerate for $75 million, though son Larry Taishoff remained in charge of day-to-day operations. In mid-1991 the magazine changed hands again, this time for only $32 million; the purchaser was a large British-based conglomerate, Reed International. Early in 1993, the magazine's title was expanded to *Broadcasting & Cable*, reflecting cable's rise to nearly equal importance. (And for the first time, the magazine adopted an editorial cover rather than selling it to an advertiser.) A weekly competitor of the magazine is *Electronic Media*, which was started in 1981 by Crain Publications in Chicago and stresses programming and advertising.

Source: Photos from *Broadcasting & Cable* magazine.

evening papers had appeared, could be used only on a sustaining (nonsponsored) basis, and had to be followed by the admonition, "For further details, consult your local newspaper(s)."

Despite all this, the Press-Radio Bureau never worked effectively. Only about a third of existing stations subscribed to it, and several independent radio news services sprang up to fill the gap. Broadcasters noted that news analysis was not covered in the agreement, so a great many radio newscasters became instant commentators. Seeking more business, United Press broke the embargo in 1935 and was soon joined by International News Service. (These two merged in 1958 to form today's UPI.) The Press-Radio Bureau finally expired, unmourned, in 1940 when the Associated Press began to accept radio stations as members.

As broadcast news matured, it became evident that, contrary to fears of newspaper publishers, radio coverage actually stimulated newspaper reading instead of discouraging it. Press services eventually acquired even more broadcasters than publishers as customers and began to offer services specially tailored for broadcast stations, including audio feeds ready to go directly on air. Central to radio's winning of the "war" was the growing strength of national networks.

FCC Investigates Networks

By 1938 most high-power radio stations were affiliated with either NBC or CBS. Then, as now, the great majority of affiliated stations were tied to networks not by ownership but by affiliation contract. The Mutual Broadcasting System, frustrated in its attempts to expand from a regional into a national network, complained to the FCC that CBS and NBC unfairly dominated the network field. After more than three years of investigation, the FCC agreed and in 1941 issued chain (network) broadcasting regulations to restrict the older networks' hold over affiliates and talent. Among other things, the new rules banned as unfair NBC's dual networks and the talent-booking agencies at both NBC and CBS. The rules stopped networks from forcing affiliates either to carry programs that they did not want

(thereby freeing stations to program more to local needs and interests) or to infringe in other ways on station autonomy.

Concerned about this dramatic intrusion into their affairs, CBS and NBC predicted total network collapse if the regulations went into effect. They fought the Commission all the way to the Supreme Court, which in 1943 decided in favor of the FCC (U.S., 1943: 190).* NBC's dual-network operation ended in 1943 with the sale of its Blue network, and in 1945 it became the American Broadcasting Company (ABC). The predicted collapse of network broadcasting did not take place, and even Mutual expanded rapidly after the war. Thus emerged radio's four-network structure, which endured until the late 1960s.

• • • • • • • • •

2.3   TV and FM

Radio listeners began to hear and read more in the 1930s about experiments involving radio-with-pictures, or television. Rumors of a new kind of radio that eliminated static also surfaced. But both innovations took far longer to achieve commercial success than their backers expected.

What Delayed TV?

Notions of wireless transmission of pictures occurred to inventors as early as wireless sound transmission. Yet even after sound broadcasting became a reality, television remained only in the experimental stage.

Television was delayed by its need for more sophisticated technology as well as by lack of agreement on a single national technical standard. Setting such a standard involved compromises

---

* The FCC extended the chain broadcasting rules to television in 1946. In 1977, after radio networks had ceased to play a dominant role, the Commission deleted the original radio chain regulations. (For more on television network rules, see Sections 9.2 and 13.9.)

among conflicting interests of patent holders, manufacturers, and government bureaucracies, each with its own economic and political concerns. Agreeing on technical details too soon might have frozen development before it peaked. And American television thus might have been cruder than necessary—or if later changes were made, the cost might have been huge as millions of receivers plus studio and transmitter equipment would have needed to be upgraded or replaced. For these reasons, U.S. television moved slowly before 1945 as standards were improved bit by bit and the FCC cautiously granted licenses for limited public tryouts.

Television's early technological development underwent two phases: initial mechanical picture scanning to the mid-1930s, followed by much-improved electronic scanning in the years since.* The latter had just begun to reach a satisfactory level when World War II (1939–1945) halted development.

TV's Mechanical Era

Experimental video that produced crude pictures interesting only for research existed long before television became a mass medium. Initial experimental equipment was mechanical in that both camera and receiver were built around the use of thin metal discs perforated with small holes in a spiral pattern.** As these discs revolved at high speed, each hole would be exposed to part of the scene being televised. As a person watched through a four- or five-inch receiver "window," the fast-moving holes created an illusion of successive patterns of light and dark lines roughly resembling the real scene. These first shadow pictures were made up of only 30 lines of picture definition, compared with 525 lines in today's American television (see Exhibit 2.c).

---

* A third era—the high-definition television of the 1990s—is detailed at Section 5.9.

** Such discs were patented in 1884 by Paul Nipkow in Germany, but he never developed the notion further. In his honor, mechanical picture-scanning systems were often said to have "Nipkow discs." A variant of Nipkow's system provided initial pictures of men on the moon in 1969. Scientists used the old system because of its ruggedness, required by the harsh conditions of broadcasting from space.

Charles Francis Jenkins in the United States and John Logie Baird in Britain both demonstrated mechanical systems and briefly manufactured and sold receivers in the 1920s. Baird's persistent efforts, along with a competing all-electronic system from British Marconi–EMI, led in November 1936 to the BBC's introduction of the first regular television service.

But by the late 1930s, mechanical television had been pushed to its limits (pictures with 240 lines of definition) while all-electronic systems, even the crude versions of that time, provided far better transmission, reception, and pictures (400 lines of definition and rapidly getting even better). The BBC soon dropped Baird's mechanical approach and focused on electronic developments, closing down in 1939 when Britain declared war on Germany.

Electronic Television

Meanwhile, two inventors figured prominently in American electronic television developments: Philo T. Farnsworth and Vladimir Zworykin (see Exhibit 2.d). Farnsworth, a self-taught genius, developed an all-electronic scanning system he called "image dissection." Still used today are basic methods he invented for suppressing the scanning beam retrace path and for inserting synchronizing pulses (as described in Exhibit 4.i on p. 135).

Zworykin emigrated to the United States from Russia in 1919 and worked as an engineer for Westinghouse. In 1923 he applied for patents covering a largely electronic television system, but he quickly found himself embroiled in a seven-party patent interference suit. One of the seven, Farnsworth, finally won a key patent decision in 1934. RCA acknowledged Farnsworth's victory five years later by paying him a million dollars to use his discoveries. Meanwhile, Zworykin won lasting fame as inventor of the *iconoscope*, an electronic camera pick-up tube.

In 1930 Zworykin became head of a celebrated research group of more than 40 engineers at RCA's laboratories in Camden, New Jersey. Merging the television research programs of General Electric, Westinghouse, and RCA, the Camden team

Exhibit 2.c ● ● ● ● ● ● ● ● ● ● ● ● ● ● ● ●

First U.S. Television Star

During the early experiments with electronic television, RCA laboratories used, as a moving object to televise, a 12-inch papier-mâché model of a popular cartoon character, Felix the Cat, posed on a revolving turntable under hot lights. The image at left shows how Felix looked on television in 1929 when picture definition was still only 60 lines per frame.

Source: Photos courtesy NBC.

systematically investigated all aspects of electronic television development, solving many technical and subjective problems of improving picture-quality standards to win full public acceptance. They progressed to ever-higher picture definition, from a 60-line standard in 1930 (see Exhibit 2.c) to 441 lines by 1939. They increased image size and brightness, introduced interlace scanning (see Section 4.9) to suppress flicker, adapted equipment to use the newly opened VHF band, and introduced sets into homes on an experimental basis.

By 1939 the Camden group felt ready for a major public demonstration. RCA chose the 1939 New York World's Fair, with its "World of Tomorrow" theme, as a suitable launching pad for RCA's 441-line demonstration. For the first time the general

Exhibit 2.d •••••• •••••••••••

American TV Innovators

Highly creative and competitive, both Philo T. Farnsworth (1906–1971), left, and Vladimir K. Zworykin (1889–1982), right, made fundamental contributions to electronic television. Farnsworth worked alone initially and then for a succession of companies that provided financial backing. Zworykin began working for Westinghouse and moved in 1930 to RCA for the remainder of his career.

Source: Photos courtesy Smithsonian Institution, Washington, DC.

U.S. public had a chance both to see and to be seen on modern television.

Industrywide agreement on television engineering standards came with recommendations of the National Television System Committee (NTSC), representing 15 major electronics manufacturers. In 1941 the FCC adopted NTSC standards for black-and-white television, including 525-lines-per-frame and 30-frames-per-second standards (to which color was added in 1953) still in effect today. A handful of stations began commercial television broadcasts on July 1, 1941. By the end of the year, however, the United States had become involved in World War II; production of civilian consumer goods was halted, and television development was shelved for the duration. Six stations remained on the air—two in New York City and one each in Schenectady (near GE headquarters), Philadelphia, Chicago, and Los Angeles. They devoted their brief schedules (only four hours a week) primarily to civilian defense programs. About 10,000 receivers existed, half of them in New York. Widespread expansion of modern television came only after war's end.

FM's Troubled Origins

The ballyhoo over television often overshadowed a radio technology promising big changes. For its first quarter-century, broadcasting meant only amplitude-modulated (AM) radio. Edwin Howard Armstrong (see Exhibit 2.e) invented a much-improved system using frequency modulation (FM) in 1933, and after years of experimentation by Armstrong, the FCC approved commercial FM radio standards at the beginning of 1941. About 50 stations were on the air when Japanese bombs at Pearl Harbor brought this country into the war and froze further FM development.

At the close of World War II in 1945, the FCC reassigned FM's prewar channels, moving them up to their present VHF location, 88–108 MHz. This rendered obsolete the half-million or so FM receivers built to receive the original FM frequencies—upsetting listeners and setting back FM progress. Still, many AM station owners obtained FM licenses as insurance against the possibility that FM might catch on. They made little attempt, however, to take advantage of FM's superior quality or even to program it as a separate service. Instead, the FCC allowed them merely to simulcast (simultaneously broadcast) AM programs on FM outlets. In the absence of high-fidelity original programming, listeners had little incentive to buy, and manufacturers little incentive to develop, FM receivers.

Initial interest in FM stations, mostly as minor partners in AM/FM combinations, peaked in 1948, with more than a thousand stations authorized and about 700 actually on the air. But fascination with television pushed FM into the background. In 1949 alone, 212 commercial FM stations went off the air,

Exhibit 2.e •••••• •••••••••••

Edwin Armstrong (1890–1954)

The inventor paces the catwalk of his 400-foot experimental FM antenna, built in 1938 on the Palisades above the Hudson River at Alpine, NJ. He opened station W2XMN on this site in 1939 as the first high-powered FM station; the only previous one had been a low-powered amateur station for demonstration purposes.

Source: Photo from *Broadcasting & Cable* magazine.

and total authorizations continued to decline until 1958 (see Exhibit 2.a). AM's future again seemed sure as FM faded away. Inventor Armstrong, fighting what appeared to be a losing patent battle with RCA and other companies, took his own life in despair in 1954.

2.4 Broadcasting at War (1938–1946)

Although wartime restrictions on civilian manufacturing, imposed in 1942, sharply cut station construction and receiver production until 1945, the number of AM stations on the air more than doubled, reaching just over a thousand by late 1946 (again, see Exhibit 2.a). By 1944, even though broadcasting had been declared an essential industry and its employees were therefore exempt from the draft, half of them had already joined the armed forces.

Radio advertising boomed during the war—helped along by paper shortages, which limited the number of ads that newspapers could print, and by government policy, which allowed manufacturers to write off most advertising costs as a business expense. Thus manufacturers were stimulated to spend freely—if not to advertise scarce products, then at least to keep their names before the public.

Wartime Entertainment

Released from competitive pressures to maximize audiences with sure-fire, mass-appeal material (inasmuch as they had no consumer products to sell), many advertisers invested in arts and cultural programming that appealed to opinion leaders in the cultural elite. Networks invested in often highly creative and artistic programs, particularly drama.

Radio developed its own playwrights, notably Norman Corwin and Arch Oboler, who won their chief literary fame in broadcasting. CBS commissioned Corwin to celebrate Allied victory in Europe with an hour-long radio play, *On a Note of Triumph*, in 1945. This distinguished program climaxed an extraordinary flowering of radio art—original writing of high merit, produced with consummate skill, and always live, for the networks still banned most recordings. However, with the

end of the war and its "artificial encouragement" of culture, competitive selling resumed, and this brief, luminous period of radio creativity came to an end.

Radio News Comes of Age

During the mid-1930s, in response to war threats in Europe and Asia, networks developed their first live overseas news reports, relayed by short-wave radio back to New York and then to network affiliates. Anxious to outdo NBC's developing European news operation, CBS decided on a bold stroke: a half-hour devoted to a CBS foreign news "roundup" on the Nazi occupation of Austria, originating live from key points—London, Paris, Rome, Berlin, and Vienna—and anchored by its man in London, Edward R. Murrow (see Exhibit 2.f). Although the networks' ban on recordings created tremendous problems of coordination and precise timing, in that historic half-hour featuring Robert Trout in New York and reports by William Shirer, Murrow, and others, "radio came into its own as a full-fledged news medium" (Kendrick, 1969: 158).

Later in 1938 came Munich—18 days of feverish diplomatic negotiations among European powers when war seemed imminent. During these tense days and nights, pioneer commentator H. V. Kaltenborn achieved fame by extemporizing a remarkable string of 85 live broadcasts from New York, reporting and analyzing news of each diplomatic move as it came in by wire and wireless. News staffers at CBS would shake Kaltenborn awake (he slept on a cot in a studio) and hand him new bulletins; going on the air immediately, he first read the bulletin, then ad-libbed his own lucid, informed commentary. He translated German and French radio speeches as they were broadcast. "Even as I talked," wrote Kaltenborn, "I was under constant bombardment of fresh news dispatches, carried to my desk from the ticker room. I read and digested them as I talked" (Kaltenborn, 1938: 9).

U.S. broadcasters escaped direct military censorship of both news and entertainment programming by complying voluntarily with common-sense rules. For example, broadcasters avoided man-on-

Exhibit 2.f ●●●●● ●●●●●●●●●●●

Edward R. Murrow (1908–1965)

CBS news reporter Murrow, shown here during World War II, often broadcast from the BBC's Broadcasting House in downtown London. He and other American reporters used a tiny studio located in a sub-basement. Once, when the building took a hit during a German bombing raid, Murrow continued his live report as stretcher bearers carried dead and injured victims of the raid past the studio to the first-aid station.

First employed by CBS in 1935 as director of talks in Europe, he came to the notice of a wider public through his memorable live reports from bomb-ravaged London in 1949, and later from even more dangerous war-front vantage points. Unlike other reporters, he had a college degree in speech rather than newspaper or wire-service experience. The British appreciated his realistic and often moving word-and-sound pictures of their wartime experiences, and American listeners liked the way he radiated "truth and concern," as William Paley put it (1979: 151).

Widely admired by the time the war ended, he became the core of the postwar CBS news organization. He served briefly as vice president for news but soon resigned the administrative post to resume daily newscasting. As an on-the-air personality, he survived the transition to television better than others, going on to appear in *See It Now* and in often highly controversial documentaries. He resigned from CBS in the early 1960s to direct the U.S. Information Agency under President Kennedy.

the-street and other live interviews and weather reports.*

* The fear was that such unscripted interviews could be used to send coded messages to enemy spies. Weather information would be useful to an enemy planning an air raid. Other than these and related guidelines, President Roosevelt refrained from using his right under the Communications Act to take over all wire and radio communications—as had happened during World War I.

Thanks to CBS's early start, Paley's enthusiastic support, and his good luck in assembling a superlative staff of news specialists, CBS set the standard for broadcast journalism during the war, establishing a tradition of excellence that lasted into the 1980s. In 1942 President Roosevelt selected well-known radio newscaster Elmer Davis to head the newly created Office of War Information (OWI), designed to coordinate release of government and military news to all media.

● ● ● ● ● ● ● ●

2.5 TV's Growing Pains

Victory in 1945 did not, as some had expected, bring an immediate surge in television activity, despite a backlog of more than 150 pending station applications. Investors held back for several reasons. The 1941 decision on standards (see Section 2.3) had left color technology unresolved, and many experts believed that all-out development should await adoption of a color system. Worried investors wondered whether people would buy black-and-white receivers that cost many times the price of radios. And would advertisers pay sharply higher costs of television programming?

Postwar TV Excitement

Two events shortly after the war increased excitement over television's future: (1) the *image orthicon* camera tube, introduced in 1945, improved camera sensitivity and thus eliminated the need for uncomfortably high levels of studio light that iconoscope tubes had required; and (2) AT&T began to install intercity *coaxial-cable links* (see Section 5.1), thereby enabling network interconnection. The New York–to–Washington link opened in 1946. By the summer and fall of 1948, with television relays reaching the Midwest, the long-predicted rush into television had begun.

In 1948 alone, the number of television stations on the air jumped from 17 to 48 while the number of cities served grew from only 8 to 23. Television sales increased more than 500 percent over 1947 levels and by 1951 had already surpassed radio-set sales. Increased program hours and stations multiplied audiences in 1948 by an astonishing 4,000 percent. CBS and NBC began regular network service that fall, and important advertisers started experimenting with television.

Freeze Imposed (1948–1952)

Television's growing pains had not yet ended, however. The FCC's go-ahead for commercial television had made only 12 VHF channels available to serve the entire United States, compared with 107 AM channels and 100 FM channels.* As more and more stations took to the air, it became obvious that (1) demand for stations would soon exceed available channels, and (2) the FCC had not required enough geographical separation between stations on the same channel to prevent serious co-channel interference.

To forestall a potentially chaotic situation, in September 1948 the FCC abruptly froze processing of new television station license applications. The freeze had no effect on applicants whose permits had already been approved, so for more than three years the 108 "prefreeze" stations that got on the air had an enviable monopoly—great advertiser demand and listener fascination and few other stations with which to compete. Many cities and some entire states had but one station on the air; a few had none at all.

Still, the freeze did not seriously inhibit television's growth. From 1948 to 1952, the number of sets in use increased from just a quarter-million to more than 17 million. After heavy losses at the outset, by 1951 stations had begun to earn back their investment. Coaxial-cable and microwave networks joined both coasts in that year, inaugurating true national television networks that soon reached 60 percent of American homes.

Sixth Report and Order (1952)

Meanwhile, the FCC held a series of hearings to settle engineering and policy questions that had brought on the freeze. The long-awaited decision, still the charter of present-day U.S. broadcast television, came on April 14, 1952, in the historic FCC *Sixth Report and Order* (FCCR, 1952: 148).** The

---

* Originally, the FCC allocated 13 channels, but channel 1 experienced too much interference from adjacent frequencies. The FCC reassigned it in 1948 to land-mobile communications. The rest were the same VHF channels, numbered 2 through 13, still in use today.

** When confronted with complex decisions, the FCC often issues preliminary "reports and orders" for public comment before producing a final version. That it took six such reports to decide a television allotment plan indicates the interrelated nature of the many problems it faced.

new rules greatly increased available channels by supplementing the existing 12 VHF channels with 70 new UHF channels. (Feasibility of using this higher range of frequencies had been demonstrated during World War II.)

A table of 2,053 allotments (individual channels assigned to each of 1,291 communities) marked a sharp contrast with prefreeze channels in only 345 cities. Two-thirds of the new allotments were UHF channels. The FCC reserved about 10 percent of total channels for noncommercial educational use, mostly in the UHF band. Exhibit 2.g shows the spacing of co-channel allotments around the country to avoid interference and also provides an example of individual city allotments. This television table of allotments has been amended many times, one of the more significant changes being an increase in educational reservations to about 35 percent of the total.*

Tremendous pressures for new stations had built up during the freeze. In less than a year after the *Sixth Report,* all outstanding uncontested applications had been granted. The number of stations more than tripled in the first postfreeze year (see Exhibit 2.h). Then began the long-drawn-out process of deciding among competing applicants for the immensely valuable channels remaining in big markets.

Despite the more than three years it took to develop, the new channel allotment plan still had serious defects. For one thing, there were too few channels to give viewers in different cities an equal number of choices. Ideally, every viewer should eventually have had a choice among at least five stations: an affiliate of each of the three commercial networks, a noncommercial station, and at least one independent station.

In practice, however—and ignoring cable television, which only later changed the picture for most Americans—70 percent of all television *households* can receive nine or more stations off the air (without cable). But only 8 percent of the *markets* in the country have five or more stations. The entire state of New Jersey, for example, had no VHF station until the 1980s, and only four or five UHF commercial stations.* The reason is that two major neighboring markets, New York and Philadelphia, blanket most of New Jersey. In several big cities, New York, Los Angeles, and Philadelphia among them, the maximum feasible number of VHF channels were licensed before the freeze, making it impossible to designate noncommercial VHF channels in those cities (New York's WNET on channel 13 grew out of a later special arrangement, as detailed on p. 281).

Trying to Save UHF

The FCC's decision to use both VHF and UHF channels for television, and, especially, to *intermix* the two in direct competition in many markets, made inequities that much worse (again, this was years before cable television reduced most viewers' dependence on over-the-air signals). The FCC had originally tried to ensure equal coverage by authorizing UHF to use more transmitter power, hoping to overcome the more limited coverage of UHF waves as compared with VHF. Even if added power could have helped (in fact, it changed little), years went by before maximum-power UHF transmitters became available.** UHF transmitters cost more than VHF to install and operate. Long after UHF television began, manufacturers were still building primarily VHF-only receivers because of national demand for VHF viewing, forcing viewers in UHF-served markets to buy often difficult-to-use converters.

Faced with such overwhelming disadvantages, UHF television declined, reaching a low point of only 75 stations in 1960. The FCC constantly tried to encourage struggling stations, most helpfully

---

* Later major changes included reallocating channel 37 to radio astronomy and, in 1970, shifting channels 70 to 83 to land-mobile use.

* The FCC reallotted WOR-TV, channel 9, from New York City to northern New Jersey in 1982 in response to strong congressional pressure. In return, the licensee, RKO General, was granted a license renewal despite some severe shortcomings. RKO sold the station a few years later.

** The pioneer commercial UHF station, KPTV (Portland, Oregon), went on the air in September 1952, using an RCA experimental transmitter. The first maximum-power (five million watts) UHF transmitter did not go on the air until 1974.

Exhibit 2.g •••••• •••••••••••

TV Channel Allotment Plan

Using channel 7 as an example (a similar map could be made for any other VHF or UHF channel), this shows the occupied channel 7 allotments (those actually on the air), except for three outside the contiguous 48 states. They are spread fairly evenly, separated from each other by a minimum of 170 miles. The list of all channels available in one of the cities is shown below. Rapid City, SD, is allotted two UHF channels (the first of which went on the air in 1988), but the town gets additional service from translators that bring in signals of several stations allotted to other cities in that region, plus cable television.

Status of channel allotments in Rapid City, SD, in 1993 (shown by a black radiating antenna on the map):

3—occupied by KOTA, an ABC affiliate

7—occupied by KEVN, an NBC affiliate

9—occupied by KBHE, a noncommercial station licensed to the state of South Dakota

15—occupied by KCLO, a CBS affiliate

21—not on the air

when in 1964 it persuaded Congress to require manufacturers to equip all receivers with UHF tuning (47 USC 303). Still later, FCC rules required UHF tuning to be as easy to use as those for VHF. These actions all helped—100 UHFs were on the air by 1966 and 200 by 1978. After 1974 UHF stations as a group managed to make an increasing profit each year.

Though over-the-air UHF stations can still achieve only 80 to 85 percent of VHF coverage at best (laws of physics that control spectrum propagation have not changed), it hardly matters now as

Exhibit 2.h

Growth in Number of TV Stations (1948–1992)

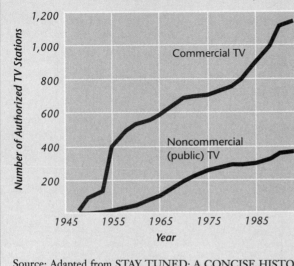

The modern TV era started in 1948, with 16 stations on the air. Just over 100 stations had been authorized when the 1948–1952 freeze imposed a temporary ceiling. After that the number shot up, reaching 400 by 1955. Growth began to slow down at that point, but has never actually stopped. Noncommercial stations developed more slowly, starting with the first two in 1954. *Not* included here are LPTV stations (1,300 by early 1993) or television translators (4,965).

Source: Adapted from STAY TUNED: A CONCISE HISTORY OF AMERICAN BROADCASTING by Sterling, C., and Kittross, J. © 1978 by Wadsworth Publishing Company, Inc. Reprinted by permission of Wadsworth, Inc.

---

attested by the existence of nearly 600 commercial UHF stations (more than VHF). Expansion of cable has served as UHF's ultimate equalizer, for on cable VHF and UHF signals appear to be identical.

Coming of Color

Even concerns about UHF took a back seat to the excitement and controversy over color television. RCA's leadership in development of black-and-white television had given its subsidiary, NBC, a head start over CBS and ABC. CBS saw an opportunity to counter NBC's advantage by taking the lead in color. During the 1940s CBS developed a partially mechanical color television system that was *incompatible* with the NTSC black-and-white standards; existing black-and-white sets could not tune

the CBS signals, even in black and white. The FCC actually approved the CBS system for public use in 1950, though few sets reached the market because of limited industry support for the system and because of Korean War (1950–1953) restrictions on some kinds of manufacturing. Meanwhile, RCA continued working on its own compatible, all-electronic color system.

The rivals eventually tired of their expensive wrangling, and in 1953 all parties accepted new standards proposed by the NTSC for an electronic system patterned closely on RCA's and thus *compatible* with sets already in use. This meant that black-and-white receivers already on the market could pick up color signals in monochrome—and new color sets could receive existing black-and-white signals.

Exhibit 2.i •••••• •••••••••••

The Coming of Color

After the FCC approved compatible color television standards in December 1953, RCA went all out to inform industry and potential set buyers about the wonders of color. Booklets, articles, and technical papers flooded broadcasters. This photo, taken from one of the earliest RCA color TV booklets (December 1953), shows the final assembly of early RCA color cameras. Because this equipment was vacuum-tube based, it was complicated to make and expensive to buy and operate. It also generated heat during use.

Source: Photo courtesy RCA.

2.6 TV Network Dominance

Television grew quickly compared to radio two decades before because developers of the new medium could build on knowledge and capital from the old. But television had no shoestring operations of the type that built small radio stations: costs of television programming and lack of recorded backlog favored a networking approach. Television networking, however, had to await building of coaxial-cable and microwave-relay links by AT&T.

Until the early 1950s, many television stations had to survive without direct network interconnection. The alternative means of distribution, *kinescopes*, recorded television pictures with a motion picture camera facing a receiver screen. These filmed recordings of network programs became available by 1948, but poor quality discouraged their use. In 1956 Ampex demonstrated a successful videotape process, which saw its first practical use that fall on CBS. In a rare spirit of cooperation, competing manufacturers put aside rivalries and opted for a single compatible broadcast *videotape* standard from the outset.

Why Three Networks?

Several factors limited national commercial television networks to only three competitors: limitations on availability of programs, on advertiser support, on hours available at affiliated stations, and, most crucial of all, on available television channels in most urban areas. To be competitive in the days before cable and satellites, a full-service commercial network needed affiliate stations with roughly equal coverage potential in all major markets. The FCC's 1952 *Sixth Report and Order* effectively limited television to three networks (though that was *not* its intent), since too few cities had been allotted more than three channels with equal coverage potential.

Even if all independent commercial stations combined to form a fourth broadcast network (by the 1990s Fox was developing just that status), it would reach only about 85 percent of the population, whereas the three older networks can each reach more than 95 percent of television homes—again, not counting cable.

Before cable so challenged broadcasters (as described at the beginning of the next chapter), there was constant pressure to create a fourth national television network for more programming and advertiser competition. Though largely forgotten today, a fourth chain *did* exist from 1946 to 1955: the DuMont Television Network, founded by pioneer receiver manufacturer Allen B. DuMont. With limited programming and advertiser support, the DuMont network survived only as long as the lack of interconnection facilities limited the other three networks. Once relays for interconnection became generally available, DuMont could not compete with CBS and NBC, or even weak ABC.

DuMont's demise prompted the FCC's second network investigation in 1955–1957, and its report the next year. It concluded that the three remaining television networks held too much economic power over their affiliates (House CIFC: 1958). Though not a policy landmark like 1941's chain broadcasting rules the 1958 study did lead eventually to substantial limits on network activity (see Section 9.2).

The "Live Decade" (1948–1957)

If many look back with nostalgia to radio's "golden era" of the 1930s and 1940s, others justifiably feel the same way about television's first decade. Networks put their first priority on stimulating people to buy sets, and only attractive programs could do that:

> It was the only time in the history of the medium that program priorities superseded all others. If there was an abundance of original and quality drama at the time . . . it was in large part because those shows tended to appeal to a wealthier and better-educated part of the public, the part best able to afford a television set in those years when the price of receivers was high. (Brown, 1971: 154)

Most programming, local and network, was live—a throwback to early radio. Videotape recording had not yet been invented. Original television plays constituted the most memorable artistic achievements of television's live decade. "Talent seemed to gush right out of the cement," wrote the pioneer New York *Times* critic, Jack Gould.

A more realistic appraisal, perhaps, came from Robert Saudek, producer of *Omnibus*, a prestigious series initiated in 1952 with Ford Foundation support as an experiment in high-quality television. Asking himself whether benefits of live production really justified the strain, Saudek concluded:

> Any sane observer would have to say no, because it is both efficient and economical to put shows on film or tape. Not only does it provide profitable reruns, but also . . . the scheduling of crews, studios, lights, cameras, sound and all the other hardware can be frozen and stored away like TV dinners to be retrieved and served up on demand. (Saudek, 1973: 22)

In short, economics of television drove it relentlessly toward shared and reused programming, and therefore toward recording, at both local and network levels.

Production Moves to Hollywood

Television programs could, of course, have been recorded by making them originally on motion picture film. Some were, but economic, technical, and social barriers delayed widespread adoption of this solution.

The slow and cumbersome single-camera production method, traditional in Hollywood, cost far too much for television. It took time to adapt film to television's physical limitations, with its lower resolution, smaller projected-picture area, and much more restricted contrast range. Solutions to these problems came slowly because of the motion picture industry's feeling of superiority. It regarded upstart television with a mixture of overt contempt and secret fear.

Many television specialists and critics counted on television to bring about a new mass entertainment genre, less trite than familiar Hollywood movies.

These two points of view were as far apart as their two production centers, television in New York and film in Los Angeles. But economics of the two media drove them ever closer together. Steadily, as technical barriers to producing television programs on film fell, production for entertainment programming shifted to the West Coast with its wealth of talent and technical expertise.

In the 1956–1957 season, 63 percent of all network programming still came from New York; nearly all of it was live, whereas most West Coast production was on film. But in 1958 CBS moved *Studio One*, most prestigious of the New York live-television drama series for a decade, to Hollywood. Away from the New York theater tradition, it died within months, symbolizing the demise of television's live decade (see Exhibit 2.j). Soap operas, however, continue to be produced in New York, drawing on the city's theatrical talent pool.

Feature Films on TV

In a replay of newspapers' earlier fears that radio would undermine news, Hollywood withheld its better and more recent theatrical feature films from television for a dozen years. The studios permitted only pre-1948 films to be seen on television, (except for some foreign imports grudgingly released by film companies in fits and starts). The cutoff year was 1948 because after that feature-film production contracts contained restrictive clauses limiting the possibility of release to television.

In the early 1950s, then, television stations had to content themselves with old "B"-grade movies produced by minor companies. Somewhat in the spirit of early radio, when networks disdained to use recorded sound, television networks in the 1950s disdained to use feature films. Not until the early 1960s did Hollywood conclude that television could be a boon because networks would pay well to show "post-48" films that no longer had value for theatrical release. Since then, Hollywood films have become a mainstay of network programming—broadcast and cable alike (see Sections 10.1 and 10.6).

Network Rivalries

CBS and NBC, with plenty of advertiser revenue, generated most of the interesting program ideas in early television. Many of NBC's early programming strategies sprang from Sylvester "Pat" Weaver's fertile imagination. Weaver became NBC's vice president for television in 1949 and left NBC only six years later as chairman of the board. In those few formative years he made a permanent mark on television programming.

He foresaw, for example, that single-sponsor shows, hallmark of big-time network radio, simply could not last in prime-time television. Program costs would eventually become far too high for any but a few rich, highly prestigious corporations to bear, and even they would be able to afford full sponsorship only occasionally. Instead, Weaver introduced *segmented sponsorship*, which enabled different advertisers to share costs of a single program. He also introduced *magazine formats*, which combine a number of separate features within a single program—as in the much later top-rated CBS show *60 Minutes*.

Like William Paley at CBS, Weaver wanted to recapture commercial entertainment from advertising agencies, which had taken control during the radio days (see Section 1.9). He recognized that advertiser control meant conservative, no-risk programming. Only networks, Weaver said in 1955, could "gamble on shows, on talent, on projects; and we will lose in doing this all too often. But only a great network can afford the risk, and that is essentially why the great network service is so important to this country." As production costs rose, fewer advertisers could afford to supply (as opposed to merely advertise within) programs. A study of prime-time program sources from 1957 to 1968 showed that advertisers declined from providing 33 percent to only 3 percent of all programs aired. Independent program packagers were increasingly active during this period, producing 81 percent of all regularly scheduled prime-time programs by 1968 (Little, 1969: 1).

Despite Weaver's innovations, however, CBS steadily gained in the *overall* ratings race with NBC.

Exhibit 2.j •••••••••••••••

Early TV Shows

Mary Martin played *Peter Pan* on NBC in 1955, an early example of the "spectacular" or special program telecast live. A 1960 version was replayed in 1989. *The Honeymooners*, starring Art Carney, Jackie Gleason, and

Audrey Meadows, was an early half-hour situation comedy built around a bumbling bus driver (Gleason) and an off-the-wall sewer worker (Carney), perennially seen in syndication to this day.

Sources: *Peter Pan* photo courtesy NBC; *The Honeymooners* photo courtesy CBS, Inc.

As a consequence, NBC let Weaver go in 1955. That same year, CBS achieved top ratings, a place it would hold undisputed for 21 years.

The American Broadcasting Company (ABC) faced an especially tough situation entering television, as even its radio network ran well behind NBC and CBS. In 1948 ABC found itself in somewhat the same position that CBS had occupied in network radio's early days. Top advertisers and performers automatically turned to CBS or NBC, regarding ABC only as a last resort. ABC began to pay more attention to audience demographics, tailoring prime-time shows to young, urban, adult-audience segments. This policy meant emphasizing action, violence, and sex. With very limited funding, ABC abandoned any serious attempt to offer the more balanced range of programming that CBS and NBC had always thought essential to their national images. Fox would follow a similar approach when it started up four decades later.

Ironically, a government-decreed corporate breakup rescued ABC in 1953. The Justice Department had forced the big Hollywood motion picture studios to sell off their extensive theater chains. One of the spun-off companies, Paramount Theaters, merged with ABC in 1953 after a long FCC proceeding, providing much-needed investment and a link with Hollywood that eventually paid off handsomely as ABC grew slowly to equal status with CBS and NBC.

In 1954 Walt Disney, first of the major studio heads to make a deal with television, agreed to produce a program series for ABC called *Disneyland* that ran until 1957 (it continued on NBC, ending only in 1981). The ABC deal gave Disney free advertising for his then-new California theme park and feature films.

• • • • • • • •

2.7 Radio in a TV Age

For radio, 1948 marked both a high-water mark and the beginning of the end for traditional network programming. In that year, radio networks earned more revenue than ever before or since, excluding profits from their own stations. For more than 15 years, networks had dominated radio, but television was about to take over.

Network Radio Tries to Adjust

After World War II, CBS's William Paley launched an all-out attack on NBC's leadership in radio programming. "I would grant NBC its greater reputation, prestige, finances, and facilities," said Paley, "but CBS had and would continue to have the edge in creative programming" (1979: 174). Paley pushed the idea that star performers could increase their income by incorporating themselves, then selling their corporation's services to a network instead of taking salaries. This was a terrific advantage to the star because corporation profits were then taxed as capital gains at only 25 percent, whereas personal salaries were taxed as high as 77 percent (Paley, 1979: 193).

Using this leverage, Paley signed up Jack Benny in 1948. Within a short time, Bing Crosby, Red Skelton, Edgar Bergen, George Burns and Gracie Allen, Groucho Marx, and Frank Sinatra all deserted NBC for greener fields at CBS. In late 1949 Paley finally achieved his dream of taking away NBC's lead and holding it for big-time network radio's brief remaining life—and building it further in television's first decades.

By 1948, Mutual, whose complaints against CBS and NBC had begun the FCC's chain broadcasting investigation nearly a decade before, had more than 500 affiliates and was advertising itself as "the world's largest network." Most MBS affiliates had low power, however, and were located outside urban centers (one reason Mutual never had the money to go into television). Under pressure to survive, MBS introduced innovative business practices, such as *cooperative advertising*—using local advertisers to help meet network program costs, originally the exclusive domain of national advertisers. Such ingenuity never succeeded in making Mutual financially stable, however, and its history was marked by frequent changes in ownership. During a four-year period in the 1950s its ownership changed six times. Today, it forms a part of Westwood One Radio Networks.

Decline of Radio Networks

Into the early 1950s national radio networks supplied a full schedule of programs—comedies, dramas, even soap operas, much as television networks do today. Advertisers sponsored (in fact, owned) many entire programs, rather than buying scattered spot announcements as they now do in television or cable. But this very identification of sponsors with network programs and stars led to the rapid drop in radio network fortunes after 1948. Television rapidly captured audience interest, luring away major advertisers and, with them, major performers. By the early 1950s complacent days for network radio had ended. William Paley, who led CBS through this transition, recalled:

> Although [CBS's] daytime schedule was more than 90 percent sponsored, our prime-time evening shows were more than 80 percent sustaining. Even our greatest stars could not stop the rush to television. Jack Benny left radio in 1958; Bing Crosby left nighttime radio in 1957 and quit his daytime program in 1962. It was sad to see them and other old-timers go. *Amos 'n' Andy*, which had been on radio since 1926 and on a network since 1929, left the air in 1960. (1979: 227)

The ultimate blow came when radio stations actually began refusing to renew network contracts—a startling change, considering that network affiliation had previously been regarded as a precious asset. But rigid network commitments interfered with freedom that stations needed to put their new tailor-made music programming formulas into effect. Only a third of all radio stations had network affiliations by the early 1960s. Meanwhile, networks scaled down their service to brief hourly news bulletins, short information features, a few public-affairs programs, and occasional on-the-spot sports events.

In 1948, as television began its phenomenal growth, radio networks and their few owned-and-operated stations earned $18 million. A decade later, radio network income had dropped to zero. Total income of radio stations dropped from $46 million to $41 million in the same period, but now twice as many stations were each claiming smaller slices of the pie. On average, each station earned only half as much in 1958 as it had in 1948.

Rock to the Rescue

If music was important to radio during the pretelevision era, after television it became all-important. With loss of network drama, variety, quiz game, and documentary programs, radio had to rely on music and news/talk, with music occupying most air time on most stations. Luckily for radio, this program-

ming transition paralleled a new musical culture, one that found radio hospitable.

Early in the 1950s a Cleveland disc jockey (DJ) named Alan Freed gained national recognition:

> [Freed] began playing a strange new sound. A sound that combined elements of gospel, harmony, rhythm, blues, and country. He called it "rock and roll." And people everywhere began to listen. . . . It transcended borders and races. It was enjoyed down South as well as in the North. The music was no longer segmented. Both blacks and whites were able to listen. . . . Rock and roll sang to the teenager; it charted his habits, his hobbies, his hang-ups. (Drake-Chenault, 1978: 1)

Radio proved perfect for this new form of expression. Rock lyrics spread slogans of the disenchanted and disestablished in a coded language, defying stuffy standards that radio had long tried to maintain.

Top-40 Radio

Radio's answer to television, "Top-40" programming, arrived in the late 1950s. The term referred to the practice of rigidly limiting DJs to a prescribed *playlist* of current best-selling popular recordings. Gordon McLendon, a colorful Dallas sportscaster and station owner, helped pioneer the format, while Todd Storz applied Top-40 formulas to group-owned stations.

Such innovators frequently moved bottom-ranked stations to top rank in their markets in a matter of months. An hour's monitoring of a Storz Top-40 station in the late 1950s yielded the following statistics: 125 program items; 73 time, weather, promotional, and other brief announcements; 58 repetitions of call letters; a 3½-minute newscast featuring accidents and assaults, each item averaging two sentences in length. The overall effect was loud, brash, fast, hypnotic—and memorable. The station acquired an instantly recognizable "sound." No other station sounded anything like a newly programmed Storz station.

The success of Top-40 came as much from its ruthlessness in turning off some listeners as from its skill in attracting others. Formula programmers relied on consistency above all else, relentlessly pursuing a limited audience segment—those under 25—no matter how many others took offense. The second "secret" in Top-40 success was an equally single-minded dedication to constant promotion and advertising. Call letters and dial position had to be uppermost in listeners' minds.

FM's Triumph

As AM was discovering rock music, FM began to recover from its decade-long slide. FM's success came not only from greater audience interest in sound quality but also from a growing lack of available AM channels and from FCC encouragement.

In 1961 the FCC approved technical standards for FM stereo. Combining FM's new stereo capability with its greater fidelity, just as public interest in high-fidelity stereo recording reached a peak, gave FM a substantial advantage over AM sound. FM rode that technical lead to become the fastest-growing broadcasting medium of the 1960s.

FCC decisions in 1965–1967 contributed further to FM's success. The *nonduplication rule* required AM/FM owners in major markets to program FM operations independent of AM sister stations at least half the time, giving an important stimulus to independent FM programming.* The rule was gradually expanded to cover smaller markets and more station time. Nonduplication proved crucial in transforming FM from a shadow of AM to an independent service with its own programming image.

At first, FM suffered from a relative scarcity of FM receivers. In the mid-1950s *transistor* radios began to make AM a truly portable medium. Though car radios soon dominated important morning and afternoon "drive time" audiences, few cars had FM receivers. In search of parity, FM lobbyists tried to persuade Congress to pass an "all

channel" bill similar to that passed for television. But growing audience demand for both radio services soon accomplished the same end without legislation. By 1974 most radios included FM, and two years later most car radios could also receive FM signals (Sterling, 1984: 225). By the early 1980s those few sets with one band were FM-only. Total national FM listening had finally surpassed AM—and kept growing into the 1990s.

• • • • • • • •

2.8   Ethical Crises

Explosive growth of television and its potential for vast profits created many temptations. And, indeed, a series of ethical crises occurred in the 1950s: political blacklisting, fraudulence in programming (including payola—payoffs to radio DJs for playing certain records), and misconduct in office by FCC commissioners.

Blacklisting

Broadcasting's social role came under political scrutiny for a decade in the late 1940s and 1950s. During this Cold War period, many Americans feared imminent communist takeover. There was an intensive hunt for evidence of procommunist, subversive influences. People in news and entertainment media became favorite targets. Many performers and writers suspected of leftist sympathies found themselves on *blacklists*—privately (and sometimes publicly) circulated rosters compiled by zealous, usually self-appointed investigators.

People so listed suddenly lost their jobs and found themselves unemployable, usually with no explanation or opportunity to provide rebutting "evidence." Networks and advertising agencies institutionalized blacklisting to avoid unfavorable publicity. According to a study commissioned by the Fund for the Republic, they assigned top executives to comb through blacklists and to compile their own "black," "gray," and "white" lists as guides to safe casting

---

* As part of its deregulation of radio and television, the FCC dropped the nonduplication requirement in 1986, by which time most FM stations were profitable largely because of their separate formats. The rule was replaced by marketplace competition, which would continue to ensure that few AM/FM combinations were programmed alike.

and job assignment decisions (Cogley, 1956). They found plenty of names in such publications as *Red Channels: The Report of Communist Infiltration in Radio and Television* (1950). Scores of innocent writers, performers, newspersons, and other employees found their careers abruptly halted. Many suffered permanent damage; some even committed suicide.

Proving such accusations false or disclaiming any communist leanings did not suffice to "clear" names once clouded. Mere innocence was not enough. Private anticommunist "consultants" demanded that suspects purge themselves of "dangerous neutralism." One of the self-appointed blacklist groups advised those who wanted to clear their names to "support anti-Communist persons, groups, and organizations" and to "subscribe to anti-Communist magazines, read anti-Communist books, government reports and other literature." Religious conversion also counted as a favorable sign of political redemption (Cogley, 1956: 136). The broadcasting industry knuckled under with scarcely a murmur of public protest. However, when the Fund for the Republic polled broadcasting executives, 67 percent said they believed that professional jealousy motivated blacklisters (Cogley, 1956: 242).

John Henry Faulk, a successful radio personality at CBS, lost his job after being blacklisted and brought suit against the blacklisters in 1956. Alleging a malicious conspiracy to defame him, Faulk proved each charge against him false. The viciousness of the libel so appalled the jury that it awarded even more damages than Faulk asked for. Louis Nizer, Faulk's lawyer, concluded: "One lone man had challenged the monstrously powerful forces of vigilantism cloaked in super patriotism" (Nizer, 1966: 464).

In point of fact, blacklisters only *seemed* monstrously powerful. They gained their strength from timidity of broadcasters, advertisers, and agencies, who generally surrendered meekly in order to avoid controversy.

Murrow Confronts McCarthy

The best-known exponent of blacklisting's style of patriotism was Senator Joseph R. McCarthy (R-Wisconsin), chair of a Senate subcommittee on investigations. McCarthy staged a series of flamboyant witch hunts soon termed *McCarthyism* as a synonym for public character assassination based on unfounded accusations.

Highly respected CBS newsman Edward R. Murrow took the risk of openly opposing McCarthy (though some critics argued that even he should have acted earlier). In television documentaries and radio commentaries, Murrow had criticized specific instances of McCarthy's unfairness, but on March 9, 1954, he mounted a direct attack on McCarthy's methods as a whole. That night, Murrow devoted his half-hour *See It Now* program to a devastating critique of McCarthyism. Murrow and his producer needed to do little more than draw upon their film files. McCarthy's own outrageous, inconsistent, illogical, opportunistic, and devious methods—all preserved on news film—condemned him.

Later in 1954, television dealt another blow to McCarthy by broadcasting in full a 36-day hearing of his Senate subcommittee, during which he attacked the patriotism of key U.S. Army officials.* As in *See It Now*, McCarthy on camera turned out to be his own worst enemy.

Murrow himself never claimed that his *See It Now* analysis played a decisive role in McCarthy's subsequent decline. Press criticism was already increasing, and the country's mood was changing. In any event, within a year McCarthy's career effectively ended when the Senate passed a motion of censure against him (he died two years later).

In doing its part to expose McCarthy, broadcasting recovered a bit of self-image from having given in so tamely to blacklister demands. Nevertheless, as Murrow said, looking back five years after the event, "The timidity of television in dealing with this man when he was spreading fear throughout the land is not something to which the art of

* In those days before CNN and C-SPAN, television networks, especially the weaker ones, often provided extended daytime coverage of news events, as viewing and advertising levels were far lower then than today. Both DuMont and ABC carried all 187 hours of the McCarthy hearings (even though ABC did not yet have complete coast-to-coast coverage). NBC carried a few days of the hearings, and CBS showed film clips in the evenings.

communications can ever point with pride. Nor should it be allowed to forget it" (quoted in Kendrick, 1969: 70).

Quiz Scandals

In the midst of this political high drama, high-stakes television quiz programs also captured national attention. They dominated prime-time ratings, becoming an obsession for audiences and programmers alike. The first such program, *The $64,000 Question,** premiered on CBS in 1955, followed in 1956 by NBC's *Twenty-One* and then by many others. At the fad's height, five new quiz shows began in a single day.

Producers milked these contests for every possible drop of suspense. Thousands of dollars hung in the balance as audiences awaited crucial answers from contestants enclosed in "isolation booths" to prevent prompting. Most glamorous of contestants on *Twenty-One* was Charles Van Doren, a bachelor Columbia University faculty member in his twenties. For 15 breathless weeks Van Doren survived one challenge after another. By the time he finally lost, he had won $129,000 (equivalent to about $700,000 in 1993) and had become a media supercelebrity.

But Van Doren, along with most other contestants, had been faking all the time, conniving with program producers to rig the outcome. Pressure to raise advertising rates by garnering huge audiences seduced producers into rigging quizzes in order to keep crowd-pleasing contestants on the air as long as possible (see Exhibit 2.k).

The first hints of quiz rigging surfaced in 1956, when several unsuccessful contestants began to speak out. Despite pious disclaimers from other contestants, producers, advertisers, and network officials, the New York district attorney began an investigation late in 1958. Ultimately, ten persons pleaded guilty to having perjured themselves by denying complicity in quiz rigging. By its end in 1959

* In 1993 dollars, the title prize would have been worth close to $350,000.

Exhibit 2.k •••••• •••••••••••

Quiz Scandals

Columbia University English instructor Charles Van Doren (left) and opponent Herbert Stempel (right) are seen in "isolation booths" used in quiz programs to prevent contestants from getting tips from the studio audience. In the investigation that followed Stempel's disclosure of rigged winning or losing outcomes, Van Doren received a suspended sentence after pleading guilty to charges of perjury. He also lost his jobs with both Columbia University and NBC television, where he had been a member of the *Today* show cast.

Source: Photos from AP/Wide World Photos.

---

the quiz craze had run its course, having earned millions of dollars for drug and cosmetic sponsors. Van Doren and others indicted by the grand jury received suspended sentences.

The ripples spread far and wide. President Eisenhower requested a report from his attorney general. Congress amended the Communications Act, threatening fines and/or jail for complicity in rigging "contests of intellectual knowledge, intellectual skill or chance" (47 USC 509). And the networks, under severe criticism for their lack of control, moved to take over programming responsibility from advertisers. For a time, network officials spoke in glowing terms of an increase in public-affairs and documentary programming, and set up a Television Information Office (TIO) to give broadcasting a better public image.*

The quiz scandals dramatized divergent views of broadcasting's role. To some, such deceptions seemed a massive betrayal of public trust, a symptom of widespread moral decay. But to others, rigging seemed no more fraudulent than a stage pistol using blanks rather than real bullets. In response to an opinion survey taken just after the disclosure of quiz rigging, a quarter of the respondents saw nothing wrong with such deception (Kendrick, 1969: 130).

FCC Payoffs

Finally, as a cap to an already dismal ethical period, two FCC commissioners were forced to resign under pressure—the only time it has happened. One withdrew in 1958 when it became known that he had accepted a bribe to vote for an applicant in quest of a lucrative television license in Florida. Two years later, the FCC chairman was forced to leave office over charges of having accepted cruises on a broadcaster's yacht when the latter was in trouble with the FCC, and of having submitted double and triple bills for official travel. These and other FCC transgressions led to a series of intensive congressional investigations of FCC operations—and such scandals have not been repeated.

Summary

2.1 Over the four decades covered in this chapter, broadcasting expanded from a small prewar business of 800 AM stations to a modern industry of nearly 9,000 radio and television stations. Throughout,

---

* The networks and the National Association of Broadcasters closed down TIO in 1989 because of "changing industry patterns, duplication of efforts by industry organizations, and declining membership," they said. FCC deregulation policy and lowered public expectations also made such expensive public-relations efforts unnecessary.

Exhibit 2.1 •••••• •••••••••••

Broadcasting Museums

That broadcasting is important and lasting is evident in the development of substantial museums devoted to its history. Two of the best known are the Museum of Television and Radio in New York, which moved into new and larger headquarters (seen here) in 1991, and the Museum of Broadcast Communications in Chicago, which occupied its new home a year later. The New York collection, begun in 1976 with major contributions by then CBS Chairman William Paley, holds one of the largest collections of video material available for public viewing. The Chicago museum, which began in 1987, features videos, broadcast receivers, and other memorabilia. Both offer extensive screenings, guest lectures, and exhibits.

Source: Photo © 1991 Norman McGrath.

---

first in radio and after 1948 in television, three national networks dominated broadcast programming and economics.

2.2 During the 1930s, controversies about broadcasting's competitive impact included battles over music licensing, union battles against use of recordings, and a brief press-radio "war."

2.3 RCA spearheaded the U.S. television system finally approved by the FCC in 1941. FM radio, brainchild of inventor Edwin Howard Armstrong, was also approved for commercial operation in 1941 but saw only limited growth until the 1960s.

2.4 Although the radio industry grew little in size during World War II, it gained enormously in stature as it reported from the world's battlefronts, laying the groundwork for postwar broadcast journalism.

2.5 Commercial television began in earnest with inception of network service in 1948, although coast-to-coast interconnections did not come until 1951. Demand for TV channels became so heavy that the FCC was forced to reevaluate its entire allotment scheme. A freeze on licensing was implemented from 1948 to 1952, ending with the *Sixth Report and Order*, which opened up UHF frequencies and set aside reserved assignments for noncommercial operation. The competitive problems of UHF dominated in the 1950s. After years of developmental work, the FCC approved color television standards late in 1953. But color did not take off commercially for another decade because of its high cost.

2.6 Networks patterned on and developed by radio networks dominated early television. Although NBC pioneered many programming practices, CBS dominated audience ratings from 1955 to 1976. ABC struggled in a weak third place, and fourth-place DuMont failed in 1955 because too few markets had four stations. Production of most network prime-time programming moved from New York to the West Coast in the 1950s, providing a closer alliance with the film industry. In 1956 videotape was introduced, making possible greater production and scheduling flexibility.

2.7 The rivalry among postwar radio networks reached a high pitch as CBS surpassed NBC in popularity; but as viewers and advertisers flocked to television, the old radio network system rapidly declined. Development in the mid-1950s of rock music, formula Top-40 radio formats, and portable transistor radios helped to build radio's new identity. FM became the fastest-growing broadcasting medium of the 1960s, encouraged by FCC decisions that established stereo standards and required separate AM and FM programming from co-owned stations.

2.8 Rapid change in and expansion of the broadcast industry, with its potential for fast and vast profits, led to several ethical crises late in the 1950s. Rock radio was shaken by DJ payola payoffs, political blacklisting was widespread, popular TV network quiz shows turned out to be deceptively rigged, and two FCC commissioners were forced to resign because of malfeasance in office. Yet usually politically timid broadcasters showed what impact they could have as CBS's Edward R. Murrow took on demagogue Senator Joseph McCarthy and helped end the senator's reign of political terror.

Chapter 3

Cable and Newer Media

• •

Traditional television and radio broadcasting continued to prosper into the 1980s, little changed from a decade or two earlier. But new multichannel delivery systems developed in the late 1970s, expanding rapidly during the 1980s and 1990s to the point that more American homes now receive their television programs by cable than from over-the-air stations. Audience demand for still more viewing options, along with technical progress and important changes in regulatory thinking that favors marketplace solutions, have combined to create a fast-changing electronic media scene. The technologies introduced here are described further in Chapters 4 (on cable television) and 5 (on relays, recording, and the digital revolution), whereas Chapter 16 looks to the future of all these services.

• • • • • • • •

3.1 *Emergence of Cable*

The television channel allotment scheme (see Section 2.5) detailed in the 1952 *Sixth Report and Order*—still the basis of over-the-air television—

severely limited the number of television signals that could be received, even in major cities. Pent-up public demand for greater access to more television signals created the need for additional and alternative means of delivery.

Extending TV Coverage

Within a few years after the *Sixth Report*, several types of low-power repeater transmitters emerged to extend television station coverage by retransmitting signals to local areas lacking service. The most common of these, *translator transmitters*, extended signals by "translating" the original signal, for example, from a nearby UHF station down to a locally unused VHF channel, to service "white" (uncovered) areas. Some 300 translator operations in 1960 grew to 2,500 by 1970 and to more than 4,000 by 1980. Despite cable's expansion, translators still play a role: more than 5,000 were operating as of the early 1990s.

Yet this means of rebroadcasting merely expanded the coverage of existing stations, one signal at a time. Few Americans could receive more than five television signals off the air, and many received three or fewer. Whole regions of the country—particularly rural areas with widely scattered populations—had no television service at all.

A new class of stations, *low-power television* (LPTV), authorized in 1982, offered little relief. Located in major population centers, these small transmitters provide some local news and other shows as well as syndicated or satellite-delivered programming, but only to limited areas (seven to ten miles from the station). LPTV stations are designed to fit into the overall allotment scheme without interfering with full-power stations already on the air.

Community Antenna TV

What eventually solved the too-few-signals problem for most Americans, *community antenna television* (CATV), emerged soon after broadcast television itself began service. Pioneering systems in the mountains of Pennsylvania and Oregon began as early as 1948. One started operating in 1950 at Lansford PA, about 80 miles northwest of Philadelphia, the nearest large market. Lansford residents could not receive any stations clearly because of distance and hilly terrain and thus were reluctant to buy television sets. Just as the sale of receivers motivated the beginning of radio broadcasting, so it was with cable. An appliance dealer, anxious to sell television sets to local residents, built a special antenna on a nearby hilltop to pick up three Philadelphia stations, then delivered the signals to houses below by means of a coaxial-cable connection. Now the dealer was in a position not only to sell receivers but also to charge customers for the new program delivery service.

During their first decade—the 1950s—CATV systems remained a local concern. Regulation, if any, came from municipal governments, which granted permission to run cables over or under public property. These authorities granted cable operators *franchises* to install and operate their systems for a fixed number of years, usually 15 or 20. Early CATV systems offered only five or six channels, carrying off-the-air signals of television stations in nearby cities. Most served from a few dozen to a few hundred subscribers.

As long as cable acted merely as a *redelivery service*, filling in "white" areas, beefing up fringe reception, and overcoming local interference, broadcasters welcomed it. Some stations eventually found their signals carried by dozens of cable systems, thus reaching substantially larger audiences than before.

Program Augmentation

Successful CATV operators sought ways to enhance—or *augment*—their service so as to sell even more subscriptions. Many looked toward larger towns and cities, where concentrations of potential subscribers could be found. Big-city dwellers might have access to several local over-the-air services, but tall-building interference often harmed direct reception. Cable operators could sell clearer reception, but they also sought to entice subscribers with more options—imported stations, original locally produced programs, and sometimes extra-cost services. After a system had repaid its installation costs, new services could be added at low additional expense.

This service augmentation took three forms. (1) Program choice and variety were increased by importing *distant signals* of stations* in other markets via microwave relays (see Section 5.2). These stations usually offered sporting events and movies. (2) With *local origination*, new and original programming (sometimes local public affairs or sports events) was provided at no extra subscriber cost. And (3) nonbroadcast program sources, a key factor in cable's growth, offered feature films, sports, and special events, sometimes at extra cost to subscribers.

Broadcaster Fears

By the mid-1960s, as CATV continued to expand in scope and audience penetration, broadcasters began to view it more as a dangerous predator than

---

*The term *distant stations* acquired a legal meaning when the FCC began regulating cable. Specifically, the term refers to broadcast stations not receivable over the air in the cable television system's market, rather than to stations at an extreme distance.

Exhibit 3.a

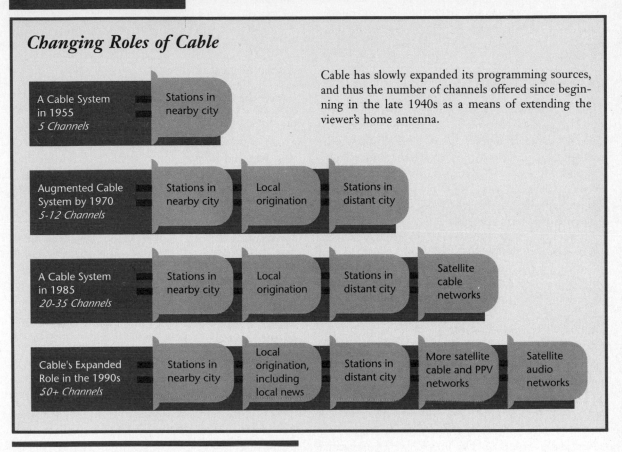

Changing Roles of Cable

| A Cable System in 1955 5 Channels | Stations in nearby city | | | |

Cable has slowly expanded its programming sources, and thus the number of channels offered since beginning in the late 1940s as a means of extending the viewer's home antenna.

| Augmented Cable System by 1970 5-12 Channels | Stations in nearby city | Local origination | Stations in distant city | |

| A Cable System in 1985 20-35 Channels | Stations in nearby city | Local origination | Stations in distant city | Satellite cable networks |

| Cable's Expanded Role in the 1990s 50+ Channels | Stations in nearby city | Local origination, including local news | Stations in distant city | More satellite cable and PPV networks | Satellite audio networks |

as a neutral extender of their audiences. The growing practice of importing "distant" signals tended to obliterate the fixed market boundaries imposed by the coverage limitations of over-the-air broadcasting. A network affiliate might find its once-unique programs duplicated in its viewing area on a CATV-imported distant station, thus dividing its audience. As the number of channels offered increased to an average of 12, CATV fragmented audiences, leaving broadcast stations with lower ratings and thus less appeal for advertisers.

Even noncommercial stations expressed concern about imported noncommercial signals from other markets, claiming that cable was dividing their already small audiences. Once-neutral and tiny CATV had emerged as a full-fledged competitor increasingly known as *cable television*—or, today, simply as *cable*.

Broadcasters began to turn to government for protection. In hearings and studies both Congress and the FCC explored cable's changing role, but they initially declined to act, seeing cable systems merely as extensions of the viewer's home antenna. As cable's presumed impact on broadcasting increased, and as broadcasters stepped up their pressure on government for protective action, the FCC began to intervene. Having nurtured UHF television for years, the commission could not afford to see that service's already shaky foundation undermined by cable expansion, which seemed to hurt the weakest stations first.

Regulation Limits Cable

Finally persuaded by broadcaster concerns, the FCC in 1962 began to impose case-by-case restrictions on cable systems that had applied for microwave-relay licenses to bring in distant stations (and thus needed access to spectrum for those relays). In 1966 it extended regulation to all cable systems, beginning what turned out to be a brief period of intensive control over cable.

The FCC required cable systems to carry all local television stations (under the *must-carry rule*) and to refrain from duplicating network programs on the same day a network offered them. No new signals could be imported into any of the top 100 markets (which include about 80 percent of the country's population) without a hearing on the probable effect of such imports on local television stations. The Supreme Court upheld this growing protectionist intervention (U.S., 1968a: 157).

The FCC, broadcasters, and cable operators carried on a heated three-way debate about cable's potential role. Broadcasters especially feared unrestricted invasion of their markets by augmented cable. They spread scare stories about *siphoning*, the draining of hitherto "free" broadcast programs (including sports specials like the World Series or Superbowl) by cable systems able to outbid broadcasters for transmission rights. They also warned that network news and station public-service programs would decline if cable cut deeper into revenues that supported such programs.

After years of arguments, the affected industries reached a compromise (everyone was equally resigned and unhappy with the result) that was codified in detailed FCC cable regulations in 1972 (FCCR, 1972b: 143). The rules severely restricted both the type and number of signals that cable could bring into major cities. Cable had to provide, on request, *access channels* for local governments, educational institutions, and the general public. Only so long as cable served primarily to expand coverage of existing television stations, or to provide new kinds of programs, would it be allowed to grow.*

Later Deregulation

The regulatory cage built to restrain cable's potential soon began to fall apart. Only five years after the FCC's "definitive" rules had appeared, a federal court decision held that the commission "has in no way justified its position that cable television must be a supplement to, rather than an equal of, broadcast television" (F, 1977b: 9). This rebuff, along with a change in administration (at both the White House and the FCC), led to reconsideration by the Commission. Under court order as well as on its own initiative, the FCC in the late 1970s began to pull back step by step from cable regulation (see Section 13.9). No longer would the FCC oversee local cable franchise standards, nor would systems have to meet federal construction standards. (These matters changed again later, however—as detailed at Section 13.8). Moreover, large cable systems no longer had to originate at least some programming locally. Under the triple pressures of court review, its own economic rethinking, and its changed political outlook on regulation, the Commission turned completely around in its perception of cable's role (see Exhibit 13.m on p. 491).**

At the same time, beginning in 1975 and accelerating after 1980, new satellite-to-cable program services—cable superstations and networks—gave cable systems an increasingly wide choice of national programming. As this new diversity coincided

---

*Precedent exists for this FCC attempt (prompted largely by competing broadcaster and motion picture interests) to restrict cable. In the short-lived press-radio "war" of the 1930s, an older medium, newspapers, tried unsuccessfully to hold back the competitive promise of a newer service, radio (see Section 2.2).

**Evidence of this regulatory cycle shows up in FCC employment records. With the issuance of the 1972 rules, the commission established a new bureau to oversee cable. Within a year, the bureau had grown to some 300 employees. But a decade later, only 30 persons remained, reflecting the FCC's declining cable role, and the operation folded into a new Mass Media Bureau.

Exhibit 3.b ••••• •••••••••••

Cable Growth Indicators (1960–1992)

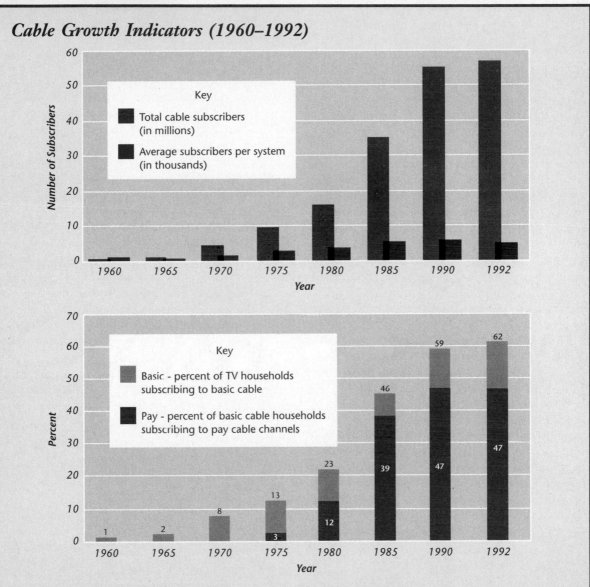

As cable grew, system size and channel capacity both increased. After 1975, pay cable spurred basic cable growth.

Source: Sterling and Kittross (1990) pp. 660–661 for data through 1985; NCTA for data since, citing various sources including *Television Factbook*, and A.C. Nielsen.

with long-time FCC objectives, the commission stopped protecting broadcasting from cable and instead encouraged competition between the two. Cable grew accordingly (see Exhibit 3.b).

•••••••

3.2 Cable Becomes a Major Player

Several developments in the late 1970s helped push small-scale CATV into large-scale cable television as an independent media service: (1) use of domestic satellite relays, (2) introduction of pay-cable services, and (3) development of television "superstations." With the 1980s came (4) dozens of new satellite-relay cable networks and (5) pay-per-view options.

Domsats' Key Role

International communication satellites were first used for occasional broadcast relays in the 1960s. They answered the demand for instant transoceanic programming. Existing national microwave- and coaxial-cable relay systems postponed demand for *domestic satellites* (domsats) designed to relay programs, voice, and data services within the country.

In 1972 an FCC deregulatory move stimulated that demand: its "open skies" policy allowed any business firm with the needed financial and technical abilities to launch one or more domsats (FCCR, 1972a: 844). Western Union's Westar I was the first American domsat in 1974. The FCC regulates satellite operators as *common carriers* (point-to-point, available-to-all, rate-but-not-content regulated communication services). Carriers lease or sell transponders (combination receiver-transmitters) to brokers and program distributors.

A second FCC decision deregulated television receive-only (TVRO) antennas in 1979, thereby eliminating a cumbersome licensing process (see Exhibit 5.f on p. 160). The dropping of such barriers opened the way for widespread use of satellites to relay program services to cable systems—and soon to broadcast stations—at less cost than with terrestrial relays. Increased TVRO sales led to greater production and lower antenna prices; nearly three million TVROs were in use by the early 1990s.

HBO and Pay Cable

Another cable innovation came with *pay cable*, led by a Home Box Office (HBO) announcement in 1975 that it had leased a transponder on RCA's Satcom I and would offer programs to any system in the country that was able to buy or lease a TVRO antenna. Satellite delivery reduced distribution costs and enabled simultaneous scheduling, which in turn made possible national promotion of the service. This one dramatic decision would ultimately transform cable into a major industry:

> Rarely does a simple business decision by one company affect so many. . . . In deciding to gamble on the leasing of satellite TV channels, Time Inc. [owner of HBO] took the one catalytic step needed for the creation of a new national television network designed to provide pay TV programs. (Taylor, 1980: 142)*

HBO charged a flat monthly payment rather than complicated per-program fees used in earlier pay-cable experiments. At first, subscribers complained about the quality of the films; but after 1978, when HBO began making a profit (and when some restrictive FCC rules were dropped), it began to show newer and better movies. Vigorous promotion increased audience demand for pay-cable services, stimulating entry of new programming entrepreneurs into the market.

Fewer than 200 cable systems had TVROs in 1977, but within a decade some 8,000 had them, with many systems using two or more to pick up

---

*In 1972 HBO introduced the idea of offering subscribers a special channel of superior entertainment for which they would pay an added fee over the *basic* fee charged for run-of-the-mill channels. HBO started in Wilkes-Barre, Pennsylvania, supplying a channel of pay-cable movies to several cable systems in the Northeast and delivering its programs to cable companies using mail or microwave relays. Lack of cost-effective relay facilities limited pay cable progress prior to satellite use.

different signals from many satellites. The superstation and pay-cable innovations pioneered by Ted Turner and HBO stimulated explosive cable system growth. Only a quarter of all cable systems carried a pay-cable channel in 1977; by the mid-1980s, virtually all did (see Exhibit 3.c).

Turner and Superstations

TVROs gave cable systems an inexpensive way of obtaining national program services with which to attract new subscribers. But the programs themselves remained in short supply until Ted Turner built on HBO's satellite idea (see Exhibit 3.c). An innovative entrepreneur who thought little of broadcast network programming and had faith in cable's future, Turner invented a way of combining local broadcasting with national cable program needs—what came to be called the *superstation*. First, he bought the lowest-ranked outlet in the five-station Atlanta market, channel 17, which became WTBS. Then, in 1976, he contracted with Southern Satellite Systems (SSS), a satellite capacity resale company, to *uplink* WTBS programs to RCA's Satcom I domsat for distribution to cable systems (again, see Exhibit 3.c). Finally, he enticed cable systems to invest in their own TVROs to *downlink* WTBS, offering systems a full schedule of sports and movie programming practically free. (Cable systems paid SSS only ten cents per subscriber; Turner's revenues came from higher advertiser rates on WTBS charged after 1979.)

WTBS programs went at first to only about 20 cable systems. By the end of 1978, more than 200 systems had downlinked WTBS; a year later, there were ten times that many. Improved TVRO technology that made antennas smaller and cheaper contributed to this record growth: today nearly all cable systems carry Turner programs.

Rise of Cable Networks

Until 1980 cable remained basically a "parasitic" medium, carrying existing broadcast programs and motion pictures to home TV sets without adding much new or original programming of its own.

HBO and Ted Turner pointed two ways to the future with their development of *cable-specific* programming—original programs produced especially for showing on cable. Both cable networks, followed soon by an increasing number of others, taped special stage shows and sports events, and commissioned original program material to expand cable services beyond just movie packages.

In cable's early years, critics predicted that cable-specific programming would develop to serve many special audience interests. But regulatory barriers and heavy cost of building cable systems delayed development of such original programming until the satellite networks made such specialization possible in the early 1980s.

One of the first to offer a format unavailable on broadcast television was Ted Turner himself, whose 24-hour Cable News Network (CNN) began in 1980 amid predictions that such a service— sneeringly called a "chicken noodle network" by TV news people—would cost far more than it could earn (see Exhibit 3.d). The pundits were wrong as, once again, Turner's flare for daring experiments paid off. He eventually forced broadcast stations and networks to expand their own news programming to meet CNN competition. Turner added CNN Headline News just 18 months later, giving news junkies two 24-hour choices.

Turner may have picked up the all-news idea from the cable consortium C-SPAN (Cable-Satellite Public Affairs Network), which began in 1979. Under founder Brian Lamb's effective leadership, C-SPAN provided coverage of floor proceedings of the U.S. House of Representatives (Senate coverage came later) as well as hearings and other public-affairs material. Its 24-hour schedule originated from Washington, DC, and was paid for by cable industry funding rather than by advertising.

Another cable-specific program innovation combined radio's music with television's pictures. MTV (Music Television) began in August 1981, each day providing 24 hours of hit recordings with matching video images, tied together by video disc jockeys (see Exhibit 10.f on p. 347). The Weather Channel followed in early 1982, providing around-the-clock weather and environmental programming. Soon

Exhibit 3.c

HBO and Turner Pioneer Satellite Relays

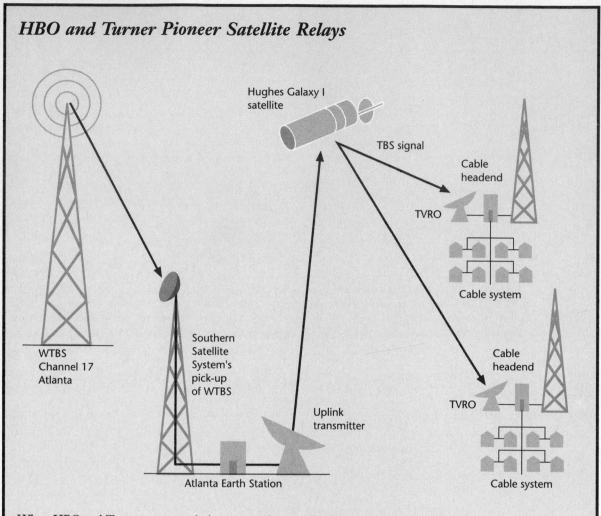

Hughes Galaxy I satellite

TBS signal

Cable headend

TVRO

Cable system

WTBS Channel 17 Atlanta

Southern Satellite System's pick-up of WTBS

Uplink transmitter

Cable headend

TVRO

Cable system

Atlanta Earth Station

When HBO and Turner announced plans to use domsats for distribution of their signals in the mid-1970s, they set a pattern used today by nearly 100 satellite-delivered cable networks, both basic and pay. While different satellites are used, the basic approach is the same.

Turner's Atlanta "superstation" WTBS is picked up by Southern Satellite Systems, a satellite carrier, and the signal is uplinked to a Hughes Galaxy I satellite. The signal is beamed down by satellite transponder for pickup at TVROs located at or near cable headends across the country.

Source: Turner Broadcasting System, Inc.

other specialized cable-only channels appeared as well: evangelical religious networks with their constant fund raising, the Nashville Network's focus on country music and variety, Nickelodeon's programming for children, and ESPN's coverage of sporting events. In the mid-1980s a flurry of home shopping networks also gave viewers a chance to order jewelry and gadgets by telephone.

By the early 1990s cable system operators could choose among nearly 100 satellite-distributed program channels offered by major superstations, pay-cable services, pay-per-view networks, and basic program services. Even more came to be offered almost weekly as video-compression technology improved their chances of reaching viewers (see Sections 5.7 and 6.3).

Scrambled Signals

As cable's extra-pay options increased, however, so did *piracy*—unauthorized reception by nonpaying viewers who could defeat the simple devices used to block such reception. Most freeloaders went directly to the source—satellites that relay programs to cable headends—and downlinked programs to their own backyard TVROS. The number of personal TVROs in service rose from about 4,000 in 1980 to more than three million in the early 1990s, many in rural areas with little or no television service of any kind, broadcast or cable. Until 1986 these backyard dish owners could freely view any satellite signals.

HBO pioneered again by electronically scrambling its video and audio signals. TVRO owners were then forced to purchase a decoder box and pay a monthly subscription fee to obtain clear signals. Soon virtually all cable and broadcast networks were scrambling their signals (see Exhibit 3.e). Despite rural voter pressure on Congress that led to hearings on the legality of scrambling signals using "public airwaves," neither Congress nor the FCC acted to curb the practice.

Pay-Per-View

In 1984 several national *pay-per-view* (PPV) services began, a throwback to per-program payments origi-nally used in experimental pay-television schemes. PPV used scrambling from the start and relied on recent feature films, before they were released to home video, as well as big-ticket special events, usually concerts and sports. PPV offered the convenience of home viewing, often at no more than theater ticket prices, and aimed at big audiences by showing the movie equivalent of best-seller books. Movie industry hostility to PPV was reduced after 1988, when releases for PPV screening were delayed until after the home video market had sold or leased copies.

But PPV services depend on subscribers having *addressable* converter boxes, which allow cable systems to send a PPV program only to those homes (addresses) that order it (PPV buys are largely impulse driven). Customers telephone the cable headend to order a program, and the system operator turns on the descrambler for that particular address. However, telephone orders can pile up, delaying execution and interfering with impulse buying. More sophisticated addressable systems permit the customer to use a touch-pad to send orders directly to headend computers that not only execute orders but also carry out record-keeping and billing operations.

Many cable operators see PPV as cable's competitive front line against expanding home video options. By getting the most popular movie and special-event fare on the air even before such pay-cable services as HBO, cable gains a leg up on the race to provide consumers with the most viewing options. As cable systems providing several hundred channels develop in the mid-1990s, thanks to both fiber relays (see Section 5.4) and video compression allowing multiple TV signals on a single channel (see Section 5.7), so, too, does their ability to offer multiple PPV channels—and thus to better compete with the local video store.

Two large-scale projects began in 1992 to further test PPV's appeal. Time-Warner's Quantum service, a 150-channel cable system in New York City's borough of Queens, devoted 55 channels to showing movies around the clock. Several channels staggered the top ten or so new hit movies, beginning every half-hour, offering what Quantum calls "video on demand." This combination of schedule availability

Exhibit 3.d ●●●●●● ●●●●●●●●●●●

Ted Turner— Cable Empire Builder

Ted Turner, board chair and president of Turner Broadcasting Systems (TBS), based in Atlanta, created SuperStation WTBS, Cable News Network, Headline News, Turner Network Television, Turner Program Services, and The Cartoon Channel. He also owns two professional sports teams—the Atlanta Braves (baseball) and Atlanta Hawks (basketball)—and is the husband of screen and exercise video star and one-time political activist Jane Fonda.

Referred to variously as "Terrible Ted," "Captain Outrageous," "The Mouth of the South," and "Man of the Year" (named by *Time* magazine in 1992), Turner is known for his outspoken opinions, his willingness to challenge the establishment, his aggressive and entrepreneurial spirit (signs reading "Lead, follow, or get out of the way" can be found on his desk, and the phrase forms the title of the one biography about him published thus far), his driving ambition (he says he'd like to own all communications media and hopes to take over a broadcast network), and his ego ("I am the right man in the right place at the right time"). Physically, he's the prototype of a southern gentleman: tall, lanky, with silver hair and mustache, a cigar in his mouth, and a Georgia drawl. He loves the movie *Gone With the Wind* so much he began his TNT network service with it, reruns it constantly, and even named one of his five children Rhett.

and popular films (plus occasional big-ticket sports events) appears to be PPV's biggest draw. In the other project, NBC, having paid $401 million for the television rights to the 1992 summer Olympics in Barcelona, provided coverage to home viewers over three different media: broadcast television for highlights; its CNBC basic-cable network for more detailed coverage; and three special PPV channels for continuous, commercial-free coverage of all events in the entire 15-day extravaganza. But the NBC "triplecast" was a bust: viewers shied away from the high price charged for the full-time PPV coverage, avoiding the many hours glued to the tube that would have made the cost worthwhile.

Turner attended Brown University and was active in debate and the yachting club. College yachting served him well: in 1977 he won the prestigious America's Cup race. But Brown threw him out of college twice for poor grades and excessive pranks—and his fraternity dropped him for burning down its homecoming display.

Turner began his business career as a salesman with his father's advertising firm in Savannah, Georgia. In 1963 he became chief executive of various Turner companies, with headquarters in Atlanta. His interest in television began in the 1970s with his acquisition of Atlanta's channel 17, then a failing independent outlet. It was there, six years later, that he dreamed up the superstation concept.

On June 1, 1980, Turner launched Cable News Network (CNN), the first live, 24-hour, cable all-news operation. Although it struggled for acceptance in its early years, CNN (including CNN Headline News, begun in 1981) now reaches virtually all of America's cable subscribers along with millions more in countries around the world. (In 1982 Turner also formed CNN Radio, a 24-hour all-news cable audio service.)

Turner does not always have the Midas touch. He stumbled in 1984 when he tried to compete with MTV. And his Cable Music Channel lasted just over a month until MTV bought its assets for about $1 million plus free advertising on Turner's other cable services. His biggest battle—also an eventual failure—came in 1985 when he tried to take over CBS (as described in the text).

Sources: Photo from AP/Wide World Photos

Within a year of the CBS debacle, Turner purchased the MGM studio's huge film library (including his beloved *Gone With the Wind*) for use on his TBS and, later, TNT cable networks. The purchase, however, pushed Turner deeply into debt, and he was forced to accept a consortium of large cable-system operators as partners. They received positions on his board of directors in return for their investment.

TNT began in October 1988, promoted as the first cable network designed expressly to challenge the major television broadcast networks. Initially reaching some 17 million subscribers, the service offered mostly movies but promised more original programs by the early 1990s. It was the fastest-growing new cable network, reaching 56 million subscribers by 1993. Among other audience-building tactics, Turner backed the computerized "colorization" of classic black-and-white films from the MGM collection. And in 1991 Turner took over the Hanna-Barbera animation studio and its film vault, which became a feeder for The Cartoon Channel begun in 1992.

By the early 1990s Turner had begun to leave most day-to-day control to managers, focusing instead on strategic planning and long-time interests—such as the environment—that he shared with Fonda. Development of the Turner cable empire continued apace. TBS helped start the first independent television station in Moscow, with five hours of daily news and entertainment, early in 1993. It will eventually expand, with advertiser support, to a round-the-clock operation.

• • • • • • • •

3.3 Niche Services

Over the past couple of decades, several alternative means of program delivery have developed to supplement mainstream broadcast and cable delivery. These *niche service options* are all provided on a subscription basis and carry programming similar to or the same as that of existing cable channels. They exist mainly in areas lacking cable service and have tiny audiences nationwide, but they may not survive competitive pressures of the 1990s. A few offer new and different content to specific audiences.

Exhibit 3.e ●●●●●●●●●●●●●●●●

Satellite-to-Home Viewing

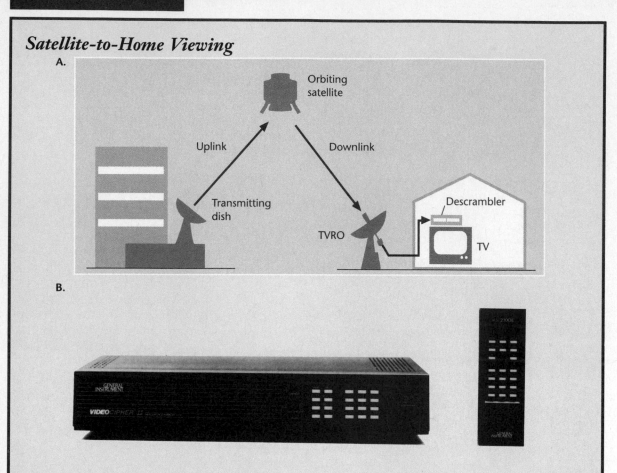

A.

Orbiting satellite

Uplink

Downlink

Transmitting dish

Descrambler

TVRO

TV

B.

(A) Satellite delivery of programs directly to viewers' homes, whether by DBS systems intended for such reception or by home pickup of relay signals designed primarily for cable system use, depends on a reliable means of scrambling the video and sound signals, to be descrambled by devices supplied only to homes that pay monthly subscription charges for the service.

(B) The descrambling device, in this case a VideoCipher II along with its hand-held remote control unit, the industry standard to the early 1990s, is installed between the viewer's TVRO and the television receiver.

Sources: Descrambler courtesy General Instrument.

STV's Brief "Window"

The first attempt to supplement broadcast television came with an over-the-air pay service—*subscription television* (STV)—proposed in the late 1940s, long before cable developed. Despite vigorous promotion by Zenith and other manufacturers, broadcast and movie theater lobbyists stymied its authorization for two decades. They played on fears that STV would siphon programming, especially big-ticket sporting events, away from "free TV"—exactly the same argument later used by broadcasters against cable television. Critics argued that many viewers should not have to pay for programming they formerly watched without charge on broadcast television. On the other hand, UHF stations in the 1950s saw STV as a potential financial life-saver, supplementing weak advertising revenue with direct viewer payments.

The FCC finally authorized STV in 1968, but under rules so restrictive as to discourage any applicants! Not until 1977, when the Commission eased many STV rules, did stations go on the air in Los Angeles and New York. By 1983, 27 STV outlets served about two million viewers. Ironically, widely advertised pay-cable programs (serving more than 20 million viewers at the time) created a temporary market for STV carriage of those same programs in cities not yet wired for cable.

STV stations operated as normal television outlets during daytime hours, scrambling pay program signals during prime-time and late-night hours. Several different technologies were used, and viewers either paid for specific programs or were charged a flat monthly fee. But as multichannel cable services expanded, single-channel STV could not survive; the last (except for some low-power stations) closed down in 1986. STV had only a narrow "window of opportunity" before multichannel competition attracted audiences in most markets.

Wireless Cable

Multichannel multipoint distribution service (MMDS) developed as a variant of the STV idea. MMDS can serve any number of buildings within reach of its short-range, line-of-sight, microwave signals. Home receivers use a set-top downconverter box to pick up MMDS signals, which are transmitted on frequencies far above those for broadcast television. Because it carries programming similar to cable, MMDS has earned the odd nickname *wireless cable*.

Originally, the FCC treated the service as a common-carrier data-delivery facility rather than as a source for entertainment. The Commission later allowed the original two-channel multipoint distribution service (MDS) to transmit television entertainment in each of the 50 largest U.S. cities. MDS began to expand in the 1980s, sparked by the same increased demand for movies and special events created by national promotion of pay-cable services that had stimulated STV development in cities not yet fully cabled. In 1983 the Commission allotted more channels (as many as 30 per market among two or more operators), thereby creating MMDS.* This development led to a crush of 16,000 applications for only 1,000 available MMDS channels, forcing the Commission to choose licensees by lottery. The first MMDS service, Capital Connection of Arlington, Virginia, began operation in December 1985.

But wireless cable faced problems that relegated it to a minor niche role (there were only 50 operators and about 200,000 subscribers nationwide in 1990). The FCC still regulates MMDS as a common carrier because of its data-only origins—meaning that license holders may not themselves control programming (wireless cable is the only entertainment medium in which this is the case). Instead, they must look to others to determine programming. In practice, this means seeking programs from the same suppliers that cater primarily to cable television. The most popular such services have frequently refused to deal with the relatively few MMDS operators, since they depend on more than

---

*Only by leasing channels from other services in the same band—chiefly Instructional Television Fixed Service (ITFS) operators, who were supposed to use frequencies for distance education—could an MMDS operator operate as many channels as this. Aware of the temptation of channel rental revenue to hard-strapped educational institutions holding ITFS licenses, the FCC limited ITFS leases to preserve their central educational role.

11,000 cable systems for their revenue—and are often at least partly owned by cable system interests. Cable legislation in 1992 removed this problem, requiring programmers to make their product available at fair market rates to MMDS and other cable competitors.*

MATV/SMATV

Looking very much like mini-cable systems, the first SMATVs (*satellite master antenna television* systems) began operation around 1980. Because they operate on private property and serve only subscribers on that property (usually a large apartment 'or condominium complex), SMATV has been exempt from regulations imposed on cable systems, including the need to have a municipal franchise.** The SMATV building-top TVRO may tie into existing master antenna television (MATV) cabling, or into cabling installed especially for the service (see Exhibit 3.f). Cable system operators, seeking to sign up as many households as possible in their franchise areas, have strongly opposed SMATV competition. By 1990 there were nearly a million SMATV home subscribers nationwide, and the market has since expanded to provide movies to hospitals, hotels, and motel chains—serving perhaps another two to three million temporary viewers.

---

*Late in 1992 a new MMDS-like competitor began experimental operation in a Brooklyn, NY, neighborhood. Able to transmit nearly 50 channels by means of many small transmitters serving small areas and using extremely high 28 GHz frequencies, "Cellular Vision" promised video, data, and voice transmission in direct competition to existing carriers. Subscribers receive signals on a tiny six-inch square antenna inside or outside—at prices half those charged for similar services by cable. The FCC moved early in 1993 to allocate spectrum for two service providers in each market.

**Applicants for cable franchises often pressure the municipalities granting the franchises either to dismantle existing SMATVs or to give cable operators equal access to SMATV buildings. SMATV competes with cable directly: each has several channels of pay programming, usually delivered by satellite. The U.S. Supreme Court overturned the legal basis for SMATV's regulatory exemption in its 1992–1993 term, as discussed at Section 13.8.

DBS—Round One

Widely touted when first announced, dismissed due to high costs and limited technology, but then once again beginning to look promising, *direct-broadcast satellite* (DBS) service seems to render any land-based delivery system obsolete by sending programs directly to consumers without the need for an intervening station or cable system. Each subscribing home would have its own small TVRO antenna to downlink signals directly from specially designed high-power DBS satellites (see Exhibit 3.e).

In late 1980 a new subsidiary of Communications Satellite Corporation (Comsat) first applied to the FCC for frequencies on which to offer a three-channel DBS service. Initially aimed at viewers lacking access to either cable or off-the-air services, Comsat's DBS would have interested mainly rural residents. Construction cost estimates ran as high as $750 million. Eight other firms soon announced similar plans. The FCC authorized commercial DBS operations in June 1982—a remarkably fast regulatory go-ahead for a totally new service. Critics (including broadcast and cable spokespersons, alarmed by the prospect of any system that would do away with the need for terrestrial stations and cable systems) questioned whether such a service—aimed principally at sparsely populated areas and competing elsewhere with cable and other services—could ever recoup its costs.

The answer came in 1984, when United Satellite Communications Inc. (USCI) inaugurated America's first DBS service using a transponder on a Canadian satellite. USCI committed $178 million for equipment, marketing, programming, and customer service—but reached only 7,000 subscribers (far below expectations) by the time it shut down in April 1985. In the meantime, several other applicants had backed away from their DBS plans.

This dim record resulted from attention to DBS technology at the expense of programming: no DBS operator could clearly describe how its service would differ from those already available from cable, broadcasting, and home VCRs. Even in rural areas beyond the reach of stations and cable, potential demand for DBS had been largely satisfied by home

Exhibit 3.f

MMDS and SMATV

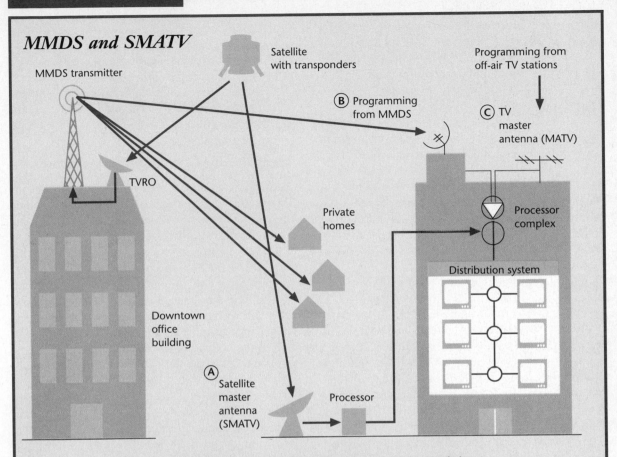

Viewers living in apartments or condominiums often receive their television signals by means of (A) a satellite master antenna television (SMATV) system, a satellite TVRO located near, as shown here, or on top of the building; (B) a multichannel multipoint distribution service (MMDS), a small terrestrial receiving antenna on the building roof; or (C) a master antenna (MATV), also on the roof, picking up off-air signals. Each of these supplies a cable distribution service within the building. Individual homes can also subscribe to MMDS services as shown here. Cable system operators pressure local franchise authorities to eliminate options (A) and (C) when they can—or at least to allow cable equal access to such buildings.

TVRO *C-band direct* reception from satellite channels that were intended as relays rather than for home reception (see Exhibit 3.e). The fact that C-band satellites require larger and more expensive receiving antennas than would higher-powered DBS satellites did not discourage their installation in more than three million households by 1992.

DBS—Round Two

Despite that dismal first round, however, technology revived interest in DBS less than a decade later. Once again, the FCC received applications from potential DBS systems, most planning service by the mid-1990s. These new American projects drew on actual experience of DBS operators in Europe and the Far East, where the service faced fewer competing terrestrial channels than it did in the United States.

The very different second-round DBS projects planned to utilize (1) less-expensive lower-power satellites, thanks to advances in the design of small TVROs; (2) video compression (see Section 5.7), which transmits multiple television signals over a single satellite transponder; and (3) both high-definition television (see Section 5.9) and digital audio (see Section 5.10). But these projects also incorporated new thinking on DBS's role, including (1) a high priority on programming, with more specialized channels to compete with cable; and (2) projects backed by cooperating groups of companies (*consortia*), each focusing on a specific aspect of the larger picture—programming, sale or lease of needed ground equipment, video compression, satellite design and launch, and so on. The huge costs of launching any DBS service would thus be spread across several partners rather than being incurred by single companies going it alone, as had been the case in most first-round proposals. One indicator that DBS may be more viable this time around is that many cable system operators are investing in DBS as insurance for the future. Also being touted is the fact that DBS costs, per home reached, are potentially much lower than those for cable.

Among contenders for DBS success in the early 1990s were two main players (others had dropped out by 1992). U.S. Satellite Broadcasting (USSB) plans to lease five high-powered transponders to begin service in mid-1994 with 15 to 20 channels and more to come. (USSB is controlled by Hubbard Broadcasting, the only round-one player still active in round two and a consistent promoter of a DBS future). Hughes DirecTv, which also plans service in 1994, projects 150 channels of service from transponders on two satellites. The French company Thomson will market consumer receiving equipment for the Hughes effort.

The Unhappy Life of Teletext/Videotex

These two services, which differ sharply in terms of capability, ownership, and the means by which they are delivered to home and office, *look* much the same to users on the screen.

Teletext, a broadcast-based information service that has not been a success in the United States, delivers print and graphic materials to television screens in homes and offices (see Exhibit 3.g). The teletext material goes out from regular broadcast television transmitters, occupying an unused portion of the channel known as the vertical blanking interval (VBI)—the dark line that separates television pictures. Viewers use a keypad to order up specific "pages" or screens of data from perhaps 200 pages continuously transmitted (and updated) from the station. The FCC authorized teletext in 1983 but declined to mandate specific technical standards, partly because of uncertainty about its appropriate role: Should teletext offer services to the mass consumer market or, as in Europe, aim largely at a narrower business and institutional market? For a while in the early 1980s, experts touted teletext as the core of a developing home information center built around the television or computer screen.

Teletext should not be confused with *videotex*, a similar-looking service as far as consumers are concerned, but with important differences behind the scenes. Videotex offers *two-way* communication over telephone or cable lines. Videotex delivery systems are thus often operated by common carriers, while actual content is created by others. Not restricted by limitations of the VBI, videotex offers unlimited numbers of information pages.

Exhibit 3.g • • • • • • • • • • • • • • • •

Teletext and Videotex

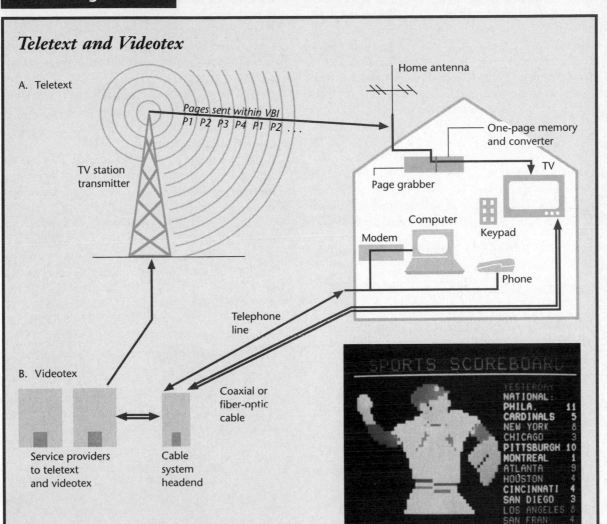

A. Teletext

Home antenna

Pages sent within VBI
P1 P2 P3 P4 P1 P2 . . .

TV station transmitter

One-page memory and converter

TV

Page grabber

Computer

Keypad

Modem

Phone

Telephone line

B. Videotex

Coaxial or fiber-optic cable

Service providers to teletext and videotex

Cable system headend

SPORTS SCOREBOARD

YESTERDAY
NATIONAL:
PHILA. 11
CARDINALS 5
NEW YORK 8
CHICAGO 3
PITTSBURGH 10
MONTREAL 1
ATLANTA 9
HOUSTON 4
CINCINNATI 4
SAN DIEGO 3
LOS ANGELES 8
SAN FRAN. 4

(A) "Pages" of *teletext* are transmitted repeatedly within the VBI (vertical blanking interval), a largely unused portion of a TV channel (see Exhibit 4.j, on p. 137.) A viewer uses a screen menu and a hand-held keypad to select a desired teletext page for viewing. When that page is transmitted, it is "grabbed" and stored in a one-page memory. The characters that make up the page are then converted into a video signal which is held on the screen until another page number is entered. (B) Videotex looks like teletext, but

(1) is sent over a coaxial or fiber-optic cable, (2) has capacity for far more "pages" of information, and (3) allows for two-way communication by use of an upstream (home to headend) cable circuit or telephone lines. In the U.S., most videotex systems, such as Compuserve or Prodigy, now use personal computers rather than television sets. Teletext and videotex can both send text and graphics, such as this sports scoreboard.

Source: Photo courtesy CBS Inc.

Despite these benefits, two large videotex operations, one in Los Angeles and the other in Florida, closed down early in 1986, having lost some $90 million because of insufficient consumer and advertiser appeal. By the early 1990s it was evident that home computers were better adapted than television sets for interactive information retrieval from such sources as Compuserve, Prodigy, and a host of other specialized business research services.*

Serving the Disabled

Making television and other media services available to those with visual or hearing impairments, or to those learning English as a new language, sparked development of several special technologies.

- *Closed captioning*, a specialized form of teletext, superimposes captions at the bottom of regular television pictures for the benefit of a hearing-impaired audience estimated at 22 million Americans. The captions are transmitted using part of the vertical blanking interval (see Section 4.9). Only viewers with a decoder can see the captions—hence the term *closed* for this variation on teletext. The service began in 1980 on a few select programs. By the early 1990s decoder costs had dropped to about $100, several firms were providing captions, and most broadcast network programs as well as PBS offerings and top-rated syndicated shows included them. A 1990 law required that by mid-1993 all new TV receivers with greater than 13-inch screens contain the computer chip necessary to make captions visible at the touch of a button, doing away with special decoders. Programs so captioned show the closed-caption symbol in a corner for the first few seconds of programming. The National Captioning Institute, one of five providers, reported

that by the early 1990s some 20 million people learning English as a second language also use closed captions as a learning aid.

- *Radio services for the blind* use an FM station's multiplexed subcarrier (described in Section 4.7) to provide a channel of selections from daily papers, magazines, and books, usually read by volunteers. One of many associations serving the blind population leases, at low rates, special receivers able to tune the subcarrier frequency. Most of the nation's top 100 markets have such a service.

- *Separate audio program* (SAP) uses a television subcarrier to carry a second language or audio description of visual action. SAP is built into newer television receivers and VCRs; it can also be tuned in with a special adaptor. SAP is used by the Descriptive Video Service (DVS), an arm of public-television station WGBH in Boston (see Exhibit 8.d on p. 274), to offer descriptions for the sight-impaired of visual portions of programs without interrupting dialog or sound effects. In the early 1990s, 35 public-television stations provided DVS.

Interacting with TV

Visionaries of the 1970s often predicted that future set owners would be able to "talk back" as an integral part of a home media center. Two-way or *interactive* cable would let customers hold an electronic dialog with cable operators, who in turn could forward communications to stores, banks, public utilities, safety agencies, and others. Other interactive schemes would use telephones for talk-back links. But for most viewers, PPV channels are as close to "interactive" television as they have come so far.

In 1977 Warner Cable began an interactive service called Qube on its Columbus, Ohio, system. Qube provided ten special channels over which viewers could respond, by means of a touch-pad, to questions aired during programs. At the experiment's height, Qube was asking viewers to respond to questions about ten times a day. But limited public demand and an economic downturn in the early 1980s brought the service, which had consistently lost money, to an end. Too few in the audience

---

*The Minitel videotex system has been highly successful throughout France. French Telecom, operator of the telephone system, initially gave away simple terminals (in the 1990s they rented at $4.00 per month) and offered electronic updated directory service to encourage use. By the early 1990s, some 20,000 independent information providers offered services through Minitel, and usage in 6.5 million homes was growing.

Exhibit 3.h • • • • • • • • • • • • • • •

Serving the Disabled

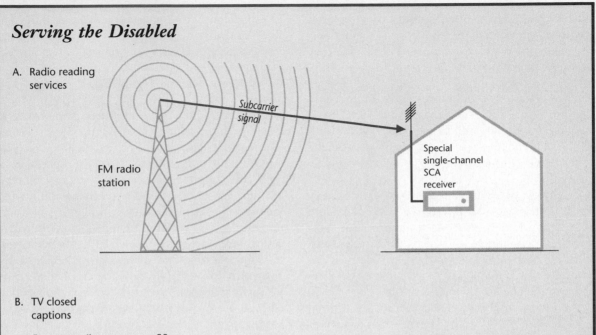

A. Radio reading services

Subcarrier signal

FM radio station

Special single-channel SCA receiver

B. TV closed captions

For system diagram, see p. 89.

Radio reading services for the blind and closed captions for the deaf allow use of electronic media by the disabled. In both cases, special signals are transmitted using a portion of a normal broadcast channel. (A) *Radio reading services* use an FM station subcarrier signal to transmit signals to special receivers designed to receive only that signal, leased to the blind. (B) *Closed captions* are a type of teletext (see Exhibit 3.g) using the VBI to send superimposed captions carrying all or most of the words spoken. While special decoder boxes have been needed up to now, Congress has required inclusion of the closed caption chip in most future television receivers, making it less expensive to receive such signals.

Source: Photo courtesy of WGBH Boston.

had made sufficient use of the interactive feature to warrant its cost.

Numerous other two-way experiments have taken place recently, often supported by research grants from government agencies or foundations; but most end when that support stops, since they lack enough subscribers to cover their ongoing costs.

Once again, however, improving technology and lower subscriber costs are leading to a "round two" for interactive television. In the early 1990s several dozen experiments were announced or actually under way. Three examples illustrate possible variations.

Beginning in 1990 Sacramento, California, saw extensive testing of an Interactive Network system with support and expertise from broadcast networks, cable operators, and the Nielsen ratings firm. The system uses signals sent by FM subcarriers to home terminals that allow viewers to answer questions, make guesses, play interactive video games, or seek more information on news stories. Late in 1991 Interactive Network began a formal market roll-out of its scheme, testing different ways of giving away, leasing, or selling home FM terminals.

Receiving wider press attention was TV Answer, a Reston, Virginia, company planning to begin service in mid-1993, with support from both Mexican and U.S. backers and a manufacturing agreement with computer maker Hewlett-Packard. Along with several competitors, TV Answer will seek one of two interactive video data service (IDVS) licenses that the FCC will grant by lottery in some 700 local market areas. The license will allow use of satellite transponders to link company headquarters with local markets, as well as high-frequency radio signals that will connect individual users to local satellite ground stations. This "double loop" communication will facilitate two-way product ordering, information retrieval, polls, and games that can be played against other system users across the country. The company has also touted itself as a "universal remote" control tied to program listings, making use of the home receiver and the VCR far easier for viewers. Fees would be paid by major information and product providers for access to the TV Answer

system as well as by viewers using the system. Meanwhile, critics have questioned the likelihood that consumers would willingly pay several hundred dollars for a converter box necessary to access the service. And indicative of the problems faced by many start-up companies, TV Answer laid off employees and tightened its operations in mid-1992, just as the FCC was beginning to pick initial licensees by lottery.

Creating considerable comment was the early 1993 announcement by media giant Time Warner that it would develop its first interactive cable system near Orlando, Florida. To be in operation in 1994, the system promised hundreds of channels, allowing subscribers to call up an almost unlimited menu of entertainment and information programming for instant viewing. Included would be interactive video telephone service, database access, distance learning, and interactive video shopping and video game capabilities. Experts hailed Time Warner's plan for its creativity and for the fact that because the system would be built around popular entertainment, wider and quicker acceptability was likely.

• • • • • • • •

3.4 Electronics Revolution

Many of the services described above are possible only because of a fundamental but steady shift from analog to digital technology in the 1990s. This ongoing "digital revolution" is based, in turn, on the rise of microelectronics. The resulting products and services are transforming all electronic media.

End of the Vacuum Tube

Our earlier discussion of the evolution of electronics ended at the stage where de Forest's improvement of the electronic tube had opened the way to broadcasting (see Section 1.3). As noted, vacuum tubes (so called because they provide an enclosed space for the manipulation of electrons in a near vacuum) are bulky, power-hungry, hot, and easily damaged.

A rack of equipment containing scores of tubes takes up a great deal of space and must be artificially cooled. Then came the *transistor,* a far more efficient means of manipulating electrons. The transistor began to supplant the vacuum tube for most applications in the 1950s. Along with later solid-state devices it has now virtually eliminated vacuum tubes, though a few persist—notably television set picture tubes and traveling-wave tubes, one source of on-board power in satellites.*

Transistors

Three Bell Laboratories engineers invented the transistor in 1947, collectively receiving the Nobel Prize in physics in 1956. In a few years, improved versions of their device had transformed the electronics industry. The transistor radio, one of the first mass-produced products based on their invention, appeared in 1954, quickly becoming the best seller in consumer product history (see Exhibit 3.i).

The transistor made possible development of the prime electronic artifact of the late 20th century, the digital computer. Experimental computers in the 1940s needed thousands of electron tubes plus miles of wires. The tubes generated so much heat that attendants had to stand by to replace the ones that blew out. Transistors solved this problem in the 1950s, at the same time enormously increasing computer speed and memory capacity.

The Chip

Anything smaller than a mainframe computer remained impractical, however, so long as thousands of separate transistors had to be meticulously wired together with hand-soldered connections. True miniaturization became possible with the invention of the *integrated circuit,* or computer "chip" (see Section 5.7 and Exhibit 3.i). Two engineers working

separately arrived at the same solution six months apart, Jack Kilby in 1959 and Robert Noyce in 1960. Each one's version had certain advantages over the other, but Kilby won the rights to the invention in a lengthy patent suit (F, 1969a: 1391).

Their epochal invention uses crystalline material, often silicon (hence the name *Silicon Valley* for the area south of San Francisco where much of the U.S. electronics industry is concentrated), to make each main electrical component needed in most circuits. Zenith first used such chips commercially in a miniature hearing-aid amplifier marketed in 1964. The chip's ability to concentrate many electronic functions in a tiny space made possible an explosion of devices such as digital watches, hand-held calculators, and personal computers.

Miniaturization

Beginning in the late 1950s, the shift from vacuum tubes to solid-state devices profoundly affected broadcast technology. Solid-state technology fed a general trend toward miniaturization in electronics, a trend driven initially by military needs for complicated communications satellites launched with rockets of insufficient thrust for the heavy loads that tube-based electronics required. The fascination with the "smallest something" grew from years of toys and hobbies to a technological revolution.*

The latest versions of this technology enable complex circuitry, incorporating thousands of transistors and other components, to be etched on a single chip an eighth of an inch in diameter. Integrated-circuit technology marries ideally with digital signal processing (detailed at Section 5.7) for the wide variety of broadcast, cable, and satellite

---

*In fact, vacuum tubes may make a comeback in the form of vacuum microelectronics. The fact that electrons flow fastest in a vacuum may be useful in design of flat-panel video display devices.

*Silicon chips, second-generation solid-state devices, are most familiar through their use in microcomputers. Apple sold the first such device in 1978 and, with the initial IBM personal computer three years later (built around a 8088 microprocessor, it had only 64k of memory and one 160k floppy-disk drive, yet initially cost nearly $3,000) began to push computers into most aspects of daily life. The Apple Macintosh introduced in 1984 made use of graphics easier and widened the computer's appeal even further (see Section 5.7).

Exhibit 3.i •••••••••••••••••••

Changing Definitions of "Portable"

A.

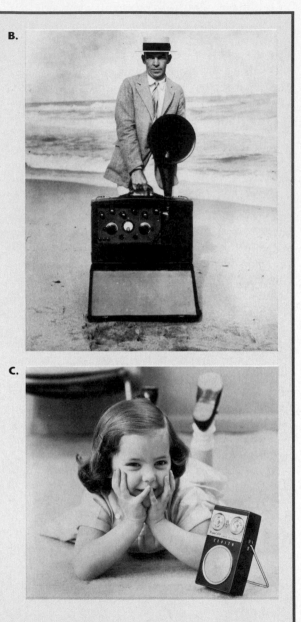

(A) The paper clip and pencil show the size of 1950s vacuum tubes in relation to 1960s transistors and current integrated-circuit chips. (B) Cumbersome vacuum-tube portable radios required either large batteries or household electric power. (C) Transistors began to replace vacuum tubes in the 1960s, leading to small, inexpensive portable radios. (D) In the late 1970s tiny portable television-receivers using integrated circuits became available.

B.

C.

D.

Source: Photo B from the Bettmann Archive; photo C courtesy Zenith Electronics Corporation; photos A and D by Janna Olson.

equipment on which all electronic media futures rest.

Remote Flexibility

Examples of the benefits made possible by this miniaturization include both ENG (electronic news gathering) and EFP (electronic field production). Formerly, when covering outside news events or when producing on-location program segments and commercials, television crews had to use cumbersome remote vehicles (see Exhibit 10.l, on p. 363). Miniaturization, however, has enabled use of lightweight equipment that is easily carried and operated by one or two persons.

The key to this development, the *time-base corrector*, contains a microcomputer that supplies accurate synchronization of sound and picture, freeing remotely operated portable equipment from dependence on studio equipment. Before the time-base corrector became available, synchronizing errors plagued remote operations, showing up as jittery pictures, skewing, and color breakup.

SNG (satellite news gathering), begun in the mid-1980s, uses portable earth stations that permit relaying of television reports from any location. Previously, live remotes depended on microwave-relay links, which require unobstructed line-of-sight paths between studio and remote unit. However, SNG-equipped stations (again, see Exhibit 10.l) can obtain short-term access to Ku-band satellite transponders (those requiring only small uplink dishes) through firms that specialize in retailing satellite capacity. Use of SNG thus enables a station or cable system to send stories from anywhere in the country back to local viewers or to a network for national delivery.

TV Improvements

Thanks to the same basic technological improvements, manufacturers have made television sets lighter, cooler, less demanding of power, less expensive to operate, with vastly improved sound (including stereo), and easier to use with digital tuning. Variety has increased, too, from tiny portable television sets, such as the Sony "Watchman," to larger-screen sets (ranging from the standard 21-inch screens of the 1960s to screens exceeding a diagonal measure of 30 inches in the early 1990s); projection screen receivers 60 or more inches across; sets better able to accommodate cable's increased number of channels; and widespread adoption of remote controls, making choices among all those added channels easier to accomplish.

All these new features had to be made compatible with existing standards—those developed in the 1940s for black-and-white television. Yet one projected improvement—high-definition television—quickly brought engineers and policy makers up against the old standards and inertia evidenced by the millions of existing sets in viewers' hands. Demonstrated in the United States for the first time in 1981, HDTV promised picture resolution twice as good as the American standard, but at the cost of incompatibility with existing receivers. (HDTV is detailed at Section 5.9.)

• • • • • • • •

3.5 Home Media Center

Improvements in television receivers have paralleled viewers' increasing ability to control their entire home electronic media environment. Home video recorders and players now allow viewers to purchase and copy programs of their own choosing—and to watch them at their leisure, instead of having to accept common signals sent to large, undifferentiated, widely dispersed audiences (see Exhibit 3.j).

VCRs: Giving Viewers Control

The home video recorder dates back to at least 1972, when Japan's Sony Corporation introduced the first *videocassette recorder* (VCR), the U-Matic, for educational and business applications. Three years later Sony marketed its Betamax machine for the home market at an initial price of $1,300. Futurists predicted a new video revolution, now that

Exhibit 3.j

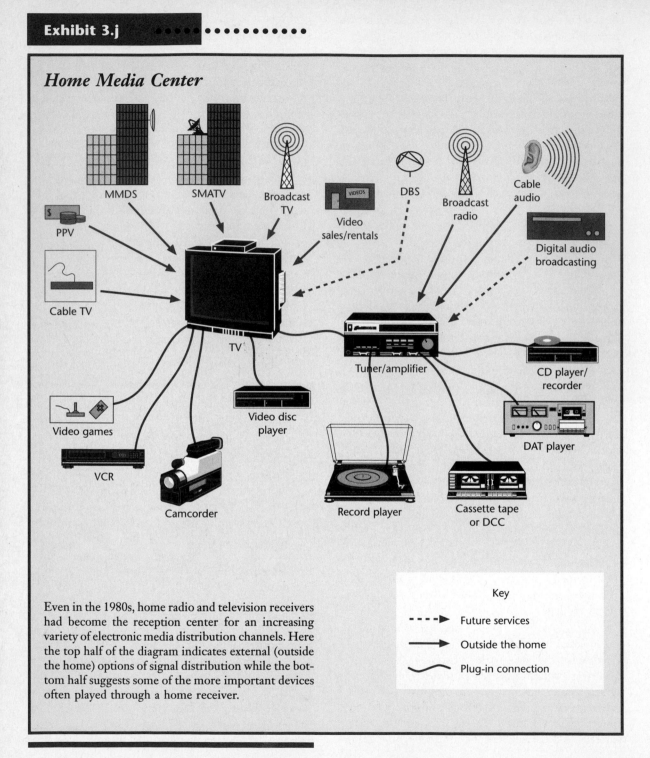

Home Media Center

MMDS   **SMATV**   **Broadcast TV**   **Video sales/rentals**   **DBS**   **Broadcast radio**   **Cable audio**

PPV   **Cable TV**   **Digital audio broadcasting**

TV   **Tuner/amplifier**   **CD player/recorder**

Video games   **Video disc player**   **DAT player**

VCR   **Camcorder**   **Record player**   **Cassette tape or DCC**

Key

- - - - ▶   Future services

——▶   Outside the home

〜   Plug-in connection

Even in the 1980s, home radio and television receivers had become the reception center for an increasing variety of electronic media distribution channels. Here the top half of the diagram indicates external (outside the home) options of signal distribution while the bottom half suggests some of the more important devices often played through a home receiver.

consumers could choose not only *when* they would view something but also *what* they would view at that time—broadcast or cable programs, prerecorded cassettes, or their own home-recorded sources (the technology is detailed at Section 5.6).

Sony's monopoly (which had angered other Japanese manufacturers) ended in 1977 when Matsushita introduced its technically incompatible VHS (Video Home System) system. By offering longer recording times, VHS gradually monopolized consumer VCR markets. Various "bells and whistles" stimulated sales, bringing prices down from an average of more than $1,000 in the late 1970s to about a third of that a decade later.

By the mid-1980s several trends had combined to create the long-promised home video revolution. Sales of VCRs after 1975 closely paralleled the 1959–1966 "take-off" years of color television receiver sales (see Exhibit 3.k). By 1992 more than three quarters of all American homes had a VCR—and about 15 percent had at least two.

As VCR penetration increased, Hollywood recognized a new market for retailing older motion pictures. Soon thousands of films could be bought (or more often rented) for home showing, thus further encouraging VCR sales. VCR users could easily duplicate tapes, leading to widespread piracy. Film distributors changed their marketing strategies to forestall illicit copying: outlets rented films for just a dollar or two a night, which was cheaper than copying. Such inexpensive rentals encouraged still more VCR buying. By the late 1980s, the purchase price of leading motion pictures on cassette had dropped from $80 to $30 or less, thus encouraging even more purchases—and still greater VCR use. When the blockbuster film *E.T.* finally reached the home-sale market, it sold a record 14 million copies at $29.95 each.

VCRs encourage *time shifting*, the recording of broadcast or cable programs (some cable networks encourage VCR use in their promotional materials)—not to keep but to view at a later time (audience data is discussed at Section 11.8). VCRs have an important psychological effect: viewers can control what they see and when. Furthermore, the machines make it easy to cut out commercials during recording (*zapping*) or playback (*zipping*)—a selling point for VCRs, but hardly popular with broadcasters and advertisers.

Cable systems see VCRs as competitors, for the same reason that TV stations view cable as competitive: the newer medium diverts viewers from the old. In fact, HBO and other pay-cable services enjoyed little audience growth after the mid-1980s, largely because of competition from VCR film rentals. As noted earlier, the addition of multiple PPV channels has been one important cable response to the VCR threat. On the other hand, cable has not had much to fear from videodiscs.

Videodiscs—Round One

Magnavox introduced the first consumer videodisc player in 1978. Although it could not record, it cost only half as much as a VCR and offered a superior picture in playback. Then RCA's incompatible *non-*laser "Selectavision" came on the market in 1981. Mass marketing brought down VCR prices faster than expected, wiping out videodisc cost advantage. Coupled with the inability to record and confusion over different standards, price competition from VCRs proved fatal to consumer potential of videodiscs, although they continued to play a role in training for education and business. In 1984 RCA pulled out of the home videodisc market, taking a loss of some $500 million. The videodisc appeared to be yet another consumer product washout.

Compact Discs

The first new audio product since tape recorders, compact disc (CD) players appeared in 1983. As described in Section 5.8, CDs use recording methods similar to video laser discs: a laser beam plays back digital musical signals, achieving nearly perfect sound reproduction with no surface noise or distortion. CD technology was expensive at first (players cost about $800 and discs at least $20 each), but mass production pushed prices down (to about $150 for players and under $10 for many discs) such that, by the late 1980s, the CD could be said to "have had the most successful product introduction in

Exhibit 3.k

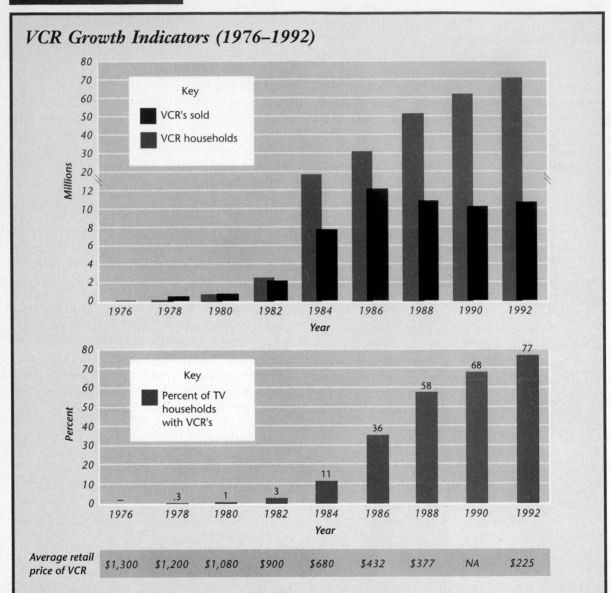

VCR Growth Indicators (1976–1992)

Key
- VCR's sold
- VCR households

Millions / *Year*

Key
- Percent of TV households with VCR's

Percent / *Year*

Year	1976	1978	1980	1982	1984	1986	1988	1990	1992
Percent	—	.3	1	3	11	36	58	68	77

	1976	1978	1980	1982	1984	1986	1988	1990	1992
Average retail price of VCR	$1,300	$1,200	$1,080	$900	$680	$432	$377	NA	$225

By 1992, virtually three-quarters of American television households owned a VCR and a growing proportion had more than one. As prices dropped in the 1980s, sales shot up. That the VCR industry is "mature" rather than growing, and that sales are now largely replacement or second-unit rather than first-purchase sales is indicated in the flat sales figures since 1986.

Source: Data from Electronic Industries Association and Television Bureau of Advertising.

consumer electronics history" (EIA, 1988: 31). By 1992 about 35 percent of homes owned a CD player (see Exhibit 3.l), and the LP record, mainstay of music recording for four decades, had virtually disappeared from store shelves.

Videodiscs—Round Two

CD technology came to the rescue of the moribund videodisc industry. Videodisc players capable of playing either audio or video appeared, and videodisc programs—mainly motion pictures—became more readily available. Most popular by the early 1990s were multifunction players able to handle standard 5-inch audio CDs as well as 8- and 12-inch laser videodiscs. Their ability to play digital stereo sound has prompted strong sales of classical and popular music video recordings. Still, this videodisc "round two" has been limited, as only about one percent of households owned a laserdisc video player by 1992 (again, see Exhibit 3.1).

● ● ● ● ● ● ● ● ●

3.6   TV Network Decline

Development of cable and other new options gave people their first real electronic media choices beyond traditional broadcasting—and the impact of those choices soon became evident. Dramatic change in fortunes of the long-dominant television networks provides one means of assessing such impact. By the end of the decade, all three had changed hands—and a new one had appeared. Thousands of employees were laid off as competition forced leaner operations. Only a decade earlier, few network leaders would have predicted any of these developments.

Traditional Competition

ABC finally achieved competitive equality with CBS and NBC, though only in the 1970s did it develop an affiliate lineup equal to those of the senior networks. It expanded its evening news to a half-hour and went fully into color. Late in the same decade, ABC for the first time moved ahead in network ratings, knocking long-time leader CBS out of the top spot for several prime-time seasons.

NBC tried to boost its ratings by hiring away ABC's program chief, Fred Silverman, as president. But NBC remained in third place until former independent producer Grant Tinker took the network presidency for five years, piloting NBC into the top spot (for the first time) by 1985.

The CBS story after 1970 centers largely on the search for William Paley's replacement. After a half-century at the helm, Paley brought in a string of potential successors, only to tire of them, forcing each out—a pattern not unknown among long-time corporate tycoons. Paley finally retired in 1983 (at 82, long past the CBS retirement limit of 65 when all others had to depart), naming Thomas Wyman as chief executive officer, only the second one in CBS's 55-year history.

FCC Studies Networks—Again

But these boardroom battles and the continuing quest for ratings success with look-alike programming masked underlying changes. Signs of those changes emerged in results of a third (and probably last) FCC broadcast network investigation. From 1978 to 1980 lawyers and economists assessed FCC network policies in light of developing technologies. With consent decrees, the Department of Justice had previously settled antitrust suits against all three networks, thereby loosening network control over independent programmers and barring them from acting as sales representatives for their affiliates.

The FCC study group reported in 1980 that most FCC network rules had little value in a rapidly changing marketplace. They merely restricted legitimate business interaction between networks and their affiliates without really protecting affiliates from network dominance. The best way to lessen three-network dominance, the report concluded, would be to eliminate FCC barriers to formation of new networks.*

---

*The study also concluded that there were only three broadcast networks not because of broadcaster anticompetitive action but because of the channel allotment decisions made in the 1952 *Sixth Report* (detailed on pp. 58–59).

Exhibit 3.1 •••••• • • • • • • • •

Penetration of Newer Media

Category	Mode		
	Broadcast/Satellite	Cable	Recordings
Universal services	Radio—98% Color TV—97% TV Remote Control—80%		Analog LP records or cassettes—about 90%
Majority services	2 or More TV sets—64% TV/VCR remote control—about 80%	Basic cable—62% Homes *passed by* cable—96%	VCR—75%
Niche services	Stereo TV—40% Projection TV—9% Home TVRO—4% SMATV } MMDS } less than 2%	Pay cable—about 45% PPV cable—about 20%	CD player—42% Camcorder—19% Laserdisc player—1%
Technologies of rising potential	HDTV } DAB } none in 1993		DAT } DDC } less than 1%
Services in decline	Teletext } STV } none MDS }	Videotex—none (by television)	Cartridge tape—none

Despite the extensive press many new services and technologies receive, few were widely available in American homes in the early 1990s. The categories suggested here merely indicate which services play what role in media delivery and recording. Figures refer to number of television households with service or technology indicated.

Source: Penetration data from Electronic Industries Association, citing information for January 1993.

New Player—Fox

The FCC report seemed vindicated five years later, when international media mogul Rupert Murdoch announced his purchase of six independent television stations to complement his purchase a year earlier of half-ownership in the 20th Century Fox film studio. Late in 1985 he announced plans to start a fourth television broadcast network—Fox.*

*This announcement marked the first such attempt since 1967, when an underfunded Overmyer/United Network effort lasted only a month (see Exhibit 3.m).

Fox was initially too small to be subject to the FCC's national network rules, so it escaped the restrictions on producing its own entertainment programs that limited its broadcast network competitors. This freedom enabled Fox to benefit from its vertical integration of Hollywood production, network relays, and owned-and-operated stations.

Under Chairman Barry Diller (until 1992, when he moved on), Fox developed toward full-fledged network status. After faltering by simply imitating existing networks with its first programs, nearly all of which failed, Fox concentrated on programs that appealed to younger audiences, such as *Married . . . with Children* and, in 1990, the biting cartoon satire *The Simpsons.* These programs, plus such lucky breaks as a 1988 writer's strike against the three big networks (which forced viewers to watch Fox shows to escape reruns), began to build Fox's audience. By 1990 Fox could reach 91 percent of all television households with its 7 owned-and-operated stations and its 126 affiliates. The program schedule was expanded from three to five nights and projected for seven in 1993. Advertisers flocked to the youthful demographics of Fox viewers. During one July week in 1992, when its older competitors were devoting some of their evening hours to coverage of the Democratic convention, Fox, for the first time ever, came in third (ahead of NBC) in overall prime-time ratings—and number one among advertiser-favored adults 18 to 49 years of age. Flush with this success, and determined to make Fox a truly "full-service" network, Murdoch announced plans for a major push into news programming and hired a former CBS news chief to lead its efforts.

Changing Hands

After more than three decades of stable ownership, the three established television networks all changed hands in less than two years. This sudden break with tradition was the result of several developments that happened to coincide: the retirement of long-time leaders, declines in ratings (due in part to upstart Fox's competition), poor financial performance, and FCC deregulation of station ownership limits. The sales suggested that all was not well at the once-dominant networks.

ABC went first. In 1985 Capital Cities Communications* announced that it would acquire American Broadcasting Companies, parent of the ABC network, in a friendly deal valued at more than $3.5 billion. Long-time ABC Chair Leonard Goldenson, moving toward retirement, said he wanted the network to have a larger financial base. The change in control created a conglomerate worth some $4.5 billion (the 1953 merger of ABC with Paramount Theaters, also engineered by Goldenson, had been valued at just $25 million). The combined firm had to shed its cable interests and several television stations to meet even the newly relaxed FCC ownership rules.

Within weeks after the Cap Cities/ABC announcement, Ted Turner revealed plans for an unfriendly takeover attempt on CBS. In a complex deal valued at about $5 billion, he offered CBS stockholders "junk bonds" (high-risk, high-yield debt securities secured by the resources of the target company) and stock in Turner Broadcasting (but no cash) in exchange for a controlling two-thirds of CBS. The network thwarted his effort by going deeply into debt to repurchase 21 percent of its own stock from shareholders. Turner withdrew his offer but left CBS reeling from debt and internal dissension. Severe cutbacks resulted, and in late 1985 the network—in need of cash—sold an owned-and-operated station.

CBS network management initially seemed relieved in 1985 when Laurence Tisch, chairperson of the Loews entertainment and investment conglomerate, bought 12 percent of CBS stock and took a seat on the board. Later in the year, Tisch enlarged his holdings to just under 25 percent and edged out Thomas Wyman as network chief. William Paley came back from retirement as a figurehead chairperson until his death five years later.

*Referred to in the industry as "Cap Cities," the name derives from the fact that the company's first two stations were located in state capitals: Albany, New York, and Raleigh, North Carolina. The merger was characterized by some as the minnow eating the whale, given how much smaller Cap Cities was than the network it took over.

Exhibit 3.m ●●●●●●●●●●●●●●

Rupert Murdoch and the Elusive "Fourth Network"

In 1985, Australian publisher Rupert Murdoch became a United States citizen almost overnight in order to acquire Metromedia's six independent major-market television stations (WNEW-TV, New York; KTTV-TV, Los Angeles; WFLD-TV, Chicago; WTTG-TV, Washington, DC; KNBN-TV, Dallas; and KRIV-TV, Houston) and one network affiliate (WCVB-TV, Boston) for $2 billion. He resold WCVB-TV to the Hearst Corporation for $450 million but picked up another Boston station, WFXT-TV.

Having purchased half-ownership of 20th Century-Fox film corporation in 1984 for $250 million, Murdoch acquired the remaining half in 1985 (after the Metromedia deal) for $325 million. He thus gained complete control over a company with an extensive film library (including such hits as *Cocoon* and *Aliens*) and rights to numerous television series (*L.A. Law* and *M*A*S*H*, for example). In 1985 Murdoch announced plans to form a new national television network, Fox Broadcasting Company. A core of six O&O stations (reaching about 20 percent of all U.S. television households) served as the network.

Fox premiered in October 1986 with *The Late Show*, starring comedienne Joan Rivers. Rivers, who had been the primary substitute host on Johnny Carson's *Tonight Show* on NBC, had credited Carson for much of her success. She became the object of Carson's ire when she switched from friend and collaborator to competitor and challenger in his time period. However, the Rivers show lasted only seven months. Fox tried several other programs before giving up on the late-night time period altogether in order to concentrate on other parts of the day.

In its first season, Fox averaged between 2 percent and 6 percent of the national audience. Fox programs typically languished at the bottom of the Nielsen list, although some fared better.

The quality of the Fox affiliate line-up remained a problem. More than 120 stations carried Fox programming, but most were UHF, some were only low-power television stations, and nearly all were the weakest stations in their markets. The network lost about $80 million in its first year of operation, but Murdoch marched on.

In December 1985 came NBC's turn. Parent company RCA, weakened by years of inept management and huge losses from unsuccessful forays into the computer and videodisc markets, welcomed a takeover by General Electric. RCA—and its then top-rated NBC subsidiary—went for $6.28 billion, the biggest nonoil acquisition to that point in U.S. history. The takeover made NBC a part of the nation's second-largest industrial corporation (excluding car manufacturers), with annual sales of more than $40 billion.* New management at NBC sold

*With the takeover, RCA returned to the company that had created it in the first place back in 1919 (see Section 1.6). But RCA was soon dismantled, becoming little more than a trade name owned by the French conglomerate, Thomson. Its respected David Sarnoff Research Center overlapped with existing GE research and development efforts and was given to another research company (for which GE earned a tax writeoff) in 1987.

His acquisition in 1988 of Triangle Publications (publisher of *TV Guide*) for $3 billion brought his U.S. magazine empire to about the same level as that of Time Inc., the largest magazine publisher in America. Indeed, Murdoch appeared well on his way to developing the most powerful communications empire in the world. He controlled 60 percent of metropolitan newspaper circulation in Australia, 36 percent of na-

tional circulation in Britain; he also had part-ownership in ten book publishers, and reached more than 13 million homes in 22 European countries with Sky Channel, a satellite broadcasting service for cable-TV viewers. He had interests in printing plants, real estate, an airline, even sheep farms.

Not everything worked. The Sky Cable venture collapsed long before any satellites were ordered. And except for *TV Guide*, Murdoch sold off his magazines in order to plow more money into Fox.

Fox had planned expanded operations to every night of the week by 1993 and Murdoch spoke increasingly of adding a news service for use by local affiliates. It would be news with a difference—something fast and in motion, to match the lifestyles of the 18- to 34-year-olds the network especially targets. He hired former CBS News chief Van Gordon Sauter to develop the news operation. Barry Diller, founding chairman and real architect of the Fox network's early years, left in 1992 to invest in and become chairman of a home shopping network. Murdoch named Lucie Salhany, former broadcaster and most recently head of Twentieth Century Fox's program production and distribution division, as Fox Broadcasting's new chair.

Meanwhile, Murdoch became increasingly involved in daily network operations—even moving his family from New York to Beverly Hills to learn more easily (what was for him) the new world of Hollywood. He concentrated on further developing his television operations and reducing corporate debt by selling many of the corporation's print properties.

Source: Illustrations courtesy The News Corporation Ltd. and Fox Broadcasting Co.

off the radio network to Westwood One and then, in separate deals, individual NBC radio stations, thus ending nearly seven decades in that business. "Radio City," NBC's long-time New York home, no longer housed a radio network, and the RCA building, centerpiece of Rockefeller Center, was renamed the GE building. WNBC radio, developed from AT&T's WEAF commercial broadcast pioneer, was sold in 1988 (and has changed hands again

since in an example of more rapid station turnover in recent years) to become WFAN, an all-sports station.

Network change was not confined to mainline networks. Univision, a Spanish-language network with nine owned-and-operated stations changed hands three times in just five years. Originally owned in large part by the Mexican firm Televisa, the network and its five stations were purchased by

Hallmark for $575 million in 1987.* Hallmark then bought four more stations for Univision in 1988–1989. But when economic (and thus advertising) decline led the operation to lose money, Hallmark sold the network and its nine stations for $550 million—much less than its own investment—to a Los Angeles entertainment investor and his minority partners (a Venezuelan company) as well as to Televisa, which thus came back into partial ownership of the company it had started.

New Network Order

For several years after the takeovers, news from all three networks was mostly bad. Profits fell, audience shares kept slipping, and thousands of employees were fired or laid off. The new owners made it clear that the days of cushy network jobs and fat expense accounts had passed. At CBS, for example, Lawrence Tisch sold off virtually all the network's subsidiaries, including extensive publishing interests, culminating with the sale of Columbia Records (the world's largest record company) to Sony in 1988 for $2 billion.**

Meanwhile, CBS and the other networks continued to tighten their belts. Driving the budget and resulting personnel cuts was a dramatic decline in the networks' combined share of prime-time viewers—from more than 90 percent in 1978 to about 70 percent a decade later, and to around 55 percent by 1993 (see Exhibit 3.n). Declines in audience levels led to parallel drops in advertiser spending on all broadcast television networks (as detailed further at Section 7.4).

These dramatic television network changes highlighted the passing of an old broadcast order. New managers working amidst a depressed national economy sought in every way to cut corners as they faced ever-stronger competition. Little of what the networks provided was unique any more: upstart CNN, for example, challenged once-invincible network news departments for audiences. CBS News, long a center of prestige, underwent a series of wrenching management changes as it thinned down. Several well-known reporters, among hundreds of others, were let go, and a spate of angry books argued pursuasively that network news would never be the same—that CBS News, especially, had lost its way from the glorious days of Edward R. Murrow. Although traditional rivalries continued to receive press coverage, somehow they seemed less important as viewers increasingly turned to cable networks or their VCRs. Rumors that GE wanted to sell NBC and that Lawrence Tisch was said to be seeking a buyer for CBS circulated widely in the early 1990s (and both networks denied the rumors), indicative of the networks' lost luster.

● ● ● ● ● ● ● ●

3.7 Broadcasting— Changing Course

Although the networks' decline dominated media news, all broadcasters faced both new and old competitors in an ever-more-fragmented marketplace. The FCC came to the industry's aid with some deregulation, offering a chance to increase revenues (see Section 13.10). Technology also helped by improving production tools and reception quality. Both cable television and VCRs—available in more than half the nation's homes—had a negative impact on television station audiences, steering them to new uses of their home television sets (as described further at Sections 11.7 and 11.8). The number of broadcast stations continued to grow in the 1970s and 1980s, but it did so at a slower rate. And for the first time since the Depression, many AM stations, losing money against more successful FM rivals, began to leave the air.

*This 1987 sale resulted in large part from FCC concern that Univision's stations had long been held by foreign nationals in violation of Communications Act requirements. Mexican ownership of the licenses had been effectively disguised for years.

**With the resulting multibillion-dollar cash hoard, CBS sought additional stations, buying first in Miami and then in Minneapolis as it refocused entirely on broadcasting.

Exhibit 3.n •••••• •••••••••••••

TV Network Decline

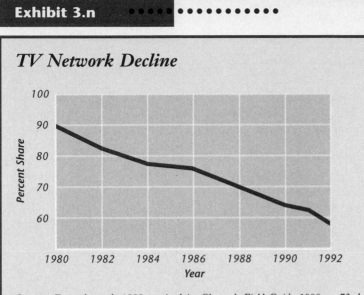

The chart shows the decline in combined three-network share (not including Fox) of total prime-time television audience for each season (1980 indicates the 1979–80 season, etc.) over the 1980–92 period.

Source: Data through 1989 as cited in *Channels Field Guide 1990*, p. 73, based on A.C. Nielsen data which is source for 1990–1992.

FM's Dominant Radio Role

Yet amidst all the new competition, radio continued to expand, dividing audiences into ever-smaller segments. The growth came in part from FCC relaxation of restraints on station ownership as well as other deregulation. The number of FM stations has risen to match that of AM (see Exhibit 2.a on p. 44). With its better sound, increasing program diversity, and often fewer commercials, FM passed AM in overall national audience popularity in the late 1970s. A decade later, FM had three listeners for every AM listener.

Demand for more FM stations forced the FCC to lower its technical standards so as to squeeze additional signals into many markets—a total of 700 new allotments nationwide. The commission also allowed limited use of directional antennas—long required in most AM operations—to help avoid interference. While some welcomed this expansion, others, including the National Association of Broadcasters, urged the FCC to limit FM growth to avoid AM's interference-prone status.

AM's Continued Problems

AM owners also pressed the FCC for a variety of technical and ownership-rule changes to better compete with FM. In the early 1980s, for example, an FCC attempt to boost the number of AM stations on the air (not, perhaps, what the business needed) by reducing channel spacing from 10 kHz to 9 kHz (the standard in all countries other than those in the Western Hemisphere) foundered largely on fears of receiver obsolescence and the costs of adjusting thousands of transmitters.

When in 1982 it approved AM stereo service, the FCC declined to select a specific standard from among five competing systems. This refusal set a precedent that would survive a decade. The commission, now controlled by marketplace ideology, argued that competition rather than government should select new standards. Individual stations, said the FCC, should pick whichever AM stereo system they wanted, and consumers could buy AM stereo sets to match. The FCC would become involved only if interference resulted.

Broadcasters argued that the lack of a recognized standard would delay the spread of AM stereo because stations and manufacturers alike would wait to see what the marketplace was going to do. They were right. By 1992, when Congress required the FCC to revisit the matter and select a system, few stereo AM radios had been sold (most were car radios), and less than 15 percent of AM stations were broadcasting in stereo, most using a Motorola-developed standard (which, in 1993, the FCC officially annointed). By then, however, AM stereo seemed moot as focus shifted to developing digital audio broadcast options (discussed at Section 5.10).

AM's problems went too deep for any single technological fix. Too many stations were chasing too few advertising dollars and listeners. Many listeners perceived AM as being full of advertising and talk (although some actually preferred the call-in formats to music). Several stations that had been on the air for decades closed down under the competitive pressure, and others were sold by long-term owners. NBC's sale of its pioneering network to Westwood One, and of its owned-and-operated radio stations indicated AM's continuing decline.

TV in Transition

Caught between improving technology and the weak economy of the late 1980s and early 1990s, commercial television stations faced a steadily tougher competitive marketplace. Television grew in one sense and remained stagnant in another. On one hand, the industry showed strength—the number of independent (nonnetwork-affiliated) stations rose from 129 in 1980 to some 400 by 1993. Fully 70 percent of stations going on the air for the first time were independents, and their proportion relative to all stations on the air increased from 18 to 35 percent. Nearly all of this growth was among

UHF outlets, helped along, ironically, by otherwise competitive cable that made the weaker UHF signal equal to VHF in cable homes (Setzer and Levy, 1991: 15–17).

On the other hand, the advertising market remained sluggish—as reflected in television station sales prices that did not increase (if inflation is taken into account) after 1985. In fact, there was little overall expansion in total advertising after 1980, and virtually no increase in what had been a steadily rising proportion of those dollars spent on broadcast television. Television's share (network, spot, and local advertising combined) has remained at about one fifth of all advertising dollars for about a decade.

Outside of the biggest markets, where profits held up well, the outlook for small-market television stations in the early 1990s was troubling. Technical change was coming fast—and to broadcasting's competitors first. Video compression (described at Section 5.7), for example, would allow the relay of several channels by each satellite transponder by 1992–1993, next would add far more channels to cable television a few years later, and only last would enable broadcasting to exceed its single-channel limitations, most likely with the arrival of digital high-definition television (Setzer and Levy, 1991: 64–65). How well stations would fare economically in the years until HDTV remains in doubt.

There was good news here, of course. Most viewers continued to identify first with (and tune most to) favorite local stations and one or more broadcast networks, supplementing those by viewing cable channels and using home VCRs.

• • • • • • • •

3.8 Sorting Out the Players

Development of new delivery systems and improvements on older systems raised questions for manufacturers, broadcasters, competing systems, and policy makers. What should be concluded from the highly expensive failures in the 1980s of RCA's videodisc, Comsat's round-one DBS proposal, several teletext and videotex experiments, STV, and Warner's Qube interactive cable system?

Competitive Confusion?

Some observers have argued that too many competitors overtaxed program creativity and confused consumers with constantly changing standards and formats. Did all these options offer a real choice or simply new means of receiving the same old programs long provided by traditional broadcasting? And do marketplace pressures encourage the wrong kind of media investment—overlapping services that provide nothing really new? (For instance, do we really need multiple home-shopping channels pushing the same stuff?)

Regulator preference for marketplace rather than government control increased after 1975. Services developed since then (pay cable, MMDS, SMATV, DBS, and VCRs) have had little or no regulatory oversight—and have brought little new programming to viewers.

Thus far, all the technological jockeying has resulted mainly in more delivery options rather than in much-increased *diversity* of choice among new programming. Most of us clearly have more options now at any given time—but they are options from a fairly narrow menu of content. Critics maintain that what is needed are new players with different ideas. One of those touted "new" potential players—AT&T—is anything but new: it played a pioneering role in radio.

Return of the Telephone Company?

For a century AT&T operated the "Bell System" as a *regulated monopoly* under varying levels of government supervision. It had created a widely admired telephone service, keeping local telephone service rates low, through a subsidy from long-distance earnings that came mainly from business users. It also earned substantial revenues by providing land-line interconnections for radio and television networks—but played no other role in broadcasting except as an occasional program spon-

sor. The 1926 settlement between AT&T and RCA (described at Section 1.8) had worked well for a half-century.

The development of microwave- and, later, satellite-relay technology, along with a general trend toward electronic miniaturization, began to revolutionize telephones and business communications in the 1970s. Firms offering specialized long-distance services began to compete with AT&T. The government grew concerned about both AT&T's anticompetitive response to these firms and its apparent suppression of some promising new technologies. AT&T's transfer of revenue from its monopoly local telephone service to help pay for development of unregulated services alarmed regulators; it meant that home telephone users were subsidizing AT&T ventures into new services for big-business users.

In November 1974 the Department of Justice brought suit to break up the Bell System on antitrust grounds. After years of wrangling and a year-long court battle, a *consent decree* settled the case in 1982.* AT&T admitted no wrongdoing (to have done so would have opened it to countless suits from competitors claiming harm) but, in the face of heavy pressure and the likelihood that litigation would drag on for years, agreed to be broken up. This momentous settlement forced AT&T to divest (give up with no payment) its regional operating companies (thereafter known as "Baby Bells" or Regional Bell Operating Companies [RBOCs]) and their local telephone service markets, while allowing the telephone giant not only to continue offering long-distance and manufacturing services but also to continue operating the world-famous Bell Labs.

On January 1, 1984, the now-independent Baby Bells began operating as seven separately owned RBOCs: NYNEX, Bell Atlantic, BellSouth, Ameritech, Southwestern Bell, U.S. West, and Pacific Telesis. Taken together, the seven controlled 80 percent of all local telephone service. Each of the companies

---

*Often called the *MFJ*, for *modified final judgment*, this 1982 agreement was legally a modification (actually a replacement) of an earlier antitrust suit result—a 1956 "final judgment" that had done little to modify AT&T behavior.

also actively began seeking a wider role in what was becoming known as the "information" market.

Telephone and Information Services

Under the provisions of the consent decree the RBOCs were restricted from many activities, including ownership and programming of such information services as cable and videotex. Within a few years of the breakup, however, pressure from the RBOCs had built in Congress and the FCC to modify the 1982 decree to allow RBOCs to become providers of information services—possibly including cable or broadcasting. The specter of huge and economically powerful telephone companies entering and quickly dominating the electronic media drew the broadcast and cable businesses together in common fear of the larger telephone menace.

More specifically, some RBOCs proposed to enter the cable television business. The FCC and Congress had long banned such activity for local telephone carriers when telephone and cable service areas overlapped. The ban grew out of concern that both businesses provide direct connections to homes. One firm owning the only such connection would have great potential power over information flow on that cable.

In mid-1992, driven by two goals, the FCC changed course and considered allowing RBOCs and other local telephone companies to transmit—but not to own—video programs over their facilities (FCCR, 1992: 5781). With this *video dial tone* decision, the commission sought to encourage (1) increased competition to cable, thus holding down exorbitant rate increases, and (2) faster development of fiber-optic cable relays (detailed at Section 5.4), to connect homes and offices to a host of developing information services in addition to media entertainment and news. Though cable may face new competition, it will easily take until the turn of the century for the full impact of this important decision to be fully felt.

In the meantime, RBOCs took their first moves toward an active video role. Late in 1992, Bell Atlantic set up Bell Atlantic Video Services (BVS) to provide all but actual program production. The company brought suit to end the federal prohibition on video and telephone service in the same area (see Section 14.5), that if successful would allow BVS to quickly develop a powerful role in news and entertainment program packaging and marketing stressing interactive applications over fiber cable installations. Shortly thereafter, Southwestern Bell became the first RBOC to purchase a U.S. cable operator when it bought two Washington DC suburban cable systems. Because the cable and telephone franchises of this RBOC were more than 1,000 miles apart Southwestern avoided the legal ban against telco/cable cross-ownership in the same service area.

In mid-1993, US West, another RBOC, purchased a 25 percent share of Time-Warner Entertainment (the huge media conglomerate is the second largest operator of cable systems in the United States), the first major collaboration between the telephone and media industries. The $2.5 billion investment will speed up development of a cable-based home entertainment and information network of services in the mid-to-late 1990s. The convergence of telephone-broadcasting-cable interests—and the appropriate regulatory aspects of each—is one of the key policy debates of the 1990s.

● ● ● ● ● ● ● ●

Summary

3.1 Since 1970 over-the-air television has faced increasing competition from new delivery systems that first develped due to TV coverage limitations, most of them traceable to the television channel allotment scheme. Community antenna television, later to become cable television, began in several rural mountain communities in the late 1940s, using a common antenna and direct cable connection to provide television signals to subscriber homes. Cable soon augmented broadcast signals with distant-station importation and some original programming in the 1960s. This development concerned broadcasters, who pressured the FCC to limit cable. The early 1970s saw heavy FCC and state regulatory control of cable.

3.2   Cable continued to expand because of post-1975 deregulation and development of domestic satellite-distributed network services, led by HBO's pay-cable pioneering use of domsats and Ted Turner's superstation. Signal piracy of pay cable and introduction of pay-per-view services led to use of scrambled signals.

3.3   Several minor niche delivery alternatives developed, including short-lived subscription television (STV) and multipoint distribution services (MDS), but these single-channel options gave way in the face of multiple-channel competition from cable, master and satellite master antenna systems (MATV and SMATV), and "wireless cable" (MMDS). None except cable served more than a tiny portion of the total audience. Direct-broadcast satellites (DBS) are likely to enter the marketplace in the mid-1990s. Technology has made possible new ways to communicate with the hearing and vision-impaired. Two-way or interactive cable and videotex experiments proved uneconomical in the 1980s. Changing technology has revived interest in interactive systems in the 1990s.

3.4   Development of the integrated circuit after 1959 led not only to the greater professional flexibility provided by ENG and SNG equipment but also to new consumer products, including improved TV sets. The most exciting and far-reaching of these options, high-definition television (HDTV) and digital audio broadcasting (DAB), were in active laboratory testing in the early 1990s, but few expect to see sets in many consumer homes before 2000.

3.5   The videocassette recorder (VCR), first introduced in 1975, could be found in about three-fourths of the nation's households by 1993. The VCR changed film distribution patterns and enabled viewers to time-shift their viewing. Digital technology initially entered most homes in the form of audio compact discs and helped revive the fortunes of videodiscs.

3.6   The FCC conducted its third investigation of broadcast television networks and concluded that most rules limiting their business operations should be eliminated. The three major networks, beginning with ABC and concluding with NBC, changed hands in the mid-1980s after three decades of stable control. The changeovers resulted in part from options opened by deregulation and concern over network television's future amidst rising competition. A new network, Fox, had emerged as a major competitor by the 1990s.

3.7   After 1975 Congress and the FCC increasingly viewed the regulation of broadcasting as excessive, especially in view of the many competing delivery systems. FM grew to dominate radio broadcasting, AM stagnated, and TV expanded even though its portion of advertising revenues remained static. Critics found too few new program ideas to match the new technological options.

3.8   The 1984 breakup of AT&T created seven new RBOCs, eager to enter an expanding information services market, including video information and entertainment. In 1992 the FCC adopted a "video dial tone" policy that began to open the door to telephone industry participation in the media industry. This participation is a key policy question for the 1990s.

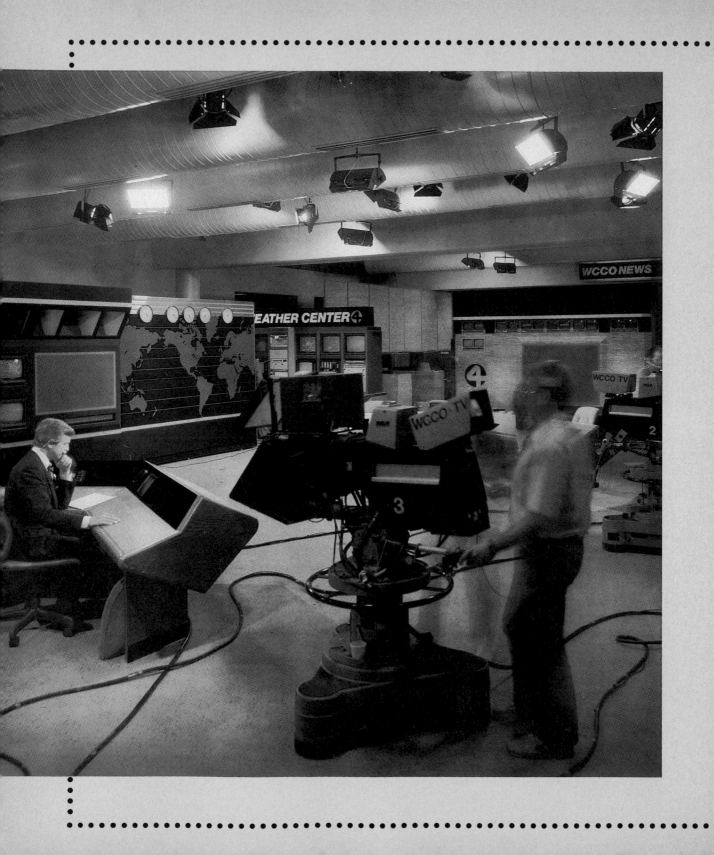

PART 2

Technology

The next two chapters provide essential background for understanding not only the physical aspects of how electronic media work at present but also the dramatic changes coming later in the 1990s. *Our theme is that technology largely determines both electronic media's potential and their limitations. Where and how far signals will travel, how much information they can carry, their susceptibility to interference, and the need for technical regulation—all of these factors depend primarily on the signals' physical nature.*

Chapter 4 surveys basic concepts involved in using radio energy for broadcasting and cable systems—the most widely used means of program delivery. Chapter 5 extends the application of these basic concepts to program relay (coaxial cable, satellite, and fiber optics), analog recording methods, and the digital revolution now transforming all electronic media.

Chapter 4

How Broadcasting and Cable Work

Technical terms and systems such as those dealt with in this and the next chapter are more easily understood if approached step by step in terms of familiar experience. Most electronic media consumers lack engineering training and have to accept some theoretical concepts on faith. Still, the basic ideas are not difficult to master. Here we begin with those basics and then extend them to traditional broadcast stations and cable systems.

4.1 *Electromagnetism— A Basic Force*

Electromagnetism is a basic natural force making possible a host of communication services, among them broadcasting. Radio,* an invisible form of

*As used in this chapter, the word *radio* (as in radio spectrum) means not just sound (audio) broadcasting but the *process* and *method* of communicating without wires. In this sense, radio transmits sounds, pictures, streams of coded data, and many other types of content including just plain noise.

electromagnetism, has the unique ability to travel through empty space, moving out in all directions without benefit of any material conductor such as wire or even air. This ability gives radio its most important advantage over other ways of communicating: radio waves can span oceans or continents, penetrate buildings, pass through people, and go to the moon (or farther) and back.

Radio Energy

All forms of radiant electromagnetic energy share three fundamental characteristics. They all (1) move at the same high speed or *velocity;* (2) assume the properties of *waves;* and (3) *radiate* outward from a source without benefit of any discernible physical vehicle.

Radio energy cannot be seen, but light is a visible form of electromagnetic energy. Light can thus illustrate some of radio's characteristics. Turn on an electric bulb and light radiates into the surrounding space, traveling 186,000 miles (300 million meters) per second. Both radio and light energy can be reflected, and both lose their strength as they travel away from their source. But radio and light differ in terms of both wavelength and wave frequency: light has much shorter waves with much higher frequency (note that inverse relationship).

Frequency refers to the fact that all electromagnetic energy has an oscillating (vibrating or alternating) motion, depicted in terms of waves. The number of separate wavelike motions produced each second determines a particular wave's frequency—a key concept inasmuch as differences in frequency determine the varied forms that electromagnetic energy assumes.

Electromagnetic Spectrum

A large number of frequencies visualized in numerical order makes up a spectrum. A piano keyboard symbolizes a *sound spectrum*, starting with keys to the left that produce low sound frequencies and progressing through higher frequencies at the keyboard's right end. We can see a *visible spectrum* when rain acts as a prism to break sunlight into its component colors. Sunlight combines "all the colors of the rainbow," which differ precisely because their frequencies differ.

To our human eye, lower frequencies of light appear red in color; as frequency increases, we see light as yellow, green, blue, and finally violet, the highest visible frequency. Above violet come *ultraviolet* frequencies; below the red visible frequency come *infrared* frequencies.

The electromagnetic spectrum is illustrated in Exhibit 4.a. Note that as frequency increases, wavelength decreases. Frequencies usable for radio communication occur near the lower end of the spectrum—where frequencies are lower and wavelengths are longer. As frequency increases, so do the practical problems of using the spectrum for communication. As communication technology improves, upper limits of usable frequencies are pushed higher. Still, there comes a point on the frequency scale at which electromagnetic energy can no longer be used for communication.

Communication satellites, for example, use the highest frequencies regularly applied to over-the-air transmission, mostly in the range from 3 GHz (3 *billion* oscillations per second) up to 15 GHz (see first footnote on p. 86 for a new experimental ser-

vice using 28 GHz). Yet even those frequencies come nowhere near those of light. Length of radio waves (see Exhibit 4.a) tells us how particular waves (and the applications that use those waves) behave.

Hertz—Expressing Frequency

Frequency is expressed in terms of *cycles per second*, or *Hertz*, abbreviated *Hz*.* The number of Hertz in higher radio frequencies rises into the billions, making for awkwardly long numbers. Thus, prefixing *Hz* with standard metric multipliers *kilo-* (thousand), *mega-* (million), and *giga-* (billion) simplifies the numbering system. Exhibit 4.a applies these metric terms to major subdivisions (*bands*) of radio-frequency spectrum and shows the abbreviations, such as VHF and UHF, used to identify such bands.

• • • • • • • •

4.2 Sound and Radio Waves

Audible sound energy differs from electromagnetic (radio) energy in fundamental ways, although sound, too, originates from oscillating sources and travels in the form of waves. By itself, sound has a limited range. (How far can you hear somebody—or even a whole football stadium crowd—shouting?) If "carried" on a radio wave, however, that sound can be carried hundreds or thousands of miles.

There's another reason for which sound is useful in illustrating the characteristics of radio waves in a tangible way: we can actually *hear* differences in sound that illustrate similar differences in radio. Understanding the nature of sound is important because sound quality and acoustics play a central role in all electronic media.

Sound as Waves

Two people talking at a party illustrate sound–wave motion principles. A speaker's vocal cords vibrate,

*Hz are so named to honor pioneer radio physicist Heinrich Hertz (1857–1894), discussed on p. 25.

Exhibit 4.a • • • • • • • • • • • • • • •

Electromagnetic Spectrum Uses

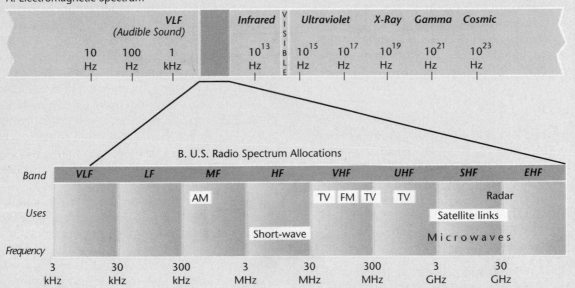

A. Electromagnetic Spectrum

B. U.S. Radio Spectrum Allocations

This diagram is not drawn to a uniform scale—as the frequencies rise, the scale gets smaller (otherwise it would be impossible to show this much spectrum in a single diagram). The usable radio spectrum with which we are concerned (B) is but a small part of the larger electromagnetic spectrum (A). The higher the frequencies, above the usable radio spectrum, the more potentially dangerous the output of electromagnetic radiation can become (infrared and ultraviolet rays), though even these can be useful (x-rays).

The radio spectrum is divided into bands by international agreement. Low frequency radio, a long-distance form of AM broadcasting, is used in Europe,

but not the United States. Though not shown here, virtually all usable spectrum is assigned to some use (aviation, land mobile, ship-to-shore, CB radio, cellular telephone, satellite uplinks and downlinks, and military applications). There is no unallocated spectrum, meaning that new services have to move older services aside (and usually upwards) in spectrum. See Exhibit 4.k for more detail on broadcast service allocations.

Changes in frequency nomenclature avoid awkwardly long numbers. Thus one kilohertz (kHz) = 1,000 Hz (Hertz, or cycles per second); a megahertz (MHz) = 1,000 kHz; a gigahertz (GHz) = 1,000 MHz.

producing word-sounds; these vocal cord oscillations set molecules of air into wavelike motion. Sound waves travel through the air to a listener's eardrums, which respond by vibrating in step with the air molecules' wave motion. Eardrum vibrations

stimulate nerve fibers leading to the listener's brain, which interprets vibrations as words.

Eardrums, unlike broadcast receivers, cannot "tune out" other voices using different frequencies; indeed, competing conversations or ambient noises often interfere with understanding. In this case, of course, the speaker can talk louder (producing stronger waves) to overcome interference.

Important wave-motion concepts can be seen in the sequence of events involved in speech. With each spoken word, vibration (alternation, oscillation) occurs. And vibration in one object (vocal cords) causes a corresponding vibratory motion in other objects (air, eardrums). In short, vibrating air molecules invisibly carry meaning from one point to another.

Wave Phases

As waves travel outward, they go through a cycle of motion. That cycle can be visualized as a wheel (which is what "cycle" means). To break a wave down into its components, consider the motion of one point on the rim of a revolving wheel, as depicted in Exhibit 4.b. A tracing of that motion results in a waveform illustrating amplitude, length, frequency, and velocity:

- The distance above and below the level of the axle represents *amplitude*, which, in the case of sound, we perceive as loudness.
- We can measure the distance the wheel travels in one revolution, which corresponds to the *length* of the wave.
- We can count the number of revolutions the wheel makes in a second, which tells us the wave's *frequency*, heard in terms of pitch (either length or frequency can be a measure of a sound's pitch).
- Finally, the distance traveled in a unit of time (in this case, a second) yields a measure of *velocity*.

As the wheel or cycle in Exhibit 4.b goes through its first, counter-clockwise, half revolution (180 degrees), the waveform rises to a maximum and then drops back to its starting level; then, during the second half of the wheel's revolution, the waveform goes through an opposite motion. Each half constitutes a *phase*, and together the two halves make up a complete *cycle*. Thus a wave consists of two opposite phases that together constitute a cycle.

When two waves of the *same* frequency exactly coincide, they are said to be *in phase*. If each has

the same amplitude, their combined amplitude is double the amplitude of just one. Conversely, if two waves of the same amplitude that are exactly halfway (180 degrees) *out* of phase combine, they cancel each other completely. Antinoise devices (such as the well-known Dolby systems), for example, eliminate unwanted sounds by generating competing sounds 180 degrees out of phase with unwanted sounds. In fact, phase plays an important practical role throughout electronic system applications. Two or more microphones fed to the same amplifier must be phased correctly to prevent their signals from interfering with each other; television relies on phase differences in processing color information; and some directional transmitting antennas use phase reinforcement and cancellation to strengthen signal radiation in one direction while weakening it in another.

Phase also has an important bearing on sound quality. A sound with a perfectly smooth, symmetrical waveform oscillates at a single frequency, creating a single tone—pure, but uninteresting. Pleasing musical tones and natural sounds, however, consist of many different frequencies of varying amplitudes, all blended together.

Sound Overtones

The frequency we hear as "the" pitch of a sound is its fundamental frequency or *fundamental*. The fundamentals of human speech have quite low frequencies, from 200 to 1,000 Hz for women and from 100 to 500 Hz for men. Complex sounds have *overtones* at higher frequencies. Overtones (also called *harmonics*) give sounds their distinctive tone quality and are formally defined as multiples of fundamentals.

Differences in distribution and amplitude of overtones account for quality differences we hear among sounds with the same pitch. We can tell a violin from a clarinet, even when the two instruments are producing exactly the same note at the same volume, because their overtones differ. Overtones can have relatively high pitch; therefore, good sound reproduction requires equipment that can reproduce the higher sound frequencies—up to 15,000 Hz.

Exhibit 4.b

Wave Motion Concepts

Tracing the rise and fall of a given point on the rim of a revolving wheel helps show the concepts of *cycle*, *phase*, *amplitude*, and *velocity*. With the axle treated as zero amplitude, movement above the axle is the point's positive phase while movement below is the negative phase. The blue curves to the right illustrate distance as the wheel travels, tracing a complete cycle of wave motion. This distance factor is measured as velocity— the distance traveled in a unit of time.

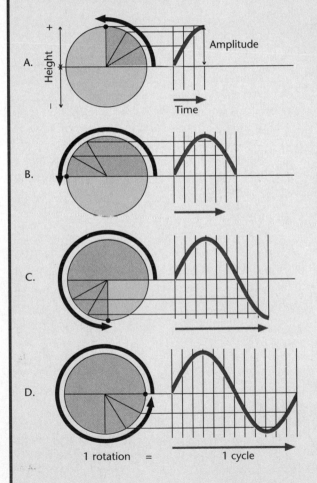

(A) Starting at zero level, the dot moves to maximum positive amplitude in one quarter-turn.

(B) In the next quarter-turn, the dot returns to zero level, completing one phase of its cycle.

(C) In its next quarter-turn, the dot moves to its maximum point of negative amplitude.

(D) In its final quarter-turn, the dot returns to its starting point, completing its second phase and one complete cycle.

Source: Adapted from SIGNALS: THE TELEPHONE AND BEYOND by John R. Pierce. Copyright © 1981 by W.H. Freeman and Company. Reprinted with permission.

Wave Attenuation

Sound waves begin to *attenuate* (weaken, or gradually lose their energy) as they travel. Drapes, human bodies, clothing, and other soft, irregularly shaped objects increase attenuation by *absorbing* sound energy. By contrast, hard, flat room surfaces *reflect* sound waves, causing reverberations or echoes (reverberations are echoes that are too closely spaced in time to be heard as separate sounds). Excessive sound absorption (though useful for recording distinct separate sounds) gives a room a "dead," uninteresting sound; reflections produce "live," bright sounds—but sometimes too much noise and echo.

The shorter the waves, the more easily small objects block their path. Long waves tend to "bend" around objects in their path. You can verify this by listening to music in another room or from around the corner of a building. As soon as you turn the corner into the area where the music originates, it immediately brightens because you begin hearing shorter-wave (that is, higher-pitched) sounds that could not get around the corner as readily as longer-wave sounds.

Sound vs. Radio Frequencies

Limitations of the human ear confine audible sound to a frequency range of about 20 to as much as 20,000 Hz (individual hearing varies a good deal, especially at the upper frequencies). By contrast, the radio spectrum runs from a few thousand Hz into the millions. Radio waves travel at 186,000 miles per second (the speed of light—the visible form of electromagnetic energy), or about 900,000 times the speed of sound in air.

Finally, radio waves need no intervening medium, such as air, in which to travel. Indeed, they travel best in a total vacuum. Sound, on the other hand, must have air, water, or some other physical conductor because sound travels as pressure waves, not electronic waves.

Carrier Waves

Radio-wave production depends upon vibration (oscillation)—but vibration of an electric current rather than of a physical object as with sound waves. An oscillating current can be envisioned as power surging back and forth (alternating) in a wire, rising to a maximum in one direction (one phase), then to a maximum in the other (the opposite phase).

A broadcast transmitter generates a basic *carrier wave*, feeding it to a transmitting antenna for radiating into space. The transmitter's carrier wave oscillates at the station's allotted frequency, radiating energy at that frequency continuously, even when no specific information (sound or picture) is going out. The carrier wave itself is usually silent on most receivers.

Frequency and Wavelength

As Exhibit 4.a suggests, the location of any wave in the electromagnetic spectrum can be stated in terms of either its frequency or its wavelength. For example, the term *microwaves* identifies a group of waves by their length, but the term *VHF* identifies a group by frequency. The number 600 (often abbreviated to 60) on an AM radio dial identifies a carrier frequency of 600 kHz.

Television stations, however, have different carrier frequencies for their video and audio components; for the sake of convenience we identify them by arbitrary channel numbers rather than by wavelength or frequency. For example, "channel 6" means a station using the 82-88-MHz channel, with a video carrier-wave frequency of 83.25 MHz and a sound carrier-wave frequency of 87.75 MHz.

• • • • • • • •

4.3 *Signal Modulation*

Modulation is the process of imposing meaningful information—such as broadcast programming—on a transmitter's carrier wave.

Signals as Energy Patterns

We can modulate a flashlight beam by turning it on and off. A distant observer could decode such a modulated light beam according to any agreed-upon meanings: a pattern of short flashes might mean "All OK," whereas a series of short and long flashes might mean "Having trouble, send help." Thus modulation produces a *pattern* that can be interpreted as a meaningful *signal*.

When radio waves carry words or music, they consist of *amplitude patterns* (loudnesses) and *frequency patterns* (tones or pitches). A microphone, responding to variations in air pressure, translates these pressure patterns into corresponding electrical patterns. The microphone's output consists of a sequence of waves with amplitude and frequency variations that closely match those of the sound-in-air pattern.

Ultimately, those AF (*audio*-frequency) electrical variations modulate a transmitter's RF (*radio*-frequency) carrier, causing its oscillations to mimic the AF patterns. At last we have a *radio signal*—patterned variations in a carrier wave that convey meaning. Note that modulation uses frequencies in two widely different ranges—low AF signal frequencies and much higher RF carrier frequencies. The RF carrier could not render sound if the carrier frequency was close to the sound frequency.

At each point where a transfer of energy from one medium to another takes place, a *transducer* (literally, a "leader across") does the job. A microphone transducer changes sound patterns into electrical patterns. A television camera transduces light patterns into electrical patterns. And a transmitter transduces electrical frequency patterns into the higher-frequency domain of RF energy.

Need for Sidebands

A carrier wave, consisting only of a single radio frequency, can carry very little information per second, whereas broadcast signals require many pieces of information per second. To convey a 500 Hz sound tone requires sending 500 pieces of information a second. Thus, modulating the carrier's single frequency involves using adjacent frequencies called *sidebands* that extend both above and below the carrier frequency. The more information conveyed, the wider the sidebands—and the channel.

Because upper and lower sidebands simply mirror each other (a phenomenon of physics), either can convey all the information imposed on a carrier wave. Many radio services, including AM and FM broadcasting, nevertheless transmit both sidebands. That wastes spectrum space, but suppressing one sideband would add considerably to the cost of both sending and receiving equipment.

Some services can and do economize on spectrum usage by suppressing one of the sidebands. Television, for instance, requires such wide channels that transmitting both sidebands would unduly consume spectrum space, seriously limiting the number of channels that could be put to use. Therefore, one of the television signal's sidebands is partially suppressed, leaving only a *vestigial* (partial) lower sideband.

Importance of Channel Width

Because of the need for sidebands, each station requires a group of frequencies in addition to its designated carrier frequency. This group makes up the station's *channel*. Broadcasting requires wide channels because stations provide a lot of information at a time. Some *non*broadcast radio services can trade slow (or lower-quality) delivery for use of a higher number of narrow channels. Some picture news services, for example, deliver video over narrow channels, taking several seconds to build up a single black-and-white still picture. A taxi-dispatching radio service needs immediate delivery but can also use narrow channels because it requires only voice understanding, not quality. Radio broadcasting needs wider channels for its *instant* delivery of quality sound, which requires overtones—and the ability to reproduce the higher frequencies from which those overtones are derived. And television channels need vastly greater information capacity (channel width) in order to pour forth instantaneous pictures as well as sound.

AM vs. FM

The chief methods for imposing patterns on broadcast carriers involve varying (modulating) either *amplitude* or *frequency*. Exhibit 4.c illustrates the differences between these carriers.* Television uses both methods: AM for the video signal and FM for the audio.** The differences in modulation lead to substantial qualitative differences for the radio stations using the two modes.

AM radio suffers from electrical interference that can distort reception when receivers pick up unwanted radio energy, including *static* caused by nature (lightning) or by people (electrical machinery and other transmitters). These unwanted signals interact with transmitted RF energy, distorting its amplitude patterns. But electrical interference has no effect on FM patterns, which rely on changes in frequency rather than in amplitude. This FM advantage is particularly useful (1) in southern states, where subtropical storms cause much natural static; and (2) in cities, where other electrical machinery creates artificial static. FM also rejects interference from other stations more readily than does AM. Good FM receivers can reproduce sound frequencies as high as 20,000 Hz. Thus they allow reproduction of those overtones necessary for high-fidelity sound, giving FM its major quality advantage over AM radio.

FM radio also has greater *dynamic range* (the loudness difference between weakest and strongest sounds) than AM. Sound-reproducing systems cannot easily match the human ear's capacity to accept extremes of loudness and softness. Very soft sounds tend to get lost in electrical noise, and very loud sounds overload the system, causing distortions. Radio stations thus use devices to limit extreme sound variations. AM broadcasting has much less dynamic range—and it sacrifices some of that by artificially compressing the signal in order to maximize average power output.***

---

*AM outlets are officially still called *standard* stations because their amplitude modulation technology was developed before frequency modulation (FM) radio.

**Sensitive FM tuners can often pick up audio from channel 6 television signals because this channel uses frequencies immediately below those used by FM radio (87.75 and 88.1 MHz, respectively).

***It's theoretically possible to build AM transmitters and receivers with full high-fidelity ability—but only in the VHF portion of the spectrum. Given spectrum congestion, that's unlikely to happen.

• • • • • • • •

4.4 Signal Propagation

Modulated signals are sent from the transmitter to an *antenna*, the physical structure from which signals radiate into surrounding space. The traveling of signals outward from the antenna is called *propagation*. We are most aware of propagation's effects when our car enters a tunnel and radio reception drops out or, while driving in a city, a radio signal suffers heavy distortion.

Station Coverage

Station coverage patterns—the areas reached by its propagated signals—usually assume uneven shapes. How far and in which directions energy travels depend on transmitter power and frequency, antenna efficiency and directionality, and varying conditions encountered in the propagation path. Physical objects and electrical interference, interference from other stations, the time of day, and even seasonal sunspot changes can affect propagation distances and patterns. Waves may be *refracted* (bent), *reflected*, *absorbed*, or *ducted* (propagated over abnormally long distances because they are trapped between layers of air of differing temperatures).

The higher the frequency, the more atmosphere absorbs wave energy and therefore the shorter distance the waves will travel. Objects that are wider than a wave's length tend to block its propagation, causing "shadows" in coverage areas. Higher frequency waves (confusingly, those of shorter length) can be interrupted by buildings and trees (detailed in Exhibit 4.m). VHF and higher waves have such short lengths that even small objects can interfere with their propagation—the shortest waves can be blocked by raindrops.

All these variables combine to create irregular shapes called *coverage contours*. Engineers draw contours on maps by measuring signal strength at various points surrounding a transmitter, showing lines of equal received power.

Frequency-related propagation differences divide waves into three types: direct, ground, and sky waves. Each has advantages and disadvantages that must be considered in matching frequency

Exhibit 4.c ● ● ● ● ● ● ● ● ● ● ● ● ● ● ●

How AM and FM Differ

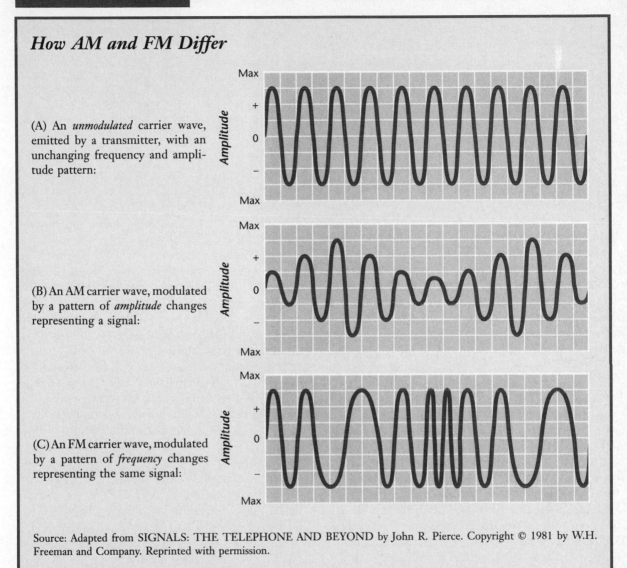

(A) An *unmodulated* carrier wave, emitted by a transmitter, with an unchanging frequency and amplitude pattern:

(B) An AM carrier wave, modulated by a pattern of *amplitude* changes representing a signal:

(C) An FM carrier wave, modulated by a pattern of *frequency* changes representing the same signal:

Source: Adapted from SIGNALS: THE TELEPHONE AND BEYOND by John R. Pierce. Copyright © 1981 by W.H. Freeman and Company. Reprinted with permission.

bands with service needs. Thus services such as international radio broadcasting need waves capable of traveling long distances, while domestic television can use waves that travel a relatively short way.

Direct Waves (FM and TV)

In FM radio, television, and microwave (that is, VHF and UHF) frequency bands, waves follow a line-of-sight path. Called *direct waves* because they travel directly from transmitter antenna to receiver antenna, they reach only as far as the horizon (see Exhibit 4.d). That's about 32 miles from a 1,000-foot-high transmitting antenna over a flat surface; the signal does not stop suddenly but, rather, fades rapidly beyond that point. Engineers place direct-wave antennas as high as possible in order to extend the "apparent" horizon. Raising a receiving antenna to a rooftop or on a hill serves the same end.

Ground Waves (AM)

Medium-frequency signals used by AM radio travel primarily as *ground waves*, propagated through the Earth's surface. They can follow the Earth's curvature beyond the horizon, as shown in Exhibit 4.d. Ground waves therefore can and often do cover greater areas than direct waves. In practice, however, a ground wave's useful coverage area depends on many factors, including soil conductivity. Dry, sandy soil conducts radio energy poorly, whereas damp soil conducts it well.*

Sky Waves (AM and Short-Wave)

Radio waves that radiate upward scatter their energy into space. However, waves in medium- (AM radio) and high-frequency (short-wave radio) bands, when they reach the ionospheric layers of the upper atmosphere, tend to bend back at an angle toward Earth in the form of *sky waves*.

The *ionosphere* consists of several atmospheric layers from about 40 up to 600 miles above the Earth's surface. Bombarded by high-energy solar radiation, the ionosphere takes on special electrical properties, causing sky waves to *refract* (bend) back toward the earth. The ionosphere's refractive effectiveness varies by time of day and frequency, so services that rely on sky waves vary accordingly. AM radio generates sky waves only at night, thus covering wider

areas than in daylight, while short-wave services often switch frequency several times daily to take advantage of changing ionospheric refraction.

Under the right frequency, power, and ionospheric conditions, refracted sky waves bounce off the Earth's surface, travel back to the ionosphere, bend back again, and so on, following the globe's curvature and traveling thousands of miles (see Exhibit 4.d).*

Antenna Differences

Whatever type of modulation and propagation may be involved, antennas are used to both transmit and receive signals. Antenna size and location have a critical influence on efficiency of transmission and reception.

Small receiving antennas built into receivers suffice to pick up strong signals. The higher the frequency, however, the more elusive the signal—and the more essential an efficient outdoor antenna becomes. Thus, in many locations, indoor "rabbit ears" pull in VHF television signals whereas UHF may require an outdoor antenna.

Transmitting antennas vary widely in size because, if they are to work efficiently, their length must be mathematically related to that of the waves they radiate (see Exhibit 4.e). Broadcast transmitter antennas usually measure one-half or one-quarter of the wavelength they radiate, depending on the frequency band used. For example, waves at the lower end of the AM band (540 kHz) have a length of about 1,823 feet; channel 2 (VHF) television transmitters radiate 20-foot waves, whereas television channel 48 (UHF) waves are less than 2 feet long.

Directional Antennas

Much as light from flashlights and car headlights can be focused by reflectors, transmitting antennas

*The FCC publishes a map showing soil conductivity throughout the United States (47 CFR 73.190). The most conductive soils have 30 times the conductivity of the least conductive. Salt water, by far the best conductor, sometimes helps to propagate AM signals for long distances along shore lines. To take advantage of this property, broadcasters try, where possible, to locate their antennas in swampy areas.

*This refraction accounts for recurring reports of receivers picking up video (AM) signals of VHF television stations hundreds of miles, even continents, away. Broadcasters who experience the phenomenon—due to several types of ionospheric conditions that are somewhat predictable—advise one another whenever it occurs.

Exhibit 4.d ●●●●●● ●●●●●●●●●

Direct, Ground, and Sky-Wave Propagation

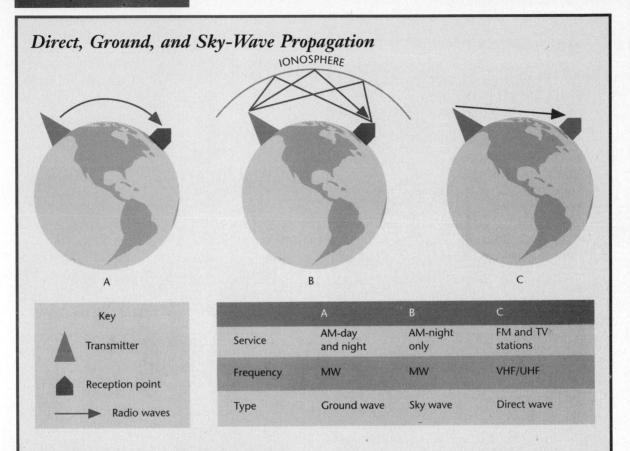

IONOSPHERE

A B C

Key	
▲	Transmitter
⬟	Reception point
→	Radio waves

	A	B	C
Service	AM-day and night	AM-night only	FM and TV stations
Frequency	MW	MW	VHF/UHF
Type	Ground wave	Sky wave	Direct wave

Because of their location in the spectrum, radio and television services have different signal propagation paths.

AM radio is most complicated because its *medium-frequency* spectrum location gives it two different means of wave propagation: ground waves in the daytime (A), and both ground and sky waves at night. Ground waves travel along the surface of the Earth. Given good soil conductivity and sufficient power, ground waves outdistance direct waves, reaching well beyond the horizon. As discussed in the text, sky waves (B) bend back toward Earth when they encounter the ionospheric layer of the atmosphere at night. Sky waves may bounce off the Earth and back to the ionosphere several times, and different frequencies are affected at different times of the day and night. In short, they are unpredictable and thus cause more interference than they provide useful service. Because of potential sky-wave interference, half of all AM stations leave the air at night. *Short-wave* international services make use of sky waves, changing frequencies to best match predicted ionospheric effects on sky waves.

FM radio and television stations, because of their *VHF* and *UHF* spectrum location, are subject only to direct line-of-sight wave propagation at any time of day or night (C). These waves are sent out from elements on top of antenna towers and directed downward toward the reception area, blocking off radiation that would otherwise scatter upward and out into space. The "horizon" limit, of course, depends heavily on local terrain.

Exhibit 4.e ●●●●●●●●●●●●●●●

Transmitting Antennas

A.

B.

C.

Antennas differ depending on the service for which they are built.

AM antennas (A) use the entire steel tower as a radiating element. For efficient propagation, the height of this tower must equal a quarter the length of the waves it radiates. Propagation of ground waves depends on soil conductivity, among other things. The photo shows heavy copper ground cables being buried in trenches radiating from the tower base to ensure good ground contact. There are three antennas here for sending out a directional signal.

Short-wave antennas (B) are very complex. Each transmitting site has many antennas to feed different HF frequencies, along with other suspended wires that act as reflectors to beam signals in specific directions to reach designated overseas target areas. The Voice of America uses scores of antennas like this one.

Television antennas (C) are similar to those designed for FM. Both use radiating elements at the top of each antenna to send out their signals.

Source: Photo A courtesy of Stainless, Inc., North Wales, PA; photo B courtesy of Voice of America, Washington, DC; photo C courtesy of CETEC Antenna Corporation.

can be designed to block propagation in some directions and reinforce it in others. In most cases, propagation in all directions is wasteful because most energy would never reach receivers. Stations in coastal cities, for example, have no need to transmit over the water. *Directional propagation* also has value for preventing interference with other stations and for beaming signals toward densely populated areas.

Concentration of radiated energy increases its effective strength. Such *antenna gain* can be very great. A microwave relay antenna concentrates its energy into a narrow beam, aimed at a single reception point. Such a beam can achieve a gain of 100,000 times the effective radiated power of an omnidirectional (all-direction) antenna. Indeed, because microwave signals attenuate rapidly, they would be of little use without this high gain, which enables them to punch through the atmosphere.

Receiving antennas are also directional, as is easily demonstrated by turning a portable AM radio in different directions. Signals from a given station come in best when the radio's built-in antenna points toward that station's transmitting antenna.

• • • • • • • •

4.5 Spectrum

Use of spectrum for communication requires meeting formal national and international technical access rules. Such rules are essential to ensure efficient use of this limited resource while minimizing interference among users. Mutual interference among stations severely limits the number that can be licensed in any particular market.

Spectrum Regulation

Most countries belong to the International Telecommunication Union (ITU), a United Nations body that coordinates worldwide radio frequency spectrum use (see Section 15.4). The ITU defines three steps in parceling out frequencies:

- *Allocation:* the setting aside of groups (bands) of frequencies for the use of specific communication services. ITU allocations apply to all countries, with slight differences among three ITU regions: (1) Europe-Africa, (2) the Americas, and (3) Asia.
- *Allotment:* the distribution of allocated frequencies to specific sub-bands or regions.
- *Assignment:* the designation of specific frequencies for the use of individual stations, usually through *licensing.* The group of frequencies assigned to a station—whether radio or television—constitutes a *channel.* Each service requires channels whose bandwidth suits the amount of information they need to carry.

The FCC has responsibility for licensing U.S. stations in accordance with ITU rules. It compiles *allotment tables* designating specific FM and television channels for use in specific communities.* However, the FCC assigns AM channels on a case-by-case basis (see Section 13.4).

Co-Channel Interference

In establishing allotment tables and assigning stations, FCC engineers know that any two stations operating on the same channel must be located far enough apart geographically to prevent their coverage contours from overlapping and causing *co-channel interference.* Signals too weak to provide reliable service may nevertheless cause such interference; a station's interference zone therefore extends far beyond its intended service area. Homes located halfway between two television stations, both operating on channel two, for example, but located too close together, would not receive a viewable picture from either station.

The FCC could prevent all co-channel interference simply by licensing only one outlet to each channel, but this would eliminate more than 90 percent of currently operating stations. As long-standing U.S. policy calls for allowing as many local communities as possible to have their own stations, the FCC makes co-channel separation rules as liberal as possible.

*Official current FCC allotment tables are annually published in the *Code of Federal Regulations* (CFR). See also Exhibit 2.g, on p. 60.

Changing day and night coverage areas of AM stations (caused by nighttime sky-wave propagation of their signals) complicates prevention of AM co-channel interference. The FCC limits that interference by requiring half of all AM stations to leave the air at local sunset; virtually all the rest use lower nighttime power.

Adjacent-Channel Interference

Near any transmitter, RF radiation is so powerful that sidebands spread far beyond the assigned channel limits, spilling over into *adjacent channels*. As the probability of such interference limits even further the number of stations that can be licensed in any one area, the FCC usually does not license consecutively numbered channels in any single market. (As Exhibit 4.k shows, some exceptions to this rule occur in television: while TV channels 4 and 5, 6 and 7, and 13 and 14 are consecutively numbered, their actual frequencies are not consecutive in the spectrum—other services intervene.)

Distance rapidly weakens signals as they travel from a transmitter, however, so adjacent-channel stations need be separated only by about the radius of their service areas. For example, the FCC imposes an adjacent-channel separation distance of only 60 miles for VHF television stations.

Spectrum Demand

Only a small portion of electromagnetic spectrum can be used with present technology. Tens of thousands of radio transmitters for different services share the usable spectrum. The threat of interference among stations, increasing demand for spectrum by new services, and further growth of established services make efficient spectrum management not only essential but also increasingly difficult as conflicting demands and changing technology must be accommodated.

Broadcasting, though it represents less than one percent of all transmitters authorized in the United States, makes especially heavy demands. *Nearly 13,000 full-power radio and television stations need con-* *tinuous access to relatively wide channels.** Broadcasters also use auxiliary facilities, such as subsidiary repeaters (translators), studio-to-transmitter links (in the 26, 153, and 450 MHz regions), and radio relays, both terrestrial and satellite, making still more demands on spectrum space. In fact, broadcasting uses more than 80 percent of the radio spectrum below 1 GHz, the region of the spectrum most in demand for all forms of terrestrial radio communication.

Conservation Measures

The need to conserve radio frequencies encourages the use of spectrum-saving processes and technologies. One of the most common, *multiplexing*, allows transmission of two or more independent signals on one channel. For example, *frequency-division* multiplex divides a channel into two or more subchannels, each with its own carrier and signal. Another type, *time-division* multiplex, rapidly samples several signals, sending short bursts of each through the same channel. This method enables the filling in of otherwise wasted time—for example, the pauses that occur between words and phrases in telephone speech. Recent experimentation has focused on the digital spectrum-saving technology of *signal compression* (described at Section 5.7), already in use by HBO and other cable services now sending two or three channels where only one was provided before 1992.

• • • • • • • •

4.6 *AM Stations*

"AM" as a class name is somewhat misleading today because *amplitude modulation* is used by many services other than radio broadcasting. The video com-

---

*Up-to-date figures on stations can be obtained from the weekly FCC statistics printed in the trade magazine *Broadcasting & Cable*. In early 1993 broadcast outlets on the air included roughly 11,300 radio and 1,500 television stations, 1,300 low-power television transitters, and 7,000 low-power FM and television translators (repeater stations). See also Exhibit 6.a, p. 186.

ponent of the television signal, for example, is also amplitude modulated.

Effect of AM's Spectrum Location

By international agreement, AM channels occupy part of the MF band. In the United States, AM broadcasting uses the 535 to 1,705 kHz band affording a total bandwidth of 1,170 kHz. The highest 100 kHz were added in 1988 by ITU action—the first expansion of the band in the United States since 1952, although the FCC restricted assignment of the new frequencies to existing stations to reduce interference, rather than licensing new facilities. Receivers with extended tuning range to pick up the new channels were just coming on the market in 1993 as the FCC began moving stations onto those frequencies.

As noted at Section 4.4, the ionosphere refracts waves propagated in the MF band at night. After sundown, therefore, AM stations can produce sky waves that reach far beyond their daytime coverage contours. However, unless they are protected from co-channel interference, AM stations rarely get consistent, improved nighttime coverage from sky waves. Indeed, sky waves from distant co-channel stations may intrude, shrinking an AM station's nighttime coverage. The AM channel classification system described below is designed to compensate for this dramatic difference between AM's daytime and nighttime coverage.

AM Band and Channels

Ideally, sound broadcasting channels would be wide enough to encompass the full range of overtone frequencies detectable by the keenest human ear—a bandwidth on the order of 20,000 Hz, eight times the bandwidth used by telephones with their adequate but low-quality voice transmission. However, AM stations in the United States make do with a quarter of that—5,000 Hz. The FCC spaces AM channels 10 kHz apart, allowing for 117 channels (that is, 1,170 kHz divided by 10). A station's carrier-wave frequency, expressed in kilohertz, identifies

the midpoint of its channel—540, 550, 560, and so on up to 1,700 kHz. The 10-kHz spacing means that channels extend 5 kHz above and below their carrier frequencies. For example, a station at 540 on the dial occupies a channel from 535 to 545 kHz.

Such 10-kHz spacing allows only 5 kHz for the actual signal, because modulation generates sidebands on each side of a carrier frequency (as discussed at Section 4.3). One 5-kHz sideband contains all the useful information. But this limitation makes AM less adequate than FM for music. Stations may modulate beyond 5 kHz on either side of their carrier frequencies if they can do so without causing interference, and many do. For some listeners this wider channel does not result in improved sound, however, because the loudspeakers in cheap AM-only receivers cannot reproduce the audible range that even a 5-kHz signal can provide.

Channel and Station Classes

The FCC classifies AM channels as shown in Exhibit 4.f.* By defining varying areas of coverage, channel classification helps the FCC license more stations while limiting interference. Local-channel stations serve small communities or parts of large metropolitan regions; regional-channel stations serve metropolitan or rural areas; and clear-channel stations serve major cities and, at night, distant rural listeners. (So-called clear channels have been "cleared" of interfering co-channel nighttime signals to enable sky-wave reception in remote areas.)

In the interests of licensing more outlets, the FCC divides AM into four station classes (shown in relation to the three channel classes in Exhibit

*These channels refer only to the long-traditional AM band of 535–1605 kHz. By 1993 the FCC had still not decided what channel or station class would be applied to the expanded AM band of 1605–1705 kHz, although it did agree that the stations assigned to that band could use 10 kw in daylight and 1 kw at night. Part of the delay came from prolonged negotiations with Mexico on shared channel use near the border.

4.f).* Class I stations are the dominant stations on clear channels. Originally, the FCC gave these stations nationwide protection from interference, but demand for still more licenses and the spirit of deregulation led to increased sharing of these channels with other primary stations in widely separated parts of the country. Class II stations must avoid interfering with Class I stations whose frequencies they share; they also must use directional antennas and either reduce power or close down entirely at night. Class III stations are less powerful and also reduce power or go off the air at night, but they can still serve metropolitan regions. Class IV stations have so little power (and therefore such short range) that they reuse the same few channels without interfering with one another.

Transmission

Higher AM transmitter power not only improves the efficiency of both ground- and sky-wave propagation for greater coverage but also helps overcome interference. Power authorizations for domestic U.S. AM broadcasting run as high as 50,000 watts (50 kw), as shown in Exhibit 4.f.** Yet the 50-kw ceiling is low relative to that in other countries, which have fewer but more powerful stations. Limiting power to 50 kw makes it possible to license more stations.

AM stations usually employ quarter-wavelength transmission antennas. The entire steel tower is a radiating element. In choosing sites, engineers look

for good soil conductivity, freedom from surrounding sources of electrical interference, and avoidance of nearby airport flight paths.* Because ground waves propagate through the Earth's crust, AM antennas are extremely well grounded, with many heavy copper cables buried in trenches radiating out from the base of the antenna tower (see Exhibit 4.e).

AM Stereo

Because of its narrower channel, stereo service on AM took a longer time to develop than on FM (see Section 4.7). AM stereo uses a "matrix mode" that melds left and right channels in a way somewhat similar to the two channels of FM stereo but without the full high-fidelity benefit. The few AM stereo stations in existence by the early 1990s had mostly chosen the Motorola C-QUAM standard finally formally adopted by the FCC a decade after AM stereo was first offered (see Section 3.7).

Carrier-Current AM

Low-power AM signals can be fed into pipes or power lines of buildings as distribution grids. Such signals radiate for a short distance into the space surrounding these conductors. Called *carrier-current* stations and operated on hundreds of college campuses, they require no license (they do not use spectrum) and may sell advertising.

A licensed carrier-current service, Travelers Information Service (TIS), uses radiation from wires strung or buried alongside highways. TIS supplies traffic information to motorists on the approaches to airports and similar congested thoroughfares. Road signs instruct motorists to tune to the relevant AM channel.

---

*The FCC is in the process of changing over from its long-standing, somewhat complicated roman-numeral designations for AM station classes (I-II-III-IV) and its three categories of AM channels, in favor of a simpler A-B-C system that designates AM station types *and* channels at the same time. The new system was first adopted in a hemispheric meeting, the Rio Agreement of 1981. See Exhibit 4.f.

**The *watt*, the term for a unit of power chosen by an 1889 international conference, is named after a man who had little to do with electricity—James Watt (1736–1819), the British scientist who improved steam engines—but was one of the first to argue for a standardized system of scientific terminology.

*Broadcasters must seek approval of tower locations from both the FCC and the Federal Aviation Administration (FAA). Antennas are often clustered in "farms" on high ground some distance from nearby airports.

Exhibit 4.f •••• •••••••••••

AM Radio Station and Channel Classes

Traditional Designation

Station Class	Channel Class	New Designation System*	Number of Channels in Class	Power Range (kw)	Percentage of Stations in Class**
I	Clear	A	60	10–50	1
II	Secondary Clear }	B	(60)***	2.5–5	33
III	Regional }		41	.5–5	46
IV	Local	C	6	.25–1	22

A large number of clear channels is needed because dominant Class I stations provide long-distance sky-wave reception and therefore have very wide geographical spacing. By the same token, only a small number of local channels is needed because many stations can occupy the same channel, prevented from interfering with one another by their low power. *Broadcasting Yearbook* lists all AM stations by channel, location, power, and antenna pattern.

*The new class designation system, replacing designations of both old station and channel class, is in the process of FCC adoption (see first footnote p. 128).

**Column does not add to 100 percent because of rounding.

***The channels shown for Class II secondary clear stations are, of course, the same channels as for Class I stations—the IIs are secondary because they must reduce power and use directional antennas especially at night to "protect" co-channel Class I outlets.

•••••••

4.7 FM Stations

FM's inherently superior quality has enabled it to outdistance AM in terms of both listeners and stations. That quality depends on the use of FM modulation in much wider channels than those used by AM.

FM Band and Channels

FM broadcasting in the United States occupies a 20-MHz block of frequencies in the VHF band, running from 88 to 108 MHz. The 20-MHz block permits 100 FM channels of 200 kHz (0.2 MHz) width each. The FCC identifies these channels by the numbers 201 to 300, but licensees prefer to identify their stations by their midchannel frequency (in megahertz) rather than by channel number (88.1 for channel 201, 88.3 for channel 202, and so on). The FCC reserves the lowest 20 FM channels (88.1 to 91.9) for noncommercial licensees. (Background information on these licensees is provided at Section 8.1.)

FM uses a relatively generous channel width (20 times that of an AM station), which allows for both high-fidelity sound (up to 20,000 Hz—four times what AM stations can provide) and multiplexing of additional signals.

Because of FM's coverage stability and uniformity, the FCC needs no elaborate channel and station classification scheme such as the one it is now phasing out for AM. The commission simply divides the country into zones and FM stations into three groups according to coverage area: Classes A, B, and C, defined in terms of power, antenna height, and zone. Class A power/height combinations enable a station to cover a radius of about 15 miles; Class B, about 30 miles; and Class C, about 60 miles.* The maximum power/height combination permits 100,000 watts of power (twice the AM maximum) and a 2,000-foot antenna height.

Transmission

Stations—including FM—that use VHF frequencies radiate direct waves, so their signals reach only to the horizon. Because of this limitation, FM escapes the nighttime sky-wave problem that complicates AM station licensing. An FM station has a stable coverage pattern, night *and* day—its shape and size depending on station power, the height of its transmitting antenna above the surrounding terrain, and the extent to which terrain or buildings block wave paths. FM signals can blank out interference from other stations more effectively than can AM. An FM signal needs to be only twice as strong as a competing signal to override it (an AM signal needs to be 20 times as strong).

FM's short wavelength calls for short radiating and receiving antenna elements, which are mounted—and polarized*—horizontally (thus putting FM reception from cars at a slight disadvantage because most car antennas are mounted vertically). To take advantage of FM's direct-wave propagation, station owners mount antenna towers on high buildings or hilltops to extend the apparent horizon as far as possible. Some FM stations use directional antennas, as do most AM stations.

FM Stereo

FM's generous 200-kHz channel width makes it easy to multiplex a second carrier to furnish stereo sound. FM stereo works as follows: Two sets of equipment corresponding to left and right channels pick up a sound source and use this signal to modulate the station's FM carrier. A control or "pilot" subcarrier and a stereo subcarrier are also transmitted. A stereo receiver (and most FM sets today are stereo) with a decoder can separate signals for delivery to left and right speakers. FM stereo is compatible in that a monaural receiver can provide a full signal, though without the separate sound of two channels.

In addition to stereo sound, FM can multiplex secondary services. A licensed *subsidiary communications service* (SCS), such as reading services for the blind (see Section 3.3) or background music for offices and stores, requires attaching a converter to an ordinary FM receiver (or leasing a special receiver) to enable reception. The subcarrier can also be used for the radio broadcast data system discussed in Section 5.10.

---

*A fourth class, D, consists of very low power (10-watts) FM educational stations, but since 1980 the FCC has sought to displace them whenever other, full-powered candidates apply for their noncommercial channels. The 10-watt stations have several options for moving to other channels requiring higher power if they do not interfere with full-power stations.

Polarization refers to the fact that radio waves oscillate *across* their propagation paths. Transmitter antenna orientation determines the direction of oscillation. Usually polarization is either horizontal (causing back-and-forth oscillation) or vertical (causing up-and-down oscillation), but circular polarization is also used.

4.8 Short-Wave Stations

Few Americans listen to short-wave (SW) broadcasting, though it plays an important role in many other countries and in international services as discussed at Section 15.9. Only a few private international SW stations, mostly religious noncommercial outlets, operate in the United States. SW services use AM and can reach distant areas by exploiting sky waves.

Location in Spectrum

Parts of the HF band between 6 and 25 MHz have been designated by the ITU for international SW services, as detailed in Exhibit 4.g. The ionosphere refracts waves in this band both day and night, enabling round-the-clock coverage thousands of miles away. However, electrical properties of the ionosphere constantly change and layers lose altitude as they cool off at night. For these reasons, a frequency that works well at ten o'clock in the morning may be entirely useless by four in the afternoon. Seasonal changes also affect short-wave broadcasting: frequencies useful for reaching a given target area in the spring can be rendered useless for that same area during other seasons. Accordingly, SW stations typically operate on more than one frequency.

Propagation

Propagation theory can predict ionospheric shifts, enabling SW engineers to schedule frequency changes throughout the day and from season to season. Unlike domestic AM stations, therefore, SW international services feed programming to several different antennas, each designed to radiate a different frequency. SW antennas are usually directional, beaming their signals toward specific target areas. The radiating elements consist of extensive arrays of suspended cables, as shown in Exhibit 4.e; in contrast to AM, SW steel towers serve only to support the cables, not to radiate the signal.

Exhibit 4.g

Short-Wave Broadcast Bands

Band Designation		Band Limits
Meters	Megahertz	Kilohertz
49	6	5,950 – 6,200
41	7	7,100 – 7,300
31	9	9,500 – 9,775
25	11	11,700 – 11,975
19	15	15,100 – 15,450
16	17	17,700 – 17,900
13	21	21,450 – 21,750
11	25	25,600 – 26,100

International broadcasters use these bands to reach distant targets by means of sky waves. Additional high frequency broadcast bands in the 5-MHz range have been allocated for domestic services in the tropical zone, where atmospheric interference caused by storms limits the usefulness of the medium wave frequencies normally used for domestic radio broadcasting. The entire HF band runs from 3,000 to 30,000 kHz. Marine, air, land mobile, amateur, and other services use the rest of the band, which is in high demand because of its long-distance capability.

Though short when compared with MF waves, HF broadcast waves still vary from 11 to 49 meters (about 36 to 160 feet) in length. Radiating elements must therefore be relatively long, as shown in Exhibit 4.e. Major SW installations (such as Voice of America antenna sites) occupy hundreds, even thousands, of acres: not only are the antenna arrays very large, but each also requires equally large reflecting elements for directional propagation.

••••••••

4.9 Electronic Pictures

Television's video technology is better understood if we look first at the principles developed for film, the original medium for pictures in motion.

Determining Picture Quality

Most photographic systems represent scenes by breaking reality down into many tiny *pixels* (picture elements or dots). Basically, the size and distribution of pixels govern picture *resolution* (also called *definition*). These terms refer to any picture system's fineness of detail—specifically, its ability to distinguish clearly two small, closely adjacent objects. Resolution in photography parallels information capacity in radio communication. High-resolution pictures demand a broadband channel, one able to handle a great many pixels each second.

The information capacity of motion pictures depends not only on film resolution but also on the size of the picture area available for each frame in the film strip and on the rate (stated in frames per second) at which film moves through the camera. Several quality standards have emerged, based on the width of film stocks stated in millimeters (mm):

- 35 mm is the professional theatrical standard (some wide-screen films use 70 mm and even larger);
- 16-mm film, originally an amateur standard, became a professional medium (thanks largely to television's demand) prior to the widespread use of videotape; and
- 8-mm (including Super-8mm) was the amateur home-movie standard before the development of home video cameras killed the film market.

In each of these formats, some space was reserved for sprocket holes, for between-frame spaces, and (usually) for a soundtrack. In television channels, some frequencies must similarly be reserved for sound and auxiliary information.

Persistence of Vision

In movies, what appears to be motion actually consists of still pictures (frames) projected in rapid succession. Each frame freezes the action at a slightly later moment than the preceding frame. The human eye retains the image of an object briefly after the object has been removed. This persistence of vision blends images together in successive frames. Thus the motion in "motion" pictures exists only as an optical illusion.

A fairly satisfactory illusion of natural motion occurs if a projector displays at least 16 frames per second (fps). For that reason, during the silent era the motion-picture industry adopted 16 fps as the standard frame rate. With the coming of sound in the late 1920s, the industry had to adopt the higher rate of 24 fps to get good sound reproduction.*

Although 24 fps gives the illusion of continuous action, at that projection rate the eye still detects the fact that light is falling on the screen intermittently. After each frame flashes on the screen, a moment of darkness ensues while the projector pulls the next frame into position for projection. The eye reacts more sensitively to these gross changes from light to dark than to small changes in positions of objects from frame to frame. A sensation of *flicker* results. In fact, early movies earned the name *flicks* because their low frame rate made them flicker conspicuously.

Increasing frame frequency can overcome the flicker sensation, but because the 24-fps rate gives all the visual and sound information required, such an increase would be wasteful. Instead, modern projectors show each frame *twice:* when the projector pulls a frame into place, it flashes the picture on the screen, blacks out the screen, then flashes the *same frame again* before blacking out to pull the next frame into position. Although it projects only 24 separate pictures, it illuminates the screen 48 times per second, thus avoiding the flicker sensation.

*The difference between the frame rate of silent and sound films accounts for the comic jerkiness of silent films shown on modern projectors; these projectors increase the original projection rate by 50 percent, speeding up the action to an unnatural degree.

Television uses a similar trick, illuminating the screen twice as many times as the number of complete pictures shown each second. So that movie sound tracks can avoid the on/off system required for the visual portion of a motion picture, audio information is separated by 26 frames from its corresponding visuals, permitting it to pass smoothly over the audio heads.

Camera Pickup Tube

The heart of the television system, the *pickup tube*,* is a transducer that converts light energy into electrical energy. An ordinary photographic camera lens focuses a live or filmed televised scene on the face of the pickup tube, which breaks down each image into thousands of pixels. Pixels start as bits of light energy distributed throughout the image; the picture tube picks them up systematically as a sequence of dotted lines, each dot representing a pixel. The picture tube converts each line of pixels into a stream of electrical impulses (voltages). Thereafter, electrons take over. Without the speed and precision of electrons, television with satisfactory definition would be impossible.

Pickup tubes come in various shapes and sizes, as shown in Exhibit 4.h. In principle, however, they all work the same way: the camera lens focuses an image on the *target plate* within the tube. The target plate, covered with thousands of light-sensitive specks, represents a single picture or *frame*. Each speck converts the light energy that falls on it into an electric charge of corresponding intensity. Thus each of the thousands of pixels on the target plate takes on an electric charge proportional to the amount of light it receives. Next, the tube releases each of the momentarily stored charges, one at a time, line by line.

*Some specialized situations, such as slow-motion sports coverage, call for the use of a solid-state imager, a tubeless camera based on a more recent technology, the CCD (*charge-coupled device*). These devices, now being adopted for professional use, were first used in home video cameras. Studio CCD cameras cost only a little more than a mere tube replacement for a standard studio color camera.

Electrons come into play as a releasing agent. Opposite to the tube's target plate, an *electron gun* shoots a stream of electrons toward the back of the plate. As the electrons fly down the length of the tube, they pass through magnetic fields generated by external *deflection coils* surrounding the body of the tube, as shown in Exhibit 4.h. Magnetic forces attract and repel the electron stream, making it move systematically in a *scanning* (reading) motion, left to right, line by line, top to bottom. Thus the electron beam "reads" the information on the target plate. The resultant string of electric pulses constitutes the pickup tube's output.

The pickup tube has no moving parts. Its electron gun remains fixed while the stream of electrons moves. Whereas a film camera must have a revolving shutter to interrupt scenes each time it draws a new film frame into place for exposure, a TV camera needs no shutter, for video pictures never exist as a complete frame, only as a sequence of pixels. Television relies on persistence of vision to blend the pixel sequence into a seemingly unbroken image in the mind's eye (see Exhibit 4.i).

Scanning Pictures

Because the television camera does not "take" a complete picture all at once, however, television could use cinema's antiflicker strategy of repeating each entire frame only at the unacceptable price of nearly doubling the width of each television channel—and thus sharply limiting the number of stations on the air.

A televised picture is scanned every 30th of a second. The picture is created by scanning first odd-numbered field lines, then even-numbered field lines. Each scanning sequence or *field* illuminates the receiver screen from top to bottom, picking up only *half* the pixels in the frame. This method, known as *offset* or *interlace* scanning, causes the electron beam to scan line one, line three, line five, and so on to the bottom of the field, then fly back to the top of the next field to fill in line two, line four, line six, and so on (again, see Exhibit 4.i). Thus, instead of film's repetition rates of 24 and 48,

Exhibit 4.h ••••• •••••••••

TV Camera Tube

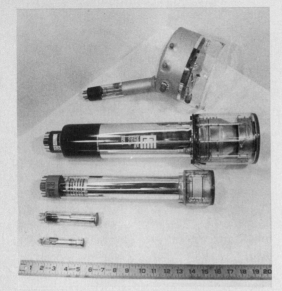

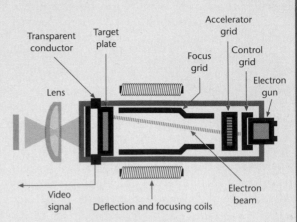

(A) As technology improved, tubes became smaller. Commercial broadcasters first used the *iconoscope*, the odd-shaped tube at the top. Then *image orthicons*, with 3-inch and 4.5-inch faces, replaced iconoscopes. Smaller tubes such as the *vidicon* and *plumbicon* in turn replaced the image orthicon.

Sources: Photo by Frank Sauerwald, Temple University. Diagram by John Fretz based on information in *Television Technology: Fundamentals and Future Prospects* by A. Michael Knoll, 1988, p. 67, Fig. 7–8. Used by permission of Artech House.

(B) The main components and functions of the vidicon type of tube are as follows: a lens focuses the image on a photoresistive plate whose electrical resistance varies with the amount of light striking its surface. At the base of the tube, three components called grids help generate and shape the electron beam. As it leaves the focus grid, it enters magnetic fields created by coils surrounding the neck of the tube. Changes in the magnetic fields, caused by changes in the voltage fed to the deflection coils, sweep the electron beam back and forth in the prescribed scanning pattern. As the electron beam scans the rear side of the plate, it causes the electric energy stored in each pixel to flow to the conductor plate as an electrical voltage. The varying amplitudes of those voltages, led by wire away from the plate, constitute the video signal (illustrated in Exhibit 4.j).

---

television uses 30 (frame frequency) and 60 (field frequency).* Engineers chose these rates to take ad-

*Special television film projectors (*film chains* or *telecine*) solve the mismatch between film and television field-frequency standards (48 versus 60 fps) by displaying every fourth film frame an extra time, thus adding 12 projections per second to film's normal 48 fields to bring the projection rate up to television's 60-field standard.

vantage of the universal timing standard available throughout the United States—the 60-Hz alternating electric current in homes.

The fact that much of the world uses 50-Hz house current accounts in part for the original differences between American television technical standards and those of many other countries. Fifty-hertz countries standardized frame and field frequencies

Exhibit 4.i ● ● ● ● ● ● ● ● ● ● ● ● ● ● ●

Scanning Fields and Frames

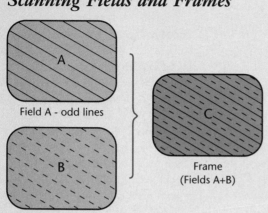

Field A - odd lines

Field B - even lines

Frame
(Fields A+B)

A complete electronic picture, or frame, is made up of two fields each of which makes up half the picture definition. One field (A) scans the odd-numbered lines and the other (B) scans the even-numbered lines (shown here as broken). Together the lines of the two fields "interlace" to make up a complete frame (C).

At the end of each scanned line, and each field, the electron beam has to fly back to start a new line or field. During these retrace times, a blanking signal prevents the beam from activating any picture elements. When the beam returns to the top of the screen at the end of each field, the time it takes, equivalent to scanning 21 normal lines, is called the vertical blanking interval (VBI). It is during this VBI that nonpicture information can be transmitted, such as closed captions and teletext (see Section 3.3).

Picture Resolution

The number of lines per frame provides a convenient index of a system's level of resolution, or picture definition. The U.S. standard of 525 lines per frame determines a picture's *vertical resolution*. However, not all 525 lines are used to convey pictures. Some time—and thus lines—must be devoted to auxiliary picture information. Also, receivers vary in the way they present pictures, necessitating use of a *mask* to standardize the visible television image. In practice, black-and-white pictures depend on only about 340 lines per frame. The color component consists of even fewer lines, about 280. This low resolution does not degrade color-picture quality because fine color-picture details ironically appear only in black-and-white. By way of comparison, a theatrical 35-mm film frame has the equivalent of 1,000 lines. High-definition television, discussed at Section 5.9, will eventually match or exceed that standard, though not the standard for 70 or 90 mm film.

Auxiliary Signals

Vitally important auxiliary signals maintain the synchronization of scanning in the receiver tube with scanning in the camera.* These *sync pulses*, originated by a special timing device in the studio (see Exhibit 4.1), ensure that each pixel in each line will appear on the receiver screen in the same location it had in the pickup tube. Even a slight loss of synchronization renders received pictures unusable.

Another type of auxiliary signal cuts off the scanning beam during *retrace* intervals, the time the electron beam needs to fly back diagonally from the end of one line to the beginning of the next (horizontal retrace) and from the bottom of

at 25 and 50. The 50 vs. 60 disparity continues to stand in the way of adopting a world television standard for emerging advanced television technologies—more so than political or economic differences among different countries (see Section 5.9).

*This synchronizing function is comparable to film *registration* mechanisms in movie cameras and projectors. They have toothed wheels (sprockets) that fit into sprocket holes along both edges of film, pulling film forward at the right speed and holding each frame accurately positioned when stopping to record or project an image.

one field back to the top of the next field (vertical retrace). During these breaks in scanning, also called *vertical blanking intervals* (see Exhibit 4.i), auxiliary signals prevent picture pickup so that the electron beam's retrace paths will not destroy an orderly scanning pattern.

Adding Sound and Color

American television uses FM for the sound carrier; the 100-kHz sound channel is located in the upper part of the television channel (see Exhibit 4.j). No synchronizing signals are needed to keep sound and picture in step, since they occur simultaneously and are transmitted in real time.

In approving television color standards in 1953, the FCC insisted that the system had to be capable of adding color information without enlarging the established 6-MHz monochrome TV channel. A committee of major U.S. manufacturers met these criteria with the system known as NTSC (National Television System Committee) color.*

The television signal mixes three primary-color signals to produce all other colors.** Filters separate primary-color information (red, blue, and green) before the image reaches the camera tube. In addition to *hue* (what we perceive as color), all colors have a brightness attribute, *luminance*. This non-color luminance component contributes all the fine detail in color pictures. A monochrome receiver interprets a color picture using the luminance signal alone and thus can display it in black and white. Multiplexing enables a color carrier to be added without enlarging the television channel, thereby fulfilling the requirement that all sets be able to receive all signals—a matter of *compatibility*. Exhibit

---

*Nearly three-quarters of foreign television services use PAL (developed in Germany) or SECAM (French-developed) color systems. PAL is the most widely used color system. Both offer more picture resolution (625 vs. 525 lines), and both were designed for color from the start—unlike NTSC, which had to adapt to existing black-and-white television.

**The colors are "primary" only in television terms, inasmuch as green is made up of yellow and blue.

4.j shows the location of the color subcarrier within a normal 6 MHz television channel.

● ● ● ● ● ● ● ●

4.10   TV Stations

Television's heavy information load requires a broadband channel. U.S. standards call for a 6-MHz channel—600 times the width of one AM radio broadcast channel and 30 times wider than an FM channel (see Exhibit 4.j). Indeed, the *entire* AM and FM broadcast bands together occupy less spectrum space than do four television channels. Even so, the NTSC standards permit what today is only fair picture resolution. Later in this decade, HDTV (high-definition television) will significantly improve resolution and other aspects of the broadcast picture (as discussed at Section 5.9).

Channel Width

The NTSC television channel allots four of its six MHz to picture information, including auxiliary signals (Exhibit 4.j details the use of the remaining 2 MHz). Even the wide 4-MHz picture channel achieves relatively low picture resolution by the standards of theatrical motion pictures and good-quality still photography.*

Current television resolution standards are compromises based on research aimed at determining the lowest quality that most viewers would tolerate. Quality had to be kept to a minimum to avoid using too much spectrum space.

Location in Spectrum

When frequencies were first allocated for television, much of the most suitable VHF band had already been allocated to other services. Room remained

---

*The average home receiver displays about 150,000 pixels per frame, whereas a projected 35-mm film frame has about a million and an 8-by-10-inch photoengraving about two million.

Exhibit 4.j   •••••• •••••••••

The TV Channel

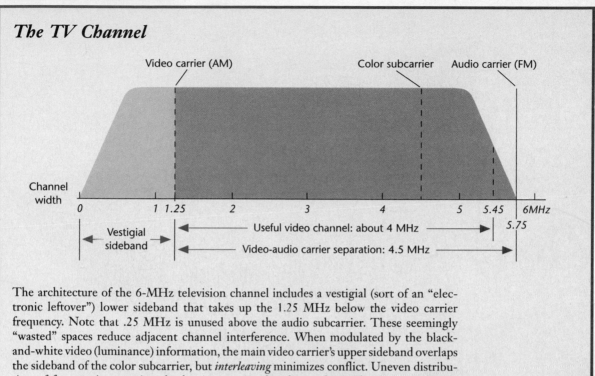

The architecture of the 6-MHz television channel includes a vestigial (sort of an "electronic leftover") lower sideband that takes up the 1.25 MHz below the video carrier frequency. Note that .25 MHz is unused above the audio subcarrier. These seemingly "wasted" spaces reduce adjacent channel interference. When modulated by the black-and-white video (luminance) information, the main video carrier's upper sideband overlaps the sideband of the color subcarrier, but *interleaving* minimizes conflict. Uneven distribution of frequencies carrying the luminance signal makes such interleaving possible. If the teeth of a comb are visualized as the frequencies occupied by the monochrome information, the color information occupies frequencies represented by the spaces between the teeth.

A 100-kHz subchannel accommodates the audio information, located near the upper end of the channel.

Source: Adapted from 47 CFR 73.699.

for only 12 (originally 13) VHF channels, numbered 2 through 13.

To find room for even those few channels, the FCC had to put VHF television into three different blocks of frequencies, as shown in Exhibit 4.k.

After discovering that 12 channels could not satisfy the demand for stations, the FCC in 1952 added 70 additional channels in the UHF band, numbered 14 through 83 (later reduced to 56 UHF channels, stopping at 69). A table allots specific channels

Exhibit 4.k　••••••• •••••••••

Summary of Broadcast Channel Specifications

This table pulls together information scattered throughout the text to allow comparison of the major channel specifications of radio and television services. Note especially the allocation of television channels into four separate frequency allotments in two different bands.

Service	AM Radio	FM Radio	VHF Television	UHF Television
Frequencies	535-1705 kHz (MF band)	88-108 MHz (VHF band)	54-72 MHz (2-4) 76-88 MHz (5-6) 174-216 MHz (7-13) (VHF band)	470-806 MHz (14-69) (UHF band)
Total channels	117	100	12	56
Bandwidth (single station)	10 kHz	200 kHz (equivalent to 20 AM channels)	6,000 kHz (equivalent to 600 AM or 30 FM channels)	6,000 kHz
Classes of stations and power limits	I Clear 10-50 Kw II Secondary Clear 2.5-50 kw III Regional 1-5 kw IV Local .25-1 kw	A about 15 miles up to 3 kw B about 40 miles 5-50 kw C about 65 miles 25-100 kw	Channels 2-6 about 65 miles up to 100 kw Channels 7-13 about 55 miles up to 316 kw	Channels 14-40 about 40 miles up to 5,000 kw Channels 41-69 about 30 miles up to 5,000 kw
Educational allocation	none	88-92 MHz (20 channels)	137 specific channel allotments	559 specific channel allotments
Factors affecting station coverage and signal quality	frequency power soil conductivity day/night (sky wave) thunderstorms directional antennas	antenna height power (to a degree) unlimited time no directional antennas high fidelity little static line of sight range	antenna height frequency power (to a degree) rigid spacing line of sight range unlimited time	antenna height frequency power (to a degree) rigid spacing more limited line of sight range unlimited time

geographically by number to specific towns and cities throughout the United States.*

Synchronization

As described above and in Exhibit 4.l, the *sync generator* plays a major role in television control rooms, ensuring synchronization of pickup and receiver tubes. It controls picture scanning by generating precise timing signals for driving camera deflection coils and inserting blanking signals. The sync generator also controls the timing of such additional video sources as tape recorders, disc recorders, computer memories, film projectors, and network feeds. A completely independent set of audio equipment handles broadcast sound.

Transmission

Video and audio signals are fed independently to the transmitter, which may be located miles from the studio at a suitable antenna site. There the two signals modulate separate audio and video transmitters. Because of its greater information load, video needs up to 20 times as much power as audio. A station's power is usually stated in terms of the *effective radiated power* (ERP) of its video signal. Signals from video and audio transmitters meet for the first time at a *diplexer*, a device that combines them into a composite signal fed to the antenna (see Exhibit 4.l).

Because television—like FM—relies on direct waves, its engineers, too, seek the highest possible locations for antenna sites, such as mountain peaks, roofs of tall buildings, or tops of tall steel towers. Direct-wave antenna towers do not radiate signals as do AM towers; they simply support radiating elements, which are quite small, in keeping with the shortness of VHF and UHF waves. Because of *horizontal polarization*, both transmitting and receiving antenna elements are mounted horizontally to the ground below (see Exhibit 4.e). Some television transmitting antennas emit *circularly polarized* waves, which travel with a corkscrew motion. When circularly polarized television signals are reflected by obstructions, the direction of rotation becomes reversed, causing the receiving antenna to reject reflected signals. This rejection helps reception in large cities, where reflections from tall buildings appear on the screen as "ghosts" (see Exhibit 4.m).

Propagation

The television transmitting antenna is designed to propagate signals directionally *downward* toward the line-of-sight coverage area, cutting off energy that would otherwise scatter into space above the horizon.

In setting television power limits, the FCC uses a formula that takes antenna height into consideration. VHF television signals have inherent advantages over UHF. Waves in the UHF band, because they are shorter than VHF waves, can be more easily blocked by objects in their path—even tree leaves. Moreover, they weaken more rapidly than VHF waves. For these reasons, the FCC allows UHF television to use very high power (up to 5 million watts) to compensate to some extent for its coverage limitations, whereas VHF stations radiate no more than 5,000 watts.

Reception

Broadcast television coverage, limited to the visible horizon (not counting cable or satellite relays, of course), depends also on receiving-antenna efficiency and height, obstructive terrain features, transmitter frequency, and power. Within about 20 miles of a powerful transmitter, indoor antennas usually suffice. Starting at about 30 miles, outdoor antennas become essential.

For regulatory purposes, the FCC classifies television station coverage in terms of Grade A and B contours. Grade A contours enclose an area in which

*For purposes of setting television co-channel separations, the FCC specifies different standards for three geographic zones (essentially, northern, midland, and south) and two channel types, VHF and UHF. As an example of the VHF-UHF distinction, in Zone 1, stations on VHF channels must be about 170 miles apart, whereas those on UHF need only be about 155 miles apart. More details on these rules can be found in the *Code of Federal Regulations*, secs. 73.606, 609–613.

Exhibit 4.l • • • • • • • • • • • • • • •

TV System Components and Signals

TRANSMITTER

Each block stands for a function that in practice may involve many different pieces of equipment. The lower portion of the diagram represents the basic items and functions involved in studio operations; the upper portion, those involved in transmission. Separate sets of equipment handle the video and audio components all the way to the diplexer, the device in transmitters that finally marries the two signals so that they can be transmitted as a composite. (Exhibit 4.j shows how the audio and video components are multiplexed in a single channel.)

Source: Based on Harold E. Ennes, *Principles and Practices of Telecasting Operations* (Indianapolis: Howard W. Sams, 1953).

Exhibit 4.m •••••••••••••••••

TV Propagation Paths

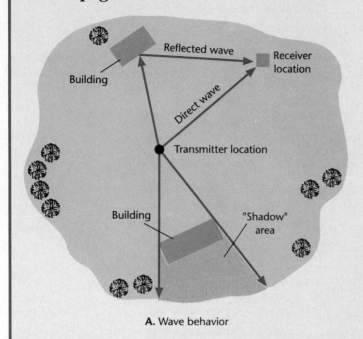

A. Wave behavior

B. Ghost image

(B) When a receiver detects both a direct wave and a reflected wave, the reflected wave will have traveled over a longer path, and will therefore arrive at the receiver slightly later than the direct wave. When the receiver displays the signal of the delayed reflected wave, the image lags slightly behind that of the direct wave, appearing as a "ghost."

(A) Simplified coverage pattern of a television station, showing some characteristics of direct-wave propagation: the waves carry only to the horizon; some may encounter surfaces that reflect signals; some may encounter obstructions that cause "shadow" areas in the coverage pattern.

---

satisfactory service can be received 90 percent of the time; Grade B contours enclose an area in which reception is satisfactory only half the time.*

Receiving antennas are designed to pick up either all channels or only the channels in one band (VHF

*These contours have no meaning for cable television subscribers, who receive their local television stations as well as cable-specific programming via cable and no longer depend on receiving antennas.

or UHF). Since they are highly directional, receiving antennas must be pointed toward the transmitters. In areas where transmitters are placed in various locations, rotatable outdoor antennas may be necessary.

Your TV Set

Like transmitters, receivers process video and audio signals separately. In most receivers, video information goes to a cathode ray tube (CRT) called a *kinescope* (see Exhibit 4.n). A phosphorescent coating on its inside face glows when bombarded with electrons. Within the kinescope's neck an electron gun (a larger version of the camera pickup tube) shoots electrons toward the rear face of the CRT. Guided by external deflection coils, the electron beam scans the rear of the tube face, releasing pixels of varying intensity line by line, field by field, and frame by frame. Synchronizing signals originated by the studio sync generator activate deflection coils, keeping the receiver scanning sequence in step with the studio camera pickup tube.

Phosphors that glow in television's three primary colors, arranged either in narrow parallel stripes or in triads of dots, coat the inside of color kinescopes. Receiver circuits decode the video signal into components representing energy levels of the three colors in each pixel. Data for each color strike the tube face separately, using one or more electron guns (again, see Exhibit 4.n). Only the primary colors appear on the kinescope. Normally the eye sees various hues as a result of the mix of primaries provided by varying energy levels in the color tube outputs. However, if you look at part of a color picture on the face of a kinescope with a magnifying glass, you see only the three primary colors.

In principle the kinescope displays only one pixel at a time, but because it takes a while for the activated phosphor to lose its glow, several pixels remain visible at any given instant. Considering the speed and precision with which primary color pixels, lines, fields, and frames must be delivered each second to create an illusion of realistic moving pictures, the color television achievement is truly remarkable.

TV Multiplexing

Several possibilities exist for multiplexing additional signals in the 6-MHz television channel. For example, no picture information goes out during the *vertical blanking interval* (VBI), the time during which the pickup tube's scanning beam returns from the bottom of the picture to the top to start scanning a new field (see Exhibit 4.i).* That interval occupies about 8 percent of the 1/60th second devoted to each field, or the equivalent of 21 picture lines. Teletext (see Section 3.3) and closed captions are transmitted on the VBI.

Another ancillary television signal, an audio subcarrier, enables telecasting of stereo and bilingual sound (again, see Section 3.3). Television sound reception, long a neglected element in receiver design, improved with FCC authorization of stereo service in 1984. While the commission did not specify a specific system, the industry generally agreed to a technical standard and moved quickly to make stereo available. Most receivers have the needed signal converters and speakers built in.

• • • • • • • •

4.11 Cable Systems

As discussed in preceding sections, television broadcasting suffers from spectrum crowding and interference inherent in any over-the-air communication. Cable systems avoid these problems by sending signals through the artificial, enclosed environment of *coaxial cable* (see Exhibit 4.o)—from which the service derives its name. Cable systems also provide multiple channel delivery.

Cable Advantages

Within the cable, a wide band of frequencies—up to 450 MHz at present, and 550–750 MHz expected soon—can be used without causing or receiving undue interference.** Because cable signals do not interfere with on-air services, cable is able to use

---

*When a receiver's vertical hold is slightly mistuned, the VBI appears on the screen as a black bar between frames of the picture.

**Coaxial cable does not enjoy total immunity from interference. When cable systems are run near transmitting antennas broadcasting on the same channels used in the cable, "ingress" from such transmitters can cause double images ("ghosts") at the home receiver.

Exhibit 4.n ● ● ● ● ● ● ● ● ● ● ● ● ●

Color Kinescope Tube

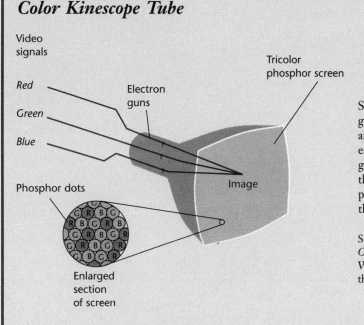

Video signals

Red

Green

Blue

Electron guns

Tricolor phosphor screen

Image

Phosphor dots

Enlarged section of screen

Some receiver tubes use three electronic guns and tricolor phosphor dots. Varying amplitudes in the modulated currents fed to each of the electron guns cause the dots to glow with varying intensities; though only the red, green, and blue primary colors appear on the kinescope face, the eye blends them together to make all the various hues.

Source: Adapted from Paul Davidovits, *Communication* (New York: Holt, Rinehart & Winston, 1972), p. 114. Used by permission of the author.

VHF channels above and below the broadcast VHF portion of the spectrum—frequencies denied to broadcasting because they are used by other services (see Exhibit 4.q). A cable system thus gives viewers a wide range of choices, usually feeding 30 or more program channels—in newer systems, more than 100—compared to an over-the-air station's single channel in the same geographical area.

Cable aids spectrum conservation and avoids some of broadcasting's other drawbacks. Confining radio energy within a cable eliminates the need for home antennas, problems resulting from co-channel and adjacent-channel interference and from different propagation paths, and varying behaviors of direct, ground, and sky waves. Cable-enclosed signals can be modulated and propagated; they retain all the radio energy characteristics already described, except those evident in open space.

Cable Drawbacks

Yet cable also sacrifices the unique asset of radio communication—the ability to reach audiences without the aid of physical connections. Cable connections are also expensive to build—and to rebuild later in order to increase channel capacity.

System construction costs exceed those for broadcast stations. Unable to use the "free" over-the-air path of broadcast signals, cable operators must physically connect each home to the system. Further, signals traveling through "wave guides" such as coaxial cable—other than those using optical fibers—attenuate rapidly, making it necessary to re-amplify signals at frequent intervals, thus increasing costs. Where possible, firms mount cables on existing utility poles; but within cities, cables are often buried underground in conduits and tunnels at even

Exhibit 4.o •••••••••••••••

Coaxial Cable

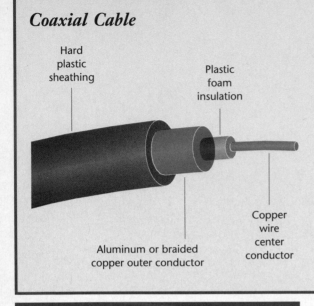

Hard plastic sheathing

Plastic foam insulation

Copper wire center conductor

Aluminum or braided copper outer conductor

Coaxial cable gets its name from the fact that it has two conductors with a common axis: a solid central conductor surrounded by a tubelike hollow conductor. Radio energy travels within the protected environment of the space between the two conductors. Cable television relies on this type of conductor, as do many terrestrial relay links that convey television signals, telephone calls, data, and other types of information. Fiber-optic relays are increasingly taking over trunk communications for this and other industries, as discussed in Exhibit 5.i on p. 164.

Source: Adapted from illustration in Walter S. Baer, *Cable Television: A Handbook for Decision Making* (Santa Monica, CA: The Rand Corporation, 1973), p. 4. Used with permission.

---

greater expense.* Cable installation over long distances to reach thinly scattered rural populations costs too much to be practical. So cable may never exceed about 75 percent penetration of American households.

The technician installing cable service usually disconnects the home's outside television antenna, if one exists; the cable system itself picks up television station signals at its headend and delivers some or all of them as part of its basic package of program channels.**

*Cable television lines can be identified by their thickness compared with other overhead wires. At frequent intervals, bulges in the cables indicate the location of repeater amplifiers. Cable lines are nearly always lowest on poles, under the thinner telephone lines.

**Unless the installation includes an *A/B switch* to enable the new cable connection to be bypassed, the subscriber cannot readily switch back to the outside antenna. Yet subscribers may need that antenna at times for direct television station reception, either to pick up stations not carried by cable or to pick up cable-carried stations when the cable system goes down.

Cable System Design

At the system's *headend*, cable assembles programs from various sources and delivers them via coaxial cable to subscriber homes. Besides reception facilities, a headend contains equipment for reprocessing incoming signals, equalizing and feeding them to a modulator for transmission over the system's coaxial-cable delivery network, and assigning each program source to a specific cable channel.*

Most cable systems have a *tree-and-branch pattern*. As Exhibit 4.p shows, *trunk cables* branch to lighter *feeder cables* that carry the signals to neighborhoods of homes, where still lighter *drop cables* connect the system to individual households. A headend can feed programs over a radius of about five miles; covering wider areas requires subsidiary headends that

*Broadcasters prefer to have the same channel number on cable as on the air, but cable operators often reposition them, changing channel numbers to suit their own programming strategies. The 1992 cable act now governs this process (see Section 13.8).

Exhibit 4.p ● ● ● ● ●   ● ● ● ● ● ● ● ●

Cable TV System Plan

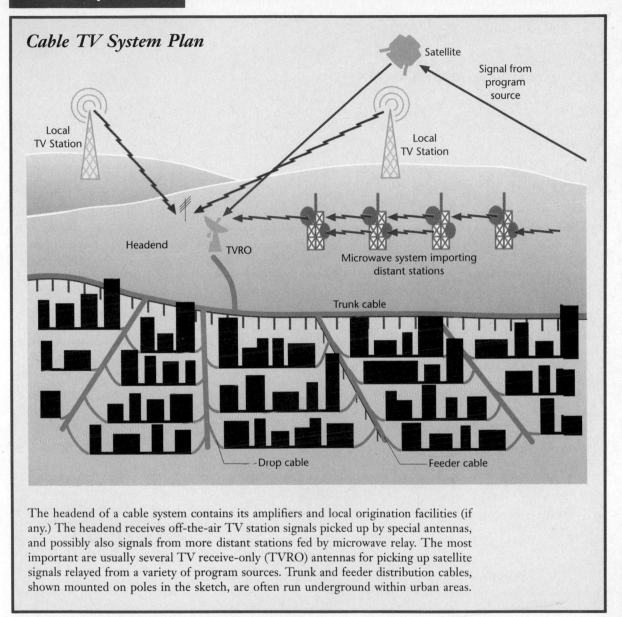

Satellite

Signal from program source

Local TV Station

Local TV Station

Headend

TVRO

Microwave system importing distant stations

Trunk cable

Drop cable

Feeder cable

The headend of a cable system contains its amplifiers and local origination facilities (if any.) The headend receives off-the-air TV station signals picked up by special antennas, and possibly also signals from more distant stations fed by microwave relay. The most important are usually several TV receive-only (TVRO) antennas for picking up satellite signals relayed from a variety of program sources. Trunk and feeder distribution cables, shown mounted on poles in the sketch, are often run underground within urban areas.

receive the programs via special *supertrunk coaxial* (or fiber-optic) cables or via microwave relays. Newer systems adopt a star pattern with a series of local hubs. This restructuring is especially useful in installing fiber trunk lines.

As also shown in Exhibit 4.p, programs for cable systems come to the headend from five sources:

- *over-the-air reception of nearby television stations,* usually from antennas near the system's headend.
- *relays of more distant stations.* To enable cable systems to pick up stations outside their local markets, the FCC has authorized a special microwave relay service, CARS (Community Antenna Relay Service), that cable systems may install to bring in signals from such stations.
- *locally produced or procured material.* Local origination facilities at or near the headend vary in complexity from simple alphanumeric news-and-weather displays to full-scale production studios.
- *satellite-to-cable networks and superstations,* received on one or more—usually several—TVROs, each aimed at a different domestic satellite.
- *audio services,* received on subcarriers of satellite-delivered television channels, directly from pay audio services, or off-the-air from nearby radio broadcast stations.

Tuning Cable Channels

Cable television uses the same radio-frequency energy as do over-the-air transmitters. Exhibit 4.q shows the broad band of frequencies fed through a 60-channel coaxial cable. A few older systems still carrying only 12 channels rely on VHF tuners in subscribers' television sets. Most systems, with more channels, must supply customers with an adapter unit—or *converter box*—that has its own tuning facility. It feeds into a receiver channel (usually 2, 3, or 4, whichever is *not* an over-the-air channel locally). In effect, the adapter supplies an expanded VHF tuner to avoid resorting to the receiver's UHF cir-

cuits, as UHF signals weaken too rapidly to be practicable for cable use.*

• • • • • • • •

Summary

4.1 Radio communication (of sound, pictures, or data) employs a form of electromagnetic energy—a basic natural force—that has some of the characteristics of sound and visible light.

4.2 Like sound, radio energy originates from an oscillating source and can be described in terms of waves that have length, frequency, phase, and velocity. These waves are subject to attenuation, refraction, reflection, absorption, and interference. However, sound waves differ significantly from radio waves in terms of velocity, frequency, and mode of travel.

4.3 Modulation imposes information on a carrier wave, creating sidebands that collectively occupy a group of frequencies called a channel. The more information a channel must deliver at the same time, the wider it must be. In traditional broadcasting, modulation of a carrier wave's amplitude (as in AM) or its frequency (as in FM) occurs in analog signal processing.

4.4 Carrier waves may be propagated as ground waves (reaching beyond the horizon), direct waves (reaching only to the horizon), or as sky waves (reaching long distances because of ionospheric refraction). Modulated carrier waves, upon being piped to an antenna, are radiated as electromagnetic energy. The length of a transmitter's antenna is

---

*Virtually all television receivers now come "cable ready" or "cable compatible," meaning that they can receive all channels offered on a cable system, including those used by cable but not by over-the-air broadcasters (so-called midband and superband channels) without need for a converter box. Some cable systems, especially those with 100 or more channels, still require converter-box use, even with such receivers—especially for encrypted pay and PPV services.

Cable TV Spectrum Architecture

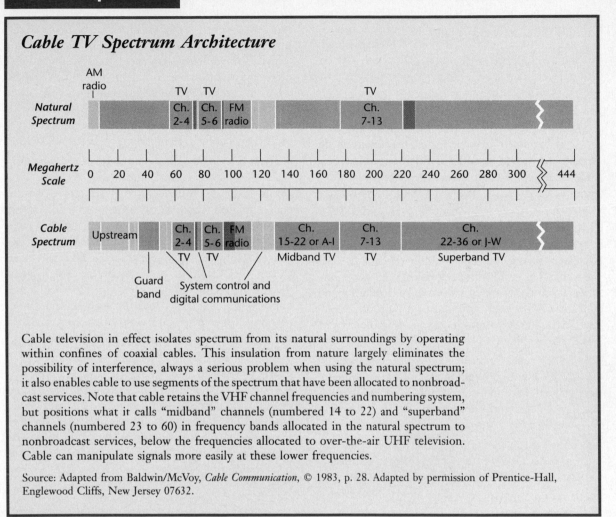

Cable television in effect isolates spectrum from its natural surroundings by operating within confines of coaxial cables. This insulation from nature largely eliminates the possibility of interference, always a serious problem when using the natural spectrum; it also enables cable to use segments of the spectrum that have been allocated to nonbroadcast services. Note that cable retains the VHF channel frequencies and numbering system, but positions what it calls "midband" channels (numbered 14 to 22) and "superband" channels (numbered 23 to 60) in frequency bands allocated in the natural spectrum to nonbroadcast services, below the frequencies allocated to over-the-air UHF television. Cable can manipulate signals more easily at these lower frequencies.

Source: Adapted from Baldwin/McVoy, *Cable Communication*, © 1983, p. 28. Adapted by permission of Prentice-Hall, Englewood Cliffs, New Jersey 07632.

proportional to the length of the waves it radiates. Directional antennas control the spread of signals, increasing signal intensity in desired directions.

4.5   Radio frequencies occupy only part of the electromagnetic spectrum; their characteristics vary according to their position in that spectrum. Inter-national agreements have grouped the radio-frequency range into bands, designated by frequency. Waves behave somewhat differently in each band. Demand for radio frequencies exceeds supply. Spectrum management matches service needs with the characteristics of the various frequency bands. Broadcasting shares spectrum with many other radio services. It uses so much spectrum space because it needs continuous access to relatively wide channels. Each broadcasting service is allocated certain frequency bands, within which each station is licensed to use a specific channel. Co-channel stations may interfere with each other—as may, at lesser distances, stations on adjacent channels.

4.6 The FCC classifies three kinds of channel and four station types for AM stations to maximize the number that may operate without causing mutual interference. AM carrier-current stations do not actually broadcast and thus do not need licenses. AM stereo has thus far seen little success.

4.7 It is easier to prevent FM radio (and television) stations from interfering with each other because their VHF or UHF transmissions do not use sky waves, as do AM stations. FM and more recent television stereo have been quite successful. The wide channels of FM and television readily accommodate multiplexing of additional information on subcarriers. Stereophonic sound and subsidiary services such as background music are examples of FM subcarrier services.

4.8 Short-wave stations reach great distances by using sky waves. Unlike domestic stations, international short-wave stations usually use several different frequencies and antennas to adjust to varying sky-wave behavior throughout the broadcast day.

4.9 Television technology uses strategies similar to motion pictures for preventing flicker and creating the illusion of continuous motion. Electronic pictures consist of pixels, lines, fields, and frames,

transmitted one pixel at a time in the form of amplitude-modulated analog signals. U.S. NTSC standards call for 525-line frames, transmitted at the rate of 30 per second, with interlaced fields transmitted at the rate of 60 per second. To limit color television's information load, the system reduces color information to three primary colors, which, when mixed in appropriate proportions, can show all hues. Color broadcasts are compatible with black-and-white sets; that is, monochrome receivers can receive color transmissions in black and white.

4.10 Television sound and pictures rely on separate equipment in both studio and receiver. The sound signal modulates an FM subcarrier within the television channel, whereas the video signal modulates an AM carrier. Television channels occupy parts of both the VHF and UHF bands. Because UHF waves attenuate more quickly than VHF waves, UHF stations have smaller coverage areas, despite the use of higher power than VHF. Cable has eliminated this variance for most viewers. Television receivers repeat the scanning sequence of the camera pickup tube, kept in step by synchronizing signals. The picture is displayed on the face of a kinescope tube.

4.11 Cable television uses the same waves and channels as broadcasting, but it encloses them within a conductor (usually coaxial cable though, increasingly, fiber-optic cable). A single cable can carry many channels simultaneously, in contrast to broadcasting's single over-the-air channel per station.

Chapter 5

Relays, Recording, and the Digital Revolution

● ●

The most dramatic recent changes in electronic media technology have come in the means of storing programs and moving them from place to place. A useful way to relate the many technologies involved is in terms of these three basic functions:

- *relay* or distribution of programs from one or more central sending points to many receiving points (stations or systems);
- *recording* or storage of programs for repeated and shared use by networks and stations or systems; and
- *delivery* of programs to the home (by broadcast station, cable system, or satellite), as described in Chapter 4.

This chapter focuses on the *convergence*, or coming together, of these functions.

● ● ● ● ● ● ● ●

5.1 *How Technologies Interrelate*

Broadcast stations and cable systems retail to their audiences programs that come mostly from distant wholesale sources. Without means of recording programs rapidly and efficiently, stations and cable systems would be limited to local and live programs—often the most expensive and least popular material. And without networks and their relays to interconnect (full time or from time to time) with local outlets, even live programs would be limited to local resources. Without external sources, there could be no mass-appeal programs, no costly entertainment, no timely world news roundups, no superstar performers, no round-the-clock schedules.

Syndication Principle

Creating programs would be useless without an efficient means of *distributing* them, nationally and internationally. Two mechanisms make centralized production feasible by conveying programs efficiently to stations and cable systems: *syndicating* (sale or lease of programs to individual stations) and *networking* (actual interconnection, usually by satellite). Both enable wholesaling of expensive program materials, *sharing* heavy costs among many local broadcast or cable systems, which provide programming to end users—listeners and viewers. Economic factors that make syndication and networking essential as well as organizational requirements for their operation are discussed at Sections 9.2 and 10.6; here we focus on technologies that make them physically possible.

International news agencies pioneered the syndication principle, enabling newspapers and, later, stations and cable systems to furnish consumers everywhere with news gathered worldwide. Only because thousands of outlets share production and distribution costs does such a news-gathering process become feasible.*

Networks as Relays

Broadcast and cable networks, though they differ from syndication in a business sense, function as a type of syndication or sharing by providing *instant* program relay. Broadcasting developed *networks* to facilitate distribution with important advantages over syndication: simultaneous relay to stations or systems and simultaneous local delivery to consumers; and a close, symbiotic working relationship between networks and their affiliates.

A *broadcast network* consists of two or more stations connected to each other so that they can put identical programs on the air simultaneously in more than one market. Likewise, a *cable network* consists of a central program production or procurement process with satellite distribution to thousands of cable delivery systems. Thus both cable and broadcast networks take advantage of electronic media's unique *instantaneous delivery* attribute. They use this attribute best when they offer live coverage of real events such as sports, weather, disasters, or the 1991 Gulf War. Even for recorded material, however, network simultaneity has great value: it gives broadcast and cable networks their unique identities, adds to the effectiveness of advertising, and enhances networks' ability to promote their programming nationally.

A broadcast or cable network can connect an unlimited number of local voices into a single, unified means of communication. Uniquely, broadcast stations can function at times as affiliates of one or more networks and at other times as local outlets. Cable systems carry this principle further in that they act as voices for many networks, in addition to offering one or more locally programmed channels. This ability to function locally, regionally, nationally, and indeed even internationally, *and to switch instantaneously from one type of coverage to another,* gives electronic media a flexibility shared by no other medium.

Recording's Role

Broadcasting and cable also depend on *storing programs*, warehousing them for later release and for repeated re-release still later. Means of storage include analog and digital disc and tape recordings, still and motion picture films, and computer memories. Virtually all programs (except for some news items, live play-by-play sports, and some special events) come to listeners and viewers *prerecorded.** National networks record even "live" programs (called live-on-tape) for *delayed broadcast* to compensate for time differences among geographic zones. And network affiliates often record live network feeds for later release. Most programs, even timely ones, thus go through one or more recording steps before reaching the public.

Convergence

Recorded program materials may be distributed to users by mail, by courier, or by various electronic network relays to local stations and systems. It has therefore become difficult in some cases to say whether a firm is functioning as a syndicator or as a specialized network when it distributes programs to stations or cable systems—not that viewers really care! Improved technology opens up possibilities for combining old and new functions into innovative and flexible configurations.

*Illustrating technology's central role, news agencies developed with the telegraph—and are still called *wire* services, although radio and satellite circuits have long since displaced wire.

*This term, though universally accepted, remains odd in that "*pre*recorded" means "recorded in advance." No one has explained how a program could otherwise be recorded at all.

Such *convergence*, a coming-together and interrelating process, blurs traditional distinctions among relaying, recording, and delivery functions, as well as between networks, syndicators, and both stations and cable systems. The superstation, familiar to cable subscribers, combines operations that once stood apart: although it is licensed as a television station to *deliver* programs to a single local market, the superstation also uses network–type relays to *distribute* its programs to thousands of cable systems for delivery to local subscribers.

As an example closer to each of us, our television sets have become general-purpose display terminals for cable, various text services, satellite downlinks, videocassette recorders, video games, and home video-cameras, as well as for their original purpose of showing broadcast programs (see Exhibit 3.k, p. 98).

Thanks to increasing digitalization, technologies are converging to permit recording, relay, and both sending and receiving equipment that can handle audio, video, voice, and even data transmission. Such technical blurring of formerly clear boundaries between industries is one important factor in revived telephone industry interest in the electronic media (see Section 3.7).

● ● ● ● ● ● ● ●

5.2 Terrestrial Relays

The oldest and still most widely used electronic means of relaying media signals are terrestrial (earth-bound) interconnections ranging from rebroadcasting to wire and more recent microwave and coaxial-cable relay systems.

Rebroadcast Relays

*Re*broadcasting combines relay and delivery functions in a single operation. If broadcast station A originates a program, station B can pick up A's signal and retransmit it to its own audience on B's own frequency (assuming it has permission—there are

legal as well as technical limits); station C picks up B and retransmits the program on C's frequency, and so on. Thus each station relays its programs to another station while, at the same time, delivering them to its own listeners. Some regional FM networks, for example, interconnect by using rebroadcasting.

But rebroadcasting used in place of separate relays has drawbacks. Each time a signal is rebroadcast, it loses some of its original quality; a series of such losses (as would happen with two or three stations in sequence) can degrade the signal below acceptable standards. Most important, if one station experiences technical problems and goes off the air, the chain breaks completely. Also, while affiliates are airing local programs, networks often use *backhaul* satellite-relay facilities to send affiliates information, preview material, promotion announcements, and programs and news items to record for later broadcast—all of which is impossible when interconnection depends only on rebroadcasting.

One specialized rebroadcast relay is the *translator*, which rebroadcasts a nearby station's signal in order to extend or improve reception in its coverage area. The name derives from the fact that these low-power (up to a few thousand watts) transmitters "translate" the station signal to another, unused, channel, for its very limited coverage area of a few square miles. A variation on translators, *low-power* television stations (LPTV) are also small (100 watts if on VHF and up to 1,000 watts if UHF), provide some original programming for a coverage area of seven to ten miles radius, and for most hours serve as a translator relay or carry programs from satellites or other network sources.

Wire Relays

Point-to-point wire circuits can also serve as electronic media relays—as they have since telegraph networks in the 1840s. Channel capacity of any circuit determines which types of relays shall be used for which purpose. For example, telephone circuits (specially equalized to compensate for rapid attenuation of higher frequencies over distance) suffice for radio programs but cannot satisfactorily handle the wide frequency band required by television.*

Microwave Relays

After techniques for efficient transmission of very short waves had been developed, AT&T supplied microwave relays to television networks for their use in distributing programs and other materials to their affiliates. Located in the UHF band and above, microwaves vary in length from one meter down to a millimeter. Waves this short attenuate in the atmosphere so rapidly that at first they seemed unusable for communication over long distances. But when a microwave signal is focused into a narrow, concentrated beam, its power can be increased by a factor of a hundred thousand. With this much strength, microwaves can punch through 30 miles of atmosphere without excessive attenuation. Because of the waves' short length, they require relatively small sending and receiving antennas (see Exhibit 5.a).

A microwave-relay system uses a series of towers spaced about 30 miles apart, each keeping the previous and the next tower in the series within line of sight. *Repeater* equipment on a tower receives a transmission from the previous tower, reamplifies it, then passes it on to the receiver on the next tower in the series. It takes hundreds of towers to span the continental United States.

Microwave-relay networks need permission from landowners to erect towers. Rugged terrain favors microwave transmission by providing high points that help in laying out line-of-sight transmission paths. Before satellites, all television networks used microwave relays as supplements to their coaxial interconnection systems.

Coaxial-Cable Relays

When fed through an ordinary copper wire, high-frequency radio energy tends to radiate from the

wire and dissipate rapidly. Coaxial cable prevents this loss, trapping the energy and moving it through an enclosed space. The cable consists of two conductors, a hollow metal tube, and a solid wire running down its center. Air or some nonconductive material insulates the wire from the tube, as shown in Exhibit 4.o on page 144. Attenuation still occurs, as it must when any radio signal travels, but repeater amplifiers, inserted at frequent intervals (typically every 1,000 feet or so in a cable television system), compensate for this loss.

Coaxial cables cost a lot to manufacture and install. In mountain terrain, installation can become prohibitively expensive (encouraging use of microwaves instead). Nevertheless, for many years, U.S. television networks reached their affiliates almost exclusively through nationwide coaxial-cable interconnection. AT&T supplied these facilities, just as it had the telephone wires for network radio.

• • • • • • • •

5.3 Satellite Relays

Because they depend on ground-based towers, microwave-relay networks cannot span oceans, as submarine cables can. Prior to the advent of fiber-optic technology, transoceanic undersea cables had limited capacity; they were suitable for telegraph and telephone communication, but not for television. Transoceanic television became possible only when communication satellites began to function as relay stations in space.* Far beyond the Earth's attenuating atmosphere, a single satellite in a sufficiently high fixed orbit can have line-of-sight access

---

*Some organizations that syndicate programs (or more usually advertising) to groups of stations use such paradoxical terms as *unwired networks*. Since they lack interconnection with their affiliates, they constitute, in both legal and practical terms, only *pseudo-networks*, using private delivery means such as UPS and Federal Express.

*From time to time, balloons and aircraft have been used as high-elevation television transmitter platforms. In 1988 Congress first authorized funds for a balloon-borne antenna in the Florida Keys to transmit television programs over the water to Cuba, supplementing Radio Martí, an existing U.S. government radio service also transmitted from the Keys. TV Martí's signal could theoretically be received directly on Cuban television sets, without the need for the ancillary receiving equipment that direct-broadcast satellites require. However, reports suggested the Cuban government effectively jammed reception of the television service, as discussed at Section 15.9.

Exhibit 5.a

Microwave Relay Antennas

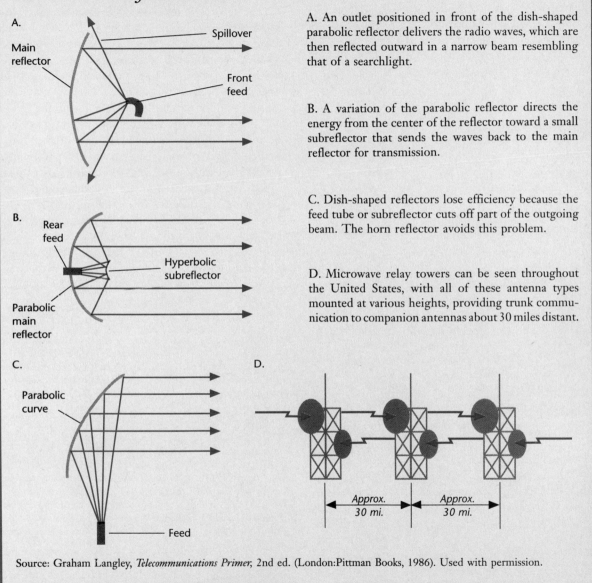

A.

Main reflector

Spillover

Front feed

B.

Rear feed

Hyperbolic subreflector

Parabolic main reflector

C.

Parabolic curve

Feed

D.

Approx. 30 mi.

Approx. 30 mi.

A. An outlet positioned in front of the dish-shaped parabolic reflector delivers the radio waves, which are then reflected outward in a narrow beam resembling that of a searchlight.

B. A variation of the parabolic reflector directs the energy from the center of the reflector toward a small subreflector that sends the waves back to the main reflector for transmission.

C. Dish-shaped reflectors lose efficiency because the feed tube or subreflector cuts off part of the outgoing beam. The horn reflector avoids this problem.

D. Microwave relay towers can be seen throughout the United States, with all of these antenna types mounted at various heights, providing trunk communication to companion antennas about 30 miles distant.

Source: Graham Langley, *Telecommunications Primer*, 2nd ed. (London:Pittman Books, 1986). Used with permission.

to some 40 percent of the globe's surface (see Exhibit 5.c).

Advantages

Although they are often likened to microwave towers thousands of miles in height, communication satellites differ fundamentally from the older relay technology. A microwave repeater can link one specific location with only two others—the next sending and receiving points in the relay network. A satellite, however, links a group of program originators or networks to an *unlimited number* of receiving Earth stations. Adding more Earth stations adds nothing to transmission costs, whereas linking up new destinations for microwave networks does.

Satellites also have the advantage of being distance insensitive—able to reach Earth stations at *any distance* within the satellite's *footprint* (coverage area). Whereas microwave signals lose quality as they go through dozens or scores of reamplifications, satellite relays need amplify a signal only once before sending it down to its destination because only a short part of the distance covered is through the atmosphere. Exhibit 5.b offers one example of how space and terrestrial relays combine in televising a major international event.

Geostationary Orbit

If satellites stay in the same spot in the sky with reference to their target ground stations, there is no need for costly tracking mechanisms to point receiving antennas at a moving signal source. Such satellites operate in a *geostationary* (or *geosynchronous*) orbit. At about 22,300 miles above the equator, objects revolve around the Earth at the same rate that the Earth revolves around its axis. The centrifugal force tending to throw a satellite outward cancels the gravitational force tending to pull it back to Earth, keeping it apparently suspended in space for years at a time.

The geostationary orbit, then, consists of an imaginary circle in space, 22,300-plus miles high. Though satellites in that enormous orbit actually move through space at about 7,000 miles an hour, from the perspective of an observer on Earth they appear to stay in one place, keeping in step with the Earth as it rotates. Actually, geosynchronous satellites tend to drift out of position, but ground controllers activate small on-board jet thrusters, making adjustments to keep them in place.*

Through the International Telecommunication Union (ITU), nations have agreed to allot each country one or more specific slots in the geosynchronous orbit for its domestic satellites. The ITU identifies positions in degrees of longitude, east or west of the prime meridian at Greenwich, England.** Exhibit 5.c shows the slots occupied by 24 U.S. domestic satellites (carrying 540 transponders) serving broadcast/cable needs in late 1992.

Each degree of arc in the geostationary orbit represents a separation of about 450 miles. Spacing for C-band satellites (defined in the subsection after next) has been reduced from the original four degrees separation to only two in order to crowd more satellites into the high-demand portion of the orbit.*** Even so, demand for orbital allotments created a potential slot scarcity analogous to the scarcity of spectrum space that holds down the number

---

*Fuel accounts for much of an orbiting satellite's weight; in turn, the amount of thruster fuel a satellite can carry limits its operational life (current communication satellites last about 10 years). It would take too much fuel to keep geosynchronous satellites *exactly* in place; ground controllers therefore let them drift slightly in and out of position, describing a small figure-eight pattern. In the future, astronauts may be able to refill fuel containers to further extend satellite life.

**The meridians, imaginary lines dividing the Earth's surface, run north and south, meeting at the north and south poles and crossing the equator at right angles. The circle of the equator, divided into 360 degrees, enables the identification of meridian positions, numbered 1 to 180 degrees east and 1 to 180 degrees west of Greenwich. ITU orbital slot allotments take into consideration the need for a satellite in a given orbital position to "look down" toward the general zone of the satellite's intended target area.

***Orbital separation prevents signal interference, not physical collision. Indeed, some satellites are *co-located*, sharing the same slot. Power, directional antennas, signal polarization, frequency differences, and Earth-station sensitivity all help in preventing satellite signals from interfering with one another. Ku-band satellites designed for direct broadcasting to homes (that is, direct-broadcast satellites) have wider spacing because their high power would otherwise cause interference among their downlink transmissions.

Exhibit 5.b

International Satellite Relay

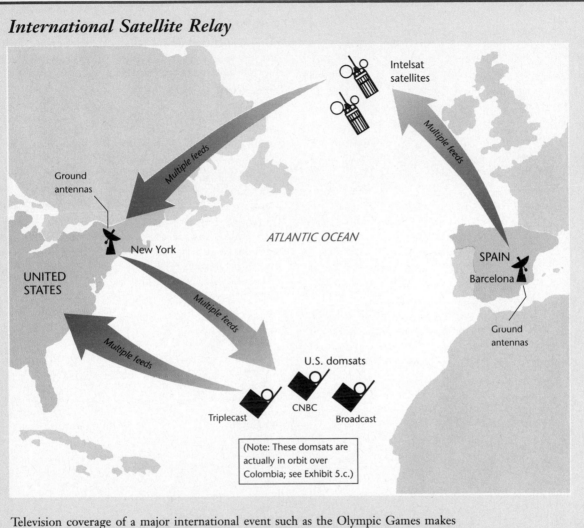

Ground antennas

New York

UNITED STATES

ATLANTIC OCEAN

Intelsat satellites

Multiple feeds

Multiple feeds

Multiple feeds

Multiple feeds

SPAIN

Barcelona

Ground antennas

U.S. domsats

Triplecast

CNBC

Broadcast

(Note: These domsats are actually in orbit over Colombia; see Exhibit 5.c.)

Television coverage of a major international event such as the Olympic Games makes extraordinary demands on relay facilities. A world audience of more than two billion people saw the 1992 summer games from Barcelona, Spain. Coverage of the 1992 games became especially complex because of NBC's "Triplecast" on its broadcast, basic cable, and PPV cable facilities (see Section 3.2, p. 82), requiring seven separate international feeds from Spain to the United States and five domestic feeds within the U.S. Shown here are only the primary trunk feeds because to show all signals beaming down from American domestic satellites to local stations and systems would virtually obliterate the rest of the diagram! Fiber-optic and microwave connections on the ground supplemented the satellite links in Spain and the United States. Major control centers in Barcelona and Manhattan stayed in constant communication.

Exhibit 5.c • • • • • • • • • • • •

Geostationary Satellite Orbit

A.

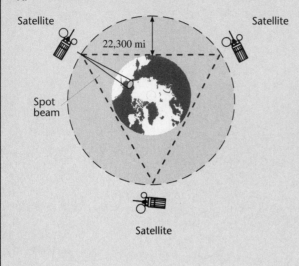

(A) Looking down from space over the North Pole, one can see how three satellites orbiting above the equator can "cover" most of the Earth ("most" because their signals fade at polar latitudes). The satellites appear to remain stationary with reference to Earth when orbited at an altitude of 22,300 miles—the geostationary (or geosynchronous) orbit (GSO). The INTELSAT international satellite system operates satellites over the Atlantic, Pacific, and Indian oceans.

(B) American domestic satellites (domsats) orbit in the GSO above Colombia, each with an assigned position expressed in degrees west from the prime meridian at Greenwich, England. Because GSO bands allotted to the United States are so crowded, Ku-band satellites are shown here at a distance from the Earth different from C-band satellites; actually *all occupy the same orbit*. The linkages between some satellites indicate they carry both Ku-band and C-band transponders.

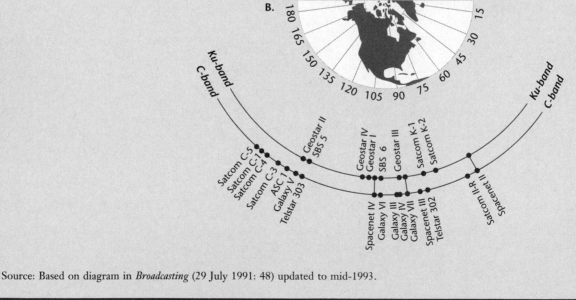

Source: Based on diagram in *Broadcasting* (29 July 1991: 48) updated to mid-1993.

of terrestrial transmitters that can be authorized. However, video compression (described at Section 5.7) provides a solution to this dilemma.

Satellite Components

Communication satellites have five essential groups of components (see Exhibit 5.d):

- *transponders*, the receive-transmit units that pick up programs, amplify them, and transmit them back to Earth;
- *antennas* for receiving uplink signals and transmitting downlink signals (for both program material and telemetering information);
- *power supplies*, consisting of arrays of solar cells and storage batteries;
- *telemetering devices* for reporting the satellite's vital signs to, and for receiving instructions from, the ground controllers; and
- small *thrusters* for orienting the satellite and holding it in its assigned position, activated on command from ground controllers.

Uplinks, Downlinks

Like Earth-based transmitters, those on satellites use ITU-allocated channels. Broadcast satellites occupy microwave frequencies between 3 and 15 GHz, most of them in the region of 3–6 GHz (*C band*) and the region of 11–15 GHz (*Ku band*). Most existing operational satellites use the C band.* Newer, more powerful satellites, intended primarily for direct reception by small home or office antennas, use the higher Ku band. The many terrestrial services that also use microwaves sometimes cause interference with Earth stations receiving C-band signals. Ku-band signals escape this drawback, but small objects such as raindrops in heavy downpours can interfere with Ku-band waves.

Each satellite needs two groups of frequencies, one for *uplinking* or on-board reception, and one for *downlinking* or on-board transmission. These frequency groups must be far enough apart to prevent interference between uplink and downlink signals. Thus satellite bands come in pairs—4/6 GHz, 12/14 GHz, and so on—with the lower frequencies used for uplinking.

The downlink frequency bands must be large enough to accommodate simultaneously transmission of several channels by the satellite's *transponders*, combination receive-transmit units. Most C-band satellites carry 24 transponders; each transponder can transmit 2 channels (more with video compression) with opposite polarizations, making a capacity of 48 television channels per satellite, or many more narrowband channels such as telephone or radio transmissions. Ku-band satellites usually carry fewer transponders, because high power means more weight per transponder. Some satellites combine both C- and Ku-band transponders for maximum flexibility.

Transmission

Satellites operate at extremely low power relative to terrestrial stations. Power per transponder varies from as little as 5 up to 400 watts (the higher power for DBS) before antenna gain. Satellite transmitting antennas focus their output into beams to create *footprints* of varying size (see Exhibit 5.e). *Global beams*, serving about 40 percent of the Earth's surface, provide transoceanic and continental coverage; *hemispheric beams*, serving about 20 percent of the surface, provide regional coverage; and for smaller footprints, *spot* beams cover about 10 percent or less. The narrower the beam, the higher the power at reception points, because directionality causes signal gain by a factor of up to 4,000.*

*Since atmospheric absorption causes signal attenuation, it may seem paradoxical that satellites send signals such great distances and yet have very low power. For most of their 22,300-mile journey, however, satellite signals travel through the near vacuum of space. When they do encounter the Earth's relatively thin atmospheric envelope, they pass almost straight down through it. Terrestrial radio signals, in contrast, are impeded by atmospheric absorption along their entire route.

*Though new launches and end-of-service-life (usually a decade or so) constantly change the totals, in mid-1992 U.S. domestic satellites in orbit numbered 24, of which 5 offered both C- and Ku-band transponders while 9 offered Ku-band transponders only.

Exhibit 5.d

Satellite Components

(A) shows that the largest part of most communication satellites is an array of solar panels (which power onboard batteries)—in this case two huge wings on either side of the electronic core of the satellite.

(B) labels the major parts of a satellite as defined in the text: transponders, antennas, power supplies (batteries and the "wing" solar panels, shown here folded up for launch), and thrusters for minor orbit adjustments.

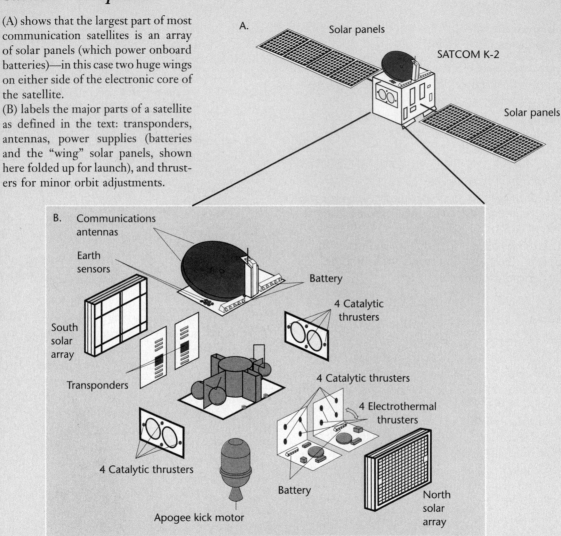

General Electric built the Satcom K-2 satellite and the National Aeronautics and Space Administration (NASA) launched it into orbit in 1986. With a useful life of about a decade, Satcom K-2 used Ku-band frequencies for—among other services—distribution of NBC television signals to the network's more than 200 affiliates, satellite news gathering (SNG) transmissions, and Conus news cooperative delivery transmissions to some 120 affiliated stations in the U.S. and abroad. A number of non-broadcast services also use its transponders.

Source: Mark Long, ed., *World Satellite Almanac: The Global Guide to Satellite Transmission and Technology*, 3rd ed. © 1993 Mark Long Enterprises, Inc., Ft. Lauderdale, FL. Used by permission.

Exhibit 5.e •••••• • • • • • • • • •

Satellite Footprints

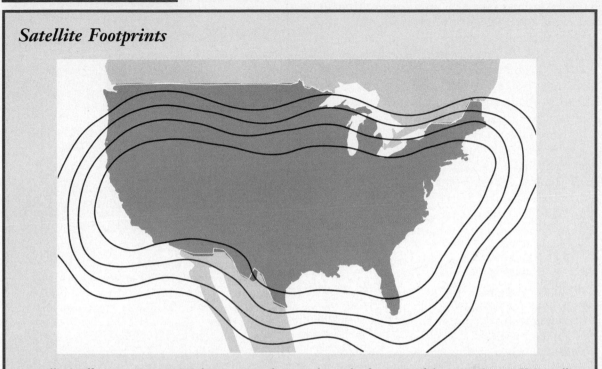

A satellite's effective coverage area, known as its *footprint*, appears on this map in terms of levels of signal strength. The inner contour defines a satellite's *boresight*, its area of maximum signal strength allowing use of smaller receiving antennas. Outlying areas beyond the borders of the country receive only *beamedge* power, beyond which satisfactory reception cannot be expected even with large receiving antennas. This map shows the footprint of the same Satcom K-2 satellite diagrammed in Exhibit 5.d, located at 81 degrees west longitude. The satellite actually orbits far to the south of the U.S., a position above the equator near the Galapagos Islands. Not shown are smaller regional beams that can be directed toward Hawaii and Alaska to serve antennas in those areas.

Source: Mark Long, ed., *World Satellite Almanac: The Global Guide to Satellite Transmission and Technology*, 3rd ed. © 1993 Mark Long Enterprises, Inc., Ft. Lauderdale, FL. Used by permission.

Orientation matters because a satellite's antennas must always point in their target direction, and its arrays of solar collectors, located on the satellite's body or on extended wings, must receive direct rays from the sun for power generation. (Most satellites hold stable orientation by means of gyroscopic spin stabilization.) The solar collectors charge on-board batteries that provide power at all times, including periods when the Earth's shadow interrupts sunlight.

Reception

The bowl-shaped antennas of satellite Earth stations have become familiar sights, but square-shaped satellite receiving antennas ("squareals"), in use commercially, may become the standard for direct-broadcast reception in homes. Antenna diameters vary from as little as 1 foot to more than 100 feet. The larger antennas, originally used for both transmission and reception, represented a deliberate tradeoff. Massive Earth receiving stations made possible lightweight satellites, necessary because of the limitations of early rocket launchers. As launch lifting capabilities improved, satellites (and their transponders) grew larger and more powerful, permitting, in turn, smaller ground antennas.*

Cable television systems and broadcast stations pick up their satellite-fed programs with TVROs (television receive-only antennas) 12 to 15 feet in diameter (see Exhibit 5.f). Reception points located near the edge of satellite footprints need larger diameters because of signal attenuation. Earth-station components include:

- *low-noise amplifiers* (LNAs), especially sensitive amplifiers capable of magnifying without distortion the extremely weak satellite signals that reach the antenna (increasing them by a factor as high as a million);
- *tuners* to select desired transponder channels; and
- *down-converters* to translate satellite frequencies into the range usable by television receivers.

Launching Satellites

A critical moment in the life of every satellite occurs when it first leaves the Earth. Dwarfed by the enormous launch rocket needed to overcome gravity and atmospheric friction in order to attain escape velocity, the fragile satellite starts its journey as a mere passenger. Only after it has traveled about 200 or more miles do its own rocket motors take over to loft it into the high geosynchronous orbit.

Most U.S. communication satellites have been launched from Cape Canaveral, Florida, by NASA (the National Aeronautics and Space Administration, a government agency created in 1958 to de-

---

*This has been especially true for VSATs (*very small antenna terminals*), which are widely and increasingly used in business.

Exhibit 5.f

TVRO Earth Station

The relatively inexpensive *television receive-only* (TVRO) Earth stations (antennas) shown here concentrate the weak satellite signal into a narrow beam directed at a small second reflector mounted on the tripod. This secondary reflector beams the signal into a horn at the center of the TVRO dish, from which it is fed, still as a very weak signal, to a low-noise amplifier (LNA).

Source: Photo by Christopher H. Sterling.

velop nonmilitary aviation and space travel). Television viewers are familiar with spectacular launches of NASA space shuttles, the reusable winged vehicles that carry satellites for the first stage of the journey. When the shuttles reach their low-orbit stations, they release satellite payloads, which then fire their on-board rockets to reach geosynchronous orbit. In the aftermath of the 1987 *Challenger* shuttle loss, NASA policy changed and commercial communications satellites were increasingly launched by disposable rockets, saving shuttle missions for military and scientific payloads. Exhibit 5.g details disposable launchers, and their roles in satellite technology.

Exhibit 5.g •••••••••••••••••

Satellite Launches

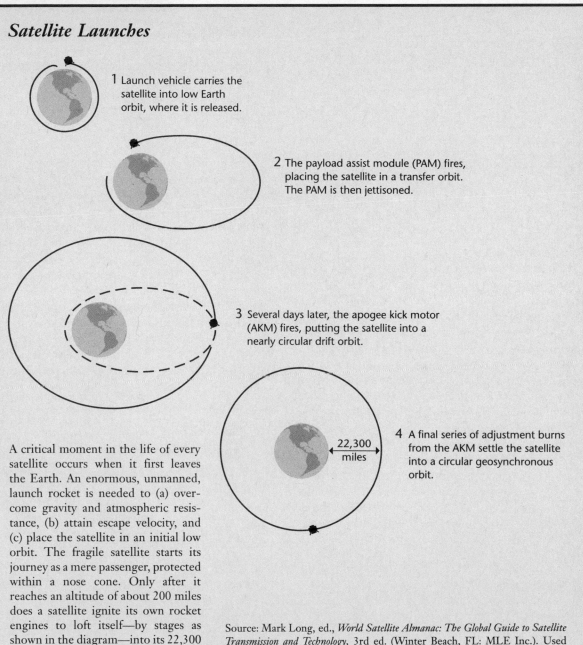

1 Launch vehicle carries the satellite into low Earth orbit, where it is released.

2 The payload assist module (PAM) fires, placing the satellite in a transfer orbit. The PAM is then jettisoned.

3 Several days later, the apogee kick motor (AKM) fires, putting the satellite into a nearly circular drift orbit.

22,300 miles

4 A final series of adjustment burns from the AKM settle the satellite into a circular geosynchronous orbit.

A critical moment in the life of every satellite occurs when it first leaves the Earth. An enormous, unmanned, launch rocket is needed to (a) overcome gravity and atmospheric resistance, (b) attain escape velocity, and (c) place the satellite in an initial low orbit. The fragile satellite starts its journey as a mere passenger, protected within a nose cone. Only after it reaches an altitude of about 200 miles does a satellite ignite its own rocket engines to loft itself—by stages as shown in the diagram—into its 22,300 mile high geosynchronous orbit.

Source: Mark Long, ed., *World Satellite Almanac: The Global Guide to Satellite Transmission and Technology*, 3rd ed. (Winter Beach, FL: MLE Inc.). Used with permission.

Direct-to-Home Delivery

An unexpected bonanza for TVRO antenna manufacturers came when hobbyists, high-tech enthusiasts, and people hungry for video programs—but beyond the reach of either television stations or cable systems—began installing "backyard dishes." About three million such dishes, on the order of 3 to 10 feet in diameter, had been installed in the United States by 1993. They can pick up as many as 150 different signals from domestic satellites, many of them private relays such as television network news feeds and other backhauls, not intended for public consumption. These home pickups became known as *C-band direct* reception because C-band satellite operators usually direct their transmissions narrowly to intermediate users such as broadcast stations and cable systems, rather than broadly to the public.

Theoretically (except for impatience and an inability to predict the future), private users could have waited for *direct-broadcast satellite* (DBS)* services designed specifically for home reception. DBS, a hybrid service combining relays and delivery functions, uses Ku-band frequencies and carries transponders ten times the power of C-band transponders (planned U.S. DBS projects promise from 100 to 400 watts per television channel). The DBS uplink leg acts like a broadcast relay; but the downlink leg acts like a broadcasting station or cable system, delivering programs directly to consumers without the intervention of ground stations or systems. The high power and shortness of Ku-band waves favor use of small receiving antennas, suitable for mounting on private homes; in some cases these antennas are only a foot in diameter, but in no case more than three feet (see Exhibit 5.h).

●●●●●●●●

5.4 Fiber-Optic Relays

Modern relay applications increasingly employ the newest kind of cable: fiber-optic conductors. A

*Also called *direct-to-home* (DTH) services, especially in Europe.

hair-thin strand of extremely pure glass in such a *fiber-optic* cable can transmit modulated light. The tremendously high frequency of light provides a bandwidth in the thousands of megahertz. A single glass filament has more than 600 times the information-carrying capacity of a coaxial cable (see Exhibit 5.i). The favorable economics of fiber-optic cable provide the first serious competition to international and domestic satellite relays.

How They Work

The frequencies present in ordinary light will not travel efficiently through an optical fiber. Instead, *lasers* (light amplification by stimulated emission of radiation) or *light-emitting diodes* (LEDs) must be used to generate what is referred to as a "coherent" light source. The modulated light does not run straight down the glass fiber like water through a pipe but, instead, reflects at an angle back and forth within the fiber (again, see Exhibit 5.i). For this reason, fiber-optic glass must be extraordinarily pure, clear of impurities that could randomly change the angle of reflection. Plastic fibers, which are cheaper, easier to install, and less fragile than glass, may slowly take the place of glass fibers.

Advantages

Optical fiber cables have many advantages for relay links, especially those carrying very heavy traffic:

- little attenuation loss occurs, thus reducing the number of repeater amplifiers needed;
- the cables are small in size and light in weight;
- the cables neither radiate energy to interfere with other circuits nor receive interference from the outside; and
- the cables consist of one of the cheapest and most abundant natural materials available—silicon.

The 1984 Los Angeles Olympic Games were an early user, employing fiber-optic cables to handle the heavy communication load within the games area. Fiber-optic cables have been permanently installed on heavy-traffic telephone routes and are increasingly used for the main distribution lines of

Exhibit 5.h •••••• •••••••••••

DBS System

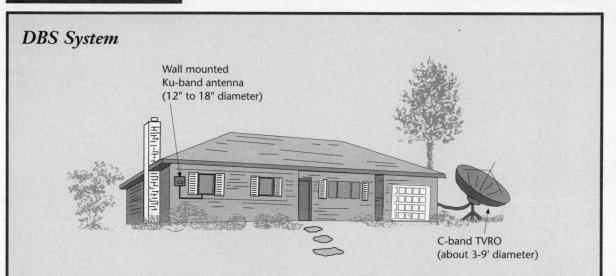

Wall mounted
Ku-band antenna
(12" to 18" diameter)

C-band TVRO
(about 3-9' diameter)

Relatively small receive-only television antennas, TVROs (see Exhibit 5.f), enable homeowners to receive satellite signals directly, without the need of being within reach of a terrestrial television station. This satellite-to-home service began in an unplanned way when hobbyists set up TVROs in their backyards to pick up relay signals never intended for public reception. This kind of satellite reception came to be known as *C-band direct.*

DBS service may begin in the United States in 1994—it has operated for years in Asia and Europe where there are fewer terrestrial television choices. DBS employs relatively small TVROs, the type and size depending on the satellite used. Some three million U.S. homes already have free-standing *C-band direct* antennas ranging up to six or more feet in diameter. True DBS service, however, will employ higher power satellites on *Ku-band* frequencies, enabling use of antennas as small as a foot in diameter, mounted on the side or roof of a house.

cable systems. Eventually, fiber-optic cables will probably replace most conventional copper wire—at least for major trunk relays—that the telephone had relied on for more than a century. Indeed, the cable and telephone industries were racing to install fiber in the early 1990s, driven by their need for stronger bargaining positions in Washington policy battles about what roles the two industries would play in information delivery (see Section 3.8).

Early in 1993, the largest cable system owner, TCI of Denver, announced plans to build a $2 billion fiber-optic network to connect some 400 of its cable systems by 1996. Combined with digital compression technology (discussed in Section 5.7), the new network will dramatically increase the viewing options and interactive capabilities available to subscribers.

International Applications

Fiber-optic cable began supplementing existing undersea copper cables in the late 1980s. A consortium dominated by AT&T installed a 4,000-mile TAT-8 transatlantic submarine fiber-optic cable in 1988; this single fiber can handle 8,000 telephone circuits. TAT-9 was added in 1991. Pacific fiber-optic cables

Exhibit 5.i ●●●●●●●●●●●●●●●

Fiber Optic Relays

A.

B.

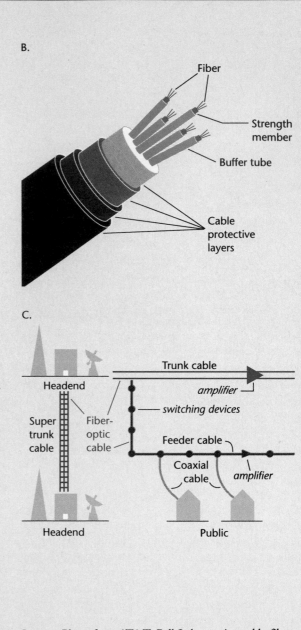

(A) The AT&T fiber-optic cable shown consists of five pairs of hair-thin glass strands, each pair able to carry some 50,000 telephone calls—or hundreds of television signals—transmitted on beams of laser light. Capacity is limited not by the small size of the fibers, but rather by the speed of the lasers that generate the information-bearing light beams, as well as the light detectors at the receiving end.

(B) Each fiber-optic cable has extensive insulation and holds many bundles of fibers each of which can carry many signals.

(C) Cable systems have begun replacing coaxial cable with optical fiber in their trunk and some feeder lines in order to compete with telephone company fiber installations as each industry seeks to be first in providing a menu of broadband services to individual households.

Sources: Photo from AT&T, Bell Laboratories; cable fiber diagram from National Cable Television Association.

have also been laid, and more are planned. Such cable facilities not only greatly increase overall capacity but also offer a cost-effective alternative to Intelsat and other satellite systems for transoceanic television relay business. Indeed, the competitive threat of fiber-optic cables has slowed the development of new satellite systems, and demand for satellite circuits has declined.

• • • • • • • •

5.5   *Analog Sound Recording*

We turn now from relays to recording technologies, beginning with the first to emerge—the art of sound recording. We deal with *analog* recording here and examine digital methods from Section 5.8 on.*

Discs

In analog disc recording, a sound source causes a *stylus* to vibrate as it cuts a concentric groove in a revolving master disc. The stylus transforms the frequency and amplitude patterns of the sound source into corresponding patterns in the form of minute wiggles in the grooves. Molds derived from pressings of the master disc can be used to mass-produce copies.

In playback, the grooves cause vibrations in a pickup-head stylus, which converts (transduces) the movements into an equivalent electrical signal that is amplified and transduced again to cause vibrations in a loudspeaker or earphones—the sounds we hear. Audio disc fidelity depends on such variables as the sensitivity of the recording and pickup styli, their accuracy in tracking grooves in the disc, the speed with which the disc revolves, and studio acoustics and equipment quality. Each operation inevitably causes imperfections, which mount incrementally.

Until the late 1940s, other than experimental recording on thin strands of wire, no alternative to discs existed. For a time, they began to lose favor as users turned more and more to tape, though digital recording methods are today reviving use of discs.

Tape

Magnetic tape recording avoids the distortions inherent in revolving turntables and stylus-and-groove contact. Unlike disc technology, tape makes recording as well as playback readily available to the consumer and combines both functions with portability. In magnetic tape recording, the tape itself is plastic, coated with tiny particles of metallic compound. The number and tiny size of the particles available per second of running time, as determined by the tape's width and speed, define storage capacity. Master sound recordings on half-, one-, or two-inch-wide tape usually call for a tape speed of 15 or even 30 inches per second (ips). In broadcasting, a playback speed of 7½ ips usually suffices. Much lower speeds can be used when quality is less crucial, as in office dictation and station output monitoring. Multitrack master recording and other specialized tasks call for tape stock that is wider than the standard quarter-inch.

Audio signals from a microphone or other source cause variations in a recording head over which tape passes. These variations create patterned arrangements of the metallic particles. On playback, the tape passes over another electromagnetic head, where the tape's magnetic patterns create a modulated electric current for delivery to amplifiers and speakers. Running the tape over a third electromagnet, an erase head, rearranges the particles to neutralize (erase) any stored magnetic patterns so that the same tape can be reused repeatedly.

Originally all tape recorders—both professional and consumer—had a reel-to-reel format, with each reel separate and accessible. Now, however, enclosed cassettes (or cartridges in automated broadcast operation) protect the tape and are more convenient to use than open reels. As discussed at Section 5.8, digital processing has overtaken analog processing in tape, as it has in disc recording.

---

*The term *analog* refers to an electronic circuit that operates with currents and voltages that vary continuously over time.

Cartridges

A cartridge, often called a *cart*, has a single hub and contains an endless recordable tape loop that repeats itself (see Exhibit 5.j). Radio stations use carts, but automated stations find them especially convenient. Many carts can be loaded into an automated player, with each cart containing a single program item (music, commercial, station ID). Computers instruct each cart when to start while inaudible cues recorded on the tape tell the playback unit to stop at the end of the item and to recue the tape for subsequent replay.

Once an important consumer format, four- and eight-track cartridge tapes were briefly popular in home stereo systems, portable recorders, and car tape players. They now have been replaced by the smaller and more convenient cassette.

Cassettes

A cassette incorporates double hubs, one each for feed and take-up reels, in a single small housing (again, see Exhibit 5.j). After playing, the cassette must be rewound. Alternatively, in the case of half-width recordings, some equipment reverses the tape direction, or the cassette may be manually flipped over to play a second "side." The cassette format lends itself equally to both analog and digital recording methods.

● ● ● ● ● ● ● ●

5.6   *Analog Video Recording*

The need for vast increases in tape's information capacity delayed tape adaptation to picture recording for almost a decade after the first experiments with audio tape.

Kinescope Recording

Surviving recordings of the earliest television shows (those prior to 1956) are all in the form of *kinescope recordings* ("kinies" for short, pronounced to rhyme with "kiddies"). A film camera, specially adapted for television's different picture-repetition rate, photographed programs by focusing on the face of a picture (kinescope) tube. But kinescope recording lost much of television's already skimpy detail: when played back, programs looked flat and hazy, far from satisfactory for use on the air. Because good broadcast quality had to await videotape, the lack of an acceptable means of video recording prolonged early television's "live decade" (see Section 2.6).

Videotape

That technology finally arrived in 1956 with the first *quadruplex* videotape recorders (VTRs), developed by Ampex. Early VTRs were costly studio recorders, nothing like home VCRs (videocassette recorders), which came much later. VTR designers needed to increase greatly the speed at which tape passes over the recording and playback heads to capture the large amount of information contained in pictures plus sound. They solved the tape-speed problem by mounting *four* recording heads on a revolving drum (hence the name *quadruplex*). The drum rapidly rotated *transversely* (across the width of tape) while the tape itself simultaneously moved longitudinally, as it does in sound recording (see Exhibit 5.k). Suction held the two-inch-wide tape against the curvature of the revolving drum to maintain head contact. The combined movements of heads and tape produced an effective head-to-tape speed of 1,500 inches per second. (If the tape itself moved at that speed, it would soon wear out the pickup heads and would require huge tape reels.)

Later, simpler and cheaper professional videotape recorders using one-inch and smaller tape stock came on the market. They retain the principle of combining head and tape movements, but use fewer heads. Instead of laying down the track transversely, the heads cross the tape at an angle, producing a *slanted* track, as shown in Exhibit 5.k. Slant-track recording allows the head to make a longer sweep than would be possible if it moved across the narrow tape transversely. The heads spin on a disc mounted

Exhibit 5.j •••••• •••••••••••

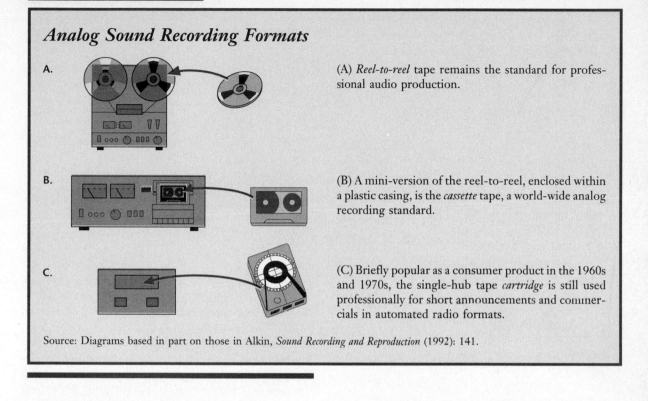

Analog Sound Recording Formats

A. (A) *Reel-to-reel* tape remains the standard for professional audio production.

B. (B) A mini-version of the reel-to-reel, enclosed within a plastic casing, is the *cassette* tape, a world-wide analog recording standard.

C. (C) Briefly popular as a consumer product in the 1960s and 1970s, the single-hub tape *cartridge* is still used professionally for short announcements and commercials in automated radio formats.

Source: Diagrams based in part on those in Alkin, *Sound Recording and Reproduction* (1992): 141.

inside a stationary drum or capstan. The tape wraps around the drum in a spiral (helical) path—hence the name *helical* for slant-track recorders.

For portable equipment, professionals opted first for three-quarter-inch tape (called *U-matic*), but as technology improved, half-inch, 8-mm (about one-third of an inch), and even quarter-inch video formats evolved. Lack of standardization among competing equipment manufacturers delayed widespread adoption of the smaller formats, despite their greater convenience and reduced cost.

Consumer VCRs

Videotape recording formats for home and small-format professional use enclose the tape within cas-settes—hence the term *videocassette recorder*. Older models recorded sound along the edge of the tape, as in the formats shown in Exhibit 5.k. More recent models incorporate high-quality stereophonic sound, interleaving slant tracks for sound with the picture tracks.

Home VCRs depend on the user's television set for playback, but they contain their own tuners to enable recording one channel off the air or from cable while the owner watches a different program. VCRs can also play or record the output of home videocameras (*camcorders*) as well as display rented or purchased tapes. Equipped with many sophisticated computer-assisted features, such as slow motion and the ability to be programmed days in advance to record a sequence of shows on different

Exhibit 5.k •••••• •••••••••••

Analog Video Recording Formats

A. *Transverse Quadruplex Format*

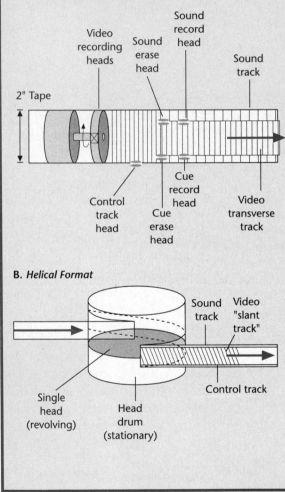

Video recording heads

Sound erase head

Sound record head

Sound track

2" Tape

Control track head

Cue erase head

Cue record head

Video transverse track

C. *One-inch Format*

Direction of tape travel

Audio track 2
Audio track 1

Video

Control track
Sync track
Audio track 3

Type C Format

B. *Helical Format*

Sound track

Video "slant track"

Single head (revolving)

Head drum (stationary)

Control track

(A) *Transverse quadruplex format:* four video recording heads mounted on a rapidly spinning wheel, shown at the left, lay down transverse tracks across the width of the two-inch tape. Sound is recorded longitudinally along one edge, auxiliary information along the other edge.

(B) *Helical format:* the tape spirals around a large, stationary drum. Within the drum, the videorecording head spins on a revolving disc, making contact with the tape as it slips over the drum's smooth surface. Because of the spiral wrap, the tape moves slightly downward as well as lengthwise, so that the combined movements of tape and recording head produce a slanting track, as shown. Some helical recorders use two heads, some use different wrap-around configurations.

(C) *One-inch format:* this is an example of one of the smaller formats. Still narrower VTR tapes are used—3/4-inch, half-inch, 8-mm, and even 1/4-inch.

Source: Courtesy Ampex Corporation. Used with permission.

stations, modern VCRs are one of the most versatile and popular of consumer electronic products. Some provide freeze-frame storage "windows" to monitor as many as nine channels at once on screen, along with a "mosaic" function that changes the video image into patterns of colored squares.

•••••••

5.7   *Digital Signal Processing*

The most striking developments in electronic media result from a fundamental change in the means by which signals are created, transmitted, and received.

Picture a traditional clock or watch that tells time by the *analog* method, using continuously rotating hands to represent the uninterrupted flow of time. The now familiar *digital* watch tells time directly in numbers, jumping relentlessly from one to the next. Digital signal processing has the same property of jumping from number to number (digit to digit).

Encoding

Digital signal processing breaks down an incoming signal into a stream of separate, individual energy pulses and assigns a numerical value to each pulse. It somewhat resembles cutting up a picture (the analog signal) into thousands of tiny pieces and assigning a number systematically to each piece. It would then be possible to transfer the picture piece by piece to another location and reassemble it there.

Digital processing breaks down an analog signal into many tiny pieces by *sampling* it at such high speed that the resulting digitized version *seems* continuous to an observer. In fact, however, the signal has been converted into a stream of separate pulses of energy. Each pulse is identified by a set of digits—hence the term *digital.*

One speaks of *digital encoding* because each pulse receives a digital code number. These code numbers consist of nothing more than the digits "zero" and "one" in various combinations. They employ the *binary* (two-part) code, a term familiar to those who use computers.* As an example, signals modulated by a microphone have a continuously varying electrical amplitude (that is, voltage). A digital processor samples, thousands of times a second, this continuous (analog) amplitude pattern, breaking it down into a series of small, discrete amplitude values. An encoder *quantizes* each value by assigning it a binary number representing the momentary amplitude. The output consists of nothing more than a pattern of "power off" signals (zeros) and "power on" signals (ones). Exhibit 5.l offers more details on digital processing and how it works. But it is

*Computer users also encounter the term *bit*, meaning *binary digit*, and *byte*, meaning a group of eight bits that is sufficient to represent a letter of the alphabet, a number, a punctuation mark, or a symbol such as the dollar sign.

enough simply to remember that digital processing converts a continuous analog signal into a series of binary numbers.

Role of Computers

Mini-computers that convert many functions of both home and studio equipment from analog to digital mode provide a familiar example of digital signal processors. Modern television studio equipment includes digitized production aids such as character generators, electronic frame stores, and special-effects generators. These computer-based units enable electronic insertion of text and graphics into ongoing programs and manipulation of images to produce an endless variety of visual transformations, familiar especially in animation, promotion announcements, title sequences, and most everywhere on MTV.

Computers play a central role in the convergence process discussed at Section 5.1, handling complex switching and other interactions among hybrid system elements. Large-scale integrated circuits on microchips, together with digital signal processing in small computers, bond different elements together into new configurations, memorizing complex instructions and storing material temporarily for special processing. Much of what one sees in broadcast programs has been extensively modified by tiny digital computers built into production equipment. Computers are also central to the operation of robotic studio cameras, controlling basic pan, tilt, zoom, and trucking and dollying moves.

Advantages

The extreme simplicity of digitized signals protects them from many outside influences that distort analog signals. Recording, relaying, and other manipulations of analog information inevitably cause quality loss; each new operation—especially recording—of a signal introduces its own distortions. Digital signals, being simply raw pulses of energy intermixed with moments of no energy, resist distortion as long as the elementary difference between "off" and "on" is preserved.

Exhibit 5.1 • • • • • • • • • • • • • • • •

More on Digital-Signal Processing

Digital-signal processing has become so pervasive in contemporary life that it's worth a little effort to learn how it works.

Actually, digital-signal processing began with the first electrical communication system, the 19th-century telegraph. Telegraph operators sent messages in Morse code by means of an on/off key that controlled electricity going down the telegraph wire. The code consists simply of varying lengths of "on" and "off," presented to the ear or eye as dots, dashes, and spaces, which in turn represent letters of the alphabet, punctuation marks, and numbers.

Modern digital-signal processing also employs simple on/off signals. They represent the elements of a *binary code*, a two-digit number system that requires only two code symbols, conventionally written as 0 and 1. All communication content can be reduced to nothing more than strings of zeros and ones.

A system that communicates digitally needs to make only one elementary distinction. "On" and "off" differ so obviously that they leave little chance for ambiguity. That simplicity makes digital signals extremely "rugged"— able to withstand external interference and imperfections in transmission and copying systems.

The familiar ten-digit *decimal* system (0 through 9) is used in everyday life. In that familiar system, the values of digits depend on their *positions* relative to one another, counting from right to left. Each new position increases a digit's value by a multiple of 10.

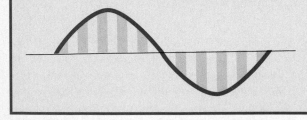

A digitized waveform looks something like this. The dark bars indicate the points at which the wave's amplitude is sampled.

Thus the number 11 means (counting from right to left) one 1 plus one 10 (1 + 10 = 11). The binary code also relies on position, but each digit's position (again counting from right to left) increases by a multiple of 2. Thus in binary code the decimal number 11 becomes 1011, which means (counting from right to left) one 1 plus one 2 plus no 4 plus one 8 (1 + 2 + 0 + 8 = 11). Here's an example converting the three-digit number 463 to binary form:

Multipliers:

$$
\begin{array}{ccccc}
 & 8 & 4 & 2 & 1 & 0 \\
\end{array}
$$

Binary numbers
$$
\begin{cases}
0\ 1\ 0\ 0\ 0 = 0 + 4 + 0 + 0 + 0 = 4 \\
0\ 1\ 1\ 0\ 0 = 0 + 4 + 2 + 0 + 0 = 6 \\
0\ 0\ 1\ 1\ 0 = 0 + 0 + 2 + 1 + 0 = 3
\end{cases}
$$

As the examples indicate, it takes more digits to express a number in the binary system than in the decimal system. Thus, although the simplicity of digital transmissions makes them less subject to error, they need larger channels than analog transmissions.

Conversion of an analog signal to a digitized signal involves *quantizing* the analog signal, that is, turning it into a number sequence. Quantizing consists of rapidly sampling an analog waveform and assigning a binary numerical value to the amplitude of each momentary item in the sample. The higher the sampling rate, the greater is the fidelity of the digitized signal. There is an equation for calculating the sampling rate necessary to avoid distortion; it usually calls for sampling thousands of times per second.

Many electronic consumer items—notably, compact disc (CD) audio recordings and digital audio tape (DAT), discussed at Section 5.8—use digital technology. It has also been applied to studio recording and other production functions, revolutionizing prebroadcast program preparation and increasing enormously the range of effects available to video directors.

Spectrum Disadvantage

Digital signals do have drawbacks. Digitally processed signals need wider channels than the same signals in analog form because a string of binary digits is needed to identify each tiny sample. The first communication modes to use digital processing, therefore, were those with relatively simple signals that made no great demands on the spectrum—data processing and telephone calls, for example. The need for high-capacity channels has thus far delayed the application of digital methods to broadcast transmission and reception. But compression and the introduction of digital audio broadcasting—all explained below—will likely overcome the disadvantage.

In addition, digital signals can be negatively affected by interference, whereas an analog signal would go right through. Some engineers have expressed concern that digital audio broadcasting may reduce signal availability from the level now possible with today's analog stations, especially in areas with high electrical interference. HDTV and DAB proponents concerned themselves with this disadvantage as they worked toward technical standards for 21st-century broadcasting.

Compression

Digital signals' hunger for frequency bandwidth drives ongoing research on *signal compression*. Compression economizes on frequencies by offering tradeoffs—more signals per channel at the cost of marginally reduced picture resolution or color fidelity. Experimenters have developed several means of squeezing multiple television signals into the space of one present television channel.

One method of band compression uses a process of selective omission. In any video transmission, not all pictures change totally from frame to frame; some picture elements remain the same over a series of frames. One video compression system transmits information only about elements that change, thus reducing the average amount of new information that has to be processed each second. Other methods achieve compression by marginally reducing picture quality (resolution) or color quality, or by slowing the pace of perceived movement (as in some video conferencing systems).

By the mid- or late-1990s, signal-compression measures will enable better-quality digital television pictures to be transmitted without a wider picture channel (see Exhibit 5.m). How *much* compression is a key question facing engineers—whether, for example, to transmit from two to six television signals on one satellite transponder or terrestrial television channel (technically feasible now), or to push technology further (and degrade picture quality somewhat) and transmit 10 or even dozens of channels. In other words, will the tradeoff of more channels per unit of spectrum provide pictures "good enough" (as opposed to the best they can be made) for most viewers?

It appears likely that whatever is decided, satellite services, and then cable television systems making use of fiber relays, will be the first media to use compression. Cable systems could then routinely carry several hundred channels. But relative cost is always important: subscriber decoder boxes able to accept compressed signals cost about $1,000 each in 1992 and are not likely to be adopted until that cost drops sharply with more efficient technology and high levels of production. For television broadcasters, video compression offers the potential for multichannel delivery services and is central to squeezing HDTV's massive information load into an existing 6-MHz channel (De Sonne, 1992: 67).

While aiding HDTV and reducing spectrum scarcity, however, video compression poses a problem for a familiar household device—the home VCR. The huge information load of digital HDTV signals (see Section 5.9) will be hard to fit into existing videotape formats without compressing

Exhibit 5.m ●●●●●● ●●●●●●●●●●

Video Compression

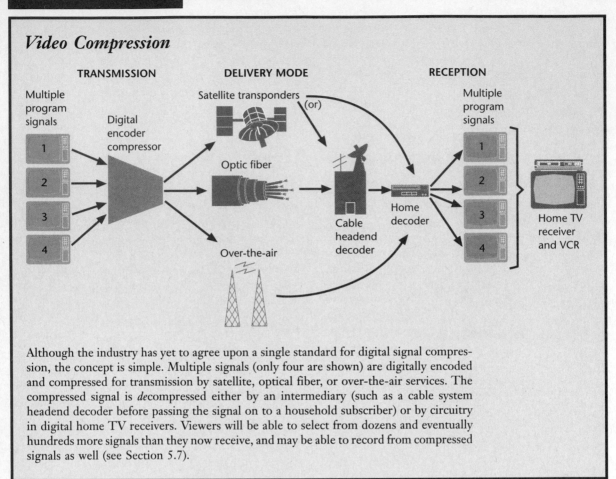

Although the industry has yet to agree upon a single standard for digital signal compression, the concept is simple. Multiple signals (only four are shown) are digitally encoded and compressed for transmission by satellite, optical fiber, or over-the-air services. The compressed signal is *de*compressed either by an intermediary (such as a cable system headend decoder before passing the signal on to a household subscriber) or by circuitry in digital home TV receivers. Viewers will be able to select from dozens and eventually hundreds more signals than they now receive, and may be able to record from compressed signals as well (see Section 5.7).

those signals. But how best to *de*compress and play those signals back?

By 1993, Japanese consumer electronics firms had spent a decade pushing development along several lines. One option, developed by Toshiba and Hitachi among others, will record a compressed signal, using the digital television receiver's decoder to play back a decompressed signal. These would be fairly inexpensive, would preserve the digital picture quality, but might not work with analog camcorders and some present features such as fast-forwarding with a visible picture. Another approach, promoted by JVC, would only record after the receiver has de-

compressed the signal, though at the cost of losing some picture definition. Still other companies sought a means of combining analog and digital recording methods in the same VCR to better bridge the late-1990's transition from analog to digital television systems.

All, however, seemed to agree that marketing success for these expensive new VCRs (initially, up to several thousand dollars per machine) would require agreement on a digital standard. One matter up for decision was whether the new machines would be tape- or disc-based. Neither industry nor consumers could afford the kind of confusion evident in the early 1980's Beta vs. VHS battle for initial VCR standards acceptance.

• • • • • • • •

5.8 Digital Recording

Distortions inherent in analog disc recording can be avoided by digital signal processing as described above. In addition, substituting *laser** beams for mechanical tracking by a stylus eliminates the wear and tear caused by physical contact of stylus on disc (see Exhibit 5.n).

Compact Discs

Digitally processed laser-produced sound in a *compact disc* (CD) format has largely replaced analog stylus recording and playback. The plastic coatings in which CDs are sealed make them almost immune to damage. They also have enormous storage capacity, recording up to 80 minutes of stereo sound on a 4 3/4-inch disc, smaller than the old 45-rpm records that held only a few minutes of music. A decade old in 1992, CDs were the first mass-marketed digital medium. In the early 1990s, however, consumers first heard about still newer standards that allow what no CD system can do—the ability to record.

Consumer Digital Recorders

Two economic pressures motivate the search for methods of digital recording at home—the constant need of industry to find a new product to market, and consumer desires to record as well as play back (evident in the success of the home VCR as compared to that of analog video discs with their superior pictures, as discussed at Section 3.4). By the early 1990s the search for a digital consumer re-

*A laser produces coherent light, a highly concentrated beam at a single frequency (or very few frequencies). In addition to their role in videodiscs, lasers supply light for transmission through fiber-optic channels and enable experimental three-dimensional television (holography) and some experimental 3-D interactive video.

cording device was moving in three quite different directions.

First announced and demonstrated was DAT (*digital audio tape*). The high cost of this product limited its consumer appeal, but it found widespread professional use. DATs initially offered users the chance to make any number of copies without the quality losses evident in duplicating analog tape. This innovation so threatened the music industry that it spoke of taking legal action and held up DAT's introduction in the United States for nearly two years until Congress agreed to a technical "fix" to prevent consumers from digitally duplicating many copies off the air or from friends. Now DATs and their more recent digital competitors all contain circuits allowing only a single digital copy to be made of any digital original—any other copy will be of analog quality.

In late 1992 Philips and other manufacturers introduced *digital compact cassette* (DCC) recorders, which differ from DAT in that they can play back analog and digital cassettes as well as record digitally. Several hundred prerecorded music titles were made available for the new machines which could also use the huge backlog of analog recordings.

Finally, substantial research developed a *recordable compact disc* for the consumer market; introduced (again, in late 1992) as the "MiniDisc" by Sony, it emphasizes portable units. Ironically, while the discs themselves are half the size of traditional CDs, the initial record/playback units were about three times as heavy as the famous Sony "Walkman." Further, the new system was incompatible with any existing digital recording mode.

Research continues on two specific formats: (1) the CD-R, which may be recorded only once but played back on any CD player—thus preventing widespread duplication; and (2) the CD-E format, which allows unlimited erasing and re-recording and playback. Each of these approaches incorporates several different technical standards.

Digital Video

Professional digital videotape recording has evolved three standards, with still others in development. The D1 standard provides the best quality because

Exhibit 5.n • • • • • • • • • • • • • •

Compact Disc System

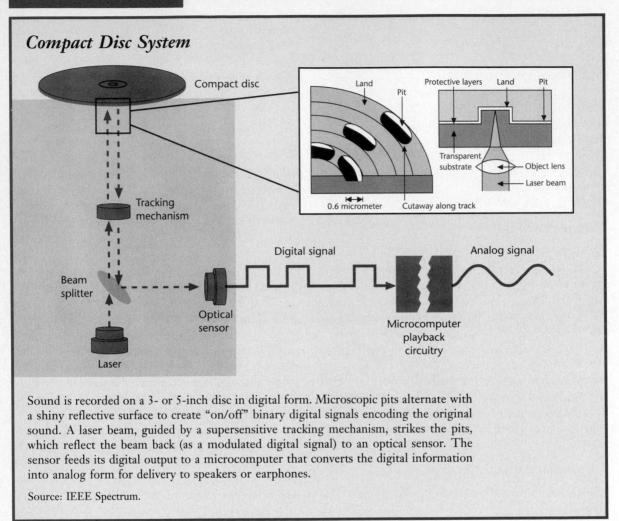

Sound is recorded on a 3- or 5-inch disc in digital form. Microscopic pits alternate with a shiny reflective surface to create "on/off" binary digital signals encoding the original sound. A laser beam, guided by a supersensitive tracking mechanism, strikes the pits, which reflect the beam back (as a modulated digital signal) to an optical sensor. The sensor feeds its digital output to a microcomputer that converts the digital information into analog form for delivery to speakers or earphones.

Source: IEEE Spectrum.

it handles the color and brightness components of the signal separately, each with its own channel. D2 uses *composite* color, meaning that it multiplexes (mixes) signal components in a single channel in the manner of an analog broadcast signal. D3, the newest standard, which also uses composite color, reduces tape width from 3/4 inch to 1/2 inch, thus making it more adaptable for lightweight field equipment. Of course, the output of all digital re-

corders must currently be converted to analog form for transmission and display on receiver screens. Higher costs will delay digital recording devices for the consumer market until some years in the future.

Laser Video

The laser recording principle used in audio CDs has been applied to picture recording, resulting in *laser video discs* with better picture-quality playbacks than those of VCRs as well as improved freeze-frame and slow-motion functions. Systems available thus far provide analog video with digital audio. Consumers already have access to combination laser playback units that play audio CDs as well as laser video discs of movies and other materials. Indeed, laser technology may eventually displace most other types of home information storage, including the magnetic floppy disks used in home computers. A single computer laser disc has 660-megabyte capacity, many times that of a computer floppy or even most hard drives.* But manufacturers still need a simple method for home recording on laser discs before they can fully rival the versatility of videotape and floppy disks.

• • • • • • • •

5.9   High-Definition Television

Larger screens, vastly improved picture resolution, and digital multichannel sound—all are expected benefits from *high-definition television* (HDTV) systems, which should become widely available by the late 1990s. HDTV, though usually described in terms of improved pictures, is actually a wholly new television transmission system that appears likely to replace the half-century-old NTSC system early in the 21st century. Right behind HDTV is digital audio broadcasting (DAB), which promises a parallel revolution in sound broadcasting (see Section 5.10).

HDTV matches the quality of 35-mm theatrical motion pictures and therefore lends itself to pro-

jected display: screens 35 inches and larger in size bring out the real improvement in picture resolution. HDTV allows comfortable viewing at a distance of only three times the picture height and can also be viewed at a much wider angle from the screen than can existing television. HDTV also permits multiple audio tracks, facilitating not only sound in stereo but also sound in several languages.

Analog Beginnings

Japanese engineers, beginning work in the 1960s, made the first significant progress with HDTV, developing a 1125-line picture with a 9-to-16 aspect ratio (see Exhibit 5.o). This analog system, called MUSE and demonstrated in the United States in 1981, required 36 MHz channels—six times wider than the U.S. 6-MHz standard. HDTV thus implied a double threat: to outmode all present receivers and transmitters, and to force many stations off the air because the spectrum lacked adequate space for HDTV. The Japanese later developed a broadcast MUSE version using a 9-MHz channel that is more—though not completely—compatible with present equipment. Since there is no additional spectrum space available in the present terrestrial television bands, HDTV must either conform to present channel specifications, be offered on fewer stations, and/or move to the higher-frequency band allocated to DBS transmission.

Until 1991 it appeared that the Japanese might dominate worldwide HDTV standards. They had a two-decade head start on any other country and by late 1991 were providing satellite delivery, eight hours a day, of MUSE service to selected viewing sites in Japan. However, the cost of receivers (about $18,000 in early 1992) drastically limited HDTV penetration. Of even greater impact was the initial appearance, beginning in 1991, of *digital HDTV*, developed as the United States moved toward selection of its own HDTV technical standard.

HDTV Standards

The FCC had felt some urgency by 1988 to adopt at least tentative U.S. HDTV standards in order to

---

*The computer version of laser video, known as CD-ROM (compact disk read-only memory), can store thousands of pages of information. CD-ROM products on the market supply small libraries of reference works on a single disk. For instance, all 12 volumes of the *Oxford English Dictionary* can be obtained on a single CD-ROM disk; far more versatile than the printed version, the laser recording permits virtually instantaneous searching for any word or combination of words within the dictionary's word definitions.

Exhibit 5.0 ● ● ● ● ● ● ● ● ● ● ● ● ● ● ●

High Definition Systems

A. NTSC - 525 lines;
analog audio

B. HDTV - 1125 lines;
digital audio

As this edition went to press, the FCC was in the final stages of selecting a technical standard for the transmission of high-definition television. Though many details had yet to be worked out, the Commission had agreed that the new service—compared to today's NTSC standard—would have more than twice as many scanning lines for improved picture definition, a much wider screen size, and both digital audio and video signal generation. The diagrams compare (A) present NTSC television with its 4:3 picture aspect ratio as approved in 1941 (and modified with color in 1953) with (B) HDTV with its 16:9 aspect ratio.

Source: Diagrams based in part on Mark Long, ed., *World Satellite Almanac: The Global Guide to Satellite Transmission and Technology*, 3rd ed. (Winter Beach, FL: MLE Inc.). Used with permission.

ensure U.S. terrestrial broadcasting's ability to (1) keep up with Japanese and European efforts in the race toward improved television, and (2) keep abreast of domestic cable, VCR, and DBS improvements. Those nonbroadcast services, not being subject to the NTSC 6-MHz channel constraint of broadcast television, could forge ahead with their own nonbroadcast version of HDTV without waiting for a compatible broadcast version to emerge.

By 1988 several producers in the United States and abroad already had television programs and motion pictures in production using MUSE-type HDTV cameras and recorders. This advanced equipment, employed as a "mastering medium," has economic and quality advantages over film. Producers of HDTV programs have been converting them for broadcast to the older analog NTSC standard, retaining the masters pending evolution of HDTV home receivers. Once these receivers become common, cable television and videocassette producers could move into HDTV production without waiting for broadcast HDTV to develop.

Given this situation, the United States' initial position at meetings of international standards-setting bodies in the late 1980s was to back the Japanese MUSE system (partly because CBS was a partner in marketing this system), in the face of seeming disinterest by American firms in developing competing standards.*

Soon, however, an FCC Advisory Committee on Advanced Television Service (ACATS), established to compare HDTV systems and recommend one to the Commission, sparked creative thinking among many domestic and foreign companies. As many as 20 potential HDTV proponents suggested technical means of achieving their common goal.

Digital Transition

By 1991 several companies and consortia had announced their shift to development of digital HDTV systems. For a year in 1991–1992 the Advanced Television Testing Center (ATTC), an industry-supported laboratory outside of Washington, DC, carefully tested five surviving applicants' HDTV systems (MUSE, which used analog transmission, and four all-digital approaches) to determine which system would work best over the long term.

While those tests showed many differences among the four competing digital systems, no one system clearly excelled in all tests above the others. Facing digital reality, however, its advocates withdrew the analog MUSE system which had once seemed the obvious standards choice. With months of further tinkering and expensive testing ahead of them, plus likely appeals from losers after any FCC decision, pressure increased on the competing digital system backers to find a means of merging. By uniting their best elements into a "grand alliance," HDTV could then be tested and more quickly

moved through final approvals to the marketplace. Debates over technical details and how to divide potential royalty income dragged on for weeks and several times negotiations nearly failed.

In late May 1993, however, the parties compromised sufficiently to reach an agreement. The new unified digital HDTV system, proponents promised, would be able to interact with both existing analog television and the digital world of computers. Indeed, HDTV was being positioned to play a central role in the convergence of capabilities from these two huge industries, as well as to revitalize American electronics.

Moving from NTSC to HDTV

One of the most difficult decisions facing the FCC amidst all this fast-moving technical change was how best to handle the transition from existing NTSC receivers and broadcast and cable production and transmission equipment to the selected HDTV standard. For example, stations will need new or additional transmission towers, but very few firms have the expertise to build them. Further, the FCC was developing a *transmission* standard, and despite a preliminary understanding in 1988, the industry had not yet reached final agreement on a *production* standard. Observers cited availability of sufficient HDTV programming as another factor in determining how quickly the new service could expand. So the problem came down to how quickly the transition could take place, and to what degree the FCC should manage the process.

The Commission decided early in 1992 on a 15-year phased transition, with both old and new systems operating side by side for a while.* Broadcasters would have to begin HDTV operations by 1999 (six years after the FCC's then-projected 1993 selection

---

*European consumer-product manufacturers, fearful of a Japanese takeover of their industry (as had long since happened in the United States), were determined to develop their own HDTV system, based on analog technology and compatible with European 50-Hz electrical standards. Philips and Thomson spearheaded a consortium to build a European system called HDMAC. Early in 1993, however, the European Community decided not to pursue its analog research in light of digital developments in the United States.

*The closest previous parallel to this situation came with FM radio's shift from 42–50 MHz up to its present 88–108 MHz band in 1945 (see Section 2.3). In that case, to allow broadcasters and consumers alike time to purchase needed equipment for the new band, the FCC allowed dual-channel operation for three years. After 1948 there were no more FM broadcasts on the old, lower, band.

of an HDTV standard) or run the risk of forfeiting access to needed spectrum. They would have to simulcast half of their programming in their second year of HDTV operation, and all of it by the third year. At the end of the transition in 2008 (15 years after an HDTV standard had been selected, when presumably a substantial portion of television homes would be HDTV receiver–equipped), stations and networks would have to convert to HDTV-only operations, all on UHF channels, and give up their old NTSC broadcast channels (VHF or UHF), which could then be reallocated to other services.

Estimates for initial television station conversion costs range between $10 million and $15 million *per station* for transmitter changes, cameras, video recorders, and related production equipment—leading some wags to suggest that HDTV really stood for "high-deficit TV." DBS and cable services face a less expensive HDTV conversion as they have less equipment to purchase.

• • • • • • • •

5.10 Digital Radio

Though the coming changes in television have earned extensive media attention, a less widely known radio revolution is not far behind.

Digital Audio Broadcasting

There is another "high-definition" development brewing, this time for audio. While few consumers have yet seen HDTV, most have heard the equivalent of digital audio broadcasting (DAB), which builds on the popularity of audio CD technology and sound quality—and of digital audio services carried on some cable systems. Despite this edge, DAB is developing more slowly than the digital HDTV version of television. It ultimately promises (or threatens, depending on one's point of view) to replace analog radio broadcasting—both AM and FM—with a single new digital system of radio.

Though selection by the FCC of a specific DAB standard remains unlikely before 1994, a good deal of planning has already begun. Estimated costs for existing stations to convert to DAB are far less than for HDTV—$20,000 to $50,000 for most stations (De Sonne, 1992: 23). As with HDTV, the FCC would likely set up a transition period during which stations would broadcast in analog AM and FM on their existing frequencies, while simulcasting DAB on new assignments (or possibly even on the existing frequencies, thanks to new multiplexing technology). Then, when sufficient homes had DAB receivers ("sufficient" to be defined sometime in the future), stations would cease their analog transmissions.

By 1992, before any formal testing and long before proposed systems had shaken out to the few that would actually be tested, about ten different technologies for achieving DAB existed, all of which fell into one of two categories. Some would require additional spectrum to achieve true digital sound quality, while the others would operate in the present combined AM and FM bands, though likely with wider channels. The latter proposals were more experimental but had the benefit of not adding to spectrum demand. Several had been demonstrated under normal field conditions by 1992 (*Broadcasting*, 7 Sep. 1992: 60, 62). Either approach offers the benefits of allowing broadcasters to "start over" with a technology that will render everyone equal in coverage and greatly reduce present interference while dramatically improving sound quality.

DAB Spectrum Needs

In the early 1990s spectrum problems threatened to delay DAB still further. The controversy centered on what frequencies were best suited to DAB's service needs.

The FCC announced in 1992 that DAB—whether transmitted by satellites or terrestrial stations (*if* the latter needed more spectrum than existing radio broadcast frequency bands)—would be allocated 50 MHz of spectrum at "S-band" frequencies, (that is, 2.3 to 2.6 GHz). That decision played into the hands of broadcasters as satellite DAB in that frequency range would be far more expensive and difficult to achieve than at lower frequencies.

Broadcasters feared that a *satellite* DAB service could eliminate need for some or all existing terrestrial broadcast operations. On the other hand, they are very interested in further developing DAB for existing stations.

Despite U.S. opposition, the ITU earlier in 1992 had established the L band (1.452 to 1.492 GHz) as the recommended location for DAB services around the world. The United States could not agree to the ITU choice because of Defense Department unwillingness to move many of its existing telemetry services off L-band frequencies. Given that virtually all other countries (many of which manufacture radios) agreed on the L-band allocation, the United States may be forced to withdraw its insistence on a different set of frequencies before any service begins, or before receiver manufacture gets under way.

In 1992 the FCC granted experimental authority for testing of in-band DAB. Both AM and FM channel tests were conducted that year. At the same time, Satellite CD Radio, the first start-up company in this area, announced plans for a 30-channel ad-free service to be launched on a subscription basis to home TVROs. By early 1993, five more firms applied to the FCC to provide satellite DAB services.

Data by Radio

In the early 1990s digital technology made possible an interesting melding of traditional broadcasting and data communications. After long debate, the broadcast industry and consumer electronics manufacturers—working through a National Radio System Committee—agreed on technical standards for a *radio data system* (RDS), transmitted on an FM station subcarrier (see Section 4.7) for receivers equipped with a special microchip. RDS transmits a digital signal—an ad slogan, information on the station's format, or other information—that can be displayed in a special receiver panel. The system would make it possible for an RDS-equipped car, for example, to tune stations by format (any one of more than 20 preset codes), with the receiver jumping to a different but more powerful signal when the tuned signal became weak—a service especially useful to listeners who come to a new area and do not know station formats. And in an emergency situation—say, a bad weather front—RDS could be used to turn on a receiver to transmit a warning message.

RDS, already available in several European countries by 1987 (though not for format scanning), was being used experimentally by about 40 American FM stations by 1993. AM stations can make use of the system only with a delay in data display. The RDS modifications to a receiver add anywhere from $50 to $100 in cost, while stations spend from $2,000 to $6,000 to add data encoders to their transmitters.

● ● ● ● ● ● ● ●

Summary

5.1 Fast-changing electronic communication technology is best characterized as *converging*, given the increasing overlap among previously separate functions and services. All of the systems discussed in this chapter serve more efficiently to distribute or store—and thus share—programming. Networks are efficient means of instant distribution from one central point to any number of local outlets.

5.2 Terrestrial relays, now used primarily for regional or local links, include rebroadcasting (rarely employed today except for translators), telephone wire (for radio), coaxial cable, and microwave (for television).

5.3 Space relays by satellites in geosynchronous orbit have greater flexibility than traditional terrestrial relays. Satellites use orbital allotments and different frequency allocations for their uplinks and downlinks, and provide different footprints depending on the service offered. Each satellite consists of transponders, antennas, power supplies, telemetering devices, and thruster motors. More powerful satellites enable smaller Earth stations. Satellite receiving antennas vary in size: cable systems and broadcasters use 12-to-15-foot receive-only antennas, whereas 3-foot dishes suffice for home satellite reception, and 1-foot antennas will work when DBS services begin.

Exhibit 5.p

World's Largest Electronic-Media Technology Marketplace

The biggest marketplace for new broadcast and cable equipment is the annual spring convention of the National Association of Broadcasters. Usually held in Las Vegas (one of few cities that can accommodate the 60,000 participants that attended in 1993), the huge display of transmission, studio, remote, and related equipment takes several days to set up and dismantle. Thousands of vendors demonstrate equipment to cable and broadcast station buyers from the United States and, increasingly, from other countries as well. Exhibitors range from the huge (Sony and Ampex have displays of several thousand square feet) to tiny start-ups with just a few square feet of the floor. The NAB display is often where new technologies first appear—as did Ampex videotape in 1956 and high-definition television in the 1980s.

Source: Photos by Christopher H. Sterling.

5.4   Fiber-optic relays, made originally of glass but increasingly of plastic, have tremendous capacity and are replacing some satellite as well as traditional terrestrial trunk relays. Fiber-optic relays also serve across both the Atlantic and Pacific oceans. Fiber cables suffer little attenuation, are small and light in weight, neither radiate energy nor receive interference, and are made from cheap, natural substances.

5.5   Analog sound recording comes in four major formats, all but the first using magnetic tape: disc, reel-to-reel, cartridge, and cassette. Audio fidelity depends on equipment and studio facilities, but any analog recording suffers imperfections.

5.6   Analog video recording began in the 1950s with kinescopes, which gave way to quadruplex magnetic videotape after 1956. For portable recording, professionals use smaller, "slant-track" formats. The latest home videocassette recorders have stereophonic sound and other advanced features.

5.7   Digital signal processing converts original continuous analog signals into discontinuous pulses of energy. Digitally processed signals are highly manipulable and resistant to distortion, but they also require greater bandwidth (more spectrum space). Signal compression techniques will overcome this drawback.

5.8   Digital recording methods suffer little distortion. Several formats are available, with more on the way. Compact disc audio recording, using laser light and digital processing, was the first major advance over conventional disc and tape recording. And video disc recording, an application of audio CD technology and analog video, greatly increases storage capacity and picture definition. In the early 1990s several mutually incompatible modes of recordable digital media were introduced on the consumer electronics market.

5.9   Digital high-definition television will arrive later in this decade, bringing better pictures and sound to home television screens here and elsewhere. HDTV development was characterized until 1991 by analog methods. The FCC will select a specific technical standard in 1994, opening the way for a transition from present NTSC to HDTV television operation phased in over many years.

5.10   Digital audio broadcasting is developing more slowly (there are many competing standards and as yet few decisions on which is best and how to integrate DAB with existing stations), but it will eventually replace both AM and FM broadcasting with CD-quality sound. Systems of sending data by radio were initially developed in Europe and began to appear in the United States in 1992.

PART 3

Business

Commercial broadcasting and cable are businesses; as such, their primary motivation is to make money. And as in any business, the way to make money is to offer a salable product and to have income exceed expense. The revenue sources that support electronic media exert a controlling influence on them. Unlike other Western democracies, the United States has allowed commercial motives to dominate broadcasting almost from the beginning.

Advertising's dominant role in financing most electronic mass media has had a profound impact on the types, number, and variety of program services offered. Cable and similar technologies rely mostly on subscriptions for their support, although advertising plays an ever-increasing role in those media as well. Part 3 describes the organization and operation of commercial electronic media in America and the influences of their economic bases. It then compares commercial with noncommercial systems.

Chapter 6

Organization and Operations

• •

Exhibit 6.a summarizes the size and scope of the electronic media industries. Although many of the numbers represented in the exhibit change almost daily, the data are representative for 1993. Networks, both radio and television, both broadcast and cable, serve important functions. But it is the individual outlets—more than 12,000 commercial broadcast stations and in excess of 11,000 cable television systems—that constitute the basic economic units of these industries. These 23,000 units function as local retailers, delivering programs to consumers and audiences to advertisers.

The terms *local station* and *local cable system* are redundant because all stations and systems are local in the sense that each of them has a license or a franchise to serve a specific local community. Despite this localism, economic efficiency favors centralization of station/system ownership and program production. Still more efficiency comes from vertical integration—common ownership of production, distribution, and delivery facilities. The large organizations that have resulted now increasingly dominate the media industry.

• • • • • • • •

6.1 Commercial Broadcast Stations

Most Americans already know, or think they know, what a broadcast station is. After all, they have been listening to them and watching them for years. But for purposes of this chapter, and for the sake of precision, we define the traditional commercial broadcast station as an entity (individual, partnership, corporation, or nonfederal governmental authority) that

- holds a license from the federal government to organize and schedule programs for a specific *community* in accordance with an approved plan;
- transmits those programs *over the air* using designated radio facilities in accordance with specified technical standards; and
- carries commercial messages that promote the products or services of profit-making

Exhibit 6.a ●●●●●● ● ● ● ● ● ● ● ●

Electronic Media Dimensions

Total U.S. Population	250 million
Total U.S. Households	94 million
Total U.S. Television Households (TVHH)	92 million

Commercial Radio stations	
AM (51 percent)	4,960
FM (49 percent)	+4,796
	9,756
Noncommercial FM stations	1,592
Total radio stations	**11,348**
(56 percent FM; 44 percent AM)	
Commercial TV stations	
VHF (49 percent)	558
UHF (51 percent)	+ 588
	1,146
Noncommercial TV stations	
VHF (34 percent)	124
UHF (66 percent)	+ 239
	363
Low-power TV stations	
VHF (36 percent)	465
UHF (64 percent)	+ 841
	1,306
Total TV stations	**2,815**
(41 percent VHF; 59 percent UHF)	
(54 percent full-power; 46 percent low-power)	
Total broadcast stations	**14,163**
(80 percent radio; 20 percent TV)	

Television Network Affiliates

ABC	223	Fox	139
CBS	223	PBS	345
NBC	205		

Cable Systems	11,254

Sources: *Broadcasting & Cable*, 1 March 1993, and *Broadcasting & Cable Market Place*, 1992.

organizations, for which the station receives compensation.

Each license encompasses both transmission and programming functions. A station therefore normally combines three groups of facilities: business offices, studios, and transmitter (including an antenna and its tower). Usually all such facilities come under common ownership, although in a few cases stations lease some or all of them.

Station Organization

Exhibit 6.b offers examples of the *tables of organization* (sometimes called *organization charts*) for both a radio and a television station. These vary widely from facility to facility, but all outline the station's personnel structure and indicate who reports to whom.

All commercial stations need to perform four basic functions: general/administrative, technical, programming, and sales. Employees perform most such functions, but stations also contract with outside consultants who offer expertise on such matters as finance, management, programming, promotion, sales, technical operations, and legal concerns.

General/administrative functions include those services (for example, payroll, accounting, housekeeping, and purchasing) that any business must provide to create an appropriate working environment. Services of a specialized nature peculiar to broadcasting usually come from such external organizations as engineering and news consulting firms and program syndicators. A network affiliate's main external contract is with its network.

Broadcasters need to keep abreast of rapidly evolving program trends, regulations, and technical developments. Many trade and professional organizations serve this need. The 1992 edition of *Broadcasting & Cable Market Place* lists more than 200 national associations and societies; in addition, each state has its own broadcasting association. Many of these groups hold annual meetings, often with elaborate hardware and software exhibits by vendors and distributors. Major management-oriented associations lobby Congress and state legislators for and against legislation that affects their interests (see Section 13.5). Managers usually join such groups as the National Association of Broadcasters, the Television Bureau of Advertising, and the Radio Advertising Bureau. Specialized station associations serve independent, UHF, and low-power television as well as farm, religious, and Spanish-language broadcasters. Individuals can join associations of engineers, program executives, promotion specialists, pioneer broadcasters, women broadcasters, and many others.

Technical functions, usually supervised by the station's chief engineer, center on transmitter operations, which must follow strict FCC rules. In the smallest stations, the chief engineer may be the only staff member with much technical expertise; but in most cases he or she supervises a staff of operational and maintenance personnel. Chief engineers at large television stations spend most of their time overseeing administration and keeping up with rapidly developing technology. Some small stations share a chief engineer; others use an outsider on a contractual basis.

Program functions involve both planning and implementation. Major program planning decisions usually evolve from interplay among the programming, sales, and management heads. Because most stations produce few programs locally, other than news and radio talk shows, the program department's major role at most broadcast facilities entails the selection of network offerings and the acquisition and scheduling of prerecorded materials—music for radio stations, and syndicated series delivered on tape or via satellite for television and cable. A program manager typically serves as the department head responsible in this area. By the 1990s, however, as economic conditions tightened and program costs soared, some television stations dispensed with that title, leaving program decisions to the general manager or combining the function with that of the promotion department. The *production* department, at some stations housed within the programming area and at others within the technical, implements program decisions, carrying out the day-to-day tasks of putting the program schedule on the air.

Promotion includes making its potential audience aware of a station's programs through advertising, on-air announcements, newspaper listings, even T-shirts and bumper stickers, and by sponsoring such special events as rock concerts. These and other promotion activities are more fully described in Section 9.7.

News, though a form of programming, usually constitutes a separate department, headed by a news director who reports directly to top management. This separation of news from entertainment makes sense because of the timely nature of news and the unique responsibilities that news broadcasting imposes on management. Often the news department also produces station editorials, if any, and public-affairs programming.

Sales departments employ their own staff members to sell time to local advertisers. To reach regional and national advertisers, however, most stations contract with a national sales firm to represent them in out-of-state business centers. Exhibit 6.c suggests some of the tasks routinely performed by a television sales manager and other executives.

One area straddles both program and sales functions—the *traffic* department. It coordinates sales with programming operations, preparing the daily *program pre-log* (usually called simply the *log*), which contains schedules for facilities, personnel, programs, and announcements. As the broadcast day progresses, operators in the station's control room "keep the log" by making entries on the pre-log to record when the scheduled events actually took place. At the end of the day, after changes have been incorporated, the program pre-log becomes the final or *official log*, providing a record of the day's broadcasts. Traffic personnel make sure that advertising contracts are fulfilled and that spot schedules start and stop on time; they also arrange for *make-goods*, the rescheduling of missed or technically inadequate commercials.

In addition, the traffic department maintains a list of *availabilities* (or, simply, *avails*), which gives sales personnel up-to-date information on commercial openings in the schedule as they become available for advertisers. Traffic personnel usually fill unsold openings with public-service or promotional announcements. At many stations, computers handle much of the complex work of the traffic department, including generating the program log; in some control rooms, computers keep the log as well (see Exhibit 6.j).

Exhibit 6.b ●●●●●● ● ● ● ● ● ● ● ● ●

Broadcast Station Tables of Organization

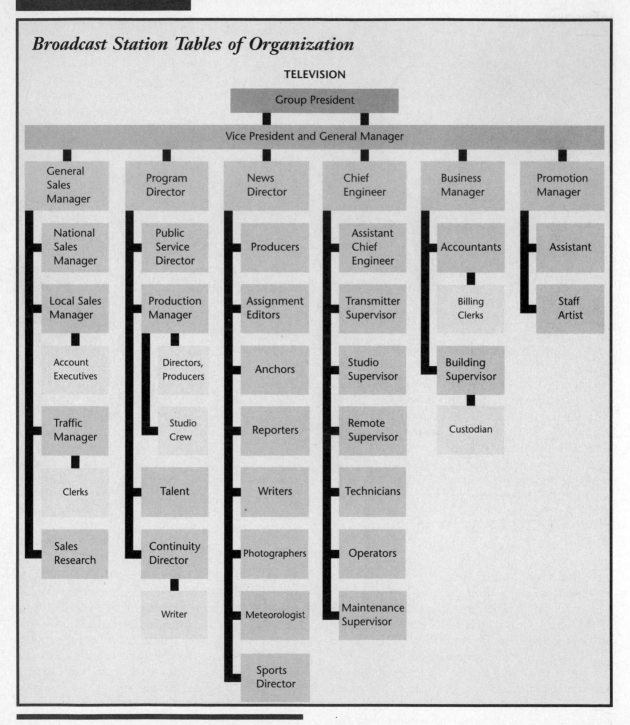

TELEVISION

Group President

Vice President and General Manager

General Sales Manager	Program Director	News Director	Chief Engineer	Business Manager	Promotion Manager
National Sales Manager	Public Service Director	Producers	Assistant Chief Engineer	Accountants	Assistant
Local Sales Manager	Production Manager	Assignment Editors	Transmitter Supervisor	Billing Clerks	Staff Artist
Account Executives	Directors, Producers	Anchors	Studio Supervisor	Building Supervisor	
Traffic Manager	Studio Crew	Reporters	Remote Supervisor	Custodian	
Clerks	Talent	Writers	Technicians		
Sales Research	Continuity Director	Photographers	Operators		
	Writer	Meteorologist	Maintenance Supervisor		
		Sports Director			

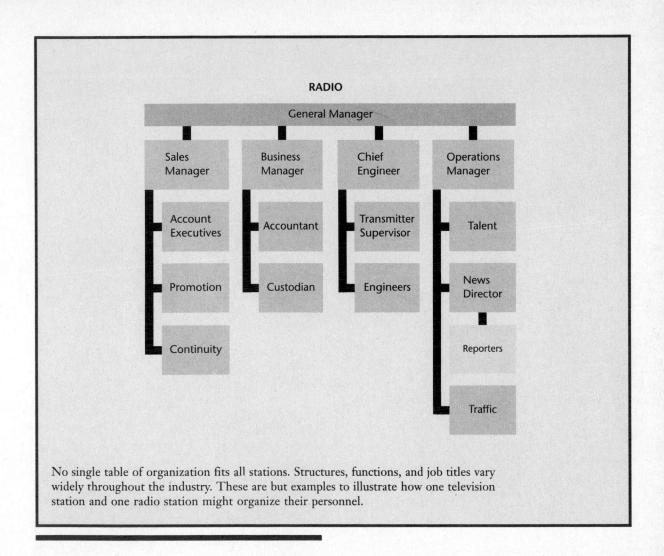

RADIO

General Manager

| Sales Manager | Business Manager | Chief Engineer | Operations Manager |

Account Executives

Accountant

Transmitter Supervisor

Talent

Promotion

Custodian

Engineers

News Director

Continuity

Reporters

Traffic

No single table of organization fits all stations. Structures, functions, and job titles vary widely throughout the industry. These are but examples to illustrate how one television station and one radio station might organize their personnel.

Low-Power TV Stations

The organizational patterns of *low-power television* (LPTV) stations often differ from those of full-power stations. Some LPTV owners elect to organize and operate their stations in traditional fashion, though with fewer employees. Others simply re-transmit the signal of a full-power station. Some affiliate with specialized low-power networks; still others belong to commonly owned groups of LPTV stations, all of which carry the same programs simultaneously—perhaps distributed by satellite.

An LPTV station's role determines its organization. If it competes with other stations in its market, or if it functions as a *mother station*, providing services for its retransmitting stations, its structure usually follows traditional lines. If it operates simply as a rebroadcaster, however, its entire staff might

Exhibit 6.c •••••• • • • • • • • • • • •

A Day in the Lives of TV Executives

	General Manager	Program Director	General Sales Manager	News Director
8:30	Open mail; dictate letters and memos.	Check Discrepancy Reports for program and equipment problems; take appropriate action.	Check Discrepancy Reports for missed commercials; plan make-goods.	Meet with Assignment Editor and producer; plan the day.
9:30	Discuss financial statements with Business Manager.	Call *TV Guide* with program updates.	Local sales meeting; discuss accounts and quotas.	Meet with Union Shop Steward; discuss termination of reporter.
10:00	Call group headquarters regarding financial status.	Prepare weekly program schedule.	Accompany local account executive on sales calls.	Read mail; screen tape of last night's 11:00 PM news.
10:30	Meet with civic group angry about upcoming network program.	Select film titles for Saturday and Sunday late movies.	More sales calls.	Discuss noon news rundown with show producer.
11:00	Call network; ask for preview of questionable show.	Meet with Promotion Manager regarding *TV Guide* ad for local shows.	Call collection agency; discuss delinquent sales accounts.	Meet with Chief Engineer regarding SNG failure.
12:00	Lunch with major advertiser.	Lunch with syndicated program saleswoman.	Lunch with major advertiser.	Monitor noon news; lunch at desk.
2:00	Department heads meeting.	Department heads meeting.	Department heads meeting.	Department heads meeting.
4:00	Meet with Chief Engineer regarding new computer system in master control.	Meet with producer/director to plan local holiday special.	Prepare speech for next week's Rotary club meeting.	Meet with producer and director; plan rundown of 6:00 PM newscast.
6:00	Dinner with Promotion Director job candidate.	Attend National Academy of Television Arts & Sciences annual local banquet.	To airport; catch flight to New York for meeting with National Sales Rep.	Monitor 6:00 PM news.

Not all television station executives work 10- or 12-hour days, but many do, especially as competition from cable and the other new media increases.

Exhibit 6.d ● ● ● ● ● ● ● ● ● ● ● ● ● ● ● ●

LPTV—In a Class by Itself?

In 1982 the FCC gave final approval to a new class of television station—low-power television (LPTV). Intended to serve local interests, LPTV facilities have limited power (10 watt, 100 watt, or 1,000 watt) and cover areas of only 15 to 20 miles in diameter. Industry observers predicted that LPTV stations would be unable to compete with their full-power counterparts, and although some even condemned the service to eventual extinction, by the 1990s more than 1,300 such stations were in operation. A survey financed by the national LPTV organization—the Community Broadcasters Association (CBA)—revealed the following figures, based on responses from a sample of 102 stations:

- Seventy-five percent of the stations broadcast 24 hours a day.
- Forty-six percent identified their markets as rural, 22 percent as urban, and the rest suburban or a combination.
- Fifty-six percent were commercial, 22 percent public/educational, 4 percent subscription, and the rest a combination.

- The stations averaged about four full-time and four part-time employees.
- Minorities owned about 12 percent of the stations.
- Eighty-nine percent used one or more of about 25 satellite-delivered program services, the most popular being Channel America. Fifty-four percent carried syndicated programs, of which more than half were barter shows. More than half of the stations said they paid nothing for programming; the others reported an average monthly cost of only $758.
- Eighty-six percent produced local programs, mostly public affairs and sports.
- Almost three-fourths were carried by cable systems, most at no charge; 14 percent paid an average of nearly $7,000 per month to cable systems.
- About two-thirds of advertising revenue came from local sources; a 30-second spot, on average, cost $52.
- Median annual revenues were $650,000; but only 6 percent of the stations reported that they were operating at a profit.

Source: Mark J. Banks and Michael J. Havice, "Selling Time in a New Medium: A Survey of the Low Power Television Industry," *Broadcast/Cable Financial Journal*, July–August 1991. Used with permission.

---

consist of a single, outside contract engineer who maintains the retransmitter's technical facilities. Exhibit 6.d takes a closer look at some LPTV operations.

Station Groups

Like other business enterprises, broadcasting can benefit from *economies of scale*. Ownership of several stations enables a company to buy programs, supplies, and equipment in bulk, to spread the cost of consultants across several stations, and generally to share experiences and new ideas.

For reasons of public policy, the FCC places limits on the number of radio and television stations one owner may control (see Section 14.5 for specific limitations). Even the largest groups fail to reach the ownership ceiling. However, the trend is toward greater concentration of ownership: 30 years ago, groups owned only half of all VHF television stations in the 100 largest markets, whereas today they own about 90 percent.

All television stations owned by a group do not necessarily affiliate with the same network—or for that matter with any network. The exceptions are those owned by the networks themselves, known as network *owned-and-operated* (O&O) stations. Each national television network O&O group reaches between 18 and 24 percent of the nation's television households (see Exhibit 6.e), thus ensuring for the

Exhibit 6.e

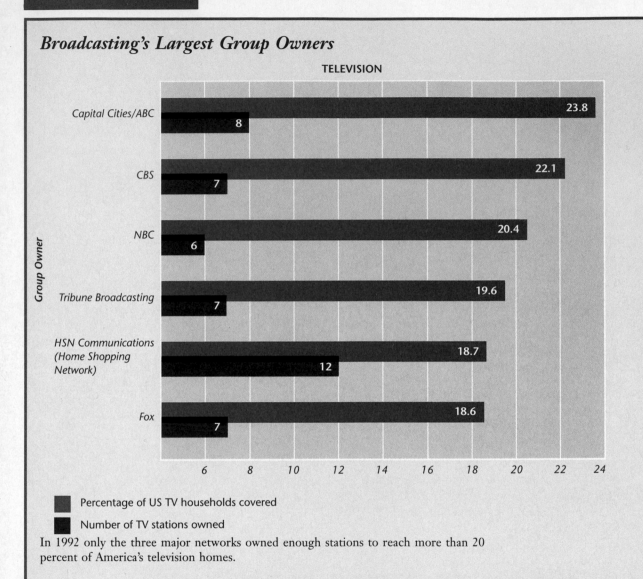

Broadcasting's Largest Group Owners

TELEVISION

Group Owner

Capital Cities/ABC	23.8 / 8
CBS	22.1 / 7
NBC	20.4 / 6
Tribune Broadcasting	19.6 / 7
HSN Communications (Home Shopping Network)	18.7 / 12
Fox	18.6 / 7

6 8 10 12 14 16 18 20 22 24

■ Percentage of US TV households covered
■ Number of TV stations owned

In 1992 only the three major networks owned enough stations to reach more than 20 percent of America's television homes.

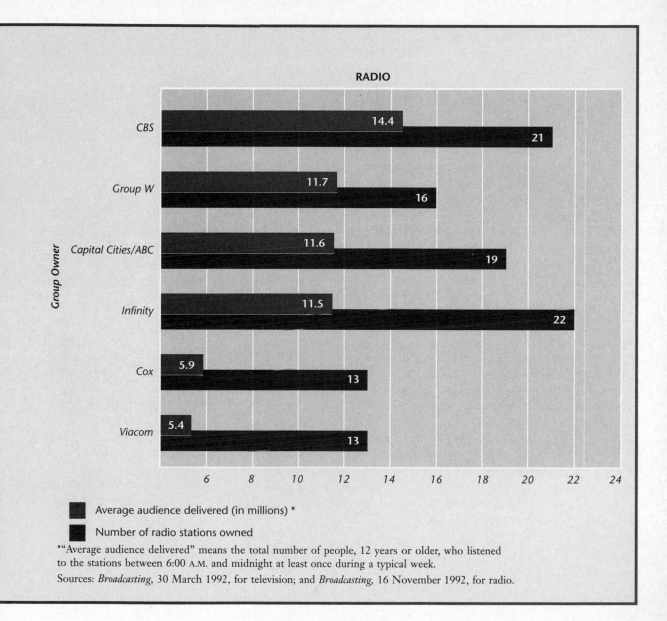

RADIO

Group Owner

Group	Average audience delivered (in millions)	Number of radio stations owned
CBS	14.4	21
Group W	11.7	16
Capital Cities/ABC	11.6	19
Infinity	11.5	22
Cox	5.9	13
Viacom	5.4	13

■ Average audience delivered (in millions) *

■ Number of radio stations owned

*"Average audience delivered" means the total number of people, 12 years or older, who listened to the stations between 6:00 A.M. and midnight at least once during a typical week.

Sources: *Broadcasting*, 30 March 1992, for television; and *Broadcasting*, 16 November 1992, for radio.

networks their own prestigious and highly profitable outlets in major markets.

Networks have administration for O&O groups separate from their network operations. A president (at ABC and NBC) or vice president (at CBS) heads each O&O station as general manager. She or he has a good deal of operational autonomy to ensure compliance with the FCC requirement that each station must serve its own community of license. Managers of O&Os have sufficient independence to reject network programs that they judge would be contrary to the interests of their local communities, though they rarely use that power.

• • • • • • • •

6.2 Commercial Broadcast Networks

Two or more radio or television stations interconnected by some means of relay (wire, cable, microwave, or satellite) so as to enable simultaneous broadcasting of the same program constitute a minimal *network*.* Networks usually provide their affiliates with programs in exchange for the stations' agreement to carry network commercials within those programs. Some radio and nearly all television networks also pay stations to carry their programs.

For years, only three major national commercial television networks existed—ABC, CBS, and NBC. Fox premiered in 1986, long after the so-called Big

*The FCC uses varying definitions of *network*, depending on the context. In its rules dealing with television affiliation agreements, the Commission defines a network as "a national organization distributing programs for a substantial part of each broadcast day to television stations in all parts of the United States, generally via interconnection facilities"; in its prime-time access rule, it defines a network as an entity "which offers an interconnected program service on a regular basis for 15 or more hours per week to at least 25 affiliated television licensees in 10 or more states" (47 CFR 73.658).

Three networks were well established (see Exhibit 3.m, page 102). In an effort to compete for advertising, and to compensate for having fewer affiliates than the Big Three (thus reaching fewer U.S. television households), Fox in 1991 formed Fox Net, which delivers Fox programming directly to about 500 cable systems in those markets where Fox has no over-the-air affiliate. In some areas without an affiliate it opened what were called *store-front* television stations—operations that do not broadcast over the air but, rather, send their programs (complete with commercials sold by the stations' sales staffs) directly to a local cable system's headend for retransmission to subscribers.

In 1992, when Fox announced plans for a seven-night-a-week program schedule, Fox Entertainment President Peter Chernin told a broadcast industry gathering: "We'd actually prefer you don't call us a 'weblet' anymore. The fledgling, almost, not-quite-a-wannabe network will become a full-service, seven-night source of programming" (*Broadcasting*, 1 June 1992: 18). Later that year, for the first time in its history, Fox's average prime-time ratings topped those of one of the Big Three; in the second week of July 1992, the four program services ranked, in order: CBS, ABC, Fox, NBC. Perhaps more important, however, Fox came in number one that week among adults aged 18 to 49, the group most sought after by advertisers. It also took steps toward establishing a national news service.

Still, Fox had a way to go before it could be considered in the same league with the other networks in terms of hours of programming offered. Indeed, so as not to run afoul of the FCC's "fin/syn" rules (see Section 9.2), which restrict "network" participation in revenues generated by television program syndication, and the prime-time access rule (see Exhibit 9.c, page 312), Fox had preferred *not* to be considered a true network—and its affiliates had agreed. Then, in April 1993, the FCC exempted Fox from all fin/syn obligations, and two months later the network added its seventh night of programming (a regularly scheduled Monday night movie).

There are more than 100 smaller networks, most of which operate part-time, usually sharing programs within a region or a single state. Some have a common program orientation, such as language (Univision), or sports (Raycom). Those formed for a limited time or special purpose are often referred to as *ad hoc* networks. Some station groups and program syndicators operate ad hoc networks in order to share special programs and feature films or to program specific parts of the broadcast day.

Here, however, we focus primarily on the three national, *truly full-service* television networks—ABC, CBS, and NBC. Each of the three has about 200 affiliates, through which they can reach virtually all television homes in the United States. Radio networks are discussed in detail in Section 10.8.

Network Organization

Like stations, networks vary in their organizational structure; yet each must fulfill the same four basic functions as stations—general/administrative, technical, programming, and sales. Networks, however, enjoy the luxury of a much higher degree of specialization. ABC, for example, has separate units, each with its own president, for productions, entertainment, news, sports, radio, the television network, and the O&O stations.

The networks appoint droves of vice presidents. At NBC, for example, VPs head up units dealing with such matters as finance, business affairs, employee relations, research, law, corporate communications, advertising and promotion, and sales. In NBC television's Entertainment Division, vice presidents supervise units specializing in prime-time programs, children's and family programs, daytime programs, specials and variety programming, movies, and miniseries.

Distinctive network responsibilities include arranging relay facilities that deliver programs to stations and maintaining good relations with affiliates. In addition to the network's Affiliate Relations department, an advisory board representing affiliates helps maintain the working relationship. In the spring, each television network organizes a convention for its affiliated stations, at which it shows pilots of new shows and unveils program plans for the coming season.

Affiliates

More than half of all full-power commercial television stations affiliate with one of the three major networks. Most function as a *primary affiliate*—the only affiliate of a given network in a given market. *Secondary affiliates*, typically those in markets with only two stations, share affiliation with more than one network. A few markets have only a single station. In Presque Isle, Maine, for example, WAGM-TV has the unusual privilege of picking and choosing programs from CBS, its primary network, or from ABC or NBC.

Affiliation does *not* mean that a network owns or operates the affiliated stations. ABC, CBS, and NBC do, of course, own television stations. But they contract with hundreds of other affiliates, agreeing with each to offer it the network's programs before offering them to any other station in the same market. The station, in turn, agrees to *clear* time for all or portions of the network schedule. However, it has the right to decline to carry any specific program, or it may offer to carry the program at a time other than that of network origination (a so-called *delayed broadcast*, or DB); the network may or may not agree to this last option.*

Traditional television networks buy affiliates' time in order to deliver station audiences to network advertisers. Affiliates sell their time to networks at a rate much lower than they charge other customers. In exchange, a broadcasting network offers its affiliates

- *monetary compensation* to the stations based on audience size and composition;

*As an example of network nonclearance consider NBC's *Tonight Show*, which has aired at various times in Nashville, Tennessee, on both the NBC and ABC affiliates, as well as on an independent station, as each tried to find the most profitable program for its late-night time period.

- a structured schedule of *network programs* at no direct cost;
- *simultaneous program distribution* so that affiliates can receive the service at the same time;
- an *advertising environment* that appeals to the affiliates' clients; and
- a *sales organization* that finds national clients to purchase advertisements that occupy the network's portion of the affiliates' commercial time.

Network-Affiliate Contract

Networks and their affiliates formalize the economic link between them through an *affiliation contract*. A clause at the heart of such a contract defines the terms on which the network will make payments—called *station compensation*—to the station for the right to use the station's time.

Each television network uses a different plan for calculating compensation. The amounts paid to affiliates vary from station to station, reflecting differences in market size, station popularity, and other factors. Rates in top markets such as New York and Los Angeles run into the thousands of dollars per hour; they go down as low as $50, and some affiliates in the smallest markets receive no compensation at all.

As increased competition and economic hard times hit the television business, networks looked to their affiliate compensation arrangements as a way to reduce costs. Each of the Big Three announced compensation cuts in the early 1990s. Some were "across the board," others related to specific dayparts (daytime, for example) or to program types (news and sports were among those hardest hit). CBS managed to reduce its total annual payments from $150 million in 1991 to about $120 million in 1992. NBC was also paying about $120 million and ABC about $103 million to their affiliates to carry their programs.

ABC and NBC tie their payment formulas to audiences delivered by an affiliate—the bigger the audience, the greater the compensation. (Fox, meanwhile, links its affiliation package to its success or failure in reaching its target viewers: 18- to 49-year-olds. As that audience increases in size, pay-ments to stations *decrease;* stations make up for the lower payments by charging higher prices for local commercials adjacent to the successful shows, while Fox uses higher payments to obtain station clearance for less-successful programs.)

In 1992, in an attempt to shave another $20 million from its compensation burden, CBS announced what it described as "the most significant change in the CBS network-affiliate economic relation in the past 25 years." Beginning in January 1993 it would (1) charge affiliates a fee for each network program they carried, (2) take back from affiliates some prime-time commercial time previously available for local sale, and (3) tie compensation amounts to program ratings (paying more for weaker programs that affiliates are more likely to decline to carry and paying less—or nothing—for hits such as *60 Minutes* and *Murphy Brown*). Later, CBS modified the plan somewhat so that fees would be offset against compensation payments.

Industry observers suggested that, especially if ABC and NBC followed CBS's lead, the basic network structure might one day look very different from what it has been. They anticipated that affiliates would increasingly pre-empt network shows for more lucrative syndicated programs. (Atlanta and Detroit's CBS stations, for example, dropped the network's low-rated *CBS This Morning;* in an attempt to plug that hole in the dike, CBS increased the number of commercial minutes in the program available for local sale.) Some even saw the possibility of CBS affiliates defecting from that network and joining Fox. Faced with a virtual civil war with its affiliates, CBS finally backed off in October 1992. Compensation cuts eventually amounted to about $10 million (about half the original goal), and affiliates recovered some of their prime-time local sales availabilities. Compensation remained tied to program performance, but with rather less drastic formulas than first announced.

Network compensation represents a surprisingly small percentage of the gross revenues of network affiliated stations—on the average, less than 5 percent. But stations measure the value of affiliation less in terms of compensation than in terms of the audiences that network programs attract. Affiliates profit from the sale of spots in the 90 seconds or so that the network leaves open for affiliate station breaks in each prime-time hour of network programming and the seven or eight minutes made available at other times of the day. Moreover, the stations' own programs (whether locally produced or purchased from syndicators) benefit from association with popular and widely promoted network programs.

Affiliation Contract Regulation

Unable to control television networks directly (because it does not license them), the FCC regulates them indirectly through rules governing stations they own and contracts affiliates make with them. Present FCC rules forbid stations from entering into contracts with networks that restrict affiliates' freedom of action in several ways:

- *Exclusivity.* A network contract may not contain exclusivity rules aimed at preventing an affiliate from accepting programs from other networks, nor may an affiliate prevent its network from offering rejected programs to other stations in its market. In practice, independent stations often enter into agreements with networks to have first call on programs that affiliates in their markets reject. For all practical purposes, however, most affiliates and their networks consider their relationships to be in fact exclusive.
- *Network ownership.* A single owner may not own two or more television networks covering the same territory. Radio networks, however, may now offer more than one service in the same market (this, too, was once prohibited). For example, several of ABC's different services, targeted to different demographic groups, may find outlets in the same market.
- *Program rejection.* A network may not coerce an affiliate in any way to ensure clearance of time for its programs. Theoretically, the affiliate has complete freedom of program choice. In reality, networks regularly apply whatever pressure they can to persuade affiliates to clear programs.

- *Rate control.* A network may not influence an affiliate's nonnetwork advertising rates.
- *Sales representation.* A network may not function as national spot sales representative for any of its affiliates other than its O&O stations.

Affiliate Relations

Networks and their affiliates experience a somewhat uneasy and paradoxical sharing of power, complicated by political and economic factors too subtle for contracts to define. In one sense the networks have the upper hand. Affiliation can play a vitally important role in an affiliate station's success. On the other hand, without the voluntary compliance of affiliates, a television network amounts to nothing but a group owner of a few stations rather than the main source of programming for some 200 stations. So in that sense affiliates have the upper hand, and woe to the network that fails to please them. The defections from other networks that occurred when ABC first forged its way into the ratings lead in the late 1970s showed what could happen. At the end of a three-year period, ABC not only equaled or topped its rivals in audience size, it also matched them in number of affiliates, having picked up more than 30 stations from CBS and NBC. However, much of ABC's success in convincing stations to change affiliation resulted from its offering (although later reducing) substantially higher compensation, rather than to affiliates' dissatisfaction with their previous network's program performance.

Networks prefer to have their programs carried by the strongest station in each television market. ABC, for example, moved in 1980 from WJKS-TV, a UHF station in Jacksonville, Florida, to WLTV, a VHF station in the same city. In 1987 ABC reduced WLTV's network compensation rate by about 25 percent. In 1988, when NBC led in the ratings, WLTV returned to NBC, and ABC had to go back to WJKS, the weaker and less desirable UHF station.

Networks cannot always predict audience reactions to affiliation changes. For example, in Miami, where several affiliation switches took place in 1989 (as described in Exhibit 6.m), WCIX, which had been an independent station, picked up only one rating point, sign-on to sign-off, when it first became a CBS affiliate; WTVJ, which moved from CBS to NBC, also improved by a single rating point; and WPLG, the continuing ABC affiliate, experienced no change (Schofield, 1991: 371).

Network Clearance

The complex relationships between networks and their affiliates hinge on the act of *clearance*—the voluntary agreement by an affiliate to keep its program schedule clear during the times the network needs to run its programs. However, even after an affiliate has cleared time for a network series, it still has the right to *pre-empt* individual episodes in that series to substitute programs from other sources.

An affiliate might fail to clear time, or pre-empt time already cleared, for several reasons. Most often a station simply wants to increase the amount of commercial time available for local sale. By substituting a syndicated program or local movie, the station can run more of its own commercials than a network show can accommodate. Such pre-emptions occur especially during the year-end holiday period, when advertiser demand peaks. Stations also drop low-rated network programs in favor of syndicated material to keep audiences from flowing to competing stations.

Networks rely on affiliates not only to carry their programs but also to carry them *as scheduled*. Delayed broadcasts erode national ratings. Networks also need simultaneous coverage to get the maximum benefit from program promotion.

In practice, affiliates accept about 90 percent of all programs offered by their networks, most of them on faith. Stations can request advance screenings of questionable programs but usually feel no need to do so, even though, as licensees, stations rather than networks have ultimate legal responsibility. Because most television programs come in series, affiliates know their general tone, so the acceptability of future episodes can usually be taken for granted.

Thus affiliates have little or no direct influence over the *day-to-day* programming decisions of their networks. In the long run, however, they exert powerful leverage. Network programming strategists take serious note of the feedback that comes from their affiliates.

Changing Network-Affiliate Relations

Starting in the late ·1980s, when rising costs and increasing competition combined to weaken ABC, CBS, and NBC, the network-affiliate relationship began to crack under the strain. Many affiliates turned against their network partners, contributing to the network decline that some in the industry predicted would cause the eventual demise of one or more of the three giants.

Both the networks and their affiliates questioned compensation rates. Networks argued that they needed relief if they were to survive. Affiliates felt that network compensation failed to reflect the real value of their time to their networks. The networks increased their own advertising time, a move resented by their affiliates. Pre-emptions reached all-time highs, costing the networks millions of dollars in lost revenues.

Technology has freed many affiliates from their former, almost total dependence on networks for nonlocal news. Using satellites and minicams, stations can now cover not only local but also regional, national, and even international news. In fact, roles have partially reversed, making the networks dependent on their affiliates. Working with reduced staffs and budgets, the networks look to stations for coverage of events that before would have been covered by now-fired network correspondents or by now-closed network news bureaus. The closing credits of a network evening newscast, listing the stations that contributed to that night's program, reflect this trend.

Television stations also turn to CNN and other nonnetwork sources for their news. Many belong to Hubbard Broadcasting's Conus Satellite Cooperative, a relatively inexpensive way of acquiring satellite news feeds. Members have access to the cooperative's satellite transponders and serve as contributors to the Conus video pool when news in their areas holds interest for stations in other markets. (See Section 9.5 for other news sources.) Attempting to minimize the adverse effects of station self-sufficiency in news, the three major networks have recently revitalized their own news-gathering efforts and news-sharing arrangements with their affiliates.

Independents

Approximately 500 stations, most of them UHF, are known as *independents*. By the early 1990s "indies" served nearly 94 percent of all U.S. television households. They do not affiliate with any of the three major networks, although they may affiliate with Fox or with one of the smaller networks. Indeed, as Fox continued to enlarge its presence, calling a Fox affiliate an independent became at best a legal technicality.*

Independents have had a remarkable rags-to-riches history. Until the late 1970s most nonaffiliated stations struggled just to survive, unable to compete with network affiliates in attracting audiences. As a group they lost money until 1975, when for the first time they averaged a small profit. In that year, independent stations received 16 percent of all nonnetwork advertising dollars spent in television; by 1980 their share had grown to 20 percent, and by 1991 to 30 percent. In terms of audience, independent stations in 1977 attracted only 9 percent of all television viewers; by 1991 that proportion had reached 24 percent.

Several factors combined to turn at least some independents into profit makers. The FCC helped by adopting the *prime-time access rule*, or PTAR (see Exhibit 9.c, page 312), which gave independents their first chance to counterprogram effectively against network affiliates in the 7:00–8:00 P.M. (Eastern and Pacific) period. PTAR gave independents the advantage of rerunning network series during that hour, a program option that PTAR denied to affiliates in the major markets. Independents gained strength in other time periods by presenting live coverage of sports events, successfully bidding against affiliates for exclusive rights to popular syndicated program series, and using aggressive promotion campaigns.

Establishment of the Association of Independent Television Stations (INTV) in 1972 also helped. In 1977 an INTV-sponsored Arbitron study provided much-needed favorable evidence about the size and character of the independent stations' audience, helping stations to overcome the negative image of independents in the minds of advertising-agency time buyers. Cable television also helped by making the signal quality of UHF independent stations equal in the eyes of cable viewers to that of the more powerful over-the-air signals of VHF affiliates.

By 1987, however, the independent rose had lost some of its bloom. One reason: in that year a decision by the U.S. Court of Appeals eliminated the *must-carry* rules that had required cable systems to carry all over-the-air stations broadcasting in their markets (see Section 13.9, as well as Exhibit 13.m, on page 491). Without must-carry restrictions, cable systems could decide which local stations to carry and which not to carry. UHF stations that are not carried lose the "VHF equality" that cable provides; more important, all stations not carried lose their ability to reach cable subscribers at all (except in those rare cable homes where *A/B switches* have been installed, allowing viewers to switch easily from cable to antenna for off-air reception). Broadcasters, cable operators, and members of Congress debated into the 1990s the possibility of restoring the must-carry rule in some form acceptable to all parties. Finally, Section 4 of the Cable Act of 1992 inserted a new Section 614 into the Communications Act of 1934, reimposing must-carry restrictions, but with obligations that varied with the size of the cable system involved. This provision too, however, faced renewed court challenges on constitutional grounds.

Some newer independents also brought problems on themselves by building in markets too small to

---

*In 1992, in what some saw as a "statement" on the subject, Fox withdrew its seven owned-and-operated stations out of the industry's Association of Independent Television Stations. Others believed the only motivation was economic: the stations paid between $150,000 and $200,000 in annual dues to the association.

support an independent or entering markets in which established, strong independents were already operating. But perhaps the heaviest blow to independents was a staggering increase in program costs. In only two years, from 1984 to 1986, with growing competition from expanding media outlets, the cost of buying programming and producing local newscasts more than doubled. Some stations, in an effort to compete, allocated nearly 50 percent of their total revenue to the acquisition of syndicated programs. By 1987, when prices had begun to level off, some 20 independent television stations had gone bankrupt. Some surviving independents tried specializing in Spanish, religious, or shop-at-home programming. A few even tried all-music-video or expensive all-news formats.

However, beginning with its premiere telecast in October 1986, the Fox network (again, see Exhibit 3.m), offered new life to independent stations. After a modest and somewhat shaky start, Fox by 1992 had become not only a major competitor for ABC, CBS, and NBC but also the source of highly popular prime-time programs for about 140 otherwise "independent" stations. Yet despite the profitability of some independents, network affiliates overall continue to dominate television viewing, and affiliation with one of the Big Three networks remains one of the most valuable assets a television station can have.

• • • • • • • •

6.3   Cable Television

The economic organization of cable television systems and networks differs substantially from that of broadcast stations and networks. Municipal franchises for cable systems impose fewer restrictions than do FCC licenses for broadcasters (see Section 13.8). Cable systems depend primarily on subscriber fees for revenue. A cable system therefore owes allegiance only to those television households in a franchise area that choose to subscribe (nearly 90

percent in some areas, but averaging about 61 percent nationwide).*

A commercial broadcaster, in contrast, depends almost entirely on advertisers and has an obligation to serve the total audience in its market area, which is usually much larger than that of a single cable system. A major television station may serve an entire metropolitan area, but most large cities divide their municipal areas into several different cable franchises. Cable systems outnumber commercial television stations nearly 10 to 1, though nearly all are monopolies in their franchise areas. Whereas most households can tune in a number of local radio and television stations, almost without exception there is only a single cable system to which they can subscribe—in the early 1990s only about 60 franchise areas offered more than one choice in cable companies.

Basic Unit: The System

In the early 1990s more than 11,000 *cable systems* served nearly 60 million subscribers living in some 23,000 cities, towns, and villages in the United States. Nine out of ten cable subscribers had access to 30 or more channels; nearly 30 percent could see 54 or more; some could view more than 100. As video compression made possible the carriage of several channels in the electronic space formerly occupied by only one, future system capacity appeared limited only by the constraints of economics.

Exhibit 6.f shows how a typical system structures its organization. Whether small, with a few hundred subscribers, or large, with hundreds of thousands, each cable system performs the same four basic functions as do broadcast stations.

• *General/administrative* functions in cable differ only a little from those in broadcasting. Rather than having an affiliation agreement with only one major television network (or at most three),

---

*Cable piracy can be risky. In 1991 a Morgan County, Alabama, court handed a jail sentence to a man who had illegally hooked up cable service to his mobile home each night and disconnected it again in the morning (see Section 14.9).

Exhibit 6.f • • • • • • • • • • • • • • •

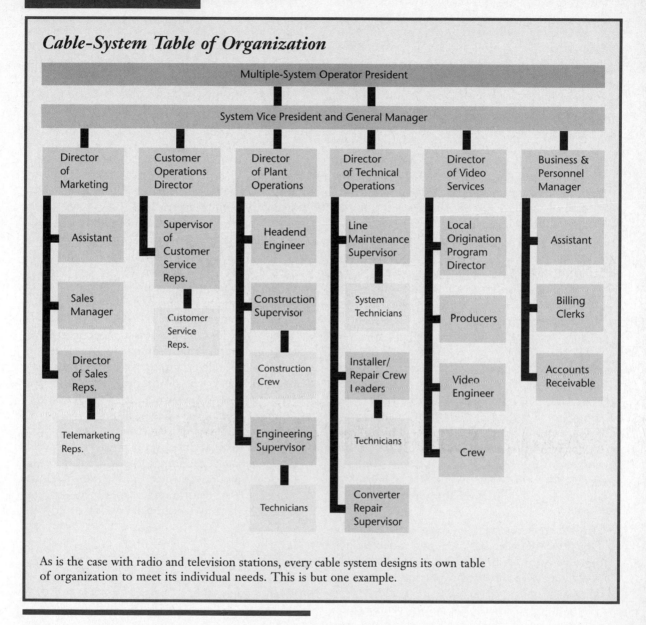

Cable-System Table of Organization

Multiple-System Operator President

System Vice President and General Manager

Director of Marketing	Customer Operations Director	Director of Plant Operations	Director of Technical Operations	Director of Video Services	Business & Personnel Manager
Assistant	Supervisor of Customer Service Reps.	Headend Engineer	Line Maintenance Supervisor	Local Origination Program Director	Assistant
Sales Manager	Customer Service Reps.	Construction Supervisor	System Technicians	Producers	Billing Clerks
Director of Sales Reps.		Construction Crew	Installer/ Repair Crew Leaders	Video Engineer	Accounts Receivable
Telemarketing Reps.		Engineering Supervisor	Technicians	Crew	
		Technicians	Converter Repair Supervisor		

As is the case with radio and television stations, every cable system designs its own table of organization to meet its individual needs. This is but one example.

cable systems typically contract with a dozen or more cable networks to fill their channels. Also, the cable business office must spend more time monitoring subscribers' accounts than those of advertisers. The National Cable Television Association (NCTA) serves as the principal professional organization for the cable industry.

- *Technical* functions at a cable system differ markedly from those at a broadcast station. First, of course, cable has no transmitter to operate and maintain. It does, however, use a complex array of equipment to receive signals from program suppliers at its *headend* and to send those and other signals, simultaneously, through a network of coaxial cables and optical fibers to homes throughout the system's service area (see Exhibit 4.p, page 145). Broadcast technicians' jobs end when the station's signal leaves the transmitter— listeners/viewers are on their own when it comes to arranging reception. Not so with cable, which often places in each subscribing home some sort of *converter* that provides an interface between the subscriber's receiver and the system's wire network.

  Because of concern for the integrity of the entire sending and receiving system, cable organizations often have both *inside-* and *outside-plant* personnel. The inside group concerns itself with equipment in the cable system's studio and headend. The outside group installs and services subscriber cable connections and converters—a critically important job because the subscriber can always discontinue a technically unsatisfactory service.

- As for the *programming* function, cable makes no distinction between affiliates and independents. Nor does broadcasting's elaborate symbiotic relationship between an affiliate and its network exist in cable.

  A radio or television station programs a single channel. A cable system, on the other hand, programs a multitude of channels. Typically, cable systems fill their channels with programs from both broadcast stations and cable networks and with some locally originated material (see Exhibit 3.a, page 75). At smaller systems, the general manager—sometimes called the system manager— may make program decisions, usually in consultation with the marketing director. Multiple-system operators may divide the programming function into specific areas, such as satellite programming and local origination, often under the direction of separate group vice presidents.

  Some cable systems offer local programming, often on channels programmed by community or educational organizations. Although some cable companies, such as Colony Communications, headquartered in Providence, Rhode Island, have made a commitment to locally produced news, most systems defer to broadcast radio and television in this expensive and personnel-intensive area, or carry news produced by regional cable news networks (see Section 10.7).

- Cable system *sales* operations might better be called *sales and marketing*. Although many systems do sell commercial time on some of their channels, marketing cable services to subscribers (typically accomplished through advertising and direct-mail solicitation) ranks as the most important function of all. Monthly subscriber fees represent the principal source of any cable system's revenue.

  The marketing department tries to convince nonsubscribers to subscribe and current subscribers to *upgrade* their service by adding more pay services,* and not to *disconnect*. Operators use the word *churn* to describe subscriber turnover—the process whereby new customers sign up for ser-

---

*Tele-Communications Inc. (TCI), the nation's largest cable operator, created a furor in 1991 when it attempted to launch its new Encore movie channel using a "negative option" strategy. Rather than providing the channel to only those customers who chose to order it, TCI delivered it to all current subscribers; those who didn't want it had to cancel the service or they would be billed for it automatically. Legal actions in at least ten states persuaded TCI to abandon the plan. Soon thereafter, one member of Congress introduced legislation that would make the practice illegal.

vice as others cancel. They calculate churn as a percentage, dividing a current month's disconnects by the prior month's total subscribers and multiplying the result by 100. The rate of churn for basic services may run from as low as 5 percent per year for established systems in stable neighborhoods to 60 percent or higher for newer systems or those in areas with more transient populations; the industry average runs between 25 and 35 percent. In contrast, the average annual churn rate for pay services such as HBO and Showtime is about 80 percent.

Customer service representatives (CSRs) have daily contact with both current and potential subscribers. CSRs answer telephones eight or more hours a day, responding to complaints from subscribers and questions from potential customers. A system's ability to handle these calls promptly and skillfully can have a profound effect on its financial success and, ultimately, even on the prospect of whether it keeps or loses its franchise. Exhibit 6.g describes NCTA's effort to improve what historically had been far-less-than-satisfactory cable system dealings with customers. Not satisfied with industry attempts at self-regulation, Congress—in its 1992 Cable Act—called upon the FCC to set service standards. In March 1993 the Commission issued its standards, which largely mirror those of the NCTA, but which, unlike the latter, are mandatory.

System Interconnection

Often several cable systems in a large market *interconnect* so that materials originated by one system can be seen on the others, providing combined advertising coverage equivalent in reach to that of the area's television stations. System interconnection may involve physically linking the systems by cable, microwave relays, or satellite (*hard* or *true* interconnections), or it may depend simply on the exchange of program and commercial tapes (*soft* interconnection).

Exhibit 6.g

Serving the Cable Customer

In an attempt to blunt long-standing public criticism of the often arrogant way some cable systems have treated their customers—and hoping to forestall congressional legislation that would address the problem—the National Cable Television Association (NCTA) in 1990 adopted a series of customer service standards. Although compliance by cable systems is voluntary, a 1991 NCTA survey found that 85 percent of responding systems were following the guidelines and about half of them had applied for the Association's "Seal of Quality Customer Service." The NCTA guidelines include the following:

- Knowledgeable company representatives must be available to respond to customer inquiries Monday through Friday during normal business hours.
- Telephone answer time by a customer service representative cannot exceed 30 seconds.
- Customers must receive a busy signal less than 3 percent of the time.
- Cable installation must occur within seven business days after an order has been placed.
- Systems must respond to service interruptions within 24 hours and to other service problems within 36 hours.
- Cable companies must provide new customers with written information on product options, prices, and how to use the cable service.
- Bills must be clear, concise, and understandable.
- Refund checks must be issued promptly.
- Customers must receive 30-day advance notice of any rate or channel change that is under the control of the cable operator.

Sources: "NCTA Sets Out Customer Service Standards for Systems," *Broadcasting*, 19 February 1990: 65; and "NCTA Surveys Customer Service," *Broadcasting*, 15 July 1991: 28.

Exhibit 6.h •••••• •••••••••••

Cable's Largest Multiple-System Operators

Multiple-system operator	Homes passed	Basic subscribers	Expanded basic	Pay units
		(in millions)		
Tele-Communications (TCI)	10.9	6.4	2.4	4.6
ATC (Time Warner)	7.9	4.8	1.4	3.4
UA Entertainment	5.0	2.9	1.1	2.8
Continental Cablevision	4.9	2.8	0.2	2.6
Warner Cable	3.7	2.0	*	1.6

*Less than 100,000

Even the largest MSO reaches fewer than 10 percent of all U.S. television households, compared to the three major broadcast networks, each of which covers more than 20 percent (see Exhibit 6.e).

Source: Data, as of December 31, 1991, from *The Cable TV Financial Databook*, Paul Kagan Associates Inc., June 1992, p. 12.

This type of local interconnection differs from national interconnectivity by satellite for distribution of program networks; system interconnection functions mainly to distribute commercials. Videopath, the cable industry's first electronic advertising interconnect, began in 1983. Using a microwave network centered in McCook, Illinois, it delivered commercials to 13 cable systems with a total of 376,000 subscribers. In 1988 Adlink, in Los Angeles, became the first to deliver commercials by satellite.

System interconnection for program distribution occurs when a municipality stipulates as a condition of its franchises that its entire municipal area have the benefit of certain public-service programs available on specific systems.

Multiple-System Operators

Cabling large urban areas far exceeds the financial means of small-system operators. Firms large enough to make the initial investments are unlikely to be attracted by the limited profit potential of a single franchise. Thus a trend emerged in the 1960s toward *multiple-system operators* (MSOs)— firms that gathered dozens and eventually hundreds of systems under a single owner. Only such firms could raise the capital required to secure politically intricate franchises and to construct and upgrade cable systems in major metropolitan areas.

About 100 major MSOs now operate in the United States. Exhibit 6.h shows the five largest, ranked by number of basic subscribers. Impressive though these numbers may be, even the largest MSO, as the exhibit notes, serves fewer than 10 percent of all television homes. By contrast, the largest group owners in broadcast television may cover as much as 18 to 24 percent of households— a scope enjoyed by only the three major networks plus Tribune, Home Shopping, and Fox.

6.4 Cable Program Services

Cable systems typically carry most broadcast television stations whose signals cover their franchise areas. In addition, some systems produce limited amounts of their own programming and offer *access channels* for programs produced locally by others. Beyond that, they draw on three main types of centralized program providers: basic-cable networks, superstations, and pay-cable networks. Despite ever-increasing channel capacity, most cable systems are unable to carry all program services available to them.

As the major cable networks began *multiplexing* operations (that is, programming multiple channels rather than only one), competition for carriage intensified. Exhibit 6.i gives data for a representative selection of cable program providers.

Basic-Cable Networks

The 1992 Cable Act requires cable operators to offer subscribers a *basic service tier* (or level) of program sources, including, at a minimum, local television stations and all public access, educational, and government (PEG) channels. (See Section 13.8 for TV stations' *must-carry* and *retransmission consent* options.) A cable operator may add other channels of programming to this minimum service. Subscribers pay a monthly fee to receive the basic tier.

The 1992 Cable Act defines *Cable Programming Service* as all video programming provided over a cable system except that provided on the basic service tier. This includes programming from such *cable networks* as USA, ESPN, and MTV, nearly all of which are *advertiser-supported*. These networks receive, on the average, about 57 percent of their total revenue from the sale of commercial time. Some cable systems include such networks in their basic service tier, others on what they call an *expanded basic* tier. Some systems have several tiers, each for a separate fee.

For virtually all basic-cable network programs (home shopping networks and Video Jukebox—now named simply "The Box"—are exceptions), a cable system pays a fee directly to each network that it carries. Fees range from just a few cents up to 50 cents and more per subscriber per month and collectively account for about 43 percent of network revenues. A basic-cable network sells commercial spots to its own advertising clients and usually leaves about two minutes of advertising time each hour for local sale by cable systems.

Advertising-supported cable networks have far smaller staffs than ABC, CBS, or NBC, and they reach smaller audiences. They maintain commercial sales departments but also must devote major attention to selling *themselves* to cable systems. Unlike major broadcast television networks, some have difficulty finding affiliates because so many cable networks compete for outlets (although a few, such as USA and ESPN, appear on virtually every system in the country). A single cable network might affiliate with several cable systems operating in different geographical areas within the same market. Conversely, other networks might find that in some markets they have no outlet at all, because competing networks have filled all available cable channels. And some cable systems simply elect to carry certain program services and not others, even though some of their channels remain empty. A program provider's marketing department must address these problems in trying to persuade cable systems to carry its programs.

Superstations

The *superstation* is a paradoxical hybrid of broadcasting and cable television—paradoxical because, although the FCC licenses each broadcast station to serve only one specific local market, superstations also reach hundreds of other markets throughout the country by means of satellite distribution to cable systems.

Cable operators usually include superstations in one of their basic packages of channels, paying a

Exhibit 6.i ●●●●●●●●●●●●●●●●●

Examples of Satellite-Distributed Cable Program Services

Basic-Cable Networks

Network (launch date)	Homes reached (millions)	Average prime-time audience (thousands)*	Content
USA Network (April 1980)	58.0	1,354	Original series, movies, specials, sports
ESPN (September 1979)	59.3	1,131	Sports events, news, and information
TNT (October 1988)	56.2	874	Movies, sports, special events, children's shows
Nashville Network (March 1983)	54.5	723	Country music and news, sports
Lifetime (February 1984)	53.4	626	Movies and series of interest to women
Discovery Channel (June 1985)	56.8	573	Nature, science, technology, history
CNN (June 1980)	58.9	546	News, weather, sports, business
MTV (August 1981)	55.0	347	Music videos and pop-culture programs
C-SPAN (March 1979)	55.0	NA**	House of Representatives sessions, public-affairs programs

Several cable systems offer some of these networks on an expanded-basic tier—at extra cost.

Superstations

Network (launch date)	Homes reached (millions)	Average prime-time audience (thousands)*	Content
TBS (December 1976)	57.7	1,314	Movies, sports, series, specials
WGN (November 1978)	34.9	NA**	Movies, sports, news, specials

Pay Services

Network (launch date)	Subscribers (millions)	Average prime-time audience (thousands)*	Content
HBO (December 1975)	17.3	1,382	Movies, sports, comedy, drama, specials
Showtime (July 1976)	7.4	493	Movies, specials, sports, concerts, series

Home Shopping Networks

Network (launch date)	Homes reached (millions)	Content
QVC Network*** (November 1986)	42.1	Electronics, jewelry, tools, cosmetics
Home Shopping Network*** (July 1985)	21.0	Electronics, jewelry, housewares, clothing

Pay-Per-View Services

Service (launch date)	Addressable homes reached (millions)	Content
Viewer's Choice (November 1985)	10.0	Movies
Request Television (November 1985)	9.1	Movies

*Mondays through Fridays, September 30, 1991, through March 22, 1992.
**NA = Not available
***In 1993 QVC and Home Shopping Network announced plans to merge, as Macy's and other retailers stated intentions to begin their own shopping channels.

(Exhibit continues next page)

Exhibit 6.i, cont. ●●●●● ● ● ● ● ● ● ● ● ● ●

Audio Services		
Service (launch date)	**Subscribers (millions)**	**Content**
Superaudio (September 1987)	10.0	Music, information, special services
C-SPAN Audio (September 1989)	4.5	International news and public affairs
Digital Cable Radio (May 1990)	2.4	Music, pay- and music-TV audio simulcasts

"Interactive" Service		
Service (launch date)	**Homes reached (millions)**	**Content**
The Box (formerly The Jukebox Network) (December 1985)	13.0	Music videos selected by viewer calls

Text Services		
Service (launch date)	**Homes reached (millions)**	**Content**
News Plus (December 1984)	2.5	News, sports, weather in text and graphic form
StoryVision (October 1983)	2.2	Children's stories in text and graphic form
Business Plus (December 1986)	1.9	Financial information, stock quotations

Sources: Program-service, homes-reached, and subscriber data from *Cable Television Developments*, National Cable Television Association (Washington, DC, May 1992). Audience data from *TV Guide*, 20 June 1992: 20.

few cents per subscriber per month for the service. The station gets most of its revenue through higher advertising rates, justified by the cumulative size of the audiences it reaches through cable systems. By the 1990s cable systems serving approximately 60 million subscribers—about two-thirds of all U.S. television homes—carried the nation's first superstation, Ted Turner's WTBS, which now calls its satellite-fed cable service simply "TBS." A score of superstations exist, some of which are listed in Exhibit 6.i.

The television superstation's huge extension of its normally limited broadcast coverage area created vexing copyright problems. In the past, copyright holders selling syndicated programs to individual stations had based their licensing charges on the assumption that each station reached a limited, fixed market. For example, syndicators formerly licensed programs to WTBS to reach only the Atlanta audience; but now that it has achieved superstation status, its programs reach audiences in hundreds of other markets, in many of which television stations may have paid copyright fees for the right to broadcast the very same programs.

Responding to complaints about the inequities created by duplicate television-program distribution on superstations, the FCC reimposed its *syndicated exclusivity* (*syndex*) rule in 1990. Syndex requires each cable system, at a local television station's request, to delete from its schedule any superstation programs that duplicate programs for which the station holds exclusive rights. The rule spawned a new industry: companies that supply programs that cable systems can insert on a superstation channel to cover deleted programs. TBS, meanwhile, worked out a *blackout-proof* schedule, free of syndicated programs subject to exclusivity clauses.

Some cable systems also carry *radio superstations*, notably Chicago's Beethoven Satellite Network (WFMT-FM), a classical music station. It is carried by several hundred cable systems serving more than a million subscribers. Listeners pay an extra fee to the cable system operator in order to receive such radio stations, as well as other audio services (see Section 7.7), which go through a special cable connection to their home high-fidelity stereo systems.

Many cable systems also carry local radio stations as background music for some of their information channels. By 1992 about 40 percent of all commercial radio stations (mostly FM) could be heard on at least one cable system.

Pay-Cable Networks

Subscribers pay their cable systems an additional monthly fee to receive *pay-cable networks*, also called *premium services*, two of which are described in Exhibit 6.i. In exchange, the subscriber gets programs (recent movies, sporting events, music concerts, etc.) without commercial interruption. Pay-cable subscription fees accumulate large sums, enabling pay-cable networks to obtain the rights to these high-priced programs.* Pay-cable subscription fees average about $10 per month for each of the more popular premium channels. The cable operator negotiates the fee with the program supplier, usually splitting proceeds 50/50. Networks rely on local systems to keep tabs on subscriber levels. Occasionally deception occurs. In 1991 an Arkansas cable operator was convicted of cheating 19 cable networks out of $1.5 million in fees, including $1 million from Home Box Office (HBO), by understating subscriber counts.

Included under pay cable are pay-per-view (PPV) networks. Instead of paying a monthly fee, PPV subscribers pay a separate charge for each program they watch, much as they would at a movie theater. Although their programs resemble those of regular pay-cable networks, PPV services offer hit movies before they are available on other channels, as well as special events that regular pay-cable networks decline to carry because of the high price tag. Like other program services, PPV networks take advantage

---

*HBO, with more than twice the number of subscribers of its nearest competitor, Showtime, has enormous *leverage* in obtaining programs on attractive terms. In 1989 Showtime's parent company, Viacom, filed a $2.4 billion antitrust suit against HBO's parent, Time Warner, charging that the latter used its market dominance to try to crush competition. Three years later, in 1992, Time Warner settled the suit by agreeing to pay Viacom an undisclosed sum and to add Viacom program services to more of its cable systems.

of *multiplexing,* offering their fare on several channels. This allows them to offer more programs and to schedule them more times each day.

Unlike advertiser-supported networks, pay-cable services do not, of course, need sales forces to sell commercial time. They do, however, have extensive marketing departments that sell the networks' services to cable operators and, often in partnership with the cable systems, convince potential customers to subscribe. As with the broadcast television networks, outside companies produce most programs, even original series, carried by pay-cable networks.

Vertical Integration

The owners of a roadside hot-dog stand might find it more efficient and more profitable to produce the hot dogs and rolls they sell, rather than buying them from others; they might find it even more profitable to raise the animals and the wheat used to produce the hot dogs and rolls. Were they to enter the businesses of raising cattle and grain, manufacturing hot dogs, and baking rolls, while continuing to operate the stand, they would have a *vertically integrated* operation. So it is with much of business.

The entertainment world finds vertical integration especially attractive. The motion picture industry set the pattern, with movie producers owning companies that distributed films and theaters that exhibited them. The federal government declared this practice to be in violation of antitrust laws and, in a series of decisions beginning in 1947 after years of legal wrangling, prohibited much of that industry's vertical integration.

Broadcasting has only limited vertical integration. Networks, as program distributors as well as producers of some programs, own some stations (the equivalent of movie exhibitors). However, laws have limited both the amount of programming a network may itself produce and still limit the number of stations it may own.

Such integration flourishes in the cable industry. Tele-Communications Inc. provides one good example. As an MSO, TCI operates the nation's largest group of cable systems. It also owns all or parts of several cable networks (among them: Showtime/The Movie Channel, ESPN, Encore, The Discovery Channel, The Learning Channel), a satellite program distribution service (Netlink), a direct-to-home satellite program service (Prime-Star), a pay-per-view operator (Request Television), an advertising sales representative firm for cable systems (Cable AdNet), and an already vertically integrated program producer/distributor/exhibitor (the Turner Broadcasting System).

● ● ● ● ● ● ● ●

6.5 *Capital Investment*

The broadcast and cable industries, though not as capital-intensive as a manufacturing industry (the automobile business, for example), nonetheless require very high investments for constructing new facilities or acquiring and maintaining existing ones.

Broadcasting

The FCC license permitting a station to operate constitutes the owner's most valuable asset. To use a license, an owner must buy equipment to receive, originate, and transmit programming, along with associated buildings and office facilities.

Radio station construction costs range from $50,000 for a simple, small-market AM or FM station to several million dollars for a sophisticated radio facility in a major market. A station in the low-power television (LPTV) class that is able to produce local programs may, under ideal conditions, cost no more than $300,000; but to rebuild a full-power, major-market television facility could cost 100 times that much.

Operating stations must maintain and, to remain competitive, upgrade their facilities. As the economic crunch hit the electronic media industry, owners in the 1990s tried to restrict their capital expenditures to only those items necessary to maintain quality services or, where possible, to create savings. But news, for example, does not come cheap. Satellite news-gathering vans cost from

$300,000 to $500,000; weather graphics equipment costs about $20,000; and newsroom computer systems run between $100,000 and $350,000. Exhibit 6.j details the use of computers in news operations as well as other areas of electronic media.

Cable

On a cost-per-home-served basis, a cable system costs even more to construct than a broadcast facility because each home must be physically connected to the cable system. Owners now pay about $500 per home when constructing new systems. To *upgrade* a system—that is, to increase its channel capacity or convert from coaxial cable to optical fiber—costs between $10,000 and $15,000 per mile.

As with a television station, a local cable system's origination equipment costs depend on the owner's operating philosophy and desired level of sophistication; a reasonably equipped color facility will cost $200,000 or more. The hardware needed to insert commercials runs about $10,000 for each channel scheduled to carry them, and to handle pay-per-view services costs about the same.

Satellite Services

Because they relay programs more efficiently and cost-effectively than terrestrial relay facilities, communication satellites have reduced the operating costs of stations, systems, and networks. Satellites, more than any other technology, have made it possible for modern cable and similar media to flourish. Although they are more economical for long-distance signal relay than traditional telephone lines and microwave relays, satellites and associated equipment remain expensive. Exhibit 6.k describes the costs—and the drama—involved in that rare instance when a satellite launch does not go as planned.

In the early 1990s ABC, CBS, and NBC each paid between $15 million and $30 million annually to lease domestic transponders, Earth-station equipment, and related satellite services. Occasional satellite use (for example, by a television station to *backhaul* or bring home live coverage of an out-of-town baseball game) costs as little as $200 per hour.

Full-power *Earth stations* that send signals up to satellites (*uplinks*) range in price from about $200,000 to $300,000; low-power uplinks (LPUs) cost between $50,000 and $70,000. Users that need transmission facilities only occasionally may rent Earth stations for about $400 an hour. Skehan Tele-video Service in Washington, D.C., one of several companies that provide portable uplinks (PUPs), will bring one, with an operator, to the user's site for $2,500 a day. TVRO (*television receive-only*) dishes* that cable systems, television stations, and others use to *downlink* satellite signals cost as little as $1,000 for simple units for residential use, and $40,000 or more for professional models capable of adjustment to enable them to "look" at several satellites.

SMATV, MMDS, and DBS

Satellite master antenna television (SMATV) construction costs depend on the size of the multiple-dwelling building it serves and the sophistication of the installation.

Multichannel multipoint distribution systems (MMDS), sometimes referred to as *wireless cable*, operate from a single transmitter that usually serves large apartment buildings or condominiums. Capital costs for such a system approximate $300 to $400 per subscriber.

Direct-broadcast satellite (DBS) systems, already established in England and Japan, send their programs directly to subscribing homes. In the mid-1980s Comsat Corp. lost more than $200 million in its unsuccessful attempt to launch and operate its American DBS service, Satellite Television Corp. As United States Satellite Broadcasting (led by Hubbard Broadcasting) and Hughes Communications prepared to launch their American systems in 1994, industry experts estimated the start-up cost of such an operation at nearly $1 billion.

One impediment to the growth of all of these services had been the unwillingness of some cable program providers to make their signals universally

*Though still referred to as "dishes," many satellite receiving antennas no longer have that characteristic shape.

Exhibit 6.j •••••• ••••••••••

How Did We Ever Get Along Before Computers?

Radio and television stations got along well without computers for years, of course. Some still do. But more and more the broadcast and cable industries depend on computer systems to increase efficiency, improve performance, reduce staff sizes, and raise profits.

In the *newsroom* computers serve as word processors for writing news scripts and for editing, organizing, producing newscasts, and making changes minutes before air time. Stations keep (*archive*) past news material and news wire services in computer storage, giving reporters speedy access to background information. Computers make daily assignments of reporters and equipment, act as a message center and automatic telephone dialing service, and even feed news scripts electronically to camera-mounted teleprompters.

In the *sales department* computers monitor commercial availabilities, store market and rating data for use in sales presentations, and make audience and cost

projections. They analyze the efficiency of commercials already run by checking against rating data. And they schedule (*traffic*) commercials, watching to ensure contract fulfillment and keeping ads for competing products from running back to back.

Program departments generate daily program prelogs by computer. They use them, with rating data entered, to analyze proposed syndicated program acquisitions and to schedule programs and movies already owned. Computers store program contracts, generate graphics (as with Quantel's Clipbox, pictured here), keep track of monthly program costs, and supply reports showing sales revenue for each program aired. Radio stations enter music playlists on computers.

In the *business office*, computers maintain records of advertisers and agencies, their credit history, and the status of their accounts. Computers calculate costs, send out bills (to advertisers and, in the case of cable, to subscribers), and follow up on receiving payment (*collections*). They store personnel files, handle payroll, and help to prepare and, once prepared, to monitor station budgets.

In the *control room*, computers execute program schedules by automatically rolling program and commercial audio cassettes or videotapes, and by inserting commercials at the right spots in cable or broadcast network programs. They make automatic entries on the daily program log, indicating which events ran when (and which didn't and why), and they insert closed captioning for the hearing impaired.

In the *studio*, robotic cameras take live electronic pictures of newscasters in their news sets. Operated by control room engineers or as part of the newsroom computer system, these cameras sometimes hang from the studio ceiling, providing shots unavailable from a traditional, human-operated camera.

Source: Photo of the new tapeless, digital Clipbox™ from Quantel.

Exhibit 6.k ••••• •••••••••••

Rescuing a Wayward Satellite

Source: Photo from NASA.

Hughes Aircraft built Intelsat VI (F-III)—at 12-by-17 feet and 9,000 pounds, the world's largest communications satellite—for $157 million. Martin Marietta received $120 million in 1990 to launch it into space. But something went wrong. The satellite failed to achieve its geosynchronous orbit and for two years wobbled aimlessly—and uselessly—some 225 miles above the earth. Finally, in 1992, the National Aeronautics and Space Administration (NASA) sent its space shuttle Endeavor to the rescue. After earlier mechanical attempts had proved unsuccessful, three astronauts donned their space suits and embarked on their own mission impossible. While they and Intelsat VI spun around the world at 17,500 miles per hour, the three men wrestled the errant satellite—by hand—into Endeavor's cargo bay. There they attached a new engine and sent Intelsat on its way into proper orbit. For its trouble, NASA received $157 million. For theirs, the astronauts received $34 over and above their regular salaries—$18 apiece for the nine days they were in orbit and $16 for the eight days spent in health quarantine back on Earth.

available to SMATV, MMDS, and DBS systems. They viewed niche services as potential competitors to cable systems, in many of which the programmers themselves held an ownership interest. Acting under provisions of the 1992 Cable Act, however, the FCC in 1993 required vertically integrated (see Section 6.4) programmers/cable operators such as TCI to offer their programming to multichannel competitors on terms equal to those given to cable operators.

High-Definition Television

The conversion to *high-definition television (HDTV)* will have a substantial financial impact on all video elements of the electronic media industry. When color replaced monochrome television, the FCC selected a system (NTSC) compatible with the black-and-white system then in use. Thus, the transition could be accomplished gradually. But because HDTV technology is incompatible with today's NTSC standard, moving to the sharper, wider pictures will require replacement of most broadcast and cable video equipment, including the home television set.

Industry experts can make only rough estimates. The first local television stations to convert to HDTV may pay $1.5 million to $2 million just for the equipment necessary to retransmit a network signal. To produce and transmit local programming may cost another $10 million to $12 million. CBS has estimated the cost to convert its facilities to be about $300 million. Some broadcasters—who oppose the new technology and thus may not be completely objective—project that the industry may pay as much as $10 *billion* for a technology that, in all likelihood, will neither increase a station's or a network's audience nor expand its advertising revenue. Whatever the investment, however, failure to make it would mean broadcast concession to such competitors as cable and DBS and, hence, audience and advertising declines.

Unlike other media, electronic mass media rely on the general public—the consumer—to supply the largest part of the industry's basic capital equipment, broadcast receivers. The public's capital investment in broadcasting amounts to many times the total investment of the industry itself. In fact, some estimates place the public's investment at more than 90 percent of the total. For consumers to be able to watch HDTV in their homes on the new, widescreen television sets (for which they may, at first, have paid anywhere from $3,500 to as much as $6,000), whether the programs come over the air or through cable or from a (now HDTV) VCR, they will pay between a conservatively estimated total of $80 *billion* and a high of $200 *billion* or more.

• • • • • • • •

6.6   Ownership Turnover

Broadcasting and cable have reached the point where investment in new outlets has largely come to a halt. Now the more likely route to ownership is through purchase of existing facilities. In the 38 years from 1954 through 1992, nearly 20,000 radio stations and more than 1,500 television stations changed ownership—some of them several times. The total value of these transactions approximated $44 billion. The weekly trade magazine *Broadcasting & Cable* (until March 1993, simply *Broadcasting*) regularly lists stations and cable systems for sale.

Although some broadcast stations and cable systems operate at a loss (see Section 7.9), most offer better opportunities to make more money than many other businesses. Supermarkets, for example,

have a notoriously low *profit margin** of perhaps 1 or 2 percent. By contrast, broadcast station profit margins have reached as high as 50 percent or more (although in the competitive marketplace of the 1990s, this level of performance became increasingly rare). For this reason, large, multifaceted *conglomerates*, many of which have no prior broadcast ownership experience, often choose to invest.

Restrictions on Ownership

The 1992 Cable Act empowered the FCC to consider the question of cable ownership limitations. In June 1993 the Commission proposed that MSOs be limited to ownership of systems whose cables pass no more than a total of 25 percent of U.S. television households, and to ownership of no more than 40 percent of the cable program services they carry. Until these proposals become final, however, a company may own as many cable systems as it likes. Not so for broadcasting. FCC rules limit the number of radio and television stations that a single entity may control. Although the Communications Act limits foreign ownership of broadcast stations, international conglomerates—especially Japanese firms—have made major investments in U.S. companies related to broadcasting and cable (see Exhibit 6.l). Before any sale of a radio or television station can become final, it must receive FCC approval. Usually a municipality controls the sale of a cable system operating under that community's franchise. (For details on legal controls and other influences on ownership and sales of broadcast and cable properties, see Section 14.5.)

Although the FCC carefully controls who may operate a broadcast station, creative arrangements exist that, if not actually circumventing Commission policy, severely test it. For example, the FCC long frowned on *time brokerage*, whereby stations sell blocks of time to brokers, who then resell it at a

---

*Profit margin means the percentage of net revenues (after sales commissions but before operating expenses have been deducted) represented by pretax profit. Thus, for example, if a television station has net revenues of $2 million and a pretax profit of $400,000, it would have a profit margin of 20 percent ($400,000 divided by $2 million).

time without an investment in programming and personnel, can make it difficult for a licensee to supervise programs closely, thus verging on surrender of control. With deregulation, however, the FCC gave broadcasters more autonomy, while still paying lip service to its long-standing position that licensee responsibility is *nondelegable*. As part of that process, the FCC actually *encouraged* time brokerage, seeing it as a desirable means of making airwaves more accessible to those who can't afford their own station or to specific ethnic groups and minorities.

In the early 1990s some station owners introduced a variation on the time brokerage theme by entering into *local marketing agreements* (LMAs). By early 1992 about 6 percent of all broadcast stations—most of them radio—were involved in LMAs, which allow one station to control all programming and advertising sales on another station in the same market, usually in return for a flat fee or a percentage of advertising revenues. Later in 1992 the FCC relaxed its radio ownership rules, raising ownership caps and allowing common ownership of more than one station of the same type in a single market. As a result, some operators who had entered into LMAs considered converting them into ownership of both stations.

The new ownership rules also encouraged some owners to buy additional stations or to merge with, or swap stations with, other owners in order to enhance their presence in a given market. By controlling more than one station in a single city—a basically illegal practice *until* 1992—broadcasters could reduce operating expenses and could dominate certain demographic groups, offering advertisers attractive multistation, reduced-rate packages. The first *acquisitions* under the new rules were the 1992 purchase by Jefferson Pilot from Capital Cities/ABC of KRXY-AM/FM in Denver, where Jefferson already owned KYGO-AM/FM, and the purchases by Infinity Broadcasting from Cook Inlet Radio Partners of WUSN-FM in Chicago, where Infinity owned WJMK-FM, and of WZLX-FM in Boston, where it already owned WBCN-FM. The first *swap:* Cox Enterprises gave up WSOC-FM in Charlotte, North Carolina, in return for EZ

markup to third parties, who in turn provide programs for brokered periods. This practice, useful to station owners as a means of filling large blocks of

Communication's WHQT-FM in the Miami market, where Cox already operated WIOD-AM and WFLC-FM; EZ then had two Charlotte FMs—WSOC and WMXC.

Station Sales

Although many radio and television stations sell at a profit, deteriorating economic conditions in the broadcast industry have resulted in more and more being sold at a loss. One example of a major loss involved Taft Broadcasting's $760 million acquisition of Gulf Broadcasting's five independent television stations in 1985, a time when "indies" enjoyed record profits. After two years that proved financially difficult for many independent stations, Taft sold the group to TVX for $240 million—a loss of some $520 million.

In recent years AM stations have declined in value compared with FM stations, AM/FM combinations, and television stations. In 1992, for example, Westwood Inc. took a $6 million loss when it sold New York City's historic WNEW-AM to Bloomberg Communications for $13.6 million. AM's failure to adopt and implement a standard system for stereo broadcasting, and thus its inability to transmit—on an equal basis with FM—the music preferred by radio's largely younger audience, has resulted in FM's capture of about three-fourths of all radio listeners.

Like real estate agents, station brokers bring buyers and sellers together. They usually receive a 5 percent commission but earn somewhat less on major transactions. Exhibit 6.m describes one of the more peculiar examples of station trading.

Pricing Methods

No reliable formulas exist for determining precisely the appropriate selling price of a station. Indeed, several factors influence what a buyer should pay or a seller should ask: market size, market location (depressed industrial city or expanding Sunbelt area), radio format or television network affiliation, equipment, competitive position within the market, financing arrangements, and so on.

As a rule of thumb, however, the selling price of a television station, an FM station, or an AM/FM combination should come to about 2.5 times the station's annual gross revenue, or 8 to 10 times its annual *cash flow;** for a stand-alone AM station the price would be closer to 1.5 times gross revenue or 5 times cash flow.

As mentioned in Exhibit 6.n, the *average* price for an operating AM radio station in 1992 was $357,000, whereas the FM station price approached $1 million. By 1993 the *record* price for an AM station stood at $70 million, the price Infinity Broadcasting paid the preceding year for New York City's all-sports outlet, WFAN. Infinity's $82 million acquisition of KVIL in Dallas had set the AM/FM combination record in 1987; because KVIL-AM accounted for only about $1 million of the price, this buy also set the FM record—$81 million. The 1989 merger of Westinghouse, Metropolitan, and Legacy Broadcasting companies to form Group W Acquisition Company—a transaction valued at $727 million—represented the all-time-high radio group deal.

The average price for a television station in 1992 exceeded $3 million. At one time, independent television stations sold for much lower prices than network affiliates, but beginning in the mid-1970s some independents had begun to increase in value. KTLA-TV, an independent station in Los Angeles, sold in 1983 for $245 million; two years later, Golden West Stations sold it to Tribune Broadcasting for a record-setting $510 million, an increase in value of some $280,000 for *each day* Golden West had owned the station. It was the highest price ever paid for any television station—affiliate, or independent—before or since.

Cable-System Sales

The usual rule of thumb for measuring the price of a cable system involves assigning a dollar value to each household that subscribes to the system. In

---

*Accountants define cash flow variously as operating revenues minus operating expenses or operating income before depreciation and amortization.

Exhibit 6.m

Miami Merry-Go-Round

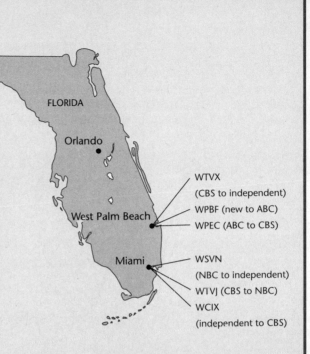

FLORIDA

Orlando

West Palm Beach

Miami

WTVX
(CBS to independent)
WPBF (new to ABC)
WPEC (ABC to CBS)

WSVN
(NBC to independent)
WTVJ (CBS to NBC)
WCIX
(independent to CBS)

In Miami, Florida, in 1988, for the only time in television history, one of the Big Three television networks owned and operated a local station that had primary affiliation with another network.

The bizarre scenario began in 1984 when Wometco sold WTVJ-TV, the Miami CBS affiliate, to the investment firm of Kohlberg, Kravis, Roberts (KKR). After a deal fell through whereby Lorimar would have bought the station from KKR for a staggering $405 million, the CBS network put in a preliminary bid of only $170 million.

While negotiating with KKR, CBS also talked to TVX, owner of WCIX-TV, a Miami independent. And while CBS was so engaged, KKR was meeting also with NBC, which for years had tried unsuccessfully to buy its Miami affiliate, WSVN-TV.

The big surprise came in January 1987, just 15 days after WSVN had renewed its NBC affiliation agreement for another two years, when NBC announced its purchase of WTVJ for $270 million. Thus, when the deal closed in September, NBC owned and began to operate a station *still affiliated with CBS.*

But the story continues. WSVN held affiliation talks with CBS, but the station refused to abandon its NBC affiliation until after the latter network's coverage of the 1988 Olympics and World Series. Fearing that WSVN's delaying tactics might leave it with no affiliate at all, CBS in August 1988 bought WCIX for $59 million—not an unreasonable price for an independent, but a steal for a station that would become a network affiliate. Because WCIX suffered signal problems, particularly in the rapidly growing areas north of Miami, CBS convinced WPEC, the ABC affiliate in West Palm Beach, 60 miles north of Miami, to change its affiliation to CBS.

But even that doesn't end the story. Observers expected WTVX, the former CBS West Palm Beach affiliate, to pick up ABC's affiliation, now that WPEC was switching to CBS. But no. ABC affiliated instead with WPBF-TV, a Palm Beach station not even on the air yet. Actually, the network *sold* the affiliation—a first in network-affiliate relations history. WPBF agreed to waive all network compensation, making a financial deal with ABC that represented an estimated overall benefit to the network of at least $1.5 million a year.

In the early morning hours of January 1, 1989, the switches went into effect. In Miami, WTVJ went from CBS to NBC, WCIX went from independent to CBS, and WSVN went from NBC to independent. In West Palm Beach, WPEC went from ABC to CBS, WTVX went from CBS to independent, and WPBF went on the air with ABC. And viewers throughout south Florida went to their *TV Guides* to try to sort out the whole mess.

Exhibit 6.n ●●●●●●●●●●●●●●●

Radio and TV Station Trading

| | Radio | | Television | |
Year	Number	Average price	Number	Average price
1984	782	$1,249,391	82	$15,268,585
1986	959	$1,553,838	128	$21,168,093
1988	845	$2,179,444	70	$25,427,971
1990	1,045	$ 831,231	75	$ 9,292,693
1992	667	$ 904,337	41	$ 3,024,488

By the early 1990s, radio and television station selling prices had dropped precipitously, reflecting both the overall national economy and the lower profitability of most broadcast properties.

Prices for individual stations vary widely. In 1992, for example, the average AM station (excluding the $70 million sale of New York City's WFAN) sold for about $357,000, the average FM for $882,000, and the AM/FM combination for $1,202,000.

Source: Based on data in *Broadcasting*, 8 February 1993, pp. 39 and 40.

the early 1980s that figure averaged about $300 per subscriber. In 1989 it peaked at between $2,000 and $2,500, but by the early 1990s it had fallen to about $1,800. Like similar formulas for determining selling prices for radio and television stations, this per-subscriber method yields only very rough estimates. It ignores such factors as geographical location, number of homes passed by the system (which represent potential subscribers), age and channel capacity of the system, amount of system construction remaining, number of pay-channel subscribers, level of subscription rates, and the influence of franchise conditions and expiration date. (For example, Southwestern Bell explained its proposed 1993 acquisition of two cable systems in the Washington, D.C. area—at a very high price of $2,800 per subscriber—by pointing to the unusually affluent nature of the systems' subscribers.) Estimates based on multiples of cash flows do account for some

of these factors. Recent selling prices have, on the average, been between 9 and 11 times cash flow.

As with radio and television station sales, brokers arrange most cable-system sales, taking fees of 2 to 6 percent of the purchase price or, in some cases, accepting part ownership of a system in lieu of a cash commission.

As of the end of 1992, the 1991 Time Warner merger, valued at $11.41 billion, constituted the largest cable-system transaction. The price equaled a cost per subscriber of about $2,000.

Cable Program Service Sales

The cable industry's settling and maturing process in the 1980s gave rise to a number of sales and mergers of cable networks. In 1984, for example, Daytime and the Cable Health Network combined to create a new advertiser-supported service: Lifetime. In the same year, HBO acquired a 15 percent interest in BET (Black Entertainment Television), which specialized in minority programming, assuming responsibility for marketing it to cable systems and advertisers.

In 1985, in a complex series of deals valued at $690 million, Viacom (a major MSO, programmer, and syndicator, and half-owner of Showtime/The Movie Channel) acquired full ownership of Showtime/TMC and of MTV Networks (operator of three cable services: MTV, VH-1, and Nickelodeon). These acquisitions made Viacom the largest cable programmer and the only programmer with significant stakes in both advertiser-supported and pay-cable services. In 1989 Viacom sold half of its Showtime cable network operations for $225 million to Tele-Communications Inc. And in 1991 Hearst bought 20 percent of ESPN for about $200 million, TCI acquired The Learning Channel for $30 million, and CNBC purchased FNN for $154 million.

These sales and mergers established a trend—already entrenched in the broadcast industry—toward concentration of control in fewer and fewer hands. Economic reality, however, prevents most entrepreneurs from starting new national services on their own. The creators of the Sci-Fi Channel, for example, had no hope of seeing their efforts reach fruition until they sold their concept in 1992 for $30 million to the financially secure USA Networks.

• • • • • • • •

6.7 Personnel

The number of people employed in an industry usually gives some indication of its importance. According to that measure, the electronic media have relatively little importance. However, the social and political significance of media lends them far greater weight than their small work force might suggest.

Employment Levels

Exhibit 6.o details employment statistics for non-network units of the broadcast and cable industries.

Overall, when networks and other related operations are included, those industries employ some 600,000 people fulltime. By way of comparison, one single manufacturing corporation, General Motors, employs nearly 800,000 people.

However, many highly specialized creative firms support the media, producing materials ranging from station identification jingles to prime-time entertainment series. Such organizations offer more opportunities for creative work—performing, writing, directing, designing, and so on—than do media themselves. Many other types of related work take place in advertising agencies, sales representative firms, program-syndicating organizations, news agencies, common-carrier companies, and audience-research organizations.

Aside from major broadcast and cable television networks, most electronic media organizations have small staffs. The number of full-time employees at radio stations ranges from fewer than 5 for the smallest markets to about 80 for the largest, with the average being 20. Television stations have anywhere from 20 to 300 employees, with a typical network affiliate employing about 90 and an independent station about 60 full-time people.

Cable systems average about 30 full-time employees but range from family-run systems in small communities with perhaps 5 or 6 employees to large city systems with staffs of well over 100. Cable MSO headquarters units average about 55 full-time employees.

Salary Levels

The huge salaries reported in the newspapers and on *Entertainment Tonight* go only to top talent, creative persons, and executives, working mostly at network, group, or MSO headquarters and at the production centers of New York and Hollywood. Average salaries for jobs at most stations and cable systems rank as moderate at best, governed by basic laws of supply and demand. Typically, those working in sales and marketing earn the highest incomes. Exhibit 6.p offers salary information for new college graduates in media or related jobs as well as for those media veterans who command top salaries, and average salaries for those working their way up in the field.

Exhibit 6.0 ••••• •••••••••••

Broadcast and Cable Employment

Medium	Full-time employees (thousands)	Percent women	Percent minorities
Commercial AM radio	55	36	14
Commercial FM radio	18	44	16
Noncommercial radio	3	40	18
Commercial television	66	37	19
Noncommercial television	9	46	20
Broadcasting headquarters	5	45	24
Total Broadcast	156	38.2	17.3
Total Cable	107	42	25

These statistics represent broadcast and cable employment in 1991 based upon reports from only those non-network units that have five or more full-time employees.

Although still larger than cable's, the broadcasting work force has been steadily decreasing (its 1987 total, for example, was 176,000) while cable's has been increasing (from 84,000 in 1987). Also, overall, representation by women and minorities in cable exceeds that in broadcasting.

Source: FCC, *Equal Employment Opportunity Trend Report*, Washington, DC, 8 June 1992.

News jobs rank among the better-paying nonsupervisory positions in television. According to the NAB reports cited in Exhibit 6.p, television news reporters on the average earned an annual salary of $29,000 in 1991, whereas news anchors earned $65,000. Radio paid a good deal less, with reporters at $19,000 and anchors at $21,000. Average annual salaries for news directors showed the same disparity, with television at $58,000 and radio at $22,000. As noted with respect to all broadcast jobs, of course, actual salaries are affected by such factors as experience and market size.

Employee benefits can represent a significant—as much as 40 percent—addition to a worker's income.

Nearly all television stations contribute to employees' health insurance, most pay for at least part of a life insurance policy, and more than half have retirement or pension plans. On the other hand, radio stations typically provide considerably less.

Employment of Women

The FCC enforces Equal Employment Opportunity (EEO) Act standards for broadcast stations, cable systems, and headquarters operations. These standards require owners to file an annual report classifying employees according to job categories, gender, and minority status.

As in all businesses, women in media often run up against corporate "glass walls" that limit their lateral movement to jobs that will provide the experience necessary for promotion to higher positions. Even when they have the appropriate qualifications, women frequently hit a "glass ceiling"—an invisible barrier that prevents their movement to the top. Exhibit 6.q, however, details the careers of three women who—to some extent, at least—broke through those barriers.

In its annual employment study of all broadcast stations with five or more employees, the FCC reported that in 1991 women occupied more than 38 percent of all jobs, up from 32 percent in 1979. Perhaps more important, women represented nearly 34 percent of employees classified as Officials and Managers (up from 23 percent in 1979) and 51 percent of those classified as Sales Workers (up from 31 percent in 1979). Exhibit 6.o offers a more detailed analysis of the FCC report.

A poll conducted by Pinnacle Communications found media management positions with the highest percentages of women to be advertising agency media directors (65 percent), followed by television station promotion managers (45 percent), program directors (42 percent), news directors (18 percent), and general sales managers (16 percent). Only 7 percent of television general managers were women (*Broadcasting*, 8 June 1992: 19).*

For cable systems with five or more employees in 1991, the FCC reports that women constituted nearly 42 percent of all employees and more than 36 percent of officials and managers. The potentially lucrative area of sales saw major improvement: women held more than 47 percent of those jobs, up from only 30 percent in 1983.

Minority Employment

EEO rules also require stations to report on their efforts to upgrade employment opportunities of minority-group members—defined by the FCC for this purpose as Aleutians, American Indians, Asians, Blacks, Hispanics, and Pacific Islanders. Although their overall progress has been slower than that of women, many have made outstanding contributions to broadcasting and cable. Exhibit 6.r describes some of them.

The FCC reported that in 1991 minorities represented about 17 percent of all broadcast employees, an improvement of only 3 percentage points over 1979. The percentage of minority members holding sales jobs increased from just over 8 percent in 1979 to nearly 12 percent in 1991. The report for officials and managers turned out slightly better in terms of progress, if not in terms of absolute numbers: minorities held more than 12 percent of the top jobs, up from just under 8 percent in 1979.

Cable has outpaced broadcasting in terms of minority employment. Of all workers at cable systems in 1991, minorities amounted to about 25 percent, compared with fewer than 12 percent in 1979. Minorities held more than 12 percent of those jobs classified as officials and managers and nearly 29 percent of those in sales.*

Unionization

Extensive unionization in broadcasting and cable exists at networks, national production centers, and

*A widely publicized sex-discrimination case involved Christine Craft, hired in 1980 as co-anchor at KMBC-TV, the Metromedia station in Kansas City, Missouri. Craft claimed that, although she had been assured her position depended on journalistic talent and not on her appearance, when her bosses critiqued her performance they spent most of their time picking apart her makeup and clothes. The station replaced her in 1981, explaining, she alleged, that she was "too old, too unattractive and not deferential to men." Craft sued for $3.5 million and in 1984 won $325,000 in damages. The court based the award on a finding of fraud; she lost on her claims of sex discrimination and equal-pay violations. In 1985 an appellate court overturned the award, and in 1986 the U.S. Supreme Court closed the case by refusing to hear Craft's appeal. Only one Supreme Court justice—Sandra Day O'Connor, the sole woman on the court—voted to hear the case.

*Broadcasters and cable-system operators also must avoid discrimination on the basis of age. For example, an Illinois radio station once fired a 51-year-old disc jockey after changing its format from beautiful music to MOR/adult contemporary. The DJ had been with the station for 9 1/2 years. Claiming he had been terminated because of his age, he brought suit against the station. The jury agreed and awarded him $194,000 in damages—double the amount of his back pay (*Broadcasting*, 19 November 1984).

Exhibit 6.p •••••••••••••••

Salary Levels

1. In the beginning . . .

Compared below are entry-level annual salaries for new college graduates in various media or related fields. These represent nationwide *median* salaries in 1991. Some graduates found jobs at higher pay, some at lower pay:

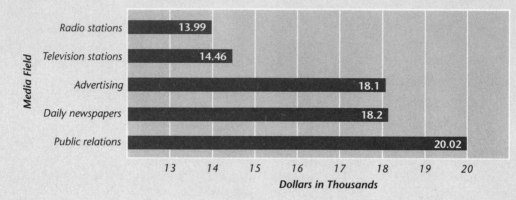

Source: Based on a survey, conducted by the Ohio State University School of Journalism, of 2,648 bachelor's degree recipients who completed their programs in journalism and mass communication in spring 1991 at one of the 79 schools participating in the survey.

2. At the top . . .

Here are estimated annual incomes of some people who have been in "the business" for a while and occupy top positions in their fields. Only their tax accountants know the exact incomes of these individuals. But these estimates indicate that media jobs can indeed be richly rewarding for those who survive the competitive pressures and find their place in the highest echelons:

Network News Anchors

Dan Rather (CBS)	$4.0 million
Tom Brokaw (NBC)	2.7 million
Peter Jennings (ABC)	2.0 million
Bernard Shaw (CNN)	0.5 million

Talk-Show Hosts

Oprah Winfrey (*Oprah*)	$80 million
Johnny Carson (*Tonight* to 1992)	30 million
Arsenio Hall (*Arsenio*)	23 million
David Letterman (on CBS in 1993)	14 million

David Letterman (on NBC to 1993)	6 million
Jay Leno (*Tonight* since 1992)	3 million
Bryant Gumble (*Today*)	2 million

Industry Executives

Michael Eisner (Disney)	$5.4 million
Bob Magness (TCI)	4.8 million
John Welch (GE/NBC)	3.2 million
Roger King (King World)	2.0 million
Laurence Tisch (CBS)	1.5 million
Ted Turner (TBS)	1.0 million
Daniel Burke (ABC)	0.8 million

Sources: *TV Guide*, 13 April 1991; *Broadcasting*, 9 December 1991, 1 June 1992, and 13 July 1992; and *Miami Herald*, 15 January 1993.

3. And on the average . . .

As they moved from entry-level to top-level positions, electronic media employees earned the following annual salaries along the way (some salaries do not appear here because broadcast stations and cable systems use somewhat different job titles). Again, these are only averages. Salaries paid by organizations in large cities tend to run higher than those in smaller communities. And because salary averages typically rise each year, the data prove most useful in comparing compensation levels for the various positions, rather than in studying specific salaries themselves:

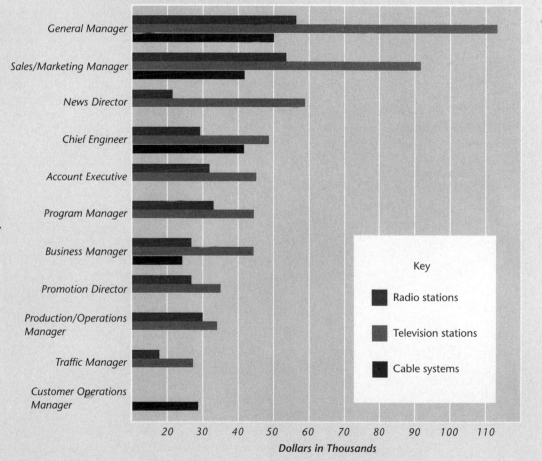

Sources: Based on data in *Television Employee Compensation & Fringe Benefits Report*, National Association of Broadcasters (Washington, DC, 1991); *Radio Employee Compensation & Fringe Benefits Report*, National Association of Broadcasters (Washington, DC, 1992); and *Cable Television Salary Survey*, Jim Young & Associates (Weatherford, TX, 1990).

Exhibit 6.q •••••• •••••••••••

A Woman's Place Is in the Newsroom

The path for women to equal job opportunity in broadcasting has been bumpy and long, but some progress has been made.

In 1948 ABC hired Pauline Frederick as the first woman network news correspondent. She remained the sole female hard-news network reporter for the next 12 years. In her early years, when assigned to interview the wives of presidential candidates at national political conventions, she was also required to apply their on-camera makeup. Later she became famous for her coverage of the UN, first as a correspondent for ABC, then with NBC. In 1976 Miss Frederick became the first woman to moderate a presidential debate, between Gerald Ford and Jimmy Carter. She died in 1990 at the age of 84.

In 1976 ABC hired Barbara Walters as the first woman anchor on a weekday evening network newscast. She shared the anchor desk with Harry Reasoner. Her salary: $1 million a year ($500,000 for anchoring and $500,000 for producing and hosting four entertainment specials a year), plus perquisites (a private office decorated to her taste, a private secretary, a makeup consultant, and a wardrobe person). Walters had established her reputation as co-host of NBC's *Today* show and as a successful, if sometimes controversial, interviewer of famous personalities as diverse as Princess Grace of Monaco, Fred Astaire, Ingrid Bergman, and Fidel Castro. Her tenure as anchor ended in 1977, and she moved on to more celebrity interviews and to ABC's news magazine *20/20*.

After earning a journalism degree in 1969, Connie Chung worked at a Washington, DC, independent station. In 1971 she was hired by CBS as a Washington correspondent. Five years later she became news anchor at CBS's O&O station KNXT in Los Angeles and was reportedly the highest paid local anchor in the country. She joined NBC in 1983 as early morning anchor, took over the Saturday *Nightly News*, and became the regular substitute for Tom Brokaw on the weekday evening newscast. In 1989 she rejoined CBS, this time as anchor of its Sunday evening newscast and of various magazine programs. In 1993 she became co-anchor, with Dan Rather, of the network's weekday evening news.

Pauline Frederick   *Barbara Walters*   *Connie Chung*

Sources: AP/Wide World Photos (Frederick); ©1989 Capital Cities/ABC (Walters); CBS, Inc. (Chung).

Outstanding African Americans in Electronic Media

Although African Americans have not yet gained full equality in the media industry, many have risen to positions of prominence in broadcasting and cable. The following are but a few.

Don Barden—president of Barden Communications, the largest black-owned cable operator, with 125,000 subscribers in the Detroit area

Karen Barnes—vice president of Fox Children's Network

Don Cornwell—chairman, president, and controlling stockholder of Granite Broadcasting, television station group owner

Ragan Henry—owner of 10 AM and 14 FM stations

Robert Johnson—founder and president of the Black Entertainment Television cable network

Jennifer Lawson— executive vice president for national programming and promotion services, Public Broadcasting Service

Michael Moye—creator and executive producer of *Married . . . with Children*

Johnathan Rogers—president, CBS Television Stations

Keenen Ivory Wayans—executive producer, cowriter, and star of *In Living Color*

Source: Reprinted with permission of BROADCASTING, September 9, 1991. © 1991 by Cahners Publishing Company.

most large-market network television affiliates, but not at the smaller-station or local-system level.

The fragmentation of the broadcast industry into so many outlets, most with relatively small staffs, usually makes unionization of such stations impracticable. For example, a small radio station cannot afford to assign two employees to record an interview, paying one as a technician to operate equipment and the other as a performer to do the talking, when the job could just as easily be done by a single employee.

Smaller cable systems, too, have relatively few unionized workers. In 1992, however, when fewer than 15 percent of cable employees belonged to unions, the Communications Workers of America announced an all-out effort to increase the number, focusing initially on such huge MSOs as TCI and Time Warner.

Electronic media draw on types of personnel first unionized in older industries—electrical work, music, motion pictures, stage, and newspapers. Most of the 40-odd unions to which broadcasting and cable employees belong cover workers in other media as well. Thus the American Federation of Musicians, whose marathon battle to control the use of recorded music is described in Section 2.2, represents every kind of professional musician, from players in symphony orchestras to pianists in bars to members of bands accompanying performers on television.

Most hourly workers in broadcasting and cable can be grouped into two broad categories, the creative/performing group and the crafts/technical group. Unions divide along similar lines; those representing the former usually avoid the word *union*, calling themselves guilds, associations, or federations.

The first pure broadcasting union, the American Federation of Television and Radio Artists (AFTRA), began (originally as AFRA) in 1937, representing that universal radio performer, the announcer. Most creative/performing unions, however, originated with stage and motion picture workers. Examples include the Writers Guild of America (WGA), the American Guild of Variety Artists (AGVA), and the Screen Actors Guild (SAG). When videotape came to rival film as a medium of production, SAG and AFTRA both claimed jurisdiction over performers recorded by the new medium. AFTRA finally won. Because they work in both fields, many actors now also belong to both unions.

Creative unions have played other significant though sometimes belated roles in forcing recognition of technological developments. For example, because filmmaking contracts had no provisions covering television, feature films were kept off the air in the 1950s. SAG went on strike in 1960 (when Ronald Reagan was its president) to force higher scales for *residuals*, the payments made to performers and others for repeated showings of recorded programs on television. SAG has collected residuals for members since 1954, much as ASCAP and BMI collect copyright payments on behalf of composers. In fact, some performers lucky enough to appear in particularly popular syndicated series became known as "residual millionaires."

New technology issues triggered strikes in 1980–1981 involving several unions. This time they fought over income from the sale of recorded programs to pay-television, videocassette, and videodisc markets. Videocassette revenue and residuals again played a role in the Writers Guild strikes of 1985 and 1988. Guild members also wanted—but failed to achieve —greater creative control over their products. The 1988 strike lasted 22 weeks, causing a delay in the start of the fall television season and a further drop in already-declining network audiences.

Technical (as opposed to creative) unions became active in broadcasting early in its history. The first successful strike against a broadcasting station may have been one in St. Louis in 1926, organized against radio station KMOX by the International Brotherhood of Electrical Workers (IBEW), a technicians' union founded in the late 19th century by telephone linemen.

In 1953 NBC technicians formed a separate association of their own that ultimately became the National Association of Broadcast Engineers and Technicians (NABET), the first union exclusively for broadcasting technicians. Later the union changed the word *Engineers* to *Employees* to broaden its scope. A third technical union, the International Alliance of Theatrical Stage Employees and Moving Picture Machine Operators of the United States and Canada (IATSE), expanded into television from the motion picture industry.

Employment Opportunities

Surveys of students enrolled in college electronic media programs indicate that most want to work either in on-camera or on-mike positions, or in "behind-the-scenes" positions. The oversupply of candidates makes these the *least* accessible to beginners. The delegation by broadcast stations and cable systems of such work to outside production companies means that these jobs concentrate in a few major cities, where newcomers face fierce competition and where unions often control entry to some of them.

News, the one field in which local production still flourishes, offers an exception to the dearth of creative jobs at stations and systems. Nearly all broadcast stations, as well as rapidly increasing numbers of cable systems and cable news services, employ reporters, photographers, writers, and so on. Competition is stiff: television news directors, for example, average 60 applications for every entry-level position they fill, and the average station hires only three new people each year. But opportunities do exist—especially in cable and broadcast outlets in smaller markets.

Sales offers another employment area likely to expand. Commercial networks and stations, and more and more cable systems, employ salespeople. Ambitious job-seekers should also note that top managerial positions historically have been filled from the ranks of sales personnel (although, in recent years, more and more general managers have come out of news). Advertising agencies and national sales representative firms offer entry-level employment opportunities as well. Nevertheless, personnel directors frequently complain that college-trained job applicants overall fail to comprehend the financial priorities of the industry and their profound influence on every aspect of operations (see Exhibit 6.s).

As technologies proliferate, competition intensifies—as does the need for creative and effective promotion. Stations, systems, and networks promote themselves and their products both to the public and to potential advertisers. Cable networks also use promotion extensively to persuade cable systems to carry their programs.

About two-thirds of all jobs in cable are technical, but marketing, customer service, research, and advertising positions are increasing. The need for creative people will also grow as more cable systems gear up for public-access and local-origination programming and, as noted earlier, news.

Exhibit 6.s ●●●●● ● ● ● ● ● ● ● ● ● ●

Advice to Job Seekers

The International Radio and Television Society, The Radio-Television News Directors Association, and The National Association of Television Program Executives commissioned the Roper Organization to conduct a survey of media executives' attitudes concerning the educational preparation received by students seeking careers in broadcasting and cable. Some examples of their opinions:

- Entry-level job applicants often have unrealistic career expectations. They expect too high a starting salary, they expect to advance too quickly, and they come to the job with a misguided impression of the industry.
- Recent college graduates will find their best opportunities in *sales* (cited by 49 percent of those responding), *news* (cited by 32 percent), and *production* (28 percent).
- Nonacademic considerations receive more weight than academic and formal credentials when broadcasters evaluate a candidate for an entry-level position. They regard as most important the applicant's *general presentation, writing skills and style, experience in the industry, and hands-on experience* in actual work situations.
- Nearly three-fourths of the respondents ranked a four-year undergraduate education as either *essential* or *important.* They placed less importance, however, on a graduate degree.

- Two-thirds of the executives considered a journalism or a communication degree as an important consideration in evaluating a prospective employee; almost half felt that way about a liberal arts background.
- Broadcasters generally expect students to come to the job knowing the *basic* elements required for work in the industry—*writing skills,* the *basics of broadcasting, knowledge of equipment operation,* and *communication skills.*

Not everyone agreed with all the findings. For example, Professor Robert O. Blanchard, chairman of the Department of Communication at Trinity University, argued that:

The worlds of the media professionals and mass communication educators overlap only minimally. The obsession of professionals, by nature, is with the present or, more likely, with the immediate past . . . What they do is based on what worked, or didn't work, last season. The university tradition reflects concern with identifying, assessing and transmitting enduring skills, principles and values, and understanding what they hold for the future . . . The future for us is symbolized for our times with the advent of the 21st century, where today's students will be living and working most of their adult lives. It will be conceptual skills and principles and values, not last season's entry-level skills, that will guide them through our fast-changing and expanding information society. (Blanchard, 1988).

Source: The Roper Organization Inc., "Electronic Media Career Preparation Study," *Executive Summary,* December 1987. Reprinted by permission of Radio-Television News Directors Association.

However, applicants who—possibly blinded by the industry's glamour—look only to broadcasting and cable for entry-level jobs seriously limit their employment opportunities. Electronic media are so central in American society that every large organization with any public contact uses them in one form or another. Countless career opportunities exist in *corporate video*—programs produced and distributed by manufacturing, service, and retail firms, educational and health organizations, foundations, government agencies, even the armed services.

Many such organizations make extensive in-house use of satellite-fed, closed-circuit television. In 1992, 80 private Business Television Networks (BTV) sent programs to more than 30,000 downlink sites in the United States. Most BTV organizations direct their materials to their own employees for product introductions, training, and corporate communications. The investment firm Merrill Lynch alone, for example, transmits three or more product-driven programs each week to its sales force in 480 offices around the country.

...is rapidly growing field of corporate video applies broadcast techniques to job skills training, management development, sales presentations, and public relations. Such nonbroadcast uses of television require trained personnel for production, direction, writing, studio operations, program planning, and similar functions. They also offer advantages over traditional broadcast positions:

- Broadcast stations are reducing their staff sizes while corporate video organizations are enlarging theirs.
- Jobs often are available for students right out of school—even in major markets.
- Even entry-level positions exist in major markets.
- Beginning salaries—and working hours—are better.
- Employees enjoy greater job stability.
- Ratings have no effect on careers.

• • • • • • • •

Summary

6.1   Broadcast stations fulfill four functions: general/administrative, technical, programming, and sales. Station organization follows the same pattern, with subheadings for news, production, traffic, and other specializations. Economic considerations encourage broadcasters to own more than one broadcast facility.

6.2   Broadcast networks organize along lines similar to stations, with added responsibilities for program distribution and station relations. Most affiliates are not owned by networks; rather, they have a contractual relationship with networks. Contracts set station compensation rates for time used for network programming and allow affiliates to refuse to clear time for network programs. The prime-time access rule limits the amount of prime time that affiliates in the top 50 markets may clear for network programs, a disadvantage that has proven beneficial to independent stations not affiliated with a network.

6.3   Cable systems perform the same four functions as commercial broadcast stations, plus marketing the systems' services to subscribers. The programming function is more extensive than at broadcast television stations because of multiple cable channels. Some systems interconnect for more efficient distribution of programs and commercials.

6.4   Cable program services are of two types: advertiser-supported and pay (or premium). Subscribers usually receive ad-supported networks as part of the system's basic or expanded-basic package of programming. They pay an extra monthly fee for commercial-free pay networks and a one-time fee for each program from a pay-per-view service. Most cable systems also carry the programming of local television stations and of superstations, independent television stations that distribute their signals by satellite throughout the country.

6.5   Capital expenditures in broadcasting and cable range from a few thousand dollars for a small radio station to many millions for cable and satellite operations. Operators face significant new costs required to implement high-definition television—as do consumers, who account for a significant portion of the total industry capital investment through purchases of radios, television sets, and VCRs.

6.6   Some broadcasting and cable profit comes from buying and selling stations and systems. Investors have been attracted to the industry because of its typically high profit margin, although prices for some stations, especially AM radio, have fallen in recent years. Many factors influence the price of a station or cable system, but buyers and sellers make rough estimates using various formulas such as multiples of projected cash flow.

6.7   Relative to their social impact, broadcasting and cable have small work forces. The percentage of jobs held by women and minorities has increased in recent years but still falls far short of the percentage held by white males. Broadcast employees are unionized at the network level and in major production centers, but not at most stations and cable systems. News and sales offer the best employment chances for newcomers to broadcasting. Technical and marketing people are most in demand in the cable industry. Other opportunities exist in corporate, nonbroadcast video.

Chapter 7

Advertising, Other Revenues, and Profits

In 1981 U.S. corporations spent a total of about $60 billion on advertising. By 1991 that figure had more than doubled to about $130 billion—or about $10 per week for every person in the nation. Radio and television broadcasting have overtaken newspapers as the nation's largest advertising medium. Television by itself ranks second behind newspapers, followed, in order, by direct mail, yellow pages, radio, magazines, cable, and outdoor (see Exhibit 7.a).

As competition intensified and the recession took its toll, however, the once-assumed profitability of broadcasting and cable became less and less assured in the 1990s. Broadcasters, for years "fat and happy" with what some referred to as "licenses to print money," looked for ways to cut costs and for new sources of revenue. Technological advances, such as fiber optics, video compression, and multiplexing, created expanded cable channel capacity and more program options, and, consequently, even greater competition for viewer attention and advertising dollars. The deregulatory stance of the Republican administration in Washington during this period, coupled with its disinclination to invoke antimonop-

oly laws, encouraged mergers and acquisitions, often involving large companies and conglomerate corporations with interests in many different aspects of the media. One result has been a continuing decline in the older commercial broadcasting culture, which at its best prided itself on its concern for the public interest and its role as the premier medium of public expression in a democratic society. Critics charge that in its place has come a "bottom-line mentality," focused not on making money while doing good, but just on making money.

7.1 Advertising

Broadcasting and cable offer advertisers unique advantages, such as broad audience reach, immediacy, and flexibility. Advertising can be as local as the area covered by a single station or cable system, or as broad as a national network with virtually universal coverage. As alternatives to local or network coverage, advertisers can choose *national spot*—an

Exhibit 7.a

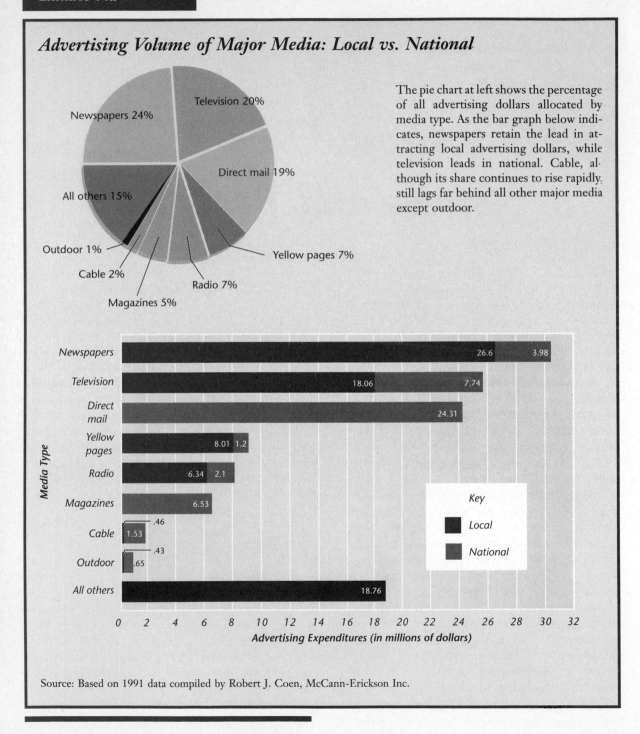

Advertising Volume of Major Media: Local vs. National

The pie chart at left shows the percentage of all advertising dollars allocated by media type. As the bar graph below indicates, newspapers retain the lead in attracting local advertising dollars, while television leads in national. Cable, although its share continues to rise rapidly, still lags far behind all other major media except outdoor.

Pie chart:
- Television 20%
- Newspapers 24%
- Direct mail 19%
- All others 15%
- Outdoor 1%
- Cable 2%
- Magazines 5%
- Radio 7%
- Yellow pages 7%

Bar graph — Advertising Expenditures (in millions of dollars):
- Newspapers: Local 26.6, National 3.98
- Television: Local 18.06, National 7.74
- Direct mail: National 24.31
- Yellow pages: Local 8.01, National 1.2
- Radio: Local 6.34, National 2.1
- Magazines: National 6.53
- Cable: National .46, Local 1.53
- Outdoor: National .43, Local .65
- All others: National 18.76

Key
- Local
- National

Source: Based on 1991 data compiled by Robert J. Coen, McCann-Erickson Inc.

arrangement that enables them to put together individual stations with any combination of coverage areas, station types, and program vehicles desired—or can place their ads simultaneously on several interconnected cable systems.

Broadcast Coverage

All stations, even network affiliates, function essentially as *local* advertising media, covering single markets, although their individual coverage areas vary a great deal. As Exhibit 7.b shows, radio depends on local advertising for more than three-fourths of its revenue, whereas television stations derive nearly half of their revenue from national spots. This difference reflects the historical fact that television captured most national advertisers, driving radio to cultivate local sources of revenue. Moreover, since radio costs far less, small local businesses find it more affordable.

Daily newspapers, broadcasting's chief rival for local advertising dollars, have far less flexibility of coverage. Most communities have only one daily newspaper. Metropolitan daily newspapers often adapt their coverage to advertisers' needs by using add-on neighborhood supplements. But in many a one-newspaper town, local advertisers may choose from among two dozen or more radio and television stations with varying coverage areas.

Local broadcast advertisers consist chiefly of fast food restaurants, auto dealers, department and furniture stores, banks, food stores, and movie theaters. When such local firms act as retail outlets for nationally distributed products, the cost of local advertising may be shared by the local retailer (an appliance dealer, for example) and the national manufacturer (such as a maker of refrigerators). This type of cost sharing, known as *cooperative advertising*, or just *co-op*, supplies radio with a major source of its revenue, so much so that some stations appoint a special staff member to coordinate cooperative advertising. It also leads occasionally to abuse—*double billing*—as described in Section 7.6.

When a station connects to a network, it instantaneously converts from a local to part of a regional or national advertising medium. For advertisers of nationally distributed products, *network advertising* has significant advantages:

- Advertisers, in a single transaction, can place messages on more than 200 stations of known quality, strategically located to cover the entire country.
- Advertisers can have centralized control over commercial messages plus assurance that ads will be broadcast within the chosen times and programs.
- Advertisers benefit from the network's sophisticated audience research.
- Networks provide convenient centralized billing for commercial-time costs.
- Advertisers gain prestige from the very fact of being on a national network.

Despite those advantages, some national advertisers find networks too costly or too inflexible. They have the option of using *national spot advertising*, working through their advertising agencies and the stations' national sales representatives, who assemble ad hoc collections of nonconnected stations. Commercial announcements go out to chosen stations by mail or satellite. Spot advertisers can choose from several program vehicles—spots within or between network programs, or in local or syndicated programs. National spots thus enable advertisers to capitalize on audience interest in local programs, something the network advertiser cannot do. Exhibit 7.e shows that the largest national advertisers use spot and network in combination to achieve better coverage than either could yield on its own, while Exhibit 7.c describes a minority audience in which advertisers have become increasingly interested.

Pros and Cons

As an advertising medium, broadcasting has unrivaled access to all family members under the changing circumstances of daily living. For example, car and portable radios allow broadcasting to compete with magazines and newspapers as an out-of-home medium. Radio and television also allow advertisers to target their audiences by scheduling commercials to coincide with listener activity (sportswear ads, for example, during a baseball game). Television is the only medium that can vividly show how a

Exhibit 7.b ●●●●●● ●●●●●●●●●●●

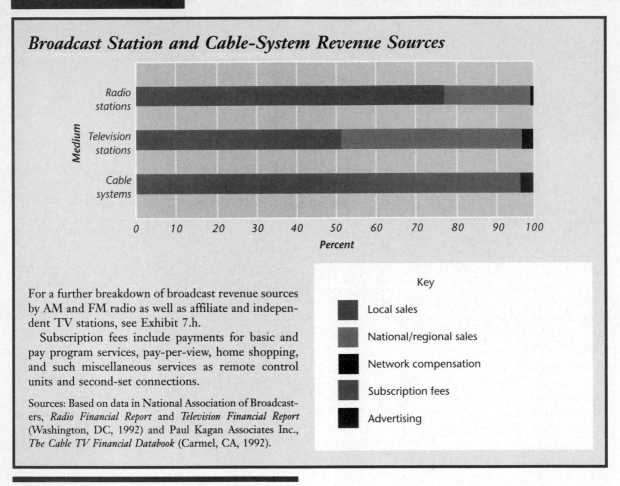

Broadcast Station and Cable-System Revenue Sources

For a further breakdown of broadcast revenue sources by AM and FM radio as well as affiliate and independent TV stations, see Exhibit 7.h.

Subscription fees include payments for basic and pay program services, pay-per-view, home shopping, and such miscellaneous services as remote control units and second-set connections.

Sources: Based on data in National Association of Broadcasters, *Radio Financial Report* and *Television Financial Report* (Washington, DC, 1992) and Paul Kagan Associates Inc., *The Cable TV Financial Databook* (Carmel, CA, 1992).

Key

- ▮ Local sales
- ▮ National/regional sales
- ▮ Network compensation
- ▮ Subscription fees
- ▮ Advertising

---

product works. Color and movement add to the effectiveness of demonstrations. Above all, the constant availability of broadcasting as a companionable source of entertainment and information gives it a great psychological advantage.

However, commercials must make their point quickly. Normally, most radio commercials last 60 seconds; most television commercials run 30 seconds, though there is a growing trend toward 10- and 15-second spots. Even the longest spot cannot duplicate the lasting utility of a large printed department-store ad or a supermarket ad with clip-out

coupons: listeners or viewers cannot set broadcast commercials aside to consult later. Nor can broadcasting compete effectively with newspaper classified sections.

Broadcasting's geographical flexibility has limits. Networks cover virtually the entire country. Yet some advertisers would rather concentrate their messages in certain regions. Sometimes (in regional feeds of football games, for example) an advertiser may be able to limit its geographical exposure. But in most cases the client must take all stations in a network's lineup or none at all. Local advertising

Exhibit 7.c ••••••••••••••••

Serving the Hispanic Audience

The Hispanic population in the United States increased some 44 percent between 1980 and 1990 and, by 1992, exceeded 22 million. Although they live and work most everywhere throughout the country, the greatest numbers of Hispanics are located in California, New York, Florida, Texas, and Illinois.

More than 300 radio stations and more than 30 full-power television stations carry Spanish-language programs in the United States. Two major television networks compete for this special audience—Univision and Telemundo—while Galavision and Cable Television Nacional operate as cable program services. The most popular television programs include Univision's variety show *Sábado Gigante* (shown here) and Telemundo's *Marielena*, a *telenovela* (soap opera), both produced in the United States.

As Hispanic media grow, so does advertiser interest. By the 1990s total ad expenditures in Spanish-language media exceeded $600 million, about one-third of which was in radio and close to half in television.

Sources: *Sábado Gigante* & Univision photos courtesy of Univision Television Network. Telemundo logo courtesy of Telemundo Group, Inc.

and national spot offer one solution, but even they sometimes force the advertiser to pay for audiences too far removed from its place of business.

The combination of limited *commercial inventory* (the list of commercial slots in the station's schedule), high demand, and large audience delivery puts television commercial prices beyond the reach of many advertisers. A single 30-second announcement in the 1993 Super Bowl, for example, cost about $850,000—affordable obviously by only the largest national advertisers. Even at the station level, television commercials, particularly those within or adjacent to programs that deliver large audiences, cost too much for small and medium-sized businesses. Section 7.4 offers details on advertising rates generally.

Brief though they may be, commercials irritate some viewers, and technology has made it all too easy (from the advertiser's viewpoint) to avoid them. Commercials typically have about a 20 percent smaller audience than the program in which they appear. And no wonder. With television remote control devices, viewers can *zap* commercials by muting the sound or changing channels when an advertising cluster begins. Or they can *flip* from channel to channel to sample other programs (a practice sometimes called *grazing* or *surfing*). Viewers with "pause" and "fast forward" features on their VCRs can zap commercials by putting their machines in "pause" when the ads run, or by speeding up their machines during playback, thus *zipping* through the messages.

The practice of scheduling several commercials together in *pods* can reduce their impact. During one break in its 8:00 P.M. movie, a Miami independent television station ran 18 consecutive nonprogram events (commercials, promotional announcements, etc.) for a total of 6 minutes and 40 seconds. Although advertisers can get the preferred positions of first or last spot in the pod, they must pay about twice the regular price. Some (Energizer batteries with their drum-thumping rabbit, for example) produce 30-second announcements in two 15-second segments, scheduling the first part at the beginning of a commercial break and the second half at the end. Broadcasters refer to these commercials as *bookends*.

A broadcasting station has only 24 hours of "space" each day, putting a limit on its commercial inventory. Moreover, only so many commercials may be scheduled without alienating the audience. Print media, on the other hand, can expand advertising space by adding pages without offending readers.

Broadcasting also is unavailable to advertise some products. Congress forbade cigarette advertising in 1971, and most broadcasters find it expedient to ban voluntarily such products as hard liquor and "adult" movies.

• • • • • • • •

7.2 *Commercial and Other Announcements*

For both legal and financial reasons, "nonprogram materials"—commercials and various other kinds of announcements—call for careful definition, scheduling, and record keeping.

Scheduling

Once a salesperson concludes an advertising sale, the contract goes to the *traffic department*, which schedules the commercials and includes them in the daily log of on-the-air activities. This department's role led to the term *trafficking*—the scattering of spots at scheduled times throughout the broadcast day, both between and within programs (not to be confused with trafficking in broadcast licenses, described in Section 7.10).

Although some stations no longer worry about *product conflicts*, others try to ensure that announcements for competing products do not appear next to each other. A Buick dealership, for example, does not want its commercial immediately followed (and thus diluted) by an ad for Fords. This concern applies also to *antithetical* products, which may be considered in conflict with one another, even if not directly competitive (beer and milk, for example). Today, at least at the large stations, computers automatically make these and many other scheduling decisions.

Sponsorship

Until the early 1960s the principal type of network advertising—full-program *sponsorship*—gave advertisers control over, and identification with, sponsored programs and their stars. However, sponsorship all but disappeared from television when most advertisers found the practice too expensive and decided instead to scatter their messages over several programs. The term *sponsor* now usually means *any* advertiser whose message appears within a program. Sponsorship in the original sense survives only for some daytime programs and for occasional specials, underwritten by large corporations that desire a particular type of image-building exposure. Sears' single sponsorship of the movie *E.T. the Extra-Terrestrial* on CBS in 1991 and again in 1992 offers one example.

Participation Programs

When networks and stations took over from advertisers the responsibility for programs, they at first maintained the fiction of sponsorship by referring to advertisers whose commercials appeared during program breaks as "participating sponsors," leading to the term *participations* (or *participating spots*). Vestiges of this concept survive in *billboards* shown at the open and close of some television programs, which give free plugs to "participating" advertisers.

Today most stations sell advertising simply as *spot announcements* (more briefly, *spots*). Most advertisers use *scatter-buying* strategies, spreading their spots over a number of different programs. This method not only avoids risking too much on any one program but also gains exposure to varied audiences.

Some programs have natural breaks where spots can be inserted without interrupting the flow—between rounds of a boxing match or between music cuts on a radio show, for example. In other cases, breaks must be artificially contrived. The art of writing half-hour situation comedies includes building plots to suspenseful break points to accommodate commercial insertions. Opinions on what qualifies as a "natural" break differ. The industry now regards breaks between stories in newscasts as natural; yet at one time interrupting news with commercials seemed not only unnatural but also highly unprofessional. Viewers often complain about arbitrary breaks in theatrical feature films, whose scripts do not, of course, provide seemingly natural climaxes in the action every ten minutes. Some also object to "television time-outs" taken during football games for the convenience not of players but of advertisers.

Sustaining Programs

Programs neither sponsored nor subject to participating spot insertions constitute *sustaining* programs, limited almost exclusively to public-affairs programs of a type that could not be commercialized without a serious breach of taste—presidential addresses, for example. Some programs are not intended to be sustaining but become so by default because they contain controversial material—and advertisers usually avoid controversy. In 1989 alone, for example, ABC lost more than $14 million when nervous clients refused to participate in certain questionable prime-time series and movies. This total included the $1 million lost when advertisers pulled out of a *thirtysomething* episode that showed two gay men in bed together. (Not surprisingly, the network decided against a rerun of that episode.)

Controversy sometimes has the reverse effect, however. Observers credit former Vice President Dan Quayle's very public criticism of *Murphy Brown* (for bearing a son out of wedlock) with moving the series to number three in the 1991–1992 season Nielsen ratings and increasing the price of a 30-second commercial from $114,000 that season to $310,000 in 1992–1993. In any case, television's most popular shows today have relatively little difficulty attracting advertisers. For example, when nine of ten scheduled advertisers dropped out of a 1992 episode of *Seinfeld* that dealt with masturbation, NBC was able to replace them immediately with no loss of revenue.

Station Breaks

Partly as a matter of law and partly as a matter of custom, stations take *station breaks*—interruptions in programming for the insertion of *station identification announcements (station IDs)*.* When they include program promotional material or, on occasion, even commercial matter, these breaks become *shared IDs*. Networks interrupt their program feeds periodically to allow affiliates to insert IDs. They also leave time for affiliates to run commercial announcements—*network adjacencies*—sold by the stations to local or national-spot advertisers.

Promos and PSAs

Two other types of announcements also occur where commercials normally appear. *Promotional announcements (promos)* call attention to future programs of networks and stations. Most broadcasters consider on-air promotion their most effective and cost-efficient audience-building tool.

Public-service announcements (PSAs), though they resemble commercials, are broadcast without

---

*The FCC requires IDs, consisting of station call letters and the community of license, at sign-on and sign-off and at hourly intervals, or at a "natural break" if a program runs longer (47 CFR 73-1201). Earlier regulation required more frequent IDs to aid in tracking down improperly operated and unauthorized stations. Today, for promotional reasons (especially during rating periods), many stations air far more IDs than legally required.

charge because they promote noncommercial organizations and causes. They give stations and networks a way of fulfilling some of their public-service obligations and, along with promos, serve also as fillers for unsold commercial openings.

The number of different commercial and other announcements within a program break has edged upward in recent years. Advertisers as well as audiences often complain about this proliferation— referred to as *clutter*.

• • • • • • • •

7.3 Cable Advertising

In the early 1990s annual cable advertising revenue totaled about $2 billion. National networks generated about three-fourths of that total; local systems, about one-fourth. Cable nevertheless had a long way to go to challenge broadcasting and newspapers, each of which accounts for about one-fourth of all advertising expenditures in all media, while cable receives but 2 percent.

Pros

Cable offers coverage flexibility, with commercial time available in

- cable systems' locally originated programs,
- cable-system interconnections, and
- ad-supported cable networks and superstations— either by way of direct national placement or through local insertion by cable systems.

Cable channels have smaller audiences than broadcast television, both because of smaller coverage areas and because cable's many channels fragment the audience. Cable therefore charges less than broadcast television, though in many cases not less than radio stations.

Cable's program specialization enables an advertiser to target a specific audience: ESPN delivers to avid sports fans, MTV to music-oriented teens, CNN to news viewers. Also, cable subscribers tend to be better educated and more "upscale" than the average television viewer.

And Cons

Larger advertisers accustomed to paying their advertising agencies to produce commercials for traditional television can easily supply these commercials to cable as well. But small, local firms may have difficulties producing commercials, even simple ones, and if done poorly they can be counterproductive. To alleviate this problem, some cable systems offer local companies commercial production services free or at reduced cost as an inducement to advertise.

Cable systems face more complexities than do broadcasters when inserting commercial messages in their programs. They have to deal with many channels, each with different timing for commercial insertions. Most cable systems now handle such procedures by using computer equipment, triggered by electronic signals, to insert commercials automatically—although not always with precision.

Perhaps more than anything else, lack of adequate statistical information about cable's audiences has impeded the growth of cable advertising—just as it did in early radio (1920s) and television (1940s). Today, radio and television stations and networks have access to sophisticated data describing their audiences. But cable's multiplicity of program choices so fractionalizes its audience that few channels attract viewers in sufficient numbers to produce statistically valid results. Rating services do make some information available for the more popular national cable networks, but not for local cable-system channels. Recognizing the need for local market ratings, an industry group called COLCAM (Committee on Local Cable Audience Measurement) in 1992 took the first step in what would be a long and expensive process by requesting proposals from Nielsen and Arbitron for a comprehensive cable-system rating service (see Section 11.7). The following year both companies announced plans for local cable measurement services that would function through personal computers.

7.4 Advertising Rates

Commercial time has value for advertisers only in terms of the audiences it represents. Audiences constantly change in size and vary widely in demographic composition. As a result, so does the value of time to the advertiser. Most large advertisers make their electronic media buys based on ratings—the statistical measurement of audiences exposed to a product's commercials (see Chapter 11). In particular, they order spot schedules designed to achieve a predetermined number of *gross rating points* (GRPs)—that is, to reach a specified number of viewers—or *target rating points* (TRPs), to reach audience subgroups such as teens or women 18 to 49 years of age.

Pricing Factors

Three relatively stable factors affect audience size and composition and, hence, prices advertisers pay for broadcast time: *market size*, *station facilities* (frequency, power, antenna location, and other physical factors that influence coverage), and *network affiliation*, if any. Station managers have no day-to-day control over these factors.

Three major dynamic variables make one station successful and another less so: *programming*, *promotion*, and *sales*. Good management can lure demographically desirable audiences away from competitors by offering attractive programs supported by effective promotion, and an efficient sales department can lure advertisers away from competitors with persuasive arguments and solicitous attention.

Cost Per Thousand

No standard formula for using all these variables to set appropriate broadcast rates exists. However, market forces—including laws of supply and demand—eventually tend to bring prices into line. The industry uses *cost per thousand* (CPM) as the main test for comparing advertising prices. CPM represents the cost of reaching 1,000 (represented by the Roman numeral "M") households or target groups such as men or teens or women aged 18 to 34.

CPM is calculated by dividing the cost of a commercial by the number of homes (in thousands) that it reached. Prime-time advertisers typically pay a household CPM of about $6 on broadcast networks and about $4 on cable networks.

CPM helps in comparing one medium with another, one station with another, and even one program with another. Occasionally stations and networks make sales "on the come," predicting and in some cases even guaranteeing a specific CPM and audience rating in advance. (NBC, for example, guaranteed its 1992 Summer Olympic advertisers an average rating of 15.3; it achieved a 16.8.) Advertisers whose commercials don't reach the promised audience level usually receive additional commercial time at no cost; only rarely does a broadcaster give refunds.

Broadcast Station Rates

Broadcast advertising depends for its effectiveness on cumulative effect. A buyer therefore contracts for spots in quantity (a *spot schedule* or a specially priced *spot package*). Most radio clients buy in groups of 6, 12, or 18—or, to reach *saturation*, 24 spots per week.

Prices vary according to the number of spots purchased (quantity discounts) and other variables such as these:

- *Time classes.* Typically stations divide their time into specific *dayparts*, and even subclasses of dayparts, with different prices for each. For example, one Ohio radio station charges $95 per one-minute spot in the 6:00 A.M. to 10:00 A.M. daypart (morning *drive time*) but only $35 between 7:00 P.M. and midnight.
- *Spot position.* For an assured place in the schedule, advertisers pay the premium rate charged for *fixed-position* spots. Less expensive *run-of-schedule*

(ROS) spots may be scheduled by a station anywhere within the time period designated in the sales contract. Some stations *rotate* spots, both *horizontally* (over different days) and *vertically* (through different time periods) to give advertisers the benefit of varying exposures for their commercials.

- *Pre-emptibility.* Stations charge less for pre-emptible spots, which they can cancel if a higher-paying customer wants those commercial positions. Advertisers do not, of course, pay for a pre-empted spot. Often, when a pre-emption does occur, the station will try to get the pre-empted advertiser to accept a spot at another time. When this happens (or if a commercial does not air for technical reasons and the advertiser agrees to run it on a subsequent date), the rescheduled spot is called a *make-good.*

- *Package plans.* Radio and television stations offer at a discount a variety of *packages*, which may include several spots scheduled at various times and on various days, or may, for example, include announcements on both an AM and a co-owned FM station.

- *Special features.* Spots associated with particular programs—sporting events, for example—often earn a higher rate. Many stations charge a premium for commercials within their local newscasts.

A television station may list more than a hundred different prices for spots, using a device known as a *rate grid.* For example, it might list 20 different time periods or program titles down the left side of its grid. Across the top it might list six different rate levels, numbered I through VI. This arrangement would create 120 cells or boxes into which specific prices can be entered.

Stations often define rate levels quite arbitrarily, enabling them to quote several different prices for the same spot. Such a grid gives sales personnel great flexibility in negotiating deals. The grid also permits a station to use the same rate card for longer periods, despite changes in audience or in advertiser demand; sales management can simply direct salespersons to negotiate within one area of the grid rather than another. Using a grid also helps in setting levels of pre-emptibility at which a commercial is likely to "hold" and not be pre-empted by a higher-paying advertiser. Exhibit 7.d compares price ranges for television spots in markets of varying size.

Broadcast Network Rates

The rate for the same spot position in a network television program changes even over the course of a single season as the audience for the program rises and falls significantly. In the early 1990s the cost for one showing of a 30-second network spot in a regular prime-time television program averaged about $100,000; low-rated programs commanded about $50,000 per spot, whereas high-rated shows sold at $250,000 or more. For example, whereas NBC priced its low-rated prime-time shows at about $55,000 per spot, a commercial in *Cheers* cost about $260,000. Fox, some of whose programs had by then become competitive with ABC, CBS, and NBC, charged as little as $90,000 for a commercial in *In Living Color* and as much as $220,000 in the high-rated *Simpsons.* Ad rates cover time charges only, not the cost of producing commercials.

Radio network ad rates also move across a wide range, influenced by daypart as well as audience reach. In the 1990s the average spot on a major national radio network ran about $1,000.

Cable Rates

Cable advertising rates vary according to three levels of audience potential: individual cable systems, interconnected systems, and networks.

As *cable systems* matured and saw little prospect of increasing their subscriber base, more and more looked to advertising as a source of increased revenue. They now offer many advertising opportunities in both locally originated programs and national program services. Ad rates vary accordingly, from as little as $2 for a listing in a system's classified ad channel to $400 and sometimes higher for a 30-second local commercial inserted into one of the more popular cable networks.

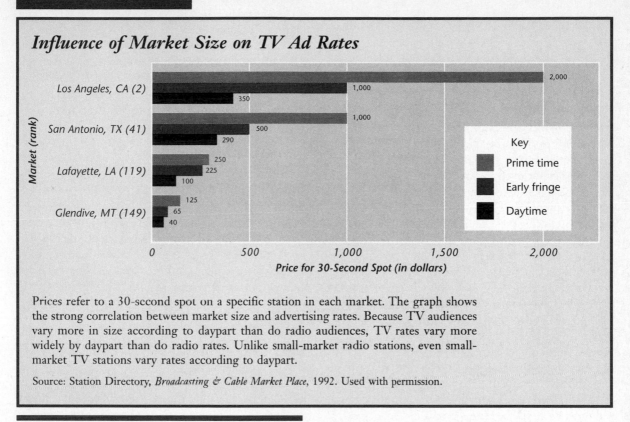

Exhibit 7.d

Influence of Market Size on TV Ad Rates

Market (rank)

Los Angeles, CA (2): Prime time 2,000; Early fringe 1,000; Daytime 350

San Antonio, TX (41): Prime time 1,000; Early fringe 500; Daytime 290

Lafayette, LA (119): Prime time 250; Early fringe 225; Daytime 100

Glendive, MT (149): Prime time 125; Early fringe 65; Daytime 40

Price for 30-Second Spot (in dollars) — 0, 500, 1,000, 1,500, 2,000

Key
- Prime time
- Early fringe
- Daytime

Prices refer to a 30-second spot on a specific station in each market. The graph shows the strong correlation between market size and advertising rates. Because TV audiences vary more in size according to daypart than do radio audiences, TV rates vary more widely by daypart than do radio rates. Unlike small-market radio stations, even small-market TV stations vary rates according to daypart.

Source: Station Directory, *Broadcasting & Cable Market Place*, 1992. Used with permission.

System interconnects differ from cable networks. A network may deliver its programs to thousands of systems throughout the nation, but interconnects involve mostly the placement of commercials on a number of systems within a geographic region. The area covered by such a group of systems may represent anywhere from as few as 13,000 subscribers, as in the case of Rock Springs/Green River, Wyoming, to more than 3.5 million in the metropolitan New York City interconnect called WNYI. WNYI links more than 45 systems in 22 counties throughout New York, New Jersey, and Connecticut, and permits advertisers to buy either the full interconnect or any of its four regional subdivisions. This wide variation in interconnect configuration results in rates that may run as low as $20 to as high as

several thousand dollars for a single 30-second spot. To increase the likelihood that viewers will see their commercials, some advertisers use interconnects to run their ads at about the same time on all available cable program services—a practice referred to as *roadblocking*.

Cable networks and *superstations*, though national in scope, do not necessarily command the highest advertising prices. Again, audience size and composition determine price. By the 1990s, on average, fewer than 3 percent of U.S. television households tuned in to any advertising-supported cable program service at any given moment. Accordingly, daytime rates varied from the low hundreds to the thousands of dollars per commercial. In prime time, A&E, for example, charged as little as $3,800 per

30-second spot while CNN and TBS charged as much as $11,000.

Alternative Ad Buys

Some commercial arrangements, used by both broadcasters and cable operators, fall outside normal rate practices.

In a *trade deal* (also called a *tradeout*), a station or cable system exchanges commercial time for an advertiser's goods or services. These might include such items as hotel accommodations, office supplies, automobiles, or even hairstyling for a news anchor. In a more specialized type of trade deal, the advertiser exchanges game-show prizes for seven- to ten-second mentions (or *plugs*) during the show. In exchange for costly prizes, the advertiser receives one or more of the short plugs; when supplying less expensive prizes, the advertiser must also pay cash to receive plugs, called *fee-spots*. This practice invokes FCC-required *sponsor identification*, usually in the form of visual or voice-over credits at the end of a program, ironically constituting yet another plug for the products. A variation involves the donation of items for use during the production of dramatic and comedy programs. At least half a dozen so-called *placement companies* offer producers such products as food, beverages, and appliances at no cost in exchange for the item's on-camera appearance. In *barter deals*, stations exchange advertising time for programs. These are discussed in detail in Section 9.2.

Per-inquiry (PI) deals, favored primarily by mail-order firms, commit the advertiser to pay not for time but for the number of inquiries—or the number of items sold—in direct response to PI commercials. Among the most successful PI promotion items have been record albums, audio tapes, CDs, and magazine subscriptions. Many broadcasters and cable operators oppose PI advertising in principle on the grounds that it underrates the value of their advertising services. Advertising's worth cannot be judged fairly by direct sales alone because well-presented commercials can produce intangible benefits as well. They can create a favorable image of the advertiser and product and imprint trade names in the audience's consciousness, thus leading to sales at a later time.

And, as described in detail in Section 6.6, some stations practice *time brokerage*—selling time in blocks to brokers, who then resell it to others at a markup. Others enter into extended brokerage deals, called *local marketing agreements*, under which one station programs and sells the commercial time on another station, often in the same market.

• • • • • • • •

7.5 Advertising Sales

Local advertising sales practices differ somewhat from regional and national practices. *Advertising agencies* play a key role in both local and national sales. National sales require additional services from network sales departments and *sales representatives*.

Local Sales

The public perceives on-air performers as the stars of commercial broadcasting, but, in an economic sense, salespeople who generate the revenue to pay those performers are the real stars. Indeed, account executives (a fancy name for salespersons) typically earn the highest incomes among radio and television employees. And historically sales has been the most common route to top management positions.

Most television sales departments employ a general sales manager, a local (and sometimes also a national) sales manager, account executives, and support staff. The number of account executives varies from station to station; about six salespeople usually suffice for a medium-market television station. At some stations a sales assistant or even a secretary does all the support work; other stations also employ research people and commercial (*continuity*) writers.

Sales managers hire, fire, manage, and train salespersons, assigning them to an *account list* of specific advertisers and ad agencies. Beginning salespeople sometimes start without benefit of such a list (except, by industry tradition, the telephone yellow pages) and must develop their own accounts by making *cold calls* on potential new advertisers.

Salespeople usually work on a *commission* rather than salaried basis, keeping a percentage of all advertising dollars they bring to the station. This arrangement gives them both an incentive to sell as much commercial time as possible and the opportunity to raise their incomes without depending on annual salary increases.

One variation of the straight-commission plan, called *draw against commission*, pays the account executive a stipulated weekly sum in anticipation of future sales. Some companies treat this arrangement as salary; others consider the payments to be salary advances, repayable by the employee. Very few stations pay a commission when a sale is made; most wait until the commercial schedule actually airs or, more likely, until the station gets paid by the advertiser.

In addition to the personal qualities needed for success in any sales job, an account executive requires one indispensable sales tool—audience research. He or she must reduce the myriad numbers contained in rating reports to terms understandable to a client and must present them in such a way as to show the station in the best possible light. Armed with these data (often displayed in attractive brochures), along with a list of commercial availabilities supplied by the traffic department, the local rate card (if one exists), and information on the advertising needs and history of each prospect, the salesperson sallies forth to do battle.

Selling aids available to the local sales department include services of the Radio Advertising Bureau (RAB), Television Bureau of Advertising (TvB), and Cabletelevision Advertising Bureau (CAB). These New York-based organizations supply sales ammunition, such as specialized audience and product data and sales-promotion materials, for their respective subscribers.

In a sense the salesperson's real job begins after a client signs the first contract. Thereafter the salesperson nurtures the client's interest in the medium through *account servicing*, seeking to ensure renewal of the first contract and, better still, to bring in bigger contracts in the future. Such servicing includes making sure the station receives the client's commercial materials on time, advising the client whenever a commercial airs improperly, and arranging make-goods. In many cases it also includes taking clients to lunch or giving them free tickets to concerts and sporting events in which the station has a sponsorship interest.

Regional and National Sales

Stations gain access to national advertising business through *national sales representative* firms (*reps* for short) and, in the case of affiliates, network sales departments. Some stations also have *regional reps* for nonnational sales outside the station's service area. A rep contracts with a string of stations, acting as an extension of the station's own sales staff in the national and regional markets. Broadcast television reps usually have only one client station in any given market, whereas radio reps often have more than one.

Reps perform many services other than sales. Their national perspective provides a broader view than that of merely local markets. Reps often advise clients on programming, conduct research for them, and act as all-around consultants. In return for their services, rep companies collect a commission of from 8 to 15 percent on the spot sales they make for their clients.

Cable systems also use sales representatives. Specialized cable reps sell local or regional advertising on individual and interconnected systems. Others, like radio and television reps, sell time on local systems to national spot advertisers. Katz Communications, one of the largest broadcast rep firms with hundreds of radio and television clients, was one of the first to move into cable representation, sometimes handling a competing television station and cable system within the same market.

Network Sales

Fox and the three major television networks maintain their own sales departments, typically headed by a vice president, usually with offices in New York and Los Angeles and sometimes in such other cities as Chicago and Detroit. They tend to organize their sales forces into specializations, such as prime time, late night, news, children's programs, sports, and so on.

Ad-supported cable networks and superstations also have their own sales departments. Advertisers who wish to place orders with many different networks often use the services of time-buying organizations, such as Cable One, which negotiate buys on their behalf for spots on all, or any combination of, cable networks.

So-called *unwired networks* offer an alternative way of selling national-spot television advertising. Under this concept, companies buy commercial time, usually in bulk and at a discount, from television stations throughout the United States, and re-sell it, at a markup, to national advertisers. This practice differs from time brokerage (discussed in Section 6.6) in that here the purchase/resale is of commercial availabilities, not of program time blocks. Most such firms offer specialized spot placement—in prime-time movies on independent stations or in major-market local newscasts, for example. Traditional sales reps strongly oppose the unwired-network concept, viewing it as a threat to their exclusive national representation of client stations.

Advertising Agencies

All regional and national advertisers and most large local advertisers deal with media through advertising agencies. Agencies conduct research; design advertising campaigns; create commercials; buy time from cable systems, broadcast stations, and cable and broadcast networks; supervise implementation of campaigns and evaluate their effectiveness; and, finally, pay media on behalf of advertisers they represent.

Agencies become intimately familiar with each client's business problems, sometimes even assisting in development of new products or redesigning and repackaging of old ones. They decide on the right *media mix* for their clients. Allocations differ widely, but no major advertiser puts all its advertising

money into a single medium. Exhibit 7.e shows how the nation's five largest advertisers allotted funds to major media, while Exhibit 7.f indicates how agencies allocated their client's money.

For decades, ad agencies traditionally received a 15 percent commission on *billings*—the amount charged by the advertising media. That is, an agency would bill its client the full amount of advertising time charges, pay the medium 85 percent, and keep 15 percent as payment for its own services. By the 1990s, however, fewer than half of all advertiser-agency arrangements were using the flat 15 percent scheme. Variations in payment method arise because a company's own advertising department may do some of the work or may retain specialist firms to do specific jobs, such as research, time buying, or commercial production. Some agencies accept less than 15 percent commission or charge fees in addition to commission; some work on a straight fee basis; and some work on a cost-plus basis.

In any event, the fact that media allow a discount on business brought to them by agencies creates an odd relationship: the agency works for its client, the advertiser, but gets paid by the medium in the form of a discount on time charges. The travel business operates similarly: a travel agency works, at least theoretically, for the traveler, but gets paid by hotels or airlines through discounts on charges.

Proof of Performance

After commercials have aired, advertisers and their agencies need evidence to show that contracts have been carried out. Broadcast stations log the time, length, and source of each commercial when it airs. These logs provide proof of contract fulfillment. Broadcast business offices rely on logs when preparing proof-of-performance warranties to accompany billing statements. At many stations today, computers do the logging automatically. Some stations also make slow-speed audio recordings of everything they air as backup in the event of a dispute.

Advertisers and agencies can get independent confirmation of contract fulfillment by subscribing to the services of Broadcast Advertisers Reports

Exhibit 7.e　●●●●●●　●●●●●●●●●●●

How Top Advertisers Allocate Their Budgets

Rank	1	2	3	4	5
Advertiser	Procter & Gamble	Philip Morris	General Motors	Sears, Roebuck	PepsiCo
Total estimated ad expenditures (in billions)	$2.1	$2.0	$1.4	$1.2	$0.9
Percentage of expenditures allocated to—					
Network TV	25	19	38	16	23
Spot TV	14	10	8	3	29
Syndicated TV	6	7	3	2	3
Network radio	*	*	1	6	*
Spot radio	*	2	2	1	2
Cable	3	1	2	2	2
Newspaper	*	*	3	7	*
Magazines	7	11	18	2	*
Outdoor	*	3	*	*	*

*Less than 1 percent

All these premier advertisers chose broadcast television for their major expenditures. Even Philip Morris, prohibited by law from advertising its cigarettes on radio or television, sells other products in sufficient quantity to warrant allocating more than a third of its budget to broadcasting. Although expenditures on cable remain relatively modest, they have increased in recent years.

Source: Reprinted with permission from the September 23, 1992 issue of Advertising Age. Copyright, Crain Communications Inc., 1992.

(BAR), a firm that conducts systematic studies of radio and television commercial performance. BAR checks on commercials by recording the audio portion of television programs in 75 markets, sending the recordings to central offices for processing, as well as actually viewing commercials in some markets. In 1991 Arbitron began market-by-market replacement of its BAR service with its new MediaWatch—an electronic monitoring system that uses frame-by-frame pattern-recognition technology to identify commercials as they appear on local television stations.

Exhibit 7.f ●●●●●●●●●●●●●●●●●

How Top Agencies Allocate Their Clients' Budgets

Rank	1	2	3	4	5
Agency	Young & Rubicam	Saatchi & Saatchi	Ogilvy & Mather	McCann-Erickson	BBDO
Total estimated agency billings (in billions)	$7.3	$5.7	$5.5	$5.4	$5.4
Percentage of expenditures allocated to					
Network TV	33	42	31	37	33
Spot TV	15	27	NA	NA	NA
Synd. TV	1	1	2	3	NA
Network radio	1	NA	2	NA	1
Spot radio	NA	NA	NA	5	5
Cable	3	4	NA	4	3
Newspaper	4	6	NA	5	7
Magazines	8	16	NA	13	NA
Outdoor	2	1	NA	2	NA

NA = Not available

Billings refers to the amounts these agencies charged their clients for media services. Some agencies tend to specialize more in one medium than in others. For example, at least two allocate more than half of their clients' budgets to medical journals, while at least four deal with only the Yellow Pages. But the top-billing agencies listed here spend most of their client's money in electronic media.

Source: Reprinted with permission from the April 13, 1992 issue of Advertising Age. Copyright, Crain Communications Inc., 1992.

Cable systems, too, must confirm that commercials ran as scheduled. Most rely for this information on equipment that not only inserts commercials into the various cable programs but also provides verification of proper performance.

●●●●●●●●

7.6 Advertising Standards

Advertising raises touchy issues of taste, legality, and social responsibility. Both legal and voluntary standards influence what may be advertised and what methods may be used.

Sponsor Identification

The Communications Act's Section 317 requires reasonably recognizable differences between radio/television commercials and programs. A station must disclose the source of anything it puts on the air for which it receives payment, whether in money or some other "valuable consideration."

This *sponsor identification rule* attempts to prevent deception by disguised propaganda or "disinformation" from unidentified sources. Of course, anonymity is the last thing commercial advertisers desire. But propagandists who use *editorial advertising* (sometimes called *advertorials*) may not always be so anxious to reveal their true identity; nor do those who make under-the-table payments to disc jockeys or others for on-the-air favors wish to be identified.

Time Standards

Constant tension exists between the urge to cram ever-more commercial material into the schedule and the need to avoid alienating audiences—and advertisers as well—with intolerable levels of interruption.

The National Association of Broadcasters, in its now-defunct radio and television codes (see Section 13.10), had established industry standards for both advertising and programs. Although full of exceptions and qualifications, the NAB Codes had set nominal limits on commercial material per hour as follows: radio, 18 minutes; network television affiliates, 9½ minutes in prime time, 16 minutes in all other times; independent television stations, 14 minutes in prime and 16 minutes in all other times.

However, contrary to what some may believe, the FCC never set a maximum number of commercial minutes per hour of programming. Until 1981 FCC license applications and renewal forms simply required applicants to state the number of commercial minutes per hour that they planned to allow, or had allowed in the past. The FCC then might ask applicants who exceeded the time standards in the industry's own codes to justify the excess. Neither the FCC nor any other authority ever suggested any time limits for commercials on cable.

The FCC once prohibited what it called *program-length commercials*—productions that interweave program and commercial materials so closely that the program as a whole promotes the sponsor's product or service. But the Commission eventually abandoned even the minimal commercial oversight it had exercised at licensing times, and dropped its program-length commercial ban as well—in 1981 for radio and in 1984 for television. The Commission argued that the marketplace could best control the problem. Apparently this deregulation did not produce a massive increase in commercial time, at least at the three major television networks. Broadcast Advertisers Reports calculated that in 1991 ABC, CBS, and NBC averaged 9 minutes and 12 seconds of commercials per prime-time hour; Fox averaged slightly more than 11 minutes; independent stations nearly 11 ½; and syndicated programs more than 13 (*Broadcasting*, 4 May 1992: 60).

Today program-length commercials, known also as *infomercials*, appear throughout the day and night—except in time periods devoted to children (see "Children's Advertising," below)—on both broadcast and cable television, touting everything from hair-loss prevention nostrums to astrology charts. Producers formed their own organization, the National Infomercial Marketing Association. And cable networks were created featuring nothing but infomercials. In all, the industry generates more than half a billion dollars a year in revenue and has paid broadcasters and cable operators as much as $20 million a month to carry the programs.

The Federal Trade Commission has forced off the air some particularly outrageous infomercials, including one promoting a diet to cure impotency, and in 1990 a congressional committee held hearings on the rising trend. Despite the aura of sleaze surrounding infomercials, some began to achieve respectability. General Motors, for example, used the form to introduce its new line of Saturn cars. And one regional telephone company, Bell Atlantic, experimented in 1992 with what it called a *sitcommercial*—an infomercial masquerading as a situation comedy.

At the time when all FCC concern for time standards had evaporated, the then FCC Chairman Mark Fowler was quoted as saying, "What's really at issue here is whether the government trusts the common man to make up his own mind about what to watch or not to watch. If a half-hour TV shop-at-home service is an annoyance, he will choose to watch—or do—something else" (*Broadcasting*, 2 July 1984: 32). Apparently that common man has made up his mind. Home shopping networks, mostly on cable but also on broadcast stations,* generate billions of dollars in revenue annually. But Congress was not satisfied, and, in its 1992 Cable Act, directed the FCC to reconsider the public-interest value of home shopping services and infomercials on broadcast television. In 1993 the Commission, by a two-to-one vote, found that home-shopping stations do operate in the public interest, at least for purposes of the Act's "must-carry" rule, which requires cable-system carriage of those local television stations that ask for it (see Section 13.8). The FCC chair said, however, that the Commission might soon reexamine overall its 1984 elimination of commercial time limitations.

Taste Standards

Some perfectly legal products and services that appear in print and on billboards never appear in the electronic media. This double standard reflects the special obligations society imposes on broadcasting and, to a somewhat lesser degree, on cable because they come directly into the home, accessible to all. Nevertheless, canons of acceptability constantly evolve. Not until the 1980s, for example, did formerly unthinkable ads, such as those selling contraceptives and those showing brassieres worn by live models, begin to appear.

*In 1992 Home Shopping Network Inc. (HSN) ranked fifth among all television group owners, with its 12 stations covering 19 percent of U.S. television homes. The stations were later spun off to Silver King Communications, a corporation owned by HSN shareholders. (See also Section 7.7.)

Congress banned the broadcasting of cigarette ads in 1971. The most conspicuous example of self-imposed advertising abstinence is the refusal to accept commercials for hard liquor (though beer and wine are acceptable). On rare occasions hard-liquor ads have appeared, but most broadcasters decline to carry them for fear of giving added ammunition to opponents of wine and beer advertising. Broadcasters also typically declined to carry ads for movies that carried a self-imposed "XXX" rating or MPAA's former "X" rating; when MPAA replaced the latter with its new NC-17 rating, most broadcasters made case-by-case decisions. In any event, in the absence of voluntary industry codes and externally applied regulation, individual broadcasters and cable programmers must gauge the tastes of the audiences they serve and set their standards accordingly.*

Self-Regulation

The ban on liquor ads and the commercial time limits are examples of the voluntary self-regulation codified by the National Association of Broadcasters (NAB) in its radio and television codes.

In 1984 the Justice Department charged that the NAB standards, even though voluntary, violated antitrust laws by urging limitations that reduced competition. The NAB promptly disbanded its Code Office, apparently relieved to be rid of a thankless task. By 1990, however, a move had developed in Congress to restore the option of industry self-regulation by exempting the NAB codes from antitrust law. ABC, CBS, and NBC in 1992 agreed on a series of broadly worded standards intended to reduce the programming of gratuitous and excessive violence, and in 1993 were joined by Fox in announcing that they would air viewer warnings when violent programs were about to appear.

Meanwhile, television networks, some group broadcasters, and a few local stations continued to set and enforce both program and advertising stan-

*A most unusual arrangement at ABC made a program's author the arbiter of good taste. Herman Wouk held control over the length and content of commercials shown during the 1988 miniseries *War and Remembrance*, based on his novel. He barred all 15-second commercials and all ads for laxatives, foot powders, and feminine hygiene products.

dards through departments variously called *Continuity Acceptance, Broadcast Standards*, or *Program Practices*, albeit with reduced staffs. (NBC, for example, had about 30 people working in standards and practices in the early 1990s, compared to about 70 in the 1980s.)

Each year the networks screen more than 50,000 commercials to determine their acceptability. Most pass muster but some are rejected. One of the more publicized rejections involved a commercial for the 1991 motion picture *The Pope Must Die*. Each of the three major networks rejected the ad because of the film's title. The producers subsequently changed the title to *The Pope Must Diet*, but they never submitted new commercials.

Deceptive Advertising

Prosecution for outright deception in advertising falls under the jurisdiction of the Federal Trade Commission (FTC) rather than the FCC. However, use of fraudulent advertising by a broadcaster can be cited by the FCC as showing lack of the character qualifications required of licensees.

Instances of possible false advertising may be brought to the FTC's attention by consumers, competitors, or the commission's staff. In recent years, however, although it has dealt with some cases, the FTC has not assumed an activist role in this area.

Children's Advertising

For years, consumer groups—notably, Action for Children's Television (ACT)—and others have contended that because young children have not yet learned to understand the difference between advertising and entertainment, they need special protection from commercial exploitation.

After years of action and inaction on the subject by courts, legislatures, and the FCC, Congress finally passed the Children's Television Act of 1990 (described in detail in Section 14.8). Under the FCC's implementation of the law's provisions, broadcast stations and cable systems must limit commercial time in programs intended for young viewers and may not carry program-length commercials directed to children.

In January 1992, after 23 years of advocacy, ACT ceased operations. Its long-time president, Peggy Charren, referring to the Children's Television Act, said, "While children's TV has never been worse, we have set in motion what is necessary to make it better" (*Broadcasting*, 13 January 1992: 128). By January 1993 the FCC had levied fines against three television stations, had admonished three others, and was considering action against at least three cable systems for violating the new rules.

Unethical Practices

Aside from issues of advertising length and content, four specific types of unethical advertising practices have proved particularly troublesome: plugola, payola, double billing, and clipping. In the past they have triggered both FCC and congressional action.

A conflict of interest occurs when a station or one of its employees uses or promotes on the air something in which the station or employee has an undisclosed financial interest. This practice, called *plugola*, usually results in an indirect payoff. A disc jockey who gives unpaid publicity to her or his personal sideline business is an example.

Direct payments to the person responsible for inserting program material usually constitutes *payola*. It typically takes the form of under-the-table payoffs by recording-company representatives to disc jockeys and others responsible for putting music on the air.

Plugola and payola violate the *sponsor identification law*. After an investigation uncovered a wide range of both plugola and payola practices, Congress strengthened the sponsor identification law in 1960 by adding Section 507 (formerly 508) to the Communications Act, prescribing a $10,000 fine or a year in jail (or both) for each payola violation. Despite these efforts, payola scandals reappear every few years.

Local cooperative advertising sometimes tempts stations into *double-billing*. Manufacturers who share with their local dealers the cost of local advertising of their products by their dealers must rely on those dealers to handle cooperative advertising. Dealer and station may conspire to send the manufacturer a higher bill for advertising than the one the dealer actually paid. Station and dealer then split the excess payment. In the past, some stations have lost their licenses for double-billing frauds that were compounded by misrepresentations to the FCC.

Clipping occurs when affiliates cut away from network programs prematurely, usually in order to insert commercials of their own. Clipping constitutes fraud, since networks compensate affiliates for carrying programs in their entirety with all commercials intact.

In keeping with deregulatory policy then in vogue, the FCC in 1986 redefined billing frauds as civil or criminal matters, not FCC violations, and left the networks to solve clipping problems. The Commission did say, however, that it would consider double-billing charges when judging a licensee's character during licensing proceedings.

●●●●●●●●

7.7   Cable Revenue Sources

In sharp contrast to broadcasting, cable television relies on monthly subscription fees for most of its revenue. In 1991 cable systems averaged about $31 total monthly revenue per subscriber. Of that amount, only about one dollar per subscriber per month came from advertising.

Cable Fee Regulation

For years most cable systems operated with relatively little control over the fees they charged their subscribers. But complaints about ever-increasing prices for cable services abounded.

Finally, in 1992, Congress enacted legislation that required the FCC to assume supervisory responsibility over most cable rates. The Commission responded in early 1993 with a series of rulings that not only would limit most cable subscriber fees but also would require some cable systems to reduce their prices and even make refunds (see Section 13.8).

Cable Service Tiers

Some cable systems charge a single monthly rate for their service. But most divide their product into several levels of program service, called *tiers*, with a separate fee for each level. They also charge for "extras" such as stereo and hookups for VCRs and second television sets.

Most modern systems offer a *basic service* that includes local television stations, one or more distant superstations, and some advertiser-supported cable networks. The monthly fee for this basic package can vary from a few dollars to $25 or more. In 1991 the average fee for basic services was $17.95 per month.* Some systems break their basic service into two or more tiers. For example, they may pull several of the more popular ad-supported networks (such as MTV and ESPN) out of the basic package and offer them separately as an *extended* or *expanded basic service* at extra cost. In 1991 the monthly fee for expanded basic service averaged $5.48. At first in anticipation of, and later in reaction to, a provision in the 1992 Cable Act calling for governmental rate regulation of the basic program tier, some systems restructured their service. Many now offer a *broadcast basic* or *lifeline* tier limited to local stations and public access, educational, and government (PEG) channels. They then offer ad-supported networks and superstations only on one or more expanded tiers.

The next level of service includes *pay-cable* or *premium* channels, such as HBO, Showtime, and Disney. By the early 1990s more than 40 million homes—about three-fourths of all cable households—subscribed to pay cable. Usually, subscribers pay a separate fee for each pay service they select. Such fees range from about $2 to $20 or more per service per month, averaging about $10. Some cable operators require that their customers subscribe not only to the basic but also to an expanded-basic tier before they can buy any premium services. The 1992 Cable Act's *Anti-buythrough* provision effec-

*Estimates of cable fees, subscribers, and revenues in this section come from *The Kagan Cable TV Financial Databook*, Paul Kagan Associates Inc., Carmel, CA, 1992.

tively prohibits this practice, although systems were given ten years to comply with the new rule.

Some systems *package* two or more pay services and offer them at a price lower than the cumulative price for the individual services. As cable matured and systems searched for ways to entice new customers or to persuade current customers to *upgrade*, they inaugurated a variety of other marketing plans. A Maryland system, for example, gave customers the chance to buy any pay service on a daily rather than monthly basis for 35 cents a day during a 30-day trial period. In Phoenix, subscribers could receive either The Movie Channel or Showtime for a meager $3.95 a month—if they promised to keep the service for a year. And on Long Island, customers could design their own packages: for $29.95 a month they could receive all broadcast stations and their choice of eight pay- and basic-cable channels.

In addition to monthly fees, most cable systems charge a one-time installation fee. They may also add a "connection" charge when a subscriber elects to add a new pay-cable channel. To induce homeowners to sign up, cable operators frequently offer reduced rates or waive these charges entirely. Partly in an effort to discourage subscribers from canceling pay services, some systems charge a fee for that privilege. The 1992 Cable Act authorized the FCC to supervise these and other fees as well.

Pay-Per-View

Cable systems with *addressable* converters dedicate one or more of their channels to *pay-per-view* (PPV) programs. A one-time PPV charge allows viewers to see a single program, either a movie or a special event such as a boxing match or a rock concert. Some industry executives distinguish between pay-per-*view* and pay-per-*event*, but most use the first term to cover all one-time-charge programs. By the early 1990s more than 20 million homes had access to PPV programs, for which they typically paid about $3 per movie and as much as $40 for each special event.

PPV programs come in one of two ways. First, individual cable systems—so-called *standalones*—ne-gotiate directly with producers for PPV movies and events. More commonly, national program services—such as Request TV and Viewer's Choice—acquire PPV rights to programs and distribute them to cable systems under an arrangement that splits revenues between the program service and the cable system. Cable networks also operate in the PPV arena. USA, ESPN, and The Nashville Network were among the first advertiser-supported program services to dip their feet into this second revenue stream.* As video compression produced greater cable channel capacity, more and more systems devoted multiple channels to PPV. Some also began to experiment with two-way, interactive *video-on-demand* (VOD), a PPV technology that would compete with neighborhood VCR rental operations by permitting subscribers to order their choice of movies at the touch of a button.

Despite its promise, PPV has its share of controversy. Critics especially deplore the likelihood that more major sports events now on "free" television will soon be *siphoned off* by (that is, move to) PPV—available only to those homes equipped to receive the service and only to those families who can afford it. The major professional boxing matches had already made the transition. Then, in 1991, Showtime and ABC made a deal for college football on PPV, and the National Football League announced it would begin experimenting with pay-per-view. In its 1992 Cable Act, Congress asked the FCC to study this growing problem of *sports migration*.

PPV fortunes vary enormously—partly because of high costs for the rights to carry some events and partly because operators remain unable to predict audience acceptance. Between 500,000 and 600,000 subscribers paid approximately $35 each to watch the 91-second heavyweight championship fight

---

*One very specialized PPV service, Video Jukebox Network (carried on about 170 cable systems and now renamed simply "The Box"), allows viewers to call a 900 telephone number and—for a dollar or two—request to see their favorite music video. Revenues are split 25 percent to the cable operator, 25 percent to the phone company, and 50 percent to The Box. When, in the early 1990s, calls proved insufficient to pay all the bills, the service began to carry advertising as well.

between Mike Tyson and Michael Spinks on June 27, 1988, producing more revenue for promoters and rights holders than did that year's Super Bowl on broadcast network television. In contrast, four years later TVKO (Time Warner's pay-per-view boxing network) lost about $3 million with Evander Holyfield's heavyweight title defense against Larry Holmes.

PPV operators usually measure success in terms of the percentage of addressable homes that order a given event. They consider a 2 percent *buy-rate* a success for typical events. By the early 1990s the most successful event ever was the Holyfield-Foreman fight in 1991, which had an 8 percent buy-rate and grossed nearly $49 million in PPV and upwards of $65 million worldwide. Among the least successful: NBC's ill-conceived Olympics Triplecast in 1992, for which some cable subscribers paid $29.95 per day or $125 for 15 days (NBC tried some 11th-hour rate cutting, which confused subscribers and infuriated participating cable systems) to watch commercial-free events on three channels. NBC had said it needed two million subscribing homes in order to break even; industry experts estimated the final tally to be about 175,000—and losses to be as high as $150 million.

Cable Audio

For years, many cable systems have offered their subscribers special hookups that bring signals of local and distant radio stations to their home stereo systems. They typically charge about $4 a month for the service. By the 1990s systems had begun to carry special digital audio services from such companies as Digital Cable Radio, Digital Music Express, and Digital Planet, which offer compact disc–quality, commercial-free music of many types on about 30 audio channels.

Some operators sell their digital audio service for about $10 a month. Others charge subscribers $200 for the required tuner plus a monthly fee of about $5. Although the services deliver mostly music, they have expanded into such other areas as children's channels and even pay-per-listen offerings.

Home Shopping Networks

The FCC's removal of its long-standing prohibition of program-length commercials produced a new revenue-generating scheme for broadcast and cable: home shopping services. Operating as many as 24 hours a day, 7 days a week, national and regional shop-at-home services sell mainly jewelry, appliances, clothing, and housewares. Some services offer their products on cable, some on low-power television, some on full-power television, and some on all three, although, as noted earlier, this became subject to possible change when the Commission in 1993 announced its intention to review generally the issue of overcommercialization on broadcast television. Whatever the medium, the method is the same: viewers see merchandise, usually offered at what the network describes as huge discounts, and call the network by telephone to place an order, paying for the goods with a credit card.

C-SPAN

Cable's public-affairs network, C-SPAN, has the distinction of being neither wholly advertiser supported nor dependent upon subscriber fees (see Section 8.5). More than 4,000 participating cable systems serving about 55 million subscribers meet most of C-SPAN's $18 million annual budget by paying three to four cents each month per subscriber to carry the service. The balance of C-SPAN's revenue comes from corporate underwriting and from such services as videotape production and sublease of satellite transponder time.

• • • • • • • •

7.8 *Other Revenue Sources*

Electronic media owners, both current and prospective, continue to search for new or different ways to generate income. Some initiate program services that compete with broadcast and/or cable. Others look for ways to expand operations already in place.

Niche Services

Multichannel multipoint distribution services (MMDS), satellite master antenna television (SMATV), and home television receive-only satellite receivers (TVROs)—all of which are described in Section 3.3—depend on subscriber fees for their revenue. However, these services show little immediate prospect of attaining financial significance.

By the 1990s MMDS monthly subscriber fees were averaging about $25, plus about $100 for installation. But by then, Microband Companies, the largest "wireless cable" owner, had filed for bankruptcy. In all, MMDS—with fewer channels than its cable competitors—had failed to attract even half a million customers nationwide.

SMATV operates as a cable system confined to private property. Many operators divide programming into a basic service and one or more tiers. Basic subscriptions usually range from about $6 to $25 a month, with the full package of basic service and added tiers priced at around $40 a month. Some building owners operate SMATV systems themselves rather than using independent suppliers, offering the service free or at cost to entice new tenants.

TVRO owners can subscribe to packages of cable channels from such direct-to-home satellite television services as PrimeStar. They pay $150 or so for a decoder and a monthly fee of about $30 to view a variety of superstations, pay-per-view networks, and audio channels. PrimeStar also makes computer data services available for an additional charge.

Direct-broadcast satellite (DBS), already in place overseas, was scheduled to begin operations in the United States in the mid-1990s. SkyPix was to have been the first, with its 80-channel system for which subscribers would pay a $150 installation fee, up to about $13 a month for service, and from 99 cents to $4 for pay-per-view movies. However, legal and financial problems delayed SkyPix, plunging it into involuntary bankruptcy in 1992. Meanwhile, Hughes and United States Satellite Broadcasting planned to launch their DBS services in 1994.

Ancillary Services

Electronic media have devised a number of ways to supplement their primary revenue bases, many of which do not relate directly to broadcast or cable.

TBS's Turner Private Networks (TPN), for example, has developed *place-based* reformatted versions of CNN Headline News, such as the Airport Channel, which it distributes to specific locations. Whittle Communications offers a similar service for doctors' offices, while TPN plans yet another—with entertainment or educational programming—for fast-food restaurants. And CNN produces *CNN Reel News*, which screens feature material—much like the newsreels of years ago—between films in movie theaters. Advertising supports all of these operations, some of which critics refer to as "ambush media."

Radio and television station signals can be used to deliver ancillary (secondary) commercial services. AM stations may multiplex inaudible secondary signals on their channels. For example, some electric power companies have arranged with AM stations to send multiplexed signals to special receivers at various business locations that turn off air conditioning units during periods of high demand. FM channels may offer subsidiary communications authorization (SCA) services.* Early SCAs provided Muzak and other background-music services, and a few stations offered farm news or business and financial information.

The FCC further expanded SCAs in 1983, permitting FM stations to use—and to lease to others—up to three subcarriers. Stereophonic sound usually occupies one, leaving the others available for such uses as paging and messenger services and transmission of computer data. Many noncommercial radio stations transmit special programming for the visually impaired and some foreign-language material. Others use SCAs for slow-scan video, a service that transmits still pictures to educational and other

---

*This term has been officially changed to *subsidiary communications services* (SCS). But most in the industry continue to refer to "SCA."

institutions for teleconferencing, instruction, and information distribution. Despite the variety of SCA uses, only about 30 percent of all FM broadcasters utilize the service.

In the early 1980s the FCC authorized television stations to exploit their unused signal capacity for *second* or *separate audio program* (SAP) technology, making possible television stereophonic sound and simulcasts of foreign-language audio to accompany English-language television programming. Television stations have the further option of using their vertical blanking intervals (VBIs) to send closed-captioned subtitles to the hearing impaired. Stations derive no direct revenue from their closed-captioned signals, seeing this activity primarily as a public service.

Production

Rather than serving as sources of added income, most locally produced nonnews programs add to expenses. Stations, cable systems, and networks produce only a very small percentage of such programs in-house; most come from independent production companies or syndicators (see Chapter 9). As for commercials, a few television stations and cable systems have production departments that produce enough spots to cover expenses and sometimes even earn a profit. But most produce commercials at a loss or on a barely break-even basis, treating this service as a necessary cost incurred to help sell advertising time.

●●●●●●●●

7.9 Profit and Loss

As they moved through the 1980s and into the 1990s, most electronic media experienced increasing financial difficulties. The nation's overall economic problems, combined with growing and ever-more diverse media players, typically resulted at best in lower profits and, at worst, in losses or even bankruptcies.

Broadcast Television Networks

In 1985 network revenues fell slightly for the first time since 1971; yet even in that year ABC, CBS, and NBC together attracted more than $8 billion in advertising and produced profits exceeding $1 billion. By 1987, however, total net revenues for the three networks had fallen below $7 billion. For the first time in its history, CBS recorded a first-quarter net loss but was able to end the year in the black; ABC lost about $15 million.

All three major networks embarked on what would become an on-going austerity program, cutting budgets and laying off personnel. Meanwhile, the emergent Fox network struggled to get into the race, losing about $90 million in its 1988 fiscal year.

Static revenues, rising costs, competition from cable, independent stations, and home video, as well the weak economy generally, took an ever-increasing toll. The three major networks, once dominant in prime time, were together able to attract only half of their potential audience during one week in July 1991. Prices paid for sports-coverage rights had hit all-time highs. Estimates placed the networks' combined cost of covering the Gulf War at $145 million and advertising losses during the Clarence Thomas Supreme Court confirmation hearings at $20 million. As shown in Exhibit 7.g, Fox, with considerably lower operating expenses than its competitors, had turned its early losses into 1991 profits of nearly $350 million. But of the three big networks, only ABC was in the black that year.

Even though the network was profitable, ABC's owners were not pleased with its overall financial performance. Cap Cities' chief executive officer, Dan Burke, pointed out in 1991 that the network, since its purchase in 1985, had taken in $450 million in profit; but he noted that this was less than the $577 million that could have been earned had the company simply invested the purchase price in a money-market fund (*Broadcasting*, 11 November 1991: 5).

Meanwhile, CBS—which in the 1990–1991 season, for the first time in its 36-year history, had finished third in network prime-time ratings— staged a never-before rebound, regaining the num-

Exhibit 7.g •••••••••••••••

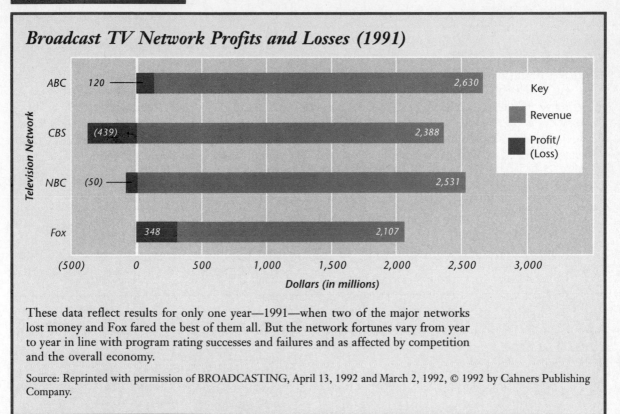

Broadcast TV Network Profits and Losses (1991)

These data reflect results for only one year—1991—when two of the major networks lost money and Fox fared the best of them all. But the network fortunes vary from year to year in line with program rating successes and failures and as affected by competition and the overall economy.

Source: Reprinted with permission of BROADCASTING, April 13, 1992 and March 2, 1992, © 1992 by Cahners Publishing Company.

ber-one spot in 1991–1992. Led by such hits as *60 Minutes* and *Murphy Brown*, the network appeared to be on its way to fiscal recovery.

NBC continued to struggle. Its nightly news dropped from second to third place, as did its prime-time ratings. It lost two of its top programs—*The Cosby Show* and *Cheers*—and, in its attempt to attract a younger audience more acceptable to advertisers, canceled three others—*Matlock, In the Heat of the Night,* and *Golden Girls,* all of which moved to ABC or CBS. The network's president, Robert C. Wright, has predicted that NBC may not again be profitable until 1994. NBC's financial predicament led to persistent speculation, usually denied by top management, that the network was for sale—for about $3.5 billion.

Looking over their shoulders, the Big Three saw Fox coming on strong. By 1991 its affiliates were carrying the newest network's programs to about 93 percent of all U.S. television households. With such highly successful programs as *Married . . . with Children, The Simpsons,* and *Beverly Hills 90210,* Fox had become fully competitive with its three senior rivals. Although his announced intention to enter Fox in the costly news business could eventually alter the picture, Chairman Rupert Murdoch predicted that profits would continue to rise.

In the 1990s ABC, CBS, and NBC intensified their cost-cutting efforts. Each tried various means of reducing affiliate compensation. They continued personnel layoffs and reduced the size of, or eliminated entirely, several news bureaus. They even cut back on programming, returning unprofitable time periods to their affiliates.

Still limited in the ways in which they can generate revenue (by rules that prevent their full participation in program syndication and by the FCC's edict that restricts network/cable-system crossownership, as discussed in Section 14.5), two of the three major networks hedged their financial bets by investing in cable program services. NBC became full or part owner of such operations as CNBC, Bravo, American Movie Classics, A&E, and Court Television; and ABC, of ESPN, Lifetime, and A&E. Only CBS remained timid, with its modest ownership of a regional (Midwest) sports channel.

Broadcast Television Stations

Exhibit 7.h indicates that, on the average, television stations nationwide earned a profit in 1991. However, about one-fourth of all network-affiliated television stations and more than half of all independents lost money. As shown in Exhibit 7.i, large-market stations tended to be profitable—though generally at lower levels than in previous years—while smaller-market stations did not.

Helping to offset poor financial performances by their television networks, the Big Three's owned-and-operated stations divisions performed well in the black. ABC's O&Os showed a profit of nearly $400 million, CBS's about $140 million, and NBC's nearly $220 million.

But overall, broadcast television's prospects remained bleak. Competition from cable and videocassettes showed no signs of diminishing, while newer technologies such as DBS threatened even greater viewer fractionalization. Although some program prices had begun to drop, most stations still carried contracts at high rates. The FCC's schedule for conversion to HDTV demanded new expenditures that likely would not produce bigger audiences. Some owners looked to the 1992 Cable Act's provision allowing stations to seek payment from cable systems for carrying their programs as a possible new source of revenue (see Section 13.8). Most observers, however, saw this measure as offering little if any relief, at least in the near term. And affiliates continued to do battle with their networks over compensation levels.

Unable to increase revenues, most stations tried to maintain profit levels by reducing costs. Personnel cutbacks became common. Total broadcast employment dropped by more than 11 percent between 1987 and 1991. Many of these cuts were in news. The CBS station in Knoxville, Tennessee, for example, dropped its late-night newscasts entirely in 1991.

Still, as in all of life, everything is relative. As the industry publication *Broadcasting* editorialized:

> The news pages of this journal last week made much of the fact that operating profit margins in over-the-air television continue to spiral downward. And, more significantly, that they're unlikely ever to spiral upward again to match the halcyon days. True, but hardly the end of the world. The fact is that television's operating margins remain several lengths ahead of most business ventures. Many broadcast groups are still in the 30-percent-plus territory, which is a fabulous place to be, and those in the 20-percent-plus range have reason to rejoice. They could be in almost any other business and be lucky to make eight percent in a good year. . . .
>
> The problem for broadcasters is that many still remember [when times were better], and now find it hard not to think the sky is falling when business is merely magnificent. (*Broadcasting*, 7 September 1992: 86)

Cable Networks

Just as the 1980s could be characterized as the decade of television network decline, so could the 1990s be the decade of decline—or at least levelling off—of cable.

As cable systems expanded their channel capacity, more and more program services arrived to fill them. Some already in operation began to multiplex their programming, offering it on not one but three channels. But because most viewers who could subscribe to cable—and who chose to do so—had already signed on by the 1990s, more channels and more cable networks meant greater fractionalizing of an essentially finite audience. Like their broadcast counterparts, cable networks experienced escalating program costs. Also, added services usually mean higher costs to subscribers who already feel they are being overcharged.

Between 1988 and 1991 some cable networks (USA and Lifetime, for example) showed increases in their prime-time ratings, others (HBO, Showtime, and MTV) showed declines, while still others (TBS and ESPN) remained flat. At times, cable programs outranked broadcast network offerings *in cable homes*. For example, throughout the 1990–1991 broadcast season, HBO outperformed ABC, CBS, and NBC on Saturday nights in those homes that subscribed to its service. Still, HBO loses about 850,000 subscribers every year and must find new ones just to stay even.

Cable network financial successes vary. MTV, VH-1, and The Movie Channel together posted 1991 profits of $88 million, The Family Channel about $43 million, and Showtime $42 million; Comedy Central, however, lost about $50 million. Turner Broadcasting's news division (CNN and CNN Headline) posted profits of about $170 million and its entertainment division (TBS and TNT), about $160 million; overall corporate profits totaled nearly $300 million.

New competition came in such forms as Court TV, the Sci-Fi Channel, and The Cartoon Channel. Other services merged (HBO's The Comedy Channel and MTV's HA! combined to become Comedy Central) or bought out rivals (CNBC acquired FNN). Still others couldn't survive: in 1987 Group W folded its Home Theater Network, one of the oldest cable services but one with only about 325,000 subscribers (it had featured only movies rated G or PG); The *Christian Science Monitor*'s Monitor Channel, launched in 1991 at an initial outlay of $250 million, operated for about a year, at a cost of $4 million a month, and finally shut down in 1992—at an additional expense of about $45 million.

As cable program services retrenched, some laid off employees. Others hoped to increase their share of the advertising pie—although, again, more channels and more networks mean more and tinier slices of that pie. Still others turned to such alternative revenue sources as Turner's Airport Channel.

Cable Systems

Although many cable systems operate at a profit, the largest multiple-system owners do not—at least on paper. Repayment of huge debts incurred to buy additional systems has resulted in ongoing MSO losses. TCI, the nation's largest MSO, has not turned a profit since 1988; in 1991 it posted a loss of more than $100 million. Time Warner, operator of American Television & Communications (ATC), the second largest, lost almost as much. In fact, of the ten highest-revenue-producing MSOs, only one—Times Mirror—showed a profit ($82 million, down 55 percent from 1990). Some (but not all) operators actually plan this unprofitability, recognizing that it is necessary in the short term in order to permit acquisitions and upgrading of systems for the long term. They remain content with technical losses on their financial statements as long as they have a positive cash flow and thus can pay their bills as they come due.

The vast majority of cable subscribers are served by systems whose typically 15-year franchises were awarded between 1979 and 1982. That means they expire between 1994 and 1997. Cable's lengthy history of poor technical performance and arrogant disregard of subscriber complaints has already led to a few franchise-renewal denials, although the 1992 Cable Act makes such results increasingly unlikely. Losing an initial franchise bid in a major market 15 years ago might have cost a company $1 million or so; losing an operating system could mean losses of ten times that amount or more. In some cases, municipalities have elected to operate their local cable systems themselves as a means of generating revenue. By the 1990s about 100 cities were doing exactly that. In other cases, municipalities approved *overbuilds*, permitting a second company to compete with the one already in place. Fewer than 100 such operations exist today, but the outlook is sufficiently rosy that overbuilders have formed their own professional association, the Competitive Cable Association. And still unclear is the effect of the 1992 Cable Act re-regulating cable system pricing and operations (see Section 13.8).

Exhibit 7.h ●●●●●● ●●●●●●●●●●● ●

Broadcast Station Revenue, Expense, and Profit

	Radio				Television	
	Daytime AM	Full-time AM	AM/FM Combo	FM	Affiliate	Independent
(dollar amounts in thousands) **Revenue**						
Total net revenue	$155	$778	$1,260	$1,262	$14,779	$15,084
Percentage derived from:						
Network compensation	0.9	1.9	1.5	1.5	4.2	0.9
National/ regional sales	11.0	21.4	21.4	22.6	44.5	46.4
Local sales	88.1	76.7	77.0	75.9	51.3	52.7
Expenses						
Total	$182	$773	$1,237	$1,288	$12,161	$14,226
Percentage spent on:						
Engineering	4.9	4.2	4.3	3.6	7.7	5.5
Program & production	23.6	22.7	21.4	19.7	24.7	51.5
News	5.4	9.4	4.2	2.3	20.3	5.3
Sales	17.1	17.9	20.0	20.2	8.6	8.3
Advertising & promotion	3.7	7.0	7.8	11.0	4.2	4.8
General & administrative	45.3	38.7	42.2	43.3	34.6	24.7

Cable systems face other attacks as well. Owners have long feared the effect of potential competition from telephone companies. Although the Cable Act of 1984 prohibits telephone companies (telcos) from owning co-located cable systems, the FCC in 1992 allowed them to introduce a "video dialtone service" (see Section 14.5), a move some observers saw as only the first step toward increased telco involvement in the cable industry. A second and potentially even more important step came early in 1993 when

	Radio				Television	
	Daytime AM	**Full-time AM**	**AM/FM Combo**	**FM**	**Affiliate**	**Independent**
(dollar amounts in thousands) Pretax Profit/ (Loss)	($27)	$5	$23	($26)	$2,618	$858
Profit margin (Profit expressed as a percentage of net revenue)	(17.4)	0.6	1.8	(2.1)	17.7	5.7

These data represent *averages* for stations operating in 1991. Many stations, of course, earned profits much higher than the average, and others suffered even greater losses.

On average, radio stations that do show a profit have very low profit margins. Although radio services allocate expenses pretty much alike, disparities in the news category occur because AMs, especially full-time AM stations, offer more news than do FMs. FMs, on the other hand, devote more resources to promotion.

Although average net revenues at independent TV stations exceeded those at network affiliates, so did expenses. Affiliates spend more on news (because they do more of it), while independents spend more on entertainment programming (because they must buy it, rather than receive much of it free from a network). As a result, independents produced lower average profits and profit margins.

Sources: Based on data in National Association of Broadcasters, *Radio Financial Report* and *Television Financial Report* (Washington, DC, 1992). Reprinted with permission.

Southwestern Bell announced it would acquire two cable systems in the Washington, D.C. area. DBS, whose future remains somewhat clouded, also stood ready to challenge cable-system dominance. And the home video industry already was persuading homeowners to watch recent movies on cassette, rather than standard fare on television.

Cable operators have reacted in many ways. They, too, have cut their payrolls. They have redoubled their efforts to attract advertisers. They have

Exhibit 7.i •••••••••••••••••

Broadcast Station Profit by Revenue and Market Size

Radio	
Station Revenue	**Average Pretax Profit/(Loss)**
More than $17 million	$6,968,684
$10 million to $13 million	$1,866,740
$6 million to $7 million	$754,238
$2.5 million to $3 million	($104,157)
$900,000 to $1 million	($204,805)
Television	
ADI Market Rank	**Average Pretax Profit (Loss)**
1–10	$13,924,986
31–40	$1,089,759
61–70	$790,259
111–120	($323,553)
131–150	($692,183)

Typically, though not universally, as market size (and, hence, revenue) goes down, so does the average annual profit for radio and television stations.

Sources: National Association of Broadcasters, *Radio Financial Report* and *Television Financial Report* (Washington, D.C., 1992). Reprinted with permission.

expanded their channel capacity—in hopes of gaining new subscribers and holding existing ones—and have increased their pay-per-view offerings. New technologies offer the promise of interactive cable with a multitude of services, including video-on-demand. And—getting back to basics—many have begun to treat their customers better.

Radio Networks

Through 1991 radio networks had largely escaped the profit declines experienced by other segments of the electronic media industry. Each year since 1982, on the average, they had posted at least modest profit increases. In 1991 ABC Radio Networks earned a profit of $38.9 million, Westwood One nearly $9 million, and CBS half a million dollars.

By 1992, however, radio network revenues had begun to drop. These networks, too, tightened their belts by watching costs and reducing staff sizes. Westwood One, for example, which reported a $24 million loss in 1992, laid off nearly 20 percent of the news personnel at its NBC Radio Network and Mutual Broadcasting System.

Radio Stations

More than half of all radio stations in the United States operate at a loss. Exhibit 7.h shows that in 1991, as a group, only full-time AM stations and AM/FM combinations showed a profit. Even they had very low profit margins. Nearly 300 radio stations have "gone dark" (closed down), more than half of them in 1991 alone. Especially dramatic evidence of radio's declining value came in 1990 when MTV offered a Georgia AM station as first prize in one of its promotional contests.

As shown in Exhibit 7.i, stations in large cities generally do well. Those in the largest markets averaged a 28 percent profit margin in 1991; those in the very smallest markets averaged a profit margin of *minus* 125 percent. Also, group owners tend to fare better than individuals. In 1991, for example, CBS earned nearly $30 million from its radio stations, ABC nearly $35 million. Overall, about 50 group owners produce about half of all radio station revenue. In what some observers saw as a possible boost for radio, the FCC in 1992 revised its ownership rules to encourage group buying (see Section 14.5).

The overall outlook for traditional radio remains gloomy. More and more cable systems offer multiple, commercial-free, CD-quality audio channels. And digital audio broadcasting (DAB) looms on the horizon as a potentially lethal competitor. When the FCC allocated spectrum space for the service in October 1992, one company, Satellite CD Radio, stood ready to launch an operation that would offer listeners—on a subscription basis—30 channels of DAB music. Two months later a second company, Digital Satellite Broadcasting Corp., announced plans for a 500-channel system that would provide national and regional as well as specific-market programming. By early 1993 the total number of organizations proposing to offer DAB had jumped to six.

Influences on Profit and Ownership

As mentioned above and as indicated in Exhibit 7.i, profitability usually depends on market size. The larger the market, generally speaking, the higher the sales revenue and, most likely, the greater the profits.

Also, the larger the organization, the more probable is its ability to achieve greater profits than those of smaller companies. A business improves profits by increasing revenue and/or by reducing expenses. Group owners and MSOs often achieve savings through bulk purchases of equipment, supplies, and programs, and by sharing employees and ideas.

Broadcasters, cable networks, and cable systems also benefit from selling intangibles—air time and subscriptions. Expenses do not increase in step with sales. For example, if an appliance dealer buys a television set for $500 and sells it for $750, a $250 profit results. Selling a second set yields another $250 profit. For every $750 in sales, the dealer must spend $500 in order to make the $250 profit. By contrast, if it costs a television station $500 to run one episode of *Three's Company*, and if one 30-second commercial within the program sells for $750, the broadcaster makes a $250 profit. But a second spot sold at the same price does not incur a second expense; the cost of the program has already been accounted for, so the entire $750 in revenue counts as profit. A third $750 sale again counts as profit. And so on. Similarly, once a system has laid its cable along a city street, it costs little more to connect and serve all the homes on that street than it would for just one. These somewhat simplistic explanations do not, of course, account for the many expenses other than direct costs, such as overhead and sales charges. But they do illustrate the advantage most electronic media have over businesses that incur substantial additional costs with each sale.

Even unprofitable media may continue to operate, because many so-called losses exist only on paper. Corporations pay income taxes on profits, not on revenues. Owners often avoid or minimize taxes by keeping profits low through the use of "creative" (though legal) accounting· procedures, while at the same time maintaining a positive cash flow. Also, failing properties attract investors, for three related reasons: first, owners have faith that they can turn the operation into a money machine, if only they can find the right formula. Second, owners who wait long enough *may* eventually realize a profit by selling to someone else. Finally, media ownership satisfies an owner's ego by conferring an aura of glamour and community prestige.

• • • • • • • •

7.10 Bottom-Line Broadcasting

Even from the public-interest standpoint, stations, cable systems, and networks *need* to earn profits, for when they operate at a loss, their public-service programs tend to suffer. And lowering of standards can be contagious. Rivals tend to reciprocate by lowering their standards in order to compete.

But obsessive concern for profitability has its dangers, too. Federal deregulation and permissive interpretation of antitrust laws have encouraged media acquisitions, mergers, takeovers, consolidations, and vertical integration. These transactions focus so single-mindedly on profit that they produce what has been referred to as the *bottom-line mentality*—executive preoccupation with profit-and-loss statements to the exclusion of all else.

Cable television, which is not explicitly required to operate in the public interest, has made little effort to modify its profit-driven goals (C-SPAN and "Cable in the Classroom" being notable exceptions). And broadcasting, which operates under the Communications Act's public-interest mandate, has fallen increasingly under the control of conglomerate officials with no broadcasting background.

Trafficking in Stations

The FCC designed its antitrafficking rule to prevent station trading at the expense of public service. It long required the holder of a broadcast station license to keep it for a minimum of three years (the then license period) before requesting its transferral to a buyer. Deletion of this rule in 1982 facilitated entry into and quick exit from the broadcast business whenever profit taking dictated.

First-time broadcast buyers began to specialize in *leveraged buyouts* of television stations, transactions that involve buying up stock to gain controlling interest in the properties. To do so, they incur huge debts that have to be repaid out of station profits, leaving little money for quality programming. Increasingly, stations turned to easy sources of income—program-length commercials, paid religion, titillating shows exploiting sex and violence, tabloid pseudo-news shows, and the like. Some even compromised the content of their evening newscasts by including such features as a cooking segment sponsored by a local supermarket.

Network Changes

Nor were the mighty networks immune. Beginning in the mid-1980s, the once all-powerful networks experienced a decline. Cable displaced over-the-air affiliates as the principal distributor of television programming. The Fox network presented added competition for the national broadcast audience. Program costs soared, exacerbated by labor union problems. Network commercial rates rose rapidly in response to rising costs, driving advertisers to seek alternative vehicles.

At the same time, new management took over at ABC, CBS, and NBC (see Section 3.6). Operating budget cutbacks caused the layoff of thousands of employees and the early retirement of others. This new austerity took its heaviest public-service toll in network news. News division budgets, roughly $85 million for each network in 1980, had grown to $300 million by 1986. This $900 million, three-network total loomed especially large when viewed in light of news division revenues of only $830 million.

At House of Representatives hearings, Congressmen Dennis Eckart of Ohio and John Bryant of Texas asserted that "the wave of cutbacks and layoffs

Exhibit 7.j •••••••••••••••

Media Ethics
(or is that an oxymoron?)

"The most pressing ethical issue facing many media executives is the continuing conflict between making money and serving the public." That was the dilemma most often cited by the 144 readers who responded to a business ethics survey conducted by *Electronic Media*, an industry magazine. Although many of the responses prove fascinating, the disappointingly low response rate puts into question the generalizability of the results.

Respondents included television and radio general managers, multiple-cable-system operators, sales managers, news directors and reporters, syndication sales executives, and television program directors.

Some specifics:

- Ninety-eight percent agreed with the statement that "Generally speaking, good ethics is good business," but 65 percent said they considered some generally accepted practices in their field of business to be unethical.
- Thirty-two percent felt that ethical standards in the television business world were lower than they had been ten years earlier.
- Eighty-seven percent believed that most people they knew would be willing to "bend the rules" to achieve success in business so long as their actions hurt no one.
- Sixty-nine percent considered it all right to do a certain amount of "hypoing" during rating periods.
- Seventy-three percent expressed belief in the honesty of corporate executives.
- Thirty-four percent said an employee should be fired for filing an expense account with $10 of falsified expenses; and 36 percent admitted they had done exactly that.

Source: *Electronic Media*, 29 Feb. 1988, p. 1. © 1989 Crain Communication, Inc. Reprinted with permission.

---

that is sweeping all three networks is alarming. . . . The American people deserve to know what the bottom line is where their news programming is concerned." Eckart said, "In this rush for profits, the public interest has been trampled on." Bryant added, "The root of my concern is that these corporate takeovers have made America's principal source of information the subject of giant corporate poker games" (*Broadcasting*, 16 March 1987: 39).

Laurence Tisch, who took over as president and chief executive officer of CBS in January 1987, had said, "I can guarantee you that the one area I will never interfere with is the delivery of news" (Vitale, 1988). He soon thereafter cut the news division's budget by $30 million and fired more than 200 employees, including such veteran reporters as Ike Pappas and Fred Graham. Despite his efforts, the first quarter of 1987 became the first in the network's modern history to record a loss.

Making an unprecedented public criticism of his own network, *CBS Evening News* anchor and managing editor Dan Rather wrote a piece for the *New York Times* entitled "From Murrow to Mediocrity?"* Rather pointed out that Tisch "told us when he arrived that he wanted us to be the best. We want nothing more than to fulfill that mandate. Ironically, he has now made the task seem something between difficult and impossible." He added,

News is a business, but it is also a public trust. . . . We have been asked to cut costs and work more efficiently and we have accepted that challenge. What we cannot accept is the notion that the bottom line counts more than meeting our responsibilities to the public. Anyone who says network news cannot be profitable doesn't know what he is talking about. But anyone

*Although the essay carried Rather's by-line, it was actually written by CBS's political producer, Richard Cohen.

who says it must *always* make money is misguided and irresponsible." (Rather, 1987)

Four years later, as network belt-tightening continued, Rather's CBS colleague, Mike Wallace, observed that Tisch had disappointed network veterans, "probably mostly by the manner in which it was done. It was done too coolly." Wallace continued,

When you've worked in an outfit 25 to 35 years and you've seen guys actually lay their lives on the line in the course of doing their job and they are tossed aside. You are led to believe that "thus far and no further will be these cuts" and suddenly it's a lot further. You begin to feel a sense of disappointment and disillusionment. (Bier, 1991)

• • • • • • • •

Summary

7.1   Broadcasting achieved relatively rapid success as an advertising medium because of its unique psychological advantages, combined with great flexibility in serving local, regional, and national advertisers. The effectiveness of broadcast advertising is offset for some users by its costs, by often reaching more people than desired, and by limits on commercial length and content.

7.2   Commercial practice has shifted from sponsorship to insertion of spots within and between programs over which advertisers have no direct control. A station's traffic department schedules commercials, as well as promotional and public-service announcements.

7.3   Compared to broadcasting, cable receives relatively little advertising revenue. Advertisers place their commercials on individual cable systems, cable interconnections, cable networks, and superstations. Cable enjoys many of television's advantages, but local systems suffer from the absence of audience research comparable to broadcast rating reports.

7.4   Advertising rates reflect the normal advertiser practice of buying time only as a means of gaining access to audiences. Because audiences change with programs and services as well as with times of day and days of the year, prices for spots tend to change accordingly.

7.5   Sales representatives and (for affiliates) network sales organizations supplement broadcast and cable sales departments in reaching some advertising clients. Advertising agencies plan most large advertising campaigns and select media outlets. Media provide proof of performance through their daily program logs, but agencies also hire specialized firms to check the fulfillment of advertising contracts.

7.6   No laws limit the amount of commercial time in and between programs, except those designed for children. Formal industry guidelines fell with the NAB codes, so that today only individual station and network standards and market pressures limit most advertising time. Standards of taste continue to evolve with changes in competition and the attitudes of society. The Federal Trade Commission has authority over deceptive advertising practices, although there has been little enforcement in recent years. Offenses that can jeopardize station licenses include network clipping, double billing, plugola, and payola.

7.7   Cable systems rely for revenue more on subscription fees than on advertising. Most make a monthly charge for basic service (some require an additional charge for expanded basic) and charge extra for pay or premium channels. Many also receive income from pay-per-view programs as well as audio services.

7.8   Other services such as MMDS and SMATV also depend on subscriber revenue. Some companies look to ancillary sources of income such as "place-based" program distribution and secondary use of their signals. Local production, other than news, rarely produces a profit.

7.9   Most segments of the American broadcasting and cable industries are structured to make a profit. The major television networks no longer enjoy the healthy profits they once did. Most television and many radio stations show profits, although at lower levels than in earlier years; some operate at a loss. While many individual cable systems show a profit, the largest multiple-system owners, on a strict accounting basis, operate at a loss. Many established cable program services have improved their financial performance; newcomers often struggle to survive.

7.10 As a result of increasing competition, rising costs, and dwindling revenue, some broadcasters operate more in the interest of profit than that of the public.

Chapter 8

Noncommercial Services

This book deals primarily with commercial electronic media because their news and entertainment programs are of primary audience and advertiser interest as well as policy concern. But as in most other countries, American commercial broadcasting's overwhelming emphasis on mass entertainment and profit making cannot fully meet all listener needs or perform the many cultural, educational, and informational roles that electronic media might—some say should—play. So over the years, alternative services have developed to fill the gap. In most countries, in fact, noncommercial or public service radio *preceded* creation of commercial broadcast services. Britain's BBC, for example, did not face commercial television competition until 1955 (Section 15.2).

Noncommercial broadcasting, programmed by motives other than profit, evolved alongside commercial broadcasting beginning in the 1920s. But it has always suffered from tiny audiences and budgets as well as from substantial disagreement about its several proper roles within a largely commercial system. More competition for noncommercial audiences and financial support has developed recently:

several specialized cable networks now also cater to cultural and educational interests.

8.1 Development

Noncommercial broadcasting began as a service narrowly confined to education and instruction. Indeed, the Federal Communications Commission still refers to *noncommercial educational* licensees, even though the 1934 Communications Act was amended by a *Public* Broadcasting Act of 1967, denoting an aim broader than "education" alone.

Rise of Educational Radio

Several colleges experimented with wireless telegraphy before World War I (see Exhibit 8.a for one example). When license applications boomed in the 1920s, other schools and religious institutions joined in the rush. They pursued varied goals: classroom and in-home education, school or church

Exhibit 8.a •••••• •••••••••

WHA—Noncommercial Pioneer

Radio station WHA at the University of Wisconsin, Madison, exemplifies how educational stations began and slowly grew. All over the Midwest, public and private universities saw a similar pattern of technical tinkering leading to an educational outlet that helped expand the college to new audiences.

Members of the University of Wisconsin physics department (shown on the left in this historical painting) had begun radio experiments as early as 1902, had built an operating wireless telegraphy transmitter by 1909, and had progressed to a licensed (though still-experimental) wireless telegraphy station, 9XM, in 1915. A year later, the station was licensed to the university and used 5,000 watts to provide regularly scheduled telegraphic (code, not voice) weather reports. During World War I, 9XM—unlike most other stations—stayed on the air to help train personnel for the U.S. Navy. After the war, 9XM provided both code and voice signals for weather purposes.

Although records are unclear, it appears that January 3, 1921, saw the start of regularly scheduled voice transmission of weather and farm market reports, with other broadcasts aired on a sporadic basis. A year later, still-experimental 9XM became regularly licensed WHA, using 500 watts of power and broadcasting about an hour a day. In academic year 1921–1922 initial faculty resistance to radio (it was "demeaning") faded as the first lectures were broadcast.

Source: Photo courtesy of Wisconsin Public Radio, Madison, WI.

The real educational role of the station began in 1931 with the appointment of H. B. McCarty (who continued to run the operation into the 1960s) and his expanded programming for schools—the "Wisconsin School of the Air." By 1933 WHA was broadcasting 53 hours a week, double the previous year's total. In 1934 it moved into a renovated heating plant, re-dubbed "Radio Hall" and sporting a Native American motif—home to the station for the next 40 years (including nearly a decade during which one of your co-authors worked there). By 1940, broadcasting nearly 60 hours a week, the station offered 13 programs weekly for School of the Air, 10 for College of the Air, and nearly 30 hours a week of music.

After World War II, WHA was the center of an expanding statewide broadcast operation. From 1947 to 1952 Wisconsin built a network of eight FM stations to provide statewide service (WHA fed all programming to those transmitters) and added WHA-TV in early 1954. Early in the 1970s the combined radio-television operation moved into Vilas Hall on the Madison campus. In 1977 the radio stations, now WHA and WERN-FM, split their programs to accommodate talk and music respectively, similar to what was happening in commercial radio. In the late 1980s the pattern was modified again—adding substantial news to FM which drew by far the greatest number of listeners. WERN now "serves a larger share of its market's radio listeners than any public radio station in America" (Giovannoni, 1991: 29).

promotion, fund raising, cultural betterment, voter awareness, and so on. Most pioneer stations operated on a financial shoestring and for only a few hours a week.

With broadcasting's advertising revenue developing by the late 1920s, commercial station owners began to seek AM frequencies used by educational licensees—many of whom then (as now) lacked funding to operate. Some schools surrendered their licenses in return for promises of educational airtime on commercial stations—promises that faded with increasing advertising value of that airtime. Educational stations that held on found themselves confined to low power, inconvenient hours (often daytime only, useless for adult-education efforts), and constantly changing frequency assignments. A majority simply gave up the struggle and left the air. In 1927 there were still 98 noncommercial stations operating; by Depression-year 1933 there were only 43; and by 1945 the number had fallen to about 25.

An observer explained the problem—a weakness of the system that persisted four decades later: "Commercial stations made money, convertible into political power; educational stations cost money. If their programming was not popular enough to attract sizable audiences, they were hard to justify politically" (Blakely, 1979: 55).

The failure of most educational institutions to defend their licenses against commercial interests confirmed what critics argued from the start: some AM frequencies should have been reserved exclusively for educational use at the outset of broadcast regulation. Educational interests could not be expected to compete for radio channels with commercial powers in an open market.

FM Channel Reservations

Faced with mounting evidence that commercial stations devoted far too little time to meeting educational needs, the FCC finally accepted the channel reservation principle when it first authorized FM service in 1941, reserving the five lowest channels for noncommercial use. In 1945 the Commission set aside 88 to 92 MHz—the lowest 20 of the 100 channels on FM's new higher band—for educational use. Disappointed by inadequate use of these reserved channels, the FCC liberalized its rules in 1948, allowing noncommercial outlets to operate at less expense—on power as low as 10 watts—thereby creating a problem for themselves later on (see footnote on p. 275).

With little program exchange and no network, educational FM stations and about 25 AM educational survivors depended almost totally on local resources. A research team that studied educational radio stations in 1971–1972 found that "no two stations are alike, and there are almost no models at which to point" (Robertson and Yokom, 1973: 115).

TV Channel Reservations

During the 1948–1952 television freeze (detailed at Section 2.5), commercial interests made a concerted effort to block proposed educational television channel reservations. The Joint Committee on Educational Television (JCET) spearheaded a counter-lobbying effort, asking the FCC not to end the freeze without adopting a noncommercial television channel reservation scheme. Commercial proponents argued—with some reason—that reserved channels would go unused while educators tried to get together funds to put stations on the air, whereas commercial firms stood ready to build stations as soon as the freeze ended. Once again, both operating and potential commercial licensees promised free time on the air for educational programs—just as they had in the 1930s with AM radio.

When the FCC ended its freeze with 1952's *Sixth Report and Order*, it reserved 242 educational television (ETV) channel allotments—80 VHF and 162 UHF—initially for only a limited time: "long enough to give . . . reasonable opportunity . . . [but] not so long that the frequencies remain unused for excessively long periods of time" (Blakely, 1979: 89). Over the years, however, the FCC made the reservations permanent and increased their number—today there are about 600 channels set aside, about 200 of which still lack operating stations.

In the decade from the end of the freeze to passage of initial federal funding for noncommercial

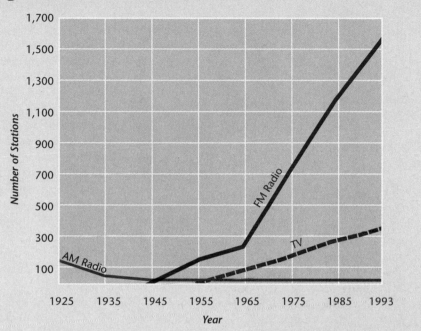

Exhibit 8.b •••••••••••••••

Growth in Number of Noncommercial Broadcasting Stations (1925–1993)

After a steady decline in the number of educational AM stations to 1945, noncommercial radio growth moved to the new FM service and eventually to television. Only a small proportion of FM stations qualify for affiliation with NPR—about 170 in 1975, and about 450 in 1992. Data refer to January 1 of each year. The figures for AM noncommercial stations are estimated because there is no official count of such operations.

Source: Data from FCC.

stations in 1962, the service grew very slowly despite concern over possible loss of reservations (see Exhibit 8.b). The few operational stations depended largely on local production and filmed programs, and programmed about half as many hours as commercial stations. After 1959 a program cooperative, National Educational Television (NET), provided a few hours a week of shared programs, sent to stations by mail in what was called the "bicycle network."

Philosophical Conflict

During the fight to obtain noncommercial channel reservations, noncommercial television grew larger and more diversified. Traditional educational radio leaders, who had kept faith over many lean years, now found themselves jostled aside by the newly saved—the national educational establishment, politicians, the Washington bureaucracy, and activist citizen groups.

Out of this matrix of forces emerged conflicting views on what form a noncommercial service should take. One group took "educational television" to imply a broadly inclusive cultural and information service; another defined it more narrowly as a new and improved audiovisual device important to schools. Some favored a strong national network and audience building, following the model of commercial broadcasting. Others stressed localism and service for specialized audiences. Some wanted high culture and intellectual stimulation; others wanted to emphasize programs of interest to ethnic minorities, children, and the poor.

As one expert who would help draft landmark 1967 legislation put it later, "It was hardly a *system* we were seeking to nurture at all, but rather a variety of broadcasting arrangements bearing a common name and yet widely differing in structure, financing, concept of role and degree of independence" (Cater, 1972: 10; emphasis added). The issue of whether national organizations or local stations should play the dominant role added to the confusion.

1967 Carnegie Study

Watershed events in noncommercial broadcasting came in 1967 with the report of the Carnegie Commission on Educational Television (CCET) and resulting legislation. Made up of top-level representatives from higher education, media, business, politics, and the arts, the privately funded commission proposed that Congress establish a "corporation for public television." The Commission chose the word *public* rather than educational to disassociate itself from what many regarded as a "somber and static image" projected by existing ETV services. It also felt that *public* would separate instructional classroom television from the broader noncommercial service intended for general viewing that Carnegie

sought. The basic structure advocated in the 1967 Carnegie report has survived, though with turf battles and changes in detail along the way, for more than a quarter-century.

Corporation for Public Broadcasting

Following Carnegie's recommendations, Congress amended the Communications Act with the Public Broadcasting Act of 1967 (*broadcasting* because Congress added public radio at the last minute), creating the Corporation for Public Broadcasting (CPB). Carnegie had recommended that the president of the United States appoint only half the CPB board (the board would then select the other half); but because Congress has power to approve such appointments, it gave all the appointive power to the president. For the same reason, Congress—retaining close control—ignored the long-term financial-support ideas recommended by the Carnegie report. These two departures from the Carnegie plan left CPB at the mercy of political pressures, sometimes with unfortunate consequences for CPB impartiality (see Exhibit 8.c).

The 1967 act gave CPB the right to dispense federal funds to stations and program producers, but not to own or operate stations or network interconnections. The ban on operation of facilities was in part an attempt to separate funding from program decisions. The act detailed the corporation's role to include the following (among a list of activities):

- facilitating "full development of educational broadcasting in which programs of high quality, *obtained from diverse sources, will be made available to . . stations with strict adherence to objectivity and balance* in all programs or series of programs of a controversial nature," and
- carrying out its work "in ways that will most effectively *assure the maximum freedom . . . from interference with or control of program content* or other activities" (47 US 396[g][1][A, D]; emphasis added).

Exhibit 8.c •••••• •••••••••••

Political Manipulation of CPB

Incidents during three conservative presidential administrations provide textbook illustrations of the difficulty of insulating a broadcast service from politics when it depends on government for substantial economic support. Section 398 of the Communications Act, added by the 1967 public broadcasting law, tries to prevent political influence by expressly forbidding any "direction, supervision, or control" over noncommercial broadcasting by officials of the U.S. government. This legal detail did not stop the Nixon administration in the 1970s nor the Reagan and Bush administrations a decade later from manipulating CPB for their own ends.

When the Public Broadcasting Service (PBS) network began beefing up its news and public-affairs programming around 1970 by hiring ex-commercial-network personnel, the White House became concerned. Regarding the PBS network as far too liberal, the administration objected to public television's concern with national affairs when, according to the administration's interpretation, it should be focusing on *local* needs. This view struck a chord with some of the station managers, who were already resentful of the increasing centralization of program decision-making by PBS and CPB. In 1973, the administration sent a more direct message when President Nixon vetoed a two-year funding measure for CPB. Several board members —ironically, all presidential appointees—resigned in protest. Long-range federal funding legislation did not finally pass until 1975.

By 1981, when the Reagan administration took office, the CPB board, never high on the priority list of political appointees, had become fertile ground for political gamesmanship. Reagan appointed several hard-right conservatives to the CPB board. In 1986, the CPB president, Edward Pfister, resigned in a dispute with Reagan-appointed CPB chair, Sonia Landau, over a proposed trip to the Soviet Union to trade programming. Less than a year later, Pfister's replacement also left CPB, which had developed a reputation for constant political infighting. Another Reagan CPB appointee advocated making a content study to determine whether public television programming leaned too far to the left. Opponents of the research felt that its sponsors merely wanted to send a signal to public broadcasters that they should adopt a more conservative agenda. The study never materialized, but the legally mandated political impartiality of the CPB had been seriously undermined.

That was evident during Bush's term (1989–1993), when CPB found itself under the combined pressure of an administration trying to trim federal funding and a Congress reviewing specific broadcasts while considering funding legislation. Late in 1991 funding for CPB for 1994–1996 was delayed for months in a controversy over both the amount of money proposed and *P.O.V. (Point of View)*, a documentary series that had presented "Tongues Untied," about gay black life (1991), and "Color Adjustment," about the role of blacks on television (1992); both aired on PBS and partially funded by the National Endowment for the Arts. In the end, Congress did pass a record authorization for the three-year period, and President Bush, in the midst of an election campaign, signed it. But all sides agreed that the constant tension over funding and programming was anything but over.

8.2 Networks

Changes in public broadcasting after 1967 continued the earlier struggle for power among several national networking organizations, and between them and local station operators. Disagreements concerned funding and who would control programming on emerging public networks.

Public Broadcasting Service

After a good deal of political wrangling arising from fears that a national television network might unduly centralize authority over station program selection and scheduling, CPB launched a national television network. Confusingly dubbed the Public Broadcasting (instead of "Television") Service (PBS), it began operating in 1970 with a budget of $7 million, serving 128 stations connected by telephone company facilities. Relationships between PBS and its member stations—as program users and, in some cases, program producers—underwent constant upheaval as PBS struggled to establish its identity and to develop a working style.

Disagreement focused on whether PBS should set *national* programming policy. Carnegie had stressed network interconnection to build audiences but also the need to avoid the program centralization evident in commercial networks. Public broadcasting was to be an alternative to commercial stations by offering "a strong component of local and regional programming . . . [and] the opportunity and the means for local choice to be exercised upon the programs made available from central programming sources" (CCET, 1967: 33).

The Carnegie report failed to appreciate the impracticality of having a national network (PBS) provide a program smorgasbord from which affiliates would choose. A variety of divisive problems emerged in the early 1970s, but disagreement over what role PBS and CPB should play continued to be *the* critical issue—and there was little agreement on what that role was.

As a means of continuing service while the philosophical debate continued, PBS program selection from 1974 until 1990 occurred through a complicated mechanism called the *Station Program Cooperative* (SPC). SPC was praised for its democratic participation by member stations (whose executives actually voted for which programs they would carry and help finance). But it was also criticized for limiting program innovation, as stations nearly always 'voted and paid for programs successful in the past, rarely investing scarce dollars in new ideas—thus fostering continuation of "the safe, the cheap, and the known" (Reeves and Hoffer, 1976). The SPC mechanism selected and paid for about half of the PBS national schedule (PBS picked the rest), including such well-known staples as *Sesame Street*, *NOVA*, and *The MacNeil/Lehrer NewsHour*. Businesses and other sources underwrote remaining PBS programming (see Section 8.5).

Late in 1989, under pressure from Congress, which was concerned about SPC's decentralized and argument-ridden decision making, PBS stations concluded that the democratic SPC system had outlived its usefulness. They dissolved the SPC and centralized all programming decisions under one PBS officer—much like the traditional commercial network model.

PBS Operations

Though now more centralized, PBS still differs from commercial networks in that it produces no programs but, rather, distributes those produced by others. Since the end of the SPC, PBS's programming chief selects the network's prime-time schedule, contracting for programs with producing stations and others (see Section 8.5), and changing program line-ups as needed.

Member stations (affiliates) contract with PBS, agreeing to pay dues determined by their respective budget and market sizes. Rather than the network paying for use of their time (long the case with commercial television network affiliates), public stations pay PBS for programs—an arrangement closer to a cable system's relationship with the many cable networks, or to program syndication in broadcasting.

In 1993 PBS served 345 stations—virtually all public television stations on the air. Its 35-member board consisted of professional station managers and members of the general public drawn from station boards. PBS staff totaled about 300 in Alexandria, Virginia (near Washington, D.C.), New York, and Los Angeles, many working on the network's satellite distribution system.

Satellite Interconnection

PBS pioneered the use of satellites for network relays. Using satellites instead of AT&T's wire and microwave facilities for relaying public television programs was first proposed by the Ford Foundation in 1966. A decade later, with government funding support, PBS announced a plan to interconnect its member stations by means of transponders on a domestic communications satellite. Benefits claimed for the system included cost savings, better-quality reception, ability to relay signals both east and west (most programs, commercial or non-commercial, had been sent from New York westward) as well as variously within given regions, and transmission of several signals at a time to allow stations to choose among more program options. Stations each had to contribute about $25,000 (a hefty sum for most) toward the cost of Earth stations. During 1978 public television stations disconnected themselves from terrestrial links and began using satellite interconnection; indeed, PBS was the first national broadcast service to do so (even before most cable networks had begun operation).

Satellite Benefits

The satellite distribution system also greatly enhances the autonomy of PBS member stations. Largely freed from the time and schedule constraints of a single-feed network, they have greater control over what they receive and use by being able to pick among a greater number and variety of programs. Satellite facilities also have opened new

fund-raising possibilities through the lease of excess transponder capacity to other users.

PBS's relay system in the 1990s relies on 178 receive-only ground antennas owned by the stations. There are 20 ground stations that can uplink programs to the satellite as well as receive them. One uplink facility, near Washington, D.C., provides the main PBS feed; others serve regional networks from centers in Colorado, Nebraska, Florida, South Carolina, and Connecticut.

As the initial satellite system was scheduled to run out of the fuel necessary for orbital corrections in the early 1990s, PBS obtained congressional support ($150 million) to help purchase six replacement transponders (five of them in the higher Ku band) on a new satellite—AT&T's Telstar 401, to be launched in mid-1993. By 1992, however, it was clear the system would not be restricted to only six channels. Compression technology (see Section 5.7) promised as many as eight or ten channels per transponder, compared to the one per transponder on the old satellite system. PBS's plans for expanded satellite capacity include more programming, multiple feeds of existing programming, interactive channels, and high-definition service (see Section 5.9).

National Public Radio

Public radio provides an interesting contrast to television operations. In 1970 CPB set up National Public Radio (NPR) both to interconnect stations (like PBS) and to produce some programs (unlike PBS). As a second Carnegie Commission report noted in 1979, NPR

combines national production and distribution capability with political representation, in a way which many feel is unthinkable for television. In addition, the production activities of NPR are funded directly by CPB and are not, therefore, entirely controlled by the licensee. Unlike the situation in public television, the public radio stations have been quite willing to have national program production and distribution centralized and under the financial oversight of CPB. Public radio stations supported the creation of NPR from the beginning, and they retain control over it through its board. Sorely underfinanced, the stations have recognized the benefits of centralizing program functions. (CCFPB, 1979: 61)

The fact that NPR can pick and choose from among a large pool of potential members (affiliated stations) gives it more clout as a network than PBS. The latter admits virtually any noncommercial television station.

NPR provides its member stations—which do not have to carry any set amount of network programming—with about 22 percent of their daily schedules. NPR also coordinates satellite interconnection with 21 uplinks and more than 300 downlinks. Satellite distribution (the world's first satellite-delivered radio network) began in 1980 with four audio channels, which by 1988 had increased to 12 channels. As with the television system, NPR can now send out a variety of simultaneous programs, allowing member stations to pick and choose from among more material than before. NPR also represents its member stations in a lobbying capacity before Congress and the CPB as needed.

CPB radio program funds go directly to NPR member stations, which support the network by paying a flat fee and then subscribing to morning and afternoon news services, NPR's musical and cultural programs, and American Public Radio programs (see Section 8.7). More than 90 percent of member stations subscribe to both news services. Stations pay anywhere from $25,000 to more than $300,000 annually for NPR's program service, depending on their revenue.

· · · · · · · ·

8.3 Stations

Local stations form the heart of all public broadcasting—unlike their commercial counterparts, which are largely local outlets for national program flows. These stations vary enormously—not only in size and resources but also in goals and philosophy. Though all are considered "noncommercial educational" stations by the FCC, some flirt with commercialism and many play no formal educational role. We deal here first with television, then radio. Their main variation comes from different types of station ownership. Noncommercial stations are exempt from most ownership limitations that restrict commercial licensees.

Most noncommercial television stations are a part of the CPB/PBS system. These outlets are of four basic types defined by ownership:

- state or municipally controlled stations;
- college and university stations;
- public school system stations; and
- community stations.

These four ownership types, with their differing structures and program goals, lead to correspondingly different programming philosophies. School- and university-run stations, for example, tend to stress education and instruction, whereas community stations provide a broad mix of cultural, entertainment, and educational programs aimed at more general audiences (though they often provide instructional programming during school hours).

State and Municipal TV Stations and Networks

About 135 stations (some 40 percent of all public television stations) come under state or municipal control. Many operate as parts of state educational networks. Among such networks, usually one station located in the state capital originates most programming; the others serve, in effect, as repeaters. Alabama began what became a nine-station network in 1955 (and later got into serious trouble, as discussed at Section 13.5); and nearly a dozen other states soon followed its example. In some states (such as Pennsylvania), stations licensed to various local groups have formed informal networks.

Several of these state networks are technology leaders. Working with local telephone companies, the Mississippi Educational Network, for example, operates "Fibernet 2000," a fiber-optic web connecting stations, two universities, and four high schools for televised distance learning. The Mississippi Educational Television Authority offers more than 150 instructional television courses per year to all the state's schools, providing detailed teacher guides for most of them. The Nebraska network produces Japanese-language courses that can equal two full-year high school course credits, offered on a live, interactive basis by satellite. Iowa built a 3,000-mile fiber-optic state network with more than 100 origination sites between 1990 and 1993. Managed by Iowa Public Television, it connects eight public stations, state agencies, 26 colleges, 350 high schools, and 500 public libraries to allow interchange of video, voice, and data. And the South Carolina Educational Television Network, which pioneered the use of multiple channels, utilizes 6 now and will soon have 20 more operating on a two-way interactive system connecting educational, state, hospital, and police entities.

University TV Stations

Some 85 stations (25 percent of all public television facilities), belong to colleges or universities, most of them publicly supported. They usually have close ties to college curricula and often complement long-established college educational radio stations (see Exhibit 8.a). These stations, at one time staffed largely by students or interns, have in recent years become more professional in employment and program practices (to the degree that at some outlets, students complain about *lack* of access). University administrations usually give only general oversight, refraining from direct meddling in station operations. Respect for academic freedom tends to prevent politically inspired interference.*

Licensed to Howard University in Washington, D.C., WHMM is still the only public television

*A notable exception to this general practice occurred at the University of Houston in Texas when it scheduled a 1980 PBS program entitled "Death of a Princess," a documentary about the execution for adultery of a Saudi Arabian princess and her commoner lover. Fearing adverse oil industry reactions, the university's vice president for public information canceled a scheduled telecast of the program on the university station, countermanding station management. When viewers mounted a legal challenge to the decision, an appellate court upheld the university, finding no violation of viewers' First Amendment rights.

station that is black owned and operated. Despite a budget of only about $4 million a year, the station produces several daily and weekly public-service programs. Broadcasting majors at Howard work in a variety of positions and produce a weekly program of their own. Some 80 percent of them go on to positions in broadcasting.

School-System TV Stations

Stations operated by, or as auxiliaries of, local school systems or school boards constitute the smallest category of public television broadcasters—only nine stations, or just under 3 percent. These stations naturally focus on in-school instructional programs produced by and for the school system. As school-system budgets became tighter in the 1980s, several such stations left the air or were transferred to other licensees. Among city school systems operating public television stations are those of San Jose, Milwaukee, New York, and Newark.

Community TV Stations

Organizations made up of representatives from various community groups, such as schools, colleges, art and cultural organizations, and the like, control 125 public television stations—just over a third of all outlets, but including some of the larger and more important program-producing stations (discussed further at Section 8.5). These nonprofit operations usually combine support from CPB with foundation, business, and listener sources.

Among the best-known community stations, because they produce much of what appears on PBS, are WNET in New York, WETA in Washington, D.C., KQED in San Francisco, KCET in Los Angeles, and WGBH in Boston. In the early 1990s more than a quarter of all public television programming came from such major producer stations, of which the Boston outlet was in many ways the most successful (see Exhibit 8.d).

WQED, in Pittsburgh, is nationally recognized for having produced the long-running *Mister Rogers' Neighborhood* for children. Its outreach programs (building programs around ideas viewers can act on

Exhibit 8.d •••••• •••••••••

WGBH—PBS "Superstation"

WGBH-TV, Boston, perhaps best known of the Public Broadcasting Service member stations, produces about a third of PBS's prime-time schedule in the early 1990s. Its annual budget totals about $120 million a year—far above those of most other public television stations.

After four years of local fund raising, WGBH licensed to an educational foundation made up of Boston's many prestigious universities and public organizations, aired its first program in May 1955. The foundation had begun operations in 1951 with

Source: Photo by Eric Roth for WGBH, Boston. Logo courtesy WGBH.

an educational FM station. Drawing on Boston's many educational and cultural activities, WGBH quickly became a major program source for other stations.

It introduced Julia Child's *The French Chef*—one of the first nationally recognized public television series—in 1970. *Masterpiece Theatre*, one of PBS's most successful and longest-running series, comes from Britain, co-produced by WGBH (which selects the material and produced 20 years of opening and closing remarks by Alistair Cooke) and British independent television companies, and underwritten from the start by Mobil. WGBH produced a multipart television history of the Vietnam War and another on the rise of the computer and its impact on society. Other WGBH-produced or co-produced programs include *Evening at Pops, Mystery!* and *NOVA* (see Exhibit 8.k).

WGBH-TV has always been entrepreneurial in its quests for new funding. In late 1991 it opened the first of what became a chain of "Learningsmith" stores in partnership with a local book and video store owner. The stores sell books, games, and other items related to WGBH programming as well as station memberships. Similar outlets, tied to other public television stations, opened in other cities. Still, raising money locally remains difficult. In 1991 the station had to abandon its 15-year-old 10:00 P.M. local newscast for lack of local underwriting support.

WGBH is also active in utilizing changing technology. In the early 1990s, for example, it explored new ways of using closed captions (see Section 4.9) for foreign-language-speaking audiences, considered how best to cooperate with cable systems to meet educational and cultural program demand, and actively packaged PBS productions for in school use with a 200-person Special Telecommunications Services unit which by 1993 was working with videodiscs and exploring applications of CD-ROM technology.

to improve their lives and community) are also well known, as it likely has developed more of them than any other station. Of special interest in this city once dependent on steel industry employment is "The Job/Help Network," operated in cooperation with local agencies and businesses to help people find new employment opportunities. WETA in Washington and WNET in New York both produce many national news and public-affairs programs for PBS.

NPR Member Radio Stations

CPB decided to build its national noncommercial radio network—NPR—around a cadre of professionally competent, full-service stations (referred to as "CPB-qualified") so the national radio service could effectively reach more people. Such stations must meet prescribed minimum standards, among them FM power of at least 3,000 watts (in recent years, CPB has granted some support to smaller stations), at least one production studio and a separate control room, five or more full-time employees, a minimum operational schedule of 18 hours a day, and an operating budget of at least $150,000 per year. In 1992 about 450 outlets (all but 28 on the FM band)—*only a third of all noncommercial radio licensees*—qualified for CPB grants by meeting or exceeding those standards.

Many public radio stations are controlled by licensees also operating public television stations. CPB-qualified public radio licensees fall into the same categories—but not the same proportions—as public television stations:

- Universities and schools own about two-thirds of all NPR-member stations (including most AM pioneers and most early postwar educational FM outlets).
- Community groups own about 31 percent.
- States and municipalities control slightly more than 4 percent of stations—including WNYC, operated by the city of New York since 1924, and its parallel FM station, which began operation in 1941.

Non-NPR Stations

A much larger group of about 900 "have-not" noncommercial stations either do not qualify for NPR membership or do not wish to join the network. These stations provide local, sometimes quite limited, services—some at very low power.* Many operate as community outlets offering some of the most original programming on the air (described at Section 8.7). Others are religious stations—still deemed "noncommercial educational" by the FCC, but with a very specific program focus. As no organization represents this large and widely varied number of radio stations, there is little broadly descriptive information available about their many different structures and audiences.

• • • • • • • • •

8.4 Economics

Ask any noncommercial broadcaster to name his or her most serious problem and the answer will almost always be: "not enough money." Because the system is *non*commercial, where it goes for its financial support on a regular basis is *the* constant and consuming concern that defines what noncommercial stations do and how well they do it.

The Money Problem

Compared to those in many other countries, America's noncommercial system, on a per-person basis,

*The FCC's 1948 decision to stimulate growth of noncommercial educational FM by licensing stations to operate with only 10 watts later proved an impediment to development of a strong NPR network. Several hundred of these low-power stations had gone on the air by the 1970s, often taking up frequencies for "electronic sandboxes" instead of giving serious broadcast training or service. Faced with growing demand for full-power public radio licenses, the FCC in 1978 began reversing course by ordering 10-watt stations to either raise their power to a minimum of 100 watts or assume a secondary status on a commercial frequency, with the possibility of having to give way entirely to an applicant for full-power service. By 1993 there were only a handful of these 10-watt stations still on the air.

Exhibit 8.e ••••••••••••••••

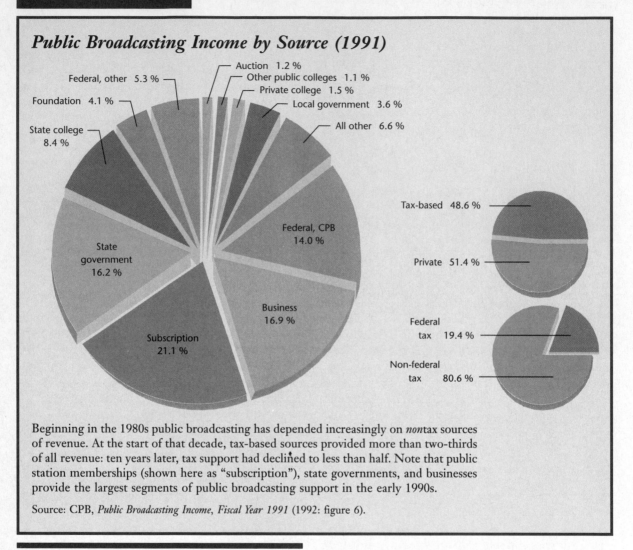

Public Broadcasting Income by Source (1991)

Auction 1.2 %
Federal, other 5.3 %
Other public colleges 1.1 %
Foundation 4.1 %
Private college 1.5 %
Local government 3.6 %
State college 8.4 %
All other 6.6 %
State government 16.2 %
Federal, CPB 14.0 %
Business 16.9 %
Subscription 21.1 %

Tax-based 48.6 %
Private 51.4 %

Federal tax 19.4 %
Non-federal tax 80.6 %

Beginning in the 1980s public broadcasting has depended increasingly on *non*tax sources of revenue. At the start of that decade, tax-based sources provided more than two-thirds of all revenue: ten years later, tax support had declined to less than half. Note that public station memberships (shown here as "subscription"), state governments, and businesses provide the largest segments of public broadcasting support in the early 1990s.

Source: CPB, *Public Broadcasting Income, Fiscal Year 1991* (1992: figure 6).

is woefully underfunded—especially given the role it is expected to fulfill. Comparing government (tax money) support of public broadcasting shows that for every government dollar allocated in America, the governments of Britain and Canada fund their BBC and CBC services, respectively, with about

$25, and Japan's NHK public network gets about $15 in government funding per person served.

After *amount* the next problem has to do with *sources* of that money. Exhibit 8.e shows the diversity of public broadcasting's funding sources, especially when compared to commercial broadcasting's al-

Exhibit 8.f ●●●●● ●●●●●●●●●●●

How Federal Tax Money Is Spent

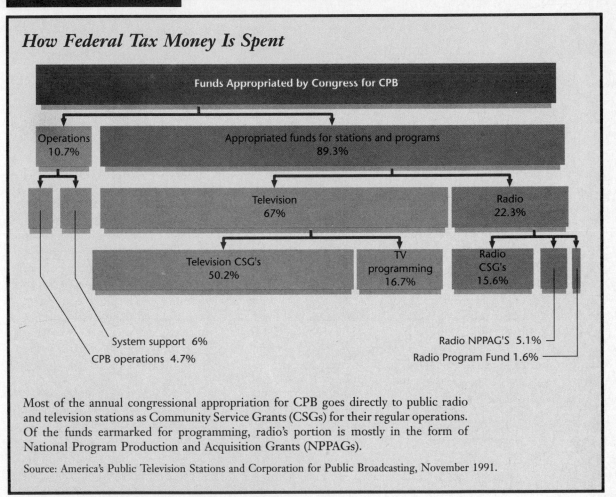

Funds Appropriated by Congress for CPB

Operations
10.7%

Appropriated funds for stations and programs
89.3%

Television
67%

Radio
22.3%

Television CSG's
50.2%

TV
programming
16.7%

Radio
CSG's
15.6%

System support 6%

CPB operations 4.7%

Radio NPPAG'S 5.1%

Radio Program Fund 1.6%

Most of the annual congressional appropriation for CPB goes directly to public radio and television stations as Community Service Grants (CSGs) for their regular operations. Of the funds earmarked for programming, radio's portion is mostly in the form of National Program Production and Acquisition Grants (NPPAGs).

Source: America's Public Television Stations and Corporation for Public Broadcasting, November 1991.

most total dependency on advertising.* But diversity has a price: each source brings different obligations with its funding, and each has its biases. Critics argue that public broadcasters, to accommodate conflicting goals of their numerous and varied con-

*Excluded from this exhibit are the 900-plus radio stations outside of CPB's purview for which there are no comprehensive or reliable data.

tributors, often resort to bland, noncontroversial programs—a weakness of much advertiser-supported programming as well. A single source of funding could be unduly restrictive, of course, but as things stand, public broadcasting executives have to serve too many masters. They spend huge amounts of time on fund raising, yet have too little financial stability to plan effectively. Exhibit 8.f shows how various public television income sources interrelate.

Government Support

Local and state governments supported educational FM from its inception in the 1940s, and many states expanded into educational television over ensuing decades. By the mid-1960s state tax funds provided about half of all public broadcasting income. In the face of rising budget shortages, however, state support declined to only a quarter of total system income by the early 1990s. State networks like those in New York and New Jersey saw their tax support cut by half, leading to substantial layoffs and program cuts. Local government (mainly school board) support fell to less than 4 percent.

In contrast, the *federal* government at first provided no financial assistance at all. With its Educational Television Facilities Act of 1962, Congress finally acknowledged a federal responsibility to support noncommercial stations with grants for construction—not operation—of (mainly television) facilities. This law helped get stations on the air to protect reserved channels against commercial pressures for reclassification.

Since 1978 this portion of total federal funding has been administered by the Department of Commerce's National Telecommunications and Information Administration (NTIA), though both the Reagan and Bush administrations tried consistently to kill the program from 1980 to 1992. Extended, revised, and updated, the public telecommunications funding program continues to provide system support three decades later. Authorized to spend anywhere from $12 million to $20 million a year, NTIA funds about half the total requests it receives, focusing mainly on getting noncommercial signals into areas thus far unreached. About 20 percent of its spending supports use of technologies other than broadcasting. NTIA will pay up to 75 percent of a total grant request; but usually it pays half the cost, the local grant applicant matching that with other funds.

Long-Range Funding

Attempts to persuade Congress to fund the Corporation for Public Broadcasting for longer than the usual federal one-year budget cycle fell victim to President Nixon's dislike of the service in the early 1970s (see Exhibit 8.c). He vetoed several bills calling for two- to three-year funding cycles, unhappy with much of the system's programming and centralization.

Only in 1975 did Congress first authorize funds for a three-year period. Such multiyear appropriations, regularly enacted since—though often with hot debate about specific programs or the overall role of the system—gave PBS more time and funds to initiate serious planning for satellite interconnection and long-term program commitments.

Then a new threat surfaced. Faced with increasing budget deficits and the Reagan administration (1981–1989) quest to reduce or eliminate federal funding for public television, Congress several times acted to *rescind* public broadcasting appropriations to which it had already agreed. Although rather passively supporting public broadcasting in principle, Reagan said that the service should look more to private sources and less to the federal government for funding. This preference echoed conservative reliance on the marketplace: those who wanted public broadcasting should be willing to pay for it more directly than through tax-supported congressional appropriations.*

This uncertain commitment by Congress and state governments (federal funding before 1992 remained basically flat while state and local tax support declined) has made it difficult for public broadcasters to plan—let alone pay—for the future. Some sought continued federal funding only until other means of support could be found. Most valuable thus far have been foundation grants and corporate underwriting of programs.

Foundation Grants

Next to tax sources, foundations provided the largest share of noncommercial broadcasting sup-

*In 1992 Congress—and a reluctant President Bush (then in a difficult reelection campaign)—agreed on legislation for 1994–1996 that increased federal funding authorization (spending ceilings) for the noncommercial system by 40 percent, though actual yearly appropriations (those that actually release money) were yet to come.

port—especially in the dry years prior to 1962. Without the backing of the Ford Foundation, educational television might not have survived its first decade. Carnegie Foundation money paid for two important studies of the system (see Exhibit 8.g).

In 1981 the largest single gift ever made to public broadcasting came from Walter Annenberg, then publisher of *TV Guide*. He donated $150 million, spread over 15 years, to fund a project to create innovative college-level courses and programs. Organized under CPB, the Annenberg/CPB project funded projects selected from dozens of applications, and some eventually aired on public television stations. The program changed focus in the early 1990s, in part because of changes in tax laws, to support programming for primary and secondary schools rather than university-level audiences. Annenberg/CPB specialized in supporting programs that made effective use of technology—interactive options for the audience, use of additional audio channels, and the like.

Corporate Underwriting

A limited form of sponsorship called *underwriting* enables program producers to secure funds from businesses to cover at least some production costs for specific projects. FCC regulations allow companies brief identifying announcements at the beginning and end of such programs. After 1981 the FCC also allowed corporations to display logos or trademarks. Sometimes several firms share in underwriting a single series; but more often, as with the well-known Mobil-supported *Masterpiece Theatre* on Sunday evenings, one company underwrites the entire production cost. Stations also seek *local* underwriting to cover their program acquisition costs.

Underwriters usually prefer noncontroversial programs that attract sizable audiences (at least in public television terms), rather than more specialized or controversial programs that might be less popular but nevertheless constitute the type of programming any alternative service should provide. It took Boston's public television station, WGBH, more than six years to find the $5.6 million needed to produce its controversial *Vietnam: A Television History*. Likewise, it took Washington, D.C.'s WETA more than five years to fund and make 1991's impressive five-part series *The Civil War*, though in the end General Motors covered a large proportion of the costs.

In 1991 corporation and foundation underwriting contributed the largest portion—37 percent—of PBS's $260 million annual budget for national programming. PBS affiliates paid 34 percent, and CPB (with federal tax money) provided 15 percent. From 1983 through 1991, such underwriting more than doubled. Aiding this increase was Public Broadcast Marketing, a private firm specialized in boosting the number and amount of tax-deductible grants from companies seeking access to public television audiences through use of "enhanced underwriting" airtime on public stations. This increasing reliance on what virtually amounts to the sale of "almost-commercial" spots concerns system critics and supporters alike who worry that public television is relying too heavily on the same funding source as commercial television—and will soon program to the same "common denominator." Their concern isn't anything new.

Commercial Experiment

As far back as the 1930s, some educational broadcasting advocates proposed *nonprofit* rather than noncommercial radio, with commercials defraying operating costs. During the FCC's 1952 hearings on television channel reservations, educational interests then saw that their hopes rested on complete avoidance of commercialism. Times change.

Nearly 30 years later, seeking alternative or additional revenue sources for public broadcasting, Congress in 1981 briefly set aside the Communication Act's ban on advertising for noncommercial stations. It established a Temporary Commission on Alternative Financing for Public Telecommunications (TCAF) to supervise an experiment with commercials as a means of support. Ten public television stations took part in a 15-month trial of on-air advertising; public radio stations decided not to participate. Legislation authorizing the test stipulated that

Exhibit 8.g •••••••••••••••••

Ford and Carnegie to the Rescue— Big Foundations and Public Television

During educational television's formative years in the 1950s, most financial support came from the Fund for Adult Education, an arm of the *Ford Foundation*. The Fund's areas of concern—American history, social anthropology, international understanding, and community self-development—automatically became educational television's topics of concern as well. The Fund's economic power determined the very nature of early educational television. The Fund also played a crucial role in securing reserved television channels by helping groups pressing for channel reservations, by supplying early stations with substantial equipment grants, and by providing a small core of nationally distributed programs for initial operations. From 1951 through 1962, the foundation gave some $82 million.

The Ford Foundation planned from the start to furnish only seed money—initial start-up grants to help a station or a service run for a few years in the hope that permanent means of support would evolve. Other money, especially from local groups to support nearby stations, was contributed in the 1950s, but Ford support was crucial. By 1983, when its direct role had been largely phased out, Ford grants to noncommercial broadcasting totaled more than $300 million.

The *Carnegie Foundation* helped to shape public broadcasting in a very different fashion—by funding two important studies of the system. The landmark 1967 study discussed in the text provided the blueprint for public broadcasting's structure. A revisit to the same issues in a 1979 study had nowhere near the same impact (it unsuccessfully called for huge increases in federal outlays at a time when the federal budget was deeply in the red) but did provide a useful report card on system progress. In late 1991 a third Carnegie-supported study emphasized television's still-unreached potential for teaching.

---

ads could not interrupt programs, could not exceed two minutes in length, and could not promote political, religious, or other ideological points of view. Station WTTW-TV in Chicago earned the most advertising income—more than a million dollars, or nearly 10 percent of its revenue that year.

Following completion of the test, TCAF concluded: (1) Limited advertising raised significant income only if labor unions and copyright holders did not demand equity treatment with commercial stations; (2) advertising produced no negative impact on viewing patterns, numbers of subscribers to public television, or other contributions; and (3) advertising had no effect on programming (though, given its short duration, the test could not fully determine this).

Still, TCAF concluded that most public television stations would not carry ads because of labor union contract requirements (commercial-level revenue would trigger calls for higher pay levels), local economic considerations, or concerns about advertising's impact on the character of public broadcasting. It added that although the experiment reduced most concerns about advertising's impact on other funding sources for public broadcasting, no experiment could demonstrate that advertising might not *eventually* cause loss of subscriber, underwriter, or government support (TCAF, 1983). The experiment ended in mid-1983 and commercials remained taboo—to the relief of commercial broadcasters.*

Creeping Commercialism?

In 1984 the Senate Communications Subcommittee held hearings to examine whether advertising on public broadcasting should be resumed. While some station executives argued for the proposal, CPB opposed the concept (as did the National Association of Broadcasters, concerned about further competition), and Congress shelved the idea. That same year, influenced by TCAF recommendations, the FCC authorized "enhanced underwriting," leading stations to carry what PBS President Bruce Christensen called "almost commercials" (Smith, 1985). The FCC tried to balance station and public needs: stations may sell 30-second announcements mentioning specific consumer products but may sell no more than two-and-a-half minutes between individual programs.

The four-station New Jersey Network, for example, permitted advertisers to talk about products, services, and locations, but drew the line at statements about product superiority. Enhanced underwriting increased New Jersey Network income from

corporations threefold in just three years—to $900,000 in 1985.*

Such commercial inroads add pressure to open advertising's door even wider—and to concern by critics and the FCC that some stations have crossed the line from enhanced underwriting to outright commercialism. The Commission has regularly warned that it will enforce its few remaining underwriting rules—and, indeed, several stations have been fined for announcements that verged on hard-sell commercials (quality and price comparisons, and encouragement to patronize specific businesses).

Critics charge that such "creeping commercialization" of public television cannot be justified. The need for an alternative service to commercial electronic media rests on the fact that commercial profit motives lead to heavily entertainment-based programming. Subjecting public broadcasting to these same motives would likely open the system to even stronger pushes for change.

Public Subscription

Individual listeners—dubbed subscribers or members—contribute a bit over a fifth (22 percent) of total public broadcasting system revenue and of public television revenue, sharing with state governments (19 percent) the largest funding role.

The constant search for money to match grants from NTIA, CPB, and corporate sources has driven public television stations to push membership drives to the saturation point. Declining income from local tax-supported sources, including school boards, has

---

*Commercial stations often assist noncommercial outlets by donating broadcast equipment and tower space for antennas, and sometimes with grants. This assistance is provided partly for public-service reasons, but even more to keep noncommercial channels from turning into commercial competitors for audience and advertisers. Further, noncommercial outlets provide public-service and minority-interest programming that commercial stations want to avoid because of their tiny audiences. In an extreme case illustrating all of this, New York City commercial stations together purchased a vacant VHF channel in 1961 and offered it for use as an educational outlet (it became today's WNET-TV), thus effectively removing a possible commercial competitor.

---

*Nevertheless, by 1992 New Jersey's statewide budget crisis had led to serious consideration of transferring management and possibly ownership of the four-station network to another noncommercial operator, New York's WNET-TV. WNET-TV proposed to operate two 24-hour networks for New Jersey, one aimed at a general audience, and the other for instructional purposes. Another indicator of economic pressure was the sale by Iowa State University of its WOI-TV, a commercial outlet, to raise money for the school.

also forced more aggressive viewer solicitation. "Membership marathons" are increasingly widespread, as station staff and volunteers operate banks of telephones while on-air personalities plead for donations in the form of paid memberships. The hard sell of these "begathons" often matches commercial station excesses. Polls indicate that most viewers dislike, though they understand the reason for, such fund raisers. As the economy weakened in 1991–1992, audience memberships fell off, as did donations, making the quest for support even harder.

Over-the-air auctions (the source of less than 2 percent of public television revenue) can be even more objectionable—one reason for their rarity. Auctions promote donated articles and services (often from commercial sources) so blatantly and at such length that they sound like program-length commercials or home shopping networks. Reacting to criticism, some stations have reduced or even eliminated on-air campaigns, relying instead on targeted direct-mail appeals. Miami's station once tried to "bribe" viewers—unsuccessfully as it turned out—by promising to shorten or even forgo auctions if they met gift quotas without waiting to be strong-armed into giving!

Seeking Alternatives

Government agencies and private think tanks have considered almost countless alternative ways of funding noncommercial broadcasting—including several suggestions throughout the years to turn the whole system over to private interests to be run on a commercial basis. More traditional ideas have included an excise tax on the sale of television receivers or license fees for their use (suggested by the first Carnegie Commission and often raised since), acceptance of limited advertising, conversion of public television to a subscription television (STV) operation, a tax on commercial broadcast revenues, leasing or auctioning spectrum space to commercial users to provide a stable fund for noncommercial operations, and—the only idea in use thus far—leasing of excess satellite capacity.

None of these proposals has received unanimous support, but all concerned agree on the need for

- *insulating* noncommercial broadcast programming from political pressures of annual congressional funding;
- an *amount* of funding adequate to allow growth;
- year-to-year *stability* of revenue; and
- funding over a *long term*, generally defined as five or more years, to allow more orderly planning of program and technical development.

No current source of money—foundations, tax support, corporate donations and underwriting, and listener contributions—meets all four of those criteria.

In 1991 a PBS-coordinated PTV Task Force on Funding concluded its most in-depth assessment of funding options in 13 years by saying there were "no magic solutions that will miraculously cause money to float down from the sky." As usual in such analyses, this one called for more federal support—but also urged expanded efforts by public broadcasters themselves to raise money needed for programs and operations.

Among the many funding ideas considered in this analysis and earlier ones—a few already used by some stations—are the following:

- selling commercial merchandise associated with programs (Children's Television Workshop generated about a third of its 1990s' *Sesame Street* revenues from such sales);
- offering closed-circuit seminar services to businesses for fees that exceed production costs;
- selling to commercial television or pay cable the rights to show newly produced programs before they are released to public television;
- renting station facilities (usually studios) to commercial producers;
- selling videotapes and other items directly to viewers (some 200,000 copies of Bill Moyers' programs have been sold, for example, with much of the income going into further program production);
- participating in other commercial tie-ins with

programs (PBS gets a portion of the income derived from the many "companion" books that are published in conjunction with PBS series);

- publishing listener magazines, or cooperating with existing city or regional magazines to raise advertising revenue (Nickelodeon cable network began such a magazine in 1993, tied to publication of program-related books);
- trading a low-number (and thus more desirable) educational UHF channel for a higher UHF commercial channel in the same market, thereby gaining an often substantial cash payment from the commercial broadcaster (the FCC has thus far disallowed potentially more lucrative trades of UHF and VHF channels that would raise more money but also badly shrink the audience reach of any educational outlet trading "down" to a UHF);
- charging commercial broadcasters a tax or fee to help pay for public broadcast needs;
- selling FM subcarrier or television vertical blanking interval (VBI) access for private uses; and
- auctioning commercial spectrum space, with proceeds going to develop a more fully competitive public broadcasting system.

• • • • • • • •

8.5   TV Program Sources

Although noncommercial broadcasting's basic purpose is to supply an alternative to commercial services, program overlap does occur. Indeed, there has even been competition for some programs in recent years. Noncommercial stations often show feature films and syndicated series obtained from the same distributors used by commercial stations. On the other hand, noncommercial outlets do more local production and experimental programming than do their commercial counterparts.

Exhibit 8.h diagrams sources of noncommercial programs. While Section 8.6 discusses programs themselves, here we focus on how and where noncommercial programs are developed.

Stations as Network Producers

A handful of major-market producer stations act as primary producers for PBS. In 1991 they provided about 37 percent of national programming, with another 10 percent coming from lesser public television stations. Major producer stations, such as WGBH-Boston (which produces the critically acclaimed science series *NOVA*, among other programs) and WNET–New York (source of *Great Performances*), have long histories of creative innovation in public television. They tend to develop specializations: WNET and WETA–Washington, D.C., for news and public affairs, for example, and WGBH for science, documentary, and drama presentations.

Foreign Sources

Some documentaries like WNET's *Nature* showcase individual programs or multipart series produced overseas. By the early 1990s nearly a fifth of all PBS series had at least some overseas material; some were co-productions with American partners, but about 12 percent came straight from such sources as British commercial and BBC television series. Best known among the latter are the long-running *Masterpiece Theatre* and *Mystery* series, both co-produced by WGBH. The foreign programs are well produced and cost a fraction of similar programs made in the United States.

Independent and Syndicated Production

PBS in the 1990s is buying more of its programs from independent producers (some of whom also sell to commercial stations and networks)—but that is a fairly recent change. In 1988 only about a tenth of national programming came from independents (that is, outside of major public television stations and producers). Under pressure from producers who claimed PBS largely ignored their output and abilities, Congress during the same year required CPB to fund an Independent Production Service,

Exhibit 8.h ● ● ● ● ● ● ● ● ● ● ● ● ● ●

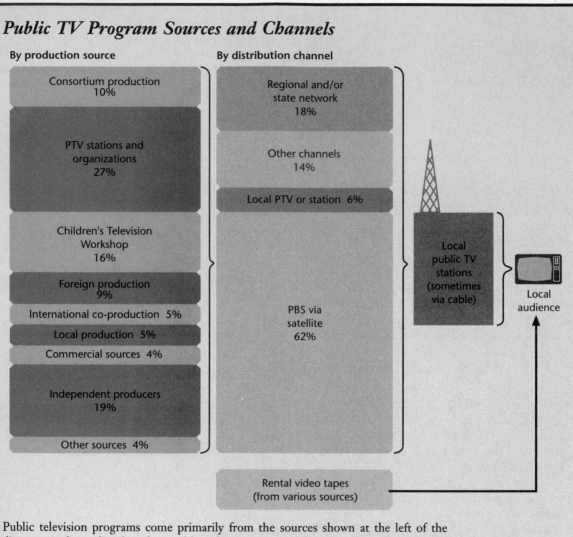

Public TV Program Sources and Channels

By production source

- Consortium production 10%
- PTV stations and organizations 27%
- Children's Television Workshop 16%
- Foreign production 9%
- International co-production 5%
- Local production 5%
- Commercial sources 4%
- Independent producers 19%
- Other sources 4%

By distribution channel

- Regional and/or state network 18%
- Other channels 14%
- Local PTV or station 6%
- PBS via satellite 62%

Local public TV stations (sometimes via cable)

Local audience

Rental video tapes (from various sources)

Public television programs come primarily from the sources shown at the left of the diagram, and are distributed to public television stations by the means shown in the middle. Note that the percentages, which vary only marginally from year to year, add to 100 for production source, and also to 100 for distribution channel. Cable and home video, of little importance in the 1970s, had grown to distribution importance by the late 1980s.

Source: Data from Corporation for Public Broadcasting.

separate from CPB, to encourage more independent program sources.* Easily the best known of these is the New York–based Children's Television Workshop (see Exhibit 8.i).

Local Production

The typical noncommercial television station produces and uses more local programming than do most commercial stations. Locally produced programs consist mainly of news and public affairs, along with some educational/instructional material telecast during daytime hours for in-school use.

However, local production is often one of the first things to go when budgets are cut, as was common during the economically difficult early 1990s. Public stations, like their commercial counterparts, found it cheaper to use syndicated and network material (even productive WGBH in Boston had to cut a popular 10 P.M. local newscast). Accordingly, stations cut local production by half from its mid-1970s level, now averaging slightly more than 5 percent of the total program schedule.

Cable Alternatives

Just as cable has increasingly taken on many of the functions of traditional broadcasting in entertainment, so has it done in education and public affairs.

In 1979 the cable industry created *C-SPAN*, the Cable-Satellite Public Affairs Network, to cover floor proceedings of the House of Representatives (see Section 12.5). Now operating two full-time cable networks, as well as two audio networks (one carries English-language radio news from other countries), C-SPAN gives first priority to covering House and Senate floor proceedings and carries between 7 and 14 other events daily, plus book reviews,

National Press Club talks, a special communications program, historical documentaries, and the like. Based in Washington, the service has an annual budget of $18 million provided by cable-system owners. It carries no advertising. C-SPAN in the Classroom, a free educational service, allows teachers to tape material for instructional use.

By 1992 more than 46,000 schools (about half of all schools in the country—and up from just over 6,000 schools in 1989) with 26 million students had been supplied with free cable service, most by local cable systems as a part of their franchises. Cable in the Classroom, a service of the commercial cable industry, provides some national coordination. Emphasizing junior and senior high schools (and having aimed to have all such institutions that are passed by cable actually connected by the end of 1992), with possible expansion to primary schools later, the service provides some 500 hours of commercial-free programming per month, supplied largely by 21 cable-delivered networks. The six most used are PBS (the only broadcast service on the list), the two CNN news services, The Discovery Channel, Arts & Entertainment, and C-SPAN. Teachers may tape and use as much or as little as they like. Cable in the Classroom also helps distribute teaching guides for various programs. The key drawback to this cable industry promotion is that many schools lack the needed television receivers and VCRs necessary to take full advantage of what is being offered.

At the end of 1992, The Learning Channel began to offer *Ready, Set, Learn!* as a six-hour, five-days-a-week block of programming for preschoolers. The weekly 30 hours consists of five series, some produced overseas, using animals, puppets, and kids to introduce very young viewers to basic social ideas.

Some cable-system operators have actively assisted in instructional development. Tele-Communications, Inc. (TCI), the largest multiple-system operator in the country, had by 1992 funded two high school projects, one in Georgia and one in Oregon, for its "High School of the 21st Century," which helps educators integrate cable programming into teaching and provides computers for classrooms.

*Late in 1992 PBS announced that it would demand first refusal of videocassette distribution rights for programs and series in which it played a large funding role. A number of independent producers protested this "blackmail," but PBS argued that it was necessary to recoup its money and invest in future programs.

Exhibit 8.i ●●●●●● ● ● ● ● ● ● ● ● ● ●

Children's Television Workshop

In the 1990s Children's Television Workshop (CTW) provided just under 12 percent of all public television programming. A nonprofit independent producer, CTW has won fame for its *Sesame Street* series, now seen in dozens of countries.

The program idea originated one evening at a dinner party in New York where several experts on education began to muse about *really* using television's acknowledged potential for reaching children. In the late 1960s all three commercial television networks turned down the initial concept for what became television's most celebrated children's program. They believed commercial sponsors would have little interest in a program narrowly focused on such a young age group. So, using seed funding from government and foundation grants, CTW turned to then-new public broadcasting.

Sesame Street premiered in late 1969 just as the transition from "educational" to "public" television took hold, bringing the first large audiences to PBS. It targeted disadvantaged children, previously ignored by television, helping to prepare them for reading and writing. Building on *Sesame Street* success, CTW later branched out with *The Electric Company* for older children, drawing on the production methods and research follow-up of *Sesame Street* but using more advanced reading concepts. In 1980 CTW began a daily science program, *3-2-1 Contact*, and later *Square One TV*, a math series for young children. To enhance its revenues, CTW also began *Encyclopedia*, a children's series for HBO. In 1991 CTW launched a $20 million multimedia literacy project called *Ghostwriter*. In addition to a television series with that name, the project included various print media and community and school outreach programs. The following year, CTW joined with the United Nation's UNICEF and Mexico's Televisa to create a Spanish-language version of its old standby, *Sesame Street*.

By the early 1990s two-thirds of CTW's budget came from ancillary commercial ventures, such as merchandising items using CTW program names and characters. Because of its independent funding, CTW rose above public broadcasting quarrels, sticking to its own research-based agenda.

Source: Photo © 1993 Children's Television Workshop. Sesame Street Muppets © 1993 Jim Henson Productions, Inc.

●●●●●● ● ●

8.6 Noncommercial TV Programming

The rationale for a largely separate, noncommercial system of broadcasting is to provide alternative programming to that offered by the mostly entertainment-oriented commercial system. Despite that fundamental difference in purpose, however, most programming basics (introduced in the next chapter) also apply here.

PBS began in 1970 with several programs either still on the air (*Washington Week in Review*) or well remembered (*The French Chef*, which featured Julia Child demonstrating that good French cooking was within everyone's reach). Many initial programs focused on news and public affairs.

News and Public Affairs

Some public broadcasters consider extended public-affairs programming to be their key advantage as an alternative service. In contrast to commercial networks, PBS found its affiliated stations receptive to long-format (more than half-hour) newscasts. More than 43 percent of all national PBS programs (and about 16 percent of total broadcast hours) in 1991 consisted of news and public affairs.

The MacNeil/Lehrer NewsHour has often been acclaimed as one of television's best in-depth information programs. Hosts Jim Lehrer in Washington and Robert MacNeil in New York City interview representatives of opposing views on significant current topics. PBS began the series in 1976 as a half-hour news program, expanding it to an hour in 1983. Despite critical praise, however, *NewsHour* has failed to build a large following, even by noncommercial standards. Public television stations have trouble agreeing on an ideal schedule position for the program, which does best when played against commercial entertainment. Still, the audience reached includes a high proportion of government and business opinion leaders, giving *NewsHour* considerable impact.

PBS provides a steady diet of other public-affairs programs as well, including *Washington Week in Review, Nightly Business Report*, and *Frontline*. (In the early 1990s this last was the only regularly scheduled documentary series on broadcast television.) The Bill Moyers specials are irregularly scheduled but get both wide coverage and high praise for their in-depth analysis of and sensitivity for social problems. So do the interviews conducted from time to time by David Frost.

When in 1992 the commercial networks abandoned full-time coverage of the quadrennial political conventions (see Section 12.4), PBS (and cable services) stepped into the breach, offering full prime-time coverage—combining Robert MacNeil and Jim Lehrer with NBC's top correspondents,

including anchor Tom Brokaw, when NBC was not airing convention news itself.

Another aspect of PBS news and public-affairs programs appeared in 1992 as well: PBS-distributed programs were now legally *required* (by CPB long-range funding legislation) to offer objective and balanced content. If an expert review panel finds questions of balance or fairness in a program, CPB may support costs of producing balancing programs. As a part of this "Open to the Public" process, CPB announced more ways for its audience to "talk back" on fairness and other issues—an 800 telephone number, quarterly meetings of the CPB Board with public groups away from Washington, and the like.

History and Culture

Documentaries and some performing arts presentations, combined, represented nearly 28 percent of national PBS programming in 1991—and includes programs watched by those who do not normally tune in on the noncommercial service. This category was exemplified by *The Civil War*, an 11-hour 1991 series, which won widespread praise and viewership—and helped sell thousands of copies of a handsome "companion" book and videotape copies of the series, proceeds from which helped meet the program's production costs (see Exhibit 8.j).

Public television's provision of such programming goes back more than two decades. The multipart *Civilization*, a review of world history and cultural development featuring Sir Kenneth Clark, ran in PBS's first season and helped to introduce the "companion book" marketing idea. As part of the American bicentennial celebrations in 1976, PBS produced a lavish six-part *Adams Chronicles* recounting the lives of the famous political and business family from Massachusetts (again, with a companion book).

Vietnam: A Television History became the highest-rated documentary of 1983 and won several awards—as well as hostile criticism from conservatives. The series, co-produced by WGBH in Boston and by French television, included fascinating

Exhibit 8.j •••••• • • • • • • • • •

Ken Burns and The Civil War

archival film from before World War II as well as a searching analysis of the peak years of U.S. involvement in that conflict. The documentary's less-than-positive assessment of America's role brought howls of protest from conservative groups—and a controversial decision by PBS to allow several critics to air their differences during an hour or so of airtime with the program's producers.

Eyes on the Prize, telecast in 1987, grippingly told the story of the American civil rights movement,

focusing on the activist days of the 1960s. *Color Adjustment*, aired in 1992, was a highly critical history of the portrayal of blacks on American television. *The American Experience* has served as host vehicle for a series of historical documentaries on American history and key historical figures—with such varied programs as those on the building of the Brooklyn Bridge, the impact of rigged television quiz shows, immigration, and several studies of recent American presidents, including a well-received

For five consecutive nights in September 1991, some 14 million viewers watched *The Civil War* unfold, making it the most-watched series in the history of public television. It earned an average rating of nine and was seen by four times the normal PBS audience.

The fruit of a five-year effort, and of some $3.2 million in support from CPB, Washington, D.C.'s WETA, General Electric (the only corporate underwriter), and the National Endowment for the Humanities, *The Civil War* was the creation of filmmaker Ken Burns. Burns had done earlier documentary programs for PBS. But this was different—an 11-hour series that brought the 1861–1865 struggle to life as most viewers had never seen or thought about it before. Combining creative use of period music, live shots of battlefields, as well as old photos over which cameras seemed to lovingly roam—and interspersed with quotes from experts—*The Civil War* took a neutral view of the war's causes. (Viewers in both North and South later complained about bias—suggesting the neutral approach had been successful.)

Syndicated newspaper columnist George Will summed up the series and its maker: "Our Iliad has found its Homer: he has made accessible and vivid for everyone the pain and poetry and meaning of the event that is the hinge of our history." Concluded producer Burns:

> There's no way that *The Civil War* could have been produced anywhere but on public television. Public television not only tolerates but encourages the kind of experimentation and risk-taking that we take as independent producers. And on public television I don't lose the viewer's attention every six to eight minutes for a commercial. The ability to hold that attention is critical to me as an artist. Public television is also the only kind of television where the creator actually retains control. (CPB,1991:44–45)

The series proved financially valuable, too. Viewer contributions to local stations rose sharply, thanks to money pleas during breaks in the program. The "companion book" sold 750,000 copies, and related video and audio recordings also sold well. Burns followed his *The Civil War* success with a 90-minute program on early radio called *Empire of the Air*, which traced the lives of Lee de Forest, Edwin Armstrong, and David Sarnoff; he also began work on a multipart documentary series tracing the history of baseball.

Source: Photo by Ken Regan/Camera 5.

two-part study of *The Kennedys* (1992) that traced the triumph and tragedy of an American political dynasty, and an assessment of President Lyndon Johnson's varied legacies. Each is hosted by historian David McCullough, who ties the pieces into their larger historical context. *Columbus and the Age of Discovery* aired in seven parts early in 1992 as part of the 500th anniversary of the explorer's first voyage. Co-produced by Spanish television (another example of increasing international co-production), the series spent as much time on Central and Latin American life today as on matters historical—and discussed both positive and negative impacts of the Spanish Conquest.

Performing Arts

All of the performing arts—drama, dance, fine music—find a home in public television, though they are now largely absent from commercial television.

Further, these series continue season after season, in contrast to the usual short lives of their rare commercial counterparts.

Among public television evening programs, *Masterpiece Theatre* is probably best known. Underwritten by Mobil and hosted for its first two decades by British-born Alistair Cooke, the Sunday evening hour-long staple provides British-made drama, ranging from short series built around historical events, famous novels, or contemporary views of the human condition, to such lengthy costume favorites as "Upstairs, Downstairs," on life in a fine Edwardian house, or "I, Claudius," a 13-part series on the bad old days of the Roman empire. Cooke offered tidbits of useful context for American viewers in his short preprogram "essays," each televised in a setting related to the drama at hand.*

American Playhouse, produced by five cooperating stations since 1982, helps balance the better-known *Masterpiece Theatre* with American productions. It provides national exposure for both major city and smaller regional theatrical companies.

Music and dance appear regularly on three PBS programs that began in the mid-1970s and are still going strong nearly two decades later: *Great Performances* (1974), *Dance in America* (1975), and *Live from Lincoln Center* (1976). A more recent series, *Evening at Pops*, features the Boston Pops Orchestra. While these are by far the best promoted and known programs of the type, many public television stations air local music and performance groups, providing them a wider audience than would otherwise be the case.

Science and Nature

About 8 percent of national programming in 1991 consisted of documentary programs and series on science and nature. One of the first, aired in the 1970s, *The Ascent of Man*, featured philosopher Jacob Bronowski's view of developing mankind in

a multipart series and yet another useful companion volume.

Since then, PBS has offered an eight-part series on *The Brain*, as well as the multipart *Cosmos*, with famous astronomer Carl Sagan introducing many Americans to the latest findings in astronomy. Some of the most popular public television documentaries, such as the *National Geographic Specials* and *National Audubon Society Specials*, proved that Americans could also produce top-notch nature films. These programs, like the societies that produce them, feature both natural and scientific topics with emphasis on dramatic pictures. Always insightful, and sometimes controversial, *NOVA* has run for nearly two decades (see Exhibit 8.k). *The Machine That Changed the World*, telecast in 1992, combined history and current research to show how computers have influenced American life (in addition to some of the cleverest television graphics at the open and close of each segment).

Children

Public broadcasting has a clear mandate to provide constructive, imaginative children's programs. Accordingly, public television stations fill a large portion of their daytime hours with in-school programs (paid for by school districts) and schedule additional special programs for children both early in the morning and again in the afternoon.*

Since 1967 Pittsburgh station WQED's *Mister Rogers' Neighborhood* has taught social skills to very young preschoolers, focusing on their values, feelings, and fears with gentle conversation and songs tailored to their cognitive needs. Second in viewing popularity only to the famous *Sesame Street* (dis-

---

*Cooke retired from the series at the end of 1992, though he continued, in his mid-80s, a weekly radio broadcast to the BBC, *Letter from America*, which may be the longest-running radio feature in history as it approaches its 50th anniversary.

*Commercial television networks used to program for children in these dayparts, with such classics as a puppet-and-human show called *Kukla, Fran and Ollie* (which aired from 1948 to 1957, with later revivals—including one on PBS in 1970–1971), until talk, game, courtroom, and quiz shows attracted advertisers uninterested in a child audience. *Captain Kangaroo* ran on CBS for a quarter-century (1955–1981) until pressure for a more appealing adult news and talk early-morning program forced it off the air. Public television now helps fill the gap left by these long-lasting pioneers.

Exhibit 8.k

Science on Public Television

In its nearly two decades as the longest-running nationally broadcast science program, *NOVA* has presented almost 400 different hour-long science documentaries over PBS. Each is devoted to a single topic—some produced by WGBH in Boston, others co-produced by the station with overseas partners. There are 20 new programs each year, six rebroadcasts, and some specials, all subject to extensive scientific review to ensure accuracy. Each week, *NOVA* draws some eight million viewers, the largest audience of any PBS weekly program.

Source: Photo and logo courtesy WGBH Boston.

cussed below), it proceeds at a snail's pace (at least by adult standards) that very young children happily endure. The Smithsonian Institution enshrined one of host Fred Rogers' sweaters in a popular-culture exhibit, commemorating his status with generations of children.

Children's Television Workshop, or CTW (see Exhibit 8.i) brought all the technical resources of television—as well as all the capabilities of educational research—to bear on *Sesame Street*. A wonderfully original group of large-scale puppets, the Muppets, became the program's hallmark. The episodes use very short segments to hold attention and employ a variety of formats, including simulated commercials ("This segment of *Sesame Street* has been brought to you by the letters A and L and the numbers 3 and 7 . . ."). Research showed that children who watched *Sesame Street* learned to read more quickly than did other children. Preschool and primary teachers began to use broadcasts of the program during the school day, doing the previously unthinkable by incorporating a popular home program into the classroom. No series on either commercial or public television has ever been given as

much scheduled air time as has *Sesame Street*. By the 1990s it had taken on classic status as the preeminent program for preschoolers. CTW recycles segments of old episodes into new ones, taking a kind of interchangeable-parts approach to production that has stretched the series into its third decade.

Other award-winning noncommercial children's programs include public broadcasting's *Villa Allegre* and *Carrascolendas*, both bilingual series aimed at Hispanic households. *Where in the World Is Carmen Sandiego?*, begun in 1991, teaches 8- to 13-year-olds about world geography by using a fast-paced search for an underground leader as the core story around which to arrange themes and features. The daily program is based on a computer game and builds on the sometimes mysterious (to adults) codes and phrases kids that age adore.

Education and Instruction

Much of the classroom programming on public television comes from educational, government, and industrial sources. Since 1977 CPB has funded 24 instructional television (ITV) series for use in classrooms, providing texts and other support for each series. A 1991 CPB survey showed that some three-quarters of the country's teachers had used instructional programs (some on videocassettes) in the previous school year, up from 54 percent in a survey eight years earlier (CPB, 1992: 11).

Beginning in 1981, PBS offered the Adult Learning Service (ALS), a cooperative effort with local stations that provides college-credit television courses for viewers at home. Some 50 courses are offered at any one time across a variety of fields. Many reach colleges directly by means of the Adult Learning Satellite Service, which began in 1988 and reaches nearly 2,000 institutions of higher learning. In parallel fashion, PBS coordinates distribution of programs for elementary and secondary schools as well.

In carrying out their classroom instruction mission, public television stations draw upon several large libraries of instructional materials that act as syndicators. Notable examples include the Agency for Instructional Television (AIT) in Bloomington, Indiana, innovative producers of interactive videodisc programs for children; the Great Plains National Instructional Television Library (GPN) of Lincoln, Nebraska, producers of well-known classroom series for children; the Annenberg/CPB Project, producers of several prime-time adult-learning series. These nonprofit agencies license program series to public television stations for in-school use.*

While more than 80 percent of public television stations provide programming to elementary and secondary schools—an average of 5.5 hours per day for classroom use—lack of equipment severely limits its impact. The average school has but one television receiver for four classrooms and fewer than four VCRs, and only 9 percent report having a satellite TVRO (APTS, 1992: 7). This shortage, made worse each year by declining school budgets,

has provided an opening for a commercial approach to education—"Channel One"—which supplies programming and the means to use it (see Exhibit 8.l).

• • • • • • • •

8.7 Noncommercial Radio Programming

Many observers of electronic media feel that public radio stations in the 1990s provide some of the most creative audio programming anywhere—news, music, and drama.

National Public Radio

Typical public radio stations affiliated with National Public Radio (NPR) and/or American Public Radio (APR), discussed below, fill about two-fifths of their weekly total airtime (an average of 146 hours per week, or about 21 hours a day) with programs from these networks and other syndicated sources.

NPR's first continuing success was its weekday late-afternoon news-and-feature program, *All Things Considered*, which began in 1971. For the first time since the demise of traditional commercial radio networks, listeners could hear national mini-documentary reports supplemented with colorful local sound. The program quickly won every radio program award in sight and became a listening addiction for its loyal fans. NPR took the same approach to news on *Morning Edition*, which premiered in 1979, and *Weekend Edition*, which debuted in 1985. During the 1991 Gulf War, these programs expanded so that, with afternoon call-in programs, some NPR stations became virtually full-time news outlets. In 1993–1994, NPR first offered around-the-clock hourly newscasts, continuing an 18 hour-a-day schedule of newscasts on weekends.

NPR's *The Thistle and Shamrock* carries contemporary Scottish and Irish music as explained by hostess Fiona Ritchie. Also highly popular is the music-and-feature *Performance Today*, which takes listeners behind recitals to learn more about composers and

---

*Generally only noncommercial users can obtain the rights to these series. However, commercial cable networks such as The Discovery Channel compete for many educational programs for children and adults, blurring the once-clear distinction between commercial and noncommercial programs.

performers through interviews and features. The controversial *World Cafe*, produced by a Philadelphia public FM station, offers two hours daily of American and other popular music. The controversy involves substantial CPB funding for a series that provides music readily available on commercial stations. Proponents pointed out that *World Cafe*, carried on about 50 public radio stations in mid-1992, appealed to an audience some 10 years younger, on average, than typical public radio listeners.

World Cafe began NPR's move away from its earlier stuffy, academic sound. The trend continued with programs such as the highly popular—as well as useful—Saturday afternoon *Car Talk* show, featuring the Boston-based Magliozzi brothers, whose answers to called-in car-maintenance questions are spiced with jokes, word play, and a general sense of fun.

American Public Radio

A second national public radio service, American Public Radio (APR), began in 1983, formed by Minnesota Public Radio chiefly as a distribution channel for the popular *A Prairie Home Companion*, featuring Garrison Keillor (see Exhibit 8.m). By the early 1990s it was the largest distributor of public radio programming.

APR transmits about 225 hours of programming each week (nearly half news and information) to 430 affiliated stations using the public radio satellite transponder managed by NPR (most APR affiliates are also NPR member stations). Unlike NPR, APR provides programs to only one station per market. Also unlike NPR, it does not produce programs but, rather, acquires them from member stations. APR also distributes original musical performance programs, including 65 hours of classical music weekly. In 1987 APR began to feed *MonitoRadio*, a one-hour (many stations used only half) weeknight news-and-feature program of the *Christian Science Monitor* newspaper. It also provides the half-hour weeknight *Marketplace* business news program produced by its University of Southern California affiliate as well as all BBC World Service programming for American listeners.

Local Public Programming

Information (the biggest attraction for most listeners) and music (usually classical, sometimes jazz) occupy the bulk of air time on most public radio stations. Classical music fills more hours than any other single content type. The primary appeal of such stations is that they offer content usually heard nowhere else—jazz, opera, local public affairs, folk music, and the like. For example, fully a quarter offer some programming in a language other than English, whereas few commercial stations (other than those directed specifically at ethnic minority audiences) do so.

More specifically, of the on-air hours of more than 500 public radio stations surveyed in 1992, 74 percent were devoted to music (34 percent classical, 14 percent jazz—and 9 percent rock!), 17 percent to news and public events, 4 percent to call-in and other public-affairs programs, and about 2 percent to non-English programs (Giovannoni, 1992: 37).

Public stations tend to differ most from their commercial counterparts in that fully half vary their content considerably each day rather than consistently hewing to a single format. They come close to the "middle-of-the-road" or "something for everybody" formats that traditional radio stations provided in the 1940s and 1950s.

Virtually all of this programming originates on some 1,500 noncommercial FM stations. Although CPB partially supports 46 public *AM* stations (12 of them operating in small Alaskan communities), they share in the general decline of AM audiences in favor of FM listening. The AM audience is older and AM program formats are thus more predictable—mostly news, public affairs, nostalgia (big band), and country music.

Instructional Radio

Overwhelmed by television and the growth of rock music, instructional radio survives in but a few cities, usually as a public school service. Only about 2 percent of stations still provide instructional programs for use in schools and other noncommercial institutions, such as churches. Radio's in-school

Exhibit 8.1 •••••• •••••••••••

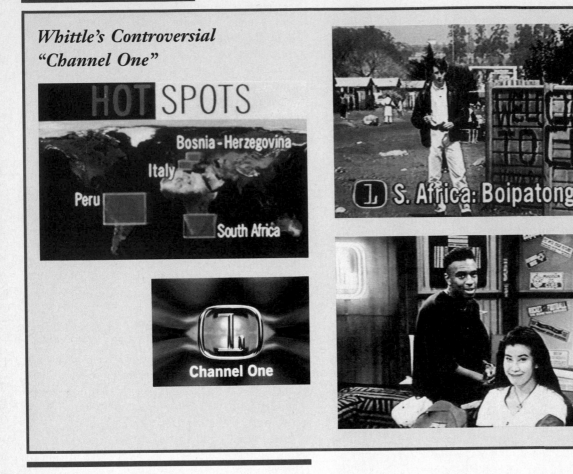

Whittle's Controversial "Channel One"

function has been largely taken over by videocassettes, which provide visuals as well as sound under the classroom teacher's direct control.

Community Radio

Several hundred noncommercial FM stations (and a few cable-only FM services) provide one or more types of community radio. In the 1960s, reacting against rigidly formatted radio and dissenting from establishment values, some small stations began the *underground* or *free-form* radio format. "Some great things were done," recalls one observer. "Tough, creative, unpolished, kinky scenes, but great. FM

radio was a world full of surprises, like the world of early television" (Pichaske, 1979: 151). Such radio is now lumped under the *progressive* format, which mixes live and recorded music and talk, usually at the whim of the presenter. Stations using anti-establishment formats have come and mostly gone, but the six-station Pacifica group described in Exhibit 8.n has survived.

Most community stations supply the bulk of their own programs. Public community stations often feature, if not progressive music, a classical, jazz, or diversified format. Small, low-salaried staffs supplemented by volunteers mean low overhead, enabling such outlets to present formats that would not be

Media entrepreneur Christopher Whittle felt he had a good idea—help expand high school student knowledge about current events, and get television teaching technology into schools that couldn't afford it. The means? *Channel One*, a ten-minute newscast supported by two minutes of advertisements, which began in March 1990. Transmitted daily by satellite directly to schools, *Channel One* uses television sets, video recorders, and a TVRO loaned by Whittle to schools as long as they regularly carry the program. Schools may use the equipment at other times for programming from other sources (see Section 8.5). Fourteen national companies financially supported the channel by running ads aimed directly at teen audiences.

By 1992 the program was being beamed into nearly 12,000 high schools (about a third of the nation's total), reaching 7.1 million students across 45 states. Another 2,000 schools awaited equipment to receive the program. But this wide acceptance was matched by heated school board and courtroom battles over the propriety of carrying advertising into school buildings. Three states—New York and California (the two biggest in terms of student population) as well as Rhode Island—banned it in public schools because of the commercials.

Texas allows parents to request that their children do something else during *Channel One* viewing time. In mid-1992 a judge in New Jersey said the advertising-supported program violated that state's compulsory-attendance free-education law. Many other county and city school boards simply rejected the Whittle equipment offer outright.

Of course, how many students actually pay attention to the program is another matter. In early 1992, in the first report from a three-year study paid for by Whittle, researchers from the University of Michigan discovered that the news program had only limited impact on students' understanding of world and national events. They found that unless the programs became a part of daily lessons to reinforce their content, they were too fast paced, fragmented, and fleeting to have lasting impact on students.

Still, many schools, especially those in rural areas and others facing ever-tighter budgets, see Whittle's equipment-for-watching deal well worth the tradeoff. For them, the ethical issue of making students watch commercials during school time has generally taken a back seat to economic concerns.

Source: Photos courtesy Channel 1—Whittle Education Network.

commercially viable. Some kind of specialization—often a narrow religious format—has become the name of the game for most of the approximately 900 noncommercial FM stations that are *not* funded by CPB or members of NPR.

Unlicensed Radio

Stations that do not actually broadcast (that is, utilize spectrum) need not seek an FCC license. Most use cable or building electrical systems—so-called radiator radio. Some nonlicensed community radio facilities exist as nonbroadcast supplements to cable television. They operate on a shoestring, with all-volunteer staffs and wildly imaginative programming that wins devoted listeners. Also, hundreds of high school and college stations operate as low-power not-for-profit stations serving a campus or school.

• • • • • • • •

8.8 *Audiences*

While overall audience research methods and findings are discussed in Chapters 11 and 12, our focus here is on the several ways in which public radio

Exhibit 8.m ● ● ● ● ● ● ● ● ● ● ● ● ● ● ●

The Mythical World of Garrison Keillor

Every Saturday evening, increasing numbers of public radio listeners across the country tune in to the soft and zany homespun humor of Garrison Keillor, creator and host of *A Prairie Home Companion* from 1974 to 1987 and, since 1989, of its successor, *American Radio Company*. The fourth season (1992–1993) offered 32 new shows and 20 repeats, most broadcast from the stage of the World Theater in downtown St. Paul, Minnesota. Produced by Minnesota Public Radio and distributed by American Public Radio, the program regularly airs on more than 225 stations to a dedicated (fanatical?) listenership of about 1.5 million.

The program's appeal centers on Keillor and a cast that includes the "Coffee Club Orchestra" and a

Source: Photo by Frederic Petters.

sound-effects expert, Tom Keith. The live variety show runs for two hours and features comedy sketches, music heard nowhere else, guests, and Keillor's monologue on the news from all those people in mythical "Lake Wobegon."

To a considerable degree, the characters and style of Lake Wobegon grow out of Keillor's own background. A Minnesota native who grew up in a small town, Keillor had aspirations—and some success—as a writer early in life. He worked as both writer and staff announcer for the campus radio station while earning a degree in English at the University of Minnesota. He wrote occasionally for *The New Yorker* after college, and it was while doing a story on radio's *Grand Ole Opry* that the notion of what would become *Prairie Home Companion* came to him in 1974. The show first aired in Minnesota that year, and went national in 1980.

Keillor explains why he likes radio:

> The beauty of radio is its comparative simplicity. We count on this. It means I can work on a show, be inventing things, right up until airtime and not be so beset with theater or transportation problems that I can't pay attention to the real job at hand.

Television, he feels, is just "the Wal-Mart of the mind. Radio is infinitely sexier." This attitude comes through in his novel *WLT: A Radio Romance* (1991). His characters are people who work at a Minneapolis station (the call letters stand for "with lettuce and tomato") in radio's golden age, an era of creativity he tries to emulate every Saturday night.

and television audiences *differ* from those for commercial channels. The differences center on overall audience size as well as demographics—and they are central to the debate about noncommercial broadcasting's place among American electronic media.

Television

For many years, a primary problem for public television was its limited reach—the number of potential viewers who could receive a signal. Until more stations went on the air in the 1970s, thanks to in-

Exhibit 8.n ● ● ● ● ● ● ● ● ● ● ● ● ● ●

Pacifica Radio— Persistent Dissenter

The original inspiration for "free-form noninstitutional radio"came from Lew Hill, an idealist who initiated the movement when he found KPFA (FM) in Berkeley, CA, in 1949, under the umbrella of his Pacifica Foundation, so named because of Hill's lifelong devotion to pacifism (Trufelman, 1979). Pacifica later acquired a second station in Berkeley and others in Houston, Los Angeles, New York City, and Washington, D.C. Pacifica stations operate noncommercially, depending on listeners and foundations for financial support, supplemented by income from a news bureau and a tape syndication service.

The stations have scheduled such unusual features as the news read in Mandarin Chinese, a reading of all the Nixon Watergate tapes of the early 1970s, recitations of lengthy novels such as Tolstoy's *War and Peace* and Joyce's *Ulysses* in their entirety, and a two-hour opera improvised on the air by phone-in singers. Absurd though some Pacifica programs have been, and limited though their audiences have remained, they have played a role in shaking up established radio. Hundreds of stations have benefited, if only indirectly, from Pacifica's challenge to the safe, the conventional, and the routine. Protesters bombed Pacifica's Houston station, putting it off the air twice in the 1970s. Pacifica stations have consistently taken the lead in defending broadcasting from encroachments on its First Amendment freedoms, often a losing battle, as in the famous "seven dirty words" indecency case to which the Pacifica name is attached (see Section 14.4). In some instances, however, even they accept that limits do exist. When KPFK-FM in Los Angeles broadcast a 30-hour "African Mental Liberation Weekend" early in 1992, it included two examples of what many complained was anti-Semitic content. A member of the CPB board of directors raised concern about the broadcast, but the Corporation took no action when the station agreed to tighten up its own procedures.

---

creased federal funding, much of the country could receive no public television service at all. By the mid-1980s, however, nearly all areas could receive at least one public television signal, usually from a nearby station.

Over the past decade, on any given evening the average public television prime-time program has reached about 2 percent of the nation's television households. On an average evening a little over half of all viewers watch commercial television network-affiliated stations, about a fifth watch an independent station, and nearly a quarter watch some cable service—leaving very few for public television.

Viewing patterns change with time of day. Thanks especially to *Sesame Street*'s wide appeal, slightly more than half of America's households will watch public television sometime during a typical week. But fewer than a third will watch in prime time over the course of that whole week. Over a typical month, about three-quarters of the country's households will have tuned in to at least one program in some daypart. These figures vary little from year to year.

Viewing patterns change as well with the educational and income status of the viewing household: as educational attainment and income rise, so does viewing of public television. Ethnic origin also helps define public television audiences—few Black or Hispanic households watch public television *except* for its children's programs. Once children grow beyond *Sesame Street* or *Mr. Rogers*, however, they are usually lost to public television.

One final indicator of the relatively small size of public television's audience is that system proponents nearly always talk of the *cumulative* audience for the service over a week, while commercial stations speak of their audiences for a given day, hour, or program. The audience for public television at any specific program or time is nearly always too small to measure effectively.

Radio

Patterns described for noncommercial television generally apply to noncommercial radio as well. Audience research for National Public Radio shows an upscale audience small in number (compared to that for popular commercial stations) but large in influence (these listeners are often society's movers and shakers).

In Arbitron's spring 1992 ratings sweep (see Sections 11.1 and 11.4), CPB-supported public radio stations achieved an aggregate share of just under 3 percent of the radio audience—with most listeners among older groups (35 years of age and above). One study of public radio stations found most of them agreed that "they appeal most strongly to white people who have been to college" and that "they don't expect to increase service greatly [to] Hispanics, native Americans, and Asians . . . [or to] people who have not (or not yet) completed high school" (Giovannoni, 1992: 66–67). Yet just like their commercial counterparts, public station managers said they were planning to focus more attention on younger listeners (aged 25 to 34) and less on those 55 and older.

Looked at another way, a small proportion of the noncommercial audience accounts for most of the listening. Just a quarter of the public radio audience accounts for two-thirds of all public radio listening—so-called heavy-core listeners. On average they tune in just over 18 hours a week. Here the differences between commercial and noncommercial radio become evident: half of heavy-core public radio listeners are between 25 and 44 years old, more than two-thirds have completed college or gone to graduate school, and a third live in households earning more than $50,000 annually (Giovannoni, 1988: 16). Commercial radio station listeners are generally younger, less educated, have lower incomes—and most (only about 5 percent in a given week) don't tune to public radio. (That number, however, jumps to a third if we look at those with

a college degree.) Politically, nearly half of public radio's weekly audience consider themselves liberal, while only a quarter classify their views as conservative.

• • • • • • • •

8.9 Changing Roles

With their small but generally upscale audiences, noncommercial stations are concerned with survival in the 1990s in at least two areas—financial support and competition from other services. But they face an even more basic dilemma as well: What can they do to justify their very existence? Years of bickering and disagreement over mission—now largely over—have left noncommercial media ill prepared to face new competition from cable networks and other sources. Perceived differences among stations and between television and radio now become very important.

New Options

A common argument heard these days is that development of alternative media, especially cable, has weakened the major rationale for public television by co-opting its once unique programming—with the possible exception of most in-class instruction (and even there, teachers often find videocassettes easier to use). Programs for children, good drama, and other cultural programming now appear on several cable networks. Given the increasing number of viewing and listening options available to most people, critics argue, narrow-appeal public services will have to find their own audience support, probably in some form of direct payment from viewers for services they choose.

The counterargument, of course, centers on the fact that about 35 percent of the population has no access to cable—either by choice (not to subscribe) or by chance (cable does not even pass their households)—while 98 percent have access to at least one public television signal. Further, audience research shows that five times as many people watch PBS prime-time programs as watch The Discovery Channel, and seven times more see PBS than Arts and Entertainment, two of the most often-cited channels offering PBS-like programming. In addition, PBS's national program budget (in 1990) was six to ten times greater than that of either of those cable channels (Carey, 1990: 3–4).

Still, it seems clear that cable competition—and increasingly widespread use of VCRs for educational material—makes public broadcasters more aware of the need to specify clearly what role they will play amidst a wider variety of viewer choices. But it remains just as clear that, for the foreseeable future, newer media cannot provide noncommercial system–type services to all who want them.

Traditional Defense

Aside from shared concerns over changing technology, supporters of public radio and television acclaim its many benefits:

- Programs usually not found elsewhere make up noncommercial radio and television's core offerings: fine arts, music, dance, important foreign-language films, superior drama, public-affairs discussions, and the like.
- The public system does better than commercial outlets at meeting needs of such subgroups in society as ethnic minorities, senior citizens, and children.
- Public stations, along with public participation in station advisory groups, are the last real bastion of localism—reflecting and projecting their local communities rather than merely passing on programs from distant centers.
- The very existence of disagreements about public television's role indicates an openness to conflicting ideas that certainly does not characterize commercial entities.
- Public broadcasting offers an essential relief from the hard-sell content of commercial networks, stations, and cable systems—although increasingly irritating fund raisers weaken this argument to some degree.
- Application of television and radio to instruction

and informal education is unmatched, with *Sesame Street* the leading example of what has been and still can be accomplished by these public services.

Noncommercial radio supporters appear to have an easier case than do supporters of noncommercial television. Those CPB-qualified stations that are NPR members provide some of radio's best news and public-affairs programs and attract consistent and loyal audiences. The 900 or so noncommercial FM stations that are not part of the larger CPB/NPR-led elite offer an almost infinite variety of programs and services—that they often rely totally on listeners and community groups for their support attests to their value.

Critical Views

In addition to citing an increasing variety of media options providing educational and cultural fare, critics in recent years have broadened their attack on the current system of noncommercial broadcasting on several related but distinct fronts:

- The funding shortage always cited by public broadcasters is largely a matter of evasion: lack of sufficient audience appeal rather than a lack of money lies at the root of their problem.
- *Public* participation in public television is in too many cases a sham because professional managers make most decisions, just as they do in commercial operations.
- Public television has little public appeal. Public television's vaunted fine arts and high culture merely serve privileged groups that are easily able to afford other sources of such material without resorting to publicly supported broadcast channels. Critics liken tax support of public broadcasting, dwindling though it is, to government support that once sustained American-flag passenger ships only the rich could afford to patronize.
- Conservatives have long targeted public broadcasting as being too liberal in news and documentary programs, presenting a one-sided view of American life. In 1991 two scheduled programs on gay lifestyles were pulled from the air (another

was delayed) because of conservative pressure. And the conservative Heritage Foundation argued again in 1992 for commercialization of public television to make it more truly tuned to public needs while at the same time cutting public tax expenditures.

Outlook

Some of these criticisms reflect the deregulatory philosophy that dominated discussions of U.S. media policy during the conservative political ascendancy of the 1980s. Similar attacks on public broadcasting surfaced in other countries, also stimulated by a market-oriented, laissez-faire approach to media regulation. Even so widely esteemed a service as the BBC came under attack as elitist and lacking in the fiscal responsibility that, according to deregulatory theory, only "discipline of the market" can impose.

In Europe, as in the United States, these attacks raise a basic question: Should all broadcasting be regarded strictly as an *economic* undertaking, with programs treated as ordinary consumer goods? Or should at least some part of any national electronic media system be regarded as a cultural undertaking, with programs treated as a significant aspect of national life? Must everything depend on that slogan of free marketers, "consumer choice"? Not everyone chooses to attend great museums, galleries, and libraries that public funds support—often in locations not far from festering slums. Yet few would advocate dismantling all such cultural treasures and diverting their government grants to public housing.

Nevertheless, market-oriented thinking and the deregulatory policies that ride its crest cannot be ignored. Leaders of national public-service broadcasting organizations readily understood and agreed with the need for in-depth self-assessments in the early 1990s. CPB worked within a constantly updated five-year plan. NPR undertook an in-depth review of its role and options. PBS tightened control over its prime-time program scheduling, seemingly modeling itself more closely on the national commercial networks than before. The whole system

Exhibit 8.0 •••••• •• •••••• •

Yet Another Look . . .

In mid-1993, a distinguished task force appointed by the Twentieth Century Fund foundation released its report "Quality Time?" suggesting, on public broadcasting's twenty-fifth birthday, changes in its structure and funding. The first such comprehensive assessment of the public system since the second Carnegie commission of 1979, the new study urged that most federal funds be applied to national programming, leaving local television stations reliant on local funding sources. Among other recommendations, the Twentieth Century task force called for increased federal funding (possibly through spectrum auctions or fees from other spectrum users); resistance to further system commercialization; and means of selecting better-qualified board members to serve the Corporation for Public Broadcasting. Both the public broadcasting establishment and members of Congress promised to consider these suggestions.

received a strong boost from these words in cable legislation of 1992:

> The Federal Government has a substantial interest in making all nonduplicative local public television services available on cable systems because . . . public television provides educational and informational programming to the Nation's citizens, thereby advancing the Government's compelling interest in educating its citizens . . . [and because] public television is a local community institution. (Cable Act of 1992, Section 2(a)(8))

•••••••

Summary

8.1 Noncommercial services include the national public radio and television systems and hundreds of other radio stations supported by communities, religious groups, and others. All share a nonprofit mission of providing program alternatives to commercial outlets. Educational radio began before World War I. After a brief boom in the 1920s, the number of noncommercial AM stations had declined by 1945 to about 25. The FCC first reserved channels for noncommercial FM radio in 1941, a reservation retained when FM changed frequency bands in 1945. After long debate, the FCC extended the reservation idea to television in 1952. Arguments about the proper mission of noncommercial services began in the 1950s and continue still.

8.2 The Carnegie Commission report of 1967 led to creation of the Corporation for Public Broadcasting, which in turn set up the Public Broadcasting Service and National Public Radio. Early years of the new system were marked by a struggle for power between stations and new national entities, a search for expanded federal funding, and political interference by Congress and the White House. By the early 1990s PBS had emerged from battles over program control and had developed a strong central programming function, though much production is done by member stations. National Public Radio produces as well as distributes news and entertainment programs to its affiliates.

8.3 Noncommercial television stations fall into four ownership types: (1) state or municipally controlled stations; (2) college and university operations; (3) public school system stations; and (4) community outlets. They differ in both approach and funding. Radio stations fall into two groups: about 300 "elite" stations, most of which are funded in part by CPB and belong to NPR; and another 900 or so smaller community stations that are not "CPB-qualified."

8.4 Insufficient financial support of noncommercial broadcasting has always been a problem. Ford and other foundations contributed to early station development. Federal funding came in 1963, and three-year funding cycles began in 1975. Government support raises concerns about insulation between funding and programming decisions. After

1981 Congress often rescinded funds already approved for public broadcasting. Nongovernment funding of noncommercial broadcasting—the largest portion of system income—comes from several sources: business funding, program underwriting, public memberships, fund-raising "begathons," and so on.

8.5 Public television program sources include individual stations, independent producers and syndicators, foreign broadcast systems, and instructional program libraries. Media systems competing for such programs include cultural cable networks, children's services, and services for schools.

8.6 Public television is most appreciated for its news and public-affairs programs, its historical and cultural documentary series, its science and nature offerings, its window on the performing arts, its classic children's programs, and the educational and instructional offerings for which the system was first created.

8.7 Public radio stations take some of their programs from National Public Radio and American Public Radio, but they produce the majority themselves, typically featuring classical or jazz music and limited instructional material.

8.8 Public broadcast audiences are tiny by commercial standards, but they are highly loyal and occupy opinion-leader positions in society. Listeners to public radio and television tend to have higher levels of education and more income than commercial outlet audiences.

8.9 Defenders of noncommercial broadcasting stress its service to groups underserved by commercial outlets: minorities, children, and those with cultural interests. Critics, on the other hand, argue that other services—especially cable—now serve these groups and that the system set up in 1952 (television channels) and 1967 (the current national structure) needs updating. But the limited reach and cost of newer media (in terms of subscriptions and advertisements) limit their replacement role for the nearly universal public broadcast system.

Part 4

Programming

Most viewers consider themselves program experts. That is, they know what they like and wonder why there isn't more of it, and they know what they don't like and wonder why there is so much. We deal here, however, not with personal preferences but with anticipation of group preferences. The collective term *programming* refers to practices used in selecting, scheduling, and evaluating programs. *Whether viewed from the perspective of broadcast or cable, the overriding purpose of commercial programming is either to attract advertisers by delivering audiences of sufficient size and appropriate composition or to attract audiences who pay monthly subscription fees—or both.* Other purposes, such as elevating or informing the public, are usually secondary. Program decision making involves risks and uncertainties uncharacteristic of most other businesses, operating as it does in the twin spotlights of intense public fascination and critical press reaction. Chapter 9 describes programming concerns and practices, program sources, and scheduling strategies commonly used by programmers. Chapter 10 examines programming at broadcast and cable networks, at local radio and television stations and cable systems, and in syndication.

Chapter 9

Programs and Programming Basics

● ●

Any broadcast or cable program schedule will have some hits, some outright failures, and many borderline successes that may tip over into failure at any time. Programmers obtain new shows to replace canceled ones, adjust the order of programs, and continuously track the ratings of them all. For those responsible for prime-time broadcast and cable network programs, success means attracting millions of television households; for small-market radio station programmers, success may mean capturing a few hundred listeners.

So many services clamor for suitable and affordable programs that they never end their search for *product*—a term, derived from the motion picture industry, that gives a hint of some programmers' disinterest in program quality. The search becomes still more intense as electronic media move to video compression and fiber optics with their promise of even more channels. Product that attracts audiences of desirable size and composition costs so much that filling all channels continuously with brand new—not to mention "good"— programs would be an economic impossibility.

● ● ● ● ● ● ● ●

9.1   Economic Constraints

Commercial programmers find themselves constrained economically in three ways: (1) programs are exceedingly expensive and prices constantly rise; (2) programmers need so much of this costly material that they must use it parsimoniously; and (3) programmers depend on advertisers or subscribers to defray costs, and so must select programs that attract those specific audiences advertisers want to reach or those willing to pay subscription fees.

Program Costs

The three major networks spend nearly $5 billion and cable networks more than $3 billion each year for the rights to limited use of programs. Networks spend up to $200 million each year on pilots for new program series, of which three-quarters fail. Exhibit 9.a outlines the steps a program takes from concept to pilot to production.

Exhibit 9.a ● ● ● ● ● ● ● ● ● ● ● ● ● ● ● ● ●

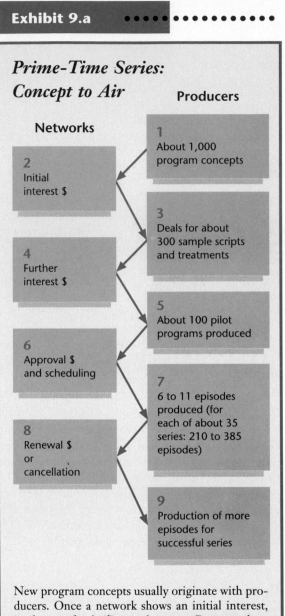

Prime-Time Series: Concept to Air

Networks

Producers

1 About 1,000 program concepts

2 Initial interest $

3 Deals for about 300 sample scripts and treatments

4 Further interest $

5 About 100 pilot programs produced

6 Approval $ and scheduling

7 6 to 11 episodes produced (for each of about 35 series: 210 to 385 episodes)

8 Renewal $ or cancellation

9 Production of more episodes for successful series

New program concepts usually originate with producers. Once a network shows an initial interest, it advances funds ($) stage by stage. Concepts drop out at each stage. In the hypothetical year depicted, nearly twenty-nine program concepts were discarded for each one actually produced. The numbers listed here typify program development from many concepts to relatively few completed episodes.

In the early 1990s the license fees that producers charged commercial broadcast networks for two showings of a new one-hour prime-time drama or action/adventure program averaged about $1 million per episode; for 30-minute shows, nearly $700,000. Very successful series cost considerably more (*Cheers*, for example, ran as much as $2.85 million).

High as these prices seem, they rarely cover the full cost of production. (Just for fun, Exhibit 9.b lists some minor items producers have to buy.) Prime-time series program production costs typically exceed license fees by anywhere from $150,000 to $300,000 per episode. Producers count on subsequent syndication sales to bring in the profits. This practice, known as *deficit financing*, capitalizes on the dynamics of the syndication market. Initial network showing enhances the future value of a series because such exposure gives a series the prestige and track record it needs for successful syndication in both domestic and foreign markets. Networks normally order only about 22 to 25 episodes of ongoing series each year, filling the balance of a time period's 52 weeks with reruns and specials. Producers of unsuccessful shows (those with fewer than 100 episodes, or about a four-year network run—the minimum usually required for syndication) have little chance to recoup their losses.

Part of network program budgets also goes to purchase rights to entertainment specials and to sports events. For example, HBO paid $2 million for Madonna's *Blind Ambition* concert and a whopping $20 million for Michael Jackson's two-hour spectacular taped in Bucharest, Romania. In sports, ABC, CBS, NBC, ESPN, and TNT shared three years of NFL professional football (from 1990 to 1993) for nearly $4 billion, while NBC paid a record $401 million for the 1992 Summer Olympics in Barcelona, Spain.

At the station level, *off-network* syndicated programs are priced according to market size, prior program performance, and other factors such as how often they have been rerun. Large-market stations commonly pay more than $10 million for four plays of a hundred or so episodes of newly released network shows, while small-market stations might

lion for the off-CBS series *Murder, She Wrote*, a record price for that network.

Parsimony Principle

To cope with high program costs, writers, producers, and programmers resort to a variety of strategies based on what might be called the *parsimony principle*. This basic rule dictates that program product be used as sparingly as possible, repeated as often as possible, and shared as widely as possible.

Sparing use of product means, for example, extending a dramatic plot over many episodes instead of burning it up in a single performance—the technique of soap opera. News directors often release news feature material as a series of mini-features. Networks prefer to package expensive sporting events, straining them to the utmost with pre-game shows, half-time shows, and post-game wrap-ups.

Writers and programmers stretch resources by *repeating* program material, using standardized openings, closings, and transitions in daily newscasts, quiz shows, weekly dramatic shows, and the like. Cartoons, movies, and television series replay endlessly over time—in fact, some cable networks repeat the same movie several times on the same day. And NBC in 1991 introduced the concept of *double-pumping*—airing the same movie (*Kindergarten Cop*) in prime time twice in the same week.

Shared use is best illustrated by networks, which enable the same programs to appear on hundreds of different stations and thousands of different cable systems. Further sharing occurs when network programs reappear in syndication. The 1990s introduced new forms of sharing that earlier would have been unthinkable in the competitive world of electronic media. Broadcast and cable networks now offer the same program series (for example, *Silk Stalkings* on both CBS and USA) and made-for-television movies (*Casualty of Love: The "Long Island Lolita" Story* on CBS and, only a few days later, on USA); cable networks share with local television stations (*Beakman's World* in syndication and on The Learning Channel, CNN on broadcast affiliates throughout the country); some cable systems carry news programs produced by local television stations;

Exhibit 9.b ● ● ● ● ● ● ● ● ● ● ● ● ● ● ● ●

How Production Pennies Add Up

Salaries of stars, writers, and producers contribute most to the cost of television program production. But every penny counts. Here are some of the items—and their prices—purchased for use in recent series:

- Each seersucker suit worn by *Matlock's* Andy Griffith (which is immediately washed to make it appear that Matlock never buys new clothes)—$2,000.
- A five-month-season's worth of Grecian Formula for The Family Channel's *Zorro*—$4,000.
- Sneakers for Fred Rogers on *Mister Rogers' Neighborhood*—$29.95.
- A guest appearance by Bubbles the Chimp (owned by Michael Jackson) on ABC's *Father Dowling Mysteries*—$800. Other animal daily rentals: zebra, $500; giraffe, $1,000 to $1,500; elephant, $1,500 to $2,000.
- The Aristo stopwatch on *60 Minutes*—$130.
- Kleenex for guests and audience members on *Sally Jesse Raphael*—$200 a year.
- Medical equipment and uniforms on NBC's *Empty Nest*—$2,000.
- Dean Stockwell's cigars on *Quantum Leap*—$185 per episode.
- Coffee consumed by ABC's *Nightline* staff—$120 a month.
- Bill Cosby's suspenders on *The Cosby Show*—$30 to $70.
- Diapers and other baby supplies on *Baby Talk*—$300 to $350 per episode.

Source: From "What Things Cost on TV," by Bill Bruns, *TV Guide*, April 13, 1991, p. 8. Reprinted with permission from TV Guide® Magazine. Copyright © 1991 by News America Publications, Inc.

---

pay as little as $100,000 for the same series. Competition between advertiser-supported cable networks and broadcast stations for the same programs has made some former network properties increasingly valuable. For example, USA Network paid $30 milsome television stations even carry the newscasts of another station in its market, while some radio stations rebroadcast the audio portion of the program. All such arrangements attempt to spread rapidly rising production costs over multiple users.

Audience Targeting

As the number of stations, cable systems, and networks grew, many program services gave up aiming at the mass audience that was the original target of broadcasting. The terms *narrowcasting* and *niche services* came into vogue, suggesting a specific alternative goal. CNN, MTV, Nickelodeon, and others now deliberately limit their appeal to specific audience segments.

Advertisers influenced the trend toward narrowcasting. They are not inclined to pay for audiences with no money to spend on their products or no interest in buying them. The need to reach people willing and able to pay the bills, whether as shoppers or as subscribers, has led to *audience targeting* and segmentation throughout the electronic media.

Although they design some of their programs for other audiences, ABC, CBS, and NBC generally—and especially in prime time—target those viewers between the ages of 18 and 49. Fox initially aimed at, and quite successfully attracted, much younger audiences—those in the 12- to 34-year-old range. In 1993, however, as it expanded its programming first to six and then to seven nights a week, Fox revised its target to concentrate on the 18- to 49-year-old viewers as well. NBC, which had drawn a susbstantial share of older viewers with such series as *Matlock*, *Golden Girls*, and *In the Heat of the Night*, cancelled those programs in an effort to attract a younger audience. Then, after it had fallen to number three in the prime-time ratings in the 1992–1993 season, the network conceded it had moved too quickly and said it would no longer try to discourage older viewers entirely. All, of course, offer programs for children, but only CBS continues actively to seek viewers 50 and older. Some cable networks (USA in particular) target a broad audience; others program for more narrowly defined groups (TNT: 30- to 50-year-olds; Lifetime: women 24–49; A&E: adults 25–54). Each service defines its audience in terms of *demographics* (age and gender) and/or *psychographics* (lifestyle and interests). Targeting women 18 to 34 years old is a demographic goal; targeting sports fans is a psychographic goal.

Even though noncommercial broadcasting and pay cable sell no advertising, they also target specific audience groups. They need to attract audience segments most likely to support them by paying membership and subscription fees. Public television favors programs that appeal to middle-to-upper-income, well-educated families. Pay cable tends to select movies that attract women or families with children.

Radio has further refined the process of targeting by using *segmentation*, which defines extremely narrow subsets of the potential radio audience. Radio usually segments audiences in both demographic and psychographic terms: teenagers-who-want-to-hear-only-hit-songs or 25-to-44-year-old-adults-who-prefer-the-music-of-the-1960s. Accordingly, most stations adopt rigid musical formats, each of which may repel great numbers of listeners but may nevertheless prove irresistible to a narrowly targeted audience segment.

9.2 Syndication

The distribution method known as *syndication* offers both a supplement and an alternative to networks as a means for financing centrally produced, high-cost product. Syndication occurs worldwide wherever broadcasting or cablecasting exists.

Distribution by syndication resembles network distribution in that the same programs go to many outlets, but it differs as to timing. Stations usually may schedule syndicated programs at any time according to their needs, whereas affiliated stations normally carry network programs at network-stipulated times. Occasionally syndicators do designate specific time slots for their programs, especially those with barter programs (see page 311). They want to be sure their clients' commercials within those programs air at appropriate times.

Definition

The FCC defines a syndicated television program as "any program sold, licensed, distributed, or offered to television stations in more than one market within the United States for non-interconnected [that is, nonnetwork] television broadcast exhibition, but not including live presentations" (47 CFR 76.5p). In practice, however, programmers classify as syndicated all *nonlocal* programs not currently licensed to a network, whether live or not, including movies.

How Syndication Works

Television program *syndicators*, also called *distributors*, obtain distribution rights for a special or series from the program producer, which may be another branch of their own company or an independent producer. They then offer the shows *in syndication*.

Like many other business specializations, syndication has its own terminology, some of which seems self-contradictory. Strictly speaking, a syndicator *licenses* a station or a cable network to show a program or program series. Ownership of the program does not change hands. However, industry people often refer to "buying" and "owning" syndicated shows.

The license grants a "buyer" the right to show the program, or each *episode** of a program series, in its local market area, a given number of times—called *runs* or *plays*—over a set period of time. A typical contract thus might call for six runs of each of 200 episodes in a series over a five-year license term. In exchange, the buyer pays a fee to the syndicator—in cash (also over time) or in free advertising time (see page 311) or in a combination of the two. After the license period expires, program rights return to the syndicator, who can recycle them over and over again. *Off-net* programs (those that origi-

*Episodes are sometimes called *titles*, acknowledging that producers give a title to each individual program in a series. In the case of hour-long dramatic series, the titles commonly appear on the air. Only rarely (in *Designing Women*, for example) is this true for 30-minute shows. One of the many delights of the short-lived but underrated series *Police Squad* was a visual opening title for each episode, accompanied by a completely different audio title from the announcer.

nally ran on one of the three major networks) sold to cable networks technically do not fit the FCC's definition of "syndicated," since a cable network is not a station, but the same programs and marketing processes are involved. Cable networks, however, obtain program licenses for national, not just local, markets.

ABC, CBS, and NBC currently own relatively few off-network programs—the result of a Federal Communications Commission (FCC) decision and a U.S. District Court antitrust consent decree. Designed to prevent network domination of program production and distribution, the *financial interest and syndication (fin/syn) rules* have severely limited each of these networks' freedom to participate in production and ownership of prime-time programs or in their domestic syndication.

The FCC modified the fin/syn rules slightly in 1991 and effectively repealed them in 1993. The financial interest portion of the rules ended immediately, permitting the Big Three networks to increase their involvement in program production. The Commission delayed repeal of the syndication portion, however, until two years after dismissal of the court's consent decree, which was expected later in the year. As part of its 1993 action, the FCC exempted the Fox network from the rules entirely. As expected, pro-fin/syn interests promised they would challenge these FCC decisions in court.

Syndicators deliver their programs by various means. A station might receive one syndicated program through a satellite feed and either broadcast it at the feed time or videotape it for later playback. The same station might receive another program by *bicycle*—a system whereby the syndicator ships perhaps two weeks' worth of program tapes to station A, which airs the shows and then forwards them on to station B, and so on.

Major television syndication firms often operate as units within vertically integrated companies—those that engage in several related activities. MCA, for example, has cable-network as well as studio and broadcasting interests. King World Productions ranks as the top syndicator, in terms of hit shows, with *Wheel of Fortune* and *Jeopardy* (typically number one and number two on Nielsen's list of most-watched syndicated shows) and *Oprah* (which usually falls within the top five). Although the company, run by brothers Roger and Michael King, has had its share of flops (*Monopoly* and an updated version of the classic *Candid Camera*), it generates annual revenues of some $500 million.

Syndicators showcase their programs at annual meetings of the National Association of Television Program Executives (NATPE—although most broadcasters more comfortably mispronounce the acronym as "NAPTE") and at other national and international program trade fairs. Although buying and selling of syndicated programs take place at these events, the process goes on throughout the year as well. Syndication firms employ sales executives whose job it is to contact stations (often assigned on regional bases), national sales representatives, and cable networks as new programs become available or earlier contracts expire. These sales people visit their customers—in person (sometimes over lunch or dinner) or by telephone—to make presentations and try to negotiate a deal. In the case of highly successful series, however, a more impersonal method—the auction—has taken over. Under this system, syndicators send all stations in a given market written notice—by FAX or otherwise—that a program is available, what the minimum acceptable bid will be, and the deadline by which bids must be submitted. Highest bidder wins.

The two major rating services, Arbitron and Nielsen, document the track records of syndicated programs (see Section 11.1). Successful programmers regularly consult rating reports, read trade magazines, screen pilots of new first-run shows, and consult with other people in the industry before committing to buy a program.

Some syndicated series have been running for more than 35 years, replayed scores of times. *Little Rascals*, a series edited from ancient *Our Gang* film shorts (they originated in 1922!), started in television syndication in 1955 and can still be seen on independent stations. *I Love Lucy* (1951–1956), perhaps the most successful off-network syndicated series ever, dates to pre-color days, yet has been syndicated in virtually every country in the world; at times there have been as many as five *Lucy* episodes on the air on the same day in a single U.S. city. (Later series also starring Lucille Ball, however, never achieved the original's level of success.) Highly popular network shows, such as *The Cosby Show* and *Who's the Boss?*, and hit programs made especially for syndication, such as *Star Trek: The Next Generation* and *Entertainment Tonight*, play in most of the 200-plus U.S. markets. This reach rivals the networks' national coverage.

Syndication Exclusivity (Syndex)

Stations may obtain from distributors *syndication exclusivity* (*syndex*)—the sole right to show a program within the buyer's own market for the term of the license. But cable program services, especially superstations, might buy the same program, bringing identical episodes into a market where a broadcast station has paid extra for exclusive rights to that very program. This duplication, of course, divides the audience and diminishes the program's value to the broadcast stations. Currently, cable networks purchase a mix of exclusive and nonexclusive national rights, depending on their budgets and programming strategy.

Responding to the program-duplication dilemma, the Federal Communications Commission in 1990 reintroduced syndex rules that it had rescinded eight years earlier in a wave of deregulation. Syndex empowers broadcast television stations to force cable systems in their coverage area to delete duplicate syndicated programs to which the stations hold exclusive rights. Cable systems must temporarily black out the offending superstation or other program service, substituting another program or a slide that explains the deletion. In some cases (WWOR-TV and WGN-TV, for example), a superstation's satellite carrier handles this task by inserting alternative programs before downlinking the station's signal to cable systems. In others (TBS), the superstation acquires only those shows that have no syndex problem and thus create a "blackout-proof" program schedule.

Syndex rules do not apply to two affiliates of the same network carried by a cable system or to very small cable systems, nor are all syndication contracts exclusive. In fact, obtaining exclusivity increases the price of syndicated programs; sometimes stations prefer forgoing exclusivity for the sake of a lower price.

Prime-Time Access

Still another FCC rule, the *prime-time access rule* (PTAR), artificially shapes the program marketplace. Before 1971 the three major commercial television networks filled nearly all prime-time hours of their affiliates' schedules. This network monopoly left little opportunity for producers to sell programs aimed at the national market but not good enough (or lucky enough) to be selected for network exhibition. On affiliated stations, only daytime and fringe hours (late afternoon and following prime time) remained open for syndicated materials. Of course, independent stations have prime time available, but in the early 1970s they could not afford to pay for recently produced, high-quality syndicated shows (later, many could, partly because of PTAR's help).

In part to enlarge the market for original syndicated and local program production, and in part to diminish the hold of the three commercial networks on the best audience hours, the FCC adopted PTAR in 1971. With some exceptions (Sundays from 7:00 to 8:00 P.M., for example) it limits network entertainment programs to no more than three of the four prime-time hours—the evening hours when the television audience reaches maximum size and, hence, when stations can pay the most for nonnetwork programs. The FCC defines prime time as the hours between 7:00 P.M. and 11:00 P.M. Eastern and Pacific time (one hour earlier in the Central and Mountain time zones, with variations during daylight saving time).

In practice, the networks had already abandoned the 7:00 to 7:30 P.M. slot to their affiliates. PTAR therefore gave the affiliates only the additional half-hour between 7:30 and 8:00 P.M. One daily half-hour may not seem like much for the networks to surrender. However, multiplying that half-hour of access time by the 260 weekdays in a year and by the 150 affiliates in the top 50 markets yields an annual large-audience market of 39,000 half-hours on major stations. Prior to 1971 syndicators and

local producers had no access to prime time on the top affiliates except in those rare instances where a station declined to carry one of its network's programs. PTAR therefore gave a significant new incentive to producers of nonnetwork programs.

With PTAR, the entire 7:00 to 8:00 P.M. hour became known as *access time*.* Affiliates in the top 50 markets can fill access time with either locally produced programs or nationally syndicated *first-run* programs (those that never aired on a broadcast network but, rather, were produced specifically for syndication), but they may not schedule either regular network feeds or former network programs. This leaves all independents and the affiliates in the 150-odd smaller markets free to use former network material during access time if they choose.** Like any rule, PTAR has exceptions, as detailed in Exhibit 9.c.

From time to time, proposals surface to repeal PTAR, based on the argument that much of the rationale for this rule (as well as for fin/syn)—network domination of television production and distribution—no longer exists. By early 1993, however, all such efforts had been unsuccessful.

Barter Syndication

In the 1970s a different way for stations to pay for some syndicated television programs emerged. Until that time, stations had normally paid cash for syndicated shows, but as program prices escalated, stations ran short of ready cash. Some program distributors responded by offering to trade (*barter*) programs for free advertising time. They presold some

---

*Arbitron and Nielsen, the principal television rating companies, rate the access hour separately for stations and advertisers, identifying as prime time only 8:00 to 11:00 P.M. and ignoring the FCC's four-hour definition.

**A station whose market rank hovers around the all-important 50th spot has special problems. Every three years, Arbitron provides the FCC with a market-rank update. Each time, some stations move into, while others drop out of, the top 50. In 1992 Albany, New York, moved out while Little Rock, Arkansas, moved in—its second flip-flop in six years. As one result, the NBC affiliate in Little Rock has had to continue bouncing reruns of *The Cosby Show*—in and out of access time.

Exhibit 9.c ●●●●●●●●●●●●●●●

PTAR: Access vs. Network Time

Time Period	Days of Week	
	Sunday through Friday	Saturday Only
Local access time 7:00–8:00 P.M. EST and PST 6:00–7:00 P.M. MST and CST	No network programs with exceptions noted and no off-network programs on affiliates in top-50 markets	No network programs except for feature films on affiliates in top-50 markets
Network prime time 8:00–11:00 P.M. EST and PST 7:00–10:00 P.M. CST and MST	All affiliates may accept all network programs	

The prime-time access rule (PTAR) is intended to give television producers outside the limited circle of network program makers a chance to sell programs during at least one of the four top-audience hours. As the FCC put it, PTAR aims

> to make available for competition among existing and potential program producers, *both at the local and national levels*, an arena of more adequate competition for the custom and favor of broadcasters and advertisers. (FCCR, 1970: 326, italics added)

The networks chose the 7:00 to 8:00 P.M. EST hour as the one to give up—known thereafter as *access time*. The rule also forbids affiliates in the top-50 markets to schedule off-network syndicated programs in that hour.

The FCC aimed to give more producers a chance to create prime-time *entertainment* programs, but not to discourage network nonentertainment programs. It therefore built several exceptions into PTAR,

Source: 47 CFR 73.658 (k).

allowing the top affiliates to accept the following types of network offerings during access time:

- Children's, public affairs, and documentary programs. (It is this exception, very broadly interpreted, that allows networks to program the 7:00 to 8:00 P.M. [Eastern and Pacific] hour on Sundays.)
- Broadcasts by political candidates.
- Reports of fast-breaking and on-the-spot news events.
- Regular network newscasts if adjacent to one-hour affiliate news or public-affairs programs.
- Runovers of live sports events.
- Feature films.

On Saturdays, however, only feature films are excepted because when the FCC adopted PTAR, affiliates favored Saturday evening for locally produced public-affairs programs, which the commission wished to encourage. The accompanying table summarizes the rule and its exceptions.

of the commercial time in barter programs to national advertisers, filling about half the spot openings with preinserted ads before delivering the series to contracting stations. Broadcasters thus obtained programs without spending cash—instead giving away for free some ad time that they might not have been able to sell anyway—and generated revenues by selling the remaining spots locally. National advertisers paid the program syndicator, getting cut-rate advertising time and an assured place in programs of their own choosing on several stations around the country.

At first, barterers mostly offered only once-a-week programs of little interest to most stations.* Generally, these were *straight* (or *full*) *barter* deals, meaning the producer/syndicator sold all the commercial time nationally and stations received a free program but no commercial time to sell locally and, hence, no opportunity for profit. Later, nearly all first-run access programs were sold as *partial barter* deals, meaning that the station retained some minutes for local advertising sales. Then syndicators discovered that former network hits could command both cash payments and advertising time. In the late 1980s most barter deals for off-net sitcoms were of this type, called *cash/barter* or *barter-plus-cash*. By the 1990s, as more and more stations became cash poor, syndicators had returned to partial barter arrangements. *Designing Women* was one of the first programs offered on the newly revived barter-no-cash deal.

In a barter arrangement, the producer/syndicator may presell perhaps three minutes of ads in each half-hour nationally, leaving three minutes for stations to sell locally. Alternatively, a national advertiser or ad agency obtains the rights to a program from the producer/syndicator, either by purchasing it or by underwriting a new production; the advertiser or agency then fills all the show's commercial time and syndicates it to stations in a full barter deal. In another variation, *time-bank syndication*, advertisers exchange programs for an inventory of spots, usually to be scheduled at a later time; toy manufacturers, for example, may bank spots during the year in order to intensify their pre-Christmas advertising.

Barter syndication truly came into its own as a method of financing program purchases when distributors of first-run access shows adopted it, notably for hit game shows such as *Wheel of Fortune* and *Jeopardy*. Soon barter included most syndicated daytime talk shows—*Oprah Winfrey* and *Donahue*—as well as first-run access magazine shows such as *Entertainment Tonight*. Then movie packages from major studios began including barter minutes, and finally off-network series did the same. *Cosby* was the first off-network series sold on a cash/barter basis, and it shattered all revenue records for a syndicated program. Licensed mostly to affiliates as a lead-in to early evening news, *Cosby* earned more money than any other syndicated series, before or since (see Exhibit 9.h). By 1992 total annual revenue for all ad-supported syndication had exceeded $1 billion.

Barter occasionally presents stations with a dilemma. A station that carries a barter program typically agrees that, if the program is moved to another, less desirable time period, the station will continue to air the syndicator's client's commercials in the original time period. This could mean that the replacement show, if it too is on a barter deal, fills with syndicators' commercials, leaving little if any time for station sales. Stations may also find that some of the most popular barter shows are too "expensive." That is, the value of commercial time given to a syndicator may be far more than the station would have been willing to pay in cash for the right to carry the program and sell all the commercial time itself.

As electronic media profits drop and program production costs escalate, it appears likely that barter will increase in popularity. Indeed, as the Big Three networks reconsider their affiliate-compensation arrangements, even they may turn to this method when offering some of their prime-time programs (NBC's *Today* and *Tonight* already give

*Three major exceptions are *Wild Kingdom*, *Hee Haw*, and *The Lawrence Welk Show*—all barter programs and each, on some stations, among their most popular.

affiliates local commercial time in lieu of cash payments). Nor is barter free from possible abuse. Although laws theoretically prohibit syndicators from doing so, some subtly force stations to accept marginal programs in order to obtain as well those that deliver big audiences.

Radio Syndication

Syndication and barter also operate in radio (Section 10.8). Syndicators use satellites and tapes to relay music, news, sports, and entertainment material to radio stations. Programmers distinguish between *syndicated formats* and *syndicated features.* A station might buy the use of a ready-made syndicated country-music format, for example, supplementing it with syndicated news and features from other sources. Thus stations can create unique programming mixes from commonly available syndicated elements. Radio feature materials—such as lifestyle inserts and stock market reports—are often bartered, whereas syndicated formats are usually cash deals.

• • • • • • • •

9.3   Program Types

As the previous sections indicate, programs can be classified according to their method of distribution as *local, network,* or *syndicated.* This section deals with other classification methods based on *content, scheduling, format,* and *genre.*

Content

Nearly all programs fall readily into one or the other of two broad categories: information or entertainment. Although most programs qualify primarily as entertainment, information programs receive special attention and deference because they enhance the electronic media's social importance.

Information programs consist of two main subtypes: *news* and *public affairs.* News includes news specials as well as regularly scheduled daily newscasts. Public-affairs programs take such forms as interviews, panel discussions, and documentaries. At one time, documentaries were a major and prestigious type of broadcast network program. By the 1980s, however, they had all but disappeared from the networks, although they became more visible in public television and on specialized cable networks such as Arts & Entertainment and The Discovery Channel. Commercial networks instead emphasize *news specials* and *news magazines,* which treat current events in detail but usually in less depth and with a less defined viewpoint than documentaries.

A hybrid class of programs became trendy in the 1980s and expanded in the 1990s. *Reality shows* such as *A Current Affair* and *Unsolved Mysteries* earned the term *infotainment* because they take on an aura of information but aim primarily at providing entertainment.

Some argue that *sports* programs should be classified as information rather than as entertainment. However, programmers classify programs according to the responsible station or network department and according to their purpose in the overall program schedule. They regard sports as primarily entertainment, not information. Network sports departments differ markedly from news departments in purpose, style, and types of personnel.

Scheduling

Professionals also classify programs according to the part of the day in which they are customarily scheduled. Prime-time programs have distinctive qualities, as do programs associated with other specific schedule positions. The same type of program scheduled in two different parts of the day takes on different colorations. Thus a daytime soap opera differs from a prime-time soap opera, and prime-time sports shows usually differ from those on weekends.

For scheduling and advertising purposes, programmers break the 24-hour day into blocks they call *dayparts.* Radio programmers generally divide the day into *morning drive, midday, afternoon drive, night,* and *overnight* segments. Morning and afternoon drive periods have the largest audiences for

Exhibit 9.d ● ● ● ● ● ● ● ● ● ● ● ● ● ● ●

TV Dayparts

The length of the TV news block varies from market to market and station to station, running as long as two or three hours on some major-market TV stations and as short as an hour elsewhere.

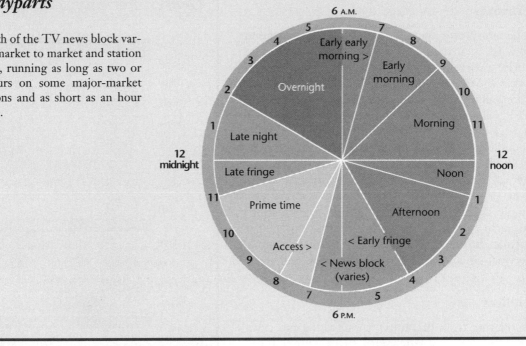

most radio stations, although some music stations draw more listeners at night.

In television, broadcast and cable networks divide the day as shown in Exhibit 9.d. *Prime time*, the most important segment, commands the largest audiences. *Access time*, the hour just prior to the network's prime-time programs, gives syndicators and station programmers their only access to the large audiences delivered by affiliated stations in the 50 largest U.S. television markets.

Most network-affiliated stations *stack* the 6:00 P.M. to 7:00 P.M. hour with local and network newscasts. Many major-market stations start local news a half-hour or even an hour or more earlier than that. The entire segment devoted to news constitutes the *news block*.

Fringe time refers to the hours preceding and following prime time when audiences, though quite large, are either building up to or dropping off from prime-time levels. Local television programmers call the late-afternoon segment, prior to the evening news block, *early fringe*, and the period after the end of network prime time *late fringe*. After late fringe comes *late night*, the domain of talk and movies, and then *overnight*, a time period filled with a mix of news, movies, and program-length commercials.

Television programs tend also to divide according to scheduling *frequency* into on-going *series*, limited-episode *mini-series*, and *specials*. The story line of an entertainment series continues from one episode to the next, whereas a special stands alone as an isolated (though often multipart) program. Specials often mark holiday seasons in the manner, for example, of *Charlie Brown's Christmas Special*. Movies, though not scripted as series with continuing story lines, may be scheduled by content type as thematic series— a "horror week" or "western weekend" series, for example.

Formats

The term *format* can refer either to the organization of a single program or to the organization of an entire program service. A program may have a "quiz-show" format. A cable channel may have a "home shopping" format. CNN's format is all-news, ESPN all-sports, and so on. Nearly all radio stations have adopted distinctive formats, such as MOR (middle-of-the-road) music, classical music, or all-news. Broadcast television stations and broadcast networks tend not to adopt single formats because they seek to appeal to a broad audience. With its single channel, a television station cannot afford to narrow its audience to followers of a particular format. In contrast, cable—as a multiple-channel service—encourages such specialization.

Genres

Borrowing from literature, broadcasting and cable programmers use the term *genre* (pronounced "zhan′-rah") to identify particular types of programs. Usually a program's content identifies its genre. Familiar entertainment genres include the *situation comedy*, the *game show*, the *western*, and the *soap opera*. Sometimes target audience rather than content type identifies the genre. Children's shows, for example, can take many different forms—not only cartoons and action/adventure but also news, discussion, quiz, and comedy.

Identifying a program by genre is a shorthand way of conveying a great deal about its probable length, seriousness, subject matter, visual approach, production method, and audience appeal. Programs that fall outside normal genre classifications often overlap two genres, leading to combined terms such as *dramedy* (a drama/comedy hybrid such as *Moonlighting*) and *docudrama* (a documentary/drama hybrid such as *Roots*). Exhibit 9.e illustrates how programmers schedule various program formats and genres.

Exhibit 9.e •••••• •••••••••••

Genres, Formats, and Dayparts

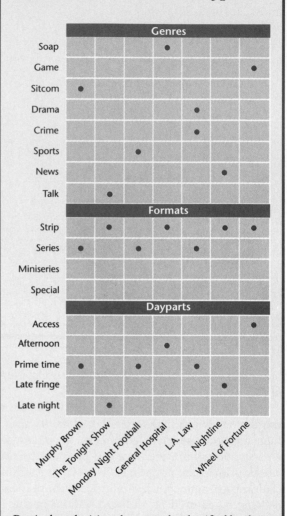

	Murphy Brown	The Tonight Show	Monday Night Football	General Hospital	L.A. Law	Nightline	Wheel of Fortune
Genres							
Soap				●			
Game							●
Sitcom	●						
Drama					●		
Crime					●		
Sports			●				
News						●	
Talk		●					
Formats							
Strip		●		●		●	●
Series	●		●		●		
Miniseries							
Special							
Dayparts							
Access							●
Afternoon				●			
Prime time	●		●		●		
Late fringe						●	
Late night		●					

Particular television shows can be classified by their content (*genre*), the way they are usually scheduled on the networks (*format*), and the time of day they are typically scheduled on the networks (*daypart*). In syndicated reruns, the methods of scheduling and daypart often differ from the original network run.

9.4 Entertainment Program Sources

Individual broadcast stations and cable systems produce little of their own entertainment programs, obtaining them instead from networks and syndicators. Broadcast and cable networks and syndicators, in turn, obtain most of their new shows from Hollywood studios and independent producers.*

In-house production by stations, cable systems, and networks consists mostly of news and sports programs (discussed in Sections 10.3 and 10.4). Television and cable networks produce some entertainment shows in-house—mainly soap operas, movies, and specials and a few prime-time series (CBS's *Rescue 911*, for example). Occasionally, networks produce programs for other networks; the CBS made-for-TV movie, *Fugitive Among Us*, for example, came from ABC Productions; and CBS's entertainment division produced the movie *Double Jeopardy*, to run first on Showtime and later on CBS. But the bulk of original entertainment programs comes from the following sources:

- The seven major Hollywood film studios, known as the *Hollywood majors* or the *Big Seven*—20th Century Fox, Paramount, Columbia, Universal, Warner Brothers, Disney, and MGM. In 1992, however, after years of operating losses and court battles over company ownership, MGM began phasing out its network production operations.
- A few smaller Hollywood studios, below the "major" rank.
- About a dozen major independent producers.
- Many other smaller, more specialized independent producers.
- Foreign syndicators distributing to the United States.

*Until the 1993 repeal of the fin/syn rules (see Section 9.2), the Big Three networks bought rather than produced most of their entertainment programs. In 1992, for example, ABC, CBS, and NBC together produced only about 24 hours of prime-time programming a week for their own and other networks.

Most program series begin as a *concept*, progress to the *pilot* stage, and finally go into production (see Exhibit 9.a). However, as production costs continued to soar in the 1990s (a half-hour pilot can now cost up to $1 million), networks moved increasingly to alternative methods of selecting new series—basing decisions sometimes on the reputation of the writer-producer, or on a few scenes from the proposed program, rather than on a full episode; producing a few episodes of a proposed series and running them during the summer as a test of their popularity; or even watching live theatrical-style presentations that cost far less than finished productions on film or tape.

Major Studios

Networks and stations value movies not only because they fill large amounts of time and generally hold the interest of audiences from beginning to end, but also because most movies appeal especially to the youthful female audiences that so many advertisers target. When television began, the major motion picture studios attempted to starve the fledgling television industry by withholding their backlog of theatrical movies. But Hollywood soon changed direction, becoming one of the networks' main sources for prime-time television series as well as for movies. Exhibit 9.f lists examples of such series, as well as some produced by other major suppliers.

In the 1970s cable began aggressively acquiring movies, bidding up prices and creating an even greater shortage of programs for broadcasters. Insatiable demands for more movies by the cable networks, television stations, and videocassette rental and sales outlets caused the studios to alter their production and release practices. They began producing more movies, aiming them at a wider variety of audiences, and releasing them not just in summer, as formerly, but throughout the year.

By definition, theatrical feature films normally reach audiences first through motion picture theaters. Thereafter, distributors release them successively to pay cable and other electronic media at

Exhibit 9.f •••••• •••••••••••

Major TV Producers and Program Examples

Company	Programs for Broadcast Networks	Programs for First-Run Syndication and Cable Networks
Columbia/Tri-Star	*Designing Women, Married . . . with Children, Who's the Boss, The Young and the Restless, Days of Our Lives*	*Wheel of Fortune, Jeopardy*
Disney/Touchstone/ Buena Vista	*The Golden Girls, Empty Nest, Home Improvement, Nurses, Dinosaurs, Blossom*	*Live with Regis and Kathie Lee, Siskel & Ebert, The Disney Afternoon*
Twentieth Century Fox	*L.A. Law, The Simpsons, In Living Color, True Colors, Doogie Houser M.D.*	*Studs*
MCA/Universal	*Murder, She Wrote; Major Dad; Coach; Quantum Leap; Law & Order; Northern Exposure; Columbo; Miami Vice*	*Out of This World, My Secret Identity, The Morton Downey Jr. Show*
MGM/UA	*In the Heat of the Night, thirtysomething, The Young Riders*	*Twilight Zone, Group One Medical, Kids Inc.*
Paramount	*Cheers, Brooklyn Bridge, Wings, Dear John, MacGyver, Young Indiana Jones Chronicles, Family Ties*	*Entertainment Tonight, The Arsenio Hall Show, Star Trek, The Maury Povitch Show, Hard Copy, The Untouchables*
Warner (a Time Warner subsidiary)	*Night Court, Growing Pains, Murphy Brown, China Beach, Life Goes On*	*Love Connection, Mama's Family*
Lorimar (also a subsidiary of Time Warner)	*Homefront, I'll Fly Away, Perfect Strangers, Family Matters, Full House, Knots Landing, Sisters*	*Time Trax*
Viacom	*Matlock, Jake and the Fatman, Perry Mason Movies*	*The Montel Williams Show, How's Your Love Life?, This Morning's Business*
Cannell	*The A-Team, Hunter, The Commish, 21 Jump Street, Wiseguy, Silk Stalkings*	*Street Justice, Renegade*
Carsey-Werner	*The Cosby Show, A Different World, Roseanne, Davis Rules*	*You Bet Your Life*

The first major television production companies began by producing theatrical motion pictures. Later, independent producers also became major players. Companies were bought and sold, merged, and otherwise created complex, vertically integrated media enterprises that owned broadcast stations and cable networks and systems, and produced and distributed a variety of programs. This list gives examples of such organizations and of programs under their control.

intervals governed by *windows* of availability, as shown in Exhibit 9.g. Despite the exhibition priority enjoyed by movie theaters, movie studios make more money from television, cable, videocassette, and foreign rights than from American theatrical exhibition. In both television and movie production, a few hits have to offset losses suffered by many failures. However, a quickly canceled television series may lose only $1 or $2 million, whereas losses from a single movie failure can run into the tens of millions. The average Hollywood movie costs more than $20 million to produce and another $10 million to $20 million for promotion and distribution. (Occasionally producers, to avoid these staggering promotion and distribution costs, will bypass theaters and sell a weak feature directly to a secondary market such as cable or videocassette.)

Producers also make movies especially for broadcast or cable television. Originally, these movies typically ran 90 minutes in length, often had limited budgets and were shot on videotape rather than the more expensive film, and were considered by some to be of overall lower quality than theatrical motion pictures. Indeed, by the 1980s, the phrase *made-for-TV* had become a derogatory expression describing anything of questionable value. In recent years, however, although some "made-fors" still fit the original descriptions, many of these movies are of excellent quality and win critical acclaim.

Independent Producers

At least half the prime-time series shown on network television come from the second major force in program production, *independent producers.* They range in size from large firms that usually have several series in production simultaneously, to small producers with only a single series under contract at any one time. Independent producers have several advantages over big Hollywood studios. Because they lease production facilities, their overhead costs usually fall below those of the studios. Lower costs in turn allow independents to charge lower license fees, a special advantage when competing to have their pilot episodes selected for trial by a broadcast network. Independents also avoid the traditional movie industry's slower-working decision-making

structures and corporate demands for quick, high profits.

In the 1970s, independent producers created some of the most innovative television series, such as *All in the Family, The Mary Tyler Moore Show,* and *Dallas.* By the 1980s and on into the 1990s, independent producers such as Spelling, Goldberg, Lorimar, Lear, Tandem, MTM, and Cannell produced an enormous number of prime-time series. Goldberg, for example, originated *Family Ties;* Aaron Spelling produced *Beverly Hills 90210* and *Melrose Place;* and a relative newcomer, Carsey-Werner, created *Cosby, A Different World,* and *Roseanne* (see Exhibit 9.f for other examples).

The 1992 *Guiness Book of World Records* recognizes Mark Goodson Productions as the most prolific producer in television history. Goodson, with countless game and other shows to his credit, claimed 38,000 episodes of programming covering more than 20,800 broadcast hours, including such classics as *Family Feud, The Price Is Right, To Tell the Truth, Concentration,* and *What's My Line,* which debuted on CBS in 1950 and ran for 17 years. When Goodson died in 1992 at the age of 77, his shows could still be seen on thousands of television stations and cable systems throughout the country.

Made-for Cable Programs

The growth of national cable program services after 1980 created an insatiable demand for more product. The leading pay-cable network, HBO, alone consumes more than 200 new movies a year.* In some years, HBO has laid claim to more than a third of all films in production, obtaining a powerful influence over movie producers. In addition, several advertiser-supported cable services—notably superstations and TNT—schedule hundreds of movies.

To increase their program supply and gain control over content and costs, cable services *co-finance* movies with producers. This investment gives them *exclusivity*—the right to show the product first on

---

*HBO's parent corporation is Time Warner, a magazine publisher and cable MSO. By the 1980s it also had become Hollywood's largest financial backer of movies.

Exhibit 9.g ● ● ● ● ● ● ● ● ● ● ● ● ● ●

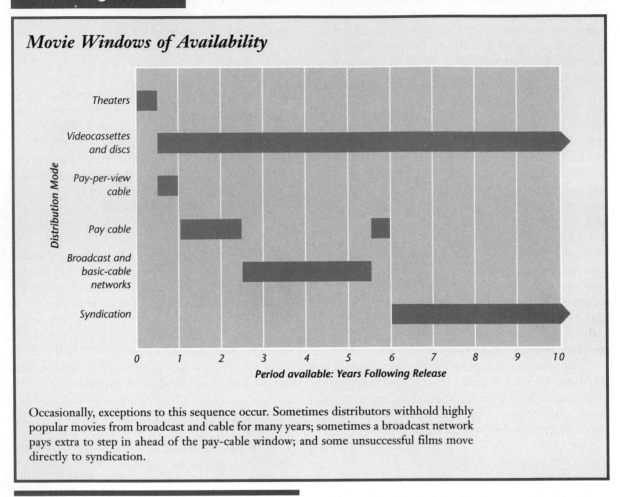

Movie Windows of Availability

Occasionally, exceptions to this sequence occur. Sometimes distributors withhold highly popular movies from broadcast and cable for many years; sometimes a broadcast network pays extra to step in ahead of the pay-cable window; and some unsuccessful films move directly to syndication.

cable—although a few of these cable-co-financed movies, such as *On Golden Pond* and *Sophie's Choice*, first had box-office success in theaters.

Each year, ad-supported as well as pay-cable services increase their investment in production activities. They develop made-for-cable dramatic, comedy, and variety programs for first-run cable use—underwriting, on average, production of at least 10 percent of their schedules annually. About a third of Showtime's schedule and nearly half of the Disney Channel's programs consist of original

cable material. The Family Channel alone spent about $125 million on nine original programs for its 1991–1992 season—including *Big Brother Jake* and *The New Zorro*. Some new products simply add fresh episodes to existing television series, as in the case of *The Days and Nights of Molly Dodd* on the Lifetime network. Others, such as HBO's *Dream On*, qualify as true made-for-cable programs. The industry recognizes the best of these shows, and the creative people involved in them, at its annual Cable ACE awards ceremony.

Made-for-cable programs counteract the old image of cable as a mere parasite on broadcast television. They also make good cable's promise to enhance program diversity. In addition, original productions enable one cable service to distinguish itself from another and thus gain subscribers seeking new program options.

Co-Production

Program creators have increasingly turned to *co-production* as a way of coping with constantly rising production costs. In co-production, two or more stations, networks, or producers agree to share the financial burden. ABC and Nickelodeon, for example, entered into an *echo* deal (so called because a program appears on one service and then, again, on another) for the series *Honey, I'm Home*. Each organization covered part of the production cost, and, in turn, each had the right to carry the program. Similarly, The Discovery Channel and NBC's affiliate in San Francisco co-produced a weekly science and technology series, *The Next Step*, to run on both the cable network and the station.

Co-productions are especially attractive when the parties involved come from different countries, because the market for the product is thereby automatically extended. Also, such deals often involve the use of foreign locations (Canada serves as a common locale), where costs generally prove lower than those in the United States. After paying some $7 million for the television mini-series rights to *Scarlett*, the sequel to *Gone With the Wind*, a consortium comprising Silvio Berlusconi Communications, the Kirch Group, CBS, and RHI Entertainment entered into a co-production deal that included a publicity-driven international search for a successor to Vivien Leigh to play the role of Scarlett O'Hara.

• • • • • • • •

9.5 News and Sports Sources

The high cost of electronic news gathering, production, and delivery has forced broadcasters and cable operators to rely on outside organizations for much of their material. At the same time, most accept the special responsibilities that accompany the presentation of information and try, to the extent possible, to reserve content control to themselves.

News Agencies

U.S. electronic media have more than a hundred news services available for their use. Many specialize. For example, on radio, ESPN offers sports and CNBC presents business news; HBO offers television stations its Entertainment Satellite Report. Other services promote corporate interests (such as The American Gas Association and The Sugar Association).

The major news services, such as Associated Press, United Press International,* Reuters, and Agence France Presse, are international in scope. They supply text, audio, video, and still pictures to subscribing networks and stations for incorporation into their newscasts and other programs.

Network News

Although broadcast networks rely on outside producers for most entertainment programs, they generally retain tight control over news and public-affairs production. At one time, the networks also produced their own sports programs, but they eventually found that regional production companies often could handle the process at lower cost.

Each of the Big Three broadcast television networks operates a news division separate from its entertainment division; each news division, in turn, employs about a thousand people. ABC, CBS, and NBC also support their own domestic and foreign news bureaus in major world cities, staffed by correspondents with in-depth knowledge of the regions they cover. In 1992 Fox announced that it would expand its operation to include news, relying largely

---

*UPI, which had been in serious financial trouble for years, appeared to have been rescued from almost-certain demise in 1992 when a Saudi Arabian company, Middle East Broadcasting Centre Ltd., bought the 85-year-old news service at auction for $3.95 million and promised to invest an additional $10 million to $20 million in the operation over the following two years.

on input from its affiliates, including its owned-and-operated stations.

In order to reduce its foreign bureau costs while still maintaining a strong international news presence, NBC in 1989 became part-owner of the Reuters television news service, Visnews. Until that move, American television networks had always competed head-on with the international news services. In 1992 Reuters repurchased NBC's interest in Visnews and entered into a 10-year agreement whereby the two companies would continue to exchange news footage. Then, in 1993, Reuter's 118 print bureaus joined with Visnews's 35 video bureaus worldwide to become Reuters Television. In the same year, ABC and the British Broadcasting Corporation entered into a partnership agreement for the exchange of television and radio news.

Broadcast networks traditionally avoided news footage or documentaries from outside sources. Independent news producers criticized this policy, but the networks maintained that they had to control news production in order to meet their responsibility for news content. This policy began to erode in the 1980s, however, when, in order to cut costs, networks began accepting news footage from affiliates and from *pool feeds*—cooperative arrangements whereby media rotate responsibility for coverage of news events, or at least share costs.*

Networks also cut back their news department operating budgets, reduced staffs, and consolidated or closed some of their news bureaus, both overseas and in the United States, relying more than ever on outside organizations such as Reuters and Worldwide Television News (WTN)—80 percent owned by ABC. In contrast, Cable News Network (CNN) expanded its presence abroad in the 1990s by opening new bureaus in Asia, Africa, and Latin America (although it, too, obtained substantial amounts of its foreign footage from WTN). CNN's success in challenging the major networks (see, for example, Exhibit 12.e on page 434) resulted in fur-

ther cable specialization, with entire channels devoted to such news genres as finance, sports, weather, and coverage of court trials (Chapter 10).

Network Sports

Except for professional football games, broadcast networks rely increasingly on production companies that specialize in televising sports. Networks simply pay the cost of national rights to the events and of producing live games, and their own announcers' salaries and travel costs. However, mega-events such as the World Series and the Super Bowl and regular-season NFL football remain exceptions to this trend. These bring in so much revenue that networks can still make profits after paying for their own very elaborate production, using numerous cameras and instant-replay machines, gigantic booms and cranes, and other specialized equipment. Cable networks and individual broadcast stations also employ sports production companies. ESPN, however, produces most of the games it carries.

For lesser sports events, such as golf and bowling tournaments, sponsors typically obtain broadcast rights and cover production costs, in addition to buying advertising time. The networks supply only the play-by-play and color announcers. Sponsors usually take part in organizing these events, lining up participants and celebrity guests, doing promotion, and even selling tickets. They hire local television stations or sports production companies to cover the events. They often recover some of their expenses by selling spots to other advertisers and peddling subsidiary coverage rights to radio stations and cable systems. Both advertisers and networks benefit from this division of labor. Sponsors retain control of costs and ensure maximum promotional value; networks gain hundreds of program hours of minor sports events too risky financially for them to cover themselves.

Station and System News Sources

The advent of electronic news gathering (ENG) during the 1970s, later supplemented by satellite news gathering (SNG), enabled local television

*The advent of the home camcorder provided yet another news source—the amateur (see Exhibit 12.k on page 451.) So much of this material now finds its way into newscasts at all levels that an organization—Amateur Video News Network (AVNN)—serves as a clearing-house and broker for amateur videographers.

news teams to fill longer newscasts and to provide more on-the-scene coverage of local events. An ENG unit can travel quickly and economically by car, van, or helicopter to the scene of an event and feed an on-the-spot news story to the studio by means of a microwave or satellite relay link (see Exhibit 10.l, page 363). Alternatively, the unit can record material for later editing at the studio. By 1992 virtually every television station that produced a newscast was equipped with some form of ENG.

A variety of syndicated sources also exist, many of which specialize in such areas as business, entertainment, and health. And television affiliates can obtain what amounts to syndicated news services from their own networks. Provided by the networks' news divisions, these services offer complete news programs during the "overnight" hours. They also feed hard-news items and features over regular network relay facilities during hours when these facilities carry no scheduled network programming. Affiliates can record these feeds, as well as regular network news programs, selecting items for later insertion in local newscasts.

Satellite relays increase the number of news suppliers, freeing affiliates from dependence on their networks and permitting some independent stations to compete for news audiences. Traditional agencies such as Associated Press supplement their wire copy with some video material. Others tailor their services specifically to television's needs. CNN, though originally a news network only for cable, now acts also as a syndicated news source for about 300 television stations, affiliates as well as independents. In 1992 CNN further increased its capacity by buying the competing Group W Newsfeed for about $2 million. CNN exchanges news stories with stations and supplies them with Headline News in 5- or 30-minute units, or continuously overnight. Another station source, Conus Communications, coordinates satellite news gathering by more than 100 stations, facilitates exchange of news footage and stories, and, with Viacom, produces its own 24-hour news service, All News Channel.

Cable systems rely primarily on CNN, CNBC, ESPN, the Weather Channel, and similar cable networks to meet their news and sports needs. In addition, nearly 30 regional networks supply sports coverage of local interest. All News Channel supplies material to some regional cable news networks (New England Cable News, for example), which, in turn, supply newscasts for cable systems. Some systems also produce their own newscasts and call upon many of the same sources as do television stations. Others use material, including even complete newscasts, supplied by local television stations.

Radio stations also avail themselves of the services of networks when meeting their news obligations. These include ABC, CBS, CNN, and Mutual (see Exhibit 10.n, page 367). Those few stations, mostly on the AM band, that still offer local newscasts (see Exhibit 10.o, page 372) use syndicated services as well for news, feature material, and weather and traffic reports. One of the more fascinating of these is Metro Traffic Control. With corporate offices in Houston, Metro supplies airborne traffic reports to stations in cities all over the country—including competing stations within the same market. In some markets, in order to maintain station individuality, a lone voice delivers on-air reports to all stations but identifies itself by a different name for each individual subscribing station.

● ● ● ● ● ● ● ●

9.6 Scheduling Practices

Whatever their program sources, stations and networks strive to organize their offerings into coherent schedules. Effective scheduling requires, among other things, coordinating program types and production tempos to complement typical audience activities. For example, light, up-tempo treatment of news and weather suits the busy early-morning period when listeners and viewers prepare for their day at work, school, or home. The less structured evening period calls for a more relaxing tempo and more in-depth treatments.

Audience Flow

Schedulers try to draw audience members away from rival channels and to prevent competing program services from enticing away some of their own audience. These efforts focus on controlling *audience flow*—the movement of viewers or listeners from one program to another. Movement occurs mostly at the junctions between programs or, on radio, after one block of songs ends and before the next begins. Audience flow includes both *flowthrough* (on the same station or channel) and *outflow* or *inflow* (to and from competing programs).

Audience research can measure the extent of audience flow. For example, Nielsen studies in the late 1980s showed that, on the average, 85 percent of a network's prime-time audience flowed through from one half-hour to the next when the same program continued. Flowthrough dropped to about two-thirds when a new program of similar type followed and to only half the audience when a program of a different type started in the next half-hour.

However, remote control channel selectors and VCRs—both now in more than three-fourths of all households—have made the tracking of television-audience flow far more difficult. A special vocabulary has evolved to describe how some audience members use these inventions: they *graze* through the available channels, *zap* unwanted commercials, *jump* between pairs of channels, *flip* around to see what's happening on nearby channels, and *zip* through the boring parts of prerecorded cassettes. But because not all viewers take advantage of this new freedom, programmers continue to employ scheduling strategies designed to control audience flow.

Scheduling Strategies

Most media products reach consumers in individually packaged physical units—a video or audio cassette, a compact disc, an edition of a newspaper or book, or an issue of a magazine. Only broadcasting and cable television offer the consumer a continuous experience. Programming unfolds, providing not merely a succession of unrelated media packages but a coherent program *service*. When scheduling this service, programmers take into account changing audience availability, changing work patterns, and changing needs and interests as the cycles of days, weeks, and seasons progress.

Programmers also take into account competition from other program services, using scheduling changes as a primary competitive weapon. Some typical scheduling strategies used by networks (television, cable, and radio) and by individual systems and stations to exploit audience flow include the following:

- *Counterprogramming* to attract the audience toward one's own station or network by offering programs different from those of the competition. For example, an independent station might schedule situation comedies against news programs on the network affiliates in its market.
- *Blocking programs* to maintain audience flowthrough by scheduling shows with similar appeal next to each other—for example, by filling an entire evening with family-comedy programs. This strategy has been expanded to include *programming marathons* during which networks and stations run several episodes of a single series back-to-back over a period of several hours or even days, or motion pictures with a similar theme (science fiction, for example) every night of the week.
- *Stripping* promotes a habit of daily viewing by scheduling episodes of a series at the same time every weekday (and sometimes on weekends as well). For example, affiliates typically strip their newscasts at 6:00 P.M. and 11:00 P.M., Eastern time.
- *Checkerboarding*, an alternative to stripping, calls for episodes from one program series on Mondays, Wednesdays, and Fridays, and from another on Tuesdays and Thursdays.
- *Leading-in* attracts a maximum initial audience by starting a daypart with a particularly strong program in the hope of retaining the audience for subsequent programs. Broadcast networks try to "grab" the prime-time audience with a hit show at 8:00 P.M.
- *Leading-out* with a strong program may similarly attract viewers to the program that precedes it.
- *Hammocking* tries to establish a new program, or to recover the audience for a show slipping in popularity, by scheduling the program in question *between* two strong programs. Flowthrough from the previous (lead-in) program may enhance the

initial audience for the hammocked program, and viewers may stick with the weak (or unfamiliar) show in order to see the strong (lead-out) program that follows it.

- *Bridging* attempts to weaken the drawing power of a competing show by scheduling a one-hour (or longer) program that overlaps the start time of the competing show. A two-hour movie scheduled at 7:00 P.M. on a pay-cable network or independent station, for example, *bridges* the 7:30, 8:00, and 8:30 P.M. program changes on competing channels.
- *Repeating*, a pay-cable strategy, makes it convenient for viewers to catch a program, such as a movie, by scattering repeat showings throughout the schedule.
- *Stunting* seeks to keep the opposing networks off balance in the short term by such tactics as making abrupt schedule changes, opening a new series with an extra-long episode, and interrupting regular programming frequently with heavily promoted specials. In NBC's 1991–1992 season, for example, the network's stunting included having stars from one of its Saturday night series (for example, Betty White of *Golden Girls*) appear on the same night's episode of another series (*Empty Nest*), and tying those episodes together with yet a third (from *Nurses*) by a plot device (a hurricane). That the regular locale of each program is Miami facilitated the project.

Two general theories, however, tend sometimes to get in the way of these scheduling strategies. One (LOP) suggests that no matter what is offered, viewers will watch the *least objectionable program* in the time period. The other, *Appointment Television*, holds that successful programs may be scheduled most anywhere because serious-minded fans will follow wherever they go.

Broadcast Network Schedules

Despite competition from cable and VCRs, the main arena of broadcast network rivalry remains the weekly 22 hours of what today most broadcasters refer to as *prime time*—the three hours from 8:00 P.M. to 11:00 P.M. each night of the week in the Eastern and Pacific time zones, an hour earlier in the Central and Mountain time zones, plus the extra hour from 7:00 P.M. to 8:00 P.M. on Sundays (EST/PST).* Actually, networks make more money on some daytime programs than on prime-time programs because of the extraordinarily high cost of the latter. Nevertheless, a broadcast network's performance in prime time establishes its prestige and defines its leadership role.

Because of high program costs, networks normally schedule prime-time series to run once a week. In other dayparts, however, they strip most of their shows Monday through Friday. Network morning magazine programs, afternoon soap operas, and evening newscasts, for example, occur at the same times each weekday.

Years ago, the Big Three networks would order 39 originals and 13 repeats of a program series to fill a prime-time period for a year. Later, deals were cut to 26 and 26. In either case, the normal pattern called for all originals to run consecutively, beginning in late August or early September, followed in the summer by reruns.

Today, television networks typically order only 22 to 25 episodes of a continuing series each year, filling the remaining slots in a time period with specials and, again, reruns. New and borderline series may receive orders for 13 or fewer episodes (not all of which may reach the air—even though paid for—if the series is a rating disaster). Hit series fare better. ABC's *Roseanne* and CBS's *Northern Exposure*, for example, obtained *two-year* renewals in 1992, as did Fox's *Beverly Hills 90210* (which also received an order for an unusual 30 annual original episodes).

Similarly, networks have changed their scheduling pattern. Instead of using all originals first,

*In the 1990s CBS and NBC allowed some California affiliates to experiment with beginning their networks' three-hours of weekday prime-time programming at 7:00 P.M. instead of the traditional 8:00 P.M. In order to carry the networks' late-night programs, especially NBC's *Tonight Show*, the stations had to request FCC waivers of the prime- time access rule, some of which were granted on a limited-time test basis and some of which were not.

networks now intersperse repeat episodes, particularly during the December holidays, saving first-runs for such periods as the February and May rating periods. (Reruns attract fewer viewers than original episodes—comedy repeats deliver about 75 percent of the audience achieved by the original episodes; dramas, only about 50 percent.)

Led by Fox, the networks now also introduce new series during the summer. Those that succeed are renewed for the following season. Examples include Fox's *Beverly Hills 90210* and CBS's *Northern Exposure*. Typically, networks pay less for summer-premiering series than for regular season programs. Actors and writers agree to accept lower salaries with guarantees of raises if a show earns renewal. Producers also cut back on production costs of such shows by reusing assets; for example, Lorimar shot *Bodies of Evidence* on existing sets from some of its other programs, including *Reasonable Doubts* and *Sisters*, that were on production hiatus.

As competition for advertiser-attractive audiences intensified in the 1990s, profit-conscious networks canceled some programs that, although they attracted large numbers of viewers, did not deliver the desired demographics. Sometimes another network rescued such series (from NBC, ABC picked up *Matlock* and CBS took over *In The Heat of the Night* and *Golden Girls*, which, in the absence of Bea Arthur, one of its stars, was renamed *Golden Palace*).

Television Station Schedules

After clearing time for its network's programs, an affiliated station still has much of its schedule left to fill with syndicated and local programs. The affiliate programmer's most important decisions concern the early-fringe and access periods.

Programmers at unaffiliated stations must fill all their airtime. Their chief stratagem, counterprogramming, capitalizes on the inflexibility of the affiliate's schedule created by its commitment to network programs. For example, an independent station can schedule sports events at times when affiliates carry major network shows. Networks can afford to devote prime time to only a few top-rated sports events of national interest. Independents, however, can schedule sports events of lesser interest, even during prime time.

Both network affiliates and independent stations utilize stripping on weekdays. Most Saturday and Sunday programs are scheduled only weekly. Many stations, however, strip their local news seven days a week. Stripping has three advantages for stations. First, daily same-time scheduling encourages the audience to form regular viewing patterns, such as the 6:00 P.M. news habit. Second, a single promotional spot can publicize an entire week's schedule for a given time slot. Finally, purchasing many episodes of a syndicated series in a single transaction earns quantity discounts from syndicators.

The practice of stripping off-network programs led to an enormous demand for television series offering many episodes already "in the can." Ideally, stripping requires 130 episodes for a half-year run (five each week for 26 weeks); series with fewer than 100 episodes have little chance in syndication. Because networks license so few new episodes of a series each year, off-network series that have generated enough episodes to warrant moving into syndication have, by definition, earned good ratings on a network over several seasons. They therefore command very high prices in syndication. As Exhibit 9.h suggests, a series can earn millions of dollars in aggregate revenue for producers and syndicators.

Network mega-hits foster intense bidding among stations for the syndication rights. Some stations paid more for *The Cosby Show* in its first release than they had paid for all the rest of their syndicated programs combined. Most stations purchasing *Cosby* could not hope to recoup the show's cost from the sale of the commercial time within it, but the expectation that it would lead to higher ratings for adjacent programs, especially local newscasts, appeared to justify the expense. As it turned out, however, such typically was not the case, as *Cosby* failed to meet rating expectations.

Most very long-running series, however, date back decades. Such network hits as *I Dream of Jean-*

Exhibit 9.h •••••••••••••••

Off-Network Syndicated Program Revenues

Series	Distributor	Estimated Revenue per Episode
The Cosby Show	Viacom	$4.8 million
Who's the Boss	Columbia	2.5 million
Cheers	Paramount	1.7 million
Magnum, P.I.	MCA	1.6 million
Webster	Paramount	1.6 million
Roseanne	Viacom	1.5 million
The Golden Girls	Disney	1.4 million
Family Ties	Paramount	1.4 million
M*A*S*H	Fox	1.1 million

Some successful programs continue in syndication virtually forever. And each new contract or contract renewal means still more income for the series. The above estimates indicate per-episode revenues as of the early 1990s for some of the more popular off-network programs. 20th Century Fox originally concluded that M*A*S*H would not perform well on local stations and, consequently, set outrageously low prices for what turned out to be one of the highest-rated—though relatively low revenue-per-episode-earning—programs in syndication history. In contrast, Viacom offered The Cosby Show at outrageously high prices, and stations, expecting results even better than those achieved by M*A*S*H, came up with the money. Unfortunately, however, Cosby did not meet local rating expectations, and industry observers do not expect to see any future series reach comparable per-episode revenues.

nie and I Love Lucy seem to run forever in syndication. But in recent years, competition made schedules more volatile. The networks nervously canceled shows at the first sign of weakening ratings. Runs became shorter, building up too few episodes for strip scheduling over the long period needed for best results. This in turn meant increasing scarcity of, and thus intensified competition for, successful syndicated series.

Cable Network Schedules

In the early 1980s, most cable networks concentrated on reaching demographic subgroups in prime time, showcasing their best product in other time periods. But by the mid-1980s, the largest cable program services, such as ESPN, USA, and TBS, had begun to compete directly and aggressively with the broadcast networks for the prime-time mass audience.

Advertiser-supported cable networks commonly adopt habit-forming strategies to build loyal audiences. The broad-appeal cable services strip many of their programs across the board both in daytime and prime time. USA and Lifetime, for example, stripped costly former network series such as *Murder, She Wrote* and *L.A. Law* in prime time, hoping to draw viewers away from broadcast stations and to build a cable-watching habit among first-time viewers. During the day they strip such programs as *Divorce Court* and *Hotel*. These program services also use counterprogramming and time-period blocking. Superstations, for example, tend to counter mass-appeal adult programs on the broadcast networks with children's shows and movies. Cable shopping and religious networks block several hours of similar programs to hold interested viewers for as long as possible with an alternative to broadcast network shows.

Pay-cable networks rely heavily on the strategy of repetition, scheduling repeat showings of their movies and variety shows in various time periods, cumulatively building audiences for each program. Each movie plays at various start times on different days. A movie may be recycled as many as a dozen times a month. For this reason, and also because cable program guides come out once a month and cable companies need to encourage monthly subscription renewals, pay networks plan their schedules in monthly cycles. Pay cable also uses bridging strategies, scheduling across the start times of other programs. HBO and Showtime movies, for example, usually start at 8:00 P.M., thus bridging the 9:00 P.M. station break, the time with the largest number of people watching television. If a movie ends before 10:00 P.M., HBO usually adds filler material to complete the hour in order to start a new program when viewers may be hunting for something to watch. Sometimes pay-cable networks try to get the jump on broadcast networks by starting their movies earlier in the evenings (at 7:00 or 7:30 P.M.). This strategy works best when broadcast schedules have been disrupted by late-running sports or political programs.

By the 1990s more and more cable systems had expanded their channel capacity. Time Warner's system in Queens, New York, was the first to offer 150 channels while others promised 500 and even more channels. Cable networks responded to the opportunities thus created. They began to *multiplex*—that is, to offer cable systems two or three program services where before they had supplied only one. HBO and MTV were among the first to test the new process. But more channels do not necessarily mean more *different* programming. Rather, the technology resulted, at least initially, in the networks offering much the same programming, but more often and at a greater variety of start times.

Cable System Schedules

Unlike programmers at television stations who concern themselves with only one channel, cable-system operators must fill multiple channels. Program decisions typically come from a committee, comprising top management and marketing executives and often representatives from the system's MSO.

Technical considerations play a major role in determining program line-ups. Despite having multiple channels, most systems cannot carry all of the 100-plus program services available to them (see Exhibit 6.i, pages 206–208), although video compression and fiber optics promised eventually to expand channel capacity almost without limit. Cable systems usually include the signals of most television stations operating in their service area—sometimes by choice, sometimes by law (see Section 13.8). Customers find convenient, and stations strongly advocate, *on-channel* carriage—that is, for example, a station broadcasting over the air on channel 2 appearing as well on the cable system's channel 2. Occasionally this proves impossible, especially in cases where a strong station signal would cause *ghosting* if carried by the system on its own channel.

Economic considerations also have an effect. Most cable networks charge systems a fee for their programming. Were systems to carry them all they would have to charge subscribers an unacceptably high monthly rate. Understandably, a system's MSO often dictates that its own systems carry those networks in which the MSO has an ownership interest. Similarly, a cable network may offer its programming at reduced prices to those MSOs that agree to carry it on all of their systems. Also, before cable, television viewers became accustomed to tuning to VHF channels 2 through 13. This habit, together with the fact that the higher the number the technically less desirable the channel becomes, moves program providers to seek placement on those lower channels—to the point where cable networks now offer lower fees to those systems that agree to carry programs on the more desirable channels and on the lowest tiers. Systems also favor ad-supported cable networks that offer the most time available for local advertising. As cable matures and systems look for sources of revenue other than subscriber fees, most dedicate one or more channels to pay-per-view services.

Some cable systems group channels together by program genre, a practice referred to as *clustering*. They schedule pay-cable networks—as well as other program services that target similar audiences—on adjacent channels as a service to customers who otherwise would have to flip through many channels to find their favorites. Where possible, MSOs try to carry the same program services on the same channels on all of their systems. By this means they facilitate both program promotion and the gathering of audience rating data.

Cable operators also consider program content and the tastes of their subscribers. Many, for example, refuse to carry the *Playboy* offering. Some have even canceled MTV.

Radio Station Schedules

Radio stations use counterprogramming, stripping, and blocking strategies even more than do television stations. Typically, radio programmers try to choose formats that appeal to groups not adequately reached by rival stations. Most stations schedule their program elements, whether songs or news stories, in hourly rotations, creating 60-minute cycles. As the day progresses, the hourly pattern is altered by daypart to match changing audience activities. Exhibit 9.i shows an hourly plan for a Top-40 for-

mat; Chapter 10 examines radio programming in more detail.

• • • • • • • •

9.7 *Program Promotion*

Having the best programs in the world means little if audiences don't know about them. Promotion therefore ranks as a major aspect of programming strategies.

On-Air Promotion

Broadcast stations and broadcast/cable networks consider on-air promotional spots the most cost-efficient way to advertise their programs. Breaks between programs contain *promos* for upcoming programs. Closing credits on shows that precede newscasts often include audio-only announcements urging viewers to stay tuned. Stations and broadcast networks also air full-video *teasers*—brief mentions of upcoming news stories—throughout prime time. Television stations and cable systems obtain from distributors, or produce themselves, promos for syndicated shows. Announcements that promote a series generally are referred to as *generic*, while those that highlight one episode in a series are called *specific* or *episodic*.

Pay-cable networks schedule elaborately produced *billboards* of upcoming programs as filler between shows. Cable systems often dedicate one or more channels entirely to program listings, channel line-up changes, and community events. A *barker channel*, like yesteryear's barker at the county fair, invites subscribers to venture into the system's pay-per-view tent and to order movies or events offered that month. New generations of television sets promise cable subscribers the ability to see program titles on-screen as they graze channels, to search for programs by theme or category, to call up a program by title, to scan a seven-day program guide organized by channel and time, and even to program their VCRs for desired programs or program types.

Exhibit 9.i •••••• ••••••••••

Radio Station Format Clock

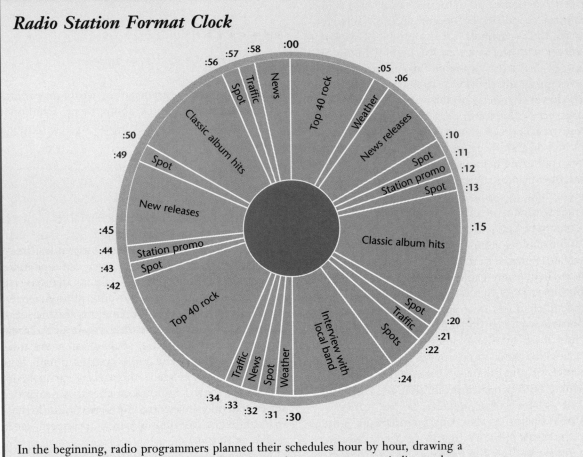

In the beginning, radio programmers planned their schedules hour by hour, drawing a circle around a 45 rpm record and dividing the circle into segments to indicate where program elements would air. Many continue to use this concept, employing different clocks to adapt to audience activities in various dayparts by incorporating changes in both the content and the tempo of presentation. The example given here represents a typical afternoon drive-time clock for a commercial station.

Promotion via Other Media

To reach nonviewers, networks, stations, and systems also advertise in newspapers and magazines, on radio, on outdoor billboards, and in other media. Radio stations promote television programs, and television stations carry spots promoting radio stations—sometimes as paid advertising and sometimes as *trade-outs*, whereby media exchange air time with no cash involved. Such cross-media promotion is not without limitations. For example, ABC, CBS, and NBC refused to carry announcements for the launch of the Fox network. And ABC, CBS, and USA won't accept ads for advertiser-supported cable networks. Most, however, will carry paid promos for pay-cable networks. The rationale: pay cable doesn't compete with broadcast networks for advertising revenue.

Still other promotion forms abound. Radio and television stations sponsor live rock concerts and ice shows and give away T-shirts and bumper stickers. Television networks send their anchors abroad to report from the locales of major news events. And broadcast and cable networks participate in joint promotional campaigns with such organizations as K-mart, Nabisco, and Six Flags theme parks.

Daily newspapers and Sunday supplements devote considerable space to broadcast and cable television listings. Some newspapers gather the data themselves; others hire outside organizations to do the job. Cable systems mail customized program guides to their subscribers; some are free, while others (*The Cable Guide*, for example) cost money (usually about one dollar a month). They also offer subscriptions to cable-network program guides (Arts & Entertainment has one, available at $18 a year). Home satellite dish owners turn to magazines such as *Satellite Orbit* to find out which transponders carry which services.

The most widely recognized printed source for program information, *TV Guide*, publishes more than a hundred different editions weekly just within the continental United States, as well as many localized editions in other countries. Exhibit 9.j tells more about this unusually successful magazine. But even *TV Guide* cannot provide full details on all available programs for viewers with access to dozens of channels.

* * * * * * * *

Summary

9.1   Broadcast and cable programmers face high program costs, scarcity of materials, and advertiser demands for effective commercial vehicles. Prices paid for premiere entertainment programs rarely cover full production costs, but the prestige conferred by network exposure makes such programs highly salable in domestic and international syndication markets.

9.2   Television stations and cable systems and networks carry syndicated programs, obtaining rights to show each episode a limited number of times over a limited number of years. "Syndex" rules protect stations from duplication of their syndicated programs by cable program services, while PTAR limits large-market television network affiliates in terms of the amount of network and off-network syndicated programs they can carry during prime time. Bartering involves trading commercial time for programs, sometimes with cash payments involved as well. Radio stations depend heavily on syndicated music, information, and feature material.

9.3   Programs are commonly classified according to several systems: by content (entertainment or information), by scheduling practices, by service formats, and by genre.

9.4   Entertainment programs come from Hollywood studios, from independent producers, and, to a small extent, from foreign sources. Expanding demand has stimulated production of feature films, and the timing of their release to theater, cassette, broadcast, and cable markets has become increasingly important. Co-production eases to some extent the problem of escalating program costs.

9.5   Broadcast networks retain control of network

Exhibit 9.j •••••• •••••••••• •

TV Guide

Every week about 16 percent of all U.S. television households turn to *TV Guide* to see what's on television, to decide what to watch, and to read articles and gossip about the television and cable industries. *TV Guide* comes in a distant third, behind weekly television supplements and daily listings in newspapers, as the source of program information most frequently cited by viewers. But these local publications cannot match *TV Guide's* estimated national readership of 40 million.

Walter Annenberg (later a U.S. ambassador to Great Britain) combined three local weekly television program guides to create the first edition of *TV Guide* in 1953. He began with 10 regional editions and a circulation of 1.5 million subscribers. Media baron Rupert Murdoch took control of *TV Guide* in 1988 when he paid $3 billion for its parent company, Triangle Publications; he already owned half of *TV Guide's* Australian counterpart, *TV Week*. By 1992 the magazine was offering 112 editions with a circulation of about 15 million (down from its 1977 peak of nearly 20 million), making it the third largest magazine in the country after *Modern Maturity* and *Reader's Digest*. Each regional edition includes the same national pages

March 27–April 2   89¢

BROOKLYN-QUEENS-S.I. EDITION

GUIDE

MR. OSCAR

PLUS Your Guide to the Academy Awards

Close-up: Can Billy Crystal Top Himself Again?

"Our Fight for a Test-tube Baby" —Tom & Roseanne

Billy Crystal and friends

---

news and public-affairs production, but they normally turn to specialist companies for the production of sports programs. ENG and SNG have greatly expanded the ability of local television stations to cover news events nationwide.

9.6 Scheduling strategies that programmers use to influence audience flow include counterprogramming, blocking, stripping, checkerboarding, bridging, repeating, and stunting, although remote tuners and VCRs somewhat undermine the effectiveness of these strategies. Broadcast networks schedule prime-time programs in weekly cycles, but in other dayparts (except for weekends) they strip programs, as do television stations generally. Advertiser-supported cable program services also strip most

of articles and news, plus special pages inserted for that region's cable and station program listings. Nearly half of all *TV Guide* copies are sold at newsstands, mostly in supermarkets.

Each week, television stations throughout the country send in upcoming program schedules; and each week, magazine editors call stations to update program information. Often, through its direct contact, *TV Guide* learns of network program changes before the network's affiliates do—an occasional source of embarrassment to the stations and a subject for acrimonious network/affiliate discussions. Refusing to list program content based on press releases from networks and other program providers, magazine staffers screen every program in advance, or read the script, or, at the very least, talk to the show's producers, writers, or talent. The magazine's computers store summaries of more than a quarter-million syndicated episodes and some 36,000 movies.

Dozens of multichannel cable systems may operate within a region covered by a single *TV Guide* edition. Because systems often carry different channel lineups, the magazine lists cable programs not by system channel but by program service. Still, more cable networks exist than could be listed in a magazine of its size (five by seven-and-a-half inches) and price (89 cents). *TV Guide* currently solves this problem by including only the most-watched services. Rarely, for example, does it offer program information for C-SPAN, CNBC, or The Learning Channel. As a possible long-term solution, the publisher is considering a larger version (seven-and-a-half by ten inches)—at a higher price.

TV Guide is designed for readers, not for media owners. Indeed, the magazine includes stories critical of the industry, though under Murdoch it is gaining more of a fan magazine image and dwelling more on personalities. Named *TV Guide*'s new editor-in-chief in late 1991, Anthea Disney (former editor at the New York *Daily News* and at *Us* magazine and, most recently, executive producer of *A Current Affair*) says the magazine exists "to really hold up the industry to the light to show the best things about it and the worst things about it. Our role is to be the absolute relentless terrier that goes after television and tries to make it better and better and better" (Walley, 1992).

of their programs, while pay-cable networks repeat their programs at various times of the day. Technical limitations force cable systems to select from a vast array of program choices and to restrict somewhat their ability to carry local television stations on the same cable channels as those they occupy over the air. Radio stations typically select a specific program format and schedule program elements in hourly rotations.

9.7 Audience promotion—using on-air announcements, advertising in other media, and program guides—is an essential component of successful programming.

Chapter 10

Network, Syndicated, Local

Programs readily fall into three broad categories—network, syndicated, and locally produced. Subcategories are based on paired differences: radio vs. television, broadcast television vs. cable television, first-run syndication vs. off-network syndication, network affiliates vs. independents, and entertainment vs. information content. Altogether, this chapter describes more than a score of program categories. Each has its own characteristic audience, its own production, distribution, and delivery methods, and its own content type.

Chapter 8 included discussion of programs in noncommercial electronic media. This chapter focuses on those in commercial broadcast and cable.

10.1 Prime-Time Network Television Entertainment

The best-known, most popular programs—consisting mostly of light entertainment—appear on television networks in prime time. Prime-time net-

work entertainment programs come as weekly series, with a sprinkling of movies and occasional one-time specials. A series can run for an indefinite number of episodes. Those designed typically with three to eight episodes are known as *miniseries*. During the 22 hours a week of television prime time, ABC, CBS, NBC, and Fox vie for huge audiences—larger than any in the previous history of entertainment. Despite their decline in audience share (Section 3.6), together the broadcast television networks still draw the most massive audiences of any medium. The rise and fall in popularity of prime-time programs regularly makes headline news. After their contractual network runs, many of those same programs travel throughout the world as syndicated off-network shows.

Situation Comedies

Long the staple of prime-time network television, situation comedies (*sitcoms*) remain highly popular with all audiences, especially women aged 18 to 49, a key demographic group that many advertisers want to reach. Stations welcome syndicated off-network sitcom shows because they want to appeal to the same target group as the networks and because sitcoms lend themselves to strip scheduling and effective promotion. Perhaps more crucial, scheduling half-hour shows such as sitcoms in early-fringe time periods allows stations to attract new viewers every 30 minutes. Stations normally prefer former-network shows to first-run syndicated material because they can better estimate the likely ratings for an off-network program.

After declining in popularity in the early 1980s, sitcoms began a comeback in 1985. The enormous success of *The Cosby Show* renewed the networks' faith in family-oriented comedy and led to fresh efforts to develop more sitcoms. By the 1990s such shows as *Cheers* (see Exhibit 10.a), *Home Improvement*, *The Simpsons*, *Roseanne*, and *Murphy Brown* topped the charts. Hit sitcoms attract large audiences and tend to rate higher than hour-long shows.

Writers of situation comedies create a group of engaging characters who find themselves in a particular situation—most often a family setting. Plots spring from the way the characters react to a specific new source of tension injected into the situation week by week. (Most quality sitcoms include a subplot in each episode as well.) The characters have marked traits that soon become familiar to the audience: habits, attitudes, quirks, and mannerisms.

Family settings work well, but sitcoms also take place in other situations—such as the tavern of *Cheers* and *Murphy Brown*'s newsroom (both family-like in their way). *The Cosby Show* presented a more traditional, if somewhat idealized, family situation—handsome middle-to-upper-class father and mother, adorable kids representing typical age groups having typical problems. On the other hand, responding to pervasive changes in work and family patterns, television series increasingly explore new social relationships, probing the boundaries of acceptable television: *Designing Women* showcased a middle-aged, all-female household; *Empty Nest* featured a motherless family; *Murphy Brown* touched some nerves (and in 1992 brought condemnation from then Vice President Quayle) when Brown,

though unwed, had a baby; and *Seinfeld* offered a variety of off-beat plots ranging from an attempt to author a television show about "absolutely nothing" to a contest to determine which of the four leading characters could survive the longest without masturbating. A variant, sometimes referred to as the *slobcom*, depicts less-than-ideal family situations. The family in Fox's *Married . . . With Children* features a frustrated housewife, a husband who fails as a provider, and outrageously undisciplined children. ABC's highly successful *Roseanne* depicts an aggressively earthy, blue-collar family—a far cry from the idyllic family situations of traditional sitcoms.

Spinoffs and Clones

A hit program with a new angle instantly begets brazen imitations. Programmers call such copies spinoffs and clones. A *spinoff* stars secondary characters from a previous hit on the same network, placing the characters in a new situation. *The Cosby Show*, for example, spun off *A Different World*, and *Golden Girls* spun off *Empty Nest*.

A *clone* closely imitates an already popular program, usually on another network, changing only the stars and details of plot and setting. Sitcoms frequently spin off new sitcoms, whereas hour-long programs tend to generate clones. Attempts to capitalize on the success of *Magnum P.I.*, the number-three prime-time show of the early 1980s, led to at least five clones in a single year, including *Hunter* and *Miami Vice* (the only ones that survived to become successes in their own right).

In the early 1980s producers began injecting comedy elements, formerly the province of sitcoms, into action/adventure shows. Series such as *Magnum P.I.* and *Moonlighting* included light-hearted comic scenes as well as warm-hearted relationships. The late 1980s series *thirtysomething* and *Beauty and the Beast* added nostalgia and fantasy to the mix. In the 1990s *Twin Peaks* and *Northern Exposure* (see Exhibit 10.b) added the word *quirky* to the vocabulary of millions of viewers. Critics referred to some of these shows as *dramedies*—hour-long blends of drama and comedy.

Exhibit 10.a ••••••••••••••••

Cheers

Set in a below-street-level Boston pub, *Cheers* was launched by NBC in 1982. In its first year, the series ranked a dismal 74th among a total of 98 prime-time programs on the air. But the network stayed with the program and, although some characters have changed over the years, it eventually became a consistent ratings winner both on NBC and in syndication. By 1992 *Cheers* had become the "most-Emmy-nominated" television show ever, with 111 total nominations, beating the record formerly held by *M*A*S*H* with 99, and had won 26 Emmy Awards, tying *Hill Street Blues* and trailing only *The Mary Tyler Moore Show*, which had 29. To the dismay of NBC, Paramount announced it would cease production of the series after the 1992–1993 season. Insiders suggested that the principal reason was the decision of the show's star, Ted Danson, to call it quits after 11 years and give up the nearly $12 million he reportedly received annually for his portrayal of bartender Sam Malone.

Source: Photo courtesy NBC.

Crime Shows

Police, lawyer, and detective dramas such as *Dragnet* and *Perry Mason* peaked in the ratings around 1960. Then they faded until the mid-1980s, when a new breed of more authentic crime shows captured top ratings. *Hill Street Blues* and *Cagney and Lacey* began a trend toward crime dramas dealing with tough social issues, using multilayered plots involving main characters.

Dramas such as *L.A. Law* use character-oriented plots, focusing on the human-interest appeal of personal moral dilemmas. *MacGyver* offered a low-key, resourceful hero who could save a damsel in distress using nothing but chewing gum and a piece of string. Shows such as *Miami Vice*, in contrast, capi-

talize on action-oriented gunfights and car chases; but even they do not depict the older, simplistic, black-and-white view of a world in which good guys always stay good guys and bad guys have no redeeming qualities. As another contrast, *Murder, She Wrote* features sanitized homicide mysteries, usually set in upper-class surroundings, solved by an unlikely detective—a well-bred, middle-aged mystery writer.

Movies

Movies include both theatrical feature films and those made for television. After being shown in theaters, feature films are licensed for release to

Exhibit 10.b ••••• ••••••••••

Northern Exposure

Referred to as "whimsical"and "quirky," *Northern Exposure* began its successful prime-time run in the summer of 1991. The very next year it received more Emmy Awards (6) and more Emmy nominations (16) than any other program that year (including the award for "Outstanding Drama Series"), and the Television Critics Association named it program of the year. Set in the mythical town of Cicely, Alaska, it features previously little-known actors playing most unusual roles—a young doctor who agrees to practice in Cicely in exchange for his government-paid education; a female air-taxi pilot whose boyfriends expire in bizarre ways; a disc jockey who sprinkles his broadcasts with quotes from Freud, Einstein, Whitman, and others; and the doctor's volunteer assistant, Marilyn, a native who seems to have all the answers but refuses to volunteer them, who appreciates different points of view, and who has no need to perceive everything in terms of right or wrong, good or bad. Plot lines, equally outrageous, include finding a long-frozen soldier who once fought in the Napoleonic wars and using a huge catapult to send hurtling through the air everything from pianos to deceased animals.

Source: Photo from CBS, Inc.

networks and other outlets in sequence, as shown in Exhibit 9.g, page 320. Made-for-television movies come in both 90-minute and two-hour lengths. Typically they have lower budgets than theatrical films and are adapted to the limitations of the small television screen.

By the 1970s the television networks were paying astronomical prices for licenses to show hit theatrical films in prime time. In 1976 the classic *Gone With the Wind* cost NBC about $5 million for a single showing, a then-record price justified by its 65 percent audience share. In 1983 a showing of *Star Wars* cost more than $10 million but attracted only 35 percent of the audience and finished second in its time period to a made-for-television movie. In the mid-1980s ABC set a new record by paying

$15 million for the right to air *Ghostbusters*, even though it had already played for two years in theaters and on pay cable.

By the 1990s, however, VCRs and pay cable had devalued network showings of movies to the point that the average licensing fee had dropped to about $3 million. Nevertheless, both broadcast and cable networks still pay huge fees for the biggest hits—movie blockbusters. These costly films rarely earn back their full rental fees in advertising revenue but can be useful for clobbering the opposing networks in the ratings.

The number of theatrical movies produced by the Hollywood studios declined in the 1970s as film production costs rose, but increased in the 1980s as cable networks and home video demanded more programs. Pay-cable networks frequently outbid the broadcast networks for top-quality theatrical films, forcing the networks to turn to related program types—made-for-television movies and miniseries. Typically, a broadcast network's rental fee for a single showing of a major theatrical feature would more than pay for making a brand-new, modest-budget feature designed for television. Sets, props, and locations need not be lavish because the small screen loses so much detail. With extravagant promotion, one well-known star supported by virtual unknowns suffices. In recent seasons, the top made-for-television movies commanded higher audience shares than any televised theatrical movie. By 1990 two-thirds of network movies were in the made-for-television category and sometimes served as pilots for prospective prime-time network series. For plots, producers often turn to actual, usually sensational events. This practice reached new heights—or exploitative depths—in 1993 when ABC, CBS, and NBC each aired a made-for-television movie based on the true story of the attempt by a teenage girl, dubbed the "Long Island Lolita," to murder her adult lover's wife.

Beginning in the mid-1980s, the major pay-cable networks (such as HBO and Showtime), as well as some other cable services (USA and TNT), also plunged into the financing of *made-for-cable* movies. Production contracts give cable networks *premiere exclusivity*—the right to air the films first. Cable networks also invest increasingly in original dramatic series, musical variety shows, and nightclub comedy. Especially as pay-per-view grows in availability and popularity, however, pay cable still relies on theatrical feature films as its bread-and-butter entertainment.

Miniseries

Roots, a 14-hour adaptation of a best seller about the evolving role of blacks in American life, ran over eight successive evenings in 1977 and began a trend toward miniseries. At the time, experts doubted the drawing power of the subject matter and its ability to sustain viewership for so many hours, but *Roots* took them by surprise. The audience increased for

each episode, breaking all records on the eighth night.

Although miniseries can be expensive (*War and Remembrance*, aired by ABC in 1988, cost about $110 million), they bring prestige and occasionally high ratings while filling the large chunks of time once devoted to blockbuster movies. In spite of its huge budget and cast of superstars, *War and Remembrance* did poorly in the ratings. On the other hand, *Lonesome Dove*, a four-part western miniseries aired by CBS in 1989, and produced at only about $20 million, attracted critical acclaim and exceptionally large audiences. Miniseries proved able to compete well against pay-cable movies and to attract new viewers, especially upscale professionals, who may otherwise watch little entertainment television.

• • • • • • • •

10.2 Non-Prime-Time Network Television Entertainment

Although broadcast networks put their best creative efforts into prime-time programming, daytime programs can yield a higher profit margin. The extraordinarily high production costs of prime-time shows and their fewer commercial minutes make them less efficient revenue earners.

Daytime programs carry more commercials than do prime-time programs—as much as 16 minutes' worth each hour. Constant switching of soap opera plot lines from the doings of one character to those of another accommodates the many interruptions that would be intolerable in most dramas.

Dayparts

Network non–prime time breaks down into the dayparts depicted in Exhibit 9.d (page 315). A characteristic program type tends to occupy each daypart:

- Networks fill the early-morning daypart with newscasts and talk, and weekends with sports, all discussed later in this chapter.
- Soaps, games, and talk shows dominate daytime

television just as they once dominated daytime radio.

- Late-night fare consists mostly of talk and comedy/variety programs.

Soap Operas

In the early days of radio, soap companies often sponsored daytime serial dramas whose broad histrionics earned them the nickname "soap operas." This genre is a classic case of frugal use of program resources. Notorious for the snail-like pace of their plots, soaps (as they came to be called) use every tactic of delay to drag out the action of each episode. Most minimize scenery costs, relying heavily on head shots of actors in emotion-laden, one-on-one dialogue.

Contemporary soaps respond to changing public tastes. They sometimes have story lines dealing with once-taboo subjects such as drug addiction, social diseases, and family violence. Women and members of minority groups began appearing in more varied roles in the mid-1970s, although the distribution of occupations, races, and sex roles by no means yet reflects society's actual norms. More women characters in modern soaps than in society at large have upper-income professions (medicine and law are favored because, while prestigious, they plausibly afford women free time for romantic involvements). Racial minorities remain underrepresented and restricted in their social interactions, though *Generations,* a trailblazing soap featuring close relations between a black family and a white family, emerged on NBC in 1989.

Changes in audience composition encouraged soap opera writers to deal with controversial topics and new social roles. First *General Hospital* and then *The Young and the Restless* stimulated a faddish interest on the part of younger viewers, including males, during the 1970s and 1980s. ABC launched *My Time for Me* during the summer of 1988 to lure young viewers during the school vacation. On-air promotion for NBC's *Santa Barbara* targeted that 15 percent of the six million daily soap watchers who are between 15 and 24 years old, trying to ingrain the soap habit early. Still, the soap opera audience core

remains housewives—an ideal target for manufacturers of household products, but a diminishing group as more women join the work force. The extraordinary loyalty of dedicated soap opera viewers of any age makes them a favored commercial target. As intense as sports fanatics in their dedication to these programs, they support several fan magazines, avidly attend shopping center appearances of soap opera stars, and consult newspapers or call 1-900 telephone numbers that give daily summaries of soap opera plots.

Soap opera fan loyalty creates its own hazards for programmers, however. Life becomes a nightmare for the broadcast executive who dares to interrupt, much less pre-empt, a soap opera to carry what most would consider an important news event.

Broad-appeal cable services such as Lifetime, TBS, and USA have yet to develop daytime soap operas that command the loyalty inspired by their broadcast counterparts. The Family Channel made the most sustained attempt to launch a cable soap opera, but it failed to capture an audience, perhaps because the program's religiously inspired "family" orientation inhibited its producers from dealing with the controversial subjects that seem essential to successful contemporary soaps.

Soap operas have highly successful counterparts on ethnic and foreign-language networks. The two principal competing U.S. Spanish-language cable/broadcast networks, Univision and Telemundo, feature imported *telenovelas.* These enormously popular soap operas reach tens of millions of viewers throughout the Spanish-speaking world. American soaps endure for decades (see Exhibit 10.c). In contrast, *telenovelas* burn themselves out in a few months. Though primarily entertainment, they often also carry educational messages, typically promoting socially approved conduct and family values.

Game Shows

Another classic, parsimonious format, audience-participation game shows, became a staple of network radio more than a half-century ago. One of the cheapest formats, game shows cost little in time, talent, effort, and money once a winning formula

Exhibit 10.c •••••• ••••••••••

Guiding Light

Guiding Light, television's longest-running soap opera, celebrated its 40th anniversary with a prime-time special in June 1992. The program, which began on January 25, 1937, as a 15-minute radio serial, made the transition to television on June 30, 1952. Its longevity attests to the enduring popularity of the soap opera genre.

Source: Photo from CBS, Inc.

has been devised and a winning emcee selected. Talent expenses are limited to the host's salary and, in some cases, to fees for show-business personalities, who usually work at minimum union scale because of the publicity value of game-show appearances. Many games capitalize also on the inexhaustible supply of amateurs willing to show off their abilities or simply anxious to be seen on television.

Some games have great endurance. *Hollywood Squares,* for example, has been around in various forms since 1966, first on network, then in syndication. *The Price Is Right* started on network television in 1956, appearing on and off in daytime and prime time and in syndication in 30- and 60-minute versions.

Game shows now turn up on almost every cable network, including even MTV, ESPN, and The Nashville Network. USA blocks several hours daily with old game shows such as *Win, Lose, or Draw* and *Joker's Wild.* Many modern game shows such as *Family Feud* use frivolous questions, often with risque overtones. But the hit game show *Jeopardy* uses the older pattern of genuinely knowledgeable contestants armed with extensive memories. Its unique gimmick is to demand that contestants come up with *questions* to the answers already given by the emcee instead of answers to the emcee's questions. The top game hit, *Wheel of Fortune* (see Exhibit 10.d), benefits both from the suspense element of the wheel's unpredictable stopping places and from the winning talent combination of emcee Pat Sajak and his assistant (referred to on the program as "co-host"), Vanna White. She won celebrity for a unique function—that of "letter turner." As she herself candidly admits, her primary role is simply to look beautiful while turning blocks on a board displaying the letters that contestants choose in their efforts to complete the words of a phrase or title.

A handful of specialists produce most of the successful broadcast and syndicated game shows. Goodson-Todman Productions, for example, grosses more than $50 million a year from game shows. Mark Goodson, one member of the team formed in 1946, once pointed out that "soap operas

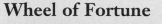

Exhibit 10.d

Wheel of Fortune

An example of a highly utilized program, *Wheel of Fortune,* aired first on daytime network television, then in a first-run syndicated version, and finally as an off network show syndicated to stations. Hostess Vanna White, looking beautiful in glamorous clothes, deftly turns letters of the alphabet as requested by game contestants. Co-host Pat Sajak's attempt in 1989 to become a talk show host did not succeed.

Source: Photo courtesy King World Productions.

and game shows are the greatest indigenous television forms, and they are alike in one important way.

There are no endings. They go on and on and on" (quoted in Buckley, 1979).

Both networks and producers profit from the enhanced commercial content of game shows. The giveaway format justifies supplementing normal advertising spots with additional *plugs*—short paid-for announcements on behalf of corporations that donate prizes and other services such as transportation and wardrobe items. The television giveaway business supports several companies specializing as prize brokers, called *schlockmeisters* in the trade. They handle the collecting, warehousing, and dispatching of game-show prize merchandise.

Most games run the half-hour length favored by syndication (that length enables flexible scheduling throughout all dayparts). Cable networks typically counterprogram the broadcast networks' afternoon soaps with game shows or movies. Affiliates often purchase first-run game shows to schedule in access time.

Underlining the overall popularity of the genre, two cable channels—The Game Channel and The Game Show Channel —planned premieres on cable in the early 1990s. Both were to feature some new programs but mostly classics. Producers planned to take the format to a new dimension as technology promised truly *interactive* game shows, permitting subscribers to play while sitting at home.

Magazine and Talk Shows

In the 1950s programmers began extending network television into hitherto unprogrammed early-morning and late-evening hours, a radical move at the time. In those days, as a chronicler of the period wrote, "Morning television was available here and there, but watching it was a taboo. . . . It was acceptable to listen to morning radio, but like sex and alcohol, television was deemed proper only after sundown" (Metz, 1977: 33). For this time period, NBC developed the *magazine format* —a medley of short features bound together by a personable host or group of hosts.

Today, NBC's pioneer early-morning magazine show, started in 1952. Continuing into the 1990s, the *Today* show shared the 7:00 A.M. to 9:00 A.M.

morning spotlight with CBS's *This Morning* (in various guises) and ABC's *Good Morning America*.

Although related to magazine shows, the talk show more closely resembles an essay than a magazine. It emphasizes the host's personality, which colors the interviews and other segments of the show. NBC's *Tonight*, a late-night companion to *Today*, was among the first and soon became the classic network talk show. Television critic Les Brown called *Tonight* "the premier desk and sofa show" (1982: 430). Exhibit 10.e describes both *Today* and *Tonight* in more detail.

Cable television also takes advantage of the relatively low production cost and flexibility of talk shows. Lifetime, for example, specializes in talk programs, carrying a dozen or so on health, consumer services, and the like. One well-publicized afternoon show, *Attitudes* features two women in an informal talk format that concentrates on fashion, beauty aids, and personal problems of women in their 30s and 40s. In addition to *Larry King Live*, CNN regularly schedules talk shows on money management, as well as news interviews and discussions, the best known of which, *Crossfire*, offers heated debates between opinionated opponents on hot political controversies. Religious networks rely heavily on inspirational talk programs, and sports channels on sports talk segments and interview shows.

Music and Variety

Except for variety shows (discussed below) and a few programs such as *American Bandstand*, which in the 1950s became one of television's first hits, and *Your Hit Parade*, which aired from 1950 to 1974, the visual medium paid little attention to popular music. That changed in 1981 with the formation of Music Television (MTV) as a cable network (see Exhibit 10.f). MTV quickly developed into a 24-hour rock-video powerhouse that targets teens and young adults aged 12 to 24. A co-owned network, Video Hits One (VH-1), aims for adults aged 25 to 49.

Originally intended to promote record sales, music videos became a television genre in their own right. Performers act out song lyrics, interpret them, provide symbolic counterpoints, or otherwise create imaginative visual accompaniments for songs. As promotional tools, many videos came free of charge to any stations or networks that would play them. But MTV changed the ground rules in 1984 by *paying* for exclusive rights to Michael Jackson's much-publicized *Thriller* video. MTV now contracts for exclusive early *windows* (periods of availability) for some videos. Utilizing barter, MTV offers free advertising time to participating record companies. These strategies essentially demolished music videos as a source of free program material.

MTV's success had wide ramifications. As one commentator put it,

> the fast pace and kaleidoscopic style of music video has ricocheted across popular culture, changing the ways people listen to music and leaving its frenetic mark on movies, television, fashion, advertising and even TV news. (Pareles, 1989)

Prime-time network programs (*Miami Vice* was among the first) added prominent musical elements. Competitors for the cable rock audience emerged, including local and regional rock video services, syndicated video countdowns and dance shows, and cable networks—such as Country Music Television—playing music videos other than rock. Even the broadcast networks scheduled MTV clones, especially in the weekend late-night time period.

By the mid-1980s music videos on television had eroded rock radio stations' audiences and threatened a key assumption about television's advertising practices. Surveys indicated that most respondents aged 12 to 24 preferred MTV to radio, and most young people in cabled homes said they always turned to MTV during commercial breaks in other television programs (Coleman, quoted in *Broadcasting*, 5 Sept. 1983: 60). Radio counterattacked by reaching out to rock music lovers in cars, at work, on the beach, while jogging with headphones, and so on. However, the grazing habits of television viewers with remote controls undermine the effectiveness of standard advertising practices such as clustering several spots in program breaks. A music video provides the perfect-length alternative to en-during spots in another program's commercial break.

Variety programs once played a role both in viewers' habits and in the world of music. Hosted by such stars as Ed Sullivan (who introduced America to Elvis and to the Beatles), Judy Garland, Frank Sinatra, Dean Martin, Perry Como, and Sonny and Cher, these programs once brought hours of music into the home. But their popularity faded as their production costs increased and as musical tastes changed. By the 1990s they had disappeared as series from network television, reappearing only occasionally as specials. CBS attempted a revival of the genre in 1991 with a new version of the *Carol Burnett* show. Audience apathy and high production costs[*] closed the show in a few weeks.

Home Shopping

Not all viewers find commercials boring, at least those that appear on home shopping networks. The broadcast/cable Home Shopping Network and its clones market consumer items such as clothing, jewelry, home appliances, and novelty ware, claiming that bulk purchasing and low overhead costs enable drastically reduced prices compared to those in-store. A cable system carrying a shopping network receives a percentage of each sale made in its service area.

Such nonstop commercialism represents a radical break with broadcast tradition. The pre-deregulation FCC enforced an arm's-length relationship between programs and advertising by penalizing stations for program-length commercials—programs that so interwove commercial and non-commercial content that audiences could not tell one from the other. The FCC reasoned that in such cases a broadcast station violated the public interest by displacing normal program functions. As discussed in Section 7.6, although the Commission's ban on such programs has long since disappeared,

---

[*]Expenses totaled about $1 million for each show. Much of this went for rights to use musical numbers—about $4,000 for any song over five seconds. One result: a 50-song medley in under five minutes with no song longer than five seconds.

Exhibit 10.e • • • • • • • • • • • • • • • •

Today *and* Tonight

Both *Today* and *Tonight* came from the creative imagination of Sylvester L. "Pat" Weaver—at the time, NBC's vice president for television. Philosophy major, Phi Beta Kappa, magna cum laude Princeton graduate, and innovative programmer, he likely is best known today as the father of actress Sigourney Weaver (whose real name is Susan but who, at 14, borrowed the more exotic "Sigourney" from a character in *The Great Gatsby* because, she says, she wanted to stand out from the crowd). His two programs also stand out from the crowd of copy-cat television shows as among the most innovative, yet most successful series ever conceived.

Today

The second-longest-running show in television history (NBC's *Meet the Press* had begun five years earlier), *Today* premiered, live, at 7:00 A.M. on January 14, 1952. It originated from a first-floor studio (with a window looking out on a mid-Manhattan street) in Rockefeller Center's then RCA Building.

Dave Garroway presided as *Today*'s first host. Subsequent anchors included newsman John Chancellor (who hated the job), Hugh Downs (who loved it), and Tom Brokaw. In the early 1960s Barbara Walters joined the program as a writer (at first limited to "women's" stories). Later, in 1974, she became its first female co-anchor—with Frank McGee—but was not allowed to participate in a studio interview until after McGee had asked the first three questions. Walters left in 1976 and now stars with Downs on ABC's *20/20*.

Only three years out of college when she started as a *Today* cast member in 1976, Jane Pauley became co-anchor with Bryant Gumbel in 1982. Willard Scott had come on board as weatherman in 1980. On the surface, the chemistry of the Gumbel/Pauley/Scott team seemed to work. Then, in 1989, Gumbel wrote a "confidential" memo—which became very public—complaining about Scott's "whims, wishes, birthdays, and bad taste." Scott subsequently moved his base of operations to Washington and away from Gumbel.

Source: Photos courtesy NBC.

Some of *Today*'s best moments: Katie Couric and Bryant Gumbel banter with sports reporter Greg Gumbel and Al Roker, the show's occasional correspondent and substitute weatherman.

In early 1990, hoping to boost the program's ratings, NBC replaced Pauley with Deborah Norville. But the viewing public expressed its support for Pauley and its unhappiness with the way she had been treated by NBC. When Norville went on maternity leave in 1991, she was replaced—at first temporarily and later permanently—by Katherine ("Katie") Couric. At last the chemistry was back—now more than ever. Couric, with more than 10 years experience as a news producer and reporter, was able to charm guests, audiences, and even Bryant Gumbel.

Pat Weaver wanted *Today* to be a "showplace for the best of everything." Appearing on *Today at 40*, a prime-time anniversary special on January 14, 1992, he explained that the show tried to "make the common man the uncommon man."

Over the years, *Today* has largely continued to pursue these same goals. Although it has had its share of guests who shamelessly hawk their latest novels or movies or their upcoming NBC programs, it has also had its moments of greatness. And during its first 40 years the program has filled some 21,000 hours with breaking news, features, and interviews of more than 60,000 guests.

Tonight

The Tonight Show began in 1950 as *Broadway Open House* with a variety of hosts. In 1951 it became *The Steve Allen Show* and, in 1954, *Tonight!* starring Steve Allen. Allen had begun his broadcast career in radio before moving into television as a regular on *What's My Line* and *Songs for Sale*. A musician and author, as well as comedian, Allen left the program in 1957 to seek his fortune (unsuccessfully) in prime time.

For about seven months the program continued as *Tonight! America After Dark*, with several different hosts, before returning as *The Tonight Show* with Jack Paar. Paar's talent lay in his ability to tell his own stories and to draw others from his guests. Nervous and shy—or at least seemingly so—he stammered and feigned deep humility, cried on the air, and complained about unfair press coverage of his daughter's weight problem. In 1960 Paar made headlines when he told what today would be considered a harmless joke about a "water closet" (a euphemism for "toilet"). When NBC edited the story out of the program, Paar the next night got up from behind his desk and literally walked off the show. He returned three weeks later and stayed with the program until 1962, when he, too, headed for prime time—and failure.

The program continued again with various hosts until Johnny Carson took over on October 1, 1962. Carson had entered show business as a pre-teen ventriloquist and magician ("The Great Carsoni"). His broadcast career began as writer and announcer in Nebraska before moving to Los Angeles with his own show—first on radio, then on television. Later, as a writer for comedian Red Skelton, Carson filled in when the star was injured. This led to his own shows on CBS and on a local station, both of which failed. He did stand-up comedy on several variety programs and served as host of ABC's daytime quiz show *Who Do You Trust?* In 1958 he was joined on the quiz program by Ed McMahon, who was to introduce him throughout his years on *The Tonight Show* with the familiar "Heeeeere's Johnny!"

For 30 years Carson reigned as King of Late Night. He hosted some 5,000 shows, talked with more than 22,000 guests (those with programs on NBC could show clips; those on competing networks could not), and ran about 100,000 commercials. He created such characters as psychic El Moldo, answer-and-question man Carnac the Magnificent, Tea-time Movie host Art Fern, and editorial spokesperson Floyd R. Turbo. He also gave jump-starts to the careers of such performers as Garry Shandling and Roseanne Arnold.

The unique qualities attributed to Carson become evident from the failure of virtually everyone to compete with him. During his tenure he successfully defended his late-night domain against assaults by Joey Bishop, Dick Cavett, Merv Griffin, Bill Dana, Joan Rivers, Pat Sajak, Rick Dees, Alan Thicke, Ron Reagan, Jr., and Dennis Miller. When Carson retired, only one serious contender had survived—Arsenio Hall, who had managed to attract a younger audience than did *Tonight*.

Carson's reign finally came to a close on May 22, 1992. During the last week, Carson abandoned his normal routine of working no more than three nights a week, greeting a veritable blizzard of guest stars who considered it a special privilege to be with him at the end. As the audience grew, so did the price of

(Exhibit continues next page)

Before becoming permanent host of *Tonight*, Jay Leno often appeared as a guest of Johnny Carson—one of his biggest fans.

Exhibit 10.e, cont. •••••• •••••••••

commercials—from about $40,000 for a 30-second spot to almost $200,000. No guests appeared on the final program. Just reminiscences by Carson, McMahon, and long-time music director, Doc Severinson. Johnny's closing words: "I bid you a heartfelt goodnight." The closing theme: "I'll be seeing you."

NBC estimated that a record 55 million people watched that final episode. The lead-in gave David Letterman the highest-ever rating for his *Late Night* program, which followed. Opening the show with clips of earlier Carson guest appearances, he acknowledged Carson's unequaled popularity by commenting: "Mating squirrels could have pulled good ratings if they had followed Johnny."

Letterman, who moved to CBS in 1993 to compete directly against the program, had aspired to move up to *The Tonight Show*. But it was James Douglas Muir Leno who sat in the host chair the following Monday. Jay Leno had spent years as a stand-up comic, in clubs and strip joints and on television. He first appeared as a *Tonight Show* guest in 1977, becoming one of several guest hosts in 1986 and exclusive guest host in 1987.

As guest host he was not, however, treated by the producers as Johnny's equal. Although the program opened with Carson's theme music, Leno had to use different music following his monologue. And he delivered that monologue in front of a drab, grey curtain, not the multicolored drapery behind Carson. When, on May 25, 1992, he premiered as permanent host of *The Tonight Show with Jay Leno* (a subtle title change from the previous *Tonight Show Starring Johnny Carson*), Leno introduced his opening visual—some 24 curtains of many colors rising and separating for the star's entrance.

Although the program essentially followed Carson's format, it had changes other than the opening—a new set and backdrop; new theme music written by new musical director, jazz saxophonist Branford Marsalis; a "cooler" eight-piece group in place of Severinson's big band; and no Ed McMahon. New, too, was Leno's pledge to do the show five times a week—at least for a while.

Leno's typical Las Vegas salary was $100,000 a week. His new job paid $3 million a year. This compared to Carson's estimated annual income of up to $30 million—a net saving for NBC that ensured the continuance of *The Tonight Show* as not only one of the most popular shows in television history but also one of the most profitable.

---

the FCC in 1993 was contemplating a review of the entire question of commercial time limits.

•••••••

10.3 Network Television Sports Programs

For true fans, sports give television and radio ideal subjects— real-life events that occur on predictable schedules but nevertheless are full of suspense. For the general audience, however, comedy and drama have wider appeal. Thus, only a few play-off events,

such as the Super Bowl* and the World Series, rank among the all-time hit programs. These exceptional events have elements of pageantry that appeal to a broader audience.

More than a third of the public watches televised professional football at least occasionally. Next in

*As if to reinforce the Super Bowl's overwhelming popularity, the Fox network conceded the time period to CBS's 1992 coverage of the event. But at the end of the game's first half, Fox presented a special, live edition of its popular program, *In Living Color*, subtitled *Super Halftime Party*. During the program, an on-screen clock counted down the time remaining before the start of the second half so viewers would know when to switch back to the game. Continuing the event's incredible success, NBC's telecast of the 1993 Dallas-Buffalo SuperBowl attracted the largest audience ever for a television program—133.4 million U.S. viewers.

Exhibit 10.f •••••••• •••••••••

MTV

MTV ushered the music-television era into the electronic-media world on August 1, 1981, at 12:01 A.M. Its very first video clip featured an obscure British band known as the Buggles.

Says Tom Freston, head of MTV Networks, "From the very beginning, we made a lot of hay out of the fact that MTV was meant to alienate a lot of people. It was *meant* to drive a 55-year-old person crazy" (Williams, 1989). MTV may well have driven the older generation crazy with worries that, like Elvis's pelvis in the 1950s, MTV would seduce their children with its hypnotic sexuality. But it does delight the young. Today, MTV is available in more than 50 million U.S. cable homes.

MTV's music videos—essentially commercials for songs—rescued the record industry, whose sales in 1981 had dropped 30 percent from their 1978 peak. Over the ensuing decade, sales hit new highs, doubling by 1991. With its fast edits, bizarre camera angles, and exaggerated colors, the MTV "look" has also influenced nearly all areas of the entertainment world. Commercials, TV shows, even movies have adopted the format.

In 1985 a sister channel, VH-1, was born, intended for an audience somewhat older than the 12-to-24-olds targeted by MTV. In addition, the network was among the first to join the compression/multiplex technology revolution so that it could offer its fare on multiple cable channels. It also has expanded beyond the all-music-video format, offering game shows, newscasts, stand-up comedy, even documentaries and its own soap opera.

But about 85 percent of MTV airtime remains devoted to music. And not just for Americans. Versions of the network are now available in Europe, Asia, Central and South America, Australia, Russia, Japan—the list goes on and on. In all, MTV beams its music videos into more than 200 million television households in more than 70 countries.

---

order of popularity come professional baseball, college football, boxing, college basketball, and pro basketball. Relatively few watch such sports as golf, auto racing, soccer, hockey, and bowling, although enough do to keep such events on network weekend schedules. Television strategists value sports programs mainly because they appeal to middle-class males, a demographic group not well reached by most other programs. The ability of sports to capture such elusive consumers justifies charging higher-than-normal rates for commercials on sports programs.

Evolution of Network Sports

In the late 1960s ABC's search for differentiation from its rival networks led to an all-out emphasis on sports. ABC already had pioneered the weekend sports anthology genre in 1961 with its *Wide World of Sports*. By combining highlights of several sports events into a single program, the anthology avoids boring audiences with overlong coverage of minor sports or games that have only regional appeal. ABC also introduced such novelties as instant replay, the controversial commentary of Howard Cosell, *Monday Night Football* (starting in 1970), and extensive Olympic coverage.

By 1990 the combined broadcast/cable rights payments for on-the-spot sports events exceeded a billion dollars annually. In the meantime, broadcast television ratings for professional and college football had begun to decline. Sports fans increasingly divided their attention among dozens of televised sports events. The major broadcast networks responded in three ways: by diversifying into cable ownership; by seeking exclusive rights to regular-season games, accompanied by limits on competing local and regional telecasts; and by purchasing rights to sports mega-events not for the profit they would generate but for their image and promotional value.

In 1984 ABC purchased ESPN (originally Entertainment and Sports Program Network), an all-sports cable network founded in 1980. ESPN became profitable by 1985 after Nabisco bought a part interest, providing ESPN with the cash to purchase rights to more popular sporting events. This 24-hour cable network now carries first-rank contests, including NFL football and Major League baseball. It provides full-length coverage of events that ABC cannot schedule in their entirety. This pairing of broadcast and cable networks enhances ABC's bidding power for rights to sports events.

Following the ABC/ESPN success, NBC in 1989 moved into cable to create supplementary sports and news outlets. It bought Tempo TV (which later became CNBC) and SportsChannel America (purchased jointly with Cablevision). SportsChannel America introduced high school sports to national television in 1990, an innovative step that expanded the pool of televisable events. In 1991 it abandoned its national service, concentrating instead on regional programming. But two years later SportsChannel America merged with another regional cable sports program supplier, Prime Network. The combined service reached more than 40 million households nationally.

CBS surprised the television industry by spending more than $1 billion on major-league baseball rights for the early 1990s and, for the Winter Olympics, $243 million in 1992 and $300 million in 1994. CBS had not carried baseball for decades; it last televised an Olympic competition in 1960. Carrying such events as the Olympics and baseball's All-Star Game and World Series gave CBS some of the prestigious sports image held first by ABC and then by NBC. Exhibit 10.g shows how sports coverage by the three major networks has changed over three decades.

Mega-events in the sporting world attract adult audiences who otherwise view little television. The Olympic Games, for example, attract millions of such light television viewers. The networks often pay more for the Olympics than they can recoup in advertising revenues, counting on the games to enhance their worldwide images, to keep the premier events off competing outlets, and to promote other programs. Events such as the Super Bowl and World Series serve the same functions, especially because they normally occur just as the broadcast networks are adding new shows to their fall and winter line-ups.

Cable and PPV Sports

The growth of sports on such cable program services as ESPN, TBS, USA, and even the Nashville Network has been a major factor in reducing the value to the broadcast networks of all but exceptional or exclusive sports events. ESPN alone reaches nearly two-thirds of all television homes.

Increases in rights charges forced the gradual migration of many outstanding sports events to pay cable. For example, broadcast television networks can no longer compete with pay cable for heavyweight boxing championships, now typically carried by HBO. Even the once-profitable NFL football packages faltered and some games moved to cable. Suffering substantial losses under their $3.6 billion, four-year contract, broadcast networks in 1992 sought a $200-million rebate from the NFL; they received only about $28 million, leading NBC to say it would not renew the contract unless the next deal was "risk free."

Exhibit 10.g ●●●●●●●●●●●●●●●

Trends in Broadcast TV Network Sports Coverage

Sports Covered

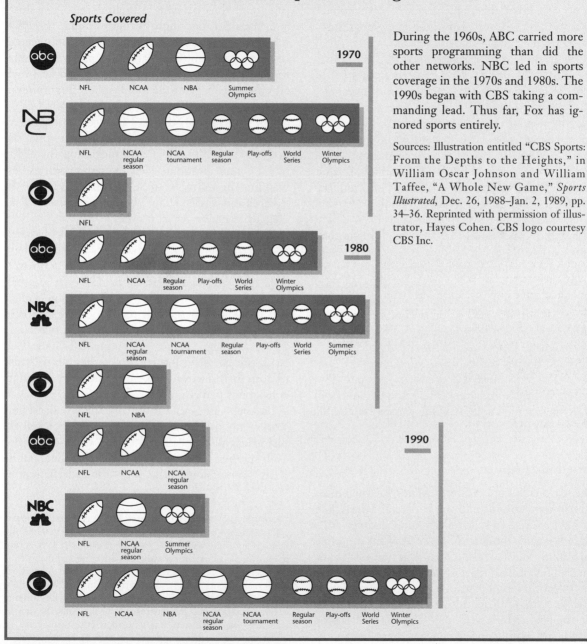

During the 1960s, ABC carried more sports programming than did the other networks. NBC led in sports coverage in the 1970s and 1980s. The 1990s began with CBS taking a commanding lead. Thus far, Fox has ignored sports entirely.

Sources: Illustration entitled "CBS Sports: From the Depths to the Heights," in William Oscar Johnson and William Taffee, "A Whole New Game," *Sports Illustrated*, Dec. 26, 1988–Jan. 2, 1989, pp. 34–36. Reprinted with permission of illustrator, Hayes Cohen. CBS logo courtesy CBS Inc.

Events such as boxing and professional wrestling have appeal for relatively small but intensely devoted and willing-to-pay audiences. These can be profitably scheduled on national pay-per-view (PPV) television. PPV programs, seen only by means of addressable cable technology in homes, bars, and hotels, have proved lucrative for some—but by no means all—sporting events.

One of the most ambitious network PPV efforts was NBC's *Olympics Triplecast* in the summer of 1992. In addition to its regular network coverage, NBC offered three PPV cable channels of continuous, commercial-free coverage of virtually all Olympic events. Although its broadcast programming (much criticized for overcommercialization) delivered large viewership, NBC's PPV channels did not, resulting in a loss estimated at about $150 million.

Also in 1992 ABC for the first time delivered college football telecasts to cable viewers on a PPV basis. The NFL promised that no pro-football games would be on PPV until at least 1994. Still, experts predict that more and more sporting events soon will be, thus reducing the general public's access to these events—a concern expressed in the 1950s and 1960s when subscription television threatened to take over coverage of major sports. By the early 1990s nearly two-thirds of all U.S. television homes had cable or satellite service, but fewer than one-third had access to pay-per-view. Although these numbers will rise, some homes will never have, or be able or willing to pay for, cable service or PPV.

Scheduling Sports

The seasonal nature of sports events and the limited control that stations and networks have over their timing give rise to scheduling complications. ABC made a daring innovation in 1970 when it started scheduling *Monday Night Football* in network prime time. This move risked—successfully, it turned out—devoting a long stretch of extremely valuable time to a single program with only selective audience appeal. Moreover, once the football season ended, successful replacement programs had to be found.

With the exception of ABC's *Monday Night* and a few other isolated cases, all major broadcast networks try to keep sports out of prime time. Not only do sports generally get lower ratings than entertainment shows in prime time, but they also often run long, thus delaying affiliates' local newscasts and network late-night programming. Football scheduling, however, is relatively uncomplicated: college games appear on Saturdays, and professional football appears on Sundays on two networks, which alternate coverage of the two leagues. Beginning in the late 1980s, ESPN also carried a weekend package of late-season NFL and college games, generally those the commercial broadcast networks did not want. By 1991 TNT had picked up the rights to pre-season and some early regular-season games. Gaining the rights to these games enhanced both ESPN's and TNT's stature with advertisers and audiences as major sports powers.

For television networks, basketball and baseball present messier problems than does football. There simply are too many games, and most are on weekdays and weeknights. Each professional baseball team plays more than 150 regular season games, and each NBA basketball team more than 80. In contrast, each professional football team plays only 16 regular league games. Thus the NFL lends itself to broadcast television network schedules because of both the limited number of games played and its convenient playing times.

Baseball games appear both on the broadcast networks and on cable. CBS and ESPN picked up major-league baseball rights for 1990–1993. But both suffered losses in the millions of dollars on the deals.* Professional NBA play-offs and champion-

---

*Two little-known elements can have a great effect on the profitability of network baseball coverage. (1) Advertising in the World Series is generally sold on the basis of six games. If a series runs fewer than six games, the network does not collect all the revenue it expected. But if a series reaches a seventh game, the network reaps real benefits because all advertising in that final game is essentially a windfall. (2) If, as happened in 1991 with Toronto, a team based in a Canadian city reaches the play-offs, the viewing audience—on which networks base their advertising rates—is underreported because rating services do not include Canada in their surveys.

ships appear on broadcast networks on weeknights during the spring. And in recent years, ABC has found a way to carry college basketball at a profit. In effect, the network sells blocks of time to an independent producer—Raycom Inc.—which handles production and sells advertising. Raycom operates more economically than a network can, primarily because it uses nonunion, freelance crews. The average cost for a network crew is about $100,000 per game; for Raycom, about $25,000.

In May 1993 broadcast television networks, having suffered both audience and revenue declines, entered into unprecedented arrangements for coverage of major sporting events. First NBC signed a four-year deal for NBA basketball at $750 million *plus* an agreement to share advertising revenues once the network reaches a certain sales level (about $1 billion). Next ABC and NBC announced a six-year contract for major-league baseball with no rights fees at all, but with immediate sharing of advertising revenue from televised games. The new baseball agreement added an extra round of playoffs but eliminated the traditional Saturday afternoon game-of-the-week on network television. Each year either ABC or NBC would carry the World Series, while the other would show the All-Star Game.

Issues in Sports Broadcasting

Television continues to increase both the coverage and popularity of sports. The downside, however, is that the enormous fees exacted for television rights have created troubling ethical issues:

- When coverage of sports events moves to cable, and especially when it moves to pay-per-view, it becomes unavailable to millions of viewers.
- Astronomical player salaries, induced by television stardom, invite press and fan criticism.
- The millions of dollars in rights fees that go to colleges have heightened the temptation to commercialize recruiting, to tolerate low graduation rates among players, and to manipulate college and NCAA rules.
- Television influences event scheduling and even the way in which some games are played. Stations and networks sometimes try to overcome the unpredictability of sports events by staging them expressly for television or by presenting videotaped coverage of a presumably live event—practices that are innocent enough when the events are clearly labeled as staged or recorded, less so when the manipulation is concealed.
- Over the protest of fans, East Coast games are played under the lights in order to maximize Pacific-time audiences. Also controversial is the delay of college basketball start times to 9:30 P.M. so that ESPN can carry double-header games on weekends. Such late starts mean that student players and fans arrive home as late as 2:00 or 3:00 A.M.
- Referees call arbitrary time-outs every 10 minutes or so to accommodate advertising spots within football and basketball games. Such artificial breaks can interrupt a team's momentum and undermine coaching strategies.
- Teams and sports associations often insist on controlling the hiring of play-by-play and color announcers. Critics regard such control as an illegal surrender of broadcaster responsibility for programs.
- Critics deplore beer sponsorship of televised college games, because such sponsorship inappropriately links the consumption of alcohol with the enjoyment of sports by underaged college students.

● ● ● ● ● ● ● ●

10.4 Network Television News and Public-Affairs Programs

The lofty network tradition of strictly separating news and public-affairs programs from entertainment began to erode as competition for audience attention became ever-more demanding in the 1980s and 1990s. Networks reacted by trying to get more value from their heavy investment in their news divisions—with more frequent news and news magazine programs and more syndication of network news product to affiliate and foreign organizations. And the show-biz culture invaded news, making much of it increasingly superficial.

At the same time, CNN emerged as the dominant international network with a global reach. But whether they receive it by broadcast or by cable, Americans turn to television as their primary news source.

Broadcast News

In 1963 CBS and NBC expanded their early-evening news programs from 15 minutes to a half-hour (actually only about 22 minutes, after subtracting time for commercials and other nonprogram elements). Still, the text of even an entire half-hour network newscast would fill less than a single page of a full-size newspaper. In 1976 the dean of American television journalism, Walter Cronkite, argued strenuously, with widespread support from the management of all three networks, for expansion to a full hour. However, affiliates overwhelmingly opposed the idea. They wanted to retain both the evening lead-in slot (usually 6:00 to 6:30 P.M.) for their own highly profitable local newscasts and the 7:00 to 8:00 P.M. access hour for revenue-producing syndicated fare. This meant networks could expand their evening news only by invading prime time at the expense of higher-rated entertainment programs, something they had no inclination to do.

All three major networks also schedule morning news or news magazine programs. In 1976 they began inserting one-minute, commercially sponsored *news capsules* in breaks between prime-time entertainment programs. However, affiliates, recognizing the revenue potential and promotional value of these micro-newscasts, soon began pre-empting the network capsules and substituting their own, many of which quickly became little more than commercially sponsored teasers for late-night newscasts.

In 1979 sizable audiences tuned to ABC's nightly 11:30 P.M. special coverage of the hostage crisis at the American embassy in Iran. This success persuaded ABC to create the permanent late-night news program, *Nightline*, featuring Ted Koppel.

The program responds with remarkable speed to same-day events, as each installment concentrates on one or two current news stories.

In the early 1980s the commercial broadcast television networks followed CNN's late-night lead by establishing their own middle-of-the-night newscasts. These services started and stopped, only to restart with different faces and a numbing variety of sound-alike titles: *News Overnight*, *Nightwatch*, *Nightside*, *World News Now*, *News Channel*, and so on. By the 1990s they were competing for affiliate and independent station clearance not only with CNN but also with such other offerings as the All News Channel.

In 1992 the Fox network announced plans to establish a national news operation. Chairman Rupert Murdoch hired veteran journalist and former CBS News president Van Gordon Sauter as president of Fox News. Murdoch also urged those Fox affiliates that were not already producing their own newscasts to invest upwards of $1.5 million each so they could do so and thus could feed some of their stories into the national news service. Murdoch explained that, by using graphic-heavy, visually oriented material—closer perhaps to music videos than to traditional network newscasts—Fox hoped to appeal to what he perceived to be an underserved audience, young people.

Television networks weigh the cost of producing newscasts and documentaries against their benefits for prestige and visibility. Huge news staffs, far-flung facilities, and regular international satellite transmission often cost more than the revenues they earn. For example, in the early 1990s NBC's news division hovered at break-even as it spent more than $1 million a day. Competition from cable news services and new, cost-conscious corporate managers encouraged networks both to tighten their traditional news belts and to expand into related ventures.

Cable News Networks

Ted Turner made what many then considered a foolhardy decision to pioneer in 1980 an all-news cable network. He launched Cable News Network

(CNN) as a fourth major television news service, providing national and international news in direct competition with ABC, CBS, and NBC. With a 24-hour schedule to fill, CNN can supply in-depth reportage as well as continuous coverage of breaking news stories.

Early doubts about CNN as a serious news service began to disappear when in 1986 it was the only network to carry live coverage of the explosion of the space shuttle Challenger. Those doubts dissolved completely in January 1991 as government officials and even ABC, CBS, and NBC turned to CNN for its coverage of the war in the Persian Gulf. After watching CNN's Peter Arnett, Bernard Shaw, and John Holliman deliver live reports by telephone from Baghdad as American planes bombed the Iraqi capital, NBC news anchor Tom Brokaw observed that "CNN used to be called the little network that could. It's no longer a little network" (Boedeker, 1991). CNN's status as the "network of record" further solidified later that same year with its gavel-to-gavel coverage of the Clarence Thomas/Anita Hill Senate Judiciary hearings on Thomas's nomination to the Supreme Court, and the William Kennedy Smith rape trial in West Palm Beach, Florida.

In 1992, after having received abysmal ratings in 1984 and 1988, the major networks conceded to CNN, PBS, and C-SPAN the gavel-to-gavel coverage of the Democratic and Republican conventions, limiting their own to a few hours each day. In fact, even cable's Comedy Central network devoted more time to convention coverage than did ABC, CBS, or NBC. Also, in a precedent-shattering arrangement, NBC's Tom Brokaw appeared on PBS at times when his own network was carrying traditional entertainment programs that had greater audience—and advertiser—appeal.

Because it does not rely on the "star" system and, hence, does not have to pay comparable salaries,* CNN competes with a much lower budget (about $200 million a year) than those of ABC, CBS, and

*Examples: CNN's Bernard Shaw's annual salary in the early 1990s was $500,000; CBS's Dan Rather earned between $3 million and $4 million.

NBC (about $300 million). As the major networks tightened their belts in the 1990s, often by closing domestic and foreign news bureaus, CNN expanded. In 1992 alone, CNN committed more than $2 million to open new overseas bureaus.

Between news roundups, CNN schedules interviews (*Larry King Live* is the best known), features on managing money, stock market analyses, sports news, and public-affairs discussions. Today more than 60 million cable television subscribers have access to CNN.

Turner's companion news service, CNN Headline News, provides news headlines and frequent updates in continuous half-hour cycles. It resembles all-news radio with pictures. More than half of all cable systems devote an entire channel to Headline News in addition to a channel for CNN. By offering discounts and ready-made promotional support, Turner makes it more economical for cable systems to take all five of his services (CNN, CNN Headline News, TBS, TNT, and The Cartoon Channel) rather than only two or three.

Some independent broadcast television stations schedule Headline News adjacent to their local newscasts; some carry it in the overnight hours, airing a half-hour, two hours, or even more. In addition, CNN syndicates news footage and narrated stories to dozens of television stations for inclusion in local newscasts. It also—through the Unistar network—supplies news services, called CNN Radio and CNN Headline, to hundreds of radio stations.

As do all conscientious news organizations, CNN must guard against the possibility of inadvertently giving *false* information. Exhibit 10.h gives one example of how this might happen.

Informational Networks

Several cable networks provide informational programming. NBC's Consumer News and Business Channel (CNBC) attempted to become a major cable player when it acquired its prime competitor, Financial News Network (FNN), in 1991. After surviving a bidding war with Dow Jones and Westinghouse Broadcasting, CNBC bought FNN for

Exhibit 10.h ●●●●●●●●●●●●●●●●

A Close Call at CNN Headline News

News organizations try to remain ever vigilant, lest they be victimized by a hoax and broadcast a story that simply is not true. As a rule, journalists insist on confirmation by more than one source. In the case of major stories, however, the rush to be first can brush caution aside—as happened at CNN in 1992.

About three hours after President Bush had collapsed at a state dinner in Japan, a man who said he was Bush's physician called CNN headquarters in Atlanta and stated that the president had died. The story was immediately entered into the computer system at CNN responsible for alerting everyone of the arrival of an important story.

A producer at Headline News instructed anchor Don Harrison to use the story. Harrison wanted confirmation that the story was true, but he was overruled and began to ad lib: "This is just in to CNN Headline News. And we say right off the bat, we have not confirmed this through any other source."

Suddenly an off-camera voice yelled, "No! Stop!"

CNN had done some checking and quickly determined the story was false. Harrison continued ad libbing, this time with the news that President Bush was resting comfortably.

Police soon arrested a man in Idaho who was identified as the caller and was later admitted to a mental hospital. As CNN executive vice president Ed Turner observed: "All news organizations fear this. Things like this give you nightmares. The people involved felt so terrible. What more could you say? All you can do is learn from it."

Source: Patrick Boyle, "CNN's Close Call," *Washington Journalism Review*, March 1992: 11. Used with permission.

cial coverage, and lifestyle programs. In addition to its cable programs, it offers CNBC Radio through the Unistar network.

The Weather Channel supplies 24 hours of general and specialized weather news, inserting local weather conditions and temperatures within each region in hourly cycles. Other cable networks that carry informational programming along with entertainment include The Learning Channel with educational programs; The Silent Channel for the hearing impaired; and The Travel Channel, which carries 24-hour travel information as well as other feature material. Some cable systems also carry any one of several alphanumeric news services, such as that provided by the Associated Press, supplying news headlines in text form.

Public-Affairs Programs

News and public-affairs programs tend to overlap. In its station license forms, however, the FCC made a distinction, defining "public affairs" as

local, state, regional, national or international issues or problems, including, but not limited to, talks, commentaries, discussions, speeches, editorials, political programs, documentaries, minidocumentaries, panels, roundtables and vignettes, and extended coverage (whether live or recorded) of public events or proceedings, such as local council meetings, congressional hearings and the like.

The Commission stressed public-affairs programs because of the traditional view that broadcasters in a democracy have a special obligation to serve the needs of citizen-voters.

Until deregulation arrived in the 1980s, pressure from the FCC, critics, and Congress spurred the production of topical *documentaries*. Expensive to produce (by comparison to, say, talk programs), they rarely attracted large audiences and often created controversies—two reasons many advertisers avoided them. By the 1990s their numbers had greatly diminished. Nevertheless, the commercial broadcast television networks and most large stations maintain at least one weekly public-affairs discussion series, sometimes also a news documentary series, and often mini-documentaries within newscasts (especially during ratings periods).

$154 million and picked up most of FNN's 35 million households. The service struggled to establish its own identity, providing a mix of hard news, finan-

Exhibit 10.i •••••••••••••••

60 Minutes

A stellar team of correspondents, originally consisting of Mike Wallace, Harry Reasoner, and Morley Safer, contributes to the *60 Minutes* success story. As a *New York Times* commentator put it:

> Their gray or graying hair, their pouched and careworn countenances, the stigmata of countless jet flights, imminent deadlines, and perhaps an occasional relaxing martini, provide a welcome contrast to the Ken and Barbie dolls of television news whose journalistic skills are apt to be exhausted after they have parroted a snippet of wire service copy and asked someone whose home has just been wrecked by an earthquake, How do you feel? (Buckley, 1978)

Later, Dan Rather joined the team; later still, Ed Bradley and (for a time) Diane Sawyer improved its ethnic/gender balance. Rather left the show in the mid-1980s to anchor *CBS Evening News*, the most prestigious news position a network can offer. In 1989 Sawyer moved to ABC, which gave her a multimillion-dollar five-year contract, and in 1991 Harry Reasoner retired. Today, Leslie Stahl and Steve Kroft, together with commentator Andy Rooney, round out the team.

The magazine format allows the program to treat a great variety of subjects in segments of varying lengths. With executive producer Don Hewitt and a staff of some 70 producers, editors, and reporters, the *60 Minutes* team develops about 120 segments annually, each of which, on the average, requires six to ten weeks to produce. The *ambush interview*, a Mike Wallace specialty, adds drama to investigative reports. Presenting his victims on camera with damning evidence

Source: Photo from CBS, Inc.

The top-rated Sunday evening newsmagazine, which has aired since 1968, now stars journalists (from left) Morley Safer, Mike Wallace, Ed Bradley, Leslie Stahl, and Steve Kroft.

of wrongdoing, Wallace grills them unmercifully. The victims' evasions, lies, and brazen attempts to bluff their way out of their predicament—often captured through extreme-close-up lenses—fascinate some viewers, while others question these tactics. Tabloid TV programs have imitated the Wallace-type confrontation to the point of turning it into a cliché.

60 Minutes is generally acknowledged to be the most successful news program—in terms of both ratings and revenues—in television history. It may well be the most successful of *any* program, news or otherwise. It is the only broadcast to have finished in the top ten Nielsen ratings for 15 consecutive seasons, and the only program to be rated number one in each of three different decades. On the revenue side: it generates a profit for CBS of between $60 million and $70 million every year, year after year after year after year. . . .

The most striking development in network public-affairs was the rise of *60 Minutes*, the weekly CBS magazine-format documentary series (see Exhibit 10.i). After a shaky start, it eventually ranked, year in and year out, as one of television's most-watched programs. That success violated all conventional wisdom, which had said that documentaries repelled

the mass audience. One reason previous documentaries had low ratings, aside from not being as well produced as *60 Minutes*, was that the networks usually scheduled them in unfavorable time slots and denied them the long-term stability they needed to build an audience. After years of wandering, *60 Minutes* finally achieved stability at a good hour—

a by-product of the prime-time access rule, which left the Sunday 7:00 to 8:00 P.M. time slot open for nonentertainment network programs. Another factor may have been the CBS counterprogramming strategy of scheduling *60 Minutes* against children's programs. Still other elements that contributed to the show's success were its magazine format and its investigative approach to controversial topics.

In the late 1980s CBS started a second public-affairs series, *48 Hours*. It turns cameras on a single topic, such as a hospital, an election, or a school. Shooting over a two-day period, it tries to reveal underlying processes and issues. *Street Stories*, a spin-off from *48 Hours*, emerged in the early 1990s. Ed Bradley of *60 Minutes* serves as host, joined by several correspondents, including Deborah Norville, formerly of *Today* and, more recently, with her own talk show on ABC radio.

ABC's *20/20*, a magazine-format show similar to *60 Minutes*, survives as a respected and modestly successful network prime-time program. Starring Hugh Downs and Barbara Walters (both of whom began their careers at NBC), *20/20* rarely makes the list of the 15 top-rated programs. Nevertheless, because of its relatively low production costs it can earn a profit with ratings in the 10s. Hoping to duplicate—or possibly even quintuplicate—*20/20's* economic success, ABC in March 1993 premiered *Day One*, hosted by Forrest Sawyer, and said it would introduce at least four additional prime-time newsmagazines by the end of the year. The network concentrates most of its other public-affairs efforts on *Nightline* and its Sunday morning public-affairs program.

NBC has had difficulty in developing a prime-time news magazine with success comparable to that of CBS and ABC. This comes not for want of trying, however. By 1993 NBC had attempted 18 times to make the format work, beginning with *First Tuesday* in 1971. Finally, 1992's *Dateline*, with former *Today* anchor Jane Pauley and former *20/20* correspondent Stone Phillips, appeared to have found an audience. Fox did not enter the news arena until the 1990s. It launched its first prime-time newsmagazine, *Front Page*, in 1993.

Each of the three major commercial broadcast networks schedules a public-affairs question-and-answer session with newsworthy figures on Sundays, usually around midday. NBC's *Meet the Press* started in 1947 and is the oldest continuously scheduled program on network television. CBS launched *Face the Nation* in 1954, and ABC began *Issues and Answers* in 1960, later replacing it with *This Week with David Brinkley*. Every politician of consequence appears on these Sunday public-affairs shows, and their remarks frequently become news on later network newscasts and in Monday newspapers.

Sunday Morning, a very relaxed public-affairs program, provides a vehicle for CBS's much-loved Charles Kuralt. It draws only low ratings, but the time slot suits Kuralt's leisurely, reflective, low-key style. With its standard closing—nature scenes accompanied not by the traditional music background but rather by natural sound—the program is considered by many to be one of the best on television.

Public Affairs on Cable

Cable television developed a unique public-affairs vehicle specifically to cultivate a positive image for its industry—an image long marred by frequent technical breakdowns, unanswered calls from subscribers, and charges of monopoly. The cable industry put its best foot forward with C-SPAN (Cable Satellite Public Affairs Network), a nonprofit corporation with the mission of originating a full, 24-hour public-affairs service. Today C-SPAN and its companion C-SPAN II offer live coverage of congressional floor sessions, hearings, political conventions, and other informative programs.

•••••••••

10.5 *Children's Programs*

Most television programs fall into recognized genres—situation comedies, movies, soap operas, game shows, sports, and so on. The *children's* program category, however, encompasses virtually all genres. Though cartoons dominate the category, most adult program types have their counterparts in children's programs. In the 1990s cable provided about 60 percent of total television hours devoted to children; Fox and independent stations, about 17 percent; and ABC, CBS, and NBC, only 3 percent. (Chapter 8 includes a discussion of children's programs on PBS, which supplies the remaining 20 percent.)

Broadcasting

Children's programming received a boost in the 1990s when the FCC initiated regulations requiring broadcasters to provide educational and informational programs for young people, as detailed in Section 14.8. ABC, CBS, and NBC already scheduled several hours of children's programming for their affiliates every week, consisting mostly of Saturday morning animated cartoons. They have been joined by the Fox Children's Network, which offers programming on weekdays as well as Saturdays. In 1992 NBC began a phase-out of its Saturday morning animated-cartoon line-up, moving instead to live-action programs that the network hoped would attract a somewhat older audience—so called "teens and 'tweens"—as well as expanding its *Today* program to seven days a week.

Broadcasters value young audiences so highly that they alter their children's program line-ups in accordance with ratings trends just as rapidly as they change their prime-time schedules. Cartoons on networks and those stripped daily by local stations reach tens of millions of children several times a week. Half-hour cartoon shows can also be re-edited into 90-minute theatrical features for theaters and videocassettes marketable in more than 100 countries around the world.

Children's programs earn a relatively small percentage of broadcast television's total advertising revenues, but most run at times that might otherwise go unsold. Toy, candy, and cereal manufacturers support most commercial children's programs.

Cable

Although the three full-service commercial broadcast networks once accounted for nearly half of all hours of children's programs on television, today cable television provides most children's programming—at least to that majority of television homes that subscribes to cable. Indeed, cable systems emphasize this service when selling subscriptions to families with young children.

Nickelodeon, Viacom's acclaimed cable network for children, originates several weekly hours of high-quality programs that avoid violence as entertainment and feature a broad range of role models. Nickelodeon targets the younger child in the mornings and teens in the late afternoons. In the evenings, Nickelodeon usually shifts to Nick at Nite, which schedules mostly off-network reruns. In 1992, however, the network began devoting two Saturday night hours to programs for its 8-to-15-year-old audience.

Nickelodeon mixes its long-running favorites such as *You Can't Do That on Television* with newer offerings such as *The Ren and Stimpy Show*. And in addition to regular series and movies, Nickelodeon imitates adult special programs by producing such children's fare as *Pop Warner's Football Superbowl*, highlighting the annual high school football championships. It even persuaded network news veteran Linda Ellerbee to bring her craft to the network.

In 1992 Ted Turner launched his new, 24-hour-a-day, all-Cartoon Network. Most of its programs come from the Hanna-Barbera library, which Turner purchased in 1991 for $320 million. That library boasts more than 3,000 half-hours of animated programs, including old television series such as *The Jetsons* and *The Flintstones*. Turner also owns about 800 MGM half-hours, including *Tom and Jerry*, as well as a collection of pre-1948 Warner Bros. cartoons.

USA Network also schedules programs for children, mostly syndicated cartoons. The Discovery Channel targets older children with original adventure and science programs, including shows on technology, history, and world exploration. About one-third of Discovery's schedule consists of nature programs, which draw its highest ratings. In 1992 The Learning Channel launched a daily six-hour block of educational shows for preschoolers, a prelude to what it hoped would eventually be a 24-hour network for the two-to-six age group.

On pay cable, The Disney Channel programs for children in the daytime and for the family in the evenings. This premium service draws on the large Disney studio library of films and off-network television series from the 1950s and 1960s, and originates several new adventure series for older children and feature films for all ages. One unique advantage over its competitors: it carries the Disney stamp but no commercials. In the 1990s Disney expanded its operation to offer *Disney Afternoon*—a two-hour block of syndicated programs for broadcast stations.

Children's Television Issues

Children have such easy access to television, they consume so much of it, and it exerts such a powerful hold on their attention that society has a special stake in the quality of programs made especially for them.*

Most foreign countries regulate children's programs in considerable detail; some forbid advertising to children altogether. The FCC, however, has imposed only minimal regulation (Section 14.8). Advocates raise such issues as these:

- The inappropriateness of much television viewed by children in terms of their needs and vulnerabilities.
- The negative impact of violent and aggressive program content (Section 12.7).
- The absence of a wide range of suitable role models on television.
- Exploitation of children by advertisers, especially by those that encourage consumption of candy and sugar-coated cereals (Section 12.8).
- The shortage of age-specific programs, especially for very young children.

*One concerned father attacked head-on the problem of excessive television viewing by his own children. He created TV Allowance, a programmable device through which parents can electronically control each child's television time. In 1992 he began to offer copies of his invention to the public—at $99 each (Morgan, 1992).

• • • • • • • •

10.6 Syndicated Television Programs

The mechanics of syndication and the ways stations and cable television use syndicated programs are discussed in Section 9.2. Here we focus on programs themselves, divided into three categories: off-network programs, first-run programs, and theatrical films (movies).

Off-Network Syndication

The programs that do best on the broadcast networks usually also excel in syndication. Most stations schedule half-hour syndicated series because they attract a desirable demographic group (typically women 18 to 49 years) and permit scheduling flexibility. As the audience of working adults builds during the afternoon time period, successive half-hour shows gain bigger audiences. Hour-long programs, on the other hand, do not attract many new viewers during their second 30 minutes. An off-network series typically earns a rating about 10 points lower in syndication on stations than it earned in its first network appearance. On cable networks, ratings for such programs may fall even lower.

Broadcast stations fill two main time periods with off-network shows: early fringe and access time (if the station is not an affiliate in one of the top 50 markets and, hence, not subject to the prime-time access rule). They strip both off-network sitcoms and hour-long adventure shows in late afternoons, with each station in a market usually choosing to block-program one genre and/or target one demographic group. Sitcoms attract both children and adult women. Stations usually put their most popular, male-appealing syndicated program, often a recent off-network show, in the slot leading into local news.

Sixty-minute action/adventure series such as *Hunter* have also had success in late afternoons because of their male demographics. Hour-long dramatic programs such as *Knot's Landing*, however, have not succeeded in that daypart because (1) they appeal to women rather than to men, and women who are at home in the late afternoon often prepare the evening meal at that time; (2) they do not appeal to children and teens, who usually control the television set in late afternoons; and (3) they require more concentrated viewing than late afternoons typically permit.

Cable networks, however, have found that some hour-long dramatic series appeal to cable viewers in access, prime-time, and late-fringe time periods. Lifetime, for example, successfully stripped both *China Beach* and *L.A. Law*, and USA stripped *MacGyver* and *Murder, She Wrote*—all in prime time. They obtained such series at relatively low per-episode rates because few stations had a suitable place in their schedules for hour-long programs.

First-Run Syndication

Shows in the second syndication category, first-run programs, are brand new when first sold to stations or cable. They are produced especially for syndication, never having been seen on a broadcast network. Viewers can hardly distinguish the best first-run syndicated programs from network programs. For example, the daily 30-minute syndicated magazine show *Entertainment Tonight* (described in Exhibit 10.j) is so slickly produced that it could easily be taken for a network program. By the 1990s producers were offering even some high-priced programs in first-run syndication. Examples include *Star Trek: Deep Space Nine* and *The Untouchables*. Sometimes, programs discarded by the networks later turn up in first-run syndication. One of the earliest examples: ABC canceled *Fame* when its ratings declined, but it came back as a syndicated series that mixed the old (off-network) episodes with new episodes (a hybrid referred to as *first-run-off-net*). *Too Close for Comfort*, *The Days and Nights of Molly Dodd*, and *Baywatch* followed the same network-to-first-run-syndication pattern.

Distributors of first-run syndicated shows target major-market affiliates, which, because of PTAR, must fill the daily, high-audience 7:00 to 8:00 P.M. hour with nonnetwork programs. Most indepen-

dents found first-run shows too costly to strip until inexpensive first-run reality shows (discussed below) became available.

Programs created especially for the access hour tend to use low-budget genres such as quizzes and games, interview programs, and magazines. The reigning king of access programs, *Wheel of Fortune*, with *Jeopardy* nipping at its heels, typically gets higher ratings than any competition in access time, including off-network shows. Some stations risk viewer outrage by running in access time a gamier type of game show, such as *Studs* (said by some to have drawn top ratings by reaching new depths of bad taste) and *Infatuation*, although most reserve such series for late night.

Syndicators and stations also favor first-run talk shows. Some, such as *Arsenio Hall*, compete with NBC's *Tonight*. But most find homes in morning or afternoon time slots. *Oprah Winfrey* and *Phil Donahue* (see Exhibit 10.k) rank at the top of the ratings ladder. But there is a constant supply of others, including *Live with Regis and Kathie Lee*, *Joan Rivers*, and *Sally Jesse Raphael*.

Also in daytime, some stations and cable networks strip a mix of off-network and first-run court shows, which typically fare best when scheduled in blocks. Several relatively inexpensive first-run shows, such as *The Judge* and *Divorce Court*, can surround hits such as *People's Court*.

A much-discussed first-run syndicated program genre emerged in the 1980s to challenge the leading access-time shows. Known variously as *reality shows*, *trash TV*, and *tabloid TV*, these programs have in common a pseudo-journalistic approach to real-life topics, usually items currently or recently in the news. *A Current Affair* started the fad in 1988 and was soon followed by *Inside Edition* and *Hard Copy*. Programs of this genre tend to cater to morbid viewer interest in the sensational and the bizarre and to exploit scandals, sex, and violence. Their blending of entertainment and journalism appeared symptomatic of a broad trend toward *infotainment*—treating news from an entertainment perspective. Even some broadcast station local newscasts have adopted a tabloid approach: "If it bleeds, it leads."

Exhibit 10.j • • • • • • • • • • • • • • •

Entertainment Tonight

Entertainment Tonight (ET) revolutionized the syndication business by proving that expensive, original, non-network programs—other than game shows—could be profitable for stations as well as for producers and syndicators. The economics of such an effort are all the more unusual in that each episode is an original—with no reruns to help spread the cost.

Introduced in the late 1970s, the program took off in 1981 when Group W began delivering the topical show by satellite. Mary Hart joined ET in 1982 (with special lighting to illuminate her legs beneath the plexiglass desk), and John Tesh arrived in 1986. By mid-1993, more than 3,000 episodes had been broadcast.

Entertainment Tonight provides a classic example of the constant innovation essential to keep a series from going stale. Initially, the program capitalized on the audience's appetite for gossip, personality exploitation, and show-biz fluff. Later the producer countered the lightweight image by introducing brief "think-pieces," some hard news, and more in-depth stories. By the 1990s, however, in order to compete with a glut of tabloid shows, the program began to turn more and more to sexually oriented items.

Among the best elements of the show are the contributions of Leonard Maltin, who became a regular contributor in 1982 and obviously knows and loves "the business." His consistently perceptive pieces are as rare on popular commercial television as is an episode of *Entertainment Tonight* that uses neither the word *exclusive* nor the phrase *behind-the-scenes.*

Movies

In addition to off-network and first-run programs, television syndicators offer movies, singly or in packages of six or a dozen or more, sometimes grouping them by genre (horror, western, science fiction). They release recent hit movies to networks on the basis of "availability windows," as shown in Exhibit 9.g on page 320.

Typically, larger packages include some box-office successes along with lesser-known films. Distributors try to sell these packages on an "all-or-none" basis—a questionable practice resembling block booking, which is legally banned in the motion picture industry. To avoid charges of block booking, distributors begrudgingly allow "cream-ing" of a package and will price films individually—placing very high prices on the desirable films and low prices on the others, to the point where it makes economic sense for the buyer simply to take the whole package. Stations and cable networks, and sometimes even cable systems, buy such packages, obtaining the right to show each movie two times (or sometimes more). Broadcast affiliates usually strip movies in late-night slots and run them on weekend afternoons; independent stations and cable networks regularly schedule them in prime time.

Syndicated Religion

Charismatic religious broadcasters contribute materially to the revenue of commercial electronic mass

Exhibit 10.k •••••• •••••••••

Phil & Oprah

Both Phil and Oprah regularly devote much of their daily program time to comments by and questions from members of their studio audiences.

Oprah departed from her daytime talk-show format for a very personal—and highly rated—prime-time interview with superstar Michael Jackson.

Phil Donahue began his broadcast career as a television journalist before undertaking his first talk show in 1967 on WLWD-TV in Dayton, Ohio. His first guest: Madelyn Murray O'Hare, the atheist who had successfully petitioned the U.S. Supreme Court to ban prayer in public schools. Eight years later the program moved to WGN-TV, the powerful independent station in Chicago; in 1976 Multimedia placed it in syndication; and in 1985 it chose New York City as its new home base. Donahue's silver-haired good looks, his wit and intelligence, and his unbridled energy soon made him a hit with daytime audiences. Some critics complain about an overabundance of sex and perversion in the programs, especially in recent years as competition has intensified. But Donahue demurs, pointing to his 20 Emmy awards, his many more-serious episodes, and his celebration in 1992 with a prime-time 25th anniversary special on NBC.

For years Donahue virtually "owned" the 9:00 to 10:00 A.M. time period on stations throughout the country and was, indeed, the Prince of daytime talk shows . . . until Oprah. Also a former journalist, Oprah Winfrey became the first personality success-fully to challenge Phil's talk-show dominance. A victim of child abuse herself, she brought to her program a special understanding of the conflict besetting the lives of her guests. Oprah began with a local show in 1984 and moved into national syndication in 1986. She also appeared in the motion picture, *The Color Purple*, earning an Academy Award nomination as best supporting actress, and executive-produced and starred in a TV miniseries, *The Women of Brewster Place*. She made headlines in the early 1990s when she lost 67 pounds on the Optifast diet, only to gain it all back. During her "slim period," *TV Guide* featured her on one of its covers—later admitting that illustrators had superimposed Oprah's head on the body of voluptuous actress Ann-Margret.

Today, the programs of both stars are carried on nearly 200 stations each, reaching nearly all U.S. television households. Oprah reigns as number one in the ratings; Phil, as number two. Each program costs relatively little—in television terms—to produce: $10 to $20 million a year. Donahue generates annual revenues of about $90 million; Oprah, more than $150 million.

Source: Photos by Scull/Globe Photos, Inc. (Donahue) and Globe Photos, Inc. (Winfrey).

media—through a curious variation on commercial syndication practice. Instead of selling programs, televangelists buy time in which to present their programs. Their revenue comes from listeners and viewers. Some, such as Billy Graham, appear to have a genuine, spiritually based mission. Most, however, offer inspirational messages generously laced with a variety of appeals for money, including the sale of religious artifacts (payments for which are disguised as "love gifts"). Many—but not all—stations welcome televangelist time-buyers because they often pay for otherwise unsalable, low-viewership hours.

Reaching each donor household costs so much that televangelists operate under tremendous pressure to maintain a continuously mounting cash flow to keep up with rising time-costs. This need helps account for the fervency of their appeals for money, accompanied by all-too-real threats of going off the air if donations fall short.

The great reach of the electronic mass media, however, enables the most effective televangelist fund raisers to pyramid donations with breathtaking ease. With so many millions of tax-free dollars pouring forth from every mail delivery, successful televangelists tend to take on commercial sidelines such as Jim Bakker's gaudy theme park, Heritage USA. But Bakker's fiscal irresponsibility and high-flying lifestyle* eventually led to his 1989 conviction and later imprisonment for fraud and conspiracy. His bankruptcy—both financial and moral—left many time-sales bills unpaid and put a dent in the entire business of syndicated religion.

• • • • • • • •

10.7 Locally Produced Television Programs

The economics of program production favor program centralization—networking and syndication. As a result, locally produced programs occupy rela-

tively little time in the schedules of most broadcast stations and cable systems. Local television consists almost entirely of news and public-affairs programming. Evening newscasts rank highest in importance among locally produced programs because of the revenue and prestige they bring.

Local News Production

Audience interest in local television newscasts escalated during the 1970s, converting many news operations from loss leaders to profit centers. Multimillion-dollar budgets for local television news departments became commonplace in large markets, enabling stations to purchase or lease helicopters, customized news vans (such as those shown in Exhibit 10.l) loaded with minicams and topped with microwave-relay dishes, movable satellite uplinks, automated newsrooms, computerized color weather maps, and other high-tech facilities for news gathering and presentation. Large stations developed their own investigative reporting and documentary units and expanded their coverage to nearby towns and cities and, in some cases, to foreign countries. Satellite technology and networking enlarged the reach of local stations, minimizing time and distance constraints. By the mid-1980s large market stations routinely dispatched local news teams to distant places to get local angles on national and international news events, sending (or *backhauling*) live stories back to home base via satellite. So important had local news become, for network affiliates at least, that being number one in its market in local news usually meant being number one overall as well.

While helpful in expanding local news capacity, improved news-gathering technology also has its down side. In particular, critics point to overuse of live relays when thoughtful in-studio reports might be more informative. There is a natural tendency to show off technical capabilities to justify expensive equipment purchases. Stations cannot arrange for major community events and natural disasters to take place between 6:00 and 6:30 P.M., during their local newscasts. As a result, they resort to marginal news stories or features that can conveniently be covered "live from the scene."

*In 1987 Bakker confessed to a sexual adventure with a woman to whom his ministry, PTL, had paid hush money. Another leading televangelist, Jimmy Swaggart, condemned Bakker, only to be tagged himself—twice—with sexual indiscretions.

Exhibit 10.1 ● ● ● ● ● ● ● ● ● ● ● ● ● ● ●

Electronic News-Gathering Equipment

The unwieldy remote-production trailer in the background contrasts with the compact, lightweight ENG (electronic news-gathering) van in the foreground. The machine gun–like object atop the van is a microwave antenna for relaying pictures back to the studio.

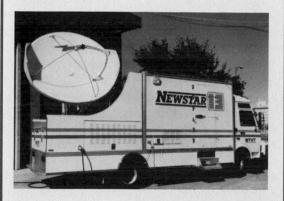

Satellite news gathering (SNG) greatly extends a reporter's range. Not limited by the "line-of-sight" requirements of microwave relays, a mobile Earth station uplinks signals to a satellite for transmission to the station.

Sources: Photo A courtesy WTVJ-TV, Miami, FL; photo B courtesy WTVT, Tampa, FL.

The 1970s also ushered in the era of *news consultants*, marketing specialists hired by stations for advice on how to improve newscast ratings. Today some stations are reluctant to alter the appearance or style of their newscasts without first seeking advice from a news consultant. Under contract to station management, news consultants move in with a battery of audience surveys and focus-group interviews. Their advice can range from wholesale replacement of news anchors to the adoption of an on-the-air dress code. They have been accused of responsibility for Ken-and-Barbie-doll news anchors and for sexist and ageist recommendations favoring men over women and young over old as news presenters. By the 1990s, however, nonstandard looks had become more acceptable to the public, and able journalists could hope to survive consultant evaluations even without a youthful appearance.

News consultants brought a more entertainment-oriented style to local newscasts. For example, "happy talk" news employs informal banter among members of the on-air news team— which now has become largely standardized with two news anchors (typically one male and one female), a sports reporter, a weather reporter, and various on-the-scene and on-set correspondents. Their synthetic light-heartedness created, as one critic put it, "an aura of exaggerated joviality and elbow-jabbing comradeship" (Powers, 1977: 35). In a similar vein, news directors contrived "happy news," stories lacking in hard-news value but inserted to relieve the gloom of real news by giving viewers the feeling that something good happened in the world that day. And nearly every market in the country has one station offering consultant-driven *action news*, a format that emphasizes visually arresting stories such as fires, accidents, and drug busts—regardless of their relative news value.

In his still-valid book critical of news consultants, Ron Powers concluded:

> When local stations create and choreograph entire programs along the guidelines supplied by researchers—toward the end of gratifying the audiences' surface whims, not supplying its deeper informational needs—an insidious and corrosive hoax is being perpetrated on American viewers. . . . The hoax is made more insidious by the fact that very few

television newswatchers are aware of what information is left out of a newscast in order to make room for the audience-building gimmicks and pleasant repartee. (1977: 234)

Local news departments sometimes capitalize on the availability of *camcorders* (relatively inexpensive hand-held video cameras/VCRs) to turn amateur photographers, at least temporarily, into *stringers* (self-employed professionals who sell individual stories to radio and television stations). Stations have used amateur footage of everything from earthquakes and tornadoes to train wrecks and traffic jams. Probably the best examples of widely used amateur footage are the 8-mm film coverage of the assassination of President Kennedy and the videotaped scenes of the Rodney King beating by police officers whose subsequent acquittal on assault charges set off the 1992 riots in Los Angeles.

Origination by Affiliates

Most affiliates originate a daily local early-evening newscast and a late-fringe newscast. Depending on the size of the market, the early news on weekdays may start as early as 4:00 P.M. or as late as 6:00 P.M.; on weekends it usually begins at 6:00. Local evening news shows either lead into network news, or both precede and follow it to form a *sandwich*. In the Eastern and Pacific time zones, network news may be scheduled from as early as 5:30 P.M. to as late as 7:00 P.M. but most commonly starts at 6:30.

Late newscasts typically appear at 11:00 P.M.. For years these programs had lasted a half-hour. By the early 1990s, however, they had expanded to 35 minutes—a network concession to affiliate desires for more local advertising time and to the networks' own efforts to improve clearances of their programs that followed: ABC's *Nightline*, CBS's *David Letterman*, and NBC's *Tonight*. Many affiliates also schedule a half-hour or hour of noon news. Network early-morning magazine shows such as *Good Morning America* provide slots into which affiliates can insert local news and weather segments. About 80 percent of affiliates also originate their own weekday early-morning newscasts or magazine/talk shows, preceding the network morning programs or even pre-empting part of them if network ratings are weak. By the early 1990s some stations had even begun producing morning news programs on weekends.

The larger the market, the more time stations are likely to devote to local news. Most broadcast brief *updates* or *news capsules* during breaks in prime-time programs, providing effective promotion for their late newscasts. Some stations also offer "news-all-night," typically from about 2:00 A.M. to 6:00 or 7:00 A.M.. Content varies from station to station, with mixes of overnight network news programs, CNN Headline and other alternative news services, and repeats of the affiliate's own late newscasts. To increase their reach, some stations produce special newscasts for, or rerun their regular programs on, independent stations or cable systems; they also offer the audio portion of their newscasts to local radio stations.

The higher rated an affiliate is within its market, the more time it will devote to local news. The number-three affiliate in many markets feels pressure from cost-conscious management to cut back on news or, in extreme cases, to eliminate it entirely.

Origination by Independents

Relatively few independent stations produce an early evening newscast. They usually counterprogram their most popular syndicated entertainment shows against local news programs on affiliates.

As noted earlier, some independents carry newscasts produced by affiliated stations in their market. Others produce their own late local newscasts, usually at 10:00 P.M. (Eastern and Pacific times) to counterprogram network stations. These often draw sizable numbers of viewers who prefer to retire early and don't want to wait until 11 o'clock for their news. Independents also carry national news programs provided by such services as CNN, scheduling them immediately before or after their late local newscasts.

A handful of independent television stations, such as KTVU in Oakland/San Franciso and WTTG in Washington, D.C., have broken from the pack, devoting enormous resources to local news and competing with affiliates for the news audience and the advertising revenues it commands. In 1992 WSVN-TV in Miami had the highest-rated 10:00

P.M. newscast in the nation. The overall success of this independent station, until 1989 an NBC affiliate, continues to astound industry observers. Not only does its 10:00 P.M. newscast sometimes achieve ratings higher than those on affiliates at 11:00, but also its 6:00 P.M. local newscast often ranks number two in the time period. And overall, from sign-on to sign-off, the station ranks second in the market. Although affiliated with Fox, WSVN promotes itself as a CNN outlet, hoping to achieve its avowed status as "South Florida's News Station."

Station-Produced Non-News Television Programs

Aside from news, broadcast stations produce relatively few programs. Affiliates generally schedule local public-affairs shows on weekday or Sunday mornings. During election years or at times when important local issues arise, they may increase local production, but normally they avoid scheduling local shows in the most valuable time periods such as early fringe, access, or prime time.

Stations that produce regularly scheduled local non-news/public-affairs shows usually choose a magazine/talk format directed to women, scheduled on weekday mornings. Some syndicated programs give the appearance of local productions, especially those that provide for live or recorded inserts by local personalities.

As in other areas of television, public broadcasting (see Chapter 8) provides a striking exception to the no-local-program-production rule. Many noncommercial stations—notably WETA-TV in Washington and WGBH-TV in Boston—produce hours of local programming and serve as major program suppliers to PBS.

Local Cable Production

Only about a quarter of the approximately 11,000 cable systems in the United States originate local programs of any kind. Those that do mostly offer either commercial *local-origination* (LO) channels, controlled and programmed by the cable operators themselves, or noncommercial *public-access* channels, programmed by private citizens and nonprofit institutions such as schools and municipal governments. Cable systems exercise little control over access-channel content, serving as traffic cops for other programmers rather than as programmers themselves.

Although some occasionally originate coverage of local sporting events, cable systems rarely undertake the expense required to produce regularly scheduled local newscasts. Exceptions include systems operated by the MSO Colony Communications. Colony produces several half-hour local newscasts (some in Spanish) on many of its systems, as well as coverage of special events. These systems, and others, also produce local news inserts in CNN's *Headline News*. Another example is Cablevision of Connecticut, whose systems' locally produced newscasts have won more than 50 news programming awards since they began in 1982, including the 1989 Associated Press award for the best newscast in the state—broadcast or cable.

An increasing number of large-market cable systems devote one channel full time to regional news services. Examples include the pioneer *News 12 Long Island*, providing a 24-hour-a-day service to more than 70 villages on New York's Long Island; *Newschannel 8* in the Washington area; and *New England Cable News Channel*, which provides around-the-clock news to an estimated one million subscribers in six northeastern states.

Local-origination channels are less common than access channels. The latter focus mostly on informational and cultural programs. About half of all cable-access shows consist of public affairs, typically school board meetings, city and county council sessions, hearings on community issues, and discussion or documentary programs on political, environmental, and educational matters. But increasingly, as described in Exhibit 10.m, access channels have begun to offer somewhat more lively fare.

• • • • • • • •

10.8 Radio Network and Syndicated Programs

Competition from television devastated the original radio networks as full-service program suppliers,

Exhibit 10.m • • • • • • • • • • • • • •

The Wacky World of Public-Access Television

Saturday Night Live's outrageous *Wayne's World*, starring Mike Meyers (left) and Dana Carvey, parodied—or in some cases emulated—public-access shows on real-life cable systems.

"You, too, can be a star!" Such is the promise of some public-access channels on local cable systems around the country.

It all started in the 1970s when, as one inducement to city fathers to grant them an operating franchise, cable operators committed to opening their facilities to virtually all comers. Many such channels carry meetings and activities of local organizations, public forums on environmental issues, and local election debates.

In the 1990s, when *Wayne's World* had progressed from a segment on NBC's *Saturday Night Live* to a hit motion picture, the access concept skyrocketed. One such program, *The Late Mr. Pete Show*, began as an access show in Los Angeles and moved to USA Network. Today, cable subscribers can see most anything on their local system's access channel—so long as it is advertiser-free and not obscene. Among the offerings:

- Environmentalists modeling shoes recycled from old tires.
- Would-be talk-show hosts with an endless parade of nervous guests and belly dancers.
- Catholics, Jews, Mormons, atheists, pagans, Peruvians, Sikhs, Democrats, Republicans, right-to-lifers, and Indian gurus.
- And hordes of *Wayne's World* wannabes, hoping for their big break.

Whether anybody watches is an entirely different matter.

Source: Photo courtesy NBC.

---

but they survived by reducing their role to that of supplements to the radio formats adopted by their affiliates. In the 1970s new networks emerged, offering their own formats. Inexpensive satellite-relay connection made this comeback possible.

No universally agreed-upon definition of "radio network" exists. Some say that any two interconnected stations constitute a network. Others maintain that a network is a network only if it serves stations in every state. Statistical Research Inc., which twice each year conducts its radio network listener survey called RADAR (Radio's All-Dimension Audience Research), defines a network as a program service that has continuity of programming; written, contractual agreements with its affiliates; the capability of an instant feed to all affiliates; and a clearance system so it can determine which affiliates carry which programs. In the early 1990s only the five commercial operations described in Exhibit 10.n met that definition, although many others—both national and regional—called themselves networks.

Exhibit 10.n

Examples of Radio Networks and Their Programs

Network	Program Samples
ABC Radio Networks: ABC FM Network ABC Contemporary Network ABC Information Network ABC Rock Network ABC Entertainment Network ABC Direction Network Satellite Music Network ABC News Radio	Music: *Real Country, Touch-Urban AC, Starstation, Stardust-MOR, Pure Gold-Oldies, Kool Gold, Country Coast-to-Coast, Heat-CHR, Classic Rock, Z Rock, Traditional Country* News/Information: *ABC News Radio, ABCData, USA Today, ABC's Morning Show, Paul Harvey News and Commentary, American Top 40 with Shadoe Stevens, ESPN, Peter Jennings Journal, This Week with David Brinkley*
American Urban Radio Networks: American Urban Radio Network STRZ Entertainment Network SBN Sports Network Urban Public Affairs Network	*Top 30 USA, Cameos of Black Women, Inside Scoop!!, Black Travel USA, Jazzmasters, To Your Health, It's the Gospel, Inside the NBA, Legends of the NFL, Major League Baseball Scorecard, Black College Football, Ringside: The Big Bout, White House Report, A Salute to Great Black Americans,* news and sports reports
CBS Radio Networks: CBS Spectrum Radio Network CBS Radio Network CBS Hispanic Radio Network CBS News Radio	*World News Roundup, Parent Profile, Healthtalk, Dan Rather Reporting, The World Tonight, Face the Nation, The Osgood File, Major League Baseball, NFL Football, NCAA Basketball, Masters Golf, Hispanic Radio*
Unistar: Ultimate Super Power CNN Headline News CNBC	Music: *AC II, Hot Country, Adult Rock & Roll, The Oldies Channel, Country, AM Only, Format 41, Super Gold, Country Gold Saturday Night, Dick Clark's Rock, Roll, and Remember* News/Information: *CNBC, CNN Radio, CNN Headline, Unistar News*
Westwood One Radio Networks: Westwood One The Source NBC Talknet NBC Radio Network Mutual Broadcasting System	*MTV News, Top 40 with Casey Kasem, Dr. Demento, American Dance Traxx with Downtown Julie Brown, The Beatle Years, Future Hits, Country Countdown, In Concert, Bruce Williams, Money Magazine Business Report, Science Update, Dr. Joyce Brothers, Don Criqui on Sports, The Media Inside, Larry King*

Like all national radio program organizations, those listed here operate several networks and offer multiple program formats. They change and adapt their programming—even create completely new networks and cancel old ones—as audience taste and, thus, station needs change.

Source: Based on data in *Broadcasting*, 13 July 1992: 36.

Network News

In 1968 the ABC radio network responded imaginatively to the needs of its formula-dominated affiliates. Recognizing the central role of audience segmentation in stations' music programming, ABC designed four network services, each for a different type of audience. Each service consisted of five-minute news-and-feature segments styled to suit specific age groups and calculated to fit smoothly into the four most popular radio formats.

The success of this approach to radio networking eventually encouraged ABC to increase its specialized services to as many as 12 music formats, six 24-hour news networks, and a host of special programs. ABC gets maximum value from its relay facilities by cycling its short news feeds to its several sets of affiliates throughout each hour, using the remaining time to feed sports and features on a closed-circuit basis for later playback by the stations. Nearly 20 years passed before affiliate pressure persuaded CBS and NBC (whose radio network was later acquired by Westwood One) to copy ABC's innovative multiple networks.

Those radio networks that are associated with television networks get the benefit of daily reports voiced by well-known television news personalities such as Peter Jennings and David Brinkley. Some television journalists anchor specific radio news reports, perhaps during morning drive time; others prerecord news stories or features for later inclusion in scheduled newscasts. Network radio's most popular journalist, however, is a radio veteran, Paul Harvey (who only briefly—and unsuccessfully—tried television). His radio career dates back to the early 1940s. Fifty years later his daily newscasts typically still rank at the top in surveys conducted by RADAR.

Talk Shows and Sports

The Mutual Broadcasting System pioneered all-night talk on network radio with *The Larry King Show*, predecessor of the CNN television program, *Larry King Live*. For years it remained the most popular talk program in its genre, though shortened and repeated in the small hours to fill out the night after King's grueling all-night schedule contributed to a heart attack. By 1992 conservative and controversial Rush Limbaugh—who tells his audience he is "the most dangerous man in America"—had taken over the number-one spot. Night-time talk had previously been regarded as a strictly local format, but King's success led to ABC's *Talkradio* with such hosts as Tom Snyder and Deborah Norville (formerly—briefly—co-host of NBC's *Today*) and NBC's *Talknet* with such hosts as Bruce Williams. In 1992, however, explaining that the format had been less successful than originally hoped, ABC abandoned its weeknight talk programming. It continued to offer its weekend talk shows, which focus on finance, gardening, and home repairs. In 1993, meanwhile, Larry King finally gave up his overnight shift, moving his radio program to weekday afternoons.

The major national radio network services fill their weekend schedules with live coverage of football, baseball, basketball, and other events. They also supply sports specials and sports talk to block-schedule with games. Mutual, now a Westwood One network, has bought radio play-by-play rights to national football for decades. It features college games on Saturdays and professional football on Sundays, supplemented by daily sportscasts and weekend sports anthologies. The sports component of radio networks is so important to affiliates that CBS paid $50 million for radio baseball rights for the early 1990s, nearly doubling the previous contract payment. The importance of radio sports became even more evident with the advent in 1992 of ESPN Radio, one of the services offered by ABC Radio networks. In addition to national networks, several regional sports radio networks supply live game coverage to hundreds of stations within a state or larger region such as the Midwest or Southeast.

Music Networks

More than a score of radio networks featuring 24-hour music developed in the 1970s and 1980s. Stations affiliated with them often also affiliate with a second network for news, another for sports, and so on. This multiple affiliation is possible because exclusivity operates only within one type of network service.

The largest music networks, such as Westwood One and Unistar, each has more than a thousand radio affiliates. Perhaps the best-known show on music radio, *Casey's Top 40 with Casey Kasem*, shifted to Westwood One in 1989 after running on ABC for nearly 20 years. Kasem's countdown technique, incorporating brief stories about the artists and their music, has become a radio standard. As is the case with sports coverage, regional radio networks supplement those of their national counterparts.

Commercial radio networking and syndication are likely to appear indistinguishable to listeners, especially since the largest organizations offer both. But each has its own characteristic type of content, delivery means, advertising procedures, and payment practices. The major networks supply news, sports, and specials, or all-talk or all-music, relaying the programs by satellite, accompanied by national advertising. Syndicators concentrate on formatted popular music and features. Radio networks often pay compensation to major-market affiliates, but syndicators usually charge for their programs.

Radio depends heavily on two types of material not always thought of as syndicated: recorded music and news services. Nevertheless, these program materials fit the syndicated definition—expensive, centrally produced program material whose high costs are shared through distribution to many users.

Format Syndication

Though stations may choose their own formats and produce their own programs, most would be lost without news services and recorded music. Local production is usually limited to record selection and disc jockey announcements between syndicated elements and commercials.

Even that limited degree of local production disappears when stations buy ready-made syndicated formats. Syndicators tailor an entire broadcast day, furnishing not only preselected program material but also a wide range of advisory services. In contrast to most radio networks, which supply only news headlines, brief features, sportscasts, and talk shows,

format syndicators typically supply a full 24-hour schedule of music, interrupted neither by national advertising nor by news. Stations that purchase syndicated formats may also affiliate with a radio network for newscasts.

More than a score of syndication companies exist, each supplying multiple formats. They design each format to target a narrowly defined demographic or psychographic group. Most companies offer several rock music variations, ranging from new-wave to hit songs to soft-album cuts, that generally fit the major format classifications of contemporary hit radio, adult contemporary, and album-oriented rock. They also offer one or more country music formats, an easy-listening or beautiful-music format, and perhaps even rap, jazz, and classical music formats.

Feature Syndication

Radio feature syndicators supply ready-made program items packaged to fit within particular formats. They range from large companies supplying hundreds of feature programs and several syndicated formats to companies marketing only a few topical specials or a single series. Stations interweave syndicated stand-alone features, consisting of either series or specials, with a locally or distantly produced music or news/talk format. Features range from sets of religious sermons to series of domestic budgeting hints to play-by-play sporting events, distributed on tape or by satellite.

Weekly country and rock countdowns of hit songs are among the popular syndicated programs, especially clones of Dick Clark's long-running *Countdown America*. Stations normally schedule syndicated countdowns on weekends, filling long hours without paying for a local, live DJ. Feature syndicators also supply brief telephone interviews with rock and country music celebrities, divided into one-minute segments for inclusion throughout the broadcast day. Such features add variety to otherwise predictable replays of fixed music playlists. Talk radio stations also vary their local sound with syndicated business, health, and other specialized reports voiced by nationally known announcers.

Role of Automation

Most radio stations use some degree of automation. More sophisticated automation systems can carry out most programming, production, traffic, billing, and engineering functions. Automated systems marry ideally with syndicated music formats, which demand precise control over content and timing. Modern radio automation uses microprocessor and digital memories, keyboards on which operators can type instructions in ordinary English, video screens that give the keyboard operator instructions and information on the status of the systems, and hard-copy printers that deliver such materials as program and commercial logs.

Increasingly, automation takes over former hands-on radio production tasks. The degree of live vs. automated production in music radio varies through three levels:

- In *live* programming, local DJs play the records and talk between songs, conduct contests, promote events, read and cue-in commercials, and so on.
- In *live-assist* programming, automatic equipment relays a syndicated music format with breaks for local DJs to add live patter between songs.
- In *automated programming* (also called *satellite* or *turnkey radio*), computers handle satellite-delivered music, commercials, and promotional and other materials without any help whatsoever from live DJs or other local staff.

In a twist that combines the advantages of both syndicated formatting and the presence of a live radio personality, a single, centrally located, on-the-air disc jockey may speak for dozens of stations. The orchestrator plays a single music tape, interspersing it with commercials, weather, and announcements appropriate to each participating station's community. Microprocessors and two-way interconnection enable the orchestrator to cue-in prerecorded local advertisements and regional weather at each station. Occasionally the orchestrator feigns the presence of a local DJ by injecting a chatty line or two heard by only one station's audience.

Critics object that this total automation by satellite radio eliminates localism and puts local radio personnel out of work. Its defenders claim that it enhances localism by giving station staff more time to produce truly local material—an opportunity that, in fact, is rarely used.

●●●●●●●●

10.9 Local Radio Programs

By and large, radio stations retain much more local program autonomy than do television stations and cable systems. Radio networks, once all-important, have receded into a secondary role. Although most stations depend almost totally on recorded music, they assemble it to fit their own, carefully crafted program formats, attuned to specific audience segments.

Music Formats

Radio is often characterized as a local rather than a national medium. However, this generalization overlooks the national scope of music recordings. Records, cassette tapes, and compact discs are syndicated media, simultaneously available all over the country. Rarely does a station have any exclusive play rights. Music promoters send free copies of recordings to stations, hoping for frequent airplay. Increasingly, stations mix syndicated formats and feature material with recordings and live DJ patter to create a unique local sound.

Most locally programmed radio stations use modified blocking, changing formats slightly to suit each daypart. For example, many stations emphasize news and weather/traffic information during drive times, shifting to recorded music at other times. Some promote on-air personalities; others suppress them. Most abide by rigid formulas, yet some favor free-form programming. Even the old-fashioned full-service program philosophy still has some followers, especially in very small towns. In major markets, however, stations typically adopt pure formats, continuing the same sound throughout the day and night. To become or remain competitive, as many as 1,000 stations—about 10 percent of the total—may change their formats every year.

Most parsimonious of all broadcast formats, the disc jockey show fully exploits the availability of recorded music, reducing local production costs to the lowest possible level. The format relies upon the ability of a DJ to build a loyal following and to comment on current events and the rapidly changing popular music scene. (Few listeners are even aware that some DJs supplement their personal wit and wisdom by using syndicated packages of such items as jokes, trivia games, and song parodies.)

Until about 20 years ago, at least some DJs had the freedom to select pretty much whatever music they wanted. Today, however, stations that still employ live DJs typically set up strict *play lists* of songs, from which the host must select. Many use sophisticated computer programs to schedule their hourly "clocks," printing every programming component on a computer log for DJs to follow, with little room for improvisation.* A form of expression once unique to radio, the DJ format has migrated to television through video jockeys (VJs) on MTV and other program services.

As Exhibit 10.0 indicates, formats based on rock music dominate radio programming. Radio draws more fine distinctions among types of rock than within other musical genres. Rock formats include *adult contemporary* (AC), a broad array of popular music and golden oldies that appeal to a wide range of adult listeners; *contemporary hit radio* (CHR), formerly known as *Top-40*, playing only the most recent hits and appealing to teens and young adults; *album-oriented rock* (AOR), a mix of rock classics and less familiar songs from popular albums; *oldies* or *classic rock*, with hits from the 1950s and 1960s; and *urban*

contemporary (UC), a blend of rock and jazz favoring black artists. Among these subformats, adult contemporary has been the most successful.

However, in the aggregate, more stations play *country music* than any other single type (except rock, if all rock subformats are added together). Though Exhibit 10.0 shows country/western as a single format, it has followed rock's trend of subdividing, splitting into urban, traditional, oldies, crossover, and other specialties. *Religious/gospel* radio, one of the top three formats, shows a steady shift to the AM band, increasingly forced out of FM by the more profitable rock music formats.

Variety/Diverse (or eclectic), as a format, refers to the full-service station that schedules a mix of news, talk, and music. Similarly, Spanish-language, black, and other ethnically oriented stations tend to mix music and informational programming as a commercial format, targeting specialized groups.

Beautiful music and *easy listening*, broad-appeal formats using mostly unobtrusive vocal or instrumental music, are broadcast in most large radio markets. They saturate waiting rooms, elevators, department stores, and other public spaces. Syndicated easy-listening, commercial-free music services, such as Muzak, go to subscribers on FM subcarriers and require special adaptors to receive the signals.

Classical music appears mostly on noncommercial FM stations, but a few commercial FM and AM stations have adopted the format, especially in the largest markets. *Jazz*, though it has a devoted following, has not proved successful commercially. *Big band*, usually a syndicated format consisting of music from the 1940s, 50s, and 60s, has been marginally successful, mostly in large and mid-sized markets as a commercial AM format. Recent fads, such as *new wave*, *hip-hop*, and *rap* have been adopted by too few stations to appear in Exhibit 10.0. Among all the various formats, adult contemporary and news/talk generally produce the most advertising revenue; easy listening and big band, the least.

The 1990s introduced a new technology to assist traveling radio listeners in finding their favorite format. The Radio Broadcast Data System (RBDS) promised listeners they could tune their car radios

*A system introduced in 1992—Radioactive Radio Music on Demand—permits *listeners* to choose (or at least *think* they choose) musical selections. An automated answering system offers callers a menu of songs from which they select one by using their touch-tone phones. When the station plays that song, listeners think it is just for them. But because a number of other callers have likely chosen the same song, the service really only creates the illusion that callers are programming the station.

Exhibit 10.o ••••••• ••••••••

Radio Station Formats by Popularity and Station Type

| Format | Popularity in Terms of: | | Station Types | | | |
	No. of Stations	Percentage of Stations	AMs	FMs	Commercial	Noncommercial
Country/Western	2,603	18%	1,391	1,212	2,585	18
Adult Contemporary	2,347	16	831	1,516	2,292	55
Religious/Gospel	1,392	9	818	574	1,009	383
Oldies/Classic Rock	1,313	9	647	666	1,275	38
CHR/Top-40	845	6	119	726	753	92
MOR	550	4	450	100	529	21
Rock/AOR	539	4	65	474	387	152
News	530	4	276	254	306	224
News/Talk	530	4	471	59	475	55
Variety/Diverse	527	4	122	405	142	385
Classical	429	3	22	407	58	371
Jazz	368	3	30	338	77	291
Talk	349	2	288	61	307	42
Spanish	331	2	242	89	309	22
Beautiful Music	289	2	98	191	251	38
Big Band/Nostalgia	285	2	228	57	268	17
Urban Contemporary	253	2	107	146	222	31
Educational	245	2	15	230	6	239
Progressive	244	2	10	234	27	217
Black	171	1	112	59	141	30
Agricultural	96	1	69	27	95	1
All Others	426	3	270	156	330	96
Total Figures	14,662	103%	6,681	7,981	11,844	2,818

Station totals exceed the number on the air because some carry more than one format.
Total percentage exceeds 100 because of rounding.

Source: Based on data in *Broadcasting & Cable Market Place* (1992): A-486.

by using a built-in scanner that picks up special signals from radio stations, identifying whether they program AOR, AC, Classical, or some other standard music format. Among the system's other features: the capacity to allow broadcasters to turn the radio on in order to deliver a weather or other emergency bulletin; automatic switching to a traffic report on another station; and a small screen that displays station call letters, song titles and artists, and—of course—advertising messages.

Information Formats

The formats listed in Exhibit 10.o include four predominantly informational types— *news, talk, educational,* and *agricultural.* Collectively, these formats occur on about 13 percent of all radio stations. Newly developed AM formats, such as *all-business* and *all-sports,* attempt to capture fresh audiences for AM radio. However, only about 20 percent of radio listeners tune to AM stations; most prefer FM. (Indeed, anecdotal evidence indicates that many young listeners avoid AM to the extent of not even bothering to "pre-set" the AM portion of automatic tuning devices on their car radios.)

Radio uses informational programming both within music formats and as a stand-alone format. Within music programming, news may consist of as little as one minute's worth of network headlines. Stations with *news/talk* formats, on the other hand, include local and network news headlines, in-depth newscasts, studio and remote interviews, informational feature stories, and telephone conversations with public figures and listeners.

The most popular informational format, *talk radio,* occurs mostly on commercial AM stations. It combines call-in and interview programs with feature material and local news. Talk content varies between the extremes of sexual innuendo and serious political or social commentary. In major markets, *shock radio* deliberately aims at outraging conservative listeners by violating common taboos and desecrating sacred cows. Shock radio's contempt for authority and social tradition tends to attract listeners younger than the usual talk radio audience. One of the best-known practitioners of the shock-radio format, Howard Stern, has had several run-ins with the FCC—in 1988, for example, when his Christmas program featured a "gay choir" singing "I'm dreaming of some light torture." Stern also had a television program for a brief period and it, too, had its problems with the FCC—as when his 1991 Christmas program included a sketch showing the host giving birth in a manger. In 1992 the FCC issued fines totaling more than $700,000 against radio stations that carried Stern's program, several of which immediately brought court challenges on constitutional grounds (see Section 14.4).

Most talk programs, however, focus on controversial issues, using guest-expert interviews and questioning by hosts and callers. Many two-way telephone call-in shows attract an older and generally conservative class of listeners—people who have both time and militant convictions that incline them to engage in discussions with talk-show hosts. Program directors have to be alert lest a small but highly vocal group of repeat callers, often advocates of extremist views, dominate the talk and kill advertiser interest. Similarly, they utilize audio-tape-delay devices that permit them to edit out obscenities uttered by a caller—or even, occasionally, by a host.

During the 1980s talk radio emerged as an important public forum in the black community, although only a few of the black-oriented stations adopted the format. *Black talk* stations provide a window through which candidates for public office, community organizations, and reporters can obtain a unique perspective on black public opinion. Politicians such as Harold Washington, Chicago's first black mayor, and the Reverend Jesse Jackson found that black talk radio gave them political input they could not get through mainstream media.

The *all-news* format costs a lot to operate, yet gets only low ratings compared with successful music formats. Still, only about 12 percent of radio newsrooms report that they lose money; the rest say they operate at a profit or at least break even. Actually, most all-news stations devote only about a quarter of their time to hard news, filling the rest with informational and service features. They count on holding attention for only about 20 minutes at a time, long enough for listeners to arm themselves with the latest headlines, the time of day, weather tips, and advice about driving conditions. To succeed, this revolving-door programming needs a large audience reservoir that only major markets can supply.

Radio farm news plays an important role in modern farming. Office and factory workers find weather reports a convenience, but farmers find them essential. Many stations piggyback farm news on another, major radio format. About 1 percent of stations, mostly commercial AM and nearly all in the Midwest, carry a full-time *agricultural format.* The U.S. Department of Agriculture uses satellites to distribute background information and taped program series, as well as responses to telephone inquiries, to keep farmers current on federal policy and agricultural data.

10.10 Program Critique

This and the preceding chapter have examined broadcast and cable programs largely from the industry viewpoint—as vehicles to carry commercial messages or to entice paying subscribers. This concluding section touches on other perspectives—those of critics and consumers.

Diversity

A persistent complaint about commercial television, especially prime-time network programming, deplores its lack of diversity—the sameness of its program types, themes, plots, production styles, and sources. Networks risk so much on each program series that they take the safe route of copying successful shows again and again. Spinoffs and clones reduce regular prime-time entertainment essentially to sitcoms, crime dramas, and movies, and daytime entertainment to talk shows, game shows, and soap operas.

The networks' homogenizing influence also affects production styles. Programs from one production company look much like those from another. Yet programmers desperately seek novelty. This seeming paradox comes from wanting to be different but fearing the consequences of taking chances. Only occasionally do new ideas escape the network straightjacket. *Twin Peaks*, for example, drew critical praise but attracted an audience too small to permit its survival. *Northern Exposure*, on the other hand, was commended for its whimsical innovation and soon became a ratings winner.

Cable television, once hailed as the harbinger of greater program diversity, has brought only limited change. The most popular cable networks depend on the same mass-appeal programs as the broadcast networks. They follow similar selection and scheduling practices. USA Network, for example, is becoming increasingly indistinguishable from ABC, CBS, and NBC. Even most specialized cable channels—The Weather Channel, CNN, ESPN, and The Cartoon Channel, for example—seldom offer anything truly new. Instead, they offer more (indeed, much more) of what is already available. Only a few—MTV, C-SPAN, and Court TV, for example—have increased viewers' program choices. Cable networks do create new material, though much of this is for pay channels, the ones best able to afford original production.

Journalism

As the public's primary news source, television has special obligations not always met in the competitive marketplace. Some observers express concern over reduced journalistic diversity resulting from the trend toward media concentration in the hands of a few corporations who have no direct accountability to the public. By 1990, 23 companies controlled most mainstream media, down from about 50 a decade earlier. As legendary press critic H. L. Mencken observed: "Freedom of the press belongs to those who own one" (quoted in Grossman, 1992).

Others contemplate the impact of television trial coverage on the rights of defendants and victims, and the adequacy of presidential election coverage (Sections 12.2 and 12.5). Traditional news programs have come under attack for seeking popularity through the incorporation of too much show business. More and more stations have reacted to the success of tabloid television by stressing violence and tragedy at the expense of more far-reaching but less visual stories.

Critics and viewers alike increasingly wonder whether journalists can be trusted. *Staged news events* continue to plague electronic journalism. In 1991 an Emmy-winning reporter for KCNC-TV in Colorado was fined $20,000 for staging a dogfight during a ratings period. At the network level, Jane Pauley and Stone Phillips, coanchors of NBC's prime-time newsmagazine *Dateline*, offered on-the-air apologies in February 1993 for a story that had been broadcast on the program the preceding November. As part of an investigative report about the safety of General Motors pickup trucks, producers had conducted a crash demonstration and—although viewers were not so informed—had ensured an explosion by placing incendiary devices under the test vehicles. Less than three weeks later, news anchor Tom Brokaw also apologized, this time for using video of dead fish from one location to illustrate an NBC Nightly News story about forest mismanagement at a different location, and for using footage of fish that appeared dead but had actually been stunned for testing purposes. In early March, NBC News President Michael Gartner resigned, largely, though not entirely, as a result of these events. The following day a *Times Mirror* poll revealed that, in the eyes of viewers, NBC News's credibility had fallen from second to last place among the four national television news organizations. Indeed, it was CNN—not one of the Big Three networks—that placed first in credibility, followed by ABC, CBS, and NBC.

Some broadcasters also deceive by not indentifying apparently live coverage as being, in fact, recorded, and by feigning authorship of video and text actually received from such other sources as corporate public-relations departments. *Digital enhancing* offers high-tech opportunities for deception. Already in use by print media, it permits a reporter to manipulate pictures in limitless ways. One print example: the *Orange County Register*'s Pulitzer prize-winning photographs of the 1988 Olympics that it doctored to achieve the desired sky color. One nationally recognized example from television that illustrates how television news might one day use the technology: the Diet Coke commercial that miraculously brings deceased entertainers Groucho Marx and Cary Grant onto the set and permits Paula Abdul electronically—though not actually—to dance with Gene Kelly.

Other ethical questions remain troublesome:

- Must television resort to "checkbook journalism"—the practice of paying for interviews? Also suspect is the practice of news subjects paying for the cost of news coverage—as when Disney

World and Delta Air Lines picked up the tab (later repaid by NBC) for the two days when *Today* originated its program from the theme park.
- Should journalists use press releases as news? One survey found that 12 percent of all responding television stations used at least one video news release (VNR) from a major political candidate during the 1992 presidential primaries, sometimes without any editing or disclaimer to identify the source. Some stations aired as many as 30 (Freedom Forum, 1992).

Exhibit 10.p lists eight television news "blindspots," as identified by a very close observer, a former chairman of the FCC.

Programs and the Public Interest

Fundamentally, the viewer/listener perspective raises the question of whether commercial motives suffice as primary arbiters of program choice and quality. That question brings up an issue around which debate has swirled ever since broadcasting began, that of commerce vs. culture. How should society balance the sometimes conflicting claims of these two goals?

Is it enough for the industry to treat programs simply as "product"—articles of trade? Those who argue otherwise regard programs as broadly cultural. In this latter view, programs contribute to the intellectual, artistic, and moral quality of national life. Seen in that perspective, programs should do more than merely entice audiences to allow themselves to be exposed to commercial messages.

"Wasteland" vs. "Toaster"

Experts and critics agree that in the final analysis the industry sells not programs but *people*. Nevertheless, as a practical matter, the industry must also think in program terms: television and radio can deliver people to advertisers only by supplying program services that interest people.

The best-known critique of the industry's program performance in public-interest terms came three decades ago from an FCC chairman appointed

Exhibit 10.p ●●●●●●●●●●●●●●

Chairman Sikes: Television News Blindspots

Although he was quick to emphasize that the FCC neither would—nor should—take any action on the matter, Alfred C. Sikes, former chair of the FCC, nonetheless identified what he perceived to be short-comings in present-day television news coverage. Sikes suggested that these eight "blindspots," as he called them, have left the American public poorly informed:

- *Visuals*—the erroneous notion that "good pictures equal good journalism."
- *Stenography*—the equally erroneous idea that news is what public officials say or do.
- *Acceptance of the Lame Response*—the failure of reporters to challenge politicians when they respond to questions with pat, simplistic answers.

- *Ignorance*—The unwillingness or inability of journalists to be well informed on matters about which they presume to report.
- *Spending*—equating government spending with government problem solving.
- *Pettiness*—television's devotion to scandal in government while core problems go virtually unnoticed.
- *Celebrity*—when television news people grow to love their status more than their duty.
- *Fickleness*—the mysterious hit-and-run, ebb-and-flow rhythm that characterizes television news coverage.

Sikes' advice: "A commitment to the public trust must now summon the television news community to rise above the limitations and conventional wisdoms, and at least partially reinvent itself."

Source: An address by Chairman Sikes at Washington State University as part of the Edward R. Murrow Symposium. Reprinted with permission from *Broadcasting*, May 11, 1992, © 1992 by Cahners Publishing Company.

by the Kennedy administration, Newton Minow (1961–1963). In an address to the National Association of Broadcasters in 1961, Minow challenged station owners and managers to sit down and watch their own programming for a full broadcast day. They would, he assured them, find a "vast waste-land" of violence, repetitive formulas, irritating commercials, and sheer boredom (Minow, 1964: 52). The "vast wasteland" phrase soon caught on and has become a part of broadcasting lore.

Some 20 years later, a Republican-appointed FCC chair, Mark Fowler, pointedly refrained from talking to the industry about program quality. In his view, the FCC had no business interfering with the workings of the marketplace. He too coined a memorable descriptive phrase when, in addresses to various broadcast industry groups, he described television as "a toaster with pictures." This dis-missive phrase reflected a then-dominant theory in Washington—that economic laws of supply and de-

mand suffice to ensure that commercial television will supply suitable programs; if it degenerates into a vast wasteland, blame not the industry but the audience.

In 1991 Newton Minow (long since an attorney in private practice) revisited television, commenting on his famous words, "vast wasteland":

Today that 1961 speech is remembered for two words—but not the two I intended to be remembered. The words we tried to advance were "public interest." To me, the public interest meant, and still means, that we should constantly ask: What can television do for our country?—for the common good?—for the American People? . . .

If television is to change, the men and women in television will have to make it a leading institution in American life rather than merely a reactive mirror of the lowest common denominator in the marketplace. Based on the last thirty years, the record gives the television marketplace an A + for technology, but only a C for using that technology to serve human and humane goals. (Minow, 1991: 9, 12)

Despite the often exaggerated charges of some critics, most would concede that television sometimes rises to peaks of excellence—even though between the peaks lie broad valleys (vast wastelands?) of routine programs. How green the valleys are depends on the viewer's personal tastes.

Taste

A continuously available mass medium such as television cannot satisfy every taste all of the time. *Most* of the time, but not *all* of the time, it must try to please *most* of the people—an extraordinary demand. In meeting it, television made apparent something never before so blatantly exposed—the low common denominator of mass popular taste as contrasted with the more cultivated standards of high taste. As Daniel Have, an authority on American cultural history, put it:

> Much of what we hear complained of as the "vulgarity," the emptiness, the sensationalism, of television is not a peculiar product of television at all. It is simply the translation of the subliterature onto the television screen. . . . Never before were the vulgar tastes so conspicuous and so accessible to the prophets of our high culture. Subculture—which is of course the dominant culture of a democratic society—is now probably no worse, and certainly no better, than it has ever been. But it is emphatically more visible. (Boorstin, 1978: 19)

From the standpoint of the middle ground between the extremes of programs-as-merchandise and programs-as-culture, it is unrealistic to expect programs always to rise above the lowest common denominator. Electronic media necessarily cater to popular tastes. That mission, however, need not preclude responsibility for serving minority tastes as well. One hallmark of a democracy is that, though the majority prevails, minorities still have rights. Public broadcasting exists in part to compensate for the omissions of commercial broadcasting in this regard. But even public broadcasting has had to increase its popular appeal in order to attract program underwriters and broaden its subscriber base.

It has thus far lacked the financial support it needs to offer an adequate alternative program service.

Promoters of the marketplace programming philosophy predicted that liberalizing the rules governing broadcasting and making things easy for new services such as cable television would automatically bring diversity and enhance quality. Deregulation did indeed give viewers more choices, but at an added price. Those who can afford, and choose to have, cable or a satellite dish (about two-thirds of all homes) can browse through scores of channels to find programs of interest. Owners of home video recorders can peruse tape inventories of video stores and use time-shifting to escape the tyranny of broadcast/cable schedules.

Thus far, however, too many of the so-called new options have turned out to be merely repetitions of the old options. With few exceptions, they have failed to make the "wasteland" bloom. After all, cable and other optional delivery methods respond to the same marketplace imperatives that drive commercial broadcasting. Significantly, the shining exception in the public-affairs field, the program service that opens a window on government in action—C-SPAN—does not operate as a self-supporting commercial venture. The cable industry subsidizes C-SPAN as a public-relations showcase of the good things television can do—when *not* constrained by the need to make money.

Popular Taste vs. Bad Taste

Although commercial broadcasters have always catered to *popular* taste, for most of their history they generally refrained from catering to the appetite for downright *bad* taste in programs. In its now abandoned Television Code, the National Association of Broadcasters (NAB) emphasized the role of television as a *family* medium, warning that "great care must be exercised to be sure that treatment and presentation are made in good faith and not for the purpose of sensationalism or to shock or exploit the audience or appeal to prurient interests or morbid curiosity" (NAB, 1978: 2).

That kind of sensitivity, along with the Television Code itself, has fallen victim to changing times. In fact, the Code's statement of what not to do accurately describes exactly what succeeded on the air, beginning in the late 1980s. " 'Raunch' on a Roll," proclaimed a headline in a trade journal over a story about the rise of what it called slobcoms—sitcoms that "stretch the bounds of what's acceptable" (*Broadcasting*, 21 November 1988). The Fox network's *Married . . . With Children*, which occasioned the article, featured plot lines dealing with such topics as premenstrual syndrome, treated with outrageously vulgar humor. Despite some complaints, the series drew high ratings, both on the network and when it moved into syndication. In the absence of any other criteria of evaluation, ratings ensured widespread imitation.

In 1992 CBS briefly offered *Grapevine*, whose series opener detailed how all of the principal characters had lost their virginity. During a single week that same year ABC offered episodes of the following established series, accompanied by their respective network advertising lines:

- *The Commish*—Tony goes undercover to bust an X-rated movie racket.
- *Life Goes On*—Jesse's nude painting of Becca makes her the talk of the town.
- *Doogie Houser, M.D.*—Doogie's caught with his pants down when he swims naked with his mom's sexy boss.
- *20/20*—How to have better sex.
- *Civil Wars*—An art photographer convinces Sydney to pose nude.

In syndication, *Studs*, which features three young women and two young men engaging in 30 minutes of sexually suggestive banter, pulled higher ratings in 1992 than *Arsenio Hall*, the first time in three years that any syndicated late-night program had beaten Hall.* Cable, which operates on a standard less strict than that of broadcast, "double-shoots" such series as HBO's *Dream On* and Showtime's

Bizarre—one version, with topless sex scenes, for the pay-cable network and foreign syndication; another, without, for ad-supported and domestic station use. The motion picture industry has used this ploy for years.

Violence, mayhem, and sociopathic behavior, long the subjects of critical debate, continued unabated into the 1990s. During a single rating sweep period, television network audiences were treated to programs that depicted Sharon Gless as a brutally beaten mother, Barbara Hershey as a seductive murder conspirator, Harry Hamlin as a berserk kidnapper, Veronica Hamel as a baby-snatching wife, Beverly D'Angelo as a murderous sexpot, Donna Mills as a vigilante mother, Elizabeth Montgomery as a wounded realtor, Lindsay Frost as an escaped convicted murderer, and Blyth Danner as yet another brutally beaten mother. These were joined by a syndicated miniseries telling the story of John Wayne Gacy who had been convicted of murdering 33 men.

One can speculate on influences that may have had a hand in bringing about this radical shift in program standards. Among the many possibilities might be these:

- The FCC's laissez-faire policy during the 1980s, which encouraged broadcasters to test the limits of public tolerance.
- Abandonment of the NAB codes, implying to some that anything goes.
- Heightened competition, encouraged in part by FCC policies, requiring ever-more strenuous efforts to capture audience attention.
- The impact of cable television, which has never been constrained either by legislated public-interest standards or by a tradition of self-restraint.
- Corporate mergers that replaced experienced broadcast and cable executives with cost-conscious managers saddled with huge debts.
- Social changes in the direction of more open and permissive behavior, marked especially by violence, sex, and rebellion against conventional standards.

As the pendulum eventually and inevitably swings in the opposite direction, reversing some of these

*Some critics suggested that Fox, which created *Studs*, operates on a double standard—this after Fox chairman Rupert Murdoch summarily fired his newly appointed president of Fox Television Stations, Stephen Chao. Chao, while delivering an address on censorship to a 1992 meeting of managers from News Corp., Fox's parent company, had attempted—unwisely, it turned out—to illustrate his point by bringing on stage a male stripper.

trends, observers will be anxious to find out whether deregulated broadcasters and cable operators regain their ability to satisfy popular taste without also pandering to bad taste.

• • • • • • • •

Summary

10.1   Prime-time programs, the most important part of television network schedules, appear mostly as weekly series, with some specials and feature films. New shows may come from original ideas but commonly are spinoffs or clones. Series divide into family and nonfamily situation comedies (the most successful program form in syndication), drama and crime shows, and miniseries.

10.2   Network soap operas attract fanatically loyal fans who resent disruptions of the daytime schedule for special events. The content of soaps has become progressively more controversial over the 'years. Game shows, talk programs, and music videos are especially parsimonious television formats, showing on both broadcast and cable services.

10.3   The dramatic nature of sporting events makes many of them ideal for live network television, both broadcast and cable. Some major events have moved to pay-per-view and critics fear others will follow, thus becoming available only to those homes able and willing to pay. Sports present scheduling difficulties for broadcast networks, but not for cable. Television's impact on both sporting events and athletes causes concerns resulting from the commercial nature of television and the large sums it pours into sports rights.

10.4   Broadcast television network news has expanded beyond traditional evening newscasts into early-morning and late-night time periods. CNN has overtaken ABC, CBS, and NBC as the leading international news network. Specialized informational cable networks include CNBC and The Weather Channel. *60 Minutes* is the most successful of the many public-affairs programs on broadcast network television. Cable relies primarily on C-SPAN to address public-affairs concerns.

10.5   Although major broadcast television networks continue to offer programs for children, cable and independent television have overtaken them as primary providers. Critics continue to worry about violence in children's programs and exploitation by advertisers.

10.6   Syndicated programs on both broadcast and cable consist of off-network shows (mostly sitcoms and action/adventure series), first-run shows (mostly games, quizzes, talk, and reality), and movies.

10.7   Most local television stations produce few programs other than newscasts. Many look to outside news consultants for ways to build audiences. Network affiliates as well as a growing number of independents are expanding their local news efforts. Some cable systems carry both local-origination programs, which they produce themselves, and public-access channels programmed by others.

10.8   Radio networks, revitalized by the advent of low-cost satellite distribution, have adapted to formula radio by supplying brief newscasts targeted to specific age groups, as well as sports, talk, features, and 24-hour music suited to selected station formats.

10.9   Most radio stations use block formats. More radio stations program rock and country than any other music type. Most FM stations feature music, whereas information formats appear primarily on AM stations.

10.10   Critics and consumers of television programs express concern about the sameness of many of them, about journalistic integrity, and about questionable program content.

PART 5

Effects

So far, we have examined electronic mass media history, technology, business, and programming. Now we reverse perspective and look at these media as causes that help produce effects. In order to do so, we first examine how research in this field tells us about audiences of electronic media; we then look at what has been learned about the media's wider impact.

Media effects, real or presumed, give significance to everything we have discussed thus far. Electronic media merit our attention only because they produce results—some good, some bad.

People buy and maintain receivers, advertisers buy time, donors help support noncommercial broadcasting—all in expectation of getting something of value in return. As we shall see in Part 6, Congress makes laws, the FCC issues rules and regulations, and other public and private forces seek to exert control—all on the assumption that media produce consequences. Seen in this perspective, everything we have examined up to this point culminates in the study of what we know, don't know, and still need to learn about the effects of electronic media.

Chapter 11

Ratings

Even if you have not been part of a ratings sample or some other audience survey, you already know something about research, as ratings are widely reported and discussed. Broadcast and cable services compete to win the popularity contest that ratings measure. If people don't watch or listen—as measured by ratings—then advertisers lose interest and programs die, to be replaced by others, or stations fail and leave the air. Program and advertising decisions (as discussed in previous chapters) are guided, in large part, by program ratings, which typically form the basis for time sales negotiations between ad agencies and media. Here we examine where ratings come from and whether they provide an accurate measure of audience behavior.

Electronic media want unbiased audience information. Further, they would like objective, consistent, and complete research. For this, broadcasters, cable services, and advertisers employ independent companies to conduct most day-to-day audience research, using scientific methods for probing into human behavior and attitudes.*

*Audience measurement constitutes *applied* research. Chapter 12 examines more theoretically oriented audience research, conducted mostly at universities and nonprofit research companies.

More than 50 such companies operate at the national level, many more at the local level. They use a variety of testing methods, first to assist in preparation of programs and advertising messages, and later to assess the impact of these messages in terms of purchasing, brand recognition, and images projected by performers, programs, stations, and networks. We hear mostly, however, about *ratings*—estimates of how many people are exposed to given programs.

We hear about ratings as part of our interest in the program battle front—which programs, stations, and networks claim to be ahead in the endless struggles for supremacy, or even survival. Because ratings play a decisive role in program selection, they merit our attention. Thus most of this chapter focuses on that one area of audience study—the theory and practice of ratings research.

11.1 Ratings Business

Practically everyone knows what television ratings are in a general sense. In the long broadcast television network battle for ratings dominance, the rise and fall of prime-time programs always make news (see Exhibit 11.a). But unlike most other industries, broadcasting and cable deliver no physical products. Program "publishing" goes on continuously, with audiences flowing at will from one program to another. Hence the need for highly specialized research.*

Arbitron and Nielsen

Two ratings firms, Arbitron and Nielsen, dominate the ratings business as sources of most measurements used by electronic media and their advertisers. The two have been locked in competition for decades. Other competitors focus more on limited types of research—or have lasted only a few years.

The two services' revenues come mainly from subscriptions by individual stations and by advertising agencies. About 90 percent of all television stations subscribe to at least one of these two firms' reports, and until recently most of those in the mid-size and largest markets subscribed to both. Because of rising costs, however, stations increasingly rely on only one. By 1992 Nielsen had far more clients than Arbitron, and the gap was widening. Station subscription rates vary according to station revenue, but actual rates are rarely disclosed.** Major ad agencies subscribe to both network and local-mar-

ratings reports, some spending close to a million dollars a year (even though agencies traditionally pay less for ratings service than do stations). Other purchasers of ratings reports include cable and broadcast networks, national sales rep firms, program suppliers, and syndicators. Most advertisers rely on their ad agencies' subscriptions.

Arbitron became a subsidiary of Control Data Corporation in 1967 and was spun off as a part of Ceridian in 1992. A. C. Nielsen, the largest market research firm in the world, became a subsidiary of Dun & Bradstreet in 1984. It has operations in a score of foreign countries as well as in the United States. Broadcast ratings, though highly visible, represent only a small portion of Nielsen's operations, which mainly involve food and drug product marketing.

Local Market Ratings

Arbitron and Nielsen compete directly as they gather and publish television data for virtually all television markets. Local reports reflect the relative position of each station among its competitors and estimate local audience size for network, syndicated, and locally produced programs. Stations use local ratings reports as primary tools in selling time to advertisers and in evaluating their programming against that of their competitors.

For all but the largest markets, it costs too much to collect data for local television ratings continuously. Instead, researchers gather data in short spurts known as *rating periods*—as many as eight scheduled for larger cities and as few as two for small markets.

Arbitron is now the primary firm providing radio market ratings—Nielsen stopped measuring radio use in 1964, and Birch Radio left the business at the end of 1991.* Arbitron covers more than 260

---

*We seldom hear about print media research, because national newspaper and magazine readership surveys are little publicized. The Audit Bureau of Circulation and several other agencies conduct specialized print media research, but few outside those media ever learn of it. This applied research is based on actual counts (circulation) and samples (readership surveys). Industry-sponsored motion picture research is nearly all based on attendance figures—box-office ticket sales—which are widely reported.

**Tidbits of rate information appear from time to time. Late in 1991, when CBS-owned television stations briefly dropped Arbitron, the service was said to be costing them about $1 million annually in the New York and Los Angeles markets (*Broadcasting*, 4 November 1991: 65). Washington, D.C., radio stations paid anywhere from $50,000 to $250,000 a year for Arbitron radio ratings, "depending on the size of their audience and the amount of information they want to receive" (*City Paper*, 11 May 1990: 17). And broadcast television networks were said to pay $5 million annually for peoplemeter service, with ad agencies paying considerably less (*Broadcasting*, 18 May 1992: 8).

*Small competitors, using different data-collection methods, pop up from time to time, but few survive. For example, Strategic Radio Research began offering its "Accuratings" to client stations in six markets in 1992, gaining stations through low pricing of its ratings research, which depends on weekly telephone calls to a sample audience aged 12 to 64. Accuratings also report a new data category—a station's most dedicated listeners, called "partisans." Other services reprocess Arbitron's numbers into reports used by stations to better position themselves.

Exhibit 11.a

Role of Ratings

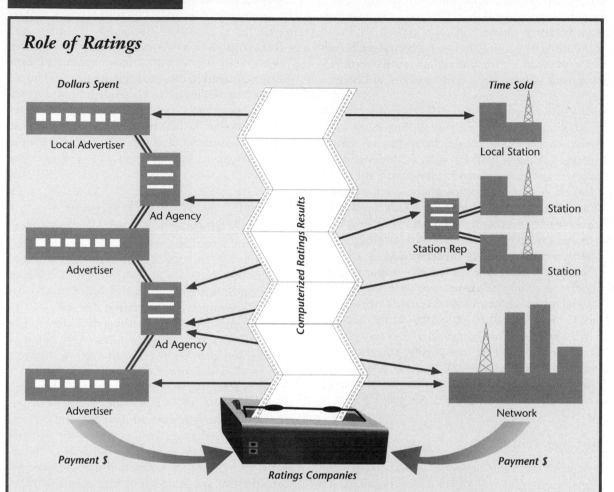

Ratings information is the oil that lubricates the process of selling electronic media advertising time. Stations and advertisers both pay ratings companies for ratings data. Advertising time buyers base their purchase decisions in large part on a station's ratings success with targeted audience groups. Put in different terms, think of ratings as a kind of neutral referee in the electronic media advertising process. Ratings provide the "common language" converting available station advertising minutes to numbers of available listeners compared with competing stations (or networks). These essential "numbers" can be compared by advertisers or their agencies before committing substantial funds to advertising campaigns.

radio markets: about 100 year-round, 70 in the spring and fall, and approximately 90 just once a year in the spring. Exhibit 11.b offers a sample page from one such report.

While Arbitron and Nielsen both produce broadcast television local-market ratings, each uses different means of measuring both markets and homes:

- Arbitron measures some 210 television markets four times a year in four-week-long *sweep weeks* (also simply called *sweeps*) by means of written diaries; a dozen markets with a combination of diaries and passive meters; and a handful of the largest markets by peoplemeter (each of these methods is described below). All metered cities also receive overnight "Arbitrend" reports. Arbitron measures metered markets continually—before, during, and after sweep weeks.
- *Nielsen Station Index* (NSI), the major Nielsen local television market measure, covers more than 200 markets—about 170 by means of written diaries, the other 30 or so (representing just over half the television homes in the country) by a combination of diary and passive household meters. Nielsen measures all markets four times a year in sweep weeks; it measures larger markets up to three additional times per year.

Network Ratings

Broadcast television networks demand faster and more frequent reporting than do local stations. But in two respects network ratings are easier to obtain: (1) not every market need be surveyed, as a sample of network markets yields a reliable picture of national network audiences; and (2) there are far fewer broadcast television networks (just four) competing at any one time than there are stations. Unlike the world of local television ratings, network ratings providers have no competition: Nielsen issues the only network television ratings, and RADAR the only ratings for network radio.

- *Nielsen Television Index* (NTI) issues television network ratings every two weeks in what is called the "pocket piece" (see Exhibit 11.d). Nielsen's

regular network reports use a national sample of 4,100 peoplemetered homes (representing the actual viewing of some 10,000 people), as described later.
- *RADAR (Radio's All-Dimension Audience Research)*, financed by the networks that contract with Statistical Research, Inc., uses telephone recall interviews (also discussed later). RADAR issues reports twice a year, each covering a sample week, based on surveys of 12,000 respondents. Unlike most telephone surveys, RADAR calls the *same* people each day, seven days in a row.

Syndicated-Program Ratings

Syndicated television programs pose special research problems; inasmuch as they are not aired simultaneously in a predictable number of markets. Despite this, program providers need to compare programs on a national basis in order to set per-episode licensing fees. Advertisers and stations also need comparative data. By using data already obtained for market ratings reports, both Arbitron and Nielsen provide regular analyses on relative performance of nationally syndicated programs.

The Nielsen *Cassandra* service (see Exhibit 11.e), acquired in 1980, provides detailed audience demographic information for both first-run and off-network syndicated programs (as well as for network and some local programs). Cassandras allow researchers to compare household demographic information for syndicated programs across markets, and to collect and measure similar data on both lead-in and lead-out programs. Arbitron's *Syndicated Program Analysis* (SPA) plays a similar role.

Special Studies

Both Arbitron and Nielsen publish many supplementary reports, drawing upon data gathered in preparing regular ratings reports. Clients can order special reports tailored to their needs. For example, to help determine when to schedule its news promotion announcements, a station might order a special "audience flow" study to discover which of its own programs attract viewers who normally watch a

Exhibit 11.b ● ● ● ● ● ● ● ● ● ● ● ● ● ●

Local-Market Radio Ratings

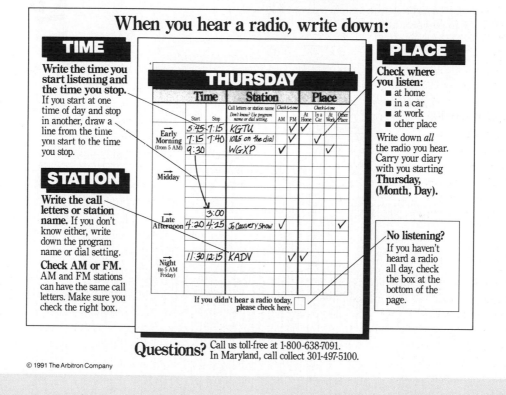

You count in the radio ratings!

No matter how much or how little you listen, you're important!

You're one of the few people picked in your area to have the chance to tell radio stations what you listen to.

This is *your* ratings diary. Please make sure you fill it out yourself.

Here's what we mean by "listening":

"Listening" is any time you can hear a radio — whether you choose the station or not.

When you hear a radio between Thursday, (Month, Day), and Wednesday, (Month, Day), write it down — whether you're at home, in a car, at work or someplace else.

When you hear a radio, write down:

TIME

Write the time you start listening and the time you stop. If you start at one time of day and stop in another, draw a line from the time you start to the time you stop.

STATION

Write the call letters or station name. If you don't know either, write down the program name or dial setting.

Check AM or FM. AM and FM stations can have the same call letters. Make sure you check the right box.

PLACE

Check where you listen:
- at home
- in a car
- at work
- other place

Write down *all* the radio you hear. Carry your diary with you starting **Thursday, (Month, Day).**

No listening? If you haven't heard a radio all day, check the box at the bottom of the page.

THURSDAY

Time		Station	Place				
Start	Stop	Call letters or station name. Don't know? Use program name or dial setting.	AM	FM	At Home	In a Car	At Work	Other Place
			Check (✓) one		Check (✓) one			
Early Morning (from 5 AM) 5:45	7:15	KGTU		✓	✓			
7:15	7:40	108.5 on the dial	✓			✓		
9:30		WGXP	✓				✓	
Midday								
	3:00							
Late Afternoon 4:20	4:15	Jo Cauvery show	✓					✓
Night (to 5 AM Friday) 11:30	12:15	KADV	✓	✓				

If you didn't hear a radio today, please check here. ☐

Questions? Call us toll-free at 1-800-638-7091. In Maryland, call collect 301-497-5100.

This instruction page from a radio diary illustrates the Arbitron system. Each individual in a household fills out a separate diary.

Source: Illustration © 1991 The Arbitron Company. Arbitron Public Relations. Used by permission.

Exhibit 11.c

Local-Market TV Ratings Report

Nielsen uses diaries and household meters to measure 211 local market television audiences. Shown here is part of a sample page of late-afternoon ratings and shares for syndicated programs in the Indianapolis market. Note how in this time period all stations strip their syndicated programs in the same dayparts. This report includes data from four weeks and shows a variety of demographic breakdowns so that station management and advertisers can obtain ratings for, say, women 25 to 49 years of age.

Source: Illustrations courtesy Nielsen Media Research. Used by permission of A.C. Nielsen.

Indianapolis, IN
Metered Market Service
May 1992
SPECIAL ETHNIC TREATMENT USED IN THIS MARKET (See Page 3)
Nielsen Station Index
Nielsen
Viewers in Profile

INDIANAPOLIS, IN

WK1 4/23-4/29 WK2 4/30-5/06 WK3 5/07-5/13 WK4 5/14-5/20

PROGRAM AVERAGES

METRO HH RTG	METRO HH SHR	STATION DAY PROGRAM	DMA HOUSEHOLD RATINGS WEEKS 1	2	3	4	MULTI-WEEK AVG RTG	SHR	HUT	DMA RATINGS PERSONS 2+	18+	12-24	12-34	18-34	18-49	21-49	25-54	35+	35-64	50+	WOMEN 18+	12-24	18-34	18-49	21-49	25-49	25-54	50+	WKG	MEN 18+	18-34	18-49	21-49	25-49	25-54	TNS 12-17	CHILD 2-11	6-11
1	2		3	4	5	6	7	8	14	15	16	17	18	19	20	21	22	23	24	25	26	27	28	29	30	31	32	33	34	35	36	37	38	39	40	41	42	43
3		*R.S.E. THRESHOLDS 25+%*	*3*	*3*	*3*	*3*	*2*			*1*	*1*	*5*	*3*	*3*	*2*	*2*	*2*	*2*	*2*	*2*	*2*	*8*	*5*	*3*	*3*	*3*	*3*	*4*	*3*	*2*	*6*	*3*	*3*	*3*	*3*	*9*	*6*	*9*
1		*(1 S.E.) 4 WK AVG 50+%*	*1*	*1*	*1*	*1*	*LT*			*LT*	*LT*	*1*	*1*	*1*	*1*	*1*	*LT*	*LT*	*1*	*1*	*LT*	*2*	*1*	*1*	*1*	*1*	*1*	*1*	*1*	*LT*	*2*	*1*	*1*	*1*	*1*	*2*	*2*	*2*
		4:00PM																																				
<<		WMCC MON HIGHWAY-HEAVEN	1	1	1	1	1	3	41	1	1	1		1				1	1	2	1							2	1	1	1	1						
<<		TUE HIGHWAY-HEAVEN	2	1	1	<<	1	3	39	1	1	1						1	1	1	1	1						2	1							2		1
<<		WED HIGHWAY-HEAVEN	2	<<	1	1	1	3	37	1	1	1						1	1	1	1	2						2	1							2	1	1
1	2	THU HIGHWAY-HEAVEN	1	1	1	1	1	2	36		1							1		1	1				1			1			1							
<<		FRI HIGHWAY-HEAVEN	1	1	1	<<	1	2	38											1								1										
<<		*AV5 HIGHWAY-HEAVEN*	*1*	*1*	*1*	*1*	*1*	*3*	*38*	*1*	*1*							*1*		*1*	*1*	*1*						*2*	*1*							*1*		
1	2	SAT COUNTRY VIDEO			1		1	3	36		1							1	1	2										1								
1	3	SAT KNIGHT RIDR SA	1	1			1	3	42	1	1	1	1	1	1	1	1			1	1	1	2	1	1	1	1	1	1							1		
2	6	SUN NEWHART		1			1	3	40	1	1		1	1	1	2	2	1	1		1		1	2	2	3	3		3		1	1	1	1	1			
<<		SUN RAT PATROL			1		1	2	28										1		1			1	1	1	1		1									
14	34	WRTV MON OPRAH WINFREY	17	14	9	13	13	32	41	7	8	5	5	6	7	7	7	9	8	10	11	8	9	10	10	10	11	13	7	4	3	4	4	4	4	3	2	3
13	35	TUE OPRAH WINFREY	12	14	12	13	13	32	39	6	8	5	6	7	7	7	7	8	8	9	10	8	9	9	9	9	10	12	8	4	4	4	4	4	4	4	2	2
12	35	WED OPRAH WINFREY	12	10	12	14	12	32	37	6	7	5	5	5	5	5	6	8	7	10	10	8	8	8	8	8	9	14	6	3	2	3	2	3	3	3		1
12	34	THU OPRAH WINFREY	12	11	9	14	12	32	36	6	7	5	5	5	6	6	6	8	7	10	10	10	8	9	9	8	9	13	6	4	2	3	3	3	3	5		1
13	35	FRI OPRAH WINFREY	11	10	16	13	12	32	38	6	7	6	5	6	6	6	7	8	8	9	11	9	9	9	9	9	9	13	7	4	3	3	3	3	3	4	1	2
13	*35*	*AV5 OPRAH WINFREY*	*13*	*12*	*12*	*13*	*12*	*32*	*38*	*6*	*7*	*5*	*5*	*6*	*6*	*6*	*7*	*8*	*8*	*10*	*11*	*9*	*9*	*9*	*9*	*9*	*10*	*13*	*7*	*4*	*3*	*3*	*3*	*3*	*3*	*4*	*1*	*2*
17	43	SAT WWOS-KY DERBY2		16			16	39	41	10	11	4	4	5	6	6	8	15	13	21	11	3	4	6	6	7	8	20	7	12	5	7	6	6	7	2	5	
6	17	SAT WWOS-PREAKNSS2				7	7	19	37	4	4	2	3	4	3	3	2	5	4	7	4	1	1	2	2	2	1	9	1	5	7	4	5	3	3		2	
4	14	SUN INTL RCE-CHAMP			4		4	12	29	2	2	1	1		2	2	3	3	3	2	2			1	1	2	2	2	1	2		2	2	3	3	2		
4	11	WTHR MON COSBY SHOW	6	4	4	3	4	10	40	3	2	6	3	2	2	2	2	1	2		2	9	3	3	2	2	2	1	1	1	2	2	2	1	1	6	6	8
3	7	TUE COSBY SHOW	2	2	3	4	3	7	37	2	1	3	2	1	2	2	2	1	2	1	2	4	2	2	2	2	2	1	1	1	1	1	2	2	1	5	2	1
3	8	WED COSBY SHOW	5	3	2	4	3	10	36	2	2	3	2	2	2	2	2	2	2	2	2	4	2	2	2	2	2	1	1	2	1	1	1	1	2	4	3	2
3	9	THU COSBY SHOW	3	4	2	3	3	9	34	2	1	3	2	1	1	2	2	2	2	1	2	4	1	2	2	2	2	1	1	1	1	1	1	1	1	5	3	3
3	8	FRI COSBY SHOW	3	4	3	3	3	8	37	2	1	3	2	1	2	1	1	2	2	1	2	4	2	2	2	2	2	1	2	1	1	1	1	1	1	4	3	5
3	*9*	*AV5 COSBY SHOW*	*4*	*3*	*3*	*3*	*3*	*9*	*37*	*2*	*2*	*3*	*2*	*2*	*2*	*2*	*2*	*2*	*2*	*1*	*2*	*5*	*2*	*2*	*2*	*2*	*2*	*1*	*1*	*1*	*1*	*1*	*1*	*1*	*1*	*5*	*3*	*4*
4	11	WTTV+MON TALE SPIN		5	4	5	4	12	38	3	1	2	2	1	1	1	1				1		1	1	1	1	1		1	1	1	1	1	1	1	4	16	18
5	11	MON TALE SPIN T≠	4				4	8	47	3	1	3	3	1	1	1	1	1	1			2	1	1	1	1	1			1	2	2	2	3	2	7	12	
4	11	TUE TALE SPIN		5	5	4	5	12	37	3		2	1	1							1	2	2	1	1	1	1		1							3	18	19
3	8	TUE TALE SPIN T≠	2				2	5	37	2		2	1	1	1	1	1					2								1	1	1	1	2	1	4	8	
4	13	WED TALE SPIN	5	4	4	4	4	12	36	3	1	2	2	1	1	1	1	1		1	1	2	2	1	1	1	1	1	1							5	13	13
3	8	THU TALE SPIN	2	3	2	6	3	10	34	2		1	1				1	1	1	1		1					1	1						1		2	13	13
3	9	FRI TALE SPIN	4	3	4	3	4	10	37	3		2	1	1							1	2	1	1	1	1	1									5	13	14
4	*10*	*AV5 TALE SPIN*	*4*	*4*	*4*	*5*	*4*	*11*	*36*	*3*	*1*	*2*	*1*	*1*	*1*	*1*	*1*			*1*	*1*	*1*	*1*	*1*	*1*	*1*	*1*	*1*								*4*	*14*	*15*
4	*10*	*AV2 TALE SPIN T≠*	*3*				*3*	*7*	*42*	*2*	*1*	*2*	*2*	*1*	*1*	*1*	*1*		*1*			*2*	*1*							*1*	*1*	*2*	*2*	*2*	*2*	*5*	*10*	
4	10	SAT SAT MOV 3	4	4	7	4	5	12	41	3	2	5	4	3	3	3	3	2	2	1	3	7	5	5	5	5	4	1	3	1	2	1	2	2	1	7	5	5
5	13	SUN SUN MOV 3	10	4	3		6	13	42	5	4	8	6	5	6	5	5	4	5	2	4	8	6	6	5	6	5	1	3	4	5	5	5	4	4	8	5	6
5	12	WXIN MON BEETLEJUCE-FOX	5	5	2	4	4	9	40	2		1	2	1	1	1	1				1	1	2	1	1	1	1		1		1			1		3	9	11
4	11	TUE BEETLEJUCE-FOX	3	3	4	3	3	9	37	2		2	2	1	1	1	1					5	1	1	1	1	1		1			1	1	1	1	5	6	6
3	10	WED BEETLEJUCE-FOX	4	4	1	2	3	8	36	1		2	2	1		1	1					1	1			1	1		1		1	1	1	1	1	5	2	1
4	12	THU BEETLEJUCE-FOX	4	2	3	3	3	8	34	1		2	1	1	1							3							1	1	1	1				4	6	7
4	10	FRI BEETLEJUCE-FOX	3	3	3	2	3	7	37	2		3	2	1								2	1						1		1		1	1	1	6	9	10
4	*11*	*AV5 BEETLEJUCE-FOX*	*4*	*3*	*3*	*3*	*3*	*8*	*37*	*2*		*2*	*2*	*1*	*1*	*1*	*1*					*2*	*1*	*1*	*1*	*1*	*1*		*1*		*1*	*1*		*1*		*4*	*6*	*7*
5	13	SAT SAT MOVIE 3	5	3	6		5	11	41	3	3	2	3	2	3	3	4	3	4	2	3	5	4	4	4	4	4	2	4	3	1	3	3	4	3	4	2	3

Exhibit 11.d •••••••••••••••

Nielsen Network Ratings Report

A-2 **Nielsen NATIONAL TV AUDIENCE ESTIMATES**   **EVE.MON. JUL.13, 1992**

TIME	7:00	7:15	7:30	7:45	8:00	8:15	8:30	8:45	9:00	9:15	9:30	9:45	10:00	10:15	10:30	10:45		
HUT	48.3	49.3	49.9	50.4	50.7	52.6	53.4	54.7	56.1	57.4	57.6	57.6	56.2	54.9	53.3	50.7		

ABC TV

					FBI: THE UNTOLD STORIES (R)		STREETS OF BEVERLY HILLS (PAE)		FBI UNTOLD STORIES SPEC. (R)		'92 VOTE-DEM NAT CONV-MON (9:30-11:26)(PAE)							
HHLD AUDIENCE% & (000)					**7.1**	6.540	**6.8**	6.260	**8.4**	7,740	**5.3**	4.880						
TA%, AVG. AUD. 1/2 HR %					*8.9*		*8.0*		*10.2*		*14.8*	5.1*		5.2*		4.9*		
SHARE AUDIENCE %					14		12		15		10	9*		9*		9*		
AVG. AUD. BY 1/4 HR %					7.2	7.1	7.0	6.7	8.0	8.9	5.3	5.0	5.5	4.9	4.9	4.9		

CBS TV

					EVENING SHADE (R)		MAJOR DAD (R)		MURPHY BROWN (R)		CAMPAIGN '92-DEM CONV-M (9:30-11:18)(PAE)							
HHLD AUDIENCE% & (000)					**7.6**	7,000	**8.0**	7,370	**10.0**	9,210	**5.7**	5,250						
TA%, AVG. AUD. 1/2 HR %					*9.6*		*9.6*		*12.7*		*16.0*	6.2*		5.1*		5.3*		
SHARE AUDIENCE %					15		15		18		10	11*		9*		10*		
AVG. AUD. BY 1/4 HR %					7.5	7.7	7.5	8.4	9.5	10.6	6.5	5.9	5.3	5.3	5.3			

NBC TV

					FRESH PRINCE OF BEL AIR (R)(PAE)		BLOSSOM (R)(PAE)		PACIFIC STATION SPCL.		MAN OF THE PEOPLE SPEC.		DECISION '92-DEM CONV MON (10:00-11:21)(PAE)					
HHLD AUDIENCE% & (000)					**9.7**	8,930	**8.7**	8,010	**5.4**	4,970	**7.3**	6,720	**5.1**	4,700				
TA%, AVG. AUD. 1/2 HR %					*11.6*		*10.6*		*6.8*		*9.2*		*10.8*	5.0*		4.7*		
SHARE AUDIENCE %					19		16		10		13		10	9*		9*		
AVG. AUD. BY 1/4 HR %					9.2	10.1	8.8	8.6	5.5	5.2	7.0	7.6	5.3	4.6	4.5	4.8		

FOX TV

					FOX NIGHT AT THE MOVIES REVENGE OF THE NERDS 3													
HHLD AUDIENCE% & (000)					**7.7**	7.090												
TA%, AVG. AUD. 1/2 HR %					*16.2*	6.4*		7.1*		8.0*		9.2*						
SHARE AUDIENCE %					14	12*		13*		14*		16*						
AVG. AUD. BY 1/4 HR %					6.3	6.6	7.0	7.1	7.9	8.1	9.4	9.0						

INDEPENDENTS
(INCLUDING SUPERSTATIONS EXCEPT TBS)

	7:00		7:30		8:00	8:30	9:00	9:30	10:00		10:30	
AVERAGE AUDIENCE	13.0	(+F)	13.0	(+F)	6.5	7.2	7.5	9.0	17.8	(+F)	15.4	(+F)
SHARE AUDIENCE %	27		26		13	13	13	16	32		30	

PBS

	7:00		7:30		8:00	8:30	9:00	9:30	10:00	10:30
AVERAGE AUDIENCE	1.5		1.9		2.6	3.3	3.4	3.2	2.8	2.7
SHARE AUDIENCE %	3		4		5	6	6	6	5	5

CABLE ORIG.
(INCLUDING TBS)

	7:00		7:30		8:00	8:30	9:00	9:30	10:00		10:30	
AVERAGE AUDIENCE	10.2	(+F)	11.6	(+F)	12.9	14.3	15.7	18.9	21.1	(+F)	19.9	(+F)
SHARE AUDIENCE %	21		23		25	27	28	33	38		38	

PAY SERVICES

	7:00	7:30	8:00	8:30	9:00	9:30	10:00	10:30
AVERAGE AUDIENCE	1.4	1.2	2.6	3.0	3.3	3.6	3.1	3.5
SHARE AUDIENCE %	3	2	5	6	6	6	6	7

U.S. TV Households: 92,100,000

For explanation of symbols, See page B.

A ratings report for a weekday evening comparing the prime-time appeal of the four national broadcasting networks with independent stations, Public Broadcasting Service, cable program services—shown here as *cable orig. (including TBS)*—and pay-cable services. Shown for each broadcast network program is the average audience in TV households (of 92 million total early in 1993), the share of audience, and the average audience rating by quarter hour. Note that for the independent stations and nonbroadcast network services, ratings show only overall average audience and share of audience, as the figures are a combination of individual market ratings, often for different programs in different cities.

Source: Chart courtesy Nielsen Media Research. Used by permission of A.C. Nielsen.

Exhibit 11.e ••••••••••••••

Syndicated Programs Ratings Report

NSI MAY 1992

CASSANDRA DMA COVERAGE AREA RANKING REPORT
RANKING BY HOUSEHOLD RATING

Program Name	Mkts	DMA Cov	DMA HH Rtg	DMA HH Sh	DMA HH Rnk	Women Total Rtg	Women Total Rnk	Women 18-34 Rtg	Women 18-34 Rnk	Women 18-49 Rtg	Women 18-49 Rnk	Women 25-54 Rtg	Women 25-54 Rnk	Women 50+ Rtg	Women 50+ Rnk	Men Total Rtg	Men Total Rnk	Men 18-34 Rtg	Men 18-34 Rnk	Men 18-49 Rtg	Men 18-49 Rnk
WHEEL OF FORTUNE (M-F)	192	98.2	15.2	28	1	12.6	1	4.8	7	6.0	3	7.2	3	24.3	1	8.2	2	3.0	10	3.8	8
JEOPARDY (M-F)	183	96.7	12.8	26	2	10.4	2	4.5	10	5.7	4	6.6	4	18.7	2	6.9	3	3.5	6	4.0	6
OPRAH WINFREY SHOW	197	98.9	11.8	34	3	10.0	3	8.7	2	8.6	2	8.7	2	12.5	4	3.5	12	2.6	13	2.6	12
STAR TREK-GENRATN-AS (C)	205	97.6	11.4	14	4	7.2	5	9.5	1	9.3	1	9.4	1	3.3	30	9.3	1	12.2	1	11.7	1
STAR TREK-GENRATN-AS (O)	205	97.6	7.9	16		5.0		6.5		6.5		6.6		2.4		6.7		8.5		8.4	
STAR TREK-GENRATN-AS (R)	117	77.8	4.3	11		2.7		3.7		3.5		3.5		1.2		3.3		4.6		4.1	
WHEEL OF FORTUNE (WKND)	159	78.8	9.2	21	5	7.6	4	2.2	51	3.0	22	3.7	14	15.8	3	4.8	4	1.6	43	2.0	22
ENTERTAINMENT TONIGHT (C)	160	93.7	8.7	16	6	6.6	6	4.9	5	5.7	4	6.4	5	8.1	6	4.6	5	3.3	7	3.9	7
ENTERTAINMENT TONIGHT (O)	160	93.7	8.1	16		6.2		4.8		5.4		6.1		7.6		4.4		3.1		3.6	
ENTERTAINMENT TONIGHT (R)	19	17.8	2.9	12		1.8		1.2		1.4		1.5		2.6		1.4		1.3		1.2	
JEOPARDY (WKND)	63	42.0	8.0	18	7	6.4	7	2.4	39	3.1	20	3.5	17	12.4	5	4.4	6	1.9	31	2.4	14
CURRENT AFFAIR (C)	155	92.2	7.5	14	8	5.4	9	3.9	13	4.3	8	4.8	6	7.3	10	4.3	7	3.1	9	3.4	9
CURRENT AFFAIR (O)	155	92.2	6.9	14		5.0		3.6		4.0		4.4		6.8		3.9		2.8		3.1	
CURRENT AFFAIR (R)	19	22.5	2.8	10		1.7		1.3		1.4		1.5		2.5		1.3		0.9		1.1	
DONAHUE	191	98.2	7.2	24	9	5.5	8	3.9	13	4.0	12	4.2	9	8.1	6	2.7	17	1.8	35	1.8	31
INSIDE EDITION	119	84.4	7.0	17	10	5.1	10	2.8	25	3.5	16	4.2	9	8.0	8	3.6	11	1.9	31	2.4	14
CHEERS	174	94.5	6.5	14	11	4.5	13	5.2	4	4.9	6	4.6	7	3.8	22	4.3	7	4.9	4	4.5	3
GOLDEN GIRLS	158	90.9	6.3	15	12	5.0	11	3.9	13	4.1	10	4.1	11	6.7	11	2.6	19	1.8	35	1.9	25
SALLY JESSE RAPHAEL	175	92.6	6.1	23	13	5.0	11	4.7	8	4.3	8	4.3	8	6.3	12	1.7	38	1.3	60	1.2	65
HARD COPY	143	88.5	5.8	14	14	4.1	14	2.6	34	3.2	18	3.6	16	5.9	13	3.0	15	2.1	23	2.3	16
MARRIED...WITH CHILDREN	155	93.7	5.8	12	14	3.6	18	5.3	3	4.5	7	4.0	12	2.1	57	3.8	10	5.0	3	4.5	3
COSBY SHOW, THE	182	95.2	5.7	13	16	3.9	15	4.5	10	4.1	10	3.8	13	3.6	25	2.4	20	2.5	16	2.3	16
FULL HOUSE	87	82.4	5.6	12	17	2.9	26	4.6	9	3.7	15	3.2	18	1.5	78	1.6	44	2.2	22	1.9	25
TEXAS COUNTRY REPORTER	15	4.5	5.2	16	18	3.5	20	1.4	88	1.6	69	1.9	46	7.4	9	3.1	14	0.9	100	1.4	47
STAR TREK NEXT GENERATION	143	85.8	5.1	10	19	2.9	26	4.1	12	3.8	14	3.7	14	1.3	90	4.0	9	5.4	2	5.1	2
FAMILY FEUD	96	68.2	4.9	11	20	3.8	17	2.8	25	2.8	24	2.9	23	5.6	16	2.3	21	1.6	43	1.7	34
LIVE W/REGIS & KATHIE LEE	184	94.0	4.8	20	21	3.9	15	2.5	37	2.8	24	3.1	19	5.7	14	1.3	70	0.7	128	0.7	123
MAURY POVICH SHOW, THE	145	91.3	4.6	16	22	3.8	18	2.4	39	2.4	38	2.5	31	5.7	14	1.9	30	2.3	21	2.0	22
WHO'S THE BOSS	148	85.3	4.6	11	22	3.0	23	3.8	16	3.3	17	2.9	23	2.5	44	1.9	30	2.3	21	2.0	22
A DIFFERENT WORLD	40	40.5	4.5	9	24	3.1	21	4.9	5	4.0	12	3.1	19	1.5	78	1.7	38	2.4	19	2.0	22
NIGHT COURT	153	91.0	4.5	10	24	2.9	26	3.3	19	3.1	20	3.0	21	2.6	41	2.7	17	3.0	10	2.8	11
COSBY SHOW II, THE	131	83.1	4.3	10	26	2.7	30	3.6	17	3.2	18	2.9	23	2.9	34	1.6	44	2.1	23	1.8	31
M*A*S*H*	13	21.5	4.3	10	26	2.9	26	3.1	20	2.9	23	2.9	23	2.9	34	2.8	16	3.2	8	2.9	10
ENTRTAINMNT TONITE 60 (C)	162	93.0	4.3	13	26	3.1	21	2.2	51	2.6	30	3.0	21	4.0	20	2.0	25	1.4	54	1.7	34
ENTRTAINMNT TONITE 60 (O)	160	92.1	3.8	13		2.8		1.8		2.3		2.7		3.7		1.9		1.3		1.5	
ENTRTAINMNT TONITE 60 (R)	13	13.4	3.4	15		2.4		3.0		2.4		2.6		2.3		1.3		0.8		1.2	
GERALDO (O)	149	89.5	4.0	14	29	3.0	23	2.6	34	2.5	33	2.6	29	4.0	20	1.4	59	1.1	73	1.0	82
WKRP (C)	198	95.9	4.0	7	29	2.5	34	2.1	55	2.2	42	2.3	36	3.0	32	2.0	25	1.9	31	1.9	25
WKRP (O)	197	93.6	2.7	7		1.8		1.4		1.5		1.6		2.3		1.5		1.3		1.3	
WKRP (R)	115	67.7	1.9	7		1.1		1.0		1.1		1.1		1.1		0.8		0.8		0.9	
STAR SEARCH	165	93.1	3.9	12	31	3.0	23	2.7	31	2.6	30	2.7	28	3.7	23	1.7	38	1.2	66	1.3	54
HUNTER	79	67.4	3.7	9	32	2.5	34	1.8	66	1.9	63	1.9	52	3.6	25	2.2	23	1.3	60	1.5	42
SAVED BY THE BELL	77	69.7	3.7	9	32	1.1	103	1.9	63	1.5	78	1.1	103	0.5	171	0.7	130	1.1	73	0.9	95
STREET JUSTICE (C)	121	80.8	3.7	8	32	2.7	30	2.9	24	2.8	24	2.8	27	2.5	44	2.0	25	2.1	23	1.9	25
STREET JUSTICE (O)	120	80.3	2.6	6		1.9		1.8		1.9		1.9		1.9		1.4		1.3		1.3	
STREET JUSTICE (R)	43	41.1	2.1	7		1.6		2.1		1.8		1.7		1.2		1.1		1.5		1.1	
CURRENT AFFAIR EXTRA	151	88.2	3.6	13	35	2.3	42	1.5	81	1.7	63	1.9	46	3.3	30	1.8	34	1.2	66	1.5	42
GROWING PAINS	117	79.1	3.6	9	35	1.8	59	2.8	25	2.3	39	1.8	52	0.9	123	1.1	85	1.7	37	1.3	54
KNIGHT RIDER	14	21.5	3.6	9	35	2.3	42	2.4	39	2.1	45	1.8	52	2.8	37	1.9	30	1.7	37	1.5	42
OUT OF THIS WORLD	15	25.5	3.6	11	35	1.6	72	2.3	46	2.0	49	1.8	52	0.8	137	1.0	94	0.9	100	1.2	65
BAYWATCH	136	85.5	3.5	9	39	2.4	40	3.0	22	2.7	28	2.5	31	1.8	68	1.9	30	2.1	23	1.9	25
HOWARD STERN SHOW	31	43.7	3.5	10	39	1.6	72	2.4	39	2.2	42	2.0	43	0.5	171	3.3	13	4.9	4	4.4	5
MAMA'S FAMILY	105	60.5	3.5	9	39	2.7	30	2.8	25	2.5	33	2.3	33	4.4	19	1.4	59	1.3	60	1.3	54
PEOPLE'S COURT	156	88.9	3.5	12	39	2.5	34	1.5	81	1.5	76	1.6	61	4.2	19	1.7	38	1.1	73	1.1	79
MONTEL WILLIAMS	52	47.6	3.4	12	43	2.5	34	2.5	37	2.3	39	2.2	38	3.0	32	1.4	70	1.1	73	1.1	79
ROGGIN'S HEROES	156	85.9	3.4	11	43	2.2	47	1.8	66	1.9	52	2.0	43	2.6	41	2.3	21	2.1	23	2.3	16
LIFESTYLS-RICH&FAMOUS (C)	144	85.8	3.4	9	43	2.3	42	1.5	81	1.7	63	1.9	46	3.4	27	1.5	49	1.0	86	1.2	65

Copyright 1992 Nielsen Media Research. Printed in the USA.

This is one page from a Nielsen "Cassandra" report with syndicated program ratings and audience demographics in early 1992. The first two columns show how many markets (and what proportion of the national market) each program reaches; the next three give each program's overall national rating, share, and rank; and the remainder show the rating and rank of each program by various audience demographic groupings.

• *DMA* refers to Nielsen's "Designated Market Area," roughly comparable to Arbitron's *ADI* ("Area of Dominant Influence").

• *COV* means coverage—the percentage of DMAs in the country where the program is carried.

• *C* = Combination—total of Original *(O)* and Repeat *(R)* airings within same week, assuming no duplication of viewers.

Rtg. means rating; *Sh* means share.

Source: Chart © 1992 Nielsen Media Research. Used by permission of A.C. Nielsen.

competing newscast. Another might commission a study to find out how much a program appeals to specific audience subgroups. Custom geographic areas can be measured in Arbitron's Trading Area Reports (TAR)—a way of defining one's own market for special needs.

• • • • • • • •

11.2 Collecting Data

Whatever electronic medium they analyze, researchers use several methods for collecting data on which to base ratings: diaries, passive household meters, active peoplemeters, and two different kinds of telephone calls. Special studies often use other methods and combinations. Each has advantages and disadvantages.

Diaries and Passive Meters

Arbitron and Nielsen researchers use a written diary method for daily gathering of most local-market data. To obtain *radio* data, Arbitron sends a separate diary to each person over 12 years of age in every sample household.* For *television* data, Arbitron uses a diary for each household television receiver and VCR. Arbitron asks diary keepers to write down for one week (beginning Thursday and ending the following Wednesday) their listening times and the stations they tune to, keeping track of away-from-home as well as in-home listening (see Exhibit 11.f).

Nielsen uses diaries for its Nielsen Station Index market television ratings outside the 29 largest markets, asking one person in each sample home to take charge of reporting all household viewing. VCR use

is measured separately (see Section 11.8). Combining diary information with set-use data measured by the passive household meter for those large markets, Nielsen can report a detailed picture of market television use.

Diaries suffer a serious drawback: people often enter inaccurate information, purposely (to show they have good taste in programs) or not (many sample families fill in a diary in "catch up" style at the end of the week rather than as listening or viewing takes place). Some also tire of making entries, suffering from "diary fatigue." Yet until development of peoplemeters, diaries were the only method that could record just which people in the household viewed what.

The *passive household meter* device (which became Nielsen's Audimeter) was the subject of considerable experimentation in several places in the 1930s, was refined and patented at MIT in 1936 and later purchased by Nielsen for further development, was first applied to report ratings in 1950, and was still actively in use in the 1990s. After several false starts (including temporary use of Nielsen Audimeters for which the rival was paid), Arbitron developed its own meter. Attached to each television set in a sample household, the so-called black box automatically records when the set is on and to which channel it is tuned. Researchers refer to the household meter as *passive* because no effort is required on the part of the viewer to record its information—it operates automatically and unobtrusively. It also provides no information as to who, if anyone, is actually watching.* In the top 15 to 25 markets, Nielsen and Arbitron therefore supplement meter data with written diary data from some of the same households to obtain demographic data on actual viewers (Webster and Lichty, 1991: 131). Demographic diary data are combined with meter viewing data in meter-diary integration. Both firms issue market ratings based

---

*Diaries led to Arbitron's creation. Originally called the American Research Bureau (ARB)—founded by James Seiler, the research director at the NBC station in Washington, D.C.—the company began issuing diary-based reports in four markets in 1949–1950, adding two more a year later. After several ownership changes, ARB became Arbitron in 1973 (Beville, 1988: 65).

*The term *passive* also distinguishes the old meter from the newer peoplemeter, which (along with the older diary method) requires an element of audience participation. The terms *passive* and *active* also distinguish *levels* of participation by peoplemeter households. A passive peoplemeter is the ideal in that viewers do nothing but watch normally: no buttons to push. As discussed below, passive peoplemeters are under development.

Exhibit 11.f ●●●●●● ●●●●●●●●●●●

Local Television Ratings Diaries

(A) One instruction page from an Arbitron weekly local-market television diary. When mailed out, the diary contains no market-specific information, and thus the sample household must enter all of that, as well as the people who watch and their gender and age, and finally, as shown here, the actual specific household viewing (panel 3). While diaries can provide considerable data in this way, critics argue that too much is asked for and many diaries come back so incomplete they cannot be used in producing the final rating report.

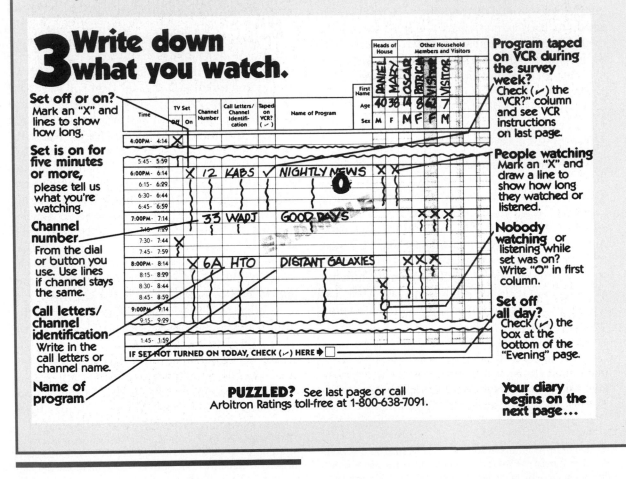

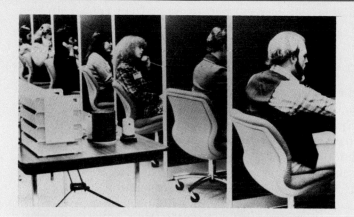

(B) Most of Arbitron's market ratings are based on diaries. (1) Telephone callers solicit households in each market to accept diaries. (2) Program titles, previously collected and verified, are matched to the ratings. (3) Computers process survey results. (4) Checkers verify the results. (5) Reports go out to stations, advertisers, agencies, and station rep offices.

Source: Diary and photos © The Arbitron Company. Arbitron Public Relations. Used by permission.

on such combined meter-diary samples. Although passive household meters were phased out of *network* rating use in 1987 with activation of peoplemeters, they remain essential for individual market ratings in the 1990s.

Peoplemeters

Changes in viewing habits caused by developing media technologies in the 1980s forced audience researchers to pay more attention to *individual* than to family viewing and listening habits. Advertiser interest combined with new computer capabilities prompted peoplemeter development. Like Nielsen's old Audimeter, this electronic device keeps a record of receiver use. To that function, the peoplemeter adds research once provided only by diaries by *simultaneously* collecting demographic data. It does this by requiring each viewer, whenever she or he watches television, to "check in" and "check out" by pushing a special handset button (see Exhibit 11.g). Several extra buttons allow household visitors to check in and out as well. Data on both receiver use and viewer identity go by telephone line to a central computer containing basic household demographic data, stored earlier when the peoplemeter was installed. Like diary keeping, however, button activity can become tedious after a time—and beyond the interest or technical capabilities of small children and many senior citizens.

Three firms—Nielsen, Arbitron, and AGB—* tested several peoplemeter variations in the mid-1980s. Nielsen began a three-year test of a peoplemeter sample in 1983 and started its peoplemeter-based national network ratings service in September 1987.

Arbitron, after conducting a lengthy market test in Denver starting in 1985, had expanded its local *ScanAmerica* peoplemeter system to six large markets by late 1992: Denver, Phoenix, Pittsburgh, St. Louis, Baltimore, and Kansas City.* Arbitron planned to—but in the end did not—replace all passive household meters with this peoplemeter system for its market ratings by the late 1990s. The company touted ScanAmerica as a three-pronged *single-source* system providing ratings, audience demographic data, and a measure of product purchasing. (Sample households pass an electronic "wand" over product codes on purchases; the wand stores that information, which is sent with set-use data for central computer processing.) ScanAmerica allowed analysis of exposure to television advertising and subsequent purchases, although it cannot show a direct connection given the many inputs into buying decisions. Late in 1992, lacking sufficient advertiser interest, Arbitron dropped use of both the wand and the name "ScanAmerica."

Introduction of peoplemeters, especially for Nielsen's network ratings, created enormous controversy. Network ratings in all dayparts dropped dramatically while ratings for many independent stations and cable channels rose. The networks understandably complained about drawbacks in peoplemeter use. In 1989 they funded an independent study that concluded peoplemeters appeared to slight such typical network heavy viewers as children and older people who might be intimidated by (or simply too impatient with) the computer-like button-pushing that peoplemeters required. Researchers also noted that, for a variety of reasons, only about half of daily peoplemeter data are fully usable. While overall viewing patterns clearly *are* changing, the reported drops in network viewing since 1987 are due in part to introduction of peoplemeters as well as to increasing use of competing services (cable) and equipment (VCRs).

---

*AGB (Audits of Great Britain), a British firm, developed the peoplemeter and pioneered its use in Europe. After a Boston market test beginning in 1985, AGB began offering a national service in 1987, forcing Nielsen to do likewise. Unable to obtain sufficient broadcaster or advertiser support, however, AGB closed its U.S. operation in 1988 after a loss of nearly $70 million. It still supplies audience data in a number of other countries.

*Spurred by financial support from CBS, Arbitron announced late in 1991 a plan to offer ScanAmerica *network* ratings in competition with Nielsen. The sample began with 1,000 homes and was to have expanded to 5,000 nationwide by 1995. But failing to get the support of other networks and of critically important advertisers, Arbitron pulled out of this brief attempt to offer network ratings just 10 months later.

Exhibit 11.g ●●●●●●●●●●●●●●●●

Peoplemeter Ratings

(A) The Nielsen national audience reporting system depends heavily on automation, from the home meter through the gathering, analyzing, and reporting processes. The peoplemeter used for network ratings consists of two parts: the hand-held unit on which each viewing member of the family and guests can "punch in," using individual keys, and the base unit on top of the receiver that stores home viewing information.

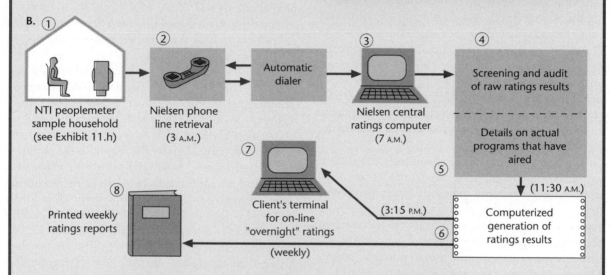

(B) The Nielsen system begins with the individual sample household (1), whose peoplemeter base unit results are (2) "read" over a telephone line (leased by Nielsen) at 3:00 A.M. local time each morning by a computer that sends the viewing results of the sample household into (3) the Nielsen central ratings computers. The collected raw ratings are (4) sent to the screening and audit process, where all ratings materials are assembled and (5) combined with the detailed program information constantly gathered by Nielsen. They are then sent for (6) computer generation of actual overnight ratings. By 3:15 P.M. the overnights are ready for (7) client (agencies, stations, networks) retrieval by computer terminal, and (8) weekly printed ratings reports. Nielsen diary and passive household meter markets go through a similar process to generate market-by-market reports.

Source: Data used by permission of A.C. Nielsen. Photo courtesy Nielsen Media Research.

Passive Peoplemeters

Intense network and advertiser pressure to improve their methods forced both Nielsen and Arbitron to announce research plans to replace peoplemeters with "passive" peoplemeters for introduction in the mid-1990s. Researchers at MIT, the David Sarnoff Research Labs, and others worked to develop systems that would not require viewers to push buttons. Using computerized image-recognition, these passive devices (again, "passive" because the viewer does nothing except watch television) presumably could "recognize" regular (family) viewers. Further, the devices could tell when viewers were actually watching the screen or doing something else. A number of variations are under consideration and being tested—including one that counts someone as watching television only if that person is actually facing the receiver. There were kinks—several demonstrations confused pets with people! But when perfected, the passive peoplemeter should be able electronically to record regular family members, and others as guests, tabulating who and how many are watching and when.*

While such systems might meet major objections to "active" peoplemeters, they raise other more troublesome concerns—chiefly viewer privacy. A device in one's home that uses visual imagery to record who is watching has at least the potential for recording anything else it "sees." The likelihood that an even greater proportion of potential sample homes would reject the new device (almost half now reject Nielsen's existing peoplemeter) would both raise the cost of research and possibly taint the sample's reliability. Demand from advertisers and agencies for better audience data (combining set-tuning,

demographic, and product purchase information) is fueling research for improved passive peoplemeters.

Coincidental Telephone Calls

Some researchers consider coincidental telephone data gathering the most accurate means of obtaining audience information.* The term *coincidental* means that researchers ask respondents what they are listening to or watching *during* (that is, coincidental with) the time of the call. Putting questions that way eliminates memory concerns and reduces possibilities of intentional misinformation. Researchers ask whether respondents have a set turned on at that moment and, if so, what program, station, or channel the set is tuned to, plus a few demographic questions such as the number, gender, and age of those watching or listening.

Because coincidental methods provide only *momentary* data from each respondent ("What are you listening to or watching *now*?"), they require many calls, spaced out to cover each daypart, to build up a complete profile of listening or viewing. Properly conducted, coincidental calls require large batteries of trained callers, making the method expensive. Nor can coincidental calls cover the entire broadcast day; information on audience activity after 10:30 P.M. and before 8:00 A.M. must be gathered during more socially acceptable calling hours, when researchers ask respondents to recall programs they listened to or viewed during these nighttime and early-morning hours.

Though many scholarly research projects use coincidental telephone surveys, no major ratings firm relies on this method for regular reports, primarily because of cost. Nielsen, Arbitron, and others do, however, offer a special coincidental service for customers who require quick answers to specific questions. For example, broadcasters often order

---

*Other passive means of measuring audiences have been tried from time to time, including special antennas that can measure emissions from receivers over a neighborhood. In mid-1992 Actual Radio Measurement (ARM) experimented with an antenna system to measure radio listening in passing cars. The system could measure to which FM outlet a radio was tuned, if on (it could not measure AM) and was used in several Southwestern cities, touted as a supplement to rather than as a replacement for Arbitron services (*Broadcasting*, 24 August 1992: 28).

*The first radio ratings used telephone methods. The Cooperative Analysis of Broadcasting (1930–1946) and Hooper (1934–1950) ratings for network and local radio relied on the telephone (Beville, 1988: 7–16), as did the Birch-Scarborough radio service, which ended in 1991.

coincidentals to measure audience preferences between sweeps, and for special-event programs.

Telephone Recall

Tricks of memory make *telephone recall* less reliable than coincidental calls, but it costs less because more data can be gathered per call. RADAR, the only source of radio network ratings, uses telephone recall, collecting samples *daily* (by prearrangement) over a period of seven days, thus minimizing memory errors while attaining a week's coverage. RADAR employs *random digit dialing*, a technique for generating telephone numbers at random by computer. It designs a national sample of individuals (not households, in this case) based on random calls.

Personal Interview

The use of in-person, door-to-door surveys has declined in recent years because knocking on doors in strange neighborhoods can be hazardous to a researcher's health. Typically, interviewers question people on the street or in shopping centers, or, for car radio listening, at stoplights (also dangerous these days!). Data gathered in these ways cannot be projected to the general population, however, because the samples are not at all representative.

Combination Methods

If cost were no object, the most reliable and valid method of audience research would be some combination of these methods. Combinations of meters and diaries, or of telephone calls and diaries or meters, provide added information while allowing checks on, and comparisons with, findings derived by different methods. For example, peoplemeters provide data equivalent to that gathered by a diary–household meter combination, albeit with the problems noted earlier.

● ● ● ● ● ● ● ●
11.3 Sampling

No matter which research method one uses, around-the-clock monitoring of all the private listening and viewing behavior of millions of people tuning to thousands of stations and scores of cable channels in more than 200 markets is obviously impossible. The task becomes possible only with drastic simplification by means of *sampling*—studying some people to represent the behavior of all. To realize that ratings based on samples *can* adequately measure overall audience behavior, we have to understand some elements of sampling.

Samples to Simplify

Sampling simplifies three aspects of ratings research: behavior, time, and number of people.

- *Behavioral sampling.* Researchers decided years ago on a minimum measurable behavioral response—turning on a receiver, selecting a station, and later turning the set off. Each ratings company has adopted an arbitrary span of time (ranging from three to six minutes per quarter-hour) that a set must be turned on to count as being "in use." This simple *set-use test*, while accurate in itself, leaves out of consideration much that we would like to know about audiences.*
- *Time sampling.* The second simplification used in ratings takes advantage of repetitive daily and weekly cycles of most broadcast and cable programming. A sample taken every few weeks or months from this continuous program stream suffices for most purposes. Ratings companies sample only network audiences and major-city audiences on a daily basis. All others are sampled only occasionally.

*Set-use data tell us nothing about whether listeners liked a program, understood what they heard or saw, chose the program after considering alternatives or merely passively accepted it because it came on the channel already tuned in, whether one family member imposed his or her choice on others, or whether *anyone* watched at all.

- *Number of people sampled.* The most controversial ratings simplification arises from the use of only a few hundred or thousand people to represent program choices of thousands or millions of others. To critics, it seems unreasonable to claim that tuning activities in a few thousand homes nationally could be used to assess tuning behavior of more than 240 million people in some 92 million households. On a local-market level, Arbitron and Nielsen use a few hundred households per market. Nielsen's national network ratings sample uses about 4,000 homes. And the RADAR national radio network surveys 12,000 people by telephone.

Random Samples

In fact, small samples *can* give reasonably accurate estimates. The laws of chance, or *probability*, predict that *random selection* of a small sample (usually households) from a large population will make that sample representative (within a predictable degree of accuracy) of the entire population. Random selection means that, ideally, *every* member of the entire population to be surveyed has an *equal* chance of being selected. Major defining characteristics of the sample will appear in about the same proportion as their distribution throughout the entire population.

However, choosing at random is not as easy as it sounds. Drawing a sample randomly from a large human population requires some means of identifying each member of the population by name, number, location, or some other unique distinguishing label. In practice, this usually means using either lists of people's names or maps of housing unit locations. Such listings are called *sample frames*. Ratings companies use either updated telephone directories or census tracts (maps showing the location of dwellings) as frames. But such frames never cover literally everybody; besides, they often go out of date even before they can be printed.

Selecting a Ratings Sample

Nielsen draws its national sample of metered television households from U.S. census maps by a method known as *multistage area probability sampling.* This method ensures that the number of sample members chosen from each geographic area will be proportional to the total population of each area. *Multistage* refers to step-by-step narrowing down of selection areas, starting with counties and ending with individual housing units, as shown in Exhibit 11.h. For local-market ratings Nielsen and Arbitron use special updated telephone directories, which include both listed and unlisted numbers, as well as new listings. About 97 percent of U.S. households have telephones, making such directories the most readily available sampling frames. *Random digit dialing* can solve the problem of reaching unlisted and newly installed telephones, but it increases the number of wasted (unused or business address) calls, thus increasing survey cost.

Ideally, each time a company such as Nielsen made a survey it would draw a brand-new sample so that imperfections in any one sample would not have a permanent effect. On the other hand, if the company uses expensive sampling and data-gathering methods, it cannot afford to discard each sample after only one use. Nielsen tries to retain each peoplemeter household in its national sample for no more than two years. Wiring of *multiset* homes for peoplemeters is especially difficult, and as a result the company has been accused of underrepresenting such households. Nielsen and Arbitron allow local-market diary families to stay in samples for up to five years, using parts of the sample for given weeks and staggering its contracts with householders, replacing part of the total each year.

Sample Size

Having established a sample universe, the researcher must next decide how large a sample to choose—the larger the sample, the higher its reliability. But reliability increases approximately in proportion to the square of sample size (the sample size multiplied by itself). For example, to double reliability requires a fourfold increase in size. Thus a *point of diminishing returns* soon arrives, after which an increase in sample size yields such small gains in reliability as not to be worth the added cost.

Exhibit 11.h ●●●●●● ●●●●●●●●●●

Multistage Sampling Method

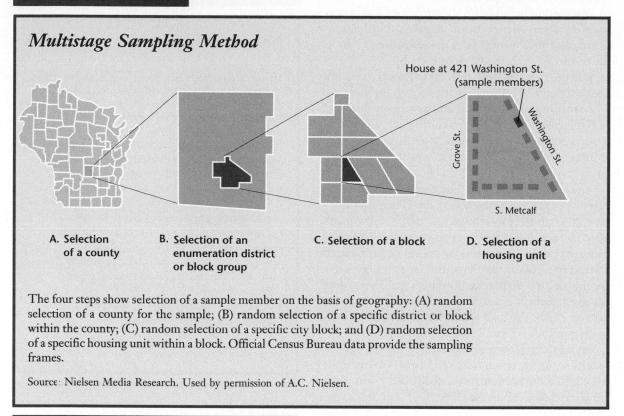

House at 421 Washington St.
(sample members)

Grove St.

Washington St.

S. Metcalf

**A. Selection
of a county**

**B. Selection of an
enumeration district
or block group**

C. Selection of a block

**D. Selection of a
housing unit**

The four steps show selection of a sample member on the basis of geography: (A) random
selection of a county for the sample; (B) random selection of a specific district or block
within the county; (C) random selection of a specific city block; and (D) random selection
of a specific housing unit within a block. Official Census Bureau data provide the sampling
frames.

Source: Nielsen Media Research. Used by permission of A.C. Nielsen.

Researchers and their clients therefore have to balance the degree of certainty desired against what they are willing to pay. At its best, *sampling yields only estimates*, never absolute certainties. Thus the real question becomes how much uncertainty can be accepted in a given sampling situation.

Sources of Error

Even when researchers carefully select their samples and sample sizes, two kinds of error can invalidate research findings. The built-in uncertainty of all measurements based on samples arises first from *sampling error*. Statistical laws of probability state that any given sample-based measurement would still be equally accurate if the sample size was in-creased or decreased by a known amount.* The *probable* amount of statistical uncertainty in ratings (that is, the amount of sampling error to be expected) can be calculated in advance (it's still only "probable" because of uncertainty even about uncertainty!).

All this is especially important for radio and cable services—because sampling error increases as ratings decrease. For radio stations or cable networks with low ratings—say, two or three percentage points in a given daypart—minor sample problems

---

*To put it another way, repeated sample measurements would vary among themselves, but the chances are that *most* (probably not all) of the measurements would be *near* the actual factor being measured.

are magnified to a degree that makes reported minor ratings differences questionable.*

The second possibly invalidating problem—*nonsampling error*—arises from mistakes, both intentional and inadvertent. Such errors produce *bias* in the results. Bias can come from lying by respondents as well as from honest mistakes. Researchers are probably consciously or unconsciously prejudiced. The wording of questionnaires may be misleading. And mistakes can occur in recording data and calculating results. Given all these pitfalls, some degree of bias is inevitable whenever researchers sample large groups.

Sometimes reports state sample size as the number of people (or households) the researcher contacted, when the key element should be how many actually *participated*. A 45 percent response rate indicates that only 45 out of 100 homes or individuals contacted actually participated. In practice, a response rate of 100 percent never occurs. Depending on the research method and purpose, a response rate of under about 85 percent for other than day-to-day ratings research is cause for concern.

Ratings companies work hard to encourage response by sample members and to ensure that those who agree to participate actually carry out their assigned tasks. Arbitron and Nielsen both stay regularly in touch with sample members and offer small cash payments to encourage them to mail in completed diaries. Arbitron pays families by the number of receivers measured—more sets mean more payment. Nielsen pays peoplemeter users in order to encourage continued participation, thereby not only improving response rates but also reducing installation costs. The company agrees to pay half of any receiver repair costs as well as a small monthly cash payment. Nielsen also contacts each metered household six times a year with either personal or telephone visits as a follow-up reinforcement measure. For two months in the spring of 1993, Arbitron experimented with on-air announcements over Atlanta radio stations encouraging listeners to com-

---

*Public consciousness of sampling error has increased in recent years. News reports of survey results almost always now add the statement "Accurate within plus or minus *x* percentage points."

Exhibit 11.i

Nonresponse Errors

Typical nonresponse errors for each of the principal methods of ratings data collection include:

- *Diaries:* refusal to accept diaries; failure to complete accepted diaries; unreadable and self-contradictory diary entries; drop-off in entries as the week progresses ("diary fatigue"); and failure to mail in completed diaries.
- *Passive (household) meters:* refusal to allow installation; breakdown of receivers, meters, and associated equipment; telephone-line failures.
- *Peoplemeters:* same drawbacks as passive meters, plus failure of some viewers (especially the very old and very young) to use the buttons to "check in" and "check out," having succumbed to "response fatigue."
- *Telephone calls:* busy signals; no answers; disconnected telephones; refusals to talk; inability to communicate with respondents who speak foreign languages.

---

plete and return diaries. This was the first time in 15 years the company tried such an approach, designed to reverse the declining rate of diary returns (from about 45 percent down to 38 percent over five years).

Despite all this, nonresponse poses a serious limitation on ratings accuracy. Some age groups, for example, have a particularly low response rate for radio diaries. Males aged 18 to 24 are especially difficult—Arbitron even considered (but didn't hire) an airplane-towed banner reading "Fill out your diary" during spring-break week! Those who do return diaries may not represent those who don't. Overall, diary and meter methods yield a usable response rate of about 40 percent ("usable" being variably defined, but meaning "returned on time," plus other measures of how completely the diary is filled in); the telephone method comes close to 75 percent. The number of such usable responses is termed the *in-tab sample*, the sample actually used in tabulating results and producing a given ratings report.

Making Up for Sampling Defects

No ratings company can afford pure probability sampling. Instead, researchers justify nonrandom sampling by taking into consideration the degrees and sources of "nonrandomness." For example, *stratified* sampling ensures that samples are drawn in such a way as to represent known population characteristics in correct proportions. Such research data as U.S. Census Bureau findings make this procedure possible. Both Nielsen and Arbitron use stratified sampling to relate subsample sizes to known population sizes in sample areas. Stratified sampling is also used to replace sample households that don't cooperate.

Another corrective, applied to data after collection, minimizes known biases by *weighting* results—giving extra numerical weight to information from certain sample members, corresponding to their known statistical weight in the total population. Ratings services usually apply weighting in an effort to improve the representativeness of their data. However, research that uses weighting assumes that the weight actually gives a representative picture of the population being measured. If data suffer from a high degree of nonresponse, as with some radio diaries in smaller markets, weighting can compound bias caused by such an unrepresentative sample.

• • • • • • • •

11.4 Determining Ratings and Shares

Defining Markets

A crucial step in ratings research is an accurate definition of the local market to be measured. Advertising depends on a universally recognized, national system of clearly defined, nonoverlapping markets.

Arbitron's *Area of Dominant Influence* (ADI), first developed in 1965, has become the most widely accepted system for defining television markets, though Nielsen has its own version, called *Designated Market Area* (DMA). An ADI consists of one or more counties in which stations located in a central town or city are the most viewed (see Exhibit 11.j). ADIs usually extend over smaller areas in the East, where cities are closer together, than in the West. Arbitron assigns each of the more than 3,000 counties in the United States to a single ADI, updating the assignments annually, although conditions change only slightly from one year to the next. ADIs range in size from No. 1 (New York City, with over 6.7 million television households) to No. 210 (Alpena, Michigan, with 15,700).*

Households

Another preliminary step in ratings research is to define what will count as "one" when measuring audience size. Researchers refer to this as the *elementary unit;* in electronic media research it is usually defined as either a person or a household.

A *household* is defined as a group of persons who occupy any housing unit, including a house, an apartment, or a single room.** Researchers can count households more easily than individuals, because households stay in one place and are fewer in

---

*Arbitron also uses three other terms to define slightly different market areas. The *home county* denotes a smaller area than an ADI, usually a station's county of license. And some markets are referred to as *metros*. This term comes from metropolitan statistical area (MSA), a geographical region defined by the U.S. Department of Commerce for census and other statistical purposes, usually consisting of one or more counties around a central city core. Both home and metro measures cover areas smaller than ADIs. On the other hand, *total service area* (TSA), the largest local region on which Arbitron reports, includes 98 percent of a market's viewing or listening audience, thus covering counties outside an ADI and overlapping with adjacent ADIs. Published ratings reports include maps of each area reported on, showing the differences between all these measures. Although counties are assigned to only one ADI or DMA, they may be shown in more than one TSA depending on viewing in that county.

**In 1992 the U.S. Census Bureau estimated that the country had slightly more than 92 million households, averaging 2.58 persons *per household*.

Exhibit 11.j • • • • • • • • • • • • • • • •

TV Market Definition Concepts

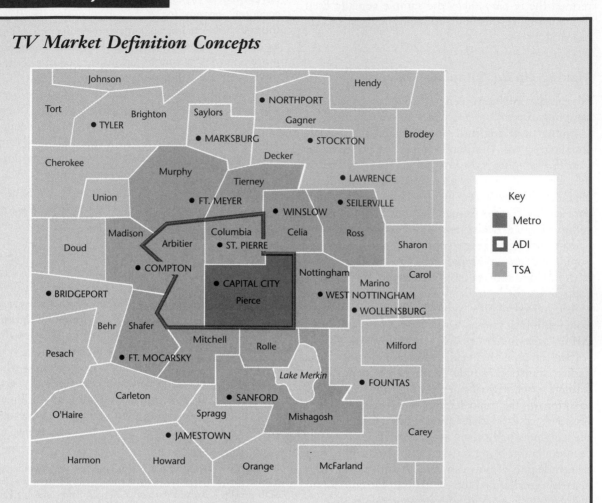

Key
- Metro
- ADI
- TSA

In this hypothetical TV market, the *Area of Dominant Influence* of stations located in or near Capital City extends to three counties—Capital City's own (also shown here as the "Metro" or home county) and two adjacent counties. Arbitron uses the term *dominant* because it assigns every county in the country to a *single* ADI. In practice, viewers often receive programs from stations in two or more markets. In those cases, Arbitron has to decide which stations dominate—that is, which are viewed most frequently by people in the market area being defined. For example, in the illustration, when viewers in Columbia County receive signals from stations in both Capital City and Northport (the large city to the north), Arbitron has determined that most of the Columbia County viewers tune to the Capital City stations. The TSA (Total Service Area) accounts for nearly all (in practice about 98 percent) of the audience of stations in the Capital City market, including counties beyond their area of dominant influence.

Source: Map © 1989 by Arbitron Ratings Company. Used by permission.

number. Households can consist not only of traditional family groups of two or more persons but also of multi-adult and single-adult households. However, household-based sampling has until quite recently failed to account for viewing in hotels, dormitories, barracks, prisons, and other institutions.

Television viewing has traditionally been a family activity, making the household a logical unit of measure, even though a majority of households now have two or more television sets, and much viewing takes place as a solo rather than family activity. A single diary or meter records viewing of each television receiver, while for radio, each listener has a separate diary. Ratings reports based on household counts thus report more or less accurately on the individual viewing or listening of all people in that household if diaries or meters cover each receiver in the home and identify individual viewers.

Radio researchers prefer to count persons rather than households because (1) radio listening usually occurs as an individual activity, and (2) much radio listening takes place outside the home, especially in autos and workplaces. As television sets become more portable and appear in cars, offices, and public places, television may also require such personal ratings. In the sections that follow, however, unless otherwise noted, we will use the household as the elementary sampling unit.

Ratings

The term "rating" is widely misused and usually confuses two quite separate industry measures: rating and share. Specifically, a *rating* is an estimate of the number of households (or persons in the case of radio) tuned to a specific channel (station, network, or program), expressed as a percentage of all television households.* It is a *comparative estimate* of set tuning in any given market (or combination of markets, for network ratings) at some specific time in the past (when the research was done). The word *comparative* tells us that a rating estimate compares *actual* audience with the *total possible* audience at that time. A rating is only an *estimate* because it is based

*Definitions used here generally conform to the National Association of Broadcasters' *Broadcast Research Definitions* (1988).

on an audience sample. Samples can yield only estimates, never absolute measurements. A rating of 100 would mean that all households with sets in a market were probably tuned to a particular channel. But this never happens: some people are not at home, some have broken receivers, and some are otherwise occupied.

The most successful nonsports entertainment program of all time, an episode of the *Roots* miniseries in 1977, had a Nielsen rating of 51.5. This means that 51.5 percent of all U.S. television households watched at least part of that episode. The Super Bowl of 1983 achieved a rating of 48.6—a record for that annual football championship. Prime-time broadcast television network shows average about a 17 rating while daytime shows average 6. HBO averages a 2 prime-time rating in terms of all *cable* television homes and an 8 rating in terms of only those homes subscribing to at least one pay cable service.* Radio stations—and public TV stations—often earn ratings of less than 1, and rarely more than 2 or 3. Such low ratings make no meaningful distinctions among stations; radio therefore relies more on *cumes* (measures of cumulative audiences) as discussed below.

Figuring ratings is pretty straightforward. You divide the number of households in a sample tuned to a given program by the total television (or radio) households in the same sample. Thus, if in a sample of 400 households, 100 tune to a given program, you find that program's rating by dividing 100 by 400 (the 400 figure is the full sample, and the 100 comes from diary or meter reports for a specific program, station, or network). This equation yields 0.25, and dropping the decimal point produces a rating of 25 percent. Exhibit 11.k illustrates basic rating concepts.

Researchers then project a rating to the total television population represented by the sample. Continuing with the above example, assume (from census data) a total market universe of 100,000 television households. Multiplying this number by the

*Note that cable-network ratings are generated as a percentage not of *all* television households but, rather, only of *all cable-subscribing* households. In 1992 the latter group (59 million) was a bit less than two-thirds the size of the former (92 million).

Exhibit 11.k •••••• •••••••••••

Ratings Concepts

A. The pie shows television set-use information gathered from a sample of 400 households, representing a hypothetical market of 100,000 households.

Note that program ratings are percentages based on the entire sample (including the "no response" households). Thus Program A, with 100 households, represents a quarter (25 percent) of the total sample of 400. The formula is 100 ÷ 400 = .25; the decimal is dropped when expressing the number as a rating.

Projected to the entire population, this rating of 25 would mean an estimated audience of 25,000 households. The formula is .25 (the rating with the decimal restored) × 100,000 = 25,000.

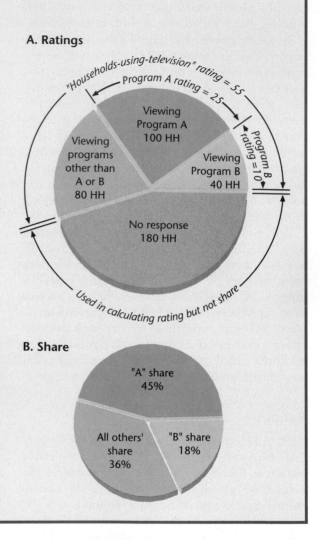

A. Ratings

"Households-using-television" rating = 55
Program A rating = 25
Program B rating = 10

Viewing
Program A
100 HH

Viewing
programs
other than
A or B
80 HH

Viewing
Program B
40 HH

No response
180 HH

Used in calculating rating but not share

B. Share

"A" share
45%

All others'
share
36%

"B" share
18%

B. The smaller pie, representing 55 percent of pie A, includes only the households using television, in this case 80 + 100 + 40 households, or a total of 220 (expressed as a households-using-television or HUT rating of 55, as shown in A). Shares are computed by treating the total number of households using television, in this case 220, as 100 percent. Thus program A's 100 households divided by 220 equals about .4545 expressed in rounded numbers as a share of 45.

rating with the decimal restored (0.25) produces an estimated total audience for the hypothetical program of 25,000 households.

Shares

A share is an estimate of the number of households (or persons for radio) tuned to a given channel, expressed as a percentage of all those households (or persons) *actually using* their receivers at that time. Recall that a rating is based on all those *owning* receivers, not necessarily *using* them.

A station's share of the television audience, on the other hand, is calculated on the basis of *households using television* (HUT). A HUT of 55 indicates that at a given time an estimated 55 percent of all television households are actually tuned in to *some* channel receivable in that market—the remaining 45 percent are not at home, busy with something else (screening videotapes perhaps), or otherwise not using television. In other words, HUT measurements combine viewing to all channels receivable in that market. HUTs vary with daypart, averaging about 25 percent for daytime hours and about 60 for prime time.

Radio research usually measures persons rather than households, yielding a *persons using radio* (PUR) rating. PUR reports usually refer to blocks of time—either individual quarter-hours or cumulative quarter-hours for a day or week—rather than to programs.

Shares are figured based on either HUT or PUR data. For television, divide each station's estimated viewing audience (in thousands) by the number of homes using television at that time, as shown in Exhibit 11.k. *A station always has a larger share than rating for a given time period.* For example, top broadcast television network prime-time programs usually average ratings of about 20, but their corresponding shares are closer to 30. (The respective shares of the two record prime-time entertainment programs noted above were 71 for *Roots* and 69 for the 1983 Super Bowl telecast.)

Television programmers use shares in making programming decisions; salespersons usually use ratings as advertising sales tools. The reason is that shares give programmers a better estimate of their competitive position within a medium, whereas ratings more readily allow comparison of advertiser exposure on radio or television with that in other media. Also, because HUT levels vary widely during different times of the year (higher in November, lower in May), programmers use share rather than rating to compare a program's competitive performance from one time of year to another.

Time of day controls overall audience size. Availability of listeners within given dayparts varies little from day to day but varies regularly by season of the year, unless extraordinary events cause people to change their normal habits. But competing programs and changes in program appeal cause audiences to tune one channel or another, increasing or decreasing the share of a given program, even though the total audience (HUT or PUR) for that time period remains about the same.

Cumes

Radio plays to such small audiences (because so many more stations divide available listeners, and because so many potential audience members choose television instead) that advertising agencies use special measures as radio (and sometimes television) buying tools. *Cumulative audience* (*cume*) figures provide a useful radio audience measurement. A radio signal reaches a relatively small number of people in any given quarter-hour, but over a period of many hours, or during the same period over a number of days, radio reaches a surprisingly large number of *different* listeners. A cume rating gives an estimate of the (cumulative) number of unduplicated persons reached by a station over a period of time, expressed as a total number of audience members or as a percentage of all potential radio listeners in a particular market. For example, during the two or four weeks that typically make up a rating period, a person who listened several times to a particular station on different days would be counted as only one person in constructing a cume figure. A person listening only once during that period would also be counted as one person, because a cume shows how many *different* people tuned to—or were reached by—the station during a given period of time.

The terms *reach* and *circulation* usually indicate cume audience measurements. Cumes are useful in commercial broadcasting because ads are often repeated. On the other hand, public television also finds cumes useful; its audiences are so much smaller than those of commercial channels that cumes over a week or month are used to report PBS and individual public television station audience reach.

Reporting Demographics

Rating reports detail audience composition in terms of gender and age. These *demographic breakouts*, or simply *demographics*, divide overall ratings into such subgroups as those for men, women, teens (aged 12–17), and children (aged 2–5 and 6–11). Adult audience age-group categories typically consist of decade units (such as men 35–44) for radio and larger units for television (for example, women 18–34 or 25–49), although "persons 12 +" serves as the basic category for determining, for example, which radio station in a given market is "number one."

In advertising's stereotyped world, most products have appeal for specific groups (acne treatments for teens, beer for men, denture products for the elderly, and so forth). Thus advertising agencies usually "buy" demographics rather than generalized audiences. Most advertisers would rather have an audience of moderate size with the right demographics for their product than a huge audience containing many members not likely to be interested.

• • • • • • • •

11.5 Use and Abuse of Ratings

Ratings and shares fill a vital function for managers and advertisers (see Exhibit 11.a)—which makes them subject to misuse. Through ignorance or misrepresentation, some users present ratings as hard-and-fast measurements instead of only estimates.

Facing Complaints

In response to complaints and investigations about ratings in the 1960s, a Broadcast Rating Council was established in 1964. Eighteen years later, in 1982, it became the Electronic Media Rating Council (EMRC), serving as an independent auditing agency representing ratings users. The EMRC accredits ratings services that meet its standards and submit to annual auditing paid for by the service provider, not by the EMRC. The procedures are sufficiently involved and costly, however, that many smaller companies don't bother to apply.

Arbitron and Nielsen disclose their methods fully, withholding from public scrutiny only some details of how they edit raw data from diaries and meters. Every ratings report contains a supplement acknowledging the multiple limitations possible in any

sampling. Arbitron, for example, lists 11 limitations in a page-long discussion of criteria for reporting station audiences.

But such candor does not stop criticism. Recent complaints have focused on the persistent failure of stations and networks to acknowledge sampling error by parading ratings "wins" of a percent or two (which are well within normal sampling error—and are thus meaningless), the tendency to underrepresent segments of society most difficult to sample, the weighting of ratings results, and the widespread station practice of trying to inflate ratings during sweeps through special programs and extra promotions.

Reliability of Ratings

Reliability in research refers to the degree to which methods yield consistent results over time. For example, the drops in broadcast television network ratings in initial peoplemeter surveys raised questions about ratings reliability, because those results clearly were *not* consistent with earlier findings. Consistent reports of lower network ratings since the peoplemeter's introduction, however, suggest that the method is generally reliable, though not necessarily valid.

Perhaps the major misunderstanding about ratings arises from thinking of them as precise measurements, rather than merely as estimates. It is important to keep in mind that ratings by their very nature provide only limited information about audiences—and do so with only limited certainty. The late Hugh Beville, Jr., former head of the then Broadcast Rating Council, suggested four guidelines that every ratings user should remember (Beville, 1981):

- Ratings are approximations.
- Not all ratings are equally dependable.
- Ratings measure quantity, not quality.
- Ratings measure [set use], not opinion.

Validity of Ratings

Validity in research refers to the degree to which findings actually measure what they purport to measure. Ratings purport to measure the *entire* broadcast audience, but in practice they can account for only the broad middle-range majority of that audience. People at ethnic, economic, and geographic extremes have less chance to be solicited by, and less inclination to cooperate with, ratings services than do people in the middle range. Thus ratings tend to underrepresent the very rich, the very poor, the very young, and ethnic minorities—and are less valid for that limitation.

Both Arbitron and Nielsen have made special efforts—including payments for completed diaries—to persuade minority respondents in their samples to participate fully. After a year's pilot project in Los Angeles, Nielsen began the first national Hispanic ratings service in September 1992, supported in part by two Spanish-language program services. It measures viewing in 800 peoplemetered homes nationwide where residents speak primarily or only Spanish. Until then, except for special studies, both Arbitron and Nielsen grouped ethnic minority viewers with white audiences.

The fact that television ratings use households rather than individuals as their measurement unit also affects validity. About a quarter of today's households consist of lone individuals whose lifestyle (and therefore broadcast use) patterns often differ from those of multiperson households.

Hyping and Tampering

A widespread industry practice known as *hyping* (or, sometimes, *hypoing*) also biases ratings. Hyping refers to deliberate attempts by stations or networks to influence ratings by scheduling special programs and promotional efforts during ratings sweeps. Radio stations hype with listener contests. Both the FTC and the FCC have investigated hyping, but with little effect. In fact, hyping efforts may cancel themselves out, since most stations resort to it. Stations feel compelled to play the hyping game because their competitors do. The arrival of 52-weeks-a-year meter ratings for television has reduced the incidence of hyping somewhat, although many stations continue the practice during sweep weeks. In any case, Arbitron and Nielsen note in ratings reports any exceptionally blatant activities so that ad-

vertisers can take them into account in market analyses.

Less commonly, ratings can be vulnerable to *tampering;* someone who can influence viewing habits of even a few households in a small sample can have a substantial impact on resulting ratings. Rating companies therefore keep sample household identities a closely held secret. Still, a few cases of outright manipulation of viewers have become public, causing ratings services to junk reports for some programs, and even entire station or market reports for a given ratings period.*

Qualitative Ratings

As long as ratings have dominated programming strategies, critics have complained that ratings encourage mediocrity by emphasizing sheer size to the exclusion of *qualitative* program aspects. Time and again, programs that are seemingly of above-average quality receive enthusiastic reviews and audiences, but fail to meet the rigid minimum-share requirements for commercial survival. Critics question whether programs that are merely accepted by large audiences should automatically win out over programs that attract smaller but intensely interested audiences. Quantitative ratings dictate this kind of judgment—the system favors "least objectionable" majority programs over possible alternatives.

In Britain and some other countries, laws require broadcasters to conduct research on qualitative aspects of programs and to take audience preferences other than mere set tuning into consideration in program decision making. Noncommercial broadcasting must, by virtue of its role as an alternative system, find evidence to support its services, which

*Sometimes the problem is sloppiness. When co-author Schofield was running a station in Tennessee some years ago, one of his top salesmen received a ratings diary. He explained the obvious conflict potential, returning the diary, for which the ratings company thanked him. During the following sweep period he received a diary again (and wouldn't tell Schofield what he did that time). Sometimes the problem is more serious than sloppy. In the same market, a syndicated program salesperson who had worked for the ratings firm told Schofield of his efforts to increase response. These efforts included visiting people in nonresponding households and helping them fill out their diaries!

often have strong appeal to only small numbers of people. The only qualitative ratings in which U.S. commercial broadcasters have shown interest seek to measure likability of performers.*

• • • • • • • •

11.6 Broadcast Audiences

Over decades of intensive ratings research, a vast amount of knowledge about electronic media listening and viewing habits has been accumulated—this is surely the most analyzed media activity in history. After examining broadcast audiences, we will turn to what is known about cable and VCR audience patterns.

Set Penetration

The most basic data about broadcast audiences, set penetration or saturation, is the percentage of all homes that have broadcast receivers. In the United States, radio and television penetration has long since peaked at more than 98 percent. Indeed, most homes have several radios and more than one television set. In short, for practical purposes the entire U.S. population of just over 92 million households constitutes the potential broadcast audience, and other services (cable, VCRs, etc.) are measured against that base.

Set Use

Households use receivers at different times and in different ways. HUT measurements tell us the average percentage of television households actually using sets at different times of the day (one set being

*Market Evaluations, Inc., regularly estimates image ratings of major performers, based on national samples of a thousand families. Using mail questionnaires, the firm constructs both familiarity and likability ratings (not necessarily the same!). The same company conducts better-known TvQ (for TV Quotient) research on the popularity of specific programs. This qualitative research uses questionnaires to determine levels of program appeal to different demographic groups.

used in a household is how Nielsen figures HUT—if more than one set is in use, that does not change the overall HUT figure). Cable has altered television HUT patterns only marginally. While the typical receiver is on about seven hours a day, few individuals actually watch more than about four hours, averaged across both demographic and daypart variables.

Television viewing climbs throughout the day from a low of about 12 percent of households at 7:00 A.M. to a high of about 70 percent in the top prime-time hour of 9:00 to 10:00 P.M. Audience levels for television change somewhat with the seasons (though less than in years past): viewing peaks in January–February and bottoms out in June, reflecting some influence of weather and leisure activity on audience availability.

On the other hand, radio listening has a flatter profile than television, with its highest peak in morning drive-time hours and little seasonal variance.

In the 1980s, with competition from cable and VCRs and then with the introduction of peoplemeter methods, combined prime-time share levels from all three broadcast television networks began to drop off—from peaks of 90 up to the late 1970s down to about 55 by mid-1992 (see Exhibit 3.n, on page 105). HUT levels remained stable, however—people were still using their sets, but often to watch cable services or VCR playbacks.

Until recently comparatively little was known about how much viewing was done away from the home. While specific network programs were studied in this regard (such as ABC's *Monday Night Football*), only in 1990 did Nielsen conduct its first national overall survey of what it then reported to be the 2 percent of overall television viewing that took place away from the household (Nielsen, 1990: 1). Early in 1993 an updated study by Nielsen (paid for by the three major broadcast networks) of the same phenomenon found that 4 percent (about six hours total) of adult weekly viewing takes place away from home. Of those over age 18, out-of-home viewing was divided primarily between workplace or college location (just over 27 percent each), with the rest in hotels or motels (17 percent), restaurants and bars (11 percent), and second homes (3 percent).* The rest (14 percent) takes place in such other locations as waiting rooms, shopping malls—even in cars! (*Broadcasting & Cable*, 15 March 1993: 54).

Another special study, this time of a specific program and its likely target audience, produced clearer results. Some two million males watch NFL weekly Monday-night football games away from home—a number large enough to raise the ratings seven percentage points per game. Many watched in someone else's home, but a third of that viewing took place in bars and clubs (*Broadcasting*, 4 May 1992: 62).

TV as Habit

Long-term trends aside, people tend to turn on their television sets day after day in the same overall numbers, with no apparent regard for the particular programs that may be scheduled. Expressed in terms made famous by Marshall McLuhan, the *medium* matters more than the message.**

Paul Klein, former CBS programming chief, proposed a similar theory, that of the *least objectionable program* (LOP). He theorized that people stay with the same station until they are driven to another station by an objectionable program. But even if they find *all* programs objectionable, according to the LOP theory, they will stay tuned to the *least* objectionable one rather than turning off the set entirely.

This accounted, wrote Klein, for the steady 90 percent of the prime-time audience gathered in by the three television broadcast networks until the 1980s. It also explained why seemingly excellent programs sometimes failed (because they were scheduled against even better programs), and why seemingly mediocre programs sometimes succeeded (because they opposed even more objectionable mediocrities). Ratings data confirmed that audience size remained stable in the 1970s, varying mostly because of changing dayparts and seasons. Rarely did a program forge ahead by enlarging the total sets-in-use figure; most succeeded only by diverting existing audience members from competing network programs.

By the late 1980s, however, this static scene changed. Competition from independent stations, cable services, and VCRs stimulated more complex and volatile audience behavior, creating problems for programmers and audience researchers, especially in prime time. Nevertheless, even with their aggregate prime-time share reduced to less than 55 percent by 1992, the three broadcast networks still had the most massive audiences of any medium and thus still constituted the most coveted national advertising vehicle.

Impact of Remote Controls

A corollary of LOP was *tuning inertia*. Whether because of viewer loyalty to a station or network, or simple laziness before widespread use of remote controls, viewers tended to leave sets tuned to the same station. For years the proportion of flowthrough viewers (those staying with the same station) remained larger than those who flowed away to different stations. Tuning inertia still strongly affects radio audiences—in large markets with as many as 40 stations from which to choose, listeners tend to confine their tuning to only two or three favorites.

By the late 1980s, however, remote control devices for television—and the increased number of cable channels—began to modify old patterns. While fewer than 30 percent of households had remote controls in 1985, by 1992 some 85 percent did—and could thus very easily change channels. The *restless viewer*, or *grazer*, has been one result—those who use a remote control to switch rapidly

---

*It was in bars that many saw their first television program back in the 1940s, first watched color television in the 1950s, and still see much of today's pay-per-view programming. Neighborhood pubs play a similar role in Britain and Ireland.

**Canadian communications theorist H. Marshall McLuhan (1911–1980), a cult figure in the 1960s, wrote a series of then-revolutionary books about the impact of media on society. In the most important statement of his thinking, *Understanding Media* (1964), he explained his view that the nature and proliferation of media said more about society than did any content carried by those media.

among several channels. They watch an average of 25 hours a week—often, they say, because they have nothing else to do. Younger viewers and males are more likely to be rapid channel switchers, and longer programs (movies rather than half-hour comedies) are most often the target of remote switching around (Arrington, 1992: 11–12).

Help for confused viewers may be on the way. The cable television act of 1992 (see Section 13.8) included provisions requiring the FCC to establish common standards for remote control devices for television sets, cable converter boxes, and VCRs by late 1993. The assumption is that the confusing number of "boxes" and remote devices now used in many homes will be sharply reduced to a single "universal" remote.

Time Spent

The total amount of time that people devote to broadcasting serves as a broad measure of its audience impact. This statistic arouses the most widespread concern among critics: any activity that takes up more time than sleeping, working, or going to school—as watching television does for many young viewers—surely, they reason, has profound social implications.

Weekly average viewing per household, combining broadcast television, cable, and VCRs, reached more than 50 hours in the mid-1980s and declined only slightly to about 48.5 hours by 1991—or nearly 7 hours a day. This total combines viewing by all members of households. As a group, women aged 18 and over spend the most time viewing, followed by children aged 2 to 11. Teenagers and college students view the least. On average, all age groups view close to the same number of hours per week; the differences between groups depend more on the accessibility of receivers than on deliberate choice. Obviously those at home have more access than those at work; and active high school or college students have less access than younger children, who spend more time at home.

Demographic Influences

Averages, however, conceal differences of detail. Demographic differences have a dramatic impact on audience set-use behavior. The following demographic variables, listed here along with examples of generalizations derived from audience research (see Exhibit 11.l), hold special interest for broadcasters:

- *Age*. Among adults, viewing increases with age.
- *Education*. Viewing decreases with education.
- *Ethnic origin*. Blacks view more than whites.
- *Family size*. Large families view more than small families.
- *Occupation*. Blue-collar workers view more than professionals.
- *Place of residence*. Urbanites view more than rural dwellers.
- *Gender*. Women view more than men.

As a practical example of how broadcasters use such information, radio programmers take into account the fact that age strongly influences format preferences. Contemporary-music formats appeal most to people in their late teens and 20s; classical, country, and MOR formats, to people in their 30s and 40s; and big-band music, news, and talk formats, to people in their 50s and older. In particular, interest in radio news and talk formats increases markedly with age. And NCAA championship basketball games, for instance, attract a much larger percentage of teens than do other sports events. In fact, gender is important for most sports events—male viewers far outnumber females.

Advertisers will pay higher prices to reach smaller but specific audiences known to buy their products than to reach larger general audiences. The more precisely an advertiser defines target-audience demographics, the higher the per-viewer cost of reaching that audience.

• • • • • • • •

11.7 Cable Audiences

Widespread use of new ways of delivering programs to viewers has complicated the researcher's task. Researching cable audiences somewhat parallels the patterns familiar in broadcast research, in terms of both methods and findings.

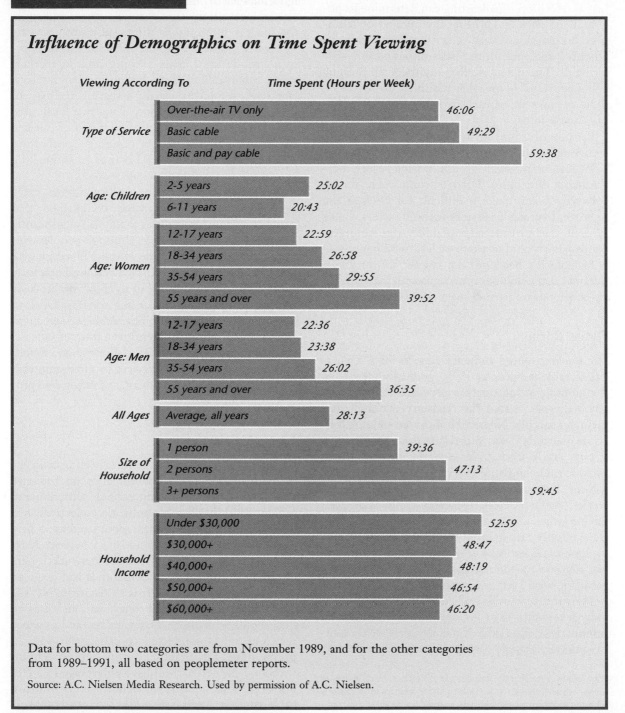

Exhibit 11.1 •••• •••••••••••

Influence of Demographics on Time Spent Viewing

Viewing According To	Time Spent (Hours per Week)

Type of Service
- Over-the-air TV only — 46:06
- Basic cable — 49:29
- Basic and pay cable — 59:38

Age: Children
- 2-5 years — 25:02
- 6-11 years — 20:43

Age: Women
- 12-17 years — 22:59
- 18-34 years — 26:58
- 35-54 years — 29:55
- 55 years and over — 39:52

Age: Men
- 12-17 years — 22:36
- 18-34 years — 23:38
- 35-54 years — 26:02
- 55 years and over — 36:35

All Ages
- Average, all years — 28:13

Size of Household
- 1 person — 39:36
- 2 persons — 47:13
- 3+ persons — 59:45

Household Income
- Under $30,000 — 52:59
- $30,000+ — 48:47
- $40,000+ — 48:19
- $50,000+ — 46:54
- $60,000+ — 46:20

Data for bottom two categories are from November 1989, and for the other categories from 1989–1991, all based on peoplemeter reports.

Source: A.C. Nielsen Media Research. Used by permission of A.C. Nielsen.

Cable Research

Just as television broadcasting can determine its potential audience by knowing the number of television households, cable television determines its potential audience on the basis of basic-cable subscribers.* Though subscriber numbers tell nothing about actual cable use, they *did* show that by 1993, cable was present in nearly two-thirds of U.S. television households.

Because of cable's many channels (and more are being added all the time), its total audience subdivides into many small groups, posing severe measurement difficulties. Further, some cable tuning converter boxes make it difficult for Nielsen and Arbitron to attach passive household meters. Cable systems that provide addressability (the ability to control and record access to each subscribing household from the headend) can resolve this problem, but only as the number of systems with that capability continues to expand in the 1990s.

Cable Ratings

Nielsen introduced audience reports for a few national cable services in 1979, gradually increasing the amount of information provided on basic and pay networks. Based on Nielsen's national peoplemeter sample, Nielsen Homevideo Index (NHI) issues quarterly *Cable National Audience Demographic Reports* and *Nielsen Cable Audience Report*s, which provide cable household viewing data in all dayparts for the largest national cable and broadcast networks. Arbitron, too, measures cable audiences, having issued its first cable audience report in 1983. Its overnight ratings from metered markets include viewing of 22 national cable services. As with Nielsen, many of its cable data are available in electronic form for local-system computer users.

However, *local* cable audiences are far more difficult to measure than national audiences. Political boundaries define cable franchise areas, often comprising only a single county or even just part of one,

whereas broadcast signals create larger markets by ignoring such artificial lines. Most individual cable-system local-origination channels attract audiences too small to interest advertisers sufficiently to warrant the cost of audience research. Nielsen and Arbitron include local cable viewing only in markets where cable audiences reach their minimum television reporting levels, usually a share percentage of three or more. This criterion means that local cable audience data appear in only about half of Nielsen and Arbitron market reports (though the proportion is increasing)—a factor that has thus far stunted the growth of advertising on cable systems.

Cable-system operators and national cable program suppliers have long complained that broadcast-based research methods significantly under-report cable viewing, although peoplemeter reports have dispelled some of these objections. In late 1992 Arbitron and Nielsen previewed new local cable ratings books designed to show market-level viewing of major national cable services. Unclear, however, was whether the new cable service might call for more sample homes, given low per-channel viewing levels. Early in 1993, both firms announced new computer-readable services to more equitably compare local, cable, broadcast, and syndicated program viewing patterns.

Uses of Cable

By the mid-1980s research showed clear evidence of national cable network influence on audience viewing patterns. Among households subscribing to cable in 1991, basic-cable networks collectively had a viewing share of 35 percent, compared to 19 percent in 1985. Pay cable hovered at a 9 percent share, down a bit from 1985. Broadcast networks' share of viewing in those same households had declined from 56 to 46 percent, across all dayparts (NCTA, May 1992: 5-A). Use of television increases in households with more than one set, and as more than one set is connected to cable television. In prime time, for example, single-set households without cable service will have an average HUT of just over 49 percent, whereas households with two cable-wired sets will have a HUT of nearly 69 per-

---

*One could argue that the number of homes *passed* by cable feeder lines—which includes many who choose not to subscribe—is a better indicator of cable's real potential.

cent (Nielsen, 1992: 75). Those latter households usually contain children, another factor producing higher HUT levels.

An interesting viewer pattern becomes clear when we look at news programming. "News is reported to be the most frequently viewed program type of those asked about, even though it is the least planned" (Heeter and Greenberg, 1989: 170). Yet despite the 24-hour availability of CNN and other news/information channels, old habits die hard—most news viewing still takes place at those times when news traditionally appears on network television stations: morning, noon, early evening, and late evening. Cable news is still thought of by many viewers primarily as a supplement to broadcast news, though cable coverage of the 1991 Gulf War and crises since has modified that view.

Some cable viewing resembles radio listening patterns—when the content is rock music. Music Television (MTV) viewers "tended to be younger, less well-educated, from larger households, and less likely to be married. Psychographically, heavy viewers were less culturally oriented, more materialistic, less conservative and tend to make use of (own) more high technology equipment. . . . Heavy MTV viewers attended more movies, watched more TV, and were newer subscribers to cable" (Paugh, 1989: 241–243). These same viewers will rent (or purchase) music videos and watch them over and over.

• • • • • • • •

11.8 VCR Audiences

Videocassette recorder use-patterns call for research approaches quite different from those for broadcasting or cable. Yet as VCRs become increasingly common (they were in three-quarters of television homes by 1992), understanding their many uses becomes vital.

VCR Research

VCRs present novel problems for media research, just as they open new options for viewers. *Time shifting* enables VCR owners to control when they watch broadcast or cable programs. VCRs also encourage skipping commercials by *zipping* or *zapping* (the latter, of course, greatly aided by remote controls). A recorded program (and possibly its advertisements) may be seen several times and by different viewers, or the ads may be seen only once if at all. To trace all of these varied patterns, Nielsen publishes a quarterly *VCR Usage Study* based on special VCR diaries filled out monthly by sample households. The time of recording of broadcast material is considered the time of viewing for purposes of determining ratings—playbacks are not counted (Nielsen, 1991: 8). Thus, even if no one ever watches the tape (a surprisingly common phenomenon), the material is *still* counted as having been viewed.

Uses of VCRs

Home VCR penetration—about 75 percent—considerably surpasses that of cable. By 1993, about a fifth of homes had more than one VCR. Five years earlier, for the first time, more VCRs were sold to homes that already had one than to homes with none (Klopfenstein, 1989: 26).

VCRs are almost twice as likely to be used to *play* tapes than to *record* them.* Although they are still used mostly to supplement real-time broadcast and cable program viewing, VCRs do give viewers more control over their time in at least four ways:

- to time-shift broadcast or cable programs for later viewing (sometimes more quickly, as in sports events, by fast-forwarding through dull spots and commercials) but not for retention after that viewing;
- to develop a permanent home video library;

*Part of the reason for playback's predominance is the difficulty of using VCRs to record—especially to time-shift. There's a standing joke in the industry that half of all VCRs in the country have their timers blinking "12:00" because owners can't even figure out how to set the time! Beginning in 1990 "VCR Plus+" offered potential relief: a remote device that, after some initial (albeit somewhat complex) programming of its own, allows users simply to punch in a three-to-nine-digit code number from television program listings and the VCR automatically records the show. Other competing systems were also being developed.

- to view purchased or rented prerecorded tapes; and
- to watch tapes made with home camcorders.

Most playback occurs during television prime-time hours. Researchers have noted that any use of a VCR (recording or playback) is usually more "purposeful" or planned than is viewing of broadcast or cable programs—in part because the VCR often is a competitor to both.

Time Shifting

In a typical week, more than half (55 percent) of VCR households record something. They record a weekly average of nearly 14 hours of programs, mostly for later viewing (what researchers call the "set off mode"). Broadcast network television is the most recorded material in both daytime (especially soap operas) and prime time. As might be expected, higher-rated shows are taped more than lower-rated programs. Independent stations come in second and original cable programming third (Nielsen, 1992: 62–65). Some researchers have found that VCR owners never watch a surprising proportion—well over half—of what they have recorded (Lin, 1990: 86–87). Further, time-shift recording has declined in recent years in favor of viewing prerecorded tapes.

Viewing Prerecorded Tapes

VCRs pull audiences away from broadcasting and cable—and movie theaters—mostly when they are used for watching rented or purchased tapes. "Half of all VCR homes rent [tapes] from once a week to twice a month" (Krugman and Johnson, 1991: 214). That rental process calls for planning, as somebody has to travel to a video outlet to obtain the tape. In part because of that more active behavior, viewing patterns for such tapes differ markedly from those for broadcast or cable programs. Usually more people together watch a rented film than would be present for a broadcast or cable program. Some research suggests that people watch rented material more intently than they do broadcast programming.

Some tapes, especially those for children, may be viewed repeatedly—even dozens of times—over fairly short periods of time. Surprisingly, perhaps, fewer people "zapped" the commercials (usually promos for other movies) that often precede prerecorded movies than zap broadcasting or cable, or time-shifted playback (Nielsen, 1992: 84–88).

Because the most convenient time to watch such prerecorded material for most people is in the evening, this application of VCRs has contributed greatly to the decline of network prime-time viewing shares. Whether such viewing is more a family or an individual matter, however, remains open for debate, as studies have shown conflicting results (Lin, 1990: 89). VCRs offer an example of history repeating itself—early studies of television viewing in the 1950s asked the same question: Does viewing bring people together, and if so, do they communicate or merely watch in silence? They found the same inconclusive results.

VCR Libraries and Camcorder Use

Building a video library (and then screening it) and using a camcorder are additional applications of the home television receiver that typically have little to do with broadcast or cable programming. One study found no demographic difference between families that had developed tape libraries and those that had not. In many cases, families display their video collections along with their books, suggesting that people increasingly see the two narrative forms of video and print as interchangeable. Indeed, both can be used repetitively and on demand (Jordan, 1990: 169). One driving factor in developing a family video library is the desire to increase viewing options for children, including their ability to replay favorite items often.

Some research shows that the longer people have VCRs, the more they use them in different ways. The VCR's fascination, in other words, does not appear to wear off much with time; if anything, it increases (Klopfenstein et al., 1991: 529). Of course, central to this phenomenon is simply understanding how to program the VCR to make it do everything the instruction manual says it will do!

As camcorder penetration increases (it totaled about 19 percent early in 1993), combination use of camcorders and VCRs also increases. The camcorder to some extent replaces still-picture cameras (especially Polaroid instant-picture cameras) and has completely replaced home-movie cameras. Thus, it produces part of a "family archive," as most owners use the device to record events such as weddings, parties, birthdays, school events, and vacations, adding sound and motion to what used to be preserved merely as still pictures in both senses of the term.

● ● ● ● ● ● ● ●

11.9 Other Applied Research

Nonratings research tries to find out what people like and dislike, what interests or bores them, what they recognize and remember, and what they overlook and forget. To study such subjective reactions, investigators usually use *attitudinal* research methods, which reveal not so much people's actions (such as set use) as their reactions—their *reasons* for action, as revealed in their attitudes toward programming.

Focus Groups

Commercial attitudinal research often makes no attempt to construct probability samples, because it usually does not try to make estimates generalizable to whole populations. Instead, investigators choose respondents informally. They assemble small panels, called *focus groups*, and gain insights about people's motivations through informal discussion-interview sessions.

Program concept research, for example, tries out ideas for potential new shows. A focus group's reactions to a one-page program description can help programmers decide whether to develop an idea further, to change details, or to drop it entirely. Advertisers often test concepts for commercials before making final commitments to full production. These tests may use simple graphic storyboards, or

they may employ *photomatics*, videotaped versions of original storyboards with camera effects and audio added to make them look and sound something like full-scale commercials.

To test new or changed programs, producers often show pilot versions to focus groups. People watch, give their reactions, and sometimes discuss reasons for their attitudes with a session director. Frequently producers, writers, and others study reactions by watching these discussions through one-way mirrors or by screening videotapes of the session.

Program Analysis

Minute-by-minute reactions to a program can be studied using a *program analyzer*—a device first developed in the 1940s and now thoroughly computerized—that enables test-group members to express favorable, neutral, or unfavorable reactions by pushing buttons at regular intervals on cue. The machine automatically sums up the entire test group's reactions, furnishing a graphic profile. A follow-up discussion can then probe for reasons why audience interest changed at given moments in a script, as revealed by peaks and valleys in the graph.

Theater vs. In-Home Testing

The movie industry has long used theater previews to gauge audience response. Several firms specialize in staging similar theater previews (sometimes called *auditorium testing*) of television programs and commercials. Investigators sometimes test advertisements under a pretext of testing programs, with commercials seeming to appear only incidentally. Viewer reactions come out in questionnaires or discussions (Exhibit 11.n).

Any staged preview has the disadvantage of being conducted outside the home. But cable television has introduced a testing method that allows researchers to test viewers in their normal surroundings, using their own receivers. One research firm owns several small cable systems that it uses for research on commercials. Two groups of subscribers receive different versions of test materials. The company asks subscribers to keep diaries of their

Exhibit 11.m ●●●●●●●●●●●●●●

Patterns of VCR Use

Research on patterns of VCR use in the early 1990s found that the device is used most often for time shifting. Taping most often occurs in the evening to record programs on network affiliates (or second most often, daytime serial dramas), and typically happens when the receiver is not otherwise being used.

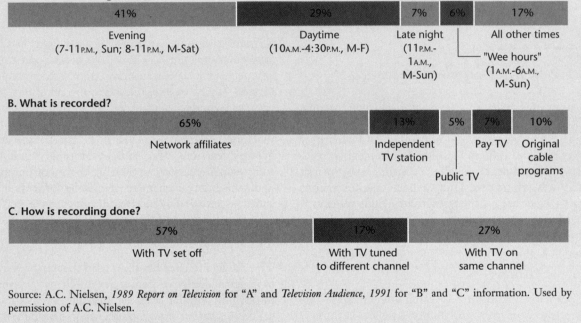

A. When is recording done?

41%	29%	7%	6%	17%

Evening
(7-11P.M., Sun; 8-11P.M., M-Sat)
    Daytime
(10A.M.-4:30P.M., M-F)
    Late night
(11P.M.-1A.M., M-Sun)
    "Wee hours"
(1A.M.-6A.M., M-Sun)
    All other times

B. What is recorded?

65%	13%	5%	7%	10%

Network affiliates   Independent TV station   Public TV   Pay TV   Original cable programs

C. How is recording done?

57%	17%	27%

With TV set off   With TV tuned to different channel   With TV on same channel

Source: A.C. Nielsen, *1989 Report on Television* for "A" and *Television Audience, 1991* for "B" and "C" information. Used by permission of A.C. Nielsen.

---

purchases, thus providing concrete evidence of the influence that commercials have on actual buying behavior.

Physiological Testing

Most of the methods described thus far depend on self-analysis by panel members. In an attempt to eliminate subjectivity and to monitor responses more subtly, researchers have identified a number of involuntary physical reactions that give clues to audience thinking. Reactions measured for this purpose include changes in brain waves, eye movements, eye pupil dilation, breathing rates, pulse rates, voice quality, perspiration, and sitting position (the "squirm test").

For example, a number of researchers have capitalized on the two-sided nature of the human brain. Each side has its own specialized functions and reacts to different stimuli. Reasoning ability seems to

Theater Television

Theater testing described on page 415 does not always provide a true indicator of program success. Famous in the industry are the poor tests of such long-running hits as *All in the Family* (12 seasons, 5 as a top-rated program), *The Mary Tyler Moore Show*, and *Married . . . with Children*. Likewise, many now-forgotten programs tested very well. The problem, according to researchers, is that theater testing tends to favor the familiar and known and to downgrade presentations that are new and different. Some producers use testing all the time—only a few have good enough reputations (or contracts) that they can pass up pilot testing.

be located in the brain's left side, and emotions in the right. It follows that product ads with emotional appeal should, if correctly designed, stimulate primarily the right side of the brain more than would commercials that appeal mainly to logic. Commercials shown to viewers wired for brain-wave recording can be tested to determine whether the messages draw the desired brain-wave responses.*

Test Markets

Test markets realistically appraise advertising effectiveness, but they call for complex and expensive planning. Researchers select two or more markets, distant from each other but well matched demographically. Viewers in each then see a different version of a proposed national advertising campaign, carried either on a television station or on a cable channel. Researchers judge the effectiveness of each version by its influence on product sales. They measure sales by keeping track of the physical movement of goods in the market or (more easily) by using *direct marketing*, offering the product for sale only through mail order or use of toll-free telephone numbers.

Research on Children

Several companies specialize in analyzing children's likes and dislikes and how these influence adult purchasing decisions. Marketers know that children have an impact on what brands or products adults buy. One research firm gains insight into children's preferences and motivations by turning a group of kids loose in a miniature supermarket. As the children go on a shopping spree, researchers secretly observe and record their behavior. But such firms avoid publicity, both to keep results confidential and to avoid criticism for taking what some would consider an unfair advantage of children.

Audience Response

Telephone calls and letters from listeners or viewers about programs, performers, and commercials provide additional audience information. Indeed, early broadcasters relied entirely on voluntary listener mail for audience information. But people who write or call a station are not a good representative sample of the entire audience. Research has shown that letter writers differ significantly from the general population in terms of race, education, income, type of job, age, and marital status—all differences important to advertisers and programmers. Further, letter-writing campaigns for or against a given point of view, product, or service can give misleading impressions about general audience reaction.

For these reasons, stations take phone calls less seriously than systematically gathered data. Nevertheless, a few strong letters of complaint, especially

---

*In the 1950s *subliminal advertising* caused a flurry of interest. Such ads consisted of simple messages of a word or two flashed on a movie theater screen so briefly as to go unnoticed. Such messages appear to have an impact below the conscious level (hence the term *subliminal*, meaning below the threshold). Subliminal messages supposedly stimulated audiences to buy greater quantities of popcorn or other foods mentioned in the messages. Fear that unsuspecting television audiences would be brainwashed by thought control led the FCC to ban it. While there is no other formal ban on such advertising in other media, subliminal approaches have not been used in television for years.

if they give the impression of a spontaneous response rather than of merely ready-made form letters, do get attention. Broadcasters and advertisers know that a few complaints of a focused kind probably represent a sizable number of dissatisfied listeners or viewers.

•••••••

Summary

11.1 Applied audience studies include those that generate program ratings and others that test subjective appeal of programs or advertising. Arbitron and Nielsen are the two most important ratings research companies. Arbitron does individual market surveys for both radio and television, whereas Nielsen does television-only surveys for both networks and local markets.

11.2 Researchers gather ratings by means of written diaries, passive household meters, peoplemeters, telephone surveys, personal interviews, or a combination of these. Network television ratings are based on peoplemeter research. Concern about audience fatigue in using peoplemeters has pushed research on a passive peoplemeter scheme in the mid-1990s. Each method has strengths and weaknesses—combinations of methods usually provide the most reliable results, but at a higher cost.

11.3 All ratings make use of three kinds of sampling: behavioral (usually a function of set tuning), time (most sampling studies are conducted occasionally, not continuously), and number of people included (all ratings use relatively small, representative cross-sections of populations). In order to be representative of a larger population, sampling requires good sample frames, high response rates, avoidance of bias, and systematic random selection of sample members. All measurements based on sampling suffer both sampling and nonsampling errors.

11.4 Ratings measure audience size in both local and national markets. The most commonly used market delineation is Arbitron's Area of Dominant Influence, or ADI. Ratings estimate the proportion—stated in percentages—of the total *possible* audience (households owning receivers) that is tuned to a particular program. Shares estimate the proportion of actual viewers or listeners (households or people using television—HUTs or PUTs—or people using radio—PURs) tuned to a program. When audiences are small, as in the case of radio or public broadcasting, "cumes" are used to show the aggregate reach of a program over a period of hours, days, or weeks. Ratings gathered through diaries and peoplemeters can best supply audience demographics—sex, age, education, income, and other characteristics.

11.5 Ratings provide a reasonably accurate picture of broadcast audiences as long as users keep in mind their severe limitations on accuracy and significance. Ratings are generally reliable but have problems with validity. Stations and networks engage in hyping and tampering during sweeps, putting the process in question. Qualitative ratings have not been widely adopted because of high cost and lack of advertiser demand.

11.6 Within given dayparts, the size of radio and television audiences remains remarkably stable, with audience members tuning from channel to channel rather than turning sets on and off. Radio use peaks during morning and afternoon drive times, while television use grows during the day and peaks in prime time. Widespread recent use of remote controls has weakened the long-held "least objectionable program" theory. Generally, broadcast audiences are those who are less educated, have lower incomes, and are urban rather than rural; further, adults tend to watch more as they age.

11.7 Development of audience ratings for cable is still relatively new. Problems include measuring audiences across the many channels available, as well as channels that carry the same program material. Most research thus far has been done on cable networks, as local-origination channel audiences are too small to warrant the cost of such research.

11.8 Research on VCRs is even more difficult, in part because of great differences in record and playback activity (mostly the latter). VCRs serve many uses, all of which empower viewers to control what they watch and when: playing of prerecorded material, time shifting, building of personal libraries, and so on.

11.9 Other applied research tests commercials, programs, and performer popularity, both during program planning and after production. Theater testing lacks the normal, everyday surroundings of in-home tests, the latter often accomplished by use of multiple cable channels showing different programs or advertisements. Sometimes entire towns become test markets. Such research, which often relies on small focus groups, probes the reactions of test subjects for personal motives and attitudes. A few specialized companies research children's product preferences.

Chapter 12

Impact

The hours we spend with electronic media—typically more each day than any other leisure activity—makes important our need to understand their varied impacts. This chapter reports some of what research has discovered about the many ways electronic media have affected our lives—and raises questions for which we don't yet have complete answers. Researchers now strongly feel that the background audiences bring to their use of electronic media is more important to understanding media "effects" than any study of media content.

12.1 Developing Effects Research

People have long assumed that spending so much time with electronic media simply had to have *some* impact, good or bad. Such assumptions take on practical significance when policy decisions are based on supposed or real media impact. For that reason, and because of scientific curiosity, research-ers have spent considerable effort to determine media effects.

Early Findings

Early "media" research focused on the impact of *mass propaganda* efforts used during World War I (1914–1918), before broadcasting arrived. After the war, the extent of deception by propagandists on all sides showed how thousands had been manipulated. The postwar advent of radio broadcasting—along with emergence of the politically threatening new communist regime in Russia—made fear of increased propaganda manipulation more alarming. This led to more research on social and psychological dynamics of propaganda.

The 1920s' concept of media impact saw messages as so many bullets of information (or misinformation) aimed at passive groups. Because researchers assumed that messages penetrated and caused specific reactions, the concept became known as the *bullet* or *hypodermic-injection* theory.

By the late 1930s researchers had realized the bullet theory was oversimplified in treating message receivers as mere passive targets. New and more sophisticated studies discovered that audiences react to messages as individuals. Media effects therefore depended on many variables within individual audience members.

Researchers labeled such factors, many not directly observable, *intervening variables* because they come between messages and effects. They vary a message's impact because of each person's previously acquired attitudes, traits, experiences, social situation, and education. Intervening variables explain why an identical message often has a different impact on different people.

World War II (1939–1945) stimulated renewed interest in propaganda research. Yale scholars studied orientation films used by the U.S. Army to indoctrinate new recruits. The research focused on measuring *attitude change*, a type of impact that lent itself readily to "before/after" laboratory tests. These studies initiated a new phase of effects research, laying the groundwork for "an attempt to set forth principles of communication effects in scientific terms backed by scientific evidence" (Schramm, 1973: 221).

One important intervening variable studied in the 1940s was the personal influence of *opinion leaders*, as contrasted to media's *im*personal influence. One theory suggested that media influence often passes through leaders to followers rather than to all individuals directly. For most people, opinion leaders play a greater role in various decisions than does direct influence of radio, newspapers, magazines, or books. Other studies confirmed and refined this *two-step flow* hypothesis of media influence (Katz and Lazarsfeld, 1955), which had great impact on research for two decades.

Selective Effects

Yet even opinion leaders are not influenced in direct proportion to the amount of persuasive media content they receive. People pay attention to messages that fit their established opinions and ignore those that don't. Researchers discovered that because of this *selective exposure*, media tend to *reinforce* existing views, rather than converting people to new ones.

Existing mindsets color how people perceive media they select. Those who select the same message may interpret it in different ways. Though the stimulus is constant, the response varies. Called *selective perception*, this variable shows that people interpret messages based on their opinions and attitudes rather than receiving them passively (as the old bullet theory had supposed).

Selective perception also accounts for a *boomerang effect*. Experiments have shown that those with strong beliefs tend to misinterpret messages with which they disagree—they distort evidence or retain only those elements that reinforce their existing attitudes, rather than allowing the message to change even slightly their preset thinking. Thus propaganda can boomerang, producing exactly the opposite of the intended effect (Cooper and Jahoda, 1947). As a classic example, many television viewers misread the antibigotry message of the "Archie Bunker" character in *All in the Family* in the 1970s. They saw an endorsement of the very prejudices of which producer Norman Lear intended to make fun.

Even lacking prejudice, people under emotional stress may have difficulty accepting evidence that contradicts an existing mindset. Striking examples of this kind of selective perception occurred during the famous Orson Welles "Invasion from Mars" broadcast (see Section 2.1). The 1938 drama simulated news reports of alien landings, fooling a number of listeners despite warnings early and midway through the drama. A later study revealed how some listeners tried to confirm the broadcast's authenticity. Even when presented with evidence that it was fiction, they turned facts around to support their conviction that the invasion was real:

- "I looked out of the window and everything looked the same as usual so *I thought it hadn't reached our section yet.*"
- "My husband tried to calm me and said, 'If this were really so, it would be on all stations', and he turned to one of the other stations and there was music. I retorted, '*Nero fiddled while Rome burned*' " (Cantril, 1940: 93).

Such stubborn refusal to forsake an existing mindset suggests that people have a kind of internal gyroscope that tends to maintain a consistent set of attitudes, opinions, and perceptions. Psychologists developed several versions of a concept known generally as *congruence theory* to account for this tendency, which is an important intervening variable in determining communication effects. Such theories hold that a person's internal state of mind is usually in balance or congruence. A message that contradicts established opinions causes dissonance, lack of congruity, or imbalance. An effort to restore balance (conscious or unconscious) follows. It might take the form of rejecting the message (saying the source is "unreliable," for example), distorting the message to make it fit the existing mindset, or, least likely, adjusting the balance by accepting the new idea—conversion to a new point of view.

These concepts all came out of the social sciences. A very different way of looking at communication came from engineering with publication of *The Mathematical Theory of Communication* (Shannon and Weaver, 1949). Here, information is seen as a transmission system, using such familiar engineering terms as channel capacity, noise, encoding, decoding, and bit (see Exhibit 12.a). *Information theory* contributed valuable insights to media research, including the concept of *feedback* (Wiener, 1950)—whereby communicators modify their messages in response to information that comes back from audiences. But because they lack the immediate give and take of face-to-face conversation, media operate at a disadvantage. It takes time for them to receive and analyze feedback and to modify their product accordingly.

More recent *accommodation theory* takes an even more contextual approach, arguing that an individual's own information system supplies raw inputs from which motives, explanations, and purposes can be developed and applied to accomplish behavioral outcomes. Media are but one part of a person's information system as evidenced by the importance of what background factors any individual brings to his or her use of media. Personal experiences and interpersonal contacts heavily color the way all of us learn from and make use of media (Anderson and Meyer, 1988: 44–45).

Research Topics

Because communication involves a chain of events, it is best explained as a *process*—as suggested by the simple model in Exhibit 12.a. A communicator initiates a process that produces an end result—if indeed definable effects occur. Study of the process can be directed to any one, or any combination, of five different elements: (1) *originators* of messages, (2) *contents* of messages, (3) *channels* through which messages travel, (4) *audiences* that receive messages, and (5) *effects* of messages. A pioneer communications researcher, Harold Lasswell, summarized these stages by saying that the objects of research could be identified by posing the question: "*Who says what in which channel to whom with what effect?*"*

- Researchers study the "who" of communication to learn about sources and shapers of media content—those who act as *gatekeepers*. FCC regulation and station or network "clearance" offices are types of gatekeeping, as is the selection, placement, and editing of all content presented. Gatekeeping studies research how controls operate, where gates in information flow occur, and what effects they have on content when it reaches its destination. Individuals and institutions are gatekeepers in mass media.

- "What" studies usually consist of content analyses of electronic media programming and thus concern us only insofar as they indicate potential impact—as with measures of the amount and types of violence present in programs of different kinds aimed at different audiences.

- As to the "which channel" question, research shows that media channels differ in their psychological impact because audiences form expectations for each medium and interpret what each

*Adapted from Smith, Lasswell, and Casey, 1946: 121. It should be understood that this single-sentence formula intentionally simplifies the communication process. A later commentator, for example, proposed that a more complete statement would ask three additional questions: *why?* (policy studies), *how?* (studies of communication techniques), and *who talks back?* (studies of feedback process).

Exhibit 12.a •••••••••••••

A Simple Communication Model

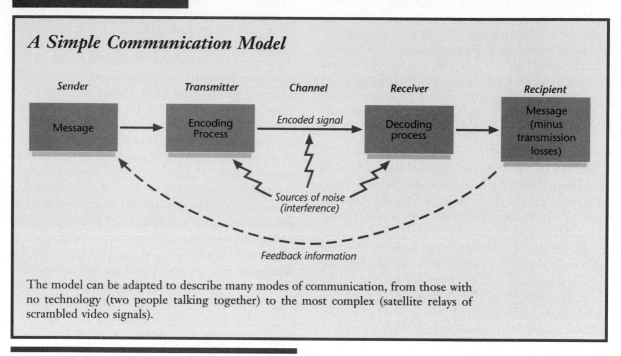

| Sender | Transmitter | Channel | Receiver | Recipient |

Message → Encoding Process → *Encoded signal* → Decoding process → Message (minus transmission losses)

Sources of noise (interference)

Feedback information

The model can be adapted to describe many modes of communication, from those with no technology (two people talking together) to the most complex (satellite relays of scrambled video signals).

delivers accordingly. Since 1959 television broadcasters have sponsored Roper Organization image studies of the medium. The surveys regularly ask respondents which of several media they would believe in case of conflicting news reports. Since 1961 they have consistently chosen television over other media by a wide margin. In 1991, 58 percent chose television, 20 percent newspapers, and 6 percent radio as the most credible medium (Roper Organization, 1991: 22).

- Ratings are an example of the "to whom" factor of Lasswell's model inasmuch as they detail media use with *media exposure* or *time-spent* data. Breakdowns of audiences into demographic subcategories give further details about the "to whom" of broadcasting. But in researching the "to whom" question, scholars use more detailed personal and social-group indicators to study composition of audiences than does ratings research. In particu-

lar, the child audience has been extensively analyzed, using such variables as race, intelligence, social class, home environment, and personality type. These analyses relate audience characteristics to effects. Researchers ask such questions as: What types of children will be most likely to believe what they see on television—and what types will imitate what they see?

- Finally, Lasswell's "with what effects?" culminates his questions because communicators, content, channels, and audiences all help determine the ultimate outcomes of communicating. Joseph Klapper summarized effects theories as of three decades ago in his influential *The Effects of Mass Communication* (1960). Summarizing more than a thousand research reports, Klapper concluded that ordinarily communication "does not serve as a necessary and sufficient cause of audience effects, but rather functions among and through a nexus of mediating factors and influences." Media largely reinforce existing perceptions and beliefs. They may persuade people to buy a product, but not to change a political allegiance or religion. The broadcasting industry welcomed this conservative conclusion, known as the *law of minimal effects*, because it gave apparent scientific sanction to the industry's argument that programs or advertisements could not be blamed for causing antisocial behavior. (Klapper went to work for CBS shortly thereafter.)

In the 1970s, however, opinion began to shift away from minimal effects concepts, largely because of intensive research on violence (discussed in Section 12.7). Researchers now even avoid talking about *effects* as such. The very word implies an oversimplification of what is now understood to be an extremely complex process. Without denying that specific media content might under specific conditions have specific effects on some specific people, researchers prefer to speak in terms of *associating* certain inputs with certain outputs. They avoid reliance on a simple, straight-line cause-effect relationship. Exhibit 12.b summarizes the stages of research development, from the simplistic cause-effect concept of early studies to our present interest in looking more deeply into the many variables involved in impact.

The People Problem

In designing studies on media impact, researchers face the frustrating problem that impact is usually made up of *subjective responses* hard to determine by direct observation and measuring instruments. Remember the point made earlier—that what people bring to their use of media is far more important than anything media bring to viewers and listeners. How can one *objectively* measure human attention, understanding, learning, likes and dislikes, and opinion formation? Some of these effects do produce observable physical cues—brain waves and other involuntary physical signals can be detected—but these signals usually reveal little about subjective experiences in human terms.

Even when communication prompts overt, observable responses, a subjective link still intervenes. In tracing the sequence of events from cause to effect, researchers lose the trail when it disappears into what the people being studied are thinking. What goes on inside the human brain obviously influences any outcome, but we can't yet study the process directly. Thus most impact research today relies in whole or in part on questioning people about their subjective experiences—how they think and feel about something—rather than on observing their reactions. Self-reporting, of course, is not altogether reliable. People are sometimes unwilling—or unable—to tell the truth about their inner experiences, or they may be forgetful or unaware of their own subconscious motivations. Furthermore, listening and viewing usually occur privately, often in situations inaccessible to an outside observer. Thus data gathering, whether based on self-reporting or direct observations, almost always introduces an element of artificiality, referred to as *intrusiveness*.

Methods of Research

Investigators usually select one of four major types of research: sample surveys, content analysis, laboratory experiments, and field studies. In the past decade or so, a fifth method, ethnography, has gained wider acceptance, though it is time-consuming and expensive, and provides results from which generalizations are difficult to derive. Each method has its own pluses and minuses in terms of the extent of its reliance on subjective data, its intrusion on respondents' lives, and—most important for researchers hard pressed to finance their project—its cost. See Exhibit 12.c for further analysis.

- *Sample surveys:* The research strategy most familiar to the general public is the sample survey used in opinion polls and audience ratings reports. Such surveys can estimate characteristics of entire populations through use of very small random samples. An additional advantage, as with ratings, is that data are gathered in settings where listening or viewing normally takes place. Commercial ratings services use sample surveys to measure that

Exhibit 12.b ●●●●●●●●●●●●●●

Development of Media Effects Research

Time Period	Prevailing Viewpoint	Empirical Basis
1. (1920s–1930s)	Mass media have strong effects	Observation of apparent success of propaganda campaigns
		Experiments show immediate attitude change after exposure to messages
		Evidence of selective perception—persons ignore messages contrary to existing predispositions
2. (1940s–1950s)	Mass media largely reinforce existing predispositions, and thus outcomes are likely to be the same in their absence	Evidence of personal influence—persons are more influenced by others than the mass media
		Evidence of little influence on voting
		No relationship observed between exposure to mass-media violence and delinquent behavior among the young
3. (1950s–1960s)	Mass media have effects independent of other influences, which would not occur in the absence of the particular mass-media stimuli under scrutiny	Evidence that selective perception is only partially operative
		Evidence that media set the context and identify the persons, events, and issues toward which existing predispositions affect attitudes and behavior
		Evidence that television violence increases aggressiveness in the young
4. (1970s–1980s)	Process behind effects so far studied may be more general, suggesting new areas for research	Research finds that under some circumstances TV may influence attitudes and behavior *other than* aggressiveness
		Many agenda-setting studies
5. (1980s–1990s)	Individual differences in audience background and needs are found central in defining media impact	Qualitative studies (including ethnographies) of media as one of many social resources

Source: First four segments adapted from George Comstock et al., *Television and Human Behavior* (Columbia University Press, 1978). Used by permission.

Exhibit 12.c ●●●●●●●●●●●●●

Media Research Strategies Compared

Strategy	Subjectivity	Typical Level of Intrusiveness	Cost
Sample survey	high	moderate	variable[a]
Content analysis	moderate[b]	nil	moderate
Laboratory experiment	variable	high	low[c]
Field study	low	low	high
Field experiment	low	moderate	high

[a]Costs of a simple local telephone survey can be low, but national telephone surveys employing sophisticated sampling and data gathering procedures (such as the commercial ratings services use) can be very high.

[b]Subjective in that coders make judgments in classifying content items.

[c]Cost can be high if sophisticated testing equipment or elaborate simulations are employed.

most basic and objective behavior—set tuning—without reference to the impact of actual listening or viewing after the set is on. Sample surveys thus tell us nothing about the *causes* of tuning. This is the major weakness of the survey strategy: "causal implications typically cannot be determined" (Comstock et al., 1978: 493).

- *Content analysis:* Classification of programs into various categories constitutes one form of content analysis. On a more sophisticated level, content analysis categorizes, enumerates, and interprets message content. Media researchers have used content analysis to study advertising copy, censors' actions, cross-national program comparisons, television specials, specific types of new content, violent acts in programs, and the portrayal of minorities in television dramas. They also study content details that reveal what electronic media are saying or implying about various subjects. One problem is deciding how to define content categories to be studied and compared

because researchers usually apply their own ideas of meaning to television programming. Thus they interpret the message when in fact they may misunderstand or fail to perceive the importance of context—the private history and set of circumstances experienced by a viewer that no researcher can see.

- *Laboratory experiments:* Regarded as the classic strategy for conducting behavioral research, laboratory experiments allow researchers to control some experimental factors precisely while excluding others. Both subjectively reported and objectively observed data can be derived from such experiments. For decades, the most popular experimental variable in studying communication was *attitude change.* A group of people is tested for current attitudes on a given topic. The experimenter then exposes them (either in a face-to-face talk or via a recording) to a persuasive message on that subject. A second test then determines if any change in attitude has occurred. One trouble with this approach is that attitudes measured in a laboratory situation do not always govern real-life actions. People often say one thing but then do another. This discrepancy has been noted in differences between expressed television program preferences and actual television viewing. Further, lab experiments put people in artificially simplified situations unlike the complex ways in which most of us actually use media.

- *Field studies:* Research projects done in more natural settings, known as field studies, record behavior in "the real world" without unduly intruding or otherwise influencing participants. In studying the impact of violent programming, for example, field-study researchers can watch children in their normal home or school environment rather than in a lab setting. A compromise between the tight controls but artificial context of the laboratory experiment and the unstructured naturalism of the field study can be achieved in field experiments. Here, researchers set up situations for testing in field or real-life situations. However, these experiments cost a great deal of time and effort to arrange, and some of their methods can be just as questionable as those used in laboratories. Thus, though especially valuable in marketing studies, they are relatively rare.

- *Ethnographic studies:* One indicator of the integration of communication research with other sociological work is the rise in the past decade or so of ethnographic media research. The researcher becomes part of the (usually small) group being studied and this *participant observation* over extended time periods allows a realistic "window" on media consumption patterns to develop, along with some sense of subtle media effects. For example, researchers might be assigned to families of different ethnic background to observe their different ways of using radio or television programming. Drawing from research traditions in anthropology and sociology, ethnographic studies take a variety of forms. They are expensive because of their intensive and time-consuming nature—and are not readily generalizable to larger groups in society because of their narrow study-group base.

• • • • • • • •
12.2 News

Because most Americans depend primarily on television for news (Roper Organization, 1991: 11), and have done so for decades, television journalism clearly plays an important role. One controversial media issue is how news is presented and consumed.

Most of us see the world beyond our own lives pretty much the way cable and television news present it to us (radio is a minor player except for breaking events). To what extent do media present an accurate news picture? Why do people feel a loss of confidence in news media—and many other institutions in American life? Are they merely blaming the messenger carrying only bad news, or is something "wrong" with those news media? Answers to these questions—and there are several—require some understanding of how "news" is defined, collected, and reported.

Gatekeeping

Media can report only a tiny fraction of everything that happens in a day. On its way to becoming neatly packaged pieces on the television screen, raw reporting of events passes through many editorial *gatekeepers*. Some open and close gates deliberately, deciding which events to cover in which places and how stories should be written, edited, and positioned in the news presentation. Some gatekeeping occurs inadvertently, depending on accessibility of news events or availability of transportation or relay facilities.

All media profoundly affect any material they transmit, both deliberately and inadvertently. Some gatekeeping has an institutional or an ideological bias—or both. Institutional biases can develop from news organization priorities ("If it bleeds, it leads"); ideological biases grow out of individual political, social, economic, or religious beliefs ("We don't reveal the names of rape victims").

Television demands pictures. This tends to bias the medium toward covering events that can be visualized, despite the fact that much news has no inherent pictorial content. Impacts of this visual bias include (1) a preference for airing stories that have dramatic pictures (fires, accidents, disasters) and (2) a forced effort to illustrate nonvisual stories with often irrelevant stock shots (as when file pictures of bidding on the floor of the stock exchange illustrate a story on financial trends). To counter—yet also to feed—this tendency, news directors increasingly use computer-based graphics to illustrate nonpictorial stories with animated symbols, charts, and other "visuals."

Agenda Setting

One example of gatekeeping's filtering and shaping process is deciding which subjects to present. Gatekeeping focuses our attention on selected events, persons, and issues temporarily in the news. The list changes frequently as old items drop out and new ones claim attention. Researchers term this overall process of selection and ranking *agenda setting*, one of the primary ways in which media shape our perception of the world. In short, while media may not tell us what to think, they do tell us what to think *about*.

A related impact is *prestige conferral*. The very fact that an event appears on the air gives it importance. Well-known anchors and correspondents lend glamour and significance to the events and people they cover personally. A former presidential press secretary described television as a giant megaphone, greatly amplifying the significance of some events (Nesson, 1980). If the story were not important, would Dan Rather, Tom Brokaw, Peter Jennings, or Bernard Shaw be covering it? Conversely, can an event really matter if television chooses *not* to be there?

In 1984–1985, for example, television helped focus world attention on starvation in parts of Africa. The drought-caused disaster had been building for two years before news reports created a public outcry that vastly increased aid efforts. In mid-1985, "Live Aid," an unprecedented satellite-fed 16-hour rock music marathon seen in more than 80 countries, led to promised contributions of some $75 million. Again television had opened the gate and set the agenda for expanded aid efforts. Unfortunately, continued reports of starvation and other disasters in Africa and elsewhere amidst a worldwide economic downturn has benumbed viewers, making it hard to repeat the "Live Aid" story.

In 1992 observers pointed out that a disastrous famine in war-torn Somalia was hardly noted by news media until it had been under way for months—making recovery that much harder and condemning thousands more to death from starvation. The delay in coverage was due in part to Somalia's distance from American concerns—European and domestic news crowded the African story off newscast agendas. Some critics argued that if Somalia had oil wells—or was not seen as simply another poor, black, African nation—the stories might have developed more quickly. Media coverage naturally increased substantially when U.S. troops landed late in 1992 to protect UN food convoys.

Covering Controversy

Similar agenda setting is evident in coverage of the AIDS epidemic. Constant television coverage of the disease's spread after 1980, health agency efforts to counter that spread, case studies of individuals who are infected and become spokespersons to warn others (especially celebrities such as basketball star Magic Johnson)—all serve to focus more attention on AIDS and the search for its cure. Coverage sharpens controversy about how the epidemic should be countered. Yet there is also a potential for backlash—heavy AIDS coverage repels many unaffected viewers.

Concern about the environment in the past few years has been encouraged by television coverage of the bad news (burning tropical forests, disappearing animal species, air and water pollution) and the good (planting of new forests, fining polluting companies, enacting tougher laws). Steady coverage of such a controversy builds public attention and concern by focusing the agenda of public discussion.

Coverage of the abortion controversy features highly vocal groups and speakers on both sides of this emotional, political, religious, and personal issue. Night after night, sparked by special protests or the latest legal decision, the issue is waved in the faces of viewers at home. Here again, television news largely *reflects* divisions evident in society at large. The camera and microphone merely record events—though in so doing, they keep a controversy at the top of the current agenda.

Media News Staging

Television's need for images creates the temptation to enhance the pictorial content of news stories artificially. Even when news crews make no move to provoke reactions, the very presence of cameras in tense situations can escalate or sensationalize ongoing action.

Legitimate exercise of news judgments in editing can raise awkward problems for electronic media. Critics often accuse news documentaries of bias and tampering with facts. Such controversy scares away advertising support—one reason for the decline of these programs in recent years.

As a practical matter, however, some artificiality is accepted as normal in news coverage. In televised interviews, for example, a camera usually focuses on the interviewee. "Reverse angle" shots of the interviewer are usually taken afterward and spliced into the interview to facilitate editing and to provide a visual give-and-take. This tactic allows a single camera to cover interviews. Even the FCC has long recognized the need for this kind of latitude, noting that

> every television press conference may be said to be "staged" to some extent; depictions of scenes in a television documentary—on how the poor live on a typical day in the ghetto, for example—also necessarily involve camera direction, lights, action instruments, etc. . . . Few would question . . . asking public officials to smile again or repeat handshakes while the cameras are focused upon them. (FCCR 1969b: 656)

Deliberate staging by reporters, however, is a far more serious violation of normal news practice. All too often we hear of a station or network carrying as news something set up by a news crew showing a drug bust, illegal betting, or the like, without any indication of the staging process. Early in 1993, NBC News got into trouble over what turned out to be a staged and partly faked story concerning General Motors truck safety. The head of the News Division was forced out and several others were fired. But the damage to NBC's credibility was still considerable (see Section 10.10).

More recent and troublesome is the ability to change photographs, film, or videotape digitally to show things that never happened. This kind of staging may merely modify a sky to make it more dramatic, or may totally alter a real event to suggest something quite different. The technology is so good than even experts are hard-pressed to discern when such manipulation has taken place. Whatever the excuse for these staged or digitally enhanced deceptions, they detract from the credibility of all electronic media journalism.

Pseudoevents

Outright staging of events by the *subjects* of news, on the other hand, grows more common every day. It occurs when press agents or public-relations counselors seek to plant stories in media or to create happenings to attract media coverage. Daniel Boorstin (1964) coined the term *pseudoevent* to describe these contrived happenings, analyzing the many forms they take, such as press conferences, trial balloons, photo opportunities, news leaks of confidential information, and background briefings "not for attribution."

Not all preplanned events are bad. For a newsworthy figure such as a president, a certain amount of ceremonial event–making is expected. Where media personnel get in trouble is with deliberate attempts to palm off such nonevents as genuine news. Organizations interested in maintaining a positive public image constantly churn out self-serving material in the guise of news. Government departments and businesses alike create and exploit pseudoevents.

Some broadcast news departments avoid using self-serving "news" handouts. But free video news releases tempt stations short on photographic material. These brief items supplied by business and government PR offices are often visually interesting, with the real message subtly buried. For example, a dramatic sequence of helicopter shots showing offshore oil drilling used to illustrate an energy story might just "incidentally" show the name of the oil company. Or a film about highway safety patrols may feature a particular make of car.

Impact on People Covered

Pop artist Andy Warhol once said that everybody is famous for 15 minutes. Media coverage makes for an instant celebrity—either positive (such as a sports figure or hero in a disaster) or negative (a serial killer brought to trial). People react differently in the often-sudden glare of media publicity: some thrive and then move back to normal lives, while others become uncomfortable and have trouble adjusting when media interest fades.

Media coverage in 1991–1992 of celebrations over the return of Americans held hostage for several years in Lebanon raises questions about the impact of media coverage on returning victims. Some critics speculated that the overwhelming barrage of media attention might cause added psychological trauma to such victims. Others countered that such coverage is *cathartic* both for victims and for the country at large, by giving expression to widespread relief.

In less unusual situations, media coverage undoubtedly does affect news subjects. Some subjects featured in *60 Minutes* reports, for example, have ended up paying fines or going to jail (or been released after wrongful jailing) after on-camera exposure by program reporters. Though the coverage itself did not cause the penalties, cameras and reporters called attention to the subjects' earlier actions in compelling fashion.

Court Trials

More widespread but also more ambiguous impact on news subjects may occur when television covers court trials (see Section 14.3, as well as Exhibit 14.c on p. 508). The long-time ban on cameras and microphones in virtually all courtrooms arose from assumptions that (1) broadcast coverage would affect behavior of participants (witnesses, lawyers, and defendants), and that (2) these effects would be detrimental to the judicial process. Later however, experience showed that once the novelty of being photographed wore off, subjects of coverage betrayed little reaction. They eventually accepted both equipment and crew as a normal part of their surroundings.

Three factors account for this minimal impact. Equipment became smaller and less obtrusive (able to operate with existing light levels, for example) than was the case when the ban first went into effect in 1935. News crews became more professional and sensitive to the need to avoid disruption. Finally, society became more tolerant, even expectant, of electronic media access to official activities.

• • • • • • • •

12.3 World Events

Electronic media are especially important in bringing distant world events to audiences—and do so with varying impact. During World War II (1939–1945), radio's first war, network news and entertainment played a highly supportive role in building morale.

Television's first war coverage came with the Vietnam conflict (the Korean War of 1950–1953 occurred during the formative years of television news, when live coverage from such a remote distance was impossible). Television coverage for the 1965–1975 decade made Vietnam a "living room war," in the words of *New Yorker* critic Michael Arlen (1969)—and the lessons learned there by both media and military have heavily affected television's impact on national morale and government policy in the conflicts since.

Vietnam

David Halberstam, who won a Pulitzer prize for his work as a war correspondent in Vietnam, supports the thesis that television had a decisive impact on the

Vietnam War and its outcome—"The war played in American homes and it played too long" (Halberstam, 1979: 507). In total, this longest war in United States history played in living rooms for 15 years. CBS sent its first combat news team to Vietnam in 1961, and news photography of the final evacuation of Saigon, showing desperate pro-American Vietnamese being beaten back as helicopters lifted off the landing pad atop the U.S. Embassy, came in 1975 (see Exhibit 12.d).

At first, Vietnam coverage tended to be "sanitized," stressing U.S. efficiency and military might and playing down the gore and suffering of actual combat. While little direct military censorship was imposed, as had been the case in previous wars, in this undeclared war generals and presidents had public relations uppermost in their minds. Thus control of access to events could serve the same end as more blatant censorship. A more violent phase of news coverage came as a result of the early 1968 "Tet" offensive, which brought fighting to the very doors of the Saigon hotels where correspondents stayed. Broadcast news from a host of network and local-station reporters turned increasingly to combat realities, and Vietnam became a real war in American living rooms, not the sanitized version of military public relations. Analyzing the contradictory images projected by television news, critic Edward Epstein wrote in *TV Guide*:

> It is no doubt true that television was to a large extent responsible for the disillusionment with the war, as those in the media take relish in pointing out. But it is also true that television must take responsibility for creating—or at least, reinforcing—the illusion of American military omnipotence on which much of the early support of the war was based. (1973: 54)

Following the Tet offensive by the North Vietnamese, several events combined to turn U.S. opinion against the war. For one thing, television's leading anchor, CBS's Walter Cronkite, gave a sharply negative assessment of the war after a visit to Vietnam (as David Halberstam put it, for the first time a war had been declared over by an anchorman). Loss of Cronkite's support for the war was said to have solidified President Lyndon John-

son's decision not to run for reelection. At about the same time, vivid photographic images from the battlefields—many carried on television—became icons of American disillusionment. Correspondent Morley Safer—later famous on *60 Minutes* but then relatively unknown—was responsible for film showing an American Marine holding a cigarette lighter to the straw thatch of a South Vietnamese hut, starting a fire that leveled 150 homes. Another image showed a South Vietnamese general calmly shooting an enemy suspect in the head. One gripping still photo showed young children running from a napalm attack, among them a girl screaming. Another lasting image showed American Marines helping the last victims escape the conquering Vietcong in 1975 (again, see Exhibit 12.d).*

More Wars

Television's effect on public perception of the Vietnam conflict raised troublesome questions about future war reporting. Could a nation at war afford to allow television freely to bring home the horror of combat night after night? A 1983 terrorist bombing that killed some 240 Americans in a U.S. Marine barracks in Beirut seemed a case in point. Television coverage of the bombing's aftermath undermined public support for the "peacekeeping" role of the Marines in Lebanon, making the venture politically untenable—American troops pulled out shortly thereafter.

On the other hand, would the public support a war that was made temporarily invisible by rigid military censorship? To the dismay of journalists, a U.S. invasion of the tiny Caribbean island of Grenada in 1984 suggested that it might. Alleging security concerns, the military barred all media access to the initial assault. For the first 48 hours, the world knew what happened only from military press releases. Subsequent press disclosures of military

---

*Controversy over the war and its coverage revived a decade later when General William Westmoreland, once a U.S. commander in Vietnam, brought suit against CBS for a *60 Minutes* report alleging a cover-up in reports of enemy troop strength, as discussed in Section 14.3.

Exhibit 12.d •••••• ••••••••

Television Goes to War

Pictures provide the most lasting media imagery of war. (A) shows victorious American Marines re-occupying the U.S. Embassy in Kuwait City in February 1991 at the height of the brief land portion of the Gulf War. (B) shows another American Embassy—this one in Saigon, then the capital of South Vietnam, which was about to fall to North Vietnamese forces in early 1975. Refugees were being evacuated to ships off shore. (C) is perhaps the best-known image of the long Vietnam War—in it, the chief of South Vietnamese policy executes a Viet Cong suspect during the 1968 "Tet" offensive. NBC also telecast this scene in its nightly news program.

Sources: Photo A from Reuters/Bettmann Archive; B from UPI/Bettmann Archive; C from AP/Wide World Photos.

bumbling in the invasion and apparent official misrepresentation of circumstances leading to the invasion came too late to dispel entirely the aura of success and righteousness surrounding the Grenada "rescue" of American civilians allegedly endangered by the volatile political situation on the island.

The public largely supported the action and applauded the administration's decision to limit media access—and impact.

Strong media criticism of this abrupt departure from prior practice led to agreement that in future actions the military would set up a news pool to cover events from the outset. When American fighter-bombers attacked targets in Libya in 1987, and again when an American navy vessel accidentally shot down an Iranian airliner over the Persian Gulf in 1988, the military reported in detail almost immediately after the conclusion of the actions. There were no news blackouts—though in the latter case investigations later suggested the full story had not been immediately told.

In the 1980s Reagan administration efforts to bring down the Sandanista regime in Nicaragua and related guerrilla fighting in several Central American countries served as testing grounds for television journalism's post-Grenada maturity. Controversy surrounded coverage of these conflicts. New Right politicians claimed that television weakened efforts to gain public support for "freedom fighters"; others, remembering Vietnam, said that aggressive television coverage might serve to keep American soldiers out of another prolonged, undeclared conflict.

Terrorism

News media problems took a vicious turn when terrorist organizations began committing crimes to gain news coverage. In the 1980s small and desperate political or religious groups seeking world attention increasingly employed violence against usually innocent third parties. Such *publicity crimes* paradoxically transform pseudoevents into real events. Bombings of airport terminals, hijackings, and kidnappings, the most common kinds of terrorist stories, pose difficult ethical dilemmas for all news media. The very act of reporting a publicity crime transforms media into accomplices, and the eagerness with which the public awaits news about it makes all of us inadvertent accomplices as well.

Publicity crimes reached bizarre new heights with the taking of American hostages in the Middle East—U.S. Embassy personnel in Iran in 1979–1980, a load of TWA airline passengers in Beirut in 1985, and other hostages in Beirut in the late 1980s, some held for more than six years. Never before had American broadcasters faced such a news dilemma. Every time they showed footage of street rallies with marchers burning American flags or of hostages paraded before cameras to mumble obviously forced "praise" for their captors, the television networks gave the terrorists priceless publicity. Newscasters develop every possible angle on such stories, including often-intrusive interviews with hostage families. Intense network competition increases the emphasis on each crisis.

Observers complain that television's massive coverage encourages future terrorists by providing them with an international forum. Criticism centers especially on coverage of news conferences staged and controlled by terrorists, whereby media appear captive to terrorist manipulation. Cable and broadcast news people often counter that they are merely serving the public's insatiable demand for more coverage.

Persian Gulf Crisis

Lessons learned in all these events heavily influenced television's coverage of and impact on the 1990–1991 Gulf War, when the United States led a successful UN effort to throw Iraqi troops out of occupied Kuwait. The Pentagon invoked strong censorship and pooling of reporters, making it almost impossible for media to report from troop sites during the months-long build-up unless a military public-affairs officer was present (SGAC, 1991).

An intense air war began in mid-January 1991 and was seen live on American East Coast television screens in prime time as CNN cameras in Baghdad focused on falling bombs and anti-aircraft fire. Reporters Peter Arnett and Bernard Shaw continued live *voice*casts from Baghdad by means of a high-tech satellite telephone (the antenna for which can fit inside a suitcase) that relayed signals to America by means of the Inmarsat satellite navigation system (costing $7–10 per minute of use). Given CNN's lack of moving pictures to go with the dramatic broadcasts, the coverage was almost a throwback to network radio during World War II.

When reporters questioned Pentagon officials the next day as to the impact of initial bombing runs, officers made clear that much of what they knew had come from the same CNN reports seen by everyone else. That pattern was evident in the first few days of the air war, when (as shown by research) 44 percent of those turning to television watched CNN coverage while 41 percent turned to one of the three traditional broadcast networks (Birch Scarborough, 1991: 9). CNN ratings jumped sharply during the brief war. (Radio, on the other hand, no longer in possession of large news budgets or staffs, fell behind.) Later analyses often attibuted CNN's "arrival" as an accepted news source to its stellar role in reporting all aspects of the Gulf conflict (see Exhibit 12.e).

During these same days, television also brought wartime uncertainty into viewer homes as Iraqi "scud" missiles began to fall on Israeli cities (though Israel was not a combatant) and U.S. bases in Saudi Arabia. Reporters donned gas masks and continued their reports looking like alien beings. Viewers could see and almost share the tension as reporters expected poison gas at any time (though in fact it never came). The missile stories added visual support to administration policy in the Gulf crisis.

Even more than had been the case with Vietnam, Operation "Desert Storm"—thanks to time-zone difference and satellite relays, as well as around-the-clock reporting—was a "living room war" in American prime time. But it was a far more *controlled* television war than Vietnam had been, the result of tight Pentagon limits on media access to troops and events—and of censorship, often directed more at the possible political impact of negative coverage than at any military security need.

Television showcased military successes, highlighting exotic hardware through the use of Pentagon-released video and making widespread use of on-air expert commentators—many of them retired military officers. There was little or no analysis or criticism of the military effort or of diplomatic efforts immediately before or after—instead, the emphasis was on live-action shots of American technological superiority. Later, in mid-1991, television covered victory parades in Washington, New York, and elsewhere. These programs projected an America throwing off old self-doubts that had lingered since the loss in Vietnam nearly two decades before.

Only months after the war was over did disquieting television reports about Iraqi civilian losses, allied soldiers killed by "friendly fire," and attempted cover-ups of other military mistakes become widely reported—but by then few were paying attention. Pentagon and administration officials called the Gulf War press pools a model for future conflict coverage, while reporters argued the opposite—that censorship had prevented their usual multifaceted job of reporting. Most public-opinion surveys, however, found that viewers were generally satisfied with

what they had seen and believed military controls to have been justified. It seemed likely the contest of wills over the "proper" role of news media in wartime would continue into the *next* war.*

Video Diplomacy

Television news has served a similar role in reporting peacetime diplomatic activities and seems to have increased impact on such efforts. From being a passive observer/reporter (with film reports delivered by air and shown hours or a day later) at world summit meetings in the 1950s and 1960s, to providing the world with live pictures relayed by satellite of President Nixon's precedent-breaking trip to the People's Republic of China in 1972, televison news teams have become an accepted participant in world affairs.

It was a participant in more ways than one when in 1978 CBS's then-anchor Walter Cronkite, while interviewing Egyptian and Israeli leaders by satellite video, sensed a willingness by two old enemies to meet face-to-face to settle long-standing differences. Egyptian President Anwar Sadat later flew to Jerusalem and Israeli Prime Minister Menachem Begin paid a return visit to Cairo. Television covered the unprecedented meetings, adding to public pressure for the two countries to reach agreement. Both leaders then joined President Jimmy Carter at his Camp David retreat for lengthy negotiations leading to a treaty between the two countries—the whole process having started with on-air "invitations" by a news anchor to two national leaders to reason with one another.

An access problem emerges when media seek to cover a dramatic story in another country, which does not want the story reported. CNN and the broadcast television networks gave extensive satellite-delivered coverage to weeks of peaceful student demonstrations in Beijing in the People's Republic of China in mid-1989—until Chinese officials "pulled the plug," fearing world reaction to live pictures of the military repression to come. Viewers then saw news reports based only on still photos, maps of the city's downtown area, and reporters' voices via telephone, rather than the on-the-spot live pictures they had come to expect. Still, even such limited reporting prompted protest demonstrations by Chinese and others in cities around the world.

CNN's growth and worldwide distribution by the late 1980s had created a new diplomatic voiceway. As political communications expert Kathleen Jamieson put it, "Once you know [the president] watches CNN, if you're a world leader, you go on CNN" (quoted in McNulty, 1991: D6). On several occasions during the build-up to the 1991 Gulf War, diplomats would see others speaking to reporters and thus would learn about new or changed positions on issues, or would go so far as to call CNN to speak out in response—all, of course, much more rapidly than with traditional diplomatic communication.

Television coverage of Soviet leader Mikhail Gorbachev's efforts after 1985 to open up the previously tightly sealed Soviet Union were instrumental in widening media access to stories formerly out of reach. The Soviet leader's several visits to the United States made him a popular figure here. Unlike his predecessors, he seemed more like a politically astute Western leader who plunged into street crowds to meet everyday people. But reports of change in the Soviet Union led to demands for change in Soviet-dominated Eastern Europe.

Revolution in Eastern Europe

Television covered the dramatic changes in Eastern Europe and the USSR in and after 1989. Indeed, television's impact seemed to speed collapse of the Soviet system. Given 45 years of Soviet control of these countries, the process was remarkably fast and free of bloodshed. Widespread availability of broadcast reports through multiple microwave and satellite links overwhelmed old regimes no longer able

*When American Marines came ashore in Somalia at the end of 1992 in an effort to restore order and assist U.N. food convoys trying to reach starving populations, there were complaints about heavy media coverage from crowds of reporters, some using bright camera lights on what looked almost like a Hollywood set. Even media proponents agreed there could be too *much* coverage.

to control communication within or among the one-time satellite nations. Nor could hardliners send out tanks and troops, as they had done in earlier revolts when television was not present—not under the steady eyes of cameras beaming scenes by satellite instantaneously around the world.

The highlight—really an icon for a revolution—was the televised scenes, many at night under harsh lights, of Berliners tearing down the hated wall that had divided their city for nearly three decades. The hardline East German regime collapsed in days as video reports carried to the world joyous scenes of Berliners demolishing remains of the concrete divider. In the following weeks, similar shifts were reported in Poland, Hungary, Czechoslovakia, and Bulgaria. In Romania a brief, bitter battle developed between forces of the long-time dictator and revolutionaries, providing television pictures of hard fighting and the eventual overthrow of communism.

In mid-1991 television highlighted the tension of what turned out to be a short-lived but frightening coup attempt in Moscow, when hardliners tried to revive the former rigid communist regime that had prevailed before Mikhail Gorbachev's more open government. For two days, television showed tanks moving in the streets of Moscow and highlighted the brave front put up by Russian leader Boris Yeltsin, leading those who challenged the coup plotters (see Exhibit 12.f). The video image of Yeltsin's defiance not only protected his position during the coup, making it harder for its leaders to defeat him, but also led to his rise to greater power in the months that followed. The weakened Gorbachev soon stepped down, as reaction to the coup hastened the end of the nearly 75-year-old USSR. The world watched in amazement as television showed the red hammer-and-sickle flag being lowered over the Kremlin on New Year's Eve 1991, to be replaced with the Russian flag—a scene previously imaginable only in spy novels.

But just as lingering and even more haunting in the months that followed was television's coverage of rising ethnic unrest in former communist-dominated countries. As had often happened in centuries past, Balkan political divisions broke into bitter civil war in what was once Yugoslavia. Viewers were treated in mid-1992 to oddly juxtaposed pictures of a war-torn Sarajevo and its devastated population (the city had been the site of the 1986 Winter Olympic games), and prosperous Barcelona hosting the 1992 games.

Night after night, television news showed the destruction of once-handsome cities and their hapless populations. Television pictures of concentration camps and reports of massive forced population shifts (ethnic or religious "cleansing" as it was called) increased pressure on other European governments to intervene to stop what struck outsiders as senseless tribal warfare.

• • • • • • • •

12.4 Politics

Early on, politicians recognized that radio could have significant impact on elections. So, in writing laws controlling broadcasting in 1927 and again in 1934, they saw to it that they would have access to radio (and, later, to television) when running for election. But beyond this self-serving consideration, electronic media have obvious impact as facilitators and reporters of democratic processes.

Election Campaigns

Radio exerted an impact on political campaigning almost from the start. Radio speeches by Calvin Coolidge, whose low-key delivery suited the microphone, may have been a factor in his 1924 reelection. Radio became especially important to Democratic candidates because it gave them a chance to appeal directly to voters, bypassing Republican-controlled newspapers. Franklin Roosevelt used radio masterfully in his four presidential campaigns, starting in 1932.

Television brought Madison Avenue sales techniques to the presidential campaign of 1952, when a specialist in hard-sell commercials, Rosser Reeves, designed television spots for Dwight Eisenhower. Commercialization of political campaigns has increased ever since. By 1968, when Richard Nixon

Exhibit 12.f

Television Covers a Revolution

A.

B.

Many observers feel the very presence of television hastened the fall of communism in Eastern Europe and the USSR in 1989–1991. Television news distributed by satellite links rapidly spread news of unrest and encouraged similar moves in neighboring countries— overthrowing once-tight control of information that had characterized the repressive regimes that ruled those countries for more than four decades. In these scenes from CNN coverage, demonstrators in late 1989 (A) celebrate the first holes punched into the three-decade-old wall that had divided Berlin, and (B) cheer Russian leader Boris Yeltsin (waving the flag) as he leads those in opposition to the short-lived, hard-line coup in Moscow in mid-1991.

won the presidential election, television had become—and remains—the most important factor in national political campaigning.

After the 1960s parties redesigned their conventions to become more effective television presentations. Convention managers began to time events

to the second, with set minutes allowed for "spontaneous" demonstrations. In reality, they left little to chance—a practice that, by 1988, had the ironic effect of forcing networks to reconsider just how much news value remained, given conventions' declining appeal to viewers. The 1992 conventions were the first the networks did not fully cover (C-SPAN, and to a lesser extent CNN, did so for those who needed their quadrennial immersion—and could receive the cable services), limiting themselves to an hour or two each evening.

Given television's impact on campaign outcomes, it might seem a forgone conclusion that candidates who buy the most time and hire the best media consultants would inevitably win. But research and experience makes clear that candidates using more television do not always prevail. One reason may be that television visualizes campaigns in two very different ways—with paid partisan advertising that candidates control, but also with objective news and public-affairs coverage. Bona fide news programs about candidates have a credibility that 30-second advertising spots and candidate-controlled appearances can never obtain.

But even campaign news suffers from television's constant need to be economically efficient. A survey of network evening newscasts during presidential campaigns from 1968 through 1988 showed that candidate comments—"sound bites"—grew steadily shorter. Whereas typical stories in 1968 included candidates speaking for more than 40 seconds, by 1988 this duration had shrunk to fewer than 9 seconds on average (Hallin, 1991: 2). Worried about the trend, CBS announced in 1992 that its evening news would use no quotations shorter than 30 seconds—only to quickly discover it had a difficult time finding sufficient news value in comments that long.

The total amount spent on television—one indicator of its predicted impact—peaked in the 1988 campaign at just under $230 million and remained about the same for 1992. Within that total, network political advertising has declined since the 1984 race, whereas national-spot and local advertising for political races has increased (*Broadcasting*, 9 January 1992: 108).

Televised Candidate Debates

Starting in 1960, televised debates between presidential candidates began to steal the spotlight from conventions and other candidate appearances. The first debates, four 1960 confrontations between candidates John F. Kennedy and Richard M. Nixon, were made possible by a special act of Congress exempting the televised event from the "equal time" law (see Section 14.6). Often called "Great Debates" (though in fact they were neither great nor debates), these carefully choreographed face-offs, especially the first one, probably decided that close race. Exhaustive research suggests that Kennedy seemed more precise and visually crisp to television viewers while Nixon sounded more persuasive to radio listeners (Rubin, 1967).

After the Kennedy-Nixon confrontations, presidential debates lapsed for 16 years because incumbent presidents (Lyndon Johnson and Richard Nixon, respectively) would not agree to give their opponents the attention a debate necessitates. Then Gerald Ford, running in 1976 for national office for the first time (having succeeded to the presidency when Nixon resigned over the Watergate scandal), agreed to debate Democratic nominee Jimmy Carter—who won the election. A pattern seemed in the making four years later, when Carter agreed to debate GOP nominee Ronald Reagan—and once again the incumbent lost (see Exhibit 12.g). But the picture changed in 1984, when Reagan faced Democrat Walter Mondale. Many believed that Reagan lost the first debate but came back much stronger in the second, recovering the momentum of his campaign and going on to win a landslide reelection.

The two 1988 televised "debates" (again, a panel of journalists questioned both candidates who rarely addressed each other directly) between President George Bush and Democratic nominee Michael Dukakis seemed to have little overall impact on that election's outcome. Bush came across as "lean and mean," whereas Dukakis seemed wooden and cold. The single vice presidential debate showed up the weakness of an ill-informed Dan Quayle, who was trounced by politically savvy Texas Senator Lloyd Bentsen.

In 1992 Bush faced Democrat Bill Clinton, who was seasoned after months of hard primary campaigns studded with televised debates among Democratic candidates. Though debates now seemed an accepted part of presidential campaigns, it appeared there might be no 1992 face-off as the two candi-

Exhibit 12.g ●●●●●●●●●●●●●●●●

Televised Election Debates

A.

B.

Nationally televised debates have become expected presidential campaign rituals. (A) John F. Kennedy debates Richard M. Nixon in one of four confrontations in 1960, with Frank McGee of NBC as moderator. The next debate would come only in 1976 when Jimmy Carter debated—and beat—Gerald Ford. Regular debates in the next several elections saw only minor format changes. (B) In 1992, however, several

debate formats were tried in three presidential candidate face-offs. In the one shown here, Bill Clinton, George Bush, and independent candidate Ross Perot (not seen in this picture) appeared in a theater-in-the-round setting answering audience questions as well as directly debating one another.

Sources: Photo A from NBC/Globe Photos, Inc. Photo B from Reuters/Bettmann Archive.

dates quarreled over dates and format.* Eventually

*After 1988 a bipartisan debate commission had recommended doing away with the traditional, but awkward panel of journalists asking questions, and having instead one moderator keeping things on track while encouraging candidates to have at each other more directly—a real debate, in other words. For the 1992 general campaign, the commission urged three debates between presidential candidates, and one between candidates for vice president. After considerable wrangling, everyone accepted the plan, though with a variety of formats. The vice presidential face-off used one moderator, whereas the three presidential debates employed varied methods, some entailing questions from journalists, others using studio audience questions or a moderator. The bipartisan commission "sponsored" them all. Had President Bush not been behind in pre-election polls, the debates might not have taken place at all. Indeed, his weak performance in all but the final debate demonstrates the danger of debates for an incumbent.

they agreed on four debates (one for the vice presidential candidates), which took place over just nine days in mid-October. A third-party candidate—independent Ross Perot—took part in the three presidential debates, adding often witty commentary on and sharp criticism of both major parties.

Talk Show Syndrome

Television's election role—and probably its impact—changed in several ways during the 1992 campaign. In addition to the decline of the conventions as televised spectacles, change was most evident in widespread use of broadcast and cable talk shows to air candidate images and ideas—or even to declare one's candidacy. During a February 1992 appearance on CNN's Larry King call-in show, Texas billionaire Ross Perot began his grassroots independent candidacy by announcing his willingness to be drafted if volunteers placed his name on all 50 state ballots. Later, in July, Perot returned to King's show to explain why he had abruptly pulled out of the race before even formally declaring his candidacy (see Exhibit 12.h). Then, in a yo-yo campaign, he came back yet again to explain his *re*entry just a month before election day. He spent about $70 million of his own money to buy network time to express his views—and to pay his many "volunteers." In a throwback to 1950s' political advertising, Perot purchased network half-hour slots in prime time to present folksy put pointed, chart-illustrated "fireside chats" (in effect, "infomercials") on his economic views.

Every candidate appeared on local and national call-in talk shows during the primaries, giving viewers an unprecedented chance to call in questions. Bush, Clinton, Perot, Quayle, and Gore all appeared on network morning programs as well as other talk shows as the campaign reached its height in October. Democratic candidate Bill Clinton even played the saxophone on the late-night *Arsenio Hall Show*, and a desperate George Bush appealed to young voters by appearing on MTV.

Election-Night Predictions

The impact of television coverage becomes especially controversial on national election-day evenings. Early television reports of voting trends in Eastern states have been blamed for lower voter turnout in the West, where polls remain open. Members of Congress have been concerned that early predictions of winners and losers—or candidate concessions—in national races adversely impact Western state and local elections, although few research findings have been reported to confirm or refute this charge. The networks agreed in 1985 not to air predictions of any state's vote until after polls in that state had closed. They largely adhered to that promise in reporting results of the national elections of and after 1986. Indeed, on election night 1992, Clinton was announced as winner only minutes after West Coast polls had closed.

Exhibit 12.h

Talking Politics

The 1992 presidential election campaign saw widespread use of a new campaign device—the topical talk show. In a pioneering example, independent candidate Ross Perot appeared with CNN's Larry King to announce his original candidacy, to explain his withdrawal six months later, and again to discuss his re-entry in the campaign. Perot used television almost in place of direct appearances as a way of reaching his supporters.

12.5 Government

Aside from coverage of seemingly endless election campaigns, television has dramatically affected the governing of America.

Presidential Television

After the campaign, a newly elected president enjoys a huge advantage over political opposition in obtaining media coverage. With easy access to television, the chief executive has endless opportunities to manufacture pseudoevents to support his policies or to divert attention from his failures. No matter how blatant this exploitation may seem, editors rarely dare ignore presidential events. Virtually everything the head of state says or does has news value.

Presidents often make foreign visits—heavily covered both here and abroad—to other heads of state as a diversionary tactic. President Kennedy may have been the first to capitalize on this ploy: "The farther he was from Washington, the less he was seen as a partisan political figure and the more he was viewed as being President of all the people" (Halberstam, 1979: 316). President Nixon applied the same tactic, making several overseas trips during his domestic Watergate crisis. Sometimes it does *not* work: President Bush's hectic Asian trip in early 1992 received bad press because of its heavy-handed U.S. business emphasis and because he became ill at a state dinner in Japan—all played out on television cameras for everyone to see.

For greatest impact, the White House can call on broadcast networks and CNN to provide simultaneous national coverage of a presidential address. National addresses can give the president a gigantic television audience—though independent television and cable channels increasingly siphon off potential viewers with entertainment programs. No law requires broadcast or cable networks to defer to presidential requests for time. Indeed, not until President Lyndon Johnson's administration (1963–1969) did these become customary. Perhaps because of the Nixon administration's Watergate troubles, networks began to evaluate such requests more critically after 1974. Presidents since Nixon have all been turned down at least once when they asked for time.

All presidents have been accused—more so recently—of dodging open confrontations with the media, preferring carefully orchestrated press conferences or "photo opportunities" to create a favorable image. Reagan was prone to embarrassing errors when ad-libbing replies to questions, obliging his staff to follow up with hasty "clarifications." Frustrated by their lack of access as the number of press conferences declined in the late 1980s, White House correspondents resorted to shouting questions at the president as he walked to or from the presidential helicopter—an undignified practice encouraged by presidential remoteness but useful to the administration as a way of making reporters appear rude.

Congressional Television

During television's formative years, veteran politicians such as House Speaker Sam Rayburn dominated Congress—and had no love for media. Lack of television coverage limited the public's image of Congress. Only when the president came to address a joint session did television enter Congress: "Then the congressmen could be seen dutifully applauding, their roles in effect written in by the President's speech writers" (Halberstam, 1979: 250).

The Senate, unlike the House, began allowing television coverage of its committee hearings (subject to committee chair approval) as early as the 1950s, leading to some notable television public-affairs coverage that had repercussions on the careers of participants. But for decades neither congressional body allowed broadcast access to its legislative sessions.

Although bills to authorize radio coverage of House debates had appeared regularly since 1941, approval for live television as well as radio coverage finally came only in 1979. Even then, the House refused to let outsiders run the show, establishing its own closed-circuit television system run by House employees. Broadcasters could carry the signal, live or recorded, at will. Unenthusiastic about coverage they do not themselves control, few broadcasters used even excerpts of House debates. Cable subscribers could see gavel-to-gavel coverage on C-SPAN, the cable industry's noncommercial public-affairs network established for this purpose.

The Senate experimented with live *radio* coverage in 1978, when National Public Radio carried some 300 hours of debate on the Panama Canal treaties. Finally, in 1986, the Senate approved television coverage of all floor sessions. Congress had at last given itself a degree of video parity with the White House. C-SPAN added a second channel to its service to cover the Senate when in session, covering other events at other times with C-SPAN I (Exhibit 12.i).

Exhibit 12.i ●●●●●●●●●●●●●●●

Congressional Television

In 1951 his role in televised hearings on organized crime catapulted Senator Estes Kefauver (D-TN) onto the Democratic ticket in the following year's presidential campaign. The televised Army-McCarthy hearings in 1954 led to the censure of Wisconsin's senator Joseph McCarthy by his colleagues and ultimately to the end of McCarthyism, the far-right communist witchhunt that he had led. The 1973 Watergate hearings chaired by folksy but astute Senator Sam Erwin (D-NC) made him a star, while the 1974 Nixon impeachment proceedings in the House propelled many members of Congress to fame—and hastened regular television coverage of congressional sessions.

The C-SPAN networks came into being originally to cover the House of Representatives (beginning in 1979) and the Senate (by C-SPAN-II, beginning in 1986). Cameras, controlled by Congress, rarely show that floor debate often takes place in nearly deserted chambers.

In 1991 the nation watched transfixed as the Senate reopened nomination hearings on Judge Clarence Thomas, a prospective member of the U.S. Supreme Court. Thomas was accused of sexual harassment by Anita Hill, an articulate law professor who had once been on his staff. Although the Senate, by a close vote, approved Thomas for the post, the hearings raised consciousness about sexual harassment: television had indeed reset the agenda of millions of Americans.

Source: Photo from UPI/Bettmann Archive.

By the 1980s both Congress and the White House had developed sophisticated facilities for exploiting television. The House and Senate maintained fully equipped studios for the personal use of members, and the White House could make news feeds and interviews available on short notice from its own studio facilities, as well as handle call-in interviews from local stations.

Other indicators of television's growing political importance to Congress include the presence of more photogenic members (the "blow-dry" look)—and the number of press secretaries on Capital Hill. A generation ago, only 30 or 35 of the most senior members of both houses had need of such a staff person. But with the decline in seniority and party importance, even newer members have more chance to be heard—if they have a savvy press-relations staff member. There is benefit here, too: individual members have more access to the media and to their own constituents, in some cases by direct video messages beamed by satellite to home districts.

Crisis Management

In times of crisis, open communication can ease panic and the stress of transition—as exemplified by the role of media during Hurricane Andrew in 1992 (see Prologue). With their immediacy and instant national scope, electronic media play a vital role in managing crisis situations.*

Television's first great test in such a crisis came when President John F. Kennedy was assassinated in Dallas in November 1963. Canceling commercials and commercial programs for "the most massive . . . concentrated broadcasting coverage in history," all networks won praise for competence, sensitivity, and dignity in handling the crisis (*Broadcasting*, 2 December 1963).

---

*Into the early 1990s, one often heard reminders of this role in radio station breaks for testing the Emergency Broadcast System, a means of letting government officials use stations in a given area, or across the nation, in case of emergency situations. In 1992 the FCC announced plans to upgrade the system and eliminate the need for interruptive tests with their loud signal tones (see Exhibit on EBS in the Prologue).

Since then, media have covered other national crises with equal distinction. For example, broadcast networks covered the historic House Judiciary Committee impeachment hearings against President Richard Nixon in full during the summer of 1974. For 54 days, they rotated the assignment day by day. It was the first time the House had permitted television coverage of any committee hearings, helping to pave the way for full-time coverage of House activity a few years later.

Increasingly since 1980, CNN has become the first source many viewers turn to for news of crisis or disaster. Airing 24 hours a day, CNN has changed viewer habits in crisis situations—as with its dramatic coverage of the short 1991 Gulf War described earlier. And the noncommercial C-SPAN network (see Section 8.5) has offered full coverage of often lengthy events that television networks can no longer afford covering. Indeed, the very existence of C-SPAN and CNN has taken much pressure off the traditional television networks, allowing them to focus on more profitable entertainment programming. Whether the resultant decline in network documentary and special-event coverage is in the public interest, however, remains in question as nearly 40 percent of households do not receive cable service.

• • • • • • • •

12.6 Entertainment

Entertainment, as well as news and public affairs, tends to reinforce the media's agenda-setting role. Any major news story that captures headlines may become grist for comment in late-night talk shows or more usefully, as the subject of a special drama or miniseries; it may also influence future episodes of established series. When President Bush suggested in his acceptance speech at the 1992 GOP convention that the country needed families more like television's old *The Waltons* and less like *The Simpsons*, the Fox program included the comment in an animated episode that appeared just 48 hours later. Docudramas, those controversial blends of fact and fiction, offer more evidence of how news can feed entertainment. Docudramas focus on dramatic events—the hijacking of planes or ships, the rescue of a child caught in an old mine, the rise and fall of a political figure—and on such historical events as the plot to kill Hitler. But by changing facts around to suit dramatic needs, docudramas add more distortions to already-simplified versions of reality presented to broadcast and cable audiences. Of course, programs not based on actual events also influence audience attitudes.

Stereotypes

Fiction influences audience perceptions by reinforcing stereotypes, versions of reality that are deliberately oversimplified to fit preconceived images, such as the stock characters of popular drama: the Italian gangster, the inscrutable Oriental, the mad scientist, the bespectacled librarian, or the befuddled father.

Even authors capable of individualized and realistic character portrayals resort to stereotypes when writing for television in order to save time, both their own and that of the medium. Stories must unfold rapidly to fit within half-hour and hour-long formats (minus time-outs for commercials, of course):

> Television dramas have little time to develop situations or characters, necessitating the use of widely accepted notions of good and evil. Since the emphasis is on resolving the conflict or the problem at hand, there is little time to project the complexities of a character's thoughts or feelings or for dialogues which explore human relationships. To move the action along rapidly, the characters must be portrayed in ways which quickly identify them. Thus the character's physical appearance, environment, and behavior conform to widely accepted notions of the types of people they represent. (U.S. Commission on Civil Rights, 1977: 27)

Stereotypical images on television clearly help perpetuate those same images in the minds of viewers. As the U.S. Commission on Civil Rights put it years ago, "To the extent that viewers' beliefs, attitudes, and behavior are affected by what they see on television, relations between the races and the sexes may be affected by television's limited and

often stereotyped portrayals." The Commission carefully avoided asserting flatly that such effects always occur, but it called for research to assess the extent to which they do.

World of Fiction

As researchers regularly examine roles in television series, they invariably find fictional characters to be markedly different from real people in the real world. Compared with life, for example, the world of fiction has far more men than women, most of them young adults, with few very young or elderly persons. Many have no visible means of support, but those who do work have interesting, exciting, action-filled jobs. Fiction therefore contains an unrealistically high proportion of detectives, criminals, doctors, lawyers, scientists, business executives, and adventurers compared with the real world, where unglamourous, dull, and repetitive jobs dominate. Most people in the real world solve their personal problems undramatically, even anticlimactically or incompletely, using socially approved methods. Fictional characters tend to solve their problems with decisive, highly visible acts, often entailing violence.

None of this should surprise us. Fact may be stranger than fiction, but fact does not occur in neatly packaged half-hour episodes, with regular commercial breaks.

Children's Socialization

Nevertheless, the make-believe world of electronic media serves as a model of reality for countless people—especially children at the very time when they are eagerly reaching out to learn about the world. Those too young to read, those who never learned the habit of reading, and those who have little access to printed sources of information and entertainment—all depend heavily on electronic media to tell them of the world outside their own immediate surroundings. Some critics have argued that television programming reveals "secrets" of the adult world—divorce, economic pressures, crime, and other negative aspects of society—and thus robs children of a protected childhood experience.

Drama has special impact because viewers and listeners identify with heroes, participating vicariously in their adventures. Research indicates that young children are especially vulnerable. They tend to believe what they see on television, making no distinction among fact, fiction, and advertising. Disadvantaged children tend to believe fiction more readily than do those whose lives contain more opportunities for learning.

Given the enormous amount of time most children spend watching television, electronic media have become major agents of socialization—the all-important process that turns a squalling infant into a functioning member of society. Socialization, though a lifelong process, occurs intensively during the first few years of life, the time when children begin to learn the language, detailed rules of behavior, and value system of their culture.

In the past, socialization was always the jealously guarded prerogative of family and religion, formalized by education and extended by peer-group experiences. Intrusion of a new, external agent of socialization—television—has been a profound change. Of course, all electronic media function as part of national culture, too, but they come from beyond the immediate family circle and its community-linked supports. The media import ideas, language, images, and practices that may be alien to the local culture.

The question of how intrusion of broadcasting and cable has affected socialization has been and continues to be widely researched and debated. Electronic media can, of course, have both good (prosocial) and bad (antisocial) effects. Producers designed such programs as *Sesame Street* and *Fat Albert and the Cosby Kids* with prosocial effects in mind. Follow-up research indicates that such programs do in fact succeed in achieving prosocial results, though each (especially *Sesame Street*) reinforces a sense that the world comes in short segments with 30-second breaks.

Much more effort, however, has gone into research to prove the *anti*social consequences of television, especially the effects of violence. In the late 1980s there was a flurry of concern about negative social impacts of some popular song lyrics (as well as music videos) that appeared to condone drugs or violence. A related topic, the impact of pornography, has also been studied intensively. This research is not discussed here because pornography, as legally defined, has thus far been effectively excluded from broadcasting and plays only a minor role in pay cable (see Section 14.4). Moralistic campaigns against sex in broadcast television that erupt periodically tend to target programs that do not remotely approach legally preventable pornography.

Influence of Time Spent

Some might well think that any activity taking up as much of people's time as electronic media do must have profound effects. "There is no more clearly documented way in which television has altered American life than in the expenditure of time" (Comstock, 1980: 29). At the very least, critics argue, time spent watching (see Section 11.6) or listening could have been spent in some other way—perhaps on some more useful, constructive activity. But no research has demonstrated that listening and watching necessarily displace more useful and active forms of recreation. In the absence of radio and television, people would do other things with their time, of course, but these would not necessarily be more beneficial.

Most researchers readily accept that by the time a young person graduates from high school, he or she has watched an average of 22,000 hours of television—more time than any activity other than sleeping. Some critics take it for granted that *anything* active would be more beneficial than passive absorption.

This criticism implies a moral judgment, the unstated feeling that it is wrong for people to waste their time staring like zombies at the television tube. One of the pioneers of social research, Paul Lazarsfeld, long ago noted this tone of moral criticism. He pointed out that intellectuals who had fought for shorter work hours and other labor reforms unconsciously resented the fact that the masses failed to take constructive advantage of their hard-won leisure. Instead they "wasted" it in passive enjoyment of broadcasting (Lazarsfeld and Kendall, 1948:

85). Indeed, many people keep their radios or television sets turned on while doing other things.

In any event, all those hours of passive listening and watching *may* be less significant than they seem. Subjectively, time is relative, dragging on interminably in some circumstances, passing all too quickly in others. Each hour on the clock has exactly the same value; not so each hour of human experience. It follows that the huge amount of time that audiences devote to electronic media may have less psychological significance than the sheer number of hours suggests.

What appears to be a developing trend in the 1990s may illustrate the point. Stations on the East and West coasts, where prime time has long been 8–11 P.M., notice an increasing drop-off in viewership in later hours. Some stations in California have received their network's permission to move prime time up an hour—to the 7–10 P.M. time period that prevails in the Central and Mountain time zones. The change, some demographers argue, is driven largely by a slowly aging population (with less energy in the evening), as well as by families in which both parents work and thus have to drop kids off at day care even before their early morning commutes. Earlier bedtimes—and less late-night television viewing—have resulted (Mathews, 1992: A7).

Importance of Television

Surveys show television as the most used of all media (see Section 11.6). For some groups it is especially important. A team of nine psychologists who spent five years assessing television stated the following conclusion in the first chapter of their report:

> Children, the elderly, ethnic minorities and women are the heaviest users of television (the elderly being the highest) because television is a default option used when other activities are not available. These populations are limited by physical restrictions and/or lack of resources. The more time people spend at home or near a television set, the more likely they will watch television. (APA, 1992: 2)

For the elderly, on which more research attention

has been focused in recent years as the overall population ages, news and information programs were most popular among those who used television as a "social network to replace the informal network previously supplied by the workplace" (APA, 1992: 3). Clearly, for some groups television is virtually indispensable—nothing else can perform the same function.

Such findings raise questions about "heavy viewers" or "television addicts." Studies suggest that anywhere from 2 to 12 percent of the population may watch up to twice the average weekly amount of television, are unhappy about that viewing, yet seem unable to do much about it. Further, they usually watch when they are sad, angry, or lonely (or just plain bored), are subject to "attentional inertia" (simply watching what's on rather than being selective), and become more passive as they watch more television.

On occasion, changes in the overall menu of media available to an audience give insight into the special impact of television. For eight months in 1992–1993, for example, a labor dispute in Pittsburgh kept the city's two daily newspapers out of readers' hands. Some new uses of electronic media were minor but curious—a funeral director's group sponsored a listing of obituaries on television to make up for the lost print version. But providing other kinds of information, for which people normally rely on newspapers, proved more difficult in the television format—real estate news and listings, detailed sports news, and performance times for movies and concerts. Theater owners noted a downturn in attendance within the first month of the strike. In October the owners put the larger paper up for sale as the strike dragged on and readers appeared permanently lost to television newscasts. Finally, on January 18, 1993, the smaller paper reappeared in what had become a one-newspaper town. But whether advertisers would return—having survived with electronic and other media—was another question.

In another example, high debt threatened to force the only radio stations in a tiny western town off the air, taking away all local news and reflection of the community. Townspeople took up a collection and bought KATQ-AM/FM so that Plentywood, Montana, could retain its local outlet. Broadcasting was so important that citizens paid anywhere from $30 to $5,000 each to retire the station debt and keep the local voice on the air (*Broadcasting*, 8 December 1991: 32–33).

One further indicator of how television has become part of our everyday landscape is the rising use of television by college students living in dormitories. Though not regularly engaged in such measurements, Nielsen estimates that fully a fifth of all viewing outside the home takes place in college rooms—usually on television sets owned by residents, not in common lounge areas as formerly was the case. As sociologist and media critic Todd Gitlin put it:

> TV is their collective dream machine, their temple, their sense of being members of a nation. It's as if they're carrying their pews with them. They've always watched *L.A. Law*. They can't imagine a world without it. It's normal. College is one episode in this unfolding normality. (quoted in Rimer, 1991: 18)

Yet many of these same committed viewers are critical of television's content, making clear in surveys that music is much more important in their lives.

The acid test, of course, would be to eliminate television—something proposed by advertising man Jerry Mander in *Four Arguments for the Elimination of Television* (1978). While researchers have conducted fairly short television deprivation experiments under controlled conditions (with varying results), they experience great difficulty in locating individuals or families willing to forgo the medium, even for a short test. It has all too clearly become an essential part of everyday living for most people.

Play Theory

Nor should we assume that time spent passively listening and watching has value only if it is devoted to programs that uplift, educate, and inform. All of us also have a need simply to relax and pass time painlessly. That, after all, is what *pastimes* are for, and use of electronic media is the most universal pastime.

Effects researchers usually study media from the point of view of serious, socially significant consequences. They want to know how media influence buying, voting, stereotyping, learning, aggression, and so on. One notable exception to this rule is a researcher who concluded that "at best mass communication allows people to become absorbed in *subjective play*." Playing, according to this researcher, does not merely substitute for some valuable activity but, rather, counts as a valuable activity in itself. It is vital to all human life—"thousands of customs, devices, and occasions are employed to gratify playing in every culture of the world, in all history" (Stephenson, 1967).

"Glow-and-Flow" Principle

The play theory helps to explain the widely acknowledged fact that programs seem of secondary importance as long as *something* fills the screen. Early in television history, one observer noted that "it is the television set and the watching experience that entertains. Viewers seem to be entertained by the glow and the flow" (Meyersohn, 1957: 347).

In a landmark 1960s study of television audience attitudes, Gary Steiner found that most people surveyed said they were more satisfied with television as a *medium* than they were with specific *programs*. He noted that "a large number of respondents were ready to say television is both relaxing and a waste of time" (Steiner, 1963: 411). Similar studies of attitudes conducted a decade or two later showed that this mixture of reactions persisted (Bower, 1973 and 1985).

The glow-and-flow principle becomes especially important when electronic media are the only companions people have. When Steiner asked respondents to describe satisfactions they derived from watching television, he sometimes received moving testimonials such as this:

> I'm an old man and all alone, and the TV brings people and talk into my life. Maybe without TV, I would be ready to die; but this TV gives me life. It gives me what to look forward to—that tomorrow, if I live, I'll watch this and that program. (Steiner, 1963: 26)

At extreme levels of deprivation—in hospitals and similar institutions—television has a recognized therapeutic function as the most valuable nonchemical sedative available.

In short, electronic media answer a compelling need of the mass audience simply to kill time painlessly, to fill an otherwise unendurable void. The media give people a highly effective way of *performing leisure*. But social critics worry that while we relax with our guard down watching television, violence and other antisocial activities portrayed in many programs may produce antisocial effects.

• • • • • • • •

12.7 *Violence*

No aspect of electronic media impact raises more worry than does the amount of violence portrayed on the air and the presumed effect of that cumulative violence. But concern that portrayals of violence and crime might have antisocial effects preceded television by many years. The first systematic research on media violence dates to film studies in the 1930s (Jowett, 1976: 220). Accusations about the potential effects of violence shifted to radio and comic books in the 1950s and, later, to television and rock videos. Along the way, emphasis shifted toward building some sort of explanatory theory, rather than merely taking effects for granted.

Direct Imitation

We occasionally see news reports of real-life violence that has apparently been modeled on similar actions in films or television programs. For example, teenagers pour gasoline on a vagrant and set him on fire—after watching a fictionalized group do the same thing in a television drama. A child watches Superman punch through a wall and tries to do the same thing, with disastrous results. It seems natural to assume that such imitation proves that televised violence sometimes causes violent behavior. Exhaustive research demonstrates, however, that view-

ing a violent act serves as a *contributing factor* to any subsequent imitation of that act. In other words, the act of viewing takes place within a larger context—one's background, education, predispositions, and the like. Taken together, all these influences *may*, in *some* circumstances, lead to violent behavior.

One ugly example of apparent imitation led to an unprecedented lawsuit. In 1974 NBC broadcast a made-for-television film called *Born Innocent*, in which inmates of a detention home for young delinquents "raped" a young girl with a mop handle. Four days after the telecast, older children subjected a nine-year-old California girl to a similar ordeal using a bottle. Parents of the child sued NBC, asking $11 million in damages for negligence in showing the rape scene, which they felt had directly incited the attack on their daughter.

The case raised a major issue: Could broadcasters be held legally responsible for the reactions of audience members to their programs? Network attorneys persuaded the trial judge to define the issue as a First Amendment question, rather than as one of negligence. The case then collapsed: it was impossible to show that NBC had *deliberately* incited the children to attack their victim and thus lost its First Amendment protection. (Cal., 1981: 888)*

General Effects

Public concern about media violence arises primarily from fear of its general impact rather than from the risk of possible direct imitation. Critics assume that adverse social effects are far more widespread and pervasive than isolated instances of imitation. This point of view emerged in another much-publicized court case in 1977.

The State of Florida charged a 16-year-old Florida boy, Ronnie Zamora, with murdering an elderly

---

*Even NBC supporters generally conceded, however, that the program's "rape" scene was unnecessarily graphic and that the network had shown poor judgment by scheduling the movie at 8:00 P.M.. The network scheduled a rerun of the film—this time at 9:00 P.M.—and it, as well as the version available later in syndication, included a much-edited version of the attack.

Exhibit 12.j ●●●●●●●●●●●●●●●●

Government Studies of TV Violence

The Surgeon General's Scientific Advisory Committee on Television and Social Behavior sponsored a group of studies in 1969–1971. Congress allotted a million dollars for the project, which in 1972 resulted in five volumes of findings and a final report. When questioned by a Senate committee, the Surgeon General said flatly:

> [B]roadcasters should be put on notice. The overwhelming consensus and the unanimous Scientific Advisory Committee's report indicates that televised violence, indeed, does have an adverse effect on certain members of our society. . . . [I]t is clear to me that the causal relationship between televised violence and antisocial behavior is sufficient to warrant appropriate and immediate remedial action. (Senate CC, 1972: 26)

A comprehensive analysis of previous research, commissioned by the committee, indicated that television's linkage to aggressive behavior had been intensively analyzed. That every research method available had been employed in these studies made evidence of television's impact even more convincing. As researchers summarized:

> The evidence is that television may increase aggression by teaching viewers previously unfamiliar hostile acts, by generally encouraging in various ways the use of aggression, and by triggering aggressive behavior both imitative and different in kind from what has been viewed. Effects are never certain, because real-life aggression is strongly influenced by situational factors, and this strong role for situational factors means that the absence of an immediate effect does not rule out a delayed impact when the behavior in question may be more propitious. (Comstock et al., 1978:13)

As a result of this work, and of research done since—including a two-volume revisit a decade later by some of the same researchers involved in the 1972 report—Congress and private groups pressured the FCC to limit televised violence. Chiefly for fear of violating the First Amendment and because of the trend toward deregulation, no lasting governmental action resulted.

Still, pressure continued. At the invitation of the Department of Health and Human Services, many researchers involved in earlier studies gathered in Washington late in 1992 to review two decades' worth of research and to assess the impact of changing technology. One study suggested that larger screens and improved picture definition made televised events more real—and thus potentially more dangerous. Others hinted that excessive television watching could impair brain development in young viewers because they would not face a sufficiently wide variety of experiences (*Washington Post*, 12 October 1992: D5).

---

neighbor during an attempted robbery. The boy's attorney tried to build his defense on the argument that Zamora could not be held responsible for his violent behavior because he had become a television addict, "intoxicated" by the thousands of murders he had seen enacted on the screen. The trial judge rejected this argument, and the jury convicted the boy of murder. Though ill-considered, his lawyer's attempt to blame television for the crime drew its inspiration from the findings of research on the generalized adverse effects of televised violence that had accumulated during the 1970s (see Exhibit 12.j).

Violence vs. Reality

A quarter-century ago, during the 1967–1968 television season, George Gerbner and his associates at the University of Pennsylvania began conducting annual analyses of television violence. From these data they constructed a violence "profile" that counted every violent act in a sample week of prime-time and weekend-morning network entertainment programs. In this way they tracked changes in the level of violence from year to year according to network and program type. The Gerbner data indicated, for example, that animated cartoons had a higher percentage of violent acts than any other program category (the coding system counted comic as well as serious acts of violence). Still being collected in the early 1990s, these data contribute to what has become a valuable long-term indicator of television content, one that adds an implied warning of possible viewer reactions to programs watched year in and year out.

Gerbner theorized that violence in programs creates anxiety in viewers because they tend to see the real world in terms of their television experience. Viewers identify with those victims of violence in fiction who resemble themselves. Gerbner found that elderly, poor, and black people have high "risk ratios," or expectations of becoming victims. This anxiety effect, he said, may be a more important by-product of television violence than the imitation effect.

Desensitization

The Gerbner risk-ratio hypothesis or *cultivation theory* seems more persuasive than older hypotheses predicting that people exposed to fictional violence would become *desensitized* to it. According to this view, when television dramatic violence becomes routine, people grow indifferent to real-life violence. Many instances of urban violence and nonresponse by passers-by in recent years lend credence to this hypothesis.

A related hypothesis argues that television violence is unrealistic because it has been deliberately *sanitized.* Consequences of fictional violence seem so neat and clean that viewers remain indifferent. They do not see what happens when real people get hurt—audiences never see or hear the revolting, bloody aftermath, the screams of agony. Joseph Wambaugh, a one-time police officer who became

a writer of police stories, withdrew from a television series based on his writings because the producers treated violence so unrealistically. He complained that if a policeman killed somebody in a television drama, viewers never saw blood or anguish—or the cop's reaction afterward. Wambaugh put his finger on a dilemma: such graphic consequences should be seen for the object lesson they would convey, but the public (and hence the media) would never tolerate their being shown.

Comparison of American culture with that of other countries, however, does not seem to bear out the assumption of a positive correlation between real and fictional violence:

> If television were the sole determinant of violent behavior, it would be difficult to explain the disparity in aggravated assault rates (almost 8 to 1) between Boston and Montreal, since these cities are both saturated with the same and similar television programs. This does not mean that there is no relationship between television violence and actual violence; it simply means that such a relationship cannot be defined explicitly at present. (Kutach, 1978: 118)

Japan offers another international contrast. Crime statistics indicate that Japan has a much lower level of social violence than the United States. Yet Japanese television regularly imports the most violent of U.S. action dramas. And these imports seem mild compared to the ferocity seen in Japanese television plays.

Violence and Urban Unrest

Some of the most extreme televised violence appears not in entertainment but in news—especially during coverage of live events. When south-central Los Angeles erupted in urban violence in April 1992 in the wake of a controversial trial verdict (see Exhibit 12.k), two examples of the violence problem emerged. First, critics argued that the jurors in the case—who acquitted police officers of a vicious assault on a black man—had become desensitized to violent behavior despite the existence of a graphic videotape of the beating taken by a bystander. Second, television newsmen again faced the balancing

Exhibit 12.k ••••• •••••••••••

Reflecting Violence in Society

Television news often brings faraway violence directly into our living rooms. When the nation viewed a home video camera recording of several Los Angeles policemen beating a drunk driving suspect in 1991, most were outraged at what appeared to be obvious police brutality. When a jury in the subsequent trial of the policemen came in with a "not guilty" verdict in the spring of 1992, the streets of south-central Los Angeles erupted in flames and racial rioting for days—all covered from both the ground and the air by local stations and national news services.

Source: Historical Still of the King beating provided courtesy of Social Reform, Inc. © 1991 by George Holliday. For more information contact Social Reform, Inc. at 1-800-ACT-HEAL.

act of how much riot coverage to show without contributing to the very violence happening in front of the cameras (see Section 12.1). Television first faced this problem in the late 1960s during repeated episodes of urban unrest nationwide brought about by racial and economic inequality, on the one hand, and by protests against the Vietnam War, on the other.

Television's technology improved between the 1960's riots and those of the 1990s. Cameras today are less intrusive and thus less likely to incite trouble by their mere presence. And they can produce pictures despite low light conditions, as evidenced by the camcorder recording of the police beating described in Exhibit 12.k. But the basic problem remains—how much to show while the rioting is actually taking place? Ironically, technological improvements have made this problem worse in that stations and networks can now put these dramatic pictures on the air almost instantly—often from helicopters—with little time to consider their potential audience impact.

Defending Violence

Given the steadily increasing range and depth of research evidence showing antisocial effects of television violence, the media business has found it increasingly difficult to defend its widespread use. Yet for television to serve as a serious medium for adult viewers, it cannot ban violence. After all, violence occurs in all forms of literature, even fairy tales for children. Bodies litter the stage when the curtain falls on some of Shakespeare's tragedies. These, however, demonstrate consequences and define true catharsis. Likewise, popular sports have always featured violence, albeit sometimes controlled.

Writers would face a difficult challenge if they had to meet television's relentless appetite for drama without resorting to violent clashes between opposing forces. A study of attitudes and opinions held by those responsible for network entertainment—the writers, producers, network executives, and program standards chiefs—supports this position (Baldwin and Lewis, 1972). A playwright illustrated the problem by explaining that authors have only four basic conflicts around which to build any plot:

- *Man against nature:* "This is usually too expensive for television."
- *Man against God:* "Too intellectual for television."
- *Man against himself:* "Too psychological, and doesn't leave enough room for action."
- *Man against man:* "This is what you usually end up with."

Only the last form of conflict can easily be shown on television; it also happens to be the one most likely to involve personal violence.

Defenders of television argue that dramatic violence merely reflects violence in real life. To ignore it or to pretend it does not exist would restrict writers unreasonably. Another justification for program violence argues that witnessing staged violence actually is good because it defuses people's aggressive instincts. The ancient Greek theory of *catharsis*, as propounded by Aristotle, held that stage tragedy cleanses the emotions of the viewer through pity and fear. According to the matching modern argument, fictional violence drains off television viewers' aggressive feelings. But such conclusions have *not* been supported by the vast majority of research.

Under growing pressure from the public, interest groups, and Congress to address—and curb—the amount of violence aired, the broadcast and cable industries took limited action in 1992–1993. The Television Program Improvement Act of 1990 had granted cable and broadcast networks and programmers a temporary antitrust exemption to encourage development of common standards to limit the total amount and some specific types of violence on the air. The broadcast networks agreed to a generalized common set of standards late in 1992, and a few months later major cable programmers agreed to try and do the same, joining the three networks in developing a national research conference to air the issues. Having commissioned Dr. Gerbner to measure a sample of cable programs (he found violence on cable to be similar to levels and types in broadcast network and syndicated shows), cable spokespersons agreed to restudy cable programs in

two years to assess the impact of their new standards. It remains to be seen whether this flurry of public relations and research would have substantial effect.

●●●●●●●●

12.8 *Advertising*

Other than violence, no aspect of electronic media impact has been more measured than that involving advertising. Advertisers demand, and receive, vast amounts of applied research on the reach and effect of their messages. Here, however, we focus on the broader, long-range social impact of advertising rather than on its immediate business applications.

Advertising as Subsidy?

At first glance, advertising appears to play a useful social role by reducing the direct cost of media to the public. In traditional commercial broadcasting, for example, advertising appears to cover the entire cost of this "free" service. In fact, however, consumers *eventually* pay the full cost, because companies include advertising expenses in the final price of their goods and services. Advertiser-supported basic cable combines two viewer charges, adding direct subscriber fees to indirect advertising costs. And for all electronic media, the audience must purchase and maintain receivers (and VCRs and other related equipment), which can be thought of as a kind of consumer subsidy of advertisers.

Advertising's General Impact

Some critics suggest that advertising actually *disserves* consumers by creating a desire for unnecessary purchases—what economist John Kenneth Galbraith termed the *synthesizing of wants*. Electronic media advertising does often stimulate widespread demand for goods and services for which consumers may have little real need. Advertising can build overnight markets for virtually useless products or "new and improved" versions of old products.

Such critics often assume from these successes that advertising can overcome most consumer resistance. Advertising practitioners find themselves wishing that were true. Failure of a high proportion of new products every year belies the assumption that advertising is all-powerful.

Not only do many products fail to catch on but, despite intensive advertising support, leading products also often give way to competitors. Marketers recognize transfer of *brand loyalty* as an ever-present threat. For this reason, much cable, television, and radio advertising aims not at moving merchandise but, rather, at simply keeping brand names visible and viable in the marketplace.

Advertising to Children

The possible impact of commercials in children's programs raises special issues. Children start watching television early in their lives and often find commercials just as fascinating as programs. Action for Children's Television (active until 1992) as well as other consumer organizations have long believed that commercials take unfair advantage of young children—especially preschoolers, who are not yet able to differentiate between advertising and programs.

Consumer groups also complain that commercials aimed at children urge consumption of sugared foods and drinks. One study, quoted by a Federal Trade Commission (FTC) staff examining the issue, counted more than 7,500 food commercials aired during weekend children's programs in the first nine months of 1976 (excluding ads for fast-food outlets). Of these ads, half promoted sugared breakfast cereals and a third pushed candy, gum, cookies, and crackers (see Exhibit 12.l). The staff concluded that the FTC had ample authority to ban such advertising. But the recommendation galvanized industry lobbyists and eventually precipitated a congressional crackdown on the idea of banning children's television advertising. The FTC has not touched the issue since.

An FCC Children's Television Task Force (FCC, 1979) and a panel of experts funded by the National Science Foundation (Adler et al., 1980) also conducted studies. The FCC group reported that some progress had been made during the 1970s in eliminating selling by program hosts and in cutting back on commercial time in children's programs, but that the industry still had a long way to go. The task force recommended encouraging alternative non-broadcast sources of entertainment for children. This advice reflected the emerging deregulatory trend; instead of forcing the industry to change its practices by regulation, the FCC relied on consumer self-discipline to prevent harmful effects.

Action for Children's Television contested the FCC viewpoint before both the Commission and the courts, finally succeeding in 1990, after two decades' effort, to get Congress to pass a new law limiting advertising in children's programs—and calling for more such programs (see Sections 7.6 and 14.8).

• • • • • • • •

12.9 Policy Making

When Congress passed the Radio Act of 1927 and the Federal Radio Commission began writing rules, neither had the benefit of research on media impact. They relied primarily on legal-historical considerations and sheer guesswork. The same guesswork was present at the creation of the FCC in 1934, as discussed in the next chapter.

Research and Policy

Today, however, major policy decisions often rely on research findings to support their goals and to predict their probable outcomes. For example:

- In defending a hands-off policy with regard to radio station format changes in the 1970s, the FCC used a study of major market formats as evidence that competition alone would ensure sufficient format variety.
- Congressional concern about the possible adverse effects of violence in programming led in 1969 to the allocation of a million dollars to the Surgeon

Exhibit 12.1 ● ● ● ● ● ● ● ● ● ● ●

Advertising and Kids

Source: Cartoon reprinted with special permission of King Features Syndicate.

General for research studies, and to funding for a follow-up survey a decade later.

- To justify its radio deregulation proposals in 1979–1981, the FCC used research on current practices of radio stations to support its theory about the effects of competition.
- During the 1980s the FCC came increasingly under the dominance of economic theorists in making decisions about the future of electronic media. Economic studies of broadcasting and cable television, along with predictions of their future interrelationships, became a growth industry. Foundations began funding such research and economists at major universities and research centers undertook numerous projects. The FCC came to rely more and more on such research in making its case for deregulation.

Private Research to Influence Policy

Several times a year Congress holds hearings on media issues and the FCC regularly considers new or revised policy initiatives. Industry and consumer groups present their views. Both now buttress their arguments with surveys of prior research on the topic, frequently adding specially commissioned research of their own. Claims need to be supported by hard evidence that research alone can supply. Some typical examples of research undertaken by private sponsors:

- Critics of broadcast news regularly conduct or cite content analysis studies to support their allegations of news bias.
- Action for Children's Television for 20 years conducted content analysis research to support its petitions for improvements in children's programming. The organization finally won action by Congress and the FCC in 1990–1991 (see Section 12.6).
- Commercial broadcasters surveyed existing research to demonstrate to Congress and others in the 1980s that bans on broadcast advertising of alcohol or legal drugs would do little to curb excessive use of these products.
- Broadcasters sponsored research showing how rapidly cable subscription rates had increased in the 1980s and used this and related studies to

urge Congress to re-regulate aspects of cable (see Section 13.8).

● ● ● ● ● ● ● ●

Summary

12.1   Communications research has steadily grown more sophisticated over the years. Early propaganda research relied on the simplistic bullet or hypodermic-injection theory of communication effects. Post–World–War–II researchers examined the personal influence of opinion leaders who used media. Still later they studied the importance of selective exposure to and perception of media messages. Information theory applied engineering concepts to communications research in the 1950s. Research on selective effects in the 1970s showed that media largely served to reinforce audiences' existing beliefs and perceptions. And most recently, researchers have emphasized intervening variables that dramatically influence how different individuals may respond to the same message.

12.2   Electronic media journalists largely define our view of the world through a combination of gatekeeping and agenda setting. Media coverage can confer prestige but, by the same token, can also be exploited through the staging of pseudoevents. That media can improve technology to provide a public view of public processes is evident in increased televising of court trials.

12.3   Television coverage of the long and frustrating Vietnam War had a strong impact on American policymakers and viewers. More recent war coverage has had a direct influence on foreign and military policymaking—but has also suffered censorship and tighter government control. Terrorists who commit publicity crimes present the media with the dilemma of supporting terrorism simply by covering terrorist activities. Television or video diplomacy helps speed up events as leaders increasingly use these media to communicate. That television's exposure helps to speed events became especially evident in the fall of communism in Eastern Europe and the USSR in 1989–1991.

12.4   Television has long exerted a strong influence on U.S. election campaigns. Televised debates have been a regular feature of national campaigns since 1976. Conventions had become less important by the late 1980s, in large part because of television. In 1992 talk shows became important forums for political issues. Election-night predictions of election outcomes before polls have closed in some states remain controversial.

12.5   Presidents have long been able to command substantial media coverage. Congress opened itself to regular television coverage (the House in 1979, the Senate in 1986), in part as a counterbalance to presidential television. Electronic media become vital in times of natural or man-made emergencies.

12.6   Television entertainment tends to reinforce stereotypes and to give a false and shallow impression of everyday life and work. Nevertheless, television can play positive roles in the socialization of children and in providing a needed leisure-time activity. Critics worry about the amount of time most people spend with electronic media, as well as about the resultant impacts of what is seen and heard in all those hours.

12.7   The extent to which television contributes to violent behavior remains controversial but, after years of intensive research increasingly obvious. Such research indicates that the medium can be a contributing factor to violent action on the part of some people in some circumstances. It may also serve to desensitize others to violence, as well as heighten people's expectation of real-life violence.

12.8   As a medium of advertising, electronic media can have a powerful impact on consumers, especially children. But as numerous business failures demonstrate, advertising alone cannot always create demand. After considerable research and lobbying, Congress and the FCC finally placed limits on advertising directed toward children.

12.9   Research results have become increasingly important in the policy-making process. Increasingly, private interests fund research to buttress their policy views, seeking to persuade government officials with results of social science studies.

PART 6

Controls

Thus far we have explored the electronic media's historical development, technical aspects, economic structure, programming, and audience impact. *We turn now to the regulatory constraints society places on electronic media, from the all-important authorization of service to more controversial limitations on media First Amendment rights.*

Chapter 13 reviews formal laws and agencies that govern electronic media, as well as less formal influences on policy making. It focuses primarily on the single most important regulatory control—licensing of stations and franchising of cable systems. Chapter 13 also discusses deregulatory trends that peaked in the 1980s and concludes with the many other kinds of regulation that can affect electronic media. Chapter 14 then turns to constitutional controversies (most involve media content) that arise when formal controls are put into effect.

Chapter 13

Regulation and Licensing

Regulation of electronic media begins with the premise that because they use public spectrum space or public right of way and have impact on their audiences, electronic media are properly subjects of public concern. *How* to regulate starts with the Constitution, on which all laws and administrative controls are based. These controls, in turn, are embedded in the Communications Act, which defines the role of the Federal Communications Commission.

13.1 Federal Jurisdiction

The U.S. Constitution gives the federal government power over specific areas (for example, international relations and declaring war), leaving all other powers to the states. Before radio broadcasting could be regulated, Congress sought constitutional justification for federal regulation.

Commerce Clause

Specific constitutional justification for Congress's taking control of electronic media comes from Article 1, Section 8(3), which gives Congress power "to regulate commerce with foreign nations, and among the several states." This commerce clause has played a vital role in American history, preventing states from erecting internal trade barriers to national unity. The provision forms a link in a chain of responsibility from Constitution to citizens, as shown in Exhibit 13.a.

Delegated Congressional Authority

It is impossible for Congress to dictate regulatory details in dozens of specialized fields. Therefore, starting with the Interstate Commerce Commission in 1887, it has delegated to a series of *independent regulatory agencies* the authority to oversee such often complex areas as power, transportation, labor, finance—and communication.

Exhibit 13.a • • • • • • • • • • • • • • •

Chain of Legal Authority

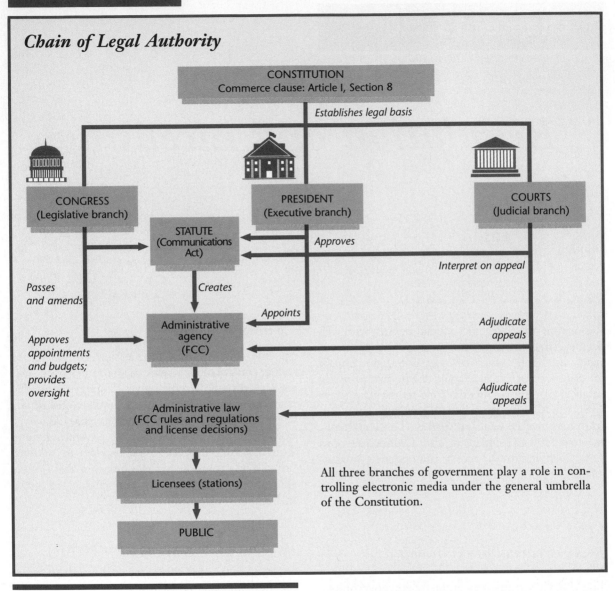

CONSTITUTION
Commerce clause: Article I, Section 8

Establishes legal basis

CONGRESS
(Legislative branch)

PRESIDENT
(Executive branch)

COURTS
(Judicial branch)

STATUTE
(Communications Act)

Approves

Interpret on appeal

Passes and amends

Creates

Appoints

Adjudicate appeals

Approves appointments and budgets; provides oversight

Administrative agency
(FCC)

Adjudicate appeals

Administrative law
(FCC rules and regulations and license decisions)

All three branches of government play a role in controlling electronic media under the general umbrella of the Constitution.

Licensees (stations)

PUBLIC

Although the president appoints FCC commissioners, with the advice and consent of the Senate, the Commission remains what some call a "creature of Congress." Congress defined the FCC's role in the Communications Act of 1934, and only Congress can change that role by amending or replacing the Act. Though commissioners have considerable leeway in determining regulatory direction, House and Senate subcommittees on communications constantly monitor the FCC, which must come back to

Congress annually for budget appropriations. Since 1983 Congress has reauthorized the very existence of the Commission every two years.*

Congress gave the FCC power to adopt, modify, and repeal rules and regulations concerning *interstate* electronic media.* These rules carry the force of federal law, deriving their power from Congress through the Communications Act. Thus an understanding of the Act is vital to understanding the FCC's day-to-day role.

• • • • • • • •

13.2 Communications Act

As described in Section 1.10, the Radio Act of 1927 ended a period of chaotic radio broadcast development. Congress for the first time crafted a statute— and created an agency—concerned explicitly with broadcasting. The 1927 Act gave the Federal Radio Commission the responsibility of defining what the public interest, convenience, and necessity would mean in practice.

---

*The change from permanent to temporary status of independent regulators grew out of congressional displeasure with the aggressive policies of the Federal Trade Commission during the Carter administration (1977–1981). The FCC's change in status resulted from congressional unhappiness with its later *de*regulatory moves in the early 1980s. Congress demands deference from "its" regulatory agencies. The reauthorization process lets Congress make changes in the Communications Act more easily when it wants to slow down or speed up FCC actions.

*Wire and cable communication differs from radio-based services in the level of government that regulates it, because it is usually limited by a specific geographical boundary. Either state or federal regulation governs telephone and related *common-carrier* services (see p. 78), depending on whether a given service crosses state lines. States have their own public-utility commissions (PUCs) that approve changes in telephone rates and service for in-state systems. Systems that cross state lines, however, have traditionally needed federal approval of rate changes. Even in the 1990s, after much deregulation, such controls still affected AT&T (as the dominant long-distance carrier) and the *interstate* operations of the seven regional Bell Operating Companies. As discussed (in Section 13.8), cable communication falls more under local than federal control for the same reason—physical cables do not cross state lines.

Passage

The Radio Act of 1927 imposed order on broadcasting, but left control of some aspects of radio and all interstate and foreign *wire* communication scattered among several federal agencies. The Communications Act of 1934 brought interstate wire as well as wireless communication under control of the FCC, which replaced the Federal Radio Commission. This change had minimal effect on broadcasting because Congress simply reenacted broadcasting provisions from the 1927 law as a part of the 1934 Act. Thus electronic media law dates back more than 65 years to the early development of radio. Although the Act has often been amended, its underlying concepts remain unchanged. Its very first paragraph specifies the reasons for the FCC's creation: "to make available, so far as possible, to all the people of the United States a rapid, efficient, nationwide and world-wide wire and radio communication service with adequate facilities at reasonable charges."

Titles

The Communications Act of 1934 is divided into seven major parts called titles.* They cover the following general subjects, among which Titles III and VI are especially important for our purposes:

I. Definition of terms; provision for setting up and operation of the FCC.
II. Common carriers.
III. *Broadcast licensing, general powers of the FCC, program controls, public broadcasting.*
IV. Hearings on and appeals from FCC decisions.
V. Penal provisions.
VI. *Cable television.*
VII. War emergency powers of the president; other general provisions.

---

*Until late 1984 the Communications Act had six titles. However, when Congress passed the "Cable Communications Policy Act of 1984" (see Section 13.8), it became a new Title VI, making the existing VI a new Title VII. References to Title VI published before 1985 refer to what we now know as Title VII.

Definitions

The Communications Act formalizes broadcasting's role (Title I, Sec. 3*) as "dissemination of radio communications intended to be received by the public directly or by intermediary or relay stations." The key phrase "intended to be received by the public" excludes from *broadcasting* any private radio communication service aimed at individuals or specific groups of individuals.*

Finally, Sec. 3 of the Act defines *radio communication* as "transmission by radio of writing, signs, signals, pictures, and sounds of all kinds, including all instrumentalities, facilities, apparatus, and services . . . incidental to such transmission." By giving the term *radio* such a broad definition, Congress made it possible for the Act to incorporate television when it became a licensed service nearly 15 years after adoption of these words in 1927.

Provision for FCC

The president appoints the five FCC commissioners to five-year terms, subject to Senate confirmation. Congress sought to minimize political bias by allowing no more than three commissioners from the same party.

Sec. 4 of the Communications Act assigns the Commission broad power to "perform any and all acts, make such rules and regulations, and issue such orders . . . as may be necessary in the execution of its functions." In a few instances Congress tied the Commission's hands with hard-and-fast requirements, such as specific station license terms and restrictions concerning foreign ownership of broadcast stations. But most provisions give the FCC wide latitude in applying its experience and expert judgment to each case.

PICON Standard

Congress drew on its earlier regulation of railway service and rates when it created a highly flexible yet legally recognized standard—*public interest, convenience, or necessity* (PICON)—to limit FCC discretion when not dictated by specific requirements of the Act. PICON occurs regularly in the Act's broadcasting sections. For example, Sec. 303 begins: "Except as otherwise provided in this Act, the Commission from time to time, as *public convenience, interest, or necessity* requires, shall. . . ." and goes on to list 19 powers, ranging from classification of radio stations to making regulations necessary to carry out the Act's provisions. The PICON phrase similarly occurs in sections dealing with the grant, renewal, and transfer of broadcast licenses.

Broadcasters tend to picture themselves as constantly facing hard decisions about what the public interest requires. But the Act does not leave them adrift in doubt as to how to interpret the phrase as that task falls to the Commission. As an appeals court put it:

> The only way that broadcasters can operate in the "public interest" is by broadcasting programs that meet somebody's view of what is in the "public interest." That can scarcely be determined by the broadcaster himself, for he is in an obvious conflict of interest. . . . The Congress has made the F.C.C. the guardian of that public interest. (F, 1975: 536)*

---

*For this and the following chapter, "Sec." refers to a section of the Communications Act or other indicated law. "Section" spelled out continues to refer to parts of this book.

*Nor is broadcasting supposed to be used to send private messages not intended for the general public. People who greet their families over the air during broadcast interviews, for example, technically violate the law. Radio messages not *intended* for the general public can, of course, be *received* by anyone with the right kind of receiver. People often tune in to police, ship-to-shore, satellite, cellular telephone, and other nonbroadcast transmissions for their own entertainment. The Act's Sec. 705(a) forbids *disclosure* of nonbroadcast messages to people for whom they were not intended. Congress, the courts, and the FCC have also made it illegal for people even to intercept some nonbroadcast signals—such as pay cable—unless they are subscribers.

*Full names and citations of all cases mentioned in the text can be found at the end of the book. Cases are listed chronologically (with suffix letters where there is more than one per year) in the main bibliography under one of five most common abbreviations used in Chapters 13 and 14: (1) *F,* for *Federal Reporter,* the official multivolume record of U.S. Appeals Court cases; (2) *FCC,* meaning a general publication of the Federal Communications Commission; (3) *FCCR,* for *FCC Reports* (changed in 1986 to *FCC Record*), the official reporter of FCC decisions; (4) *US,* meaning decisions of the Supreme Court as found in *United States Reports,* its official record; and (5) *USC,* meaning United States Code. The page given in citations is that for the specific quotation; the bibliography list shows the page on which the case actually begins.

The public-interest standard chosen by Congress to give the FCC flexibility in meeting unforeseeable situations invites charges of vagueness. But as an appeals court judge pointed out decades ago:

> It would be difficult, if not impossible, to formulate a precise and comprehensive definition of the term "public interest, convenience, or necessity," and it has been said often and properly by the courts that the facts of each case must be examined and must govern its determination. (F, 1946: 628)

In sharp contrast, important 1984 cable amendments to the Communications Act nowhere use the phrase "public interest," giving the FCC discretionary powers that *could* have been made subject to the same public-interest test that controls broadcasters—had Congress so chosen. But because of its strongly deregulatory nature, the 1984 amendments relied far more on marketplace than on PICON decision making. Cable amendments in 1992 *did* make reference (in a new sec. 628(a)) to promoting "the public interest, convenience, and necessity by increasing competition and diversity in the multichannel video programming market," suggesting that deregulatory thinking may have slowed down, at least in Congress.

Amendments

The cable amendments of 1984 and 1992 (detailed below) are the most substantial examples of a process that has gone on regularly since the passage of the 1934 Act—revisions and updates of the Act by amendment. Although the 1934 Act's basic principles remain little changed, many specifics have been modified to deal with a much larger and more complex electronic media business.

From 1977 through 1981 Congress made several attempts to replace the 1934 Act with entirely new legislation that would fully take into account many new media and common-carrier services developed since 1934. Called *rewrites*, these legislative proposals went far beyond the patch-ups brought about by both earlier and subsequent amendments. The efforts failed, largely because many affected groups (broadcast, cable, and common carrier) could not come to a consensus on such broad changes. The debate, however, paved the way for cable legislation.

The 1984 cable act amended the Communications Act by adding a new Title VI, and defined cable television as *neither* a common carrier *nor* a broadcasting service. Congress left the FCC with little responsibility for cable, far less than it had for broadcasting and interstate wire services, and limited the power of states to regulate cable programming and subscriber rates. But as detailed in Section 13.8, Congress amended the Act again in 1992, reinstating many cable regulatory powers to the FCC and local authorities—yet another example of the Act being constantly adjusted to meet current social and political needs.

• • • • • • • •

13.3 FCC Basics

As a creation of Congress, the FCC acts on behalf of the legislative branch. When it makes regulations, the Commission acts in a quasi-legislative capacity. It functions as an executive agency when it puts the will of Congress and its own regulations into effect. And when the FCC interprets the Act, conducts hearings, or decides disputes, it takes on a judicial role.

Budget and Organization

In the early 1990s Congress appropriated about $125 million annually for the FCC. This budget makes the Commission one of the smaller federal agencies, employing about 1,800 persons. The Field Operations Bureau, Common Carrier Bureau, and Mass Media Bureau have the largest staffs, about 350 members each. The unit of most interest here, the Mass Media Bureau, has four divisions, the duties of which can be summarized as follows:

• *Audio services.* Directs processing of applications for construction permits, licenses, and license renewals for radio stations and related auxiliary operations.
• *Video services.* Directs processing of applications for construction permits, licenses, and license renewals for television stations and related auxiliary operations. Also maintains a staff for the FCC's growing cable responsibilities.

- *Policy and rules.* Handles FCC proceedings that produce new rules and conducts studies needed for policy-making decisions.
- *Enforcement.* Processes public complaints, ensures compliance with statutes and rules, issues interpretations of rules, and represents the Bureau at hearings within the Commission.

Several offices service all FCC operational bureaus: the Office of Plans and Policy, largely an economic research unit; the Office of Chief Engineer, which provides most FCC engineering expertise and runs an FCC laboratory that grants type acceptance of broadcast transmitters and other equipment; the Office of International Communications, which coordinates FCC with other agency policies on worldwide telecommunication; and the General Counsel, which represents the FCC before other agencies and the courts and gives the Commission internal legal advice (see Exhibit 13.b).

Commissioners

The president appoints (with the consent of the Senate) the five commissioners (there were seven until 1982) who serve five-year terms and may be reappointed.* Members often resign before serving a full term (replacements fill only the unexpired period of a term), with the result that two or more seats may come up for appointment in a given year, giving a president considerable power to change the Commission's makeup and direction. Additionally, the Communications Act gives the president authority to designate the agency's chair. Commissioners must be citizens, may not have a financial interest

*Robert E. Lee holds the FCC longevity record, having served for 28 years (1953–1981), the last few months as chairman. The first woman commissioner, Frieda Hennock, served from 1948 to 1955. The next woman was not appointed until 1971, but since 1979 at least one commissioner has been a woman. The first African-American commissioner was Benjamin Hooks (1972–1977), a Memphis attorney, county judge, and later the long-time head of the NAACP. Hispanics as well as African-Americans have been appointed often since.

in any type of communications business, and must devote full time to the job. They meet several times each month in sessions open to the public, though much administrative decision making is handled behind the scenes "on circulation" among commissioners' offices. Commissioners and their staff are often referred to collectively as "the eighth floor" for their location atop the FCC headquarters building in downtown Washington.

Commissioners seldom originate policy. The FCC staff generates most policy initiatives, with commissioners shaping and sometimes rejecting or altering proposed staff drafts of FCC orders. Each commissioner has three assistants, usually lawyers, to help analyze the flood of complex issues presented at each meeting.

Strict *ex parte* rules often govern contact with outsiders. Such rules require a public record of meetings between commissioners and other key policy makers and individuals directly affected by a decision's outcome. To avoid unfair last-minute one-sided lobbying, FCC commissioners may not meet with anyone concerned—other than FCC staff members—in the week prior to an FCC public meeting at which decisions will be made.

Staff Role

References to "the Commission" usually include not only the five commissioners but also senior staff of FCC bureaus. Staff members handle inquiries and complaints, which seldom come to the commissioners' attention. The staff handles thousands of letters, applications, and forms from FCC-regulated industries. Deregulation reduced paperwork considerably during the 1980s.

Except for top administrators (bureau chiefs), whom the chair appoints, Commission staff is part of the federal civil service. Many serve for decades, developing in-depth expertise on which commissioners depend. After several years of closely observing the Commission, researchers noted that "staff members who are accomplished politicians and wily empire builders may find themselves with greater power than any single commission member—key staff members have the power to decide what infor-

Exhibit 13.b ●●●●●●●●●●●●●●●●

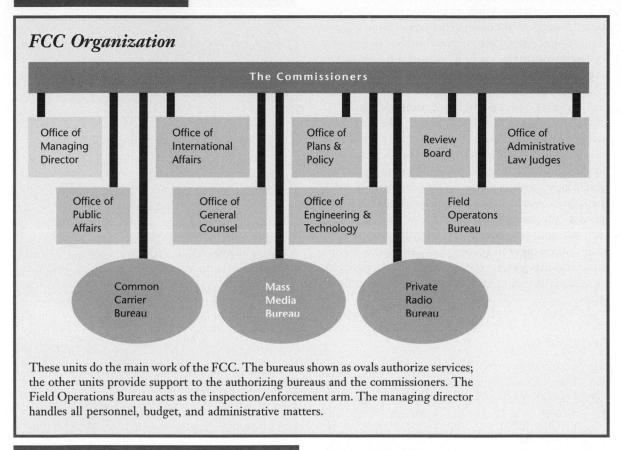

FCC Organization

These units do the main work of the FCC. The bureaus shown as ovals authorize services; the other units provide support to the authorizing bureaus and the commissioners. The Field Operations Bureau acts as the inspection/enforcement arm. The managing director handles all personnel, budget, and administrative matters.

mation to bring to the Commission's attention and in what form" (Cole and Oettinger, 1978: 11).

To make decisions, FCC staff uses authority formally delegated from the commissioners in the form of *processing rules*. These spell out which decisions staff may settle and which must go to the commissioners. Staff recommendations accompany all items forwarded for formal commission consideration. The professional staff thus exerts considerable influence on day-to-day operations as well as long-term policy, somewhat reducing commissioners (in common with many politicians) to being creatures of their own staff.

Rule-Making Process

The rule-making function generates a large body of FCC administrative law called *rules and regulations* (there is no difference between the two—the phrase is traditional). Whether the Commission acts on a petition to consider a certain action (petitions of little merit are dismissed quickly) or acts on its own, it often begins with a *notice of inquiry* (NOI) for a subject that needs preliminary comment and research, or a *notice of proposed rule making* (NPRM) when offering specific new rules for public comment, or a combination of both. These notices invite comment from interested parties, mostly attorneys representing affected individuals, stations, companies, or industries. A few public-interest and consumer groups sometimes participate as well. Parties often submit research studies to buttress arguments for or against intended FCC action. On rare occasions, proposed rule changes of special significance or of a controversial nature may be scheduled for oral argument before the five commissioners.

After digesting outside comments, the staff prepares a proposed decision for the commissioners, usually as a recommended *report and order* with background discussion explaining and defending the action. Once a proposed report and order is adopted, that action becomes subject to petitions to the Commission for reconsideration and/or appeal to the U.S. Courts of Appeals, as suggested in Exhibit 13.c. Increasingly in recent years, one party or another appeals nearly every "final" FCC decision, sometimes delaying implementation by months or years.

Adjudication

The second type of FCC decision making is adjudication, which settles specific disputes—whether between outside parties (for example, rival applicants for a television channel) or between the FCC and an outside party (such as a broadcaster who protests a fine). The staff may settle simple disputes quickly, but others become the subject of hearings.

Electronic media owners avoid hearings if at all possible. Such hearings nearly always take place in Washington, require expensive legal representation and documentation, and can take a long time. And unexpected additional problems can be raised while the hearing is under way.

Informal Pressure

In addition to formal rule making and adjudication, the FCC has often influenced licensee conduct through an informal "raised eyebrow" approach. The FCC once used such approaches to warn of action it would take if broadcasters did not put their own house in order. This regulatory style sometimes

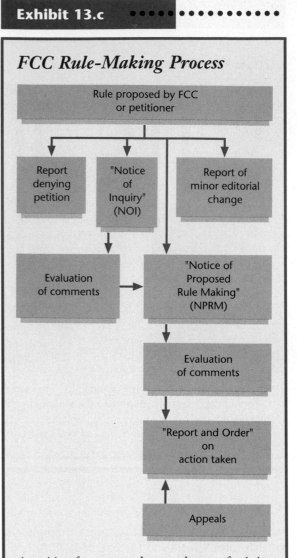

Exhibit 13.c

FCC Rule-Making Process

A petition for a new rule or a change of existing rules can come from the general public (rare), the regulated industries (common), another part of the executive branch, or a unit within the FCC itself. Parties who are dissatisfied with denials or new rules often appeal for reconsideration by the FCC and, if still not satisfied, to the courts. Each step of the process must be documented in the *Federal Register* so that all interested parties can keep themselves informed of rule-making actions.

Exhibit 13.d ●●●●● ●●●●●●●●●●●●

A Persistent Petition

The most persistent letter-writing and telephone campaign to afflict the FCC—one still evident nearly two decades later—began in 1975 in reaction to a petition asking the FCC to stop exempting noncommercial FM and television stations from the multiple-ownership rules. It also asked for a freeze on licensing of such stations to religious groups, pending an investigation of the extent to which they complied with the fairness doctrine and fulfilled the educational purposes of the non-commercial allocations.

The FCC's staff rejected the petition less than a year after it had been submitted. That should have closed the episode, but the dismissal of the petition had no effect whatever on the flood of mail and calls opposing it from those who had somehow been misled into believing that the petition asked for an outright ban on all religious programs.

By late 1992 (the last time a count was issued) more than 22 *million* complaints had been received by letter and telephone—and they continue to roll in despite efforts to stanch the flow. This mindless outpouring carried a double irony: not only had the petition long since been denied, but the writers had no understanding of what it would have accomplished even if it *had* been accepted by the FCC.

And on into the 1990s . . . those calling the FCC's public information number (202-632-7000) hear an electronic message providing several options. Option three offers a brief statement of further information on the religious broadcasting petition, which has been a regulatory "dead letter" for nearly two decades but seems to have an endless life of its own.

---

went further to become *jawboning*, or, given FCC licensing power, what courts have held to be a kind of "forced persuasion."

In the deregulatory era after 1980, the FCC employed this pressure far less often. To the contrary, public statements, speeches, and articles by FCC commissioners in the 1980s more often argued for a decreasing FCC role or for other deregulatory notions.

FCC Critique

Over its six decades, the FCC has been among the most frequently analyzed and scathingly criticized of all federal regulatory agencies. Official investigations and private studies of the Commission and its methods reach negative conclusions with monotonous regularity. A few criticisms are recurrent:

- The political process for choosing commissioners often fails to select qualified people. FCC appointments do not rank high in the Washington political pecking order. The president often uses appointments to regulatory commissions to pay off minor political debts.
- As a consequence, commissioners usually lack expertise and sometimes the dedication assumed by the Communications Act. Most appointees have been lawyers. People with experience in engineering, the media, or common carriers—or in relevant academic specialties—rarely receive appointment because they lack the political constituencies required for serious consideration.
- Commissioners' hopes for future employment with regulated industries may underlie their usually narrow reading of "the public interest." Not many stay in office long enough to attain great expertise; the more ambitious and better-qualified appointees soon move on to higher-paying positions, usually in private legal practice, specializing (of course) in communication law.
- Taken as a whole, the regulatory process long had an air of make-believe. Until the late 1970s, it set high-sounding public-interest goals that neither media owners nor the Commission seriously tried to achieve. Since then, however, deregulation has gone to the opposite extreme, eliminating not only the pretense but seemingly also much concern for protecting any larger public interest.

13.4 Licensing

The *authorizing of service*—licensing of broadcasting stations—is the FCC's single most important function. (Local authorities that franchise cable systems—see Section 13.8—play a parallel role.) All other regulation grows out of this licensing process. The FCC acts as gatekeeper, using its licensing power to offer station operation to some and not others. Most licenses are granted and renewed routinely. Sometimes the Commission makes comparative licensing decisions only after extensive investigation; with newer services such as MMDS and LPTV, it simply awards licenses by lottery. Licensing plays a key role in determining the nature of broadcasting, which inevitably reflects the character and standards of people who own and operate stations.

Channel Ownership

No one can legally "own" any part of the electromagnetic spectrum. Conscious of both real and potential claims to the contrary, the Communications Act repeatedly codifies the ban on channel ownership. For example, Sec. 304 requires licensees to sign a waiver "of any claim to the use of any particular frequency or of the ether as against the regulatory power of the United States because of the previous use of the same."

There is increasing political and economic pressure, however, at least to experiment with spectrum ownership—through auction by the government—in services other than broadcasting (see Section 4.5). Economic theory holds that such ownership will lead to far more efficient spectrum use. But as of early 1993, despite extensive debate in Congress, neither Congress nor the FCC had moved to change the "no ownership" basis of spectrum access. The Clinton administration strongly promoted spectrum auctions, as had the Bush administration earlier—one indication that much of communication policy is bi-partisan in nature.

Finding a Channel

A would-be licensee applies for specific facilities (channel, power, coverage pattern, antenna location, time of operation, and so on). Because the FCC has allotted all FM and television channels to communities in advance, the applicant consults allotment tables to find a vacant channel (47 CFR 73.201, 73.603; see also Exhibit 2.g, p. 60). Alternatively, the applicant may petition for a change in the allotment tables to move—for a short distance—an available channel or, less likely, to "drop in" a channel at a specific location. In the case of AM radio, however, no such tables exist. Applicants use engineering consultants to search out locations where an AM channel could be activated without causing interference.

Most desirable commercial channels had long been assigned by the 1970s, so that a would-be licensee nearly always had to buy an existing station. In the past decade, however, several new opportunities developed in both television and radio. The Commission approved a new service in 1982—low-power television (LPTV)—whose channel use could fit in among existing outlets, inasmuch as LPTVs are limited in power so as not to interfere with full-power television stations. In the mid-1980s the FCC created nearly 700 new FM allotments made possible by improved technology limiting interference with stations already on the air. Finally, early in the 1990s, the FCC extended the AM band to 1705 kHz, adding 10 new medium-wave channels to which existing AM outlets could migrate, thus cutting down on existing interference (see Section 4.6).

But in a strong shift away from earlier policy, the Commission restricted access to some of these "new" services to old players—existing broadcasters. It used the expanded AM band, for example, to spread out existing broadcasters, thereby reducing interference, rather than allowing still more new operators into what many feel is an overcrowded service. Likewise, as the FCC considered policies for high-definition television and digital audio broadcasting (see Sections 5.9 and 5.10), it made clear its intention to restrict access to those services to existing stations before any consideration might be given to new entrants. The Commission argued that such an approach would allow for a transitional period of dual-channel broadcasting of the present services while newer technology is introduced. Once that transition is completed and the old service terminated, new applicants might then be considered. Any spectrum space freed may eventually be transferred to nonbroadcast uses.

Construction Permit

To ensure that transmitters behave exactly as planned and authorized, the Communications Act requires would-be licensees to apply first for *construction permits* (CPs). The holder of a CP applies for a regular license to broadcast only after submitting satisfactory proof of performance of transmitter and antenna. Given present-day solid-state technology, this is almost never a problem; but when the Act was written, 1930s' technology needed to be proof-tested. Although many broadcasters argue that this CP requirement is long out of date, Congress has not seen fit to change it.

A CP gives its holder a limited time (usually 24 months for television and 18 for radio) to construct and test the station. The CP holder then files a record of technical testing, to apply for a regular license. With FCC permission, a permittee may (and most do) begin on-air program testing pending final approval of the license.

Licensee Qualifications

Sec. 308(b) of the Communications Act allows only *U.S. citizens* who qualify as to *character, financial resources*, and *technical ability* to receive a license. Congress left the FCC with wide discretion in implementing and interpreting these basic requirements, and applicants nearly always meet the minimum statutory qualifications. Sec. 310(b) forbids foreign control of a broadcast license (most other countries have similar rules).

- *Character.* Applicants should have personal and business histories free of evidence suggesting defects in character that would cast doubt on their ability to operate in the public interest. Criminal records and violations of antitrust laws may constitute such evidence. Any previous history of misrepresentation to the FCC would be an almost-fatal defect (see Exhibit 13.e).
- *Financial resources.* Applicants must certify that they have "sufficient" financial resources. The FCC has issued varied definitions over time as to what "sufficient" means; in the early 1990s it meant the ability to construct and operate facilities for 90 days without reliance on station revenue.
- *Technical ability.* Most applicants hire engineering consultants to prepare technical aspects of their applications. Such consultants specialize in showing how a proposed station will get maximum physical coverage (including primary service coverage in the proposed community of license) without causing objectionable interference to existing stations.

Mutually Exclusive Applications

In any comparative proceeding (two or more applications for the same facility), the FCC exercises its right under the Act to specify "other qualifications," such as the degree of local ownership and/or the role of minorities and women in station management. These FCC-generated criteria become crucial when, as usually happens in major markets, the Commission has to choose among competing applicants. The FCC can make a choice among them only after conducting comparative hearings—an often drawn-out and costly process for all concerned.

License by Lottery

So many thousands of competitive applications piled up for LPTV stations in the early 1980s that, responding to the FCC's plea, Congress amended the Act in 1982 to authorize selection of new (*not* renewal) LPTV licensees by means of a *lottery* rather than time-consuming comparative hearings (47 USC 309[i]). Using lotteries, the FCC could check an LPTV (or MMDS) applicant's qualifications to

Exhibit 13.e •••••• ••••••••••

RKO—Licensee Qualification Gone Wrong

In 1965, a license renewal challenge to Los Angeles television station KHJ began a bizarre series of events that tested two FCC licensing concepts: licensee "character" qualifications and the comparative renewal hearings process. KHJ-TV was one of 16 stations then owned by RKO General, a subsidiary of General Tire (renamed GenCorp in 1982). Although no serious complaints had been lodged against KHJ-TV during the preceding license period, the challenger had discovered that the parent of RKO General, General Tire, had been investigated by a federal agency for numerous alleged financial irregularities, including bribing foreign officials, maintaining secret overseas bank accounts, and misappropriating corporate funds. While such allegations, even if true, had no direct bearing on the operation of the Los Angeles station or of its parent, RKO General, they gave the opposing applicant, Fidelity Television, a chance to argue to the FCC that renewal should be denied on the ground that General Tire's alleged financial irregularities constituted "character" defects that disqualified it as a broadcast licensee.

Similar renewal challenges to the other RKO stations followed, against WNAC-TV in Boston in 1969, and WOR-TV in New York in 1972. Attacks on RKO's character qualifications snowballed, eventually placing all 16 of its licenses in jeopardy. In 1980, the commission declined to renew the Boston, New York, and Los Angeles television stations. On appeal, RKO managed to retain two, losing the Boston outlet, then worth more than $200 million. In 1983, 18 years after the KHJ-TV case began, the FCC turned the whole affair (now including over 150 other applicants for RKO facilities) over to one of its Administrative Law Judges to make a definitive finding on the RKO character qualification issue, among others.

Delays and expense continued. It took the ALJ four years to explore such issues as whether RKO General had tried to deceive the FCC about the charges brought against General Tire, and whether such transgressions should endanger the broadcast stations which were not directly involved. While the legal fees and delay mounted, the head of General Tire, presumably the one responsible for its past irregularities, retired. This raised a new question: can character defects be tied to a corporation separate from its responsible officers?

Finally, in 1987, the ALJ concluded in a strongly worded report that renewal of all remaining RKO stations should be denied. RKO, he said, had set a record of dishonesty in dealing with the FCC. Of course, RKO appealed, admitting to only minor failings, pointing out that the changes in top management ensured future compliance with FCC rules, and stating its intention to sell all its stations as soon as the FCC cleared its licenses (owners may not sell stations while their licenses remain under investigation).

By 1989, after a quarter-century of hearings, appeals, court cases, and remands, the RKO licenses remained up in the air. RKO still operated all but two of its stations—the Boston television station lost in the 1980 decision, and the New York television station which had been sold (despite pending renewal issues by a special act of Congress aimed at granting New Jersey its first commercial VHF channel).

Over the years, RKO had spent $27 million in legal fees. The legal costs of all parties totaled close to $100 million. As for Fidelity Television, the company that had started it all back in 1965, it agreed to drop its application in favor of an offer of the Walt Disney studios to buy the station, with $103 million of the sale price going to Fidelity to cover its accumulated expenses. But even this was contingent on a final FCC decision as to RKO's overall status as a licensee. In early 1991 the dragged-out process finally closed down as the FCC approved the last of the several sales RKO had lined up over the preceding several years (RR, 1991: 1341).

The marathon RKO case dramatizes the absurd lengths to which the character test of licensees, and the comparative renewal hearings process of the FCC can go when complex corporate entities are involved.

be a licensee *after* the applicant had already been chosen by the lottery, going back to choose another applicant if the first winner was deficient in some way.

Critics object to lotteries, charging that they allow the FCC to evade its responsibility—that is, by granting licenses only if the recipients show intention to serve the public interest. Further, and ironically, lotteries have frustrated rapid licensee diversification by creating an unforeseen paperwork monster. Thousands filed the simplified application forms for the new services. And complaints about lottery "mills"—investors being duped into putting their money in a "sure thing" that was anything but—became common. In the early 1990s the FCC, FTC, and Better Business Bureau—along with nearly 20 state agencies—were investigating such mills and trying to promote investor caution (*Broadcasting*, 20 April 1992: 42). By 1985—just two years after lotteries were first used—the FCC had been inundated by 20,000 LPTV, 16,000 MMDS, and 5,000 cellular telephone applications that took years to resolve even with lotteries.

Regulators expressed fears that more lottery scams would develop as they opened newer services or reallocated spectrum. With that in mind, the FCC asked Congress to give it authority to switch lotteries to outright *auctions*, which, because of the higher costs involved, would greatly reduce the number of lottery "players"—though no legislation had resulted by 1993.

Meanwhile, lotteries had eliminated the application back-up for LPTV, MMDS, and cellular telephone service licenses. The FCC said it would apply lotteries to regular broadcast applications only if comparative hearings resulted in ties—which by 1992 had happened only once or twice.

Minority/Diversity Preferences

The FCC designed its LPTV service as a means of diversifying television programming. In keeping with that goal, the lottery amendment included a provision awarding a two-to-one *preference* to applicants more than half owned by minorities and/or to applicants with no other media interests. These minority and diversity preferences could be combined to give a minority-controlled entity new to the media field a four-to-one preference.* The first LPTV lottery, held in 1983, resulted in 23 grants, 8 to minority applicants.

Services Requiring No License

Stations that use subcarriers for auxiliary services not related to broadcasting and not received on regular receivers need not apply for FCC licenses for such services. Carrier-current radio stations (found on many college campuses) also operate without licenses as they are not propagated over the air.

● ● ● ● ● ● ● ●

13.5 Operations

To encourage operation in the public interest, the FCC could monitor station operations constantly, ensuring fulfillment of licensee promises and compliance with regulations. Realistically speaking, however, budget and personnel limits (plus deregulatory thinking) make it impossible for the Commission to monitor the nearly 14,000 broadcasting stations in any detail.

Instead, complaints from the public, competitors, and would-be competitors call attention to most violations. Insofar as the FCC does exercise oversight, matters of concern tend to be those that are easily identifiable and objectively verifiable—for example, engineering and employment practices—rather than such less tangible matters as quality or variety of programs wherein regulatory (and public) tastes change.

---

*The FCC conducts lotteries by assigning a number to each applicant, mixing the numbers randomly before drawing enough of them to fill the current quota of licenses. It enhances the chances for both minority applicants and media newcomers by duplicating their numbers, thus doubling the probability that their numbers will be drawn. An applicant who qualifies for preference on both counts enjoys the statistical benefit of quadruplicated numbers.

Employment Practices

Broadcast licensees and cable franchisees proposing to employ five or more persons full time must set up a "positive, continuing program of practices assuring equal employment opportunities." These *equal employment opportunity* (EEO) requirements refer to women in all cases, and to minority ethnic groups in cases where they form 5 percent or more of the work force in a station's or cable system's service area. The CP application includes guidelines for establishing EEO programs, which require statements about plans or practices with regard to

- general EEO policy,
- the official responsible for implementing that policy,
- methods of publicizing the policy,
- methods of recruitment and training,
- an analysis of the racial composition of the population in the station's or system's service area (usually obtained from Census Bureau or Department of Labor records), and
- personnel promotion policies.

Stations and cable systems with five or more full-time employees must submit to the FCC annual employment reports that must be kept in the station's or cable system's public file (discussed below). The FCC reviews a licensee's recent EEO record when considering its license renewal, and periodically also examines cable system reports.

To help pin down EEO policy requirements, the Commission has issued detailed processing guidelines (see Exhibit 13.f). Congress extended broadcast EEO requirements to cable systems in the 1984 cable act; 1992 amendments expanded those requirements further—to "any multichannel video programming distributor." The 1992 changes also prohibit the FCC from revising (deregulating) EEO requirements then in place, making EEO one area where deregulation failed to make inroads.

Public File

Beginning in 1971 the FCC required stations to keep license-renewal applications and other relevant documents in a file, readily available for public in-spection. Three years later, the Commission issued a procedure manual explaining how the FCC handled complaints and how citizens could participate in its proceedings, as well as detailing what intervening parties needed to do to build sound legal cases (FR, 1974: 32288). Though now a quaint and outdated indicator of pre-deregulation attitudes, the manual still must be included in every station's public file.

Applicants and licensees are required to assemble specified documents and keep them ready to show, during business hours, to any member of the public on request. All stations, commercial and non-commercial, must maintain such a file, retaining some documents for seven years in the case of a radio station and five in the case of television. Cable systems have to maintain a public file of employment-related documents. The more inclusive broadcast public file includes the following:

- The latest construction permit or license application, including any for major changes.
- The latest license renewal application, as well as ownership reports and annual employment reports.
- The EEO model program, if required (see Exhibit 13.f).
- The now-obsolete pamphlet entitled "The Public and Broadcasting—A Procedural Manual," issued in 1974.
- A record of the disposition of any political-broadcast time requests for the preceding two years.
- A quarterly listing of programs the licensee believes provided the most significant treatment of local community problems of public importance.
- Records required by the Children's Television Act of 1990 concerning programming for and advertising to children under the age of 16 (see Section 14.9 for details).
- Any time brokerage agreements in force (see Section 6.6 for details).
- Copies of (television) station decisions concerning must carry and retransmission consent governing its relationship with any local cable systems (see Section 13.8 for details).
- Letters received from members of the public (to be kept for three years) and any agreement with citizens groups.

Exhibit 13.f ●●●●●●●●●●●●●●●●●

EEO Mandates and Staff Size

Number of Full-Time Employees	EEO Requirements
1 to 4*	Need not file an EEO plan.
5 to 10	The FCC will review system or station EEO programs unless the percentage of minority and women employees equals half of their representation in the local labor force. In other words, if a market's labor force, as defined by the Census Bureau, if half black, at least one-quarter of a station's or cable system's employees in that market should be from that minority group. In the top job categories (officers and managers, professionals, technicians, and salespersons), a station or system should have a minority-employee ratio of at least one-quarter of that minority's representation in the local labor force. If half of the local labor force is black, at least one-eighth of the top 4 station or system jobs should be held by blacks.
11 or more	Should employ at least half as many minorities and women as are represented in the local labor force overall *and* in the top-4 job categories (officers and managers, professionals, technicians, and salespersons).
50 or more†	Same as for stations or systems with 11 or more employees but in addition, EEO programs are regularly reviewed.

*This category consists mainly of radio stations.
†Most of these are television operations.

Deregulatory decisions such as the abandonment of formal ascertainment of community needs, deletion of programming guidelines (detailed in Section 13.9), and reduction of renewal applications to postcard form (see Exhibit 13.g) reduced the public file's size, but media owners still regard it as a waste of time. Indeed, members of the public rarely ask to see it.*

*Students in university electronic media courses are sometimes assigned inspection of station public files as a course project. But they often get blank stares or flat refusals because even top station personnel seem to know little or nothing about the FCC public-file requirement.

Keeping Up with Washington

Station and cable system managers must keep current with changes in FCC regulations. Trade organizations and publications and an army of communications attorneys in Washington help licensees with this task. Well over 1,000 attorneys representing electronic media clients are members of the Federal Communications Bar Association (FCBA). Personal contacts with FCC staff members enable Washington lawyers to get things done faster than can distant licensees unfamiliar with the federal bureaucracy. The National Association of Broadcasters, National Cable Television Association, and

Exhibit 13.g ●●●●●●●●●●●●●●●●

Renewal Paperwork Before and After Deregulation

(A) In 1971, before deregulation, it took more than 16 pounds of paperwork to file for renewal of four Nebraska stations. (B) In 1983, this small stack of papers along with (C) a double-sided renewal postcard did the same job.

Source: Photos from *Broadcasting & Cable* magazine; postcard from FCC.

other trade associations offer legal clinics and regular publications on FCC rules.

From all of these sources, stations and systems receive continuous advice on what is new and what not to forget. For example, licensees often seem unaware of differing federal or state requirements on such things as employee drug use and over-the-air use of live or recorded telephone conversations. The timely filing of regular ownership, EEO, and other reports required by the Commission is a mundane but important aspect of using legal counsel.

Monitoring Performance

The FCC rarely monitors electronic media. Inspectors from the Field Operations Bureau check technical aspects of station and cable-system operations, but only occasionally and in random fashion. Questions about programming and commercial practices,

if they arise at all, usually come to FCC attention through complaints from the general public, consumer groups—or competing licensees or applicants at renewal time.

The Mass Media Bureau's Enforcement Division receives more public comments than any other federal agency except those dealing with environmental protection and consumer product safety. A complaints and compliance office was created in 1960 in the aftermath of quiz and payola scandals. Originally planned as an active FCC monitoring arm, it soon settled into a passive role—perfunctorily disposing of thousands of cards and letters sent to the FCC each year by the general public.

Few complainers seem to understand the FCC's legal limitations—most complaints are discarded because they ask the Commission to violate the First Amendment by censoring material that writers personally dislike. The leading topics vary only

C.

Federal Communications Commission
Washington, D.C. 20554

**APPLICATION FOR RENEWAL OF LICENSE FOR
COMMERCIAL AND NONCOMMERCIAL AM, FM OR TV BROADCAST STATION**

Approved by OMB
3060-0110
Expires 5/31/91

For Commission Fee Use Only	
	FEE NO:
	FEE TYPE:
	FEE AMT:
	ID SEQ:

For Commission Use Only: File No.

For Applicant Fee Use Only

Is a fee submitted with this application?   ☐ Yes ☐ No

If No, indicate reason therefor (check one box):

☐ Nonfeeable application

Fee Exempt (See 47 C.F.R. Section 1.1112)

☐ Noncommercial educational licensee

☐ Governmental entity

1. Name of Applicant

Mailing Address

City	State	ZIP Code

2. This application is for: ☐ AM   ☐ FM   ☐ TV

(a) Call Letters: _____   (b) Principal Community:
City _____   State _____

3. Attach as Exhibit No. _____ an identification of any FM booster or TV booster station for which renewal of license is also requested.

4. Have the following reports been filed with the Commission:

(a) The Broadcast Station Annual Employment Reports (FCC Form 395-B) as required by 47 C.F.R. Section 73.3612?   ☐ Yes   ☐ No

If No, attach as Exhibit No. _____ an explanation.

(b) The applicant's Ownership Report (FCC Form 323 or 323-E) as required by 47 C.F.R. Section 73.3615?   ☐ Yes   ☐ No

If No, give the following information:
Date last ownership report was filed _____
Call letters of station for which it was filed _____

FCC 303-S
May 1988

5. Is the applicant in compliance with the provisions of Section 310 of the Communications Act of 1934, as amended, relating to interests of aliens and foreign governments?   ☐ Yes   ☐ No

If No, attach as Exhibit No. _____ an explanation.

6. Since the filing of the applicant's last renewal application for this station or other major application, has an adverse finding been made or final action been taken by any court or administrative body with respect to the applicant or parties to the application in a civil or criminal proceeding, brought under the provisions of any law relating to the following: any felony; broadcast related antitrust or unfair competition; criminal fraud or fraud before another governmental unit; or discrimination?   ☐ Yes   ☐ No

If Yes, attach as Exhibit No. _____ a full description of the persons and matters involved, including an identification of the court or administrative body and the proceeding (by dates and file numbers) and the disposition of the litigation.

7. Would a Commission grant of this application come within 47 C.F.R. Section 1.1307, such that it may have a significant environmental impact?   ☐ Yes   ☐ No

If Yes, attach as Exhibit No. _____ an Environmental Assessment required by 47 C.F.R. Section 1.1311.

If No, explain briefly why not.

8. Has the applicant placed in its station's public inspection file at the appropriate times the documentation required by 47 C.F.R. Sections 73.3526 or 73.3527?   ☐ Yes   ☐ No

If No, attach as Exhibit No. _____ a complete statement of explanation.

The APPLICANT hereby waives any claim to the use of any particular frequency or of the electromagnetic spectrum as against the regulatory power of the United States because of the previous use of the same, whether by license or otherwise, and requests an authorization in accordance with this application. (See Section 304 of the Communications Act of 1934, as amended.)

The APPLICANT acknowledges that all the statements made in this application and attached exhibits are considered material representations and that all the exhibits are a material part hereof and are incorporated herein as set out in full in the application.

CERTIFICATION: I certify that the statements in this application are true, complete, and correct to the best of my knowledge and belief, and are made in good faith.

Name	Signature
Title	Date

WILLFUL FALSE STATEMENTS MADE ON THIS FORM ARE PUNISHABLE BY FINE AND IMPRISONMENT. U.S. CODE, TITLE 18, SECTION 1001.

slightly from year to year, often influenced by organized letter-writing campaigns as well as by program trends (see Exhibit 13.d).

• • • • • • • •

13.6   Renewal

Under the Communications Act, licenses may be awarded for only "limited periods of time" (since 1981, five years for television and seven for radio) and must regularly come up for renewal—a requirement that at least theoretically enhances the power of the FCC's licensing authority. Although the FCC renews *more than 98 percent* of all licenses without asking any searching questions, possible nonrenewal seems always to be lurking in the background. Challenges to renewal applications can come from the FCC but are far more likely to be lodged by other would-be licensees who want to displace the incumbent, or by dissatisfied citizens in the licensee's community. Even if the incumbent wins a contested renewal (and they usually do), defending it can be both expensive and time consuming.

Application Routes

Sec. 309 of the Communications Act stipulates that "licenses shall be renewed if the public interest, convenience, and necessity would be served" by renewal. Before deregulation of renewal procedures, applications often required piles of supporting documents showing how the licensee had served—or would serve—the public interest (see Exhibit 13.g). In 1981 the FCC began using a simple postcard-sized renewal form, submitted four months before the expiration of the current station license. Still, most applicants supplement their "postcard" with additional multipage exhibits. The FCC staff investigates any minor problems by mail or telephone.

In deciding whether a renewal would be in the public interest, the FCC considers any information in the FCC's licensee file that may have arisen from complaints or penalties during the license period.

Whether or not this evidence affects renewal decisions depends on the route the renewal application takes through the FCC bureaucracy. As shown in Exhibit 13.h, renewal applications take one of three paths: uncontested, petition-to-deny, or the mutually exclusive application route.

- Some 98 percent of all renewal applications fall in the *uncontested* category. In the absence of serious complaints about a station, major penalties assessed against it during the preceding license period, and filed objections, the FCC staff uses its delegated authority to renew the station almost automatically. In fact, consumer advocates complain that the Mass Media Bureau merely "rubber-stamps" uncontested applications, no matter how mediocre a station's past performance may have been.
- The now rare *petition-to-deny renewal* comes from a citizen group or other party that opposes an incumbent licensee without itself wanting to take over the license. Such groups claim that incumbents have failed to meet public-interest standards (most often allegations about EEO compliance) and therefore should not be allowed to retain their licenses.
- *Mutually exclusive applications* arise when would-be licensees try to displace incumbents, claiming they can do a better job serving the public interest.

Comparative Renewals

Contested renewals present the FCC with difficult and controversial decisions. Two goals, desirable but opposite, compete for priority: (1) giving incumbent licensees a "legitimate renewal expectation," but at the same time (2) ensuring that incumbents nevertheless feel a "competitive spur" to better serve the public interest.

On one hand, incumbent licensees need a reasonable assurance of continuity to justify investments in equipment, personnel, and programming. Without a strong expectation of renewal at the end of a license period, no prudent investor would be willing to build a station. On the other hand, if incumbent

Exhibit 13.h ●●●●●●●●●●●●●●●●

License Renewal Routes

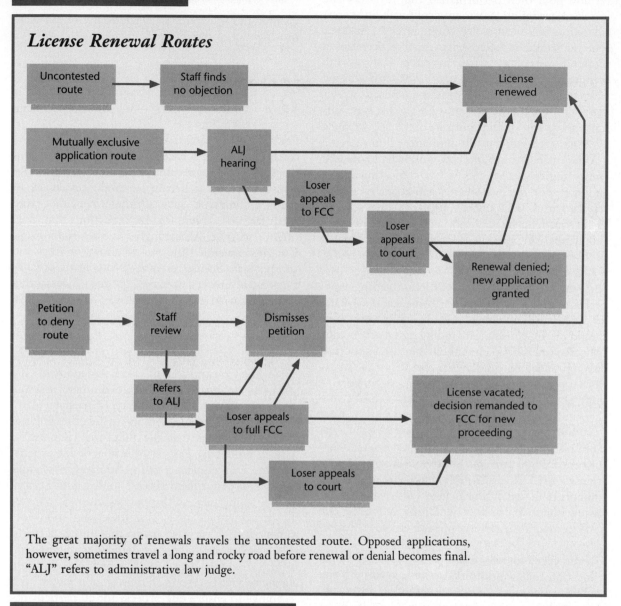

The great majority of renewals travels the uncontested route. Opposed applications, however, sometimes travel a long and rocky road before renewal or denial becomes final. "ALJ" refers to administrative law judge.

licensees feel assured of automatic renewal, no matter how poor their performance, they may take the low road, wringing maximum profit with little consideration for the broader public interest. Assured renewal would in effect give existing licensees a monopoly on channels, freezing out possibly worthy competitors (exactly the situation that critics argue exists today). Even though the Communications Act plainly rejects this solution by stating that renewals must serve the public interest, deregulation since 1980 has created virtually permanent licensees.

When it has to decide between incumbents and competing applicants, the FCC is comparing apples and oranges—the incumbent's actual past record of service with a competitor's *proposed* future service. What sort of performance by an incumbent licensee should the FCC accept in preference to a would-be licensee's glowing promises to do even better if given a chance? Should "merely average" past performance ensure renewal? "Better than average" performance? "Superior" performance? And what do such words mean in practice? What evidence should the FCC weigh in grading past performance to decide whether an incumbent deserves a superior, passing, or failing grade? Significantly, these questions typically involve programming. And programming is the one—admittedly crucial—licensee role that the FCC least wants to appraise.

When faced with a comparative renewal, the Commission relies in part on criteria issued a quarter-century ago for comparative hearings for new licenses (FCCR, 1965: 393) and considered for modification many times since (with yet another review under way as this book went to press). The 1965 comparative criteria include consideration of

- technical factors (for example, a proposed antenna location that would serve more people than the present one).
- ownership and management issues (diversification of media ownership—not owning other media or not owning other nearby media; localism—active participation by the owner in management; and ownership by members of a minority).
- past broadcast record (of the incumbent and, if applicable, the opposing applicant).

- program service proposals (especially the amount and type of nonentertainment programming).

Exhibit 13.i illustrates a "David and Goliath" case in which all of these criteria played a part.

• • • • • • • •

13.7 Enforcement

For several decades, Congress and the FCC relied solely on threat of license loss to enforce its rules and the Communications Act. The FCC either could refuse to renew a license or could revoke it. In practice, however, such ultimate penalties were often far too extreme for the infractions that most often occurred. Accordingly, in the early 1960s Congress amended the Act to allow for fines and shorter-term license renewals. None of these sanctions can be invoked without legal due process, often beginning with a formal hearing.

Due Process

A fundamental safeguard of individual liberties under the Constitution, the Fifth Amendment's *due process clause*, guarantees that government may not deprive a person of "life, liberty, or property without due process of law." Among many other applications, this means that the FCC may not use its powers arbitrarily. Fairness, the goal of due process, requires that applicants and petitioners have ample opportunity to argue their cases under nondiscriminatory conditions and that parties adversely affected by decisions may appeal for review by authorities other than those that made the initial decision. Many due process rights are detailed in the *Administrative Procedure Act* of 1946, which specifies how agencies such as the FCC must conduct their proceedings to ensure due process for all participants. For example:

- The Commission must advise unsuccessful license applicants of its reasons for rejecting their applications. The applicants may reply, and if the Commission still decides against them, it must then set the matter for a hearing.

Exhibit 13.i ●●●●● ●●●●●●●●●●●●

David v. Goliath—
The Simon Geller Renewal

Simon Geller, the eccentric owner and sole staff member of classical music station WVCA-FM in Gloucester, MA, a fishing and resort community north of Boston, was a folk hero to his loyal listeners. Geller, who put his station on the air in 1964, adopted a wall-to-wall classical music format that ran 15 hours daily, interrupted only with barely enough advertising to keep the station solvent. In fact, many of his 90,000 appreciative listeners sent in donations to keep the station afloat. Geller did not let news or public-affairs programs interrupt the music; he felt that the Boston stations that put signals over the Gloucester area took care of those needs.

Grandbanke Corporation, a group owner of radio stations in Massachusetts, became interested in the potential of the Gloucester market. As no other FM channels were allotted to the small town, Grandbanke tried to buy Geller's station, offering to keep him on the payroll. Geller, for whom the station was a way of life, turned down the offer. Grandbanke thereupon filed a competing application for the facility when Geller's license came up for renewal. The corporation assembled a textbook set of management and program promises closely paralleling the FCC's 1965 comparative renewal criteria. It promised to devote nearly 29 percent of the station's overall schedule to news and public affairs, while retaining the classical music format the rest of the time. The management would work closely with Gloucester groups to air community issues.

The FCC administrative law judge who heard the case initially approved Geller's renewal. However, the commission, concerned about Geller's total lack of news and public affairs programs, set the case for an oral argument before making a final decision. Geller, who was unable to pay for an attorney, came to Washington and gave the FCC an emotional defense of his stewardship, noting that the station had to go off the

air while he appeared before the FCC because there was no one else to run it. Unmoved, the FCC found Grandbanke's several attorneys persuasive in proving that their client could better fulfill the public interest as defined by the FCC's 1965 statement.

Geller appealed the case, meanwhile keeping his station on the air. In 1985, the court of appeals returned the case to the FCC, telling the commission that it had been inconsistent in applying its own 1965 statement of comparative criteria to this case. Specifically, Geller should be awarded a preference for his absolute integration of ownership and management and for localism (the station was in Geller's two-room apartment). Finally, late in 1985, the FCC reversed itself and renewed Geller's license (FCCR, 1985c: 1443). David had faced Goliath in unequal combat and had won. In 1988, Geller had the last laugh: he sold his station for a cool million dollars—and not to Grandbanke—and retired to the movie theaters and delicatessens of the Upper East Side of Manhattan. The new owner promised to keep the classical format—and to hire 10 people to run the station 24 hours a day.

Source: Photo by Rick Friedman/New York Times Pictures.

- On the other hand, if the Commission grants a license application *without* a hearing, for the ensuing 30 days (after a public notice announcing this action) the grant remains open to protest from "any party in interest." If the FCC finds that some party raises pertinent issues, the Commission must then postpone the effective date of the grant and hold a hearing.
- If the Commission wishes to fine a licensee, it must invite the licensee to "show cause" why such action should *not* be taken.

FCC Hearings

When an issue arises that requires presentation of opposing arguments, the FCC may hold a hearing to settle the dispute. Senior staff attorneys called *administrative law judges* (ALJs) preside over initial FCC hearings. They conduct the proceedings somewhat like courtroom trials, with sworn witnesses, testimony, evidence, counsel for each side, and so on. Initial decisions of ALJs (who act as both judge and jury, in contrast to many courtroom trials) are reviewed, first by the FCC's Review Board and then by the commissioners themselves. When opposing sides exploit all possibilities for reviews and appeals, as they often do, final decisions take a long time.* Procedural rules head off frivolous interventions and intentional delays by carefully defining circumstances that justify hearings and qualifications of parties entitled to *standing*—that is, the right to participate.

*The longest-running case in FCC annals began in 1941. Among other matters, it entailed arguments over nighttime use of the 770-kHz AM radio channel used by both KOB in Albuquerque and WABC in New York. After more than 30 years of appeals, the FCC in 1977 again confirmed WABC's primary status on the channel. KOB's "final" objections appeared to be quashed by a 1980 appeals court affirmation of the FCC order that the Supreme Court declined to review. In 1981, however, KOB's irrepressible licensee filed still another petition, this time asking the FCC to reclassify the channel, giving him yet another avenue of appeal. That also failed, and, after *four decades* of legal proceedings, the station was sold in 1986. For another example of marathon proceedings, see Exhibit 13.e.

Court Appeals

Even after all safeguards in FCC hearings and re-hearings have been exhausted, the Communications Act gives parties adversely affected by FCC actions still further recourse. The Act provides that all appeals concerning station licenses must go before the U.S. Court of Appeals for the District of Columbia Circuit, in Washington, D.C. This court consists of nine judges, but panels of only three hear most cases. The court may confirm or overturn Commission actions, in part or in whole. It may also *remand* a case, sending it back to the FCC for further consideration in keeping with the court's interpretation of the Communications Act and other laws (see Exhibit 13.j). Given all its experience, this appeals court has become expert on FCC matters, as was intended by the Act's framers six decades ago.

Appeals from FCC decisions in cases that do not involve licensees may be initiated in any of the 12 other U.S. Courts of Appeals. Each serves a specific region of the country and is known as a *circuit court of appeal*.

From any of the federal circuit courts, final appeals may be sought before the Supreme Court of the United States. A request for consideration by the Supreme Court, called a *writ of certiorari*, may be turned down ("cert. denied"). If that happens, the appeal process is over. Refusal to hear a case does not necessarily mean that the Supreme Court agrees with lower court findings, but the earlier decision holds nonetheless, though without standing as a compelling nationwide legal precedent.

Loss of License

From the FCC's creation in 1934 through 1990, only about 140 stations involuntarily lost their licenses. *Nonrenewal* accounts for two-thirds (98) of these losses. Outright *revocation*—not waiting for the current license to expire—occurred only 41 times in nearly 60 years. The average rate of *involuntary deletions* (either nonrenewals or revocations) was less than three stations per year. FCC records show but two revocations and only nine nonrenewals in

Exhibit 13.j •••••••••••••••••

Citizen Involvement—
The Landmark WLBT Case

Until the late 1960s, a broadcast station's audience members had no right to take part in regulatory proceedings concerning that station. That situation changed as a result of a court case that began in 1955 when a group of citizens made the first of a series of complaints to the FCC about the conduct of WLBT, a VHF television station in Jackson, MS. The group accused the station of blatant discrimination against blacks, who formed 45 percent of its audience. The FCC dismissed the citizens' complaints, saying that they had no legal right to participate in a licensing decision. When WLBT's license again came up for renewal in 1964, local groups obtained legal assistance from the Office of Communications of the United Church of Christ (UCC) in New York.

The UCC petitioned the FCC on behalf of the local groups for permission to intervene in the WLBT renewal application proceeding, but the FCC again rejected the petition, saying that citizens had no *legal standing* to intervene. At that time the commission recognized only signal interference or economic injury (to another broadcaster) as reasons to give parties the right to participate in renewal hearings. Thus only other broadcasters had standing to challenge existing licensees.

The UCC went to the Court of Appeals, claiming that the FCC had no right to bar representatives of the viewing public from intervening in renewals, or to award a renewal without a hearing in the face of substantial public opposition. The court agreed, directing the FCC to hold hearings on WLBT's renewal and to give standing to representatives of the public (F, 1966). The FCC held a hearing and grudgingly permitted UCC to participate as ordered. However, it once again renewed WLBT's license.

The UCC returned to court and in 1969 an exasperated appeals court reconsidered the case—14 years after the first complaints had been recorded. In the last opinion written by Warren Burger before he became Chief Justice of the Supreme Court, the court rebuked the FCC for "scandalous delay." It ordered the FCC to cancel WLBT's license and to appoint an interim operator pending selection of a new licensee (F, 1969). But ten *more* years passed before the FCC finally selected a new permanent licensee. Altogether, the case dragged on for more than a quarter of a century.

As the FCC had feared, the WLBT case triggered many petitions to deny renewal of other licenses. However, this "reign of terror," as a trade magazine put it, resulted in few actual hearings and still fewer denials. Of the 342 challenges filed in 1971–1973, only 16 resulted in denials of license renewal. An exacting standard of evidence established by the FCC and approved by the court ensured this high rate of petition failure. Only after an opponent presented overwhelming evidence would the FCC schedule a license-renewal hearing (F, 1972).

---

all of the 1980s. In short, though an ever-present background threat, loss of license only rarely becomes a reality.* The drop-off in the pace of involuntary deletions appears to be a result of the liberalized standards that flow from deregulation.

*Data extracted from FCC, *56th Annual Report, Fiscal Year 1990* (pp. 33–34), which reports information through September 30, 1990.

Nonrenewal of broadcast licenses occurs more frequently than revocation because the burden of proof for showing that the renewal would be in the public interest falls on the licensee. In contrast, revocation puts the burden of proof on the FCC. The Commission typically treats violators with extraordinary leniency as long as they candidly admit error and contritely promise reform. In those few cases where revocation or nonrenewal did occur, most involved a history of *willful misconduct* by a station.

A review of reasons for involuntary deletions shows that program infractions, such as news slanting, rarely result in loss of license. In the great majority of cases, the FCC cites nonprogram violations related to character standards (such as misrepresentation and concealment of ownership), technical violations, and fraudulent billing of advertisers. One can safely assume that the almost complete absence of program infractions does not mean that the deleted stations had faultless program records—the FCC simply felt on safer constitutional ground when exacting the maximum penalty for *non*program violations.

If hearings delay renewal, the license remains in effect pending resolution of the case. Even if a station loses its final appeal, the FCC gives it a grace period in which to wind up its affairs, though it may no longer attempt to sell its license (it *can* sell its equipment, buildings, and land). Following this, a new applicant may arrive on the scene to make a fresh start, or the Commission may appoint an interim operator if comparative hearings delay grant of the channel to a new licensee.

Lesser Penalties

Not all offenses, of course, warrant the capital punishment of license loss. For lesser offenses, the FCC inflicts milder sanctions of short-term renewals, conditional renewals, forfeitures (fines), or letters placed in the station's file.

- *Short-term renewal* (usually a year or two instead of the full renewal term) puts a licensee on a kind of probation pending correction of deficiencies evident during its preceding license period.
- *Conditional renewal* is granted pending correction of some specific fault. Either this or a short-term renewal can have a "green light" effect—encouraging competing applications at renewal time.

- *Forfeitures*, or *fines*, ranging up to a maximum of $250,000 for repeated violations may be assessed for infractions of FCC rules. Most forfeitures come from technical violations, few from program violations—and most are for much less than the maximum amount. As cable systems have no license which the FCC can threaten, fines are the agency's chief means of enforcing cable rules. FCC fine levels greatly increased in 1991, as did Commission flexibility in determining specific fines. Most per-violation fines range from as little as $1,250 up to $20,000, with considerable FCC discretion (adjustment up or down by 20 to 90 percent) depending on circumstances (*Broadcasting*, 5 August 1991: 24).
- Relatively minor infractions may result in a *letter* being placed in the station's file for consideration when it applies for license renewal.

But when contrasted with some 14,000 broadcast stations on the air, the relatively low use of any of these penalties reflects generally lenient FCC treatment of licensee wrongdoing. Commissioners tend to sympathize with problems of marginal stations struggling to survive, just the ones most likely to commit punishable infractions.

●●●●●●●●

13.8   *Cable Franchising*

Cable "licensing," or *franchising*, follows a pattern totally different from broadcast licensing. Franchises are issued by local rather than federal authorities because cable systems use streets and other public property that is subject to municipal jurisdiction, rather than federally controlled airways. Federal cable laws contain provisions covering crossownership, equal employment opportunities, program obscenity, customer service, and technical standards. Passed in 1984 and 1992, both laws amended the Communications Act.* It's useful to understand their general thrust before turning to the specifics of franchising.

Cable Acts—General Provisions

The "Cable Communications Policy Act of 1984" created a new Title VI of the Communications Act which established a loose federal *de*regulatory framework for cable television. Key parts of that act were reversed in the strongly *re*-regulatory "Cable Television Consumer Protection and Competition Act of 1992," which amended Title VI. This 1992 legislation grew out of public and congressional anger over sharp increases in cable subscription rates—in some cases three times the rate of inflation—in the five years before it became law. The combined result of the two acts includes the following key provisions:

- The 1984 act defined cable television as a one-way video programming service; neither it nor the 1992 revisions regulate two-way (interactive) services.
- The 1992 act is transforming the relationship between broadcasters and cable systems. Under this act, each commercial television station has the right every three years (beginning in October 1993) either to charge cable systems within the same ADI a negotiated fee for use of its signal (termed *retransmission consent*) or simply to require that cable systems carry its signal (this provision—the *must-carry rule*—is discussed at Section 13.9). If a station and cable system cannot reach agreement on terms, that station will not be carried on that system for at least three years. Stations that fail to choose between must-carry and

retransmission consent will, by default, come under the must-carry option. MMDS and SMATV systems are also subject to retransmission consent rules.*

- A television station may also demand carriage on the same channel number on cable that it uses over the air. (Increasingly controversial in the years prior to passage of the 1992 act had been the decision by some cable systems to shift broadcast stations' locations on their cable spectrum; by carrying a station on a channel number different from its broadcast channel, they confused viewers and made it difficult for the station to promote itself to cable viewers. Cable argued that most prime channel locations do go to broadcasters, but the increasing number of cable services in demand by viewers makes channel assignments increasingly difficult. The 1992 act gave stations the upper hand by requiring that they be carried on the same channel as that on which they broadcast—or at least on a channel agreed to by both system and station).
- Reversing a key aspect of the 1984 law, the 1992 act required local authorities or the FCC to regulate subscriber rates for the basic tier of cable service.** Both cable acts reinforced an existing FCC ban on *local* regulation of pay-cable rates.

*The 1984 and 1992 cable acts do not directly control private cable systems that avoid using public rights of way—such as SMATV systems, that serve large apartment complexes and are entirely on private property. In mid-1993, the Supreme Court upheld FCC rules requiring "external" SMATV systems (those connecting buildings with different owners) to be considered as cable systems requiring franchises (*Communication Daily*, 2 June 1993:2).

*The "retransmission consent" and "must-carry" provisions were the most controversial aspects of the 1992 act and led to heavy cable industry lobbying against the bill as well as to President Bush's veto, which Congress quickly overrode. The "must-carry" requirement, once an FCC regulation, had been twice overturned on First Amendment grounds by a federal appeals court in the late 1980s. As this book goes to press, both provisions have been appealed to the Supreme Court, having been initially upheld at the appeals court level, and the outcome of that review is uncertain. While awaiting judgment by the Supreme Court, several large cable MSOs have made clear they will *not* negotiate retransmission consent fees with broadcasters. As written, the law requires that cable systems with 12 or fewer channels must devote at least three to local broadcast signals. Systems with more than 12 channels may be required to devote up to a third of their capacity to carrying such broadcast signals. None of this applies to the relatively few cable systems with fewer than 300 subscribers.

**For details on cable system program tiers, see Section 6.4, page 205.

(Cable systems are exempt from rate regulation *if* (1) they serve fewer than 30 percent of the households in their area or (2) are subject to "effective competition" from some other multichannel competitor (MMDS, SMATV, or, eventually, DBS) that is *available* to at least 50 percent—and actually *subscribed* to by at least 15 percent—of an area's households.)

- In May 1993, the FCC issued a 450-page decision detailing how fair cable subscription rates were to be determined. Critics argued the FCC approach was as confusing as income tax regulations—and that it would be years before the true extent of government oversight of cable subscriber rates became clear, thanks to the likelihood of extensive appeals and litigation.
- Cable program providers (for example, ESPN or HBO) that are owned even in part by cable-system operators must make their services available to multichannel cable competitors (such as SMATV, MMDS, and DBS) at the same prices offered to cable systems. This provision, which expires in 2002, is designed to give competing delivery systems a chance to get an audience foothold. Its initial impact was evident within months as pending DBS operators signed agreements with dozens of popular (formerly cable-only) program services.

Cable Acts—Franchising

Whereas the 1984 act severely limited regulatory powers of state and local authorities, the 1992 law reinstated many of those same powers and added new FCC oversight of many aspects of cable franchising.

- Local franchising authorities may require public, educational, and governmental access ("PEG") channels over which the cable operator has little editorial control.
- The 1992 act added protection for children against indecent programming on commercially leased access channels. System operators may require that any such programming be limited to a single scrambled channel to be unblocked only on written request by a cable subscriber. This provision of the 1992 law, and FCC rules to enforce it, were appealed in 1993 on grounds that they amounted to unconstitutional censorship (see Section 14.4. p. 509).

- The 1984 act called for cable systems with more than 36 channels to set aside 10 to 15 percent of those channels for leased access to outside parties. The cable owner sets rates for leasing access channels but has no editorial control over their content—other than enforcement of obscenity and indecency limitations (as discussed later). The 1992 act requires the FCC to set maximum rates for use of such channels.
- Reinforcing existing practices and FCC guidelines, Congress allowed local franchise authorities to charge annual franchise fees of up to 5 percent of cable-system gross revenues to cover the cost of negotiating the franchisee's subsequent oversight.
- When granting franchise renewals, local authorities may require operators to upgrade cable facilities and channel capacity.
- The FCC may require that specific customer service levels and technical standards be included in new and renewal franchise agreements. Initial detailed FCC rules were issued early in 1993.
- The 1992 act required the FCC to evaluate every franchise-granting authority in the country (some 20,000 cities, counties, and other political units) and to certify that each had authority and capacity to issue and enforce such franchises—and that the franchise provisions agree with all requirements in the amended Communications Act. If any franchise authority is *not* so certified, then the FCC itself is to act as authority for cable in that market until a local franchise authority is certified.

Franchise Process

Because cable systems nearly always have effective monopoly status within their service areas, they fall under state and community *utility regulations*, which govern installation, standards of service, and complaint procedures for such services as telephone, power, and transportation.

When a local franchising authority (city, town, or county) decides it wants cable service, it first develops an *ordinance* or legal codification describing the conditions under which a cable system will be allowed to operate. Drawn up in many cases with the advice of outside experts, ordinances typically stipulate

- the term of the franchise (usually 10 to 15 years, but sometimes longer);
- the quality of service to be provided;
- technical standards, such as the minimum number of channels to be provided, time limits on construction, and interconnection with other systems;
- the franchise fee; and
- PEG channel requirements, if any.

Bidders base their offers on the design and timetable outlined in the franchise authority's *request for proposals* (RFP). Although franchisers usually grant a franchise to only one bidder, multiple awards (termed *overbuilds* if they cover the same region) are possible. During the 1980s controversy arose when successful bidders made grand promises that they later could not fulfill, so that the franchise agreement had to be renegotiated, with a lower quality of service resulting. A few communities avoided such problems by choosing to operate cable systems themselves as a municipal service, an arrangement common in Europe.

Renewals

As with original awards, local authorities handle franchise renewals. A local authority need not find that renewal will serve the public interest or meet any other standard but, rather, may simply renew a franchise without ceremony. If, however, the local authority wants to deny renewal, the Communications Act requires that it hold a hearing, in effect raising public-interest issues by deciding whether the incumbent operator has (1) complied with the law; (2) provided a quality of service that is "reasonable in light of the community needs"; (3) maintained the financial, legal, and technical ability to operate; and (4) prepared a renewal proposal that is "reasonable to meet the future cable-related com-

munity needs and interests" (Sec. 626). The Act does not require consideration of proposals from competing would-be franchisees during the course of renewal grants or renewal hearings.

• • • • • • • •

13.9   Deregulation

The widespread effort to deregulate—in communications and several other economic sectors—has many motives. Least controversial is the recognized need to discard outdated rules, to simplify unnecessarily complex rules, to ensure that those rules that remain can actually achieve their objectives, and to lighten administrative agency loads. Deregulation based on these motives began in the 1970s with wide political support.

A more controversial drive to deregulate stems from ideological motives growing out of a specific vision of a limited governmental role in national life. This view opposes government intervention, advocating instead reliance on the marketplace as a nongovernmental source of control over private economic behavior. This approach first emerged as a force on the national agenda in the late 1970s under President Jimmy Carter, escalated when Republican Ronald Reagan came to the White House in 1981, and continued to the end of the Bush administration in early 1993.

Theoretical Basis

Deregulatory theory holds that marketplace economic forces can stimulate production of better, more varied, and cheaper consumer goods and services without official guidance from above. Where government regulation may be necessary, on the other hand, it should be tested by a cost-benefit formula to make sure that the costs of such regulation do not outweigh its gains. As a case in point, the FCC explained its initial move to deregulate radio this way:

> Producers (providers) of goods and services must be responsive to consumers' desires in order to compete

successfully with rival producers. Consumers, by their choice of purchases, determine which producers (providers) will succeed. Moreover, not only does the competition among producers for consumers lead to the production of the goods and services that consumers want most, the same competitive process forces producers continually to seek less costly ways of providing those goods and services. As a result, parties operating freely in a competitive market environment will determine and fulfill consumer wants, and do so efficiently. (FCCR, 1979: 492).

The FCC did not go so far as to advocate abandoning *all* regulation. It divided rules into behavioral and structural categories. *Behavioral regulation*, which deregulators seek to discard or at least minimize, controls what licensees may or may not do in conducting their businesses; *structural regulation* controls the overall shape of the marketplace and terms on which would-be licensees can enter. Rules requiring a licensee to limit advertising in children's programs or banning indecent program material are examples of behavioral regulation; rules preventing a licensee from owning another related communications business or from owning more than *x* number of stations are examples of structural regulation. Deregulation, however, tilts toward the structural regulation approach, which enhances competition by making marketplace entry easier, preserves competition by preventing monopoly—and stays away from program-based decisions. Critics argue that deregulation serves mainly to enrich a few companies and individuals, often at the expense of broader public concerns.

Even theorists favoring deregulation admit that *market failure* can occur. Sometimes competition fails to produce expected favorable results. Indeed, uncontrolled competition may produce corporate giants that suppress competition (major airline control of most departure gates at "hub" airports is one example). And some public "goods," as economists call desirable services, may fall outside the realm of marketplace economics and therefore fail to materialize. If, for example, public television is thought desirable but costs too much to produce with limited private support, marketplace economics may have to be supplemented by giving such broadcasters government aid.

Broadcast Deregulation

While the FCC did away with many minor regulations in the 1970s, during the 1980s it began removing more substantive rules (see Exhibit 13.k), focusing first on commercial radio. In 1981, after an inquiry begun four years earlier, the Commission deleted four long-standing constraints on radio licensees (FCCR, 1981: 968)—and later did the same for educational radio and television (FCCR, 1984b: 746) and finally commercial television (FCCR, 1984c: 1076):

- the prescribed formal process for *ascertaining local community needs* that stations once underwent as a basis for making programming decisions (only the requirement of having a general knowledge of the local community remains);
- rules for comprehensive *program-log* keeping; though most stations still maintain logs for commercial reasons and still must put quarterly lists of "issue responsive" programs in public files;
- guidelines maintaining at least a certain level of *nonentertainment programs* per week; and
- guidelines on the maximum allowable amount of *advertising time* on the air.

The removal of these constraints caused heated controversy, especially because some critics erroneously believed that the FCC had once imposed formal rules (rather than guidelines) on programs and advertising. For example, many mistakenly feared that deregulation might mean the end of religion on the air, thinking that the FCC had always required such programs.*

In some cases the FCC substituted less demanding procedures for its former regulations. For example, in place of the old ascertainment rule, the Commission required all licensees to place in their public files

*The FCC had delegated to its licensing staff the authority to enforce guidelines on nonentertainment programming and advertising. Contrary to general opinion, the FCC never had *rules* mandating specific amounts of nonentertainment programming or limiting the maximum amount of advertising time. Instead, it had *guidelines* and allowed its staff to grant applications unless licensees failed to follow the guidelines. Only applications in violation of the guidelines had to go before the full commission. In practice, the guidelines became virtual quotas because applicants sought to avoid the close scrutiny and delay that would result if the staff referred a decision to the commissioners.

quarterly statements of community problems or issues along with a list of programs the licensee had offered about those problems (FCCR, 1984a: 930).*

Network Deregulation

Television networks underwent an intensive FCC special inquiry in 1979–1980, the third (and probably last) broadcast network study. A special staff exhaustively researched the potential for new television networks, FCC jurisdiction over networks,** issues of station and cable-system ownership, the impact of specific FCC rules, and the degree to which cable and newer media then just appearing had increased competition. A staff report concluded that prior network regulation had utterly failed to bring about its stated goal of fostering increased diversity of programming. Indeed, it had actually stifled competition, often by protecting networks from such new technologies as cable. It recommended that the Commission undo most of its existing network rules—including both PTAR and syn/fin rules, as discussed in Section 9.2 (FCC, 1980a: 491). When the Commission tried to follow the network deregulation recommendations, however, industry lobbyists limited the effort and the debate continued into the early 1990s.***

*In practice, many broadcasters backed into compliance with this rule by first examining what programs they carried in the preceding three months and then determining what problems or issues the programs seemed to fit best.

**Bear in mind that the Communications Act gives the FCC no explicit power to regulate networks. Sec. 303(i) does grant the Commission the right to *"make special regulations applicable to radio stations engaged in chain broadcasting"* (emphasis added), but not to regulate networks directly. The FCC does control broadcast networks indirectly, however, through its licensing authority over stations, including O&Os, that affiliate with them.

***The FCC could not, however, undo the chief factor behind the existence of only three national television networks, even though hundreds of new stations had been licensed since ABC, CBS, and NBC had begun television operations. The FCC's post-freeze 1952 television channel allotment plan made it virtually impossible for a fourth network to recruit enough affiliates to compete equally. The Fox network demonstrates this; even by 1993, seven years after it started, its largely UHF station line-up reached just over half of the national audience served by the three older networks (see Section 6.2), though Fox parlayed its smaller audience potential to considerable success just the same.

Cable Deregulation

The FCC had more success in streamlining procedures and requirements for newer delivery services. As discussed at Section 3.1, cable television took the brunt of the FCC's traditional policy of protecting the broadcasting status quo. The Commission sought especially to protect UHF television, which it feared would suffer irreparably from rapid cable expansion. A series of court reverses, followed by the economic rethinking noted above, caused the FCC to drop most cable regulation by 1980, as shown in Exhibit 13.1. Congress initially followed suit with its 1984 cable act limiting both local franchise and FCC authority.

By 1993, the Supreme Court was considering one aspect of cable regulation which had been eliminated twice before. Back in the mid-1980s, the only important FCC restriction on cable was the *must-carry rule*, which required each cable system to carry the signals of all "significantly viewed" television stations within that system's franchise area. The FCC intended to protect broadcasters from discriminatory treatment by cable operators and to help nonnetwork UHF and public outlets by equalizing the reach of all stations' signals in cable-covered areas.

The must-carry rule, however, penalized cable systems, as mandatory television signals filled many of their available channels, leaving few for cable-specific programs. Systems whose service areas straddled two or more broadcast markets sometimes had to carry several affiliates of the same network, stations that duplicated all but a few local programs.

In 1985 an appeals court agreed with cable interests that the rule violated the Constitution (F, 1985b: 1434). The FCC rewrote the rule, but in 1987 the same appeals court also found this version unconstitutional (F, 1987: 292). Cable systems did drop some independent and public stations available in larger markets and some television stations paid cable systems to continue carrying their signals—adding to pressure already building for re-regulation of cable. The 1992 cable act reinstated must-carry, triggering the new constitutional challenge to the Supreme Court (see Section 13.8).

Exhibit 13.k ●●●●●●●●●●●●●●●

Before and After Deregulation

The FCC modified or eliminated many broadcasting and cable rules during its deregulatory drive in the 1980s. Unchanged, however, were rules on equal employment opportunity, political broadcasting access, and PTAR. Moving against the deregulatory tide, Congress mandated limits on advertising in children's programming, requiring minimum amounts of such programming (1990), and moving to substantial reregulation of cable (1992). The FCC reversed its syndicated exclusivity (1988), and its own deregulatory course on technical standards with HDTV (1993–94).

Before 1980	Changes Since 1980
Licensing	
License runs three years for any broadcast station	License lasts five years for television, seven for radio (action by Congress, 1981)
Comparative hearings required for choosing among competing applications	Applicants for newer services (LPTV, MMDS, etc.) chosen by lottery (action by Congress, 1982; by FCC, 1983)
Ownership	
Limit of seven AM, seven FM, and seven television outlets	Limit raised to 12-12-12 (action by FCC, 1985); radio limits raised again to 18-18 (action by FCC, 1992)
Duopoly rule: Only one station of each kind per market	May own more than one radio station in larger markets (action by FCC, 1992)
Trafficking rule: Must hold a station at least three years	May sell license (with FCC okay) at any time (action by FCC, 1982)
Programming	
FCC application processing guidelines (not rules) call for minimum amounts of nonentertainment programming	No qualitative program guidelines (action by FCC for radio, 1982; for television, 1985)
Specific rules requiring determination of local program interests, needs (ascertainment)	Rules dropped; must file a quarterly "programs/problems" list in public file (action by FCC for radio, 1982; for television, 1985)
(no requirement)	Requirement to program some educational and cultural programs for children (action by Congress, 1990; by FCC, 1991)
Controversial issues must be aired and opposing sides treated fairly (fairness doctrine)	Fairness doctrine dropped (action by FCC, 1987)

Before 1980	Changes Since 1980
Advertising	
Guidelines (not rules) on maximum amount of advertising time allowed	Guidelines dropped (action by FCC for radio, 1982; for television, 1985)
(no requirement)	Specific limits on advertising in children's programming set (action by Congress, 1990)
Technical Rules	
Specific technical standards selected/mandated for each new service (e.g., color TV, FM stereo)	Starting with AM stereo decision, standards left to marketplace forces (action by FCC, 1982; Congress mandates FCC to select a specific standard, 1992); HDTV standard chosen (action by FCC, 1993/1994)
Engineers ranked by class, and specific classes required for certain jobs	Engineers no longer ranked by class (action by FCC, 1981)
Rules requiring signal quality and avoiding interference	Stations may use own methods (actions at various times by FCC)
Cable Television	
Cable systems must carry all local television stations	Must-carry rule dropped (U.S. Appeals Court, 1985, 1987); rules reinstated (action by Congress, 1992)
Syndicated exclusivity rules allow a station to force local cable systems to black out syndicated programs on superstations which are also carried by the local station	Rules dropped (action by FCC, 1980); then reinstated (action by FCC, 1988, effective 1990)
Local communities may control rates charged by cable systems	Local regulatory role largely eliminated (action by Congress, 1984); then reinstated (action by Congress, 1992)

Technical Standards

Though electronic media owners agreed with most aspects of broadcast and cable behavioral deregulation, they became uneasy when the FCC began deregulating technical standards. The issue was defined when the Commission declined to select a specific standard for AM stereo in 1982, a precedent

for a decade of future refusals to impose standards. Similar "nondecisions" followed regarding DBS, teletext, and other standards, indicating that economists had superseded engineers in Commission policy making, even in largely technical matters.

The "marketplace" in each case actually consisted, of course, not of consumers buying receivers but of station owners, operators, and manufacturers

Exhibit 13.l ••••• •••••••••••

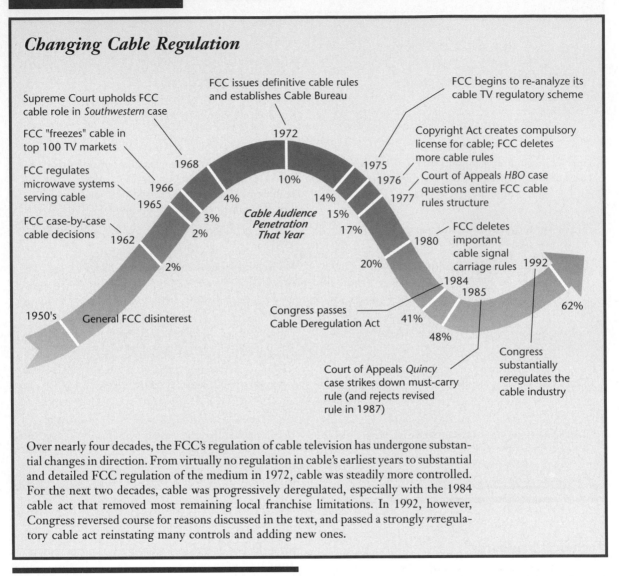

Changing Cable Regulation

Supreme Court upholds FCC cable role in *Southwestern* case

FCC issues definitive cable rules and establishes Cable Bureau

FCC begins to re-analyze its cable TV regulatory scheme

FCC "freezes" cable in top 100 TV markets

1972

FCC regulates microwave systems serving cable

1968

1975

Copyright Act creates compulsory license for cable; FCC deletes more cable rules

1966

10%

1976

Court of Appeals *HBO* case questions entire FCC cable rules structure

FCC case-by-case cable decisions

1965

4%

14%

1977

1962

3%

Cable Audience Penetration That Year

15%

2%

17%

1980

FCC deletes important cable signal carriage rules

1992

2%

20%

1984

1950's   General FCC disinterest

1985

62%

41%

Congress passes Cable Deregulation Act

48%

Court of Appeals *Quincy* case strikes down must-carry rule (and rejects revised rule in 1987)

Congress substantially reregulates the cable industry

Over nearly four decades, the FCC's regulation of cable television has undergone substantial changes in direction. From virtually no regulation in cable's earliest years to substantial and detailed FCC regulation of the medium in 1972, cable was steadily more controlled. For the next two decades, cable was progressively deregulated, especially with the 1984 cable act that removed most remaining local franchise limitations. In 1992, however, Congress reversed course for reasons discussed in the text, and passed a strongly *re*regulatory cable act reinstating many controls and adding new ones.

choosing equipment. Broadcasters would have to decide for themselves which transmission standard to use, hoping that set makers would eventually gear up to supply receivers that consumers would buy.

In AM stereo's case, that did not happen—a decade later few stations were broadcasting in stereo and few consumers had stereo-equipped AM receiv-

ers. In late 1992 Congress ordered the Commission to reopen the AM stereo question and select a specific standard within a year (see Exhibit 13.m).

Industry debate over the FCC's approach to technical standards rose to a fever pitch over high-definition television (see Section 5.9). At issue were the same questions: Should government help industry

Exhibit 13.m ● ● ● ● ● ● ● ● ● ● ● ● ● ●

The AM Stereo Experiment

In April 1961, when the FCC approved technical standards for FM stereo broadcasting, it turned aside proposals for stereo AM in order to allow the then-weaker FM service a chance to get on its feet. Two decades later, with AM and FM fortunes reversed, the AM industry sought to implement a stereo system of its own to compete better with now-dominant FM.

As had happened with FM and television standards years earlier, manufacturers made comparative tests of several different systems as a basis for recommending a decision to the FCC. But the five systems that emerged from testing, while different in design and thus incompatible with one another, offered little basis for choosing one over the other. The industry could not make a recommendation to the Commission.

Early in 1980, after some testing of its own, the FCC announced selection of a Magnavox-developed system. Broadcast engineers challenged the FCC's tests and questioned the validity of its choice. The Commission withdrew its decision pending further research. When the issue came to a vote two years later, deregulation (and several new commissioners) had changed the approach of the FCC. In March 1982, with only one dissent, the Commission voted to approve AM stereo operations—but to leave the choice of system to "the marketplace," setting only minimal standards to prevent interference (RR, 1982: 51[1]). Because of antitrust laws, the radio industry could not simply get together and select a standard, because to do so would freeze out other standards, constituting restraint of trade in the eyes of the law.

By 1990 only about 700 AM stations (of more than 5,000 on the air) had taken the trouble to invest in stereo broadcasting. Most used a Motorola system, while a few used one developed by Leonard Kahn. All agreed that the service had been fatally crippled by lack of a definitive FCC decision, which at the least would have removed confusion and might have spurred equipment manufacturers to build and actively market the needed receivers. As noted in the main text,

Source: Advertisement courtesy Motorola, Inc., AM Stereo.

however, the FCC took the AM stereo nondecision as a precedent to follow in other technical standards decisions.

By the early 1990s, however, the seeming precedent became a mere experiment. Pressed by radio broadcasters, Congress mandated the FCC to select a specific AM stereo technical standard by late 1993. The Commission seemed likely to choose the Motorola system already used by nearly all of the (few) AM stations offering stereo service. Combined with the FCC's moves to select a standard for HDTV (see Section 5.9), the Commission's experiment with letting "the market" choose electronic media technical standards seemed at an end.

select specific standards, and would selection of a standard stifle technical development? But HDTV's financial stakes were far higher—the probable replacement of all the country's broadcast and consumer television equipment beginning in the mid-1990s if HDTV succeeded and related concerns about our balance of international trade if HDTV devices were largely imported. Thus HDTV loomed as *the* media standards question to be resolved, with a final FCC choice due in early 1994 with billions of dollars riding on the outcome (see Section 6.4).

Newer Technologies

The FCC's reluctance to mandate technical standards reflects the deregulatory theory that market competition should lead to technological development. For decades the Commission had zealously protected traditional broadcasting, delaying entry of new services and limiting competition. Examples of such FCC discouragement of new services include its early restrictions on cable television and its even longer delay of over-the-air subscription television.

Although its full impact was not foreseen at the time, the FCC's 1979 decision to deregulate licensing of television receive-only (TVRO) satellite antennas had far-reaching effects. The Commission had required a complicated and often expensive licensing process for these antennas, nearly all of which then belonged to cable systems or broadcast stations. Elimination of licensing meant that anyone could buy or build an antenna without burdensome red tape. Demand for antennas increased, prices came down, and demand surged. TVRO deregulation directly fueled expansion of cable networks and the potential for DBS. On the other hand, TVROs also led directly to more signal piracy (as detailed in Section 14.9).

By the 1980s, however, FCC deregulatory policy encouraged as many services as the market would bear, letting competition, not government, decide which new technologies would survive and how fast they would develop. FCC authorization of DBS

services, discussed in Section 3.3, is a good example of this process. From the first filing for a DBS service in 1980 to final authorization in 1982, the Commission moved with unaccustomed speed to authorize a wholly new service. And the agency moved ahead despite strong opposition from a broadcast industry fearful of potential competition.

In the case of low-power television, the FCC moved *too* fast, creating the huge application-processing problem discussed in Section 13.4. In this case, deregulatory zeal *delayed* emergence of a new service.

The FCC's permissive approach to newer technologies has thus far failed to realize another deregulatory goal, the so-called *level playing field* among media services. Broadcasting, despite extensive deregulation, remains the most heavily regulated medium. Cable, once tightly controlled, operated under little regulation in the late 1980s and early 1990s, only to have regulation reinstated in 1992 because of poor service and high rates. Some newer services, such as DBS and MMDS, are also regulated lightly.

More Deregulation?

Deregulation after 1980 had many positive effects. It greatly speeded FCC actions, eliminated outdated rules, encouraged development of new technology, and gave audiences more program choice. The Commission in the 1990s is more open to new ways of getting things done—as well as to benefits of new technology-based competition. Seeing deregulation's gains, many people pushed for more.

But deregulation had negative results as well. While too much regulation can prove harmful, some areas still need closer governmental oversight. Congress, always cool to deregulation, has shifted fundamentally toward a more traditional oversight role for government—and in several areas has forced the FCC to take a more active regulatory stand. Some FCC actions, and speeches by FCC commissioners, suggest that the broadscale ideological push for deregulation may have peaked—that specific situations will now define the pace of regulation or deregulation. Indeed, the FCC can see limits on some of its own earlier decisions:

- FCC refusal to adopt a mandatory standard for AM stereo inadvertently stunted its growth, to the detriment of the declining AM broadcasting service. This precedent may have had a similar impact on teletext and initial DBS, among other services. A congressional mandate a decade later to make a selection while the FCC was moving to adopt an HDTV standard, seemed tacit agreement that the AM stereo "market" experiment had not worked.
- Abandonment by the FCC of many record-keeping requirements as a money-saving tactic in the early 1980s, left blanks in knowledge about electronic media. For example, discontinuation of annual broadcasting and cable financial reports limited the FCC's own understanding of the changing financial health of broadcasters and cable systems amidst substantial transition— as evidenced in some of its own reports, which could only guess at some trends for lack of official "numbers."
- Deregulation—no matter what the source—tends to put business interests ahead of those of the public. With its 1984 cable act, for example, Congress curbed the right of cities to control cable subscription fees, allowing systems to raise rates freely, given their monopoly status in most markets. Subsequent cable price increases and poor service pushed Congress to reinstate FCC cable oversight eight years later, though the Commission argued against the renewed powers, fearful of the multimillion-dollar cost and staff time they would require.
- The FCC's 1980s vision of all human activity reduced to simplistic economic terms ("the marketplace") treated programs as the equivalent of manufactured goods with little concern for diversity, quality, or cultural content—what then-chairman Mark Fowler called "a toaster with pictures." Its lax enforcement of program requirements in the 1990 Children's Television Act (discussed in Section 14.8) suggests that this hands-off role may continue for program concerns. By contrast, the Commission intensified its investigation of complaints regarding broadcast indecency (discussed in Section 14.4).
- In its long-standing acceptance of program-length commercials aimed at children, the FCC once considered allegations of harm only upon a specific showing of provable damage; the Commission regarded a mere lack of benefit in such programs as irrelevant. Only a 1990 law from Congress limiting advertising in such programs forced the FCC to take a harder look at industry practice.

• • • • • • • •

13.10   Other Regulation

International treaties, press law, general business and advertising regulation, antitrust regulation, and lottery restrictions—as well as state and local laws on a variety of topics—also affect electronic media.

Treaties

Agreements between the United States and other nations (concerning electronic media or anything else) have the status of treaties. After the executive branch reaches treaty agreements with foreign countries, ratification by the Senate gives these treaties the force of federal law. Sec. 303 of the Communications Act assigns the FCC the task of carrying out treaties that affect its work. The United States and its neighbors have entered into separate regional treaties governing AM, FM, and television broadcasting. AM agreements cover the widest territory, because long-distance sky-wave propagation affects the scattered islands of the Caribbean as well as the two common-border nations, Canada and Mexico; agreements on simpler FM and television allocations have also long been in place with both countries (see Section 15.6).

The FCC works closely with the National Telecommunications and Information Administration

(NTIA)* and the State Department on American international telecommunications policy. The FCC provides technical expertise and helps coordinate private-sector participation.

Press Law

Electronic media share with print media a body of laws, precedents, and privileges known as the law of the press. Press law relies heavily on tradition and case-law precedents built up over many generations. Typical areas of common concern include defamation, obscenity, trial coverage, freedom of access to information, right of privacy, labor laws, and copyright (many of which are discussed in Chapter 14.)

One other, *reporters' privilege*, concerns the asserted right of news personnel to withhold the identity of news sources and to refuse to surrender personal notes, including any audio and video "outtakes." Journalists argue that only with such protection can the media safeguard their right to seek sources other than official handouts. This and many other aspects of press law fall under state jurisdiction, with results varying widely from state to state.

Regulation of Advertising

The Federal Trade Commission (FTC), established in 1914, regulates business practices and advertising, both of which have a long tradition of common law that greatly complicates FTC regulatory activity. The FTC was originally designed to protect businesses from unfair competition, not consumers from unfair business practices. A 1938 amendment to the FTC Act made it unlawful to use "unfair methods

of competition in commerce, and unfair or deceptive acts or practices in commerce" (15 USC 45). The amendment gave the FTC a basis for regulating deceptive broadcast advertising, even if no harm to a competitor could be shown.* In the past, the FTC acted against misleading broadcast ads but, as a result of the deregulatory atmosphere of the 1980s, stopped asserting that authority.

Only one category of commercial product has been legally banned from the airwaves—tobacco goods, notably cigarettes. In 1965, as a result of the first of what became an annual series of reports from the U.S. Surgeon General on the health dangers of smoking, Congress mandated health warnings on all print and broadcast cigarette ads (15 USC 1333 [2]). Five years later, with more health evidence at hand, Congress banned electronic media advertising of cigarettes or little cigars, effective at the start of 1971 (15 USC 1335) and added smokeless tobacco to the ban in 1986. Broadcasters claimed that they had been unfairly singled out because cigarette ads continued to appear in print media and outdoor advertising. Still, health warnings, and the electronic media ban as well as limits on places where one could smoke, had impact; cigarette smoking has declined in the United States since the 1970s.

Lottery Laws

In 1948 Congress moved from the Communications Act to the U.S. Criminal Code laws that forbade lottery advertising and obscenity in broadcasting. However, the FCC still had to develop its own rules against both in order to invoke these Criminal Code provisions.

Electronic media advertising for or information about *commercial lotteries* may subject a licensee to a base fine of about $6,000 (meaning, it could be less for mitigating circumstances, or far more for a repeated or egregious violation) and/or a year's

---

*NTIA, an agency of the U.S. Department of Commerce established in 1978, acts as the president's chief adviser on telecommunications questions and as spokesperson for the administration. NTIA plays three important roles: (1) as a research "think tank," helping to develop policy initiatives and prepare filings with the FCC; (2) as assigner of spectrum to federal users, through the Interdepartmental Radio Advisory Committee (IRAC); and (3) as a disbursement agency for facility grants in support of public telecommunications systems. NTIA has about 200 employees and an annual budget approaching $20 million, plus another $30 million for the grants.

---

*The Communications Act gives the FCC no authority to punish licensees for unfair advertising, except insofar as a licensee's character qualifications might be brought into question as a result of FTC actions. Thus the FCC leaves most broadcast advertising regulation to the FTC.

imprisonment for each day's offense (15 USC 1304). This provision created a dilemma for media when individual states began legalizing their own *state lotteries*. Congress amended the law effective in 1990 to permit licensees to carry any lottery information and advertising (including casino gambling on Indian reservations), if such lotteries are legal within their own state.

The antilottery statute, however, has long had special application to broadcasters who frequently use contests in advertising and promotional campaigns. Care must be taken that such contests do not turn into illegal lotteries. Three elements must be present to turn a harmless contest or promotion into an illegal lottery: a *chance* to win a *prize*, for a *price*. A contest that requires participants to pay any kind of fee or calls for them to go considerably out of their way (price or *consideration*), that chooses the winner by lot (chance), and that awards the winner something of value (prize) constitutes a lottery and has frequently meant trouble for stations with the FCC.

State and Local Laws

Under the Constitution, federal laws prevail over state laws in subject areas designated as being of federal concern. This means that a state law cannot rise above the Communications Act. Nevertheless, state laws govern many electronic media activities that are not covered by federal statutes. Scores of state laws affect print and electronic media, especially those concerned with

- individual rights (regarding defamation and privacy, as discussed in Section 14.3);
- advertising of specific products and services;
- noncommercial broadcasting (many states have commissions to coordinate statewide public radio and television activities);
- standard business operations (state taxes, for example); and
- aspects of cable television—including franchising or cable right-of-way disputes, theft of service, and the attachment of cable lines to utility poles. Municipalities, too, have enacted many local regulations on cable franchising.

Informal Controls

Many outside influences, beyond formal regulation, have impact on electronic media. Some consist of lobbying and participating in hearings and court cases, while others apply more direct social and economic pressure to force changes in media operations.

We have seen how all three branches of government—executive, legislative, and judicial—participate in the formal regulatory process. These forces divide the FCC's allegiance. The Commission finds itself under constant and often conflicting pressures not only from the White House, Congress, and courts but also from industries it regulates, lobbyists representing special interests, and the general public.

Although Congress gave the FCC a mandate in the Communications Act of 1934 to act on its behalf, it continually brings the Commission up short if it wanders far afield. In addition to Senate approval of nominations to the FCC and congressional control of federal budgeting, Congress conducts frequent *oversight* hearings on the Commission's performance and plans. In fact, it tends to second-guess the FCC on virtually every major regulatory issue that arises—a process known in Washington as *micromanagement*.*

Since the 1920s the White House has found ways, usually indirect, to influence electronic media policy. Most such efforts to influence the FCC take place behind the scenes, which makes them difficult to document. In the early 1990s the Bush administration slowed the pace of federal regulatory efforts—including new FCC rules—through the activities of the "Council on Competitiveness," a

---

*The best—or worst—example of such micromanagement concerned another regulatory agency. In the space of only 16 months, Representative John Dingell (D-MI), the powerful chairman of the House Commerce Committee (which also oversees the FCC), sent no fewer than 176 letters or fax messages to the commissioner of the Food and Drug Administration, 45 of them—regarding medical devices—sent in 1992 alone (*Washington Post*, 11 September 1992: A-21). These "Dingellgrams" sought information, faster FDA action, or questioned FDA decisions.

pro-business group chaired by Vice President Dan Quayle and abolished by the Clinton administration in early 1993. The overall effect of White House pressure varies with each administration and its interest in communications matters.

Consumer Action

The highlight event that crystallized interest in broadcast reform came in the consumerism heyday of the 1960s. For the first time, the WLBT case (see Exhibit 13.j) gave a station's audience the legal right to file complaints on and participate in license renewal proceedings. Hundreds did, though with little lasting impact.

During the Reagan and Bush administrations (1981–1993), however, consumerism faced its most hostile political climate in 30 years. A reaction had set in against what many regarded as excessive government concern for consumer interests. Even then, consumer pressure helped to expand fair employment policies in electronic media even as consumer-interest support activities suffered in budget cuts at both the FCC and FTC. Many consumer groups closed up shop, and those that remained seemed sometimes out of touch. Groups that once promoted broad public-service uses of cable faded when most municipal governments and cable operators failed to pay them much attention.

Nevertheless, in recent years consumer action has increasingly taken the form of single-issue groups with an ax to grind. And, because lobbying the FCC or Congress to intervene can take a long time, the *boycott* has become the strongest action such groups can take to try to influence electronic media behavior. Boycotts involve refusal to buy advertised products. In a pluralistic society, boycotters have difficulty achieving sufficient consensus and discipline to do substantial economic damage. Were it not for the fact that advertisers and media often surrender without attempting to call the boycotters' bluff, boycotts would rarely have any discernible success.

Boycotts most often arise because programs or proposed programs offend church groups, ethnic minorities, or single-issue groups. For example, a widely publicized attack on immorality on television emerged in the 1980s, spurred by success of fundamentalist religious broadcasters in the political campaigns of 1980 and later. Advertisers disliked by these critics were earmarked for boycotts. But with the exception of occasional advertiser capitulation—markedly similar to sponsor compliance with black-listing during the 1950s—the pressure had little impact. Ethnic awareness greatly increased during and after the 1970s. Common television stereotypes of Native Americans, Chinese, Irish, Italians, Japanese, Jews, Mexicans, and Poles all came under attack. Programmers now routinely edit old feature films to remove the gross ethnic slurs they often contain.

Concern over abortion, gun control, prayer in the schools, and other "family values" issues heightened after 1980 (indeed, they were central to the 1992 campaign). Programs and ads debated them all. Protests stimulated widespread news coverage. Complaints under the fairness doctrine (in effect until 1987) flooded the FCC. Ironically, a New York group's vociferous complaint about a local station's programs on nuclear power led the FCC to abolish the fairness doctrine altogether, closing one means of access for consumers (discussed in Section 14.7).

Even noncommercial broadcasting, supposedly freer to present more points of view because it does not cater to advertisers, has succumbed to group pressure. Programs on gay lifestyles, avant-garde art, and Third World political movements have all been criticized—and sometimes temporarily removed from the air. And conservative advocacy groups concerned about the so-called liberal tilt of public television public-affairs programs are often active before congressional hearings on budget appropriations for public broadcasting.

Self-Regulation

Many professions and industries adopt voluntary codes of conduct to cultivate favorable public relations and forestall abuses that might otherwise bring on government regulation. But such codes can have a down side. Those that affect the freedom to compete run afoul of antitrust laws.

The National Association of Broadcasters (NAB) began developing a code for radio programming and advertising practices in the late 1920s, and extended them to television in 1952. Necessarily voluntary, these codes used broad generalizations and many "shoulds" and "should nots," but left most decisions to the discretion of station management. Nonetheless, the codes reinforced generally observed standards, especially as to the amount of time broadcasters should devote to advertising. They were also designed in part to ward off FCC rules or congressional investigations (but see Section 14.8).

Despite NAB precautions to avoid any hint of coercion, the Department of Justice brought suit against the Television Code in 1979. The suit alleged that code time standards "artificially curtailed" advertising, repressing price competition and "depriving advertisers of the benefits of free and open competition." In 1982 a federal district court approved a consent decree by which the NAB disbanded its code-making activities.

The demise of industrywide NAB codes seemed to have little impact, however. For a time, networks and many stations continued to follow their own internal standards—some even tougher than the former NAB codes. Marketplace competitive pressures seemed to help hold the line on the total amount of prime time devoted to advertising, though program-length commercials in fringe times increased.

By the 1990s, however, the networks had cut back their program standards departments as part of more stringent budget controls, despite the fact that together they screen some 50,000 commercials each year to determine which may be used (a few advertisers knowingly submit something a network will be unlikely to use—just for the publicity boost such a rejection can give). Broadcasters still announce most theatrical films as "edited for television"—though the editing is more usually for length (to allow time for commercials) than to meet content concerns. Cable television enjoys more relaxed standards than broadcast television. Pay cable regularly shows films with uncut violence, profanity, and nudity. These episodes cause complaints, but nowhere near as many as such material on over-the-air television would elicit.

As for self-regulation by broadcast personnel, aside from engineers the broadcast employees that come closest to being self-policing professionals are those belonging to the Radio-Television News Directors Association (RTNDA). Members subscribe to a Code of Broadcast News Ethics. The code stresses the importance of accurate and comprehensive presentation of broadcast news, no matter how such presentation might affect station or network public relations. Article 6 of the RTNDA code appears to require that news directors refuse to distort the news to suit their own political preferences—or the whims of owners or managers:

> Broadcast journalists shall seek actively to present all news the knowledge of which will serve the public interest, no matter what selfish, uninformed or corrupt efforts attempt to color it, withhold it, or prevent its presentation.

As discussed in Sections 10.4 and 12.2, NBC experienced serious trouble with distortion of news reports in 1992–1993. Instances of news personnel denouncing attempts of owners to control the news do surface, but only rarely.* It appears that responsible journalists tend to leave stations that bring unethical pressures on them, rather than to challenge their employers openly.

Press Criticism

Coverage of electronic media in both the trade and popular press often affects policy. Congress, the White House, the FCC, and other agencies closely follow reporting about the media, seeking reports of their actions. Certain prestigious writers and trade newsletters play a special role because how a new

---

*In late 1992, during intense lobbying over what became the 1992 cable act, National Association of Broadcaster's officials sent a memo to its thousands of member stations urging them to "tell it like it is—generate the news stories!" in support of the pending legislation. The head of the RTNDA and many others questioned the use of news programs for industry lobbying.

policy or rule "plays" in the trade press gives a foretaste of how the industry itself will react.

As for program criticism, reviewers in major newspapers and magazines seem to have more impact on news and public-affairs programs than on entertainment shows. Further, they influence producers of such programs more than they do the general audience. The agenda-setting role of critics can, however, sometimes focus government and industry attention on areas of controversy, such as violence, questionable advertising, and copyright violations. Tom Shales, the incisive television critic for the Washington *Post*, Walter Goodman and John O'Connor of the New York *Times*, and a few others often have impact on industry leaders and Washington lawmakers.

• • • • • • • •

Summary

13.1 Electronic media come under control of Congress because of the Constitution's "commerce clause." Through the Communications Act of 1934, Congress delegates supervisory responsibility to the FCC, using the broad guideline of the "public interest, convenience or necessity" (PICON) to define FCC discretionary powers.

13.2 Although many attempts have been made to rewrite or replace the 1934 Communications Act, amendments have been remarkably few for an act so old and a field going through such rapid change. Cable television was substantially deregulated by a 1984 amendment to the Communications Act and *re*-regulated by 1992 legislation.

13.3 The FCC consists of five presidentially appointed commissioners and a professional staff of about 1,800. It organizes into bureaus and offices, among which the Mass Media Bureau has jurisdiction over electronic media. The FCC regulates through formally adopted rules, processing standards, guidelines, and adjudicatory decisions. It also uses "raised eyebrow" and "jawboning" techniques to influence licensees.

13.4 Licensing of broadcasting stations and franchising of cable systems are the most important regulatory functions—all other regulation flows from this process of authorizing service. Broadcast license applicants must be American citizens and qualify in terms of financial resources, technical ability, and character. Licensees do not own the spectrum channels they use. In the 1980s and 1990s the FCC increased the number of broadcast stations by adding new AM, FM, and television channels to those already in use.

13.5 Broadcast licensees must establish equal employment opportunity programs, maintain a public file that includes listings of community problems and related programs, and keep up with FCC rule changes.

13.6 Most broadcast license renewals are uncontested, and licenses are granted almost automatically. Contested renewals usually arise because of competing applications.

13.7 The threat of license loss is the FCC's ultimate enforcement weapon. However, the Commission deletes few licenses through nonrenewal and fewer still through outright revocation. Lesser penalties include short-term renewals and fines. Few stations suffer any of these sanctions. Due process and the Administrative Procedure Act give those accused many avenues of appeal.

13.8 Local authorities franchise cable systems, subject to regulations established by the 1984 and 1992 cable acts. A cable franchise usually runs for a decade or more and its holder usually operates as a monopoly in its service area. Cable's basic rates and conditions of service were re-regulated in 1992.

13.9 After 1980 the FCC took a strong deregulatory stance, abolishing long-existing rules and guidelines governing broadcasting and cable and encouraging new services to emerge with little or no regulation. The FCC's role in mandating electronic media technical standards appeared to end with its AM stereo decision of 1982 but was revived for both AM stereo and HDTV a decade later. The FCC's deletion of outmoded rules and removal of barriers to emergence of new media services has benefited consumers—but has also reduced incentives to serve the public interest.

13.10 Electronic media are also subject to many other laws, among them international treaties, press law, advertising regulation, antitrust laws, and equal employment opportunity rules. Further, regulation of broadcasting and cable is affected by White House and congressional intervention, court reviews of FCC actions, consumer activism (now in decline), network and station self-regulation, professional self-regulation, and trade-press criticism.

Chapter 14

Constitutional Controversies

The First Amendment to the U.S. Constitution prohibits government regulation of speech and press—yet the Communications Act imposes federal licensing and other limitations on those who own electronic media. This paradox isn't unique, as society often demands a balance between the ideal of *absolute* individual freedom and the practical need to limit speech that might harm others (for instance, don't cry "fire" in a crowded theater if it isn't true). The essence of the constitutional controversies discussed here is how to compromise between these opposing goals.

14.1   First Amendment

The freedoms of speech and press included in the First Amendment were intended from the start—and the courts have construed them since—to encourage a wide-open *marketplace of ideas*. First Amendment theory holds that ideas and opinions

from different sources should compete in such a marketplace. As the Supreme Court noted in a landmark electronic media decision, "It is the purpose of the First Amendment to preserve an uninhibited marketplace of ideas in which truth will ultimately prevail, rather than to countenance monopolization of the market" (US, 1969: 390).

Although freedom of expression is only part of one of the ten amendments that make up the Bill of Rights, that freedom has played a pivotal role in the American political system (see Exhibit 14.a). In the words of Supreme Court Justice William O. Douglas, the First Amendment "has been the safeguard of every religious, political, philosophical, economic and racial group amongst us" (US, 1951: 584).

"No Such Thing as a False Idea"

"Under the First Amendment," said the Supreme Court, "there is no such thing as a false idea. However pernicious an opinion may seem, we depend for its correction not on the conscience of judges

Exhibit 14.a ••••••• ••••••••••••

"Congress Shall Make No Law. . . ."

The First Amendment protects four fundamental rights of citizens that governments throughout history have had the most reason to fear and the greatest inclination to violate—freedom to *believe*, to *speak*, to *gather together*, and to ask rulers to *correct injustices*.

Source: Photo by Kerwin B. Roache/FPG.

The amendment conveys all this in only 45 words, of which just 14 guarantee freedom of expression:

> Congress shall make no law respecting an establishment of religion, or prohibiting the free exercise thereof, or abridging the freedom of speech, or of the press; or the right of the people peaceably to assemble, and to petition the Government for a redress of grievances.

These words limit not only Congress but also state and local governments, thanks to the Fourteenth Amendment, passed in 1868, which says, "No state shall make or enforce any law which shall abridge the privileges or immunities of citizens of the United States. . . . " Section 326 of the Communications Act of 1934 explicitly extends the First Amendment's protection to broadcasting:

> Nothing in this Act shall be understood or construed to give the Commission the power of censorship over the radio communications or signals transmitted by any radio station, and no regulation or condition shall be promulgated or fixed by the Commission which shall interfere with the right of free speech by means of radio communication.

and juries, but on the competition of other ideas" (US, 1974: 339)—again, the marketplace metaphor.

The First Amendment *encourages* disagreement. "A function of free speech under our system of government is to invite dispute," wrote Justice Douglas. "It may indeed best serve its highest purpose when it induces a condition of unrest, creates dissatisfaction with conditions as they are, or even stirs people to anger" (US, 1949: 4). Anger certainly arose during the 1980s in Dodge City, Kansas, when station KTTL-FM broadcast daily hour-long sermons by two fundamentalist ministers attacking Jews, blacks, and other groups. They urged listeners to ignore police officers and attack such groups at

will. The invective poured out in such abundance that several local groups protested renewal of KTTL's license when it expired in May 1983.

A huge media uproar resulted, with a congressional subcommittee hearing in August 1983 and extensive press coverage of the station owner's extremist conservative views favoring local armed vigilantes. In mid-1985 the FCC designated the license for a comparative hearing with another applicant for the same frequency. At the same time it imposed a fine on the station for several rule violations. But in a controversial decision to renew, the FCC said that the First Amendment protected the broadcasts, offensive though they might be to many listeners

(FCCR, 1985a). The Commission found that because the material did not present a *clear and present danger* to the public, a test long established by the U.S. Supreme Court, it qualified as protected speech (US, 1919: 52). Such incitement to take illegal or dangerous actions did not, as the FCC had said in an earlier case, "rise far above public inconvenience, annoyance, or unrest" (FCCR, 1972c: 637).

Government Censorship

Many assume that the First Amendment also provides protection from private parties. But in fact the amendment aims at protecting people only from government (censorship), not from one another (broadcaster or cable editorial decisions). Station, system, and network officials who edit, cut, bleep, delete, revise, and otherwise mangle programs may be guilty of bad judgment, excessive timidity, and other faults, but editorial control is not censorship, and it does not violate the First Amendment.

Such control becomes a violation only when it results from the kind of government intrusion known as *state action*. In promoting the "family viewing" concept in the 1970s, for example, the FCC attempted to reduce television violence not by rule but by "jawboning"—pressuring the television industry to regulate itself. When the NAB responded to this pressure by amending its Television Code, a court construed this private action as state action in violation of the First Amendment (F, 1979: 355).

Religious Freedom

Another First Amendment clause guarantees religious freedom. The active role of television evangelists in the national elections of 1980 and since (especially the candidacy of Pat Robertson for the GOP nomination in 1988, and some GOP platform planks in 1992) disturbed many people who were sensitive to First Amendment concerns about establishment of any specific religion. Yet the same amendment protects the evangelists' right to have their say. Doubly protected by the freedoms of speech *and* religion, however, stations owned by religious groups have claimed near-immunity from FCC requirements because they regard their right of religious freedom (from any government action) as absolute. Though the FCC has held religious licensees to the same standards of regulation for all broadcasters, it has resisted close monitoring of any licensees.

• • • • • • • •

14.2 Broadcasting's Limited Rights

Just what do the First Amendment words *speech* and *press* mean in today's context? Speech encompasses not only that amplified by public-address systems but also film, broadcasting, videos, and cable. And the press includes pornographic magazines. Can *all* ways of expressing oneself and *all* forms of the press claim equal First Amendment rights?

Broadcasting vs. Print

More specifically, should regulated electronic media have First Amendment *parity*—equality—with unregulated media, especially the printed press? Until recent years, the answer has generally been "no." Many argue that electronic media have at least three unique attributes that justify limitations that would violate the First Amendment if imposed on print:

- The *scarcity of channels* (on the federally-controlled frequency spectrum) makes it necessary to reject some applications for broadcast licenses.
- In deciding which applicants deserve *licensing* in the public interest, the FCC must take programming into consideration.
- Broadcasting's unique role—its *intrusion* into the home and especially its availability to children—brings with it obligations for some government oversight to protect the public.

Channel Scarcity

Not everyone who wants to own a station can do so, because intolerable interference would otherwise result—as occurred before passage of the 1927 Radio Act. Because of this channel scarcity, the government (the FCC) has to choose among applicants. Where mutually exclusive applications seek facilities whose activation would cause interference, only one license can be granted—thereby abridging the freedom of other applicants. In contrast, anyone who can afford it can publish a newspaper or magazine without limit or license. And the cost need not be high—one can use desktop publishing or even duplicating machines.

Development of new and improved services *has* decreased scarcity as a justification for regulating broadcasting. The huge increase in the number of stations since Congress wrote the 1927 Radio Act—from about 600 to nearly 14,000 plus more than 11,000 cable systems—makes scarcity a relative factor at best. And while demand for channels in major markets continues, cable provides virtually unlimited additional channels—converting scarcity into abundance. Some argue that *all* media should be counted when determining "scarcity," so that diversity of print and other information sources more than offsets any scarcity of over-the-air media.

In contrast, others point to the many applicants for desirable stations that become available—and the huge prices often paid for them—to suggest that scarcity continues. They argue that availability of cable channels does not fully relieve scarcity because cable reaches a little over 60 percent of the population while broadcasting reaches virtually everyone. In any event, cable differs sharply from "free" broadcasting in requiring subscription fees over and above receiver expenses.

Conflict in Licensing

When writing the Communications Act, Congress explicitly confirmed "the right of free speech by means of radio communication" (see Exhibit 14.a). Yet the Act also required the FCC to grant or renew licenses only if they serve the public interest. It also told the FCC to ensure that candidates for public office had equal opportunities to use broadcasting. In defining its duty to see that broadcasting serves the public interest, the FCC established guidelines for programming, particularly with regard to *localism*.

Any such requirements—by definition—place limits on licensees' freedom of speech. That fundamental contradiction came before the Supreme Court in the 1943 *NBC* case, where broadcasters argued that the FCC had the right to regulate only *technical* factors, and that any further regulation violated the First Amendment. But the Court emphatically rejected this argument, saying:

> We are asked to regard the Commission as a kind of traffic officer, policing the wave lengths to prevent stations from interfering with one another. But the Act does not restrict the Commission merely to supervision of the traffic. It puts upon the Commission the burden of determining the composition of that traffic. (US, 1943: 215)

By "determining the composition of that traffic" the Supreme Court referred to the choices the FCC makes in licensing. In deciding which of several would-be licensees will best serve the public interest, the FCC necessarily takes programming into account (at least in theory). The Court has frequently cited the composition-of-the-traffic rationale of this landmark decision as legal precedent for upholding limited FCC control over programs. Of course, use of lotteries to select licensees (see Section 13.4) undermines this whole rationale.

Intrusiveness

The third argument for regulating broadcasting more than other media rests on its intrusiveness. Radio and television enter directly into virtually every household, readily available to people of all ages and types. Some content acceptable in other media—indecency, for example (see Section 14.4)—would be regarded as intolerable in broadcasting. First Amendment purists respond that where such distinctions need to be made, the marketplace can make them better than government. If people object to a program, they can—and do—complain to station and system operators, networks, or advertisers. All of these, in turn, impose their own restraints in order not to lose public confidence. As an example, broadcasters have passed up ready income by refraining from advertising hard liquor—not because of any government rule, but in their own self-interest, knowing that to present such advertising would evoke such a storm of protest that regulation might result, banning the advertising of *all* alcoholic beverages.

To sum up, while many electronic media claim they should be just as free of government control as newspapers, others—including some broadcasters—believe that a special public-service responsibility (operating in the PICON, as discussed in Section 13.3) accompanies their use of scarce channels, government licenses, and intimate access to any home. While this "social responsibility" view long dominated regulatory thinking, deregulation has, of late, considerably weakened it in practice.

• • • • • • • •

14.3   *Things You Can't Say*

Despite that seemingly strict First Amendment command "Congress shall make no law. . .," government *does* in fact make laws that punish *unprotected* speech. This refers to defamation (libel),* obscenity, invasion of privacy, and incitement to insurrection. These punishable types of speech fall outside the First Amendment's protection from government interference, for they contribute nothing to the marketplace of ideas and can cause great harm.

Libel—Protecting Reputations

The practice of libel law is a good example of how a *chilling effect* (fear of potential punishment) can

---

*Libel is *defamation* by published words that may expose its subject to public hatred, shame, or disgrace. Spoken defamation is called *slander*, but because electronic media spread spoken words far and wide (and because the words are often preserved on tape), broadcast or cable defamation is treated as *libel*. If defamation can be proved—not an easy thing to do (in part because of widely different state laws), as discussed below—victims may be able to collect for damages.

undermine First Amendment goals. Criticism of those in power is a good test of whether a society enjoys true freedom of expression. Democratic societies encourage aggressive news reporting to uncover government wrongdoing or incompetence, even at the highest political levels. But such reporting cannot survive in a society in which harsh, easily invoked libel laws threaten journalists with huge fines or imprisonment if they criticize public officials.

Libel laws constitute another example of conflicting social interests. While libel should be punishable because society has an interest in protecting its citizens, society also needs to expose official corruption and incompetence. Harassing libel suits can serve as a screen to protect dishonest politicians. In the United States all public figures—not just politicians—must be prepared to face harsh, sometimes even unfair and ill-founded criticism from the media, because it is extremely difficult to prove the *actual malice* standard necessary for their libel suit to succeed (see Exhibit 14.b).

In 1979, and again six years later, libel cases arising from television interviews about the Vietnam War tested the "actual malice" standard created by the *Sullivan* case. Both grew out of interviews conducted by CBS reporter Mike Wallace. In the first, *Herbert v. Lando*, an army officer (Herbert) sought to find out whether the *60 Minutes* interview producer (Lando) believed the officer was lying. If Lando did not, the program's charges about Herbert's role in the war could have constituted actual malice—saying something Lando knew was not the case. Lando refused to answer, claiming a journalist's privilege to keep news sources and editorial processes confidential. But to the media's collective dismay, the Supreme Court upheld Herbert's request, agreeing that access to material that could reveal Lando's state of mind while preparing the story was essential to prove actual malice as required by the *Sullivan* case (US, 1979: 169).

This decision—despite Herbert's eventual failure in his suit—threatened severely to limit journalists' defenses against libel actions. Complainants could now rummage through tape archives, correspondence files, and program outtakes to determine the "state of mind" of reporters and editors. Later cases extended the ruling, making "journalists nearly as vulnerable for what they did not say as for what they did" (*Time*, 4 March 1985: 94).

The second case against CBS never reached a jury but had wide impact. Early in 1982 CBS aired a documentary alleging that the military lied about enemy troop strength in the late 1960's to encourage support at home for pursuing the war. Wallace interviewed the top American military commander in the war, General William Westmoreland. In May, *TV Guide* accused CBS News of violating reportorial standards and the network's own policies in an attempt to "get" Westmoreland (Kowet and Bedell, 1982: 10). CBS undertook a comprehensive internal investigation, which concluded that the producers *had* violated network news standards but upheld the program's cover-up allegation (Benjamin, 1988). In September, Westmoreland filed suit against CBS, claiming that his reputation had been ruined. Conservative foundations underwrote most of Westmoreland's $3 million legal costs for the five-month trial in 1984–1985. After it became clear that most of the testimony supported the CBS program, however, Westmoreland abruptly withdrew his suit, settling for a mild apology from CBS that admitted no wrongdoing. The libel principle established by the *Sullivan* case, that malicious intent must be proved, survived the *Westmoreland* case, as did most of CBS's journalistic credibility; but defending the suit cost the network millions. These decisions contributed to a rising number of libel cases filed against the media.

By the early 1990s the primary sources of libel trouble for electronic media were radio "shock jocks" such as Howard Stern and radio call-in shows (because licensees are liable for any defamation spoken over the air by those calling in). A 1992 study by the Libel Defense Resource Center traced some 300 libel trials dating back to 1980 and found that the media won only a quarter of the jury trials in those 12 years—though only 58 of 167 initial awards were finally upheld on appeal and judgments paid. The same study found that awards averaged more than $8 million in the last two years, whereas earlier the average had been only $1.5 million (cited in

Television Digest, 31 August 1992: 4). In fact, about 90 percent of all such libel suits are dropped or settled long before they reach trial. Even where the media win, they spend a lot of money defending themselves. More important, such suits have a "chilling effect" on investigative reporting. Critics argue that many media libel cases should go to arbitrators rather than to juries, to encourage both public correction of erroneous stories and more moderate monetary awards. Moreover, arbitration would consume far less time and money than suits and their appeals, while still protecting those who felt libeled.

Preserving Privacy

Privacy as an individual right, though not spelled out in the Constitution, is implied in the Fourth Amendment: "The right of the people to be secure in their persons, houses, papers, and effects . . . shall not be violated." As a legal concept, *invasion of privacy* closely relates to libel. As with libel, laws on privacy vary among states. Individuals have several privacy rights:

- the right to physical solitude;
- protection from intrusion on private property or publication of the details of one's personal life (for example, an investigative television team seeking pictures of a restaurant kitchen found in violation of local health standards may run up against the owner's right to limit access to his or her private property);
- protection from being presented in a "false light" (for example, being photographed walking on campus and then being included in a visual accompanying a television feature about drug use in college); and
- protection from unauthorized use of one's name or image for commercial gain.

Taken together, the personal protections afforded by libel and privacy laws impose limits on media access. Although the courts have held that public officials, performers, and people involved in news events have a lesser right to privacy because of legitimate public interest in those persons or events,

Exhibit 14.b ●●●●●●●●●●●●●●●●

Times *v.* Sullivan—
Libel Landmark

The leading case establishing the relative protection of media from libel suits filed by public figures occurred during the civil rights protests of the 1960s. By chance it involved an instance of "editorial advertising," not investigative reporting. Supporters of the Montgomery, Alabama, bus boycott protesting segregation bought a large display advertisement in the *New York Times* (most of which is shown on the next page) that criticized Montgomery officials. Some of the statements in the advertisement were false, although they apparently were not *deliberate* lies. Sullivan, one of the officials, sued for libel in an Alabama court (all libel suits have to be brought at the state level). The court awarded Sullivan a half-million dollars in damages, and the Alabama Supreme Court affirmed the decision.

On appeal to the U.S. Supreme Court, however, the *Times* won a reversal. Criticism of public officials, said the Court, had broad First Amendment protection. Even though some of the allegations against the unnamed officials were untrue, they did not constitute libel. Argument over public officials, the Court continued, should be "uninhibited, robust, and wide-open." It may include "vehement, caustic, and sometimes unpleasantly sharp attacks on government and public officials." Such freewheeling debate would be discouraged if, in the heat of controversy, the critic must pause to weigh every unfavorable word:

> The constitutional guarantees require, we think, a federal rule that prohibits a public official from recovering damages for a defamatory falsehood relating to his official conduct unless he proves that the statement was made with "actual malice"—that is, with knowledge that it was false or with reckless disregard of whether it was false or not. (US, 1964: 279).

Subsequent libel cases broadened the term *public officials* to include anyone who, because of notoriety, could be classed as a *public figure*. People so classified have little chance of bringing a successful libel suit against the media. Even when stories about public figures are false, plaintiffs find it exceedingly difficult to prove deliberate malice.

---

privacy laws still limit the media by generally supporting individual rights.

Restricting Court Coverage

Protecting constitutional rights of individuals can pose other challenges to media First Amendment rights. The due process clause of the Fifth Amendment ensures fair play to persons accused of crimes. The Sixth Amendment also spells out some of the elements of due process, among them the right to a fair and public trial. Ordinarily, news media freely cover trials, but that coverage can subject participants to such extensive publicity that a fair trial becomes impossible. In this *free press vs. fair trial* confrontation, the constitutional rights of the media sometimes have to give way to the constitutional rights of defendants.

Electronic media become deeply involved in this thorny issue when they attempt to cover highly publicized trials or pretrial proceedings. For decades there was virtually no live or recorded radio or television coverage of trials. After messy coverage of the Lindbergh kidnapping trial (see Exhibit 14.c), the American Bar Association (ABA) recommended in 1935 that judges discourage radio and photo coverage because it tended "to detract from the essential dignity of the proceedings, degrade the court, and create misconceptions with respect thereto in the mind of the public." The 1960s trial of convicted

Heed Their Rising Voices

As the whole world knows by now, thousands of Southern Negro students are engaged in widespread non-violent demonstrations in positive affirmation of the right to live in human dignity as guaranteed by the U. S. Constitution and the Bill of Rights. In their efforts to uphold these guarantees, they are being met by an unprecedented wave of terror by those who would deny and negate that document which the whole world looks upon as setting the pattern for modern freedom....

In Orangeburg, South Carolina, when 400 students peacefully sought to buy doughnuts and coffee at lunch counters in the business district, they were forcibly ejected, tear-gassed, soaked to the skin in freezing weather with fire hoses, arrested en masse and herded into an open barbed-wire stockade to stand for hours in the bitter cold.

In Montgomery, Alabama, after students sang "My Country, 'Tis of Thee" on the State Capitol steps, their leaders were expelled from school, and truckloads of police armed with shotguns and tear-gas ringed the Alabama State College Campus. When the entire student body protested to state authorities by refusing to re-register, their dining hall was padlocked in an attempt to starve them into submission.

In Tallahassee, Atlanta, Nashville, Savannah, Greensboro, Memphis, Richmond, Charlotte, and a host of other cities in the South, young American teenagers, in face of the entire weight of official state apparatus and police power, have boldly stepped forth as protagonists of democracy. Their courage and amazing restraint have inspired millions and given a new dignity to the cause of freedom.

Small wonder that the Southern violators of the Constitution fear this new, non-violent brand of freedom fighter ... even as they fear the upswelling right-to-vote movement. Small wonder that they are determined to destroy the one man who, more than any other, symbolizes the new spirit now sweeping the South—the Rev. Dr. Martin Luther King, Jr., world-famous leader of the Montgomery Bus Protest. For it is his doctrine of non-violence which has inspired and guided the students in their widening wave of sit-ins; and it this same Dr. King who founded and is president of the Southern Christian Leadership Conference—the organization which is spearheading the surging right-to-vote movement. Under Dr. King's direction the Leadership Conference conducts Student Workshops and Seminars in the philosophy and technique of non-violent resistance.

Again and again the Southern violators have answered Dr. King's peaceful protests with intimidation and violence. They have bombed his home almost killing his wife and child. They have assaulted his person. They have arrested him seven times—for "speeding," "loitering" and similar "offenses." And now they have charged him with "perjury"—a *felony* under which they could imprison him for *ten years*. Obviously, their real purpose is to remove him physically as the leader to whom the students and millions of others—look for guidance and support, and thereby to intimidate *all* leaders who may rise in the South. Their strategy is to behead this affirmative movement, and thus to demoralize Negro Americans and weaken their will to struggle. The defense of Martin Luther King, spiritual leader of the student sit-in movement, clearly, therefore, is an integral part of the total struggle for freedom in the South.

Decent-minded Americans cannot help but applaud the creative daring of the students and the quiet heroism of Dr. King. But this is one of those moments in the stormy history of Freedom when men and women of good will must do more than applaud the rising-to-glory of others. The America whose good name hangs in the balance before a watchful world, the America whose heritage of Liberty these Southern Upholders of the Constitution are defending, is *our* America as well as theirs ...

We must heed their rising voices—yes—but we must add our own.

We must extend ourselves above and beyond moral support and render the material help so urgently needed by those who are taking the risks, facing jail, and even death in a glorious re-affirmation of our Constitution and its Bill of Rights.

We urge you to join hands with our fellow Americans in the South by supporting, with your dollars, this Combined Appeal for all three needs—the defense of Martin Luther King—the support of the embattled students—and the struggle for the right-to-vote.

Your Help Is Urgently Needed . . . NOW!!

Exhibit 14.c ● ● ● ● ● ● ● ● ● ● ● ● ● ● ● ●

Covering Courts—Changing Pictures

A.

B.

Alleged Victim   CNN LIVE

Broadcast coverage of court trials began with the 1925 Scopes case, and reached the height of overkill with the 1935 trial of Bruno Hauptmann for the kidnap and murder of Charles Lindbergh's son. Reaction to that intrusive coverage by radio and film led to the ABA's "Canon 35," which banned trial coverage for decades. (A) An experiment in television coverage in the 1960s, Billie Sol Estes' trial for fraud, led to a

Supreme Court reversal because of television intrusiveness. (B) As restrictions on trial coverage declined in the 1980s, sometimes lurid trials came into people's homes—such as the 1992 rape trial of William Kennedy Smith. The jury found him not guilty, but the trial became known for its often graphic testimony and the media's use of a fuzzy dot over the victim's face to protect her identity.

Source: Photo A from UPI/Bettmann Archive; B from AP/Wide World Photos.

swindler Billie Sol Estes in Texas (for a time, one of only two states that did not follow the ABA recommendation) seemed to support this stand; an appeals court reversed the lower court's guilty verdict because of the circus atmosphere created by 12 cameras and attendant lights and crews. The Supreme Court narrowly upheld the appeals court decision in the *Estes* case (US, 1965: 532).

But during the 1970s, with less intrusive equipment and seemingly more mature broadcast journalism judgment, the ABA recommended that judges be given wider latitude in allowing photo

and video coverage of trials. In 1981 the Supreme Court—although it bans cameras and microphones in its own proceedings—noted the improved technology, holding that "the risk of juror prejudice . . . does not warrant an absolute constitutional ban on all broadcast coverage" (US, 1981: 560). By the early 1990s all but a handful of states either allowed cameras in their courtrooms or had conducted experiments to that end. But federal courts remained off limits to such coverage, despite repeated media attempts to breach that barrier. After a study group recommended it in 1990, a three-year experiment with television coverage of civil cases in six federal district and two appeals courts began in mid-1991.

Another indicator of the easier relationship between courts and the media was the launch in mid-1991 of Court TV, a national 24-hour cable service that *depended* on coverage of interesting trials to attract listeners. Attorneys were hired to act as informed anchors. The service's first year was highlighted by several spectacular trials and congressional confrontations that attracted listeners. Trials from some 30 states and 78 municipalities were included, and features about the legal system were developed.

Broadcast Hoaxes

While the broadcasting of "news" that isn't really news dates back at least to the 1938 Orson Welles' broadcast of *War of the Worlds*, there have been relatively few cases of intentional news hoax broadcasts—until recent years. Indeed, a rash of cases in the early 1990s convinced the FCC that it needed stronger rules and a means of fining stations rather than just sending letters of concern. Several stations broadcast stories of false murders, one station said a nearby trash dump was about to explode because of methane gas build-up, another used the Emergency Broadcast System and said a nuclear attack was under way, and still another reported that a volcano had erupted in a suburban Connecticut town. All were presented as real events, and emergency forces responded accordingly.

In 1992 the Commission adopted a rule against such "harmful" hoaxes—those that might divert police or fire or other safety forces from real events. The FCC made clear that it had the First Amendment in mind as the rule was developed and, hence, limited its actions to cases where "broadcast of such information will cause substantial public harm, and broadcast of the information does in fact directly cause such harm." Such broadcasts can result in fines of up to $25,000 for each day on which a harmful hoax occurs—to a maximum FCC fine of $250,000 for repeated violations. Several broadcast-

ers agreed that the industry had not adequately policed itself and thus had brought about this action.

Improved technology has made another type of hoax readily available. As cameras get smaller and operate at lower light levels, options for use of hidden cameras increase. Of growing concern in the early 1990s are the number of station and network or syndicated "undercover investigations" in which reporters using hidden cameras impersonate another person (*not* a reporter) to obtain information. This process of omission (not making clear that a reporter is asking questions) raises substantial questions of ethics.

• • • • • • • •

14.4 Obscenity and Indecency

One of the most controversial topics regarding electronic media content is how far programming can go without coming up against a variety of limitations on obscenity and indecency.

What Is Obscene?

Prior to the 1930s obscenity in literature and art could be arbitrarily suppressed at the whim of officials and censorship boards. But the successful defense in 1933 of James Joyce's literary masterpiece *Ulysses* initiated a series of court decisions that protect media from suppression by zealous moral watchdogs.

Current obscenity law dates to the 1973 *Miller* case in which the Supreme Court upheld a California obscenity law. The decision emphasized that *community standards* vary from place to place: "It is neither realistic nor constitutionally sound to read the First Amendment as requiring that the people of Maine or Mississippi accept public depiction of conduct found tolerable in Las Vegas or New York City."

Nevertheless, the Court warned, state laws must carefully confine what they classify as *obscene* to "works which, taken as a whole, *appeal to the prurient interest in sex, which portray sexual conduct in a patently offensive way, and which, taken as a whole, do not have serious literary, artistic, political, or scientific value*" (US, 1973b: 24; emphasis added).

The *Miller* case, along with later decisions that added minor modifications, restricted obscenity censorship to "hard-core" materials, leaving it to the states to define obscenity—a task impossible to carry out to everyone's satisfaction. In any event, current guidelines rule out abuses of power freely committed by censors in the past. For example, courts now interpret the First Amendment as preventing censors from taking such arbitrary action as

- condemning an entire work because of a few isolated obscene words;
- using outdated standards no longer common to the local community;
- applying as a standard the opinions of hypersensitive persons not typical of the general public; or
- ignoring serious artistic, scientific, literary, or political purpose in judging a work.

Generally speaking, courts must consider the "average person" when applying contemporary community standards to potentially obscene material. Of course, those standards will be stricter for material available to children.

Limiting Indecency in Broadcasting

Sec. 1464 of the U.S. Criminal Code reads:

> "Whosoever utters any *obscene, indecent,* or *profane* language by means of radio communication shall be fined not more than $10,000 or imprisoned for not more than two years, or both." (18 USC 1464; emphasis added)

Note the use of *indecent* and *profane* in the statute. As with *obscene,* definitions and degrees of control have varied for these terms over the years. In a 1992 policy statement, the Commission defined indecency as "Language or material that, in context, depicts or describes, in terms patently offensive as measured by *contemporary community standards for the broadcast medium,* sexual or excretory activi-

ties of organs" (FCCR 1992b: 6464, note 4, emphasis added).

The Commission long remained in doubt as to its power to enforce the Criminal Code provision. Because of ready availability of electronic media to children, material acceptable in other media might be regarded as unacceptable by many in the audience. Furthermore, because broadcast and cable network services have national reach, they confront a great variety of local standards.

Broadcasting's traditional conservatism delayed its response to the tolerant social climate of the 1960s, but the liberalization of standards in other media had its effect. In the 1970s a "topless radio" fad triggered thousands of complaints to the FCC. The format invited women to call in and talk on the air about intimate details of their sex lives. Although such talk shows are commonplace today—on television as well as radio—one Illinois radio broadcast in 1973 triggered a flood of complaints. The FCC imposed what was then a fairly steep $2,000 fine on the offending FM station (FCCR, 1973: 919). The Commission had actually hoped that the station would contest the fine, thus precipitating a test case, but the station dutifully mailed in a check instead (for an amount equal to only a few minutes' advertising revenue in a major market).

Pacifica Decision

That same year, the FCC finally got its test case. A noncommercial station, WBAI-FM in New York, included in a discussion of social attitudes about language a recording of a nightclub act by comedian George Carlin. Called "Filthy Words," the monologue satirized society's hang-ups about seven sexually oriented words not likely to be heard on the air. This time, though, they were heard—no fewer than 106 times in 12 minutes. The single complaint came from a man who, as it later turned out, was associated with a group called Morality in Media. He heard the early afternoon broadcast with his teen-age son—a crucial element in the case.

On the basis of that lone complaint, the FCC advised station management that the broadcast appeared to violate the obscenity statute. The licensee,

Pacifica (see Exhibit 8.n on page 297), challenged the ruling as a matter of First Amendment principles. The FCC received an initial setback in the appeals court but won Supreme Court approval of its reasoning. Focusing its argument on the Carlin monologue as *indecent* rather than obscene (as the Supreme Court had defined obscenity), the FCC stressed that the broadcast came when children would normally be in the audience.

The FCC argued that children need protection from indecency. Instead of meeting the First Amendment directly by flatly banning such material as the Carlin monologue the FCC said it should be *channeled* to a part of the day when children are least likely to be in the audience.*

The channeling concept has precedence in nuisance law, which recognizes that something acceptable in one setting could be an illegal nuisance in others. The Supreme Court agreed with this rationale when, recalling that a judge had once said that a nuisance "may be merely a right thing in a wrong place—like a pig in the parlor instead of the barnyard," the Court added that if the FCC "finds a pig has entered the parlor, the exercise of regulatory power does not depend on proof that the pig is obscene." The Court also accepted the FCC's narrowing of community standards in adding the words *for broadcasting*, saying, "We have long recognized that each medium of expression presents special First Amendment problems. . . . And of all forms of communication, it is broadcasting that has received the most limited First Amendment protection" (US, 1978: 748).

Political Football

A decade later, in 1987, a rising flood of complaints about perceived obscenity or indecency on the air caused the FCC to issue a statement announcing plans to enforce Sec. 1464 of the Criminal Code. The Commission reprimanded three stations for

using overly explicit language, especially at times when children might be in the audience (FCCR, 1987a: 2726). In an interview, the FCC's general counsel argued that marginal program material (indecent, perhaps, but not obscene) might be scheduled during the midnight to 6 A.M. period. For some time, the FCC had informally allowed such material to begin as early as 10 P.M. The narrower definition of allowable time led to a court appeal.

Several broadcasters joined in challenging the FCC decision and in 1988 won reversal of the Commission action on the grounds that limiting indecent language to the midnight-to-6-A.M. hours violated the First Amendment. The court remanded to the FCC the question of how best to "promote parental—as distinguished from government—control" of children's listening (F, 1988: 1332).

Thereupon Congress entered this hotly controversial arena. In approving the FCC budget for the 1989 fiscal year, legislators (mindful that they were in the midst of an election campaign) ordered the FCC to ban indecent material at *all hours* of the day. The FCC complied, though observers questioned whether such a blanket ban would survive an appeal based on First Amendment principles. While the controversy raged in the courts, the FCC took action against a score of radio stations, fining them for various obscenity violations, but only if they fell in the 6-A.M.-to-8-P.M. period. In early 1992 the Supreme Court declined to review an earlier appeals court ruling that the 24-hour ban *was* too broad a limit on freedom of expression (F, 1991: 1504).

The FCC then initiated a rule-making procedure to define and justify a "safe harbor" for such programming, and stepped up its prosecution of indecency violations at a number of radio stations. Meanwhile, it received "advice" on defining proper "channelling" time in the 1992 funding act for public broadcasting, which included a provision restricting indecent programming on all stations, commercial and public, to the midnight-to-6-A.M. period—right back where the FCC was in 1987. Adding to the pressure was an appropriations bill containing just such a definition of safe harbor, signed by the president late in 1992. In early 1993 the FCC rule-making concluded (sagely) that the

---

*In considering the channeling rationale, however, remember that ratings data indicate that nearly as many children watch television in late prime time as during the traditional Saturday morning hours.

midnight-to-6-A.M. safe harbor seemed the best compromise for all concerned.* Yet another appeal, however, knocked the safe harbor back to 8 P.M. to 6 A.M. while arguments pro and con raged in court.

Late in 1992 the FCC fined "shock jock" Howard Stern's employer, Infinity Broadcasting, a record-high $600,000 for Stern's consistent use of indecent speech in his highly popular radio show. Infinity had already appealed a 1988 fine of $6,000 for another Stern broadcast, and appealed the new fine as well, arguing the FCC standard was vague.**

Regulating Indecency in Cable

Because states as well as the federal government regulate cable, concern over obscenity and indecency on cable has caused conflicts of jurisdiction as well as of substance. The cable act of 1984 provided for fines or imprisonment for anyone who "transmits over any cable system any matter which is obscene or otherwise unprotected by the Constitution" (47 USC 639).

The 1992 cable act made system operators liable for any obscene material carried on their leased access channels and empowered system operators to enforce written policy on such programming (47 USC 612, 638). Under both cable acts and according to FCC rules, cable systems were required to gather together any such programming on a single channel, and to block viewer access to that channel unless a subscriber requested it in writing. How these restrictions square with limits imposed on broadcasting and with First Amendment protec-

tions remains to be fully tested. While the Supreme Court has held that cable television *does* have First Amendment protection, it has also said that such protection must be balanced against what it called "competing social interests," without specifying what those interests may be or how that might be done (US, 1986: 488).*

States had previously tried to go even further by applying the Supreme Court's *Miller* and *Pacifica* decisions to questionable cable content. Four federal court decisions in the mid-1980s, three initiated in Utah, concluded that state laws banning cable indecency violated the First Amendment because they were too broad in scope. Because cable does not use open spectrum, the scarcity argument that had supported indecency limits in broadcasting could not be applied. The courts reasoned that cable is not as "uniquely intrusive" as broadcasting, nor as available to children, because subscribers pay for the service—and that *Pacifica* therefore did not apply to cable. The judge in one case suggested that the real responsibility for preventing children from seeing such programming rested with parents (F, 1985c: 989), a finding that echoed deregulators' arguments against government intervention.

To monitor the situation better, the FCC and the Justice Department agreed in 1991 to divide up their overlapping concerns about obscenity and indecency. Justice would take primary responsibility for any actions against cable or pay-cable services, whereas the FCC would concentrate on broadcast cases (Ferris et al., 1983–1992: 8-38/9).

Seeking a Balance

Obscenity/indecency law as applied to electronic media will evolve as society's standards evolve. After three decades of increasing liberalization, during which many taboos fell and audiences grew more tolerant of explicit language and scenes, the

---

*FCC decisions on individual indecency/obscenity complaints go through several layers of staff legal review (after quick dismissal of those lacking any substantiation, in the form of a tape or transcript) before finally reaching the commissioners for a final decision. The review process took about a year in 1992 (*Broadcasting*, 31 August 1992: 24).

**The fine had escalated because of the cumulative number of stations carrying Stern's broadcasts—Infinity stations in New York, Philadelphia, Washington, and by tape in Los Angeles.

*As this edition goes to press, a federal court of appeals has stayed (delayed) the 1992 act's limits on indecent programming on PEG and leased access channels pending a final decision on the law's constitutionality.

Exhibit 14.d • • • • • • • • • • • • • •

I Know It When I See It. . . .

Is broadcast or cable television too racy? Is it loaded with sexual content either active or heavily implied? Some conservatives and/or religious critics have long thought so and have tried to organize boycotts against

Source: Photo from Stephane Sednaoui/Warner Bros. Records Inc.

sponsors of such programs. In recent years their targets have included most of the nationally syndicated talk shows that seem fascinated with cross-dressing, odd marital crises, strippers (of both genders), cops-turned prostitutes, and the like. Even some audience participation shows—*Studs*, for example—have raised eyebrows about what is acceptable content for television. Ironically (as few seem to complain), the most prominent sexual situations show up daily in soap opera dramas with their steamy scenes of illicit sex or pretty clear implications of what is happening just outside of camera range. While there is disagreement over what is "too much" reference to sex, there is broad agreement that young children must be protected from the occasional overt sex that *does* show up—especially on uncut movies shown on pay cable and pay-per-view. And sexual content on radio talk shows is also controversial—remember that it was a radio program that resulted in the landmark *Pacifica* decision discussed in the text. Judges have long found it difficult to clearly define just what is obscene or indecent in all cases. As one Supreme Court Justice admitted years ago when asked to define what was illegal, "I know it when I see it. . . "

---

pendulum for a while swung to a more conservative standard—restrictions aimed at preserving "family values." The country's trend toward political conservatism in the 1980s inclined in that direction despite another conservative article of faith—reliance on the marketplace to set any rules.

On the other hand, no indication of a disappearing market for programs that pushed limits was evident in the early 1990s. Syndicated shows (such as *Studs* and certain other Fox network series) and even traditional network shows (such as one *Civil Wars* episode in late 1992 showing a semi-nude Mariel Hemingway) suggested that

the search for what was acceptable—how far one could go—continued.

The 1990s' trend seemed to be toward more permissive interpretation of laws dealing with sexuality for cable as compared to broadcast programming. This difference arises largely because cable lacks the universal reach of broadcasting and comes into the home only after a conscious decision to subscribe—a decision reviewed monthly when the bill comes in. Still, the all-out invasion of X-rated cable programs—once predicted—has not occurred. Even such a mildly liberated home service as the Playboy pay-cable channel drew relatively few subscribers—so few that in 1989 it switched to pay-per-view status in some markets.

• • • • • • • •

14.5 Ownership

First Amendment theory stresses the value of many diverse and antagonistic sources of information and opinion. Unregulated competition, however, can lead to monopoly control. Thus, government seeks a positive First Amendment role by limiting media monopoly. *Diversification* of ownership and control, for example, has long been a major FCC goal. This *structural* regulation contrasts with the *behavioral* regulation discussed in most of the remainder of this chapter. But the *intent* of such structural regulation matches the more direct behavioral approach—to enhance First Amendment interest in diverse opinions. Examples of structural regulation include rules limiting

- the number and kind of stations licensed to any one owner,
- concentration of control over program production and distribution, and
- cross-media ownership (stations, systems, and other media under common control).

Every broadcast station enjoys a limited monopoly—exclusive use of a given channel in a particular market. Cable, a monopoly service in most markets, has more far-reaching control. Once viewers subscribe, installers usually disconnect rooftop antennas so that home owners receive even broadcast stations only (or at least primarily) by cable. A cable operator thus has control over *all* video signals coming into some homes, other than rented or purchased tapes. Is such a situation a regulatory problem? For answers, we begin with a look at antitrust law.

Antitrust Law

The Sherman Act of 1890 and the Clayton Act of 1914 together aim to prevent monopolies. They provide the basis for such government actions as the one that led to the 1984 breakup of the giant telephone monopoly, AT&T.

Courts have long held that despite the First Amendment, business law—including antitrust statutes—may be applied to media. Sec. 313 of the Communications Act requires the FCC to consider revoking licenses held by companies found guilty of violating antitrust laws. However, the deregulatory atmosphere of the 1980s weakened enforcement of antitrust (the suit to break up AT&T had been initiated years earlier). The Justice Department rarely questioned either the huge media mergers and take-overs during the 1980s or the trend toward ever-larger combinations in cable television. Yet such consolidations tend to undermine the First Amendment goal of preserving competition in ideas through diversification of media ownership.

Multiple Ownership

Because of the monopolistic nature of each licensee's use of a broadcast channel, the FCC limits the total number of stations anyone may control. As of mid-1993 those limits confined a single owner to no more than 18 AM, 18 FM, and 12 television stations nationwide (for the latter only, there is an additional limit of reaching markets totaling no more than 25 percent of the television homes in the country). Radio limits will increase to 20 in each service in 1994. Owners can have a noncontrolling interest in up to 3 additional stations if these are controlled by small businesses or minority interests.*

---

*Prior to 1985 the FCC had for three decades limited multiple ownership to no more than 7 stations of each type—an arbitrary ceiling. In view of the increasing number of stations during those decades, the Commission tried to remove all ownership limits, but pressure from Congress led to a "12-12-12" compromise—also an arbitrary ceiling—in 1985. The FCC had raised the radio ownership limit to 30 AM and 30 FM early in 1992, but it retreated under a storm of congressional (and some industry) protest that the number was too high. The Commission was considering raising the television limit as this book went to press, but given the protest over radio and the smaller number of television stations overall, any increase is likely to be small—perhaps to 14 or 15 stations nationwide.

During the 1980s the FCC eliminated a number of other ownership limitations: an *antitrafficking* rule that had required a licensee to hold a station at least three years before selling it, a limitation on regional concentration of ownership, and rules that defined passive financial holdings in broadcast companies as "ownership." These changes reflect the FCC's policy of relying more on marketplace competition than on structural regulation to safeguard the public interest.

Duopoly

On the individual market level, a *duopoly* rule issued by the FCC in 1940 and enforced for half a century held that no single owner could have more than one station of the same type (for example, more than one AM station) in the same market. Originally one owner could control a single-market AM-FM-TV combination, but the Commission banned such combinations in 1970, while *grandfathering* existing combinations.*

In 1992, however, while changing its radio ownership rules, the FCC struck down the duopoly limitation. A single owner can now own up to two AM and two FM commercial stations in markets with 15 or more radio stations. In markets with fewer than 15 stations, any single owner can have up to three such stations, two in the same service.** While some critics argued that this new measure would further weaken diversity of views, others suggested it might increase program variety if owners of several stations programmed each one to a different audience for the largest possible cumulative reach.

---

*To "grandfather" means to let a once-legal practice continue after a law or rule is changed. The FCC will typically grandfather media outlets from having to meet an ownership rule change until or unless they are sold, by which time they must abide by current regulations.

**Noncommercial stations are not counted in determining the total number of stations in a market. Nor do these rules limit noncommercial station ownership, because the FCC wants to foster expansion of the noncommercial service. Several states have developed networks of FM and/or television stations under this exemption (see Section 8.3).

Cable Systems

None of this regulatory complexity limits ownership of newer electronic media such as cable systems, although anit-trust law does, of course, apply. The possibility of a limit on *multiple-system operators* (MSOs) or a ceiling on how many cable subscribers one MSO may serve has been discussed by various agencies at least since the mid-1970s. But deregulatory policy and cable industry lobbying had long fended off such limits.

However, while the 1984 cable act *allowed* the FCC to establish cable ownership rules if it chose (it didn't), the 1992 cable act *mandated* an FCC proceeding in 1992–1993 to set up "reasonable limits" on the number of cable systems or subscribers any one entity could have, and on the number of channels on a system that could be programmed by a source in which the cable system had a financial interest (Sec. 613). By early 1993, drawing from decades of broadcast station ownership rules and guidelines, the FCC was considering a 25 percent limit of cable subscribers for any one owner. (The largest MSO at the time, TCI, controlled systems with about 17 percent of all cable subscribers.) There are no controls on cable-system ownership of cable program services, though the 1992 act also required the FCC to "consider the necessity and appropriateness of imposing limitations" on such vertical integration.

Other Media

LPTV has no ownership limitation, nor is there any limit on MMDS ownership (other than only one per market of two available) or DBS (other than obtaining FCC approval and both orbital slot and uplink and downlink frequencies). Full-power broadcasters argue—with some reason, though thus far unsuccessfully—that rules applicable only to them fly in the face of establishing parity among competitive media services (see Exhibit 14.e).

Cross-Media Ties

Ownership by the same entity of more than one medium in the same market reduces the variety of viewpoints in that market. The oldest example of

Exhibit 14.e •••••••••••••••••

Who Can Own What?

	May co-own any of the following:						
	Broadcast Stations			Broadcast Networks		Cable	
The Owner of a(n)	AM	FM	TV (A)	Radio	TV	Systems	Networks
AM radio station	17	18	12	no limit	1	no limit	no limit
FM radio station	18	17	12	no limit	1	no limit	no limit
TV station	18	18	11	no limit	1	no limit*	no limit
Radio network	18	18	12	no limit	1	none	no limit
TV network	18	18	12	no limit	none	(B)	no limit
Cable system	18	18	12*	no limit	none	no limit (C)	no limit
Cable network	18	18	12 (but not in same market with co-owned cable system)	no limit	1	no limit**	no limit
Local telephone company	(D)	(D)	(D)	(D)	(D)	no limit*	(D)
Foreign entity	(E)	(E)	(E)	no limit	no limit	no limit	no limit

(A) For television stations only, the total potential national audience reach of all co-owned stations must not exceed 25 percent (only half of a UHF station's reach counts in the total). Thus the actual limit on the number of television stations licensed to a single owner may be lower, especially if the stations are in top markets. As many as 14 stations may be licensed by minority groups.

(B) Television broadcast networks may own systems reaching, in any given market, no more than 10 percent of homes passed by cable or up to 25 percent of all cable homes.

(C) Under provision of the 1992 cable act, as discussed in the text, the FCC was considering imposition of some ceiling limit in 1993—perhaps 25 percent of all cable subscribers nationwide.

(D) At present, a combination of statute, FCC rules and regulation, and tradition prevents local telephone companies from owning and operating any electronic medium in the same market area as where they provide local exchange telephone services. There is considerable 1990s' debate regarding the potential for cable ownership and operation of cable systems.

(E) Under Section 310(a) of the Communications Act, no foreign entity can own more than 20 percent of any domestic U.S. broadcasting station.

Not shown here is the effect of the FCC's 1992 relaxation of its radio duopoly rule allowing ownership of more than one radio station of a type in a single market (see Section 14.5).

*if not in same market   **if not in same market with co-owned TV stations such *crossownership* is where a broadcast license or cable franchise is granted to a local newspaper publisher. This reduction in alternative information sources (sometimes called media *voices*, as opposed to actual *outlets* such as stations or systems) is especially undesirable in small communities, in which the only newspaper might own the only broadcast station or cable system. The FCC issued rules banning new newspaper/broadcasting crossownership in 1975, but grandfathered all but a very few existing combinations. Though both the FCC and Congress have considered limits on newspaper/cable crossownership on several occasions, no such limits have been adopted.

In 1970 the Commission prohibited broadcast television network ownership of cable systems as well as crossownership of telephone companies or television stations and cable systems in the same market area (except in rural areas of fewer than 5,000 people). This ban was intended to prevent older services from controlling programming to the detriment of cable, then in its early stages of development. On the other hand, with cable a far stronger player two decades later, the 1992 cable act banned crossownership by a cable system of any MMDS or SMATV service in its franchise area, so as to encourage growth by those cable competitors. The FCC, as usual, grandfathered combinations existing when the act was passed (Sec. 613(a)(2)).

Video Dial Tone

At the end of the 1980s, pushed in part by technical and structural changes in the telephone industry (see Section 3.8), a new crossownership controversy developed that found broadcasters and cable owners on the same side. Both groups feared that the FCC might allow local telephone companies to own cable systems—and possibly even broadcast stations—within their telephone service areas. A ban on such crossownership in the 1984 cable act keeps the regulated common-carrier and media businesses apart in the same market, but telephone industry representatives increasingly seek a share in the *information* or content business.

In the early 1990s the FCC sought to increase telephone company participation in electronic media ownership for three reasons:

- to develop competition with largely monopoly cable systems,
- to hasten installation of fiber-optic transmission lines with their high-quality broadband capacity (see Section 5.4), and
- to encourage development of two-way (interactive) video services.

The FCC's video dial tone (VDT) decision of 1992 allows telephone companies to provide means of audio and video program delivery, though they may control no more than a 5 percent interest in the programs themselves (FCCR, 1992a: 5781).* Through this common-carrier approach, the Commission tried to balance the public's interest in more competing service providers against protective demands from three monopoly industries—telephone, cable, and broadcast. The FCC decided that, because local telephone companies were not to be programmers, they would not be required to hold a franchise in order to provide VDT. On the other hand, the Commission prohibited them from buying an existing cable system in their service area because that would simply replace one monopoly provider with another.

Initial reaction to the VDT decision was predictable. Telephone companies felt it did not go far enough: it limited them to no more than a 5 percent participation in programming. They argued that only the revenues from program ownership would warrant the enormous expenditures required to build fiber networks for video, voice, and two-way interactive services. Broadcast and cable interests, on the other hand, worried about this telephone industry foot in the electronic media's door.

Whether this FCC decision takes on landmark status, as many at the Commission expect, will

---

*The Regional Bell Operating Companies, or RBOCs (see Section 3.8), which control 80 percent of the nation's telephones, had been banned from participating in the information business by a court-mandated restriction growing out of the break-up of AT&T. Court decisions in 1991 eliminated that barrier.

depend on how local telephone companies move into this area in the next few years, and whether Congress removes the 1984 ban on same-market cable-telephone crossownership. Several telephone firms are already testing different kinds of video delivery (some under experimental exemptions from FCC limitations), seeking the right mix that attracts customers and provides revenue sufficient to invest in fiber-optic networks and other needed technologies. Not to be outflanked, some large cable MSOs are investigating different kinds of voice and data services they might provide. Video compression (see Section 5.7) and other technological developments aid the competing industries as they move onto one another's turf. How regulators will control the shifting alliances and technologies promises to feed major electronic media policy debates in the 1990s.

Minority Ownership

For many years, the FCC ignored minority status of owners as an aspect of diversifying media control. A series of court reversals in the 1960s and early 1970s, however, forced it to reexamine its position, and it slowly began to give an advantage to minority applicants.

Spurred initially by Carter administration policies on aid to minorities, the FCC since 1978 has taken several steps to enhance opportunities for members of ethnic and racial minority groups (African-Americans, Hispanics, Asians, American Indians) to become licensees:

- *Tax Certificates:* These encourage sales of stations to minorities by allowing sellers to defer paying capital gains taxes on their profits; sellers can further defer the taxes if they purchase another station within two years (they must be paid when the "replacement property" is sold). In their first 15 years of use, tax certificates helped place more than 240 stations into minority hands (some were later sold). An average of 12 such certificates were issued per year through 1986, a figure that jumped to at least 30 for each of the next five years (*Broad-*

casting, 8 April 1992: 68). Minority purchasers must hold the property for at least one year. Critics argued many then sold out for big profits, diminishing the point of certificates to increase long-term minority control.

- *Distress Sales:* Normally the Commission will not permit an owner whose license is in serious danger of nonrenewal to sell anything other than the station's physical assets (equipment, buildings, land). But to encourage sales to minority applicants, the FCC permits endangered licensees to recover some, though not all, of the market value of "intangible assets" (effectively the station license and the operation's public image). When the FCC agreed in 1979 to drop fraudulent billing charges against a small AM station in Connecticut after the incumbent offered to sell the property to a minority group for 75 percent of its appraised value, that 75 percent figure became a de facto standard for future distress sales. By 1991, 27 sales involving 38 stations had been approved (*Broadcasting,* 8 April 1991: 70).

- *Minority minorities:* In 1982 the Commission sought to further encourage minority ownership by allowing members of a racial minority holding as little as 20 percent of the equity in a licensee to take advantage of both certificates and distress sales rules—provided that the minority owner had voting control. At the same time, the FCC made cable-system sales eligible for tax certificate consideration (16 had changed hands under this provision by early 1991). On the other hand, when the Commission raised radio ownership limits in 1992 (see "Multiple Ownership," page 514), it dropped a former provision allowing more stations to be owned if they were minority controlled.

- *Lotteries:* Use of lotteries in choosing LPTV and MMDS licensees gives preference to minority ownership, as detailed in Section 13.4.

Total minority ownership of stations increased sharply during the 1970s, and more slowly since—from 31 stations (only one of which was a television station) in 1976, to 256 radio and 31 television stations in mid-1991 (NTIA, 1991b). The National

Black Media Coalition reported that to achieve ownership of stations in proportion to their actual numbers in society, some 1,250 broadcast stations would have to be owned by African-Americans and about 450 by Hispanics. The industry has a long way to go before minorities achieve such ownership parity.

Despite this record, the deregulatory-minded FCC briefly suspended the distress sale minority preference option in the 1980s because of ideological opposition to "reverse discrimination," as opponents called special breaks for minorities. However, pressure from Congress soon forced the Commission to reinstate it. Several legal attacks on this and other minority preference policies were consolidated into one case but rejected by the Supreme Court, which held that such preference policies "do not violate equal protection principles" (US 1990: 547).

Networks as Owners

As the once-chief producers, purchasers, and distributors of broadcast programs, television broadcast networks were long the target of FCC structural controls. Network ownership of stations and of other media was a specific subject of concern. Networks, like all other broadcast group owners, fall under the multiple-ownership rules discussed above. But only in 1992 were they finally allowed to own cable systems (they had always been allowed to own cable networks).

Reasoning that broadcast networks had lost much of their economic power during the 1980s, the FCC allowed them to build or purchase cable systems, though with limitations that apply to no other owners. The 1992 rules allow networks to own systems to a ceiling of 10 percent of all homes passed by cable nationally, and 50 percent of all homes passed by cable in any given market, unless there is a competing cable system already operating there. The FCC plans to review these rules in 1995.

The rise in number of cable networks after 1980—and the drop in broadcast television network audiences—reduced FCC concern about the former three-network control over broadcast television program origination. But despite strong FCC attempts to reduce or eliminate them, several old behavioral rules for television networks remain, strongly supported by elements of the broadcast and motion picture industries. Notable examples are the prime-time access and syndication/financial interest rules (see Section 9.2). Designed originally to increase diversity by opening network affiliate time to independent producers, these rules built up independent television stations and their program suppliers. Having grown under the protection of those rules, independent producers successfully put pressure on Congress—and the Reagan White House in the mid-1980s—to make the FCC retain the rules. Increasing financial pressure on the networks, however, pushed the FCC to modify its thinking—and consider again changing or eliminating the rules in 1993.

Foreign Control

Sec. 310(a) of the Communications Act forbids control of a U.S. radio or television broadcasting station by a foreign entity. Specifically, no more than 20 percent of the station's stock or other means of control can be in the hands of foreign investors.* Most other countries have similar restrictions on broadcast ownership by other than their own nationals. No other electronic medium is restricted this way: Canadian and other foreign interests own many cable systems.

• • • • • • • •

14.6 Political Access

The Communications Act regulates programs most explicitly when they involve candidates for public office. Congress correctly foresaw in 1927 that

---

*It was this statute that caused media mogul Rupert Murdoch to give up his Australian citizenship and become a naturalized American in 1985 in order to purchase the Metromedia television stations that would become the heart of his later Fox network (see Exhibit 3.m on page 102).

broadcasting would one day exert a major influence on voters. If the party in power could monopolize electronic media, opposing candidates would stand little chance of winning elections. The First Amendment goal of diversified points of view again needed an "assist" in the case of electronic media.

"Equal Time"

In order to equalize the political benefits of broadcasting, Congress wrote the *equal opportunities** provision—Sec. 315—into the Act:

> If any licensee shall permit any person who is a legally qualified candidate for any public office to use a broadcasting station, he shall afford equal opportunities to all other such candidates for that office in the use of such broadcasting station; *Provided,* That such licensee shall have no power of censorship over the material broadcast under the provisions of this section. No obligation is imposed under this subsection upon any licensee to allow the use of its station by any such candidate. (47 USC 315a)

Originally, the "no obligation" clause in the last sentence meant that licensees could avoid demands for equal time by refusing *all* applicants for time. A series of amendments adopted to bring the Communications Act in line with the Federal Election Campaign Act of 1971 closed this option, at least for candidates for federal office (the House, Senate, vice president, and president). One of the 1971 amendments *mandated* access by adding as a new basis for license revocation the "willful or repeated failure to allow reasonable access to" federal candidates (47 USC 312a(7)).

Buying Political Time

One of the trickiest problems in political broadcasting is defining what constitutes a station's "lowest

*The commonly used term *equal time* does not appear in the Act. Indeed, *equal opportunities* requires more than just equal time. A literal interpretation of equal time would permit a broadcaster to run a 30-second commercial for a favored candidate during prime time and run another for the opponent at 4:00 A.M.—a ploy not permitted under the broader equal opportunities rule.

unit charge." This phrase in Sec. 315(b) of the Communications Act defines the maximum rate that licensees may charge candidates (federal, state, or local) who buy time for political purposes shortly before elections (45 days in the case of a primary, 60 days for a general election). In effect, stations may charge a political candidate no more for a given commercial than would be charged to the lowest-paying advertiser for the same spot. For example, a commercial advertiser might have to buy several hundred spots to qualify for the maximum quantity discount, but a political candidate benefits from that discount even when buying only a single spot. Also, when a station proposed charging a candidate more than five times its rate for a one-minute spot for a five-minute program (on the grounds that program rates differ from spot rates), the FCC ruled that the lowest-unit-charge provision limited charges to no more than five times that of a one-minute spot. This "lowest unit charge" remains one of the most contentious aspects of the political broadcasting rules and leads to new FCC guidelines with nearly every election.

Candidates in the News

At first, Sec. 315's equal opportunities mandate left licensees free to make normal news judgments in deciding between self-promotion and bona fide news in covering candidate activities. In 1959, however, the FCC ruled that even a bona fide (good faith) news-related broadcast involving a candidate counted as a political "use" of broadcasting, triggering equal opportunity obligations (FCCR, 1959: 715). That action created a furor and set Congress to amending the Act to exclude news programs:

> Appearance by a legally qualified candidate on any
>
> (1) bona fide newscast,
> (2) bona fide news interview,
> (3) bona fide news documentary (if the appearance of the candidate is incidental to the presentation of the subject or subjects covered by the news documentary), or
> (4) on-the-spot news coverage of bona fide news events (including but not limited to political conventions and activities incidental thereto),

shall not be deemed to be use of a broadcasting station within the meaning of this subsection. (47 USC 315(a); emphasis added)

While the amendment liberated news coverage from political equal-time harassments, it also left the FCC with many knotty problems of interpretation. Questions regarding political candidates' rights are among those most frequently asked by licensees seeking interpretation of FCC rules. Some examples of the issues confronting stations are detailed in Exhibit 14.f.

In addition to providing paid-for access, electronic media have a responsibility to inform the electorate about political issues in a nonpartisan way. This tricky combination of enforced cooperation (which does not exist for newspapers or other print media), profit making, and the obligation to journalistic objectivity continues to create problems for media managers.

• • • • • • • •

14.7 Public Access

Not everyone with an idea to express can own a station or cable system—nor can everyone expect access to stations or systems owned by others. The FCC long struggled with this problem by trying to provide access to broadcasting for *ideas* rather than for specific *people*. But even access for ideas has to be qualified. It would be impractical to force stations to give time for literally every idea that might be put forward.

The FCC mandated access only for ideas about *controversial issues of public importance*, thus emphasizing another First Amendment value—an open marketplace of differing ideas. This approach had two advantages: (1) it allowed licensees to retain general responsibility for programming, leaving to their discretion decisions about which issues have public importance and who should speak for them, and (2) it obligated licensees, though in an unstructured way, to provide access to ideas other than their own. Thus licensees' First Amendment rights were generally preserved along with those of the public at large.

Rise of the Fairness Doctrine

The FCC slowly elaborated its access ideas into a formalized set of procedures called the fairness doctrine. In first announcing the concept in 1949, the FCC said:

> It is the right of the public to be informed, rather than any right on the part of the Government, any broadcast licensee or any individual member of the public to broadcast his own particular views on any matter, which is the foundation stone of the American system of broadcasting.
>
> This affirmative responsibility on the part of broadcast licensees to provide a reasonable amount of time for the presentation over their facilities of programs devoted to the discussion and consideration of public issues has been reaffirmed by the commission in a long series of decisions. (FCCR, 1949: 1249)

Congress in 1959 endorsed FCC thinking in an incidental way when it amended Sec. 315 to exempt bona fide news programs about political candidates from equal opportunities requirements, as described in Section 14.6. After listing the four exempt program types, the amendment included the fairness doctrine's concern with "controversial issues of public importance":

> Nothing in the foregoing sentence shall be construed as relieving broadcasters, in connection with [the exempt news programs], from the obligation imposed upon them under this Act to operate in the public interest and *to afford reasonable opportunity for the discussion of conflicting views on issues of public importance.* (47 USC 315(a); emphasis added)

In the 1960s and 1970s the Commission continued to refine its view of the doctrine. It obligated stations to (A) schedule time for programs on controversial issues of public importance, and (B) ensure expression of opposing views on those issues. Both stations and the FCC largely ignored (A), focusing their attention on (B), seen by many as a right of reply. In practice, therefore, most fairness doctrine complaints came as reactions to ideas that had already been discussed on the air, rather than as complaints about the failure to initiate discussion of issues. Stations needed to monitor their programs

Exhibit 14.f •••••••••••••••••

What Does "Equal Opportunities" Mean?

- *Who gets equal opportunities?* Candidates for nomination in primary elections and nominees in general elections get equal opportunities. But equal opportunities can be claimed only by candidates for the same specific office; purchase of time by a candidate for Congress, for example, entitles all other candidates for that post in that district to equivalent opportunities, but not candidates for other districts or other offices.

- *Do presidential news conferences count as bona fide news programs?* Yes—they are exempt from equal opportunities claims.

- *Do presidential candidate debates count as news?* Though the rules have changed many times, the answer is "yes." However, third-party candidates are less likely to be heard (networks or other sponsors exclude them as being of little interest—Ross Perot in 1992 being an exception)—a news exception that flies in the face of Sec. 315's intent to let voters hear all the candidates.

- *Are regularly scheduled interview and talk programs exempt from equal opportunity requests?* Yes—including "infotainment" programs such as *Donahue* and *Oprah Winfrey*.

- *How much time constitutes "reasonable access"?* The FCC refuses to provide any set amount, but stations are prohibited from limiting candidates for federal office to set numbers of spots or amounts of program time, even when their schedules do not easily allow extended political speeches.

- *May live news appearances be recorded for later playback and still be exempt?* Yes.

- *Is a candidate entitled to whatever time of day he or she wants?* No. Candidates cannot decree when they appear. Stations may keep political spots out of particular periods—such as the times scheduled for news programs.

- *Must a station broadcast a candidate's use of obscene material?* No. When in 1984 *Hustler* publisher Larry Flynt threatened to use arguably obscene material in a possible campaign for the presidency, licensees asked the FCC for policy guidance. The Commission held that the ban on obscenity overrode the "no censorship" provision of Sec. 315.

- *Are photos of aborted fetuses in political ads obscene, and therefore not allowed?* No. During the 1992 elections, several candidates ran on anti-abortion platforms and some used graphic pictures of aborted fetuses in their advertising. Yielding to both viewer and licensee concerns, the Commission held that such depictions, while well within the rights of candidates' uncensored access, might be indecent and thus could be restricted to the "safe harbor" hours of midnight to 6 A.M. A federal court in Atlanta found that such ads were obscene and thus *should* be so restricted. Stations could also run a disclaimer that federal law required the ad to be carried.

- *Must a station carry potentially libelous material by a candidate?* Yes. *Is the station legally liable?* No.

- *May electronic media endorse political candidates in editorials?* Yes; but if they do, they must notify opposing candidates for the same office and offer reply time, even if the editorial occurs within a newscast.

- *Are cable systems held to the same regulations?* Regulations apply only to channels on which the cable operator *originates* programming. Cable systems are not responsible for political content of stations or services whose programs they carry but over which they have no content control.

- *May a licensee evade political broadcasting problems by banning all political advertising?* No—at least not for federal candidates (who must receive "reasonable access").

- *Is any appearance of a candidate a "use" of broadcast facilities?* No. Until 1992, however, any time a candidate appeared on the air—even in an entertainment or other non-political situation—that time counted as "use." In 1992, the FCC narrowed the definition to cover only time which is authorized or otherwise controlled by a candidate or his or her committee—in other words, overtly political use of time.

to make sure that if anyone introduced a controversial issue, opposing interests had a chance to reply. If licensees themselves introduced such issues in station editorials, they had to offer time for the expression of opposing views.

In complying with the fairness doctrine, licensees had great latitude in deciding whether or not a subject qualified as both a controversial issue and one of public importance, how much time should be devoted to replies, when replies should be scheduled, and who should speak for opposing viewpoints (except, of course, for those replying to personal attacks, as discussed on page 525).

In 1969 the Supreme Court upheld the FCC's fairness doctrine, as well as its related personal attack and political editorializing rules, in its landmark *Red Lion* decision (see Exhibit 14.g). By unanimously supporting the FCC in this case, the Court strongly affirmed the fairness doctrine concept in an opinion that emphasized four key principles relevant to broadcasting's First Amendment status (US, 1969: 367):

- *On the uniqueness of broadcasting:* "It is idle to posit an unabridgeable First Amendment right to broadcast comparable to the right of every individual to speak, write, or publish."
- *On the fiduciary principle:* "There is nothing in the First Amendment which prevents the Government from requiring a licensee to share his frequency with others and to conduct himself as a proxy or fiduciary."
- *On the public interest:* "It is the right of the viewers and listeners, not the right of the broadcasters, which is paramount."
- *On the scarcity factor:* "Nothing in this record, or in our own researches, convinces us that the [spectrum] resource is no longer one for which there are more immediate and potential uses than can be accommodated, and for which wise planning is essential."

End of the Doctrine

Fifteen years later, in a footnote to another decision (US, 1984b: 364), the Supreme Court implied that it would be receptive to reviewing relevancy of the scarcity factor in view of the many new services available to listeners (no such case reached the Court before the FCC dropped the doctrine). In the meantime, legal appeals continued—unsuccessfully—against FCC fairness doctrine decisions.

Despite the fairness doctrine, a few broadcasters used their stations to promote extreme positions on controversial issues, oblivious to the fact that as licensees they had an obligation to offer opportunities for rebuttal. One of the most publicized instances of licensee one-sidedness, and the only case in which fairness violations led to loss of a license, involved a religious broadcaster. The licensee of WXUR, an AM/FM radio operation in Media, Pennsylvania, defied the fairness doctrine and lied to the FCC about its intent to comply with the doctrine. Licensed to an organization headed by Carl McIntire, a cantankerous right-wing fundamentalist preacher, the stations carried his *Twentieth Century Reformation Hour,* a syndicated series noted for its intemperate attacks on opponents of his philosophy. In 1970 the FCC, after receiving many citizen complaints, refused to renew the license, alleging not only fairness violations but also failure to fulfill program promises and to ascertain local needs. An appeals court upheld the FCC action, and the stations left the air (F, 1972: 16).

No other fairness complaint had such drastic consequences. The FCC dismissed most others out of hand either because complainants cited no legally definable controversial issue of public importance or because they failed to show how the overall programming of accused stations had in fact denied reasonable opportunities for opposing sides to be argued. Still, almost every year brought another controversial case and kept broadcasters concerned about the highly unpopular doctrine. Broadcasters complained how differently they were being treated from any other medium.

By 1985 the FCC, by then largely made up of Reagan administration appointees dedicated to deregulation, had joined the mounting chorus of opposition to the fairness doctrine. After a lengthy proceeding, the Commission concluded:

Exhibit 14.g • • • • • • • • • • •

A Place and a Case Called Red Lion

An unlikely small-town station formed the setting for one of the leading Supreme Court decisions on electronic media. During the 1960s right-wing preachers inundated radio with paid syndicated political commentary, backed by ultraconservative supporters such as Texas multimillionaire H. L. Hunt through tax-exempt foundations. Purchased time for these religious/political programs provided much-needed radio income in small markets.

The landmark case got its name from WGCB, a southeastern Pennsylvania AM/FM outlet licensed to John M. Norris, a conservative minister, under the name Red Lion Broadcasting. In 1964, one of the Reverend Billy James Hargis's syndicated broadcasts, carried by the station, attacked author Fred Cook, who had criticized defeated Republican presidential candidate Barry Goldwater and had written an article on what he termed the "hate clubs of the air," referring to the Hargis series *Christian Crusade*, among others. Hargis attacked Cook on the air, charging him with communist affiliations and with criticizing the FBI and the CIA—the standard litany of accusations Hargis routinely made against liberals.

Cook then accused the station of violating FCC rules by failing to inform him of a personal attack. When he wrote asking for time to reply, the station responded with a rate card, inviting him to buy time like anyone else. Cook appealed to the FCC, which agreed that he had a right to free airtime for a reply. It ordered WGCB to comply.

It would have been easy for the Reverend Mr. Norris to grant Cook a few minutes of time on the Red Lion station, but he refused on First Amendment grounds,

Fred Cook   *Billy James Hargis*

appealing the Commission decision. The court of appeals upheld the FCC, but Norris took the case to the Supreme Court, which, in 1969, also upheld the FCC, issuing an opinion strongly defensive of the FCC's right to demand program fairness.

Several years later, Fred Friendly, a former head of CBS news but by then a Columbia University journalism professor, began looking into the background of this well-known case for a book about the fairness doctrine (Friendly, 1976). He discovered that Cook had been a subsidized writer for the Democratic National Committee and that his fairness complaint had been linked to a systematic campaign mounted by the Democrats to discredit right-wing extremists such as Hargis. According to Friendly, the Democrats set out to exploit the fairness doctrine as a means of harassing stations that sold time for the airing of ultraconservative political programs. Cook and the Democratic National Committee claimed that Friendly had misinterpreted their activities, maintaining that Cook acted as a private individual, not as an agent of the Democratic party.

Source: Photos from George Tames/New York Times Pictures.

[Based on] our experience in administering the doctrine and our general expertise in broadcast regulation, we no longer believe that the fairness doctrine, as a matter of policy, serves the public interest. . . . Furthermore, we find that the fairness doctrine,

in operation, actually inhibits the presentation of controversial issues of public importance to the detriment of the public and in degradation of the editorial prerogatives of broadcast journalists. (FCCR, 1985b: 143)

However, the FCC felt it lacked authority to abolish the doctrine unilaterally because Congress had included reference to the concept in its 1959 addition to Sec. 315. In a 1986 fairness doctrine case, a federal appeals court removed this doubt by concluding, "We do not believe that the language adopted in 1959 made the fairness doctrine a binding statutory obligation; rather it ratified the Commission's longstanding position" (F, 1986: 501). Thus armed, the FCC concluded that an open marketplace of ideas made the doctrine unnecessary. Acting on yet another court remand requiring the FCC to reconsider an earlier fairness decision, the Commission instead abolished the doctrine entirely (FCCR, 1987b: 5043). The personal attack and political editorializing rules, however, remained in place, as discussed below.

That should have ended the matter, but the FCC's defiance in ending a practice that Congress had gone on record as favoring enraged key legislators. They vowed to reinstate the fairness mandate, in the meantime making their dissatisfaction known by holding up approval of appointments to vacant FCC seats. Bills reinstating the doctrine were introduced and passed twice, but were vetoed both times by President Reagan. When President Clinton stated early in 1993 that he would sign a fairness doctrine reinstatement bill if it reached his desk, many predicted renewed congressional action.

A *Right* of Reply?

Two specific fairness-related requirements, the personal attack and political editorializing rules (both adopted in 1967 and retained even after the fairness doctrine's demise in 1987), continue to cause concern to opponents of FCC program interference. These rules require stations to give those individuals affected by explicit political editorials or personal attacks over the air copies of relevant materials within specified time limits as well as an opportunity to respond.

The *personal attack rule* requires stations to inform individuals or groups of personal attacks on their "honesty, character, integrity or like personal qualities" that occur in the course of discussions of controversial public issues. Within a week after the offending broadcast, licensees must advise those attacked, explaining both the nature of the attack and how replies can be made. Specifically exempted from the right of reply are on-the-air attacks made against foreigners, those made by political candidates and their spokespersons during campaigns, and those occurring in news interviews, on-the-spot news coverage, and news commentaries (47 CFR 73.1920)

The *political editorializing rule* requires that all candidates be given a chance to respond if a licensee endorses any of their opponents. If a station editorially opposes a candidate, that candidate must, likewise, be given an opportunity to respond. A station must inform such candidate(s) of their rights to respond within 24 hours of such editorials. The rule does not apply to use of a station's facilities by opposing candidates, a situation covered by the equal opportunities procedures discussed in Section 14.6. This rule is one reason why few licensees editorialize for or against political candidates (another, obviously, is that stations don't want to offend viewers or advertisers who hold opposing views).

Rights for Advertisers

Access by advertisers to broadcasting has been governed more by considerations of taste and public acceptance—and income potential—than by government regulation. However, cigarette advertising became the subject of a famous fairness doctrine complaint. In 1968 the FCC decided that the Surgeon General's first report on the dangers of smoking, as well as Congress's 1965 act requiring a health warning on cigarette packages, justified treating cigarette advertising as a unique fairness doctrine issue. Therefore, stations would have to carry antismoking spots if they carried cigarette commercials. These counter-ads ended, of course, after Congress banned all broadcast advertising of cigarettes in 1971, though occasional public-service announcements concerning smoking still appear.

Editorial advertising or "advertorials," however, posed a different kind of problem. Traditionally, electronic media have declined to let advertisers use commercials as vehicles for comment on controversial issues, arguing that

- serious issues cannot be adequately discussed in short announcements;
- selling larger blocks of time for editorializing by outsiders involves surrender of editorial responsibility; and
- not everyone can afford to buy time, so selling to those with funds is inherently unfair.

The Supreme Court upheld the principle of licensee *journalistic discretion* in a case dealing with a fairness doctrine demand for access to editorial advertising:

> Since it is physically impossible to provide time for all viewpoints . . . the right to exercise editorial judgment was granted to the broadcaster. The broadcaster, therefore, is allowed significant journalistic discretion in deciding how best to fulfill the Fairness Doctrine obligations, although that discretion is bounded by rules designed to assure that the public interest in fairness is furthered. (US, 1973a: 111)

Despite deletion of the fairness doctrine, the question of editorial advertising continually reappears. Controversies arise periodically between advertisers and broadcasters. In several cases, ads that were turned down for television have appeared on cable or in print—with pointed commentary about the refusal of broadcasters to sell time for such advertising. The controversy over advertising of condoms is but one recent example: few broadcasters accepted condom advertising or editorial statements calling for their use to prevent AIDS, for fear that substantial parts of their audiences would be offended by such messages.

Editorial Discretion

By their nature, news and public-affairs programs necessarily involve controversial issues, often leading partisans to bring charges of unfairness. It becomes difficult for broadcasting and cable journalists to deal with serious issues if their corporate bosses prefer to avoid controversy. Yet electronic media cannot win full public respect and First Amendment status without taking risks similar to those the printed press has always faced.

The FCC and courts generally assume that reporters and editors use editorial discretion, which calls for fair and considered news treatment of events, people, and controversies. No one believes that journalists always use the best judgment or that they totally lack bias or prejudice. First Amendment philosophy holds, however, that it is better to tolerate journalists' mistakes—and even their prejudice and incompetence—than to set up a government agency as an arbiter of truth. The Supreme Court reaffirmed this notion in confirming yet another FCC decision rejecting a fairness complaint:

> For better or worse, editing is what editors are for; and editing is selection and choice of material. That editors—newspapers or broadcast—can and do abuse this power is beyond doubt, but that is not reason to deny the discretion Congress provided. Calculated risks of abuse are taken in order to preserve higher values. (US, 1973a: 124)

News Bias

Critics often accuse electronic media, especially television network news departments, of news bias. CNN discovered in an ironic way that it had "arrived" as a widely used news source when, in the wake of its 1991 Gulf War coverage, many complained of its alleged bias by keeping reporters in Baghdad.

Such charges usually come from political conservatives, many of whom regard all news media as too liberal in outlook. They argue that the cumulative effect of alleged liberal bias over time tends to build up one-sided perceptions of issues. Professional gadflies, such as the misnamed Accuracy in Media (which seems always to find *in*accuracy and bias in every media report it investigates), regularly take up conservative causes against alleged television bias. Reagan and Bush administration elements lent support to such complaints, particularly after Bush's reelection defeat in 1992. Content-analysis research is used to support both sides of the bias question, depending on who finances the studies. The debate continues.

Localism

The public needs access to diverse voices—but they also need voices of their own. The notion of a broad right of public access has two aspects—access to ideas of others and to the means of expressing those ideas. The widespread availability of stations and cable systems can facilitate such two-way access—especially within local market communities.

From its inception well into the 1960s, the FCC encouraged *localism*—reflection of the local community's needs and interests—by distributing as many local outlets to as many localities as possible, and by issuing guidelines that encouraged airing of programs reflecting community needs and interests. The Communications Act gives the Commission its own localism guidelines when it acts on applications for new stations:

> The Commission shall make such distribution of licenses, frequencies, hours of operation, and of power among the several States *and communities as to provide a fair, efficient, and equitable distribution of radio service to each of the same.* (47 USC 307(b); emphasis added)

This policy of localizing stations has provided listeners in major markets 40 or more radio stations from which to choose, whereas people in rural areas have far fewer or, in some cases, none at all. As cable expanded, it equalized and increased television channel choices in most urban and suburban areas; but it, too, underserves rural areas.

Yet cable does serve to take pressure off commercial broadcasters, inasmuch as coverage of meetings and local events has largely transferred to local cable government and access channels. Most cable systems have "PEG" (public, educational, and governmental) channels as encouraged by federal law and often required by local franchise. Though budget problems facing most local governments and school systems have restricted their use, the potential of cable's growing number of channels to serve a variety of local concerns has increased greatly in the past decade.

Still, when threatened by changing technology—direct broadcast satellites or telephone industry takeover, for example—broadcasters immediately cite their unique public interest in providing locally relevant programs. They argued long and hard to the FCC and Congress, though to no avail, that cable and DBS are almost entirely national services, whereas broadcasters still hold to the ideal of station-based localism. However, as any discerning listener can attest, while broadcasting and cable do have local *outlets*, the *voices* they carry are increasingly the same nationwide.

• • • • • • • •

14.8 Serving Children

First Amendment theorists understand well that the free marketplace of ideas does not always work. This is perhaps nowhere else so true as with audiences unable to influence that market directly, yet strongly affected by its operations. After years of debate before Congress, the FCC, and the courts, proponents of improved programming for children finally achieved success in 1990 with legislation that created new requirements for broadcast and cable-system operators. Because these represent the industries' first specific program *requirements* (aside from the political broadcasting rules), broadcasters and cable-system owners—accustomed to years of *de*regulation—read them very closely.

Seeking a Balance

Programming for children involves two policy issues dating back to the heyday of network radio: how much and what to *program* for children, and how much *advertising* should such programming carry. In its landmark program reports of 1946 on radio (FCC, 1946) and 1960 on television (FCCR, 1960: 2303), the FCC included children's programming as part of the program mix required for a balanced approach to meeting the public interest, but it issued no special requirements. Then, in the 1970s, the FCC revisited the subject, releasing a report in 1974 that again issued no specific requirements but simply outlined licensee responsibilities in general. One of the groups complaining that this meant no improvement in programming for children was the Boston-based Action for Children's Television (ACT), begun in the late 1960s by a number of mothers concerned over their children's television fare. ACT lost its appeal of the FCC's conclusions (F, 1977a: 458).

A far more extensive report appeared in five volumes in 1979 under FCC Chairman Charles Ferris (FCC, 1979). It found that broadcasters had not provided the minimal amount of programming called for five years earlier and offered considerable detail on broadcasting's poor record. At almost the same time, the Federal Trade Commission issued a strong staff report calling for removal of all advertising in programs aimed at children. ACT and others felt that, finally, some serious remedial action to improve children's programs, and to limit advertising in them, was imminent.

But the deregulatory 1980s killed off this activism as both the FCC and FTC switched gears and began to favor less regulation, rather than more. A 1983 FCC report terminated a 13-year inquiry into children's programming by yet again rejecting any mandatory programming or advertising limits, a conclusion upheld on appeal (F, 1985a: 899). But when the Commission made clear that its deregulation of radio and television advertising guidelines (see Section 13.9) included advertising in children's programs, the stage was set for an historic reversal of years of government inaction.

Children's Television Act

Reacting to constant pressure from ACT and others concerned about lack of governmental action, Congress first passed legislation in 1988 regulating the amount of advertising in children's programs as well as establishing a general obligation to serve child audiences. President Reagan vetoed the bill, calling it an infringement on broadcasters' First Amendment rights. Two years later, much the same bill, the Children's Television Act of 1990, reached the White House and President Bush allowed it to become law without his signature. Among its major provisions:

- Advertising per hour of children's programs is limited to no more than 10½ minutes on week-

ends and 12 minutes on weekdays. (This is the first time there has been any *law* restricting the overall amount of advertising airtime.) This "limitation" (far more liberal than what most protesting groups wanted and, in fact, merely reflecting the existing informal time limits used by most broadcasters) applies to broadcast licensees *and* cable systems—for all programming produced and broadcast primarily for children.

- At license renewal, the FCC must consider whether stations have served the "educational and information needs of children" through their overall programming, which must include "some" (otherwise undefined) programming specifically designed to meet children's needs.

- Establishment of a National Endowment for Children's Educational Television was proposed, to be funded at $2 million for fiscal year 1991 and $4 million for fiscal 1992.* The endowment was eventually funded at about half this rate, and administered by NTIA.

Licensee Duties

With the basic provisions of the Children's Television Act having set the stage, the FCC conducted rule makings in 1990–1991 to put more specific regulations in place. After considerable input from the broadcast and cable industries and others, the Commission arrived at the following decisions:

- It took a very wide view of *programming* by defining "children" as those 16 and younger, thus

*A year earlier, Congress had passed the Television Violence Act of 1989, which exempted television networks and program producers from antitrust laws for a three-year period in order to encourage development of voluntary guidelines limiting violent content in programming—primarily as a protection for children. Only at the very end of the period did three networks (ABC, CBS, and NBC) agree to a 15-point joint set of guidelines. Among them: "all depictions of violence should be relevant to the development of character or to the advancement of theme or plot. . . . [programs] should not depict violence as glamorous, nor as an acceptable solution. . . . scenes showing excessive gore, pain or physical suffering are not acceptable [yet at the same time] . . . realistic depictions of violence should also portray . . . the consequences of that violence. . . . [and] portrayal of dangerous behavior which would invite imitation by children . . . should be avoided" (as quoted in *Television Digest*, 14 December 1992: 6).

allowing stations to include music and dance programs aimed at teens—not what Congress had in mind (the congressional limitation on *commercials*, for example, affects programs aimed at children 12 and under).

- It prohibited program-length commercials for children. A program built around a fantasy hero may no longer include advertising for products related to that hero—they must run in another, unrelated children's program. (The FCC had earlier banned "host selling" and for nearly two decades had prohibited close intermixing of program and advertising elements.)

- It defined the "educational and cultural" programming called for in the Children's Television Act to mean "programming that furthers the positive development of the child in any respect, including the child's cognitive/intellectual or emotional/social needs." The FCC made clear that it would read this mandate quite broadly, leaving considerable latitude to licensees.

- It declared that stations need not program for all children—if desired, they may select one or more age groups. (Several broadcast attorneys have warned their clients not to read this provision too narrowly; in essence, their licenses are not jeopardized by appealing to large numbers of young people.)

- It encouraged (but did not require) licensees to "assess" the needs of children in their communities by reviewing (1) circumstances in that community, (2) other available programming on the station, (3) programming on other stations, and (4) other programs for children available in the market (presumably on cable).

- It declined to set minimum amounts of time for children's programming, although the Children's Television Act and the FCC rules call for "some." While public-service announcements will be seen in a positive light, "some" means programs of traditional length—a half-hour or hour—though they need not be regularly scheduled. (Again, broadcast attorneys recommend that regular scheduling, while not required, is perhaps the best way to fend off potential complaints later.)

- It required keeping of records, in a form chosen by the licensee, that must be made a part of the station's public file. These records, which may be updated quarterly or annually, have to include programs, nonprogram efforts in support of the Children's Television Act's goals, and amounts of advertising carried. In addition, a summary of activities during the license period must accompany renewal applications.

- It decided that while public broadcasters must meet the programming requirement, they are not held to the specific record-keeping regulations. Cable systems are not obligated to meet either the programming or record-keeping requirement, but they are bound by all advertising limits.

- Finally, it established a fine of $10,000 for each violation of any of the rules growing out of the Children's Television Act (47 CFR 73.660).

The Commission began to review compliance with this list of requirements in 1992 and found that 95 percent of monitored program hours met the commercial limits within weeks of their being put in place. But several television stations and cable systems *did* run afoul of these limits and became widely publicized examples of the FCC's intent to enforce the new rules rigidly (*Broadcasting*, 13 July 1992: 38).

As for the programs themselves, one consumer group reported in late 1992 that a sample of broadcasters were meeting the letter of the law's requirements (and those of the loose FCC reporting rules) simply by claiming positive aspects of existing cartoon or rerun comedy shows, or by placing what few new programs were being produced at very early morning hours when few would watch (*New York Times*, 30 September 1992: 1, B8). That study, and rising consumer group and congressional displeasure with broadcaster performance, led to 1993 hearings in Congress and inception of an FCC inquiry into whether its children's program requirements should be made more specific. Several station license renewals were held up by the Commission pending further evidence that their children's programming met the intent of the 1990 law. At the same time, the seeming revival of 1970s-style program concerns underlined how differently broadcasting and cable are regulated, as no such children's program requirements exist for cable.

14.9 Copyright

The Constitution recognizes the fundamental importance of encouraging national creativity. Article I, Section 8, the same passage that gives Congress the right to regulate interstate commerce, also calls on it to "promote the progress of science and the useful arts, by securing for limited times to authors and inventors the exclusive right to their respective writings and discoveries." This measure resulted in patent, and copyright, and trademark laws that enable investors and creative people to profit from their achievements while also ensuring reasonable public access to those achievements.

When broadcasting began, authors and composers had to rely on the Copyright Law of 1909, which dealt primarily with printed works and live performances. Congress amended the 1909 law from time to time to adapt it to the many new recording, duplication, distribution, and reproduction technologies that emerged throughout the years. But the old act never caught up with the times, and after two decades of study and debate, Congress finally passed a new copyright law in 1976, effective for works published in 1978 and later. The compromising necessary for its passage delayed the new law such that it was largely out of date concerning technology by the time it finally went into effect.

Basics

Key provisions of the 1976 Copyright Act, administered by the Copyright Office (part of the Library of Congress), include the following:

- *Purpose.* Copyright holders license others to use their works in exchange for payment of *royalties.* "Use" consists of making public by publishing, performing, displaying—or broadcasting.
- *Copyrightable works.* In addition to traditionally copyrightable works—books, musical compositions, motion pictures, and broadcast programs— such works as sculptures, choreographic notations, and computer programs can be copyrighted. Things *not* copyrightable include ideas, slogans, brand names, news events, and titles. (However, brand names, logos, and slogans can be protected under trademark regulations.)
- *Length of copyright.* In general, a copyright lasts for the life of the work's creator plus 50 years. After that, a work enters the *public domain* and can be used without securing permission or payment of royalties.
- *Compulsory licensing.* In some cases copyright owners *must* license their works on a fixed-royalty basis. The 1976 law mandated compulsory licensing of cable systems, for example. Owners of copyrighted material who license television stations to use their work must grant *retransmission consent* to cable systems that lawfully pick up such programs off the air and deliver them to subscribers. Cable systems, in turn, must pay a preset small proportion of their revenue for these rights.* (See Exhibit 14.h). The 1992 cable act gave broadcast stations the right either to demand carriage by any local cable system or to charge the cable system directly for having their signal carried (see Section 13.8).
- *Fair use.* Absolutely rigid enforcement of copyright restrictions would defeat the object of copyright law—the promotion of new creative activities. For example, it would prevent a student from photocopying a magazine article, or a scholar from quoting other writers, without securing permission. The new act retained the traditional copyright concept of fair use, which permits limited uses of copyrighted works without payment or permission for certain educational and critical or creative purposes (such as reviews of books and musical works).

Each of these provisions proved controversial, with electronic media often struggling among themselves as well as against copyright owners for favorable interpretations.

*Copyright owners of broadcast programs imported from distant markets by cable systems receive two payments: one directly from the initial carrier (the network or, in the case of syndicated programs, the station) and another—indirectly from the Copyright Royalty Tribunal—from the cable system as a retransmitter.

Exhibit 14.h • • • • • • • • • • • • • • • •

How Copyright Works

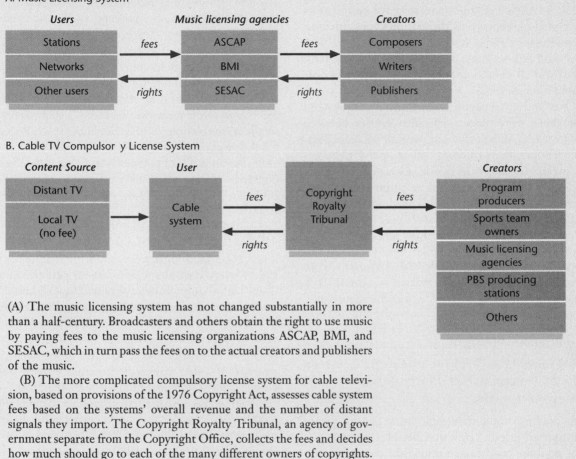

A. Music Licensing System

Users — **Music licensing agencies** — **Creators**

(A) The music licensing system has not changed substantially in more than a half-century. Broadcasters and others obtain the right to use music by paying fees to the music licensing organizations ASCAP, BMI, and SESAC, which in turn pass the fees on to the actual creators and publishers of the music.

(B) The more complicated compulsory license system for cable television, based on provisions of the 1976 Copyright Act, assesses cable system fees based on the systems' overall revenue and the number of distant signals they import. The Copyright Royalty Tribunal, an agency of government separate from the Copyright Office, collects the fees and decides how much should go to each of the many different owners of copyrights.

Music Licensing

Broadcast and cable programmers obtain rights to use recorded music by reaching agreements with the copyright licensing organizations ASCAP, BMI, and SESAC.* Most stations hold *blanket licenses* from these agencies, which allow unlimited use of any music in their catalogs in return for payment of an annual percentage of the station's gross income. Though some radio stations, especially those with news and talk formats, pay on a per-use basis, most radio and all television stations and networks hold blanket licenses.

Over the years, payment rates and billing systems have been the subjects of court battles between broadcasters and performing-rights societies. Stations cooperate in creating "all-industry" negotiating groups that annually negotiate rates with ASCAP and BMI. Stations negotiate individually with SESAC. Deadlocks often result, leading to court proceedings, but rates climb each year nevertheless. Early in 1985 the Supreme Court let stand an appeals court ruling that use of a blanket license did not violate antitrust laws, as television broadcasters had contended in a six-year legal battle (F, 1984: 217). Television networks had earlier lost the same battle.

Cable and Copyright

The Copyright Act of 1976 established a Copyright Royalty Tribunal (CRT). For cable television, the CRT has three tasks:

- to establish rates that cable must pay for use of imported distant television broadcast signals,
- to pool the resulting revenue (just over $200 million in 1990), and
- to divide pooled royalty money among copyright holders.

*ASCAP, the American Society of Composers, Authors and Publishers, was founded in 1914 by, among others, composer Victor Herbert. In 1939 some radio stations set up BMI, Broadcast Music Inc., as a means of balancing ASCAP's demands (see Section 2.2). American broadcasters still own BMI, which is the largest such agency. In Europe, in 1930, a German publisher formed SESAC, the Society of European Stage Artists and Composers, the smallest agency.

The process of apportioning payments has been snarled in legal proceedings from the day the CRT began work. Program syndicators (and owners of those programs) receive about 75 percent of each year's pool from the start whereas broadcasters receive only 3 to 5 percent, sports rights holders (usually the professional teams themselves) about 12 percent, PBS just over 5 percent, and music licensing agencies about 5 percent. Broadcasters and other aggrieved parties have regularly tied up the annual proceedings in court appeals.

This lack of revenue for broadcasters was central to their support of new regulation of cable calling for *retransmission consent*, whereby cable systems would have to come to each broadcaster whose signal they wanted to carry and negotiate permission—and possibly a direct payment—for that right. Such consent was a controversial centerpiece of the 1992 cable act (see Section 13.8).

CRT Controversy

The CRT added controversy when it fixed the copyright royalty rates that cable systems paid for using distant television station programs. Copyright holders and broadcasters complained about extremely low levels of payment—two-thirds of all cable systems (those earning less than $76,000 annually) pay only $59 in royalty a year. On the other hand, 98 percent of cable copyright revenue comes from about 2,000 large systems serving 90 percent of cable subscribers. All these payments average out to about 36 cents per subscriber per month, totaling more than $200 million in 1990. The total has risen threefold since the mid-1980s as more systems develop and older systems grow larger—and thus pay more (Picard, 1991: 8–9). The CRT can raise rates because of inflation only every five years.

Throughout its short history, the CRT has lacked sufficient staff and expertise to carry out its contentious assignments. In 1982 the agency's chairperson called the whole process unworkable and unfair, and urged Congress to reconsider the treatment of cable in the Copyright Act of 1976. A successor repeated the same charge in 1985. Bills introduced in Congress into the 1990s called—thus far unsuccessfully—for changes in or replacement of the CRT as well as for changes in cable's compulsory license system. The 1992 Cable Act, discussed in Section 13.8, added pressure for CRT change.

Cable Piracy

The 1976 Copyright Act allows limited use of copyrighted materials without payment under the *fair-use* principle. But not everyone agrees as to what constitutes fair use. Fair-use controversies have involved not only reception of cable television or satellite programs without payment of required fees but also unauthorized recording of broadcast and other media.

Until the mid-1980s *signal piracy* chiefly involved illicit hookups to cable television feeder lines, enabling cable reception without payment of monthly subscriber fees. As pay cable developed, illegal "black boxes" (decoders) made possible the reception of even scrambled signals. The cable industry estimated in 1992 that an equivalent of a quarter of cable revenue was lost to pirate reception. Indeed, the early 1990s saw a great increase in the theft of premium channels. The cable industry found at least a partial solution to the problem of direct theft of pay-cable services by switching from easily circumvented "traps" for pay channels to much more secure addressable converter systems. Still, creative minds can—and do—break just about any scrambling system. Digital compression technology held the promise of reducing piracy due to the complexity of its signals.

Pirated cable reception violates Sec. 705 of the Communications Act, which defines penalties for unauthorized "publication" of communications intended for reception only by subscribers paying to use special unscrambling devices. Several cable systems prosecuted violators under the provisions of Sec. 705 and publicized the resulting felony convictions, which entailed jail terms and fines of up to $25,000 for the first violation and $50,000 for subsequent violations. More than half the states have passed antipiracy laws prohibiting the manufacture, sale, or use of unauthorized decoders or antennas.

TVRO Piracy

Piracy increased when the prices of television receive-only (TVRO) Earth stations began to fall in the 1980s, making them affordable by ordinary households. Both pay- and basic-cable operators began to scramble satellite signals to protect their investments from pirates. In hearings before Congress, the cable industry and pay-system operators complained of the fast-growing home receiver antenna industry (up to three million TVROs by 1993) and the freeloading users.

As a result, Congress modified Sec. 705 to allow individuals to pick up any *nonscrambled* satellite programming if they have obtained authorization, usually for a fee. The authorization applies only to satellite programming intended for personal use, not for resale. By the early 1990s nearly all satellite channels were scrambled. Since the cable industry had long refrained from marketing its services to such scattered audiences, a number of third-party brokers had already begun by the late 1980s to assemble packages of cable services for sale to TVRO users.

VCR Piracy

A second major fair-use issue concerns home video recording off the air, off cable, or from rented cassettes. In 1976 a number of program producers brought suit against Sony, the pioneering manufacturer of home video recorders, for "indirect" copyright infringement.* A district court found in favor of Sony, concluding that home recordings of broadcast programs not sold for a profit fell within the fair-use provision of the new copyright law. The Supreme Court affirmed the decision by a 5 to 4 vote (US, 1984a: 417). The high court cited audience research showing that people record broadcast signals primarily for time-shifting purposes, which it regarded as a "fair use."

The decision, however, left unresolved the legality of recording cable or pay programming, for the

---

*"Indirect" because Sony provided the *means* of infringement—the machines that made possible such recording.

Sony case covered only recording of over-the-air or "free" broadcast material. The legality of showing a taped copy of a copyrighted film or program to a group outside the home remained in question, a problem intensified by increasing numbers of video rentals. Hollywood producers pressured Congress to modify the Copyright Act once more, this time to extract from those who did home recording such indirect royalty payments as a surcharge on recorders or blank tapes at the time of purchase, or on rental fees paid by customers to video rental stores. Congress had not acted by early 1993.

The *Sony* decision, the unexpected proliferation of TVROs, and the growth of the video rental business all illustrate the difficulty of keeping copyright laws abreast of technology and its newer applications.

Digital Audio Piracy

Late in 1992 Congress enacted into law an industry compromise on digital audio home recording devices. The music and consumer electronics industries had taken years to agree on a royalty to be paid record companies, music artists, and publishers for home recordings made on the coming generation of digital recorders (see Section 5.10). Digital audio tape (DAT) and Digital compact cassette (DCC) as well as future hardware systems, would include a 2 percent royalty fee (from $1 to $8 per machine), whereas blank tapes and discs would include a 3 percent fee on their wholesale price. The funds raised would go to the Copyright Office and be disseminated to copyright holders.* The new law also supported the industry's Serial Copy Management System (SCMS) technical standard, which prevents a second-generation digital dub from being made on any of these machines (in other words, an owner can make a copy, but not a copy of a copy) (*Television Digest*, 28 September 1992: 10).

---

*In the early 1990s, about 38 percent went to record companies, 26 percent to artists, 17 percent to songwriters, 17 percent to music publishers, and the rest to other rights holders. No royalties were due for analog recordings.

14.10 *Changing Perspectives*

The writers of the Constitution saw the marketplace of ideas in 18th-century terms, as a forum in which small traders in the spoken and printed word competed pretty much equally. They expected a leisurely self-righting process to occur as citizens heard, read, and digested diverse viewpoints. But technology and deregulation have changed that, challenging old assumptions about how the First Amendment applies to modern media.

In the late 20th century, numerous media compete for attention and consumer dollars, but more can too often become less in a marketplace dominated by giant corporations. These well-financed communicators blanket the nation, limiting the diversity of competing voices and narrowing windows of opportunity within which the self-righting process occurs.

Two totally different approaches to this problem are actively being debated in this final decade of the century. Here stands the *deregulator*, confident that the marketplace will regulate itself, given maximum competition and unconstrained consumer choice. There stands the *regulator*, demanding that government intervene once more to oppose monopolistic media tendencies and protect the public interest from effects of unrestrained competition. The first argues for media to compete on an "even playing field," whereby all are equally protected from government interference—a matter of First Amendment "parity." The other wants a more flexible interpretation of the First Amendment, to take into account the fact that different media have different impact, reach, and accessibility. One side sees the communication marketplace largely in economic terms; the other regards "marketplace" as a metaphor, seeing communication more in cultural terms.

In this and earlier chapters, many practical examples of this fundamental clash of views have been discussed:

- Should indecency in electronic media have the same First Amendment protections it has on newsstands and in movie theaters? If so, how best can children be protected from such content?

- Does violence in electronic media have such potentially damaging social effects as to justify tilting the regulatory playing field against it? Other than tepid network statements about curbing violent content, should more be done—and if so, by whom?
- Should electronic media have special responsibilities with regard to airing controversial issues of social importance? If so, why—and to what degree—should they be treated differently than print media that bear no such responsibilities?
- Does the impact of these media on children warrant special regulation? If so, again, how much control and by whom?

The very capacity of broadcasting to survive in the traditional sense comes under question—as is discussed in our final chapter. At one time, broadcasting enjoyed special status because it played a central informational role and made its services available equally to all at minimum cost. It was protected from cable competition, the latter more costly and less universal than broadcasting. But that special status temporarily evaporated with the 1984 cable law and subsequent court decisions. For example, in striking down the FCC's must-carry rule (see Section 13.9), an appeals court clearly found broadcasting's role less important than cable's freedom of speech. The 1992 cable law at least partially reinstated a special role for broadcasting when must-carry was restored (see Section 13.8) and retransmission consent applied. Congress very specifically cited the importance of local broadcasting as the reason for these requirements.

In sum, as the 20th century winds down, the continued conservatism of the FCC and growing conservatism of the courts suggest intensifying media competition. How well the public will be served by this overflow of technological options remains to be seen. Certainly traditional broadcasting's long-time primacy in American lives continues, though with a lesser public responsibility role than it once played.

• • • • • • • •

Summary

14.1 Freedoms of speech and press have as their goal a robust and wide-open marketplace of ideas. The First Amendment protects even inflammatory, hateful, and false ideas from government censorship, but it does not prevent private interference unless such interference is carried out on behalf of government.

14.2 Broadcasting has not had First Amendment parity with other media because of a scarcity of channels, the fact that the FCC must consider programming in its licensing decisions, and the medium's intrusive role in the home and access to children.

14.3 Unprotected forms of speech, such as libel, invasion of privacy, and obscenity, are punishable after the fact; but punishment must not be so easily imposed as to have a chilling effect on freedom of speech and press in general. Former restrictions on cameras in courtrooms have given way in state courts, but electronic media are currently only experimentally allowed in a few federal courts.

14.4 Attempts to define a late-evening portion of the broadcast day for possibly indecent material created a huge political and legal battle in the late 1980s and early 1990s. Court, congressional, and FCC decisions cleared the way for a limited window (midnight to 6 A.M.) into which such programs can be channeled. And Congress in its 1984 and 1992 cable acts included strong limits on cable programming of indecent or obscene material.

14.5 FCC regulation of electronic media ownership is the major means of structural control—limiting the number of broadcast stations under any one owner, restricting crossownership, and limiting network control of programming—designed to increase diversity of points of view through diversifying ownership. Even with substantial deregulation of ownership rules in 1992, remaining regulations try to encourage a variety of viewpoints. Cable television is subject to few ownership rules, though

1992 legislation called for close FCC study of the question. Limited telephone company participation in program delivery has been approved; still hotly debated is the telephone companies' role in program (and electronic media outlet) control.

14.6   Sec. 315 of the Communications Act requires that opposing candidates for public office be given equal opportunities for use of broadcast and cable facilities. Bona fide news and public-affairs programs are exempt. Sec. 312(a)(7) mandates access for candidates for federal office. Varying definitions of complicated "lowest unit charge" pricing and other FCC rules result in varying political broadcast regulation every few years.

14.7   Localism—the right to hear and express ideas of interest to a community—has become largely obsolete because of economic centralization of programming and ownership. The fairness doctrine had its roots in localism and was formalized in a 1949 FCC decision allowing station editorializing, enhanced by legislation in 1959, and upheld by the *Red Lion* decision of 1969. In 1987, after intensive study, the FCC abolished the doctrine, and Congress failed to reinstate it. Related personal attack and political editorializing rules remain in force. Only one commercial product—tobacco—has ever been subject to provisions of the fairness doctrine. Few stations or systems accept paid editorial advertising ("advertorials").

14.8   The Children's Television Act of 1990 limited advertising in programs for children 12 and under, and FCC rules now require "some" educational and informational programming for children up to age 16. Initial studies suggested little compliance with the spirit of the law, though lax FCC rules on programming proved easy to meet.

14.9   The 1976 Copyright Act ensures creative artists payment for use of copyrighted works. When cable systems carry broadcast programs for which copyright fees have already been paid, copyright holders must grant compulsory licenses for which they receive reimbursement from fees paid by cable operators to the Copyright Royalty Tribunal. Several kinds of copyright piracy have developed with the emergence of newer technologies, all of which put pressure on the copyright regime under the 1976 act. Potential piracy of copyrighted works by means of cable, TVROs, home video recording, and newer digital audio recording have led to a variety of remedies to protect copyright owners.

14.10   Conflicts between the deregulator and the regulator help define changing regulatory perceptions of electronic media. The two schools of thought have sharply differing views on the proper role of government amidst rapid technical advancement.

PART 7

World of Electronic Media

Having discussed American electronic media, we turn finally to the operation and role of broadcasting and newer services in other countries, and to the likely future of electronic media here and abroad. *Our themes are (1) how foreign electronic media systems differ from American practice, and (2) how the world of electronic media is changing even more rapidly than before.*

Driven in part by political changes and economic pressures, several countries have begun to adopt many American electronic media characteristics: private ownership, more entertainment programming, greater dependence on advertising support, and deregulation. Yet as discussed in Chapter 15, considerable and lasting differences remain between American and foreign electronic media systems. Further, although considerable international cooperation does occur, national interests often get in the way of efficient worldwide communication.

Our evolutionary view of the future of electronic media, presented in Chapter 16, is determined largely by trends in technology and economics. While media change slowly from year to year, by the end of this decade we will enjoy a world of electronic media considerably different from what we know today.

Chapter 15

Global View

Americans remain largely unaware that most other countries operate their electronic media systems quite differently from the way we do. Further, because radio waves ignore national boundaries (especially when sent from satellites that cover most of the globe), electronic media are truly international. Countless organizations here and abroad participate in the global exchange of equipment, programs, and training.

Truly understanding broadcasting in America requires at least brief attention to broadcasting and newer media elsewhere. An examination of foreign electronic media, which developed as unique combinations of national character, geography, language, economics, and legal systems, provides added insight to our study of systems here at home.

Each country starts with the same potential for electronic media, yet adopts a system uniquely adapted to serve its own conditions and needs. Three attributes of these media—already discussed in the American context—promote a mirror-like relationship between a nation's character and its electronic media:

- Broadcasting invites *government regulation* be-

cause it uses the electromagnetic spectrum, which all governments view as public property. Each government interprets its responsibility to control spectrum use in accordance with its own history, geography, economics, culture, and—most important—political philosophy.

- Radio-frequency transmissions can cause *interference*, creating a need for international and national regulation of transmission. Again, political philosophy affects how, and how much, a country chooses to regulate.

- Electronic media have *political and cultural impact* because they can cover one or more nations instantly. They can bypass government entities, going directly to people at home and abroad. Whatever its politics, no nation can afford to leave such persuasive media totally unregulated.

15.1 Controlling Philosophies

Controls that any nation imposes on electronic media reflect the attitude its government takes toward its own people. Approaches generally fall into

541

three broad categories: permissive, paternalistic, and authoritarian.

Permissivism

Electronic media in America provide the classic example of a predominantly permissive or *laissez-faire* system. The U.S. Constitution makes freedom of communication a central article of faith and encourages free enterprise. Resulting all-out commercialism creates more lively, popular, and expertly produced programs than are usually found elsewhere.

Generally speaking, countries now or once within the traditional U.S. sphere of influence, such as the Philippines or many nations in Latin America, have adopted similar permissive, profit-driven systems. Many other countries deplore American commercialism because it focuses almost exclusively on what people *want* rather than on what critics, experts, and government leaders think they *need*.

Paternalism

Lacking America's avowed melting-pot character, most other countries perceive electronic media as playing a positive social role: preservation and enhancement of national culture. They take a paternalistic approach, putting special emphasis on preserving national language, religious, and social norms by ensuring a "balanced" program diet— meaning not too much light entertainment at the expense of information and culture. And many nations take special care with children's programs, ensuring positive and culturally relevant examples.

The British Broadcasting Corporation (BBC) offers the classic example of paternalism. Growing out of a brief period of commercial operation, the BBC converted to a public-service role in 1926, seeking to avoid America's "mistake" of radio commercialization. BBC funds today come primarily from government-imposed license fees on television receivers, relieving the service of advertising dependence.

A well-articulated ideal of *public-service broadcasting* emerged from the BBC experience. Adopted by

many other countries, public-service broadcasting includes such principles as

- balanced programming, representing all the main genres;
- control by a public body, independent of both political and commercial pressures;
- relative financial autonomy, usually secured by partial or complete dependence on receiver license fees;
- program services that can be received by, and that hold interest for everyone including rural dwellers and minorities;
- strict impartiality in political broadcasts; and
- respect for the artistic integrity of program makers.

This public-service broadcasting philosophy, adapted to varying national circumstances, spread worldwide. Thousands of broadcasters from scores of countries have visited the famous Broadcasting House in London, discussed in Exhibit 15.a. Many take BBC training courses in all aspects of production, engineering, and management. Other national services modeled to some extent on BBC traditions include Australia's ABC, Canada's CBC, and Japan's NHK.

While the BBC is a widely influential broadcasting service, other countries have tried but failed to replicate it. This is so because the BBC developed out of special characteristics intrinsic to Great Britain, evidence that electronic media systems uniquely adapt to their own national settings.

Authoritarianism

Traditionally, communist and many Third World countries take an authoritarian approach to electronic media. The state itself finances and operates the systems, along with other telecommunication services. Indeed, governments own and operate most of the world's broadcasting systems, although the number of privately owned services began to increase during the 1980s.

Because communist ideology stresses the importance of media in mass political education, the former Soviet Union embraced broadcasting early,

Exhibit 15.a ••••• •••••••••••

Broadcasting House, London

In pretelevision days, broadcasters from all over the world journeyed to this famous art deco building in the heart of London as a kind of broadcaster's mecca. The BBC moved here from its original quarters on the bank of the Thames in 1932. Though Broadcasting House tripled the corporation's previous space, the new building proved too small for BBC activities even before its completion. The giant BBC television center is located in a London suburb—and BBC radio and television own or lease many other buildings around the city. Brits often refer to their world-respected broadcast service simply as "the Beeb."

Source: Photo from BBC.

embarking on a vigorous "radiofication" program. The Russian masses, however, failed to invest in home receivers as eagerly as did Western audiences, because of low incomes and government programming that offered little incentive to buy.

The authoritarian approach generally ignores popular taste. Programs have a propaganda, or perhaps an educational, goal. Broadcasting officials pay little attention to marketing techniques that permissive and even paternalistic broadcasters employ to ensure attractive and cost-effective programs. Indeed, authoritarians look on broadcasting as a one-way medium—all give and no take. Either they do not understand or they actively suppress its potentially democratic nature as a medium that depends on free-will cooperation from audiences.

Third World Authoritarianism

Lack of purchasing power limits ownership of even simple radio sets in many Third World countries. And absence of rural electrical power as well as of relay facilities for networking further restricts

growth—especially for line-of-sight television service. Neither receiver license fees nor advertising (alone or in combination) can bring in enough revenue to support broadcasting adequately. Therefore, most Third World governments own and operate their broadcasting systems. In any event, dictators heading often shaky regimes such as some of those in Africa, Latin America, or the Far East dare not allow broadcasters the free rein to interact with illiterate masses. Prudence—even more than ideology—dictates tight authoritarian control.

•••••••

15.2 Pluralistic Trend

In the 1990s none of these three regulatory philosophies— permissive, paternalistic, or authoritarian— exists anywhere in its pure form. Compromise leads to combinations of features to create a fourth approach: pluralism.

Role of Competition

Seventy-five years' experience has proved that pluralistic electronic media systems work best in most national circumstances. Pluralism means more than simply competition among rival services; given that similar motives drive all services, media would tend only to imitate one another in the absence of pluralistic competition.

Pluralism means putting a variety of motives to work, each with approximately equal status—usually a mix of commercial and public-service motives. Healthy competition between differently motivated broadcasting organizations stimulates creativity, encourages innovation, and ensures variety. The result is usually a wider range of genuine program choices than any single-motive system could produce.

British Pluralism

The British eventually developed a widely admired pluralistic system based on control by two non-commercial public authorities: the BBC and the Independent Broadcasting Authority (IBA), which was set up in the 1950s. Though this "comfortable duopoly"—a benign, paternalism of two—ended in 1990, it is worth review for its historic achievements as a model for others.

The IBA, a nonprofit, government-chartered corporation, selected and supervised regional commercial television companies known collectively as Independent Television (ITV), as well as specialized national television networks and, eventually, local radio stations.

Like the BBC, IBA owned and operated its own transmitters, so commercial motives could not distort geographical coverage by placing outlets only in major cities. Unlike the BBC, however, IBA had no programming function. Instead, privately owned commercial companies provided programming and sold advertising time.

True pluralism requires national network competition on a more or less equal footing. IBA therefore allowed its regional program companies to join forces most of the time in the ITV cooperative network. A commonly owned nonprofit subsidiary, Independent Television News (ITN), supplied news programs. The five most lucrative companies furnished most network entertainment programs. American viewers know some ITV companies from seeing such imported series as *The Benny Hill Show* (Thames Television) and *The Jewel in the Crown* (Granada Television).

A fourth British network (after BBC's two and ITV), appropriately called Channel Four, began in 1982. IBA again supplied the transmitter facilities. Channel Four acts as an "electronic publisher," buying all of its programs from others. One of Channel Four's innovations was to introduce American professional football to audiences devoted to soccer. IBA required ITV companies to subsidize Channel Four, but the companies recovered some of that subsidy through commercials they were allowed to schedule on Channel Four.

Although British viewers until recently had only four television signals from which to choose, all four could be received throughout the country. Further, each usually offered distinctly different programs, thus ensuring genuine choice. British viewers lacked local outlets, although BBC and ITV companies supplied regional programs, especially news.

By the 1960s BBC and IBA were earning similar audience ratings, although the BBC offered more programs appealing to cultural and intellectual minorities. The BBC-1 mass-appeal network competed against ITV entertainment while BBC-2 aimed at smaller, more specialized audiences, as did (in the 1980s) the semicommercial Channel Four.

BBC's national and regional radio services had little competition. Its networks feature pop music (Radio 1), middle-of-the-road programs (Radio 2), serious music and talk (Radio 3), and news/current affairs (Radio 4). In 1991 it added Radio 5 to bring instructional/educational programs to schools as well as to provide such programming as African music to underserved audiences. Today, some 40 BBC local radio stations compete with an increasing number of local commercial radio stations.

A 1990 law ended the "comfortable" British broadcasting duopoly, as described in the next section.

15.3 Deregulation

During the 1980s U.S.-inspired deregulatory practices swept the telecommunications world. Although it was not American influence alone that caused this deregulatory trend, foreign experts studied the American experience intensively, while U.S. government and media officials promoted deregulation and private ownership abroad. Deregulation appealed overseas as it did in the United States for another reason—no control mechanism could adequately keep up with the options provided (or problems created) by fast-changing technology.

Impact on Public-Service Broadcasting

With deregulation, traditional public-service broadcasting organizations faced unaccustomed competition. Cable television, satellite-distributed programs for both cable and direct-to-home viewing, videocassettes, and new commercial broadcasting channels fought for audiences, advertisers, and programs. Critics argued that excessive competition might force public-service broadcasters to lower program standards as they struggled to maintain viable audience shares.

American deregulators found enthusiastic support from Britain's Conservative government under Prime Minister Thatcher (1980–1991) because it disliked the BBC's elitist political neutrality. A government-appointed committee suggested that BBC television should be converted to a subscription service: only those willing to pay would receive BBC programs (Great Britain, 1986).

Though Parliament did not go that far, a 1990 broadcasting law reflected the report's deregulatory approach. Major features included the following:

- The BBC would continue as the "cornerstone of public-service broadcasting," still deriving revenue from receiver license fees, at least for the time being. Because its Royal Charter comes up for renewal in 1996, however, further detailed analysis of all BBC operations has already begun.
- ITV's network became Channel 3 at the beginning of 1993, with the BBC's two networks renamed Channels 1 and 2. Channel Four retained its character as an "electronic publisher" but could now sell its own commercial time. The ITV/Channel 3 companies remained responsible for Channel Four's financial health.
- A new commercial Channel 5, able to reach about 70 percent of the population, was established. It will air by 1994 with a 10-year franchise and program requirements similar to Channel 3.
- The IBA and a separate Cable Authority merged into a new "light touch" regulatory authority called the Independent Television Commission (ITC). A separate Broadcasting Standards Council was created to develop a program code controlling program sex and violence.
- The new ITC auctioned regional franchises for ITV/Channel 3 and the new Channel 5 to the highest bidders, subject to the bidders' ability to meet program-quality requirements. The auctions took place in 1991–1992. The ITC also franchises local MDS and SMATV operations.
- A new Radio Authority would auction 200 to 300 new local commercial radio station franchises in the 1990s.

The 1990 law reflected changes taking place with varying speed and completeness worldwide—increases in competition, local services, private ownership, advertising support, and newer media services, including DBS and cable (discussed in Sections 15.9 and 15.10, respectively).

Privatization

The process of converting state-owned facilities to private ownership and creating new privately operated facilities is known as *privatization*. This form of deregulation in the media world rapidly took hold in France and Italy. Other European countries, as well as Australia, Canada, Japan, and New Zealand, have taken similar, though usually less drastic, deregulatory steps.

The government once operated all of France's broadcasting stations and networks. In 1984, a French socialist government began licensing private stations and networks. Two years later, conservatives won control and took the unprecedented step of selling off France's leading public-service television broadcasting network, TF1, and of authorizing competition from new privately owned television networks.

Privatization came earlier in Italy and by a different route. In the 1970s the official Italian broadcasting monopoly, RAI (Radio Televisione Italia) went to court to suppress unauthorized cable operations. The Italian Constitutional Court ruled in 1975 that RAI's legal monopoly covered only *national network* broadcasting. RAI could prevent neither local cable nor local broadcast operations by private owners. This decision opened the floodgates to thousands of private stations. In the early 1990s these stations were still operating without benefit of formal regulation because the Italian Parliament, though always seemingly about to pass a new law, could not agree on the form it should take.

Former Communist States

In the former Soviet Union and (to an even greater degree) in its then East European client-states, democratization brought parallel liberalizing moves in different political settings. In 1985 the new Soviet leader, Mikhail Gorbachev, announced a radical policy change, called *glasnost*—roughly translated as "candor" or "openness." In addition, electronic media spillover signals from neighboring countries, insistent penetration by official external services such as the Voice of America (described in Section 15.8), satellite-borne programs from Western Europe, and videocassettes all played a major role in pushing communist societies toward change. Radio and television played an active part in the actual revolutions of 1989–1991 (see Section 12.3).

Mismanagement by Soviet media of news about the Chernobyl atomic power plant disaster hastened drastic reforms.* Soviet broadcasters, along with other journalists, began profound changes. They started covering hitherto banned subjects—other domestic disasters, the Soviet—Afghan War, runaway environmental pollution, and even public criticism of government officials.

In the late 1980s American-Soviet broadcast "bridges" frequently enabled citizens in both countries to exchange uncensored views by satellite. Soviet broadcasters scheduled more live shows, spontaneous interviews (in place of the obviously rehearsed recitals formerly used), and telephone call-in programs. They extended schedules into early-morning and late-night dayparts. For the first time, broadcasting—the most democratic of media—began to fulfill its mission of pleasing and informing the Soviet public instead of lecturing to it.

Even more dramatic changes took place in USSR-supported regimes as in 1989 they toppled domino-like in the wake of Gorbachev's reforms. The 1989 revolt against Romania's dictator provides an extreme example. Nicolae Ceausescu had exploited the Romanian state television apparatus for years as a means of personal glorification. During the short but bloody revolution, rebels turned television cameras around, documenting his crimes and eventual execution. A U.S. State Department committee that studied communication conditions in Eastern Europe in the spring of 1990 described broadcasting's role:

> Romanian TV was in many respects the central nervous system during the bloody December [1989] revolution. . . . In the months following the revolution, television consolidated its role by broadcasting the trials of those accused of genocide, and also offering hours every day of public access commentary and political campaigning to all political parties. (USDOS, 1990: 39)

Nothing in broadcast history matches the startling suddenness with which 40-year-old rigid communist control, like the Berlin Wall, crumbled almost overnight in country after country—culminating with the collapse of the Soviet Union itself in late 1991 (see Exhibit 12.f, p. 437).

International Telecommunication Union

As with changes in individual countries, many international controls underwent revision during the 1980s. Most nations belong to the International

---

*The atomic power plant explosion in 1986 devastated not only the surrounding countryside but also the credibility of Soviet media, which simply failed to cover the disaster, one of the biggest international news stories of the decade. The Soviet government finally released a statement after Sweden demanded an explanation of why nuclear contamination, drifting over its territory from the USSR, had reached a dangerous level.

Telecommunication Union (ITU), an affiliate of the United Nations, headquartered in Geneva, Switzerland.* As sovereign nations, its members cannot be forced to obey ITU regulations—though they usually find it in their best interests to meet ITU requirements and to adopt ITU standardized terms and procedures.

Acting together, ITU member-states allocate frequency bands to specific services to avoid interference. Throughout the world, AM and FM radio, television, and broadcast satellite services have similar spectrum allocations. The ITU also issues initial letters for station-identification call signs—hence the *K* or *W* used by American stations, while Canadian station calls begin with *C* and Mexican outlets with *X*.

In the 1980s the ITU expanded its aid to help developing nations improve their telecommunication facilities. At the same time, with many newly independent Third World members, ITU conferences became more politicized. Third World countries argue that ITU spectrum and orbital allocations should be planned for the long term. In other words, they want channels and slots reserved for their future use, even though decades might pass before most developing nations could activate them. The United States and most other heavy users of satellite communications, however, need immediate access to these resources in order to meet current needs and to foster technological development. Clashes of will on this controversial issue occur at each ITU meeting.

In the early 1990s the ITU underwent its most dramatic reorganization in a half-century—evidence that its dozens of Third World members were having an impact on ITU decisions and processes alike. In a substantial restructuring of its responsibilities, the ITU elevated assistance to Third World countries to an equal status with technical standard setting and frequency allocations.

Competing Technical Standards

Thanks to uniform spectrum allocations by the ITU, a traveler taking a portable radio receiver

*The ITU, formed in 1865 as a European telegraph union, expanded to include radio services of all kinds in the 1930s. The United States became a member at the same time.

abroad can pick up stations almost anywhere. But although the ITU and other world bodies encourage the international cooperation that makes such radio portability possible, national chauvinism often gets in the way.

While television has similar channel allocations throughout the world, its technical standards are *not* uniform. No fewer than 14 monochrome and 3 principal color technical standards require converters in order to interchange programs or to use one country's television equipment elsewhere.

The three basic color television systems—NTSC, PAL, and SECAM—reflect American, German, and French government decisions made in the 1960s. Each country lobbied frantically to persuade other governments to adopt its standard. Adoptions meant not only national prestige but also tremendous profits from international sales by manufacturers of equipment using the favored system. PAL is most widely used; the American NTSC system is nearly universal in North and South America and Japan, whereas France, the former USSR, and their close allies or former colonies adopted SECAM.

A clean start on world television standards could develop out of forthcoming ITU decisions on direct-broadcast satellite (DBS) and high-definition television (HDTV) system technologies. Universal, ITU-approved DBS and HDTV–signal processing standards could result. Certainly satellite-to-cable and DBS services designed to cover many countries simultaneously cry out for such standardization.

But national interests may win out again. By 1990 Europe, Japan, and the United States each had different and incompatible analog HDTV standards on the drawing boards. The American breakthrough on digital HDTV (see Section 5.9) led early in 1993 to the end of Europe's attempt to develop its own analog standard, although Japan continued promoting and using its MUSE analog system.

PTT Deregulation

Deregulation has also had a widespread effect on common-carrier services, loosening the grip of highly centralized national post, telephone, and telegraph (PTT) monopolies. In addition to their telephone operations, PTTs have long held exclusive rights to install and operate broadcast transmitters and relays, as well as cable facilities. However, in many countries, transmission and programming supervision came under separate government authorities.

For cable, marketing and promotion play key roles: consumers need a persuasive explanation of how this strange and, in many countries, new service will benefit them. Lack of experience in facing competition, however, generally deprives such monopolies of marketing expertise. Progress in cable installations has often languished under PTT leadership. Rising public demand for cable and other services has helped to break down PTT controls in country after country since the mid-1980s.

••••••••

15.4 Access

That all electronic media can inform, persuade, and cultivate values makes access to them a jealously guarded prerogative. Traditionally, most countries limited access to professional broadcasters, experts on subjects of public interest, people currently in the news, and politicians.

Politicians

Democratic political ideology requires preserving fairness in political uses of electronic media— without at the same time crippling their role as a means of informing voters.

In keeping with American broadcasting's permissive orientation, the weakest parties and candidates have the same access rights as the strongest—provided they can afford to buy advertising time. No other industrialized democracy permits such broad access for candidates and such commercialization of elections. In most European countries, for example, despite strict fairness regulations on paper, ruling political parties often evade rules by controlling appointments to state broadcasting services and regulatory agencies.

Britain, however, severely limits political broadcasts, while providing them free of charge. Campaign broadcasts focus on parties rather than on individual candidates (in keeping with the parliamentary system in which party membership is more important than in American elections).* Given that British national campaigns last only 30 days, voters are spared endless merchandising of candidates. Nor do candidates have to beg for donations and accept money from lobbyists to pay for expensive broadcast advertising.

Britain is also one of the few countries that allow live televising of Parliament debates, similar to C-SPAN's coverage of Congress here. That sort of political access helps bring voters closer to the process of governing.

Citizens

During the 1960s people in many countries began to ask why ordinary citizens had no airways access. They argued that if spectrum really does function like a national park or other shared natural resource, then everybody should get a chance to use it. This access movement paralleled a widespread rise in ethnic and regional awareness. Today's electronic media are still adapting to access demands that began three decades ago.

The access movement had less initial impact in Europe than in America because broadcasting there was for many years more centralized, affording little chance for local access. Those seeking access could hardly expect national or regional networks to open their studios if they had nothing of national or regional significance to say. Access seekers therefore petitioned authorities to create small local and (even smaller) community stations, exempt from many regulations that govern larger stations and network services.

Most democracies responded in the 1970s and 1980s by authorizing such stations. France, for ex-

*In recent years, only British parties offering 50 or more parliamentary candidates received television time at all. Each party had from one to five free broadcasts of five to ten minutes' duration, the number depending on each party's strength in the previous election.

ample, legitimized more than a thousand small, privately owned FM radio stations following passage of a new broadcasting law in 1982. Many had started as pirate stations, which the French government had suppressed rigorously. The 1990 British broadcasting law regulated only slightly some 300 new local radio stations as well as new commercial networks first permitted under the new law. In Scandinavia, governments finance low-power FM *när radio* (neighborhood stations), inviting local groups to cooperate in programming them, free of virtually all regulation.

Groups

Another way of dealing with access demands is to shift emphasis from individuals to the groups to which individuals belong. The now-defunct FCC fairness doctrine applied such a strategy (as detailed in Section 14.7).

The uniquely structured access system of the Netherlands has gone farthest in assuring groups their own programs on nationally owned broadcasting facilities. The government turns over most program time on government-run networks to citizen broadcasting associations. Some represent religious faiths; some have a nonsectarian outlook. Even very small constituencies, such as immigrant workers or people from Dutch colonies, can regularly obtain airtime.*

An umbrella organization, NOS (Netherlands Broadcasting Foundation) coordinates Dutch time-sharing and produces programs of broad interest, such as national and international news and major sporting events. Another central organization handles sales of advertising time, revenue from which goes to a central program fund. For years, program associations had not been allowed to insert advertisements in their programs (though some did so surreptitiously).

Access can also work in a negative fashion. The white-controlled government of South Africa attempted for a time to limit black access to outside sources of news. Radio news directed at tribal groups in their own languages was channeled on FM radio. As FM and short-wave tuning were not ordinarily available in the same receiver, the use of FM for controlled domestic news limited black listeners' access to external news sources.

• • • • • • • •

15.5   Economics

Economics comes in second only to politics in determining the shape of a country's electronic media system. National systems vary widely in audience size, facilities, revenue sources, and the ability to produce homegrown programs. Economic constraints account for these differences, though political and cultural factors also play an important role.

Audience Size

Some 200 countries and dependencies have their own radio broadcasting systems. By 1992 Switzerland led in television set penetration with 78 per 100 people, followed by the United States and Britain with 73 and 72, respectively. Fewer than 40 countries (mostly small islands) lacked any television stations by the early 1990s.* High penetration levels depend only partly on economics—important as well are programs popular enough to motivate set purchase, and a policy of licensing local stations.

The governments of former communist countries invested heavily in transmitters, relays, and production facilities. Nevertheless, set penetration remained disproportionately low. The former Soviet Union, for example, had 37 sets per 100 people in 1992. And the People's Republic of China did not begin television broadcasts until 1958. A quarter-century later it still had pitifully few receivers for a

---

*Often referred to as "pillarization" for the many pillars of society, this system developed after World War II as one means of ensuring that all citizens would have access to and a voice in the Netherlands' newly reconstituted democracy.

*International set-penetration comparisons use sets-per-hundred or -thousand population figures rather than household-based statistics. The data here come from the BBC (1992).

nation of more than a billion population—only 13 sets per 100 people.

In tropical Third World countries, many radio sets do not work because of humidity and a shortage of batteries. Government investment in transmitters and production facilities can therefore prove extremely uneconomic. It costs just as much in program and transmission expenses to reach a few scattered individuals as to reach everyone within a transmitter's coverage range. Lack of communications infrastructure—electric power, telephones, and relay facilities for networks—further impedes Third World electronic media development. However, a few of the oil-rich Middle East states have achieved high radio set penetrations—for example, 70 per 100 people in Kuwait and 55 per 100 in Bahrain.

Revenue Sources

Electronic media support comes from three main sources: government appropriations, receiver license fees, and advertising. Most countries still depend on government funds, in whole or in part.

In industrialized democracies, however, substantial support depends on receiver license fees. This source insulates broadcasting organizations from inevitable biases caused by dependence on either direct government funding or advertising. But the protection is only partial. Governments write the laws requiring fee payments and setting fee levels. And most fee-supported systems gain part of their revenue from advertising, though theoretically advertising contributes too small a part to give advertisers any real influence over programs.

Because of currency exchange fluctuations, it is difficult to assign exact U.S. dollar values to color television set licenses in Europe. In 1993, however, such licenses averaged about $150 per year. In most countries, licensing of radio sets has been either dropped or combined with the television fee.

Color television brought increased production costs, causing serious financial problems for systems that rely heavily on receiver fees. As set penetration reached near saturation, the license-fee revenue curve leveled off as operational expenses kept rising.

Moreover, politicians, who control fee levels, tend to delay the unpopular task of authorizing increases as long as possible.

Though Marxist doctrine frowned on advertising as a capitalistic device for exploiting workers, even communist countries found broadcast commercials useful for moving consumer goods that sometimes piled up because of central-planning errors. In a sharp change of policy, China began introducing Western-style advertising in 1979, in collaboration with U.S. companies such as CBS. Prior to its collapse, even the USSR became more tolerant of advertising. In 1990, for example, a USSR state television network contracted with CNN to supply news services on a commercially supported basis, agreeing to split revenues 50/50.

Program Economics

Television consumes expensive programs at such a rate that even developed nations with strong economies cannot afford to program several different television networks exclusively with homegrown productions. Britain is unusual in having as many as four full-scale broadcast television networks (with another soon to begin), but even it imports some entertainment programs. British channels impose a voluntary ceiling of 14 percent of their airtime on such imports.

In smaller European countries, the dearth of programs from domestic sources stimulated growth of cable even before satellite-to-cable program networks came into being. Community antennas in small countries such as Holland can pick up a half-dozen services from neighboring countries.

Most imported programs come from the United States (as discussed in Section 15.7), though many come from Britain. A few Third World countries (Brazil, Mexico, and India, especially) increasingly display their wares at international program fairs.

No simple solution to shortages of television programs—other than international syndication—has emerged, although various forms of cost and talent sharing have helped. For example, the European Broadcasting Union (EBU), an association of official broadcasting services in Europe and nearby countries, shares programs through Eurovision, which arranges regular exchanges (mainly sports and news) among its members. Similar associations exist in Asia, the Middle East, and the Caribbean, although they are not as active as the EBU in handling program exchanges.

Co-production is increasingly used as a means of covering high program costs. Producers from two or more countries combine financial and other resources to co-produce television series or movies. They divide capital expenses and profits from assured distribution of programming in two or more participating countries.

• • • • • • • •

15.6 Geography

A nation's size, shape, population distribution, nearness to neighbors, and historical development all affect the kinds of electronic media that evolve. Geography plays an especially prominent role.

Coverage Problems

Cost-effective coverage of a country depends on both its shape and its size. The continental United States has a roughly rectangular land mass insulated on two sides from spillover programs by large bodies of water. Alaska, Hawaii, and offshore territories had to await satellites to enjoy coverage simultaneously with the mainland.

In contrast, Japan, for example, is an archipelago of mountainous islands extending across nearly 2,000 miles of ocean. The Indonesian archipelago's 6,000 or so widely scattered inhabited islands with diverse populations speaking many different languages present even more formidable coverage problems. And Russian territory extends so far east and west that national broadcast schedules have to be adapted to serve 11 different time zones (contrasted with only 4 in the continental United States). Program distribution needs have prompted Russia to become one of the first countries to use domestic satellites.

Spillover

Geography insulates most American listeners and viewers from programs spilling over from foreign countries. But spillover from the United States has strongly influenced not only broadcasting but also satellite and cable development in neighboring Canada. Most Canadians live near the American border and can easily receive American radio and television signals off-air and/or by cable (and vice versa, of course). As a result, Canada became the first heavily cabled country in the world. In the 1980s some American programs were produced in Canada to save costs.

To avoid being overwhelmed by American programs—and to ensure work for its own creative community—Canada imposes quotas limiting the amount of syndicated programming that Canadian broadcasters and cable operators may import. To help fill the gap, it also subsidizes Canadian production, leading to a vibrant Canadian popular music industry, for example.

• • • • • • • •

15.7 Programs

Interchangeability of programs reflects inherent technical, economic, and social aspects of electronic media that lead to similar program formats throughout the world. News, commentary, public affairs, music, drama, variety, studio games, sports events—such program types appeal everywhere. National differences are evident only in the way these genres are treated.

News and Public Affairs

Prime-time daily news programs are universally popular, but their content and style differ among countries. Parochialism, chauvinism, and ideology affect the choice, treatment, and timing of news stories. Each country emphasizes its own national events, few of which hold interest elsewhere.

In authoritarian countries such as Iraq and Cuba, news focuses heavily on the national leader to the virtual exclusion of all else. Some broadcasting systems devote their external pickup facilities entirely to following the head of state around, reporting on his every public move.

Program Balance

Audiences everywhere prefer light entertainment to more serious content. Accordingly, wherever popular demand controls programs—as through audience ratings—entertainment dominates. Most industrialized democracies other than the United States try to strike a balance among light entertainment and news, information, culture, and educational programs.

Those parts of society that pay for services, buy most consumer products, and enjoy access to political and legal entities will see and hear far more of themselves through electronic media than will the poor and powerless. Accordingly, electronic media depict a largely urban, fairly well-educated, affluent people, whether fictional or real.

Third World nations cannot afford many homegrown productions with popular appeal. Therefore, they lease foreign syndicated entertainment that attracts audiences for a fraction of what it would cost to produce programs locally. But imports throw schedules out of balance (as discussed below) by overemphasizing entertainment and playing up foreign cultures.

Schedules

Though common in America, broadcast days of 18 to 24 hours rarely occurred even in other developed countries until recently. Traditionally, less affluent radio services would broadcast a short morning segment, take a break before a midday segment, then another break before evening programs, closing down for the night relatively early. Even in Britain, the BBC began 24-hour radio only in 1979, when Radio 2 filled in the previously silent hours of 2:00 to 5:00 A.M.

Television in much of the world begins only late in the afternoon, signing off by about 11:00 P.M. Extending programming into early-morning and late-night hours in the 1980s became one sign that new networks, stations, and cable systems were adding competition. A 1987 European conference on "breakfast television" was titled "Morning Has Broken: An Idea Whose Time Has Come" (EBUR, 1987).

International Syndication

Cultural differences often impact programming. One major difference between American and foreign television (especially in Europe) is the tolerance of nudity in programs and advertising. Full frontal nudes are not uncommon on German, Swiss, Dutch, and Scandinavian television channels.* Alternatively, some Japanese quiz shows seem focused on debasing contestants. What is acceptable in one country often is not in another, creating problems for program exchange or syndication. American programs, for example, are often criticized abroad for being excessively violent.

U.S. programs, always dominant in world syndication, came to new prominence with added demand from new satellite-distributed cable networks, direct-broadcast satellite channels, and VCRs (discussed in Sections 15.9 and 15.10). These services vacuum up programs from whatever sources they can find. Their enhanced demand has intensified old fears of American cultural domination. The low cost of American programs (because their original cost has already been repaid through domestic sales) and their almost sure-fire mass appeal keep them in demand. Exhibit 15.b shows typical prices paid overseas for syndicated American programs.

By the 1990s, however, American international syndicators had begun experiencing slower growth of sales abroad. In response, many American firms invested in overseas media, but these ventures often encountered legal and cultural opposition to rapid adoption of American cost-effective operating methods. Nor could investors count on quick or easy profits from newly introduced, advertiser-sup-

---

*A German service even offered a strip quiz show in 1989—missing a question meant removing an item of clothing. Some contestants stripped to nothing.

Exhibit 15.b •••••••••••••••

Program Bargains from U.S. Syndicators

Prices for U.S. syndicated material vary widely according to potential audience and ability to pay. As an extreme example, note that a British outlet can pay hundreds of times as much for a feature film as an outlet in Iceland.

		Cost per Program (U.S. Dollars)			
		Series		Movies	
Purchasing country	Television specials	Half hour	Hour	TV	Theatrical
Iceland	$ 900–1,000	$ 250–300	$ 500–600	$ 1,200–1,300	$ 500–1,000
Botswana	1,100–1,300	250–300	500–600	1,110–1,300	na
Israel	1,100–1,300	550–650	950–1,000	2,000–3,000	1,200–4,000
Venezuela	4,000–6,000	2,000–3,000	4,000–5,000	4,000–6,000	4,000–7,000
Mexico	12,000–15,000	4,000–5,000	6,000–10,000	10,000–12,000	10,000–50,000
Italy	20,000–50,000	4,500–10,000	10,000–30,000	15,000–50,000	20,000–750,000
Japan	35,000–50,000	4,000–6,000	14,000–16,000	25,000–75,000	60,000–200,000
Britain	30,000–50,000	8,000–16,000	15,000–100,000	40,000–100,000	50,000–2,000,000
France	30,000–50,000	10,000–20,000	25,000–50,000	30,000–50,000	30,000–150,000
Australia	20,000–60,000	12,000–18,000	24,000–60,000	80,000–110,000	50,000–400,000
Canada*	30,000–70,000	15,000–35,000	45,000–60,000	145,000–165,000	20,000–60,000

*English soundtrack films; French soundtrack prices vary but are less.

Source: Based on data in "Global TV Programming Prices," *Variety* (April 6, 1992): 42. Reprinted with permission from Variety Inc. Variety is a registered trademark of Variety Inc.

ported, privately owned media services. Rundown economies of former communist countries, for example, needed cash for the most basic economic necessities, leaving audiences with little ability to purchase media-advertised goods.

Cultural Imperialism

American dominance of international syndication has long caused Third World concern about cultural imperialism. Critics argue that images and values depicted in imported television undermine local cultures. Such shows encourage excessive consumption, materialism, and disregard for indigenous traditions. Further, every program purchased from abroad denies locals opportunities to showcase their own talents. Thus cheap imported programs can perpetuate dependence on foreigners.

Nor do such complaints come only from the Third World. Even developed nations with extensive production of their own limit the amount of entertainment their national systems may import. In 1992 the 12-nation European Community (representing a market larger—though less unified—than America) imposed program-import restrictions, erected over strong American objections.

The United States strongly resists such attempts by other countries to limit program imports. Americans successfully advocated a *free-flow* international communication policy when the United Nations was created in 1945. But more than 70 new nations, most of them extremely conscious of their prior histories as colonies of developed countries, have since joined the UN. They ask what value free flow has for them when it runs almost entirely in one direction—*from* the United States and a few other industrialized countries *to* the Third World. Instead, they call for "balanced" rather than "free" flow—defined as news that treats Third World countries and stories fairly and in proportion to their population significance.

UNESCO's Role

Much of this debate came to a head in the 1970s and 1980s at the Paris-based UN Educational, Scientific and Cultural Organization (UNESCO), which led in defining and calling for establishment of a *new world information and communication order* (NWICO). American media leaders and politicians saw this development as an attack on journalistic independence and free-enterprise advertising. Claiming that UNESCO wasted money (a quarter of its budget came from the United States) and had become hopelessly politicized, the U.S. government withdrew from UNESCO in 1984, leaving an agency that America had helped to establish four decades earlier.

As a result of NWICO claims, however, Western news agencies have become somewhat more sensitive to Third World feelings, and Western governments and the ITU have increased aid to Third World communications systems. But the news imbalance continues.

15.8 Transborder Broadcasting

The ability to use radio to overcome political boundaries added a potent new factor to diplomatic relations. Never before had it been possible to talk directly to masses of foreigners, crossing even the most heavily defended national borders. By the 1990s more than 80 countries were operating official external services—programs aimed at foreign countries.

BBC's World Service

Colonial commitments first prompted nations to broadcast internationally. The Dutch and Germans started in 1929, the French in 1931. After experimenting for several years, Britain's BBC began what was first called the Empire Service in 1932. It initially broadcast only in English, primarily seeking to maintain home-country ties with expatriates around the world.

Two years later, Italy began radio propaganda in Arabic aimed at the Middle East. The BBC countered with its own Arabic programs—the BBC's first foreign-language broadcasts—and soon Allied and Axis powers were locked in a multilanguage war of words. During World War II, foreign listeners came to regard the BBC service as having the most credibility among external broadcasters, and it has retained that reputation ever since. Worldwide listeners automatically tune to what is now called BBC World Service, especially when they doubt reports from other sources.

BBC World Service has more than a million American radio listeners; some listen via short wave, but many tune in via American Public Radio. Europeans can also hear it as a direct-to-home satellite service. BBC World Service Television (WSTV) began in 1991 as a cooperative effort of domestic television news and World Service radio.* Intended

*Early in 1993 ABC News and the BBC signed a wide-ranging agreement to exchange radio and television news reports and share use of correspondents and production teams.

to compete internationally with CNN, it aimed first at a huge potential audience in Asia via the Hong Kong–based Star TV satellite service and soon programmed to Africa, the Middle East, and Canada as well.

Radio Moscow

The Soviet Union had no overseas colonial empire, but it used radio to explain its revolution to sympathizers in Europe and elsewhere. From the inception of Radio Moscow in 1929, the Soviets recognized the importance of foreign-language radio as a means of gaining and influencing friends abroad.

Radio Moscow developed fewer overseas relay stations than major Western external broadcasters, though in the 1960s it built one such station in Cuba aimed at the Americas. Like radio services in all communist states, Radio Moscow tended to be relentlessly propagandistic; however, it lightened its tone to gain wider appeal in the 1980s, even before *glasnost* took hold. It even initiated a 24-hour English-language service. Under Boris Yeltsin's regime, Radio Moscow leased its surplus transmitters to Deutsche Welle and other groups to improve its reach into China. It even began to accept advertising—and faced its first internal competition from Radio Russia, set up prior to the failed communist coup of mid-1991.

Voice of America

The United States joined the growing battle of words with Voice of America (VOA) early in 1942. Wary of creating a federal domestic propaganda agency, however, Congress forbade VOA to release programs in the United States. Anyone with a short-wave radio can pick up VOA programs aimed at overseas listeners, but to this day only scholars, journalists, and government agencies can gain access to VOA scripts and recordings.

In 1993 VOA used 48 languages in addition to English, broadcasting 1,034 hours a week, about 85 percent devoted to American events and news. VOA programs originate in Washington, going overseas via leased satellite channels and 114 VOA short-wave transmitters located in Greenville, North Carolina, and several secondary U.S. sites. The VOA also leases sites in a dozen foreign countries, where it maintains transmitters for rebroadcasting programs to listeners in nearby areas.

VOA news and public-affairs programs reflect official American policies. News commentaries are explicitly labeled as coming from the United States government. For the sake of credibility, however, VOA tries to observe the spirit of its original 1942 policy: "Daily at this time we shall speak to you about America. . . . The news may be good or bad. We shall tell you the truth." Truth telling continues to be VOA policy, despite occasional lapses when partisan officials bend facts to suit momentary political objectives.

Worldnet

The short range of broadcast television makes it useless for external services aimed at distant targets in the manner of short-wave radio. The United States Information Agency (USIA), VOA's parent organization, used to rely entirely on persuading foreign broadcasters to carry American television programs on their own domestic television services.

In 1983 USIA created Worldnet as a daily television service distributed abroad by satellite. To entice foreign broadcasters into using its material, Worldnet offers interactive teleconferences with U.S. government officials responding to live questions from foreign news personnel. American interviewees speak from a Washington studio to questioners in other countries. Participation by a recipient country's own broadcasters makes the American presence more acceptable on that country's television service.

Worldnet fills most of its schedule with "passive" programs—news and general information minus the interactive feature. American diplomatic posts throughout the world pick up Worldnet on some 230 TVROs, as do foreign cable systems and broadcast stations in about 200 cities in more than 125 countries. Worldnet is available via INTELSAT (discussed in Section 15.9) to any foreign broadcasting or cable television operation that wishes to use it.

However, the costs of the service, as well as audience research showing very small audiences, led to congressional budget cuts for Worldnet in the early 1990s, thus limiting its ability to provide original programming.

RFE and RL

In addition to conventional external broadcasting, the United States has long provided a type of programming referred to as *surrogate* domestic services. Such broadcasts simulate domestic networks, bypassing censored domestic media in targeted authoritarian countries.

Beginning in the early 1950s, Radio Liberty (RL) targeted the Soviet Union while Radio Free Europe (RFE) aimed at Eastern European states then under Soviet control. CIA support of these services was revealed only in the early 1970s, leading to their reorganization under the Board for International Broadcasting. RFE and RL initially built studios and transmitters in Munich, Germany, and additional transmitters in Portugal, and in Spain at sites favorable for sky-wave transmission to their target countries. Broadcasting by radio, entirely in the languages of the target countries, RFE and RL provided domestic and foreign news from the listeners' perspective, often with strong messages encouraging resistance to communist thinking and governments. The United States spent more on operating these two surrogate services than on VOA.

The dramatic political changes in Russia and Eastern Europe in 1989–1991 led to major adjustments in RFE and RL. Both stepped up their activity now that listening to them was no longer illegal, and they soon added transmitters and news bureaus in their target countries—something undreamed of in Cold War days. RFE's and RL's 1,600 employees produced more than 800 hours of programming per week, about half transmitted to Russia. At the same time, however, proposals appeared from several U.S. government commissions to combine the two European radio services with VOA in a unified world radio service. Driven by budget concerns and

Clinton administration proposals, Congress in 1993 was considering some kind of merger that might eliminate separate RFE/RL funding by 1995.

Radio/TV Martí

In May 1985 the United States introduced Radio Martí, a new surrogate service aimed at giving Cuba news and information free of Castro-regime bias. Supporters claim that it has had a powerful effect, heightening dissatisfaction with the Castro regime by revealing facts it conceals from its own people. The expatriate Cuban community in south Florida, with strong Republican political ties in Washington, strongly supports the operation.

Congress authorized funds in 1988 to start experiments with a television version of Radio Martí, using a transmitter hung from a balloon tethered 10,000 feet above Cudjoe Key in Florida. This height enabled television line-of-sight signals to reach Havana 110 miles away. Tests conducted in 1990 incited Cuba to *jam* TV Martí transmissions and to interfere with American AM radio stations.* The Cuban government appealed to the ITU, claiming TV Martí violated ITU allocation rules that designate television channels for domestic use only. Many American broadcasters also objected to the scheme, which was characterized by one *Broadcasting* editorial as a "huge, disastrous silliness" (9 April 1990: 98).

Yet the idea of bringing news reports to places otherwise unlikely to hear them took hold on the other side of the world. In the early 1990s Congress considered establishing a "Radio Free China" service aimed at potential audiences in the People's Republic of China.

Religious Broadcasters

A different ideological motivation led to transborder religious broadcasting. International radio gave evangelicals their first opportunity to deliver their

---

*Jamming is the operation of radio transmitters to send electronic noise that renders incoming radio signals unlistenable. For much of the postwar period, Soviet and East European communist governments jammed RFE and RL, and sometimes VOA signals as well.

messages directly to potential converts in closed societies dominated by state religions. Official hostility—in some Moslem countries toward Evangelical Christians, for example—can prevent the setting up of on-site missions but cannot easily bar radio messages. Well-funded conservative religious broadcasters have so saturated short-wave bands that listeners can pick them up almost anywhere in the world, 24 hours a day.

Peripherals

Commercial motives account for transborder broadcasters known as *peripherals*. Several European mini-states bordering large countries have long operated such stations, capitalizing on unfulfilled demand for popular music and broadcast advertising. Both audiences and advertisers, frustrated by severely regulated domestic services, have welcomed these alternatives.

Peripherals beam commercial radio services in appropriate languages to neighboring countries. They specialize in popular music formats, sometimes supplemented by objective news programs, which are welcome where ruling political parties dominate broadcast news.

The Grand Duchy of Luxembourg, ideally located for peripheral transmitters at the intersection of Belgium, France, and Germany, gets much of its national income from international commercial television as well as radio broadcasting. Exhibit 15.c gives further details. Other notable transborder commercial radio stations operate in the German Saar (Europe No. 1), Monaco (Radio Monte Carlo), Cyprus (Radio Monte Carlo Middle East), Morocco (Radio Mediterranean International), and Gabon (Africa No. 1).

Peripherals tend to be rather staid operations, tolerated by their target countries, some of which even invest in them. They still leave some commercial and program demands unsatisfied, creating a vacuum filled by pirate radio outlets.

Pirates

The first offshore pirate stations began broadcasting from a ship anchored between Denmark and Sweden in 1958. They were often financed by American interests and copied American pop-music formats, advertising techniques, and promotional gimmicks. They quickly captured large and devoted youthful audiences—their very illegality adding spice to their attractiveness.

Some pirates made a lot of money, but at considerable risk. They suffered from storms, raids by rival pirates, and stringent laws that penalized land-based firms for supplying or doing other business with them. In spite of suppressive legislation, offshore pirates occasionally still crop up.

The appetite for pop music whetted by pirate stations forced national systems to take notice of ignored musical tastes. The BBC, for example, reorganized its national radio network offerings, adding a pop-music network (Radio 1) imitative of the pirates. Some of the offshore DJs ended up working for the BBC and other established broadcasters.

Controversy over pirate broadcasting caused the fall of a Dutch government, and the Netherlands reorganized its broadcasting system as a result. It permitted two former pirate organizations to come ashore and develop into leading legitimate broadcasters. As national systems became more pluralistic in program appeal, the rationale for pirate stations declined. Few operate today.

• • • • • • • •

15.9 International Satellites

In recent years commercial services have crossed borders by use of satellite-to-cable networks and DBS facilities.

INTELSAT

The United States led the 1964 founding of the International Telecommunications Satellite Organization (INTELSAT). With relay satellites stationed above the Atlantic, Indian, and Pacific oceans, INTELSAT eventually made possible instant worldwide distribution not only of television

Exhibit 15.c •••••• •••••••••

Luxembourg: Home of Peripherals

The tiny Grand Duchy of Luxembourg granted a broadcasting monopoly to a hybrid government/private corporation, now known as RTL (Radio-Télé-Luxembourg), back in 1930. A year later, it began operating as what the French called a *radio peripherique* (peripheral radio). In those days, when official European radio services tended to be rather highbrow and stuffy, listeners far and wide avidly tuned in to its pop-music programs. Legend has it that Radio Luxembourg, received in Liverpool, England, gave the Beatles their first taste of pop music.

Today, RTL has high-power long-wave (2,000 kw), medium-wave (1,200 kw), and short-wave (500 kw) radio transmitters radiating across the borders, carrying programs in Dutch, French, and German. It broadcasts television in both the PAL and SECAM systems in order to reach both French and German viewers. RTL holds shares in a number of European privately owned broadcasting services and owns extensive production facilities in Luxembourg.

Television's short range made it impossible for the Grand Duchy of Luxembourg to repeat its radio coverage with the newer medium, but it overcame this problem in part by setting up jointly owned broadcasting services in neighboring countries, notably RTL Plus in Germany (both a broadcast and a satellite-to-cable service), TV (French-speaking Belgium's first commercial broadcast channel), and RTL-Veronique (Holland's first privately owned commercial broadcasting channel).

The ITU's 1977 allocation of DBS orbital slots to European countries offered Luxembourg a chance to extend its television coverage to the whole of Europe. SES (Societé Européénne des Satellites), founded in 1985, launched ASTRA in 1988—the first privately

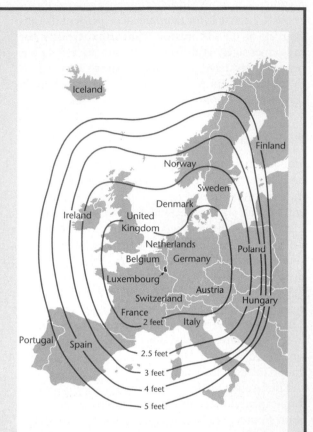

owned European communication satellite. The numbers on the second map indicate the diameter of home TVROs needed to receive ASTRA in the zone defined by the contour lines.

ASTRA contracted with a variety of direct-to-home and satellite-to-cable services to occupy its 16 channels, including Disney and MTV-Europe. It also down linked the first British DBS service, Sky Television, later known as BSkyB.

---

programs but also of telephone conversations, news agency stories, and business data.

More than 100 countries have part-ownership of INTELSAT, but the United States owns the largest block of its shares (about 25 percent), houses its

headquarters (in Washington, D.C.), and has provided the last three of its director-generals. Communications Satellite Corporation (Comsat) initially operated INTELSAT's network under contract on behalf of the rest of the consortium until

Exhibit 15.d ●●●●● ● ●●●●●●●●●●

INTELSAT and "Separate Systems"

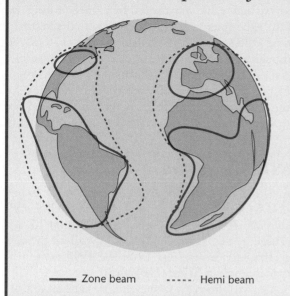
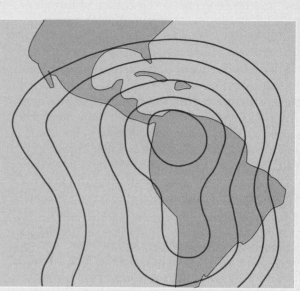

—— Zone beam   ----- Hemi beam

The globe shows an example of INTELSAT coverage. INTELSAT V (F-15), located above the Atlantic Ocean, beams both to the east and to the west. The west hemispheric beam (unbroken line) covers all of Africa and Western Europe.

American satellite firms, strongly backed by the American government, argue that INTELSAT's monopoly is inefficient, that its rates do not reflect actual costs, and that its sheer size make it inflexible. Competition from smaller, nimbler satellite firms, they contend, would lower prices for all, enhance services, and encourage innovation. The first private American "separate system" to launch a satellite, Pan American Satellite Corporation (PAS), offers both domestic and international satellite services. It links the United States and countries of the Hispanic world—Central and South America and the Caribbean—with Europe, and serves Hispanic domestic needs as well.

Peru became the first PAS customer, followed by the Dominican Republic and Costa Rica on this side of the Atlantic, and by Britain, Ireland, Luxembourg, Sweden, and West Germany on the other, with more yet to come. CNN and other U.S. satellite-to-cable networks contracted with PAS to relay their programs to countries to the south.

Source: Satellite footprints courtesy INTELSAT and Pan American Satellite. Used by permission of INTELSAT.

INTELSAT itself took over in 1979. In the early 1990s the former Soviet Union and its onetime client-states of Eastern Europe abandoned their Intersputnik rival network and became members of INTELSAT. Exhibit 15.d offers more details on INTELSAT and its recently emerged competition.

Though primarily an international carrier, INTELSAT also leases satellite capacity at reasonable rates to Third World countries for their *domestic* use. Thus INTELSAT enables many such nations to vault directly into the satellite era, avoiding costly construction of microwave and coaxial-cable circuits throughout their territories.

Satellite Launching

The U.S. government's National Aeronautics and Space Administration (NASA) long monopolized the West's capacity to launch communication satellites. In 1984, however, a consortium of European countries began to challenge NASA's monopoly with their own launch facility, Arianespace (named for *Ariane*, the rocket used). Ariane rockets operate from a site in French Guiana on the northern coast of South America, near the equator. That location gives Arianespace better conditions for attaining equatorial orbit than does NASA's more northerly location at Cape Canaveral, Florida.

After the *Challenger* shuttle exploded on takeoff in 1986, the American government decided to confine NASA operations to government projects. This decision opened the launch market to private U.S. and foreign rocket makers. China and Russia made their government launch facilities available to foreign commercial users—although American national security concerns limited U.S. participation (we did not want to give away expensive technology information to potentially hostile countries). China's first customer for the use of its *Long March* rocket was a Singapore consortium. It launched AsiaSat in 1990, using one of two satellites that had been rescued by U.S. shuttles after being stranded in low orbit (see Exhibit 6.k, p. 213).

Domsats

The Soviet Union took the lead in domestic satellite (domsat) development. In 1965 it began launching the *Molniya* satellite series that enabled relaying of Soviet television throughout its vast territory. Canada's *Anik* domsat series followed, starting in 1972. Anik preceded the first U.S. domsat, Westar, by two years.

The 1970s also saw the launching of domestic and regional satellite services in several other countries: Indonesia's *Palapa*, the first Third World satellite; Europe's *Eutelsat* forerunner, the first of a regional satellite series; and Japan's first satellite. France, first among the European countries with its own domsat, launched *Telecom* in 1985, in part to enable relays to French overseas territories.

DBS Services

DBS services have shown promise in countries, such as Australia and Japan, where these services do not have to compete with deep cable penetration. Japan forestalled cable expansion by concentrating on DBS experiments. It led the world with the first full-time DBS service in 1987. And Australia's *AUSSAT*, though a general-purpose satellite rather than a specialized DBS vehicle, transformed Australian broadcasting in the late 1980s. It brought television for the first time to remote areas too thinly populated to support either terrestrial relay or cable systems.

ASTRA and BSkyB

In 1989 a Luxembourg corporation launched *ASTRA*, Europe's first privately owned satellite suitable for DBS services, described in Exhibit 15.c. It is used by Sky Television (called BSkyB on the air), a DBS service resulting from the 1990 merger of two competing British DBS firms.

The first direct-to-home satellite venture in Britain, Rupert Murdoch's Sky Television, began in 1989, based on that country's pioneer satellite-to-cable network, Sky Channel. A second British DBS service, British Satellite Broadcasting (BSB), launched a true high-power, Ku-band DBS satellite in 1990; but the two services could not continue the costly competition for home subscribers—a competition costing Murdoch $3.2 million a week. The merged Sky service provides sports, general programming, films, and an all-news channel.

Radio by Satellite

Americans tend to think of DBS services exclusively in television terms, but Europeans can receive some 60 radio services from satellites. In addition to the major public-service broadcasters, such as the BBC, a number of colorfully named private radio stations can be received by satellite—Kiss FM, Radio Radio, Fun FM, and Skyrock, for example. Europeans receive satellite radio services directly by means of home TVROs or indirectly via cable systems and FM radio stations.

•••••••

15.10 Cable and Newer Media

Many European countries had primitive community antenna television (CATV) for years before the emergence of modern cable. However, these early systems merely extended domestic broadcast station coverage, sometimes adding a few channels for the purpose of carrying neighboring foreign broadcast networks. Most operated noncommercially, often owned by municipalities. They offered few channels, no local origination, and no pay television.

Cable

Modern cable has developed most extensively in Canada, the United States, and well-developed small countries such as Belgium (where cable penetration of television households had reached about 93 percent by 1990) and the Netherlands (around 80 percent). Larger European countries still have relatively low cable penetration.

Although cable penetration continues to increase, public demand in larger countries remains sluggish. If basic cable systems do not offer a wide variety of popular programs, subscribership remains low. High-appeal cable services delivered by satellite did not begin in Europe until 1982 with the launch of Sky Channel, the London-based English-language service noted earlier. After that, satellite networks grew rapidly. More than 50 were serving European cable systems by 1990. Some targeted only a single country; some, several countries that had a common language. Exhibit 15.e provides details on the major multinational satellite networks.

VCRs

Both as alternative and as supplement to cable and DBS, videocassette recorders (VCRs) have proved a boon to viewers in countries where broadcast services failed to satisfy demand. They offer a relatively inexpensive short cut to programs banned from, or otherwise not available on, national broadcast or cable channels.

In formerly communist countries, rigid political censorship created appetites only VCRs could help satisfy. Clandestine VCR tapes hastened the end of those repressive regimes. VCRs also abound in Britain, not primarily because of frustration with available programs but in order to time-shift desired programs to more convenient viewing hours as well as to view feature films. In 1992 the BBC reported just under 80 million VCRs in all of Europe. But penetration varies from a high in Switzerland of 40 per 100 people to Britain with 31, the Netherlands with 24, Turkey with 2, and the former USSR with 1 (BBC, 1992).

VCRs help make up for often inadequate Third World television schedules and poor program quality. Few individuals in such countries can afford to buy a VCR outright, but rentals, club purchases, and group viewing in bars, coffee houses, and even on buses resolve cost problems. In some cases heavy censorship encourages VCR growth—as in Saudi Arabia, where puritanical Moslem standards severely limit broadcast television. A worldwide underground market in VCRs and tapes defeats most government attempts to limit sales and rentals. It also undermines profitability of video sales.

Teletext and Videotex

The BBC and the IBA invented teletext, which has proved far more successful overseas than in the United States (see Section 3.3). Though not a runaway success, it has nevertheless found greater acceptance in Britain and Europe generally than in this country, where too many alternative media choices exist.

France leads the world in videotex development. Its *Minitel* system is available in more than six million French households. The government telecommunications monopoly promotes Minitel, offering the hardware at a low monthly rent ($4) to consumers. Telephone subscribers forgo printed telephone directories, instead paying about six cents a minute for Minitel's many services, which include, in addition to telephone directory assistance, thousands of independent electronic services such as transportation schedules, banking, and personal "chat lines."

Exhibit 15.e • • • • • • • • • • • • • • • •

Major European Multinational Satellite Program Channels

Dozens of satellite-delivered channels are available to European viewers who have the proper TVRO equipment or cable connections.

Service	Owner	Programming	Language	Remarks
BBCTV Europe	BBC	General	English	
SVT1/SVT2	Sveriges TV	General	Swedish	
TVE Int'l	RTVE	General	Spanish	
RAI1/RAI2	RAI	General	Italian	
A2	Antenne 2	General	French	
3-Sat	ZDF/ORF/SRG	General	German	3-nation; German language
TV5 Europe	TF1/A2/SRC/TVA/ FR3/RTBF/SSR	General	French	Multinational; French language
La Sept	French Government	Culture	French	
Sky One	News Int'l	Entertainment/news	English	
Superchannel	BetaTV/Virgin	Entertainment/news	English	
RTL Plus	CLT/Bertelsmann	Entertainment/news	German	
Sat 1	Kirch/Springer	Entertainment/news	German	
Pro 7	Kirch/Ackermann	Entertainment/news	German	
Tele 5	Telemünchen/CLT	Entertainment/news	German	
TF 1	Bouygues/Maxwell	Entertainment/news	French	
Canal Plus	Havas	Movies/sport	French	Pay-TV
M6	CLT/Lyonnaise	Entertainment	French	
TV3	Scansat	Entertainment	Swedish, Danish, Norwegian	Scandinavian
KTL 4 Veronique	CLT	Entertainment	Dutch	
Galavision	Euro Visa Ltd.	Entertainment	Spanish	
Nordic Channel	Karissima AB	Entertainment	Swedish	
FilmNet	Esselte	Movies	English	Pay-TV

Service	Owner	Programming	Language	Remarks
Sky Movies	News Int'l	Movies	English	Pay-TV
Teleclub	Kirch/Ringier	Movies	German	Pay-TV
SF Succe	Svensk Film Time-Warner	Movies	Swedish	Pay-TV
TV 1000	Kinnevik	Movies	Swedish, Danish, Norwegian	Pay-TV
Children's Channel	British Telecom	Children	English	
Kindernet	W.H. Smith	Children	Dutch	Pay-TV
Canal J	Hachette	Children	French	Pay-TV
Eurosport	News Int'l	Sports	English, German	
Screen Sport	Smith, ESPN	Sports	English	
Sport Kanal	Smith, MHV, CCR	Sports	German	
TV Sport	Smith, GDE	Sports	French	
EBC	AWF	Business inform'n	English, German	
MTV Europe	Viacom, Mirror	Pop videos	English	
CNN Int'l	Turner	News	English	
Worldnet	USIA	News	English	
Lifestyle	W.H. Smith	Women's	English	
Discovery Channel	UAE, Discovery Channel	Nature documentaries	English	Pay-TV

Source: *SZV/ASE Bulletin* (1990), no. 3, p. 13, as reprinted in Blumler (1992: 26–27).

Subscription TV

Subscription television (STV), an over-the-air pay service, failed in the United States (see Section 3.3) but has succeeded brilliantly in France. The French STV service, Canal Plus, features recent movies (many from the United States) and major sports events. It has succeeded so well that it has helped launch clones in Belgium, Germany, and Spain.

• • • • • • • •

Summary

15.1 Though broadcasting has universal characteristics, each nation develops its own unique features. Three controlling philosophies of electronic media have emerged over the years: permissive, paternalistic, and authoritarian.

15.2 Britain's system of broadcasting offers a good example of a pluralistic system that melds features of permissive and paternalistic philosophies by introducing competition. Pluralistic systems are the most successful worldwide and are becoming more common.

15.3 American communications deregulation has heavily influenced similar moves in other countries, many of which are privatizing formerly government-owned services. Public-service broadcast services are increasingly threatened by entertainment-based competition. The International Telecommunication Union has become more politicized in its development of technical standards and world cooperation in spectrum and orbit allocations.

15.4 Access to the airwaves varies greatly by country, with some nations giving political candidates limited free time and others providing blocks of airtime to various societal and cultural groups.

15.5 Foreign electronic media revenues come mainly from government appropriations, receiver license fees, advertising, or a combination of these sources. The high—and rising—cost of programming is a central feature of electronic media economics.

15.6 The size, terrain, population distribution, neighbors, and location of a nation greatly influence the nature and extent of electronic media systems. Border areas typically experience spillover of broadcast or satellite signals from one country to another.

15.7 While basic program types are universal, nations vary in the extent to which they require balance among types. Few countries can afford 24-hour transmissions, though the amount of airtime is increasing worldwide. America is the largest syndicator of television programming in the world. Many countries have adopted limits on program imports to protect their cultural traditions. The free-flow communications doctrine long supported by the United States encounters stiff opposition from many Third World countries more interested in a balanced view of news and equal access to technical facilities.

15.8 Major countries exploit transborder broadcasting—much of it by short wave—as a form of public diplomacy. The BBC's World Service is recognized as the most believable of official external services. American services include the Voice of America and Radio Free Europe/Radio Liberty, as well as more recent services directed to Cuba and a projected service to the People's Republic of China.

15.9 The INTELSAT consortium has operated international satellites since 1965, steadily improving its capabilities and capacities. Both American and foreign rockets launch international satellites. Private satellites carry a growing number of DBS and radio services worldwide.

15.10 Cable television and VCRs are steadily increasing their presence among the electronic media audience around the world. Teletext and videotex services, thus far unsuccessful in the United States, have achieved limited market acceptance in other countries, especially France and Britain.

Chapter 16

Tomorrow

Experience proves that predicting electronic media futures is at best a risky task. Many media executives and often their companies have failed in trying to foresee what lay ahead. And countless innovations (both programs and hardware) have misfired while relatively few have made millions. Indeed, a review of past predictions of how television might develop reveals that even entire industries have miscalculated their own futures.

Throughout the 1920s and 1930s, popular press articles (and some inventors) described commercial television as "just around the corner." It turned out, however, to be a distant corner. Television evolved very slowly as press releases moved faster than technology.

In the 1940s, smug Hollywood film studios ignored postwar television, viewing the upstart as but a passing fad. Then, threatened by its growing appeal in the 1950s, film as well as print competitors sought to slow television's development by stressing some of its problems, especially its high cost.

As late as the 1970s, television broadcasters arrogantly proclaimed that cable would serve only as a means of enlarging their own audiences—and promoted government policies they hoped would keep cable in what they saw as its proper place.

Part of the "prediction problem" is that experts too often base their forecasts primarily on existing technologies and on those institutions that pay for futures research. These approaches are potentially flawed:

- Predictors often assume the public will eagerly embrace whatever new technology or service comes along. But such technological determinism greatly overestimates "wants" and largely ignores social needs and economic realities. Examples such as the public rejection of early videotex, video discs, and first-generation direct-broadcast satellites confirm the likelihood of failure when suppliers take consumers for granted. People want to make life easier and more fulfilling, not more complicated. Most have little patience with expensive "bells and whistles" that often prove difficult to use while offering no real improvement over existing products or services.
- Only rarely can predictors forecast fundamental scientific or technical breakthroughs. Arthur C.

Clarke stood virtually alone in foreseeing geosynchronous-orbit satellites when he predicted them in 1945, well in advance of technology's ability to build or launch such devices. In the 1960s few experts foresaw personal computers or the revolution they would spawn. And a decade ago no one even dreamed of digital video compression, a technology now at the center of media planning.

Today, some industry observers forecast that current media will rapidly give way to more individualized technologies, allowing huge but now-passive audiences to become truly interactive. Others feel that electronic media will evolve more gradually and that most or all of today's major companies, technologies, and services will, in at least some form, be around tomorrow. In the final analysis while its pace has increased dramatically, major change seldom comes as quickly or totally as many futurists often predict.

The following pages offer our vision of the *most likely* trends in electronic media, especially for the balance of this decade, arranged parallel to previous parts of the book. Specific predictions appear in *italics*. We realize all too well that some of what we suggest here may not take place, at least not when or how we see it. But even our admittedly cloudy crystal ball may stimulate the reader's own ideas.

• • • • • • • •

16.1 Technology

Much of what exists today will survive the 1990s, with dramatic changes more likely after the turn of the century. Central to our evolutionary rather than radical view is the huge investment in existing technology that serves to reinforce the status quo. One scholar created a "law of the suppression of radical potential" to describe how those with the most to lose from change intentionally retard new and competing technologies (Winston, 1986: 23). Indeed, established industries, seeking time to develop new roles within a changing system, often urge restrictive policies to control or suppress growth of new

competitors—as did the movie studios with television, and broadcasters with cable.

Industry and consumer investments in today's analog technology will temporarily retard the growth of high-definition television and digital audio services. For the next several years, these new services will suffer the same "chicken and egg" dilemma that limited the growth of early television and FM radio a half-century ago. Should media firms invest in equipment and programs to entice audiences to buy new receivers and recorders? Or should they wait, hoping that audiences will grow sufficiently on their own (in expectation of improved service) for advertising and subscription revenues to offset digital conversion costs as they occur?

Personal communication services will further modify electronic media in the coming decade. Most such devices build on earlier efforts (see Exhibit 16.a) to enhance our individual ability to pick and choose among an increasing number of options. Many readers will remember when cable service or a videocassette machine first dramatically increased their control of, and choice among, more channels (and perhaps enlarged a circle of admiring friends!). Likewise, widespread adoption of remote control devices in the late 1980s made those options easier to access.

As new products come on line, they will be marketed at prices dropping, or at least rising more slowly than, the overall cost of living. Thanks to fierce competition and more efficient technology, prices of home television receivers and VCRs, in terms of constant dollar value, have actually dropped over the past decade. While some of the newest digital technology-based equipment (such as HDTV) will be expensive at first, the same price-reducing pressures will operate to force costs down in a relatively short time.

Telephone companies, increasingly competitive with one another and with cable firms in the early 1990s, will rapidly develop new ways of using their extensive networks and digital switches to deliver audio, video, and data services. At the same time, cable will step up its pace of installing fiber-optic lines to better compete with telephone companies.

Competition between at least two direct-broadcast satellite (DBS) services will be available throughout the

Exhibit 16.a ●●●●●●●●●●●●●●●●●

The More Things Change . . .

Just as kids today use headphones, so, too, did their grandparents in the earliest days of radio. Headphones were then the only means of listening, whereas today, given their tiny size, they are a way for an individual to take radio with him or her where radio couldn't go before—public transit, libraries, and, yes, even classrooms.

Sources: Left photo from the Bettmann Archive; right photo from Michael Grecco/Stock, Boston.

United States by 1995. As happened in Britain, however, there is at least an even chance that competing DBS operators may merge. Each will at first offer dozens of channels of entertainment and information, aimed primarily at areas underserved by cable. The prospect that DBS can effectively compete head-on with established cable systems, however, seems less likely.

More new ways of transmitting and receiving information will emerge to compete with existing modes. As this book went to press, a high-frequency microwave means of distributing multiple information and entertainment channels (more cheaply than by broadcast, cable, satellite, or possibly even fiber networks) was in experimental use in New York. If successful, it could offer cost-effective competition for existing cable and even telephone monopolies.

Building on Dick Tracy's classic wrist radio, technological advances will soon have us carrying pocket communication devices connecting us—digitally—to distant points by voice, video, and data from home, car, or office (see "Interacting," below). Voice and data interactive communication from cars may be possible by mid-decade.

Increasing

Media digitalization, accelerating in the 1990s, will dramatically increase capability and capacity.

Thanks to digital signal compression, cable and satellite media have entered an era of almost unbelievable capacity expansion that will soon make hundreds of channels available to millions of viewers. Newly developed digital switches and set-top decoders will soon allow the hundreds of digital channels to reach homes without expensive replacement of present telephone and coaxial-cable "last mile" connections. Fiber-optic cable will increasingly dominate trunk communication links.

New digital means of storing massive numbers of different movies or television programs will allow computer-controlled "video on demand" which in turn will further reduce viewer dependence on the scheduling practices of broadcast or cable firms. Such systems will be offered experimentally by mid-decade and should be widespread by the year 2000, at least in major markets.

Digital HDTV is coming, though its major impact will not be evident until after the turn of the century. Market forecasts suggest that perhaps one-fifth of American households will be capable of receiving digital HDTV by the year 2000 and that half of all homes may be so equipped a few years later. Note in Exhibit 16.b that some homes will receive HDTV on wall-size screens that may eventually eliminate the bulky television receiver we have known for decades. Little more than a few inches thick, such screens may use laser or plasma technology under active development by Japan's NHK and others in the early 1990s.

On the other hand, there were by 1993 a rising number of HDTV naysayers increasingly making themselves heard. One broadcaster called DBS the "cinerama of television," referring to the high cost and limited consumer (or broadcaster) gain from the system.* Others noted how little consumer research had been done on DBS's appeal and future—the

*Cinerama was a wide-screen and stereo sound system for theatrical movies, popular in the late 1950s and into the 1960s. The cost of converting theaters to its complicated multi-projector and multi-track sound technology and very wide screens discouraged widespread adoption.

research focus, as with the first round of DBS fascination a decade ago, has been on the technology and not on programming or consumer appeal factors.

With its promise of more, and better-quality, radio signals *digital audio broadcasting (DAB) will first (in the next three to five years) supplement and then (early in the next century) likely replace existing analog AM and FM radio stations.*

Interacting

After years of rather vague predictions, the early 1990s finally saw considerable experimentation—and even more hype—about "talk-back TV" and "interactive media." We doubt that many of these audience-empowering technologies will develop widely before the turn of the century. Lack of agreement on technical standards, content, financial support, and control impedes progress—another example of Winston's "suppression law." Far more optimistic is the outlook for a new means of interacting: personal communication services (PCSs).

PCSs will further blur the present boundaries between mass and personal media. Under active development in the 1990s, PCSs physically resemble small, portable cellular telephones, easily carried in pocket or purse. (Some radical futurists go so far as to predict that we will be wearing future communication terminals like jewelry by the beginning of the next century!) Despite unresolved policy questions (including allocation of sufficient frequencies to make systems truly national and multichannel, and determination of who will be allowed to own and operate such services), *PCS devices will eventually connect individuals into an integrated national network allowing interactive communication and computing from virtually any urban location, perhaps as soon as the end of this decade.*

Eventually, the combining of multiple interactive channels with home shopping services, information, and entertainment will further blur the distinctions between advertising and programming. Viewers will be able to roam shopping malls, rapidly spending down their credit cards without leaving home.

Under development for television and in actual use in some computer applications in the early 1990s

Exhibit 16.b • • • • • • • • • • • • • • •

Tomorrow's Multimedia Home

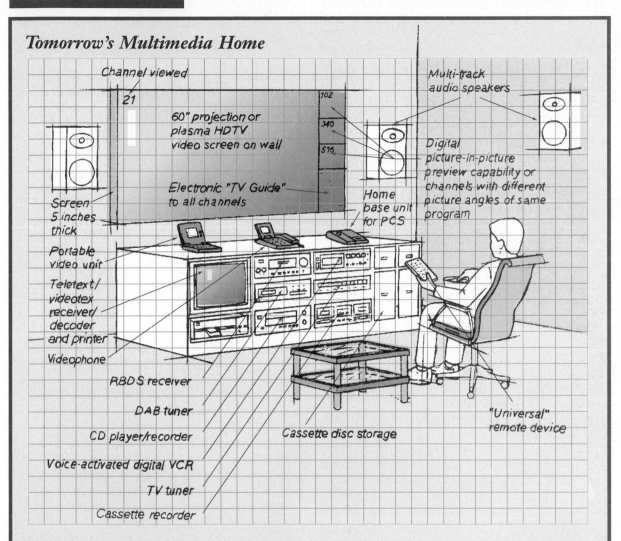

Channel viewed

21

60" projection or plasma HDTV video screen on wall

Electronic "TV Guide" to all channels

Screen 5 inches thick

Portable video unit

Teletext/ videotex receiver/ decoder and printer

Videophone

RBDS receiver

DAB tuner

CD player/recorder

Voice-activated digital VCR

TV tuner

Cassette recorder

102
340
575

Multi-track audio speakers

Digital picture-in-picture preview capability or channels with different picture angles of same program

Home base unit for PCS

Cassette disc storage

"Universal" remote device

By the turn of the century, a home multimedia center may become a common feature in some households. The potential size of the projection, wall-mounted HDTV video screen (five feet across or even more), as well as the capacity of digital multi-track sound systems will force multimedia use to take over an entire room. The center features an integrated and fully-digital set of devices to offer multiple video and audio inputs through integrated decoders at the flick of a universal remote button. Not shown here, but an important part of any such room, will be interactive audio and video services allowing consumers to "talk back" to program producers. Home units for interactive video telephone and personal communication services (PCS) may be a part of such rooms. Inputs will include many of those illustrated in Exhibit 3.j on p. 96, and probably others.

are talk-back media where users literally *tell* equipment what to do. Based on computer technology and a limited vocabulary of machine-recognized words, *by the end of the decade some electronic equipment will allow consumers to use verbal commands to turn sets on and off, change channels, and program audio and video recordings.*

• • • • • • • •

16.2 Business

Electronic media industries now more than ever are driven by their search for innovation and sufficient capital to stay competitively (and profitably) alive. Identification of future "winner companies" becomes challenging because there exist at least two schools of thought on the subject.

Satellite communication and the production of television series, for example, require huge investments that only multifaceted, vertically integrated companies can afford. Some observers predict that only huge multinational conglomerates will be able to compete effectively in worldwide markets. The Time Warners, Turner Communications, and Rupert Murdochs of the world will, by this line of thinking, increasingly dominate media trends and developments, operating across dozens of countries.

Others argue that small start-up companies can more quickly generate creative ideas and develop new markets. Many interactive television projects, for example, come from firms new to this field.

Employment patterns offer one indicator of change. *The decline in available broadcast positions will continue,* in part because of management shifts and huge debts resulting from earlier mergers, but mostly because of a weak economy, depressed advertising revenue, and increased competition. *At the same time, other services—corporate video, direct-broadcast satellite, programming, and personal communications—will continue to expand.*

Overall employment levels across all electronic media will probably remain steady for the next few years. Distribution of jobs among services will continue to shift, however, reflecting changing competitive strengths as new technologies and services arise and older ones fade.

Merging

Of the two schools of thought, the "big company" concept comes closer to likely future electronic media development. While many good ideas originate in smaller firms, most lack the capital or managerial prowess to market their innovations effectively and thus sell out to or become a part of one of the mega-companies.

The trend toward bigger, conglomerate media firms with expanding worldwide scope will continue and its pace may well quicken. Government policies as implemented by such FCC decisions as allowing a single owner to control more stations, facilitate such consolidations. The major impetus to merge and grow is both economic and circular—to accumulate capital required to operate existing outlets and build or acquire new facilities, while applying economies of scale to compete more effectively with other well-heeled (and often foreign-based) firms.

However, as was true a century ago, when business "trusts" dominated many aspects of American life, *actions of huge conglomerate media companies will raise policy concerns as firms concentrate ownership in fewer hands.* Consolidation reduces the variety of points of view—the voices—available to audiences. It also contributes to the increasing sameness of programs as profit-driven media compete for similar segments of the audience.

Individual nations will find it increasingly difficult to monitor firms that operate worldwide. Such companies take on a kind of global independence, arising in part from their very size and multiple locations. Rupert Murdoch's News Corp.—parent of the Fox network and television stations in the United States, of a DBS service, and several newspapers in Britain, and of other print and electronic media operations around the world—offers the classic example.

Networking

Electronic media's first experience with consolidation produced national radio networks. Later television moved into networking, as have, most recently, cable and satellite services. Centralized decision making and distribution of programs to many outlets has dominated each of these delivery modes in turn because of networking's economic efficiency. If DBS services are successfully established in the United States (as we think at least one will be), they will form the latest version of networking—this time, directly to individual households rather than to intervening media outlets.

As for the traditional broadcast television networks, perhaps two or three of them will survive in recognizable form. Given their diminishing role, and hence their reduced advertiser support, it seems likely that at least one will not be around by the turn of the century. While one or two runaway hit programs could dramatically change the picture, as of early 1993 ABC appears the strongest and NBC the weakest—although CBS could be the first to go because it has not hedged its bets as well as the other two by moving into cable. Fox will survive, but with slower growth than it has experienced in recent years.

Networks will survive to the degree that they capitalize on their unexcelled programming expertise, regardless of the means of delivery—becoming, in effect, recognized "brand-name" syndicators while trimming their reliance on and traditional loyalty to increasingly obsolete over-the-air transmission.

At the very least, the Big Three traditional networks will originate less programming in some dayparts over the next few years. They will no longer be able to afford filling quite so many hours with sometimes marginal-appeal programs as they do now. Instead they will concentrate their competitive efforts in high-viewing hours, leaving less profitable periods for their affiliates to program.

On the other hand, *network radio and cable audio services will continue to expand as they convert to digital service.*

Subscribing

As program costs rise—and as more channels lead to still more programs—financial support of electronic media will begin a fundamental shift.

Well into the coming century, advertising will continue to provide most of the support for broad-cast stations, and for broadcast and non-premium cable networks. There is no danger that advertising will disappear.

At the same time, *direct audience payment by either subscription or pay-per-view will steadily become more prevalent*, bringing electronic media practice more in line with that of print and film. Increasing use of direct payment will parallel wider availability of specialized program channels. Exactly how all of this will work remains unclear, however—given NBC's substantial loss from mixing advertising and direct payment for varied levels of 1992 Olympics coverage.

Meanwhile, the unique element of cable premium services will begin to disappear. *At least limited advertising will appear on some pay-cable channels within the next five years.* The temptations to accept advertising revenue in order to offset rising program costs will become too strong to resist.

Surviving

Some media face an uphill battle simply to survive at all. The single-channel radio or television broadcaster is at an increasingly competitive disadvantage against multichannel services. Changes in broadcast ownership rules allowing one owner to control multiple local over-the-air services treat only the symptoms of this problem, not the problem itself.

Many broadcast stations will not survive the decade. The downward trend is already evident: hundreds of AM stations, lacking sufficient advertiser support, have already left the air. This decline in stations results in part from their reduced usefulness.

As more and more programming (and virtually all entertainment) is produced and distributed nationally, provision of *local* news-weather-sports offers insufficient rationale to support the costs of nearly 14,000 separate broadcast outlets—even without competition from newer services. More extensive coverage of local sports may help some stations survive, but only a few.

Public broadcasting's national organizational structure (CPB, PBS, and NPR) will evolve over the next few years. The present structure seems too cumbersome, elitist, and expensive to survive the rapidly expanding channel choices becoming available to most viewers.

A more cohesive structure—perhaps one combining several modes of delivery (broadcast, cable, satellite, and home video) for cultural, arts, educational, and informational television programming—may emerge instead. The result could be an amalgamation, in effect, of such present cable and broadcast services as Arts & Entertainment, Discovery, PBS, and C-SPAN.

What is now public television will operate with increasing reliance on underwriting if not actual advertising. Ultimately advertising revenue is essential to cultural programming's viability. Other means of support (except for direct audience payment) are too small and too scattered.

Public radio will prosper, comparatively speaking, while public television faces the double whammy discussed in Chapter 8: more competition, on the one hand, plus tighter state and federal budget constraints, on the other.

• • • • • • • •

16.3 Programs

Although we are already basking in program plenty compared to most other countries, still more choices are coming. The content of these new programs remains unclear, however, because of what cannot readily be predicted—artistic trends. Nobody could have foreseen, for example, that the Beatles in the 1960s, or Michael Jackson two decades later, would suddenly and dramatically change the music of the times. Nor can we know in advance what other creative breakthroughs may appear, let alone what impact they may have on media futures. Even so, we can confidently predict that the vast increase in the number of available channels will have great impact, some good and some less so. Furthermore, *the pace of television will quicken as digital editing allows fast-changing pictures and sound in commercials today and some programming tomorrow.*

The availability of dozens, and soon hundreds, of additional channels provides opportunities—"blank slates"—for creative minds to cater to more specialized audience needs and desires. *No longer faced with limited channels or artificial regulatory concerns, programmer access to audiences will increasingly be determined by economics, audience interest, and producer creativity.*

Some media outlets—local video stores and movie theaters especially—will see their profits dramatically reduced in the next few years as people gain a wider choice from their own television sets. Movies on demand will be offered over cable and satellite services, saving viewer trips to video stores—some of which might become cable service providers instead.

Entertaining

Clearly one thing will *not* change—the mass entertainment basis of most broadcast, cable, and satellite-delivered programming. Entertainment's proven audience appeal acts as bait attracting investment in new technology—what some have called "digital entertainment." As one example, several states have already developed fiber-optic networks by initially using entertainment programming to attract investment and viewers, then piggybacking cultural and educational channels on top of entertainment's appeal.

The basic sameness of most electronic media programming will continue. Most "new" programs will vary only the same few basic themes evident since network radio, if not since Shakespeare. We will see far more repetition of existing themes (and of popular old programs and movies) than new niche programs for specific audiences, though the latter will multiply as well.

On the other hand, *there will be more cross-media co-production and shared ownership of programs.* As programming expenses continue to rise, broadcast and cable interests will increasingly share production costs, working out "windows" within which different delivery modes can make use of resulting programs.

This sharing trend, in turn, will be accelerated by the demise in the next few years of remaining FCC restrictions on broadcast network/production company coopera-

tion and co-ownership (the fin/syn rules were largely relaxed in 1993; PTAR faces a similar fate soon).* The artificial limits of those rules, which date to pre-cable days when three networks dominated television, cannot survive in the face of expanding numbers of channels and outlets.

Over the next several years, an increasing proportion of sports coverage will shift to pay services including PPV. The never-ending financial demands of professional sports, fueled by outrageously high salaries for top athletes, have already changed the face of televised sports. Broadcast networks can no longer absorb costs that advertising revenue no longer covers. This change will likely begin at the margins—with minor sports or teams made available at fairly low cost on local PPV channels, following the precedent set decades ago by televised boxing. By the end of the 1990s, the practice may extend even to such popular and expensive staples as the World Series.

Informing

Information programming will also experience considerable change in the 1990s. Because of their relative low cost and popularity, *more news feature magazine programs will appear on local cable and broadcast outlets in the next few years.* But the rising *amount* of news does not necessarily mean more quality or depth in that news. *The readily apparent trend toward more sensational "shake and bake" news with its emphasis on people, entertainment, sex, and violence will accelerate,* given tighter competition for audiences.

Already blurred distinctions between "national" and "local" news will fade further as multiple news sources and modes of delivery make virtually all news coverage available around the clock to "local" outlets. Similarly, worldwide events will become more widely available. *Each year we will see more live television coverage from around the world.* Our sense of time

and space will continue to shrink as once-distant places intrude into our lives.*

Network evening newscasts will become more feature- and theme-oriented, offering less breaking news—just as newspapers had to adjust to radio and then to television. Indeed, *at least one broadcast television network will likely abandon its early evening newscast altogether,* choosing instead to strip a magazine show at 10:00 P.M. on weeknights, each edition featuring a brief review of that day's top news stories.

Specializing

One of the most common yet wrong-headed predictions in past years has been that mass media would completely give way to *non*mass services aimed at focused-interest audiences (sometimes called *narrow*casting to differentiate the approach from *broad*casting). As cable began to expand a quarter-century ago, futurists saw it as a means of breaking network broadcasting's mass entertainment mold. But cable's evolution has produced yet another service that mostly programs the same kind of mass entertainment—and for the same reason: to deliver as many viewers as possible to potential advertisers.

Nonetheless, *with the explosion of channel capacity will come a gradual increase in program specialization.* As one indicator of what is coming, some program-listing services already organize cable's dozens of channels into such larger program categories as information, music, movies, and shows for children to allow easier scanning of what is available at any given time. Moreover, *TV Guide* and others are seeking electronic ways of making this information available on an interactive basis, thus easing rapid program choice across hundreds of channel options.

Among those options (only wishfully predicted a decade ago) are at least some highly specialized electronic services, offered *along with* (not replacing) mass entertainment channels (see Exhibit 16.c).

---

*With the fin/syn rules finally disappearing totally over the next two years or so, chances have improved that at least one of the networks, possibly NBC, will be acquired (rescued?) through takeover by a program producer or distributor such as Paramount.

*As an example, one of the authors, while in Warsaw, Poland, early in 1993, watched live Pentagon briefings held in Washington D.C., thanks to the wide availability of CNN worldwide. For that matter, people around the globe could have watched President Clinton's inauguration live—if they didn't mind staying up at odd hours.

Exhibit 16.c ●●●●●●●●●●●●●●●●

Soon, On a Screen Near You . . .

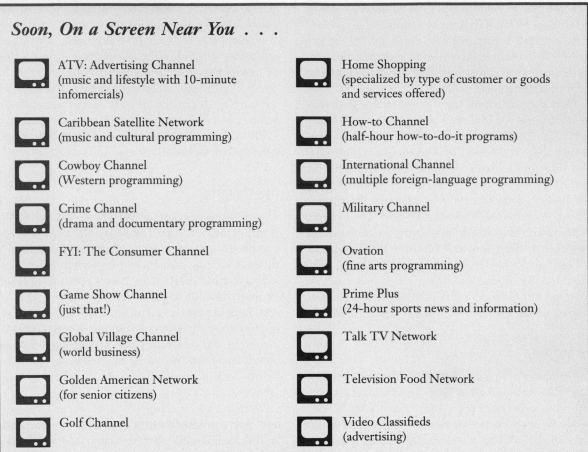

ATV: Advertising Channel
(music and lifestyle with 10-minute infomercials)

Caribbean Satellite Network
(music and cultural programming)

Cowboy Channel
(Western programming)

Crime Channel
(drama and documentary programming)

FYI: The Consumer Channel

Game Show Channel
(just that!)

Global Village Channel
(world business)

Golden American Network
(for senior citizens)

Golf Channel

History Channel
(drama and documentaries)

Home Shopping
(specialized by type of customer or goods and services offered)

How-to Channel
(half-hour how-to-do-it programs)

International Channel
(multiple foreign-language programming)

Military Channel

Ovation
(fine arts programming)

Prime Plus
(24-hour sports news and information)

Talk TV Network

Television Food Network

Video Classifieds
(advertising)

Wellness Channel
(exercise and health)

Among the many proposed program services designed to fill the soon-to-expand number of available channels are these, some of which may be available by the time you read this. Their variety indicates the expansion of niche programming given the many channels available. *Not shown* are program service spinoffs such as MTV-2, MTV-3, MTV-4, electronic bulletin boards, and computer data channels, all of which will offer additional choices.

Sources: *Broadcasting* (30 November 1992) 39; *Time* (12 April 1993): 56.

Once again, economics will determine which of the start-ups survive.

On the other hand, *standards of program taste will continue to decline as more channels compete to attract pieces of the total audience.* Broadcast program standards, already at the edge, will soon match those of cable, non-premium cable channels are already moving toward the looser standards of pay channels, and PPV (and likely DBS) delivery modes already include scrambled adult channels.

The ultimate in specialization, *video on demand,* is already here in limited form. The great increase in available channels—and the limited creativity evident thus far in programming those channels—suggests that *many new channels, especially those devoted to PPV, will increasingly be given over to repeating popular programs at varied starting times.*

● ● ● ● ● ● ● ●

16.4   Effects

Even as we learn more about the many ways media influence our lives, we realize how much remains a mystery. The reason is related, in part, to the way research is paid for, a pattern unlikely to change in the next few years.

Measuring

Audience measurements will continue to be driven more by commercial needs than by broad social science research interests or concerns. As in the past, those willing to pay for research results—advertisers selling goods and services—will largely define the progress in audience measurement.

While the commercial ratings-driven system will still be in use by the year 2000, it will differ in detail as it adjusts to the dramatic increase in channels. Greater audience fragmentation across more viewing options will make valid and reliable audience ratings increasingly difficult to obtain.

Rating companies will introduce passive peoplemeters over the next few years to meet advertiser demands for less intrusive information-gathering about *who* watches *what* and *when.* Despite measurement improvements, however, researchers will still know precious little about the all-important *why* we spend time with these services.

Researching

With the exception of audience measurement, *the pattern of electronic media research—what is researched and how that research is funded—seems unlikely to change much during the rest of the 1990s.* Given budget deficits, it seems unlikely that government will again fund major research efforts to match those of two decades ago examining television's impact on children. Research will therefore continue to be based in academic and other nonprofit centers, which will have to seek external funding for such work.

In the next few years, such social science research will likely focus on the impact of media on special audiences, including senior citizens, the very young, and those with mental handicaps.

Polling

Some observers have suggested that electronic media should build on existing rating and other research methodologies to become more directly a part of social and political decision making. Electronic polling has been widely predicted—and techniques and technologies for large-scale instant polling already exist. (Recall that Ross Perot, while campaigning for president in 1992, called for regular national and local electronic meetings as a truly democratic application of media technology.) Others refer simply to "electronic democracy."

We think such *electronic decision making will not happen—at least not in the 1990s.* For one thing, Americans tend to trust more traditional means of measuring public opinion—from voting booths to man-on-the-street interviews. For another, a system for accessing and maintaining a valid and reliable national sample for regular electronic polling has no apparent means of financial support.

Waiting

Unfortunately, not everyone will have access to the host of new service options being developed, at least not right away. New products and services are usually expensive until mass adoption brings prices down. Any programming service reliant on direct audience payment will bypass those lacking means. But a more serious problem of "haves" and "have-nots" is brewing, dividing rich and poor as well as urban and rural.

Absent an effective national policy to require or at least encourage equal access for people to at least a minimal menu of media channels, *a minority made up of rural residents, urban poor, and ethnically defined minorities risk being left behind, waiting for new media options already being enjoyed by others.* Far more people worldwide already have access to television than have indoor plumbing. What even more harmful choices will new media force on these have-nots?

Traditional broadcasting has long been the one service available to virtually everyone—provided one has access to a receiver, radio and television reception are "free." But with networks and stations under growing competitive stress from newer services, broadcasting's ability and motivation to serve marginal audiences (rural residents, urban poor, and minorities) will likely decline. This shortcoming may—and should—trigger a national policy debate on how to fill the void.

• • • • • • • •

16.5 Controls

The needs of society's have-nots and the pace of technological development indicate considerable re-evaluation of regulatory bodies in coming years. We believe that *regulation will become less important as a day-to-day concern for media, although government may play a larger role in developing national communication strategies.*

Crumbling

The traditional foundation for electronic media regulation—channel scarcity—has long since crumbled. The "public interest, convenience, or necessity" (PICON) rationale holds that a limited number of outlets requires closer regulation of electronic than of print media. But this reasoning no longer makes much sense. When PICON first appeared in the 1927 Radio Act, only about 600 radio stations were on the air. Today there are nearly 14,000 radio and television outlets, plus more than 11,000 cable systems—as well as dozens of other electronic sources of entertainment and information. In the meantime, the number of daily newspapers continues to decline.

When Congress tried to replace PICON with a market-driven standard, however, it found little agreement on how such a replacement might function in a practical fashion. Memories of that fruitless battle will keep Congress from another such comprehensive attempt in the near future.

Policing

Given the small likelihood of congressional action, the focus for change over the next few years will be on the FCC. Indeed, the Commission had already begun playing a more active regulatory role during the early months of the Clinton administration than it had played for a dozen years before.

The FCC will continue to be the primary shaper of day-to-day licensing and regulation. The relationship between the Commission and those media it licenses or otherwise oversees is, however, changing.

Given the decline of channel scarcity as a rationale, *the FCC will play less of a day-to-day administrative "traffic cop" role. Instead, it will increasingly act more as a referee among competitors, trying to find politically and economically acceptable ways for industry segments to coexist and provide improved service.* This objective will entail a difficult balancing act of seeking and shaping economic and political compromise among powerful warring parties.

Congress will continue to provide oversight (and political noise), only occasionally rising to fulfill its constitutional role of creating broad national policy—as it most recently did with the 1992 Cable Act. Business, more than Congress, will shape the needed compromises that will define the future.

We do feel, however, that *Congress will finally act*, though it may take several years, *to bring protection of intellectual property ownership up to date with technology*. The ability to protect creative ideas has long been eroding. Intellectual property (including but not limited to copyright) comes under increasing threat as digital technology makes it easier to create exact copies of programs, songs, and movies.

We also predict that Congress will restore the Fairness Doctrine—in at least some form—requiring broadcasters (and perhaps others) to cover controversial public issues and, in so doing, to cover them impartially.

Dialing

Compromise seems unlikely in one of the hottest communications policy debates of the 1990s, one already well under way. The battle over the extent to which common-carrier telephone companies ("telcos") should be allowed to participate in (or own) electronic media is one of vital concern to both industries. The outcome may well determine which industry segment ultimately achieves domestic information-age leadership. Media and telephone industries differ in outlook, regulation, technology, and purpose. Somehow those gaps will have to be bridged in the next few years.

We believe that *telcos will be allowed (or will otherwise gain) a much larger role in media*, bringing new competition to broadcasters and cable operators, and broader information-age thinking to help merge media and common-carrier concerns. The FCC's "video dial tone" scheme of the early 1990s is but the beginning of that process.

The question of whether common carriers achieve actual ownership or creative control of programming, however, remains more problematical,

especially in the near term. But certainly by the year 2000 the formerly clear distinctions between telephone and media firms will have largely disappeared.

● ● ● ● ● ● ● ●

16.6 Worldwide

Changes in the United States will be echoed in—and sometimes led by—other countries. American interests alone neither control nor limit the futures of electronic media. Technology plays a major role abroad, as it does here; but foreign political and economic shifts also have substantial impact on overseas media operations.

Evolving

Indeed, structural changes overseas will be more radical than those here. Most foreign countries are quickly moving away from their tradition of government control and operation and toward the privately owned, commercial electronic media model we have long used. While some countries—mostly former communist nations and Third World dictatorships—are changing more slowly than others, the overall trend has become clear.

By the turn of the century, most media systems around the world will look more like ours than they do now—entertainment driven and advertiser supported, operating as businesses rather than as arms of government.

This business orientation will create a snowball effect: more demand for programming (especially entertainment) on added channels in countries that until now have operated but a handful, more advertising (to pay for all those new channels), and more concern over cultural independence of those countries that produce little of their own program material.

Sharing

Our sense of time and distance continues to change as electronic media bring once-isolated places into our living rooms.

Exposure to foreign entertainment will continue to grow. Co-production will increasingly lead not only to shared costs but also to a breaking down of cultural barriers. As more channels become available around the world, so will co-production opportunities for those nations—including the United States—that have substantial production capacity.

Likewise, chances to share technology will increase. *Some countries will bypass cable television*, with its high installation costs, *opting instead for participation in a cooperative DBS service* (as is already operating in Europe and parts of Asia). The demand to develop such modern systems, especially in the countries of Central and Eastern Europe, will fuel joint research, manufacturing, and cooperative planning efforts.

Protecting

Despite these sharing trends, cultural and economic protectionism will give way only reluctantly, if at all. There is far too much at stake—economic power, employment, social and cultural self-image—for most nations to submerge their systems and industries (and, to a large extent, their very identities) in a worldwide media market. *Government policies to protect domestic media will continue to limit total free flow and trade in at least three areas:*

- *business* (consumer electronics manufacturers in France and Germany, for example, do not want to lose existing markets to Japanese competition as did the United States years ago);
- *programming* (most countries—especially such English-speaking nations as Canada and Australia—have regulations limiting how much programming may be imported); and
- *technical standards* (control of a new system being adopted worldwide is immensely valuable in itself—but often it means control of manufacturing and programming markets as well).

Choosing

Only now are many foreign countries beginning to offer audiences the degree of choice among multiple media channels that Americans have long enjoyed. Most European nations had but three or four television channels on the air in the 1970s, a situation relieved only in the 1980s with the addition of cable, satellite broadcast, and VCR options.

This trend toward more choice will accelerate—and will put additional pressure on traditional quasi-governmental broadcasters to provide more popular fare. Changes considered for and ultimately adopted by the BBC when its charter is renewed in 1996 will be a bellwether for other countries.

Added channels in many countries will boost program demand and expand larger potential markets for American and foreign production.

• • • • • • • •

16.7   Summary

Summing up our predictions on earlier pages, how different will electronic media be by the end of the decade? Two overall themes emerge as dominant.

Digital Choice

Development of digital technologies will continue at an increasingly rapid pace. In early 1993, the National Association of Broadcasters' convention showcased a "Multimedia World" demonstrating how the scope of computers and electronic media increasingly overlapped. While few broadcasters knew much about computers—and few computer programmers knew much about broadcasting—the exhibition helped pinpoint why and how fast that was changing.

Summing up the principal impacts of this increasing use of digital technology for the rest of the 1990s, we feel that:

- High-definition television, available in some homes by the year 2000, will deliver clearer, sharper pictures, especially on large-screen receivers. Likewise, digital audio broadcasting, to begin in the next few years, will deliver CD-like quality to home, auto and portable tuners.

- Direct-broadcast satellite services will bring information and entertainment to homes inadequately served by cable and broadcast television—and may compete with cabled areas as well.
- Digital signal compression will virtually eliminate the present delivery bottleneck, making space for hundreds of program channels. Viewers will be able to choose from almost limitless audio, video, and data services—some passive, some interactive—delivered by a variety of satellite and terrestrial services.

Convergence

Once-clear lines that historically have separated delivery services—radio, recording, television, cable, telephone—will continue to fade and eventually disappear. The digital revolution will both speed this process and in large measure dictate its direction.

- To meet the challenges and seize opportunities offered by digital technology, media organizations will continue their trend toward consolidation, expansion, and vertical integration.
- Some entities (many AM stations, at least one of the Big Three broadcast television networks, and possibly public television), unable to keep up, either will not survive or will change so radically in their structure and purpose as to be virtually unrecognizable.
- Former competitors (cable systems, broadcasters, telephone companies), facing constantly rising costs and growing audience fractionalization, will work more closely together in common ventures.
- Despite these developments, most audio and video programs (regardless of how delivered) will resemble what exists today—tailored to mass-entertainment tastes. These will be supplemented by a growing number of niche services filling newly available channels for special-interest audiences.

- Direct audience payment for this new abundance of programs (especially pay-per-view niche and entertainment services) will grow in importance, though advertising will remain essential.
- By decade's end most programming for most people will still be, as now, nationally distributed, advertiser supported entertainment.

And . . . looking forward to the early 21st century . . . foundations are being laid for even more dramatic changes. Key protagonists are already lining up business and technical alliances to compete better after the year 2000 when today's media and information industries will steadily converge into some form of unity. At the same time, government is seeking ways to encourage business-driven technological progress while simultaneously protecting privacy and intellectual property rights.

Which specific product and service combinations will succeed after the turn of the century is hard to discern today as we stand only at the threshold of a watershed digital revolution. As in the past, however, the key to success remains economic—predicting what people want and will be willing to pay for. Entertainment will continue to be the initial bait attracting users to help pay for technological progress.

Increasingly after 2000, media will combine interactive capacity with multimedia capabilities integrating text, sound, video, and data forms. The media as we know them now will increasingly give way to more personal means of communicating, working, buying, entertaining, and interacting. Users will communicate at least as much as they listen and watch. Miniature receiver/transmitters, multiple modes of transporting information, and universal individual identification codes will keep us in touch whether at home, work, school, or as we travel (indeed, versions are already in service—consider cellular telephones, fax modems, and televisions in airplanes).

In whatever form or format, ownership patterns, or economics, these future electronic media will remain an influential element in American life. And despite present and future flaws, they will remain largely unequaled around the world.

Further Reading

A Selective Guide to Literature on Electronic Media

Christopher H. Sterling

• •

This guide parallels text chapter and section headings offering suggestions for further reading on most topics. Limited space allows for only a representative selection of the most recent titles from a huge and growing literature. Included are the most important book-length publications as of mid-1993. Following the chapter-by-chapter sections are lists of recommended bibliographies and relevant periodicals. Although the text mentions many books included here, this guide independently assesses each title. The Bibliography details every work here and in the text.

• • • • • • • •

Prologue: Hurricane Andrew: Electronic Media in a Crisis

Because this chapter introduces ideas covered in detail in later chapters, citations for further reading are listed below. For more on "Andrew" and its aftermath, see Florida newspapers for late August and early September 1992,

as well as such national papers as the *New York Times* and *Washington Post*, and such newsweeklies as *Time* and *Newsweek*.

CHAPTER 1

Rise of Radio

1.1 Precedents Csida and Csida, *American Entertainment* (1978), provides a text and picture scrapbook approach to popular culture taken from the pages of *Billboard*, while Toll, *The Entertainment Machine* (1982), offers a concise tracing of American show business, including vaudeville, in this century. A handbook of historical statistics and trends for all media is found in Sterling and Haight, *The Mass Media* (1978). *Wonderful Inventions* (1985) is a lavish picture and recorded history of movies, recorded sound, and early broadcasting. A highly insightful analysis of the telegraph, motion picture, and radio and their impact on America is offered in Czitrom,

Media and the American Mind from Morse to McLuhan (1982).

Regarding specific media, Emery and Emery, *The Press and America* (1992), is the standard history of newspapers and magazines, while Stephens, *A History of News from the Drum to the Satellite* (1988), offers a broad-stroke review of the changing definitions of news—and of the ways it has been disseminated. Advertising's development is covered in Pope, *The Making of Modern Advertising* (1983). The two standard histories of the phonograph are Gelatt, *The Fabulous Phonograph* (1977), and the more detailed and equipment-oriented Read and Welsh, *From Tin Foil to Stereo* (1976). Useful histories of American film include Jowett, *Film* (1976), and Gomery, *Movie History: A Survey* (1991).

1.2   Wire Communication   Marvin, *When Old Technologies Were New* (1988), is one of the few studies on the impact of 19th-century electrical communication. An early but still useful survey of electrical communication history is in Harlow, *Old Wires and New Waves* (1936), covering telegraph, telephone, and radio. Davis, *Electrical and Electronic Technologies* (1981–1985), provides a technical chronology by year and by topic. Coates and Finn, *A Retrospective Technology Assessment: Submarine Telegraphy* (1979), is a fascinating analysis of the 1866 trans-Atlantic cable's impact. Brooks, *Telephone* (1976), offers an informal history of AT&T, while Pool, *The Social Impact of the Telephone* (1977), and Fischer, *America Calling* (1992), show how that impact has varied with time. Development of telecommunications industry and policy is related in Brock, *The Telecommunications Industry* (1981), while the best analysis of AT&T's breakup and its causes is Temin with Galambos, *The Fall of the Bell System* (1987).

1.3   Invention of Wireless   The premier study of patent conflict in radio is Maclaurin, *Invention and Innovation in the Radio Industry* (1949), which carries the story to early television. FTC, *Report on the Radio Industry* (1924), focuses on patents in RCA's rise. Development of GE and Westinghouse is detailed in Passer, *The Electrical Manufacturers: 1875–1900* (1953).

The definitive treatment of early wireless is the two-volume work by Aitken, *Syntony and Spark: The Origins of Radio* (1976), which relates Hertz and Marconi's work, and *The Continuous Wave* (1985), which continues the story to 1932. Leinwoll, *From Spark to Satellite* (1979), is a brief survey of radio development. Dunlap, *Radio's 100 Men of Science* (1944), provides short biographies on inventors discussed in the text. Jolly, *Marconi* (1972), is the

most recent biography of the key inventor. One of the few really good company histories in this field is Baker, *A History of the Marconi Company* (1971).

1.4   Early Wireless Services   Because of the predominant role of the U.S. Navy in this period, Howeth's *History of Communications-Electronics in the United States Navy* (1963) is essential to an understanding of nonmilitary events and international and domestic regulation as well as the cover topic. For the general role of shipboard radio, see Hancock, *Wireless at Sea* (1950), a Marconi company history of technical applications. Radio's role in the *Titanic* disaster is best told in Marcus, *The Maiden Voyage* (1969).

1.5   Radio Experimenters   Fessenden, *Fessenden* (1940), is a good biography of the inventor by his wife. Tyne, *Saga of the Vacuum Tube* (1977), is a very detailed study of the subject to about 1930. Lacking modesty but providing human-interest detail is de Forest, *Father of Radio* (1950). Compare it to Lessing, *Man of High Fidelity* (1956), a biography of Edwin Armstrong. Lewis, *Empire of the Air* (1991), offers an insightful and readable biography of early radio through the lives of de Forest, Armstrong, and Sarnoff. See also Aitken's two volumes under 1.3.

1.6   Government Monopoly: The Road *Not* Taken   See Howeth as noted under 1.4, the FTC report under 1.3, and the Archer histories under 1.8, all of which detail formation of RCA and its patent pool. For the final government ownership debate, see House CMMF, 1919.

1.7   The "First" Broadcast Station   Inception of amateur radio is related in De Soto, *Two Hundred Meters and Down* (1936). The major histories of American broadcasting include the three-volume Barnouw, *A History of Broadcasting in the United States* (1966–1970), Sterling and Kittross, *Stay Tuned: A Concise History of American Broadcasting* (1990), Hilliard and Keith, *The Broadcast Century* (1992), and the anthology edited by Lichty and Topping, *American Broadcasting* (1975). All cover both radio and television beginning with technical developments and carrying to recent years, though each is arranged differently. Best analysis of "Broadcasting's Oldest Station" is the article of that name by Baudino and Kittross (1977).

1.8   Emergence of an Industry   Ponderous in tone and not clearly organized, yet still important for its inside view of the "radio group" side of the debate, is the two-volume history by Archer, *History of Radio to 1926* (1938) and *Big Business and Radio* (1939), both biased toward RCA's point of view. For a balancing telephone company view, see Banning, *Commercial Broadcasting Pioneer* (1946), which is the story of WEAF to 1926.

1.9 How the Networks Began See the discussion of the early years of NBC and CBS in Archer's histories noted under 1.8, and also Bergreen, *Look Now, Pay Later: The Rise of Network Broadcasting* (1980). For biographies of the key leaders, see Bilby, *The General* (1986), and Smith, *In All His Glory: The Life of William S. Paley* (1990), as well as Paley, *As It Happened* (1979).

Best analysis of the early development of (mainly network) radio advertising is Hettinger, *A Decade of Radio Advertising* (1933), which includes data and documents found nowhere else. The first books on how to advertise with the new medium were Felix, *Using Radio in Sales Promotion* (1927), and Dunlap, *Advertising by Radio* (1929), both filled with fascinating detail about early network and station operations.

1.10 Developing Government's Role An overview of the period is Rosen, *The Modern Stentors: Radio Broadcasters and the Federal Government 1920–1934* (1980). Howeth, under 1.4, covers the 1910 and 1912 acts. Best study of the 1927 act is Davis, *The Law of Radio* (1927). See also House CIFC, *Regulation of Broadcasting* (1958b).

CHAPTER 2

Radio to Television

2.1 Radio in the Depression (1929–1937) For a year-by-year retrospective, see *The First 50 Years of Broadcasting* (1981), published by *Broadcasting* Magazine. Codel, *Radio and Its Future* (1930), is an anthology suggesting likely future directions for the industry. Hettinger and Neff, *Practical Radio Advertising* (1938), reflects organization and practices in the 1930s. For reference and specific data, see U.S. Bureau of the Census, *Radio Broadcasting* (1935), the first in-depth national government survey, and *Broadcasting/Cablecasting Yearbook*, an annual that began in 1935. See also the general titles listed under 1.7.

MacDonald, *Don't Touch That Dial!* (1979), and Settel, *A Pictorial History of Radio* (1967), both stress network programming, as does Slide, *Great Radio Personalities in Historic Photographs* (1982). The best analysis of the first hugely popular network program is found in Ely, *The*

Adventures of Amos 'n' Andy: A Social History of an American Phenomenon (1991).

2.2 Early Radio Controversies Late in the 1930s a whole literature criticizing radio's direction began to appear: Frost, *Is American Radio Democratic?* (1937), and Brindze, *Not to Be Broadcast: The Truth About Radio* (1937), are examples. The most detailed narrative of radio's ASCAP and AFM troubles is found in chapters 12–14 of Warner, *Radio and Television Rights* (1953). On the rise of LP recordings, see the phonograph histories under 1.1.

Several books detail radio at its pretelevision peak: Rose, *National Policy for Radio Broadcasting* (1940), is the best early analysis of structural and regulatory problems; White, *The American Radio* (1947), offers critical analysis pleading for more public service and education applications; and Landry, *This Fascinating Radio Business* (1946), describes network radio development and the peak years. The definitive official analysis of radio network structure and operations is FCC, *Report on Chain Broadcasting* (1941), which is analyzed in Robinson, *Radio Networks and the Federal Government* (1943). See as well the early chapters of Bergreen, noted under 1.9.

2.3 Television and FM Radio Emerge The best history of television's technology is Abramson, *The History of Television, 1880 to 1941* (1987), while the rise of the industry through 1941 is related in Udelson, *The Great Television Race* (1982). Winston, *Misunderstanding Media* (1986), details the inventive history of the medium as he develops a model of the innovative process. For a life of Farnsworth, see Everson, *The Story of Television* (1949). For FM's early development, see Lessing, under 1.5, and Siepmann, *Radio's Second Chance* (1946).

2.4 Broadcasting at War (1938–1946) A fascinating analysis of early radio news and comment impact is found in Culbert, *News for Everyman* (1976), while a more popular treatment is Fang, *Those Radio Commentators!* (1977). Individual biographies abound—best of the lot is Kendrick, *Prime Time: The Life of Edward R. Murrow* (1969). For television developments, see Abramson, under 2.3.

2.5 TV's Growing Pains A solid analysis of television allocation up to the late 1950s is found in House CIFC, *Network Broadcasting* (1958a). The famous "Sixth Report and Order," which ended the freeze, is found in its entirety in FCCR (*FCC Reports*), Vol. 41. That same volume includes the 1950 and final 1953 color decisions. Slide, *The Television Industry: A Historical Dictionary* (1991), is just that, stressing business organizations and their development.

2.6 Era of TV Network Dominance Three good general surveys of television development are Barnouw, *Tube of Plenty* (1990); Greenfield, *Television: The First Fifty Years* (1977), a coffee-table illustrated program history with an intelligent text; and MacDonald, *One Nation Under Television* (1990). Sturcken, *Live Television: The Golden Age of 1946–1958 in New York* (1990), helps illustrate why the period is still called "golden," while Boddy, *Fifties Television: The Industry and Its Critics* (1990), takes a broader view of the decade's developments and impact. Likewise, Watson's *The Expanding Vista: American Television in the Kennedy Years* (1990) carries the story into the early 1960s. Shulman and Youman, *How Sweet It Was* (1966), is the best picture treatment of the first 15 years of network television programming; see also Marschall, *The Golden Age of Television* (1987). For network developments, see House CIFC under 2.5; Smith and Paley under 1.9; Metz, *CBS* (1975); Goldenson, *Beating the Odds: The Untold Story Behind the Rise of ABC* (1991); and Campbell, *The Golden Years of Broadcasting* (1976) for NBC. For directories of network program series, see titles under 10.1.

2.7 Radio in an Age of Television Early textbooks offering good insight into radio industry structure and operations in this important transitional period include Siepmann, *Radio, Television and Society* (1950), focusing on impact of the media; Wolfe, *Modern Radio Advertising* (1949); and Midgley, *The Advertising and Business Side of Radio* (1948). Changes forced by television are evident in three later text or professional books: Head, *Broadcasting in America* (1956), the first edition of the present textbook; Seehafer and Laemmar, *Successful Television and Radio Advertising* (1959); and Reinch and Ellis, *Radio Station Management* (1960).

Network radio programming is described in Dunning, *Tune in Yesterday* (1976), an alphabetical guide to most program series; Stedman, *The Serials* (1977), detailing that genre on radio, films, and television; and Wertheim, *Radio Comedy* (1979). A general survey of music and radio developments is provided in Eberly, *Music in the Air: America's Changing Tastes in Popular Music, 1920–1980* (1982).

2.8 Ethical Crises of the 1950s Treatment of the quiz scandals is found in Anderson, *Television Fraud* (1978), which includes transcripts of several programs, and in Stone and Yohn, *Prime Time and Misdemeanors:*

Investigating the 1950s TV Quiz Scandal (1992), an inside account by one of the investigators. Blacklisting is discussed in Vaughn, *Only Victims: A Study of Show Business Blacklisting* (1972). Important contemporary books include the original broadcast blacklist by Counterattack, *Red Channels* (1950), Cogley's *Report on Blacklisting II: Radio-Television* (1956), and Faulk's telling of his own case in a suspenseful narrative, *Fear on Trial* (1964). FCC program regulation in this era is discussed in Baughman, *Television's Guardians: The FCC and the Politics of Programming 1958–1967* (1985).

CHAPTER 3

Cable and Newer Media

Reference statistics on trends in broadcasting and cable are found in Sterling, *Electronic Media* (1984). Useful broad background on the topics in this chapter is provided in Compaine, *Understanding New Media* (1984); Gross, *The New Television Technologies* (1991); and Singleton, *Global Impact: The New Telecommunication Technologies* (1989).

3.1 Emergence of Cable Any book on cable prior to the early 1980s is useful today only as history. Land Associates, *Television and the Wired City* (1968), is one of the earliest views of cable's potential—albeit from a broadcast point of view. Among books designed as history, the most useful is LeDuc, *Cable Television and the FCC* (1973), which carries the story through the 1972 rules.

3.2 Cable Becomes a Major Player Important policy decisions leading to approval of domestic satellites are reviewed in Magnant, *Domestic Satellite* (1977). There is as yet no overall history of pay cable (but see Mair's *Inside HBO* [1988] for part of the story). Ted Turner is profiled in Williams, *Lead, Follow, or Get Out of the Way* (1981), while Whittemore's *CNN: The Inside Story* (1990) relates the first several years of Turner's news network. Most literature on interactive cable is in research reports, but see Bretz, *Media for Interactive Communication* (1983), for a sense of both technical basics and applications. Whiteside's "Cable" (1985) is an excellent narrative of cable's development. Survey overviews of most aspects of cable are found in Roman, *Cablemania* (1983), and in Baldwin and McVoy, *Cable Communications* (1988).

3.3 Niche Options The most complete study of STV is Howard and Carroll, *Subscription Television* (1980). A substantial number of reports appeared during DBS's original early 1980s heyday; of them, the best are Taylor, *Direct-to-Home Satellite Broadcasting* (1980), and NTIA, *Direct Broadcast Satellites: Policies, Prospects, and Potential Competition* (1981). See also Gross and Singleton, listed in the introductory note for this chapter section.

3.4 Electronics Revolution There is a growing literature on the development of computers and microelectronics. One good survey is Augarten, *Bit by Bit: An Illustrated History of Computers* (1984). Queisser, *The Conquest of the Microchip* (1988), offers a brief history of the "chip" and its impact. A readable popular account is Forester, *High-Tech Society: The Story of the Information Technology Revolution* (1987). Williams, *The New Telecommunications: Infrastructure for the Information Age* (1991), relates the broad social, cultural, and political impacts of these changes.

3.5 Home Entertainment Center Inglis, *Behind the Tube: A History of Broadcasting Technology and Business* (1990), offers an RCA-biased view of broadcast and related service history. Development of video recording is detailed in Marlow and Secunda, *Shifting Time and Space: The Story of Videotape* (1991); Nmungwun, *Video Recording Technology* (1989); and Lardner, *Fast Forward: Hollywood, the Japanese, and the VCR Wars* (1987), the last focusing on the legal issues between movie studios and VCR makers. Economic and political assessments of home video are found in Noam, *Video Media Competition: Regulation, Economics, and Technology* (1985). Graham, *RCA and the VideoDisc: The Business of Research* (1986), suggests how the company fumbled the technology. EIA, *The U.S. Consumer Electronics Industry in Review* (annual), is a free booklet of statistics and text showing trends in electronic media components. There is a large literature, much of it now badly dated, on teletext and videotex. One comprehensive assessment is offered in Tydeman et al., *Teletext and Videotex in the United States* (1982). Wilson, *Technologies of Control: The New Interactive Media for the Home* (1988), reviews the potential for videotex. HDTV titles are covered under 5.9.

3.6 TV Network Decline The FCC network investigation is covered in FCC (Network Inquiry Special Staff), *New Television Networks* (1980a), which provides a great deal of economic information on television network structure and operations as they existed before incursions of cable and other services. Good analyses of network problems are found in two books stressing how the shift in network ownership changed their outlook and operations: Auletta, *Three Blind Mice: How the TV Networks Lost Their Way* (1991), which offers incisive behind-the-scenes details, and Williams, *Beyond Control: ABC and the Fate of the Networks* (1989), focusing on the dramatic shifts within one network. Block, *Outfoxed* (1990), relates the rise of the Fox network, while Shawcross, *Murdoch* (1993), is the best study of the man behind Fox and many other media.

3.7 Broadcasting—The Rest of the Story Useful analysis of the modern radio business appears in Fornatale and Mills, *Radio in the Television Age* (1980); see also the books listed under 2.7. McLean, *RadioOutlook II: New Forces Shaping the Industry* (1991), is an insightful industry view of the current market. Turow, *Media Systems in Society: Understanding Industries, Strategies, and Power* (1992), investigates the factors in rapid media changes in the 1990s. Hunn, *Starting and Operating Your Own FM Radio Station* (1988), details the process amidst all these changes.

3.8 Sorting It Out Useful background on the fast-changing "telco"-in-the-media scene is found in the following: Johnson and Reed, *Residential Broadband Services by Telephone Companies* (1990), and Johnson, *Telephone Company Entry into Cable Television* (1992), both of which review the technology, economics, and public policy issues involved; Brotman, *Telephone Company and Cable Television Competition* (1990), an anthology of key articles and documents; and NAB, *Telco Fiber and Video Market Entry* (1989b), a protectionist broadcast industry view.

CHAPTER 4

How Broadcasting and Cable Work

A good dictionary of media technology will help in Chapters 4 and 5. Among several available are Graham, *The Facts on File Dictionary of Telecommunications* (1983); Weiner, *Webster's New World Dictionary of Media and Communications* (1990); Jones, *Jones Dictionary of Cable Television Terminology* (1987); Diamant, *The Broadcast Communications Dictionary* (1989); Ellmore, *NTC's Mass Media Dictionary* (1991); Penney, *The Facts on File Dictionary of Film and Broadcast Terms* (1991); and Browne, *Film Video Terms and Concepts* (1992). Several of these include business as well as technology terms.

Pierce and Noll, *Signals: The Science of Telecommunications* (1990), details technical basics; it includes some history but assumes no prior knowledge. Ebersole, *Broadcast Technology Worktext* (1992), uses text and graphics to introduce many topics discussed here. Pavlik and Dennis, *Demystifying Media Technology* (1993), is a useful anthology survey. In-depth background on all topics discussed in this and the next chapter is provided in *NAB Engineering Handbook* (1992), which *does* assume a technical background on the part of readers.

4.1–4.2 Electromagnetism: Sound and Radio Waves A fascinating discussion of the kinds and impact of sound is found in Schaefer, *The Tuning of the World* (1977). Truax, *Acoustic Communication* (1985), deals with all aspects of sound. A good diagram-illustrated discussion of sound modulation is offered in Beck, *Words and Waves* (1967). Alten, *Audio in Media* (1990), details waves and many other aspects of electromagnetism discussed in this chapter.

4.3–4.4 Modulation and Propagation Technical details on these topics can also be found in *NAB Engineering Handbook* (1992).

4.5 Spectrum Use and Abuse Levin, *The Invisible Resource: Use and Regulation of the Radio Spectrum* (1971), which after two decades remains the definitive study, deals equally with technical, economic, and political aspects of the topic. The official detailed record of frequency use and management in the United States is provided in NTIA, *Manual of Regulations and Procedures for Federal Radio Frequency Management* (regularly updated). Glatzer, *Who Owns the Rainbow?* (1984), is a simplified discussion of spectrum-use tradeoffs. NTIA, *U.S. Spectrum Management Policy: Agenda for the Future* (1991), offers a good review of current thinking.

4.6–4.7 AM and FM Stations See materials under introductory note to this chapter.

4.8 Shortwave Broadcasting The standard annually revised sourcebook for all radio "hams" is American Radio Relay League, *The Radio Amateur's Handbook*. Two useful guides including considerable technical background are Helms, *Shortwave Listening Guidebook* (1991), and the annually revised *Passport to World Band Radio*.

4.9–4.10 Electronic Pictures, TV Stations There is a substantial technical literature on television, including NAB, as listed in the introductory note for this chapter section. Two of the best introductions to television basics are the dated but still valuable Fink and Lutyens, *The Physics of Television* (1960), directed at the layperson, and Noll, *Television Technology: Fundamentals and Future Prospects* (1988b), which uses graphics and clear text to survey all of this material and assumes no prior knowledge. Hartwig, *Basic TV Technology* (1990), also offers clear diagrams and brief text descriptions. Jackson and Townsend, *TV and Video Engineer's Reference Book* (1991), as the title suggests, does assume a fair bit of background. Zettl, *Television Production Handbook* (1992), is a standard text.

4.11 Cable Systems See Baldwin and McVoy, *Cable Communications* (1988), and Harrell, *The Cable Television Technical Handbook* (1985).

CHAPTER 5

Relays, Recording, and the Digital Revolution

Given the rapid pace of change, periodical articles are essential to stay current with the increasing digitalization of electronic media; see the periodicals listing on pages 599–600. Lyle and McLeod, *Communication Media and Change* (1993), offers an excellent nontechnical introduction to the topics discussed in this chapter. Grant and Sung, *Communication Technology Update* (1992), is the first version of what will be an annual review.

5.1 How Technologies Interrelate A dated but interesting approach to topics considered in this chapter is found in Bretz, *A Taxonomy of Communication Media* (1970), which compares interrelationships of transmission and recorded technologies and their applications. A social science research approach to many of the same questions is found in Rogers, *Communication Technology: The New Media in Society* (1986). See also the titles discussed under 3.4 and 3.5. Regarding ENG equipment, see Yoakam and Cremer, *ENG: Television News and the New Technology* (1988).

5.2 Terrestrial Relays See the material discussed under Chapter 4.

5.3 Satellite Relays For an excellent and clear introduction to how communication satellites work, see Pelton, *The "How To" of Satellite Communications* (1991), and

Wood, *Satellite Communications and DBS Systems* (1992b). Prentiss, *Satellite Communication* (1987), and Binkowski, *Satellite Information Systems* (1988), are other good choices for initial background reading that don't require much prior knowledge. The annual reports of NASA, Comsat, and Intelsat are good current data sources. Two useful annuals with very detailed directories of all current satellites (including capacity and coverage patterns) are Long, *World Satellite Almanac*, and *International Satellite Directory*, either of which can update what is provided in this section.

5.4 Fiber-Optic Relays For background on fiber, including applications, see Chaffee, *The Rewiring of America: The Fiber Optics Revolution* (1988); Reed, *Residential Fiber Optic Networks: An Engineering and Economic Analysis* (1992); and Yates et al., *Fiber Optics and CATV Business Strategy* (1990), each of which details both the technology and the many ways it is being used.

5.5 Analog Sound Recording Alten, *Audio in Media* (1990), is a detailed guide to all aspects of sound, including recording methods and techniques. One useful diagram-illustrated guide is Overman, *Understanding Sound, Video and Film Recording* (1978).

5.6 Analog Video Recording For background on all these systems, see the titles under 3.5.

5.7–5.8 Digital Signal Processing and Recording A very useful introduction for those without any technical background is provided in Lebow, *The Digital Connection: A Layman's Guide to the Information Age* (1991).

5.9 High-Definition Television The literature here is only just beginning to appear. Initial studies, all issued prior to selection of an American technical standard in 1994, include Benson and Fink, *HDTV: Advanced Television for the 1990s* (1991); Stan Prentiss, *HDTV: High-Definition Television* (1990); and Rice, *HDTV: The Politics, Policies, and Economics of Tomorrow's Television* (1990). See also NAB, *NAB HDTV World Conference Proceedings* (1991–1993), for largely technical papers leading to selection of a technical standard. As soon as the standard is picked, more books will appear in short order.

5.10 Digital Radio As this book goes to press, nearly all information on DAB is restricted to periodicals; but see De Sonne, *Digital Audio Broadcasting: Status Report and Outlook* (1990), for an industry assessment.

CHAPTER 6
Organization and Operations

Useful background reading on media structure and operations, the subjects of Chapters 6 and 7, is found in two books by Turow: *The Media Industries* (1984) and *Media Systems in Society* (1992). Picard, *Media Economics* (1989); Vogel, *Entertainment Industry Economics: A Guide for Financial Analysis* (1990); and Owen and Wildman, *Video Economics* (1992), also offer valuable assessments of how the media industry marketplace operates.

6.1 The Commercial Broadcast Station Pringle et al., *Electronic Media Management* (1991), and Sherman, *Telecommunications Management: The Broadcast and Cable Industries* (1987), shed useful light on day-to-day operations of stations. Keith and Krause, *The Radio Station* (1993), and Hilliard, *Television Station Operations and Management* (1989), are concise handbooks of current thinking about station management.

6.2 Commercial Broadcast Networks The last official—and now seriously out of date—analysis is the FCC Network Inquiry Special Staff, *New Television Networks* (1980a). The economic and political lessons of that two-year study are clearly brought out in Besen et al., *Misregulating Television: Network Dominance and the FCC* (1984). This material is useful historically in terms of what experts predicted would happen as new media developed.

6.3 Cable Television The standard annual reference directories of systems, networks, and owners are *Broadcasting/Cablecasting Yearbook* (with various titles over the years), and *Television Factbook*, both of which include large cable sections and statistics. Baldwin and McVoy, *Cable Communications* (1988), is the best overall survey of the industry and its operations.

6.4 Capital Investment Other than investment company and corporate annual reports and books cited in the introductory note to this chapter, about the only general information on this topic appears in the NAB's *Radio Financial Report* and *Television Financial Report*, issued annually. These detail expenses and investments for different sizes of stations in different sized markets, based on an annual national survey. NAB ceased publishing the radio report in 1993.

6.5 Ownership Turnover Each year in a January or

February issue, *Broadcasting* reviews major sales and transfers of broadcast licenses and cable operation in the previous year. A very clear and detailed guide to the process is Krasnow et al., *Buying or Building a Broadcast Station in the 1990s* (1991). Industry structure and FCC rules are discussed in Besen and Johnson, *An Assessment of the Federal Communication Commission's Group Ownership Rules* (1984); see also Sterling, in Compaine, *Who Owns the Media?* (1982). A strong attack on what it describes as an overly concentrated media ownership is found in Bagdikian, *The Media Monopoly* (1992). *The Knowledge Industry 200* (1987) provides a detailed breakout of holdings of the major media firms in the 1980s, along with some sense of corporate structure and operation.

6.6 Personnel A useful descriptive guide to career options is found in Reed and Reed, *Career Opportunities in Television, Cable, and Video* (1990); see also Napier, *Looking for Employment in the Broadcasting Industry: Getting Started* (1991). Until 1981, the FCC collected and reported annual broadcast and cable television employment information—the only official source now is the Bureau of Labor Statistics of the Department of Labor. The Commission does annually compile minority employment information.

CHAPTER 7

Revenues and Profits

See the titles noted at the beginning of Chapter 6—they are useful here as well.

7.1–7.2 Advertising and Commercial Announcements Barnouw, *The Sponsor* (1978), offers a critical essay on development of the advertiser's role in radio and television, supplemented with photos and text in Hall, *Mighty Minutes: An Illustrated History of Television's Best Commercials* (1984). Poltrack, *Television Marketing: Network, Local, and Cable* (1983), remains a valuable guide to the buying and selling of video time. Latest practices are evident in Zeigler and Howard, *Broadcast Advertising* (1991), and in Warner and Buchman, *Broadcast and Cable Selling* (1993), both of which offer details on how the process works. Any of several advertising texts can usefully supplement this material.

7.3 Cable Advertising Three books review cable advertising: Batra and Glazer, *Cable TV Advertising: In Search of the Right Formula* (1989), is a compilation of 11 papers

by academics and business leaders; Jones et al., *Cable Advertising: New Ways to New Business* (1986), is a concise "how to do it" guide; and Kaatz, *Cable Advertiser's Handbook* (1985), offers a more detailed approach. See also Warner and Buchman, under 7.2.

7.4–7.6 Advertising Rates, Sales, and Standards Duncan, *American Radio* (annual), provides comparative rate information for most radio markets. Regular issues of *Standard Rate and Data Service* reprint some radio, television, and cable rate cards for many markets—though most stations began to hold back on printing rate cards in SRDS in the 1980s because of rapid changes in the industry.

7.7 Alternative Revenue Sources For the latest developments on cable subscriber fees and home shopping networks, see the periodicals listed on pages 599–600.

7.8–7.9 Profit and Loss and Bottom Line Broadcasting See the NAB reports under 6.4.

CHAPTER 8

Noncommercial Services

The literature on noncommerical and public radio and television is very thin: little new writing has appeared in recent years.

8.1 Development Gibson, *Public Broadcasting: The Role of the Federal Government, 1912–1976* (1977), details the growing federal financial support function, while Blakely, *To Serve the Public Interest* (1979), provides an overall historical picture. CCET, *Public Television* (1967), is the landmark Carnegie report. The second Carnegie report is CCFPB, *A Public Trust* (1979). The shape of public broadcasting after a decade of the new structure is discussed in Wood and Wylie, *Educational Telecommunications* (1977). The debate behind the national organizations is covered in Avery and Pepper, *The Politics of Interconnection* (1979). A good assessment of the early political battles is found in Stone, *Nixon and the Politics of Public Television* (1985).

8.2 Networks The many statistical reports issued by the Corporation for Public Broadcasting (901 E St. NW, Washington, D.C. 20004)—especially *Status Report on Public Broadcasting* (title varies; issued every several years) and the CPB *Annual Report*, which details spending and the overall shape of public radio and television—are invaluable. The most detailed discussion of public radio is found in NAPTS's *Public Television and Radio and State Governments* (1984).

8.3   Stations   See the titles listed under 8.2.

8.4   Economics   Current information will be found in the most recent hearings before the House Committee on Energy and Commerce regarding the budget request of the Corporation for Public Broadcasting, and in the CPB *Annual Report*. The TCAF *Final Report* (1983) is a still-useful source of data on the advertising experiment and other funding ideas.

8.5–8.6   TV Program Sources and Programming See NAPTS, *FYI: Facts About America's Public TV Stations* (1992), for the latest summary information. See also the CPB *Annual Report*.

8.7   Noncommercial Radio Programming   Giovannoni, *Radio Intelligence 1988–1990* (1991a), and Giovannoni et al., *Public Radio Programming Strategies* (1992), offer the most current thinking on this topic. Every two years a detailed content analysis of the major public radio stations appears in the form of CPB's *Public Radio Programming Content by Category*.

8.8   Audiences Giovannoni, *AM Radio Listening* (1991), and Giovannoni et al., *Audience 88: A Comprehensive Analysis of Public Radio Listeners* (1988), are the best sources for radio. Frank and Greenberg, *Audiences for Public Television* (1982), is a useful, though now dated, assessment based on a national survey.

8.9   Changing Roles   Two early and thoughtful traditional analyses of what public television can and should be are found in Blakely, *The People's Instrument: A Philosophy of Programming for Public Television* (1971), and Macy, *To Irrigate a Wasteland* (1974). The latest assessment is the Twentieth Century Fund's *Quality Time?* (1993).

CHAPTER 9

Programs and Programming

A number of books are useful for this and the following chapter. Among them, Eastman's *Broadcast/Cable Programming* (1993) is the most inclusive assessment dealing with strategies for all types of stations and systems. For another detailed analysis, see Carroll and Davis, *Electronic*

Media Programming (1993). Brown, *Les Brown's Encyclopedia of Television* (1992), is a very good reference with entries on all aspects of programming. Altschuler and Grossvogel, *Changing Channels: America in TV Guide* (1992), assesses television through the eyes of the weekly magazine.

9.1   Economic Constraints   The best discussion of traditional network program economics is found in the FCC Network Inquiry report (see 3.6). Included are documents and analysis of network-affiliate contracts, compensation schemes, program procurement, etc. Owen and Wildman, listed in the introductory note for Chapter 6, is a valuable study of the program distribution market as it operates today.

9.2   Syndication   See the titles under 10.6.

9.3   Program Types   For this category, all of the titles listed for Chapter 10 are appropriate.

9.4   Entertainment Program Sources   A unique study of the writers behind most television entertainment is found in Stempel, *Storytellers to the Nation* (1992). Another title, which speaks to the huge amount of *non*success in television, is Goldberg, *Unsold Television Pilots 1955 Through 1988* (1990). Marc and Thompson, *Prime Time, Prime Movers* (1992), focuses on program producers past and present, while Kuney, *Take One: Television Directors on Directing* (1990), interviews ten key examples.

9.5   News and Sports Sources   A highly useful overview of how radio and television news developed is provided in Bliss, *Now the News* (1991). Frank, *Out of Thin Air* (1991), also takes an historical view (specifically of NBC news, which the author long headed), commenting on sources and approaches.

9.6   Scheduling Practices   Several books describe the seasonal programming process in television, among them Gitlin, *Inside Prime Time* (1983), and Cantor, *Prime-Time Television* (1992), a pioneering study of the production process. All of them deal with the institutions and major players in program decision making. For more on the strategies discussed here, see Eastman plus Carroll and Davis listed in the introductory note for this chapter section.

9.7   Program Promotion   Promotion in broadcasting is assessed and described in Eastman and Klein, *Promotion and Marketing for Broadcasting and Cable* (1991), and in Bergendorff, *Broadcast Advertising and Promotion* (1983).

CHAPTER 10

Network, Syndicated, Local

Books on the programming process are listed in the previous chapter section. Here we include titles on specific program types or formats—and can only briefly sample a substantial and fast-growing literature. Basic reference (little narrative information, but a host of detailed charts and tables allowing the tracing of network schedules), is found in the two books by Shapiro: *Television Network Prime-Time Programming, 1948–1988* (1989) and *Television Network Daytime and Late-Night Programming, 1959–1989* (1990), which provides hard-to-find information. Inman, *The TV Encyclopedia* (1991), and Parish and Terrace, *The Complete Actors' Television Credits, 1948–1988* (1989–1990), detail specific credits of actors, actresses, and other creative people.

10.1 Prime-Time Network Television Entertainment As one might expect, there is a massive literature on this topic, with at least one book for every popular series. For series program reference, see Brooks and Marsh, *The Complete Directory to Prime Time Network TV Shows* (1992), or McNeil, *Total Television* (1991), which includes some cable coverage; for details of specific episodes, see the six-volume Gianakos, *Television Drama Series Programming* (1978–1992). Two recent case studies of comedy programs are Alley and Brown, *Murphy Brown: Anatomy of a Sitcom* (1990), and Fuller, *The Cosby Show* (1992). Eisner and Krinsky, *Television Comedy Series: An Episode Guide to 153 TV Sitcoms in Syndication* (1984), details the enduring television genre. Turow, *Playing Doctor: Television, Storytelling and Medical Power* (1989), assesses one popular dramatic format. Two broad surveys of recent prime-time programming that assess what television tells us about ourselves are McCrohan, *Prime Time, Our Time* (1990), and Taylor, *Prime Time Families* (1989).

10.2 Non-Prime-Time Network Television Entertainment The literature on daytime serials is large: Stedman (listed under 2.4) offers the best history of serials in films and broadcasting; Matelski, *The Soap Opera Evolution* (1988), compares and contrasts plots, characters, audiences, and theme trends of major programs; and Williams, *"It's Time for My Story": Soap Opera Sources, Structure, and Response* (1992), seeks out the patterns within such programming. DeLong, *Quiz Craze: America's Infatuation with Game Shows* (1991), offers an informal history of the format. Matelski, *Daytime Television Programming* (1991), is a concise review of all daytime formats.

10.3 Network Television Sports Programs O'Neil, *The Game Behind the Game: High Stakes, High Pressure in Television Sports* (1989), reviews the changing role of professional sports, as does Klatell and Marcus, *Sports for Sale: Television, Money, and the Fans* (1988). Chandler, *Television and National Sport: The United States and Britain* (1988), compares and contrasts specific sports and their coverage in the two countries. Wenner, *Media, Sports, and Society* (1989), is a collection of 13 academic research papers. Details of how the games get on the air are found in Wyche et al., *Sports on Television: A New Ball Game for Broadcasters* (1990), and Hitchcock, *Sportscasting* (1991).

10.4 Network Television News and Public-Affairs Programs Here again, the literature is huge and growing—some sources are descriptive, some scholarly; many are highly critical. Among the best are Bliss, *Now the News* (1991), which offers a detailed overall history of radio and television news; Frank, *Out of Thin Air* (1991), which relates the development of NBC News as seen by a long-time head of that department; Goldberg and Goldberg, *Anchors: Brokaw, Jennings, Rather and the Evening News* (1990), which details the key people and their backgrounds; and the earlier but still useful Matusow, *The Evening Stars* (1983), a very readable narrative on development of the network news anchor. Ellerbee's *"And So It Goes"* (1980) is better than most news memoirs. The rise and decline of network television documentaries are detailed in three histories: Bluem, *Documentary in American Television* (1965), covering the years through the early 1960s; Hammond, *The Image Decade* (1981), for the 1965–1975 period; and Einstein, *Special Edition* (1987), which details all such programs through 1979.

10.5 Network Children's Programs A massive study of the quantity of programming provided for young children is FCC, *Television Programming for Children* (1979), which found little to cheer about. Definitive directories include Woolery's two-volume *Children's Television: The First Thirty-Five Years, 1946–1981* (1983–1984) and the same author's *Animated TV Specials: The Complete Directory to the First 25 Years, 1962–1987* (1989).

10.6 Syndicated Television Programs As no book-length analysis of the syndication process exists, see Eastman and Carroll and Davis as listed in the introductory note for Chapter 9. For an annotated directory, see Erickson, *Syndicated Television: The First Forty Years, 1947–1987* (1989). The very special world of syndicated religion is discussed in Hoover, *Mass Media Religion: The Social Sources of the Electronic Church* (1988), and in Bruce, *Pray*

TV: Televangelism in America (1990). Abelman and Hoover, *Religious Television: Controversies and Conclusions* (1990), is a compilation of nearly 30 scholarly analyses on all aspects of the topic. Ferre, *Channels of Belief: Religion and American Commercial Television* (1990), includes discussion of religious news and advertising spots as well as of religious watchdog groups.

10.7 Locally Produced Television Programs Shaffer and Wheelwright, *Creating Original Programming for Cable TV* (1983), includes a discussion of access programming. Henson, *Television Weathercasting: A History* (1990), is the only available coverage of this topic.

10.8–10.9 Radio Network, Syndicated, and Local Programs The inception of rock music on radio is the subject of Smith, *The Pied Pipers of Rock 'n' Roll: Radio Deejays of the 50s and 60s* (1989), and of Garay, *Gordon McClendon* (1992), which details the life of an important pioneer in station program innovation. Modern approaches—especially to music—are evident in MacFarland, *Contemporary Radio Programming Strategies* (1990). Levin, *Talk Radio and the American Dream* (1987), gets behind this increasingly hot format. Halper, *Full-Service Radio: Programming for the Community* (1991), and the same author's *Radio Music Directing* (1991) are current views of the programming process. See also the titles under 2.7 and 3.7.

10.10 Program Critique Berg and Wenner, *Television Criticism: Approaches and Applications* (1991), is the definitive treatment of what is being, and can be, done. Lemert, *Criticising the Media* (1989), reviews scholarly analyses of critical writing. Mander's *Four Arguments for the Elimination of Television* (1978), while old, remains useful, highly critical, and thought provoking—even though some of its arguments are pushed to the extreme.

CHAPTER 11

Ratings

Good background reading for all parts of this chapter is found in Webster and Lichty, *Ratings Analysis: Theory and Practice* (1991). See also the definitive historical treatment by a long-time practitioner: Beville, *Audience Ratings: Radio, Television, Cable* (1988). Both discuss major firms and their development, methods used, problem areas, and likely directions. Buzzard, *Electronic Media Ratings:*

Turning Audiences into Dollars and Sense (1992), is a brief survey. For terminology, see Fletcher's *Broadcast Research Definitions* (1988).

11.1–11.3 Ratings Business: Collecting Data and Sampling Arbitron and Nielsen provide detailed and regularly updated booklets regarding their radio and television data-gathering methods on request. See also the titles described in the introductory note for this chapter.

11.4 Determining Ratings and Shares Heath and Harshorn, *Numbers to Dollars: Using Audience Estimates to Sell Radio* (1991), is a practical guide aimed at station personnel. A useful station workbook on how to use ratings is found in Fletcher, *Squeezing Profits Out of Ratings: A Manual for Radio Managers, Sales Managers and Programmers* (1985).

11.5 Use and Abuse of Ratings See the titles listed in the introductory note for this chapter.

11.6 Broadcast Audiences The literature on this topic is rapidly expanding and greatly improving in overall quality. Barwise and Ehrenberg, *Television and Its Audience* (1988), is a concise survey of a wealth of research. Meyrowitz's *No Sense of Place: The Impact of Electronic Media on Social Behavior* (1985) is a popularly written survey, covering all aspects of television's role. Kubey and Csikszentmihalyi, *Television and the Quality of Life: How Viewing Shapes Everyday Experience* (1990), applies an "experience sampling" method for its current assessment of how we use the tube and what that use does to us. Condrey, *The Psychology of Television* (1989), is a valuable assessment of previous research organized into a new approach. Wober, *The Use and Abuse of Television: A Social Psychological Analysis of the Changing Screen* (1988), takes a critical approach. Ang, *Desperately Seeking the Audience* (1991), compares and contrasts European and American television audience information and research methods.

Changes in television audience make-up and preferences can be traced through Steiner, *The People Look at Television* (1963), Bower, *Television and the Public* (1973), and Bower, *The Changing Television Audience in America* (1985), which report, respectively, on parallel national surveys taken in 1960, 1970, and 1980. See also the books cited for Chapter 12.

11.7 Cable Audiences Heeter and Greenberg, *Cableviewing* (1988), is a compilation of some 20 papers on different aspects of watching cable in the 1980s.

11.8 VCR Audiences Dobrow, *Social and Cultural Aspects of VCR Use* (1990), and Levy, *The VCR Age: Home Video and Mass Communication* (1989), are pioneering collections of research papers by several authors on most applications of VCRs.

11.9 Other Applied Research Dominick and Fletcher, *Broadcasting Research Methods* (1985), is a compilation of 20 original articles on all aspects of electronic media research, both scholarly and business oriented. Broader instruction in methods across all media is found in Wimmer and Dominick, *Mass Media Research: An Introduction* (1991); Adams, *Social Survey Methods for Mass Media Research* (1989); Jensen and Jankowski, *A Handbook of Qualitative Methodologies for Mass Communication Research* (1991); and Hsia, *Mass Communications Research Methods: A Step-by-Step Approach* (1988). A short survey guide to writing research papers with different methods is Berger, *Media Research Techniques* (1991).

CHAPTER 12

Impact

Of value throughout this chapter is the review of current research that appears every several years in *Annual Review of Psychology* and in the occasional volumes (about every other year) in the series edited by Dervin et al., *Progress in Communication Sciences* (1979–1991). Harris, *A Cognitive Psychology of Mass Communication* (1989), offers a useful assessment of current thinking.

A good introduction to communication theory is De-Fleur and Ball-Rokeach, *Theories of Mass Communication* (1988); see also McQuail, *Mass Communication Theory* (1983), and the graphic approach in McQuail and Windahl, *Communication Models for the Study of Mass Communications* (1993).

12.1 Development of Effects Research Books taking an historical look at audience research include Lerner and Nelson's *Communication Research—A Half Century Appraisal* (1977) and Lowery and DeFleur's *Milestones in Mass Communication Research* (1988). A dated but classic overview of early research is Klapper, *The Effects of Mass Communication* (1960).

12.2 News There is a huge literature on all aspects of television news impact. Among the most recent studies are Weaver and Wilhoit, *The American Journalist: A Por-*

trait of U.S. News People and Their Work (1991), a comparative survey of print and broadcast journalists and their backgrounds; Campbell's *60 Minutes and the News: A Mythology for Middle America* (1991), a study of the continuingly popular CBS program; and Dayan and Katz, *Media Events: The Live Broadcasting of History* (1992), which describes how media cover and effect historical events.

12.3 World Events Of the many books on America's experience in Vietnam, two stand out for their media treatment: Braestrup, *Big Story: How the American Press and Television Reported and Interpreted the Crisis of Tet 1968 in Vietnam and Washington* (1977), which dissects the turning point in the war, and Hallin, *The "Uncensored War": The Media and Vietnam* (1986), which divides wartime coverage into two segments: before and after 1965, when American intervention dramatically increased. Regarding more recent military actions, see Dennis et al., *The Media at War: The Press and the Persian Gulf Conflict* (1991); Fialka, *Hotel Warriers: Covering the Gulf War* (1991); and H. Smith, *The Media and the Gulf War* (1992).

Terrorism and the media are discussed in Dobkin, *Tales of Terror: Television News and the Construction of the Terrorist Threat* (1992), and in Alali and Eke, *Media Coverage of Terrorism: Methods of Diffusion* (1991).

12.4 Election Politics A standard text treatment is found in Graber, *Mass Media and American Politics* (1993), while Jamieson, *Packaging the Presidency: A History and Criticism of Presidential Campaign Advertising* (1992), provides an historical account. Diamond and Bates, *The Spot: The Rise of Political Advertising on Television* (1992), focuses on television's role. Entman, *Democracy Without Citizens: Media and the Decay of American Politics* (1989), argues that media play too negative a role and that many improvements are needed.

Of the large literature devoted to media in specific campaigns, see Dennis et al., *The Media and Campaign '92: A Series of Special Election Reports* (1992–1993). Sabato, *Feeding Frenzy: How Attack Journalism Has Transformed American Politics* (1991), details a fairly recent trend. Hirsch, *Talking Heads: Political Talk Shows and Their Star Pundits* (1991), details another relatively new media phenomenon.

Presidential candidate debates are discussed in a veritable shelf of books, among them Jamieson and Birdsell, *Presidential Debates: The Challenge of Creating an Informed Electorate* (1988); Hellweg et al., *Televised Presidential Debates* (1992); and Lemert et al., *News Verdicts, the Debates, and Presidential Campaigns* (1991).

12.5 Government The best historical survey of research prior to 1975 is Kraus and Davis, *The Effects of Mass Communication on Political Behavior* (1976). Donovan and Scherer, *Unsilent Revolution: Television News and American Public Life* (1992), is a measured treatment of media coverage of elections and government in the 1948–1991 period. Foote, *Television Access and Political Power: The Networks, the Presidency, and the "Loyal Opposition"* (1990), reviews media policies regarding coverage of the White House. Tebbel and Watts, *The Press and the Presidency* (1985), assesses noncampaign relationships historically. The struggle over television coverage of Congress is detailed in Garay, *Congressional Television: A Legislative History* (1984). Government as communicator is the subject of Shoemaker, *Communication Campaigns About Drugs: Government, Media and the Public* (1989).

Greenberg and Parker, *The Kennedy Assassination and the American Public* (1965), is a classic analysis of media in a national crisis. More recent crises are reviewed in Nimmo and Combs, *Nightly Horrors: Crisis Coverage in Television Network News* (1985), and in Walters et al., *Bad Tidings: Communication and Catastrophe* (1989).

12.6 Entertainment Studies of minorities, stereotyping, and media include MacDonald, *Blacks and White TV: African-Americans in Television Since 1948* (1992), and Greenberg, *Mexican-Americans and the Mass Media* (1983). Marc's *Demographic Vistas: Television in American Culture* (1984) reviews the general impact of television entertainment programming. Winn's *The Plug-In Drug: Television, Children, and the Family* (1985) is sometimes overwrought, but suggests that parental control of "kidvid" is crucial.

Scholarly research on children's use of television is reviewed by Comstock and Paik, *Television and the American Child* (1991), and Liebert et al., *The Early Window: The Effects of Television on Children and Youth* (1987). See also Van Evra, *Television and Child Development* (1990); Bryant, ed., *Television and the American Family* (1990), which includes recent scholarly assessments of television's impact; and Lull, *Inside Family Viewing: Ethnographic Research on Television's Audiences* (1990), which reviews studies here and overseas.

12.7 Violence The Surgeon General's committee's work is found in Surgeon General, *Television and Growing Up* (1972). The second such government committee reported its work in *Television and Behavior: Ten Years of Scientific Progress and Implications for the Eighties* (1983). The APA study cited in the text, which summarizes a decade of research after the reports above, is Huston et al., *Big World, Small Screen: The Role of Television in American Society* (1992).

12.8 Advertising Any good survey text on advertising will provide an overview of recent research findings. See also the titles listed for Chapter 7.

12.9 Policymaking The definitive study of the impact of scholarly research on policy is Rowland's *The Politics of TV Violence: Policy Uses of Communication Research* (1983), which focuses on the first Surgeon General's committee. Two other studies relating research to policy are Donnerstein et al., *The Question of Pornography: Research Findings and Policy Implications* (1987), and Linsky, *Impact: How the Press Affects Federal Policymaking* (1986).

CHAPTER 13

Regulation and Licensing

Note A: General Background Several books provide background for Chapters 13 and 14. For the history of early broadcast regulation, see the titles noted under 1.10. In addition, the following two-volume works are excellent for tracing early broadcast policy development: Socolow, *The Law of Radio Broadcasting* (1939); and Warner, *Radio and Television Law* (1948) and *Radio and Television Rights* (1953). A chronological collection of some of the most important legal cases and other documents is provided in Kahn, *Documents of American Broadcasting* (1984). Recent casebooks on broadcast and cable regulation that include extensive excerpts from FCC and court decisions as well as congressional actions are Carter et al., *The First Amendment and the Fifth Estate* (1993), and Ginsburg et al., *Regulation of the Electronic Mass Media* (1991). An excellent primer for all the subjects discussed in this chapter is Krasnow et al., *The Politics of Broadcast Regulation* (1982). Two important economic critiques of regulatory trends are Owen and Wildman, *Video Economics* (1992), and Levin, *Fact and Fancy in Television Regulation* (1980), both of which are wide ranging and reflect deregulation's impact. For background on general media law, see the following, all regularly updated: Gillmor et al., *Mass Communication Law: Cases and Comment* (1990); Zuckman et al., *Mass Communications Law in a Nutshell* (1988), an inexpensive paperback; and Carter et al., *The First Amendment and the Fourth Estate* (1991). For a more journalistic than legal orientation, see Pember, *Mass Media Law* (1993).

Note B: Staying Current While documentation of administrative agencies, courts, and Congress can seem forbidding, some tips on staying current should prove useful. The definitive but unofficial source for keeping up with electronic media regulation is Pike and Fischer, *Radio Regulation*, a loose-leaf reporter service that is updated weekly and carefully indexed (instructions on use appear in its "Current Service" volume). *Media Law Reporter* is another loose-leaf commercial service that rapidly reports matters of journalism law, including those relating to electronic media. The annual volumes of PLI, *Communications Law* (typically two or three), provide a compendium of cases, decisions, and analyses of media issues over the previous year. The *NAB Legal Guide to Broadcast Law and Regulation* (1988) is a single-volume desk reference aimed at station managers. Official government sources of cases and decisions are detailed in the footnote on p. 462 of this book.

13.1–13.2 Federal Jurisdiction, Communications Act The official chronological compilation of all U.S. laws (legislation) on telecommunications from the 1910 act to date is found in U.S. Congress, House of Representatives, *Radio Laws of the United States*, which is revised by the addition of new material every several years. The compilation includes the 1962 Communications Satellite Act (which created Comsat), the 1967 Public Broadcasting Act (part of Title III of the 1934 Act), and the cable acts of 1984 and 1992. (Most of these cable amendments appear as Title VI of the 1934 Act.)

Of considerable historical interest is the book written by the senator most responsible for the 1934 Act: Dill, *Radio Law* (1938). Paglin, *A Legislative History of the Communications Act of 1934* (1989), is a compilation of the key documents in creation of the landmark Communications Act.

13.3 FCC Basics A fascinating account of the development of the regulatory agency idea, told through the lives of four key individuals, is offered in McGraw's *Prophets of Regulation* (1984). Kittross, *Administration of American Telecommunications Policy* (1980), is a compilation of important documents on development and criticism of the FCC.

A useful introduction to the present Commission is Hilliard, *The Federal Communications Commission: A Primer* (1991). Cole and Oettinger, *Reluctant Regulators: The FCC and the Broadcast Audience* (1978), is a very insightful—though now dated—view of the policy-making process and general Washington environment for that

process. Regarding FCC trends and key decisions, see FCC, *Annual Report*.

FCC rules and regulations are annually revised in CFR (Code of Federal Regulations), *Title 47: Telecommunications*. Of its five volumes, the first deals with FCC organization and procedures, the second and third with common carrier, the fourth with broadcasting, and the fifth with cable and emergency procedures. The FCC's proposed and final rules appear in daily issues of FR *(Federal Register)* and are gathered chronologically in FCC and FCCR *(Federal Communications Commission Reports;* the first and second series run through 1986 and are continued by the *Federal Communications Commission Record* from that time forward). They accumulate at the rate of four to six fat volumes each year. See also Pike and Fischer under Note B.

13.4–13.6 Licensing, Operating and Renewal Titles listed in Note B include material on licensing, of which the NAB legal guide is most specific.

13.7 Enforcement See works on the FCC under 13.2. Hixson, *Mass Media and the Constitution: An Encyclopedia of Supreme Court Decisions* (1989), and Campbell, *The Supreme Court and the Mass Media: Selected Cases, Summaries, and Analyses* (1990), are compilations of major decisions, with commentary. See also the titles under 14.1.

13.8 Cable Franchising Definitive legal information on cable is the three-volume Ferris et al., *Cable Television Law* (1983–present), which is updated twice annually and offers details on both the 1984 and 1992 cable acts.

13.9 Deregulation Tunstall, *Communications Deregulation* (1986), offers a useful critique of early deregulatory moves. LeDuc, *Beyond Broadcasting: Patterns in Policy and Law* (1987), argues that deregulation has not gone far enough—that electronic media are still unfairly controlled. Horwitz, *The Irony of Regulatory Reform* (1989), suggests that all the deregulatory noise did not accomplish very much in either media or common carrier. Ray, *FCC: The Ups and Downs of Radio-TV Regulation* (1990), strongly attacks the deregulation of the 1980s as having gone too far.

13.10 Other Regulation For information on international treaties, see 15.3. Press law is covered in the general texts discussed under Note A, while advertising law is well reviewed in Petty, *The Impact of Advertising Law on Business and Public Policy* (1992). The best recent assessment of pressure-group activity is found in Montgomery, *Target: Prime Time—Advocacy Groups and the Struggle Over Entertainment Television* (1989). A case study of government and industry self-regulatory interaction is related in Cowan's *See No Evil* (1979) on the "family viewing" case. Media responsibility is the focus of the collection in Dennis et al., *Media Freedom and Accountability* (1989). Of the many books on media ethics and self-regulation, the best include Fink, *Media Ethics: In the Newsroom and Beyond* (1988), and Christians et al., *Media Ethics: Cases and Moral Reasoning* (1991).

CHAPTER 14

Constitutional Controversies

14.1 First Amendment Powe, *The Fourth Estate and the Constitution: Freedom of the Press in America* (1991), is a fine current survey of the past, present, and likely future of First Amendment protections. Emord, *Freedom, Technology, and the First Amendment* (1991), is a valuable current view of how technology is changing our views of the 200-year-old amendment. Parsons, *Cable Television and the First Amendment* (1987), discusses the various pressures on cable. See also the guides to Supreme Court decisions under 13.7.

14.2 Broadcasting's Limited Rights Powe, *American Broadcasting and the First Amendment* (1987), argues for treatment of electronic media in a fashion more equal with print.

14.3 Things You Can't Say See the titles under Note A for Chapter 13. Detailed analyses of changes in libel law are found in Rossini, *The Practical Guide to Libel Law* (1991). The Westmoreland case is analyzed in Brewin and Shaw, *Vietnam on Trial: Westmoreland vs CBS* (1985), which includes the trial and aftermath. For the question of reporter privilege, see Van Gerpen, *Privileged Communication and the Press* (1979). Freedman, *Press and Media Access to the Criminal Courtroom* (1988), provides a review of recent changes.

14.4 Obscenity and Indecency Spitzer, *Seven Dirty Words and Six Other Stories: Controlling the Content of Print and Broadcast* (1986), discusses reasons for control of some kinds of content.

14.5 Ownership See the titles listed under 6.5.

14.6 Political Access The NAB regularly revises booklets guiding station managers on how best to treat access by political candidates.

14.7 Public Access Barron, *Freedom of the Press for Whom?* (1973), remains the strongest published argument in favor of a right of public access. Of the many sources on the defunct FCC fairness doctrine, two stand out: the reasoned argument that the doctrine had long outlived its usefulness, by an author with both legal and network reporting background—Rowan, *Broadcast Fairness: Doctrine, Practice, Prospects* (1984); and a solid history of its development in Simmons, *The Fairness Doctrine and the Media* (1978). For viewpoints generally critical of networks, see research monographs issued by such conservative think tanks as Accuracy in Media, American Enterprise Institute, and The Media Institute, all based in Washington, D.C.

14.9 Protecting Copyright As this is a fast-changing field, books are useful more for background than for current specifics. Strong, *The Copyright Book: A Practical Guide* (1993), offers just that. See also OTA, *Intellectual Property Rights in an Age of Electronics and Information* (1986), an excellent assessment of technological pressures on the present legal regime, as well as Lawrence and Timburg, *Fair Use and Free Inquiry: Copyright Law and the New Media* (1989), a compilation of more than 20 papers reviewing aspects of the problem.

14.10 Changing Perspectives See earlier sections.

CHAPTER 15

Global View

Useful background for this chapter is found in Fortner, *International Communication: History, Conflict and Control of the Global Metropolis* (1993), which provides a good historical approach to all the topics we deal with here; Head, *World Broadcasting Systems: A Comparative Analysis* (1985), on which much of this material was originally based; the United Nations' *World Media Handbook* (1990), and Unesco, *World Communication Report* (1989), plus the statistics updated annually in Unesco's *Statistical Yearbook*.

Turning specifically to Europe, Donow, *European Media Markets* (1992), offers details on 15 western nations and, Noam, *Television in Europe* (1992), is the most detailed description and analysis of Europe's changing TV systems. Silj, *The New Television in Europe* (1992), provides considerable depth on Italy, France, and Germany, among others, as does Sepstrup, *Transnationalization of Television in Western Europe* (1990).

15.1 Media Control Philosophies The development of British radio and television is well documented in Briggs, *The BBC: The First Fifty Years* (1985), based on his four-volume definitive history of the BBC. The variations evident to our north are detailed in Raboy, *Missed Opportunities: The Story of Canada's Broadcasting Policy* (1990).

For more on the former Soviet system, see Mickiewicz, *Split Signals: Television and Politics in the Soviet Union* (1988), written on the eve of dramatic changes in the former Soviet sphere; and USDOS, *Eastern Europe: Please Stand By: Report of the Task Force on Telecommunications and Broadcasting in Eastern Europe* (1990), issued soon after the political changeovers.

15.2 Pluralistic Trend The best comparative analyses of broadcasting among developed nations—nearly all examples of paternalistic systems converted to pluralistic ones—include: Browne, *Comparing Broadcast Systems: The Experiences of Six Industrialized Nations* (1989); Blumler and Nossiter, *Broadcasting Finance in Transition: A Comparative Handbook* (1991); and Kuhn, *The Politics of Broadcasting* (1985), a comparative study of eight nations. Lewis and Booth, *The Invisible Medium: Public, Commercial and Community Radio* (1990), compares and contrasts radio systems around the world.

For pluralism in Britain, see Paulu, *Television and Radio in the United Kingdom* (1981), which explores the rise of competing commercial channels to the long-time BBC monopoly; and the two volumes by Sendall, *Independent Television in Britain* (1982), which take the story to the late 1960s.

15.3 Deregulation Etzioni-Halevy, *National Broadcasting Under Siege: A Comparative Study of Australia, Britain, Israel and West Germany* (1987), assesses national systems as they adjust under deregulation. Hills, *The Democracy Gap: The Politics of Information and Communication Technologies in the United States and Europe* (1991), also evaluates fundamental changes in government regulatory approaches.

Headrick, *The Invisible Weapon: Telecommunications and International Politics 1851–1945* (1991), provides useful historical background on ITU developments in that era. The modern ITU is detailed in Codding and Rutkowski, *The International Telecommunication Union in a Changing World* (1982), updated by Savage, *The Politics of International Telecommunications Regulation* (1990), on the modern ITU role. A good analysis of the development of three conflicting systems of color television is in Crane, *The Politics of International Standards* (1979). A collection of important documents from world agencies is gathered and annotated in Ploman, *International Law Governing Communications and Information* (1982). Ungerer, *Telecommunications in Europe: Free Choice for the User in Europe's '92 Market* (1988), reviews early PTT deregulation. Barnett et al., *Law of International Telecommunications in the United States* (1988), is the best survey of the American approach to these issues.

15.4 Access See titles discussed under 15.5–15.7.

15.5–15.6 Economics and Geography Start with the Unesco publications detailed in the note at the beginning of this chapter. For a good overview of how *what* is communicated depends in part on *who* owns the media, see Tunstall and Palmer, *Media Moguls* (1991), which details multinational companies, and Shawcross, *Murdoch* (1992), the best study of the man and his companies.

Even after all these years, Katz and Wedell, *Broadcasting in the Third World* (1977), is still the best overview of the subject. Sussman and Lent, *Transnational Communications: Wiring the Third World* (1991), includes 13 papers on different parts of the developing world. Mowlana and Wilson, *The Passing of Modernity: Communication and the Transformation of Society* (1990), takes a very broad view, focusing on the development process.

For specific regions, see Head, *Broadcasting in Africa* (1974), Lent, *Broadcasting in Asia and the Pacific* (1978), Boyd, *Broadcasting in the Arab World* (1993), and Alisky, *Latin American Media* (1981), though three are badly dated. Unfortunately, few such regional analyses are published.

15.7 Programs and Impacts The standard annual of information on broadcasting systems and programming is *World Radio-TV Handbook*. Paterson, *TV and Video International Guide*, is also issued annually but takes a descriptive rather than directory approach. Wildman and Siwek, *International Trade in Films and Television Programs* (1988), and Negrine and Papathanassopoulos, *The Internationalization of Television* (1990), are two of the few available studies on program flows. Johnston, *International Television Co-Production from Access to Success* (1992), details how the process works. The relatively recent development of local service is examined in Jankowski et al., *The People's Voice: Local Radio and Television in Europe* (1992).

Much of the cross-cultural debate literature is highly emotional. A recent government view of America's role is found in NTIA, *Globalization of the Mass Media* (1993). The best international statement of the free- versus the balanced-flow issue is found in Unesco's McBride Commission, *Many Voices, One World* (1980), while Nordenstreng, *The Mass Media Declaration of Unesco* (1984), reviews that agency's increasing activity in this area. Giffard, *Unesco and the Media* (1989), reviews the activist role played in world media, and Preston et al., *Hope & Folly: The United States and Unesco 1945–1985* (1989), details the deteriorating relationship that led to American withdrawal from the world body.

A calm overview of news-flow questions is found in Hachten, *The World News Prism: Changing Media of International Communication* (1992). Wallis and Baran, *The Known World of Broadcast News* (1990), details the actual content and sources of world-news information.

15.8 Transborder Broadcasting   There is a large literature on propaganda, much of it based on World War II experiences. Two good starting points for the changing role of international transmission are Brown, *International Radio Broadcasting* (1982), and Wood, *History of International Broadcasting* (1992a). Both cover major countries with a stress on recent developments, the latter being somewhat more technical. For books on shortwave technology, see 4.8.

The BBC's role is discussed in Mansell, *Let Truth Be Told: 50 Years of BBC External Broadcasting* (1982), updated by Tusa, *Conversations with the World* (1990). Activity in the former Soviet Union is reviewed in Mickewicz noted above as well as in Bittman, *The New Image Makers: Soviet Propaganda & Disinformation Today* (1988), and Ebon, *The Soviet Propaganda Machine* (1987). The beginnings of a concerted American effort are discussed in Shulman, *The Voice of America: Propaganda and Democracy, 1941–1945* (1991). RFE and RL activities are detailed in the annual reports of the Board for International Broadcasting, as well as in Mickelson, *America's Other Voice: The Story of Radio Free Europe and Radio Liberty* (1983). For a sense of post–Cold War realities, see the President's Task Force on U.S. Government International Broadcasting, *Report* (1991).

The many European and British "pirate" broadcasters are detailed in Harris, *Broadcasting from the High Seas* (1977), and Chapman, *Selling the Sixties: The Pirates and Pop Music Radio* (1992).

15.9 World Satellites   For INTELSAT, see its annual reports; Snow, *The International Telecommunications Satellite Organization (INTELSAT)* (1987); and M. Smith, *International Regulation of Satellite Communication* (1990). Woods, *Satellite Communications and DBS Systems* (1992b), offers a clear study of changing technology and its impact. Collins, *Satellite Television in Western Europe* (1992), details some of the dramatic changes such technology has created. Howkins and Foster, *Television in 1992* (1989), reviews changes in Europe.

15.10 Cable and Newer Media   One indicator of technological change is the VCR—two useful studies are Boyd et al., *Videocassette Recorders in the Third World* (1989), and Alvarado, *Video World-Wide* (1988), a study done for Unesco.

CHAPTER 16

Tomorrow

For two earlier views of likely futures for communication, see Doyle, *The Future of Television* (1992); Didsbury, *Communications and the Future* (1982); and Haigh et al., *Communications in the Twenty-First Century* (1981). Toffler's key works include *Future Shock* (1970) and *The Third Wave* (1980). Brody, *Communication Tomorrow: New Audiences, New Technologies, New Media* (1990), offers a broad-scale series of predictions of what is happening, and will happen.

16.1 Technology   Heldman, *Future Telecommunications* (1993), lays out dramatic changes to come. While badly dated, Martin's *Future Developments in Telecommunications* (1977) is still useful in terms of the background it provides; note, too, that many of the developments it predicted have actually taken place. For more current and less technical guides, see Williams, *The New Telecommunications* (1991), which covers media and common carrier, suggesting ways in which they will increasingly merge, and Arlen, *Tomorrow's TVs: A Review of New TV Set Technology, Related Video Equipment and Potential Market Impacts, 1987–1995* (1987).

16.2 Business   Penzias, *Ideas and Information: Managing in a High-Tech World* (1989), is a Nobel Laureate's idea of the likely future of business through communication. On a far more specific level, one of the most useful industry predictive publications is *The Veronis, Suhler &*

Associates Communications Industry Forecast, issued annually with projected financial data for nine industry segments.

16.3 Programs Cook et al., *The Future of News* (1992), looks to likely changes in print, news agency, and television news entities and operations, while Koch, *Journalism for the 21st Century* (1991), details the increasing use of online information and databases in reporting news.

16.4 Effects Neuman, *The Future of the Mass Audience* (1991), is a thoughtful assessment of what may be coming, given changes in technology. Cross and Raizman, *Telecommuting: The Future Technology of Work* (1986), suggests how communication technology will do far more than merely entertain or inform.

16.5 Controls Pool, *Technologies Without Boundaries: On Telecommunications in a Global Age* (1990), and his earlier *Technologies of Freedom: On Free Speech in an Electronic Age* (1983) take an essentially optimistic view of how a future of plentiful channels and voices will ease regulatory burdens.

16.6 Worldwide A forward-looking assessment is offered in NTIA, *Globalization of the Mass Media* (1993). Though written before the dramatic changes in Eastern Europe and the USSR, McPhail, *Electronic Colonialism: The Future of International Broadcasting and Communication* (1987), remains a useful assessment.

● ● ● ● ● ● ● ●

Recommended Bibliographies

Following are the most useful book-length bibliographies for seeking further reading on electronic media. Full citations are in the Bibliography. Libraries should have most of these bibliographies, but readers should also check library availability of electronic data bases for more efficient literature searches.

Block and Bracken, *Communication and the Mass Media: A Guide to the Reference Literature* (1991), is compiled by two experienced librarians. Details nearly 500 sources, divided by format and well indexed.

Blum and Wilhoit, *Mass Media Bibliography* (1990), is a standard overall annotated guide, divided by medium and including nearly 2,000 domestic and foreign citations plus good subject, author, and title indexes.

Brightbill, *Communications and the United States Congress: A Selectively Annotated Bibliography of Committee Hearings, 1870–1976* (1978), remains the only guide to all congressional hearings on media and common-carrier communications.

Carothers, *Radio Broadcasting from 1920 to 1990: An Annotated Bibliography* (1991), is a useful listing of sources, though with often weak annotations and confusing categories. More than 1,700 sources are indexed by author and title.

Cassata and Skill, *Television: A Guide to the Literature* (1985), provides an intelligent assessment of books on the topic, well divided by subject categories.

Comstock et al., *Television and Human Behavior* (1975), is a three-volume bibliography of the research literature: a main list, detailed annotations for 50 key studies, and a list of work in progress, along with an integrative review. Invaluable for the material published to that point.

Cooper, *Bibliography on Educational Broadcasting* (1942), is far more inclusive than the title suggests—it's the best annotated survey of some 1,800 pre–World War II works on domestic broadcasting.

Cooper, *Television and Ethics: A Bibliography* (1988), details some 1,100 resources divided into multiple topics and clearly indexed.

Finn, *The History of Electrical Technology: An Annotated Bibliography* (1991), when used with Shiers (see below), offers a window onto the history of technology literature.

Fisher, *On the Screen: A Film, Television, and Video Research Guide* (1986), details more than 700 sources, many of which relate to electronic media and all of which are well indexed by author and subject.

Flannery, *Mass Media: Marconi to MTV—A Select Bibliography of New York Times Sunday Magazine Articles on Communication, 1900–1988* (1989), is just that—divided by year and then by medium, with long subtitles serving as annotations.

Garay, *Cable Television: A Reference Guide to Information* (1988), is the best single place to begin, given the logical divisions of topic and the wealth of material in all formats.

Godfrey, *Reruns on File: A Guide to Electronic Media Archives* (1992), details hundreds of collections of recordings, arranged by state, with information on access and use—the only such guide available.

Gordon and Verna, *Mass Communication Effects and Processes: A Comprehensive Bibliography, 1950–1975* (1978), is not annotated, but its 2,700 entries provide a useful context for electronic media studies in that quarter-century.

Greenfield, *Radio: A Reference Guide* (1989), is a valuable combination of text and bibliography on most aspects of radio, past and present. Beginning with a discussion of networks and stations, it details specific program genres in the remaining sections.

Hill and Davis, *Religious Broadcasting: An Annotated Bibliography* (1984), details the increasing amount of descriptive and research writing on this topic.

Johnson, *TV Guide 25 Year Index* (1979), is just that, covering the period 1953–1977.

Lent, *Women and Mass Communications: An International Annotated Bibliography* (1991), includes more than 3,200 sources, many of them annotated, arranged by region and country. Well indexed.

"Mass Communication" (title varies), in *Annual Review of Psychology*, appears every several years with a review article and appended list of research studies for the period covered. See Vol. 13 (1962): 251–284 for writings up to 1960; Vol. 19 (1968): 351–386 for research published in 1961–1966; Vol. 22 (1971): 309–336 for 1967–1970; Vol. 28 (1977): 141–173 for 1970–1976; and Vol. 32 (1981): 307–356 for 1976–1979. No further articles were published through the 1993 volume.

Matlon and Ortiz, *Index to Journals in Communication Studies Through 1990* (1992), includes chronological tables of contents and subject/author indexes for 15 journals, including those of the Speech Communication Association, *Journalism Quarterly*, and *Journal of Broadcasting*. The latter issued its own 25-year index in 1982.

McCoy, *Freedom of the Press* (1968 and 1979), is wide ranging, with thousands of excellent annotations covering two centuries, all well indexed.

NAB, *Broadcasting Bibliography* (1989a), is an invaluable booklet of subject-divided listings, plus a periodicals listing.

Nuessel, *The Image of Older Adults in the Media: An Annotated Bibliography* (1992), includes more than 550 references under 21 categories, with indexes.

Performing Arts Books: 1876–1981 (1981) is a massive card catalog, supplemented by an index of serial publications.

Pringle and Clinton, *Radio and Television: A Selected, Annotated Bibliography* (1989), covers the 1982–1986 period with some 1,300 entries arranged by subject. Well indexed.

Rubin et al., *Communication Research: Strategies and Sources* (1993), offers something different—a unique guide on how to do research and use the many helpful sources available toward this end. The best introduction to research in media.

Shearer and Huxford, *Communications and Society: A Bibliography on Communications Technologies and Their Social Impact* (1983), emphasizes various kinds of electronic media impact.

Shiers and Shiers, *Bibliography of the History of Electronics* (1972), offers some 1,800 detailed annotations on the history of telegraph, telephone, radio, television, and related services. (Compare with Finn, above.)

Signorelli, *Role Portrayal and Stereotyping on Television: An Annotated Bibliography of Studies Related to Women, Minorities, Aging, Sexual Behavior, Health, and Handicaps* (1985), covers just that, with more than 400 sources detailed.

———, *A Sourcebook on Children and Television* (1991), breaks the topic into a dozen subject categories and discusses each, along with good indexes to the hundreds of resources noted.

——— and Gerbner, *Violence and Terror in the Mass Media: An Annotated Bibliography* (1988), includes nearly 800 sources abstracted under four major headings. Includes good author and subject indexes.

Smith, *U.S. Television Network News: A Guide to Sources in English* (1984), is still the most inclusive guide to the topic.

Sova and Sova, *Communication Serials: An International Guide to Periodicals in Communication, Popular Culture, and the Performing Arts* (1992), is a massive and exceptionally detailed guide to some 2,700 magazines and journals, with more than a dozen different indexes to finding everything!

• • • • • • • •

Electronic Media Periodicals

This brief list includes the more important and/or useful electronic media-related periodicals, most of which should be in any good library. Given the rate of change in this field, these are the best sources for current developments.

Advertising Age (1929, weekly) is the main trade paper for the industry, with details of new accounts and agency doings as well as periodic statistical summaries.

Broadcasting & Cable (1931, weekly) is the single most important trade paper for the business; although it usually takes a strong pro-industry stance, it is indispensable for understanding current events, especially those concerning management and relations with government. Added *Cable* to title early in 1993.

Broadcasting/Cablecasting Yearbook (began in 1935; title has varied) is a directory of stations and systems, and of support industries as well.

Cablevision (1975, biweekly) provides coverage of all aspects of cable.

Columbia Journalism Review (1962, bimonthly) specializes in critiques of print and electronic journalism.

Critical Studies in Mass Communication (1984, quarterly) focuses on content studies and criticism across all media.

Current (1982, biweekly) details public radio and television trends and issues.

EBU Review (1949, monthly) provides in-depth articles and news notes on Europe's broadcast services.

Electronic Media (1981, weekly) focuses on programming and advertising, often with in-depth interviews. Large, tabloid format.

Federal Communications Law Journal (1946, triannual) specializes in detailed legal analysis of current concerns regarding regulation of electronic media by the FCC.

Gannett Center Journal, later *Media Studies Journal* (1987, quarterly), provides theme issues with a combination of research and commentary articles on all aspects of media.

Intermedia (1970, bimonthly) reviews worldwide communication trends and issues in short news pieces and longer essays, concentrating on Western Europe.

Journalism Quarterly (1924, quarterly) contains academic research on print and broadcast media, with excellent book-review sections.

Journal of Broadcasting & Electronic Media (1956, quarterly) provides scholarly research on all electronic media.

Journal of Communication (1951, quarterly) has focused since 1974 on mass communication with research, opinion, and reviews.

Journal of the SMPTE (1930, monthly) is an excellent source for historical and current discussions of the technology by authors with the Society of Motion Picture and Television Engineers.

Multichannel News (1980, weekly) is a tabloid-size newsmagazine on cable services, MMDS, and related newer technologies.

Public Opinion Quarterly (1937, quarterly) is a respected source of research on polls, media, opinion measurement, etc.

Telecommunications Policy. (1976, quarterly; later, nine times a year) offers scholarly work on media and broader telecommunication concerns, emphasizing U.S. and foreign policy development.

Television Digest (1945, weekly) is an excellent newsletter on policy, business, and technology that includes a section on consumer electronics. Supplemented by an annual three-volume *Television Factbook*.

Television News Index and Abstracts (1972, monthly) lists the exact content of network evening newscasts, indexed by topic. Includes an annual overall index.

Topicator (1965, monthly) selectively indexes 18 broadcast and advertising periodicals. Includes an annual index.

TV Guide (1953, weekly) is the standard guide to programs, with often excellent articles and an annual Fall Preview issue.

Variety (1905, weekly) is the major trade paper for show business, including stage, screen, music, television, and foreign developments.

Bibliography

ABC *Nightline*. 1984 (December 21). Transcript.

Abel, John A., et al. 1970. "Station License Revocations and Denials of Renewal 1934–1969," *Journal of Broadcasting* 14 (Fall): 411.

Abelman, Robert, and Hoover, Stewart M., eds. 1990. *Religious Television: Controversies and Conclusions*. Ablex, Norwood, NJ.

Abramson, Albert, 1987. *The History of Television, 1880 to 1941*. McFarland, Jefferson, NC.

Abramson, Jeffrey B., et al. 1988. *The Electronic Commonwealth: The Impact of News Media Technologies on Democratic Politics*. Basic, New York.

AD (Appellate Division, New York Supreme Court). 1963. *John H. Faulk v. AWARE, Inc. et al.* 19 AD 2d 464.

Adams, R.C. 1989. *Social Survey Methods for Mass Media Research*. Erlbaum, Hillsdale, NJ.

Adler, Richard P., et al. 1980. *The Effects of Television Advertising on Children*. Lexington Books, Lexington, MA.

Agostino, Don. 1980. "New Technologies: Problem and/or Solution," *Journal of Communication* 30 (Summer): 198.

Aitken, Hugh G. 1976. *Syntony and Spark: The Origins of Radio*. Wiley, New York (reprinted by Princeton U. Press).

———. 1985. *The Continuous Wave: Technology and American Radio, 1900–1932*. Princeton U. Press, Princeton, NJ.

Alali, A. Odasuo, and Eke, Denoye Kelvin, eds. 1991. *Media Coverage of Terrorism: Methods of Diffusion*. Sage, Newbury Park, CA.

Alisky, Marvin. 1981. *Latin American Media*. Iowa State U. Press, Ames.

Alley, Robert S., and Brown, Irby B. 1990. *Murphy Brown: Anatomy of a Sitcom*. Delta, New York.

Alten, Stanley R. 1990. *Audio in Media*, 3d ed. Wadsworth, Belmont, CA.

Altschuler, Glenn C., and Grossvogel, David I. 1992. *Changing Channels: America in TV Guide*. U. of Illinois Press, Champaign.

Alvarado, Manuel, ed. 1988. *Video World-Wide: An International Study*. John Libbey, London.

American Radio Relay League. Annual. *The Radio Amateur's Handbook*. A.R.R.L., Newington, CT.

Anderson, James. 1987. *Communication Research: Issues and Methods*. McGraw-Hill, New York.

———, and Meyer, Timothy. 1988. *Mediated Communication: A Social Action Perspective*. Sage, Beverly Hills, CA.

Anderson, Kent. 1978. *Television Fraud: The History and Implications of the Quiz Show Scandals*. Greenwood, Westport, CT.

Ang, Ien. 1991. *Desperately Seeking the Audience*. Routledge, New York.

Annual Review of Psychology. Annual. Annual Reviews, Inc., Palo Alto, CA.

APA. 1992. "APA Task Force Explores Television's Positive and Negative Influences on Society." News Release. American Psychological Association, Washington, DC.

Applebone, Peter. 1988. "Scandal Spurs Interest in Swaggart Finances," *New York Times* (27 February): 8.

Archer, Gleason, L. 1938. *History of Radio to 1926*. American Historical Society, New York (reprinted by Arno Press in 1971).

———. 1939. *Big Business and Radio*. American Historical Company, New York (reprinted by Arno Press in 1971).

Arlen, Gary H. 1987. *Tomorrow's TVs: A Review of New TV Set Technology, Related Video Equipment and Potential*

Market Impacts, 1987–1995. National Association of Broadcasters, Washington, DC.

Arlen, Michael J. 1969. *Living-Room War.* Viking, New York.

Arrington, Carl. 1992. "The Zapper: All About the Remote Control," *TV Guide* (August 15): 8.

Augarten, Stan. 1984. *Bit by Bit: An Illustrated History of Computers.* Ticknor and Fields, New York.

Auletta, Ken. 1991. *Three Blind Mice: How the TV Networks Lost Their Way.* Random House, New York.

Avery, Robert K., and Pepper, Robert. 1979. *The Politics of Interconnection: A History of Public Television at the National Level.* National Association of Educational Broadcasters, Washington, DC.

Bagdikian, Ben H. 1971. *The Information Machines: Their Impact on Men and Media.* Harper and Row, New York.

———. 1992. *The Media Monopoly,* 3d ed. Beacon Press, Boston.

Baker, W. J. 1971. *A History of the Marconi Company.* St. Martin's, New York.

Baldwin, Thomas F., and Lewis, Colby. 1972. "Violence in Television: The Industry Looks at Itself," in Comstock and Rubenstein, eds. 1972: 290–365.

Baldwin, Thomas F., and McVoy, D. Stevens. 1988. *Cable Communications,* 2d ed. Prentice-Hall, Englewood Cliffs, NJ.

Bandura, A. D., et al. 1963. "Imitation of Film-Mediated Aggressive Models," *Journal of Abnormal and Social Psychology* 66: 3.

Banks, Mark J., and Havice, Michael J. 1991. "Selling Time in a New Medium: A Survey of the Low-Power Television Industry," *Broadcast/Cable Financial Journal* (July–August).

Banning, William P. 1946. *Commercial Broadcasting Pioneer: The WEAF Experiment, 1922–1926.* Harvard U. Press, Cambridge, MA.

Barnett, Stephen R., et al. 1988. *Law of International Telecommunications in the United States.* Nomos Verlagsgesellschaft, Baden-Baden, Germany.

Barnouw, Erik. 1966. *A Tower of Babel: A History of Broadcasting in the United States to 1933.* Oxford U. Press, New York.

———. 1968. *The Golden Web: A History of Broadcasting in the United States, 1933–1953.* Oxford U. Press, New York.

———. 1970. *The Image Empire: A History of Broadcasting in the United States Since 1953.* Oxford U. Press, New York.

———. 1978. *The Sponsor: Notes on a Modern Potentate.* Oxford U. Press, New York.

———. 1990. *Tube of Plenty: The Development of American Television,* 2d rev. ed. Oxford U. Press, New York.

Barron, Jerome A. 1973. *Freedom of the Press for Whom? The Right of Access to Mass Media.* Indiana U. Press, Bloomington.

Barwise, Patrick, and Ehrenberg, Andrew. 1988. *Television and Its Audience.* Sage, Newbury Park, CA.

Batra, Rajeev, and Glazer, Rashi. 1989. *Cable TV Advertising: In Search of the Right Formula.* Quorum, New York.

Baudino, Joseph E., and Kittross, John M. 1977. "Broadcasting's Oldest Station: An Examination of Four Claimants," *Journal of Broadcasting* 21 (Winter): 61.

Baughman, James L. 1985. *Television's Guardians: The FCC and the Politics of Programming 1958–1967.* U. of Tennessee Press, Knoxville.

BBC (British Broadcasting Corporation). 1928–1987. *BBC Handbook* (title varies). Annual. BBC, London.

———. 1992. "World Radio and Television Receivers." BBC, International Broadcasting Audience Research, London.

Beck, A. H. 1967. *Words and Waves: An Introduction to Electrical Communication.* McGraw-Hill, New York.

Benjamin, Burton K. 1988. *Fair Play: CBS, General Westmoreland, and How a Television Documentary Went Wrong.* Harper and Row, New York.

Benson, K. Blair, and Fink, Donald G. 1991. *HDTV: Advanced Television for the 1990s.* McGraw-Hill, New York.

Berg, Leah R. Vande, and Wenner, Lawrence A. 1991. *Television Criticism: Approaches and Applications.* Longman, White Plains, NY.

Bergendorff, Fred, et al. 1983. *Broadcast Advertising and Promotion.* Hastings House, New York.

Berger, Arthur Asa. 1991. *Media Research Techniques.* Sage, Newbury Park, CA.

Bergreen, Lawrence. 1980. *Look Now, Pay Later: The Rise of Network Broadcasting.* Doubleday, New York.

Berke, Richard L. 1992. "Presidential Candidates to Get 3-Second Minimum on CBS," *New York Times* (July 3): A13.

Besen, Stanley, et al. 1984. *Misregulating Television: Network Dominance and the FCC.* U. of Chicago Press, Chicago.

———, and Johnson, Leland. 1984. *An Assessment of the Federal Communication Commission's Group Ownership Rules.* Rand, Santa Monica, CA.

———, 1986. *Compatibility Standards, Competition, and Innovation in the Broadcasting Industry.* Rand, Santa Monica, CA.

Beville, H. M., Jr. 1981. "Understanding Broadcast Ratings," 3d ed. Broadcast Ratings Council, New York.

———. 1988. *Audience Ratings: Radio, Television, Cable*, 2d ed. Erlbaum, Hillsdale, NJ.

BIB (Board for International Broadcasting). Annual. *Annual Report*. GPO, Washington, DC.

Bier, Tom. 1991. "What Makes '60 Minutes' Tick?" RTNDA *Communicator* (September).

Bilby, Kenneth. 1986. *The General: David Sarnoff and the Rise of the Communications Industry*. Harper and Row, New York.

Binkowski, Edward S. 1988. *Satellite Information Systems*. G. K. Hall, Boston.

Birch Scarborough. 1991. "How America Found Out About the Gulf War: A Birch Scarborough Study of Media Behavior," Birch Scarborough Research, Coral Springs, FL.

Bishop, John. 1988. *Making It in Video: An Insider's Guide to Careers in the Fastest-Growing Industry of the Decade*. McGraw-Hill, New York.

Bitting, Robert C., Jr. 1965. "Creating an Industry," *Journal of the SMPTE* (November): 1015.

Bittman, Ladislav, ed. 1988. *The New Image-Makers: Soviet Propaganda and Disinformation Today*. Pergamon-Brassey's, McLean, VA.

Blakely, Robert J. 1971. *The People's Instrument: A Philosophy of Programming for Public Television*. Public Affairs Press, Washington, DC.

———. 1979. *To Serve the Public Interest: Educational Broadcasting in the United States*. Syracuse U. Press, Syracuse, NY.

Bliss, Edward, Jr. 1991. *Now the News: The Story of Broadcast Journalism*. Columbia U. Press, New York.

Block, Alex Ben. 1990. *Outfoxed: Marvin Davis, Barry Diller, Rupert Murdoch, Joan Rivers, and the Inside Story of America's Fourth Television Network*. St. Martin's, New York.

Block, Eleanor S., and Bracken, James K. 1991. *Communication and the Mass Media: A Guide to the Reference Literature*. Libraries Unlimited, Englewood, CO.

Bloomquist, Randall. 1990. "Mysteries of the Arbitrons Revealed," [Washington, DC] *City Paper* (May 11): 17.

Bluem, A. William. 1965. *Documentary in American Television: Form, Function, Method*. Hastings, New York.

Blum, Eleanor, and Wilhoit, Frances Goins. 1990. *Mass Media Bibliography: An Annotated Guide to Books and Journals for Research and Reference*. U. of Illinois Press, Urbana.

Blumler, Jay G., ed. 1992. *Television and the Public Interest: Vulnerable Values in West European Broadcasting*. Sage, London.

———, and Nossiter, T. J. 1991. *Broadcasting Finance in Transition: A Comparative Handbook*. Oxford U. Press, New York.

Boddy, William. 1990. *Fifties Television: The Industry and Its Critics*. U. of Illinois Press, Champaign.

Boedeker, Hal. 1991. "For Drama, Surprise, Americans Tune in to CNN," *Miami Herald* (December 29): 2-I.

Boorstin, Daniel J. 1964. *The Image: A Guide to Pseudo-Events in America*. Harper and Row, New York.

———. 1978. "The Significance of Broadcasting in Human History," in Hoso-Bunka Foundation, *Symposium on the Cultural Role of Broadcasting*, The Foundation, Tokyo.

Bower, Robert T. 1973. *Television and the Public*. Holt, Rinehart and Winston, New York.

———. 1985. *The Changing Television Audience in America*. Columbia U. Press, New York.

Boyd, Douglas A., ed. 1993. *Broadcasting in the Arab World*. 2d ed. Iowa State U. Press, Ames.

———, et al. 1989. *Videocassette Recorders in the Third World*. Longman, White Plains, NY.

Braestrup, Peter. 1977. *Big Story: How the American Press and Television Reported and Interpreted the Crisis of Tet 1968 in Vietnam and Washington*, 2 vols. Westview, Boulder, CO.

Bretz, Rudy. 1970. *A Taxonomy of Communication Media*. Educational Technology, Englewood Cliffs, NJ.

———. 1983. *Media for Interactive Communication*. Knowledge Industry, White Plains, NY.

Brewin, Bob, and Shaw, Sydney. 1987. *Vietnam on Trial: Westmoreland vs. CBS*. Atheneum, New York.

Briggs, Asa A. 1965. *The Golden Age of Wireless: The History of Broadcasting in the United Kingdom*. Vol. 2. Oxford U. Press, Oxford.

———. 1985. *The BBC: The First Fifty Years*. Oxford U. Press, Oxford.

Brightbill, George D. 1978. *Communications and the United States Congress: A Selectively Annotated Bibliography of Committee Hearings, 1870–1976*. Broadcast Education Association, Washington, DC.

Brindze, Ruth. 1937. *Not to Be Broadcast: The Truth About Radio*. Vanguard, New York.

Broadcasting (after 1992, *Broadcasting & Cable*). (Note: The articles listed here are special reports. Citations for shorter specific articles are found only in the text.)
1963. "A World Listened and Watched" (Dec. 2): 36.
1970. "A Play-by-Play Retrospective" (Nov. 2): 74.
1979. "CBS: The First Five Decades" (Sept. 19): 45.

1979. "Minorities in Broadcasting: The Exception Is No Longer the Rule" (October 15): 27.

1979. "Children's Programming" (October 29): 39.

1980. "The Washington Lawyer: Power Behind the Powers That Be" (June 16): 32.

1984. "State of the Art: Technology" (October 8): 54.

1984. "The New Order Passeth" (December 10): 43.

1984. "Perspectives 1985" (December 31): 72.

1987. "Television's Shifting Balance of Power" (October 12): 40.

1991. "Satellites '91: Launching a Higher-Tech Future" (July 29): 33.

1992a. "Broadcasting's Top 100 Companies in Electronic Communications" (June 22): 43.

1992b. "Satellites '92" (July 27): 37.

1992c. "The State of the First Amendment" (October 19): 44.

1992d. "Talk! Look Who's Talking" (December 14): 22.

1993a. "Satellites '93" (February 22): 22.

1993b. "News Services: Filling Changing Needs and Niches" (May 31): 27.

Broadcasting/Cablecasting Yearbook. (Title varies.) Annual. Broadcasting, Washington, DC (to 1991); Bowker, New Providence, NJ (1992–present).

Brock, Gerald W. 1981. *The Telecommunications Industry: The Dynamics of Market Structure.* Harvard U. Press, Cambridge, MA.

Brody, E. W. 1990. *Communication Tomorrow: New Audiences, New Technologies, New Media.* Praeger, New York.

Brooks, John. 1976. *Telephone: The First Hundred Years.* Harper and Row, New York.

Brooks, Tim, and Marsh, Earle. 1992. *The Complete Directory to Prime Time Network TV Shows: 1946–Present,* 5th ed. Ballantine, New York.

Brotman, Stuart N. 1990. *Telephone Company and Cable Television Competition: Key Technical, Economic, Legal and Policy Issues.* Artech, Norwood, MA.

Brown, James A. 1980. "Selling Air Time for Controversy: NAB Self-Regulation and Father Coughlin," *Journal of Broadcasting* 24 (Spring): 199.

Brown, Les. 1971. *Televi$ion: The Business Behind the Box.* Harcourt Brace Jovanovich, New York.

———. 1992. *Les Brown's Encyclopedia of Television,* 3d ed. Facts on File, New York.

Browne, Donald. 1982. *International Radio Broadcasting: The Limits of the Limitless Medium.* Praeger, New York.

———. 1989. *Comparing Broadcast Systems: The Experiences of Six Industrialized Nations.* Iowa State U. Press, Ames.

Browne, Steven E. 1992. *Film Video Terms and Concepts.* Focal, Stoneham, MA.

Bruce, Steve. 1990. *Pray TV: Televangelism in America.* Routledge, New York.

Bruns, Bill. 1991. "What Things Cost on TV," *TV Guide* (April 13): 8.

Bryant, Jennings, ed. 1990. *Television and the American Family.* Erlbaum, Hillsdale, NJ.

Buckley, Tom. 1978. "Popularity of '60 Minutes' Based on Wide-Ranging Reports," *New York Times* (December 17): 99.

———. 1979. "Game Shows—TV's Glittering Gold Mine," *New York Times Magazine* (November 18): 49.

Buzzard, Karen. 1992. *Electronic Media Ratings: Turning Audiences into Dollars and Sense.* Focal, Stoneham, MA.

Cable Television Developments. Semimonthly. National Cable Television Association, Washington, DC.

The Cable TV Financial Databook. Annual. Paul Kagan Associates, Carmel, CA.

Cal. (California Reporter). 1981. *Olivia N. v. National Broadcasting Co.,* 178 Cal. Rptr. 888 (California Court of Appeal, First District).

Campbell, Douglas S. 1990. *The Supreme Court and the Mass Media: Selected Cases, Summaries, and Analyses.* Praeger, New York.

Campbell, Richard. 1991. *60 Minutes and the News: A Mythology for Middle America.* U. of Illinois Press, Urbana.

Campbell, Robert. 1976. *The Golden Years of Broadcasting: A Celebration of the First 50 Years of Radio and Television on NBC.* Scribner's, New York.

Cantor, Muriel G., and Cantor, Joel M. 1992. *Prime-Time Television: Content and Control,* 2d ed. Sage, Newbury Park, CA.

Cantril, Hadley. 1940. *The Invasion from Mars: A Study of the Psychology of Panic.* Princeton U. Press, Princeton, NJ.

Carey, John. 1990. "Public Television and Specialized Cable Channels," Association for Public Broadcasting, Washington, DC.

Carothers, Diane Foxhill. 1991. *Radio Broadcasting from 1920 to 1990: An Annotated Bibliography.* Garland, New York.

Carroll, Raymond L., and Davis, Donald M. 1993. *Electronic Media Programming: Strategies and Decision Making.* McGraw-Hill, New York.

Carter, T. Barton, et al. 1991. *The First Amendment and the Fourth Estate: The Law of Mass Media,* 5th ed. Foundation, Westbury, NY.

———. 1993. *The First Amendment and the Fifth Estate: Regulation of Electronic Mass Media*, 3rd ed. Foundation, Westbury, NY.

Cassata, Mary, and Skill, Thomas. 1985. *Television: A Guide to the Literature*. Oryx, Phoenix, AZ.

Cater, Douglass. 1972. "The Politics of Public TV," *Columbia Journalism Review* (July/August): 8–15.

CCET (Carnegie Commission on Educational Television). 1967. *Public Television: A Program for Action*. Harper and Row, New York.

CCFPB (Carnegie Commission on the Future of Public Broadcasting). 1979. *A Public Trust*. Bantam, New York.

CFR (Code of Federal Regulations). Annual. *Title 47: Telecommunications*, 5 vols. GPO, Washington, DC.

Chaffee, C. David. 1988. *The Rewiring of America: The Fiber Optics Revolution*. Academic Press, Orlando, FL.

Chandler, Joan M. 1988. *Television and National Sport: The United States and Britain*. U. of Illinois Press, Champaign.

Chang, Won Ho. 1989. *Mass Media in China: The History and the Future*. Iowa State U. Press, Ames, IA.

Chapman, Robert. 1992. *Selling the Sixties: The Pirates and Pop Music Radio*. Routledge, London.

Christians, Clifford, et al. 1991. *Media Ethics: Cases and Moral Reasoning*, 3d ed. Longman, White Plains, NY.

Coates, Vary T., and Finn, Bernard. 1979. *A Retrospective Technology Assessment: Submarine Telegraphy—The Transatlantic Cable of 1866*. San Francisco Press, San Francisco.

Codding, George, and Rutkowski, Anthony. 1982. *The International Telecommunication Union in a Changing World*. Artech, Dedham, MA.

Codel, Martin, ed. 1930. *Radio and Its Future*. Harper, New York (reprinted by Arno Press in 1971).

Coen, Robert J. 1992. "Estimated Annual U.S. Advertising Expenditures, 1990–91 (revised)." McCann-Erickson, Inc., New York.

Cogley, John. 1956. *Report on Blacklisting II: Radio-Television*. Fund for the Republic, New York (reprinted by Arno Press in 1971).

Cole, Barry, and Oettinger, Mal. 1978. *Reluctant Regulators: The FCC and the Broadcast Audience*. Addison-Wesley, Reading, MA.

Collins, Richard. 1992. *Satellite Television in Western Europe*, rev. ed. John Libbey, London.

Communications: Understanding Computers. Time-Life Books, Alexandria, VA.

Compaine, Benjamin M., et al. 1982. *Who Owns the Media? Concentration of Ownership in the Mass Communications Industry*, 2d ed. Knowledge Industry, White Plains, NY.

———, ed. 1984. *Understanding New Media: Trends and Issues in Electronic Distribution of Information*. Ballinger, Cambridge, MA.

Comstock, George, et al. 1975. *Television and Human Behavior*, 3 vols. Rand, Santa Monica, CA.

———, and Rubenstein, E., eds. 1972. *Television and Social Behavior: Media Content and Control I*. Government Printing Office, Washington, D.C.

———, et al. 1978. *Television and Human Behavior*. Columbia U. Press, New York.

———. 1991. *Television in America*, 2d ed. Sage, Beverly Hills, CA.

———, and Paik, Haejung. 1991. *Television and the American Child*. Academic Press, New York.

Condry, John. 1989. *The Psychology of Television*. Erlbaum, Hillsdale, NJ.

Cook, Philip S., et al., eds. 1992. *The Future of News: Television, Newspapers, Wire Services, Newsmagazines*. Johns Hopkins U. Press, Baltimore.

Coolidge, Calvin. 1926. "Message to Congress," 68 *Congressional Record* 32.

Cooper, Eunice, and Jahoda, Marie. 1947. "The Evasion of Propaganda: How Prejudicial People Respond to Anti-Prejudice Propaganda," *Journal of Psychology* (January 23): 15.

Cooper, Isabella. 1942. *Bibliography on Educational Broadcasting*. U. of Chicago Press, Chicago (reprinted by Arno Press in 1971).

Cooper, Thomas W., et al. 1988. *Television and Ethics: A Bibliography*. G. K. Hall, Boston, MA.

Counterattack. 1950. *Red Channels: The Report of Communist Influence in Radio and Television*. New York.

Cowan, Geoffrey. 1979. *See No Evil: The Backstage Battle Over Sex and Violence on Television*. Simon and Schuster, New York.

CPB (Corporation for Public Broadcasting, Washington, DC).

Annual. *Annual Report*.

Annual. *Summary Statistical Report of CPB-Qualified Public Radio Stations* (title varies).

Annual. *Public Broadcasting Income* (title varies).

Biennial. *Public Radio Programming Content by Category*.

Biennial. *Public Television Programming Content by Category*.

1981. *Status Report on Public Broadcasting*. (Earlier editions: 1973 and 1977.)

Annual. *Public Broadcasting Directory*.

Crane, Rhonda J. 1979. *The Politics of International*

Standards: France and the Color TV War. Ablex, Norwood, NJ.

Cross, Thomas B., and Raizman, Marjorie. 1986. *Telecommuting: The Future Technology of Work*. Dow Jones Irwin, Homewood, IL.

Csida, Joseph, and Csida, June Bundy. 1978. *American Entertainment: A Unique History of Popular Show Business*. Billboard, New York.

Culbert, David H. 1976. *News for Everyman: Radio and Foreign Affairs in Thirties America*. Greenwood, Westport, CT.

Czitrom, Daniel. 1982. *Media and the American Mind from Morse to McLuhan*. U. of North Carolina Press, Chapel Hill.

Danielian, N. R. 1939. *AT&T: The Story of Industrial Conquest*. Vanguard, New York (reprinted by Arno Press in 1974).

Davis, Henry B. O. 1981–1985. *Electrical and Electronic Technologies: A Chronology of Events and Inventors*, 3 vols. Scarecrow, Metuchen, NJ.

Davis, Stephen, 1927. *The Law of Radio*. McGraw-Hill, New York.

Dayan, Daniel, and Katz, Elihu. 1992. *Media Events: The Live Broadcasting of History*. Harvard U. Press, Cambridge, MA.

DeFleur, Melvin, and Ball-Rokeach, Sandra. 1988. *Theories of Mass Communication*, 5th ed. Longman, White Plains, NY.

de Forest, Lee. 1950. *Father of Radio*. Wilcox and Follett, Chicago.

DeLong, Thomas A. 1991. *Quiz Craze: America's Infatuation with Game Shows*. Praeger, New York.

Demac, Donna A. 1986. *Tracing New Orbits: Co-operation and Competition in Global Satellite Development*. Columbia U. Press, New York.

Dennis, Everette E., et al. 1989. *Media Freedom and Accountability*. Greenwood, Westport, CT.

———, et al. 1991. *The Media at War: The Press and the Persian Gulf Conflict*. Freedom Forum, New York.

———. 1992–1993. *The Media and Campaign '92: A Series of Special Election Reports*, 4 vols. Freedom Forum, New York.

Department of Commerce. 1922. "Minutes of Open Meeting of Department of Commerce on Radio Telephony." Mimeo. Washington, DC.

———. 1924. *Recommendations for Regulation of Radio*. GPO, Washington, DC.

Dervin, Brenda, ed. 1979–1993. *Progress in Communication Sciences*, 12 vols. Ablex, Norwood, NJ.

De Sonne, Marcia L. 1990. *Digital Audio Broadcasting: Status Report and Outlook*. National Association of Broadcasters, Washington, DC.

———. 1992. *Advanced Broadcast/Media Technologies: Market Developments and Impacts in the '90s and Beyond*. National Association of Broadcasters, Washington, DC.

De Soto, Clinton. 1936. *Two Hundred Meters and Down: The Story of Amateur Radio*. ARRL, West Hartford, CT.

Diamant, Lincoln, ed. 1989. *The Broadcast Communications Dictionary*, 3d ed. Greenwood, Westport, CT.

Diamond, Edwin, and Bates, Stephen. 1992. *The Spot: The Rise of Political Advertising on Television*, 3d ed. MIT Press, Cambridge, MA.

Didsbury, Howard F., ed. 1982. *Communications and the Future: Prospects, Promises, and Problems*. World Future Society, Bethesda, MD.

Dill, Clarence C. 1938. *Radio Law: Practice and Procedure*. National Law Book, Washington, DC.

Dobkin, Bethami A. 1992. *Tales of Terror: Television News and the Construction of the Terrorist Threat*. Praeger, New York.

Dobrow, Julia R., ed. 1990. *Social and Cultural Aspects of VCR Use*. Erlbaum, Hillsdale, NJ.

Dominick, Joseph R., and Fletcher, James F. 1985. *Broadcasting Research Methods*. Allyn and Bacon, Boston.

Donnerstein, Edward, et al. 1987. *The Question of Pornography: Research Findings and Policy Implications*. Free Press, New York.

Donovan, Robert J., and Scherer, Ray. 1992. *Unsilent Revolution: Television News and American Public Life*. Cambridge U. Press, New York.

Donow, Kenneth R. 1992. *European Media Markets: Commercial and Public Media in Fifteen Countries*. National Association of Broadcasters, Washington, DC.

Doyle, Marc. 1992. *The Future of Television: A Global Overview of Programming, Advertising, Technology and Growth*. NTC Business Books, Lincolnwood, IL.

Drake-Chenault Enterprises Inc. 1978. "History of Rock and Roll," Drake-Chenault, Canoga Park, CA.

Duncan, James. Quarterly. *American Radio*. Duncan Media, Indianapolis, IN.

Dunlap, Orrin E., Jr. 1929. *Advertising by Radio*. Ronald, New York.

———. 1944. *Radio's 100 Men of Science*. Harper, New York.

Dunning, John. 1976. *Tune in Yesterday: The Ultimate Encyclopedia of Old-Time Radio, 1925–1976*. Prentice-Hall, Englewood Cliffs, NJ.

Dyson, Kenneth, and Humphreys, Peter. 1986. *The Politics of the Communications Revolution in Western Europe.* Frank Cass, London.

Eastman, Susan Tyler, and Klein, Robert. 1991. *Promotion and Marketing for Broadcasting and Cable*, 2d ed. Waveland, Prospect Heights, IL.

Eastman, Susan Tyler, ed. 1993. *Broadcast/Cable Programming: Strategies and Practices*, 4th ed. Wadsworth, Belmont, CA.

Eberly, Philip K. 1982. *Music in the Air: America's Changing Tastes in Popular Music, 1920–1980.* Hastings, New York.

Ebersole, Samuel E. 1992. *Broadcast Technology Worktext.* Focal, Stoneham, MA.

Ebon, Martin. 1987. *The Soviet Propaganda Machine.* McGraw-Hill, New York.

EBUR. 1987. "Morning Has Broken: An Idea Whose Time Has Come," *European Broadcasting Union Review* (Sept.): 12.

———. 1988. "Statistics on European Programmes and News Exchanges," *European Broadcasting Union Review* (May): 27.

EIA (Electronic Industries Association). Annual. *The U.S. Consumer Electronics Industry in Review* (title varies). EIA, Washington, DC.

Einstein, Daniel. 1987. *Special Edition: A Guide to Network Television Documentary Series and Special News Reports, 1955–1979.* Scarecrow, Metuchen, NJ.

Eisner, Joel, and Krinsky, David. 1984. *Television Comedy Series: An Episode Guide to 153 TV Sitcoms in Syndication.* McFarland, Jefferson, NC.

Elbert, Bruce R. 1987. *Introduction to Satellite Communication.* Artech, Norwood, MA.

Ellerbee, Linda. 1986. *"And So It Goes": Adventures in Television.* Putnam, New York.

Ellmore, R. Terry. 1991. *NTC's Mass Media Dictionary.* NTC Business Books, Lincolnwood, IL.

Ely, Melvin Patrick. 1991. *The Adventures of Amos 'n' Andy: A Social History of an American Phenomenon.* Free Press, New York.

Emerson, Thomas L. 1972. "Communication and Freedom of Expression," *Scientific American* (September): 163.

Emery, Michael, and Emery, Edwin. 1992. *The Press and America: An Interpretive History of the Mass Media*, 7th ed. Prentice-Hall, Englewood Cliffs, NJ.

Emord, Jonathan W. 1991. *Freedom, Technology, and the First Amendment.* Pacific Research Institute, San Francisco.

Ennes, Harold E. 1953. *Principles and Practices of Telecasting Operations.* Sams, Indianapolis.

Entman, Robert M. 1989. *Democracy Without Citizens: Media and the Decay of American Politics.* Oxford U. Press, New York.

Epstein, Edward J. 1973. "What Happened vs. What We Saw," *TV Guide* (Sept. 29, Oct. 6, Oct. 13): 7, 20, 49.

Erickson, Hal. 1989. *Syndicated Television: The First Forty Years, 1947–1987.* McFarland, Jefferson, NC.

Ettema, James S., and Whitney, D. Charles, eds. 1982. *Individuals in Mass Media Organizations: Creativity and Constraint.* Sage, Beverly Hills, CA.

Etzioni-Halevy, Eva. 1987. *National Broadcasting Under Siege: A Comparative Study of Australia, Britain, Israel and West Germany.* Macmillan, London.

Everson, George. 1949. *The Story of Television: The Life of Philo T. Farnsworth.* Norton, New York (reprinted by Arno Press in 1974).

F (*Federal Reporter*, 2d Series). West, St. Paul, MN.
  1926. *U.S. v. Zenith Radio Corp.*, 12 F2d 614.
  1946. *WOKO v. FCC*, 153 F2d 623.
  1969a. *Kilby v. Noyce*, 416 F2d 1391.
  1969b. *Office of Communication v. FCC*, 425 F2d 543.
  1971. *Citizens Communication Center v. FCC*, 447 F2d 1201.
  1972. *Brandywine–Main Line Radio v. FCC*, 473 F2d 16.
  1973. *TV 9 v. FCC*, 495 F2d 929.
  1975. *Natl. Assn. of Independent TV Distributors v. FCC*, 516 F2d 526.
  1977a. *ACT v. FCC*, 564 F2d 458.
  1977b. *Home Box Office v. FCC*, 567 F2d 9.
  1979. *Writers Guild v. ABC*, 609 F2d 355.
  1981. *RKO v. FCC*, 670 F2d 215.
  1984. *Buffalo Broadcasting Co. v. FCC*, 744 F2d 217.
  1985a. *Action for Children's Television v. FCC*, 756 F2d 899.
  1985b. *Quincy Cable TV Inc. v. FCC*, 768 F2d 1434.
  1985c. *Jones v. Wilkinson*, 800 F2d 989.
  1986. *Telecommunications Research and Action Center v. FCC*, 801 F2d 501.
  1987. *Century Communications Corp. v. FCC*, 835 F2d 292.
  1988. *Action for Children's Television et al. v. FCC*, 852 F2d 1332.
  1991. *Action for Children's Television v. FCC*, 932 F2d 1504.

Fang, Irving E. 1977. *Those Radio Commentators!* Iowa State U. Press, Ames.

Farhi, Paul. 1992. "Broadcasters' Group Causes Static," *Washington Post* (September 12): C-8.

Faulk, John H. 1964. *Fear on Trial.* Simon and Schuster, New York.

FCC (Federal Communications Commission). GPO, Washington, DC.

Annual. *Annual Report* (1934–1955 issues reprinted by Arno Press in 1971).

1939. *Investigation of the Telephone Industry in the United States.*

1941. *Report on Chain Broadcasting.*

1946. *Public Service Responsibilities of Broadcast Licensees* ("Blue Book").

1979. (Children's Television Task Force). *Television Programming for Children,* 5 vols. FCC.

Irregularly revised. *The Law of Political Broadcasting and Cablecasting: A Political Primer* (title varies).

1980a. (Network Inquiry Special Staff). *New Television Networks: Entry, Jurisdiction, Ownership and Regulation. Final Report,* Vol. 1. *Background Reports,* Vol. 2.

1980b. *Staff Report and Recommendations in the Low-Power Television Inquiry.* FCC, Washington, DC.

1989. *Equal Employment Opportunity Trend Report, Radio and Television* (January 13).

FCCR (*FCC Reports,* 1st and 2d Series; and *FCC Record*).

1949. *Editorializing by Broadcasting Licensees.* 13 FCC 1249.

1952. *Amendment of Sec. 3.606* [adopting new television rules]. . . Sixth Report and Order. 41 FCC 148.

1959. *Columbia Broadcasting System.* Interpretive Opinion. 26 FCC 715.

1960. *En Banc Programming Inquiry.* Report and Statement of Policy. 44 FCC 2303.

1965. *Comparative Broadcast Hearings.* Policy Statement. 1 FCC2d 393.

1968. *Broadcasting in America and the FCC's License Renewal Process: An Oklahoma Case Study,* 14 FCC2d 1.

1969a. *Application . . . for Renewal of License of Station KTAL-TV, Texarkana, Tex.* Letter. 19 FCC2d 109.

1969b. *Network Coverage of the Democratic National Convention,* 16 FCC2d 650.

1972a. *DOMSAT.* Report and Order. 35 FCC2d 844.

1972b. *Cable Television.* Report and Order. 36 FCC2d 143.

1972c. *Complaint by Atlanta NAACP.* Letter. 36 FCC2d 635.

1973. *Apparent Liability of Stations WGLD-FM* [Sonderling Broadcasting]. News Release. 41 FCC2d 919.

1974. *Handling of Public Issues Under the Fairness Doctrine and the Public Interest Standard of the Communications Act.* Fairness Report. 48 FCC2d 1.

1979. *Deregulation of Radio.* Notice of Inquiry and Proposed Rulemaking. 73 FCC2d 457.

1980. *Application of RKO General, Inc. (WNAC-TV), Boston, Mass., for Renewal of Broadcasting License.* Decision. 78 FCC2d 1.

1981. *Deregulation of Radio.* Report and Order. 84 FCC2d 968.

1984a. *Deregulation of Radio.* Second Report and Order. 96 FCC2d 930.

1984b. *Revision of Program Policies and Reporting Requirements Related to Public Broadcasting Licensees.* Report and Order. 98 FCC2d 746.

1984c. *Revision of Programming and Commercialization Policies, Ascertainment Reports, and Program Log Requirements for Commercial Television Stations.* 98 FCC2d. 1076.

1985a. *Cattle Country Broadcasting [KTTL-FM].* Hearing Designation Order and Notice of Apparent Liability. 58 RR 1109.

1985b. *Inquiry into . . . the General Fairness Doctrine Obligations of Broadcast Licensees.* Report. 102 FCC2d 143.

1985c. *Application of Simon Geller.* Memorandum Opinion and Order. 102 FCC2d 1443.

1987a. *New Indecency Enforcement Standards to Be Applied to All Broadcast and Amateur Radio Licenses.* Public Notice. 2 FCC Rcd 2726.

1987b. *Complaint of Syracuse Peace Council Against Television Station WTVH.* Memorandum Opinion and Order. 2 FCC Rcd 5043.

1989. *Catoctin Broadcasting Corp. of New York (WBUZ).* Memorandum Opinion and Order. 4 FCC Rcd 2553.

1992a. *Telephone Company–Cable Television Cross-Ownership Rules.* Second Report and Order, Recommendation to Congress and Second Further Notice of Proposed Rulemaking. 7 FCC Rcd 5781. ("Video Dial Tone")

1992b. *Enforcement of Prohibitions Against Broadcast Indecency in 18 USC 1464.* 7 FCC Rcd 6464.

Federal Radio Commission. Annual. *Annual Report.* 1927–1933. GPO, Washington, DC (reprinted by Arno Press in 1971).

Felix, Edgar. 1927. *Using Radio in Sales Promotion.* McGraw-Hill, New York.

Fenby, Jonathan. 1986. *The International News Services.* Schocken, New York.

Ferre, John P., ed. 1990. *Channels of Belief: Religion and*

American Commercial Television. Iowa State U. Press, Ames.

Ferris, Charles, et al. 1983–present. *Cable Television Law: A Video Communications Guide*, 3 vols. Matthew Bender, New York.

Fessenden, Helen. 1940. *Fessenden: Builder of Tomorrows*. Coward-McCann, New York (reprinted by Arno Press, 1974).

Fialka, John J. 1991. *Hotel Warriers: Covering the Gulf War*. Woodrow Wilson Center Press, Washington, DC.

Fink, Conrad C. 1988. *Media Ethics: In the Newsroom and Beyond*. McGraw-Hill, New York.

Fink, Donald G., ed. 1943. *Television Standards and Practice*. . . . McGraw-Hill, New York.

———, and Lutyens, David M. 1960. *The Physics of Television*. Anchor, Garden City, NY.

Finn, Bernard S. 1991. *The History of Electrical Technology: An Annotated Bibliography*. Garland, New York.

The First 50 Years of Broadcasting. 1981. Broadcasting Magazine, Washington, DC.

Fischer, Claude S. 1992. *America Calling: A Social History of the Telephone to 1940*. U. of California Press, Berkeley.

Fisher, Glen. 1987. *American Communication in a Global Society*, 2d ed. Ablex, Norwood, NJ.

Fisher, Kim. 1986. *On the Screen: A Film, Television, and Video Research Guide*. Libraries Unlimited, Littleton, CO.

Flannery, Gerald V., comp. 1989. *Mass Media: Marconi to MTV—A Select Bibliography of New York Times Sunday Magazine Articles on Communication, 1900–1988*. U. Press of America, Lanham, MD.

Fletcher, James. 1985. *Squeezing Profits Out of Ratings: A Manual for Radio Managers, Sales Managers, and Programmers*. National Association of Broadcasters, Washington, DC.

———. 1988. *Broadcast Research Definitions*. National Association of Broadcasters, Washington, DC.

Foote, Joe S. 1990. *Television Access and Political Power: The Networks, the Presidency, and the "Loyal Opposition."* Praeger, New York.

Forester, Tom. 1987. *High-Tech Society: The Story of the Information Technology Revolution*. MIT Press, Cambridge, MA.

Fornatale, Peter, and Mills, Joshua A. 1980. *Radio in the Television Age*. Overlook, Woodstock, NY.

Fortner, Robert S. 1993. *International Communication: History, Conflict and Control of the Global Metropolis*. Wadsworth, Belmont, CA.

Fox, Elizabeth, ed. 1988. *Media and Politics in Latin America: The Struggle for Democracy*. Sage, Newbury Park, CA.

FR (*Federal Register*). The following two FCC releases were published in FR:
1974a. *Program Length Commercials*, 39 FR 4042.
1974b. *The Public and Broadcasting: A Procedure Manual*, rev. ed. 39 FR 32288.

Frank, Reuven. 1991. *Out of Thin Air: The Brief Wonderful Life of Network News*. Simon and Schuster, New York.

Frank, Ronald, and Greenberg, Marshall G. 1982. *Audiences for Public Television*. Sage, Beverly Hills, CA.

Freedman, Warren. 1988. *Press and Media Access to the Criminal Courtroom*. Quorum Books, New York.

Friendly, Fred. 1967. *Due to Circumstances Beyond Our Control*. . . . Random House, New York.

———. 1976. *The Good Guys, the Bad Guys, and the First Amendment: Free Speech vs. Fairness in Broadcasting*. Random House, NY.

Frost, S. E., Jr. 1937. *Is American Radio Democratic?* U. of Chicago Press, Chicago.

F Sup (*Federal Supplement*). West, St. Paul, MN.
1979. *Universal City Studios v. Sony*, 480 F Sup 429.
1985. *Community Television of Utah v. Wilkerson*, 611 F Sup 1099.

FTC (Federal Trade Commission).
1924. *Report on the Radio Industry*. GPO, Washington, DC.
1978. *Staff Report on Television Advertising to Children*. FTC, Washington, DC.

Fuller, Linda K. 1992. *The Cosby Show: Audiences, Impact, and Implications*. Greenwood, Westport, CT.

Ganley, Gladys D., and Ganley, Oswald H. 1987. *Global Political Fallout: The VCR's First Decade*. Ablex, Norwood, NJ.

Garay, Ronald. 1984. *Congressional Television: A Legislative History*. Greenwood, Westport, CT.

———. 1988. *Cable Television: A Reference Guide to Information*. Greenwood, Westport, CT.

———. 1992. *Gordon McClendon: Maverick of Radio*. Greenwood, Westport, CT.

Gelatt, Roland. 1977. *The Fabulous Phonograph: 1877–1977*, 2d rev. ed. Macmillan, New York.

Gerbner, George. 1972. "Communications and Social Environment," *Scientific American* (September): 153.

———, et al. 1977. "The Gerbner Violence Profile . . . ," *Journal of Broadcasting* 21 (Summer): 280.

———, et al. 1986. *Television's Mean World: Violence Profile 14–15*. Annenberg School of Communications, Philadelphia.

Gianakos, Larry J. 1978–1992. *Television Drama Series Programming: A Comprehensive Chronicle*, 6 vols. Scarecrow, Metuchen, NJ.

Gibson, George H. 1977. *Public Broadcasting: The Role of the Federal Government, 1912–1976.* Praeger, New York.

Giffard, C. Anthony. 1989. *Unesco and the Media.* Longman, White Plains, NY.

Gillmor, Donald M., et al. 1990. *Mass Communication Law: Cases and Comment,* 5th ed. West, St. Paul, MN.

Ginsburg, Douglas H., et al. 1991. *Regulation of the Electronic Mass Media: Law and Policy for Radio, Television, Cable and the New Video Technologies.* West, St. Paul, MN.

Giovannoni, David G. 1991a. *AM Radio Listening.* Corporation for Public Broadcasting, Washington, DC.

———. 1991b. *Radio Intelligence 1988–1990: An Anthology of Essays on the Meaning, Design, Management, and Use of Public Radio's Audience and Programming Research.* Corporation for Public Broadcasting, Washington, DC.

———, et al. 1988. *Audience 88: A Comprehensive Analysis of Public Radio Listeners.* Corporation for Public Broadcasting, Washington, DC.

———, et al. 1992. *Public Radio Programming Strategies: A Report on the Programs Stations Broadcast and the People They Seek to Serve.* Corporation for Public Broadcasting, Washington, DC.

Gitlin, Todd. 1983. *Inside Prime Time.* Pantheon, New York.

———. 1987. *Watching Television.* Pantheon, New York.

Glatzer, Hal. 1984. *Who Owns the Rainbow? Conserving the Radio Spectrum.* Sams, Indianapolis.

Godfrey, Donald G., comp. 1992. *Reruns on File: A Guide to Electronic Media Archives.* Erlbaum, Hillsdale, NJ.

Goldberg, Lee. 1990. *Unsold Television Pilots 1955 Through 1988.* McFarland, Jefferson, NC.

Goldberg, Robert, and Goldberg, Gerald Jay. 1990. *Anchors: Brokaw, Jennings, Rather and the Evening News.* Birch Lane, New York.

Goldenson, Leonard H., with Wolf, Marvin J. 1991. *Beating the Odds: The Untold Story Behind the Rise of ABC—The Stars, Struggles and Egos That Transformed Network Television.* Scribner's, New York.

Goldmark, Peter C., and Edson, Lee. 1973. *Maverick Inventor: My Turbulent Years at CBS.* Saturday Review, New York.

Gomery, Douglas. 1991. *Movie History: A Survey.* Wadsworth, Belmont, CA.

Gordon, Thomas F., and Verna, Mary E. 1978. *Mass Communication Effects and Processes: A Comprehensive Bibliography, 1950–1975.* Sage, Beverly Hills, CA.

Graber, Doris A. 1993. *Mass Media and American Politics,* 4th ed. CQ Press, Washington, DC.

Graham, John. 1983. *The Facts on File Dictionary of Telecommunications.* Facts on File, New York.

Graham, Margaret B. W. 1986. *RCA and the VideoDisc: The Business of Research.* Cambridge U. Press, New York.

Grant, August E., and Sung, Liching. 1992. *Communication Technology Update.* Technology Futures, Inc., Austin, TX.

Great Britain, Command (Cmnd.) Papers.

1977. *Report of the Committee on the Future of Broadcasting* ["Annan Report"], Cmnd. 6753. Her Majesty's Stationery Office, London.

1986. *Report of the Committee on Financing the BBC* ["Peacock Report"], Cmnd. 9824. Her Majesty's Stationery Office, London.

1988. Home Office. *Broadcasting in the 90s: Competition, Choice and Quality* ["White Paper"], Cmnd. 517. Her Majesty's Stationery Office, London.

Greenberg, Bradley S., ed. 1983. *Mexican-Americans and the Mass Media.* Ablex, Norwood, NJ.

———, and Parker, Edwin B., eds. 1965. *The Kennedy Assassination and the American Public: Social Communication in Crisis.* Stanford U. Press, Stanford, CA.

Greenfield, Jeff. 1977. *Television: The First Fifty Years.* Abrams, New York.

Greenfield, Thomas A. 1989. *Radio: A Reference Guide.* Greenwood, Westport, CT.

Gross, Ben. 1954. *I Looked and I Listened.* Random House, New York (expanded edition issued in 1970).

Gross, Lynne Shafer. 1991. *The New Television Technologies,* 3d ed. Brown, Dubuque, IA.

Grossman, Ann. 1987. *The Marketer's Guide to Media Vehicles, Methods, and Options.* Quorum, New York.

Grossman, Lawrence K. 1992. "Television and the Future of the First Amendment," *Television Quarterly* (25:4): 65.

Hachten, William A. 1992. *The World News Prism: Changing Media of International Communication,* 3d ed. Iowa State U. Press, Ames.

Hadden, Jeffrey K., and Shupe, Anson. 1988. *Televangelism: Power and Politics on God's Frontier.* Holt, New York.

Haigh, Robert W., et al., eds. 1981. *Communications in the Twenty-First Century.* Wiley, New York.

Halberstam, David. 1979. *The Powers That Be.* Knopf, New York.

Hall, Jim. 1984. *Mighty Minutes: An Illustrated History of Television's Best Commercials.* Harmony, New York.

Hallin, Daniel. 1986. *The "Uncensored War": The Media and Vietnam.* Oxford U. Press, New York.

———. 1991. "Sound Bite News: Television Coverage of Elections, 1968–1988," Media Studies Project, Woodrow Wilson International Center for Scholars, Washington, DC.

Halper, Donna L. 1991. *Radio Music Directing*. Focal, Stoneham, MA.

———. 1991. *Full-Service Radio: Programming for the Community*. Focal, Stoneham, MA.

Hammond, Charles M. 1981. *The Image Decade: Television Documentary 1965–1975*. Hastings, New York.

Hancock, Harry. 1950. *Wireless at Sea: The First 50 Years*. Marconi International Marine, Chelmsford, England (reprinted by Arno Press, 1974).

Hanson, Jarice. 1987. *Understanding Video: Applications, Impact, and Theory*. Sage, Newbury Park, CA.

Harlow, Alvin. 1936. *Old Wires and New Waves: The History of the Telegraph, Telephone, and Wireless*. Century, New York (reprinted by Arno Press, 1971).

Harrell, Bobby. 1985. *The Cable Television Technical Handbook*. Artech, Dedham, MA.

Harriss, Richard Jackson. 1989. *A Cognitive Psychology of Mass Communication*. Erlbaum, Hillsdale, NJ.

Hartwig, Robert L. 1990. *Basic TV Technology*. Focal Press, Stoneham, MA.

Head, Sydney W. 1956. *Broadcasting in America: A Survey of Radio and Television*. Houghton Mifflin, Boston.

———, ed. 1974. *Broadcasting in Africa: A Continental Survey of Radio and Television*. Temple U. Press, Philadelphia.

———. 1985. *World Broadcasting Systems: A Comparative Analysis*. Wadsworth, Belmont, CA.

Headrick, Daniel R. 1991. *The Invisible Weapon: Telecommunications and International Politics 1851–1945*. Oxford U. Press, New York.

Heath, Julie, and Harshorn, Gerald G. 1991. *Numbers to Dollars: Using Audience Estimates to Sell Radio*. National Association of Broadcasters, Washington, DC.

Heeter, Carrie, and Greenberg, Bradley S., eds. 1988. *Cableviewing*. Ablex, Norwood, NJ.

Heldman, Robert K. 1993. *Future Telecommunications: Information Applications, Services and Infrastructure*. McGraw-Hill, New York.

Hellweg, Susan A., et al. 1992. *Televised Presidential Debates: Advocacy in Contemporary America*. Praeger, New York.

Helms, Harry L. 1991. *Shortwave Listening Guidebook*. Hightext, San Diego, CA.

Henson, Robert. 1990. *Television Weathercasting: A History*. McFarland, Jefferson, NC.

Hettinger, Herman S. 1933. *A Decade of Radio Advertising*. U. of Chicago Press, Chicago (reprinted by Arno Press, 1971).

———, and Neff, Walter J. 1938. *Practical Radio Advertising*. Prentice-Hall, New York.

Hill, George H., and Davis, Lenwood. 1984. *Religious Broadcasting: An Annotated Bibliography*. Garland, New York.

Hilliard, Robert L. 1989. *Television Station Operations and Management*. Focal, Stoneham, MA.

———. 1991. *The Federal Communications Commission: A Primer*. Focal, Stoneham, MA.

———, and Keith, Michael C. 1992. *The Broadcast Century: A Biography of American Broadcasting*. Focal, Stoneham, MA.

Hills, Jill, and Papathanassopoulos, Stylianos. 1991. *The Democracy Gap: The Politics of Information and Communication Technologies in the United States and Europe*. Greenwood, Westport, CT.

Hirsch, Alan. 1991. *Talking Heads: Political Talk Shows and Their Star Pundits*. St. Martin's Press, New York.

Hitchcock, John R. 1991. *Sportscasting*. Focal, Stoneham, MA.

Hixson, Richard. 1989. *Mass Media and the Constitution: An Encyclopedia of Supreme Court Decisions*. Garland, New York.

Hoover, Herbert. 1952. *Memoirs*, 3 vols. Macmillan, New York.

Hoover, Stewart M. 1988. *Mass Media Religion: The Social Sources of the Electronic Church*. Sage, Newbury Park, CA.

Horwitz, Robert Britt. 1989. *The Irony of Regulatory Reform*. Oxford U. Press, New York.

House CIFC (U.S. Congress, House of Representatives: Committee on Interstate and Foreign Commerce). GPO, Washington, DC. (Committee was renamed Committee on Energy and Commerce in 1981.)

1958a. *Network Broadcasting*. Report of the FCC Network Study Staff. House Report 1277, 85th Cong., 2d Sess.

1958b. *Regulation of Broadcasting: Half a Century of Government Regulation of Broadcasting and the Need for Further Legislative Action*. 85th Cong., 2d Sess.

1960. *Responsibilities of Broadcast Licensees and Station Personnel (Payola and Other Deceptive Practices in the Broadcast Field)*. Hearings in 2 parts. 86th Cong., 2d Sess.

1963. *Broadcast Advertisements*. Hearings. 88th Cong., 1st Sess.

1963, 1964, and 1965. *Broadcast Ratings: The Methodology, Accuracy, and Use of Ratings in Broadcasting*. Parts

1–3, 88th Cong., 1st Sess.; Part 4, 88th Cong., 1st and 2d Sess.

1971. *Subpoenaed Material re Certain TV News Documentary Programs*. Hearings. 92nd Cong., 1st Sess.

House CMMF (U.S. Congress, House of Representatives, Committee on Merchant Marine and Fisheries). GPO, Washington, DC.

1919. *Government Control of Radio Communication*. Hearings. 65th Cong., 3d Sess.

1924. *To Regulate Radio Communication*. Hearings. 68th Cong., 1st Sess.

Howard, Herbert H., and Carroll, S. L. 1980. *Subscription Television: History, Current Status, and Economic Projections*. National Association of Broadcasters, Washington, DC.

Howeth, L. S. 1963. *History of Communications-Electronics in the United States Navy*. GPO, Washington, DC.

Howkins, John, and Foster, Michael. 1989. *Television in 1992: A Guide to Europe's New TV, Film and Video Business*. Coopers and Lybrand Deloitte, London.

Hsia, H. J. 1988. *Mass Communications Research Methods: A Step-by-Step Approach*. Erlbaum, Hillsdale, NJ.

Hunn, Peter. 1988. *Starting and Operating Your Own FM Station: From License Application to Program Management*. TAB, Blue Ridge Summit, PA.

Huston, Aletha C., et al. 1992. *Big World, Small Screen: The Role of Television in American Society*. U. of Nebraska Press, Lincoln.

Inglis, Andres F. 1990. *Behind the Tube: A History of Broadcasting Technology and Business*. Focal, Stoneham, MA.

Inman, David. 1991. *The TV Encyclopedia*. Perigee/Putnam, New York.

International Satellite Directory. Annual. Design Publishers, Sonoma, CA.

IRE (Institute of Radio Engineers). 1962. *Proceedings of the IRE*. 50 (May): entire issue celebrates 50th anniversary, with articles covering 1912–1962.

Jackson, K. G., and Townsend, G. B. 1991. *TV and Video Engineer's Reference Book*. Butterworth, Oxford, England.

Jamieson, Kathleen Hall. 1992. *Packaging the Presidency: A History and Criticism of Presidential Campaign Advertising*, 2d ed. Oxford U. Press, New York.

———, and Birdsell, David S. 1988. *Presidential Debates: The Challenge of Creating an Informed Electorate*. Oxford U. Press, New York.

Jankowski, Nick, et al., eds. 1992. *The People's Voice: Local Radio and Television in Europe*. John Libbey, London.

Jensen, Klaus Bruhn, and Jankowski, Nicholas W., eds. 1991. *A Handbook of Qualitative Methodologies for Mass Communication Research*. Routledge, New York.

Johnson, Catherine E. 1979. *TV Guide 25 Year Index: By Author and Subject*. Triangle, Radnor, PA.

Johnson, Leland L. 1992. *Telephone Company Entry into Cable Television: Competition, Regulation, and Public Policy*. Rand, Santa Monica, CA.

———, and Reed, David P. 1990. *Residential Broadband Services by Telephone Companies: Technology, Economics, and Public Policy*. Rand, Santa Monica, CA.

Johnson, Nicholas. 1970. *How to Talk Back to Your Television Set*. Little, Brown, Boston.

Johnston, Carla B. 1992. *International Television Co-Production from Access to Success*. Focal, Stoneham, MA.

Jolly, W. P. 1972. *Marconi*. Stein and Day, New York.

Jones, Glenn R. 1987. *Jones Dictionary of Cable Television Terminology*. Jones International, Englewood, CO.

Jones, Kensinger, et al. 1986. *Cable Advertising: New Ways to New Business*. Prentice-Hall, Englewood Cliffs, NJ.

Jowett, Garth. 1976. *Film: The Democratic Art*. Little, Brown, Boston.

Kaatz, Ronald B. 1985. *Cable Advertiser's Handbook*, 2d ed. Crain, Lincolnwood, IL.

Kahn, Frank J., ed. 1984. *Documents of American Broadcasting*, 4th ed. Prentice-Hall, Englewood Cliffs, NJ.

Kaltenborn, H. V. 1938. *I Broadcast the Crisis*. Random House, New York.

Katz, Elihu, and Lazarsfeld, Paul F. 1955. *Personal Influence: The Part Played by People in the Flow of Mass Communications*. Free Press, Glencoe, IL.

———, and Wedell, George. 1977. *Broadcasting in the Third World: Promise and Performance*. Harvard U. Press, Cambridge, MA.

Keith, Michael C., and Krause, Joseph M. 1993. *The Radio Station*, 3d ed. Focal, Stoneham, MA.

Kendrick, Alexander. 1969. *Prime Time: The Life of Edward R. Murrow*. Little, Brown, Boston.

Kittross, John M., ed. 1980. *Administration of American Telecommunications Policy*, 2 vols. Arno, New York.

Klapper, Joseph T. 1960. *The Effects of Mass Communication*. Free Press, Glencoe, IL.

Klatell, David A., and Marcus, Norman. 1988. *Sports for Sale: Television, Money, and the Fans*. Oxford U. Press, New York.

Klein, Paul. 1971. "The Men Who Run TV Aren't That Stupid . . . They Know Us Better Than You Think," *New York* (January 25): 20.

Kline, F. Gerald. 1972. "Theory in Mass Communication Research." In Kline and Tichenor, 1972: 14–40.

———, and Tichenor, Phillip J., eds. 1972. *Current Perspectives in Mass Communications Research*. Sage, Beverly Hills, CA.

Klopfenstein, Bruce C.; Spears, Sara C.; and Ferguson, Douglas. 1991. "VCR Attitudes and Behaviors by Length of Ownership," *Journal of Broadcasting & Electronic Media* 35 (Fall): 525.

Knowledge Industry Publications. 1987. *The Knowledge Industry 200, 1987 Edition: America's Two Hundred Largest Media and Information Companies*, 2d ed. KIP, White Plains, NY.

Koch, Tom. 1991. *Journalism for the 21st Century: Online Information, Electronic Databases and the News*. Praeger, New York.

Krasnow, Erwin, et al. 1982. *The Politics of Broadcast Regulation*, 3d ed. St. Martin's, New York.

———, et al. 1991. *Buying or Building a Broadcast Station in the 1990s*, 3d ed. National Association of Broadcasters, Washington, DC.

Kraus, Sidney. 1988. *Televised Presidential Debates and Public Policy*. Erlbaum, Hillsdale, NJ.

———, and Davis, Dennis. 1976. *The Effects of Mass Communication on Political Behavior*. Penn State U. Press, University Park, PA.

Krugman, Dean M., and Johnson, Keith F. 1991. "Differences in the Consumption of Traditional Broadcast and VCR Movie Rentals," *Journal of Broadcasting & Electronic Media* 35 (Spring): 213.

Kubey, Robert, and Csikszentmihalyi, Mihaly. 1990. *Television and the Quality of Life: How Viewing Shapes Everyday Experience*. Erlbaum, Hillsdale, NJ.

Kuhn, Raymond, ed. 1985. *The Politics of Broadcasting*. St. Martin's, New York.

Kuney, Jack. 1990. *Take One: Television Directors on Directing*. Praeger, New York.

Kutash, Irwin L., et al. 1978. *Violence: Perspectives on Murder and Aggression*. Jossey-Bass, San Francisco.

Land, Herman W., Associates. 1968. *Television and the Wired City*. National Association of Broadcasters, Washington, DC.

Landry, Robert T. 1946. *This Fascinating Radio Business*. Bobbs-Merrill, Indianapolis.

Lardner, James. 1987. *Fast Forward: Hollywood, the Japanese, and the VCR Wars*. Norton, New York.

Lasswell, Harold D. 1952. "Educational Broadcasters as Social Scientists," *Quarterly of Film, Radio, and Television* 7: 150.

Lawrence, John Shelton, and Timburg, B. 1989. *Fair Use and Free Inquiry: Copyright Law and the New Media*, 2d ed. Ablex, Norwood, NJ.

Lazarsfeld, Paul F., et al. 1944. *The People's Choice: How the Voter Makes Up His Mind in a Presidential Campaign*. Duell, Sloan and Pearce, New York (2d ed. published by Columbia U. Press in 1948).

———, and Kendall, Patricia L. 1948. *Radio Listening in America*. Prentice-Hall, New York.

Lebow, Irwin. 1991. *The Digital Connection: A Layman's Guide to the Information Age*. Computer Science/Freeman, New York.

LeDuc, Don. 1973. *Cable Television and the FCC: A Crisis in Media Control*. Temple U. Press, Philadelphia.

———. 1987. *Beyond Broadcasting: Patterns in Policy and Law*. Longman, White Plains, NY.

Leinwoll, Stanley. 1979. *From Spark to Satellite: A History of Radio Communication*. Scribner's, New York.

Lemert, James B. 1989. *Criticising the Media: Empirical Approaches*. Sage, Newbury Park, CA.

———, et al. 1991. *News Verdicts, the Debates, and Presidential Campaigns*. Praeger, New York.

Lent, John A., ed. 1978. *Broadcasting in Asia and the Pacific: A Continental Survey of Radio and Television*. Temple U. Press, Philadelphia.

———, comp. 1991. *Women and Mass Communications: An International Annotated Bibliography*. Greenwood, Westport, CT.

Lerner, Daniel, and Lyle Nelson, eds. 1977. *Communication Research: A Half Century Appraisal*. East-West Center, Honolulu.

Lessing, Lawrence. 1956. *Man of High Fidelity: Edwin Howard Armstrong*. Lippincott, Philadelphia (reprinted by Bantam Books in 1969).

Levin, Harvey J. 1971. *The Invisible Resource: Use and Regulation of the Radio Spectrum*. Johns Hopkins Press, Baltimore.

———. 1980. *Fact and Fancy in Television Regulation*. Russel Sage Foundation, New York.

Levin, Murray B. 1987. *Talk Radio and the American Dream*. D. C. Heath, Lexington, MA.

Levy, Mark R., ed. 1989. *The VCR Age: Home Video and Mass Communication*. Sage, Newbury Park, CA.

Lewis, Peter M., and Booth, Jerry. 1990. *The Invisible Medium: Public, Commercial and Community Radio*. Howard U. Press, Washington, DC.

Lewis, Tom. 1991. *Empire of the Air: The Men Who Made Radio*. HarperCollins, New York.

Lichty, Lawrence W., and Topping, Malachi, eds. 1975.

American Broadcasting: A Source Book on the History of Radio and Television. Hastings, New York.

Liebert, Robert M., et al. 1988. *The Early Window: The Effects of Television on Children and Youth*, 3d ed. Pergamon, New York.

Linsky, Martin. 1986. *Impact: How the Press Affects Federal Policymaking.* Norton, New York.

Little, Arthur D., Inc. 1969. *Television Program Production, Procurement, Distribution and Scheduling.* Arthur D. Little, Inc., Cambridge, MA.

Long, Mark, ed. Annual. *World Satellite Almanac.* MLE, Winter Beach, FL.

Lowery, Shearon, and De Fleur, Melvin L. 1988. *Milestones in Mass Communication Research: Media Effects*, 2d ed. Longman, New York.

Lull, James. 1990. *Inside Family Viewing: Ethnographic Research on Television's Audience.* Routledge, New York.

Luther, Sara Fletcher. 1988. *The United States and the Direct Broadcast Satellite.* Oxford U. Press, New York.

Lyle, Jack, and Douglas McLeod. 1993. *Communication, Media and Change.* Mayfield, Mountain View, CA.

MacDonald, J. Fred. 1979. *Don't Touch That Dial! Radio Programming in American Life, 1920–1960.* Nelson-Hall, Chicago.

———. 1992. *Blacks and White TV: African-Americans in Television Since 1948.* 2nd ed. Nelson-Hall, Chicago.

———. 1990. *One Nation Under Television: The Rise and Decline of Network TV.* Pantheon, New York.

MacFarland, David T. 1990. *Contemporary Radio Programming Strategies.* Erlbaum, Hillsdale, NJ.

Maclaurin, W. Rupert. 1949. *Invention and Innovation in the Radio Industry.* Macmillan, New York (reprinted by Arno Press in 1971).

Macy, John Jr. 1974. *To Irrigate a Wasteland: The Struggle to Shape a Public Television System in the United States.* U. of California Press, Berkeley.

Madow, William G., et al. 1961. *Evaluation of Statistical Methods Used in Obtaining Broadcast Ratings.* House Report 193. 87th Cong., 1st Sess. GPO, Washington, DC.

Magnant, Robert S. 1977. *Domestic Satellite: An FCC Giant Step Toward Competitive Telecommunications Policy.* Westview, Boulder, CO.

Mair, George. 1988. *Inside HBO.* Dodd, Mead, New York.

Mander, Jerry. 1978. *Four Arguments for the Elimination of Television.* Morrow, New York.

Mansell, Gerard. 1982. *Let Truth Be Told: 50 Years of BBC External Broadcasting.* Wiedenfeld and Nicolson, London.

Marc, David. 1984. *Demographic Vistas: Television in American Culture.* U. of Pennsylvania Press, Philadelphia.

———, and Thompson, Robert J. 1992. *Prime Time, Prime Movers: From "I Love Lucy" to "L.A. Law"—America's Greatest TV Shows and the People Who Created Them.* Little, Brown, Boston.

Marcus, Geoffrey. 1969. *The Maiden Voyage.* Viking, New York.

Marcus, Norman. 1986. *Broadcast and Cable Management.* Prentice-Hall, Englewood Cliffs, NJ.

Markey, Edward J. 1988. "Statement Accompanying Congressional Research Service Letter to House Subcommittee on Telecommunications and Finance. Cases Involving the Federal Communications Commission That Were Reversed . . ." (March 21). Library of Congress, Washington, DC.

Marlow, Eugene, and Secunda, Eugene. 1991. *Shifting Time and Space: The Story of Videotape.* Praeger, New York.

Marschall, Ken. 1987. *The Golden Age of Television.* Exeter, New York.

Martin, James. 1977. *Future Developments in Telecommunications*, 2d ed. Prentice-Hall, Englewood Cliffs, NJ.

Marvin, Carolyn. 1988. *When Old Technologies Were New: Thinking About Electric Communication in the Late Nineteenth Century.* Oxford U. Press, New York.

Matelski, Marilyn J. 1988. *The Soap Opera Evolution: America's Enduring Romance with Daytime Drama.* McFarland, Jefferson, NC.

———. 1991. *Daytime Television Programming.* Focal, Stoneham, MA.

Mathews, Jay. 1992. "More People Not Ready for Prime Time," *Washington Post* (January 18): A1.

Matlon, Ronald J., and Ortiz, Sylvia P. 1992. *Index to Journals in Communication Studies Through 1990*, 2 vols. Speech Communication Assn., Annandale, VA.

Matusow, Barbara. 1983. *The Evening Stars: The Making of the Network News Anchor.* Houghton Mifflin, Boston.

McCombs, Maxwell E., and Shaw, Donald L. 1977. *The Emergence of American Political Issues: The Agenda-Setting Function of the Press.* West, St. Paul, MN.

McCoy, Ralph E. 1968. *Freedom of the Press: An Annotated Bibliography.* Southern Illinois U. Press, Carbondale, IL.

———. 1979. *Freedom of the Press: A Bibliocyclopedia Ten-Year Supplement (1967–1977).* Southern Illinois U. Press, Carbondale, IL.

McCrohan, Donna. 1990. *Prime Time, Our Time: America's Life and Times Through the Prism of Television.* Prima, Rocklin, CA.

McGraw, Thomas K. 1984. *Prophets of Regulation: Charles Francis Adams, Louis D. Brandeis, James M. Landis, and Alfred E. Kahn.* Harvard U. Press, Cambridge, MA.

McLean, Austin J., ed. 1991. *RadioOutlook II: New Forces Shaping the Industry.* National Association of Broadcasters, Washington, DC.

McLuhan, H. Marshall. 1964. *Understanding Media: The Extensions of Man.* McGraw-Hill, New York.

McNeil, Alex. 1991. *Total Television: A Comprehensive Guide to Programming from 1948 to the Present,* 3d ed. Penguin, New York.

McNulty, Timothy J. 1991a. "In Mideast, Leaders Confer via Sound Bites," *Chicago Tribune* (December 24): 1.

———. 1991b. "Bush Taking Direct Route to Viewers," *Chicago Tribune* (December 25): 1.

McPhail, Thomas L. 1987. *Electronic Colonialism: The Future of International Broadcasting and Communication,* 2d ed. Sage, Newbury Park, MD.

McQuail, Denis. 1983. *Mass Communication Theory: An Introduction.* Sage, Beverly Hills, CA.

———, and Windahl, Sven. 1993. *Communication Models for the Study of Mass Communications.* 2d ed. Longman, New York.

———, and Siune, Karen. 1986. *New Media Politics: Comparative Perspectives in Western Europe.* Sage, Newbury Park, CA.

Metz, Robert. 1975. *CBS: Reflections in a Bloodshot Eye.* Playboy Press, Chicago.

———. 1977. *The Today Show: An Inside Look* . . . Playboy Press, Chicago.

Meyersohn, Rolf B. 1957. "Social Research in Television." In Rosenberg and White, 345–357.

Meyrowitz, Joshua. 1985. *No Sense of Place: The Impact of Electronic Media on Social Behavior.* Oxford U. Press, New York.

Mickelson, Sig. 1983. *America's Other Voice: The Story of Radio Free Europe and Radio Liberty.* Praeger, New York.

Mickiewicz, Ellen P. 1988. *Split Signals: Television and Politics in the Soviet Union.* Oxford U. Press, New York.

Midgley, Ned. 1948. *The Advertising and Business Side of Radio.* Prentice-Hall, New York.

Minow, Newton N. 1964. *Equal Time: The Private Broadcaster and the Public Interest.* Atheneum, New York.

———. 1991. "How Vast the Wasteland Now?" Gannett Foundation Media Center, Columbia University, New York (May 9).

Montgomery, Kathryn C. 1989. *Target: Prime Time: Advocacy Groups and the Struggle Over Entertainment Television.* Oxford U. Press, New York.

Morgan, Curtis. 1992. "Father of 3 Devises Box to Control TV," *Miami Herald* (March 10): 1-E.

Mowlana, Hamid, and Wilson, Laurie J. 1990. *The Passing of Modernity: Communication and the Transformation of Society.* Longman, White Plains, NY.

NAB (National Association of Broadcasters), Washington, DC. Annual. *Radio Financial Report* (to 1992).

Annual. *Television Financial Report.*

Semiannual. *Broadcast Regulation* (title varies).

1978. *The Television Code.*

1988. *NAB Legal Guide to Broadcast Law and Regulation,* 3d ed.

1989a. *Broadcasting Bibliography,* 3d ed.

1989b. *Telco Fiber and Video Market Entry: Issues and Perspectives for the Future.*

1991–1993. *NAB HDTV World Conference Proceedings.*

1992. *NAB Engineering Handbook,* 8th ed.

Napier, Sabrie L. 1991. *Looking for Employment in the Broadcasting Industry: Getting Started.* National Association of Broadcasters, Washington, DC.

NAPTS (National Association of Public Television Stations; also called America's Public Television Stations). Washington, DC.

1984. *Public Television and Radio and State Governments,* 2 vols.

1992. *FYI: Facts About America's Public TV Stations.*

NCTA (National Cable Television Association), Washington, DC. 1992. *Cable Television Developments* (October).

National Institute of Mental Health. 1982. *Television and Behavior: The Years of Scientific Progress and Implications for the Eighties,* 2 vols. GPO, Washington, DC.

Negrine, Ralph M., ed. 1985. *Cable Television and the Future of Broadcasting.* St. Martin's, New York.

———, ed. 1988. *Satellite Broadcasting: The Politics and Implications of the New Media.* Routledge, New York.

———, and Papathanassopoulos, Stylianos. 1990. *The Internationalization of Television.* Pinter, London.

Nesson, Ron. 1980. "Now Television's the Kingmaker," *TV Guide* (May 10): 4.

Neuman, W. Russell. 1991. *The Future of the Mass Audience.* Cambridge U. Press, New York.

Newcomb, Horace. 1987. *Television: The Critical View,* 3d ed. Oxford U. Press, New York.

Newman, Mark. 1988. *Entrepreneurs of Profit and Pride: From Black-Appeal to Radio Soul.* Praeger, New York.

Newsweek. 1963. "As 175 Million Americans Watched." (December 9): 52.

New Yorker. 1985. "Talk of the Town," *The New Yorker* (16 September): 29.

New York Times.
1984. "Television Surpasses Radio News in Survey." (September 1): Y13.
1985. "And Now, the Media MegaMerger." (March 24): 3:1.

Nielsen Media Research. 1990. "Nielsen Reports Results from First Out-of-Home Viewing Study," Nielsen Media Research, New York.

Nielsen Television Index. 1992. *Television Audience 1991*. Nielsen Media Research, New York.

———. 1991. *Television Audience 1990*. Nielsen Media Research, New York.

Nimmo, Dan, and Combs, James E. 1985. *Nightly Horrors: Crisis Coverage in Television Network News*. U. of Tennessee Press, Knoxville.

Nizer, Louis. 1966. *The Jury Returns*. Doubleday, New York.

Nmungwun, Aaron Foisi. 1989. *Video Recording Technology: Its Impact on Media and Home Entertainment*. Erlbaum, Hillsdale, NJ.

Noam, Eli M., ed. 1985. *Video Media Competition: Regulation, Economics, and Technology*. Columbia U. Press, New York.

———. 1992. *Television in Europe*. Oxford U. Press, New York.

Noll, A. Michael. 1988a. *Introduction to Telecommunication Electronics*. Artech, Norwood, MA.

———. 1988b. *Television Technology: Fundamentals and Future Prospects*. Artech, Norwood, MA.

Nordenstreng, Kaarle. 1984. *The Mass Media Declaration of UNESCO*. Ablex, Norwood, NJ.

NTIA (National Telecommunications and Information Administration, U.S. Department of Commerce). GPO, Washington, DC.
Regularly updated. *Manual of Regulations and Procedures for Federal Radio Frequency Management*.
1981. *Direct Broadcast Satellites: Policies, Prospects, and Potential Competition*.
1991a. *U.S. Spectrum Management Policy: Agenda for the Future*.
1991b. "Compilation by State of Minority-Owned Commercial Broadcast Stations," Minority Telecommunications Development Program (October).
1993. *Globalization of the Mass Media*.

Nuessel, Frank. 1992. *The Image of Older Adults in the Media: An Annotated Bibliography*. Greenwood, Westport, CT.

Nye, Russel B. 1970. *The Unembarrassed Muse: The Popular Arts in America*. Dial, New York.

O'Donnell, Lewis B., et al. 1989. *Radio Station Operations: Management and Employee Perspectives*. Wadsworth, Belmont, CA.

Ohio State University. School of Journalism. 1988. *1987 Journalism and Mass Communications Graduate Survey: Summary Report*. Ohio State University, Columbus, OH.

O'Neil, Terry. 1989. *The Game Behind the Game: High Stakes, High Pressure in Television Sports*. Harper and Row, New York.

Oringel, Robert S. 1989. *Audio Control Handbook for Radio and Television Broadcasting*, 6th ed. Focal, Stoneham, MA.

Orlik, Peter B. 1988. *Critiquing Radio and Television Content*. Allyn and Bacon, Boston, MA.

Osborn, J. Wes., et al. 1979. "Prime Time Network Television Programming Preemptions," *Journal of Broadcasting* 23 (Fall): 427–436.

OTA (Office of Technology Assessment, U.S. Congress). 1986. *Intellectual Property Rights in an Age of Electronics and Information*. GPO, Washington, DC.

Overman, Michael. 1978. *Understanding Sound, Video and Film Recording*. TAB, Blue Ridge Summit, PA.

Owen, Bruce, and Wildman, Steven. 1992. *Video Economics*. Harvard U. Press, Cambridge, MA.

Paglin, Max. 1989. *A Legislative History of the Communications Act of 1934*. Oxford U. Press, New York.

Paley, William S. 1979. *As It Happened: A Memoir*. Doubleday, New York.

Palmer, Edward L. 1988. *Television and America's Children: A Crisis of Neglect*. Oxford U. Press, New York.

Pareles, Jon. 1989. "After Music Videos, All the World Has Become a Screen," *New York Times* (10 December): E6.

Parish, James Robert, and Terrace, Vincent. 1989–1990. *The Complete Actors' Television Credits, 1948–1988*, 2 vols., 2d ed. Scarecrow, Metuchen, NJ.

Parsons, Patrick. 1987. *Cable Television and the First Amendment*. Lexington, Lexington, MA.

Passer, Harold C. 1953. *The Electrical Manufacturers, 1875–1900*. Harvard U. Press, Cambridge, MA.

Passport to World Band Radio. Annual. International Broadcasting Services, Penn's Park, PA.

Paterson, Richard. Annual. *TV and Video International Guide*. Tantivy, London.

Paugh, Ronald. 1989. "Music Video Viewers." In Heeter and Greenberg, 237–245.

Paulu, Burton. 1981. *Television and Radio in the United Kingdom*. U. of Minnesota Press, Minneapolis.

Pavlik, John V., and Dennis, Everette E., eds. 1993. *Demystifying Media Technology: Readings from the Freedom Forum Center*. Mayfield, Mountain View, CA.

Pelton, Joseph N. 1991. *The "How To" of Satellite Communications*. Design Publishers, Sonoma, CA.

Pember, Don R. 1993. *Mass Media Law*, 5th ed. Brown, Dubuque, IA.

Penney, Edmund F. 1991. *The Facts on File Dictionary of Film and Broadcast Terms*. Facts on File, New York.

Penzias, Arno. 1989. *Ideas and Information: Managing in a High-Tech World*. Norton, New York.

Performing Arts Books: 1876–1981. 1981. Bowker, New York.

Petty, Ross D. 1992. *The Impact of Advertising Law on Business and Public Policy*. Quorum, New York.

Phillips, Mary Alice Mayer. 1972. *CATV: A History of Community Antenna Television*. Northwestern U. Press, Evanston, IL.

Picard, Robert C. 1989. *Media Economics: Concepts and Issues*. Sage, Newbury Park, CA.

———. 1991. "Copyright Royalty Payments Top $200 Million as Payments by Cable Triple," *Broadcast Cable Financial Journal* (July–August): 8.

Pichaske, David. 1979. *A Generation in Motion: Popular Music and Culture of the Sixties*. Schirmer Books, New York.

Pierce, John R., and Noll, Michael. 1990. *Signals: The Science of Telecommunications*, 2d ed. Scientific American Library, New York.

Pike and Fischer. *Radio Regulation*. Washington, DC.

PLI (Practicing Law Institute). Annual. *Communications Law*. PLI, New York.

Ploman, Edward, ed. 1982. *International Law Governing Communications and Information*. Greenwood, Westport, CT.

Poltrack, David. 1983. *Television Marketing: Network, Local, and Cable*. McGraw-Hill, New York.

Pool, Ithiel de Sola, ed. 1977. *The Social Impact of the Telephone*. MIT Press, Cambridge, MA.

———. 1983. *Technologies of Freedom: On Free Speech in an Electronic Age*. Harvard U. Press, Cambridge, NIA.

———. 1990. *Technologies Without Boundaries: On Telecommunications in a Global Age*. Harvard U. Press, Cambridge, MA.

Pope, Daniel. 1983. *The Making of Modern Advertising*. Basic Books, New York.

Powe, Lucas A., Jr. 1987. *American Broadcasting and the First Amendment*. U. of California Press, Berkeley, CA.

———. 1991. *The Fourth Estate and the Constitution: Freedom of the Press in America*. U. of California Press, Berkeley.

Powers, Ron. 1977. *The Newscasters*. St. Martin's Press, New York.

Prentiss, Stan. 1987. *Satellite Communication*, 2d ed. TAB, Blue Ridge Summit, PA.

———. 1990. *HDTV: High-Definition Television*. TAB, Blue Ridge Summit, PA.

President's Study Commission on International Broadcasting ("Stanton Commission"). 1973. *The Right to Know*. GPO, Washington, DC.

President's Task Force on U.S. Government International Broadcasting. 1991. *Report*. GPO, Washington, DC.

Preston, William, Jr., et al. 1989. *Hope and Folly: The United States and Unesco, 1945–1985*. U. of Minnesota Press, Minneapolis.

Pringle, Peter K., and Clinton, Helen H. 1989. *Radio and Television: A Selected, Annotated Bibliography, Supplement Two: 1982–1986*. Scarecrow, Metuchen, NJ.

Pringle, Peter K., et al. 1991. *Electronic Media Management*. 2d ed. Focal, Stoneham, MA.

Queisser, Hans. 1988. *The Conquest of the Microchip*. Harvard U. Press, Cambridge, MA.

Raboy, Marc. 1990. *Missed Opportunities: The Story of Canada's Broadcasting Policy*. McGill-Queen's U. Press, Montreal.

Rather, Dan. 1987. "From Murrow to Mediocrity?" *New York Times* (March 10): A27.

Ray, William B. 1990. *FCC: The Ups and Downs of Radio-TV Regulation*. Iowa State U. Press, Ames.

Read, Oliver, and Welsh, Walter. 1976. *From Tin Foil to Stereo: Evolution of the Phonograph*, 2d ed. Sams, Indianapolis.

Reed, David P. 1991. *Residential Fiber Optic Networks: An Engineering and Economic Analysis*. Artech, Norwood, MA.

Reed, Maxine, and Reed, Robert. 1990. *Career Opportunities in Television, Cable, and Video*. 3d ed. Facts on File, New York.

Reeves, Michael G., and Hoffer, Tom W. 1976. "The Safe, Cheap and Known: A Content Analysis of the First (1974) PBS Program Cooperative," *Journal of Broadcasting* 20 (Fall): 546–566.

Reid, T. R. 1984. *The Chip*. Simon and Schuster, New York.

Reinsch, Leonard, and Ellis, Elmo. 1960. *Radio Station Management*. 2d ed. Harper, New York.

"Report Prompts 176th Dingellgram to FDA," 1992. *Washington Post* (September 11): A21.

Rice, John F., ed. 1990. *HDTV: The Politics, Policies, and Economics of Tomorrow's Television*. Union Square, New York.

Rice, Ronald, et al. 1984. *The New Media: Communication, Research, and Technology*. Sage, Newbury Park, CA.

Rimer, Sara. 1991. "Television Becomes Basic Furniture in College Students' Ivory Towers," *New York Times* (October 27): 18.

Roberts, Donald F., and Bachen, Christine M. 1981. "Mass Communication Effects." In *Annual Review of Psychology*: 307–356.

Robertson, James, and Yolcum, Gerald C. 1973. "Educational Radio: The Fifty-Year-Old Adolescent," *Educational Broadcasting Review* 7 (April): 107–115.

Robinson, Thomas P. 1943. *Radio Networks and the Federal Government*. Columbia U. Press, New York.

Rogers, Everett M. 1986. *Communication Technology: The New Media in Society*. Free Press, New York.

Roman, James. 1983. *Cablemania*. Prentice-Hall, Englewood Cliffs, NJ.

Roper Organization. 1991. *America's Watching: Public Attitudes Toward Television*. National Association of Broadcasters, Washington, DC.

Rose, Brian G., ed. 1985. *TV Genres: A Handbook and Reference Guide*. Greenwood, Westport, CT.

———. 1986. *Television and the Performing Arts: A Handbook and Reference Guide to American Culture Programming*. Greenwood, Westport, CT.

Rose, C. B., Jr. 1940. *National Policy for Radio Broadcasting*. Harper, New York (reprinted by Arno Press in 1971).

Rosen, Philip T. 1980. *The Modern Stentors: Radio Broadcasters and the Federal Government 1920–1934*. Greenwood, Westport, CT.

———. 1988. *International Handbook of Broadcasting Systems*. Greenwood, Westport, CT.

Rosenberg, Bernard, and White, David Marining, eds. 1957. *Mass Culture: The Popular Arts in America*. Free Press, Glencoe, IL.

Rossini, Neil J. 1991. *The Practical Guide to Libel Law*. Praeger, New York.

Rowan, Ford. 1984. *Broadcast Fairness: Doctrine, Practice, Prospects*. Longman, New York.

Rowland, Willard. 1983. *The Politics of TV Violence: Policy Uses of Communication Research*. Sage, Beverly Hills, CA.

RR (*Radio Regulation*).
  1982. *AM Stereophonic Broadcasting*, 51 RR2d 1.
  1991. *RKO General Inc. (KFRC)*, 68 RR2d 1341.

Rubin, Bernard. 1967. *Political Television*. Wadsworth, Belmont, CA.

Rubin, R. B., et al. 1993. *Communication Research: Strategies and Sources*, 3d ed. Wadsworth, Belmont, CA.

Sabato, Larry J. 1991. *Feeding Frenzy: How Attack Journalism Has Transformed American Politics*. Free Press, New York.

Sabine, Gordon A. 1980. *Broadcasting in Virginia: Benchmark '79*. Dept. of Communications, Virginia Polytechnic, Blacksburg, VA.

Safran, Claire. 1980. "Children's Television: What Are the Best—and Worst—Shows?" *TV Guide* (August 9): 2.

Sanders, Marlene, and Rock, Maria. 1988. *Waiting for Prime Time: The Women of Television News*. U. of Illinois Press, Urbana.

Sarnoff, David. 1968. *Looking Ahead: The Papers of David Sarnoff*. McGraw-Hill, New York.

Saudek, Robert. 1973. "Omnibus Was Like Running Five Broadway Openings Every Week," *TV Guide* (August 11): 22.

Savage, James G. 1989. *The Politics of International Telecommunications Regulation*. Westview, Boulder, CO.

Schaefer, R. Murray. 1977. *The Tuning of the World*. Knopf, New York.

Schneider, Cy. 1987. *Children's Television: The Art, The Business, and How It Works*. NTC, Chicago.

Schofield, Lemuel B. 1979. "Don't Look for the Hometown Touch," *TV Guide* (April 14): 39.

———, and Driscoll, Paul D. 1991. "Effects of Television Network Affiliation Changes: A Miami Case Study," *Journal of Broadcasting & Electronic Media* 35 (Summer): 367.

Schonfeld, Reese. 1983. "Pop News: TV's Growth Industry," *Channels* (September/October): 33.

Schramm, Wilbur. 1973. *Men, Messages, and Media: A Look at Human Communication*. Harper and Row, New York.

Seehafer, Gene F., and Laemmar, Jack M. 1959. *Successful Television and Radio Advertising*, 2d ed. McGraw-Hill, New York.

Senate CC (U.S. Congress, Senate Committee on Commerce). GPO, Washington, DC. (Title of committee has varied.)

1930. *Commission on Communications.* Hearings. 71st. Cong., 2d Sess.

1944. *To Amend the Communications Act of 1934.* Hearings. 78th Cong., 1st Sess.

1948. *Progress of FM Radio.* Hearings. 80th Cong., 2d Sess.

1972. *Surgeon General's Report by Scientific Advisory Committee on Television and Social Behavior.* Hearings. 92nd Cong., 2d Sess.

1980. *Amendments to the Communications Act of 1934.* Hearings. 96th Cong., 1st Sess.

SGAC (Senate Government Affairs Committee). 1991. *Pentagon Rules on Media Access to the Persian Gulf War.* Hearing. 102nd Cong., 1st Sess.

Sendall, Bernard. 1982–1983. *Independent Television in Britain,* 2 vols. Macmillan, London.

Sepstrup, Preben. 1990. *Transnationalization of Television in Western Europe.* John Libbey, London.

Settel, Irving. 1967. *A Pictorial History of Radio,* 2d ed. Grosset and Dunlap, New York.

———. 1983. *A Pictorial History of Television,* 2d ed. Ungar, New York.

Setzer, Florence, and Levy, Jonathan. 1991. *Broadcast Television in a Multichannel Marketplace.* FCC Office of Plans and Policy (Staff Study No. 26, June).

Shaffer, William D., and Wheelright, Richard. 1983. *Creating Original Programming for Cable TV.* Communications Press, Washington, DC.

Shannon, Claude E., and Weaver, W. 1949. *The Mathematical Theory of Communication.* U. of Illinois Press, Urbana.

Shapiro, George H., et al. 1983. *"CableSpeech": The Case for First Amendment Protection.* Law and Business, New York.

Shapiro, Mitchell E. 1989. *Television Network Prime-Time Programming 1948–1988.* McFarland, Jefferson, NC.

———. 1990. *Television Network Daytime and Late-Night Programming, 1959–1989.* McFarland, Jefferson, NC.

Shawcross, William. 1992. *Murdoch.* Simon and Schuster, New York.

Shearer, Benjamin F., and Huxford, Marilyn. 1983. *Communications and Society: A Bibliography on Communications Technologies and Their Social Impact.* Greenwood, Westport, CT.

Sherman, Barry L. 1987. *Telecommunications Management: The Broadcast and Cable Industries.* McGraw-Hill, New York.

Shiers, George, and Shiers, May. 1972. *Bibliography of the History of Electronics.* Scarecrow, Metuchen, NJ.

Shoemaker, Pamela J., ed. 1989. *Communication Campaigns About Drugs: Government, Media and the Public.* Erlbaum, Hillsdale, NJ.

Short, K.R.M. 1986. *Western Broadcasting Over the Iron Curtain.* St. Martin's, New York.

Shulman, Arthur, and Youman, Roger. 1966. *How Sweet It Was: Television—A Pictorial Commentary.* Shorecrest, New York.

Shulman, Holly Cowan. 1991. *The Voice of America: Propaganda and Democracy, 1941–1945.* U. of Wisconsin Press, Madison.

Sieber, Robert. 1988. "Industry Views on the People Meter: Cable Networks," *Gannett Center Journal* 2 (Summer): 70.

Siepmann, Charles. 1946. *Radio's Second Chance.* Atlantic-Little, Brown, Boston.

———. 1950. *Radio, Television and Society.* Oxford U. Press, New York.

Signorelli, Nancy. 1985. *Role Portrayal and Stereotyping on Television.* Greenwood, Westport, CT.

———. 1991. *A Sourcebook on Children and Television.* Greenwood, Westport, CT.

———, and Gerbner, George, comps. 1988. *Violence and Terror in the Mass Media: An Annotated Bibliography.* Greenwood, Westport, CT.

Sikes, Rhea G. 1980. "Programs for Children: Public Television in the 1970's," *Public Telecommunications Review* 8 (September/October): 7.

Silj, Alessandro. 1992. *The New Television in Europe.* John Libbey, London.

Simmons, Steven J. 1978. *The Fairness Doctrine and the Media.* U. of California Press, Berkeley.

Singleton, Loy. 1989. *Global Impact: The New Telecommunication Technologies.* Ballinger, New York.

Slide, Anthony. 1982. *Great Radio Personalities in Historic Photographs.* Dover, New York.

———. 1991. *The Television Industry: A Historical Dictionary.* Greenwood, Westport, CT.

Sloan, William David. 1989. *American Journalism History: An Annotated Bibliography.* Greenwood, Westport, CT.

Smith, Bruce Lannes, et al. 1946. *Propaganda, Communication and Public Opinion.* Princeton U. Press, Princeton, NJ.

Smith, F. Leslie. 1974. "Hunger in America Controversy: Another View," *Journal of Broadcasting* 18 (Winter): 79.

Smith, Hedrick, ed. 1992. *The Media and the Gulf War: The Press and Democracy in Wartime.* Seven Locks, Washington, DC.

Smith, Milton L. 1990. *International Regulation of Satellite Communication*. Martinus Nijhoff, Dordrecht, The Netherlands.

Smith, Myron J. 1984. *U.S. Television Network News: A Guide to Sources in English*. McFarland, Jefferson, NC.

Smith, Richard A. 1985. "TV: The Light That Failed," *Fortune* (December): 78.

Smith, Sally Bedell. 1990. *In All His Glory: The Life of William S. Paley—The Legendary Tycoon and His Brilliant Circle*. Simon and Schuster, New York.

Smith, Wes. 1989. *The Pied Pipers of Rock 'n' Roll: Radio Deejays of the 50s and 60s*. Longstreet Press, Marietta, GA.

Snow, Marcellus S. 1987. *The International Telecommunications Satellite Organization (INTELSAT)*. Nomos Verlagsgesellschaft, Baden-Baden, Germany.

Socolow, A. Walter. 1939. *The Law of Radio Broadcasting*. 2 vols. Baker, Voorhis, New York.

Soley, Lawrence C., and Nichols, John S. 1987. *Clandestine Radio Broadcasting: A Study of Revolutionary and Counterrevolutionary Electronic Communication*. Praeger, New York.

Sova, Harry W., and Sova, Patricia L. 1992. *Communication Serials: An International Guide to Periodicals in Communication, Popular Culture, and the Performing Arts*. Sovacomm, Virginia Beach, VA.

Spitzer, Matthew L. 1986. *Seven Dirty Words and Six Other Stories: Controlling the Content of Print and Broadcast*. Yale U. Press, New Haven, CT.

SRDS (Standard Rate and Data Service, Skokie, IL) Monthly. *Spot Radio Rates and Data*. Monthly. *Spot Television Rates and Data*.

Standard & Poor. 1988. "Networks' Dynasty Dims" (July 4): 16.

Stedman, Raymond W. 1977. *The Serials: Suspense and Drama by Installment*, 2d ed. U. of Oklahoma Press, Norman.

Stein, Harry. 1979. "How '60 Minutes' Makes News," *New York Times Magazine* (May 6): 28.

Steiner, Gary A. 1963. *The People Look at Television: A Study of Audience Attitudes*. Knopf, New York.

Stephenson, William. 1967. *The Play Theory of Mass Communication*. U. of Chicago Press, Chicago.

Stempel, Tom. 1992. *Storytellers to the Nation: A History of American Television Writing*. Continuum, New York.

Stephens, Mitchell. 1988. *A History of News from the Drum to the Satellite*. Viking, New York.

Sterling, Christopher H. 1982. "Television and Radio Broadcasting," Chapter 6; and "Cable and Pay Television," Chapter 7, in Compaine et al., 299–450.

———. 1984. *Electronic Media: A Guide to Trends in Broadcasting and Newer Technologies, 1920–1983*. Praeger, New York.

———. 1988. "Billions in Licenses, Millions in Fees: Comparative Renewals and the RKO Mess," *Gannet Center Journal* (Winter): 53.

———, and Haight, Timothy R. 1978. *The Mass Media: Aspen Institute Guide to Communication Industry Trends*. Praeger, New York.

———, and Kittross, John M. 1990. *Stay Tuned: A Concise History of American Broadcasting*, 2d ed. Wadsworth, Belmont, CA.

Stone, David M. 1985. *Nixon and the Politics of Public Television*. Garland, New York.

Stone, Joseph, and Yohn, Tim. 1992. *Prime Time and Misdemeanors: Investigating the 1950s TV Quiz Scandal—A D.A.'s Account*. Rutger's U. Press, New Brunswick, NJ.

Strong, William S. 1993. *The Copyright Book: A Practical Guide*, 4th ed. MIT Press, Cambridge, MA.

Sturcken, Frank. 1990. *Live Television: The Golden Age of 1946–1958 in New York*. McFarland, Jefferson, NC.

Surgeon General, Scientific Advisory Committee on Television and Social Behavior. 1972. *Television and Growing Up: The Impact of Televised Violence*. GPO, Washington, DC.

Sussman, Gerald, and Lent, John A., eds. 1991. *Transnational Communications: Wiring the Third World*. Sage, Newbury Park, CA.

Tan, Alexis S. 1986. *Mass Communication Theories and Research*. Macmillan, New York.

Tannenbaum, Percy H., and Kostrich, Leslie J. 1983. *Turned-On TV/Turned-Off Votes*. Sage, Beverly Hills, CA.

Tannenwald, Peter. 1985. "Selling Off the Spectrum," *Channels* (Jul.–Aug.): 41.

Taylor, Ella. 1989. *Prime Time Families: Television Culture in Postwar America*. U. of California Press, Berkeley.

Taylor, John P. 1980. *Direct-to-Home Satellite Broadcasting*. Television/Radio Age, New York.

TCAF (Temporary Commission on Alternative Financing for Public Telecommunications). 1982–1983. *Alternative Financing Options for Public Broadcasting* (Vol. 1); *Final Report* (Vol. 2). FCC, Washington, DC.

Tebbel, John, and Watts, Sarah Miles. 1985. *The Press and the Presidency*. Oxford U. Press, New York.

Temin, Peter, with Louis Galambos. 1987. *The Fall of the Bell System: A Study in Prices and Politics*. Cambridge U. Press, New York.

Thomas, Cal. 1988. "End of the Moral Majority?" *Los Angeles Times Syndicate* (November 9).

Toffler, Alvin. 1970. *Future Shock*. Random House, New York.

———. 1980. *The Third Wave*. Morrow, New York.

Toll, Robert C. 1982. *The Entertainment Machine: American Show Business in the Twentieth Century*. Oxford U. Press, New York.

Truax, Barry. 1985. *Acoustic Communication*. Ablex, Norwood, NJ.

Tunstall, Jeremy. 1984. *The Media in Britain*. Columbia U. Press, New York.

———. 1986. *Communications Deregulation: The Unleashing of America's Communications Industry*. Basil Blackwell, New York.

———, and Walker, David. 1981. *Media Made in California: Hollywood, Politics, and the News*. Oxford U. Press, New York.

———, and Michael Palmer. 1991. *Media Moguls*. Routledge, London.

Turow, Joseph. 1984. *Media Industries: The Production of News and Entertainment*. Longman, New York.

———. 1989. *Playing Doctor: Television, Storytelling and Medical Power*. Oxford U. Press, New York.

———. 1992. *Media Systems in Society: Understanding Industries, Strategies, and Power*. Longman, White Plains, NY.

Tusa, John. 1990. *Conversations with the World*. BBC Books, London.

Twentieth Century Fund Task Force on Public Television. 1994. *Quality Time?*

Tydeman, John, et al. 1982. *Teletext and Videotex in the United States: Market Potential, Technology, and Public Policy Issues*. McGraw-Hill, New York.

Tynan, Kenneth. 1979. *Show People: Profiles in Entertainment*. Simon and Schuster, New York.

Tyne, Gerald F. J. 1977. *Saga of the Vacuum Tube*. Sams, Indianapolis.

Udelson, Joseph H. 1982. *The Great Television Race: A History of the American Television Industry 1925–1941*. U. of Alabama Press, University, AL.

UNESCO (United Nations Educational, Scientific and Cultural Organization), Paris.

Annual. *Statistical Yearbook*.

1980. *Many Voices, One World: Communications and Society Today and Tomorrow* ("MacBride Commission").

1987. *Latest Statistics on Radio and Television Broadcasting*.

1989. *World Communication Report*.

Ungerer, Herbert. 1988. *Telecommunications in Europe: Free Choice for the User in Europe's '92 Market*. European Community, Brussels.

United Nations. 1990. *World Media Handbook: Selected Country Profiles*. UN, New York.

US (*United States Reports*). GPO, Washington, DC.

1919. *Schenk v. U.S.*, 249 US 47.

1942. *Marconi Wireless Telegraph Co. of America v. U.S.* 320 US 1.

1943. *NBC v. U.S.*, 319 US 190.

1949. *Terminiello v. Chicago*, 337 US 1.

1951. *Dennis v. U.S.*, 341 US 494.

1964. *New York Times v. Sullivan*, 376 US 254.

1965. *Estes v. Texas*, 381 US 532.

1968a. *U.S. v. Southwestern Cable*, 392 US 157.

1968b. *Fortnightly Corp. v. United Artists Television*, 392 US 390.

1969. *Red Lion v. FCC*, 395 US 367.

1973a. *CBS v. Democratic National Committee*, 412 US 94.

1973b. *Miller v. California*, 413 US 15.

1974. *Miami Herald v. Tornillo*, 418 US 241.

1978. *FCC v. Pacifica Foundation*, 438 US 726.

1979. *Herbert v. Lando*, 441 US 153.

1981. *Chandler v. Florida*, 449 US 560.

1984a. *Universal Studios v. Sony*, 464 US 417.

1984b. *FCC v. League of Women Voters of California*, 484 US 364.

1986. *City of Los Angeles and Department of Water and Power v. Preferred Communications, Inc.*, 476 US 488.

1989. *Sable Communications v. FCC*, 492 US 115.

1990. *Metro Broadcasting v. FCC*, 497 US 547.

1993. *FCC v. Beach Communications, et al.* — US —.

USACPD (U.S. Advisory Commission on Public Diplomacy). Annual. *Report to the Congress and the President of the United States*. GPO, Washington, DC.

U.S. Bureau of the Census. 1935. *Radio Broadcasting*. GPO, Washington, DC.

USC (*United States Code*). Regularly revised. GPO, Washington, DC.

U.S. Commission on Civil Rights. 1977, 1979. *Window Dressing on the Set: Women and Minorities in Television*, 2 vols. GPO, Washington, DC.

U.S. Congress, House of Representatives. Regularly revised. *Radio Laws of the United States* (title varies). GPO, Washington, DC.

USDOS (U.S. Department of State). 1990. *Eastern Europe: Please Stand By—Report of the Task Force on Telecommunications and Broadcasting in Eastern Europe*. GPO, Washington, DC.

Van Evra, Judith. 1990. *Television and Child Development*. Erlbaum, Hillsdale, NJ.

Van Gerpen, Maurice. 1979. *Privileged Communication and the Press: The Citizen's Right to Know Versus the Law's Right to Confidential News Source Evidence*. Greenwood, Westport, CT.

Vaughn, Robert. 1972. *Only Victims: A Study of Show Business Blacklisting*. Putnam, New York.

Vitale, Joseph. 1988. "Sad News at Black Rock, Good News from the Field," *Channels Field Guide 1988*: 36

The Veronis, Suhler & Associates Communications Industry Forecast: Historical and Projected Expenditures for 9 Industry Segments. Annual. Veronis, Suhler, New York.

Vogel, Harold L. 1990. *Entertainment Industry Economics: A Guide for Financial Analysis*, 2d ed. Cambridge U. Press, New York.

Walley, Wayne. 1991. "Nielsen Beefing Up Minority Ratings," *Electronic Media* (July 15): 14.

———. 1992. "Editor: TV Guide Still Soldiering On," *Electronic Media* (January 20): 56.

Wallis, Roger, and Baran, Stanley. 1990. *The Known World of Broadcast News: International News and the Electronic Media*. Routledge, New York.

Walters, Lynne Masel, et al., eds. 1989. *Bad Tidings: Communication and Catastrophe*. Erlbaum, Hillsdale, NJ.

Warner, Charles, and Buchman, Joseph. 1993. *Broadcast and Cable Selling*. Updated 2d ed. Wadsworth, Belmont, CA.

Warner, Harry P. 1948. *Radio and Television Law*. Matthew Bender, Albany, NY.

———. 1953. *Radio and Television Rights*. Matthew Bender, Albany, NY.

Watkinson, John. 1988. *The Art of Digital Audio*. Focal, Stoneham, MA.

Watson, Mary Ann. 1990. *The Expanding Vista: American Television in the Kennedy Years*. Oxford U. Press, New York.

Weaver, David H., and Wilhoit, G. Cleveland. 1991. *The American Journalist: A Portrait of U.S. News People and Their Work*. Indiana U. Press, Bloomington.

Weaver, Sylvester L. 1955. "The Form of the Future," *Broadcasting-Telecasting* (May 30): 56.

Webster, James. 1985. "Program Audience Duplication: A Study of Television Inheritance Effects," *Journal of Broadcasting & Electronic Media* 29 (Spring): 121.

———, and Lichty, Lawrence W. 1991. *Ratings Analysis: Theory and Practice*. Erlbaum, Hillsdale, NJ.

Weiner, Richard. 1990. *Webster's New World Dictionary of Media and Communications*. Prentice Hall, Englewood Cliffs, NJ.

Welch, Randy. 1985. "The Builder of Cable Empires," *Channels* (January/February): 45.

Wenner, Lawrence A., ed. 1989. *Media, Sports, and Society*. Sage, Newbury Park, CA.

Wertheim, Frank. 1979. *Radio Comedy*. Oxford U. Press, New York.

White, David M. 1950. "The 'Gate Keeper': A Case Study in the Selection of News," *Journalism Quarterly* 27 (Fall): 383.

White, Llewellyn. 1947. *The American Radio*. U. of Chicago Press, Chicago (reprinted by Arno Press in 1971).

White, Rita Lauria, and White, Harold M., Jr. 1988. *The Law and Regulation of International Space Communication*. Artech, Norwood, MA.

Whiteside, Thomas. 1985. "Cable," *The New Yorker* (May 20): 45; (May 27): 43; (June 3): 82.

Whittemore, Hank. 1990. *CNN: The Inside Story*. Little, Brown, Boston.

Wiener, Norbert. 1950. *The Human Use of Human Beings*. Houghton Mifflin, Boston.

Wildman, Steven S., and Siwek, Stephen E. 1988. *International Trade in Films and Television Programs*. Ballinger, Cambridge, MA.

Williams, Carol Traynor. 1992. *"It's Time for My Story": Soap Opera Sources, Structure, and Response*. Praeger, New York.

Williams, Christian. 1981. *Lead, Follow, or Get Out of the Way: The Story of Ted Turner*. Times Books, New York.

Williams, Frederick. 1991. *The New Telecommunications: Infrastructure for the Information Age*. Free Press, New York.

Williams, Huntington. 1989. *Beyond Control: ABC and the Fate of the Networks*. Atheneum, New York.

Williams, Margorie. 1989. "MTV as Pathfinder for Entertainment," *The Washington Post* (December 13): A1.

Wilson, Kevin G. 1988. *Technologies of Control: The New Interactive Media for the Home*. U. of Wisconsin Press, Madison.

Wimmer, Roger, and Dominick, Joseph. 1991. *Mass Media Research: An Introduction*, 3d ed. Wadsworth, Belmont, CA.

Winn, Marie. 1985. *The Plug-In Drug: Television, Children, and the Family*, 2d ed. Penguin Books, New York.

Winston, Brian. 1986. *Misunderstanding Media*. Harvard U. Press, Cambridge, MA.

Witherspoon, John, and Roselle Kovitz. 1987. *The History of Public Broadcasting*. Current, Washington, DC.

Wober, J. Mallory. 1988. *The Use and Abuse of Television:*

A Social Psychological Analysis of the Changing Screen. Erlbaum, Hillsdale, NJ.

Wolfe, Charles H., ed. 1949. *Modern Radio Advertising.* Funk and Wagnalls, New York.

Wonderful Inventions—Motion Pictures, Broadcasting and Recorded Sound at the Library of Congress. 1985. Library of Congress, Washington, DC.

Wood, Donald N., and Wylie, Donald G. 1977. *Educational Telecommunications.* Wadsworth, Belmont, CA.

Wood, James. 1992a. *History of International Broadcasting.* Peter Peregrinus/Science Museum, London.

———. 1992b. *Satellite Communications and DBS Systems.* Focal, Stoneham, MA.

Woolery, George W. 1983–1984. *Children's Television: The First Thirty-Five Years, 1946–1981,* 2 vols. Scarecrow, Metuchen, NJ.

———. 1989. *Animated TV Specials: The Complete Directory to the First 25 Years, 1962–1987.* Scarecrow, Metuchen, NJ.

World Radio-TV Handbook. Annual. Billboard, New York.

Wurtzel, Alan, and Acker, Stephen R. 1989. *Television Production,* 3d ed. McGraw-Hill, New York.

Wyche, Mark C., et al. 1990. *Sports on Television: A New Ball Game for Broadcasters.* National Association of Broadcasters, Washington, DC.

Yates, Robert K., et al. 1990. *Fiber Optics and CATV Business Strategy.* Artech, Norwood, MA.

Yoakam, Richard, and Cremer, Charles. 1988. *ENG: Television News and the New Technology,* 2d ed. Southern Illinois U. Press, Carbondale.

Zeigler, Sherilyn K., and Howard, Herbert H. 1991. *Broadcast Advertising,* 3d ed. Iowa State U. Press, Ames.

Zettl, Herbert. 1992. *Television Production Handbook,* 5th ed. Wadsworth, Belmont, CA.

Zuckman, Harvey, et al. 1988. *Mass Communications Law in a Nutshell,* 3d ed. West, St. Paul, MN.

of, 512; and ownership, 515, 517; and telcos, 256

Cable Guide, The, 331

Cable Health Network, 218

Cable in the Classroom, 285

Cable Music Channel (Turner), 83

Cable National Audience Demographic Reports, 412

Cable News Network. *See* CNN

Cable-Satellite Public Affairs Network. *See* C-SPAN

Cabletelevision Advertising Bureau (CAB), 241

Cable Television Consumer Protection and Competition Act of 1992, 410, 483–484, 487

Cable Television Nacionale, 233

Cable TV: advantages and drawbacks, 16, 142–144; advertising, 204, 236, 238–240; audience, 202–203, 205, 209, 410, 412, 413; basic-cable networks, 205; basic unit, organization of, 200, 201 (exhibit), 202–204; in Canada and other developed countries, 551, 561; capital investment in, 210–214; changing roles of, 75 (chart), 76; for children, 357–358; and competition, 97, 106, 108, 298–299; construction cost, 211; and convention coverage, 353; and DBS, 88; defined, 483; deregulation of, 76, 487, 490 (exhibit); design of, 144–146; emergence of, 58, 73–78; employment in, 219–228, 472; in Europe, 561; FCC and, 75–76, 78, 203, 213, 214, 248, 343, 410; and format, 316; franchising for, *see* Franchises; future of, 566–568, 571–572; growth indicators, 77 (chart); Hurricane Andrew and, 6, 13; impact of, 104; interactive, 90, 92, 107, 342, 568–570; interconnected systems, 203–204, 239; licensing of, 76, 85, 86; as major player, 78–82; movies acquired by, 317–319; multiple-system operators, *see* MSOs; must-carry rule, 76, 199, 205, 246, 483, 487, 535; news networks, 352–353; ownership of, 214, 216–219, 515; pay and pay-per-view, *see* Pay cable; PPV; piracy of, 200*n*, 533; profitability of, 254–258; programming for, 79, 81, 202, 374; program services, 205, 206–208 (exhibit), 209–210, 218–219; program sources, 146, 365; promotion on, 329; public access channels, 76, 364, 365; public affairs on, 356; public broadcasting, 285; ratings of, 412; as redelivery service, 74; regulation of, *see* Regulation; retransmission consent, 205, 483; revenue sources, 205, 232 (exhibit), 236, 248–250, 254; rise of networks, 79–81; sales and sales reps of, 202,

241; satellites and, 78–81, 206–208 (exhibit), 561; schedules, 327–329; scrambled signals in, 81, 84, 533; service tiers, 248–249; shipping network, 343; SMATV vs., 86; spectrum architecture, 147 (exhibit); sports on, 348, 350; and syndex, 310–311; system sales, 216–219; talk shows on, 342; telephone companies and, 108; tuning facilities, 146; VCRs as competition for, 97; VHF and UHF signals on, 61, 106; "wireless," 85–86. *See also* Coaxial cable relays; Fiber-optic relays; HBO (Home Box Office); Networks, TV; Superstations

Cablevision, 348, 365

Cagney and Lacey, 336

Camcorders, 167, 364, 415. *See also* VCRs

Cameras: home video, 133*n*; motion picture (kinetoscope), 22

Camera tubes, 58, 133, 134 (exhibit), 142

Canada, 350*n*; and cable TV, 351, 561; and domsat, 560; movies located in, 321; treaties with, 493

Canal Plus (French STV), 564

Candid Camera, 310

Cannell (independent producer), 319

"Canon 35" (ABA), 508 (exhibit)

Capital Cities Communications ("Cap Cities")/ABC, 101, 215, 252

Capital Connection (MMDS service), 85

Capital investment, 210–214. *See also* Economic constraints

Captain Kangaroo, 290*n*

Carlin, George, 510, 511

Carnegie Commission on Educational Television (CCET), 268, 270, 271, 282

Carnegie Foundation, 279, 280 (exhibit)

Carney, Art, 65 (photo)

Carol Burnett Show, 343

Carrascolendas, 291

Carrier-current stations, 128

Carrier waves. *See* Waves, radio

CARS (Community Antenna Relay Service), 146

Carsey-Werner (independent producer), 319

Carson, Johnny, 102, 222, 345 (exhibit)

Cart (recording cartridge), 166

Car Talk, 293

Carter, Jimmy, 224, 435, 461*n*, 485, 518; debates, 438, 439 (exhibit)

Cartoon Channel, The, 82, 83, 255, 353, 374

Cartoons, 357

Casey's Top 40 with Casey Kasem, 369

Cash flow, 216

Cassandra service (Nielsen), 386, 390 (exhibit)

Cassettes, tape, 166

Castro, Fidel, 556

Casualty of Love: The "Long Island Lolita," 307

Catharsis, Greek theory of, 452

Cathode ray tube (CRT), 142

CATV (community antenna TV), 74–75, 78; augmentation of service, 74; in Europe, 561

Cavett, Dick, 345

C-band. *See* Signal(s)

CBC (Canadian Broadcasting Corporation), 276, 542

CBS (Columbia Broadcasting System) network, 44; affiliates, 51, 60, 195, 196, 197, 198; blacklisting at, 69; created, 37–38; drops recording ban, 49; and early color TV, 61; music schedule, 48; network rivalry, 46, 61, 64–66, 99, 104, 200; and news, 49, 323; and sports, 368; subsidiaries sold, 104; and sustaining programs, 38, 48, 67; takeover attempt by Turner, 83, 101; in World War II, 56, 57

CBS Evening News, 15, 261, 355

CBS News, 57, 104, 505

CBS Radio Network, 259

CBS (TV): audience share, 334; for children, 290*n*, 308, 357; costs, 211, 253–254, 306, 307, 321; and cross-media promotion, 331; future of, 571; libel suits against, 69, 504, 505; and Miami stations, 217 (exhibit); and minorities, 47*n*; and movies, 338; network service begins, 58; and news, 342, 352, 353, 356, 364, 438; and off-network programs, 309; program sources, 317, 319, 321; and public affairs, 355–356; quiz shows, 70; scheduling by, 325, 326; and sports, 346*n*, 348, 349 (exhibit), 350, 368; Turner attempts takeover, 83, 101; and variety shows, 343; videotape first used by, 62; and violence, 246

CCD (charge-coupled device, TV camera), 133*n*

CDs (compact discs), 97, 99, 175 (exhibit); and CD-ROM, 175*n*; recordable, 173

Ceausescu, Nicolae, 546

"Cellular Vision" (subscription TV), 86

Censorship, 434, 474, 484; government, 502; of obscenity, 510. *See also* First Amendment

Census Bureau, U.S., 401

Chain broadcasting. *See* Networks, radio

Challenger satellite, 160, 560

Chancellor, John, 344

Channel(s), 119; allotment of FM, *see* FM radio; allotment of TV, 136–137, 279, 468–469, 483; AM, FCC classification,

264, 463, 483, 520–521; enforcement of, 478–482, 484; and foreign ownership, 214, 469; free speech confirmed in, 503; and license renewal or revocation, 476, 478, 494*n*, 514; and piracy, 533; and politics, 269, 519, 520; set aside, 279; sponsor identification rule, 245; and treaties, 493; and unions, 49

Communications Satellite Corporation. *See* Comsat

Communications Workers of America, 225

Communism, fears of, 68–69, 524

Community: needs, ascertaining, 486; radio, 294–295; TV stations, 273, 275

Community Antenna Relay Service (CARS), 146

Community Broadcasters Association (CBA), 191

Community Service Grants (CSGs), 277

Como, Perry, 343

Compact discs. *See* CDs

Compatibility of monochrome with color TV, 61, 95, 136

Competition: from cable services, 254–255, 327; early radio, 46; from new technologies, 254, 566–567; press-radio, 49, 51; and prices, 566; radio station, 33, 35, 258; role of, 544; TV and TV network, 61–66 *passim*, 99, 101–108 *passim*, 200, 260, 327

Competitive Cable Association, 255

Composite color (digital video), 174

Compression technology, 271. *See also* Signal(s)

Compuserv (videotex system), 89, 90

Computers, 175, 212 (exhibit); and computer "chip" (integrated circuit), 93, 94; role of, 169, 187; transistors and, 93

Comsat (Communications Satellite Corporation), 86, 106, 211, 558

Concentration, 319

Concept (of program series), 317

Conductivity. *See* AM radio

CONELRAD (Control of Electromagnetic Radiation), 8

Conglomerates, investment by, 214

Congress, U.S.: and advertising, 494; and closed captions, 91; C-SPAN coverage of, 79, 441; and DATs, 173; and documentaries, 354; and FCC, 460, 462–463, 468–471 *passim*, 495, 503, 511, 521; future actions by, 577; and media issues, 454, 493; and public broadcasting, 270, 278, 279, 281, 283; and radio, 31, 68, 106, 268; and regulation/deregulation of commerce, 459–461, 492, 493, 495; and scrambling signals, 81; and telegraph services, 23;

and TV (cable), 75, 202*n*, 203, 455, 463, 472, 484. *See also* Communications Act of 1934; Radio Act(s)

Congressional TV, 441, 442 (exhibit), 443

Congruence theory (opinion surveys), 422

Conrad, Frank, and KDKA, 31–32

Consent decree, 107, 309

Constitution, U.S., 495, 542; chain of legal authority under, 460 (exhibit); changing perspectives and, 534–535; commerce clause, 459; controversy over, 500–534; must-carry rule violates, 587; and privacy, 505. *See also* First Amendment; Fifth Amendment

Construction permits (CPs), 469

Consumer action, 496, 513. *See also* Citizen

Contemporary hit radio (CHR), 371, 372 (chart). *See also* Top-40

Content analysis (of programs), 426

Continuity: acceptance (network), 246–247; writer, 240

Contours. *See* Station coverage

Control Data Corporation, 384

Controlling philosophies, 541–543

Control room, computer use in, 212

Controls on media, 576–577. *See also* Regulation

Controversial issues of public importance, 521

Controversy: over advertising, 526; over Constitution, 500–534; coverage of, 428–429, 526; effect of, 235; over radio programming, 48–51

Conus Communications, 323; Satellite Cooperative, 158 (exhibit), 198

Conventions, political, 101, 287, 353, 437–438, 443

Convergence, technological, 150, 169, 579

Converter box (cable TV), 146; addressable (PPV), 81, 249

Cook, Fred, 524 (photo)

Cooke, Alistair, 274, 290

Cook Inlet Radio Partners, 215

Coolidge, Calvin, 36, 41, 436

Cooperative advertising, 66, 231, 247

Cooperative Analysis of Broadcasting, The, 396*n*

Co-production. *See* Production

Copyright, 530–534; how it works, 531 (exhibit); live music, 48; syndicated program, 29

Copyright Act of 1976, 530–534

Copyright Law of 1909, 530

Copyright Royalty Tribunal (CRT), 531, 532–533

Cornwell, Don, 225 (exhibit)

Corporation for Public Broadcasting. *See* CPB

Correll, Charles, 46, 47

Corwin, Norman, 56

Cosby Show, The; 311*n*, 319 335; NBC loses, 253; popularity of, 310, 313; revenue from, 326, 327 (exhibit)

Cosell, Howard, 348

Cosmos (series), 290

Costa Rica, 559

Cost per thousand (CPM) as test for advertising prices, 237

Costs. *See* Advertising rates; Economic constraints; Prices; Production costs; Programming, programs and; Salary levels

Coughlin, Father Charles, 46

Countdown America, 369

Counterprogramming, 324, 328. *See also* Programming, programs and

Country Music Television, 343

Country/western music, 371, 372 (chart)

Couric, Katherine ("Katie"), 344

Courts of Appeals, U.S., 199, 466, 480, 481 (exhibit), 487

Court trials, coverage of, 430, 506, 508

Court TV, 254, 255, 374, 509

Coverage. *See* Station coverage

Cox Enterprises, 215

CPB (Corporation for Public Broadcasting), 297, 300; Annenberg and, 279, 292; funding by, 268, 277 (exhibit), 278, 279, 281, 287, 289, 298; future of, 571; Independent Production Service of, 283; and instructional TV, 291–292; launches PBS, 270; and NPR, 271–272, 273, 292, 299; politics and, 269 (exhibit)

C-QUAM standard (stereo), 128

Craft, Christine, 221*n*

Credibility of news, 374–375, 429, 505; Voice of America and, 555

Crime shows, 336

Criminal Code laws, 494, 510, 511

Crisis management, 1–17, 28, 40, 443

Cronkite, Walter, 352, 431, 435

Crosby, Bing, 49, 66, 67

Crosley "Pup," 34 (photo)

Crossfire, 342

Cross-licensing. *See* Patents

Cross-media: ownership, 108, 515, 517; promotion, 331

C-SPAN (Cable-Satellite Public Affairs Network) I & II, 374, 443; in the Classroom, 285; covers Congress, 79, 356, 441; covers conventions, 353, 438; future of, 571; subsidization of, 250, 377

Cuba, 152*n*, 551, 555, 556

Cultural imperialism, 553–554

gram, 317; public broadcasting, 283–285, 286–292, 296; ratings and, 405; responsibility in, abused, 70–71; sources of, 146, 283–285, 323, 365, 550; syndication and, 149–150, 309, 358–362; weather and environmental, 79; and wireless cable, 85–86

Program practices department, 247

Promotion, program, 329–331; and advertising prices, 237; commercial broadcasting, 187; cross-media, 331; on-air, 329; other media, 331; promotional announcements (promos), 235, 329

Propaganda: boomerang effect of, 421; research on, 420–421

Propagation, signal, 120–125; directional (radio and TV), 125, 139; propagation theory, use of, 131; TV paths, 141 (exhibit). See also Antenna(s); Signal(s)

Protectionism, 578

Pseudoevent, 429–430

Pseudo-networks, 152n

Psychographics (in audience targeting), 308

PTAR (prime-time access rule). See Prime-time

PTT (post, telephone, telegraph monopoly) deregulation, 547–548

Public access, 521, 523–527, 524 (exhibit), 548–549; access time, 311, 312 (exhibit), 315, 359; channels, 76, 365, 366 (exhibit); political, 519–521, 548

Public affairs programs, 314, 354–356; on cable, 356; global, 551–552

Public broadcasting, 264–300; and advertising, 279–281; audiences for, 276 (chart), 281–282, 295–298, 308; bilingual, 291, 293; cable competition with, 298–299; cable TV, 285; changing roles of, 298–300; children's programs, 290–291, 297; commercial station aid to, 281n; community stations, 294–295; Corporation for, see CPB; criticism and defense of, 299–300; education and instruction on, 291–292; in Europe, 300; FCC and, 266, 272, 275, 279, 281; formats in, 294–295; funding of, 268–274 passim, 275–283, 286–289 passim, 293, 298; future of, 571–572; ownership of, 272–275; and performing arts, 289–290; politics and, 269 (exhibit); and popular taste, 377; radio programming, 292–295; science and nature programs, 290, 291 (exhibit); stations, 272–275; TV programming, 283–285, 286–292, 296; unlicensed, 295. See also PBS

Public Broadcasting Act of 1967, 264, 268

Public Broadcast Marketing (private firm), 279

Public domain, 530

Public file (of license-renewal applications), 472–473

Public interest, convenience, or necessity standard. See PICON

Public interest, programming for, 375–379

Publicity crimes, 433

Public officials (legal definition), 506 (exhibit)

Public-service announcements (PSAs), 235–236

Public-service broadcasting, 542; deregulation and, 545

Pulitzer prize: and deception, 375; Halberstam wins, 430

PUPs (portable uplinks), 211

PUR (persons using radio), 405

Quadruplex VTRs, 166

Qualitative program aspects, 407

Quantizing (in digital processing), 169, 170 (exhibit)

Quantum cable system, 81

Quayle, Dan, 438, 440, 496; and *Murphy Brown*, 235, 335

Qube interactive service, 90, 107

Questionable programs. See Taste, popular

"Quirky," 335

Quiz scandals, 70–71

Racism in radio, 47

RADAR (Radio's All-Dimension Audience Research), 366, 368, 386, 397, 398

Radio: data by, 179; digital, 178–179; as electromagnetic force, 113; radio energy, 113–114. See also Signal(s); Waves, radio

Radio (broadcasting): advertising, 35–36, 38, 56, 64, 66, 231; audience, 33, 298, 308, 408; for the blind, 90, 91 (exhibit), 130; British, 544; cable audio service, 83; chain, see Networks, radio; changing course of, 104–106; Congress covered by, 441; comedies, 46–47; competition in, 33, 35; Depression era, 43–47; digital audio, see DAB; disc jockeys in, see DJs; emergence of industry, 35–37; ethical crises in, 68–71; in Europe and Third World, 179, 548–549, 550; evolution of, 21, 22, 27–31; "first" station, 31–35; formats in, 294, 330 (exhibit), 370–374; government role in, 33, 38, 40–47 passim; legislation, see Radio Act(s); licenses for, 33, 35; local pro-

grams, 293, 370–374; low-frequency, 115; minorities and women in, 47; networks begin, 37–38; noncommercial, 292–295; and political campaigns, 436; racism in, 47; recordings used in, 67–68; rock music on, 343; schedules, 329; short-wave, 122, 123 (exhibit), 131; superstations, 209; toll, 35, 36; transition from, to TV, 43–71; in World War II, 56–57, 433, 554. See also Programming, radio; Public broadcasting; Wireless

Radio (technology): AM and FM, see AM radio; FM radio; automation, 370, 371n; evolution of, 21–35, 92–93; miniaturization in, 93–95; precedent technologies, 21–23; radio energy, 113–114; radio signals, 118–125. See also Waves, radio

Radio Act(s): of 1912, 33n, 40, 41; of 1927, 41, 45, 461, 519, 520, 576

Radioactive Radio Music on Demand, 371n

Radio Advertising Bureau (RAB), 7, 187, 241

Radio astronomy, 59n

Radio Broadcast Data System (RBDS), 371

Radio Free Europe (RFE), 556

Radio-frequency. See Frequencies Radio Group stations, 35, 36, 37

Radio Liberty (RL), 556

Radio Martí, 152n, 556

Radio Moscow, 555

Radio Radio (Europe), 560

"Radio Recovery"(Army station), 6

Radio Russia, 555

Radiotelegraphy, Radiotelephony. See Telegraph; Telephone

Radio-Television News Directors Association (RTNDA), 227 (exhibit), 497

Radio waves. See Waves, radio

RAI (Radio Televisione Italia), 546

Random selection (in sampling), 398

Rap format, 371

Rates, advertising. See Advertising rates

Rather, Dan, 355; covers disasters, 15, 17 (exhibit); criticizes CBS, 261–262; salary of, 222 (exhibit), 353n

Ratings, 383–418, 423; concepts, 404 (exhibit); as criteria, 378; defined, 403; diaries, 391, 392–393 (exhibit), 394; future measurement of, 575; gross and target rating points (GRPs and TRPs), 237; local market, 384, 386, 387 (exhibit), 388 (exhibit), 412; network, 194, 255, 386, 389 (exhibit); polls and, 575; qualitative, 407; rating periods, 384; reliability and validity of, 406–407; shares, 404–405; syndicated programs, 386,

peals to, 480; and fairness doctrine, 523, 524, 526; and free speech, 502, 503, 504; landmark decisions, 500, 506 (exhibit), 523, 524 (exhibit); and must-carry rule, 76; and networks, 51; nomination hearings, 252, 353, 442; and obscenity law, 509–510, 511, 512; and piracy, 533; and regulation, 487, 519; and SMATV, 483*n*; and TV intrusion, 508 (exhibit)

Surfing. *See* Grazing (through channels)

Surgeon General, U.S., 494, 525; study of violence by, 449 (exhibit), 453–454

Surrogate domestic services, 556

Surveys. *See* Media effects research

Sustaining programs, 36, 38, 48, 67, 234. *See also* Programming, programs and

Swaggart, Jimmy, 362*n*

Sweden, 559

Sweep weeks, sweeps (Arbitron ratings), 386

Switzerland: TV and VCR penetration in, 549, 561

Synchronization: of pickup and receiver tubes (sync generator), 139, 142; of scanning (sync pulses), 135; of sound and picture, 22–23

Syndex rules (FCC), 209, 310–311

Syndicated Program Analysis (SPA), 386

Syndication, 307, 308–314; barter, 311–314, 343; defined, how it works, 308–310; exclusivity (syndex), 209, 310–311; feature, 369; fin/syn rules, 194, 309, 311, 317*n*; first-run, 311, 359; format, 314, 369, 371; international, 552, 553 (exhibit); news service, 323, 369; off-network programs, 306–307, 327 (exhibit), 358–359; prime-time access, 311; principle of, 149–150; radio, 314; rating of programs, 386, 390 (exhibit); of religion, 360, 362; time-bank, 313; TV, 309, 358–362

Synthesizing of wants (advertising), 452

System interconnects. *See* Interconnection (of cable systems)

Tabloid TV, 359

Taft Broadcasting, 216

Taishoff, Larry, 50

Taishoff, Sol, 50

Talkies, 22. *See also* Motion pictures

Talknet, 12, 368

Talkradio, 368

Talk shows, 342, 356, 368; news/talk, 372 (chart), 373; shock radio, 373; talk radio, 372 (chart), 373; talk show syndrome, 439–440

Tampering (with ratings), 407

Tandem (independent producer), 319

Tape recording, 165

Targeting audience. *See* Audience

Target plate (within pickup tube), 133

Target rating points (TRPs), 237

Taste, popular, 377–379; and questionable programs, 235, 335; standards of, 246, 575

Tax certificates, 518

TBS (Turner Broadcasting Systems), 82–83 (exhibit), 101, 210, 327, 348, 353; advertising prices, 240; audience for, 209, 339; and CBS, 101; profits of, 255; TPN of, 251

TCAF (Temporary Commission on Alternative Financing for Public Telecommunications), 279–281

TCI (Tele-Communications Inc.): building plans, 163; as cablesystem owner, 210, 219, 515; losses by, 255; programming by, 202*n*, 213; in schools, 285; unions and, 225

Teasers (promotion), 329

Technical functions: cable TV, 202; station, 187

Technologies. *See* Electronic technologies

Telecine film projector, 134*n*

Telecom (France), 90*n*, 560

Tele-Communications Inc. *See* TCI

Telefon Hirmondo ("Telephonic Newspaper," Budapest, Hungary), 24*n*

Telegraph, 151; development of, 23; wireless (radiotelegraphy), 23*n*, 27, 28, 31, 265 (exhibit)

Telemetering devices (satellite), 157

Telemundo (Spanish-language network), 7, 233, 339

Telenovelas, 339

Telephone: coast-to-coast, 24, 26; European service, development of, 24*n*; invention of, 23–24; participation in media, 517–518; and radiotelephony, 23*n*, 27, 29, 30, 31

Telephone companies (telcos), 107–108, 517–518; future of, 151, 256–257, 566, 577. *See also* AT&T

Telephone Group radio stations, 35, 37

Telephone recall (in surveys), 397

Telephonic newspaper, 24*n*

Teletext/Videotex, 88, 89 (exhibit), 90, 107, 142, 561

Televangelists. *See* Religious broadcasts

Televisa (Mexico), 103, 104, 286

Television (broadcasting): advertising, 58, 101, 106, 204, 231; AM and FM used in, 120; antisocial results of, 445; audience, 73, 78, 408–418; changes in, 104, 106; channel numbers, 118; commercial, beginning of, 54; delay of, 51–52; for disabled, 90, 91 (exhibit); feature

films in, 64, 85, 97, 336–338; growth of, 61 (chart), 106; importance of, 446–448; interacting with, 90, 92, 107, 342, 568–570; international agreements on, 493; licensing of, *see* Licensing; "live decade" of, 63; locally produced, 74, 146, 285, 362–365; noncommercial, 272–275 (*see also* Public broadcasting); nonnews, 365; and political campaigns, 436–440; profitability of, 253–254; regulation and deregulation of, 76, 78, 101, 104; in Russia (Moscow), 83; schedules, 326–327; set penetration and use, 408–409; station-produced, 365; subscription, *see* STV; syndication, 309, 358–362; tabloid approach in, 359; time spent watching, 410, 411 (exhibit), 423, 445–446; transition from radio to, 43–71; transmission and reception of, 139, 140 (exhibit), 141–142; and TV as habit, 409. *See also* Networks, TV; News coverage; Programming, TV

Television (cable). *See* Cable TV

Television (color): basic systems, 136*n*, 547, 558; coming of, 61, 62 (exhibit); composite color, 174; FCC standards, 136; kinescope, 142; luminance in, 136, 137 (exhibit); monochrome compatibility with, 61, 95, 136; phosphor dots, 142, 143 (exhibit); "primary" colors, 136*n*, 142; production costs of, 550; replaces monochrome, 213; tube for, 142, 143 (exhibit)

Television (technology): antennas, 124 (exhibit); cable relays, *see* Coaxial cable relays; Fiber-optic relays; channel requirements, 125–126, 136, 137 (exhibit); and compatibility of monochrome and color, 61, 95, 136; components and signals, 140 (exhibit); coverage extended, 73–74; early development, 51–55, 58–61; FCC and, 52, 58–60, 139; film projectors, 134*n*; high-definition, *see* HDTV; improvements in, 95; location in spectrum, 136–137; mechanical era, 52; miniaturization in, 93–95; newer-media, penetration of, 100 (exhibit); news gathering, overuse of, 362; niche services, 83–92, 213, 251; post–World War II, 58–61; propagation, 139, 141 (exhibit); remote control devices, 409–410; SAP, 90, 252; sound and color, 136; standards adopted, 54; stations and station coverage, 73–74, 83, 120–121, 136–142, 194; transmission and reception, 139, 140 (exhibit), 141–142, 177; U.S. standards, 134, 135, 136; VHF-UHF signals, 61, 106, 123 (exhibit); video-compression, 81, 106,

U-Matic (VCR), 95
U-matic VTR tape, 167
Uncontested applications for license renewal, 476. *See also* Licensing
Understanding Media (McLuhan), 409*n*
Underwater cables, 23, 163
Underwriting, program, 279, 289; local, 279
Unethical practices. *See* Ethical crises
Unions, 221, 225–226; and live music, 48, 49
Unistar network, 353, 354, 369
United Arab Emirates, 12
United Church of Christ, 481 (exhibit)
United Nations, 125, 547, 554; UNESCO, 554; UNICEF, 286
United Press, United Press International, 49, 51, 321
United Satellite Communications Inc. (USCI), 86
United States: and free-flow policy, 554; Information Agency (USIA), 57, 555; land mass of, 551; syndicated material from, 552, 553 (exhibit); TV set penetration in, 549
United States Satellite Broadcasting. *See* USSB
Universal Pictures, 215 (exhibit)
Universal Studios, 215 (exhibit), 317
University: of Houston, 273*n*; of Michigan, 295; of Southern California, 293; of Wisconsin, 265
University TV stations, 273
Univision (Spanish-language network), 103–104, 195, 233, 339; during hurricane, 7, 12
Unsolved Mysteries, 314
Untouchables, The, 359
Unwired networks, 152*n*, 242
UP, UPI (United Press, United Press International), 49, 51, 321
Updates (news), 364
Upgrading of cable services, 202, 249
Uplinks (satellite), 157; low-power (LPUs), 211; portable (PUPs), 211
Urban contemporary (UC) music, 371, 372 (chart)
USA cable network, 219, 255, 307, 331; audience targeting by, 308; competition by, 327; and made-for-cable movies, 338; ownership of, 215 (exhibit); and PPV, 249; programming by, 339, 341, 348, 357, 374; and public access, 366; stripping by, 328, 359
USCI (United Satellite Communications Inc.), 86
USIA (United States Information Agency), 57, 555
Us magazine, 333 (exhibit)

USSB (U.S. Satellite Broadcasting), 88, 211, 251
U.S. West (telco), 107, 108

Vacuum tube, 62 (exhibit), 94 (photo); development of, 24, 26; end of, 92–93; mass production of, 27; revival seen, 93*n*
Vacuum tube oscillator, 26
Van Doren, Charles, 70 (photo)
Variety/Diverse (or electric) format, 371, 372 (chart)
Variety shows, 343
Vaudeville as precedent technology, 22
VBI (vertical blanking interval), 88, 89 (exhibit), 135 (exhibit), 136; and closed captions, 90, 91 (exhibit), 142, 252; and sale for private use, 283
VCRs (videocassette recorders), 90, 107, 233; audience for, 413–415; consumer, 92, 106, 167–168; impact of, 104, 173, 324, 337, 394, 408, 409, 414; introduction and growth of, 95, 98 (exhibit); libraries and camcorders, 167, 364, 414–415; piracy by, 533–534; prices of, 566; remote control for, 410; school use of, 292, 299; Third World use of, 561; and time shifting, 97, 413, 414; use patterns, 416 (exhibit); video compression and, 171–173
Vertical blanking interval. *See* VBI
Vertical integration (of industry), 210
Vertical resolution, 135. *See also* Electronic pictures
VHF band, 120*n*, 121, 123; antennas for, 122; FCC restrictions, 55, 58, 59–60, 126, 137, 139, 283; FM use of, 55, 129, 130; signal quality of, 120, 199; "translation" from UHF to, 73, 106; TV use of, 53, 58–61 *passim*, 126, 136–137, 141, 143, 146, 329; VHF as term, 118
VH-1 (Video Hits One network), 255, 342, 347
VHS (Video Home System), 97
Viacom, 209*n*, 219, 323, 327 (exhibit), 357
Video, digital, 173–175; laser, 174–175
Videocassette recorders. *See* VCRs
Video-Cipher II descrambler, 84 (exhibit)
Video-compression. *See* Signal(s)
Video dial tone (VDT) decision, 108, 517–518, 577
Videodiscs, 99; failure of, 97, 106
Video Hits One. *See* VH-1
Video Jukebox Network, 205, 249*n*
Videopath (advertising interconnect), 204
Videotape, 63, 166–167; first use of, 62; quadruplex recorders (VTRs), 166

Videotex. *See* Teletext/Videotex
Vidicon camera tube, 134 (exhibit)
Vietnam: A Television History, 274, 279, 287–288
Vietnam conflict, 430–431, 432 (exhibit), 433, 434; interviews and documentaries about, 504–505; protests against, 451
Viewer's Choice (PPV operator), 249
Villa Allegre, 291
Violence on TV, 246, 378, 448–452; British program code on, 545; desensitization to, 450; government studies of, 449 (exhibit); reflected in society, 451 (exhibit); U.S. programs criticized abroad, 552; Violence Act passed, 528*n*
Visnews (Reuters service), 322
VJs (video jockeys), 371
VLF signal, 27
Voicecasts, 433
Voice of America (VOA), 124, 131, 546, 555, 556
Voices, media, 517, 527
VTRs (quadruplex videotape recorders), 166

WABC, 37, 480*n*
WAGM-TV, 195
"Walkman" (Sony), 173
Wallace, Mike, 262, 355 (exhibit), 504, 505
Walters, Barbara, 224, 344, 356
Waltons, The, 443
Wambaugh, Joseph, 450
War: TV coverage of, 430–436. *See also* Gulf War; World War I; World War II
War and Remembrance (Wouk), 246*n*, 338
Warhol, Andy, 430
Warner Brothers, 317, 357
Warner Cable, 90, 107
War of the Worlds (radio play), 45, 509
Washington, Harold, 373
Washington *Post*, 498
Washington Week in Review, 286, 287
"Wasteland" epithet, 375–377
Watergate scandal, 438, 441, 442
Waves, radio, 113, 114–118; antennas and, 120, 122, 124 (exhibit), 125; attenuation and absorption of, 118, 120, 143; carrier, 118, 119, 121 (exhibit), 127, 128; direct (FM and TV), 121–122, 123 (exhibit), 130, 139; frequency and wavelength, 116, 118; ground (AM), 122, 123 (exhibit); phases or cycles of, 116; refracted, reflected or ducted, 120, 122; sky (AM and short-wave), 122, 123 (exhibit), 130, 131; wave-motion concepts, 116, 117 (exhibit); "wave guides," 143. *See also* Frequencies; Signal(s)
Waves, TV, 139